West Kent College

This book is due for return on or before the ~~date~~
stamped below unless an ext~~ension~~

Handbook of Crime Prevention and Community Safety

Edited by

Nick Tilley

WILLAN
PUBLISHING

Published by

Willan Publishing
Culmcott House
Mill Street, Uffculme
Cullompton, Devon
EX15 3AT, UK
Tel: +44(0)1884 840337
Fax: +44(0)1884 840251
e-mail: info@willanpublishing.co.uk
website: www.willanpublishing.co.uk

Published simultaneously in the USA and Canada by

Willan Publishing
c/o ISBS, 920 NE 58th Ave, Suite 300
Portland, Oregon 97213-3644, USA
Tel: +001(0)503 287 3093
Fax: +001(0)503 280 8832
e-mail: info@isbs.com
website: www.isbs.com

ISBN 1-84392-146-4 paperback
ISBN 1-84392-147-2 hardback

British Library Cataloguing-in-Publication Data

A catalogue record for this book is available from the British Library

Project management by Deer Park Productions, Tavistock, Devon
Typeset by GCS, Leighton Buzzard, Beds
Printed and bound by T.J. International, Padstow, Cornwall

Contents

List of abbreviations

ACPO	Association of Chief Police Officers
ANPR	automated number-plate recognition
APA	Association of Police Authorities
APACS	Association for Payment Clearing Services
ASBO	anti-social behaviour order
ATF	(Bureau of) Alcohol, Tobacco and Firearms
BBBS	Big Brothers/Big Sisters
BCC	British Chambers of Commerce
BCS	British Crime Survey
BCU	basic command unit
BPD	Boston Police Department
BRC	British Retail Consortium
BVPI	best-value performance indicator
CAP	(California) Civil Addict Program
CAPS	Chicago Alternative Policing Strategy
CBRN	chemical, biological, radiological and nuclear
CCA	crime-centred analysis
CCO	conjunction of criminal opportunity
CCP	Comprehensive Communities Program
CDA	Crime and Disorder Act 1998
CDRP	Crime and Disorder Reduction Partnership
CDT	child development trainer
CEA	crime environment analysis
CJS	criminal justice system
CMOCs	context, mechanism, outcome (pattern) configurations
CPS	Crown Prosecution Service
CPTED	crime prevention through environmental design
CRARG	Co-ordinated Response and Advocacy Resource Group

CRAVED   concealable, removable, available, valuable, enjoyable, disposable
CRP   Crime Reduction Programme
CVS   Commercial Victimization Survey

DAC   design against crime
DARE   Drug Abuse Resistance Education
DAT   drug action team
DICE   Design Improvement Controlled Experiment
DRR   drug rehabilitation requirement
DTTO   drug treatment and testing order
DV   domestic violence
DVLC   Driver and Vehicle Licensing Centre
DYP   Dalston Youth Project

ED   enumeration district
EPSRC   Engineering and Physical Science Research Council

FPB   Forum of Private Business

GIS   geographic information system
GPS   global positioning system

HIMOs   houses in multiple occupancy
HMIC   Her Majesty's Inspectorate of Constabulary
HVP   high-visibility policing

ICE   in-car entertainment
ICT   information and communication technology
ICVS   International Crime Victims Survey
IDAP   Integrated Domestic Abuse Programme
ISSP   Intensive Supervision and Surveillance Programme
IT   intermediate treatment

JDI   Jill Dando Institute
JLBx   Juvenile Liaison Bureaux
JOLT   Juvenile Offenders Learning Tolerance

LAPD   Los Angeles Police Department
LGBT   lesbian, gay, bisexual or transgender
LGC   Laboratory of the Government Chemist
LSP   Local Strategic Partnership

MAPPA   multi-agency public protection arrangement
MAPPP   multi-agency public protection panel
MAPS   Mapping and Analysis for Public Safety
MARAC   multi-agency risk assessment conference
MO   modus operandi

MRA	market reduction approach
NAAG	National Association of Attorneys General
NCIS	National Crime Intelligence Service
NCRS	National Crime Recording Standard
NCVS	National Crime Victimization Survey
NHTCU	National Hi-Tech Crime Unit
NIJ	National Institute of Justice
NIM	National Intelligence Model
Nnh	nearest neighbour hierarchical
NOMS	National Offender Management Service
NPD	Newark Police Department
NPM	new public management
NRPP	National Reassurance Policing Programme
NSPCC	National Society for the Prevention of Cruelty to Children
NTORS	National Treatment Outcome Research Study
OAG	Office of the Attorney General
ODPM	Office of the Deputy Prime Minister
OJJDP	Office of Juvenile Justice and Delinquency Prevention
PAT	problem analysis triangle
PCT	primary care trust
PESSTLE	political, economic, social, scientific, technological, legal, environmental
PITO	Police Information Technology Organization
PLC	public limited company
PNC	Police National Computer
POA	problem-oriented approach
POP	problem-oriented policing
PSA	public service agreement
PSDB	Police Scientific Development Branch
RAT	routine activities theory
RBI	Reducing Burglary Initiative
RJ	restorative justice
RTT	resource targeting table
RV	repeat victimization
SACSI	Strategic Alternatives to Community Safety Initiative
SARA	scanning, analysis, response, assessment
SBC	Scottish Business Crime (survey)
SBCI	Small Business and Crime Initiative
SBD	secured by design
SCP	situational crime prevention
SDVC	specialized domestic violence court
SIC	standard industrial classification
SOCOs	scene of crime officers

STAC   spatial and temporal analysis of crime

TASC   Tackling Alcohol-related Street Crime
TPI   Targeted Policing Initiative

VAP   violence against the person
VED   Vehicle Excise Duty
VIVA   value, inertia, volume and access

WSU   women's safety unit

YAR   Youth At Risk
YI   youth inclusion
YIP   Youth Inclusion Programme
YJB   Youth Justice Board
YLS   Youth Lifestyle Survey
YOP   youth offender panel
YOT   youth offending team

ZTP   zero-tolerance policing

Notes on contributors

Kate J. Bowers is Senior Lecturer at the Jill Dando Institute of Crime Science, UCL. She has worked in the field of environmental criminology for ten years. Prior to becoming a full-time crime scientist, she completed a BSc in natural science at Durham University and an MA and PhD at the University of Liverpool. Her research has generally focused on applying quantitative methods to crime analysis and to studies of crime prevention. Some of her previous work has involved examining spatial and temporal patterns in crime, evaluating the effectiveness of crime prevention schemes and investigating business crime. Her work has been funded by a variety of organizations, including the Home Office, the police, the DfES and the ESRC. She has published over 30 research papers and book chapters in criminology, has guest edited a special edition of a journal and co-edited a book on crime mapping.

Fiona Brookman is a principal lecturer in criminology and Deputy Director of the Centre for Criminology at the University of Glamorgan. She has a BSc (Hons) from the University of Glamorgan and an MSc and PhD in criminology from the University of Cardiff. She is a member of the Homicide Research Working Group and Secretary and Chair of the British Society of Criminology, Wales and West Branch. Her main areas of research are homicide and violence. She has conducted several Home Office research projects including an inquiry into the potential for reducing homicide in the UK (with Mike Maguire); an examination of why certain homicide cases 'fail' at court; and an evaluation of Operation Tarian Regional Drugs Task Force (with Trevor Bennett and Mike Maguire). She recently published a single-authored book entitled *Homicide in the UK* (Sage, 2005). Fiona is currently conducting an ESRC-funded qualitative study of the role of violence in street crime. Recent publications include articles on homicide (*Journal of Interpersonal Violence, Journal of Crime, Law and Social Change* and *Australian and New Zealand Journal of Criminology*) and street robbery (*British Journal of Criminology*).

John Burrows is a partner in Morgan Harris Burrows (MHB), a consultancy group specializing in crime risk management and crime reduction. He formerly worked at the Home Office and in the retail world as Security Adviser for the Dixons Group. He set up MHB (with others) in 1991. Between 1993 and 1995 he was Director of the British Retail Consortium's 'Crime Initiative'. This is an ongoing programme which aims to provide authoritative data on the extent to which crime affects the retail sector and town-centre environment and to foster the development of retail/town-centre perspectives in interagency crime prevention programmes. He was also head of the Small Business and Crime initiative – a three-year programme of work aimed at combating the crime problems facing small businesses in two high-profile 'demonstration schemes'. As well as focusing on crime affecting business, he has published widely on a range of issues relating to policing, youth crime, drugs and the criminal justice process. He has held visiting fellowships at Cranfield Institute of Technology, Leicester University and Surrey University, and is currently a visiting professor at Nottingham Trent University.

Ronald V. Clarke is University Professor at the School of Criminal Justice, Rutgers University, and is also a visiting professor at the Jill Dando Institute of Crime Science, UCL. He was employed for 15 years in the Home Office Research and Planning Unit, where he had a significant role in the development of situational crime prevention and the British Crime Survey. He has held faculty appointments at the State University of New York at Albany and at Temple University, Philadelphia. He has been Visiting Fellow at the National Police Research Unit in Australia, the Norwegian Police Academy and the US National Institute of Justice. Ronald is the founding editor of *Crime Prevention Studies* and is author or joint author of about 200 books, monographs and papers, including *The Reasoning Criminal* (Springer-Verlag, 1986), *Situational Crime Prevention: Successful Case Studies* (Harrow & Heston, 1997), *Superhighway Robbery* (Willan Publishing, 2003) and *Become a Problem-solving Crime Analyst* (Jill Dando Institute, 2003).

Jason Ditton is Professor of Criminology in the School of Law at Sheffield University, and Director of the Scottish Centre for Criminology. A full list of all the things he has written is on his website at www.ditton.net/scotcrim and he can be contacted at jasonditton@lineone.net. He is currently completing the analysis of data gleaned from a three-wave longitudinal panel survey of the fear of crime conducted with Derek Chadee of the University of the West Indies in Trinidad, and designing the instrumentation for a second similar three-wave survey they intend to begin there in 2006. He is also working on the design of new fear-of-crime questions that could be used to measure the fear of crime with greater sensitivity at the local level.

John E. Eck is a professor in the Division of Criminal Justice of the University of Cincinnati where he teaches graduate courses on research methods, police effectiveness, crime prevention and criminal justice policy. John is internationally known for his studies on problem-oriented policing, the prevention of crime at places, the analysis and mapping of crime hotspots, drug dealing and trafficking control, and criminal investigations. He was a member of the National Academy of Sciences Committee on Police Policy and Research, and a former Director of Research for the Police Executive Research Forum, where he helped pioneer the development and testing of problem-oriented policing. John has served as a consultant to the Office of Community Oriented Policing Services, the National Institute of Justice, the Police Foundation, the Police Executive Research Forum, the Royal Canadian Mounted Police and the London Metropolitan Police. He earned his PhD in criminology from the University of Maryland and his bachelors and masters degrees from the University of Michigan.

Adam Edwards is Lecturer in Criminology and Criminal Justice in the School of Social Sciences, Cardiff University. He is also a director of the European Society of Criminology's working group on the European Governance of Public Safety, the remit of which is to compare the social contexts and political construction of crime prevention within Europe. Contributions to this working group are published in the 2005 special issue of *Theoretical Criminology* (Volume 9, issue 3), co-edited with Gordon Hughes. He has also made the case for a political analysis of crime prevention in two co-edited volumes of papers, one on local crime prevention strategies in England, entitled *Crime Control and Community* (Willan Publishing, 2002) and another on the international policy response to serious and organized crime, entitled *Transnational Organised Crime* (Routledge, 2003), and in numerous chapters and articles, including contributions to the *British Journal of Politics and International Relations*, *Contemporary Politics*, *Crime, Law and Social Change*, *Crime Prevention and Community Safety* and the *International Journal of Risk, Security and Crime Prevention*. His current research interests include the import–export trade in crime prevention policies, the politics of science in the 'what works' debate and the implications of urban renewal programmes for crime prevention.

Paul Ekblom has recently become Professor of Designing Out Crime at Central St Martins College of Art and Design, University of the Arts, London, and Associate Director of the nascent Research Centre in that field. This follows a long career in the UK Home Office which took him from the beginnings of situational crime prevention research, through early demonstration projects, the industrial-scale evaluation of the Safer Cities Programme, developing and managing the Design against Crime initiative within the UK Crime Reduction Programme, contributing to international work with the EU, Council of Europe and UN, and supporting the development of foresight/futures work in policing, crime and cybercrime. During the course of his career he has developed/contributed to a range of conceptual frameworks for use by researchers, evaluators, policy-makers, educators and practitioners, including the police, planners, designers and community safety workers. These include the 'conjunction of criminal opportunity' for analysis of the immediate causes of criminal events and specification of preventive interventions in contexts ranging from volume crime to organized crime and terrorism; the 5 Is for capturing and transferring knowledge of good practice by a detailed breakdown of the preventive process; the 'misdeeds and security' framework for forecasting crime risks and crime preventive opportunities from new technology; and (with a Council of Europe expert group) a 'logic model' for defining partnership in crime prevention.

Graham Farrell (PhD Manchester, 1993–4) is Professor of Criminology in the Midlands Centre for Criminology and Criminal Justice at Loughborough University. He realized he had been studying repeat victimization for around 17 years after working at the Home Office Crime Prevention Unit in 1988–9. Amongst other research on crime prevention and criminal justice, he has published research on racial incidents in prisons (whilst at Oxford University) and on a range of studies on international drug policy which developed from work undertaken at the United Nations office in Vienna. He taught as a visiting assistant professor at Rutgers, the State University of New Jersey, and was an associate professor at the University of Cincinnati. But before all this he was an undergraduate at the University of Surrey where he studied economics and sociology, went to Bolton School and began his education at Greenmount County Primary School where, as one peer recently reminded him, he was the fastest runner in the under 10s.

Martin Gill is Director of Perpetuity Research and Consultancy International (PRCI), a 'spin out' company from the University of Leicester where he is a professor of criminology. The company specializes in research and consultancy in the areas of security and risk management, crime prevention and evaluation studies. Martin has been actively involved in a range of evaluation projects, including the causes of false burglar alarms, the effectiveness of CCTV, the generators of illicit markets, the effectiveness of security guards and the causes of indiscipline in schools. He has a special interest in offender-based studies, including work on the perspectives of armed robbers and shop thieves, and he is currently interviewing fraudsters who have stolen over £50,000 from their employers. He has recently been returning offenders to the scenes of their crime and filmed their views and experiences on environmental and security triggers that facilitated and impeded their offending. He has published 11 books (*Managing Security* and *CCTV* were published in 2003), and he is currently working on the *Handbook of Security*. Martin is a fellow of the Security Institute, a member of the Risk and Security Management Forum, the Company of Security Professionals (and a freeman of the City of London), and he is Chair of the ASIS Research Council.

Daniel Gilling is a principal lecturer in criminal justice studies at the University of Plymouth, and is currently Head of the CJS Subject Group. From his PhD research into the implementation of the much-lauded Kirkholt Project, through to the present, he has been actively researching the field of crime prevention, focusing particularly upon its institutional architecture and upon the wider impact of crime prevention technologies and rationalities. He has published a text on crime prevention (*Crime Prevention: Theory, Policy and Politics*, UCL Press, 1997), as well as a number of other research-based journal articles and chapters. He served until 2004 as an academic adviser to researchers with the Crime Reduction Team at the Government Office South West, and is currently working on a book which will explore developments in crime prevention under New Labour.

Niall Hamilton-Smith is currently a senior research officer in the Organised Crime Research Team in the UK's Home Office. He joined the Home Office in 1999 having completed a PhD in criminology at Nottingham Trent University. Until early 2005 he worked in the Acquisitive Crime Research Team, with a specific responsibility for helping to manage the evaluation of Reducing Burglary Initiative projects funded as part of the UK's £250 million crime reduction programme. Recent publications include editing and co-authoring *The Reducing Burglary Initiative: Design, Development and Delivery* (*Home Office Research Study* 287, available at http://www.homeoffice.gov.uk/rds/horspubs1.html) and a chapter on utilizing criminological theory to target the measurement and interpretation of crime displacement/diffusion of benefits (in N. Tilley (ed.) *Evaluation for Crime Prevention*, Willan Publishing, 2002). His current research interests include the measurement of harm caused by organized crime and organized immigration crime.

Alex Hirschfield is Professor of Criminology and Director of the Applied Criminology Group at the University of Huddersfield. He is also Visiting Professor in the Centre for Investigative Psychology at the University of Liverpool and an associate of the Jill Dando Institute of Crime Science at UCL. His research interests include environmental criminology and crime analysis, the evaluation of crime prevention strategies, technologies for crime reduction and links between crime and public health. He has secured research funding from the ESRC, the EPSRC (Technologies for Crime Prevention and Detection), the Home Office, the Department of Health, the Department for Transport and ODPM. Between 1999 and 2002 he led a Home Office-funded consortium to evaluate the Reducing Burglary Initiative in the north of England and subsequently led the 'Crime Theme' in the national evaluation of the New Deal for Communities Programme. He was awarded honorary membership of the Faculty of Public Health in July 2000. Since 2002 he has been the Home Office's Senior Academic Adviser to the Crime Reduction Director and team in the Government Office North West.

Ross Homel is Foundation Professor of Criminology and Criminal Justice at Griffith University in Brisbane, Australia, and Director of the Key Centre for Ethics, Law, Justice and Governance. He served as editor of the *Australian and New Zealand Journal of Criminology* from 1992 to 1995, and was a part-time commissioner of the Queensland Criminal Justice Commission from February 1994 to April 1999. In July 2003 he took on a half-time role for 12 months with the Australian Research Alliance for Children and Youth to help develop a set of national research priorities to advance the well-being of children and young people, and to set up a new Australian Research Council research network on behalf of the alliance. In 2004 he was elected a fellow of the Academy of the Social Sciences in Australia. Ross's career focus is the theoretical analysis of crime and associated problems, such as violence and injury, and the prevention of these problems through the application of the scientific method to problem analysis and the development, implementation and evaluation of interventions. He is particularly interested in prevention projects implemented through community development methods at the local level, and is co-director of a large early intervention project in a disadvantaged area of Brisbane (the Pathways to Prevention Project). In 2004 this project, which he developed in partnership with Mission Australia, won equal first prize in the National Crime and Violence Prevention Awards.

Matt Hopkins is a consultant for Morgan Harris Burrows. He was formerly a lecturer in criminology at Nottingham Trent University where he completed his PhD thesis on abuse and violence against small business. He has experience of academic research and evaluation in relation to both crimes against business and crime reduction in general. He has published in the *British Journal of Criminology*, *International Review of Victimology*, *Security Journal* and *International Journal of Risk, Security and Crime Prevention*. He has also completed book chapters on *Crime at work* (edited by M. Gill, 1998), *Violence at Work* (edited by M. Gill *et al.*, 2002) and *Crime Reduction and Problem-Oriented Policing* (with Mike Maguire edited by Bullock and Tilley, 2003).

Mike Hough is Director of the Institute for Criminal Policy Research at the School of Law, King's College London. The ICPR has a staff of 16, carrying out policy research for central and local government and for independent funders. Mike has extensive experience in quantitative research methods, especially large-scale sample surveys such as the British Crime Survey and the Policing for London survey. He has published extensively on topics including crime prevention and community safety, anti-social behaviour, policing, sentencing, probation and drugs. He also works as Senior Adviser to the Home Office Regional Crime Reduction Director in the Government Office for London. The unit's current work includes evaluations of intermittent custody, of witness services and of programmes for drug-dependent offenders.

Gordon Hughes is Professor of Criminology at the International Centre for Comparative Criminological Research at the Open University. He is Co-director of the European Society of Criminology's working group on the European Governance of Public Safety. His current research interests include communitarianism and crime control, comparative geohistorical analysis of the politics of safety in Europe, the sociology of crime prevention and community safety expertise. Recent publications include *Crime Control and Community: The New Politics of Public Safety* (with Adam Edwards, Willan Publishing), *Crime Prevention and Community Safety: New Directions*, *Criminological Perspectives* and *Youth Justice* (with Eugene McLaughlin and John Muncie, both with Sage). He is currently completing a book of essays entitled *The Politics of Crime and Community* (Palgrave, 2006). He is also co-editor (with Adam Edwards) of the special edition of *Theoretical Criminology* (2005, Volume 9, issue 3) on 'The governance of safety in Europe'.

Martin Innes is Senior Lecturer in Sociology at the University of Surrey. He is author of two books, *Investigating Murder* (Oxford University Press, 2003) and *Understanding Social Control* (Open University Press, 2003), together with a number of articles and reports. Between April 2003 and July 2005 he led the research for the National Reassurance Policing Programme sponsored by the Home Office and the Association of Chief Police Officers. His current research includes continued development of his work on signal crimes, an empirical study of the role of social control in urban development trajectories and research on the role of intelligence in counter-terrorism policing.

Shane D. Johnson is a senior lecturer at the Jill Dando Institute of Crime Science, UCL. Shane was previously a lecturer in forensic psychology and, before that, a senior research fellow at the University of Liverpool. He has worked within the fields of criminology and forensic psychology for over 10 years, and currently has a particular interest in the spatial and temporal distribution of crime and crime forecasting. He has conducted work for a variety of sponsors, including the Home Office, the DfES and the police, and currently co-ordinates an international collaborative research network funded by the British Academy. He has published over 30 papers within the fields of criminology and forensic psychology and recently guest edited a special edition of an international journal concerned with environmental criminology and crime analysis.

George L. Kelling is a professor in the School of Criminal Justice, Rutgers-Newark University, Faculty Chair of the Police Institute, a senior fellow at the Manhattan Institute, professor emeritus at Northeastern University and a former fellow in the Kennedy School of Government, Harvard University. His major works include the Kansas City Preventive Patrol Experiment, the Newark Foot Patrol Experiment, 'Broken windows' with James Q. Wilson in *The Atlantic*, and 'Fixing broken windows', with Catherine Coles. He has widely consulted with, and lectured in, police departments both in the USA and other countries. Currently, he is conducting the Greater Newark Safer Cities Initiative, consulting with the Boston and Los Angeles Police Departments and working on a book with William Bratton, formerly Commissioner of the New York City Police Department and currently Chief of the Los Angeles Police Department.

Andrew Kent is a research officer currently embedded within the Acquisitive Crime Research Team. He joined the Home Office in 2003, initially supporting the regional research Home Office programme, then moved to the central Home Office working with Paul Ekblom on best practice 'capture' frameworks, specifically the 5 Is framework and wider 'what works' knowledge management. He has been involved in a number of evaluation strands, including the small retailers in deprived areas project and looking at interventions to tackle anti-social behaviour and vehicle-related crime. Prior to the Home Office, Andrew worked on a range of research projects at the University of Surrey, including an evaluation of new key workers in the Child and Adolescent Mental Health Service and a study of public attitudes to date and relationship rape for the Sentencing Advisory Panel.

Gloria Laycock graduated in psychology from University College London in 1968 and completed her PhD at UCL in 1977. She worked in the Home Office for over 30 years, of which almost 20 years were spent on research and development in the policing and crime prevention fields. She established and headed the Home Office Police Research Group and edited its publications on policing and crime prevention for seven years. She has extensive research experience in the UK and has acted as a consultant on policing and crime prevention in North America, Australia, New Zealand, Israel, South Africa and Europe. She is currently an adviser to HEUNI – a UN-affiliated crime prevention organization based in Helsinki. In 1999 she was awarded an international visiting fellowship by the US Department of Justice based in Washington, DC. She returned to the UK in April 2001 from a four-month consultancy at the Australian Institute of Criminology in Canberra to become Director of the Jill Dando Institute of Crime Science at UCL.

Mike Maguire is Professor of Criminology and Criminal Justice at Cardiff University. He was formerly a research fellow at the Oxford University Centre for Criminological Research. He has published in many areas of crime and justice, including burglary, victim issues, complaints systems, sexual and violent offenders, policing, prisons, probation, parole and resettlement. He conducted several studies under the Home Office Crime Reduction Programme, and his recent work on policing includes studies of criminal investigation and intelligence-led policing. He is a co-editor of *The Oxford Handbook of Criminology* (OUP, 2002) and editor of a book series published by Open University Press. He was formerly a member of the Parole Board and is currently a member of the Correctional Services Accreditation Panel and South Wales Probation Board. He is also Senior Academic Adviser to the Home Office research team based in the Welsh Assembly.

Tim McSweeney is a research fellow at the Institute for Criminal Policy Research, School of Law, King's College London. He is currently part of a consortium evaluating the Drug Interventions Programme and also leads fieldwork in London as part of a European Commission-funded study (QCT Europe) in partnership with eight organizations from six countries examining the processes and effectiveness of court-ordered treatment for drug-dependent offenders. The study represents the first systematic, comparative, cross-national research project of its kind conducted in Europe, and is tracking the progress of 845 people who have entered drug treatment, 427 (51 per cent) having been mandated by the courts.

Tim Newburn is Professor of Criminology and Social Policy and Director of the Mannheim Centre for Criminology at the London School of Economics. His main research interests include the sociology and governance of policing and security, youth crime and youth justice, criminal justice and penal policy, and comparative policy-making. He is the author or editor of over 20 books, the most recent of which are *Handbook of Policing* (Willan Publishing, 2003), *Policing: Key Readings* (Willan Publishing, 2004) and *Dealing with Disaffection* (Willan Publishing, 2005). His current work includes a study of the impact of the Stephen Lawrence Inquiry on British policing and an ongoing study of penal policy in the USA and UK, and he is about to embark on a comparative study of police governance in New York, Paris and London. He is editor of the international journal *Criminal Justice*, general editor of the Longman *Criminology Series* and the *Key Ideas in Criminology* series published by Routledge. Tim is President of the British Society of Criminology.

Ken Pease is Visiting Professor at the University of Loughborough and at University College London, although he has retired from full-time work. He was previously Professor of Criminology at the University of Manchester and Associate Professor in the Department of Psychiatry, University of Saskatchewan. A chartered forensic psychologist, he has published widely on diverse topics within criminology, but has found his interests moving towards the deployment of science generally in the crime reduction enterprise – a movement hastened by his membership of the DTI Foresight Crime Panel and his involvement in the setting up of the Jill Dando Institute of Crime Science at UCL, which enshrines a pan-science approach to crime. He is a member of the Home Office's Science and Technology Reference Group.

Tim Read is Senior Lecturer and Award Leader on the post graduate Community Safety and Crime Prevention Programme at the University of the West of England, Bristol. Until April 2001, Tim worked as a principal research officer for the Policing and Reducing Crime Unit (PRC) at the Home Office, latterly managing the evaluation of the Targeted Policing Initiative (TPI), part of the government's Crime Reduction Programme. Prior to this, Tim undertook and managed research for the PRC on a variety of police-related subjects, notably in the areas of crime pattern analysis, problem-solving, problem-oriented policing and racially motivated crime. Prior to working at the Home Office, he worked as a researcher for the Middlesex Area Probation Service.

Michael S. Scott is Director of the Center for Problem-oriented Policing and Clinical Assistant Professor at the University of Wisconsin Law School, specializing in research and teaching in policing. Michael was formerly Chief of Police in Lauderhill, FA, served in various civilian administrative positions in the St Louis Metropolitan, Ft Pierce, FA and New York City Police Departments, and was a police officer in the Madison, WI Police Department. He was a senior researcher at the Police Executive Research Forum (PERF) in Washington, DC. He was the 1996 recipient of the PERF's Gary P. Hayes Award for leadership in improving police service. He is the author of several publications, including *Problem-oriented Policing: Reflections on the First 20 Years*, several of the *Problem-oriented Guides for Police*, *Managing for Success: A Police Chief's Survival Guide* and co-author of *Deadly Force: What We Know. A Practitioner's Desk Reference to Police-involved Shootings in the United States*. He holds a JD from Harvard Law School and a BA in behavioural science and law from the University of Wisconsin-Madison.

Henry Shaftoe is the Award Leader for the Community Safety and Crime Prevention Open Learning Programme at the University of the West of

England, an international distance-learning course with over 150 students worldwide. He has also worked as a consultant with the Safe Neighbourhoods Unit (a national not-for-profit organization) and undertakes research into many aspects of crime prevention and urban security. With a background in social work, community development and architectural design, he is a proponent of the importance of integrating social and environmental factors in any strategy to create safer communities. This is reflected in the wide range of publications he has contributed to, from a schoolteacher's curriculum pack (*Safe for Life*, Nelson), a handbook of security detailing (*Design for Secure Residential Environments*, Longman), to a general overview of crime prevention policy and practice (*Crime Prevention: Facts, Fallacies and the Future*, Palgrave Macmillan). He has carried out work for the European Commission and government departments in Britain and France and is an expert on comparative approaches to urban security in European countries.

Anna Souhami is a research fellow in the Department of Social Policy, London School of Economics. She currently holds a British Academy post-doctoral fellowship in which she is exploring the emergent system for the governance of youth crime in England and Wales. Her previous research in this area explored the radical restructuring of the youth justice system under the Crime and Disorder Act 1998 and questions of occupational culture and identity amongst youth justice professionals, and she is currently completing a book provisionally entitled *Transforming Youth Justice: Occupational Identity and Cultural Change*, which will be published by Willan Publishing in early 2006. She has recently completed a two-year study (with Tim Newburn and Janet Foster) examining the impact of the Stephen Lawrence Inquiry on policing in England and Wales, which will be published by the Home Office in late 2005.

Mike Sutton is Reader in Criminology at Nottingham Trent University. He is Founding Director of the Nottingham Centre for the Study and Reduction of Hate Crime Bias and Prejudice and General Editor of *Internet Journal of Criminology*. The market reduction approach (MRA) originated from research he first conducted in 1993 and subsequently developed whilst working as Senior Research Officer for the Home Office. Mike continues to work with police services to implement the MRA to reduce stolen goods markets with an aim to reduce theft. His other areas of teaching and research interest are hi-tech crimes, general crime reduction, race relations and hate crimes. Researching a number of issues around the theme of what might be termed the bent society, and incorporating many ideas from the rapidly evolving field of cultural criminology, he is currently undertaking and managing a broad programme of research activities with an aim to consolidate knowledge of the dynamics of illicit markets, harmful/illegal business practices and the exploitation of new communications media.

Nick Tilley is Professor of Sociology at Nottingham Trent University and Visiting Professor at the Jill Dando Institute of Crime Science at UCL. He was seconded to the Home Office Research Development and Statistics Directorate as a research consultant for 11 years from 1992. He continues to be Senior Adviser to the Home Office research team based in the Government Office for the East Midlands. His research interests lie in policing, crime prevention and programme evaluation methodology. He is author or editor of eight books and more than 100 reports, book chapters and journal articles. The books include *Realistic Evaluation* (with Ray Pawson), *Crime Reduction and Problem-oriented Policing* (with Karen Bullock), *Crime Science* (with Melissa Smith) and *Gangs* (with Jackie Schneider).

Barry Webb is Deputy Director of the Jill Dando Institute of Crime Science at UCL. He has published on a range of crime topics, particularly car crime, designing out crime and 'what works' evaluations. He has also commissioned a good deal of research on crime and policing in his previous role as a programme director in the Home Office Research Development and Statistics Directorate.

Preface

This book was not originally my idea. Brian Willan (Director of Willan Publishing) suggested that I prepare a proposal, which I duly did. He sent it out for comment and as a result of the responses he received I made quite a large number of changes to both the structure and the authors who would be invited to provide chapters. I'm indebted to those who fed in suggestions for improvements, most though not all of which I followed. I should mention Ron Clarke, Gloria Laycock, Rob Mawby, Ken Pease, Keith Soothill and Martin Wright in particular, since they all bear some credit for what has been produced here. I'd like also to blame them for remaining flaws, but I'm afraid I can't do that since some will be thinking, 'He should have paid more attention to me!'

All but three of the original invitees agreed to take part in this project. And all bar one who promised chapters delivered on their promises, despite illness, floods, job changes, computer failures, diverse competing commitments, hassles with employing organizations, childbirth and all the other distractions of everyday life. Of those who subsequently contributed to the book, though with no disrespect to the individuals first asked, for the most part I think the chapters are at least as good, and in one case certainly far better, than I could ever have hoped for from the person originally invited.

I am hugely grateful to all those who have contributed. Brian Willan and I had hoped that this big book would provide an accessible and authoritative snapshot of where we now are with crime prevention and community safety. Notwithstanding the inevitable gaps that attend any overview, though I may be *parti pris* I do not believe that there is currently a better single source. Moreover, many of the chapters seem to me to take thinking further, and to comprise important statements in their own right.

The idea was that the chapters should be interesting enough for any general reader, thorough enough for the student first coming to crime prevention and community safety, stimulating enough for those already in the field and close enough to practice to be usable by that vast array of people for whom crime prevention and community safety are at least part of their responsibility.

Amongst the latter could be included most of those in central government, many manufacturers, most within service industries, all retailers, most involved in transportation of people and things, all architects and planners, most involved in designing and delivering public services, the preponderance of those working in health and education, many working in the mass media, most of those working across the criminal justice system, as well as those groups with statutory and specified responsibilities – most obviously people within the police and local authorities, and all members of the extended police family. Some capacity constructively to think about crime, crime prevention, order maintenance and feelings of security is, we think, relevant to the work of all those who (often unwittingly) create conditions for crime or suffer its consequences. There is food for thought here, as well as in some cases rather direct implications for action, for all of them. I am proud that the contributors to this volume have provided so rich a set of materials for the broad scope of readers to whom it is pitched.

It should be clear that I am immensely pleased with the way this book has turned out. I hope you, dear reader, for whatever reason you find yourself between its covers, will be enlightened by what you meet. And, if not enlightened, then I hope you will be sufficiently exasperated that you become determined to do better.

Nick Tilley
July 2005

Part I

Background and Context

Chapter 1

Introduction: thinking realistically about crime prevention

Nick Tilley

I began to write this introduction on 4 February 2005. The *Guardian* newspaper had a page-six item with the headline: 'The simple truth: get complex.' It described the efforts of two Danish artists to hand out 1,000 pieces of art in London, each bearing the message: 'Keep life complicated.' These artists had already staged a similar event in Copenhagen and were planning another in New York. In all cases they were trying to repudiate a 'Simple Living' crusade that had evidently begun in California, but then spread into Europe. The artists, Jan Egesborg and Claus Rohland, argued that people found the simple-living message stressful. It failed to match their experience. At the same time the impetus to simplify life, to look at what is fundamental and to cut to the heart of what really matters is, of course, a strong one that is reflected in the influence of the Californian crusade.

As with the rest of life, crime prevention can be seen to be both disarmingly simple and bewilderingly complex. The disarmingly simple side relates to the prosaic, obvious, everyday, commonsense measures that are routinely and widely taken to minimize threats of victimization. They include avoiding seemingly threatening people and places, watching out for danger, trying to protect property from predators and keeping an eye open for those dear to us. The disarmingly simple side relates also to the popular notion that sufficiently severe punishment will either deter or incapacitate wicked offenders, though this version of simplicity is not much addressed in this volume. The bewilderingly complex side relates to the definition and prioritization of 'crime' for preventive attention; the prediction of future crime problems; the choice between differing means of control; the language used to discuss and describe prevention; the processes involved in the implementation of preventive measures; the ethics and aesthetics of differing preventive activities; the politics of agency and organization competency, responsibility and involvement; the measurement of crime patterns and of the intended and unintended consequences of preventive interventions; estimating the costs and benefits of using resources for crime prevention as against other issues; and estimating the costs and benefits of different methods of crime prevention.

The simple side of prevention is not, of course, without appeal or interest, and complexity soon sets in. The prosaic, everyday, lay tactics and strategies we adopt as a matter of course are remarkably akin to those used to provide for biological survival (Farrell 2000). Plants and animals with no protection from threats to their survival clearly perish. It seems likely that we are preprogrammed in the interests of survival to try to side step predation. Many methods – from property marking to barrier creation to surveillance to guardianship, to socialization of the young, for example – go back as far as we can see in history, with adaptations in the details as conditions alter. What gets watched and how in the twenty-first century may differ from what was watched in the first, but watching (surveillance) in the interests of avoiding predation occurred just the same. There can be and perhaps need to be technologically complex means of delivering traditional techniques of prevention in the complex circumstances of modern life stressed in Egesborg and Rohland's art (see Tilley 1995). Contriving property marking, barrier creation, surveillance and guardianship in cyberspace creates different challenges from those faced in twenty-first-century physical space (see Newman and Clarke 2003), just as the nature and meaning of physical space in the twenty-first century differ in a host of respects from those of the first. So, though much that is done in crime prevention may at heart be quite simple, the complex conditions for it make even the simple complex in contemporary contexts. Understanding the moves and countermoves by those trying to avoid predation and would-be predators in a fast-changing technological environment offering new opportunities to both is, in itself, a substantial challenge, even if the underlying logic of what each does is easy to grasp (Ekblom 1997).

But the technical complexity of delivering fundamentally simple means of crime prevention is only the start of the complications of crime prevention policy and practice. Crime prevention methods can be classified in a variety of ways. Brantingham and Faust (1976) distinguish 'primary', 'secondary' and 'tertiary' prevention, referring respectively to the prevention of the crime event in the first place, the prevention of criminality amongst those at risk of becoming involved and the prevention of continued criminal behaviour amongst those already involved in it. Tonry and Farrington (1995) distinguish between 'situational', 'community' and 'developmental' prevention. Tilley *et al.* (2004) differentiate between 'policing and criminal justice mechanisms', 'social intervention mechanisms', 'individual treatment mechanisms' 'and 'situational mechanisms' in the prevention of crime. Ekblom (2005) has attempted to map out the full range of preventive possibilities in his 'conjunction of criminal opportunity'. This distinguishes between eleven generic types of preventive intervention, each of which may address more immediate ('proximal') or more remote ('distal') causes of crime. The classes of cause addressed include: criminal predisposition, lack of resources to avoid crime, readiness to offend, resources for committing crime, decision to offend, offender presence in the situation for offending, the crime target, the crime target enclosure, the wider environment, crime preventers and crime promoters. Each of these has its subtypes and each presents a raft of preventive possibilities. The potential scope of prevention is vast and the means of capturing it highly various. This presents a challenge for the practitioner attempting to reduce crime, for the crime scientist trying to develop effective means of reducing crime and for the criminologist attempting critically to make sense of policies and practices defining crime problems and responding to them.

Much crime prevention effort has gone into trying to lessen dispositions to commit crime. The apparently simple methods already alluded to referred to the sorts of precaution taken by prospective victims. The supply of offenders minded to commit crimes was rather taken for granted. Indeed, for some the disposition to commit crime is uncomplicated: in the absence of any external inhibitors, is it not perfectly natural to take what one wants, or to strike someone one dislikes provided one can get away with it? Proudhon's famous aphorism, 'Property is theft,' implies that it is the institution of private property that constitutes theft as a crime. Using what one wants is otherwise quite natural and non-criminal. Commonly, though, the disposition to commit crimes and more generally to behave in an anti-social manner is deemed problematic and open to a variety of interventions relating to the educational, social, economic, cultural, developmental, genetic or nutritional conditions fostering criminality, or at any rate comprising 'risk factors' associated with criminality (see Farrington 1996, 2002). The biographical, social structural and biological interactions can be complex in relation to specific individuals and their crime careers. There are potentially costly decisions with interventions targeting the 'false positives', those identified as likely offenders who would in any case not commit crime or, worse still, whose disposition to commit crime might be enhanced by labelling and by the engineered association with fellow likely offenders created by some programmes. The potential benefits are maximized the earlier in the process intervention is begun, but the targeting can become more precise, as the revealed anti-social behaviour by some reduces the focus on the false positives. Fine judgement will be needed, though of course relatively light-touch, broad-based, non-stigmatizing interventions do not preclude more intensive interventions amongst the subset who reveal actual criminal dispositions.

The status and underpinnings of the practices and policies of crime prevention raise complex issues. The crime scientists referred to earlier comprise a recently formed group, self-consciously addressing crime prevention using the language and methods of science, and wanting to do for crime what medical scientists aspire to do for disease (see Smith and Tilley 2005). They are interested in formulating hypotheses and testing techniques for preventing crime to discover effective means of pre-empting, inhibiting or reducing it. Others perceive this to be contentious. Crime and its prevention is essentially a social and moral issue. Crime is socially defined, socially committed and elicits social responses. Dominant values (perhaps reflecting the interests of dominant groups) define classes of crime, crime seriousness and responses to crime. Subterranean values (perhaps reflecting patterns of social exclusion) inform criminal behaviour. The shape of particular responses to crime at particular times and in particular places reflects the local contingencies of place, perhaps in terms of the power, interests and values of those involved in criminal behaviour and responses to it. Even those lining up with crime science are unlikely to deny that there are important ethical and aesthetic issues in making judgements on ways of attempting to prevent crime. Ways of preventing crime may be effective but that does not make them acceptable in other ways (see von Hirsch *et al.* 2000). There are, for example, proper concerns about the potential threats to civil liberties from intrusive surveillance methods or from brutal forms of punishment designed to deter, and about the aesthetics of fortresses to keep out the unwanted.

One of the key technical and moral issues for crime prevention relates to its side-effects. And the side-effect most often mentioned relates to displacement. The assumption that some hold seems to be that there is a fixed volume of crime that will come out one way or another. Preventive efforts that fall short of addressing fundamental sources of criminality generally do no more than redistribute the suffering from crime. At worst they may actually increase suffering as determined offenders, repelled from simple, non-violent crimes, out of desperation adopt forcible means. The implications of this 'hydraulic' view of crime prevention (that if it goes down here it must go up somewhere else) are sometimes overlooked. One is that there can be no net impact on crime levels. There would be no more crime were we to abandon all preventive efforts save those directed at criminality. Locks, bolts, safes, airport security, cheque countersignature, credit card chips, security guards and so on, might protect those able to afford them or to afford the best of them but have no net effect on the total volume of crime. They affect only crime distribution. If people are free to use these means, however, the consequential crime distribution is a function of the resources available to and used by different people and groups to protect themselves (see Barr and Pease 1990). Crime distribution becomes a function of variable capacity to resist crime. Pure free-marketers might be happy with that, as might the very rich who are well able to protect themselves. Those of a more egalitarian persuasion ought presumably to come to rather different conclusions about public investment in prevention, even if they believe that the effects of preventive efforts are only to displace! In the event, the evidence about displacement is pretty clear. Whilst it is not possible to be absolutely certain of its extent, studies have consistently failed to find that the displacement of prevented crime has matched measured reductions achieved (see Hesseling 1994). Moreover several studies have shown preventive interventions to have preventive effects beyond their operational range (Clarke and Weisburd 1994). The displacement hypothesis, the non-displacement hypothesis and the diffusion of benefits hypothesis all point towards the utility of preventive interventions, even where they do not address underlying causes of criminality. Except, of course, for the extreme proponent of the free market, where crime and conditions affecting its distribution become a function of market forces.

Michael Tonry suggests a further potential side-effect of crime prevention efforts on public temper and from thence to the expansion of the criminal justice system to try to control crime. He says:

> Now, I think England's massive and continuing investment in crime prevention a mistake. People who are constantly reminded that they should be fearful and protect themselves from criminals become fearful: and that may make them more likely to be more mistrustful and more receptive to populist anti-crime appeals. And, having through assiduous crime prevention programmes created a more fearful populace, England is now busily expanding its criminal justice system to address these fears. The worst of both worlds (Tonry 2004: 56).

This is an interesting piece of speculation by a distinguished American criminologist based at the time of writing at the Institute of Criminology at Cambridge University. Though at first sight plausible, there is no direct evidence for this causal link. Moreover, it would seem doubtful that (rarely reported) piecemeal preventive efforts could compete with the widespread and often alarming news coverage of crime and the profile given to it by populist politicians, as an influence over public opinion concerning crime and punishment. The otherwise excellent book in which Tonry makes this casual comment does, though, rightly highlight the growth of punishment in England as a way of responding to crime, mimicking earlier developments in the USA.

So far in this introduction, the language has all been of 'crime prevention'. Yet this is problematic. The terms 'community safety', 'crime reduction, 'public protection' and 'security' are used too at different times and in different jurisdictions, with substantial overlap but also some variation in meaning. Should the title of this book have referred only to 'crime prevention'? Or should a wider term have been used, to signify relevance to a wider potential readership? The nuances have some political significance. Crime prevention has been deemed a police term, whilst community safety is preferred in local authorities in Britain to signify a broader set of interests in crime consequences, social forms of crime prevention and, at any rate to some, also a set of non-crime hazards as well as those from crime (see Ballintyne *et al.* 2000). In the event as readers will realize we called this book *Crime Prevention and Community Safety*. The coverage certainly goes beyond police crime control competences and includes associated crime harms as well as crime *per se*. Yet it does not extend to issues unrelated to crime. This decision, whilst giving the book a reasonably clear focus, omits some issues that could be included within some of the ways in which community safety can be construed.

Even sticking to crime prevention and associated harms produces dilemmas of coverage. The offence set included in this volume, though quite broad, relates only to a subset of crimes and harms that might form the focus of preventive attention. Professional malpractice, corporate malfeasance, terrorism, fraud, environmental crime, traffic offences, political crimes, anger about crime and most victimless crime, for example, are either not discussed at all or are mentioned only in passing. Instead the bias follows that of both literature and most present practice and policy, in homing in on volume property crime, violence, criminality, drugs and fear of crime. The subsets of crime and disorder that become objects of attention are not arbitrary but reflect, amongst other influences, variations in power and popular assumptions about what matters most. Whilst much that is said about the means of preventing crime may be as applicable to the types of crime that are not discussed explicitly and whilst no volume could cover all crime types, the selection included here largely reflects dominant assumptions about what matters most for policy and practice, and that is properly a matter for analysis and debate.

For the policy-maker or practitioner, the practical selection of approaches to try to prevent crime and avert its damaging side-effects is tricky. Some of the difficulty relates to the identification and analysis of problems, some to the determination of potentially effective means of responding to them, some to the implementation of the measures selected to try to address the problem, some to persuading those capable of acting that they should do so and some to the assessment of the effectiveness of the measures put in place in order that valid and reliable lessons can be learnt for future practice. The commonsense problem-solving approach to crime issues suggests that we first scan the environment for existing and future problems, then subject them to careful analysis to figure out what might be done about them, and on the basis of this develop a strategy to address them, which is then systematically evaluated so that practice may be refined and failed approaches abandoned. This is much easier said than done. Data on problems are often hard to access, partial and inaccurate. Teasing out real patterns to identify underlying problems requires substantial understanding and skill. Finding effective points of intervention and ways of applying them can seem child's play for armchair critics and self-evident after a successful intervention has been put in place, but in practice is difficult and requires subtle analysis of the presenting problem. Moreover, the initially 'obvious' can be quite mistaken, and ill-thought through but well intentioned responses are capable of producing perverse and damaging effects. That possibility is one of the strongest grounds for instituting systems of evaluation, though tracing the consequences of interventions in the messy open-air world of projects and communities is hugely challenging, and the appropriate methods highly contentious.

It has become a commonplace that the effects of efforts to prevent or reduce crime should be evaluated. So-called experimental methods, with randomized control trials taken to be the 'gold standard' (see Sherman *et al.* 1997), vie with so-called realist approaches that question the validity of findings from attempted experiments and aim to devise, test and refine context, mechanism, outcome pattern configurations (CMOCs) (Pawson and Tilley 1997). The experimental methods stress the exclusion of threats to internal validity, trying to be as certain as possible that the measure put in place was associated with producing the outcome to the exclusion of all other plausible possibilities. Realist methods stress the need to know what it was about the intervention that produced its effect(s) and the conditions needed for the effect(s) to be brought about. Both these approaches (and there are others) agree that discerning real from apparent effects is difficult in practice in open-air settings where what is done often differs from what was planned, where a multitude of interventions relating to a multitude of interconnected problems often take place simultaneously, where there can be a wide range of different types of side-effect that need to be balanced against intended effects and where there are understandable calls for inputs and outcomes fully to be costed so that cost-benefit analysis can allow valid comparisons across different patterns of resource allocation. Identifying the time course for effects to kick in and then to fade, and taking account of differences in impact across space and time, add to the complexity in providing useful and valid answers to simple-sounding questions over whether an initiative did or did not represent good value for money. Moreover, by common consent many of the studies that have been produced fail to meet even minimum standards of technical adequacy (Ekbolm and Pease 1995; Sherman *et al.* 1997; Her Majesty's Inspectorate of Constabulary 1998, 2000).

There is a variety of levels at which to pitch crime prevention: the particular target at risk of repeat victimization (and perhaps near-neighbours), the local neighbourhood in which crime problems are most concentrated, the local authority or police force area with responsibilities and some resources to prevent crime, national government with leverage over a range of conditions and behaviours that may facilitate or inhibit crime, or more global organizations and institutions that may shape crime opportunities such as multinational companies whose products and practices may be criminogenic (Read and Tilley 2000). The sale of contraband cigarettes, fuel drive-offs, the theft of high-value, mass-produced electrical goods, the theft of motor vehicles, drugs trafficking and the theft of parts from motor vehicles, for example, all present preventive challenges and opportunities at a variety of levels. Identifying, mobilizing, connecting and implementing multi-level responses to problems that manifest themselves at multiple levels is highly complex and difficult.

In England and Wales, local Crime and Disorder Reduction Partnerships (CDRPs), including the police, local authorities, probation, health and sundry other public, private and voluntary sector invitees, have a statutory responsibility to identify and address local crime and disorder problems. Lining up the organizations and agencies involved, where there is no one lead body and where each organization has its own aims and interests, turns out to be fraught with difficulties, even though the logic of required arrangements seems impeccable. Each organization has much to bring to the crime prevention table; each is typically well intentioned; none on its own has the capacity to address the full range of conditions giving rise to local crime problems; and collectively they promise synergy and the potential to devise and implement short and long-term strategies to address local priority crime and disorder problems. Yet the reality of the conditions for co-operation, for 'joining up' policy and practice, make it deeply difficult: competing demands on the organizations and individuals belonging to them; differences in philosophy, culture and organizational style; lack of dedicated resources; differences over leadership; historic lack of trust; apparent indifference or apathy amongst some; and so on, all conspire to create obstacles to the operation of effective formal partnerships. Efforts to involve the community create a host of further puzzles about whom to involve, how to engage them, what they can do and the means by which they can relate to local formal organizations. Partnership thus raises substantial and knotty theoretical and empirical research questions for students of crime and crime prevention. They also raise complex practical difficulties for those attempting to bring off effective prevention in local settings.

There are widely varying contexts for the application of crime prevention strategies and methods. What might work or be possible in one place or at one time might not be possible or effective in another place and time. 'Policy transfer' describes the adoption in one jurisdiction of policies originating in another (Newburn and Sparks 2004). Processes of globalization mean that crime prevention ideas and methods can travel fast, especially where they have surface plausibility or are ideologically attractive. Neighbourhood Watch, Zero Tolerance Policing, Situational Crime Prevention, Community Policing, Problem-oriented Policing, Crime Prevention through Environmental Design, Drug Abuse Resistance Education (DARE), Scared Straight, COMPSTAT, Family Group Conferences and Restorative Justice, the Boston Gun Project and Communities that Care are just a few of the crime prevention and community safety ideas that have crossed national borders. Though the term 'policy transfer' refers strictly to transnational transfers, parallel processes occur within nation-states as apparently successful projects are 'rolled out' within wider areas or replicated in other places. Issues of policy transfer, programme roll-out and project replication pose a series of theoretical, empirical and practical questions. What counts as a 'real' replication or 'transfer' (Tilley 1996)? How similar must the copy be to the original? In what respects must there be similarity? Will the name alone do? Is the name necessary? Is the only needed similarity the action taken, or does it include the classes of people taking the action? Or does the similarity need to lie in the underlying causal mechanisms though the intervention is expected to produce its effects, regardless of what is done or who does it? Must similar resource levels be included? Must the recipients of the intervention in the copy be akin to those in the original and, if so, in what respects? Normatively, under what conditions and how should replication, roll-out and transfer be attempted? The study, as well as practice of policy transfer, roll-out and replication, requires answers to those tricky and complex questions. Even if they are not made explicit, the practical accomplishment of policy transfer, roll-out and replication will necessarily incorporate assumptions about them that at least the scholar needs to unpack.

It should be clear from the foregoing that crime prevention is ineluctably complex. This means that those for whom crime reduction or community safety is a specialist responsibility either as policy-maker or practitioner need to have a broad grasp of the theory, evidence, circumstances, options, contexts, ethics and possible consequences of varying responses if they are to make informed decisions. The chapters brought together here should provide them with many of the resources they need more fully to think through what they should do or recommend. Policy-makers and practitioners do not have the luxury enjoyed by the student or researcher to stand back and pass lofty judgements about what is being done in the name of crime prevention and the underlying assumptions behind it. They can, though, usefully draw on critical commentaries in efforts to improve what is delivered and to make decisions more knowingly, even if they have to balance a wider range of considerations than those of us inhabiting the ivory towers of academe.

There are, of course, some benefits in simplification. Much insightful scholarship penetrates behind surface complexity and variety to uncover simple structures and processes animating the apparent complexities that are apt to bemuse us. There are some theories that repeatedly crop up in this collection that may help bring some of the confusing complexity to order. The ideas of situational crime prevention, routine activities theory, crime pattern analysis and repeat victimization, in particular, are called on to bring crime patterns to order and to find points where interventions appear promising. But they relate to only part of the complexity of crime prevention and perhaps only a particular means of applying purchase to problems of crime and criminality. Moreover, the scope that these theories have for finding means of controlling crime has as yet been explored in only quite limited ways. There is much room for applying those theories we do have much more fully to a growing range of crime and disorder problems, as there is also scope for theoretical developments aimed at finding further points of leverage on crime problems. Much of this will involve scratching behind a confusing and complex surface to find stable patterns offering potential pinch-points for intervention. Newman and Clarke's study of e-commerce crime and situational means of preventing it comprises a recent example of the former (Newman and Clarke 2003). The chapter by Ross Homel in this volume (Chapter 4), suggesting fresh ways of looking for interventions relating to emerging criminality, comprises an example of the latter.

Some of the chapters in this volume report pessimistic findings over the effectiveness of crime prevention measures that have often been put in place. Few, if any, responses are found universally to be effective. No panaceas have been found. Because of this, because the circumstances for crime and criminality change, and because over time offenders adapt to efforts to thwart them, it may make more sense to try to develop, test and then flexibly to apply strong theories than to look for or expect standard measures mechanically to produce standard effects. Though there may be science in the development and critical test of theories for crime prevention, there is likely to be both art and craft in their deployment (in particular, varying real-world conditions), bringing us back to complexity in practice.

A month after starting this introduction, in early March, I returned to finish it off from a Home Office meeting about 'knowledge management' for crime prevention and community safety. A senior official, though a neophyte to this area of responsibility, asked passionately for one-page summaries laying out simple messages about what local partnerships should do to address crime problems. The urge is understandable. The impatience with academics and academic research is unsurprising. The commitment to effectiveness is commendable. But, as the contributions to this volume make obvious, complexity is unavoidable. In the end Egesborg and Rohland are right. The inescapable complications of crime prevention and community safety need to be acknowledged by researchers, students, practitioners and policy-makers alike. The purpose of this book is to help all those groups better find their way round, to bring at least some order to the ideas and activities involved, but without descending to the misleading and sometimes dangerously simplistic.

The following chapter, by long-time observers of what has been happening to policy and practice in crime prevention and community safety, takes a broad temporal and geographical view of the field, whist focusing on England and Wales as a case study. Drawing on critical realist ideas, Gordon Hughes and Adam Edwards pay particular attention to the importance of context in conditioning the ways in which crime prevention and community safety activities operate. They fetch up with a critique of what they refer to as 'false universalism' and 'false particularism'. The former underestimates the significance of variations in context and the latter the commonalities in conditions faced.

Part II includes a series of chapters that describe major, broad and influential approaches to crime prevention and community safety: situational crime prevention, developmental prevention, community crime prevention, repeat victimization and the mobilization of science. Most of these pick themselves. The odd one out may appear to be the last on mobilizing science. That is included here less because of what has been done historically, and more because of the potential that many see for future improvements in prevention, making use of a broader range of disciplines than have traditionally been much drawn on.

Whilst Part II is about general approaches, the chapters in Part III refer more specifically to means that have been used to prevent crime. There are three chapters on what can be done to design out crime, focusing respectively on products, places and procedures. These are followed by chapters on what the police can effectively do in involving third parties; what might be possible in targeting the market for stolen goods; the potential for focusing on resources for committing crime; the use of publicity in the service of crime prevention; the diversion of youth from crime; and policing for public safety.

Part IV considers what has been done and what achieved in efforts to address some of the types of problem most often focused on in crime prevention and community safety work, though the chapters do not and could not include every crime and crime-related issue that has been addressed. There are chapters on domestic burglary, vehicle crime, crimes against businesses, violent and sexual crime, drugs and alcohol, and issues related to the fear of crime.

The final part of the book focuses on key processes involved in preventing crime or achieving community safety. There are chapters on ways of identifying and analysing crime and disorder problems, methods of deciding what to do about them, means of evaluating the effectiveness of what has been put in place and the partnership context in which much that is done to reduce crime is supposed to take place.

References

Ballintyne, S., Pease, K. and McLaren, V. (eds) (2000) *Secure Foundations: Key Issues in Crime Prevention, Crime Reduction and Community Safety*. London: IPPR.

Barr, R. and Pease, K. (1990) 'Crime placement, displacement and deflection', in M. Tonry and D. Farrington (eds) *Crime and Justice. Vol. 12*. Chicago, IL: University of Chicago Press.

Brantingham, P. and Faust, F. (1976) 'A conceptual model of crime prevention', *Crime and Delinquency*, 22: 284–96.

Clarke, R. and Weisburd, D. (1994) 'Diffusion of crime control benefits: observations on the reverse of displacement', in R. Clarke (ed.) *Crime Prevention Studies. Vol. 2*. Monsey, NY: Criminal Justice Press.

Ekblom, P. (1997) 'Gearing up against crime: a dynamic framework to help designers keep up with the adaptive criminal in a changing world', *International Journal of Risk, Security and Crime Prevention*, 2: 249–65.

Ekblom, P. (2005) 'How to police the future', in M. Smith and N. Tilley (eds) *Crime Science*. Cullompton: Willan Publishing.

Ekblom, P. and Pease, K. (1995) 'Evaluating crime prevention', in M. Tonry and D. Farrington (eds) *Building a Safer Society. Crime and Justice. Vol. 19*. Chicago, IL: University of Chicago Press.

Farrell, G. (2000) 'Crime prevention', in C. Bryant (ed.) *Encyclopaedia of Criminology and Deviant Behaviour*. London: Taylor & Francis.

Farrington, D. (1996) 'The explanation and prevention of youthful offending', in J. Hawkins (ed.) *Delinquency and Crime*. Cambridge: Cambridge University Press.

Farrington, D. (2002) 'Developmental criminology and risk-focused prevention', in M. Maguire *et al.* (eds) *The Oxford Handbook of Criminology* (3rd edn). Oxford: Clarendon Press.

Her Majesty's Inspectorate of Constabulary (1998) *Beating Crime: HMIC Thematic Review of Crime and Disorder*. London: Home Office.

Her Majesty's Inspectorate of Constabulary (2000) *Calling Time on Crime: A Thematic Inspection on Crime and Disorder*. London: Home Office.

Hesseling, R. (1994) 'Displacement: an empirical review of the literature', in R. Clarke (ed.) *Crime Prevention Studies. Vol. 3*. Monsey, NY: Criminal Justice Press.

Newburn, T. and Sparks, R. (eds) (2004) *Criminal Justice and Political Cultures: National and International Dimensions of Crime Control*. Cullompton: Willan Publishing.

Newman, G. and Clarke, R. (2003) *Superhighway Robbery*. Cullompton: Willan Publishing.

Pawson, R. and Tilley, N. (1997) *Realistic Evaluation*. London: Sage.

Read, T. and Tilley, N. (2000) *Not Rocket Science? Problem-solving and Crime Reduction. Crime Reduction Research Series Paper 6*. London: Home Office.

Sherman, L.W., Gottfredson, D., MacKenzie, D., Eck, J., Reuter, P. and Bushway, S. (1997) *Preventing Crime: What Works, What Doesn't, What's Promising*. Washington, DC: US Department of Justice, Office of Justice Programs.

Smith, M. and Tilley, N. (eds) (2005) *Crime Science*. Cullompton: Willan Publishing.

Tilley, N. (1995) 'Seeing off the danger: threat, surveillance and modes of protection', *European Journal of Criminal Policy and Research*, 3: 27–40.

Tilley, N. (1996) 'Demonstration, exemplification, duplication and replication in evaluation research', *Evaluation* 2: 35–50.

Tilley, N., Smith, J., Finer, S., Erol, R., Charles, C. and Dobby, J. (2004) *Problem-solving Street Crime*. London: Home Office.

Tonry, M. (2004) *Punishment and Politics: Evidence and Emulation in the Making of English Crime Control Policy*. Cullompton: Willan Publishing.

Tonry, M. and Farrington, D. (1995) 'Strategic approaches to crime prevention', in M. Tonry and D. Farrington (eds) *Building a Safer Society. Crime and Justice: A Review of Research. Vol. 19*. Chicago, IL: University of Chicago Press.

Von Hirsch, A., Garland, D. and Wakefield, A. (eds) (2000) *Ethical and Social Perspectives on Situational Crime Prevention*. Oxford: Hart.

Chapter 2

Crime prevention in context

Gordon Hughes and Adam Edwards

Introduction

Debates over crime prevention, in particular evaluative arguments over 'what works, what doesn't and what's promising' (Sherman *et al.* 1997; Petrosino *et al.* 2000), have been preoccupied with the problem of generalization. Counterpoised to those seeking universal claims about the applicability of crime prevention strategies and criteria for their evaluation are those who emphasize the 'indigenous' qualities of crime and control (De Haan 1992; Willis *et al.* 1999). It has been argued, perhaps most influentially by David Garland (2001), that this tension between generalization and specificity is unavoidable; either one aims at eliciting the broad structural patterns of crime and control, whilst inviting the criticism that the patterns so identified obscure particular local experiences, or one conducts detailed local case studies which may provide rich descriptions of such experiences but are limited in their broader significance for criminological thought and practice. Whilst individual authors cannot escape this dilemma in their own analyses, the best that can be hoped for is that the 'scholarly community as a whole' encompasses a division of intellectual labour between researchers in which 'Sweeping accounts of the big picture can be adjusted and revised by more focussed case studies' and 'An accretion of small-scale analyses eventually prompts the desire for more general theoretical accounts' (Garland 2001: vii–viii).

Conversely, we wish to argue that the trade-off between generalization and specificity is a false one, premised on a predominant but misleading conception of explanation in the social sciences. Social scientists have, according to philosophical realists, too often adopted the natural scientific model of causation as a premise for studying social relations. The 'Humean' or 'successionist' model of causality, in which generalizations inform and are informed by the observation of regular events, misunderstands the qualitatively different character of the objects of social as opposed to natural science. Whereas the latter are sometimes capable of being observed in controllable, laboratory conditions, social relations are 'open systems' that are subject to change and alteration precisely because their objects

– human beings and their inter-relationships – are reflexive and thus capable of altering their behaviour on the basis of monitoring their own actions (Sayer 2000: 10–17). Reflexivity implies that we should expect observations of regularity in social relations to be scarce and therefore alternative criteria of explanation are needed. This, we believe, can be found in the critical realist method of articulation whose key features are worth sketching out as a justification for our belief in the importance of contextual knowledge about crime prevention and as a prelude to our illustration of contextual analysis in relation to contemporary crime prevention policy-making in England and Wales.

Certain implications for explanation follow from an acknowledgement that social relations, like crime and its prevention, are open-ended. Whether the real causal powers or mechanisms that social relations necessarily have, by virtue of their structure, are actually activated is a contingent feature of the different conditions these relations inhabit (Bhaskar 1975). It can be argued, for example, that any crime event is structured by the necessary presence of certain mechanisms, such as a supply of motivated offenders and suitable targets, and the absence of others, such as capable guardians or controls (Cohen and Felson 1979). The activation of these mechanisms depends, however, on the particular conditions in which they are exercised, these conditions being other mechanisms, such as changes in local labour and housing markets (cf. Hobbs 2001), the manufacture of high-value and highly portable consumer durables (Clarke 1995), the decisions of public authorities to expand or reduce the provision of leisure and educational facilities for young people, changes in the tolerance for and censure of transgressive behaviour and so on and so forth.

These conditions are not simply the backdrop to, but are *constitutive* of, interactions between crime and control. From a critical realist perspective they cannot, therefore, be 'controlled' for in some quasi-natural scientific experiment. Rather, explanation of these interactions proceeds through a focus on concrete processes of crime and control in particular places and certain moments, articulating what causal mechanisms were activated in these concrete instances and identifying how, in turn, they were generated by the structure of crime control interactions. As Sayer (2000: 15) notes, 'events arise from the workings of mechanisms which derive from the structures of objects, and they take place within geo-historical contexts'.

Context, then, is central to any evaluative understanding of crime prevention because it is constitutive of concrete crime prevention events and processes not just the tangentially relevant vessel in which such activity occurs. To view context as constitutive is, however, to attribute a particular technical meaning to this concept. Context is not restricted to the determinant effect of macro-social transitions, such as the 'rise of market society' (Taylor 1999) or 'late modernity' (Young 1999). Rather, it is to acknowledge the spatial and temporal scales of social relations, which can include such macro-theoretical concerns but can also accommodate the local conditions of crime and control (Sayer 2000: 133). A key insight of 'geohistorical' explanations of social relations is an understanding of their 'uneven development' not only between but within national territories (Massey 1984).

It is this insistence on geohistorical accounts that distinguishes the evaluative

15

understanding of crime prevention that we wish to cultivate from both the broad-sweeping research into 'general' patterns of crime control (Petrosino *et al.* 2000; Garland 2001) and idiographic studies of particular localities (Keith 1993) that have hitherto polarized arguments over crime prevention.[1] In the remainder of the chapter, we wish to illustrate the conceptual gains that can be made through this focus on the geohistories of crime prevention, specifically the need for research to be self-conscious about the spatial and temporal scales of its analysis and its putative relationship to insights that can be gleaned from research conducted at other spatial and temporal scales.

We begin with an account of key policy shifts in England and Wales over the past three decades in recognition of the continuing importance of the national scale of analysis, not least because it is the level at which criminal legal codes and justice systems are constituted. The very logic of crime prevention, however, is to take control beyond criminal justice simultaneously exhorting civil society to assume greater responsibility for its own security. Our contention is that as soon as this twin movement is accepted, the implication for research is that the constitutive effects of the extra-legal, political, economic and cultural contexts of crime become even more compelling. Further and apropos findings from other geohistorical research, we can expect a regional unevenness in the constitutive effects of these contexts at the subnational level. We conclude with a discussion of the future challenges for producing contextual knowledge of crime prevention.

The British experience: from the crisis of criminal justice to the preventive solution?

For much of the twentieth century the criminal justice system in Britain was largely insulated from overt political criticism and public scrutiny, being celebrated for its 'difference', being 'above party politics', 'unique' in character and best left to 'the experts'. This was related to the hegemonic and symbolic presence of the legal discourse surrounding criminal justice. As McLaughlin (1998: 162–4) notes, it meant that all governments had to tread very warily because the criminal justice system deals with fundamental symbolic issues of principle – rights, duties, order, equity, justice and punishment – that lie at the heart of a social order that is governed by the rule of law.

Alongside this privileged presence for criminal justice, the postwar social democratic welfare state was also committed to state-sponsored social reform, and the eradication of the causes of criminality, by means of both social and individualized programmes of rehabilitation, inside and often beyond the correctional system. Such preventive programmes in turn were experiments devised by social scientific experts. There was much optimism about the potential capacity and desirability of the state to engineer social change and to usher in an end to poverty, deprivation and discrimination by direct state intervention. Looking back, the mid-twentieth-century regimes of prevention via treatment and rehabilitation and community development now appear as part of an age of criminological optimism. By the post-Second World War period and the rise of the social democratic welfare state, positivist thinking, both psychological and sociological, on crime and its prevention was an integral part of the institutions of government and of the welfare state's programme of national reconstruction. There was a widespread belief that the political will and scientific means now existed to remould and improve virtually all aspects of society. The new professions of the welfare state were given the responsibility to intervene proactively in society's whole range of social ills, not least in treating crime and its prevention scientifically. Positivist crime prevention strategies, particularly those targeted at juvenile delinquency and the 'problem family', were thus an important element in the postwar welfare settlement in the UK and across many Western societies (Hughes 1998). Here we have the social democratic moment of crime prevention in the UK which proponents of the post-1970s crime prevention often ignore.

The last decades of the twentieth century witnessed a growing strain on the criminal justice system, and the allied correctional and rehabilitative regimes of the 'welfare-penal complex' (Garland 2001). This was in part as a consequence of the broader crisis tendencies affecting capitalist societies and their states but it was also due to the ideological marriage of neoliberal individualism and authoritarian conservatism. This crisis of the welfare-penal complex was associated with:

- the increasing rate of recorded crime and the numbers of people passing through the different parts of the system, despite the growing affluence and the welfare state;

- overload combined with a crisis of efficiency (e.g. the declining clear-up rates of the police, overloaded courts and the overcrowding of prisons);

- a growing awareness of extensive social and economic costs of crime; and

- the increasing recognition that formal processes of criminal justice (i.e. detection, apprehension, prosecution, sentencing and punishment of offenders) have only a limited effect on controlling crime.

This pessimism has also been connected with a crisis of confidence, most notably across the USA and UK, in the effectiveness of the social democratic rehabilitative ideal, captured in the phrase, 'nothing works'.

In response to the widespread acknowledgement of this crisis of the criminal justice system, two preventive logics have come to the fore internationally since the 1980s, namely, primary situational crime prevention and social crime prevention. These logics capture a key problematic which remains at the heart of crime prevention theory and practice, namely, the possible tension between reducing opportunities through situational measures and social modes of intervention (see Crawford 1998: 140). Situational crime prevention chiefly concerns 'designing out' crime and opportunity reduction, such as the installation of preventive technologies in both private and public spaces. Social crime prevention, on the other hand, is focused chiefly on changing targeted social environments and the motivations of offenders, and 'community' development initiatives. Social crime prevention measures thus tend to focus on the development of schemes, such as youth clubs and activity-based projects, to deter potential or actual offenders from future offending. Common to both elements of situational and social crime prevention is their claim to be less damaging and more effective than traditional (reactive and 'law and order') justice approaches. They also share a new emphasis on targeted risk management and a commitment to a strategy of 'responsibilization' for all actors and agencies in civil society. According to Tim Hope (2004), the new crime prevention objective – in which situational crime prevention is the dominant logic – is to maximize private security and social conformity in a liberal democracy which inscribes values of responsibility and personal liberty. As a consequence, Hope contends that the pursuit of individual self-interest is assumed to aggregate into a common good.

Both situational and social approaches have long submerged histories (Hughes 1998), but recent decades have witnessed a key shift in terms of their political salience in the field of crime control, both within Britain and beyond it. As Adam Crawford has noted (1998: 35):

> the 'nothing works' pessimism has precipitated a criminological shift away from the offender as the object of knowledge towards the offence – its situational and spatial characteristics – as well as the place and role of the victim ... As a consequence, a new prominence began to be accorded to crime prevention and community safety, with appeals to informal control and wider responsibility.

In turn David Garland (2001) is even bolder in his assertion of the new preventive consciousness associated with late modernity. According to Garland (2001: 17), the new preventative sector is not to be understood merely as an annex or extension of the traditional criminal justice system:

> On the contrary. The new infrastructure is strongly oriented towards a set of objectives and priorities – prevention, security, harm-reduction, loss-reduction, fear-reduction – that are quite different from the traditional goals of prosecution, punishment and 'criminal justice' ... Today's most visible crime control strategies may work by expulsion and exclusion, but they are accompanied by patient, ongoing, low-key efforts to build up the internal controls of neighbourhoods and to encourage communities to police themselves (but see also Hughes 2004d).

The national context: manufacturing the new 'local' governance of crime reduction and community safety in Britain

In this section, and continuing with our national case study of England and Wales, the main features of the contemporary legislative and institutional contexts are outlined in order to help unpack the discursive movements from 'crime prevention', to 'community safety' and latterly on to 'crime and disorder reduction' in recent years. There is a highly prescriptive and directive central government shaping of the contemporary reductive landscape in Britain with simultaneously both enabling and constraining consequences for a whole range of actors and agencies. Furthermore, this is indicative of what may be termed a sovereign state strategy which stresses greater control alongside the diffusion of responsibility for crime control (Stenson and Edwards 2004).

Central government shaping of the field

The local governance of this field has been on a statutory footing since the Crime and Disorder Act (CDA) 1998 in England and Wales. However, its roots can be found in Home Office and Conservative government developments since the 1980s and most clearly in the report of the Morgan Committee of 1991, set up by the Home Office to review the local delivery of crime prevention (Edwards and Hughes 2002). Two of the latter's recommendations have emerged as the foundation for the central government approach: 1) the introduction of the two concepts of community safety and (increasingly) crime and disorder reduction to signify a comprehensive and targeted local approach to crime control (as against crime prevention more narrowly defined); and 2) a clear statutory responsibility for local authorities, alongside the police, for delivering the multi-agency partnership approach.

Two further features of the approach instituted in the CDA 1998 illustrate a general concern to avoid overt political considerations in the framing of local prevention strategies. They are associated with the virtual exclusion of elected representatives from effective involvement in managing crime in the community (Hughes 1998). First, there has been a concern to develop an executive administration for crime prevention within a multi-agency framework, through the involvement of the office of local authority Chief Executive, who along with the Chief Officer of Police, acts as the responsible authority for crime prevention. The CDA was thus in Hope's (2004) terms a 'politically satisficing' solution to a long-term dilemma, namely, how to incorporate local authorities into crime reduction without antagonizing the police and threatening their operational autonomy. Secondly, the official guidance since the CDA has emphasized the primacy of objective data analysis and the model of rational, 'evidence-based' policy-making, as the cognitive basis for partnership strategies, disseminated from central government by new expert criminologists of everyday life in the Home Office (Hope 2004). As a consequence, there has been an emphasis on the administrative and managerial rather than the political nature of crime prevention and community safety activity. However, changes associated with central government's 'modernizing agenda' on local government, particularly with regard to local political leadership, since the turn of the present decade, may well be increasingly disturbing the administrative and managerial partnership settlement of the local governance of crime, disorder and safety.

The key elements of the post-1998 framework include legislation requiring and enabling local government to address issues of crime and disorder, and the establishment of local Crime and Disorder Reduction Partnerships (CDRPs), resting upon the new statutory duties imposed upon local government (for a fuller discussion, see Gilling, Chapter 25, this volume). However, this framework is also associated with a new regime for public auditing of local government performance and service delivery ('Best Value') arising out of the Local Government Acts 1999 and 2000. This auditing element may have the most significant impact on the future governance of crime and disorder given that the regime of incentives and penalties associated with Best Value scrutiny constitutes a powerful disciplinary tool to bring about compliance (McLaughlin *et al*. 2001; Hope 2004). This noted, it is possible that this may in practice often be 'paper' compliance rather than genuine compliance (Hughes and Gilling 2004).

Changing discourses of prevention, safety and reduction

There now exist well established legislative and institutional arrangements for bringing about the compliance of local government to deliver services concerning crime and disorder. And yet there remains uncertainty about the question of towards what purposes, standards and values of 'community safety' is such compliance being directed (Hope 2004)? The official definition of the primary purpose of the new local governance of crime is that of crime (and increasingly disorder) reduction. However, there is another response to the insecurity of the private citizen that has also characterized the recent history of local government in Britain – that of community safety (Hughes 2002a). The implementation of these arguably different policy objectives may be producing an underlying tension in the resulting local practices which have not been acknowledged sufficiently by either legislators or researchers to date. As Tim Hope (2004) observes, whilst the goal of crime and disorder reduction is associated with concerns about the performance and delivery of services that would attain the aim of reducing the incidence of crime (including anti-social behaviour that has 'crime-like' consequences), in contrast, the goal of community safety reflects an aspiration to construct a new public good of safety in response to a range of actual and perceived risks and harms. The attainment of such a 'public good' (Jordan 1996) aspires to contribute to the 'quality of life' of citizens and consequently is associated with identifying and addressing community needs for safety rather than a narrower obsession with targeted crime reduction. The scrutiny and disciplinary logic arising from the introduction of the new public management into central-local government relations is thus uncovering a struggle to conceptualize and develop values, criteria and standards for the goods of safety and security to be delivered to citizens which remain contested and profoundly unfinished. These struggles too can be seen as a consequence of the contradictions and ambiguities between the contrasting notions of 'crime (and disorder) reduction' and 'community safety'.

According to Ken Pease (Wiles and Pease 2000; Byrne and Pease 2003), community safety is a misnomer as the function circumscribed within the CDA for it deals only with the sources of danger occasioned by human agents acting criminally or in disorderly ways. This:

> distorts the recognition and prioritisation of all the threats to safety which a community may encounter, and neglects the distributive justice which is appropriately achieved by the equitable sharing of unavoidable risks ... Rather than start with crime per se we believe it would be more useful to start with the broader issue of hazard and hazard management, of which crime and disorder are then sub-sets (Byrne and Pease 2003: 287–8).[2]

Despite this important clarification of the distinction between the two terms, the dominant discourse promoted by the Home Office agenda remains one where community safety is a subset of crime and disorder reduction rather than vice versa.

Further legislative and institutional developments from national government have occurred since the watershed legislation of the 1998 CDA and the Local Government Acts 1999 and 2000. The Police Reform Act 2002 included amendments to the CDA with tackling the levels and patterns of drug misuse established as a new statutory responsibility for CDRPs. In turn the Anti-social Behaviour Act 2003 has further extended the tasks and legal responsibilities of partnerships with regard to anti-social behaviour. From 2003, the cross-government National Drug Strategy is to be delivered (in part) by local partnerships. From 2005, responsible authorities via their CDRP/Drug Action Team (DAT) will have to produce two strategies, one relating to crime and disorder and one relating to drug misuse. In turn, there is now a Home Office national Public Service Agreement (PSA) target for reducing crime and the fear of crime. National targets to be met by 2006 with regard to reducing vehicle crime, domestic burglary and robbery have also been set and local partnerships are required to prioritize these alongside local crime and disorder targets.

Local partnerships continue to be seen as being at the forefront of work associated with the central government's stated commitment to delivering a reduction in crime, the fear of crime, anti-social behaviour and in reducing the harm that drugs cause to communities, individuals and their families. Partnerships are also meant to make a significant contribution to a number of other central PSA targets associated with the communitarian-inspired civil-renewal agenda, such as increasing voluntary and community sector activity and making sure that the views of local people are taken into account.

Finally, recent years have witnessed the growing importance of regional government structures across Britain. There are now nine regional offices in England each with a Home Office team dedicated mainly to supporting crime reduction. The National Assembly for Wales is responsible for comparable monitoring and advice in Wales. Their main tasks in formal terms are liaison between local CDRPs and the Home Office; co-ordinating bids from the region and identifying regional priorities; and acting as the first point of contact for partnerships within the region. The regional government office crime reduction teams have been given a mandate to monitor work of CDRPs in meeting the evolving national targets and modernization agenda. According to some commentators (Byrne and Pease 2003: 295), the regional government offices should be viewed primarily as the agencies which act as conduits for central government funds and thus enable central government oversight of CDRPs to an extent not hitherto possible. In our view it is too early to be certain of the consequences of this piece of the jigsaw although the centralizing thrust of national government is difficult to ignore. Further research on the emergent regional infrastructure around crime reduction and community safety, the possibility of divergent regional political cultures and thus different translations of the problems of crime control and public safety remains to be done.

Taking stock of the national experiment

In any overview of the changing national context of crime control in the UK, it is difficult to ignore the growing salience of the developing local and, increasingly, the regional institutional architecture and allied institution-building associated with the new governance of crime and disorder. Partnership has become both a key technique of the new local and regional governance and more specifically a vital rhetorical principle of 'prevention' and 'safety' policies, involving, on the surface, the rearrangement of responsibilities between central government, public services and local government, the sharing of responsibilities between the police and local government, alongside a dispersal of responsibilities between public and voluntary agencies and private interests in local communities.[3]

The processes associated with the rise of local preventive partnerships and the increasingly strident appeals to 'community' as the site, agency and effect of governance has been termed the new 'community governance of crime control' (Edwards and Hughes 2002). As already noted, this political project is heavily influenced by managerial ideas. However, an equally significant source of ideological inspiration is that of moral authoritarian communitarianism (Hughes 1996, 2004b). The British state is at the forefront of contemporary attempts both to 'modernize' and 're-moralize' the nation, not least by appeals to governing through communities as simultaneously the site, agency and effect of the local governance of crime.

Such developments raise major questions about where the new institutional expertise and its division of labour may be heading. Central to the argument here is the contention that the debate on the future of these new forms of expertise is not one that can be treated as a purely technical exercise. Rather, the governmental projects associated with CDRPs, embedded in 'arm's length' relations and requiring new agencies and agents ('partnerships'), are both structurally unstable and morally and politically volatile: about the very definition of the field; about the forms of power and professional domination within the field; about which communities get to be 'safe'; etc. (Clarke 2002: 12; Hughes 2004a). For example, as a result of the recognition that effective crime control strategies must be rooted in the dynamics of local communities, and New Labour's determination to clamp down on disorder and the 'anti-social', we appear to be witnessing an intensive re-territorialization and re-moralization of highly localized crime control strategies (see McLaughlin 2002; Stenson and Edwards 2004).

What lessons may be drawn from the British experience and its national 'context'? The discussion has shown that a managerial and auditing culture is pronounced across most agencies and sites in which discourses of evaluation, audit, monitoring, target-setting and performance measurement have a pervasive presence and influence. A local partnership approach is widely promoted as the most effective and 'economic' means of both promoting crime reduction and alleviating the consequences of social exclusion. There is a renewed enthusiasm for the state, both nationally and locally, having a communitarian mission to reconstruct and remoralize the nation, and especially those 'anti-social' and 'socially excluded' populations. There is a consensus across politicians, policy-makers and practitioners with regard to the importance – at least rhetorically – of informal, 'community-based' social control mechanisms as well as formal criminal justice measures. In turn crime prevention is increasingly promoted as needing to be pluralized and dispersed throughout the social fabric. Finally the logic of 'managing' crime and disorder coexists alongside the persistent punitive vision of control. The extent to which these national and international trends are unsettled and reworked in subnational, local contexts will be addressed in the next section.

Looking elsewhere: defining and refining contexts

In this section the chapter changes 'gear' conceptually and empirically. First it moves beyond the British nation-state frame of reference both in its focus on other national cases but also more crucially in highlighting other contingent and determinate contexts than that of the national. This discussion begins by outlining in brief the international trends in crime prevention, focusing in particular on three comparative ideal types on crime prevention or security regimes. However, we also contend that the retention of the nation-state frame in comparative criminological work on crime prevention and public safety is itself inherently limiting if superficially neat. As a consequence the chapter goes on to discuss the potential importance of both supranational and subnational contexts as well as the national, drawing on examples across a range of political and cultural traditions as well as sociospatial localities across Europe.

Three logics of security

Much recent criminological literature confirms that crime prevention and the new local politics of public safety appear to be achieving a global, if uneven, pre-eminence as a pattern of crime control in part as a reaction to the growing doubts about the capacity of the nation-state to guarantee and supply order and security to citizens in their everyday lives (Hughes 1998; Garland 2001). Much is also made in contemporary social and political theory of the emergence of a new world order following the collapse of the Soviet bloc and the rise of a global economy (Giddens 1998). Whatever the merits and limitations of these grand narratives, it is widely accepted in the social sciences that important transformations in the ordering of societies are both clearly evident and significant. In particular, it has been argued that there has been a shift across 'late modern' societies in the way in which crime and disorder is governed. And how we govern crime and disorder is of course related to how we govern ourselves. In turn there are strong arguments that crime prevention and the politics of security are becoming increasingly 'Americanized' rather than globalized (Hughes *et al.* 2002a; Stenson and Edwards 2004).

In an important intervention in the comparative criminology of crime prevention and of the new politics of security, Hebberecht and Duprez (2002) has suggested that three basic logics of security, may be distinguished across Europe.

1. *Neoliberal security* – premised on an individualized, actuarial logic of risk assessment and management.

2. *Social democratic security* – premised on a logic of collective solidarity that presumes safety will be produced through a more egalitarian redistribution of economic and political resources.

3. *Moral conservative security* – premised on a cultural logic that presumes safety will be produced by the presence of morally authoritative formal and informal controls on otherwise debased individuals.

Hebberecht and Duprez suggest that these strategies are present throughout Europe, albeit the admixtures of these strategies vary from country to country in accordance with the changing political contexts in which they were promoted and challenged.

Convergence and divergence in strategies of prevention

Comparative criminological research suggests that there are convergent and divergent processes at play as a result of which there is a redefinition of the governance of security and crime control occurring across Europe and in particular at the local level. Institutionally there is now a growing number of new actors and emergent occupational practices involving new methods and technologies – not least through the technique of partnership – of 'policing' and 'security' across many European nation-states (Crawford 2000; Hughes 2004c). Alongside these institutional developments there is the parallel articulation of new problems, ranging from the control of local disorders and incivilities and minor but persistent street crimes, to the management of the volatile mobilities of migrant peoples. And in turn, we see the rise of locality-based policies which attempt to get the public authorities closer to local populations and their fears.

Amongst some of the key points of policy and political convergence across contemporary European nations are the pluralization of local policing and the rise of multi-agency partnerships, the growth of crime prevention and reduction strategies alongside historically dominant criminal justice policies. We are also witnessing the common recognition of wider social harms and problems in addition to crime *per se* alongside technical approaches to the management of risks. More worryingly for liberals and human rights supporters alike these developments coexist alongside populist communitarian appeals for order and safety in the wake of the new global mobilities, with the conflation of 'migrant'/'asylum seeker'/'terrorist' (Hughes 2004b). Perhaps, the latter is the most striking of all shared European trends, including the demonization of the 'anti-social' outcast within (van Swaaningen 2005).

However, the story is not a simple one of political and policy convergence. There remain, for example, significant differences in the degree to which the rhetoric and practice of 'evidence-based policy-making', the 'whole of government' mantra and the 'what works' paradigm of policy evaluation has crossed the Channel and the Atlantic from the UK and the USA, despite current attempts by the European Union's Crime Prevention Network to disseminate this brand of policy transfer thinking and practice. Nelken (2000: 3) has also suggested that Garland's analysis of the ways in which the state in 'Anglo-American' countries is divesting itself of some of its responsibilities in crime control has less obvious and general application in 'the state-centred societies of Continental Europe where, in some respects, it is only now that the state's responsibility to protect its citizens from street crime is becoming a top priority'. Another key divergence between nations and localities is over the very vocabulary used to translate problems of 'crime reduction', 'community safety', 'social harm', 'public security', etc., in different European societies and regions. Suzanne Karstedt's (2004: 19–20) comments on the different 'translations' of 'community' in Germany as against the UK and USA are especially instructive here:

> Crime policies comprise more than a technology, a practice or a strategy. They have to be conceptualised as integrated concepts, which have emerged in a particular institutional setting and in a legal and public culture of crime prevention and control. They are decisively local and national. Specific values and symbolic meanings are as much part of them as are particular institutional designs. The difficulty of even literally 'translating' these concepts … make the problem of 'transport', 'import' and 'export' obvious. There is no proper term in German for 'community crime prevention' that can grasp its semantic, in particular not the context of the social fabric of a neighbourhood and community. The translation only refers to the political body of the municipality, but misses out on the sense it has in the context of the UK and the USA.[5]

Crime prevention is therefore as much a matter of cultural meaning as what David Nelken (2002: 175) describes as 'instrumental effectivity'. The conceptual and practical problems of translation thus remain central and pressing despite superficial similarity across nations (Newburn and Sparks 2004: 7). None the less there is currently a fast-growing 'export and import' trade and flow in ideas involving criminologists, criminal justice experts, policy-makers and practitioners – or what Karstedt (2004) refers to as 'epistemic communities' – in this field. The 'policy transfer' debate on the question of 'how does crime prevention *and safety* policy travel?' has now entered the critical academy (see Hughes *et al.* 2002; Newburn and Sparks 2004). The collection of studies in Newburn and Sparks' edited text lend support to the editors' claim that 'it is the socio-political and cultural context in which "transfer" occurs, or is attempted, that has the most profound effect on the eventual shape and style of the policy concerned' (Newburn and Sparks 2004: 5). Such debates open up the investigation of the *intra-* and *trans-*national, as well as *inter-*national developments in the governance of public safety as one of the most exciting and challenging fields for criminological research. It is clear that we may learn as much from diversity as from uniformity, within the nations, across Europe and globally.

The subnational and local contexts of crime control

The above typology of three security logics (or crime prevention and security regimes) should not be read as describing specific nation-states and their logics of security. However, most comparative research to date in the area does commit this cardinal error of focusing on the national level, whether in terms of nation-state, or national culture.[6] In the league table of advanced capitalist democracies, to paraphrase Gosta Esping-Andersen (1990: 1), states vary considerably with regard to their accent on crime control and law and order, with the USA as a truly exceptional case in its deployment of punitive and exclusionary strategies as well as privatized preventive technologies. Whilst accepting this unevenness between nation-states, it is also crucial to note that differences *within* nation-state territories in terms of local political cultures can be greater than the differences between them. Furthermore, nation-states are often 'default units of analysis in debates on policy transfer in crime control because criminal justice is used as the organizing framework for understanding policy change' (Stenson and Edwards 2004: 228). This critique of existing comparative research is especially important in alerting us to the distinction between criminal justice and crime control. Crime control, of course, impacts on the entire social policy spectrum and it will also have more 'histories' to it than just the legal history. Again, Stenson and Edwards (2004: 229) point to the importance of the local political, economic and cultural, as well as legal histories.

This theme of the localities effect is developed in an intriguing case study of a 'Middle England' small town by Girling *et al*. (2000). Noting that most criminology is mesmerized by the 'drama, romance, glamour and degradation of the city', Girling *et al*. study the 'criminological terra incognito' of a medium-sized English town. As a result of their 'place-sensitive sociology of public sensibilities toward crime', they show that much of the 'fear of crime' and concerns over community safety is largely about 'the protection of certain places or territories (houses, streets, communities, nations) against incursions, usually seen as arising from elsewhere' (2000: 10). Furthermore, their local 'place-sensitive' research shows that the conflicts that pervade the debates on crime and its prevention or control – such as the responses to the perceived limitations of local public policing and the possible support for the privatization of patrol and guardianship functions – are played out in specific places 'to particular and not entirely predictable conclusions' (2000: 164).

The collection of local case studies in Hughes and Edwards (2002) lend support to the argument for treating appeals to community in public safety practices as irreducibly political in nature. These case studies also suggest that this local politics of community governance is necessarily spatialized and its understanding needs to be 'place-sensitive'. It is contended that a crucial limitation of most commentaries on the national politics of crime control in 'Britain' is that they ignore the effect the diverse social, economic and political histories and the consequent cultural milieux that particular localities have on the generation of problems such as crime and disorder and on the governmental responses to these problems. As a consequence, such commentaries provide relatively indeterminate accounts of the actual conduct of crime control 'on the ground', since all centres of political authority, whether supranational, national, regional or local, encounter an 'implementation gap' between their legislative and policy commands and the practice of government. It is clear that central authorities are dependent on subordinate policy actors to enact their commands and it is in the interstices of this interdependent relationship that local actors can resist, contest and manipulate central commands to fit their own agendas and 'translations' (see also Hughes and Gilling 2004). In Newburn and Sparks' (2004: 9) words, 'Influential models and dictions meet resistances, counter-discourses and extant traditions and sensibilities'.

According to Edwards and Hughes (2002: 10–13), local case studies suggest that what is often most insightful about the actual conduct of community governance is its diversity. For example, in Roy Coleman *et al.*'s (2002) study of the Safer Merseyside Partnership, the latter's role in reasserting the sovereign authority of commercial and corporate interests in the regeneration of Liverpool city centre is plotted. The authors contend that this reassertion of sovereign authority is 'translated' through the coercive policing and surveillance of those disenfranchised populations that are believed to threaten capital accumulation. This coercive strategy is bought at the cost of public investment in services for the socially excluded and in turn neglects the social harms perpetrated by corporations.

A very different local political context is highlighted in Kevin Stenson's (2002) research on 'Middle England'. In his study of the affluent Thames Valley area, Stenson documents the consequences of the shift from a universal provision of public services to the targeting on 'hotspots' of crime and social disadvantage. The use which departments in Whitehall make of various audits of crime and social exclusion in deciding the allocation of grant-aid and other sources of public investment may disadvantage partnerships located in affluent regions. For, whilst High Wycombe is ranked as the fifteenth wealthiest local authority district in the UK, it none the less has pockets of high crime, victimization and poverty that are visible only through audits conducted at the level of enumeration district. Given their consequent exclusion from access to government funding programmes through these processes of audit, local agencies and policy coalitions in the Thames Valley region have had to lever in resources through 'experimental' crime control programmes on, for example, restorative justice, problem-oriented policing and domestic violence. Notwithstanding its location in a region dominated by Conservative Party politics, the Thames Valley Police and associated partnership initiatives, for example, have, as a result, acquired a considerable reputation for their liberal and innovative ethos.

In his comparative analysis of community governance in the cities of Leicester and Nottingham in the East Midlands of England, Edwards (2002) examines the strategic dilemmas of the partnership approach to crime control. Such dilemmas include the problem of how co-operative agencies within partnerships can be, when forced to compete amongst themselves and other local partnerships for limited financial and other resources, or how open a partnership can be to the complex milieu of interests in a locality without compromising its capacity to act. Whilst there are formal similarities in the recent political economy of these two localities, there were, in the mid 1990s, significant differences in their apprehension of these dilemmas. These local strategic dilemmas emphasize the analytical and practical importance of political agency in understanding the powers of partnerships.

Finally, Simon Hallsworth (2002) draws upon his research into responses to street crime in southeast London to explore further the rhetorical nature of appeals to community governance and challenge the tendency, in both administrative and critical criminological research, to misrepresent the practice of crime control partnerships. Based on his analysis of practices in southeast London, Hallsworth argues that both critics and supporters of crime reduction strategies overestimate the rationality of policy-making and implementation 'on the ground'. In reality local partnership practice is more chaotic and 'labyrinthine' not least because it is characterized by a 'deficit' of the political resources that would be needed to deliver either the empowerment or coercion of local communities.

Understanding the importance of localities is, or at least should be, central to debates over the transferability of crime control and public safety policies across diverse social contexts. Furthermore, an appreciation of this effect is necessary if policy-makers are to anticipate and minimize any unintended consequences of emulating imported practices that originate in very different contexts and circumstances, ranging from New York ('zero tolerance policing') to Kirkholt or Huddersfield ('repeat victimization') (Edwards and Hughes 2002: 14). Adam Crawford's (2000) comparative research into victim–offender mediation initiatives across specific localities in France and England lends further support to the claims made above, given his finding that specific initiatives were 'pulled in different, and often competing, directions as they try to meet the multiple aims and objectives and satisfy the divergent demands of the different constituencies' (Crawford 2000: 207).

Context, locality and indigenous criminology

The standard dictionary definition of indigenous is 'native born, originating or produced naturally in a country, not imported'. In contemporary comparative criminology the term has been used either to describe ways of criminological thinking in countries outside the USA (Willis *et al.* 1999) or to describe the modes of governance associated with indigenous peoples in several post-colonial societies (Cuneen 2003). Our use of the term is distinct from both these in important respects. Following Willem De Haan's (1992) initial exploration of the idea, the 'indigenization' of criminological thought is used to describe theory that is 'naturally produced in a region' and that reflects 'local or group specific experiences'. Although there are some difficulties with De Haan's notion of 'natural production', we suggest this emphasis upon locality may play an important role in moving criminology on from a comparative design set in nation-state terms and towards a greater, though not exclusive, focus on the subnational.

Such a comparative indigenous criminology would begin to ask such questions as: 'if a person lives in London, might he or she not have a greater affinity in many respects with residents of capital or "global" cities in other European countries (Berlin, Paris, Rome, etc.) than with residents in provincial towns (let alone rural localities) in his or her own country of residence?' This conceptual reframing may have profound implications for the predicates of comparative criminological research. A leading comparativist, David Nelken (1994, 2000), for example, is careful to delineate the predicates of his comparative research to that of legal culture and criminal justice institutions and actors. Of course it makes sense to organize comparative research into criminal justice on inter-national terms. However, if the predicates of comparison are shifted from the strictly legal to the political, economic and cultural contexts of control and ordering more generally (and as is necessary in studying crime prevention and security policies), it becomes more difficult and more problematic to sustain the exclusive use of nations as the common denominators of comparison. Does it not make greater sense to compare capital cities with other capital cities, and in turn port cities, large industrial second cities, small towns or rural communities with others in other countries? We would speculate that the political, economic and cultural history and trajectory of Liverpool, for example, may potentially have more in common with Bilbao, Rotterdam, Hamburg and Marseilles than it has with London or much of 'middle England'. It may be that this is a mistaken claim and that the differences between European countries are more significant for the purposes of comparative criminology than the differences between localities within them. None the less, taking the proposition that there may be distinct local political cultures of crime control is a necessary prerequisite of testing the continued preoccupation with inter-national comparison. The argument for this proposition is strengthened further by current debates over the 'hollowing-out' of the nation-state as a consequence of so-called processes of 'glocalization' in which the growth of increasingly global relations, political, economic and cultural, acts to emphasize local differences, not least in the differential capacity of localities to adapt to the global economy.

Finally is it legitimate to ask whether comparative research should restrict itself to what Adam Crawford (2000: 205) has termed the excavation of 'the cultural embeddedness of particular strategies of crime control'? There is no easy or definitive answer to this question. However, it is indicative of what we may term the 'cultural anthropological' turn in criminology. Perhaps if we replace the search for either uniformity or uniqueness with the search for necessity and contingency, a comparative criminology may be built that delivers concrete studies of crime and control in particular localities that illuminates the generic aspects of crime and control whilst producing explanations of how these aspects are configured in particular places and moments.[7]

Conclusion

This chapter has offered a critique of both the false universalism and acontextuality of much policy transfer literature on crime prevention and the false particularism of postmodernist accounts of crime control. In turn it has been argued that contexts are not just 'containers' of the real stuff of prevention and safety practices, but instead are constitutive of the very structure and content of these practices. The discussion in this chapter also confirms that crime policies in general and preventive policies specifically are as much about politics, economics and cultures, and the normative and ideological, as about rational debates about techniques that work according to evidence-based evaluation. There cannot be in Nelken's (1994) terms 'a culture-free theory of crime' and nor can there be a culture-free theory of crime prevention. Furthermore, there is in Pat O'Malley's (2004) words, a 'constitutive role for politics' in the governance of harm and risk. And just as there can be no 'pre-political' mode of risk management, so there can be no pre-political techniques of crime prevention and public safety. In accord with the political and normative goals of critical and progressive scholarship, we need to follow the advice of the Australian criminologist, Adam Sutton (forthcoming), in arguing that advocates of crime prevention as a viable political alternative to 'law and order' need to recognize that crime prevention and community safety must 'work' at the symbolic and normative levels (for example, associated with the advocacy of social inclusion, social justice and non-punitive and restorative principles) as well as at the technical and cost-effective levels.

Selected further reading

A highly influential text on the importance of understanding the place of context in evaluating 'what works' in crime prevention is Ray Pawson and Nick Tilley's *Realistic Evaluation* (1997). The most sustained statement on the critical realistic perspective in the social sciences which underpins the arguments in this chapter is Andrew Sayer's *Realism and Social Science* (2000). For an introduction to the critique of the seemingly context-free, apolitical paradigm of crime prevention, see Gordon Hughes' (1998) *Understanding Crime Prevention: Social Control, Risk and Late Modernity* (Chapter 1) or Tim Hope's 'Introduction' to *Perspectives on Crime Reduction* (2001).

There is a growing number of texts which provide detailed accounts of the socioeconomic and political contexts of crime prevention in Britain. These include Dan Gilling's *Crime Prevention* (1997); Gordon Hughes (1998 – see above); Adam Crawford's *The Local Governance of Crime* (1997); and Gordon Hughes and Adam Edwards' *Crime Control and Community* (2002). For a discussion of both UK and international trends in safety and the preventive turn, see Les Johnston and Clifford Shearing's *Governing Security* (2003); Gordon Hughes, Eugene McLaughlin and John Muncie's *Crime Prevention and Community Safety: New Directions* (2002); and Adam Edwards and Gordon Hughes' 'Comparing safety in Europe: a geohistorical approach' (2005). For a compelling account of the late-modern cultural, political and economic contexts behind the rise of the new crime control complex, see David Garland's *Culture of Control* (2001). For a critique of Garland, which draws on the research findings from the national and local contexts of preventive partnerships in England and Wales, see Gordon Hughes' 'Straddling adaptation and denial: crime and disorder reduction partnerships in England and Wales' (2005).

Notes

1. With the notable exception of the work of Pawson and Tilley (1994, 1997, *inter alia*), who have applied realist philosophy to an understanding of how and under what conditions policy mechanisms can block criminal acts. Whilst Pawson and Tilley's

scientific realism is compatible with the *critical* realist philosophy of explanation that we wish to advance, it has been criticized as a 'limited instance' of realist explanation because it focuses on the policy mechanisms rather than on 'the structures and circumstances from which the mechanisms derive' (Sayer 2000: 23). It is in questioning the structural properties of crime prevention that we are interested in its political, economic and cultural contexts. For a full discussion of these questions see Edward and Hughes (2005, and forthcoming).

2. Ken Pease's position on the difference between the two signifiers 'crime reduction' and 'community safety' is one the authors have previously articulated and endorsed but with different conclusions drawn (Hughes 2000a; Edwards and Hughes 2002).

3. For a full discussion of the practice of partnership as a vehicle for delivering effective and ethical crime prevention, see Gilling (Chapter 25, this volume).

4. With regard to contemporary European 'nightmares', Timothy Garton Ash (2004) has argued that Britain faces a 'Janus dilemma' today. According to Garton Ash, Britain has four faces. 'The back and front faces can be labelled "island" and "world"; the face on the left says "Europe" and that on the right "America". No wonder Britain's head aches' (2004: 4). Island and world appear opposites (as virulently articulated around the new migrations and mobilities) but the connection is direct and simple. 'The world has now come to the island because the island first went to the world' (Garton Ash 2004: 5). This peculiarity is not unique to Britain but is shared, with important local differences, across most if not all European countries. As Garton Ash (2004: 6) notes, 'Every other European country has its own version, though usually less extreme, of island versus world, if one takes "island" to mean not the mere condition of being land surrounded by water (a physical fact of ever-diminishing importance) but the nurtured peculiarities of a real or claimed exceptionalism'.

5. See also Crawford's (2000) analysis of the crucial differences in the uses of appeals to 'community'/'communauté' in Britain and France.

6. This is the case for the literature generated from otherwise very different ends of the administrative/positivist and critical/interpretivist continuum of criminology. See, for example, Graham and Bennett (1995) from the administrative side to Hebberecht and Duprez (2002) from the critical end.

7. For a fuller discussion of the critical realists distinction between necessity and contingency, see Edwards (2002) and Edwards and Hughes (2005).

References

Bhaskar, R. (1975) *A Realist Theory of Science*. Leeds: Leeds Books.

Byrne, S. and Pease, K. (2003) 'Crime reduction and community safety', in T. Newburn (ed.) *Handbook of Policing*. Cullompton: Willan Publishing.

Clarke, J. (2002) 'Reinventing community? Governing in contested spaces.' Paper presented at the 'Spacing for social work' conference, Bielefeld, 14–16 November.

Clarke, R. (1995) 'Situational crime prevention', in M. Tonry and D. Farrington (eds) *Building a Safer Society*. Chicago, IL: University of Chicago Press.

Cohen, L. and Felson, M. (1979) 'Social change and crime rate trends: a routine activity approach', *American Sociological Review*, 44: 588–608.

Coleman, R., Sim, J. and Whyte, D. (2002) 'Power, politics and partnerships: the state of crime prevention on Merseyside', in G. Hughes and A. Edwards (eds) *Crime Control and Community: The New Politics of Public Safety*. Cullompton: Willan Publishing.

Crawford, A. (1997) *Local Governance of Crime*. Oxford: Clarendon Press.

Crawford, A. (1998) *Crime Prevention and Community Safety*. London: Longman.

Crawford, A (2000) 'Contrasts in victim-offender mediation and appeals to community in France and England', in D. Nelken (ed.) *Contrasting Criminal Justice*. Aldershot: Ashgate.

Cuneen, C. (2003) 'Thinking critically about restorative justice', in E. McLaughlin *et al.* (eds) *Restorative Justice: Critical Issues*. London: Sage.

De Haan, W. (1992) 'Universalism and relativism in critical criminology', *The Critical Criminologist*, 14: 7–8.

Edwards, A. (2002) 'Learning from diversity: the strategic dilemmas of community-based crime control', in G. Hughes and A. Edwards (eds) *Crime Control and Community: The New Politics of Public Safety*. Cullompton: Willan Publishing.

Edwards, A. and Hughes, G. (2002) 'Introduction: the new community governance of crime control', in G. Hughes and A. Edwards (eds) *Crime Control and Community: The New Politics of Public Safety*. Cullompton: Willan Publishing.

Edwards, A. and Hughes, G. (2005) 'Comparing safety in Europe: a geohistorical approach', *Theoretical Criminology*, Special Edition, 9(3)1: 345–63.

Edwards, A. and Hughes, G. (forthcoming) 'The politics and ethics of transferring prevention'.

Esping-Andersen, G. (1990) *Three Worlds of Welfare Capitalism*. Cambridge: Polity Press.

Etzioni, A. (1995) *The Spirit of Community*. London: Fontana.

Garland, D. (2001) *The Culture of Control*. Oxford, Oxford University Press.

Garton Ash, T. (2004) 'Janus-faced Britain', *Guardian*, 6 June.

Giddens, A. (1998) *The Third Way*. Cambridge: Polity Press.

Gilling, D. (1997) *Crime Prevention: Theory, Policy and Politics*. London: UCL Press.

Girling, E., Loader, I. and Sparks, R. (2000) *Crime and Social Change in Middle England: Questions of Order in an English Town*. London: Routledge.

Graham, J. and Bennett, T. (1995) *Crime Prevention Strategies in Europe and North America*. Helsinki: Helsinki United Nations Institute.

Hallsworth, S. (2002) 'Representations and realities in local crime prevention: some lessons from London and lessons for criminology', in G. Hughes and A. Edwards (eds) *Crime Control and Community: The New Politics of Public Safety*. Cullompton: Willan Publishing.

Hebberecht, P. and Duprez, D. (eds) (2002) *The Prevention and Security Policies in Europe*. Brussels: VUB Brussels University Press.

Hobbs, D. (2001) 'The firm: cultural logic on a shifting terrain', *British Journal of Criminology*, 41: 549–60.

Hope, T. (ed.) (2001) *Perspectives on Crime Reduction*. Aldershot: Ashgate.

Hope, T. (2004) 'The new local governance of crime reduction', in M. Emmerich (ed.) *Public Services under New Labour*. London: IPPR.

Hughes, G. (1996) 'Communitarianism and law and order', *Critical Social Policy*, 16: 17–41.

Hughes, G. (1998) *Understanding Crime Prevention: Social Control, Risk and Late Modernity*. Buckingham: Open University Press.

Hughes, G. (2000a) 'Community safety in the era of the risk society', in S. Ballintyne *et al.* (eds) *Secure Foundations: Issues in Crime Prevention, Crime Reduction and Community Safety*. London: IPPR.

Hughes, G. (2000b) 'In the shadow of crime and disorder: the contested politics of community safety', *Crime Prevention and Community Safety*, 2: 47–60.

Hughes, G. (2002a) 'Plotting the rise of community safety: critical reflections on research, theory and politics', in G. Hughes and A. Edwards (eds) *Crime Control and Community: The New Politics of Public Safety*. Cullompton: Willan Publishing.

Hughes, G. (2002b) 'The audit culture and crime and disorder partnerships: exorcising the wicked issue of community safety', *Crime Prevention and Community Safety*, 4: 9–18.

Hughes, G. (2004a) 'The community governance of crime, justice and safety: challenges and lesson-drawing', *British Journal of Community Justice*, 2: 7–20.

Hughes, G. (2004b) 'Communities, crime prevention and the politics of articulation', *Australian and New Zealand Journal of Criminology*, 37: 1–12.

Hughes, G. (ed.) (2004c) 'The prevention and safety politics in Europe', *Community Safety Journal* (special edition), 3(1).

Hughes, G. (2004d) 'Straddling adaptation and denial? Crime and disorder partnerships in England and Wales', *Cambrian Law Journal*, 34(4): 1–22.

Hughes, G. and Edwards, A. (2002) (eds) *Crime Control and Community: The New Poltics of Public Safety*. Cullompton: Willan Publishing.

Hughes, G. and Edwards, A. (2004) 'Beyond community safety?' *Community Safety Journal* (special edition), 3(1): 1–7.

Hughes, G. and Gilling, D. (2004) 'Mission impossible: the habitus of community safety manager and the new expertise in the local partnership governance of crime and safety', *Criminal Justice*, 4: 129–49.

Hughes, G. and McLaughlin, E. (2002) 'Together we'll crack it: partnership and the governance of crime prevention', in C. Glendinning *et al.* (eds) *Partnership, New Labour and Governance of Welfare*. Bristol: Policy Press.

Hughes, G., McLaughlin, E. and Muncie, J. (2002a) 'Teetering on the edge: the futures of crime control and community safety', in G. Hughes *et al.* (eds) *Crime Prevention and Community Safety: New Directions*. London: Sage.

Hughes, G., McLaughlin, E. and Muncie, J. (eds) (2002b) *Crime Prevention and Community Safety: New Directions*. London: Sage.

Johnston, L. and Shearing, C. (2003) *Governing Security*. London: Routledge.

Jordan, B. (1996) *A Theory of Poverty and Social Exclusion*. Cambridge: Polity Press.

Karstedt, S. (2004) 'Durkheim, Tarde and beyond: the global travel of crime policies', in T. Newburn and R. Sparks (eds) *Criminal Justice and Political Cultures*. Cullompton: Willan Publishing.

Keith, M. (1993) *Race, Riots and Policing: Lore and Disorder in a Multi-racist Society*. London: UCL Press.

Massey, D. (1984) *Spatial Divisions of Labour*. London: Macmillan.

McLaughlin, E. (1998) 'Probation, social work or social control', in G. Hughes and G. Lewis (eds) *Unsettling Welfare*. London: Sage.

McLaughlin, E. (2002) '"Same bed, different dreams": postmodern reflections on crime prevention and community safety', in G. Hughes and A. Edwards (eds) *Crime Control and Community: The New Politics of Public Safety*. Cullompton: Willan Publishing.

McLaughlin, J., Muncie, J. and Hughes, G. (2001) 'The permanent revolution: New Labour, new public management and the modernisation of criminal justice', *Criminal Justice*, 1 (3): 301–18.

Nelken, D. (1994) 'Whom can you trust? The future of comparative criminology', in D. Nelken (ed.) *The Futures of Criminology*. London: Sage.

Nelken, D. (ed.) (2000) *Contrasting Criminal Justice*. Aldershot: Ashgate.

Nelken, D. (2002) 'Comparing criminal justice', in M. Maguire *et al.* (eds) *Oxford Handbook of Criminology*. Oxford: Oxford University Press.

Newburn, T. and Sparks, R. (2004) 'Criminal justice and political cultures', in T. Newburn and R. Sparks (eds) *Criminal Justice and Political Cultures*. Cullompton: Willan Publishing.

O'Malley, P. (2004) 'The uncertain promise of risk', *Australian and New Zealand Journal of Criminology*, 37.

Pawson, R. and Tilley, N. (1994) 'What works in evaluation research', *British Journal of Criminology*, 34: 291–306.

Pawson, R. and Tilley, N. (1997) *Realistic Evaluation*. London: Sage.

Petrosino, A., Farrington, D., Weisburd, D. and Sherman, L.W. (2000) 'Proposal for a Campbell Criminal Justice Group.' Paper presented at the February meeting of the Campbell Collaboration, University of Pennsylvania, 24–25 February (http://www.campbellcollaboration.org/FraAbout.html).

Sayer, A. (2000) *Realism and Social Science*. London: Sage.

Sherman, L., Gottfredson, D., Mackenzie, D., Eck, J., Reuter, P. and Bushway, S. (1997) *Preventing Crime: What Works, What Doesn't, What's Promising. A Report to the United States Congress*. College Park, MD: University of Maryland, Department of Criminology and Criminal Justice.

Stenson, K. (2002) 'Community safety in Middle England – the local politics of crime control', in G. Hughes and A. Edwards (eds) *Crime Control and Community: The New Politics of Public Safety*. Cullompton: Willan Publishing.

Stenson, K. and Edwards, A. (2004) 'Policy transfer in local crime control: beyond naïve emulation', in T. Newburn and R. Sparks (eds) *Criminal Justice and Political Cultures*. Cullompton: Willan Publishing.

Sutton, A. (forthcoming) *Understanding Crime Policy: The Honest Criminologist's Guide*.

Sutton, A. and Cherney, A. (2003) 'Crime prevention and reduction', in A. Goldsmith *et al.* (eds) *Crime and Justice*. Pyrmont, NSW: Thomson Legal.

Taylor, I. (1999) *Crime in Context: A Critical Criminology of Market Societies*. Cambridge: Polity Press.

Van Swaaninigen, R. (forthcoming) 'Public safety and the management of risk'.

Wiles, P. and Pease, K. (2000) 'Crime prevention and community safety: Tweedledum and Tweedledee', in S. Ballintyne *et al.* (eds) *Secure Foundations*. London: IPPR.

Willis, C., Evans, T. and Lagrange, R. (1999) '"Down home criminology": The place of indigenous theories of crime', *Journal of Criminal Justice*, 27: 227–38.

Young, J. (1999) *The Exclusive Society*. London: Sage.

Part II

Approaches to Prevention

Nick Tilley

The chapters in Part II describe some major approaches to preventing or reducing crime. Each describes a different broad way of looking at crime and crime problems and what that has already meant, or might in the future come to mean, for effective prevention.

The first (Chapter 3) is by Ronald Clarke. Though now based in the USA, Clarke previously conducted research in the Home Office in Britain, where he developed the theory of situational crime prevention in the late 1970s and profoundly influenced a generation of researchers and practitioners. The notion that opportunity caused crime and that reducing or removing opportunities for crime could effect reductions of it without equivalent displacement, was and is a radical one, challenging many assumptions about 'root causes' of criminality and the need to address them to have an impact on crime levels. Clarke's influence is evident in many other chapters in this handbook, where use is made of the typology of preventive techniques which he has developed over the past quarter century. In his chapter Clarke answers seven criticisms of situational crime prevention: that it is simplistic and atheoretical; that it has been shown not to work; that it diverts attention from the root causes of crime; that it comprises a conservative, managerial approach to crime; that it promotes an exclusionary society; that it promotes Big Brother and restricts personal freedoms; and that it blames the victim.

Australian Ross Homel has long been interested in crime prevention and has previously made major contributions to the literature on situational crime prevention and policing. More recently he has led studies of pathways to crime and their disruption. In Chapter 4 he examines the way in which criminality develops and the means by which that development might be averted. Homel distinguishes between interventions that focus on risk factors that have been found to be associated with the future development of criminality, from those that focus on 'pathways' and 'transitions' which may be critical to the stimulus or inhibition of emergent criminality. The former approach is more familiar and Homel reviews the literature relating to it. He highlights the need for early intervention in what is often seen as a linear development of criminality, which is set in motion in early years. The latter, though not denying the importance of cumulative and connected developments through life, describes a subtle effort to trace patterns in the uneven development of contingencies which occur as we grow up and which may mark turning points leading us towards or away from criminal careers. Certain transitions, for instance those associated with changing schools, are highlighted as potential branching points, where existing trajectories may either be maintained or altered, either leading towards or away from criminal involvement. This way of looking at criminal development suggests points at which there may be a need as well as opportunity for intervention in relation to criminal careers.

George Kelling has been for many years writing influentially about communities and crime prevention in the USA. He is, perhaps, best known for his Broken Windows theory developed with James Q. Wilson. In Chapter 5 Kelling describes in some detail a 'Safer Cities' initiative in Newark, New Jersey, in which he and Rutgers University have played a major part. This scheme has been operating for five years, has involved numerous agencies and organizations, and has succeeded in drawing in members of the community. Kelling describes the slow and at times painful way in which the group developed. He also describes the problem-oriented approach that was adopted, and the need in that for prolonged analysis properly to define and understand issues prior to taking action. He identifies several features that he believes to have been especially important in the initiative. Administratively, these include bi-weekly meetings of a fistful of agencies and community members; case conferences relating to high-risk individuals; and face-to-face 'schmoozing' to contrive to get things done, overcome blockages and build trust. The 'treatment modalities' include: 'notification sessions' that identified problem people must attend, where they are told that their continued behaviour will elicit concentrated enforcement attention, that the difficult conditions in which they live are appreciated, and that they will be helped to turn their lives around; 'accountability sessions' to which notified problem people would return to check on their behaviour and on that of others supposed to help them; '"rev up" sessions' where local clergy with moral authority prepare the ground for practical support; 'enhanced enforcement and service' to improve collaborative, targeted delivery; a 'gun strategy' that requires all individual cases to be reviewed to determine needs, and also involved the local community; and 'public awareness and outreach' promoting the message that violence is unacceptable.

In Chapter 6 Graham Farrell, a pioneer in repeat victimization research on both sides of the Atlantic, provides an up-to-date review of what is now known about patterns of repeat victimization and the ways in which repeat victimization provides points of potential intervention to prevent crime. He describes the consistent and by now quite well established research findings identifying repeat patterns of crime across a wide range of offence types, which provide indications of promising points for preventive intervention. This work has largely focused on repeats of same offence types against the same target, for instance repeat burglary. Farrell highlights in addition other important but less widely recognized repeat patterns, including repeat tactics, repeat offence times, repeat nearby offences, and repeat targeting of the same victim but across different crime types. He also describes the overlaps between varying forms of repeat. Farrell notes the main, though not exclusive, emphasis so far given to residential burglary as a focus for repeat victimization reduction, and the scope for findings more often to be applied much more widely. He also refers to the shortage so far of well implemented and evaluated initiatives to ascertain best methods of reducing crime by attending systematically to repeat patterns. This may in part follow from a variety of 'tricky issues', which Farrell identifies, in bringing off successful repeat victimization work and learning from it.

Ken Pease has, like Graham Farrell with whom he has written widely, been a pioneer in repeat victimization research. He was also the inspiration behind the development of 'crime science' and the foundation of the Jill Dando Institute of Crime Science at University College London. In Chapter 7 he discusses what the natural sciences have ostensibly done and what science and engineering might do in the future to inform means of controlling crime. He notes, in particular, the scope for much greater and much better integrated application of science and engineering to issues of crime control. He highlights the ways in which crime problems change with new opportunities, the challenges these chronically present to those wishing to prevent crime and the scope there is for science and engineering to be mobilized in the service of crime reduction. He deems it more likely that we shall be able to anticipate and forestall new crime opportunities than to deal effectively with the recurrent stimuli and dispositions to behave criminally. Crime, as he puts it, 'will remain the hum in the machine of emotional, social and economic life'. Science and technology can, he believes, help reduce or eliminate criminal opportunities.

If Pease is right, the social sciences are not the only academic disciplines that can contribute to understanding and preventing crime. Indeed, the other sciences may in the end be found to have as much or more to offer. There may be benefits from the co-operation of those working in the social and physical sciences. There are some signs that this may be happening in the UK through streams of work that are being funded by the Engineering and Physical Sciences Research Council. Time will tell.

Chapter 3

Seven misconceptions of situational crime prevention

Ronald V. Clarke

Situational crime prevention has its origins in research undertaken by the Home Office Research Unit in the 1970s. At its most simple, it can be described as the art and science of reducing opportunities for crime – 'science' because a large body of theory and research now buttresses situational prevention, and 'art' because, despite this research, practitioners still have to rely heavily on their own judgement and experience in implementing projects. In fact, situational prevention is now almost a synonym for opportunity reduction, and most of the work done in its name is implemented without any detailed knowledge of its scientific underpinnings. In brief, these consist of the following:

1. A strong body of theory concerning the relationship between situational factors and crime.

2. An action research methodology that begins by focusing on a highly specific form of crime and then follows through with a) an analysis of the contributory factors; b) the identification of responses tailored to these factors; c) the selection and implementation of those responses most likely to be effective and accepted; and d) the assessment and dissemination of the results.

3. A classification of 25 situational prevention techniques.

4. A collection of evaluated case studies, including findings about displacement.

Lack of familiarity with this research base has not impeded the growth of situational prevention – some commentators believe it is the fastest-growing form of crime control worldwide – but it has resulted in some poorly thought-out initiatives whose failures have fuelled criticisms of the approach, especially by criminologists. This chapter reviews the most frequent criticisms and argues that they are overstated and generally misconceived. They flow from the ideological positions of the critics buttressed by a limited view of the causes of crime.

The first section of the chapter deals with theoretical criticisms of the approach and the second with related criticisms of its effectiveness. The subsequent sections deal more briefly with ethical criticisms and supposed social harms. Each section begins by briefly outlining the criticism without attributing it to particular individuals because in every case it is common and widely expressed. Then, the defence is mounted in considerably more detail. Table 3.1 serves as guide to the structure of the chapter and an aide-memoire of the main points argued.

Situational prevention is simplistic and atheoretical

This is the criticism that situational prevention ignores the vast body of criminological research establishing that the 'root' causes of crime lie in deprivation resulting from genetic inheritance, personality and upbringing, or from social, cultural, racial and economic disparities. This deprivation results in the development of delinquent or criminal dispositions that are the primary drivers of criminal behaviour. Situational and opportunity factors might help to

Table 3.1 Seven misconceptions of situational crime prevention

Criticism	Rebuttal
1. It is simplistic and atheoretical	It is based on three crime opportunity theories: routine activity, crime pattern and rational choice. It also draws on social psychology
2. It has not been shown to work; it displaces crime and often makes it worse	Many dozens of case studies show that it can reduce crime, usually with little displacement
3. It diverts attention from the root causes of crime	It benefits society by achieving immediate reductions in crime
4. It is a conservative, managerial approach to crime	It promises no more than it can deliver. It requires that solutions be economic and socially acceptable
5. It promotes a selfish, exclusionary society	It provides as much protection to the poor as to the rich
6. It promotes Big Brother and restricts personal freedoms	The democratic process protects society from these dangers. People are willing to endure inconvenience and small infringements of liberty when these protect them from crime
7. It blames the victim	It empowers victims by providing them with information about crime risks and how to avoid them.

determine when and where crime occurs, but they do not play a role in whether crime occurs. This being so, opportunity reduction is largely irrelevant. The only effective way to prevent crime is to deal with its root causes through psychological, social or political interventions. This requires theoretical understanding of the complex relationships between the various forms of deprivation and the development of criminal dispositions. Generating this theoretical understanding is the core focus of criminology. To suggest (as do the advocates of situational prevention) that there is a direct link between opportunity and crime is to oversimplify the determinants of human behaviour.

This criticism of situational prevention may have had more legitimacy when first expressed because the early papers outlining the approach based it on a simple 'choice' model of crime (e.g. Clarke 1980). Quite soon, however, this basic model was expanded into the more developed rational choice perspective (Cornish and Clarke 1986; Clarke and Cornish 1985, 2000) and supplemented by routine activity theory (Cohen and Felson 1979; Felson 2002) and crime pattern theory (Brantingham and Brantingham 1993) to give situational prevention a stronger theoretical base. The focus of each of the theories is somewhat different, as follows:

- Routine activity is a 'macro' theory that seeks to explain how changes in society expand or contract opportunities for crime. These opportunities are mediated by the supply of suitable targets for crime (such as the proliferation of high-value, light-weight electronic goods) and the availability of capable guardians who protect targets (custodians, park keepers, shop assistants and so forth).

- Crime pattern theory has a 'meso' neighbourhood or community focus, and seeks to explain how offenders seek or stumble across opportunities for crime in the course of their everyday lives.

- The rational choice perspective, a 'micro-level' theory, deals with the decision-making processes that result in an offender choosing to become involved in crime and selecting specific crimes to commit.

Because these theories give an important role to situational factors in crime they are sometimes called *opportunity* theories. Because they differ from most other criminological theories in that they seek to explain the occurrence of crime, not the development of criminality, they are sometimes called *crime* theories. Finally, David Garland (2000) has called them the 'criminologies of everyday life' because they treat the occurrence of crime as theoretically unproblematic, resulting from normal human impulses of greed and selfishness.

In their original formulations, these theories stopped short of arguing that opportunity causes crime. However, this claim was made more recently by Felson and Clarke (1998) in *Opportunity Makes the Thief*, a pamphlet written for the Home Office. The claim strengthens the case for reducing opportunities for crime because it helps to explain why displacement does not inevitably result from situational prevention. The grounds for making the claim are therefore reviewed below.

The role of opportunity in crime

Nobody familiar with criminology, including the advocates of situational prevention, could deny the importance of the commonly regarded 'root' causes of crime. But those advocates believe that immediate situational and opportunity factors have an equally important causal role in crime. In fact, crime is the outcome of an interaction between criminal dispositions and situational temptations and opportunities, and the offender's decision-making is the medium through which these two sets of factors bring their influence to bear. Dispositional factors might make the offender more prepared to break the law, but the perception of crime opportunities (temptation) also motivates the offender to commit crime. In this model, opportunity not only plays a determining role in the time and place of crime, but it also plays a vital role in eliciting criminal behaviour. It does so in four main ways:

1. Criminally disposed individuals will commit a greater numbers of crimes if they encounter more criminal opportunities.

2. Regularly encountering such opportunities could lead these individuals to seek even more opportunities.

3. Individuals without pre-existing dispositions can be drawn into criminal behaviour by a proliferation of criminal opportunities and temptations.

4. More particularly, individuals who are generally law-abiding can be drawn into committing specific forms of crime if they regularly encounter easy opportunities for these crimes.

In this model, opportunity has a much stronger causal role in crime than the advocates of situational prevention first thought. In a radical departure for the day, they claimed only that opportunity plays an important part in crime. This claim can now be amply documented, but proof is still lacking of the causal role of opportunity outlined in the four points above, partly because few studies have sought to examine this role and partly because experiments to increase opportunities for crime would be considered unethical. 'Lost letter' experiments (Farrington and Knight 1980), the laboratory studies of Stanley Milgram (1974) on obedience, and Hartshorne and May's (1928) early experiments on deceit with children do indicate that a wide range of subjects will take opportunities to behave dishonestly and even cruelly when these are presented to them, but it would be questionable to generalize from these findings to serious forms of crime.

What, then, are the grounds for believing that opportunity is a cause of crime? There are several different sources of evidence, none of which is incontrovertible, but which together provide strong grounds for asserting a causal relationship. First, a large body exists of evaluated case studies (briefly reviewed below) showing substantial reductions in specific forms of crime following situational interventions. Few of these studies employ strong evaluative designs, and all could be criticized on methodological grounds, but taken together they establish that removing opportunities can reduce crime – sometimes dramatically. Secondly, offenders often report in interviews with researchers that opportunity led them to commit particular crimes (see, for example, Box 3.1). Whilst these statements might be doubted, they do provide strong presumptive evidence that encountering specific opportunities caused the offenders to commit crimes that they would otherwise not have done. Thirdly, many studies have found much stronger than expected relationships between situational factors and the occurrence of specific forms of crime. One example is provided in Table 3.2 that uses British Crime Survey (BCS) data to show the risks of vehicle crime for cars parked in different locations. Thus, the risk of vehicle crime is 20 times greater for cars parked in an owner's driveway or carport compared with those parked in the owner's garage. And cars parked on the street outside the owner's home are nearly 60 times more at risk than those in the garage. Strictly speaking, these

Box 3.1 Perceptions of opportunities for burglary as reported in interviews with burglars

---

Usually when I get in my car and drive around I'm thinking, I don't have any money, so what is my means for gettin' money? All of a sudden I'll just take a glance and say, 'There it is! There's the house'.

I got a friend that do burglaries with me. He usually the one that sets them up. If he ain't got one set up, then I might go off into somethin' else.

When I was reconnecting the cable line, I overheard the lady talking on the phone and saying they be out of town for a few days. And when I heard that, I knew what time it was, time to come back and help them out; watch they house for them.

I was with this dude. He went to these people's house and took me with him. Just visiting, you know … So we went in [and we were just sitting around] and I unlocked the window … There wasn't nobody in the room when I did it … The next morning I woke up, after I had thought about it all night, and I decided that I was gonna get 'em. So I just woke up, went to they house, raised the window up and didn't have to break nothing. I just went in.

I know a lot of people and they know my game, so they put me up on certain people: 'So and So's leavin' town next week' … they want something out of the deal, they ain't doing it for nothing.

Then I seen [a well-known regional furniture store] bring another living room set in. Then I said, 'This a pretty livin' room set here. These folks got some money'. So that's what made me decide to [check them out].

Yeah, [I'm and opportunist] cause I find myself walkin' down the street with no intentions on doing a burglary. But I may see somebody leavin' the house and, at that time, the idea [to break in] may pop into my head, right at that instant … Lots of times I may do it right there on the spot

Well lately I haven't did any [robberies]. But when I was doin' it, I robbed every Friday … I ain't got no pistol, that's the only reason [I haven't been doing them], … I swear.

Source: Wright and Decker (1994).

data show only that situational factors determine which cars are victimized, not whether they are victimized, but the findings are so strong that they are consistent with a stronger causal relationship.

A fourth set of examples consistent with the causal role of opportunity is provided by the accumulating research (Clarke and Eck 2003) showing that crime is remarkably concentrated at particular addresses (hotspots), on particular victims (repeat victims), on particular products (hot products) and within different kinds of establishments and facilities (risky facilities). Thus, Sherman *et al.* (1989) found in their classic paper on hotspots that 4 per cent of addresses in Minneapolis in 1986 accounted for 53 per cent of the calls for police service, and Farrell and Pease (1993) reported that 43 per cent of the victimizations reported in the 1992 BCS were experienced by just 4 per cent of the population. Hotspots result partly from the fact that offenders live or spend time at those addresses and some repeat victimization is the result of ongoing interactions or relationships between victims and offenders. But the regular presence of offenders is only part of the explanation for these crime concentrations. Thus, some victims are repeatedly targeted because they live in poorly secured premises and thus provide easy pickings for offenders. Hot products also attract offenders because of the rewards they provide. For example, the Nissan Maxima generates seven to eight times the average number of insurance claims for new US automobiles because its high-intensity headlights can be fitted to older Nissan models originally supplied without them (Highway Loss Data Institute 2004). The theft risk for livestock carriers (including small horseboxes) was found in Home Office research to be 56 times greater than for refuse disposal trucks – almost certainly because there is a much stronger second-hand market for the former vehicles than the latter (Brown 1995). Some shops qualify as risky facilities because shoplifters are attracted to the goods they carry – cigarettes, designer jeans and cassettes or DVDs (Clarke 1999). Once again, it is not the existence of crime concentrations that constitutes support for a causal link between situational opportunities and crime. Rather, it is the *degree* to which crime is concentrated which suggests that the opportunities giving rise to these concentrations are so rewarding, or so lacking in difficulty and risk, that they tempt people into crime.

Table 3.2 Car thefts and parking place, England and Wales, British Crime Survey

Where parked	Car crimes* per 100,000 cars per 24 hours
Garage at home	2
Drive/carport	40
Street outside home	117
Public parking lot	454

*Includes theft of, theft from, attempts and deliberate damage.
Source: Clarke and Mayhew (1998).

Unexpectedly, the strongest evidence of the casual role of opportunity comes from studies of suicide and homicide. Suicide is not a crime though it was once treated as such. But, like much crime, it is commonly regarded as a deeply motivated act committed by desperate people. However, there is conclusive evidence that the detoxification of the gas supplied to people's homes brought about a reduction of about one quarter in the number of suicides in England and Wales between 1958 and 1977 (Clarke and Mayhew 1988). In 1958 almost exactly half the 5,298 people who committed suicide poisoned themselves with gas – to use the common expression, they put their heads in the gas oven. Changes in the manufacturing process for gas in the 1960s substantially reduced the amount of carbon monoxide in the domestic gas supply and then the replacement of manufactured gas by natural gas from the North Sea in the 1970s completely removed carbon monoxide. As a result, in 1977, only 0.2 per cent of the 3,944 suicides in that year made use of domestic gas. This means that whilst there was some displacement to other means of suicide, many people who would otherwise have killed themselves did not do so. The reasons lie in the particular advantages of domestic gas as method of suicide. It was readily available in everyone's home. It required little preparation, older people could readily make use of it and it involved no pain, blood or disfigurement, which are all features that made it attractive to suicides.

Suicide may not be a crime, but homicide is universally regarded as one of the most serious criminal acts. The primary evidence that situational/opportunity variables play a large part in its causation comes from a comparison of homicide rates between England and Wales and the USA. It is well known that the homicide rate is higher in the USA and widely believed that the much greater availability of guns there (a situational variable) provides the explanation. However, it is the details of the comparison that make a compelling causal argument. A study of the two countries made in the 1980s showed that the overall rate of homicides was 8.5 times higher for the USA, the gun homicide rate was 63 times higher and the handgun homicide rate was 75 times higher (Clarke and Mayhew 1988). Most telling of all is that the average number of handgun murders for the USA in the mid-1980s was a little over 9,300; that for England and Wales was just under 12!

For those wishing to deny the causal role of handguns in homicide, it was possible to argue in the 1980s that the USA was a much more crime-ridden and violent society than England and Wales. However this argument is no longer credible. Steady declines in crime in the USA have resulted in crime rates for most common offences now being lower, sometimes markedly so, than those of England and Wales. More particularly, comparative victimization surveys, not available in the 1980s, show that the rates of assault in England and Wales are higher than in the USA (Langan and Farrington 1998). Whilst rates of homicide have declined in the USA, they are still six times higher than in England and Wales and greater handgun availability still provides the explanation. This does not mean of course that the availability of a weapon is the sole determining reason for homicide, but it clearly establishes that opportunity is a powerful cause of homicide. If this is true of homicide, it must also be true of the remainder of crime, which is generally considered to be less deeply motivated than homicide.

45

Table 3.3 Twenty-five techniques of situational prevention

Increase the effort	Increase the risks	Reduce the rewards	Reduce provocations	Remove excuses
1. *Target harden* • Steering column locks and ignition immobilizers • Anti-robbery screens • Tamper-proof packaging	6. *Extend guardianship* • Go out in group at night • Leave signs of occupancy • Carry cell phone	11. *Conceal targets* • Off-street parking • Gender-neutral phone directories • Unmarked armoured trucks	16. *Reduce frustrations and stress* • Efficient lines • Polite service • Expanded seating • Soothing music/muted lighting	21. *Set rules* • Rental agreements • Harassment codes • Hotel registration
2. *Control access to facilities* • Entry phones • Electronic card access	7. *Assist natural surveillance* • Improved street lighting • Defensible space design • Support whistle-blowers	12. *Remove targets* • Removable car radio • Women's shelters • Pre-paid cards for pay phones	17. *Avoid disputes* • Separate seating for rival soccer fans • Reduce crowding in bars • Fixed cab fares	22. *Post instructions* • 'No Parking' • 'Private Property' • 'Extinguish camp fires'
3. *Screen exits* • Ticket needed for exit • Export documents • Electronic merchandise tags	8. *Reduce anonymity* • Taxi-driver IDs • 'How's my driving?' deals • School uniforms	13. *Identify property* • Property marking • Vehicle licensing and parts marking • Cattle branding	18. *Reduce temptation and arousal* • Controls on violent pornography • Enforce good behaviour on soccer field • Prohibit racial slurs	23. *Alert conscience* • Roadside speed display boards • Signatures for customs declarations • 'Shoplifting is stealing'

4. *Deflect offenders*
- Street closures
- Separate facilities for women
- Disperse pubs

5. *Control tools/ weapons*
- 'Smart' guns
- Restrict spray-paint sales to juveniles
- Toughened beer glasses

9. *Use place managers*
- CCTV for double-deck buses
- Two clerks for convenience stores
- Reward vigilance

10. *Strengthen formal surveillance*
- Red-light cameras
- Burglar alarms
- Security guards

14. *Disrupt markets*
- Monitor pawn shops
- Controls on classified ads
- Licensed street vendors

15. *Deny benefits*
- Ink merchandise tags
- Graffiti cleaning
- Disabling stolen cell phones

19. *Neutralize peer pressure*
- 'Idiots drink and drive'
- 'It's OK to say No'
- Disperse trouble-makers at school

20. *Discourage imitation*
- Rapid repair of vandalism
- V-chips in TVs
- Censor details of modus operandi

24. *Assist compliance*
- Easy library checkout
- Public lavatories
- Litter receptacles

25. *Control drugs and alcohol*
- Breathalysers in bars
- Server intervention programs
- Alcohol-free events

Sources: Clarke and Eck (2003), Cornish and Clarke (2003).

The role of excuses and provocations

As mentioned above, an important component of situational prevention is a classification of preventive techniques. This classification has grown in step with the expanded theoretical base of situational prevention. Originally, it grouped the techniques under three main categories drawn from rational choice theory: increasing the risks and the effort of crime, and reducing the rewards (Clarke 1992). Some of the specific techniques falling into these categories were derived from other theories – for example, 'deflecting offenders' from routine activity theory and 'reducing inducements' from social psychological theorizing by Berkowitz and by Zimbardo. Some years later, a fourth category of techniques was added, removing excuses for crime, which derived from Sykes and Matza's (1957) neutralization theory and Bandura's (1976) closely related concept of self-exoneration (Clarke and Homel, 1997). The techniques falling under this heading may be most effective in preventing everyday offences that many people commit, such as drunk driving and evading taxes.

The latest modification of the classification was made in response to Wortley's (1998, 2001) critiques of situational prevention, which, he argued, had focused too exclusively on opportunity reduction and had neglected a whole range of situational precipitators factors that can provoke, prompt, permit and pressure people to commit crime. In making this critique, Wortley drew on a social psychological framework that emphasizes the role of environmental cues in evoking behaviour and research in bars (Homel *et al.* 1997) and prisons (Wortley 2002), which showed that assaults, fights and a variety of other problematic behaviours in these closed environments were partly the result of poor design and management. Consequently, a fifth major category, removing provocations, has been added to the classification, which now consists of 25 techniques of situational prevention (see Table 3.3). This means the approach is extremely flexible and is applicable to the full range of crimes. Not all techniques are applicable to every crime, but there will always be enough techniques applicable in any particular case to allow practitioners to make some choice amongst them. Long past are the days when critics could get away with describing situational prevention as no more than target hardening.

Summary

When first described, situational prevention was dismissed as atheortical and simplistic, but quite soon its theoretical base was strengthened by the development of three 'crime' theories: the rational choice perspective, routine activity theory and crime pattern theory. Those who continue to dismiss the approach on theoretical grounds can therefore only mean that situational prevention fails to make use of the theories that they favour. In recent years, recognition has grown that 1) opportunity is a cause of crime, such that an increase in opportunity leads to more crime; and 2) situational factors can also precipitate crime. The latter insight has led to an expansion of the classification of opportunity-reducing techniques, whilst both insights together have important implications for displacement – discussed in the following section.

Situational prevention has not been shown to work: it displaces crime and often makes it worse

It would be tedious, and probably unnecessary, to list all the examples of successful situational prevention reported in the literature since the concept was first described 25 years ago (Clarke 1980). Some are mentioned below, and they have been regularly reviewed in previous publications (e.g. Clarke 1982, 1992, 1995, 1997; Smith *et al.* 2002). They involve common property offences of burglary, car theft and vandalism, but also various forms of fraud, robbery, assault, street prostitution, drug dealing and domestic violence. Smith *et al.* listed 142 situational prevention case studies at 211 sites, most of which reported reductions, sometimes dramatic, in the specific crime problems addressed. To take two examples of dramatic reductions, a plague of bus robberies in New York and 18 other US cities in the early 1970s was largely eliminated by the introduction of exact fares systems coupled with the installation of drop safes in buses (Stanford Research Institute 1970; Chaiken *et al.* 1974). This form of 'target removal' meant that there was no longer any point in attempting to rob the driver. More recently, US cell phone companies largely wiped out cloning by the introduction of five new anti-cloning technologies (Clarke *et al.* 2001); at its height, this problem had been costing the companies about $800 million per year in fraudulent phone calls (see Figure 3.1).

Probably no other form of crime control can claim such a record of evaluated successes, but some critics continue to dispute the evidence. They focus on failures – see the 'Introduction' to Clarke (1997) for examples – resulting from skipping the diagnosis of the problem, use of flawed measures such as Neighbourhood Watch, the blanket application of measures such as CCTV surveillance in unsuitable locations, and a variety of other implementation mistakes and failures (Grabosky 1996). They argue that situational prevention has been evaluated using only weak research designs; that the reductions claimed are negated by displacement (i.e. the offenders shift their attention

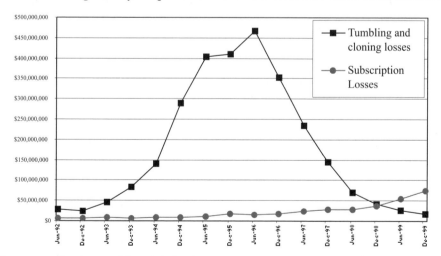

Figure 3.1 Semi-annual fraud dollar losses, USA, June 1992–December 1999
Source: Clarke *et al.* (2001).

to other places, times and targets, use different methods or commit different crimes); that situational prevention results in escalation (i.e. offenders resort to more harmful methods to gain their ends); and that even if displacement does not occur immediately, the criminal population adapts in the long run to reduced opportunities by discovering new ways to commit crime.

Displacement and escalation

The most persistent of these criticisms concerns displacement, which is not surprising considering the extent to which dispositional assumptions pervade professional and lay theorizing about crime ('bad will out'). However, the displacement thesis was always overblown. It is credible for some crimes, but not for all. Thus, it is highly unlikely that motorists prevented from speeding on a particular stretch of road would look for another road on which to speed, or that shoppers prevented from shoplifting at their local supermarket by new security measures would shop instead at some more distant store where they could continue to steal, or would turn to mugging senior citizens. Shoplifting is easier to rationalize and much less risky than mugging.

In fact, almost by definition, any instance of escalation is more costly for offenders. Some of them may be prepared to make more difficult rationalizations or run additional risks, but they will be in a minority. In fact, there are few documented cases of escalation in the literature. Ekblom (1988) found some evidence of increased use of firearms by robbers following the introduction of anti-bandit screens in London post offices, but these attacks were less successful than ones with sledge-hammers or baseball bats, and resulted in no more harm to postal workers. A few years ago, the police and others claimed that improved vehicle security, which had made it more difficult to steal unattended cars, had resulted in increased numbers of 'carjackings'. In fact, carjackings might have increased, but the number of vehicles stolen by these means is a tiny fraction of the reduced number of car thefts by other means. (This might also be true of thefts and burglaries to obtain car keys, which is also said to be a consequence of improved vehicle security.) Any calculation of increased harm resulting from improved vehicle security would have to take account of these differences in the number of incidents. It is also possible that carjackings might have increased anyway, irrespective of improved security. Organized offenders can accomplish them quickly and might more easily obtain a high-value car by this method than by looking to find one left unattended on the street.

The developments in theory underlying situational prevention have further undermined claims about the inevitability of displacement and the risks of escalation. If it is the case that opportunity increases the amount of crime, and that crime can result from a variety of situational precipitators, there is every reason to believe that reducing these opportunities and inducements will result in real reductions in crime. In fact, this is the message of the empirical research. Three separate reviews of the evidence on displacement found that it does occur, but it is not inevitable. In the most recent review, Hesseling (1994) found no evidence of displacement in 22 of the 55 studies he examined; in the remaining 33 studies, he found some evidence of displacement, but in no case was there as much crime displaced as prevented.

Quite often, no real evidence of displacement is found even when those close to the preventive action assert that it has occurred. For example, London Underground officials believed that the appearance of a £ slug soon after ticket machines were modified to prevent use of a 50p slug was the result of displacement. However, Clarke *et al.* (1994) showed that this was unlikely to be the case. The £ slugs required metal working facilities, whereas any schoolchild could make the 50p slugs by wrapping a 10p coin in silver foil. Moreover, the two kinds of slugs were found in different stations suggesting that they were the work of different groups of offenders.

Similar results to Hesseling's would likely be found if his review were repeated today. Many more studies of displacement have been reported, many of which have reported little or no displacement. For example, little displacement seems to have occurred to other forms of cell phone fraud when cloning was largely eliminated in the USA. The lower line in Figure 3.1 shows the numbers of 'subscriber frauds' reported during the rise and fall of cloning. These were the second most common form of fraud during the period. They involved obtaining a telephone service through the provision of a false name and/or address. These frauds increased throughout the period, in line with increases in cell phone use and apparently quite independently of cloning frauds. Always at a relatively low level, they showed little sign of increasing to compensate for the reduction in cloning that began in 1996, probably because they would be difficult to reproduce on a wide scale and would therefore not be attractive to criminal groups. On the other hand, cloned phones were 'mass produced' by criminals who had learnt how to acquire hundreds of legitimate phone numbers and program them into stolen phones.

Whilst this study clearly shows that there was little if any displacement to other forms of cell phone fraud, it illustrates an inherent weakness of research on displacement – it is nearly always impossible to prove conclusively that displacement has not occurred, at least if one were willing to argue that displacement can occur to any form of crime. To quote Barr and Pease (1990: 293):

> If, in truth, displacement is complete, some displaced crime will probably fall outside the areas and types of crime being studied or be so dispersed as to be masked by background variation. In such an event, the optimist would speculate about why the unmeasured areas or types of crime probably escaped displaced crime, while the pessimist would speculate about why they probably did not. No research study, however massive, is likely to resolve the issue. The wider the scope of the study in terms of types of crimes and places, the thinner the patina of displaced crime could be spread across them; thus disappearing into the realm of measurement error.

Thus, in the cloning example above, it is possible that the offenders involved might have turned to fraud not involving cell phones; it is also possible, however, that many of them were not exclusively dependent on crime for a living. It might have been a sideline for them, or merely a way of making money for a time.

When cloning was closed down, they might have had to make do with reduced income – like we all must from time to time – or they might have turned their energies to legitimate ways of making money. Such positive outcomes from the application of situational prevention become conceivable once freed from dispositional assumptions about crime.

Diffusion of benefits and anticipatory benefits

Another positive outcome of situational prevention is diffusion of benefits. Sometimes described as the reverse of displacement, the term refers to the fact that situational prevention can often bring about reductions in crime beyond the immediate focus of the measures introduced (Clarke and Weisburd 1994). This greatly enhances the practical appeal of situational prevention, especially as the phenomenon is quite general as shown by the following examples:

1. Security added to houses that had been repeatedly burgled in Kirkholt reduced burglaries for the whole of the estate, not just for those houses given additional protection (Pease 1991).

2. When street lighting was improved in a large housing estate in Dudley, crime declined in both that estate and a nearby one where the lighting was not changed (Painter and Farrington 1997).

3. When 'red light' cameras were installed at some traffic lights in Strathclyde, not only did fewer people 'run the lights' at these locations, but also at other traffic lights nearby (Scottish Office Central Research Unit 1995). (In a smaller city, with more local traffic, this effect might be short lived as people learnt exactly which junctions had cameras.)

4. CCTV cameras installed to monitor car parks at the University of Surrey reduced car crime as much in one not covered by the cameras as in the three that were covered (Poyner 1991).

5. As expected, electronic tagging of books in a University of Wisconsin library resulted in reduced book thefts. However, thefts also declined of videocassettes and other materials that had not been tagged (Scherdin 1986).

6. When a New Jersey discount electronic retailer introduced a regime of daily counting of valuable merchandise in the warehouse, employee thefts of these items plummeted – but thefts also plummeted of items not repeatedly counted (Masuda 1992).

7. When vehicle-tracking systems were introduced in six large US cities, rates of theft declined citywide, not just for car owners who purchased the tracking devices (Ayres and Levitt 1998).

8. Widespread ownership of burglar alarms in an affluent community near Philadelphia resulted in reduced burglary rates for the community at large (Hakim *et al.* 1995).

Potential offenders often know that new prevention measures have been introduced, but they may be unsure of their precise scope. They may believe the measures are more widespread than they really are, and that the *effort* needed to commit crime, or the *risks* incurred, have been increased for a wider range of places, times or targets than in fact is the case.

Diffusion of benefits was identified as a regular outcome of situational prevention only ten years ago and little is known about ways deliberately to enhance it (Clarke and Weisburd 1994). An important method may be through publicity. Thus, a publicity campaign helped to spread the benefits of CCTV cameras across an entire fleet of 80 buses in the north of England, although these were installed on just a few of the buses. One of the buses with CCTV was taken around to schools in the area to show pupils they could be caught if they vandalized the bus, and the first arrests resulting from the cameras were given wide publicity in the news media (Poyner 1988).

The benefits of diffusion are likely to decay when offenders discover that the risks and effort of committing crime have not increased as much as they had thought. Research has shown that this occurred in the early days of the breathalyser in the UK, which had a greater immediate impact on drunk driving than expected given the actual increase in the risk of getting caught (Ross 1973). However, as drivers learnt that the risks of being stopped were still quite small, drunk driving began to increase again. This means that ways will have to be found of keeping offenders guessing about the precise levels of threat, or quite how much extra effort is needed if they are to continue with crime.

Just as offenders often overestimate the reach of situational prevention, they often believe that prevention measures have been brought into force before they actually have been. This results in what has been called the 'anticipatory benefits' of prevention. Smith *et al.* (2002) found evidence of anticipatory benefits in 40 per cent of situational prevention studies whose data could have revealed such benefits. Once again, this provides 'added value' to situational prevention. Once again, however, little is known about how to enhance these benefits deliberately, though advance publicity of measures can undoubtedly help to achieve this.

Adaptation

The concept of criminal adaptation further complicates any consideration of the outcomes of situational prevention (Ekblom and Tilley 2000). It refers to the process through which offender *populations* discover new crime vulnerabilities after preventive measures have been in place for a while. Paul Ekblom (1999) has used the analogy of an arms race between preventers and offenders to describe this concept. It is a longer-term process than displacement, which refers to the ways that *individual* offenders find to circumvent preventive measures. One clear example of adaptation is found in the work of Levi and colleagues (1991, 1998) on the prevention of credit card fraud. They have shown how a partnership between the police, the Home Office and the banks led to successful action in the mid-1990s to reduce credit card frauds. The measures included new lower limits for retailers for seeking authorization of transactions and tightened procedures for mailing new credit cards to customers. As Figure

3.2 shows, these measures brought about a sharp reduction in fraud losses. In recent years, however, losses have begun to climb again. This is due principally to the growth in 'card not present' frauds (due to the expansion of Internet sales) and in the counterfeiting of cards (said to be the work of organized gangs in East Asia). Both these reasons for the recent increase in frauds illustrate offender adaptation rather than displacement.

Evaluation strategies

Situational prevention has been criticized for the quality of the research designs employed in evaluations, specifically for making so little use of random allocation. In fact, it is very difficult to employ random allocation in this field. Those seeking to introduce situational measures are not scientists, but are managers in municipal authorities, public transport companies, businesses and shops, whose primary concern is to reduce crime and victimization as rapidly and as inexpensively as possible. For them, it will usually be apparent quite soon whether the preventive measures have worked. They might on occasion be willing to share data to permit a more formal evaluation, so long as this has some benefit for them and involves few costs of time, effort or possible loss of competitive advantage. Only in very rare cases would they be willing to endure the inconvenience and cost of randomly allocating measures to an

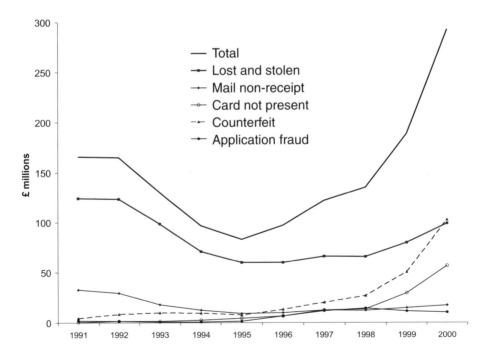

Figure 3.2   Credit card fraud losses, UK

experimental and control group in the interests of scientific study. Even when there might be greater interest in a scientific evaluation, as for example when central government sponsors preventive measures, the logistic (and political) difficulties of incorporating random allocation into the evaluative design will generally be seen as too great.

For the foreseeable future situational prevention will therefore have to rely mainly on evaluative designs involving before and after comparisons and matched control and experimental groups. Fortunately, the results of situational prevention are often so dramatic that this may not matter much. For example, Figure 3.1 showing the time course of cloning provides very persuasive evidence that the anti-cloning technologies introduced in the mid-1990s were effective. To the critics, however, this would be regarded as a weak evaluation. No comparison group, whether randomly selected or not, was employed; no statistical tests are reported of the significance of the decline; and, finally, no replication of the study has been published. To expect this would of course be quite silly. The opportunity to undertake the evaluation only arose serendipitously after the measures had been in place for some time; they were introduced (at great cost) wholesale across the country in co-ordinated action by the phone companies, which means that no control group would have been possible; it was once-and-for-all experiment, not to be repeated even in other countries because of different phone technologies; and given the huge numbers of frauds involved and the dramatic fall in their incidence, statistical tests of significance would be redundant.

Similar points could be made about most other evaluations of situational prevention. Rarely is it possible to use random allocation or to replicate interventions since these have to be tailored carefully to the specific crime problem and the precise circumstances of the setting or environment. In fact, given the highly idiosyncratic nature of situational interventions, and given that the effect of particular measures may be partly dependent on others introduced at the same time in the same package, replication probably serves a much smaller role in building knowledge about what works in situational prevention than it may do in other fields. More important than to accumulate research on the effects of specific measures used in a variety of settings and circumstances is to develop theoretical understanding of the effects of interventions so that informed choices can be made amongst them when dealing with a new crime problem.

Nevertheless, there are several ways in which evaluations of situational prevention should be improved. First, research designs that simultaneously allow displacement and diffusion to be detected should be used whenever possible (Bowers and Johnson 2003). Secondly, more attention needs to be paid to detecting possible anticipatory benefits. Thirdly, longer follow-ups are needed to permit assessment of any criminal adaptation. With the notable exception of Webb's (1997) 30-year follow-up of the effectiveness of steering-column locks, few evaluations of situational prevention have studied outcomes for more than a year or two. Finally, more cost-benefit studies of situational prevention are needed. When undertaken, as in the cloned phone example discussed above, they can show that highly cost-effective results were achieved.

Situational prevention diverts attention from the root causes of crime

Criminology is a highly fragmented discipline, united by little more than its dispositional bias. Whilst criminologists might disagree about the source of criminal dispositions, most of them agree that the only effective form of prevention is to tackle these root causes through the provision of improved nursery schooling, financial support and counselling for families at risk, leisure activities for youth and so forth. They believe that situational prevention diverts attention (and funds) from these efforts to eliminate disadvantage by offering quick and superficial 'fixes' to crime symptoms.

A conciliatory response to this criticism would deny any conflict between situational prevention and addressing disadvantage. These actions are focused at different places in the causal chain. They are the responsibility of different agencies and they can be pursued quite independently, without interfering with one another. Situational prevention measures, which can bring about immediate reductions in crime, can even be regarded as buying time for measures to tackle disadvantage whose results will be apparent only in the longer term. And an undertaking to introduce longer-term measures to tackle disadvantage might sometimes make short-term situational measures more palatable to local communities.

However, there is no necessary symmetry between the causes of crime and effective action to prevent it. Whilst disposition and opportunity act together to produce crime, it does not follow that prevention must address both equally. In fact, there are several reasons for focusing preventive effort on crime opportunities rather than criminal dispositions. First, we know more about how to reduce opportunities and provocations than how to reduce dispositions, despite the much greater investment of research in the latter. Secondly, situational changes are more likely to be effective because these are directed to the near, rather than the distant, causes of crime. There are too many intermediary links between distant causes and crime to be sure that action directed at these causes will be effective. Thirdly, it is much easier to demonstrate the results of situational changes because they are expected to have an immediate impact. On the other hand, the benefits of changing dispositions, particularly of young children, can only be expected to appear many years later. Proving that such action had been effective would be almost impossible without conducting intrusive and possibly unethical experiments.

So instead of diverting attention from criminology's central mission of reducing crime through improving social institutions, situational prevention can help rescue criminology from an impossible quest. In any case, it seems wrong-headed for criminologists to define themselves as social reformers. Surely, the policy role for society's crime experts would be more appropriately defined as finding effective ways to reduce crime, by any socially acceptable and just means? On present evidence, situational prevention offers far more promise of meeting this goal than social reform. The goal of creating a more equal and just society is worth pursuing in its own right and is ill-served by dubious promises of crime reduction. Criminologists can make their greatest contribution to meeting this goal by finding effective and ethical ways to reduce the crime which plagues the lives of poor and deprived people.

Situational prevention is a conservative, managerial approach to crime

Many of the same critics who believe that situational prevention diverts attention from the root causes of crime also accuse it of being a fundamentally conservative approach to crime, content to manage the problem and keep it from overwhelming the forces of law and order. It is damned as 'administrative criminology' because of it origins in Home Office research. It is castigated for its lack of social awareness in its choice of crimes to address and it is accused of paying too much attention to protecting the property and interests of the powerful, whilst neglecting crimes against women and minorities. Finally, it is said to be a creature of the times, lacking any vision and social purpose. In other words, left-leaning criminologists hate it.

It is true that the early applications of situational prevention involved common property crimes of theft and vandalism, but this was little different from the focus of most criminologists of the day. In any case these are volume crimes, which directly affect the lives of many people, particularly those living in the poorest areas of towns and cities. Gradually, the crimes addressed by situational prevention have expanded to include many forms of robbery, violence and fraud, as well as everyday offences of speeding, drunk driving, shoplifting and employee theft. Situational prevention projects have addressed robberies and assaults of taxicab drivers (Smith in press), bus drivers (Stanford Research Institute 1970), convenience store staff (Hunter and Jeffrey 1997) and immigrant shopkeepers (Ekblom *et al*. 1988). Other projects have attempted to apply the principles of situational prevention to reducing crime on the Internet and identity theft (Newman and Clarke 2003). One project has even employed situational prevention in finding new ways to prevent deaths of illegal immigrants on the US/Mexican border (Guerette 2004). Today, it is difficult to see any particular pattern in the applications of situational prevention. This is not surprising because no government (or any other entity) has a monopoly on the approach. It can be employed by any agency or organization that seeks to reduce a specific form of crime. Which agencies decide to do so is still largely a matter of chance and is likely to remain so until the approach becomes more broadly accepted.

As for the cosy relationship between advocates of situational prevention and government, it can only be said that there is little evidence of this in government policy. Senior officials are just as likely to buy in to dispositional assumptions about crime as criminologists themselves and, whilst situational prevention did originate in the Home Office in the 1970s, that ministry has given it only sporadic and limited support in subsequent years. During the mid-1980s, for example, all mention of the term was studiously avoided in official documents because of its supposedly simplistic approach. The government is now devoting many more resources to prevention than 25 years ago when situational prevention was launched, but in an attempt to be even-handed, it gives as much support to so-called social prevention (for which there is little evidence of effectiveness) as to situational prevention. In any case, the government resources devoted to all forms of crime prevention still constitute a small fraction of the crime and justice budget.

Finally, there is scant evidence that situational prevention appeals to conservative values. True, there is a superficial fit between situational prevention and conservative ideas of 'small government', value for money, individual responsibility and so forth. In addition, conservatives might tend to agree that crime is chosen, but for them crime is a moral choice not an economic or instrumental one. Consequently, they generally have little interest in situational prevention. They are more likely to see it as an inadequate response to crime because it neglects the punishment of those who have broken the law and caused harm to society.

Situational prevention promotes a selfish, exclusionary society

When first introduced, situational prevention was seen as the harbinger of a fortress society in which citizens, terrified of crime, will lock themselves in their homes, shun their neighbours and emerge only for work and other essential business. It was claimed that the increased use of situational prevention would result in the growing alienation of the population and the destruction of communities. In fact, much situational prevention practice has exactly the opposite objective of strengthening community ties and reinforcing social controls by enabling people to keep watch on the neighbourhood around their homes. This is the purpose of the 'defensible space' designs that Oscar Newman (1972) proposed for public housing estates in the early 1970s. Fears of a fortress society have also receded as crime rates have begun to decline, but critics still contend that situational prevention promotes a selfish concern of the wealthy and powerful with protecting themselves from crime. This criticism takes three specific forms: that the poor will suffer as the result of self-protective action taken by the wealthy; that the increase in affluent gated communities, fuelled by fear of crime, will lead to a further polarization of the rich and poor in society; and that the use of situational prevention results in the exclusion of those labelled as 'undesirables' (vagrants, minorities, the unemployed and gangs of youths) from places such as shopping malls, parks and entertainment centres and, in the case of gated communities, from residential streets.

The poor will suffer

Having purchased protection in the form of alarms, guards, CCTV cameras, it is claimed that the rich will gradually withdraw their support for public law enforcement, just as they have for nationalized medicine and publicly funded schooling. To date, there is little evidence of this occurring. Wealthy people can afford to protect their homes from burglars, but only the super-rich can buy protection in the wider world. This means that even the wealthy depend upon the public police in their daily lives. In any case, wealthy people have a strong interest in an orderly society, since order is a basic requirement for the production of the goods and services that they consume and the generation of the wealth from which they profit. It therefore seems unlikely that they would support reductions in public spending on law enforcement.

A second charge is that self-protection by the wealthy will drive crime to the doors of the poor. Thus, the rich man's burglar alarm will displace burglary to his poorer neighbour. As argued above, the displacement argument is overstated and, in fact, there is no clear evidence of crime being displaced from the rich to poor, though, for a time, vehicle-tracking devices to prevent car theft seemed to carry this risk. Because of their cost, these devices are mostly fitted to expensive cars. They also require a receiver to be installed on police cars to pick up the signals from stolen vehicles. As a result, police attention could become concentrated on the more expensive stolen cars fitted with tracking devices to the detriment of those without the devices. Consequently, many municipalities in the USA now make it a condition of police co-operation that cars fitted with the tracking device do not use decals to advertise this fact. Thieves therefore do not know which cars have the devices and which do not, which may help to produce a more general deterrent effect. Indeed, an evaluation of these devices in the northeastern USA suggests that they helped to bring down overall levels of a car theft in the communities concerned (Ayres and Levitt 1998). If so, poorer car owners would have collected 'free rider' benefits from the preventive efforts of more wealthy owners. Felson and Clarke (1997) have argued that similar benefits may diffuse to nearby poorer communities as the result of increased crime prevention in more wealthy neighbouring communities.

Gated communities

In 'gated communities', access is restricted to residents in the hope of keeping out offenders who cruise neighbourhoods looking for crime opportunities. Access is controlled by walled or fenced perimeters, by gates and sometimes by security guards. The number of gated communities has increased rapidly in the USA, South Africa, South America and elsewhere in the past couple of decades. A recent estimate puts the numbers of American families now living in some form of gated community at about 2.5 million (Blakely and Snyder 1998). Gated communities are criticized for limiting freedom of movement and public access to the streets (von Hirsch and Shearing 2000) and, because they are assumed to be only for the rich, they are considered to be exclusionary.

However, many if not most of the gated communities being built in the USA are intended for middle-income residents, who are hoping to avoid traffic, litter and other incivilities of modern life, as much as they are seeking protection from crime (Blakely and Snyder 1998). In fact, there is no clear evidence that gated communities do protect the well-off from crime. If the community is located in a high-crime area and security is tight, then they might, but rather few gated communities fulfil these conditions. They are being built in the outer suburbs where crime is already low. They might begin by employing security guards, but often give these up because of the expense.

Gated communities have their analogues in poorer parts of the city where streets have been closed or alley gates installed to keep out burglars and other offenders. Evaluations have shown that these measures can reduce crime. For example, Matthew's (1986, 1993) work in London suburbs has shown that street closures helped to reduce street prostitution, and Lasley (1998) has shown that, when installed in an impoverished area of Los Angeles, they reduced a variety of crimes including drive-by shootings by gang members. More recently, Bowers *et al.* (in press) have shown that the installation of 3,178 alley gates, protecting 106 blocks of housing in Liverpool, produced a decline of approximately 37 per cent in the gated areas. A simple cost-benefit analysis indicated that once the gates had been in place for a year or more, they became cost-beneficial, with a return of around £1.86 for every £1 spent.

As so often turns out, therefore, the truth about gated communities is more complex than portrayed by the critics. Gated communities are not merely for the wealthy. They do not simply consist of walled residential neighbourhoods with guarded entrances. Barriers to entering can often be more symbolic than real, and may inconvenience rather than prohibit entry. If their development has been encouraged at all by situational prevention, this is in *poorer* rather than in wealthier neighbourhoods. It is in these poorer neighbourhoods that their crime prevention benefits may be greatest. They may strengthen community bonds rather than weaken them, and they might enhance rather than impede informal controls. Because they might help to reduce fear, they may even reduce the perceived need for other, more harmful forms of self-protection such as (in the USA) purchasing guns.

Exclusion

Two situational techniques in particular, controlling access to facilities and deflecting offenders, have been criticized for promoting exclusion, but both are used in a closely targeted way that avoids this risk. Access controls are designed to keep people out of private facilities, such as office blocks or factories, who have no right of entry. They are not designed to keep groups of 'undesirables' out of public places such as shopping malls or municipal gardens because situational prevention assumes that anybody might exploit opportunities for crime in these places. Where the purpose is to exclude 'troublemakers' from public and semi-public spaces it would more likely be served by 'order maintenance' policing undertaken by the public police or private security guards. Similarly, the use of deflecting offenders is closely targeted to particular problems and settings. One example would be the co-ordination of last buses with pub closing times, which is designed to get late-night drinkers out of the city centre before they get into trouble. Another example would be closing off cut-throughs and alleyways near schools to prevent pupils from vandalizing cars or stealing items left in back gardens on their way to and from school. In neither case is exclusion a likely result of the implementation of these measures. Where a measure does carry this risk, it is likely to be identified at the pre-implementation stage, which (at least in the scientific form of situational prevention) requires that measures be carefully scrutinized for their social costs and acceptability, including exclusion, before they are implemented.

Situational crime prevention promotes Big Brother and restricts personal freedoms

Just as the fortress society has haunted situational prevention from the start, so has the spectre of Big Brother and the threat of intrusive surveillance – a threat given greater credibility by recent developments in technology. CCTV raises fears of being snooped on by the police as we go about or daily business. Speed cameras can give the authorities information about where we drive and when. Caller-ID can reveal our whereabouts against our wishes. In the minds of the critics, these technologies put too much power into the hands of governments that are only too willing to employ repressive forms of crime control.

This fear might be justified in a totalitarian society, but it ignores the reality of the democracies in which we live. Democratic freedoms combined with widespread suspicion of technology would make it very hard to impose blanket governmental surveillance, though people are willing to surrender some freedoms or endure inconvenience in specific contexts if they gain protection from crime. For example, the security that must be endured when checking in for airline flights can be very irksome, but baggage screening and other measures introduced in the 1970s largely eliminated hijackings (Landes 1978; Wilkinson 1986). Travellers have accepted the need for the additional precautions introduced since 9/11 because they recognize that the new breed of terrorist hijackers are willing to die when they seize an airliner and might know how to fly the aircraft themselves.

Self-appointed custodians of liberty often overstate the dangers of technology and, short of outright bans, fail to consider ways of averting the risks. When infringements on liberty seem unavoidable, they rarely consider whether these costs are outweighed by crime reduction benefits. As a consequence, some valuable preventive technologies are underutilized or underdeveloped. For example, despite their demonstrated value in reducing accidents and saving lives (Bourne and Cooke 1993), the New Jersey State Senate banned speed cameras on the populist grounds that they result in impersonal law enforcement (it would no longer be possible to bribe the traffic cop) or in raised insurance costs (resulting from the accumulation on driving licences of 'points' for speeding). In the UK, the cameras have been painted yellow to make them more visible to speeding motorists. A second example is that, despite the capacity of Caller-ID to deter obscene and harassing phone calls (Clarke 1990), many states in America would only permit its introduction if callers could block display of their numbers on Caller-ID devices. This preserved the privacy of the caller at the expense of those called.

In time, greater familiarity with the technology and more realistic analysis of the actual threats posed to individual liberty can lead to its greater acceptance and ways may be found to reduce the technology's risks without impeding its effectiveness. For example, Caller-ID devices are now being marketed which reject calls from blocked numbers. This restores some of Caller-ID's preventive benefits and gives more privacy to those called.

Much of the new surveillance is introduced not by governments but by businesses. People recognize that businesses must protect their assets from crime and that, if they did not, the costs of crime would be passed on to the consumer. Consequently, few people protest about CCTV cameras in banks or refuse to provide their addresses when registering at a hotel. Some of the precautions instituted by businesses help to protect the customer as well. These precautions can be irksome, such as using a PIN for one's bank card, but without PINs, bank cards would quickly become unusable, and the conveniences would be lost of carrying around less cash and of obtaining money at any time of the day or night.

Of course, people should not be subjected to inconvenient or annoying security precautions without such compensatory benefits. One egregious example concerns other people's car alarms sounding at night. Nobody should have to endure this kind of cost (Duff and Marshall 2000), particularly as the deterrent value of these alarms has never been established. In fact, some cities have banned car alarms and it would be possible to replace them by alarms that roused only the vehicle's owner. In attempting to prevent fraud, insurance companies and government bureaucracies also sometimes unduly inconvenience people who are legitimately claiming benefits or compensation. In the world of commerce, business competition ensures that irksome and unnecessary precautions are quickly eliminated. In state-run or public enterprises lacking competition, other avenues exist for procuring change in tiresome rules, including elected representatives, the press, complaint lines, ombudsmen and other devices of a democratic state. The process of change may take longer, but the problem of bureaucratic roadblocks and delays is not unique to crime prevention. At worst, a higher price will be paid for security, for longer than needed, but there is no reason to be saddled with unnecessary regimentation for ever.

Situational prevention blames the victim

It is sometimes argued that citizens have a right to expect governments to protect them from crime (Kleinig 2000), but David Garland (2001) has described how governments have come increasingly to recognize that they cannot deliver public safety without considerable help from a variety of community partners. These include ordinary members of the public who are increasingly enjoined to take some elementary precautions against crime. Whilst it is indefensible to blame rape on short skirts and other 'sexually provocative' conduct, there is certainly a place for giving people information about behaviours that put them at risk of crime and many people welcome such advice. For example, tourists often ask whether it is safe to use the local taxis or to walk in the streets at night. It is also useful for car owners to know (see Table 3.2) that, if they put their cars away overnight in their garages and do not leave them on the driveway, they can reduce by twenty-fold their risks of vehicle crime (Clarke and Mayhew 1998). They can then decide whether the reduced risk is worth the effort of putting the car away.

In general, if people decide to take a known risk, they must bear some of the responsibility for the consequences. When risks are taken in blatant disregard of the costs for others, responsibility can shade into blame, as in the case of shopkeepers who refuse to alter practices – such as displays to encourage impulse purchases – that they know increase the risks of theft. Despite this, they might continue to expect the police and the courts to deal firmly with any shoplifters. Blaming and shaming them may be a way of getting these shops to change. This may be all the more important since many persistent shoplifters are feeding drug habits and negligent retailers may therefore be helping to fuel the drug trade.

Other business victims deserving their share of blame include managers of low-cost apartment complexes in the USA who increase the risks of crime to their own property and persons, and to that of other tenants, by failing to establish codes of conduct (Clarke and Bichler-Robertson 1998). Some pubs create conditions that lead to drunken fights by failing to serve alcohol in a responsible manner or by employing aggressive bouncers (Homel *et al.* 1997). And some convenience store owners save money, but expose their employees to robbery, by employing inexperienced and young staff at night (Hunter and Jeffrey 1997).

Blame as a tool of crime prevention can be used legitimately not just against these business victims, but also against those who produce criminogenic products. Many cities in the USA are currently engaged in suing gun manufacturers for the irresponsible overproduction of weapons, which has led to enormous criminal justice and healthcare costs (Fields 2000; Butterfield 2002). The British government shamed car manufacturers into improving vehicle security by publishing league tables of the most stolen cars (Laycock 2004) and this approach is being broadened to include a wider range of criminogenic products (Pease 2001; Ekblom, Chapter 8, this volume; Clarke and Newman in press).

Conclusions

From the start situational crime prevention has had an uneasy relationship with its parent discipline of criminology. The first academic paper describing the approach criticized criminology for its dispositional bias and argued that explanations of crime would be incomplete unless situational factors were incorporated (Clarke 1980). Though radical, this critique was not developed in detail and the paper went largely unnoticed by mainstream criminologists. In any case, criminologists have become accustomed to accommodating a wide range of theoretical explanations in their fragmented discipline and, despite its burgeoning literature and policy impact, most still seem to regard situational prevention as just one more perspective on crime, alongside many dozens of others. If covered at all, this is generally how it is treated in textbooks. As mentioned, some left-leaning criminologists are hostile to the approach, but most other criminologists seem to regard it as peripheral to their main interests. Consequently, few of the criticisms of situational prevention discussed in this paper have been spelt out in detail though they commonly arise in informal discussions. The only in-depth critique (mostly rather benign as it turns out) is contained in von Hirsch *et al.* (2000), which reports the proceedings of two small conferences on the ethical and social issues raised by situational prevention.

Consequently, the development of situational prevention has taken place in relative isolation from the remainder of criminology. This is to the detriment of both. Situational prevention has lacked the informed, critical commentary from outside its small group of adherents that would serve to refine it and help it fulfil its primary mission of reducing the harms of crime. For its part, criminology has not fully benefited from the body of research that situational prevention has generated on specific kinds of crime and their situational determinants; nor has it properly accommodated the 'crime' or 'opportunity' theories that would help correct its lopsided, dispositional bias. It has also turned its back on a highly effective form of crime control – one that also avoids many of the serious problems of formal sanctioning – to which it could have laid claim.

So what does the future hold? There is little risk that situational prevention will follow the path of many other 'radical' critiques of criminology and become a footnote in the discipline's history. It has too many crime reduction successes to ignore and these will grow as its links are strengthened with problem-oriented policing (Tilley 1999). Its literature is too large (including more than 100 relevant Home Office reports and nearly 20 volumes of *Crime Prevention Studies*, a book series devoted to situational prevention). Its advocates (including some contributors to this volume) are a tightly knit group actively involved in research and teaching. Its consumers include a growing body of crime analysts and crime prevention specialists (numbering in the hundreds if not thousands) in local government and the police. Its research future is guaranteed by the development of greatly improved databases on crime incidents, sophisticated crime mapping software and the growing availability of low-cost computing.

There seems equally little prospect of situational prevention moving any closer to the centre-stage of criminology. Apart from the dissonances of causal theory, situational prevention does little to promote the welfarist, social reform agendas of most criminologists. It also offends many of their attitudes, which include suspicion of governmental authority, distaste for business, fear of corporate power, distrust of wealth and sympathy for the criminal underdog. Moreover, many criminologists are uncomfortable with situational prevention's crime control agenda. Most see their own roles as being simply to understand and explain crime, leaving others to draw out the policy implications. In their view, situational prevention threatens to turn criminology into a technical discourse more in tune with the police and the security industry than with academia.

Nor does it seem likely that the advocates of situational prevention, and those of related theories such as problem-oriented policing and CPTED (crime prevention through environmental design), will remain content with their peripheral status in a discipline of which they are increasingly critical. This is particularly the case now that an alternative is being offered them in crime science. When the trustees of the Jill Dando Fund decided to establish an academic department at University College, London, they were quite clear that this would not be merely another institute of criminology, conducting research on crime that might (or might not) have long-term implications for prevention. Rather, the Jill Dando Institute of Crime Science was founded to undertake work, including situational crime prevention, which would bring about immediate reductions in crime.

Many differences of emphasis exist between crime science and criminology in their missions, theories and methodologies (Table 3.4), but it is unclear whether these will prove sufficient justification for establishing crime science as a discipline taught widely in universities, separate from criminology. Universities are generally reluctant to establish new departments, but there are two reasons for thinking that crime science might be an exception. First, universities need increasingly to attract research funds. If more academic departments of crime science were established in universities, with explicit crime reduction goals, they would be likely to win more research grants than conventional departments of criminology. This would almost certainly be true if they subsumed terrorism

Table 3.4 Differences of emphasis between criminology and crime science

Criminology	Crime science
Mission	
Understand criminals	Understand crime
Long-term social reform	Immediate crime reduction
Help the criminal underdog	Reduce harm to victims
'Pure'	'Applied'
Theory-led	Problem-led
Shun policy	Embrace policy
Theory	
Distant causes paramount	Near causes paramount
Opportunity secondary	Opportunity central
Crime pathological	Crime normal
The *why* of crime	The *how* of crime
Criminal dispositions	Criminal choice
Criminal motivation	The rewards of crime
Anomie, subcultures and conflict theory	Routine activities, rational choice
Sociology, psychiatry, law	Economics, geography, biology, planning, computer science
Research methods	
Cohort studies	Crime patterns
Criminal careers	Hot spots
Regression analysis	Crime mapping
Self-reported delinquency	Victim surveys
Randomized control trials	Crime-specific case studies
Long-term studies in depth	Rapid appraisal techniques
Applications and audience	
Crime and delinquency in general	Specific crime and disorder problems
Sentencing/treatment/social prevention	Detection/deterrence/situational prevention
Social workers/probation officers	Police, planners and security industry
Social policy-makers	Business and management
Scholarly treatises	Policy briefs
Careers in academia	Careers in prevention/security/police

Source: Clarke (2004).

under the crime reduction remit. (It is difficult to see how dispositional theorizing could assist in preventing terrorism, but the potential contribution of situational thinking is much more apparent.) Secondly, dissatisfaction with criminology also helped fuel the mushrooming growth of criminal justice in American universities during the past few decades. These departments were established to undertake operational studies of the criminal justice system (and train those working in the system) – again work disdained by many criminologists as being 'atheoretical' and mundane. Whether this experience will serve as a model or as warning only time will tell.

Selected further reading

Crime Prevention Studies (Criminal Justice Press and Willan Publishing), of which 18 volumes have now been published, is a book series covering research and practice in situational crime prevention. *Situational Crime Prevention: Successful Case Studies* (1997) contains 22 case studies with an introduction by the editor, Ronald V. Clarke. For an appraisal of ethical issues, see *Ethical and Social Issues in Situational Crime Prevention* (2000), edited by Andrew von Hirsch, David Garland and Alison Wakefield. Marcus Felson's *Crime and Everyday Life* (2002) provides an accessible account of some of the theoretical underpinnings of situational prevention. For the fit between situational crime prevention and problem-oriented policing, see Anthony Braga's *Problem-oriented Policing and Crime Prevention* (2002).

References

Ayres, I. and Levitt, S.D. (1998) 'Measuring positive externalities from unobservable victim precaution: an empirical analysis', *Quarterly Journal of Economics*, February: 43–77.

Bandura, A. (1976) 'Social learning analysis of aggression', in E. Ribes-Inesta and A. Bandura (eds) *Analysis of Delinquency and Aggression*. Hillsdale, NJ: Erlbaum Associates.

Barr, R. and Pease, K. (1990) 'Crime placement, displacement and deflection', in M. Tonry and N. Morris (eds) *Crime and Justice: A Review of Research. Vol. 12*. Chicago, IL: University of Chicago Press.

Blakely, E.J. and Snyder, M.G. (1998) 'Separate places: crime and security in gated communities', in M. Felson and R. Peiser (eds) *Reducing Crime through Real Estate Development and Management*. Washington, DC: Urban Land Institute.

Bourne, M.G. and Cooke, R.C. (1993) 'Victoria's speed camera programme', *Crime Prevention Studies. Vol. 1*. Monsey, NY: Criminal Justice Press.

Bowers, K. and Johnson, S. (2003) 'Measuring the geographical displacement and diffusion of benefit effects of crime prevention activity', *Journal of Quantitative Criminology*, 19: 275–301.

Bowers, K., Johnson, S. and Hirschfield, A. (in press) 'Closing off opportunities for crime: an evaluation of alley-gating', *European Journal on Criminal Policy and Research*.

Braga, A. (2002) *Problem-oriented Policing and Crime Prevention*. Monsey, NY: Criminal Justice Press.

Brantingham, P.L. and Brantingham, P.J. (1993) 'Environment, routine and situation: toward a pattern theory of crime', in R.V. Clarke and M. Felson (eds) *Routine Activity and Rational Choice*. New Brunswick, NJ: Transaction Press.

Brown, R. (1995) *The Nature and Extent of Heavy Goods Vehicle Theft. Crime Detection and Prevention Series Paper 66*. London: Home Office Police Research Group.

Butterfield, F. (2002) 'Suit against gun makers gains ground', *New York Times*, 3 January: A16.

Chaiken, J.M., Lawless, M.W. and Stevenson, K.A. (1974) *The Impact of Police Activity on Crime: Robberies on the New York City Subway System. Report R-1424-N.Y.C.* Santa Monica, CA: Rand Corporation.

Clarke, R.V. (1980) 'Situational crime prevention: theory and practice', *British Journal of Criminology*, 20: 136–47.

Clarke, R.V. (1982) 'Situational crime prevention: its theoretical basis and practical scope', in M. Tonry and N. Morris (eds) *Crime and Justice. Vol. 4*. Chicago, IL: University of Chicago Press.

Clarke, R.V. (1990) 'Deterring obscene phone callers: preliminary results of the New Jersey experience', *Security Journal*, 1: 143–8.

Clarke, R.V. (1992) 'Introduction', in R.V. Clarke (ed.) *Situational Crime Prevention: Successful Case Studies*. Guilderland, NY: Harrow & Heston.

Clarke, R.V. (1995) 'Situational crime prevention', in M. Tonry and D. Farrington (eds) *Building a Safer Society. Strategic Approaches to Crime Prevention. Crime and Justice: A Review of Research. Vol. 19*. Chicago, IL: University of Chicago Press.

Clarke, R.V. (ed.) (1997) *Situational Crime Prevention: Successful Case Studies* (2nd edn). Monsey, NY: Criminal Justice Press.

Clarke, R.V. (1999) *Hot Products: Understanding, Anticipating and Reducing the Demand for Stolen Goods. Police Research Series Paper 98*. London: Home Office.

Clarke, R.V. (2004) 'Technology, criminology and crime science', *European Journal on Criminal Policy and Research*, XXX: 1–9.

Clarke, R.V. and Bichler-Robertson, G. (1998) 'Place managers, slumlords and crime in low rent apartment buildings', *Security Journal*, 11: 11–19.

Clarke, R.V., Cody, R. and Natarajan, M. (1994) 'Subway slugs: tracking displacement on the London Underground', *British Journal of Criminology*, 34: 122–38.

Clarke, R.V. and Cornish, D.B. (1985) 'Modeling offenders' decisions: a framework for research and policy', in M. Tonry and N. Morris (eds) *Crime and Justice. Vol. 6*. Chicago, IL: University of Chicago Press.

Clarke, R.V. and Cornish, D.B. (2000) 'Rational choice', in R. Paternoster and R. Bachman (eds) *Crime Theories*. Los Angeles, CA: Roxbury.

Clarke, R.V. and Eck, J. (2003) *Become a Problem-solving Crime Analyst – in 55 Steps*. London: Jill Dando Institute of Crime Science, UCL.

Clarke, R.V. and Homel, R. (1997) 'A revised classification of situational crime prevention techniques', in S.P. Lab (ed.) *Crime Prevention at a Crossroads*. Cincinnati, OH: Anderson.

Clarke, R.V., Kemper, R. and Wyckoff, L. (2001) 'Controlling cell phone fraud in the US: lessons for the UK "Foresight" prevention initiative', *Security Journal*, 14: 7–22.

Clarke, R.V. and Mayhew, P. (1988) 'The British gas suicide story and its criminological implications', in M. Tonry and N. Morris (eds) *Crime and Justice. Vol. 10*. Chicago, IL: University of Chicago Press.

Clarke, R.V. and Mayhew, P. (1998) 'Preventing crime in parking lots: what we know and what we need to know', in M. Felson and R. Peiser (eds) *Reducing Crime through Real Estate Development and Management*. Washington, DC: Urban Land Institute.

Clarke, R.V. and Newman, G. (in press) 'Modifying criminogenic products: what role for government?', in R.V. Clarke and G. Newman (eds) *Designing out Crime from Products and Systems. Crime Prevention Studies. Vol. 18*. Monsey, NY: Criminal Justice Press.

Clarke, R.V. and Weisburd, D. (1994) 'Diffusion of crime control benefits: observations on the reverse of displacement', in R.V. Clarke (ed.) *Crime Prevention Studies. Vol. 2*. Monsey, NY: Criminal Justice Press.

Cohen, L.E. and Felson, M. (1979) 'Social change and crime rate trends: a routine activity approach', *American Sociological Review*, 44: 588–608.

Cornish, D.B. and Clarke, R.V. (eds) (1986) *The Reasoning Criminal: Rational Choice Perspectives on Offending*. New York, NY: Springer-Verlag.

Cornish, D.B. and Clarke, R.V. (2003) 'Opportunities, precipitators and criminal decisions', in M. Smith and D. Cornish (eds) *Crime Prevention Studies. Vol. 16*. Monsey, NY: Criminal Justice Press.

Duff, R.A and Marshall, S.E. (2000) 'Benefits, burdens and responsibilities: some ethical dimensions of situational crime prevention', in A. Von Hirsch *et al.* (eds) *Ethical and Social Issues in Situational Crime Prevention*. Oxford: Hart Publications.

Ekblom, P. (1988) 'Preventing post office robberies in London: effects and side effects', *Journal of Security Administration*, 11: 36–43.

Ekblom, P. (1999) 'Can we make crime prevention adaptive by learning from other evolutionary struggles?', *Studies on Crime and Crime Prevention*, 6: 27–51.

Ekblom, P., Simon, F.H. and Birdi, S. (1988) *Crime and Racial Harassment in Asian-run Small Shops: The Scope for Prevention. Crime Prevention Unit Paper* 15. London: Home Office, Crime Prevention Unit.

Ekblom, P. and Tilley, N. (2000) 'Going equipped: criminology, situational crime prevention and the resourceful offender', *British Journal of Criminology*, 40: 376–98.

Farrell, G. and Pease, K. (1993) *Once Bitten, Twice Bitten: Repeat Victimisation and its Implications for Crime Prevention. Crime Prevention Unit Series, Paper* 46. London: Home Office Police Research Group.

Farrington, D.P. and Knight, B.J. (1980) 'Stealing from a "lost" letter', *Criminal Justice and Behavior*, 7: 423–36.

Felson, M. (2002) *Crime and Everyday Life* (3rd edn). Thousand Oaks, CA: Pine Forge Press.

Felson, M. and Clarke, R.V. (1997) 'The ethics of situational crime prevention', in G. Newman *et al.* (eds) *Rational Choice and Situational Crime Prevention: Theoretical Foundations*. Aldershot: Dartmouth.

Felson, M. and Clarke, R.V. (1998) *Opportunity Makes the Thief: Practical Theory for Crime Prevention. Police Research Series, Paper* 98. London: Home Office.

Fields, G. (2000) 'Gunmakers fight back', *USA Today*, 27 April: 1.

Garland, D. (2000) 'The new criminologies of everyday life', in A. Von Hirsch *et al.* (eds) *Ethical and Social Issues in Situational Crime Prevention*. Oxford: Hart.

Garland, D. (2001) *The Culture of Control: Crime and Social Order in Contemporary Society*. Chicago, IL: University of Chicago Press.

Grabosky, P.N. (1996) 'Unintended consequences of crime prevention', in R. Homel (ed.) *The Politics and Practice of Situational Crime Prevention. Crime Prevention Studies. Vol. 5.* Monsey, NY: Criminal Justice Press.

Guerette, R. (2004) 'Toward safer borders: extending the scope of situational crime prevention.' Paper presented at the American Society of Criminology annual meeting, Nashville.

Hakim, S., Gaffney, M.A., Rengert, G. and Shachmurove, J. (1995) 'Costs and benefits of alarms to the community: burglary patterns and security measures in Tredyffrin Township, Pennsylvania', *Security Journal*, 6: 197–204.

Hartshorne, H. and May, M.A. (1928) *Studies in the Nature of Character Vol. I. Studies in Deceit*. New York, NY: Macmillan.

Hesseling, R.B.P. (1994) 'Displacement: a review of the empirical literature', in R. Clarke (ed.) *Crime Prevention Studies. Vol. 3.* Monsey, NY: Criminal Justice Press.

Highway Loss Data Institute (2004) *Insurance Theft Report 2001–2003: Passenger Vehicles.* Arlington, VA: Highway Loss Data Institute.

Homel, R., Hauritz, M., McIlwain, G., Wortley, R. and Carvolth, R. (1997) 'Preventing drunkenness and violence around nightclubs in a tourist resort', in R.V. Clarke (ed.) *Situational Crime Prevention: Successful Case Studies* (2nd edn). Albany, NY: Harrow & Heston.

Hunter, R. and Jeffrey, C.R. (1997) 'Preventing convenience store robbery through environmental design', in R.V. Clarke (ed.) *Situational Crime Prevention: Successful Case Studies* (2nd edn). Albany, NY: Harrow & Heston.

Kleinig, J. (2000) 'The burdens of situational crime prevention', in A. Von Hirsch *et al.* (eds) *Ethical and Social Issues in Situational Crime Prevention*. Oxford: Hart.

Landes, W.M. (1978) 'An economic study of US aircraft hijacking, 1961–1976', *Journal of Law and Economics*, 21: 1–32.

Langan, P.A. and Farrington, D.P. (1998) *Crime and Justice in the United States and in England and Wales, 1981–96*. Washington, DC: US Department of Justice, Office of Justice Programs, Bureau of Justice Statistics.

Lasley, J. (1998) *Designing-out Gang Homicides and Street Assaults. Research in Brief, National Institute of Justice*. Washington, DC: US Department of Justice.

Laycock, G. (2004) 'The UK car theft index: an example of government leverage', in M.G. Maxfield and R.V. Clarke (eds) *Understanding and Preventing Car Theft. Crime Prevention Studies. Vol. 17*. Monsey, NY: Criminal Justice Press and Cullompton: Willan Publishing.

Levi, M., Bissell, P. and Richardson, T. (1991) *The Prevention of Cheque and Credit Card Fraud. Crime Prevention Unit Paper* 26. London: Home Office.

Levi, M. and Handley, J. (1998) *The Prevention of Plastic and Cheque Fraud Revisited. Home Office Research Study* 182. London: Home Office.

Masuda, B. (1992) 'Displacement vs. diffusion of benefits and the reduction of inventory losses in a retail environment', *Security Journal*, 3: 131–6.

Matthews, R. (1986) *Policing Prostitution: A Multi-agency Approach. Centre for Criminology Paper* 1. London: Middlesex Polytechnic.

Matthews, R. (1993) *Prostitution and Multi-agency Policing. Crime Prevention Unit Paper* 43. London: Home Office.

Milgran, S. (1974) *Obedience to Authority: An Experimental View*. New York, NY: Harper & Row.

Newman, G.R. and Clarke, R.V. (2003) *Superhighway Robbery: Preventing E-commerce Crime*. Cullompton: Willan Publishing

Newman, O. (1972) *Defensible Space: Crime Prevention through Urban Design*. New York, NY: Macmillan (London: Architectural Press, 1973).

Painter, K. and Farrington, D. (1997) 'The crime reducing effect of improved street lighting: the Dudley Project', in R.V. Clarke (ed.) *Situational Crime Prevention: Successful Case Studies* (2nd edn). Albany, NY: Harrow & Heston.

Pease, K. (1991) 'The Kirkholt project: preventing burglary on a British public housing estate', *Security Journal*, 2: 73–7.

Pease, K. (2001) *Cracking Crime through Design*. London: Design Council.

Poyner, B. (1988) 'Video cameras and bus vandalism', *Journal of Security Administration*, 11: 44–51.

Poyner, B. (1991) 'Situational prevention in two car parks', *Security Journal*, 2: 96–101.

Ross, H.L. (1973) 'Law, science and accidents: the British Road Safety Act of 1967', *Journal of Legal Studies*, 4: 285–310.

Scherdin, M.J. (1986) 'The halo effect: psychological deterrence of electronic security systems', *Information Technology and Libraries*, September: 232–5.

Scottish Office Central Research Unit (1995) *Running the Red: An Evaluation of the Strathclyde Police Red Light Camera Initiative*. Edinburgh: Scottish Office.

Sherman, L., Gartin, P. and Buerger, M. (1989) 'Hot spots of predatory crime: routine activities and the criminology of place', *Criminology*, 27: 27–55.

Smith, M.J. (in press) *Robbery of Taxicab Drivers. Problem-oriented Guides for Police*. Office of Community Oriented Policing Services. Washington, DC: US Department of Justice.

Smith, M.J., Clarke, R.V. and Pease, K. (2002) 'Anticipatory benefits in crime prevention', in N. Tilley (ed.) *Analysis for Crime Prevention. Crime Prevention Studies. Vol. 13*. Monsey, NY: Criminal Justice Press.

Stanford Research Institute (1970) *Reduction of Robbery and Assault of Bus Drivers. Vol. III. Technological and Operational Methods*. Stanford, CA: Stanford Research Institute.

Sykes, G. and Matza, D. (1957) 'Techniques of neutralization: a theory of delinquency', *American Sociological Review*, 22: 664–70.

Tilley, N. (1999) 'The relationship between crime prevention and problem-oriented policing', in C. Solé Brito and T. Allan (eds) *Problem Oriented Policing: Crime-Specific Prooblems and Making POP Work*. Washington, DC: Police Executive Research Forum.

Von Hirsch, A., Garland, D. and Wakefield, A. (eds) (2000) *Ethical and Social Issues in Situational Crime Prevention*. Oxford: Hart.

Von Hirsch, A. and Shearing, C. (2000) 'Exclusion from public space', in A. Von Hirsch *et al.* (eds) *Ethical and Social Issues in Situational Crime Prevention*. Oxford: Hart.

Webb, B. (1997) 'Steering column locks and motor vehicle theft: evaluations from three countries', in R.V. Clarke (ed.) *Situational Crime Prevention: Successful Case Studies* (2nd edn). Guilderland, NY: Harrow & Heston.

Wilkinson, P. (1986) *Terrorism and the Liberal State* (2nd edn). New York, NY: New York University Press.

Wortley, R. (1998) 'A Two-stage Model of Situational Crime Prevention', *Studies on Crime and Crime Prevention*, 7: 173–88.

Wortley, R. (2001) 'A classification of techniques for controlling situational precipitators of crime', *Security Journal*, 14: 63–82.

Wortley, R. (2002) *Situational Prison Control: Crime Prevention in Correctional Institutions*. Cambridge: Cambridge University Press.

Wright, R.T. and Decker, S.H. (1994) *Burglars on the Job*. Boston, MA: Northeastern University Press.

Chapter 4

Developmental crime prevention

Ross Homel

Introduction

> People are not like rockets whose trajectory is established at the moment they are launched. Indeed, it is the lifelong capacity for change and reorganization that renders human beings capable of dramatic recovery from early harm and incapable of being inoculated against later adversity. This lifelong plasticity renders us both adaptive and vulnerable (Shonkoff and Phillips 2000: 90).

> But not even great talent and industry can ensure life success over adversity without opportunity (Elder 1998: 9).

Developmental prevention involves the organized provision of resources in some fashion to individuals, families, schools or communities to forestall the later development of crime or other problems. Doing something about crime early, preferably before the damage is too hard to repair or crime becomes entrenched, strikes most people as a logical approach to crime prevention. The twin challenges, of course, are to identify exactly what it is in individuals, families, schools or communities that increases the odds of involvement in crime, and then to do something useful about the identified conditions as early as possible.

The good news is that we now have persuasive scientific evidence that this approach might really work. Indeed, this chapter would probably not have been written if it were not for the solid evidence produced in the last few years by an influential series of experiments that it is possible to work with young children and their families in such a way as to head off future health, behaviour and crime problems (Farrington and Welsh 2002). There is quite impressive evidence for long-term effects from a range of studies that commenced in the USA before the 1980s, such as the Perry Preschool Project (Schweinhart 2004), the Elmira Prenatal/Early Infancy Project (Eckenrode *et al.* 1998; Olds 2002) and the Seattle Social Development Project (Hawkins *et al.* 1999). As Brooks-

Gunn *et al.* (2003) have observed, a more recent generation of interventions, again mostly from the USA, has confirmed that early intervention programmes can have positive effects for children from low-income backgrounds, with 'initial gains in intellectual and achievement scores, and longer term outcomes reflecting more successful school experiences...Reduction of behavior problems and delinquency have also been reported' (p. 10) (see also Shonkoff and Meisels 2000; Farrington and Welsh 1999, 2000).

In most of the successful experiments the systematic delivery to disadvantaged families with young children of basic services or resources that are taken for granted by middle-class populations in many countries eventually resulted in surprisingly large reductions in crime involvement amongst those targeted. Of equal or greater importance, a variety of studies have found improved outcomes in terms of educational performance (mother and child), child maltreatment, maternal workforce participation, child and youth behaviour, income, substance abuse and similar measures (Hawkins *et al.* 1999; Reynolds *et al.* 2001; Olds 2002; Brooks-Gunn *et al.* 2003; Schweinhart 2004). So it seems that simple things that everybody believes in and can feel good about, like baby healthcare or preschool, if they are done 'right', might be an important component not only of successful crime policies but also of policies that promote many aspects of the health and well-being of disadvantaged populations.

The aim of this chapter is to help people interested in developmental prevention to think more clearly about how to understand crime problems and how to apply a developmental perspective in formulating preventive responses. My starting point is the literature on risk-focused prevention and early-in-life interventions since these approaches are currently dominant, but I take the view that in fact developmental prevention is more general in its scope and methods than either of these approaches. One noteworthy feature of the criminological literature, for example, is that despite a bias towards early prediction and child-focused models (Sampson and Laub in press), there is considerable interest in prevention programmes in the primary and high-school years (Gottfredson 2001). This extensive literature is one of several reasons, discussed later in this chapter, for a broader focus when thinking about developmental prevention than interventions restricted to preschool and early childhood.

So in this chapter we explore how the boundaries of developmental prevention can be extended by thinking from a developmental and life-course perspective about crime problems in diverse contexts, drawing extensively on the literatures on risk factors and early-in-life interventions, but not being limited by them. Given the emphasis on conceptual issues, neither the review of risk factors nor prevention programmes is complete or systematic; my aim rather is to use these literatures to elaborate concepts and to raise issues. For readers interested in narrative and systematic reviews and overviews, some excellent references are outlined at the end of this chapter in the selected further reading.

In the next section we look at risk-focused and early-in-life prevention approaches in a little more detail, emphasizing their promise whilst asking what processes lie behind the long-term changes that have been observed. This leads, in the following section, to a consideration of some of the core conceptual issues and debates that underpin the theory and practice of developmental prevention. These include most fundamentally the notions of 'development' and 'criminality', as well as what 'early' means in 'early intervention', and the strengths and limitations of a risk-focused approach. A case study (Jack's story) is used as a vehicle further to elaborate developmental prevention concepts, particularly life phases and life transitions, turning points, ecological-transactional analysis and prevention programmes suitable for different life phases. We conclude by suggesting some new directions for the field.

Early intervention and risk-focused prevention

The term *early childhood intervention* (or, sometimes, *early-in-life* or simply early intervention) is used to label a vast body of literature concerned with the study of multidisciplinary services designed to enhance the health and well-being of children aged from birth to five, and their families (Shonkoff and Meisels 2000). Partly as a result of the successful experiments cited above there has been an enormous increase in interest in recent years in early childhood as a site for social interventions (Brooks-Gunn *et al.* 2003), especially in English-speaking countries where there is a historic emphasis on individual family rather than collective responsibility for child raising.

Hertzman (2002: 1), for example, observes that in 'Canada, the past ten years have been a time of renewed focus on early childhood and the challenge of making a strong collective commitment to our young children'. Fraser Mustard, the Founding President of the Canadian Institute for Advanced Research, has been extremely influential in Ontario and internationally in highlighting the critical importance of the early years for a healthy and competent population (McCain and Mustard 1999). In the UK, enormous resources have been directed through Sure Start to the needs of families with children under the age of four, especially in disadvantaged communities (Glass 1999; Tunstill *et al.* 2002). In the USA, programmes like Head Start attracted increased resources in the 1990s, despite general cutbacks in public expenditure on social programmes (Kamerman 2000). By contrast with the USA, as part of a general increase in social expenditure from a low base (Saunders 1998; Kalisch 2000; Australian Government Taskforce on Child Development 2003), Australia has increased expenditure on family support and early-in-life intervention programmes through a National Agenda for Early Childhood (Australian Government Task Force on Child Development 2003) and the Stronger Families and Communities Strategy.[1] Internationally, the World Bank, the OECD and UNICEF have all issued reports in recent years on the importance of investment in early childhood for building human and social capital (McCain and Mustard 2002).

The Elmira (New York) home-visiting study by David Olds and his colleagues is an excellent example of an influential, policy-relevant prevention programme that is usually classified as 'early intervention' since many outcomes related to babies and young children, although the target population was actually young mothers. This work is also usefully viewed as a good example of risk-focused prevention. Olds' research has shown that for teenaged first-time mothers from very disadvantaged backgrounds regular prenatal and postnatal home visits by trained health professionals can, under some circumstances, have long-term benefits not only to the mothers but also to their children. Although many elements of this intervention can be found in community child health programmes around the world, what is distinctive about the Olds approach is the fact that the programme is explicitly grounded in theories of human ecology, self-efficacy and human attachment and the nurse home visitors systematically and rigorously addressed risk factors associated with poor birth outcomes, child abuse and neglect, welfare dependence and poor maternal life course (Olds *et al.* 1999). Early evaluation of this randomized trial showed a decrease in recorded child physical abuse and neglect during the first two years of life, and in a 15-year follow-up both mothers and the children had fewer arrests than control groups where the mothers were not visited. In fact the children had less than half as many arrests as children of control mothers, and also smoked and drank less and had had fewer sexual partners (Olds *et al.* 1998).

The term 'risk factor' captures an emphasis on the identification, measurement and manipulation of key variables correlated with future crime as the basis for programme design and delivery. Risk factors are essentially commonsense notions that have been put through the wringer of exact measurement and statistical analysis, often in longitudinal surveys where the same individuals are followed for some years (sometimes from birth). Longitudinal studies, such as the Mater University of Queensland Longitudinal Study of Pregnancy and its Outcomes (Bor *et al.* 2001), permit the study of statistical associations between conditions at one time (such as being aggressive at the age of four) and outcomes at a later time (such as involvement in delinquency at the age of 13). The language of risk factors is used to avoid the epistemological and scientific challenges posed by the language of causation (Susser 1998) and to highlight the essentially correlational nature of our knowledge. We know rather more about factors that are associated in a statistical sense with crime than we do about 'causal processes' (Farrington 2002).

Risk factors that have been found most commonly to predict youth crime include childhood anti-social behaviour, low self-control (impulsiveness, hyper-activity, a poor ability to plan ahead, etc.), low levels of parental supervision, harsh and inconsistent discipline, child maltreatment (abuse and neglect), offending by parents and siblings, parental conflict, a large family size, and weak parental and school attachment (Farrington 2002; Sampson and Laub in press). All these have been the focus of preventive efforts in recent years on the assumption that we do not require a full understanding of causal processes in order to do effective prevention work, especially if an 'omnibus' or 'scattergun' approach is adopted that targets as many risk factors as possible in the hope of scoring some hits on some key causes. According to Farrington (2002: 660): 'The basic idea of this approach is very simple: Identify the key risk factors for offending and implement prevention methods designed to counteract them. There is often a related attempt to identify key protective factors against offending and to implement prevention methods designed to enhance them.' As Farrington notes, this approach became enormously popular in the

1990s, and in fact there is now a strong tendency in the literature to equate developmental prevention with risk-focused prevention.

Risk-focused prevention does seem to work. Although based on different theories and methods from the Olds programme of research (Olds 2002), the findings from a number of other experiments are equally noteworthy. Table 4.1 summarizes the evaluations of a sample of five well-known interventions, including the Elmira Project. Although many projects could have been selected, the five projects in Table 4.1 serve our present purposes since their focus ranges from the prenatal and infancy periods to the late teens, they use a variety of approaches underpinned by different processes, they involve work in multiple contexts, and they have all been well evaluated. Projects are classified using terminology first proposed in 1994 by the US Institute of Medicine (Marshall and Watt 1999): *universal* interventions are provided for the general population or for all members of a specified collectivity like a local community, a school or a workplace; *selected* interventions are directed at groups judged to be at increased risk; and *indicated* interventions are directed at individuals already manifesting a problem such as disruptive behaviour.[2]

The Perry Preschool Project is probably the most widely cited and influential early intervention project ever implemented, with follow-ups of the 123 study children annually at the ages of 3 to 11 and then at at ages of 14, 15, 19, 27 and 40. The goal of the project, which was implemented in the years 1962–7, was to enhance intellectual development and subsequent school achievement in disadvantaged 3 and 4 year-old children (Schweinhart *et al.* 1993; Schweinhart 2004). A daily preschool programme was provided in addition to weekly home visits by teachers. The aims were to 'encourage children in effective decision making, self discipline (setting and achieving goals), working effectively with others and recognising their views, self-expression, reasoning, having an enquiring spirit and in understanding and accepting people's differences' (Pirani 1994).

Although cognitive gains for children in the programme were not maintained, the programme participants' school achievement and behaviour were significantly better than those of control children. They were more likely to graduate from high school and continue to further education. By the ages of 27 and 40, they had higher incomes and were more likely to be home-owners and, at the age of 40, more programme-group males than controls were employed (70 vs. 50 per cent). The impact of the preschool programme on later offending was impressive: at the age of 15, programme children had lower self-reported offending; at 19, they were less likely to have been arrested; at 27, the control group had twice the number of arrests; and at 40 the programme group had significantly fewer lifetime arrests than the no-programme group (36 vs. 55 per cent arrested five or more times). As summarized by Schweinhart (2004: 3): 'The study presents strong evidence that the Perry Preschool program played a significant role in reducing overall arrests and arrests for violent crimes as well as property and drug crimes and subsequent prison or jail sentences over study participants' lives up to age 40.'

Family support was the key intervention component in the *Syracuse Family Development Research Program* (Lally *et al.* 1988) with the provision of child care as a supplementary feature. Home visitation was conducted

Table 4.1 Summary of five major prevention programme evaluations

Programme	Level	Focus/outcome	Life phase	Participants	R	Duration	Content	Outcomes	Economic outcome
Elmira Prenatal/Early Infancy Project (Olds 2002)	S	Poor birth outcomes, child maltreatment, welfare dependence, poor maternal life course	Prenatal/infancy and late teens	400 first-time young, single and/or low SES mothers	Yes	2 yrs	Family support	Improved pregnancy outcomes, better parenting skills. At the age of 4: higher maternal employment, fewer and more widely spaced pregnancies, more mothers returned to education, less abuse/neglect. At the age of 15: fewer arrests (mother and child), less smoking and drinking, fewer sexual partners	Cost-savings analysis: high-risk families, programme cost US$6,083 (1996 dollars), savings to government US$24,694 (1996 dollars), net savings $18,611. 80 per cent of savings ($20,384) attributed to higher employment rates for mothers and reduced welfare usage. $4,310 attributed to less crime over the child's lifetime
Syracuse Family Development Research Program (Lally *et al.* 1988)	S	Cognitive	Prenatal/infancy	108 low-income families	No	5 yrs	Family support, early education	Initial cognitive gains not maintained. 10-year follow-up (children aged 13–16): lower delinquency, better school attendance and performance for girls	Cost-savings analysis: findings demonstrate savings to government do not break even with programme costs. Programme cost US$45,092 (1998 dollars). Taxpayers receive $0.19 in criminal justice system benefits for every dollar spent. Combined taxpayer and crime victim receive $0.34 for every dollar spent

Programme		Focus	Level	Sample	R	Duration	Components	Outcomes	Cost-benefit analysis
Perry Preschool Program (Schweinhart 2004)	S	Cognitive	Preschool	58 disadvantaged 3–4-year-olds	Yes	1–2 yrs	Family support (teacher visits) Enriched early education	Intellectual gains not maintained, but higher school achievement, higher rates of literacy and employment, less offending (especially fewer arrests) and anti-social behaviour, less welfare dependency (up to the age of 40)	Cost-benefit analysis: programme cost US$12,356 (1993 dollars), savings to government $108,002, net savings $95,646. Most savings to government due to reduction in criminal justice costs $49,044, then reduction in health services, taxes from increased employment, reduction in welfare
Montreal Prevention Project (Tremblay et al. 1995)	I	Anti-social behaviour	Early primary	250 disruptive boys aged 7–9 yrs	Yes	2 yrs	Parent training Child training	At the age of 12: lower delinquency, less anti-social behaviour, higher school achievement	
Seattle Social Development Project (Hawkins et al. 1999)	U	Anti-social behaviour; connectedness to school, family and community	Early primary	500 Grade I children; late intervention for Grades 5 and 6	No	2 yrs	Parent training Child training Teacher training	After programme: intervention group less aggressive. Fifth grade: intervention group less delinquent, better family communication and parent management, higher attachment to school. Age of 18: intervention group less delinquent, less heavy drinking, less sexual activity and fewer pregnancies	Cost-benefit analysis: cost per participant US$3,017 (1998 dollars), taxpayers receive $0.90 in criminal justice system benefits for every dollar spent (per participant benefit $2,704). Crime victims save average $2,695 per participant. Combined taxpayer/crime victim benefit of $1.79 for for every dollar spent

Notes:
R = Randomized design: at recruitment families were randomly allocated to treatment and non-treatment groups.
U = Universal: programme offered to general population or group.
S = Selected: participants were chosen on the basis of membership of a group judged to be at increased risk.
I = Indicated: participants were selected because they displayed behaviours that were precursors to aggressive/offending outcomes.

by paraprofessionals, often from similar backgrounds to the programme participants. Known as child development trainers (CDTs), they had the role of a knowledgeable friend, advisor and advocate. All CDTs attended weekly training sessions which included case reviews and group problem-solving. Intensive annual two-week training programmes were conducted for all programme staff, including cooks, bus drivers and secretaries. During weekly home visits, CDTs performed ten activities that are important features of home visitations. These included teaching families games, language interactions and learning tasks appropriate to the child's level of development; nutritional information; positive support and encouragement for the mother; and encouraging the mother to take an active role in the child's schooling. At the age of 15, only 6 per cent of programme children compared to 22 per cent of a control group had official juvenile delinquent records. The children in the control group had more serious and chronic offences compared with those of the programme children. Charges included burglary, robbery, physical assault and sexual assault.

In the *Montreal Prevention Project*, boys identified by their preschool teachers as the most disruptive learned social skills and self-control strategies (Tremblay *et al*. 1995). Their parents received training in monitoring behaviours, using effective discipline and encouraging prosocial behaviour. Evaluations at the age of 12 showed that boys in the programme were achieving more highly at school and displaying less anti-social behaviour (e.g. fighting) than the non-intervention group. Self-reported delinquent behaviour (e.g. burglary and theft) was significantly lower and the differences between programme and non-intervention boys increased with time (from the ages of 10 to 12).

Instead of targeting an indicated group, the *Seattle Social Development Project* (Hawkins *et al*. 1991, 1992, 1999) provided a universal programme of teacher training and supervision, child training in cognitive problem-solving, peer-group sessions and parent training for effective behaviour management. The focus was Grade 1 children, but there was also a late intervention for children in Grades 5 and 6. There was an underlying belief that offending would be discouraged in children who established strong bonds with their families, schools and communities. Following the programme, teachers rated children as less aggressive, although this effect was only apparent for white children. Subsequent evaluations when the children were beginning Grade 5 showed that fewer experimental children reported alcohol use or delinquent behaviour. In addition, programme children displayed greater attachment to school, and their parents demonstrated better management skills, greater involvement in their children's development and more effective family communication. At the age of 18, fewer students receiving the full intervention (compared with the controls) reported violent delinquent acts, heavy drinking, sexual intercourse, having multiple sex partners and pregnancy or causing pregnancy. The positive results observed earlier for school attachment and achievement were maintained. Late intervention in Grades 5 and 6 only did not appear to affect these outcomes.

Significantly, these and similar interventions seem in most cases not only to have yielded reductions in crime and a range of other problem behaviours, but also to have done so in a cost-effective manner (see the last column of

Table 4.1) (Karoly *et al.* 1998; Aos *et al.* 2001; Welsh 2001). For example, a cost-savings analysis of the Elmira Prenatal/Early Infancy Project for high-risk families estimated the total cost per participant as US$6,083 (1996 dollars) with estimated net savings of US$24,694 to the government. Cost-benefit analysis of the Perry Preschool Program (Barnett 1993) yielded the oft-quoted figure of US$7.16 return per dollar spent. The biggest 'bang for the buck' were reductions in crime (an estimated $49,044 per participant), followed by increased taxes on earnings (26 per cent), a decrease in the need for special education for participating children (25 per cent) and reduced welfare assistance (9 per cent) (Karoly *et al.* 1998).

Contrary to these positive results, cost-savings analysis of the Syracuse Family Development Research Program demonstrated that savings to the government did not exceed programme costs. Programme costs per participant (1998 dollars) were estimated to be US$18,037, outweighing the combined benefits of criminal justice costs avoided ($3,953) and crime victim costs avoided ($3,842). This resulted in a total net cost to taxpayers per participant of minus $10,242 (Aos *et al.* 1998). However, these findings only demonstrate the programme's savings in terms of criminal justice and crime victim costs avoided. Although savings to the government did not match the programme's costs, the overall intervention could well be considered a success. This is evident from the lower failure rates of participating students, higher grades, lower rates of juvenile delinquency and greater family unity (Manning 2004). Thus the Syracuse programme is a good example of why net savings to the government should not be the only indicator of a programme's viability or worthiness for funding. This is particularly salient given that some costs are very difficult to monetize, and so are not usually included in economic analysis.

It is important to note that positive outcomes are not limited to the early 'classic' studies. Farrington and Welsh (2003) have, for example, shown in a meta-analysis of the effectiveness of 40 family-based crime prevention programmes, some of which commenced more recently than those in Table 4.1, that the majority had an impact on delinquency and anti-social child behaviour. The mean effect size was .321, which corresponds roughly to a decrease in offending from 50 per cent in a control group to 34 per cent in an experimental group.

How is it that these outcomes were achieved? What were the processes involved? Many possibilities are suggested by the studies reviewed. Of fundamental importance, all the interventions were well resourced and were carefully implemented by staff who were well trained. All were based on explicit theories, although these were rather varied in nature suggesting that there is no one 'correct approach'. All involved some form of development of parental capacities, resources and skills, sometimes through parent 'training' and sometimes more broadly through family support. All illustrate the importance of working simultaneously in multiple domains, most commonly involving children, their parents and their teachers. Some studies suggest that improvements in children's cognitive abilities (such as IQ) are crucial, others that improvements in social skills or in the extent of the child's attachment to family, school or community are the key. Significantly, some studies found that effects were not universal, indicating complex interactions between the programme elements and the characteristics of participants and the groups from which they come. In the Elmira study, for example, positive outcomes were restricted to the high-risk mothers and their children; in the Seattle study, black children did not improve in their behaviour.

It would be easier to understand what underlies improved outcomes, or their absence, if evaluations of interventions collected more data on intervening mechanisms, but unfortunately often little can be learnt from major interventions about the specific processes of change (Brooks-Gunn *et al.* 2003). Even when interventions have been well evaluated, not many studies (until very recently) have collected rich qualitative or quantitative data on the multiple sources of influence on individual pathways, or on the amount, intensity and variety of services children or families receive. This is a major challenge for the field.

It is certainly the case that one is left with the impression from some studies that 'getting in' before the age of five is crucial, or at least highly desirable. For example, Schweinhart (2004) presents a path model linking the Perry Preschool intervention at the ages of 3 and 4 with outcomes at the age of 40, with post-programme IQ serving as a crucial predictor of school achievement and commitment in the mid-teens linking to the later outcomes (admittedly with attenuated predictive power by the age of 40). This could be taken to mean that to some extent the intervention acted as a 'magic bullet', boosting IQ (at least temporarily) and hence later-life performance. The failure of the 'late' intervention on its own in the Seattle project could also be interpreted as evidence that intervening at an earlier age is essential in order to bring about sustained changes in individual characteristics or 'propensities'. We now turn to a more detailed examination of these and related issues.

Concepts and controversies

Perhaps Laub and Sampson (2003: 33–4) have most clearly articulated the debates about 'development' and the associated concept of 'propensity' or 'criminality' from the perspective of their analyses of the life histories of 52 men up to the age of 70 from the original sample constructed by Sheldon and Eleanor Glueck (1950):

> Developmental accounts, especially from developmental psychology, focus on regular or lawlike development over the life span ... The resulting emphasis is on systematic pathways of development (change) over time, with the imagery being one of the execution of a program written at an earlier point in time ... In contrast, life-course approaches, while incorporating individual differences and notions of lawlike development such as aging, emphasize variability and exogenous influences on the course of development over time that cannot be predicted by focusing solely on enduring individual traits ... or even past experiences ... A life-course focus recognizes emergent properties and rejects the metaphor of 'unfolding' that is inextricably part of the developmental paradigm.

Whilst the intensity and extent of the preprogrammed deterministic view of human development in modern developmental psychology are debatable (Lerner 2002), Laub and Sampson's critique is nevertheless useful for identifying some of the key tensions underlying the developmental approach to prevention. If a propensity to commit crime is established before the age of five (Gottfredson and Hirschi 1990), or if more generally early childhood development 'is a key step in human development trajectories that are set in the early years and tend to carry on through education into adult life in respect to health, learning and behaviour' (McCain and Mustard 2002), then logically the main focus of prevention efforts should be the early years. If on the other hand Laub and Sampson are correct in their arguments that childhood risk factors have very modest predictive power into adulthood and that human agency, situational factors and chance events are of much greater importance than previously believed in terms of understanding the enormous variability and diversity in life histories (including the process of desistance from crime), it follows that one would devote resources to prevention efforts across the life course, be sceptical about relying too much on risk factor analyses and offender typologies in designing interventions, and give weight to routine activities theory and to situational approaches to prevention as well as to developmental research.

Some years ago the Developmental Crime Prevention Consortium (1999) prepared a report for the Australian government that anticipated many of these issues. This interdisciplinary group that I had the privilege to convene evolved a view of developmental pathways and of developmental prevention that took a life-course approach and did not presuppose the existence of a propensity to offend, although the possibility of enduring individual traits that predispose some people to crime was by no means dismissed. This stance contrasted with the definition of developmental prevention adopted by Farrington (1996), which makes criminality reduction (or inhibiting 'the development of criminal potential in individuals') the central focus of prevention efforts. The concepts and models proposed in this chapter have developed from the foundations we laid in our earlier work.[3]

Developmental pathways

Life, according to this perspective, is not marked by one steady march towards adulthood whose direction becomes fixed after early childhood, or one steady line of change, either for better or for worse. Instead, what occurs is a series of phases, a series of points of change, a series of transitions. These points of transition are when intervention can often occur most effectively, since at times of change individuals are both vulnerable to taking false steps and open to external support or advice. In the course of becoming an adult, for example, most people move from home to school, from primary to secondary school, from school to seeking entry into the paid workforce, acquiring a driver's licence, being legally able to buy alcohol, possibly leaving home. Throughout adulthood, further transitions occur: making commitments to other people, possibly becoming a parent, coping with shifts in employment status, being faced with the evidence that one's child is in various kinds of trouble, to a time of standing back and allowing one's children to bring up the next generation.

Consistent with the analysis of Laub and Sampson, the nature of these transitions becomes increasingly hard to predict as time passes since they depend on life events and on how individuals understand and react to these events, and indeed how they help to shape them. Many transitions require a person to come to grips with new social institutions, and many involve new developmental tasks and challenges. Extensive literatures have developed around many of these life phases and transitions. For example, the transition from home to school is well researched, with a special focus on the concept of 'readiness for school' and how such readiness can be understood and perhaps improved through planned interventions (Ramey and Ramey 1998).

Life phases are not 'stages' in the sense that they represent the unfolding of a predetermined developmental blueprint, but are socially constructed and highly variable, depending as much on individual choices and happenstance as on normative or biological timetables. At each time of transition there is the possibility of more than one outcome. For some children, the transition from home to school is unproblematic, especially if they have had the advantage of a happy preschool experience and a family that values education and understands how to get the best out of the school system. Others soon learn that school is a place to stay away from as much as possible, since the main lesson is that one is a failure who doesn't belong. Again, some people negotiate the transition from school to the paid workforce with a minimum of effort, whilst others never make the transition.

Essentially, developmental approaches are characterized by a pervasive emphasis on *pathways* and on aspects of time and timing. Pathways are understood not just as unique individual biographies, but as roads through life – from conception to death – that fork out in many directions (often unpredictable) at the kinds of crucial transition points that mark new experiences and relationships. A person may follow an easy path to respectable middle age, or a painful path through teenage substance abuse, homelessness and early death. In contrast to earlier generations when, for most people, fewer choices were available, increasingly there is no set timetable or established societal route for many children and young people. Youth pathways in particular tend now to be characterized by 'non-linearity' and by complex patterns of transition in which, through force of circumstance and an increased societal emphasis on individualism, young people enter a 'new adulthood' earlier and choose their own timetables for achieving goals such as a steady job or finishing school (Wyn 2004).

Crucially, developmental pathways in the sense discussed here should be distinguished from the kind of pathways models proposed by Hertzman (1999) and others who write from a medical or epidemiological background, where there is a much stronger (although mostly implicit) emphasis on what might be characterized as 'linear causal chains of events'. In these conceptions, one condition (such as a lack of readiness for school) tends to lead inexorably to another (such as disability and absenteeism in the fifth decade of life) via intermediate events (such as being stuck in a high-stress, low-control job). According to this model, much of the social gradient effect in health outcomes arises from the amplification and reproduction by social processes of the effects of differences in individual traits and in life circumstances at (or before) birth. Both conceptualizations – the causal pathways model and the developmental pathways model – obviously have many points in common, but the developmental model has a greater place for human agency and the possibility that people can 'reinvent themselves' in the light of social circumstances and opportunities that arise over the life course (Elder 1998).

Whatever the role of agency and happenstance, quantitative analysis of developmental pathways would not be possible without some degree of underlying regularity and predictability. Since patterns in pathways are largely constructions out of correlational data, it is important to ask what may underlie the statistical connections. From a developmental perspective three kinds of answers are possible.

The most familiar explanation is in terms of proposing a variety of processes or 'carrier mechanisms' that may account for connections over time. These processes are most often placed within the individual, as Laub and Sampson complain. The experience of particular events, for example, establishes some predisposition to react with hostility, to lie, to steal, to think only in terms of one's own pleasure or of the short term. The recent work by Caspi and Moffitt and their colleagues (Caspi *et al.* 2002) on genetic factors that appear to moderate the effects of child maltreatment illustrates one way this kind of process could operate, whilst also highlighting the importance of 'environmental insults' to children (p. 851). Using data from the Dunedin Multidisciplinary Health and Development Study, this research team found that 'maltreated children with a genotype conferring high levels of MAOA [monoamine oxidise A] expression were less likely to develop antisocial problems' (p. 851). This is consistent with the hypothesis that genetic factors are part of the carrier mechanism linking the early experience of abuse with later violent behaviour, although the possibility that the same genetic factors drive both parental abuse of children and child aggression cannot be discounted.

The interaction between individual and environmental factors found by Caspi and his colleagues suggests another general way of thinking about what underlies patterns in pathways. This consists of seeing the particular processes as contained in the interactions between people, a point we return to later in discussing the case study. The best known example, based on observations of behaviour sequences, is the concept of 'coercive cycles' proposed by Patterson and Dishion (1988). A child starts off, for example, with a low-level aggressive action. The parent responds ineffectively, reinforcing the child's negative behaviour and moving it up a notch. The parent then finds it even more difficult to respond effectively, and so problems intensify. In effect, each party's response to the other both perpetuates and escalates the connection between a prior event and a later behaviour.

Perhaps the least familiar approach to understanding connections over time is the one taken by Sameroff and his colleagues (Sameroff *et al.* 1993). They observed that a number of environmental conditions were negatively related to a child's IQ scores at the age of 4, and that these scores were in turn correlated with IQ scores at the age of 13. They took as well, however, the unusual step of measuring for the presence of the same risk conditions at the age of 13. The correlations between the two sets of risk conditions were quite high (around 0.7) and taking that into account effectively halved the correlation between the IQ scores at the two ages. In effect, what might appear to be some disposition carried forward within the individual could well reflect continuity in the conditions that are being encountered. This is an important insight since, as Elder (1998: 5) has emphasized, 'longtitudinal studies *seldom* examine the stability and nature of children's social environments over time … As a result, sources of behavioral continuity and change remain poorly understood' (emphasis in original).

Do these possibilities matter for the task of prevention?

These alternative explanations matter for the choice of what to change. Prevention, it has been argued, should target what we think of as causally related to crime – what we see as the underlying process – rather than be aimed at what is simply correlated (Tremblay and Craig 1995; Farrington 2000). They matter also for our interpretation of any effects we obtain. What we see as change within the individual (and as then likely to persist even if circumstances change) may in fact be a change in the individual's circumstances, making it likely that the old behaviour will appear again as soon as the circumstances swing back to where they were. So when we come to evaluate whether what we have done has made a difference we should check both for changes in individuals *and* in circumstances, something that is, as we have seen, too seldom done.

The timing of interventions

One crucial consequence of a focus on developmental pathways is that 'early intervention' means *intervention early in the pathway*. This may or may not mean early in life. What a person does at a particular time does depend heavily on current circumstances as well as on chance events and the exercise of individual choice, as Laub and Sampson (2003) emphasize. However, behaviour is also influenced by earlier events, as they also acknowledge. Decisions in the present depend at least to some extent on how earlier problems have been coped with and on the extent to which they have equipped the person involved with the skills, the strategies, the energy and the openness to advice or opportunity that are now called for. A first-time offender, for example, needs to be ready to listen, to feel shame, empathy and embarrassment. His or her family also need to have developed sufficient will and trust to be able to cope with this particular false step and to move on effectively. Whether they can do so depends on what has happened at earlier points in life. If those earlier situations have led to distrust, alienation or entrenched and unproductive strategies for dealing with difficulty, then success in working through this new problem will be all the more difficult to achieve.

There are, then, good reasons for intervening early in life. Families with babies and preschoolers who suffer the consequences of poverty, relationship breakdown and abusive or inept parenting styles are more likely to produce teenagers who participate in crime and substance abuse (Farrington 2002). Once it is accepted that some conditions and situations at an early age have multiple consequences later in life – they alter the 'baggage' one carries – it follows that successful intervention at an early age should be a cost-effective preventive strategy.

In summary, there are two main reasons for taking early-in-life interventions seriously. One key reason is that early in the pathway frequently equates to early in life, especially for children living in disadvantaged areas. Some sequences of offending, for example, are manifest in the preschool years through aggressive and hostile behaviour. In these cases, early interventions have more immediate as well as long-term goals, especially since dealing with behaviour problems in a reactive fashion even at a young age can be extremely costly (Manning 2004). The second reason for considering an early-in-life approach is that it is likely to be strategically effective to attempt to divert people from harmful pathways before maladaptive patterns of behaviour are well entrenched. Protective and anticipatory action is more powerful and less painful than clinical or punitive interventions after a history of offending, even if such interventions can be very cost-effective (as is the case for example with multisystemic therapy; Aos *et al.* 2001).

Much crime prevention work, however, also means intervening with those who have made a false start (so developmental prevention encompasses what is usually regarded as 'offender treatment'). Creating *pathways to recovery* is probably as important as keeping people on the straight and narrow, given the prevalence of offending in western societies compared with developing countries (Wei *et al.* 2004). Moreover, firm foundations in early life do not guarantee a problem-free adolescence. Wikström and Loeber (2000) have, for example, demonstrated that well adjusted adolescents from well functioning, loving families can be more likely to become engaged in late-onset serious crime (including violence and drug dealing) if they grow up in high-crime public-housing areas. A broad view of developmental prevention is that it involves interventions early in developmental pathways that might lead to problems (or the escalation of problems), not only interventions in early childhood. The nature and timing of intervention depend, from the developmental perspective, not just on the individual's age, but on the identified pathways to offending and the critical transition points that characterize those pathways. The first offence – the first contact with the criminal justice system – is one of those critical transition points in a person's life.

Risk-focused prevention

Sampson and Laub (in press) argue that child risk factors have very limited predictive power across the life course. Risk is not destiny. Moreover, recent evaluations in the UK by Crow and his colleagues (2004) of implementations of *Communities that Care*, a prominent exemplar of risk-focused prevention, underline the considerable practical difficulties entailed in identifying, measuring and changing risk factors in local communities. On the other hand, the examples of risk-focused prevention we examined earlier suggest that it would be foolish to abandon prevention initiatives that aim to influence child and family risk factors. The evidence, after all, is that this approach can work very well. What, then, to make of risk factors and risk-focused prevention?

Much of the inspiration for risk-focused preventive approaches in criminology derives from experience in public health, with programmes designed to reduce heart disease or cancer through a focus on such factors as smoking, exercise and diet being viewed as models for how crime prevention programmes should be constructed and evaluated (Hawkins *et al.* 1992). Amongst its many virtues, this approach maximizes the likelihood that programmes will be implemented that really influence some of the key factors that lead to crime and violence, whilst building on individual and family strengths through an emphasis on protective factors. Randomized clinical trials emerge in this paradigm as the gold standard to which other study designs aspire, since they produce the highest-quality evidence concerning the causal impacts of interventions (Weisburd *et al.* 2001).

It is the case, however, that whilst criminologists have been embracing public health models as an enlightened scientific alternative to the traditional preoccupation with largely ineffective, punishment-oriented criminal justice remedies (Moore 1995), a growing number of public health researchers have been expressing serious dissatisfaction with the dominant perspective and direction of their own discipline. McKinlay and Marceau (2000), for example, take stock of the state of public health in the USA, arguing that it is preoccupied with methods to the exclusion of philosophical orientation and theory development, and that established epidemiology is hamstrung by its adherence to 'an individualistic/medical natural science paradigm' (p. 25). They are especially critical of 'risk factorology', likening epidemiology to a maze of risk factors with no opening or exit in sight. Mining of extant databases produces the phenomenon of 'the risk factor du jour' (p. 28), with a thicket of single factor associations measured at the individual level obscuring the view of the larger landscape of environmental and social structural forces that have the more profound influence on population health. As Keating and Hertzman (1999: 3) put it, 'the development of health and well-being is a population phenomenon rather than a purely individual affair. Particularly striking is the discovery of a strong association between the health of a population and the size of the social distance between members of the population'.

The problem of 'levels of explanation' is a recurrent theme in recent public health writings, with a plea for epidemiology to rediscover its population focus and to use methods that fit the problem rather than making the problem fit the method. And the problem is increasingly understood as requiring an analysis of 'the historical and social context and … the importance of diversity and local knowledge rather than only searching for universal relationships' (Pearce 1996). In an analysis of the implications of the results of community intervention trials, Sorenson and colleagues (1998) call for the targeting of multiple levels of influence (moving beyond a focus on individual behaviour change); addressing social inequalities in disease risk; involving communities in programme planning and implementation; tailoring interventions to the unique needs and cultures of communities (avoiding a one-size-fits-all approach); and utilizing rigorous process tracking (understanding better what is inside the intervention 'black box'). They also call for the use of the full range of research phases and methods, from hypothesis generation and methods development to dissemination research. As Pearce and many others have argued, the randomized clinical trial is no doubt the most appropriate design for studies of the impact of individual factors or specific programmes where control can be maintained by the researcher, but is ill-suited to other kinds of problems, such as complex community trials incorporating multiple programmes that develop and change as participants are incorporated into the research process as partners, not just as subjects.

Thus there is a strong current of thinking in contemporary public health that acknowledges the remarkable achievements of the field in the past century in tackling the causes and consequences of illness, disability and death, but that questions the continued appropriateness of risk-focused prevention initiatives for every problem, at least as conventionally understood. There is a plea for increased attention to history, community context and social structure, particularly to the malign impact on population health and well-being of the steepening social gradient – the social distance between rich and poor – in most developed countries. There is a concomitant discontent with conventional research methods that elevate certain techniques to gold class whilst relegating others to steerage, regardless of the nature of the problem.

Of course this kind of critique has not bypassed the crime prevention community. Many of the issues that trouble our health colleagues have their echoes in the criminological literature. There is for example a vigorous debate around the methodology of community trials (Farrington 1998; Pawson and Tilley 1998; Laycock 2002), and the need to intervene at multiple levels – individual, parent, family, school, community – has been recognized for many years (Wasserman and Miller 1998). Nor has the necessity of community involvement and empowerment escaped attention, although such emphases are still not central to most crime prevention initiatives. As noted earlier, Hawkins and his colleagues are the most prominent exponents of a community mobilization approach within a risk-focused framework, drawing on experience with cardiovascular disease and smoking-prevention programmes. Their *Communities that Care* model is undoubtedly one of the most influential community crime and drug abuse prevention programmes, with trials and evaluations in the USA (Hawkins *et al.* 1992; Harachi *et al.* 1996), the UK (Communities that Care 1997; Crow *et al.* 2004); and Australia (Toumbourou 1999). This approach involves intervening at the community level as well as at the levels of individuals and families, using mobilization techniques that promote community ownership of programmes and that empower diverse groups to take control of efforts to assess, prioritize and address risk and protective factors. Unfortunately, as with the majority of community-based prevention programmes designed to promote health and welfare, the evidence is not yet in that Communities that Care 'works' to reduce crime and related problems.

Perhaps one of the key lessons to be drawn from the various literatures is that risk factor research is an essential tool in any analysis, but that it is also essential to draw on any historical data on how a community has arrived at the point of social dislocation, or on qualitative data that tell us about how people view their situations and the challenges they face (Peel 2003). Such analyses are, for example, the beginning of wisdom in attempts to understand the needs of indigenous communities (Homel *et al.* 1999; Burns *et al.* 2000).

There is also a need to better understand the human stories and processes that lie behind statistical indicators.

Jack's story

To explore further the meanings of development prevention, in this section we consider Jack's story (Box 4.1). This is a story about one individual's pathway to tragedy, but it is also a story about his society and key social institutions, about missed opportunities and misunderstandings. The story therefore helps to 'flesh out' some of the processes that could only be hinted at in the previous section. Although we know less than we might like about Jack's life, particularly his early years, some features of what we do know about his experiences will ring bells amongst those who have studied the development of problem behaviours, particularly conduct disorder. As Stewart-Brown (1998) observes, behaviour problems have now become the most important cause of disability in childhood.

In our analysis of Jack's experiences we draw for inspiration on the transactional-ecological model proposed by Sameroff and Fiese (2000), although the detailed application of this approach to the case study probably goes somewhat beyond what can be supported by systematic empirical research. A key feature of the transactional-ecological model is that not only does the environment in its many facets affect child development, the child influences and takes from the environment: 'the development of the child is seen as a product of the continuous dynamic interactions of the child and the experience provided by his or her family and social context' (Sameroff and Fiese: 142).

Box 4.1 Jack's story

> 'Jack' as a 14-year-old boy caused the deaths of two young people when the BMW he stole crashed during a high-speed police pursuit. The victims, a 24 year-old female accountant and her 25-year old doctor boyfriend, were immolated when their vehicle burst into flames after Jack hurtled through red traffic lights at perhaps 100 km/h. Jack was critically injured but not killed, sustaining head injuries that prevented him remembering what happened. His young female passengers also survived.
>
> Stories about the 'Killer Youth' made headlines all around Australia. Jack's record of crime and drug abuse was contrasted with the promising lives of his victims, with the young woman's father lamenting that 'it is tragic that two people with so much to give can be blotted out by a bunch of losers'. Radio airwaves crackled with demands to get tough on teenage crime. Community outrage became even more intense some months later when Jack, having recovered from his injuries, was sentenced to six years in a detention centre, with a minimum of three years and three months for good behaviour. Eighteen months for each life was universally seen as too little, the legal system – according to a local psychiatrist – having 'colluded with evil rather than dealing with it'.
>
> Jack's parents were a working-class couple, married for 20 years and reasonably prosperous as a result of hard work in their own business. Jack himself seems to have been a happy, normal kid, 'cheeky and bright'. However, things began to go wrong when he went to school. A mild hearing impairment that necessitated

a hearing aid occasioned some teasing by other children, but taunts about AIDS, arising from hepatitis B that was contracted from his father (who in turn had acquired the disease when he was tattooed) was the major form of persecution. Jack began to exhibit behavioural and concentration problems, for which support was provided by the school.

But it was in Grade 5, at the age of 9, that Jack's behaviour suddenly and inexplicably deteriorated. Only years later was it revealed that at that time Jack had been sexually abused by an older and much bigger boy. He told no one and ran away from home, a pattern of behaviour that occurred frequently over the next few years. His father eventually gave up chasing him. Nevertheless, in Grade 6 it seemed that some kind of recovery might be underway: Jack had a good year with a teacher who cared a lot, and his reports were full of praise and promise. However, the promise was not fulfilled in high school, where after only a few months not one teacher had a good word to say about this student who was characterized as disobedient, abusive and unable to develop healthy peer relationships. At home his father increasingly responded to bad behaviour with physical punishment, in contrast to his mother's attempts to rely more on discussion and persuasion.

By the age of 13 Jack was facing a long suspension from school and his parents were at their wits' end, having consulted the Education Department endlessly about special residential schools or centres. Apparently Jack was deemed too young for such treatment, but in the end his parents found a private centre run by an ex-minister of religion that was prepared to take him in. This experience proved a disaster, since it provided the ideal environment for the rapid escalation of Jack's drug usage from experimentation with marijuana to the regular use of a range of drugs 'beyond his wildest dreams'. He returned, ill with hepatitis, to a household under enormous stress. His mother kept him out of school to avoid expulsion, but he ran away all the time. By the age of 14 he was living on the streets, at which time he first appeared in court charged with assault on a taxi driver. The court remanded him to live with his aunt and uncle on their farm 500 kilometres away, the first of a series of court-ordered attempts to make 'a fresh start'. Jack repeatedly breached these court orders, living with four different sets of relatives as well as in a refuge and a special learning centre.

The state department responsible for child welfare was sympathetic but depressing, officers seemingly unable to offer meaningful assistance. Jack's father started to act violently towards his wife, so that she was forced to seek a court restraining order. They separated briefly before reconciling, but by now Jack was out of control. He threatened to burn the house down, provoking a strong physical response from his father, then threatened suicide when the sexual assault incident was finally revealed through his grandmother. A psychiatrist decided that in fact Jack was not likely to kill himself, and in desperation his parents had him charged with stealing 80 cents from his grandmother in the hope that the court would remand him in custody and order counselling. In fact despite interviews about the sexual assault by a psychiatrist and a joint investigation team, the court sent him away to his uncle's farm again, from which he ran away (again). Shortly after this came the accident and hospitalization, and only then the detention his parents had sought. Unfortunately two people lost their lives along the way. Jack summed it all up best when he faced the families of the dead couple after sentencing: 'I am very sorry...I have destroyed your families and I have destroyed my own family'.

Source: Condensed from Wheatley (1999).

The journalist who wrote about Jack, Jane Wheatley, raises two questions critical to the developmental perspective on prevention. The first is simply:

> How did it come to this? How does it happen? How does the child of two ordinary, well-intentioned parents with a strong and supportive network of family and friends go so badly out of control that he ends up causing two deaths and, in his own words, destroying the lives of three families? (Wheatley 1999: 15).

The second question Wheatley poses arises directly from the first: 'So how did he manage to fall through all the cracks?' What went wrong with the systems that were supposed to stop this kind of thing from happening?

One way of approaching this question is to organize what we know about Jack's story in terms of life phases and transitions, identifying the associated developmental challenges and the problems, difficulties or obstacles encountered in meeting these challenges. We can then contrast the responses of Jack, his family and societal institutions with examples of the kinds of responses (programmes, services and resources) that, had they been available, might have helped Jack and his family to overcome the difficulties. Table 4.2 sets out the results of a simple analysis along these lines, based on selected aspects of Jack's story. It should be emphasized that the table is designed to illustrate a method of analysis rather than present the results of an exhaustive examination of what went wrong and what should have been done (for which clinical data would be required). The suggested preventive responses at each life phase are also only a small sample of possible approaches.

In the table institutional responses have been placed immediately after the listing of problems, before the responses of Jack and his family. This is because many of the problems Jack encountered, and his reactions to those problems, related both to his failure to negotiate key transitions between social institutions (chiefly primary and high school), and the failure of institutions to respond adequately to his needs. In reality, however, we could place institutional, individual and family responses in different orders at different life phases, depending on the nature of the interactions at different times.

An attempt has been made, in the spirit of Sameroff and Fiese's (2000) ecological analysis, to represent with arrows some of these interactions or transactions between Jack and his family and other institutions. Using this approach, there is no single 'cause' of Jack's behavioural problems but a series of person–environment transactions extended over time and embedded in an interpretive framework. For example, Jack's behaviour suddenly deteriorates causing conflict with his puzzled parents, leading to a sense of rejection by Jack who runs away but is brought back by an angry and hurt father who inadvertently accelerates the downward spiral. Experiences are constructed, interpreted and reinterpreted over time in ongoing interactions, making it impossible to think of the environment as independent of the child. The transactional-ecological model implies that continuity in individual behaviour is a systems property rather than a characteristic of individuals like 'criminal propensity', thus providing a rationale for an expanded focus of intervention efforts.

One striking aspect of Jack's experience is how problems seemed to start, or to intensify, after he commenced both primary and high schools. School served as an arena in which it seemed that his many defects and failures were progressively identified, denounced and punished, so that for him schooling became an increasingly isolating experience. Problems at school, in the form of aggressive behaviours, academic failure, low commitment and truancy, are known to be associated with juvenile crime, violence and mental health problems (Hawkins *et al.* 1998; Marshall and Watt 1999). In particular, Jack's experiences point to the importance of making a successful transition to school, and later to high school.

Transition points, as we have seen, mark the boundaries or markers between life phases. Each life phase brings with it related developmental tasks (e.g. for preschoolers, regulating one's social behaviour; in adolescence, establishing one's identity and independence), and moving from one phase to another usually involves movement between social institutions (e.g. family to school). Jack clearly had trouble very early in primary school in mastering the new tasks required such as making friends, a problem that was compounded by chronic ill-health. Both these factors are commonly implicated in the development of problem behaviours in the early stages of school (Marshall and Watt 1999), although there are many other material, cognitive, social and emotional influences on a child's readiness for school (Lipps and Yiptong-Avila 1999).

In Jack's case the school provided support in the early years, which might have been reasonably effective since it was only in Grade 5, after the sexual abuse incident, that his behaviour really started to get out of control. Nevertheless, it is likely that since childhood peer rejection is known to contribute to anti-social behaviour (Coie and Miller-Johnson 2001), a more concerted effort by schools to manage such problems in the early years would have general benefits. One obvious way of preventing or mitigating the effects of teasing and associated behaviours (McCarthy and Carr 2002) is through a whole-school bullying prevention programme (Olweus 1993). An equally attractive approach would be to implement a version of the Seattle Social Development Project (Table 4.1). Whatever specific approach is adopted, the points emphasized by McCarthy and Carr in their review apply: programmes should be routinely introduced into primary and secondary schools according to programme guidelines, supported by extensive training and consultancy resources. The key to success is rigorous implementation.

Universal programmes of this nature should be supported by selected interventions that address the needs of specific subgroups, such as those (like Jack) with sensory impairments. For example, there is evidence that daily school lessons that teach deaf children interpersonal problem-solving skills are effective in promoting social-emotional understandings and behavioural adjustment (Kusche and Greenberg 1994; Fahey and Carr 2002). Once again, however, such a programme must be underpinned by systematic screening procedures and a commitment to a range of initiatives that meet the diverse needs of children and their parents.

Sexual abuse is known to have devastating short and long-term consequences for both men and women, including the risk of subsequent juvenile crime, sexualized behaviour, school-based attainment problems, relationship

Table 4.2 Jack's story: life phases and transitions, challenges, obstacles and responses

Life phase	Developmental challenges	Problems/ obstacles	Institutional responses	Jack's responses	Family's responses	Resources needed (examples)[1]
Transition to school						
Middle Childhood and primary school	Peer relationships Adjustment to school	Teasing about hearing aid Taunts about AIDS	School 'support' for behaviour problems No apparent response to teasing	Poor behaviour Lack of concentration	Concern	Whole-school bullying prevention programme School-based programme to teach sensory-impaired children interpersonal problem-solving skills
Grade 5 (aged 9)	Trust in others Self-esteem	Sexual abuse by an older boy	Conflict with teachers Labelled as a problem child	Told no one Deterioration in behaviour Ran away from home Ran away	Increased concern Conflict with parents Brought home by father, more conflict Father gives up chasing by the age of 13	School-based multi-modal-multisystemic child sexual abuse prevention programme, targeting children in all grades, parents, teachers, others
Grade 6	Preparation for high school		Supportive and caring teacher	Problem behaviour Improved behaviour		Whole-school focus on preparing children for transition to high school

Transition to high school

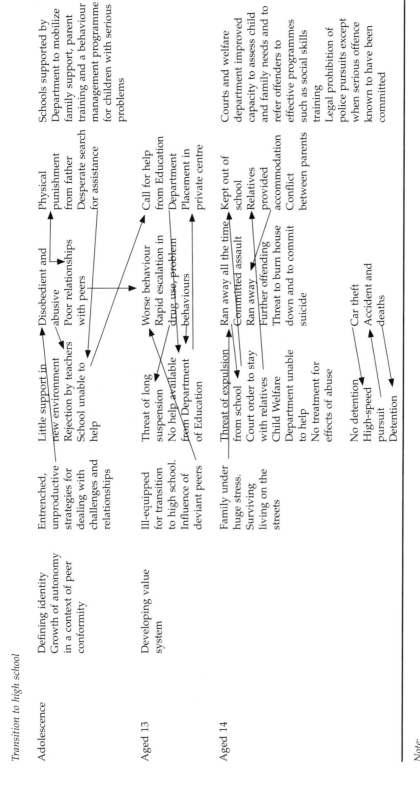

Note:
1. See text for details of the proposed interventions.

difficulties, violent behaviour by males, further sexual victimization for females and running away for both males and females (Maxfield and Widom 1996; Kaufman and Widom 1999; Weatherburn and Lind 2000; Duane and Carr 2002). The specific effects on a boy of sexual victimization by a larger and older boy are less well researched. In Jack's case, the experience constituted a major turning point in his life.

Unlike transitions, turning points are personalized, non-normative life events that instigate a radical change in a particular person's pathway (Laub and Sampson 2003).[4] Nearly everyone goes to school and faces the maturational and institutional demands entailed, but not everyone is sexually abused. Sexual abuse takes on significance in developmental terms because it usually has radical and far-reaching impacts on the psychological well-being and subsequent behaviours of the affected individuals. In other words, it occasions a major change in direction, with life taking a different (and worse) course thereafter. Turning points can of course take many forms. They need not be negative in their effects, as Sampson and Laub (1993) found in some cases for juvenile institutionalization. They may (and often do) coincide with life transitions, and so are not just milestones in individual biographies. Some turning points involve choice, and some open up options rather than closing them down.

All these features – the coincidence, on occasion, with points of transition, their possible positive consequences and the potential opening up of doors previously shut – make turning points particularly important to those interested in preventive interventions. Indeed, one way in which interventions may bring about change is by facilitating individual experiences that serve as positive turning points for at least some in the targeted groups or populations. Alternatively, and perhaps more commonly, an intervention may assist in the avoidance of negative turning points. Prevention programmes with a specific target, like sexual abuse or bullying, are obviously of the latter type. One effective approach to the prevention of child sexual abuse across all primary grades uses multimodal behavioural skills training techniques including video modelling, didactic instruction and discussion, and targets multiple members of children's social systems (including parents and teachers). Duane and Carr (2002) recommend that such programmes span at least one school term, be developmentally staged and comprise a routine part of primary school curricula.

Jack did not benefit from any routine sexual abuse prevention programme, and there was nothing positive about the 'intervention' that took place in Grade 5. However, his life was not marked even then by a completely steady descent into drugs, crime and violence. It seemed that in Grade 6 (the year before high school), through kindness, a teacher's professional skill and constant encouragement, Jack might recover from his trauma. This 'lifelong capacity for change and reorganization' (Shonkoff and Phillips 2000) is what makes the science of prevention possible.

Jack's improved behaviour did not survive the transition to high school, for reasons that are not entirely clear from the published record but can almost certainly be guessed at with some accuracy. In reality, the transition to high school often involves three kinds of transitions simultaneously: the transition to a new, larger, more demanding and less supportive school structure; the transition to puberty, with the associated need to establish one's own identity as an adult, independent of parents; and a transition to a new neighbourhood or peer group. Probably Jack had difficulties in all three areas, and the school failed to provide the supports that might have maintained his record of positive achievements in primary school. The Developmental Crime Prevention Consortium (1999) found that of all major transitions in childhood, the transition to high school is least often the focus of prevention programmes in Australia, despite the strong and universal evidence for big increases in participation rates and accelerated rates of offending in early adolescence (Gottfredson and Hirschi 1990; Moffitt 1993).

Like most serious offenders, by early high school Jack was engaging not only in frequent acts of crime like car stealing, he was using drugs, frequently running away from home so that he was sometimes homeless, he was becoming more difficult to control at home, school and elsewhere, beginning to commit acts of physical violence (such as the assault on the taxi driver), and exhibiting mental health problems such as depression and suicidal ideation. In fact, he illustrates in a single case the phenomenon of intertwined and escalating psychosocial problems stemming from common risk factors (Durlak 1998; Huizinga and Jakob-Chien 1998; Farrington 2002). According to Huizinga and Jakob-Chien's analysis, interventions that deal effectively with school problems such as low grades, truancy, suspensions or dropping out – all part of Jack's colourful history – may be especially valuable for serious, violent juvenile offenders like him.

So, how should we evaluate the attempts that were made throughout Jack's life to help him and to steer him into more positive pathways? Certainly, despite Jack's headlong rush to disaster once he hit high school, it is not correct to conclude that no one cared about him or that responsible individuals and agencies did not attempt to slow him down or divert his path. The published account suggests that his parents did just about all that one could reasonably expect of normal, untrained people in the absence of meaningful external supports, almost becoming casualties themselves on a few occasions. This is not to say that their parenting styles were perfect. For example, Jack's father sometimes reacted with harsh physical discipline that did not appear to produce positive results, whilst his mother's 'good cop' style of discipline might have sent contradictory and confusing messages to a boy who already had serious emotional problems. Nevertheless, the family is portrayed as essentially functional, loving, long-suffering and desperate to co-operate with whatever agency could offer assistance to Jack. Unfortunately, like Jack, they seemed to become increasingly isolated.

A fatal mistake, precipitated by the perceived failure of the Education Department to offer any form of practical help, was the decision to send Jack at the age of 13 to a mission on a farm, run by an ex-minister. The disastrous outcomes in terms of escalating drug use and intensified problem behaviours seem to be in line with a growing literature on the iatrogenic effects of peer-group interventions, particularly for high-risk youths, like Jack, who are in the 13–14 age range (Dishion et al. 1999). The evidence adduced by Dishion and his colleagues comes both from analysis of videotapes of interactions between boys aged 13–14 who were then followed up as part of the Oregon Youth Study, and from the results of two experimental interventions that included group training of adolescents. The phenomenon of 'deviancy training', defined as 'the process of contingent positive reactions to rule-breaking discussions' (Dishion *et al.* 1999: 756), is a possible explanation for the long-term negative effects of the Cambridge–Somerville prevention experiment for youths who were sent to summer camp on at least two occasions (McCord 2002).

Perhaps the main conclusion is that Jack had particular needs that mainstream institutions, including the criminal justice system, could not meet with existing knowledge or resources. Even positive institutional responses were often the outcome of an individual initiative, such as a teacher taking a particular interest, rather than a reflection of adequate systems based on evidence. Systemic responses failed to deal with the real problems. For example, in the light of the results of the Montreal Prevention Project (Table 4.1), if the courts or child welfare department had been able to refer Jack and his family to a social skills programme instead of ordering ineffectual care by relatives, or if adequate support and guidance for his family had been available, then outcomes for both Jack and the family might have been very different.

Some system responses were positively destructive. High-speed pursuits are a routine response by police agencies to suspected law breaking. In nearly every case there is no evidence of a serious crime when they are commenced, but from the police point of view it's who might be caught or what might be found that is the real justification for pursuing. Every pursuit is a fishing expedition with the potential to end as tragically as did Jack's (Homel 1990). Since pursuits are a primary and frequent manifestation of a deeply engrained police culture that takes for granted the absolute primacy of catching crooks over maintaining order or preventing crime and injuries, firm legislative action banning such destructive practices would, from a developmental perspective, be highly desirable.

Unfortunately, political realities make such legislation very unlikely. Police pursuits can be viewed as a highly socially valued component in the dominant policy response to problem behaviours. This dominant orientation dictates reasonably indulgent responses to malefactions in a person's early years, tinged with the threat that if the individual does not take advantage of the second chances provided and mend his or her troublesome ways he or she will increasingly be held personally accountable. The responses typically progress from laissez-faire, unco-ordinated and under-resourced helping programmes to interventions that increasingly abandon the rehabilitative ideal for the more pragmatic goals of containment, exclusion or punishment. The image of the 'killer youth' is a totally logical social construction from this point of view, as is the depiction of the legal system as having 'colluded with evil' through its manifest leniency.

New directions

Jack's story reminds us that prevention based on science must compete with other political priorities based on very different views of the world. It also highlights the fact that children and families need help – sometimes a great deal of help – to overcome difficulties posed by problem behaviours and by the obstacles thrown up by the social institutions that should be part of the solution. Where was the community in Jack's case? Why was the family apparently so isolated? Where were the programmes that could have made a difference to Jack and many other children?

The major lesson from the literature on developmental crime prevention is that it *is* possible to make a difference, in the short term and in the long term, especially for disadvantaged and vulnerable children and young people. Starting in early childhood is good, but much can be done later in the life course. In general the rule is, 'never too early, never too late' (Loeber and Farrington 1998). Of course, the extent to which a society is prepared to go down the track of intervening early in developmental pathways instead of relying on popular 'end of the line' law-and-order policies is a matter of political choices. It is at this point that the deep cultural attachment to notions of childhood determinism noted by Sampson and Laub (in press) could be harnessed by social scientists in support of policies that embody the principles of development prevention. The distinguished Canadian medical scientist Fraser Mustard has, as noted earlier, been particularly effective in tapping into societal concerns about early childhood, although in his home province of Ontario success so far in moving public policy forward appears to have been mixed (McCain and Mustard 2002).

Unfortunately mixed success is the current state of the field. If the good news is that science now provides some foundation for optimism about developmental approaches, the bad news is that not all appealing ideas work, some backfire (they increase crime involvement), and even techniques that 'work' (such as home-visiting programmes) don't do so consistently across all the settings in which they have been studied (Chaffin 2004). Moreover, nearly all community-based implementations of early intervention initiatives have encountered major problems in engaging successfully with families and children, especially in disadvantaged areas. They have also faced difficulties in moving beyond a sole focus on the child to include family, school and community systems, and most have struggled with long-term funding and sustainability (Farran 2000; Halpern 2000). Social scientists are therefore faced with a pretty tough challenge if asked to advise policy-makers. On the one hand they can point to the success stories, emphasizing the scientific rigour of the experiments and the solid data on outcomes and cost-effectiveness they have yielded, but on the other hand they cannot guarantee that the results will be reproducible if adopted, perhaps many years later, in different communities, cultures or countries in a routine fashion by agencies that, perhaps, lack the knowledge, expertise and commitment of the original experimenters.

The risk-factor paradigm may not be perfect as a tool for extending the reach of developmental prevention, and certainly needs to be deposed from its position as 'the one true way' of proceeding, but it has at least provided a bridge between longitudinal and prevention research that has helped move prevention policies from the realm of good ideas to evidence-based practice. Reference to risk factors should help to ensure that interventions deal effectively with some of the baggage that people carry and the barriers they face, so increasing the odds that some developmental pathways will take a more positive direction. What is needed now is a creative dialogue between risk-factor analyses and approaches based on different methodologies, especially those that situate communities in their social and historical context and endeavour to take seriously the voices of children and young people and those who care about them.

Based on personal experience in designing, implementing and evaluating (with colleagues) a large community-based developmental prevention programme in a disadvantaged area of Brisbane (Homel *et al.* 2001; Freiberg *et al.* 2005), several conclusions can be asserted with confidence.

One conclusion is based on the observation that the local community exerts a pervasive influence on families and children, sometimes supporting but often undermining the efforts of parents and schools. Programmes cannot just be introduced by outsiders based on their expert knowledge without some understanding of local issues and without engaging with parents, community leaders, teachers and principals, and many other people. Partnerships at many levels are essential, and steps must be taken at an early stage to try to understand the world through the eyes of programme participants and key community 'influentials' so that meaningful interventions can be devised. It follows from this that there is no royal road, no magic carpet. Partnerships, governance arrangements and specific programmes must be tailored to the needs of the community and to individual families whilst maintaining scientific integrity. This requires creative methodologies of the kind recommended by Sorensen *et al.* (1998), underpinned by an unwavering commitment to quantitative measurement. There is no one right way of doing all this, and our experience is that a great deal of trial and error is involved. One useful principle, discussed earlier in this chapter, is the strategic value of focusing on life transitions (such as starting school) when parents are open to support because they have a felt need.

Perhaps the most important conclusion from our work in Brisbane is that communities cannot 'do it all'. Whilst it is essential to work in partnership, disadvantaged communities in particular need a wide range of tangible external resources to overcome the numerous barriers faced every day by parents who, to a man and woman, want their children to succeed at school and in life but who frequently do not have the knowledge, skills and resources to achieve this goal. Attempting to bridge the significant gap between needs and resources from a developmental perspective helps to keep the focus on institutions and social arrangements, not just the deficiencies of individuals. As Arnold Sameroff (2003) has observed, the fact that the death rate for women in third-class cabins on the *Titanic* was about 45 per cent compared with 3 per cent for women in first-class cabins could be interpreted to mean that poorer women don't swim as well or are less resilient. The reality, of course, is that stewards were told to lock the doors on the lower decks.

Unlocking doors, or making them more attractive or easier to go through, is what development prevention is all about. The steepening social gradient in many countries has increased the number of young people who are denied the opportunity to participate fully in social and economic life. Programmes such as quality preschool education and home visiting, as well as broader initiatives such as poverty alleviation and public housing, are strategies which attempt to compensate for the impact of these trends and promote the attachment of individuals and communities to mainstream social supports and developmental institutions. These social institutions form an essential backdrop to crime prevention programmes through the creation of a 'child friendly' society, a society which fosters meaningful developmental pathways for its citizens.

Acknowledgements

I am particularly indebted to Matthew Manning for his assistance with the references and with the economic analyses of early intervention programmes. Colleagues from the Developmental Crime Prevention Consortium have been enormously important over the years in shaping my thinking, although the ideas in this chapter are my own version of what it all means. I should also like to thank especially Nick Tilley and Alan France for helpful comments on earlier drafts of this chapter.

Selected further reading

It is useful to have a nodding acquaintance with several literatures in order to get a grip on what developmental prevention is about. In criminology, David Farrington is undoubtedly one of the most prolific and influential scholars. In the third edition of the *Oxford Handbook of Criminology*, Farrington (2002) presents an excellent overview of developmental criminology and risk-focused prevention as they are commonly understood, including a comprehensive discussion of individual, family and school risk factors. For a more detailed examination of family-based interventions, his systematic review with Brandon Welsh in *Children and Society* in 1999, and his meta-analysis in 2003 (also with Welsh) in the *Australian and New Zealand Journal of Criminology*, are recommended. An older review, but worthy of serious study for the manner in which it links a comprehensive review of developmental interventions with theoretical issues around causal pathways, is by Richard Tremblay and Wendy Craig in Volume 19 of the annual *Review of Research in Crime and Justice* in 1995. The Australian report produced by this author and colleagues in 1999, *Pathways to Prevention: Developmental and Early Intervention Approaches to Crime in Australia*, is also still a useful and comprehensive resource on how to think about developmental crime prevention and how to relate it to broader literatures in developmental psychology, sociology and human services.

For readers interested in the broader field of developmental research and early-in-life interventions, a wealth of literature is available. Particularly useful is the US report published by the National Academy Press in 2000 on behalf of the Committee on Integrating the Science of Early Childhood Development, chaired by Jack Shonkoff. Titled *From Neurons to Neighborhoods*, this book provides a good introduction to developmental research and its social and policy contexts. Equally useful is the second edition of the *Handbook of Early Childhood Intervention*, edited by Jack Shonkoff and Samuel Meisels in 2000. A more recent edited publication by Jeanne Brooks-Gunn and colleagues published in 2003, *Early Child Development in the 21st Century*, contains an account of several 'families' of contemporary large-scale studies of early development, including evaluations of large-scale intervention programmes.

A third literature that is important for developmental crime prevention is influenced by medical and public health research, although its interdisciplinary nature makes this too narrow a characterization. Noteworthy is the book edited in 1999 by Dan Keating and Clyde Hertzman, *Developmental Health and the Wealth of Nations*, which brings together biological, psychological and sociological perspectives and introduces the concept of 'developmental health' as representing the true wealth of a nation. An Australian publication, *Child Behaviour Problems* written by Dr Jann Marshall and Paula Watt, is an excellent resource for understanding child behaviour problems and appropriate interventions. It was published by the Interagency Committee on Children's Futures in Western Australia in 1999.

Notes

1. See http://www.facs.gov.au/internet/facsinternet.nsf/aboutfacs/programs/sfsc-sfcs.htm.
2. Contrary to the usage proposed here, Farrington and Welsh (2002) argue that programmes that target all children in a high-crime area should be called selective, not universal, since these children are as much at risk as those living in (say) low-income families. If this approach is adopted a new term is required for 'universal' programmes restricted to specific collectivities like an entire school. This is because the dynamics of such programmes are very different from those that target at-risk individuals, and also because (as Farrington and Welsh acknowledge) there are very few truly universal programmes in their sense of the term.
3. The Developmental Crime Prevention Consortium comprised (at the time the Pathways report was prepared) the convenor Ross Homel (Griffith University), Judy Cashmore (NSW Child Protection Council), Linda Gilmore, Ian O'Connor, John Western and Jake Najman (University of Queensland), Jacqueline Goodnow and Alan Hayes (Macquarie University), Jeanette Lawrence (University of Melbourne), Marie Leech (Uniya: Jesuit Social Justice Centre) and Tony Vinson (University of NSW). The project was funded by the Commonwealth Department of the Attorney General through its National Crime Prevention Program.
4. I am indebted to Jeanette Lawrence for these insights on turning points.

References

Aos, S., Barnoski, R. and Lieb, R. (1998) 'Preventive programs for young offenders effective and cost-effective', *Overcrowded Times*, 9(2): 1–11.

Aos, S., Phipps, P., Barnoski, R. and Lieb, R. (2001) *The Comparative Costs and Benefits of Programs to Reduce Crime*. Washington, DC: Washington State Institute for Public Policy.

Australian Government Taskforce on Child Development, Health and Welfare (2003) *Towards the Development of a National Agenda for Early Childhood* (consultation paper). Canberra: FACS.

Barnett, W.S. (1993) 'Benefit-cost analysis of preschool education: findings from a 25 year follow-up', *American Journal Orthopsychiatry*, 63(4): 500–8.

Bor, W., Najman, J.M., O'Callaghan, M., Williams, G.M. and Anstey, K. (2001) *Aggression and the Development of Delinquent Behaviour in Children*. Canberra: Australian Institute of Criminology.

Brooks-Gunn, J., Fuligni, A.S. and Berlin, L.J. (2003) *Early Child Development in the 21st Century: Profiles of Current Research Initiatives*. New York, NY and London: Teachers College Press.

Buchanan, A. and Hudson, B.L. (eds) (1998) *Parenting, Schooling, and Children's Behaviour*. Sydney: Ashgate.

Burns, A., Burns, K. and Menzies, K. (2000) 'Strong state intervention: the stolen generations', in J. Bowes and A. Hayes (eds) *Children, Families, and Communities*. Melbourne: Oxford University Press.

Caspi, A., McClay, J., Moffitt, T.E., Mill, J., Martin, J., Craig, I.W., Taylor, A. and Poulton, R. (2002) 'Role of genotype in the cycle of violence in maltreated children', *Science*, 297(2): 851–4.

Chaffin, M. (2004) 'Is it time to rethink healthy start/healthy families?', *Child Abuse and Neglect*, 28: 589–95.

Coie, J.D. and Miller-Johnson, S. (2001) 'Peer factors and interventions', in R. Loeber and D.P. Farrington (eds) *Child Delinquents: Development, Intervention, and Service Needs*. Thousand Oaks, CA: Sage.

Communities that Care (1997) *Communities that Care (UK): A New Kind of Prevention Programme*. London: Communities that Care.

Crow, I., France, A., Hacking, S. and Hart, M. (2004) *The Evaluation of Three Communities that Care Demonstration Projects in England and Wales*. Sheffield: University of Sheffield.

Developmental Crime Prevention Consortium (1999) *Pathways to Prevention: Developmental and Early Intervention Approaches to Crime in Australia*. Brisbane: National Crime Prevention, Commonwealth Attorney-General's Department.

Dishion, T.J., McCord, J. and Poulin, F. (1999) 'When interventions harm: peer groups and problem behaviour', *American Psychologist*, 54: 755–64.

Duane, Y. and Carr, A. (2002) 'Prevention of sexual abuse', in A. Carr (ed.) *Prevention: What Works with Children and Adolescents: A Critical Review of Psychological Prevention Programmes for Children, Adolescents and Their Families*. Brighton: Brunner-Routledge.

Durlak, J.A. (1998) 'Common risk and protective factors in successful prevention programs', *American Journal of Orthopsychiatry*, 68: 512–20.

Eckenrode, J., Olds, D., Henderson, C.R., Kitzman, H., Luckey, D., Pettitt, L.M., Sidora, K., Morris, P., Powers, J. and Cole, R. (1998) 'Long-term effects of nurse home visitation on children's criminal and anti-social behaviour', *Journal of the American Medical Association*, 280: 1302.

Elder, G.H. (1998) 'The life course as developmental theory', *Child Development*, 69: 1–12.

Fahey, A. and Carr, A. (2002) 'Prevention of adjustment difficulties in children with sensory impairments', in A. Carr (ed.) *Prevention: What Works with Children and Adolescents? A Critical Review of Psychological Prevention Programmes for Children, Adolescents and their Families*. Brighton: Brunner-Routledge.

Farran, D.C. (2000) 'Another decade of intervention for children who are low income or disabled', in J.P. Shonkoff and S.J. Meisels (eds) *Handbook of Early Childhood Intervention*. New York, NY: Cambridge University Press.

Farrington, D.P. (1996) *Understanding and Preventing Youth Crime*. York: Joseph Rowntree Foundation.

Farrington, D.P. (1998) 'Evaluating "Communities that Care": realistic scientific considerations', *Evaluation*, 4: 204–10.

Farrington, D.P. (2000) 'Explaining and preventing crime: the globalization of knowledge – the American Society of Criminology 1999 Presidential Address', *Criminology*, 38: 1–24.

Farrington, D.P. (2002) 'Developmental criminology and risk-focused prevention', in M. Maguire *et al.* (eds) *The Oxford Handbook of Criminology* (3rd edn). Oxford: Oxford University Press.

Farrington, D.P. and Welsh, B.C. (1999) 'Delinquency prevention using family-based interventions', *Children and Society*, 13: 287–303.

Farrington, D.P. and Welsh, B.C. (2002) 'Family-based crime prevention', in L.W. Sherman *et al.* (eds) *Evidence-based Crime Prevention*. London: Routledge.

Farrington, D.P. and Welsh, B.C. (2003) 'Family-based prevention of offending: a meta-analysis', *Australian and New Zealand Journal of Criminology*, 36: 127–51.

Freiberg, K., Homel, R., Batchelor, S., Carr, A., Lamb, C., Hay, I., Elias, G. and Teague, R. (2005) 'Pathways to participation: a community-based developmental prevention project in Australia', *Children and Society*, 19: 144–57.

Glass, N. (1999) 'Sure Start: the development of an early intervention programme for young children in the United Kingdom', *Children and Society*, 13: 257–64.

Glueck, S. and Glueck, E. (1950) *Unraveling Juvenile Delinquency*. New York, NY: The Commonwealth Fund.

Gottfredson, D.C. (2001) *Schools and Delinquency*. Cambridge: Cambridge University Press.

Gottfredson, M.R. and Hirschi, T. (1990) *A General Theory of Crime*. Stanford, CA: Stanford University Press.

Halpern, R. (2000) 'Early childhood intervention for low-income children and families', in J.P. Shonkoff and S.J. Meisels (eds) *Handbook of Early Childhood Intervention*. New York, NY: Cambridge University Press.

Harachi, T.W., Ayers, C.D., Hawkins, D.J., Catalano, R.F. and Cushing, J. (1996) 'Empowering communities to prevent adolescent substance abuse: process evaluation results from a risk and protection-focused community mobilization effort', *Journal of Primary Prevention*, 16(3): 233–54.

Hawkins, D.J., Catalano, R. and associates (1992) *Communities that Care: Action for Drug Abuse Prevention*. San Francisco, CA: Jossey-Bass.

Hawkins, D.J., Catalano, R., Kosterman, R., Abbot, R. and Hill, K. (1999) 'Preventing adolescent health-risk behaviours by strengthening protection during childhood', *Archives of Pediatrics and Adolescent Medicine*, 153: 226–34.

Hawkins, D.J., Catalano, R.F., Morrison, D.M., O'Donnell, J., Abbott, R.D. and Day, L.E. (1992) 'The Seattle Social Development Project: effects of the first four years on protective factors and problem behaviours', in J. McCord and R.E. Tremblay (eds) *The Prevention of Anti-social Behaviour in Children*. New York, NY: Guilford Press.

Hawkins, D.J., Herrenkohl, T.I., Farrington, D.P., Brewer, D., Catalano, R. and Harachi, T.W. (1998) 'A review of predictors of youth violence', in R. Loeber and D.P. Farrington (eds) *Serious and Violent Juvenile Offenders*. Thousand Oaks, CA: Sage.

Hawkins, D.J., Von Cleve, E. and Catalano, R.F. (1991) 'Reducing early childhood aggression: results of a primary prevention program', *Journal of American Academy of Child and Adolescent Psychiatry*, 30(2): 208–17.

Hertzman, C. (1999) 'Population health and human development', in D.P. Keating and C. Hertzman (eds) *Developmental Health and the Wealth of Nations: Social, Biological, and Educational Dynamics*. New York, NY: Guilford Press.

Hertzman, C. (2002) *An Early Child Development Strategy for Australia? Lessons from Canada*. Brisbane: Queensland Government Commission for Children and Young People.

Homel, R. (1990) *High Speed Police Pursuits in Perth: Report to the Police Department of Western Australia*. Perth: WA Police Department.

Homel, R., Elias, G. and Hay, I. (2001) 'Developmental prevention in a disadvantaged community', in R. Eckersley *et al.* (eds) *The Social Origins of Health and Well-being.* Cambridge: Cambridge University Press.

Homel, R., Lincoln, R. and Herd, B. (1999) 'Risk and resilience: crime and violence prevention in Aboriginal communities', *The Australian and New Zealand Journal of Criminology*, 32: 182–96.

Huizinga, D. and Jakob-Chien, C. (1998) 'The contemporaneous co-occurence of serious and violent juvenile offending and other problem behaviours', in R. Loeber and D.P. Farrington (eds) *Serious and Violent Juvenile Offenders: Risk Factors and Successful Interventions.* Thousand Oaks, CA: Sage.

Kalisch, D.W. (2000) 'Social policy directions across the OECD region: reflections on a decade of change', *Social Policy Research Paper, Department of Family and Community Services*, 4: 1–32.

Kamerman, S.B. (2000) 'Early childhood intervention policies: an international perspective', in J.P. Shonkoff and S.J. Meisels (eds) *Handbook of Early Childhood Intervention* (2nd edn). Cambridge: Cambridge University Press.

Karoly, L.A., Greenwood, P.W., Everingham, S.S., Hoube, J., Kilburn, M.R., Rydell, C.P., Sanders, M. and Chiesa, J. (1998) *Investing in Our Children: What we Know and Don't Know about the Costs and Benefits of Early Childhood Interventions.* Santa Monica, CA: Rand.

Kaufman, J.G. and Widom, C.S. (1999) 'Childhood vicitmization, running away, and delinquency', *Journal of Research in Crime and Delinquency*, 36: 347–70.

Keating, D.P. and Hertzman, C. (1999) 'Modernity's paradox', in D.P. Keating and C. Hertzman (eds) *Developmental Health and the Wealth of Nations: Social, Biological and Educational Dynamics.* New York, NY: Guilford Press.

Kusche, C.A. and Greenberg, M.T. (1994) *The PATHS Curriculum.* Seattle, WA: Developmental Research and Programs.

Lally, R.J., Mangione, P.L. and Honig, A.S. (1988) 'The Syracuse University Family Development Research Program: long-range impact on an early intervention with low-income children and their families', in D.R. Powell (ed.) *Parent Education as Early Childhood Intervention: Emerging Directions in Theory, Research and Practice.* Norwood, NJ: Ablex.

Laub, J.H. and Sampson, R.J. (2003) *Shared Beginnings, Divergent Lives: Delinquent Boys to age 70.* Boston, MA: Harvard University Press.

Laycock, G. (2002) 'Methodological issues in working with policy advisors and practicioners', in N. Tilley (ed.) *Analysis for Crime Prevention.* London: Criminal Justice Press.

Lerner, R.M. (2002) *Concepts and Theories of Human Development.* Mahwah, NJ: Erlbaum Associates.

Lipps, G. and Yiptong-Avila, J. (1999) *From Home to School: How Canadian Children Cope: Initial Analyses Using Data from the Second Cycle of the School Component of the National Longitudinal Survey of Children and Youth.* Culture, Tourism and The Centre for Education Stati.

Loeber, R. and Farrington, D.P. (1998) 'Never too early, never too late: risk factors and successful interventions for serious and violent juvenile offenders', *Studies on Crime and Crime Prevention*, 7: 7–30.

Manning, M. (2004) 'Measuring the costs of community-based developmental prevention programs in Australia.' Unpublished Masters dissertation, Griffith University, Brisbane.

Marshall, J. and Watt, P. (1999) *Child Behaviour Problems.* Perth: Interagency Committee on Children's Futures.

Maxfield, M.G. and Widom, C.S. (1996) 'The cycle of violence: revisited 6 years later', *Archives of Pediatric and Adolescent Medicine*, 150: 390–5.

McCain, M.N. and Mustard, J.F. (1999) *Reversing the Real Brain Drain: Early Years Study: Final Report*. Toronto: Government of Ontario.

McCain, M.N. and Mustard, J.F. (2002) *The Early Years Study Three Years Later. From Early Child Development to Human Development: Enabling Communities*. Toronto: The Founders' Network of the Canadian Institute for Advanced Research.

McCarthy, O. and Carr, A. (2002) 'Prevention of bullying', in A. Carr (ed.) *Prevention: What Works with Children and Adolescents? A Critical Review of Psychological Prevention Programmes for Children, Adolescents and their Families*. Brighton: Brunner-Routledge.

McCord, J. (2002) 'Counterproductive juvenile justice', *Australian and New Zealand Journal of Criminology*, 35: 230–37.

McKinlay, J.B. and Marceau, L.D. (2000) 'To boldly go...', *American Journal of Public Health*, 90: 25–33.

Moffitt, T.E. (1993) 'Adolescence-limited and life-course-persistent antisocial behavior: a developmental taxonomy', *Psychological Review*, 100: 674–701.

Moore, M.H. (1995) 'Public health and criminal justice approaches to prevention', in M. Tonry and D.P. Farrington (eds) *Strategic Approaches to Crime Prevention: Building a Safer Society*. Chicago, IL and London: University of Chicago Press.

Olds, D. (2002) 'Prenatal and infancy home visiting by nurses: from randomized trials to community replication', *Prevention Science*, 3: 153–72.

Olds, D., Henderson, C.R., Kitzman, H.J., Eckenrode, J.J., Cole, R. and Tatelbaum, R.C. (1999) 'Prenatal and infancy home visitation by nurses: recent findings', *The Future of Children*, 9: 44–64.

Olds, D., Pettitt, L.M., Robinson, J., Henderson, C.R., Eckenrode, J., Kitzman, H., Cole, R. and Powers, J. (1998) 'Reducing risks for antisocial behaviour with a program of prenatal and early childhood home visitation', *Journal of Community Psychology*, 26: 65–83.

Olweus, D. (1993) *Bullying in Schools: What We Know and What We Can Do*. Oxford: Blackwell.

Patterson, G.R. and Dishion, T.J. (1988) 'Multilevel family process models: traits, interactions and relationships', in R. Hinde and J. Stevenson-Hide (eds) *Relationships and Families: Mutual Influences*. Oxford: Clarendon Press.

Pawson, R. and Tilley, N. (1998) 'Caring communities, paradigm polemics, design debates', *Evaluation*, 4: 73–90.

Pearce, N. (1996) 'Traditional epidemiology, modern epidemiology, and public health', *American Journal of Public Health*, 86: 678–83.

Peel, M. (2003) *The Lowest Rung: Voices of Australian Poverty*. Cambridge: Cambridge University Press.

Pirani, M. (1994) 'High/Scope, preschool curriculum', in C. Henricson (ed.) *Crime and the Family Conference*. London: Family Policies Study Centre.

Ramey, S.L. and Ramey, C.T. (1998) 'The transition to school: opportunities and challanges for children, families, educators, and communities', *Elementary School Journal*, 98: 293.

Reynolds, A.J., Temple, J.A., Robertson, D.L. and Mann, E.A. (2001) 'Long-term effects of an early childhood intervention on educational achievement and juvenile arrest: a 15 year follow-up of low income children in public school', *Journal of the American Medical Association*, 285: 2339–46.

Sameroff, A. (2003) *Families Who Need Services Most: Promoting Positive Outcomes in the Context of Multiple Risks* (http://64.233.167.104/search?q=cache:vLrBipsE-p4J: www.harrisschool.uchicago.edu/Centers/chppp/pdfs/sameroff_spring2003. pdf+Sameroffandhl=en).

Sameroff, A. and Fiese, B. (2000) 'Transactional regulation: the developmental ecology of early intervention', in J.P. Shonkoff and S.J. Meisels (eds) *Handbook of Early Childhood Intervention* (2nd edn). Cambridge: Cambridge University Press.

Sameroff, A., Seifer, R., Baldwin, A. and Baldwin, C. (1993) 'Stability of intelligence from preschool to adolescence: the influence of social and family risk factors', *Child Development*, 64: 80–97.

Sampson, R.J. and Laub, J.H. (1993) *Crime in the Making: Pathways and Turning Points Through Life*. Cambridge, MA: Harvard University Press.

Sampson, R.J. and Laub, J.H. (in press) 'A general age-graded theory of crime: lessons learned and the future of life-course criminology', in D.P. Farrington (ed.) *Advances in Criminological Theory. Volume 13. Testing Integrated Developmental/Life Course Theories of Offending*. New Brunswick, NJ: Transaction Publishers.

Saunders, P. (1998) 'Global pressures, national responses: the Australian welfare state in context', *Social Policy Research Centre Discussion Paper*, 90: 1–18.

Schweinhart, L.J. (2004) *The High/Scope Perry Preschool Study through Age 40: Summary, Conclusions, and Frequently Asked Questions*. Ypsilanti, MI: High/Scope Educational Research Foundation.

Schweinhart, L.J., Barnes, H.V. and Weikart, D.P. (1993) 'Delinquency and crime', in *Significant Benefits: The High/Scope Perry Preschool Study through Age 27. Vol. 10*. Ypsilanti, MI: High/Scope Press.

Sherman, L.W., Farrington, D.P., Welsh, B.C. and MacKenzie, D.L. (eds) (2002) *Evidence-based Crime Prevention*. London: Routledge.

Shonkoff, J.P. and Meisels, S.J. (eds) (2000) *Handbook of Early Childhood Intervention*. Cambridge: Cambridge University Press.

Shonkoff, J.P. and Phillips, D.A. (eds) (2000) *From Neurons to Neighborhoods: The Science of Early Childhood Development*. Washington, DC: National Academy Press.

Sorensen, G., Emmons, K., Hunt, M.K. and Johnston, D. (1998) 'Implications of the results of community intervention trials', *Annual of Review Public Health*, 19: 379–416.

Stewart-Brown, S. (1998) 'Public health implications of childhood behaviour problems and parenting programmes', in A. Buchanan and B.L. Hudson (eds) *Parenting, Schooling and Children's Behaviour*. Sydney: Ashgate.

Susser, M. (1998) 'Does risk factor put epidemiology at risk? Peering into the future', *Journal of Epidemiology and Community Health*, 52: 608.

Swanston, H., Parkinson, P., O'Toole, B., Plunkett, A., Shrimpton, S. and Pates, K. (2003) 'Juvenile crime, aggression and delinquency after sexual abuse', *British Journal of Criminology*, 43: 729–49.

Toumbourou, J. (1999) 'Implementing communities that care in Australia: a community mobilisation approach to crime prevention', *Australian Institute of Criminology: Trends and Issues in Crime and Criminal Justice*, 122: 1–6.

Tremblay, R.E. and Craig, W.M. (1995) 'Developmental crime prevention', in D.P. Farrington (ed.) *Strategic Approaches to Crime Prevention: Building a Safer Society*. Chicago. IL: University of Chicago Press.

Tremblay, R.E., Pagani-Kurtz, L., Masse, L.C., Vitaro, F. and Pihl, R.O. (1995) 'A bimodal preventive intervention for disruptive kindergarten boys: its impact through mid-adolescence', *Journal of Consulting and Clinical Psychology*, 63: 560–8.

Tunstill, J., Allnock, D., Meadows, P. and McLeod, A. (2002) *Early Experiences of Implementing Sure Start*. London: London University.

Wasserman, G.A. and Miller, L.S. (1998) 'The prevention of serious and violent juvenile offending', in R. Loeber and D.P. Farrington (eds) *Serious and Violent Juvenile Offenders: Risk Factors and Successful Interventions*. London: Sage.

Weatherburn, D. and Lind, B. (2000) *The Role of Economic Social Support in Crime Prevention*. Sydney: NSW Bureau of Crime Statistics.

Wei, Z., Homel, R., Prichard, J. and Xu, J. (2004) 'Patterns of juvenile offending in Shanghai and Brisbane', *Australian and New Zealand Journal of Criminology*, 37: 32–51.

Weisburd, D., Lum, C.M. and Petrosino, A. (2001) 'Does research design affect study outcomes in criminal justice?', *The Annals*, 578: 50–70.

Welsh, B.C. (2001) 'Economic costs and benefits of early developmental prevention', in R. Loeber and D.P. Farrington (eds) *Child Delinquents: Development, Intervention, and Service Needs*. London: Sage.

Wheatley, J. (1999) 'Before that night in June…', *Sydney Morning Herald Good Weekend Magazine*, 13 February: 14–21.

Wikström, P.O.H. and Loeber, R. (2000) 'Do disadvantaged neighborhoods cause well-adjusted children to become adolescent delinquents', *Criminology*, 38: 1109–42.

Wyn, J. (2004) *Youth Transitions to Work and Further Education in Australia* (http://www.edfac.unimelb.edu.au/EPM/YRC/documents/AERA.doc.pdf).

Chapter 5

Community crime reduction: activating formal and informal control

George L. Kelling

The police at all times should maintain a relationship with the public that gives reality to the historic tradition that the police are the public and that the public are the police; the police are the only members of the public who are paid to give full-time attention to the duties which are incumbent on every citizen in the interest of the community welfare (Sir Robert Peel 1829).

Introduction

This is a chapter about community attempts to prevent crime. It is based on my own experiences and research as well as reflections based on the literature. At its heart is a violent crime reduction effort in Newark, New Jersey that I am involved in that is called the Greater Newark Safer Cities Initiative (Safer Cities). I believe it deserves attention for at least two reasons: it is inspired by the Boston 'pulling levers' hypothesis that has gained so much attention in the USA and, different from Boston itself and most of the replications (e.g. Minneapolis and Baltimore), it has not only sustained itself for five years, it is gaining momentum (see Kennedy and Braga 1998). At least 40 agencies and community groups are involved; more are being added as the programme evolves; the majority of the agencies and groups have been involved continuously; the nature of agency or group involvement varies widely; and even some agencies that were originally hostile to the effort are now enthusiastic supporters. Although we have evidence that we have helped control a population of high-rate offending and dangerous probationers and parolees, we have no evidence that we have had an impact on homicides.

Over the five years of its existence Safer Cities has survived four state governors, four attorneys general, three superior court assignment (chief) judges, three US attorneys, three county prosecutors, four heads of the parole board, three directors of the Newark Police Department – each of whom has considerable influence over the effort. Moreover Newark, Essex County and New Jersey have no shortage of interagency hostilities, corruption, professional rivalries, 'thinking *inside* the box' and political dealings. None the less Safer Cities has survived and thrived. We are now replicating Safer Cities in two other cities in New Jersey: Camden and Trenton.

Before discussing Safer Cities I will briefly discuss the dominant role of police in the US history of problem-solving and the shift to a community justice strategy

Police, problem-solving and the community

During the past decade or so, I have been directly involved in major problem-solving activities in three cities in the USA: New York City, Newark, NJ and Los Angeles, CA. I have also consulted with, observed and evaluated such efforts in many other cities.[1] The problems with which I have been involved have ranged from 'squeegeemen' in New York City to homicides in Newark. Some have been spectacular successes: restoring order in the subway and controlling squeegeeing in New York City are examples (see Kelling and Coles 1996: 141). Other problems have been more intransigent: homicide in Newark, for example.

In all these cases a prolonged problem analysis preceded implementation of any set of tactics to address the problem(s). In fact, in several of these efforts, the problem analysis phase was longer than the problem management period. Analysing and figuring out how to handle the 'squeegeemen' problem in New York City, for example, took four months.[2] Handling it took three weeks. Likewise, it took over a year to figure out how to manage the disorder problem in New York's subway, but it took a matter of a few months to resolve it (Kelling and Coles 1996). The essential idea that I wish to convey here, however, is that *in every problem-solving effort in which I have been involved some form of interorganizational relationship was required to solve the problem –* and it did not matter how minor or grave the concern was. (I use the term *interorganizational* here advisedly because at times the relationship was with relatively informal non-structured groups.) In other words, no one agency could 'own' the problem.

This reality – that no one agency can own a problem – originally came as a shock to most criminal justice practitioners and policy-makers, especially police. The Los Angeles Police Department (LAPD), for example, historically has viewed itself as a self-sufficient organization that could operate independently, with little need for relationships with other organizations or citizens. More than this, since the 1950s, the LAPD has presented itself, and has been widely recognized as, a national model for truly 'professional' policing: highly mobile, small relative to area and population, independent from political oversight, remote and detached – 'Just the facts, ma'am' – self-regulating and autonomous. My current contacts with other agencies in Los Angeles confirm this reputation: many are pleasantly surprised to be invited to the table to work with the LAPD; others, especially minorities, are overtly sceptical.

This change is coming fairly late to the LAPD in comparison to other leading US police departments. Police departments in the USA have been developing strong relationships with 'outsiders' and other organizations at least since the 1970s. As an example, virtually all the 'big ideas' that are revolutionizing US police departments came about as a result of interorganizational efforts between police and individuals in universities or 'think tanks.' Three examples: *problem-solving* developed out of work during the 1970s between Herman Goldstein of the University of Wisconsin Law School and police departments, especially Madison Wisconsin (Goldstein 1990). Likewise, *broken windows* – at least my contribution to it – evolved from research on foot patrol conducted in the Newark Police Department during the 1970s whilst I worked for the Police Foundation (Wilson and Kelling 1982). *Pulling levers* grew out of a relationship among the Boston Police Department, prosecutors and David Kennedy of the Kennedy School of Government at Harvard University during the 1990s (Kennedy 1997).

In fact, police are leading the ongoing reform in criminal justice. They have led in problem-solving, the movement towards a community model of justice, in shifting criminal justice from a reactive law enforcement model to a proactive crime prevention model, in developing relationships outside the traditional silos and in establishing accountability in communities. Prosecution, probation and parole, and the courts have, with some exceptions, been dragged into this new thinking and practices. This is not to say that all police departments have gone through this shift or that many police departments operate at an ideal level. But the paradigm shift is complete: virtually no police department will do less than give lip service to this new thinking and practice. Moreover, this new thinking and practice has bubbled up from local, city, police departments rather than from state or federal police. There is not a single 'big idea' in policing that has emanated from sources other than local.

The origins of the rather remarkable circumstance of local police usurping criminal justice leadership (especially since police are the least well educated and least 'professional' of the occupations when, for example, compared to lawyers) are to be found in the total defeat of US police during the 1960s and 1970s. Whether it was the reaction of the Supreme Court to the conduct of criminal investigations, the inexorable rise in crime, the ongoing demand in cities to restore order, the rejection of police in the form of rioting by African-American communities or the findings of research into police tactics, the dominant police strategy and tactics were simply found to be without support. And police leaders knew it: policing in the USA was literally an occupation in search of a core competence by the end of the 1970s.

What explains policing's success in reforming itself, at least conceptually? Whilst one can only surmise with dealing with history, a fairly convincing explanation can be found. First, the first generation of iconoclastic police leaders like Patrick V. Murphy (Washington DC and New York City), Lee Brown (Atlanta GA, Houston TX and New York City), Robert DeGrazia (Boston) and others experimented with team policing, sensing even during the 1970s that all was not well with the then-current reactive strategy. Team policing, of course, was a precursor of community policing with its emphasis on understanding neighbourhood needs, decentralization and devolution of authority. Whilst team-policing was generally short-lived in most police departments, many who were involved in team policing innovations or experiments found it a compelling, although not then coherent, alternative to the then-current strategy. Secondly, some community relations programmes – widespread 1960s and 1970s efforts to improve the relationship between minorities and police – shifted from public relations to problem-solving. Egon Bittner has documented this shift in San Francisco CA, in an interesting but not well-known article (Bittner 1979). Thirdly, these two developments, especially team policing, meant that police departments were developing an institutional capacity – that is, a cadre of young and up-and-coming police officers – to deal with communities in new ways. William Bratton (Boston, MA, New York City, Los Angeles) and 'Joe' Santiago (Newark, NJ, New Jersey State Police, Trenton, NJ) are but two examples: young, well educated officers who were given leadership positions in experiments in team policing who later became chiefs. Fourthly, these, and other police leaders, in turn, maintained strong working relationships with academic and consultant types: Lee Brown with Robert Wasserman and Mary Ann Wycoff; David Couper (Madison, WI) with Herman Goldstein and Mary Ann Wycoff; Tony Bouza (Minneapolis, MN) with Larry Sherman; William Bratton with Robert Wasserman and me; Willie Williams (Philadelphia, PA and Los Angeles) with Jack Greene and Mark Moore – the list could go on. Fifthly, the ongoing citizen demand to 'do something now' about crime and disorder in cities gave rise to political leaders who tired of hearing the old saw that police could do little to prevent crime and led them to turn to many of the names mentioned above. Mayor 'Rudi' Giuliani of New York City was the best known but, in many respects, he was just one example of a political sense in the USA during the late 1980s and early 1990s that enough was enough. In those respects, the new message to chiefs was 'Don't tell me what you can't do; tell me what you can do'. And by the 1990s knowledgeable police leaders knew at least three things: police departments had to solve problems, they could not solve problems alone and they had to structure opportunistic relationships with citizens and public and private sector organizations and agencies to succeed. This new ethos penetrated even departments that had successfully isolated themselves in the past (e.g. the LAPD and state police). Increasingly, prosecutors, probation and parole, and courts became subject to the same demand. My own interpretation of what happened is that because police in the USA are subject to local control, decentralized in neighbourhoods and 'on the streets' they simply could not withstand the citizen and political demands for reform. Other criminal justice agencies were not as exposed to this demand and consequently were able to resist even consideration of reform until the very late 1990s and early 2000s – although, having said this, there are earlier examples of community prosecution, courts, and probation and parole.

The Greater Newark Safer Cities initiative

Shortly after I arrived at Rutgers–Newark University in 1996, Newark's Director of Police, Joseph 'Joe' Santiago, asked me if I could help the Newark

Police Department (NPD) deal with violence. The department was doing well in dealing with some problems: in fact, the overall declines in crime, whilst starting somewhat later than most cities, were amongst the steepest in the nation during 1996 to 1998. Figure 5.1 shows the violent crime rate[3] per 100,000 residents for Newark, Jersey City, Boston, New York and Philadelphia.

Clearly, Newark had a higher level of violent crime during the formative stages of Safer Cities. Boston, for example, a city with nearly 560,000 people, had just 35 murders in 1998. Newark, a city with 269,000 people, experienced 60 murders – a rate nearly four times that of Boston.

Arguably, these declines were linked to Santiago's implementation of Compstat – the accountability/crime analysis administrative mechanism developed in New York City under William Bratton. Director Santiago was completely sold on Compstat and, with his colleague Anthony Ambrose who became Newark's Police Director in 2004, had installed one of the more robust and thoroughgoing Compstat programmes in the country. Yet violence, especially homicides, was unresponsive to NPD tactics. Linked to the director's concerns were two other problems: the NPD's inability to get any 'good press' and its deteriorating relationship with the Essex County Prosecutor's Office.

Several factors shaped my decision to help: first, I had been interested in the role of universities in dealing with urban problems since the 1960s. More recently my colleagues at Harvard – Frank Hartmann, Mark Moore, David Kennedy and others – and I had talked often about developing the equivalent of a 'teaching hospital' in criminal justice. Secondly, although I had not been involved in Operation Ceasefire – the unusually successful gang violence reduction effort in Boston – I had strong relations with many of its principals in the Boston Police Department, the Suffolk County District Attorney's office (especially District Attorney Ralph Martin) and in the Kennedy School of Government at Harvard University (especially David Kennedy). My own

Figure 5.1 Violent crime index

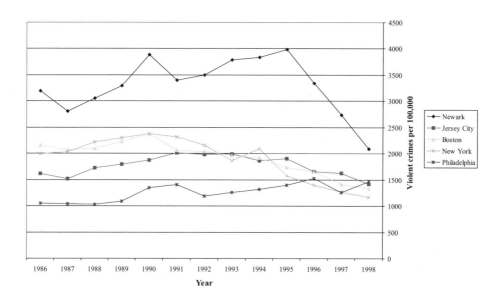

view was that 'pulling levers' was truly one of the 'big ideas' revolutionizing criminal justice. Yet, I was aware already in 1997 that the powerful interagency coalition that gave rise to Operation Ceasefire had fallen apart, indeed with some acrimony. I was interested in whether such efforts could be sustained over time. Finally, I 'owed' the NPD – it had been instrumental in the evolution of the 'broken windows' theory that James Q. Wilson and I had developed (Police Foundation 1981). Moreover, Director Santiago seemed genuinely committed to a multi-agency approach.

I want to digress slightly at this point and elaborate on the idea that universities can and should contribute to problem-solving. The view in the USA that universities can contribute to society by solving problems has its origins in the success of land grant universities in assisting farmers during the early twentieth century. Attempts to replicate this success in urban settings were popular during the 1960s – *à la* 'War on Poverty's' Model Cities programme. However, they were largely unsuccessful, especially in crime control. Part of the difficulty was that crime prevention thinking during this era was closely linked to the ideas of the war on poverty. Crime prevention was largely thought to be only attainable through large-scale social change: obtaining social justice, eliminating racism and remedying societal inequities. As worthy as these goals were, it was questionable whether they had much to do with preventing crime. Moreover, such change, if it was to be obtained, could only be achieved through political and social action, often pitting social scientists and criminologists against 'city hall' and politicians. 'Manning the barricades' in the cities in the name of crime prevention was a far cry from the rural farm agent.

There were other problems with applying the analogy of the rural farm agent helping farmers to ameliorating urban problems. For example, the farm agent had to deal with individuals around farming practices; those who want to attempt crime prevention have to influence the conglomeration of agencies that deal with urban crime: police, prosecutors, courts and so on. Moreover, it was not until the 1990s that crime control theories had developed to the point that were translatable into anti-crime policies and practices. These 'action' theories included problem-solving, broken windows, crime prevention through environmental design, situational crime prevention, pulling levers and variations of opportunity reduction theory.

But there was an additional idea about the role that universities can and should play a role in urban problem-solving. As mentioned above, this is the analogy of a 'teaching hospital' – a mix of physicians and scientists – in which advanced students can simultaneously learn, conduct relevant research, and inform and shape criminal justice policy and practice. This idea, too, has shaped Safer Cities and the subsequent evolution of the Police Institute at Rutgers–Newark University. Although a criminal justice teaching hospital was a far cry from responding to Director Santiago's request for help, responding systematically to such a request none the less positioned a school of criminal justice *vis-à-vis* the community quite differently from that which had been traditional.

To return to Safer Cities, my first move in response to Director Santiago's request for help was to ask the then-Provost of Rutgers–Newark University,

Norman Samuels, to convene a meeting among key stakeholders. (The details of the chronology of events is documented in Table 5.1).

Implicit in my request to the Provost were two assumptions. First, we assumed that all the parties would return a call from the Provost. The Director of Police certainly would return a call from me, but I was not at all certain that the US Attorney or the County Prosecutor would. The second was that I believed that the university could play the role of the 'neutral convener'. Frank Hartmann, Executive Director of the Program in Criminal Justice Management in the Kennedy School of Government, first labelled this important function. This role not only assumes that the university has something to say about urban problems and how to deal with them, it also assumes that universities are outside the normal hurly-burly of interorganizational relationships and, as such, able to pull together agencies and interests that often had what were seen as conflicting agendas. Although not entirely true – think of many of the town and gown struggles between communities and universities – it was close enough to being true that it became an important organizing and sustaining factor. (At one point, after the group was pretty well formed, we wondered out loud if the group wanted to rotate meetings to agencies. The 'no' was universal and forceful. The university was neutral territory – a safe place for representatives of agencies and groups that had a history of conflict to meet.)

During the first months we had a lucky break. I was invited to attend and speak at a meeting of the National Association of Attorneys General (NAAG). Attending as well was Thomas 'Tom' O'Reilly, the Administrator of New Jersey's Office of the Attorney General (OAG). Tom and I had worked happily and successfully together when I headed the research team that conducted the Newark Foot Patrol Experiment, but we had fallen out of touch. By now, he was an 'old hand' in New Jersey, in what was arguably one of the most powerful positions in criminal justice in the country. The power is derived from that fact that New Jersey has a relatively unique political and criminal justice system. In contrast to practically every other state in the USA, New Jersey has only one statewide elected officer, the Governor. Again, in contrast, the Governor appoints the Attorney General. Likewise, the Attorney General appoints county prosecutors. This centralized system is unique in the USA. Of significance to us, it gave the OAG enormous and exceptional influence in counties. With Tom deeply committed to innovation and reform in criminal justice, Safer Cities found a 'godfather.'

Over the long haul, this would result in fairly high levels of financial support for the evolving Police Institute – created by Acting Governor Donald DiFrancesco in 2001 – but of more immediate importance during the early phases of Safer Cities O'Reilly provided access to key players. For example, the project had three early needs: access to criminal histories and juvenile records, and the permission of the New Jersey Supreme Court for probation to become involved in a project that included police (probation is considered a judicial function in New Jersey and the courts are leery of any joint police/probation activities). Consequently, O'Reilly set up meetings between me and the Chief Justice regarding access to juvenile records and the Attorney General for access to criminal histories so that, when local representatives forwarded our

Table 5.1 Safer Cities: chronology

Phase I: start-up
Establishing a partnership and building a foundation

Goals:

1. Obtain a commitment from key community and criminal justice leaders.
2. Create a planning partnership amongst criminal justice stakeholders.
3. Begin research and analysis activities aimed at identifying the problem to be addressed.

Process components	Description	Timeline	Comments/high points
Step 1: recruit neutral convener to host initial meetings of critical stakeholders	Criminal Justice Professor George Kelling asks Rutgers–Newark Provost Norman Samuels to convene, and the university to host, a series of meetings with critical criminal justice leaders	Completed 1997	The Provost is supportive and eager to have Rutgers–Newark become more active in local community
Step 2: form exploratory task force, Criminal Justice Stakeholders Group, to consider prospects for concerted action and take initial steps towards a formal project	Included in this group are US Attorney Faith Hochberg, Newark Police Director Joseph Santiago and NJ Attorney General Peter Verniero	Completed 1998	The initial meeting marks the first time the US Attorney and Newark Police Director meet together during their respective tenure
Step 3: develop formal relations with criminal justice agencies	The group included the Newark Police Department, the NJ Attorney General's Office, Office of the US Attorney for the State of NJ and the School of Criminal Justice, Rutgers University–Newark	February–March 1999	23 February 1999: meeting held with key NJ Criminal Justice leaders at Rutgers–Newark to formalize partnership. All pledge support

Step 4: Rutgers-based staff for the Safer Cities initiative begin data collection on best practices nationally regarding crime control and prevention, and establish links with initiatives in other locations using problem-solving approaches to violence and crime prevention	Project staff visit and communicate with Operation Ceasefire in Boston, the federally funded SACSI (Strategic Approaches to Community Safety Initiatives) programme, and the Office of Juvenile Justice and Delinquency Prevention (OJJDP), in Washington, DC	March 1999 (task ongoing)	17 March 1999: follow-up meeting with criminal justice leaders establishes liaisons between Safer Cities initiative and agencies Current NJ Attorney General John Farmer and Acting US Attorney Robert Cleary replace their predecessors when Verniero and Hochberg are appointed to judgeships. Judge Joseph Falcone joined after coming to Essex County as the new Assignment Judge for the vicinage 15 November 1999: meeting with criminal justice stakeholders held to update on project activities. Essex County Acting Prosecutor Donald Campolo added as CJ Stakeholder.
	Staff members visit and observe initiatives in Boston, Indianapolis and Memphis		
	OJJDP staff participate in a crime prevention seminar hosted by the Safer Cities initiative and the Newark Boys' and Girls' Club on 30 November 1999		

Table 5.1 continued overleaf

Table 5.1 continued

Process components	Description	Timeline	Comments/high points
Step 5: initiate efforts to link schools, service providers and the faith community with Safer Cities initiative	Meetings held with service agencies, school representatives, youth representatives, the faith community and the business community. Pledges of support received. All staff are involved in working with community representatives	July 1999 (task ongoing)	30 June 1999: George Kelling meets with Commissioner of Education David Hespe 17 August 1999: Safer Cities initiative meet with local school officials at Rutgers–Newark to discuss project. Newark Superintendent Marion Bolden attends February 2000: Reverend Eugene Rivers of the National Ten-point Coalition speaks to representatives of the Newark faith community Safer Cities initiative hires an outreach co-ordinator to promote integration of the faith community into project efforts 13 September 2000: local PTA holds monthly meeting at the School of Criminal Justice. PTA president asks to hold all future meeting at the school
Step 6: Safer Cities initiative staff begin general data collection on violence in Newark to initiate problem-identification process	Convene data management working group consisting of representatives from Newark Police Department, US Attorney's Office, Bureau of Alcohol, Tobacco and Firearms, Administrative Office of the Courts and New Jersey Transit	March 1999 (task ongoing)	Quantitative data gathered from a variety of sources, chiefly from the Newark Police Department. Project staff begin receiving weekly updates of department's crime data 23 November 1999: Violence Institute of NJ at UMDNJ awarded grant from Healthcare Foundation of NJ to develop and begin emergency room surveillance

system to collect data for use by Safer Cities initiative

Initial qualitative data collection: including observational data from police ride-alongs, interviewing of staff in criminal justice partner agencies and review of police homicide files

Phase II: building operational capacity
Structures and procedures.

Goals:

1. Build structures through which partnerships between and within criminal justice, service, faith and community sectors can be implemented and operate.
2. Establish and refine data collection/analysis procedures to facilitate problem analysis and problem-solving.
3. Identify and analyse violence and crime problem in Newark.

Process components	Description	Timeline	Comments/high points
Step 1: Create Criminal Justice Working Group as ongoing forum for problem identification and development of overall violence reduction strategy	Consists of operational-level personnel from the Newark Police Department, US Attorney's Office, Essex County Probation Department, Essex County Sheriff's Department, Essex County Prosecutor's Office, NJ State Police, NJ Transit Police, FBI, ATF, DEA, Newark Housing Authority, Division of Parole, School Security for Newark Public Schools and Irvington Police Department	Began December 1999 (task ongoing)	Meetings held bi-weekly until late February 2000, then weekly. The group has continued to expand its membership. The Irvington Police Department joined early in the year – motivated by its proximity to Newark and the potential displacement effect an intervention might have

Table 5.1 continued overleaf

Table 5.1 continued

Process components	Description	Timeline	Comments/high points
Step 2: develop and maintain feedback and evaluation capacity at Rutgers	Evaluation staff recruited and hired; preliminary evaluation protocols are developed	Began October 1999 (evaluation activities ongoing for remainder of project)	Positions include: 1) an evaluation co-ordinator responsible for the outcome evaluation of the Safer Cities initiative; and 2) a project ethnographer/process evaluator, to oversee qualitative data collection/analysis and evaluate processes by which the project proceeds
Step 3: develop and strengthen ties to the community; work towards incorporating their participation and input into the Safer Cities initiative	Safer Cities initiative Rutgers staff hold informational meetings in the community to describe project efforts. Follow-up meetings held with key groups and leaders establish partnership. Safer Cities Initiative staff provide data and assistance to local groups preparing grant applications	July 1999–May 2000	10 May 2000: meeting between Safer Cities initiative senior staff and Judy Diggs, local PTA president, West Side Park resident, and Weed and Seed Executive Board Member. She pledges support and agrees to join working group. 7 March 2000: meeting between Safer Cities initiative staff and Dr Verner, Rev. Simmons and other prominent clergy to elicit support of Black Minister's Council. 9, 11, 16 May 2000: meetings sponsored by Community Agencies Corporation of NJ held with community residents in local schools to discuss Safer Cities initiative

Step 4: Rutgers staff for Safer Cities initiative undertake systematic collection and analysis of data obtained from participating criminal justice agencies.	User Agreement signed with State of NJ granting permission for Safer Cities initiative to obtain adult criminal records New Jersey Supreme Court grants permission for Safer Cities initiatives to obtain confidential juvenile records	February 2000 May 2000	User agreement allows Safer Cities initiative staff to move ahead with data collection for problem identification/analysis Request submitted through Judge Joseph Falcone, Assignment Judge, Essex Vicinage, March 2000
Step 5: Criminal Justice Working Group members deliberate on the nature of the violence problem(s) in Newark	Safer Cities initiative staff provide results of data collection and analysis to the working group, facilitating its discussion of the nature and dimensions of violence in Newark Working group members assist researchers in refining data analysis and developing an understanding of crime by applying their practical and street knowledge	Begun spring 2000 (ongoing)	Safer Cities initiative Rutgers staff also provide information to working group members on strategies for addressing similar crime configurations in other locations around the country
Step 6: communicate basic findings regarding the crime problem in Newark to heads of partner agencies, funders, community groups and local government	19 June 2000: Safer Cities initiative staff present results of crime data analysis to criminal justice stakeholders Similar presentations follow for funders, community groups (such as West Side Park Weed and Seed group), representatives of the faith community and Mayor Sharpe James. Mayor James pledges commitment to the project	June–July 2000	Safer Cities initiative Rutgers staff also hold meetings (21/3/00, 9/5/00, 18/7/00) with media consultants and public information representatives from criminal justice agencies, to begin planning a strategy for communicating working group findings and the intervention strategy to wider target and general audiences in the community

Table 5.1 continued overleaf

Table 5.1 continued

Phase III: strategy building and implementation
Develop, implement and evaluate outcomes of the intervention strategy.

Goals:

1. Craft intervention strategy to reduce/prevent violence based upon problem-solving analysis.
2. Prepare protocol to define roles of participating agencies and schedule initial activities.
3. Implement pretest/pilot intervention activities.
4. Assess and evaluate pretest intervention activities; provide feedback to partner agencies.
5. Adjust intervention strategy as needed and plan/implement further intervention activities.
6. Formally announce implementation of strategy and Safer Cities initiative in media.

Process components	Description	Timeline	Comments/high points
Step 1: Obtain formal commitment to Safer Cities initiative and participation in intervention strategy by partner agencies	Memorandum of understanding circulated to partner agencies for signature	August–September 2000	
Step 2: Criminal Justice Working Group crafts overall violence reduction strategy and specific tactics to be implemented with adult population	Proposed components of intervention strategy are identified. Discussions at working group meetings establish goals, objectives and parameters for each component; and consider anticipated roles of individual partner agencies/forms of co-operation amongst them Working group subcommittees established to design protocols for implementing specific	June–August 2000	19 June 2000: Safer Cities initiative senior staff brief Newark Police Director Joseph Santiago, US Attorney Robert Cleary, NJ Attorney General's Office representatives, Essex County Acting Prosecutor Donald Campolo, Essex County Sheriff Armando Fontoura, Commissioner of Parole Jack

| | | components, including follow-up handling of cases that will be generated | Terhune, Director of Irvington Police Robert Rankin, Essex County Assignment Judge Joseph Falcone, representatives of the Department of Probation and representatives of federal law enforcement agencies on tentative strategy components
20 June 2000: Safer Cities initiative senior staff brief Mayor Sharpe James on working group findings and on tentative strategy components
20 July 2000: Safer Cities initiative senior staff meet with Essex County Assignment Judge Joseph Falcone to discuss strategy components |
| Step 3: add community input to planning the intervention. | July–August 2000 | Community representatives begin attending working group meetings in order to craft non-law enforcement portions of the intervention strategy, as well as provide insight in planning, and approval for, law enforcement portions | Safer Cities initiative staff attend community meetings in Newark to describe plans for the intervention and inform community members
In July, representatives of the faith community and service agencies join the working group in their deliberations
In August, community representatives join intervention subcommittees |

Table 5.1 continued overleaf

Table 5.1 continued

Process components	Description	Timeline	Comments/high points
Step 4: Criminal Justice Working Group members/ agencies and community representatives review legality and morality of overall intervention strategy and specific tactics	Plans are reviewed within the context of the values of participating organizations and community representatives, and legal parameters for the activities of law enforcement partners who will join in the intervention	July–September 2000	Safer Cities initiative staff consult with staff at sites around the country concerning legal issues they confronted in planning and conducting interventions. A committee is convened by the NJ Attorney General's Office to consider legal issues pertaining to intervention strategies. AGO staff are assigned to conduct a formal legal review
Step 5: finalize all components and phases of the intervention strategy	Working group members finalize plans for the first intervention components to be implemented and schedule dates for pilot/ pretests	August–September 2000	Safer Cities initiative Rutgers evaluation staff develop specific protocols for monitoring/evaluating each pretest intervention component, including a timetable for evaluation activities
Step 6: implement pretest/pilot for intervention components The intervention will target probationers and parolees at risk of becoming offenders and victims of violence	During the pilot, evaluation staff monitor and evaluate pretest activities and provide ongoing feedback to the working group and individual agencies so that they can address problems or concerns immediately, and adjust or refine tactics as they are employed in the pilot Probationers and parolees who have extensive and serious criminal charges are put on specialized, reduced caseloads	October 2000	Safer Cities initiative is successful with Essex County Probation and the State Parole Board to create specialized, reduced caseloads

Step 7: Working group member agencies adjust/refine/add specific tactics and reassess overall intervention strategy based upon feedback/ findings of Safer Cities initiative evaluation staff. Final plans and schedule are determined for continuation of the intervention strategy	At the conclusion of the pretest, evaluation staff will brief working group members on the overall process and outcomes that can be determined by that time. This information can be used by the working group in determining how to proceed with full implementation of the strategy	October 2000
Step 8: formal public announcement of Safer Cities initiative and implementation of the violence prevention strategy	Preparations undertaken through consultation with media representatives of partner agencies and funders. An extensive press briefing is held as part of the announcement	25 October 2000	The formal announcement was attended by heads of participating law enforcement and governmental agencies, funders, service providers, clergy, the business community and other community representatives
Step 9: Safer Cities initiative develops a notification session to alert the probation and parolees that violence will not be tolerated in Newark	Agency representatives from the Superior Court, US Attorney's Office, Essex County Prosecutor's Office, police, clergy, social service and treatment providers collectively inform the cohort that these agencies are working together and are paying special attention to this cohort	January 2001 (ongoing)	Though initially held in a court room, later notification sessions are moved to community churches to make the session more neutral and welcoming to clients Notification sessions are held quarterly

Table 5.1 continued overleaf

Table 5.1 continued

Process components	Description	Timeline	Comments/high points
Step 10: Safer Cities initiative develops monthly accountability sessions to hold clients, officers, and parole and probation administrators accountable for their actions	Chairman of the State Parole Board and Chief of Essex County Probation held sessions with their respective clients where clients discussed their progress on supervision. The chairman and chief had the ability immediately to impose and lift sanctions	April 2001 (ongoing)	Clients repeatedly look forward to meeting with these high-level officials, seeing themselves and these officials as partners working together
Step 11: Social service and treatment providers express their concern to other Safer Cities initiative partners that clients have substance abuse and mental health problems but officers may not be identifying these needs	Officers and social service and treatment providers meet every other Wednesday to discuss troubled clients and to ensure that officers and providers communicate on the progress of clients at providers' programmes.	June 2001 (ongoing)	Case conferencing brings truth to the credo that all Safer Cities initiative partners share responsibility in the at-risk caseload
Step 12: Safer Cities initiative partners express their concern that gun violence is increasing and additional mechanisms are needed to address this issue	Rutgers staff conducts research that reveals repeat gun offenders in the greater Newark area receive relatively low bail Titled 'gun strategy', Safer Cities initiative develops a strategy in which the Newark Police and the Essex County Superior Court implement better information sharing techniques, enabling judges to set appropriate bail for repeat gun offenders	November 2001 (ongoing)	Gun strategy deals with a small cadre of offenders that continue to threaten Newark's neighbourhoods by carrying guns and committing crimes with firearms, but who are not under probation or parole supervision To date gun strategy has assisted in over 30 repeat gun offenders, who receive federal prosecution under Triggerlock

Step 13: Safer Cities initiative social service and treatment providers as well as clergy discuss the culture of violence and the reluctance by many at-risk participants to attend treatment	Working group members add a component to the at-risk caseload. One week after notification session, newly notified clients assemble in a church to have a dialogue with clergy and providers on taking advantage of available services and the need to resist violent tendencies	28 June 2004 (ongoing)	Clients responded positively to the dialogue and express desire to receive treatment
Step 14: Safer Cities initiative partners express concern on the emerging gang phenomenon and partners feel the initiative should address this trend	Rutgers research evaluation staff conduct focus groups with various law enforcement agencies to understand the 'gang problem' including the number of gangs, gang sets, members and activities. It is discovered that a major gang area is on the Newark and Irvington border	January 2003–May 2004	Jean McGloin, primary researcher for this project, completes her dissertation on her gang analysis and receives recognition from Rutgers University winning the Dean's Dissertation Award
Step 15: Safer Cities initiative charge Rutgers outreach staff with discussing the 'gang problem' with community members for 'community-based solutions'	For nearly a year the group works on creating a proposal that includes reach-in centres in Newark and Irvington open during non-traditional hours and outreach workers to motivate community members not to engage in violent activity or associate in dangerous areas	February 2004 (ongoing)	This proposal assists the Safer Cities initiative in reviewing similar strategies in the country, particularly public health models on violence reduction Safer Cities initiative is visited by Dr Deborah Prothrow-Stith on 3 November 2004 and Dr Gary Slutkin on 1 February 2005 to discuss Boston and Chicago's public health models respectively

Table 5.1 continued overleaf

Table 5.1 continued

Process components	Description	Timeline	Comments/high points
Step 16: Safer Cities initiative members create Operation Ceasefire Newark and Operation Ceasefire Irvington	Criminal justice partners including Newark Police Department, Irvington Police Department and NJ State Police create a task force to investigate vigorously shootings on the Newark and Irvington border	February 2005 (ongoing)	Healthcare Foundation of NJ pledges $125,000 for the creation of reach-in centres and outreach teams
	Clergy and social service providers pledge their support in speaking with victims and victims' families to lend support and advice on stopping retaliatory violence		
	Community members continue their quest in securing funding for reach-in centres and outreach teams		

official requests, the Chief Justice and Attorney General would have already been backgrounded. Likewise, when Judge Joseph Falcone was about to be appointed as Assignment Judge (Chief Judge) in the Essex County Superior Court, Tom arranged for a meeting amongst Director Santiago, himself, me and Judge Falcone to brief Falcone about Safer Cities even before he took office.

The workings of Safer Cities

Safer Cities comprises four administrative processes, problem analysis (research) and five treatment modalities. The administrative processes include bi-weekly meetings, case conferences and face-to-face 'schmoozing.' The treatment modalities include notification sessions, accountability sessions, 'rev'-up sessions, enhanced services and supervision and the gun strategy. Two additional complementary modalities are now under development, outreach and public education. The notification sessions are patterned after Boston's Operation Ceasefire; the 'rev'-up sessions are inspired by New York City's Midtown Community Court; and the accountability sessions are patterned after drug courts. The services, treatment and law enforcement, are traditional but targeted and co-ordinated. The soon-to-be-implemented outreach and public education modalities are based on a public health model, akin to that developed in Chicago by a public health physician, Dr Gary Slutkin. They were due to be in place by April 2005.

In the section that follows, I will briefly discuss each of the admininstrative processes, the problem analysis and the treatment modalities. The chronology and salient features of the progress of Safer Cities are presented in Table 5.1 and the details will not be repeated. The following discussion will highlight what I consider to be some of the more important events or processes.

Administrative processes

Bi-weekly meetings
The central process of the Safer Cities initiative is the bi-weekly meeting of agencies and representatives. The participants include several police departments (local and state); county, state and federal prosecutors; probation and parole; the public defender; social service, employment, mental health, and drug and alcohol abuse agencies (public and private); clergy; and community voluntary organizations (as represented by a full-time community organizer who is part of the staff of Safer Cities). The meetings are held in the School of Criminal Justice and chaired by Michael Wagers, the Executive Director of the Police Institute. During the formative and problem analysis stages, the group met weekly. Later, as the programme rolled out we adjusted to bi-weekly meetings. This group, generally 30–40 participants, but often ranging as high as 50 or 60, consists of administrative and operational personnel from the agencies and groups discussed above. We wanted decision-makers at the table, so we asked agency administrators to send operatives whom they trusted and who had sufficient authority to make decisions. During the initial

problem analysis phase of its activities, whilst relationships were being formed and tested, the group was restricted to criminal justice agencies. (Actually we had two reasons for this: first, as noted, we wanted to work out inter-criminal justice agency relationships outside public view. Also, we wanted to ensure that no confidential information about suspects or juveniles would be available to inappropriate persons.) Within six months, however, public and private social service agencies, clergy, the public defender and community representatives were invited to the table. This six-month lead-time gave the group the opportunity to get a pretty good picture of the violence problem in Newark and to resolve most of the conflicts.

The most intense resistance to the process came from assistant county prosecutors who, quite frankly, thought that I was mad: the idea that they can and should do other than case processing was simply out of their frame of reference. Their challenge to the process took the form of blocking access to homicide files. (In New Jersey, investigators in the County Prosecutor's office conduct investigations of homicides.) Their position was that as long as a case might be appealed, researchers could not have access to the files. (By this time, the students and I had already been cleared by the New Jersey Supreme Court for access to juvenile records and by the New Jersey Attorney General for access to criminal histories.) The struggle became so heated, and the prosecutors became so intimidating ('tough lawyer stuff' at the table), especially to the police who had access to and wanted to share the files, that we finally asked the county prosecutors to leave the table and appealed the matter to the Attorney General. The Attorney General over-ruled the local prosecutors and we obtained access to the files. (We collect data on all homicides to this day. A doctoral student is scheduled to complete a dissertation in May 2005 based on these data. This database will be broadened in April 2005 to include all shootings.)

Case conferences
Safer Cities now has a caseload of some 200 or so probationers and parolees who have been identified as at risk of killing or getting killed. It has maintained such a caseload for well over three years. Case conferences are held bi-weekly, meeting during the alternate weeks of the bi-weekly meetings. Social service agencies, clergy, probation and parole officers, prosecutors, and public defenders attend these meetings. The meeting, like the bi-weekly meeting, is held at the university and chaired by Sean Kelly (a student who received his MA in criminal justice and who is now studying part time in the law school).

A major issue in projects like Safer Cities is that of discretion. From the beginning of Safer Cities, we emphasized that agencies and groups maintained their discretion in every respect. Operationally, the issue of discretion affects the case planning in case conferences more than in any other aspect of the intergroup relationship. In practice, this means that, for example, the decision to return a probationer to court for an infraction is solely that of the probation officer/department. All participants in the case conference understand this. Yet, probation officers rely heavily on the advice of participants in the case conference – in fact, given the current set of relationships, it is rare that either probation or parole officers reject the recommendations of the case conference.

Moreover, the court now expects and relies on recommendations from Safer Cities at all hearings regarding youths who are on the caseload. (By the way, all stereotypes go out the window: it is often clinical operatives who want sterner action than their law enforcement colleagues.)

Face-to-face 'schmoozing'

Face-to-face interactions were the base of relationship building. At first, spinning off the influence of the Provost and whatever reputation I might have had, we met with stakeholders – political and organizational leaders whose co-operation would be necessary if the project were to go forward. Tom O'Reilly's involvement accelerated this process. Our first goal was to get them to trust us – that we had good ideas, that we could deliver, that we would not get their agencies or organizations in trouble either internally or in their environment and that we would not 'play favourites' in the normal interorganizational struggles that characterize criminal justice. In other words, we had to convince them that we were responsible and neutral.

The issue of trust covered many dimensions. For example, law enforcement agencies simply did not trust each other regarding the media and news – either good (who gets the credit) or bad (who gets the blame). All, however, came to believe that Rutgers would ensure that policies and practices would be developed in Safer Cities to assure fairness in handling the media. (All ultimately agreed that I would handle all media inquiries. The rationale for this was that we would have nothing to say for quite a while and 'Kelling says nothing better than anybody else around'.) Achieving face-to-face trust in this and other dimensions required a seemingly endless round of breakfast, lunch and dinner meetings. Developing trust with was especially sensitive in dealing with clergy as we were starting Safer Cities just as the New Jersey State Police were in the middle of their racial profiling controversy. It was not hard to misinterpret or misrepresent what we were proposing as 'locking up black kids'. (My association with broken windows and New York City was a mixed blessing: for some it gave me considerable credibility; for others, it was a liability.)

When we tried to replicate Safer Cities by ourselves in Camden, NJ – a very troubled city approximately 100 miles from Newark – the importance of face-to-face contact was evident. Because of the distance, we simply could not do the kind of trust building that was required to allow agencies and groups to make an initial investment in us. We just could not do all the 'schmoozing' that is required between meetings in order for the meetings to be a success. Sensing this very early, we recruited a local university institute, the Rand Institute, to replace us and diverted some of our funds to it. Within the past months, they have implemented a variation of Newark's Safer Cities.

Ultimately in Newark, the operatives developed trust amongst themselves. The role that Mike and I now play in solving any problems among agencies or groups is small. A fascinating sign of the change is that even after the bi-weekly meetings are adjourned, virtually nobody leaves for another half hour or so. Reverend D wants to talk to Deputy Chief Z about a problem he is having in the neighbourhood. Social agency Director S wants to talk to staff member of Office of the Attorney General about the problems of getting referrals of newly released prisoners to state-funded programmes. In other words, operatives are using the bi-weekly meetings and case conferences to settle other problems. Occasionally, a major crisis will develop – one agency representative is undermining a key Safer Cities process, for example – that will require our intervention, but this is rare.

In other words, one important feature of face-to-face 'schmoozing' is that it is an essential transitional process during which individual trust is developed between neutral conveners and agencies and groups. Face to face does not always work. There are agencies, churches and groups who simply want no part of me, Rutgers, the Police Institute or Safer Cities. A few view themselves as our competitors. Most of those who joined in and stayed with us, however, have gone beyond their trust in us and have extended it to each other – at least around the problem of violence. The need for face-to-face interaction does not end, however, once a well functioning group is formed. Perhaps it does not require the same level of intensity, but trust has to be constantly renewed, especially with agencies like the courts that believe they have a lot on the line. We have been 'spanked' several times by powerful officials who felt that we were being neglectful.

Research (problem analysis and evaluation)

From the beginning of Safer Cities, we maintained a position that we would not begin any programme without gaining a clear understanding of 'who was doing what, to whom, where, when and how'. Three factors are involved in this stance: first, we mean it – we really believe Herman Goldstein's admonition that problems are rarely what they seem; secondly, even if we had a good idea of the shape of the problem when Safer Cities began to meet, the group was not ready to work together; and we used this rationale to fend off demands from funders and supporters that we 'get going' with some action. (By the end of several months we had obtained funds from several foundations and the Office of the Attorney General. One foundation, which continues to be very generous in dealing with us, was especially demanding. Tom O'Reilly of the OAG would often try to push us to get going, but would back off quickly, understanding from his own bureaucratic experience the difficulty of what we had come to refer to as 'herding cats' – that is, taking a group of disparate agencies and getting them going in the same direction.)

The research was interesting: we found both similar and different patterns when compared to Boston. First, a few oddities about homicide in Newark: few juveniles kill or are killed, homicides tend to be a late-20s phenomenon. Secondly, few spouses, lovers or family members kill each other. Domestic homicides are rare. Generally, the following homicide patterns emerge: a small number of African-American youths who carry guns, deal drugs, have lengthy histories of criminal and violent behaviour, and drape themselves in gang colours, kill each other over trivial incidents – insults, 'dissing' and minor disputes. The criminal histories of the killers and those killed are virtually identical – it really does appear to be the 'luck of the draw' that determines who is killed and who kills. Although a few tightly knit small 'sets' of gang members exist, gangs are loosely organized and only marginally territorial.

It probably is even a misnomer to call them gangs if they are compared to Boston, Los Angeles or Chicago. In Newark, 'Crips' kill 'Crips' and 'Bloods' kill 'Bloods'. It is only a small exaggeration to say that Newark does not really have 'hotspots'; it has two 'cool spots' – homicides are widely spread throughout the city. Complicating the issue, to the extent that there are hotspots, they overlap political boundaries and jurisdictions. Irvington – a small troubled city that juts into Newark dividing two of its large areas – for example, simply was unwilling and unable to 'come to the table' until recently. The organizational (bad rift in the Police Department between the Director and Chief) and political (no leadership) factors that gave rise to this have been resolved and Irvington is now at the table and will be at the heart of our continuing effort. (I believe this partially explains our apparent inability to have an impact on homicide, but this is arguable.)

I call attention to one characteristic identified above, race. Sixty-five per cent of the citizens of Newark are African-American, yet over 80 per cent of the killers and those killed are African-American. I will discuss race in the concluding section.

The implications of the research were several. We believed that homicide was too widespread and the jurisdictional issue so complicating that attempting to focus on hotspots would be futile. Also (although we did not confirm this with data until much later), our view was that the gangs were so disorganized that we could not leverage them to get them to control their own members. We decided then to concentrate on parolees and probationers who matched the criminal history profile of killers and those killed. Race would not be a factor in this decision but we had little doubt that we would be working primarily with a male African-American population.

Treatment modalities

Notification sessions

Our notification sessions are loosely patterned after Boston's Operation Ceasefire. Youths with a history of serious repeat offences that include violent offences who are on probation or parole are identified as an 'at risk' population. They are ordered by the court or by their probation or parole officer to attend a notification session – generally in groups of about 10 or 15. The intent of the session is to send two messages: the community will no longer tolerate your violent behaviour – if you continue to be violent the entire weight of the criminal justice system will come down on you. The second message, hopefully sent as powerfully, is that the community understands that life has been tough for you and we will try to give you first shot at whatever you need to turn your life around: jobs, education, drug treatment, mental health assistance or whatever. Speakers at the notification session include a judge, police officers, clergy, social service personnel, prosecutors, and probation and parole representatives. The 'neutral conveners' play no role whatsoever.

Our first notification session was held in January 2001 in a courtroom. It was a disaster. Although some of the speakers were African-American the overall impression was, as I described in the debriefing later, like 'a lot of honkys hollering at black youth'. The helping message was largely lost.

Moreover clergy, who at this time were still quite wary about involvement, had agreed to participate only if they would be assured that no one would be taken into custody during the session unless they were wanted for something approaching homicide. As it turned out, because the session was held in the courtroom, several probation officers attended the session as observers who were not involved in Safer Cities. One saw a probationer who was wanted on a technical violation and, without consultation with his peers or involved supervisors, proceeded to make an arrest – or at least attempt to. The ensuing brawl, ultimately involving probation officers, sheriff deputies and police, was carried out practically in the laps of attending clergy. Needless to say, few of the Safer Cities operatives present enjoyed the pizza served at the debriefing.

Not surprisingly, the start of the following bi-weekly meeting was tense. Several clergy and at least one service agency refused to attend (and has not attended since). The probation officer in charge asked to speak as soon as the meeting began. He turned to the clergy, apologized, explained what happened but accepted full responsibility and assured them it would never happen again. The clergy accepted the apology and the matter was closed. It was an important moment: trust among participants was starting to develop.

In the following discussion, one of the clergy – a soft-spoken and generally quiet participant – spoke up and suggested that we try holding the next notification session in his church and that he host and, in effect, emcee it. The more we talked about it, the better this idea sounded. Like the discovery that there were no hotspots in Newark, only two cool spots, this was one of those 'Aha' moments: the implicit message of holding the session in the courtroom, and having it chaired by a probation officer, was that the criminal justice agencies were taking action and were being supported by the community and service agencies. Holding the session in a neighbourhood church, chaired by the pastor of that church, sent a very different message. This message was the *community* would no longer tolerate violent behaviour and *it* was being *supported* by criminal justice and service agencies. Moreover, the programme of the notification session was limited to 'talking heads' – the speakers from the respective organizations and agencies. This was hardly the first step in developing some kind of relationship with the youth. So, we decided that rather than have Safer Cities participants have pizza after the session, as we did after the first session, we would have the participants and the offenders mingle, sit together and eat. Many youths got to 'talk' to a judge for the first time.

We have now conducted notification sessions along the lines suggested by our clergy partners for five years. Word has spread in the community and many of the youths who attend are ahead of us, anticipating the process. (One of the speakers, a prosecutor with a thunderous base voice, uses the phrase: 'Don't bring me no bad news' (a line from the musical *The Wiz*). Several times recently, as this prosecutor has walked into the church prior to the session, youths have anticipated the phrase, humorously greeting him with 'Don't bring me no bad news'.

Accountability sessions
Accountability sessions were the idea of Mario Paparozzi who was the chair

of the New Jersey's Parole Board during the early days of Safer Cities and who regularly attended the bi-weekly meetings. It was routine that after a notification session youths would be referred to a local social service agency for a needs assessment. After this, however, except for contacts with probation or parole agents, the youths would have no identifiable relationship with Safer Cities. Paparozzi's idea was to run 'accountability sessions' that, like drug courts, would give youths an opportunity to report on how they were doing, what services they were receiving and their perceptions of their ongoing needs and problems. In a sense, these accountability sessions held both the youth and Safer Cities accountable, in that lapses of services or supervision could be identified as well as adjustment problems on the part of the youths. Moreover, youths who were succeeding and who attended the accountability sessions provided excellent examples for some of the newcomers. Like many drug courts, many youths received well deserved applause for their successes. (We now have alumni who regularly attend accountability sessions.) As significant as this was for the youths, it was also a milestone for Safer Cities: for the first time Safer Cities had a caseload – a concept that, perhaps more than anything else, bound the group comprising Safer Cities and gave it an ongoing responsibility. The accountability sessions were, I believe, crucial to the continuity and persistence of Safer Cities.

'Rev'-up sessions

The rev-up sessions are new, having been implemented at the beginning of 2005. 'Rev' is a take-off on 'Reverend' – a title, of course, for clergy. Two points: first, the idea of clergy involvement in social programmes is popular and has achieved considerable political attention. Converting this into programmes, however, has not been easy.[4] Except for those who have received special training, say in pastoral counselling, their special competence is not clear. Mentoring is often mentioned as a legitimate role. However, such programmes are difficult to establish and carry with them concerns about liability. Secondly, as Winship and Berrien (1999) suggest, the clergy's 'umbrella of legitimacy' is important and we in Safer Cities have clearly benefited from it. Their claim to a special role in guiding the morality of programmatic efforts is also important and has shaped several of our efforts. Moreover, youths have identified with some of our clergy and sought their help and guidance. But for the most part, although involving clergy seems like a good idea (and it certainly is important in maintaining credibility), just exactly what clergy could offer programmatically was not clear.

The clergy and social service partners, not always in close agreement about issues, none the less identified a serious gap in our efforts. This awareness grew more acute after members of Safer Cities visited New York's Mid Town Community Court. What struck them was that offenders, after their hearing, were taken immediately to service providers who had offices in the court building. This meant that at a vulnerable moment in the lives of offenders, service providers were immediately present. Our problem was that after the notification session it might be several weeks before clients had their needs assessment and a month before they attend an accountability session or got to a service agency. Any vulnerability to help could easily be lost during this time. The question the group was asking was: 'How do we ready these youths to be ready?' The social service group and the clergy proposed rev-up sessions as a means of preparing clients to accept help – and the kind of help that they need. For example, practically every offender 'wants a job'. The sad reality is that many, if not most, of them are simply not prepared for work. Clergy, with their special role in the African-American community, assisted by ex-offenders who have been 'through it' and succeeded, are in a unique position to cut through the resistances and unrealistic self-perceptions that characterize many offenders and ex-offenders. Consequently, clients now attend a rev-up session within a week of their notification session. Like the notification session it is conducted in a neighbourhood church. At the first, members of the church prepared 'soul food' for all the participants – sending, in my mind, an additional message about the 'caring' of the community. Again, trying to send and reinforce the message that although we were prepared to be very assertive if offenders brought us 'bad news', we were also determined to send a message of caring and opportunity.

Enhanced enforcement and services

With one exception, I see no need to detail this set of activities. They include reduced and special caseloads for probation and parole, vertical prosecution, the gun strategy (discussed briefly below), needs assessment and a variety of social, drug and mental health services. I do want to emphasize, however, one new aspect of our programme as it is an example of the extent to which *collaboration* – a word I have not yet used in this chapter and will discuss below – has become 'business as usual'.

This chapter began with an assertion that, whilst we believe we have controlled the at-risk probation and parole youths, we have not had an apparent impact on the homicide rate. Figure 5.2 illustrates this.

Our ongoing homicide analysis and our gang analysis, however, revealed an emerging pattern. Youths similar to those described above, however, not under supervision of any kind, were regularly killing each other. Most had

Figure 5.2 Newark homicide rate, 1986–2004

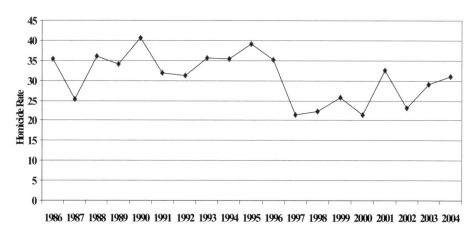

'maxed out': that is, they had either completed probation or parole or had served their full time in prison. This was a consequence of the national trend in the USA of 'truth in sentencing' and other such political phrases turned into sentencing policy that appeared to be tough but, in reality, turned angry and troubled youth out of prison at the end of their sentence without any form of community supervision or control.

This ongoing problem, and a crisis that was created when four youths were executed in Newark in late 2004, gave rise to our determination to roll out community outreach efforts. The starting point is that police and prosecution will investigate every shooting as if it were a homicide. Every Monday morning the involved law enforcement agencies will meet (again, at the university). The group will include Newark and Irvington Police, New Jersey State Police, the Sheriff's Department, prosecutors and investigators from the Essex County Prosecutor's Office and parole agents. (It is not clear whether probation officers can participate as they are viewed as officers of the court. We will visit this issue with the New Jersey Supreme Court.) Because of confidentiality concerns, other groups will not be included in this part of the meeting. This law enforcement group will analyse all shootings and homicides, informed by our gang analysis (a network analysis of the internal workings of gangs) (McGloin 2004, forthcoming), and whatever other information is relevant from investigatory or intelligence sources. A co-ordinated criminal investigation plan will be devised.

Once an investigative strategy has been put in place, outreach workers (well trained ex-gang members) and clergy will join the law enforcement group. Using whatever data are appropriate, the entire group will devise a community outreach effort that could include, to give just two examples, gang interventions to reduce the possibility of a revenge cycle setting in and clergy marches to dramatize the community indignation with violence.

I use this example because it is really a collaboration – that is, it is an example of agencies and groups mutually modifying their routines and breaking down the boundaries that normally characterize their activities.

Gun strategy

The gun strategy, briefly mentioned above, grew out of an awareness that many youths who were carrying guns were not only not under probation or parole supervision but also were not being treated seriously by the courts (often because of poor information sharing between police, prosecutors and the courts). Yet, many arrested for gun carrying or shooting were serious repeat offenders. For example, one youth in his mid-twenties was arrested wearing body armour and armed with a 9-mm automatic pistol with dum-dum bullets. He had already shot somebody once before and had been shot once himself. Obviously, he was 'hunting' or 'being hunted' when arrested. Yet he was released under a $1,300 bail. Safer Cities could not intervene because he was not under any form of supervision. He was shot and killed two weeks after his release. Consequently, because of the data available to Safer Cities and the leverage it had developed, Safer Cities managed to persuade the courts to review all gun arrests to determine, first, if this was more than a first arrest with a gun and, secondly, if the arrestee had a history of violence. If these criteria were met, a superior rather than a municipal court judge reviewed his or her case. Average bail for those who met these criteria increased from approximately $1,000 to around $100,000. Offenders who are not imprisoned, and who meet the other qualifications, are included in Safer Cities as a condition of probation.

A final note about the gun strategy: as it evolved our community organizer, Lori Scott-Pickens, worked closely with neighbourhood and community groups. Because we were 'changing the rules of the game' and using criminal justice authority more assertively we believed that it was important to keep the community involved and seek its support. The response of some groups was, at first, cynical: 'Let 'em kill each other.' But all finally agreed that they would support our effort providing that we reinstated a gun buy-back programme and a hot line so that citizens could confidentially report gun carrying. A coalition of community groups called a press conference and explained the three aspects of the programme – more stringent bail review, gun buy-back and a hot line. They then called upon Safer Cities officials to provide details. Again, we were seeking to send the message that the community was being supported by criminal justice and other agencies.

Public awareness and outreach

The public health modality, now being implemented, will concentrate on two initiatives: public awareness and outreach. Although Safer Cities has had a modest public education element, it has not sent a consistent and powerful message to the community that violence is unacceptable – along the lines of anti-smoking and drunk-driving campaigns. Additionally, ex-gang members have been recruited and will be trained to reach out to the community in an attempt to end the cycle of violence: someone is shot, someone else seeks revenge, *ad infinitum*.

Discussion: defining the terms of the relationship and lessons learned

Defining the terms of the relationship

Note that throughout this chapter, with the exception of the discussion about collaboration above, I have used the term 'relationship' to characterize interorganizational efforts. I have deliberately avoided terms like 'collaboration', 'partnership' or 'co-operation'. This is because it is essential to understand the *terms, or conditions, of interorganizational relationships*. In common conversation, terms like partnership and collaboration might mean the same thing but, for analytical purposes, they might indicate quite different relationships. If we think about it, organizations/units can relate in a variety of levels ranging from the extremes of active opposition to collaboration. This awareness, and the need to articulate the differences, grew out of my evaluation of what was called the Comprehensive Communities Program (CCP) – a favourite programme of the Department of Justice during the Clinton administration (Kelling *et al.* 1998). During the administration of this project, the 16 cities involved would regularly be convened by the Department of Justice to share ideas. What became clear during these meetings was that terms like partnership and collaboration would be thrown around glibly, but have imprecise meanings.

Moreover, it became clear that organizations and citizens could simultaneously be involved in very different kinds of relationships, usually depending upon the nature of the problem at hand. In Boston, one of the cities studied as part of the CCP evaluation, an organization called the Ten Point Coalition – started by African-American clergy to deal with gangs and violence – concurrently had two dissimilar reactions to the Boston Police Department (BPD). Their relationship to the 'pulling levers' programme, that so successfully constrained the violent activities of gangs in Boston, was one of 'consent' – that is, to use Winship and Berrien's (1999) metaphor, they offered an 'umbrella of legitimacy' to law enforcement activities in the community that were quite assertive. At the same time, clergy in the Ten Point Coalition led demonstrations against Boston police officers when, in their view, they were excessively violent in African-American neighbourhoods. Simultaneously, to use my terms, they were offering *consent* to one element of the BPD whilst *actively resisting* another.

Consequently, I developed a continuum of interorganizational relationships and attempted to define and differentiate them.[5] To be sure, there are elements of arbitrariness about this. For example, the word 'partnership' could be substituted for 'collaboration.' Moreover, the terms of the relationship can change over time: in the example I gave above from Safer Cities, for example, the relationship of the clergy to Safer Cities began, and for several years remained, at the *consent* stage; it now operates at the *collaboration* stage given their role in the rev-up sessions. None the less, Box 5.1 portrays a continuum of interorganizational relationships ranging from active opposition to collaboration. It also includes definitions of the terms/conditions of the relationship.

Box 5.1 Continuum of interorganizational relationships

**Collaboration–Co-ordination–Co-operation–Consent–Indifference–Objection–
Passive protest–Defiance–Active resistance**

Definitions

- *Collaboration:* an implicit or explicit contract between two entities, by which each agrees to implement, conduct or refrain from certain activities, in ways that depart from each organization's traditional 'business as usual' and that permeate traditional boundaries.

- *Co-ordination:* two entities identify a common problem, adjusting and aligning their activities in light of it and each other; however, the traditional organizational boundaries remain intact.

- *Co-operation:* two entities conduct their traditional respective activities, whilst agreeing to support each other and to ensure that their programmes do not overlap, conflict or cross jurisdictional or professional boundaries.

- *Consent:* an ongoing public declaration that one entity approves of the activities of another.

- *Indifference:* two organizations that may or may not be aware of each other's activities but, if aware, believe them not to be significant for the other.

- *Objection:* an ongoing public declaration that one entity disapproves of the activities of another.

- *Passive protest:* one entity attempts to stop the activities of another through public declarations and information dissemination.

- *Defiance:* one entity attempts to block the other's programme implementation or maintenance by advocating, implementing and maintaining conflicting programmes.

- *Active resistance:* active hostility between two entities enacted through political, legal or violent attempts to stop each other's activities.

Above, I presented an example of planned collaboration amongst investigatory agencies, clergy and outreach workers. It is a good example because it modifies a core competence of police agencies: the conduct of criminal investigations. Note that this is not just a particular high-profile case but a new way to do business around a particular problem. I could give examples for each of the stages on the continuum of relationships. For example, we co-operate with one agency in dealing with the issue of prisoner re-entry. They rarely come to the table, but we co-ordinate activities. At times, around special events they come to the table, but there is no expectation of more than that. Likewise, another agency is developing a community outreach effort. Because we have resources for training in outreach techniques (this will be co-ordinated with Gary Slutkin, mentioned above, from Chicago), we are offering to train their staff.

My purpose is more than semantic here. If we are to analyse and understand the nature of relationships in interorganizational and community crime control efforts, some uniformity of language is required. Another scheme might be even more helpful. None the less I put this scheme forward because it has been useful to me in understanding community efforts.

Lessons learned

The following are the lessons I think I have learnt from my experiences and research into formal and informal means of crime prevention:

- *Organize around an urgent problem, not around system change.* System change probably will occur if continuity can be developed, but it should not be pushed. It should grow out of the realization that to deal with the urgent problem change must take place. Had I suggested five years ago that the law enforcement agencies, including parole officers, would be regularly meeting every Monday to deal with shootings and homicides and that following this meeting they would meet with clergy and outreach workers, it would have been considered one more example of my madness. Moreover, if the problem is urgent, it is very hard for agencies not to participate initially or to back away later.

- *Get the high moral ground.* In criminal justice we are dealing with the power of the state. In fact, in Safer Cities we were concentrating it on a small number of offenders. We were doing this in Newark at a time when racial profiling was at the centre of attention. At virtually every meeting, the group discussed not just the legality of our enterprise, but its morality.

- *Deal with race.* At least in the USA, one cannot deal with crime without confronting the race issue. The proportion of African-Americans who were killing each other in Newark was way out of proportion to their representation in the community. We had to learn to talk about this. It was not easy. Whites may talk to whites about race and blacks may talk to blacks about race, but few have experience talking about race across racial lines. It took time, it took practice and it took forgiveness, but we succeeded. Echoing a comment David Kennedy once made to me, we too 'deracialized the homicide problem'.

- *Find a common language.* Various professional groups approach the table with different theories, ideologies, languages and stereotypes about other disciplines. Keeping the group focused on the data during the problem analysis tends to overcome these divisions. The stereotypes do not hold true once problems get specific. In Safer Cities a 'tough cop' – and he is – got more jobs for our clients than any other single person or agency. The esoteric languages of professions and disciplines get in the way when generalities are on the table; when specifics are, they largely vanish.

- *Work with what you have got.* Despite our success in bringing important agencies and groups to the table, we miss the participation of the federal agencies (the US Attorney co-operates with us – I mean it in the sense defined above – but has not really made the kind of commitment that US Attorney Donald Stern did in Boston's Operation Ceasefire), of Newark's city government agencies and of adjacent cities. Whilst this places limitations on Safer Cities, we have been able to work around these gaps. Having said this, the local police department and the county prosecutor were absolutely essential, at least in Safer Cities with its focus on violent crime. But this would change depending upon the problem.

- *Fall on the sword.* Mistakes, failures, problems are always the fault of the convener, not any of the agencies or groups. Success is always credited to the group. Part of this is linked to local media. Agency heads, politicians and other local groups can live or die by the media. (Academics and blooming academics, on the other hand, live or die by their publications.)

- *Respect discretion.* This is discussed above. The more agencies are assured that they maintain their discretion, the more likely is that they will not use it.

- *Keep the process open.* We have very few written agreements protocols and or memos of understanding. It has become a mantra of Safer Cities that because we are aiming at a moving target, we have to remain loose and flexible.

- *Keep schmoozing.* This has been discussed above at length.

- *Keep the community and community groups up front.* This may sound manipulative, but I really doubt that it is. For generations we have professionalized crime control to the extent that citizens and citizen groups have forgotten their responsibilities as citizens in a democracy. Both citizens and criminal justice agencies have forgotten Sir Robert Peel's admonition when he created the London Metropolitan Police in 1829 – with which I began this chapter.

- *Take your time.* Good problem analysis often takes longer than solving or managing the problem. Moreover, thorough problem analysis allows agencies to get beyond their traditional rivalries, allows participants to develop collegial relations around a problem rather than around an agency or profession and helps develop a common language. My own view is that the Strategic Alternatives to Community Safety Initiative (SACSI), federal attempts to replicate Boston's Operation Ceasefire in a group of cities, fell short of its potential because of the pressure from the Department of Justice to start prematurely, even before cities understood fully the nature of the problem or had formed the relationships that could lead to success. (Newark was not one of the communities. We attended their meetings because we were implementing a similar programme, however, without federal funds.)

In closing, this chapter has defined the 'success' of Safer Cities in terms other than outcomes. I believe that we will be able to show that we helped control a dangerous and aggressive population. So far, we have not had much luck reducing homicides, but we remain at the drawing boards, adapting and experimenting with new approaches. I think that we still might make a difference with homicides. But even if we do not, I do not want to hold community-based approaches to higher standards than the old professional – in the USA, Progessive – model, that has largely failed. The genius of Anglo-Saxon policing is that it is a serious shot at people policing themselves rather than being policed by a central government. We lost this idea in the USA for most of the twentieth century. The outcome was bad policing and bad citizenship. We now are developing better policing and better citizenship.

Good policing, like good research, is policing that is done well, not that gets any specific outcome. (The same could be said of all criminal justice practice.) There are good reasons to suspect in the USA that it also has positive outcomes in terms of crime prevention. This is, of course, a hotly debated issue now in the US – one that is not likely to subside quickly. None the less, Safer Cities has produced better policing and better criminal justice practice. (I do hope, however, that we can reduce homicides as well.)

Selected further reading

The notion of community is notoriously slippery. Community crime prevention has been conceptualized in a variety of ways and is rooted in a variety of theories. The following will give the reader a good idea of what has been said and done. Hope and Shaw's collection, *Communities and Crime Reduction* (1988), remains a useful set of background papers. Hope's 'Community crime prevention' (1995) provides an accessible, authoritative overview. Skogan's collection, *Community Policing: Can it Work?* (2003), includes a variety of readable papers dealing with efforts to address community crime problems. Utting and Langman's *A Guide to Promising Approaches* (2nd edn, 2005) summarizes research-based lessons about means of addressing community-based problems of crime and criminality. Kelling and Coles' *Fixing Broken Windows* (1996) is highly accessible and sets community crime prevention in the context of broken windows. Sampson *et al.*'s 'Neighbourhoods and violent crime: a multilevel study of collective efficacy' (1997) is technically difficult, though the ideas are quite simple and the paper has been highly influential well beyond Chicago where the study was set. Hancock's *Community, Crime and Disorder* (2001) comprises a readable ethnography describing community crime problems and ways of responding to them in Merseyside. Skogan and Hartnett's *Community Policing: Chicago Style* (1997) provides an account of the largest-scale study to date of efforts to address local crime problems through community-based policing.

Notes

1. For example, I was the principal evaluator of the US Department of Justice's Comprehensive/Communities Program. The evaluation included 16 sites throughout the USA (see Kelling *et al.* 1998).
2. 'Squeegeemen' refer to youths who extort money by insisting on 'washing' car windows at intersections – often by spitting on windows and wiping them with filthy rags – regardless of the wishes of the driver.
3. The violent crime rate is composed of the crimes of murder, robbery, aggravated assault and rape.
4. I have discussed this in some detail in Kelling (2001).
5. I first used this continuum to describe the complex relationship between faith-based organizations and the government in Kelling (2001).

References

Bittner, E. (1979) 'The impact of police–community relations on the police system,' in D.P. Geary (ed.) *Community Relations and the Administration of Justice*. New York, NY: Wiley.

Goldstein, H. (1990) *Problem-oriented Policing*. Philadelphia, PA: Temple University Press.

Hancock, L. (2001) *Community, Crime and Disorder*. Basingstoke: Palgrave.

Hope, T.J. (1995)'Community crime prevention', in M. Tonry and D.P. Farrington (eds) *Building a Safer Society. Crime and Justice. Volume 19*. Chicago, IL: University of Chicago Press.

Hope, T.J. and Shaw, M. (eds) (1988) *Communities and Crime Reduction*. London: HMSO.

Kelling, G.L. (2001) 'Defining the terms of collaboration: faith-based organizations and government in criminal justice', in E.J. Dionne and M.H. Chen (eds) *Sacred Places, Civic Purposes: Should Government Help Faith-based Charity?* Washington, DC: Brookings Institution.

Kelling, G.L. and Coles, C.M. (1996) *Fixing Broken Windows: Restoring Order and Reducing Crime in our Communities*. New York, NY: Free Press.

Kelling, G.L. *et al.* (1998) *The Bureau of Justice Assistance Comprehensive Communities Program: A Preliminary Report. National Institute of Justice, Research in Brief*. Washington, DC: US Department of Justice.

Kennedy, D. (1997) 'Pulling levers: chronic offenders, high-crime settings, and a theory of prevention', *Valparaiso University Law Review*, 31: 449–84.

Kennedy, D. and Braga, A. (1998) 'Homicide in Minneapolis: research for problem solving', *Homicide Studies*, 2: 263–90.

McGloin, J.M. (2004) *Associations among Criminal Gang Members as a Defining Factor of Organization and as a Predictor of Criminal Behavior: The Gang Landscape of Newark, New Jersey*. Ann Arbor, MI: University of Michigan Press.

McGloin, J.M. (forthcoming) 'Policy and intervention considerations of a network analysis of street gangs', *Criminology and Public Policy*.

Police Foundation (1981) *The Newark Foot Patrol Experiment*. Washington, DC: Police Foundation.

Sampson, R.J., Raudenbush, S.W. and Earls, F. (1997) 'Neighbourhoods and violent crime: a multilevel study of collective efficacy', *Science*, 277: 918–24.

Skogan, W.G. (2003) *Community Policing: Can it Work?* Belmont, CA: Wadsworth.

Skogan, W.G. and Hartnett, S.M. (1997) *Community Policing: Chicago Style*. New York, NY: Oxford University Press.

Utting and Langman (2005) *A Guide to Promising Approaches* (2nd edn). London: Communities that Care.

Wilson, J.Q. and Kelling, G.L. (1982) 'Broken windows,' *Atlantic Monthly*, February.

Winship, C. and Berrien, J. (1999) 'Boston cops and black churches', *The Public Interest*, 136: 52–68.

Chapter 6

Progress and prospects in the prevention of repeat victimization

Graham Farrell

Introduction

This is a *handbook* of crime prevention and community safety, so this chapter does not seek to examine the entirety of knowledge relating to repeat victimization. Rather, it takes stock of developments in research and practice relating to its prevention. It identifies problem areas and outlines prospects for future research and prevention efforts. Readers interested in documenting progress from earlier reviews are referred to *Repeat Victimization: Taking Stock* (Pease 1998, available free online), which is the definitive work covering the period prior to its publication.

Some facts relating to repeat victimisation are particularly relevant to crime prevention and are now largely accepted:

- Crime surveys find an average of 40 per cent of crimes against individuals and households are repeats against targets already victimized that year, with variation by crime type and place.[1]

- Repeat victimization against the same target often occurs quickly.

- The same offenders are more likely to commit repeat victimization (after learning that a target is suitable for further crime).

- Risks of repeat victimization vary by crime type and context but high rates are typically found for personal crimes including domestic violence, sexual victimization, abuse of elders and children, racial attacks, bullying and assaults and threats.

- Amongst property crimes, high rates of repeat victimization are often found in crimes against businesses, including commercial burglary, robbery and shoplifting.

For those crime types typically referred to as 'street' or 'common' crimes that often take place in residential neighbourhoods:

- rates of repeat victimization are, on average, higher for personal crime than property crime;

- when a house is burgled, nearby neighbours experience a heightened risk. The risk declines with time and distance from the crime site;

- rates of repeat victimization are disproportionately higher in high-crime areas for the relevant property and personal crimes; and

- repeat victimization often underpins, or disproportionately contributes to, apparent geographical hotspots of crime.

All of the above points can inform decisions about where, when and how to allocate crime prevention resources. Several projects aiming to prevent repeat victimization have been evaluated and are discussed in more detail later. Some efforts have proven more effective than others, and key practical lessons have been learnt. Of particular importance are those lessons relating to implementation:

- It is not necessarily easy to identify appropriate areas or contexts in which to tackle repeat victimization (partly because some data are of limited use, and partly because some analysts find it difficult to measure repeat victimization).

- Identifying appropriate preventive measures to introduce is still difficult for many types of crime.

- Where known prevention measures exist, victims or others involved can be difficult to contact.

- When contacted, some victims (or others involved) do not want, or do not have the means, to adopt preventive measures.

Amongst other key issues is the fact that practice and evaluation to date have focused disproportionately on repeat residential burglary. There is a pressing need for a broader agenda in relation to the many types of crimes that might be fruitfully addressed by this approach. Some crime types, as diverse as sexual victimization and computer network attacks, have hardly begun to be approached via this prevention strategy.

The next section of this chapter defines repeat victimization, discusses developments in terminology and presents a preliminary typology. After a brief look at the types of crime that are repeated and the extent of repetition, the chapter examines why repeat victimization is an attractive crime prevention strategy. A section on how to prevent repeat victimization includes a summary of findings from evaluations. This facilitates the identification of 'what works' and 'what does not work' which in turns leads to an examination of specific 'tricky issues' relating to the development and implementation of prevention efforts. Towards the end of the chapter, repeat victimization is suggested to be integral to other strategies that can be used to focus prevention efforts, including targeting hotspots, repeat offenders and hot products. The conclusion suggests that the prevention of repeat victimization needs to be undertaken in relation to far more types of crime than it has been to date. It proposes that repeat victimization should be treated not as a short-term fad but as a fundamental shift in the manner in which society understands and handles the problem of crime.

What is repeat victimization?

Repeat victimization (or rv) is usually used to refer to various types of repeatedly victimized targets. Restricting the term to victims (people) is inappropriate because a repeatedly victimized target can be a business, a vehicle, a household, a building with several households, a person or other type of target however defined. The unit of analysis should be that which works best to promote crime prevention. So, whether repeats are counted as occurring against, say, the owner or the vehicle (if it changes ownership) or the household or its occupants (if they relocate), should be determined by what best serves prevention of any further crime. Thus viewed, the flexibility and adaptability of the definition are not only unproblematic but can promote crime prevention.

Definitions have developed alongside research and practice. Pease (1998) proposed 'virtual repeat victimization' or virtual-repeats to refer to instances where targets are selected because offenders have already offended against similar or identical targets. For example, the same make and model of car offer similar prospects to offenders. If the car is parked in a similar location or situation, the virtual-repeat is all the more identical. Nearby households with the same layout are prone to virtual-repeats because, for the offender, there is a good chance that the same types of effort and skills are needed, and the risks and rewards are similar to those of the previous target. These virtual-repeats provide a useful angle for thinking about crime prevention: whether virtual-repeat victimization occurs due to a target's design (easy to break into), its location (in an unlit area) or its high resale value and low traceability (a laptop, a portable MP3 player), can influence the choice of tactics for a preventive response.

The term 'near-repeat' was coined to refer to the victimization of targets located near to one that is victimized (Townsley et al. 2003; Johnson and Bowers 2004; Johnson et al. 2004). For example, households close to a burglary have an increased likelihood of experiencing that crime type. The increased risk declines with distance from the initial target. Townsley et al. found that burglaries are 'infectious' – that is, they can spread like a disease across an area. They found this to be particularly the case in areas with similar housing type and layout, with repeat rates in areas of more diverse housing type. The likely explanation is that many offenders prefer easy pickings – that is, more familiar targets where they have a better knowledge of likely risk, effort and rewards.

Johnson and Bowers have developed 'prospective hotspotting' which utilizes near-repeats as the trigger for area-based preventive interventions. They demonstrate that '[T]he risk of burglary is communicable, with properties within 400 metres of a burgled household being at a significantly elevated risk of victimization for up to two months after an initial event.' (Johnson *et al.* 2004: 641). Johnson and Bowers suggest prospective hotspotting can increase the predictability of future crime compared with traditional hotspotting. In the popular press, the comparison was made between these crime analysis efforts and the futuristic prediction/prevention effort of a Hollywood blockbuster: 'Every police force in the country has been ordered to develop hi-tech crime maps – as seen in sci-fi blockbuster film *Minority Report* – to predict future offending... In *Minority Report*, starring Tom Cruise, criminals are caught before the crimes they commit' (Roberts 2005). Prospective hotspotting has fewer ethical problems than its fictional counterpart, and is an emerging area of rv research. In the present context, virtual-repeats and near-repeats can be viewed as specific instances from a more general typology. The defining characteristics of the virtual-repeat is the replication of the modus operandi of an earlier crime. The repetition is of a particular tactic or skill. For instance, if an offender only knows how to pick locks of a certain type or brand then this modus operandi is the defining characteristic of what might more precisely be termed a *tactical repeat*. However, the primary characteristic of a 'near-repeat' is spatial proximity to a previous crime. Hence it is a *spatial repeat* even though it is likely to combine elements of the tactical repeat (since nearby houses are more likely to be similar in layout, guardianship and likely rewards). From these building blocks, a preliminary typology of rv is set out as Table 6.1. Each type is defined by the predominant characteristic that underpins repetition. In reality they will rarely be so distinct (that is, the types overlap with more than one involved in a repeat crime). Hence a neighbouring household may be burgled the same night because it is nearby (spatial repeat) at the opportune time (temporal repeat), has a similar layout and level of security requiring identical skills in its commission (tactical repeat). Bowers and Johnson (forthcoming) examined the modus operandi of near-repeats to find similarities suggesting they are committed by the same offenders. (Note that the type referred to here as 'repeat targets' are those traditionally framed as rv in most previous work. This preliminary typology is intended to assist the process of developing crime prevention responses that are appropriately tailored to the crime.)

What types of crime and disorder are repeated?

Though it is more intuitively obvious that rv occurs for domestic violence, racial attacks and bullying, frequent repetition has been demonstrated for many types of crime and disorder. Property crimes include:

- bank robbery;
- commercial burglary;
- computer network hacking;
- computer theft;
- credit card fraud;
- criminal damage and vandalism;
- fraud and other white-collar crimes;
- graffiti;

Table 6.1 Typology of repeat victimization

Repeat type	Characteristics	Example(s)
Target	Crime against the same target	Crime against same person, building, household, vehicle or other target however defined
Tactical (virtual)	Crimes requiring the same skill, or modus operandi, to commit. Often the same type of target	Particular type of locks picked (on different types of property); websites with particular types of security are repeatedly targeted; theft of same model of car; burglary of property with same layout
Temporal	An offending spree – temporal proximity is the defining characteristic	Multiple burglaries of different properties in the same night; theft of car, then a robbery and getaway
Spatial (near)	Crime in nearby location due to proximity and characteristics	High crime areas; hotspots
Crime type	The same target victimized by different types of crime	The same person is burgled, assaulted, robbed at different times
Offender	Victimization of same target by different offenders	A property appears attractive to different offenders; any easy or rewarding target

Note:
This table owes much to typologies of displacement (Repetto 1974; Barr and Pease 1990).

- property crime against schools;
- residential burglary;
- shoplifting;
- theft of and from vehicles;
- computer network attacks; and
- other types of property crime.

Personal or violent crimes and disorder where extensive rv has been shown to date include:

- common assault;
- domestic violence;
- elder abuse;
- neighbour disputes;
- robbery of shops and stores (commercial);
- sexual victimization (including rape, other physical, verbal and visual sexual victimizations);
- serious assault;

- stalking;
- child abuse (physical, sexual and emotional, including neglect as a repeated or ongoing crime of omission);
- street robbery (including 'muggings', stick-ups, robbery at cash machines);
- threats of violence;
- shooting and stabbings; and
- other personal and violent crimes

The aggregate information that a review essay of this type necessarily presents risks losing vital information relating to the experience of victims. Although at best a limited effort to overcome this, Box 6.1 presents a case study of domestic violence lest the reader forget the damage that rv can cause or the potential reward from its prevention.

The list of crime types above is not exhaustive, but demonstrates some crime types that prevention efforts need to tackle.[2] However the list is useful

Box 6.1   A survivor of domestic violence

This is a brief case history of a woman and her children who experienced repeated domestic violence for at least ten years. She received an emergency police alarm (mobile phones are now more typically used, though they remain to be formally evaluated). The case history was related by a local domestic violence agency worker. Ms Everton is a pseudonym.

Ms Everton
The violence against Ms Everton by her (ex-) husband has been going on for at least 10 years. She left home with her four children aged 8 to 16 and spent two nights in the open, as she did not know where to go. Eventually she spent a few weeks with her two youngest children in a refuge and she returned home when the Housing Office put the house solely in her name. The house had been damaged by her husband and furniture and clothes destroyed. Ms Everton said that her husband has said he wants to murder her. Before the installation of the police alarm he used to arrive unexpectedly. He would smash his way into the house and usually become violent. The two eldest children are terrified of him.

Since the installation of the alarm he has only called once. He knows that Ms Everton has an alarm, as the letter offering the alarm arrived whilst she was in the refuge and he was still living in the property. Ms Everton thinks this knowledge has deterred him from making any more visits. She says that the police response when she activated the alarm was excellent: two officers went after her husband who ran away, and he did not have time to do any damage. Unfortunately they did not succeed in catching him. She said the police took only about two minutes to arrive and were sympathetic and helpful.

Ms Everton believes that the alarm may have prevented her murder or his (she feels that when defending either herself or the children she could kill him). Her son, aged 13, has stabbed the father once, in an effort to stop him attacking her. Since this event the boy has become withdrawn and nervous. Ms Everton thinks that the alarm has given greater confidence to the children, as well as to herself and says that they are no longer living under quite the same amount of pressure. She carries the alarm everywhere with her.

Source: Adapted from Lloyd *et al.* (1994: 14–15).

because, when contrasted with current evaluated practices discussed further below, it quickly becomes apparent that efforts to prevent rv are in their infancy. Relatively few crime types have been tackled by prevention efforts (or if they have, they have not been evaluated). It is also the case that prevention policy and practice to date have embodied a particular focus upon residential burglary. Possible explanations for the bias towards residential burglary are suggested in Box 6.2. What is clear is that far more attention needs to be paid to the prevention of repetition of other types of crime.

Box 6.2   Why has repeat residential burglary usually been the focus?

Despite the fact that residential burglary has, on average, lower rates of rv than many types of crime, to date it has received the most preventive attention. The reasons for this are likely to include the following:

- The success of the influential Kirkholt Burglary Prevention Project (Forrester *et al.* 1988, 1990) which reduced burglary by 70 per cent and provoked much interest in rv.

- Burglary is a high-volume crime in recorded crime statistics and a high-profile crime in the media.

- Burglary has relatively high rates of reporting to the police (for insurance purposes). This contact can be used to initiate preventive activities by police and other agencies.

- Burglary is uncontentious as a target for prevention.

- There is a broader range of known preventive tactics against burglary compared with many crime types (including locks and bolts, alarms, grilles, tracking devices for property, property marking, local property-watch).

- Burglary may be less likely to involve difficult interpersonal negotiations.

- Burglary takes place at a known and fixed location (whereas, say, street robbery and assaults 'move around' with the victim).

The extent of repeat victimization

The extent of rv will only be covered briefly. It is taken as given that rv contributes disproportionately to the overall crime count. Pease (1998: 3) found that, in one year:

- 16 per cent of the UK population experience property crime, but 2 per cent of the population experience 41 per cent of property crime; and
- 8 per cent of the UK population experience personal crime, but 1 per cent of the population experienced 59 per cent of personal crime.

With variation by crime type time and place, rv contributed disproportionately to all types of crimes adequately studied to date. Box 6.3 lists some key findings from the International Crime Victims Survey (ICVS).

From the mid-1990s there was an exponential increase in the number of studies examining rv. By the start of 2005 they number in the hundreds and

Box 6.3   Key findings from the International Crime Victims Survey

---

- Patterns of rv are remarkably similar in the 17 western industrialized countries that were studied.

- Repeated sexual incidents against women are typically the crimes most likely to be repeated, with close to half of all incidents being repeats against the same women.

- Rates of repeat personal crimes were generally higher than those of repeat property crime. Rates of repeat 'assault and theft' and robbery were particularly high.

- The ICVS findings on rv are remarkably consistent for survey sweeps covering more than a decade.

Source: Farrell and Bouloukos (2001).

document the extent of rv for various crime types, using various methods and in many countries and contexts. Yet whilst there is now little doubt about the contribution of rv to the overall makeup of crime, this does not necessarily mean that practical prevention efforts have made the same degree of progress.

The significance of rv continues to be revealed in relation to new and different types of crime as they are studied. For example, a recent study by Soumyo Moitra and Suresh Konda (2004), investigating network attacks on computer systems, demonstrated extensive rv. It is summarized in Box 6.4 which also makes some preliminary suggestions regarding the implications of the findings for prevention.

Box 6.4   Network attacks on computer systems as an example of an emerging area of rv research

---

With the widespread use of the Internet, e-commerce, business and other networks, the security of such networks is increasingly important. Yet attacks and incidents against networks are increasingly common. Potential crimes include fraud, theft (of funds, knowledge and information, or other), account break-ins, malicious damage to users, institutions or networks.

Over a quarter (27 per cent) of the 6,684 computer sites studied experienced at least three attacks and a mean of twelve attacks each. The ten most victimized sites experienced an average of 369 attacks! Repeat attacks were far more likely to occur soon after a prior attack, particularly in the first week. Some types of attack were likely to occur more quickly than others, and repeats were more likely to be the same type of incident (perhaps suggesting the same offenders). Some network domain types experienced more rapid repeats (those ending '.edu' were fastest and those ending '.com' were slowest).

Though prevention was not the primary focus of the research, the potential is evident. Focusing network security on sites already hacked could prevent a lot of hacking (and the displacement literature suggests that, for various reasons, much

---

of it will not simply move to other networks). Security should be put in place quickly and certain types of domain such, as educational institutions (.edu sites), should be particularly proactive in prevention. There could exist the potential to track and detect returning hackers who, in turn, may well be the most prolific and serious hackers.

Source: Adapted from Moitra and Konda (2004).

The next section examines why the prevention of rv is an attractive crime prevention strategy, followed by sections examining actual prevention efforts that have taken place to date.

Why prevent repeat victimization?

Seventeen reasons underpinning efforts to prevent rv are summarized in Box 6.5. The list of reasons touches on various aspects of economics, philosophy, politics and practice, reflecting both theoretical and empirical research. Setting these diverse reasons alongside each other gives clearer insight into why the prevention of rv is an attractive crime prevention strategy with much potential.

Box 6.5   Seventeen reasons for policing to prevent repeat victimization

1. Preventing rv is a crime prevention activity and hence pursuant to the most fundamental of police mandates as defined since Robert Peel's original list of policing principles outlined in 1829.
2. Targeting rv is an efficient means of allocating, in time and space, scarce police resources to crime problems.
3. Preventing rv is an approach that is relevant to all crimes with a target. It has been shown to be a feature of crimes including hate crimes, domestic and commercial burglary; school crime (burglary and vandalism); bullying; sexual assault; car crime; neighbour disputes; credit card fraud and other retail sector crime; and domestic violence and child abuse. Even murder can be the repeat of attempted murder.
4. Police managers can use rv as a performance indicator (Tilley 1995; Farrell and Buckley 1999). These can range from the national to the local level.
5. Preventing rv naturally allocates resources to high-crime areas, crime hotspots and the most victimized targets (Bennett 1995; Townsley *et al.* 2000).
6. Preventing rv may inform the allocation of crime prevention to nearby targets (near-repeats) and targets with similar characteristics (virtual repeats; Pease 1998).
7. Preventing rv is a form of 'drip feeding' of prevention resources (Pease 1991). Since all crime does not occur at once, police resources need only be allocated as victimizations occur from day to day.
8. Preventing rv is even less likely to result in displacement than unfocused crime prevention efforts (Bouloukos and Farrell 1997; Chenery *et al.* 1997).

9. Offenders will be made uncertain and more generally deterred by changed circumstances at the most attractive and vulnerable targets. Hence preventing rv may be even more likely to result in a diffusion of crime control benefits than more general crime prevention.

10. Preventing rv can generate common goals and positive work between police and other agencies (such as housing, social services and victim organizations) which may in turn facilitate broader co-operation.

11. Focusing on rv empowers police officers to do something tangible and constructive to help crime victims and for policing to become more generally oriented towards victims who are arguably its core consumers (Farrell 2001).

12. Efforts to prevent rv can lead to positive feedback from victims. This is still a relatively rare reward for police in the community. It may promote good community relations.

13. Preventing rv is triggered by a crime being reported. Since victims can be asked about prior victimizations, a response does not necessarily require data analysis.

14. Preventing rv can sometimes – but not always – use off-the-shelf prevention tactics rather than requiring inventive and sometimes difficult problem-solving.

15. Preventing rv can be used to enhance the detection of serious and prolific offenders. Police officers like detecting offenders.

16. Preventing rv presents possibilities for preventing and detecting organized crime and terrorism that focuses on vulnerable and rewarding victims and targets – including protection rackets, forced prostitution, loan-sharking, repeat trafficking via certain low-risk locations, art and other high-value thefts and robberies, and terrorist bombings.

17. Targeting rv can inform thinking on repeat crimes typically perceived as 'victimless' where the repeatedly victimized target is the state or nation.

Source: Adapted from Laycock and Farrell (2003).

The list of reasons for preventing rv given in Box 6.5 is a summary of a large amount of information gleaned from research and practice. However, it also highlights some of the potential for work on rv to extend into areas that are currently largely uncharted, such as the prevention of organized crime and terrorism. These are areas where, although there may be clear potential, to our knowledge there has been little research to date.

How to prevent repeat victimization

A recent review of evaluated efforts to prevent repeat residential burglary produced findings that are likely to apply to other types of crime. The review examined ten evaluations that met the criteria of being able to compare the rate of rv before and after an intervention in both a project area and a comparison group (see Farrell and Pease in press for further details). Some evaluations do not meet the evaluation quality standards for such a review or are otherwise patchy, inconsistent, opaque, or poor in various respects to the extent they cannot be included.[3] The types of interventions that were introduced varied quite widely between projects. Some projects were able to contact a large proportion of victims and implement a wide range of security upgrades and other prevention measures (from mini-neighbourhood watch to focused police patrols) at and around victimized properties. Some projects offered only advice and recommendations to victims on what measures to take – that is, they did not actually assist victims with the implementation of preventive measures. This was for various reasons such as predefined project protocols or restrictions upon the funding of security equipment. Some projects had problems contacting victims so that, regardless of the nature of the preventive intervention, overall implementation rates were necessarily low.

The ten evaluated anti-burglary projects are summarized in Table 6.2. Each evaluation is detailed across one row of the table. The table has six columns that detail critical information: project name and key publications or reports; the nature of the comparison area(s); summary details of the intervention and funding; implementation rates; outcome measures; and the rate of displacement. The two outcome measures detailed are the change in repeat burglary and the change in overall burglary, though both were not always available. The final column detailing displacement also gives any relevant information deemed critical to the overall assessment of the project.

The evaluated projects were not all successful in reducing crime. Depending on how a 'project evaluation' is defined, between half and two thirds of the projects were assessed to have prevented burglary.[4] This is not necessarily the whole picture, however. Perhaps the most important information to be gleaned from such review work relates to insight about best and worst practices. Such information can be used to inform (that is, to revise and improve) further research and prevention efforts. It could only be claimed that preventing rv often does not work if the practice is viewed in a vacuum whereby future revision and improvement of the practices cannot occur. In reality, research and practice take place as an iterative learning process whereby current research informs future practice. The review detailed in Table 6.2 highlighted a series of findings about projects, from which conclusions can be drawn about what works and what does not in preventing rv. Such conclusions should be used to inform future research and practice. The remainder of this section summarizes the conclusions and is followed by a section that expands upon the lessons learned with a particular focus upon various 'tricky issues' encountered during the development and implementation of efforts to prevent rv.

The main conclusions of the review of residential burglary efforts are summarized in Boxes 6.6 and 6.7 where they have been adapted to apply more generally. To prevent rv, something must be changed to reduce risk against the target where crime has occurred. If nothing is changed (even if someone is trying but failing to change something) then risk is not reduced. It is also possible that something is changed but risk of further crime is still not reduced.

Table 6.2 Ten evaluations of the prevention of repeat residential burglary

Study (main publications)	Comparison area	Intervention (and who paid?)	Implementation rates and issues	1. Reduced repeat burglary? 2. Reduced overall burglary?	1. Displacement? 2. Any other key issues?
Kirkholt (Forrester et al. 1989, 1990; Farrington 1992)	Remainder of police subdivision; lower burglary rate	Focused security upgrades; coin-box removal; Cocoon Neighbourhood Watch. Debt counselling for offenders; arrests (free for victims)	68% for security upgrading; close to 100% for Cocoon Watch	1. Repeat burglary fell to zero in sequence with implementation 2. Burglary fell 60% in 6 months and 75% over 3 years	1. No displacement found
Site ?R1 (Tilley 1993a)	Remainder of police subdivision	Target-hardening security measures (locks and Cocoon Watch – also at some non-burgled 'vulnerable' properties) (free for victims)	Cocoon Watch achieved 25% coverage (p. 7)	1. Not measured 2. A 24.3% fall relative to comparison area (but increase in absolute terms)	1. Displacement not measured
Site ?R3 (Tilley 1993a)	Remainder of police subdivision	Target-hardening security measures (free for victims)	55% of victims received target hardening	1. 40% fall in proportion relative to comparison; increased time to repeats; no drop in secured properties without prior burglary 2. 54% drop in incidence relative to comparison area	1. Displacement not measured
Huddersfield (Anderson et al. 1995; Chenery et al. 1997)	Remainder of police force area except contiguous areas to measure displacement	Graded response according to risk, with multiple tactics (some free, some part-sponsored)	'[I]mplementation a factor in any repeats' (p. 17)	1. Reduction in silver and gold responses suggested reduced repeat burglaries 2. A 30% drop in incidence relative to comparison area	1. No displacement found

Cambridge (Bennett and Durie 1999)	Matched non-contiguous areas plus computer-generated groups	Combined package of security, guardianship and offender-based measures (p. 19) (means-tested eligibility or purchase by victims)	Low rates for key tactics: 3.5% of victims received door locks; 9% received loan alarms (p. 36)	1. No reduction 2. No reduction	1. Not measured 2. 'The right medicine but the wrong dosage' (p. 41) suggests implementation failure
Baltimore (Weisel et al. 1999)	Matched non-contiguous area (p. 25)	Advice cards for victims and neighbours; security surveys, property registration, police patrols (p. 27) (free advice but no funding for security)	Few process measures; police 'distributed' cards and 'alerted' neighbours (p. 27)	1. No reduction 2. A 5.2% decrease in treatment and 24% increase in comparison (p. 91)	1. Not measured 2. No explanation for why reduction occurred
Dallas (Weisel et al. 1999)	Matched non-contiguous area	Advice letter to victims, security surveys, apartment managers notified of risks (p. 35) (free advice but no funding for security)	13% of victims bought alarms; 9% boarded windows; 18% locks; 27% moved/moving (p. 107)	1. No change relative to comparison group 2. Slight burglary increase relative to control (p. 91)	1. Not measured 2. Advice to victims did not lead to implementation of prevention tactics
San Diego (Weisel et al. 1999)	Matched non-contiguous area (p. 39)	Improved investigations; security checks and brochure for victims (pp. 40–1) (free advice but no funding for security)	Few process measures; police personnel 'sceptical' (p. 43)	1. No reduction 2. Incidence fell 12% relative to comparison area (p. 92)	1. Not measured 2. No explanation for why reduction occurred
Beenleigh (Budz et al. 2001)	Matched non-contiguous area (p. 12)	Three-tiered response for one-time victims (security advice and materials), two-	Victims more likely than controls to	1. Repeat victims fell 16% and repeat incidents 15%, and increased in	1. 'Possible' displacement within treatment area (p. 21)

Table 6.2 continued overleaf

Table 6.2 continued

Study (main publications)	Comparison area	Intervention (and who paid?)	Implementation rates and issues	1. Reduced repeat burglary? 2. Reduced overall burglary?	1. Displacement? 2. Any other key issues?
		time victims (more extensive prevention materials) and hotspots areas (security assessments, property marking) (free to victims)	implement tactics but still unlikely overall (p. 22)	comparison areas 2. Burglaries increased relative to comparison group	2. Low burglary rate with prominent random and seasonal effects (p. 14)
Tee Tree Gully (Ball PR and Walters 2002; Henderson 2002)	Matched non-contiguous area; contiguous areas to measure displacement	Security audit; informal support, referral to other agencies; referral for property marking; links to neighbours (free advice to victims)	Advice at 32% of properties (p. 9) resulted in locks and alarms at 8% and 4% respectively	1. Repeats reduced relative to control (stable in absolute terms) 2. Incidence increased relative to comparison area	1. No displacement found

Note:
Page references refer to the relevant main report.
Source: Adapted from Farrell and Pease (in press).

Box 6.6   What works in preventing repeat victimization?

Evaluation research to date suggests that what works to prevent rv is the following:

1. *A strong preventive mechanism.* Specific prevention tactics need to be tailored to the context and target because the nature of crime varies from one place to the next.
2. *Multiple tactics.* The currently available evidence suggests multiple tactics working together can produce a synergistic effect. Whilst there is little conclusive evidence regarding the effectiveness of particular tactics, opportunity-blocking aimed at preventing rv by the same modus operandi seems the most likely candidate for effectiveness.
3. *Strong implementation.* Some prevention efforts failed because the preventive mechanism was not introduced.
4. *A focus on situations with high rates of rv.* Those crimes, times and places where repeat rates are highest are clearly an appropriate focus for prevention efforts.

Source: Adapted from Farrell and Pease (in press)

Box 6.7   What doesn't work in preventing repeat victimization?

Evaluation research to date suggests that what causes some efforts to fail to prevent rv is the following:

1. *Weak or inappropriate preventive tactics* fail to prevent crime. Further, the same prevention tactic in a different context does not necessarily bring prevention if the nature of the crime problem is different.
2. *Poor implementation* fails. In particular, education or advice for victims is an indirect route which, even if well meaning, does not necessarily mean that security and other measures are implemented: victims may be unable or unwilling to spend money on crime prevention. This suggests better sources of funding for security and other equipment, and better motivation and incentives for victims, are required.
3. *Replicating tactics without attention to context* does not necessarily work. The most transferable aspects tend to be methods or strategies. For example, security upgrades to prevent repeat burglary by the modus operandi of the prior burglary require different tactics to be adopted as necessary.
4. *Overall impact is less where rv rates are low.* Attempting to prevent rv in circumstances where none is likely to be present cannot be said to fail *per se,* because it is a non-starter.

Source: Adapted from Farrell and Pease (in press)

Existing evaluation research suggests there is reasonable evidence that a package of prevention measures often works better than a single measure. So, for example, locks and bolts on the point of entry, a household alarm, smart property marking, encouraging neighbours to keep watch, satellite-tracking of high-value items (cars, some electrical goods), other efforts to detect revisiting offenders, increased police patrols and other efforts seem to work better as a team. Teasing out the independent and interaction effects of multiple interventions in different contexts may prove a difficult task for future research.

Preventing repetition of other types of crime

The focus on residential burglary does not mean that there has not been some effort to prevent the repetition of other types of crime. Efforts have been undertaken in relation to the prevention of repeat commercial burglary (Tilley 1993b; Taylor 1999; Bowers 2001), repeat domestic violence (Hanmer *et al.* 1999), repeat family violence (David and Taylor 1997), repeat elder abuse (Davis and Medina-Ariza 2001) and repeat sexual victimization (Breitenbecher *et al.* 1998). Other evaluations have included an element of the prevention of rv. For example, the series of domestic violence arrest experiments evaluated the impact of a single tactic (arrest) in the prevention of repeat domestic violence (see, e.g., Sherman and Berk 1984; Sherman 1992), whilst evaluations of police domestic violence units are justified in examining their effectiveness in preventing repeat calls to domestic violence incidents (Farrell and Buckley 1999).

The nature and type of efforts to prevent crime types other than residential burglary, as well as the nature of the evaluations, have varied widely. Broadly speaking, however, they have met with less success than the evaluated anti-burglary efforts detailed previously. However, the types of problems encountered by the variety of prevention efforts are remarkably similar. In particular, those projects where the intervention was the small-scale education of victims or the leafleting of households appeared to produce little change in the crime rate. Presumably nothing changed that would be likely to prevent further crime, and such issues are discussed below.

Several of the projects undertaken as part of the recent Crime Reduction Programme have contained elements that seek to prevent rv. However, there is little published information available on rv for individual projects at the time of writing, whilst that which is available appears to suggest a situation broadly similar to that represented by the previous evaluations of burglary projects shown in Table 6.2.

The apparently straightforward nature of the aspects of 'what works' in preventing rv does not chime well with the lack of success in some projects. The most common weakness of projects was in the identification of appropriate preventive tactics and in the implementation of tactics, and the next section addresses these 'tricky issues' in more detail.

Tricky issues in preventing repeat victimization

The main stumbling blocks to the prevention of rv can be broken down into five distinct issues. They are presented in Box 6.8 in roughly the chronological order that they occur in the development and implementation of a crime prevention project. Repeat victimization can be tricky to measure, it is sometimes tricky to know what to do to prevent it, tricky to get victims or others to do anything, tricky to copy successful efforts from elsewhere, and tricky to sustain successful efforts and make them part of routine practice. Problems with any one of these tricky issues can lead to failure to prevent further crime (or, in the case of evaluation failure, of being found to have succeeded).

Box 6.8 Tricky issues in the prevention of repeat victimization

---

Evaluated efforts to prevent rv suggest that it is tricky to:

1. measure rv and, hence, to identify it or evaluate the impact of prevention efforts (the *measurement and evaluation problem*);
2. know what to do to prevent rv (the *intervention or tactical problem*);
3. get people, including victims, to adopt preventive measures (the *implementation problem*);
4. copy prevention efforts from elsewhere because local burglary problems can vary (the *transferability and replicability problem*); and
5. maintain prevention efforts once a funded intervention project has completed its funding cycle (the *sustainability problem*).

The issues presented in Box 6.8 warrant identification and the space that is given to them here in order that they might be overcome. They are discussed in turn in more detail below.

The measurement and evaluation problem

It is now well known that rv can sometimes be difficult to measure. The issue remains important because measurement can directly influence the perceived need for prevention, the preventive policies and tactics developed, plus the findings of an evaluation. Measurement problems are particularly acute when recorded crime data are used, yet this is the data source most commonly utilized by police, other practitioners and researchers (because it is routinely recorded and therefore most easily and cheaply available). The main reasons that rv is difficult to measure are summarized in Box 6.9 for the key types of data that are typically utilized.

Box 6.9 The measurement and evaluation problem for different data sources

---

Recorded crime data
Under-reporting and recording is disproportionate
Under-reporting and recording of crime disproportionately reduce the rate of rv found in police data. For example, if there is 50 per cent likelihood or 0.5 probability of a burglary being reported to the police then there is only 25 per cent likelihood (i.e. $0.5 \times 0.5 = 0.25$ probability) of two burglaries being reported from the same household and, therefore, of them being represented in the police dataset (assuming, for simplicity, that the likelihood of reporting is consistent across burglaries).

Address and name-linking issues

Most police databases seek to trace rv by tracing the same addresses or names. This means that if the same person or place is typed-in differently, they may not be identified as repeats (so, instead of two crimes against one target, the data identify two crimes against different targets). Differences in spelling, syntax, abbreviations or even in the use of upper and lower-case letters may (depending on the IT system) serve to understate the rate of repeats and overstate the apparent rate of single-incident victimizations. Linking victims' locations and offenders is also difficult with most current police information technology (Pease 1998: 32–3).

The time-window problem (relevant to any data type)

This is an issue relevant to any type of data. It is most acute in datasets covering only a few months. Repeat Victimization occurs over time, so when any period of data is examined it will contain some crimes that are repeats of crimes that occurred before the period in question, as well as some crimes that are precursors of crimes that will occur after the time period. One year of data was found to capture, proportionately, over 40 per cent more repeats than six months of data (Farrell *et al.* 2002).

Victim survey data

The main problem with survey data is often a problem with researchers who refuse to count rv accurately. This is particularly the case with the National Crime Victimization Survey in the USA (see Box 6.10 dedicated to the NCVS). Many surveys place an artificial limit on the number of crimes that a victim is 'allowed' to report to the survey, and then often reclassify or place an upper limit on the number of crimes that are counted.

Source: Adapted from Farrell and Pease (1993, 2003).

Site selection error can be the result of measurement error. Some sites have received funding to prevent rv when, in reality, they may have had low rates of rv. In some instances relating to the recent Crime Reduction Programme sponsored by the Home Office, it has been suggested that some bids for funding may have claimed artificially high rates of rv in order to attract monies. Rather than suggest fraudulent activities, the lesson that might be learnt is that if measurement can be manipulated, it needs to be transparent with respect to method.

One problem usually identified as evaluation failure can be the result of problems in the measurement of rv. If rv is poorly measured, then an evaluation is unlikely to be precise enough to detect a change in the level of rv. The result may be that some successful prevention efforts go undetected because of measurement error, although the extent to which this occurs remains unknown. Victim surveys are more likely to elicit more accurate measures of rv than recorded crime data, and should be the measurement tool of choice where feasible.

A particularly important instance of the measurement problem is manifest in the National Crime Victimization Survey (NCVS) of the USA. It is detailed in Box 6.10. The NCVS systematically under-counts rv with the result that the national crime rate in the USA is significantly misrepresented. Due to the prominence and influence of the NCVS, it is difficult to estimate the overall impact upon crime prevention policy that is due to this counting error. Although the problem has been recognized for many years, it is hard to modify a survey such as the NCVS without making it difficult to continue the time-series of data that has resulted, and so it is possible that the problem has been swept under the carpet. A recent study by Mike Planty (2004) suggests that, if estimates by victims of their actual annual victimization rate were to be included in the NCVS crime counts, the violent crime rate in the USA would treble!

Box 6.10   Repeat Victimization in the USA – a conspiracy of silence?

> The National Crime Survey is the main annual survey of crime in the USA. It has long been known grossly to under-represent rv – and, thereby, crime in the USA overall. However, little has been done to address the problem:
>
> - As far back as 1980, Albert Reiss of Yale University noted that the inclusion of series incidents in the national crime count would increase the number of crimes by 18 per cent. Since then, Reiss's words and their implications have been largely ignored.
>
> - Most NCVS-based reports continue to exclude RV where the person says the crimes were very similar and occurred in a series. As a result, most US government crime reports ignore the experiences of these repeat victims, silencing their voices and systematically under-counting crime in the USA.
>
> - The NCVS uses a six-month recall period which is a short window of time to measure rv. Different methodologies find that a six-month recall period captures around 40 per cent less RV than a one-year recall period (Farrell and Sousa 1997; Farrell et al. 2002).
>
> - A major recent piece of work concludes that the survey is poor at measuring rv (Ybarra and Lohr 2002).
>
> - The International Crime Victims Survey find similar rates of rv in the USA to those found in other countries (Farrell et al. forthcoming).
>
> - Dr Michael Planty (2004) examined the impact of the exclusion from NCVS reports. He found that, on average, *including repeat victimisation as rv reported by victims produced a 313 per cent increase for all violent victimizations in the USA between 1993 and 2002. Put another way, the current counting rules which exclude rv serve to exclude 79 per cent of all violent victimizations!*

The intervention problem

What prevention measures should be put in place to prevent rv? One reason burglary has been the focus of much rv research to date is probably because there is a fairly broad repertoire of existing prevention tactics. These include locks and bolts and other forms of target-hardening security, movement detectors and other alarms, police patrols, tracking systems for high-cost targets, CCTV and other measures. Securing the target with locks and bolts, with extra measures to prevent entry to premises by the same modus operandi, may appear relatively straightforward. In contrast, however, the existing repertoire to prevent many types of personal crime appears relatively limited. Improvements have been made in the repertoire of tactics to tackle some types of crime including domestic violence, bullying, assaults and disorder in pubs and clubs, some forms of commercial burglary and robbery, and shoplifting. However, generally speaking, the pool of techniques is less well known and more difficult to implement than those for burglary (if, say, they involve changes to the design, layout or working practices of a store or business). For some types of crime that are frequently repeated, such as sexual victimization of women, and the abuse of children and elders, the development of prevention tactics remains in its early stages. Further research into rv may assist and promote the development of such prevention tactics. However, it is arguable that the strategy is also hostage to the need to expand further the repertoire of prevention tactics available for different crime types.

The implementation problem

Knowing what to do and where to go is all well and good. Getting people actually to do something is a different issue. Ensuring that an appropriate alarm or CCTV is purchased, correctly sited and adequately monitored is not always straightforward. Ensuring that victims buy and install secure locks can be difficult in areas without public funding for equipment and labour. Sometimes implementation problems occur due to communication problems between agencies and victims. Some efforts to prevent repeat burglaries have failed to make a substantive contact with many of the victims (that is, anything more substantial than sending them a letter). In Box 6.11, implementation problems are split into those relating to responders (agency officials) and victims.

Box 6.11   The implementation problem

Evaluation research to date has highlighted a number of implementation issues which are here separated into those relating to responders (police or other agencies) and those relating to victims or owners/managers of targets.

Responder implementation problems:

1. Poorly formulated policy guidance and protocols. This means agency workers on the ground do not know what to do.
2. Poorly supervised protocols that are allowed to slip – so little or no effort is made to contact victims.
3. Police try but fail to contact victims. Repeated calls, letters and even visits do not necessarily result in contact.
4. Contact is made, but only advice is given. The result is that no real preventive intervention occurs.

Victim/target implementation problems:

1. Victims do not know what action to take to prevent further crime.
2. Victims are unwilling to take action. This may occur if they do not trust the police, or if they do not think it is worth the effort or expense.
3. Victims sometimes cannot afford to take recommended preventive action. Alarms and other security hardware can be expensive for low-income households.
4. Businesses do not realize that it may be cost-efficient to invest in security upgrades. It may appear that insurance eliminates the need for prevention even if this is rarely the case.

To date, however, there is little research examining which type of implementation problem is most prevalent. This may be a prerequisite to tackling implementation problems. An additional side of implementation that is rarely considered is unrecognized implementation. In the wake of a crime, there are some victims who will take action to reduce future risk even if they do not receive advice from an outside agency. In such instances, rv may be less likely to occur. Such independent efforts were recognized in the research of Weisel *et al.* (1999) in the USA but may warrant further examination to determine their extent and importance as well as those factors that make some actors more likely to undertake prevention than others. More generally, the identification of factors that facilitate or generate implementation may prove a fruitful line of inquiry for research.

The transferability and replicability problem

In the 1980s, the highly successful Kirkholt Burglary Project eliminated repeat burglaries in an area of public housing, and reduced overall burglary by 70 per cent (see Forrester *et al.* 1988, 1990; Pease 1991; Farrington 1992). It catalysed research on rv and inspired several efforts to replicate its success. Yet the success proved somewhat elusive. This was because the prevention tactics adopted in Kirkholt were developed to tackle the particular burglary problem that existed in Kirkholt. Other areas had burglary problems with different characteristics. For example, properties vary between areas, so the choice of target, means of entry and type of property stolen can vary widely (amongst other factors). Subsequent replications, and a particular theme of Tilley's work (since Tilley 1993a), has been that prevention needs to cut the cloth to match the coat, and that tailor-made prevention can require much time and skill.

Although some prevention tactics are not transferable, others may be. Clearly, those tactics that can be most easily and widely replicated in different circumstances are highly desirable. Those prevention tactics that are likely to prove unique to a particular area may be the most difficult to identify and introduce because of the level of expertise required. Hence in practice there is a trade-off between the relative ease of adopting proven tactics that are highly replicable (for instance, secure doors and window frames to reduce risk of repeat burglary), and the more arduous task of undertaking crime analysis to identify problem-specific tactics that address issues in a local context.

Efforts to prevent rv are often, and quite rightly, combined with other strategic crime prevention efforts. Hence, for example, a burglary prevention project may have many components of which one is to aim to prevent rv. From the perspective of building a knowledge base this can introduce difficulties, as teasing out the contributions of different prevention components can be difficult. Subsequently, identifying those components that worked best in order that they might hopefully be adopted elsewhere is a difficult task.

Whilst the replication of specific tactics may appear efficient, it is not always appropriate. The most replicable aspect of many successful projects appears to be their analytical or methodological approach. This is typically an action research, crime analysis, targeted policing or problem-solving approach. Such approaches encounter a range of issues relating to the identification of appropriate tactics which are outside the scope of this chapter. Suffice to say that although there have been significant steps towards providing problem-solving tools to practitioners, such as Clarke and Eck's guide to *Become a Problem-Solving Crime Analyst in 55 Small Steps* (Clarke and Eck 2003), there is still a long way to go. However, the identification of tactics is in large part an issue which, whilst critical to efforts to prevent rv, is a more general issue relating to crime prevention.

The sustainability problem

This is arguably a problem that is applicable to crime prevention generally rather than specific to the prevention of rv. Many crime prevention evaluations or development projects receive funding from local or central government. The funding is typically for a fixed period of time in which the crime prevention effort is developed, implemented and evaluated. The usual scenario is that funding then ceases which, in turn, means that prevention efforts cease.

The development of routine practices, based on written protocols for police and other agencies that are then enforced, is a key effort to overcome this problem. The development and institutionalization of performance indicators based on rv is another effort to ensure longevity. However, even written police policies may sometimes appear to pay only lip-service to the issue. A survey of UK police forces in 2000 found that, although all of them had written policies to prevent rv, there was relatively little evidence of thorough implementation of prevention efforts. Some crime prevention officers who responded to the survey appeared unable to distinguish tactics to prevent repeat victimization from more general crime prevention tactics (Farrell *et al.* 2000). More generally, sustaining momentum among high-level government policy-makers, police chiefs and others can be difficult with changes in staff and operational priorities in addition to competing political and other demands.

Concluding note on the tricky issues

Some efforts to prevent rv, most notably residential burglary, have been located in areas with few repeats, whilst others have become mired in implementation problems. Despite government-backed national policies and performance indicators, some police policies and protocols appear to pay only lip-service to the problem. Contacting victims has sometimes proven difficult and, when contact is made, there are instances of inadequate or inappropriate advice, equipment or funding. Knowing what to do to prevent crime is not always obvious. Victims, for their part, have sometimes been sceptical, either unable or unwilling to take crime prevention advice or adopt crime prevention security or other prevention tactics. Some victims appear to prefer to run the gauntlet whilst others cannot afford to do otherwise. Research on the prevention of rv needs to continue to adopt innovative approaches to address these issues as new types of crime are addressed.

Allocating crime prevention effort using a range of indicators

Repeat victimization research and practice can be located within a more general picture of efforts to improve the efficiency and effectiveness in the allocation of crime prevention resources. Repeat victimization sits alongside efforts to target hotspots, hot products and repeat offenders as a means of allocating society's limited crime control resources.

Crime is grossly unevenly distributed in almost every dimension from which it is approached. This includes the following:

- *Hot products* – consumer products that are frequently stolen.
- *Hotspots* – geographical areas of varying size where crime is located.
- *Repeat victimization* – particular people, places, vehicles or other targets which experience a disproportionate amount of crime.
- *Prolific offenders* – those repeat offenders who commit a disproportionate amount of crime.

Figure 6.1 is a crude hypothetical illustration showing the overlap between the concepts of rv, repeat offending, hotspots and hot products. The relative size of each phenomenon and the extent of the overlaps are not intended to be to scale. Whilst each of the four foci can be used to allocate prevention resources, there is a case to be made that resource allocation is even more efficient at the points of overlap. A complementary interpretation is that rv can be used to provide inroads into the other three phenomena. Repeat victimization allocates resources to hotspots and can be used as a means of detecting prolific offenders. Since insurance means hot products are often replaced in the same location, targeting rv may provide a natural means of identifying and preventing the theft of hot products. The four foci identified here should ideally be viewed as complementary tools for focusing crime prevention and detection resources, but a case can be made for the use of rv as a spearhead. It has been argued elsewhere that rv might also be used as a natural spearhead for victim-oriented policing (Farrell 2001) – that is, policing which has more of an overall focus upon the needs and rights of crime victims.

Crime control policy and strategies are slowly adapting to reflect the fact that crime is concentrated in various dimensions. Repeat offenders are the target of focused detection, special sentencing considerations, in-prison behavioural and other treatments regimes, and intensive probationary supervision. Hot products are gradually achieving attention from product designers as well as from legislators who realize that crime-free product design may pre-empt much crime. Hotspots draw police and other resources like moths to the

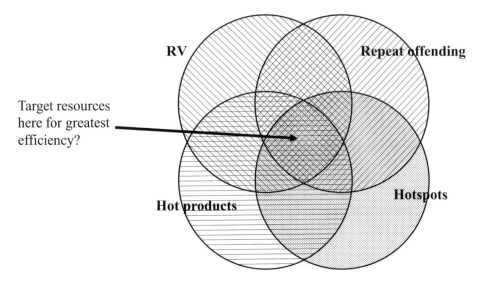

Target resources here for greatest efficiency?

Figure 6.1 Overlap between rv, hotspots, repeat offending and hot products
Note: Figure not to scale.

flame, and repeatedly victimized targets receive post-victimization advice and assistance to avoid further crime. Which of these various strategies is the most cost-effective is probably a moot question. Specific strategies or combinations of strategies will be more appropriate at particular times and locations, and must evolve and adapt to meet the constantly changing shape of crime.

Conclusions

Little or no efforts to prevent rv have been evaluated for most types of crime. This is the most glaring conclusion of this chapter. Much practice and research needs to be developed. Those efforts which have taken place to date have disproportionately focused on residential burglary and, in some instances, have been poorly developed or poorly implemented. Yet if the wrong areas are identified, if few victims are contacted or if few appropriate prevention measures are introduced, it is hardly surprising that some efforts do not succeed in preventing crime. Such lessons are emerging from the preliminary knowledge base relating to the prevention of rv.

By 2005 there are signs that the Home Office is beginning to throttle back on research and development relating to rv. In some recent policy-related debates and documents, rv is conspicuous by its absence. Some of this shift in emphasis may be attributed to the lack of institutional memory which occurs when key personnel change post. Perhaps some of it is due to political whim. Perhaps some of it is due to a greater emphasis on competing crime control strategies (even though most should be viewed as complementary). Perhaps some ignorant policy-makers think that rv can be handled as a fad rather than as a fundamental revision to the manner in which society understands and deals with crime. Such change – that is, if it is true that there is reduced pressure from government researchers to pursue rv strategies – is clearly not evidence-based. Whilst it is clear that there are implementation issues to overcome, this is a normal step in the learning process, and should not be allowed to hinder the development of further new and innovative research-driven practices to prevent rv. Such prevention efforts will be for the betterment of crime victims.

Selected further reading

Overviews of repeat victimization are provided in Farrell and Pease (1993) and Pease (1998). A bibliography of repeat victimization studies (albeit now somewhat dated) is given on the International Victimology website at http://www.victimology.nl/onlpub/otherdocs/rv-bibliography.pdf. In addition, a range of PDF-downloadable publications on repeat victimization is available on the above author's websites via the Midlands Centre for Criminology and Criminal Justice at Loughborough University.

Notes

1. This is a conservative estimate based on crime types found in 17 countries from the International Crime Victims Survey (Farrell and Bouloukos 2001). This average includes repeats across as well as within crime types.
2. The lists do not use legal categories, and it is clear that some of the 'types' are overlapping (for example, assault and domestic violence) and imperfect (for example ' sexual victimization' can include a further extensive list of crimes against adults and minors that is only hinted at here – see, e.g., Fisher et al. 2000).
3. See Tim Hope's evaluation work on the Reducing Burglary Initiative for a recent example (Hope 2004).
4. Table 6.2 lists ten evaluations of which five prevented burglary according to the outcome measures. However, the three evaluations in Baltimore, Dallas and San Diego were all part of a single project run by the Police Executive Research Forum (Weisel et al. 1999). The three sites had similar characteristics and themes and resulted in one main evaluation report. Hence the case could be made that they should count as a single evaluation, in which case, five of eight or 62.5 per cent of projects would be deemed to have prevented crime. In contrast, Tilley's (1993a) report contains three evaluations of projects undertaken separately.

References

Anderson, D., Chenery, S. and Pease, K. (1995) *Biting Back: Tackling Repeat Burglary and Car Crime. Crime Detection and Prevention Series Paper 58.* London: Home Office.

Ball Public Relations Pty Ltd and Walker, C. (2002) *The South Australian Residential Break and Enter Pilot Project Evaluation Report – Summary Volume.* Canberra: Commonwealth Attorney-General's Department.

Barr, R. and Pease, K. (1990) 'Crime placement, displacement and deflection', in M. Tonry and N. Morris (eds) *Crime and Justice. Vol. 12.* Chicago, IL: University of Chicago Press.

Bennett, T. (1995) 'Identifying, explaining, and targeting burglary "hot spots"', *European Journal on Criminal Policy and Research*, 3: 113–23.

Bennett, T. and Durie, L. (1999) *Preventing Residential Burglary in Cambridge: From Crime Audits to Targeted Strategies. Police Research Series Paper* 108. London: Home Office.

Bouloukos, A.C. and Farrell, G. (1997) 'On the displacement of repeat victimization', in G. Newman *et al.* (eds) *Rational Choice and Situational Crime Prevention.* Aldershot: Ashgate.

Bowers, K. (2001) 'Small business crime: the evaluation of a crime prevention initiative', *Crime Prevention and Community Safety: An International Journal,* 3: 23–42.

Bowers, K.J. and Johnson, S.D. (2004) 'Who commits near repeats? A test of the boost explanation.' London: Jill Dando Institute of Crime Science.

Bowers, K.J., Johnson, S.D. and Pease, K. (2004) 'Prospective hot-spotting: the future of crime mapping?' *British Journal of Criminology,* 44: 641–58.

Breitenbecher, K.H. and Christine, G.A. (1998) 'An empirical evaluation of a program designed to reduce the risk of multiple sexual victimization', *Journal of Interpersonal Violence,* 13: 472–88.

Budz, D., Pegnall, N. and Townsley, M. (2001) *Lightning Strikes Twice: Preventing Repeat Home Burglary.* Queensland: Criminal Justice Commission.

Chenery, S., Holt, J. and Pease, K. (1997) *Biting Back II: Reducing Repeat Victimization in Huddersfield. Crime Detection and Prevention Series Paper* 82. London: Home Office, Police Research Group.

Clarke, R.V. and Eck, J.E. (2003) *Become a Problem-solving Crime Analyst in 55 Small Steps.* Cullompton: Willan Publishing.

Davis, R.C. and Medina-Ariza, J. (2001) *Results from an Elder Abuse Prevention Experiment in New York City. Research in Brief.* Washington, DC: National Institute of Justice.

Davis, R.C. and Taylor, B.G. (1997) 'A proactive response to family violence: the results of a randomized experiment', *Criminology,* 35: 307–33.

Farrell, G. (1995) 'Preventing repeat victimization', in M. Tonry and D.P. Farrington (eds) *Building a Safer Society: Strategic Approaches to Crime Prevention, Crime and Justice.* Chicago, IL: Chicago University Press.

Farrell, G. (2001) 'How victim-oriented is policing?', in A. Gaudreault and I. Waller (eds) *Tenth International Symposium on Victimology: Selected Symposium Proceedings.* Montreal: Tenth International Symposium on Victimology.

Farrell, G. and Bouloukos, A.C. (2001) 'A cross-national comparative analysis of rates of repeat victimization', in G. Farrell and K. Pease (eds) *Repeat Victimization. Vol. 12. Crime Prevention Studies.* Monsey, NY: Criminal Justice Press.

Farrell, G. and Buckley, A. (1999) 'Evaluation of a UK police domestic violence unit using repeat victimization as a performance indicator', *The Howard Journal,* 38: 42–53.

Farrell, G., Hobbs, L., Edmunds, A. and Laycock, G. (2000) *RV Snapshot: UK Policing and Repeat Victimization. Crime Reduction Research Series. Policing and Reducing Crime Unit Paper* 5. London: Home Office.

Farrell, G. and Pease, K. (1993) *Once Bitten, Twice Bitten: Repeat Victimisation and its Implications for Crime Prevention. Crime Prevention Unit Paper* 46. London: Home Office (available at www.homeoffice.gov.uk/prgpubs/fcpu46.pdf).

Farrell, G. and Pease, K. (2003) 'Measuring and interpreting repeat victimization using police data: findings from repeat burglary in Charlotte, North Carolina', in M. Smith and D. Cornish (eds) *Theory for Practice in Crime Prevention. Vol. 16. Crime Prevention Studies.* Monsey, NY: Criminal Justice Press.

Farrell, G. and Pease, K. (in press) 'Preventing repeat residential burglary', in B.C. Welsh and D.P. Farrington (eds) *Preventing Crime: What Works for Children, Offenders, Victims, and Places.* Belmont, CA: Wadsworth.

Farrell, G. and Sousa, W. (1997) 'Repeat victimization in the United States…and in ten other industrialized countries.' Paper presented at the National Conference on Preventing Crime, Washington D.C.

Farrell, G., Sousa, W.H. and Lamm Weisel, D. (2002) 'The time-window effect in the measurement of repeat victimization: a methodology for its measurement and an empirical study', in N. Tilley (ed.) *Analysis for Crime Prevention. Crime Prevention Studies. Vol. 13*. Monsey, NY: Criminal Justice Press.

Farrell, G., Tseloni, A. and Pease, K. (in press) 'Repeat victimisation in the ICVS and the NCVS', *Crime Prevention and Community Safety: An International Journal*.

Farrington, D.P. (1992) 'Evaluation of the Kirkholt Burglary Project.' Unpublished report to the Home Office. Cambridge: Institute of Criminology, University of Cambridge.

Fisher, B.S., Cullen, F.T. and Turner, M.G. (2000) *Sexual Victimization of College Women. Research Report*. Washington, DC: National Institute of Justice (available at http://www.ncjrs.org/pdffiles1/nij/182369.pdf).

Forrester, D., Chatterton, M. and Pease, K. (1988) *The Kirkholt Burglary Prevention Project, Rochdale. Crime Prevention Unit Paper* 13. London: Home Office.

Forrester, D., Frenz, S., O'Connell, M. and Pease, K. (1990) *The Kirkholt Burglary Prevention Project: Phase II. Crime Prevention Unit Paper* 23. London: Home Office.

Hanmer, J., Griffiths, S. and Jerwood, D. (1999) *Arresting Evidence: Domestic Violence and Repeat Victimization. Police Research Series Paper* 104. London: Home Office.

Henderson, M. (2002) *Preventing Repeat Residential Burglary: A Meta-evaluation of Two Australian Demonstration Projects*. Barton Act: Commonwealth Attorney-General's Office.

Hope, T. (2004) *SDPs in the Yorkshire and the Humber, East Midlands and East Regions. Report to the Home Office*. Keele: Department of Criminology, Keele University.

Johnson, S.D. and Bowers, K.J. (2004) 'The burglary as a clue to the future: the beginnings of prospective hot-spotting', *The European Journal of Criminology*, 1: 237–55.

Johnson, S.D., Bowers, K.J. and Pease, K. (2004) 'Predicting the future or summarising the past? Crime mapping as anticipation', in M. Smith and N. Tilley (eds) *Launching Crime Science*. Cullompton: Willan Publishing.

Laycock, G. and Farrell, G. (2003) 'Repeat victimization: lessons for implementing problem-oriented policing', in J. Knutsson (ed.) *Problem-oriented Policing: From Innovation to Mainstream. Crime Prevention Studies. Vol. 15*. Monsey, NY: Criminal Justice Press.

Lloyd, S., Farrell, G. and Pease, K. (1994) *Preventing Repeated Domestic Violence: A Demonstration Project on Merseyside. Police Research Group, Crime Prevention Unit Paper* 49. London: Home Office.

Moitra, S.D. and Konda, S.L. (2004) 'An empirical investigation of network attacks on computer systems', *Computers and Security*, 23: 43–51.

Pease, K. (1991) 'The Kirkholt project: preventing burglary on a British public housing estate', *Security Journal*, 2: 73–7.

Pease, K. (1998) *Repeat Victimisation: Taking Stock. Crime Detection and Prevention Series Paper* 90. London: Home Office.

Pease, K. and Laycock, G. (1996) *Revictimization: Reducing the Heat on Hot Victims. Research in Action*. Washington, DC: National Institute of Justice.

Phillips, C. and Sampson, A. (1998) 'Preventing repeated racial victimization: an action research project', *British Journal of Criminology*, 38: 124–44.

Planty, M. (2004) 'Understanding the role of repeat victimization in the production of annual victimization rates.' Paper presented at the American Society of Criminology Annual Meeting, Nashville, TN, November.

Repetto, T.A. (1974) *Residential Crime*. Cambridge, MA: Ballinger.

Roberts, B. (2005) 'Computer maps "will beat crime"', *Daily Mirror*, 12 February (available at: http://www.mirror.co.uk/news/allnews/page.cfm?objectid=15129313&method=full&siteid=50143).

Sherman, L.W. (1992) *Policing Domestic Violence: Experiments and Dilemmas*. New York, NY: Free Press.

Sherman, L.W. and Berk, R.A. (1984) 'The specific deterrent effects of arrest for domestic assault', *American Sociological Review*, 49: 261–72.

Taylor, G. (1999) 'Using repeat victimization to counter commercial burglary: the Leicester experience', *Security Journal*, 12: 41–52.

Tilley, N. (1993a) *After Kirkholt: Theory, Method and Results of Replication Evaluations. Crime Reduction Unit Paper 47*. London: Home Office.

Tilley, N. (1993b) *The Prevention of Crime against Small Businesses: The Safer Cities Experience. Crime Prevention Unit Series Paper 45*. London: Home Office.

Tilley, N. (1995) *Thinking about Crime Prevention Performance Indicators. Crime Detection and Prevention Series Paper 57*. London: Home Office.

Townsley, M., Homel, R. and Chaseling, J. (2000) 'Repeat burglary victimisation: spatial and temporal patterns', *Australian and New Zealand Journal of Criminology*, 33: 37–63.

Townsley, M., Homel, R. and Chaseling, J. (2003) 'Infectious burglaries: a test of the near repeat hypothesis', *British Journal of Criminology*, 43: 615–33.

Weisel, D.L., Clarke, R.V. and Stedman, J.R. (1999) *Hot Dots in Hot Spots: Examining Repeat Victimization for Residential Burglary in Three Cities. Final Report to the National Institute of Justice*. Washington, DC: Police Executive Research Forum.

Ybarra, L.M.R. and Lohr, S.L. (2002) 'Estimates of repeat victimization using the National Crime Victimization Survey', *Journal of Quantitative Criminology*, 18: 1–21.

Chapter 7

Science in the service of crime reduction

Ken Pease

Klaus Schmidt...burst into a bank in Berlin in August 1995, waved a pistol and screamed 'Hand over the money'. Staff asked if he wanted a bag, to which he replied 'Damn right it's a real gun'. Guessing Schmidt was deaf, the manager set off the alarm, saying later 'It was ridiculously loud, but he didn't seem to notice'. After five minutes, punctuated by Schmidt occasionally shouting 'I am a trained killer', police arrived and arrested him. Schmidt then sued the bank, accusing them of exploiting his disability (Moore 1996: 11).

The idea of outsmarting criminals has general appeal. Television programmes such as *America's Dumbest Criminals* permit a feeling of superiority in the viewer. We find newspaper stories of burglars who photograph themselves at the scene of their crime, and bank robbers who write their demands for cash on the back of self-addressed envelopes. These invite ridicule of those who might otherwise be feared, and feeling superior to the inept criminal sits uneasily with feeling threatened by and vulnerable to them.

A less direct but still powerful means of asserting superiority over criminals is to outwit them. Within police work, the usual instrument is the 'sting' operation, where (for example) those on outstanding arrest warrants are notified that they have won a lottery prize, and are invited to collect it. At the collection point, they are arrested.

A still less direct means of asserting superiority involves the use of science. If the techniques of this most admired of human activities can be brought to bear on crime reduction, then (the citizen opines) virtue may yet prevail. The writer knows of no research which clarifies such beliefs and feelings. Speculatively, stories of offender ineptitude and police stings have the attraction of being accessible. What happened is clear. Stories of science applied to crime are less accessible, but have a compensating glamour and mystery and feature extensively in television schedules (there were two such programmes in the schedules on the night when this was written, 31 January 2005).

This chapter aspires to do three things. First, it seeks to outline the range of scientific endeavours which are self-consciously applied to crime control; in other words what is the science currently deemed relevant. Secondly, it considers whether there are other areas of scientific endeavour which are potentially relevant, or other ways of thinking about the application of disciplines already seen as relevant. Thirdly, it addresses the issue of how 'hard' science may interact with conventional criminology to increase its impact. *En passant*, it notes:

- the extensive self-protective effort expended in military and commercial contexts, and considers how such applications may 'trickle down' to general application in crime control; and

- the obstacles to bringing science-inspired crime reductive products to market.

The current range and status of science within the Home Office

The Home Office is the government department which is responsible for crime control within England and Wales. The first three of its declared aims are as follows. The first two are deemed central to the coverage of this chapter, the third marginally so. To:

1. reduce crime and the fear of crime, tackle youth crime and violent, sexual and drug-related crime, anti-social behaviour and disorder, increasing safety in the home and public spaces;

2. reduce organized and international crime, including trafficking in drugs, people and weapons, and to combat terrorism and other threats to national security, in co-operation with EU partners and the wider international community; and

3. ensure the effective delivery of justice, avoiding unnecessary delay, through efficient investigation, detection, prosecution and court procedures. To minimize the threat to and intimidation of witnesses and to engage with and support victims.[1]

Its website[2] is therefore as good a place as any to see how it invokes science in its work. Searching on the keyword 'science', we read as introduction:

The Home Office undertakes a huge range of scientific projects to support its work. Recent projects include measuring the effect of treatment initiatives on drug users, researching biometrics for ID cards and investigating whether tasers can be used safely by the Police. The results of this scientific work are used to inform policy and make sure that the Home Office is making the best use of new technologies.

Seven of the first ten matches 'by relevance' feature the Forensic Science Service. Thus forensic science seems to have primacy at least in terms of this simple check. However, the links from science in the Home Office home page invokes a number of other Home Office locations as having science relevance. These are listed in Table 7.1, which is thus a crude enumeration and description of science-based activities done by and for the Home Office. In some of the linked sites the activity is transient and concentrated on training (as in the forensic pathology case), in some cases it focuses more on social than physical or biological science (exclusively so in the Youth Justice Board site, and overwhelmingly in the Research Development and Statistics Directorate). In some cases the relevance of the cited science to the Home Office aims centred upon crime and noted above is not detailed. The Immigration and Nationality Directorate's involvement with science seems limited to its choice of iris recognition as the intended biometric means of unique personal identification.

Exploring the relevant websites and downloadable documentation makes two things clear. First, it seems that the research programmes are not substantially cross-referenced. The cynic's view of this state of affairs would be that the programme is not fully integrated. The apologist's view would be that each group serves a particular market precisely. That there are recurring themes across at least some of the units and groups mentioned here is clear, the three most obvious being the unique identification of people (and to a lesser extent things, especially drugs), the tracking of people (and to a lesser extent things, especially consumer products) and the development of telecommunications. The lack of cross-referencing across parts of the Home Office even when the theme is the same inclines one towards the cynic's view.

Limiting discussion in this chapter to the role of the Home Office neglects the wider issues of integration across government departments, since many crime issues are facilitated or constrained by the decisions of departments of state from education to the Exchequer. It may be that the prospect of the possibly cataclysmic effects of CBRN (chemical, biological, radiological and nuclear) attack will expedite cross-departmental co-operation, and that this will operate through (or incidentally affect) the regulation of volume crime. For the moment, attention will be restricted to intra-Home Office matters.

It is certain that the Home Office recognized the fragmentation of scientific effort as sub-optimal. Three recent events support such an interpretation:

1. The Head of the Research, Development and Statistics Directorate was designated Chief Scientific Adviser to the Home Office, with overarching responsibility for all science activities.

2. The Police Scientific Development Branch is to be retitled the Home Office Scientific Development Branch, with a correspondingly wider mandate for applied research.

3. Two police 'science strategy' documents were published.

Table 7.1 Home Office science links

Name	Description	Web address (prefixed by http://www)
Animal Scientific Procedures Division	Regulates use of animals in scientific procedures	homeoffice.gov.uk/inside/org/dob/direct/aspd.html
The Forensic Pathology Review Implementation Team	Concerned with the provision of forensic pathologists	homeoffice.gov.uk/inside/science/forensic.html
Forensic Science Service	Supply of forensic science services to police forces in England and Wales	forensic.gov.uk/forensic_t/inside/about/index.htm
Information and Communications Technology Unit	Responsible for support of police telecommunications, information technology and radio engineering	homeoffice.gov.uk/inside/org/dob/direct/ictu.html[1]
Immigration and Nationality Directorate	Responsible for immigration control	Ind.homeoffice.gov.uk/content/ind/en/home.html
Police Information Technology Organization	Provides information technology and communication systems to the police and criminal justice organizations	pito.org.uk/
Police Scientific Development Branch	Provides impartial and accurate scientific and technical advice to the police and ministers; improving police operational effectiveness and efficiency	homeoffice.gov.uk/inside/org/dob/direct/psdb.html
Research, Development and Statistics Directorate	Maintains statistics published by the Home Office, conducts economic analyses and carries out and commissions social science research	homeoffice.gov.uk/inside/org/dob/direct/rds.html
Science Policy Unit	Develops and delivers policy on police use of science and technology	homeoffice.gov.uk/inside/org/dob/direct/spu.html
Youth Justice Board	Researches what works in reducing youth crime	youth-justice-board.gov.uk/YouthJusticeBoard/Research/

Note:
1. This may no longer exist by the date of publication. Mention of it is retained to give the fullest possible depiction of the state of affairs at the time of writing.

Whilst these changes will doubtless diminish fragmentation of effort somewhat, they represent, as the Home Office would certainly acknowledge, only a promising first step in its ongoing process of integrating science activities. For example, the Crime and Disorder Act 1998 conferred responsibility for local crime and disorder reduction upon local partnerships (CDRPs), including local authority and police representation. In logic, the science strategy mentioned above should incorporate CDRP interests. If the partnership is the responsible agency, the partnership should receive scientific support. In partial mitigation, the restriction of the document to police concerns stems from its origins in the police reform process.

Although one may question its restriction to the police as a customer agency, the science strategy is admirable in its integrative intent (and future orientation, the first explicitly covering a period to 2008 and establishing a future scanning function) and merits discussion at some length. Information and communications technology (ICT) and forensic science are the areas singled out for special mention, with the catch-all 'other technologies' added. The primacy of these topics is evident in the specific goals for policing technology which are mentioned, and in the areas identified as profitable for Home Office research sponsorship (Home Office 2003: 13), which are all concerned with the unique identification of people, products or drugs:

> Over the period of the plan the police service, working as necessary with its criminal justice partners, should by:
>
> - 2003 have secure e-mail facilities across the Criminal Justice System.
>
> - 2004 have the profiles of the whole active criminal population on the national DNA database (currently projected to be 2.6 million offenders by 2004).
>
> - 2005 complete the roll-out of Airwave, the new police radio communications service.
>
> - 2005 have begun to enable victims to track progress of their case on-line.
>
> - 2005–06 ensure that the Case and Custody system is implemented in every force, with links to courts and the Crown Prosecution Service. (Home Office 2003: 9).

Figure 7.1, reproduced from the strategy, details 'key stakeholders'. The figure is interesting for several reasons. First it acknowledges the role of a large range of agencies[3] recognizing the basic argument, to be developed later in this chapter, that the levers on crime incidence are primarily outside the police and criminal justice networks. Secondly, it assigns 'stakeholders' to one of two roles, either service providers or 'key links'. Service provision is clear from agencies like the Forensic Science Service to the police. The area of remaining doubt in making such service as up to date as possible is how the key links might work. What services do 'academia, industry, and international sources' provide directly to the police? Why are there are no updating or other services

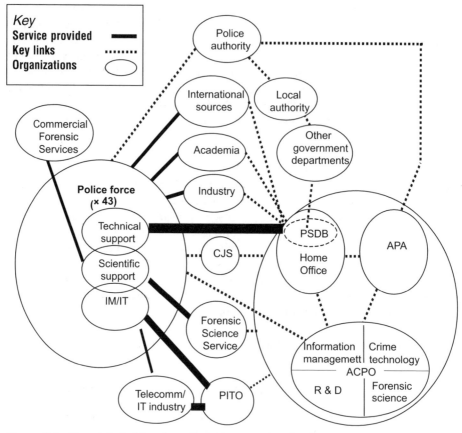

Figure 7.1 Key stakeholders in police science and technology
Source: Adapted from Home Office (2003).

to the Home Office? Why are the constituent parts of the Home Office linked to each other and the constituent parts of the police service not similarly linked? Why does the telecommunications industry (depicted separately from industry generally) have no identified links to the Home Office? One could continue to dissect the figure and identify more unresolved issues and oddities, but the purpose here is not to bury the strategy but to praise it as a very useful first step in a hitherto fragmented domain. The figure reflects that and, as the strategy document makes clear, was intended only as 'a much-simplified representation of the complex relationships between the key organisations involved in the provision of police science and technology' (p. 8). Further, some modest clarification of the figure is provided in the text.

The successor strategy document does not, in the accompanying letter from the Minister of State, 'represent a dramatic change of direction from the original'. The emphasis on post-crime science is maintained, but the report's Appendix 4 does represent both an increased diversity of projects and a higher proportion of them under the 'Crime Reduction' heading. The enhanced role of automatic number plate recognition is notable and welcome, together with the emphasis on the real-time establishment of identity.

A crude measure of the relative emphasis on reduction and investigation can be gleaned from the number of items listed in Appendix 4 as components of police science and technology capabilities classified under 'Reduce Crime' relative to those listed under 'Investigate Crime'. There are 16 under the first and 22 under the second, and arguably many of those classified as 'Reduce Crime' involve action after a crime has taken place (e.g. those involving the monitoring of known offenders and the use of CCTV in detection and prosecution). In the strategy document's Appendix 7, we find the conclusions of the Future Scanning Sub-group, which identifies 'those developments which are most likely to impact on policing over the next five years' (p. 41). These (with brief illustrative quotations) are as follows:

- *Biometrics:* 'The threat of criminal subversion of biometric systems...could make identity theft a much greater threat'.

- *Electromagnetic imaging*: 'These are emergent technologies...whose value could be great, particularly for security applications. One of the main opportunities for application is in screening for weapons, explosives etc. in airports.'

- *Encryption:* 'The use of encryption provides capabilities that can be viewed as...negative when employed by the criminal.' The debate concerns the police right to hold encryption keys for secure communications between citizens, and the possible criminal use of steganography and quantum cryptographic techniques.

- *Geo-location:* 'This term encompasses...technologies to locate people, vehicles and other assets.'

- *Lab-on-a-chip:* 'the miniaturisation of existing chemical or biochemical synthesis, detection and analysis procedures.' This would allow rapid crime scene analysis of forensically relevant material. Noteworthy is the recommendation that a 'working group should be set up to keep the crime relevance of the technology in the minds of the developers'.

- *Third generation of mobile phones*: New software will enable a reduction of the number of stolen mobiles purchased for criminal activity, by detection of theft and de-activation. 'It is important to work with industry and existing bodies to identify threats and opportunities at an early stage.'

Although the second strategy document moves towards integration, a developing theme of the chapter is that the thrust of hard science is primarily directed towards a narrow range of topics, amongst which unique identifiability and telecommunications in the service of the police and courts are pre-eminent. This was anticipated some 30 years ago by Leslie Wilkins. In an astonishingly prescient paper in 1973 entitled 'Crime and criminal justice at the turn of the century', he bewailed the application of science to the establishment of guilt rather than to crime prevention. He wrote as if he were already at the turn of the century, and concluded that

There has been little development of technology which makes crime more difficult; techniques have been concerned with the various aspects of the finding of guilt and the allocation of blame. Fingerprints, voice-prints, lie-detectors and the like help only in pinning the blame more certainly upon the person who has already been suspected. Even the modus operandi index is used to identify persons who may have committed the crime, rather than for the purposes of preventing further crimes of a similar nature (p: 22).

The primary reasons for the state of affairs which Wilkins foresaw are twofold. First, his was a soaring intellect. Secondly is the nature of the market in crime reductive products, which is driven directly and indirectly by the police service. The direct role comes via its own procurement of systems like the Airwave radio system and advanced fingerprint analysis. Its first indirect role comes through its demand for forensic services, primarily through the Forensic Science Service, the Forensic Alliance and the LGC (as the Laboratory of the Government Chemist is now known). Its second indirect role comes through its (generic) recommendation of products and services available to the public or commercial organizations, for example by its incorporation into the advice of police crime reduction officers. The service is scrupulously careful about endorsing individual products in a competitive market, but recommendation of products with particular technical features and meeting standards drives the range of available products.

First stirrings of a wider view of science relevance

The contrast between the first and second editions of the police science technology strategy lies in a movement towards a wider and more balanced use of science in crime reduction and crime investigation.[4]

Marcus Felson's routine activity theory (see Felson 1998) identifies three necessary conditions for a crime to occur. They are the coincidence of:

- a motivated offender, and
- a suitable victim, in the
- absence of a capable guardian.

Although this formulation seems anodyne, even self-evident, its implications are surprisingly profound. As science and engineering transform society, each of the three necessary conditions changes, as does the meaning of coincidence. For example, victims of theft are suitable when they carry items with particular characteristics, summarized by the acronym VIVA. To be attractive to thieves, objects must be high in **V**alue, low in **I**nertia and **V**olume, and moderate in **A**ccess.[5] Mobile phones in the 1990s and i-Pod devices at the time of writing are classic VIVA items, with the i-Pod having the advantage of a distinctively coloured headset so as to be identifiable even when the device itself is out of sight, presumably so as to confer prestige on the wearer. Ekblom (2004: x) puts it well:

Social and technological change moreover constantly creates new opportunities for offending – new targets (mobile phones and laptops), new environments (cash machines, shopping centres, financial networks in cyberspace), new business models (e-tailing), new tools (such as cordless drills, spray cans, colour photocopiers or easy-to-fly airliners) and new information sources (how to pick locks or make explosives, courtesy of the Internet) which may mean a wider circle of offenders acquire 'expert' techniques.

The other profound change of recent years has been in the possibilities for coincidence of offender and suitable victim. The potential afforded by the postal service, the telegraph and the telephone in bringing offender and victim together have paled into insignificance alongside that afforded by the exploitation of cyberspace. The migration of crime from meatspace to cyberspace is one of the major features of the modern world,[6] with the following advantages for the offender:[7]

- The ready and simultaneous access to millions of potential victims or potential co-offenders, whose interests and sensitivities are reflected in their presence in chatrooms and user groups (for example adolescents in 'flirty' chatrooms, vulnerable to sexual predation; people interested in synthesizing narcotics; see Schneider 2005; people competing as a skill to gain illicit access to services, such as satellite TV; see Mann and Sutton 1998).

- The ready and simultaneous access to millions of computer systems which can be compromised by Trojans, worms, etc., either to yield money or as an expression of malice.

- Ease of dissembling about oneself (and perhaps adopting multiple identities), for example a sexual predator pretending to be of similar age to potential victims, or a fraudster pretending to require money to release a huge legacy.

In short, the scope of science and engineering relevance is potentially much wider than as a means of intervening after the fact. The simultaneous recognition of the wide implications of science change and the relatively narrow focus on policing response is encapsulated in the first two paragraphs of the Minister of State's Foreword to the first Home Office strategy document cited above:

i.   Society, as a whole, is experiencing rapid and accelerating change. In a relatively short space of time our reliance on science and technology has increased dramatically in both the work place and in our homes. Mobile phones, the Internet (and computers more generally), laptops and electronic organisers are for many part and parcel of daily life. These new technologies provide many benefits – but they also provide new opportunities for abuse and criminal exploitation.

ii. I want to ensure that the police service is equipped with the best tools and techniques available to enable them to work with maximum effectiveness and efficiency. From the very start of the police reform process it has been clear that a more strategic approach to science and technology was needed and we made this one of our key commitments in the white paper: *A Blueprint for Reform*. For the first time this strategy presents an overarching vision of how we will address not only our immediate policing needs, but also the capabilities the police will need in the future (p. i).

It may be unfair to label this Foreword as schizoid, since the strategy outlined was a policing strategy specifically, and indeed one of the elements in the strategy was an orientation towards future trends. However, it should perhaps have pointed to the need for a wider strategy on science wherein police investigative needs featured less and crime reduction needs featured more. To the observer, the migration of crime to cyberspace calls into question the whole balance of effort between crime reduction organized territorially and globally. One police officer friend spoke with appropriate contempt of a questionnaire he had been invited to complete asking 'How much Internet crime takes place in your area?' The establishment of the Hi-Tech Crime Unit (NHTCU)[8] is one straw in the wind suggesting that the balance of effort is changing to meet the changed challenge. The direction of change in the second police science strategy compared with the first is an even more important one.

Perhaps a crucial element in seeing science as aiding policing rather than shaping crime has been the pace of change in crime, and the way in which shoe-horning the rich diversity of criminal action into the arid and uninformative crime categories used by the Home Office serves to obscure what actually happened; who did what to whom in what context. The recognition that standard crime categories are fundamentally unhelpful for purposes of crime reduction (including the involvement of science to that end) is so central as to merit some expansion.

Whilst the first nine decades of the twentieth century showed a consistent year-on-year increase in the volume of recorded crime, and whilst any short period does not yield major qualitative change in crime, it is possible to overlook the fact that over the centuries the acts that get squashed into relatively unchanging crime categories have altered almost beyond recognition.

Table 7.2 details what is stolen in offences coming to the attention of Black Country courts in 1835–60. It will be seen that the theft of animals predominates, with theft from employer and theft of fuel also major reasons for coming before the court. There was no instance of theft of or from motor vehicles, or theft of video equipment, which together now account for nearly half of all thefts suffered according to the British Crime Surveys of recent years.

Until perhaps a decade ago, thinking about future crime tended to focus on future criminality and its detection rather than on the crime event. This tendency to focus on the future of criminality and responses to it, rather than to anticipate changes in crime itself, even extends to fiction. The science fiction and fantasy literature concentrates upon criminal justice (see, for example, Olander and Greenfield 1977). The best-known science fiction work is Isaac

Table 7.2   Black Country theft 1835–60

Type of theft	%
Theft from place of work	28
Theft of food or clothing	25
Theft of animals	7
Theft of or from motor vehicles	0
Theft of video/audio equipment	0

Source: Modified from Philips (1977).

Asimov's detective Elijah Bayley, and his robotic sidekick. Prediction of crime types and extents is thus, for all practical purposes, not part of criminology, traditionally conceived. The one book whose subtitle suggests that its contents should deal with future crime rather than future justice is *Visions for Change: Crime and Justice in the Twenty-first Century*. This book (by Muraskin and Roberts 1996) does not fulfil the promise of its title.

Whilst the self-conscious anticipation of crime trends is almost wholly missing from criminology literature, some work is usable for prediction purposes and may have been carried out with half an eye to prediction. For example, Simon Field's demonstration that economic cycles bring crime consequences, with property crimes rising at times of recession, and crimes of violence during more prosperous crimes (Field 1990), affords a predictive tool of sorts. However, even this operates with gross measures of crime and its predictive use is only implicit.

Just as criminologists have by and large neglected the future, so futurologists have largely neglected crime. None of the books in the World Future Society's bookshop bears a title which suggests it deals with crime (*Future Times* 1998). None of that Society's 'Sixty-five forecasts about your future life' deals with crime (*Futurist* 1998). Peter Cochrane is perhaps currently the UK's leading futurologist. His writing is unfailingly stimulating and shrewd. However, in his *108 Tips for Time Travellers* (Cochrane 1998), crime appears only twice in the index of the 227-page book, once in relation to encryption, and once about pornography.

In the future, human cupidity and aggression, distributed unevenly across people, can be assumed. People will pursue self-interest by force or fraud. Many of the ways in which they do so will be familiar from the past. Partners will still assault each other. People will steal from each others' homes and places of work. They will do so to a large extent rationally (see, e.g., Cornish and Clarke 1986). They will steal away from the gaze of people and cameras, they will steal goods which they will themselves enjoy using or can sell on. They will arm themselves with weapons which, whilst not exciting, are capable of causing harm of at least the level desired. Because of their rationality, the extent to which and the ways in which they commit crime will depend upon the kinds of behaviour which social and physical arrangements favour. Crime will remain the hum in the machine of emotional, social and economic life. It is unquestionably more profitable to examine the criminal opportunities which a future society will offer, and the ways in which science and technology can reduce or eliminate these, than to look at possible people change, either through socialization or the effects of criminal justice.

The group within the Home Office which brings the broadest range of sciences to bear upon policing is without doubt the Police Scientific Development Branch, soon to be redesignated as the Home Office Scientific Development Branch, in line with the trend discerned above in recognition of the fact that progress shapes crime as well as responses to it.

The Foresight programme

The Foresight Crime Panel was one of three cross-cutting panels which the Department of Trade and Industry established in its second phase of work in 1999 (the rationale for the panel is spelled out by Rogerson *et al.* 2000). Conventionally, such panels cleaved to industry divisions (such as insurance, financial services and the like) which sought to identify developments in science and technology which would alter the industry landscape. Crime was included as a special case in that, as Marcus Felson (1998) makes clear, trends in every segment of commerce would determine the supply of criminal opportunities. The two reports of the panel (DTI 2000a, 2000b) remain of relevance both in their own right and as stimulating later developments.[9]

The paraphrased recommendations of the panel will be listed, with an indication in each case of how the recommendation was reached.

That a dedicated funding stream be established to focus science and technology attention on crime reduction. This recommendation flowed from the recognition that work funded by the research councils and which were specifically crime oriented were overwhelmingly concentrated in the Economic and Social Research Council. This was recognized as an over-statement of the position, in that work of crime relevance was done elsewhere but classified under another heading. However, researchers from other science disciplines commented on the absence of a crime motif in their work. The lack of a funding focus for such work was implicated, as was the difficulty of obtaining sympathetic peer review for cross-cutting work, since reviewers were (almost by definition) selected for the distinction of their work within a discipline. The recommendation led, more or less directly, to a funding stream established by the Engineering and Physical Science Research Council, whose content will be illustrated later in the chapter. The procedure by which the Police Science and Technology Steering Group works to keep focal the crime relevance of lab-on-a-chip development is also an indication of the same process of thought as the Foresight group displayed. In parallel, the involvement of the Design Council and the Royal Society of Arts in stimulating work into crime-reductive design are also developments which were set in train or speeded by the Foresight work.

That a national e-crime strategy be established for all levels of e-crime. The panel noted initiatives in this direction, but contended that the work primarily focused on high levels of organization of such crime (for example, the National Crime Intelligence Service (NCIS) Operation Trawler). It was not convinced that comparable attention was given to crimes against individual citizens, and saw such crime as hampering the development of e-commerce. The establishment of the national office of E-Envoy is a step towards this, with a private company, Entrust, contracted to manage government Internet security. However, the risk in card-not-present frauds[10] suggests that, in relation to e-commerce, the panel's concerns were well founded.

That the wider impact of new technology on the criminal justice system (CJS) be reviewed – including training, equipment, funding, co-ordination and consistency, and action taken to address the issues identified. The absence of connectivity amongst police forces and between police and other players in criminal justice concerned the panel. The independent purchasing decisions of police force areas were seen as problematic, delaying integration of data across the police service as a whole. The lack of understanding of evidence in cybercrime cases by lawyers (including judges) and jurors was a cause for concern. This recommendation was no doubt wholly unsurprising to the Home Office (including the Police Information Technology Organization – PITO) and informed others.

That thinking on crime reduction be incorporated into the mainstream of central government and business decision-making. Similarly, ongoing programmes to encourage 'horizon scanning' to identify and prepare for future threats should be established. This recommendation reflects the Felson perspective on crime. Ways in which it could be concretized include the application to central government of the obligation imposed on local government by s. 17 of the Crime and Disorder Act 1998 to consider the crime consequences of any decision taken. The relevance of this recommendation to science and technology development is indirect but important. There is good reason for obligations placed on local government to be placed on central government also, if only on a 'what's sauce for the goose is sauce for the gander' basis. However, there are practical reasons for s. 17 to apply to national government. The first is to remove anomalies. For example, as in the Aquariam Investments case in Brighton (see Moss 2005), planning applications rejected locally on s. 17 grounds are appealable to the Planning Inspectorate, an arm of central government. Thus (as in the Aquariam Investments case) a decision properly taken locally on s. 17 grounds will be overturned centrally because s. 17 considerations do not apply – the two-act charade all taking place at public expense. As for science and technology, making s. 17 nationally applicable would require crime thinking to be incorporated into decisions on science strategy no less than elsewhere. Under Freedom of Information Act provisions, adherence to this requirement would become transparent (or at least more transparent than it is now).

That a programme be developed to address crime at all stages of a product's life-cycle. This recommendation incorporates the following sub-elements:

1. Identifying the roles of manufacturers, retailers and customers in developing secure products.

2. A voluntary standards system within manufacturing which would show that the criminogenic capacity of a product had been addressed to diminish criminal misuse and stealability.

3. The contribution of the retailer, particularly the impact on crime of e-commerce and home delivery of products purchased electronically.

4. How to encourage a climate of demand for secure products amongst consumers.

5. An annual award for new products which have been designed with crime reduction in mind.

It would be untrue to say that this process is substantially advanced at the time of writing. The annual competitions of the Royal Society of Arts for crime-reductive design give instances of where novel engineering solutions to diverse crime problems (from bicycle theft to ATM robberies) may be found. There is ongoing research funded by the European Commission about the crime-proofing of products and services (Project MARC), and there are evaluations demonstrating the crime-reductive effects of building design (see Armitage 2000), but there is no wholesale movement towards engineering and science solutions to crime problems. This will have to await action on Recommendation 4, above, which is the most fundamental of the recommendations.

The Police Scientific Development Branch (PSDB)

Of all the current science facilities within the Home Office, PSDB comes closest to a pan-science approach (see PSDB 2004a, 2004b). Whilst proclaiming that it is 'not a research institute', visitors are likely to conclude that it is indeed a research institute doing high-quality applied and operational research across a range of topics from the establishment of standards of stab resistance for police body armour through devising the Battenburg design to maximize the visibility of police vehicles, to the use of Raman spectroscopy in explosive and drug detection. A major strand of its work currently concerns the tracking of people and substances, which is applied in contexts as varied as primary schools and political party conferences (although perhaps the contrast is not so extreme, after all).

A particular strength of PSDB is ingenuity in choosing from a range of technologies to address particular problems in novel ways. For example, it addressed the problem of prison suicides by the development of a life signs monitoring system. This locates low-power microwave sensors in the cells of prisoners deemed at risk of suicide, and monitors movement. If all movement ceases (or presumably if there are periods of frenzied activity) prison officers are alerted. One project is noteworthy in that it takes criminological research showing that the probability of burglary is very high in the wake of prior burglary to design alarm technology which can be conveniently installed for short periods after a burglary (Griffiths *et al.* 1998; PSDB 2004c).

There is something very endearing about an outfit where people with PhDs in theoretical physics and expertise on black holes are working on tracking technologies. Their breadth of imagination is admirable and refreshing. However, PSDB work is instigated primarily by demands from the police service. The question inevitably presents itself as to whether there are modes of thought within science which would be applicable to crime reduction if they were brought to bear. Put another way, is there science support that police and local Crime and Disorder Partnerships would like to have but do not know that they could have?

To rehearse the argument so far, Home Office science strategy has, acknowledging some outliers particularly in the work of PSDB, concentrated on a limited number of topics, notably unique identifiability and telecommunications. There have been recent signs of a broader conception of science relevance, evident in both the Foresight Crime Panel recommendations and the Engineering and Physical Science Research Council's (EPSRC) initiative which flowed from that. In the next section, the EPSRC initiative will be outlined, together with the work of the Jill Dando Institute of Crime Science at University College London. Thereafter the idea of trickle down from military applications will be introduced. In the concluding section, the notion of discipline blind spots will be mooted, with some suggestions about how these might be eradicated.

The EPSRC initiative

Following the recommendation of the Foresight Crime Panel, the Engineering and Physical Science Research Council (EPSRC) launched its 'Think Crime' initiative on 1 November 2002.[11] Table 7.33 summarizes the general areas of projects funded in the first two rounds of the initiative, and it will be seen once more that projects addressing preventive (rather than forensic or offender tracking) technologies are in the minority. Projects within each of the categories are exciting in their own terms, including the first attempt at using nanotechnology to identify the presence of illicit substances and the development of an algorithm to aid classification of deaths as murder, suicide or accident.

None the less, the balance of work substantially reflects the activity suggested by the police science strategy document discussed earlier. The quality and commercial possibilities of the projects are substantial. Even though, in terms of general category, they tread well worn paths, they more than justify the

Table 7.3 Projects and networks funded in the first two rounds of the EPSRC crime initiative

	First round	Second round
Forensics	8	7
Surveillance/tracking	6	5
Preventive	3	3

initiative of EPSRC. Parallel initiatives by the other research councils would be welcome.[12]

Glass ceilings and crime science

The reader who has accepted the chapter's argument to this point will be persuaded that science enters the lists against crime primarily in the form of:

1. forensic analysis (wherein evidence is generated which uniquely identifies and locates an individual, object or substance); and

2. telecommunications (wherein relevant information is collected, stored, processed and analysed in ways which aid criminal justice).

There is an overlap between these areas (one may instance CCTV and vehicle tracking). Less developed in the public arena at least is science deployed in making the crime event less likely to occur. There are three questions which can be posed about this state of affairs, all of which imply 'glass ceilings' of different kinds. The glass ceiling is the concept coined to reflect invisible limits on achievement. The first question concerns whether there already exist science solutions which have not been commercially realized. The second is whether there is effort to prevent crime events which impact upon business or state security of a scale which makes science applied to crime reduction look relatively feeble. The third is whether the disciplines contributing to crime reduction are the 'natural' ones, or whether there are others which could make a contribution, which have not yet been considered.

One person's solution in another person's pocket

It seems clear to the point of self-evident that some useful crime-reductive products remain commercially unrealized. None of the winning entries to the annual Royal Society of Arts crime-reductive design competition has yet been taken up commercially. Many ingenious devices produced by students of the Royal St Martins School of Design remain without a commercial developer. The Stealthguard research team within BT in the late 1990s, which explored the development of location-aware electronic products, did not translate into commercial reality. The instances could be multiplied many times. The obstacles include the selling of products by association with criminal victimization, and the sometimes limited scale of anticipated demand. Discussion of tax and other inducements in the translation of science ideas into crime-reductive products seems urgently necessary.

If it matters to a nation or a business, science will be deployed to prevent it

During the first Gulf War, amongst the most arresting images were those of Cruise missiles lumbering above a street in Baghdad towards their target. With that image, the potential of global positioning system (GPS) became clear. Yet ten years later, this had not surfaced in the continuous tracking of tagged offenders. Multinational companies have emerged to address particular crime forms which are mission critical for companies and states. De La Rue, for example, is 'a global company employing over 6,600 people across 31 countries, is the world's largest commercial security printer and papermaker, involved in the production of over 150 national currencies and a wide range of security documents'.[13] The effort expended to control counterfeiting is immense because of its potential to compromise national economies. Conversations with those responsible for military aircraft and nuclear power stations make clear the sophistication of perimeter security in those contexts. Entering into the Google search engine the keywords 'Critical Infrastructure Assurance' yields 259,000 results, perhaps a record for a phrase not involving sex or popular culture. In brief, there is a shadowland of crime-reductive effort expended in national and commercial interests. Although difficult to be precise, there seems to be some trickle down of preventive technologies from such applications to the public domain, and this appears to be the result of personal contacts and spin-offs from military and commercial contracts. The fact of a dual standard can be instanced by reference by global positioning technologies. The levels of GPS performance the USA allows to civil agencies are fully documented (US Department of Defense 2001).

Respecting confidences makes this section difficult to write. Put succinctly, there is a range of security measures deployed in national and commercial interests. It would certainly be helpful if more attention could be paid to identifying techniques which are obsolete in military and commercial terms which would none the less offer an improvement on more generally available crime reduction technology. The first step in achieving this is recognizing it and creating a national government awareness of the issue. The present situation was expressed to the writer as follows: 'the transit of technology from more secure to less secure applications is most often controlled by those who currently use the technology.'

The disciplines which have traditionally contributed to an understanding of crime have been only a subset of those which could be brought to bear. This insight led to the establishment of the Jill Dando Institute for Crime Science at University College London (hereinafter JDI). Considering crime as being the result of the supply of opportunities and the demand for opportunities (otherwise thought of as criminal inclination, transient or enduring), the work of the institute has primarily centred upon the supply of opportunities, and its control.[14] However, its mission statement encompasses both: 'Our mission is to change crime policy and practice. The Institute plays a pivotal role in bringing together politicians, scientists, designers and those in the front line of fighting crime to examine patterns in crime, and to find practical methods to disrupt these patterns.' The work of JDI will be mentioned later in the attempted rapprochement of quantitative criminology and epidemiology.

As an article of faith, all science disciplines may contribute to the mission. This was put to the test in a simple way (see Giles 2003) when papers from diverse science research groups within University College London were submitted for identification of their crime relevance. These were deliberately challenging (for example one was about temperature variation in the Gulf Stream) but in the writer's view, plausible parallels were drawn in each case.

Ekblom (2004) also takes this as a starting point, seeking 'to alert, motivate and empower the wider science and engineering community to act as "scouts" in this task – to systematically "think crime"'. Ekblom's (2004) developments of his tests for crime risks and crime prevention opportunities are too extensive to be detailed here, but provide an elegant scout's handbook for those in the science and technology community wishing to accept his challenge.

For present purposes, two examples must suffice. The first is ecology, the second behaviour genetics (and its close relative evolutionary psychology). Ecology is interesting in that its central components are similar to the elements of Marcus Felson's depiction of crime, with motivated offender (predator), suitable victim (prey) and capable guardian (predator on predator) operating in a habitat where the balance of factors makes for ecological niches for crime. Shifts in crime rates can be conceptualized as co-evolutionary struggles. Ekblom (1999) brilliantly outlines some of the possible implications. He writes

> Crime prevention faces a perpetual struggle to keep up with changing opportunities for crime and adaptable offenders. To avoid obsolescence, it has to become adaptive itself. The task of keeping prevention up to date resembles other 'evolutionary struggles' such as biological co-evolution between predator and prey (eg continually sharper teeth versus continually tougher hide) (p. 27).

The specific lessons drawn by Ekblom *include* the following (the Ekblom piece should be read in the original for its dazzling variety of implications):

1. The incorporation into crime reduction of engineering principles from struggles in nature. One example is the use of predetermined fracture points (as in a lizard's detachable tail). This principle was (after Ekblom wrote) incorporated into one entry into the Royal Society of Arts annual student competition on designing out crime, where mobile phones were attached to one's belt or bag in such a way that, if snatched, the most valuable part of the phone, the chip, remained on the lanyard rather than was taken. A variant of the method comes with cases used to prevent loss in cash theft, where the act of detaching the case from its carrier sprays a permanent dye on the cash, rendering it worthless. Another example which postdates the Ekblom paper is the product 'Smokecloke'[15] which sprays non-toxic smoke into secure environments when under attack, as the squid sprays ink to thwart predators.

2. Threats should be perceived distally. It is, for example, contended that animals did not die in large numbers in the East Asian tsunami which claimed (according to the estimate at the time of writing) 200,000 human lives.[16] 'Sri Lankan wildlife officials have said the giant waves that killed over 24,000 people along the Indian Ocean island's coast seemingly missed wild beasts, with no dead animals found. "No elephants are dead, not even a dead hare or rabbit. I think animals can sense disaster. They have a sixth sense. They know when things are happening," H.D. Ratnayake, deputy director of Sri Lanka's Wildlife Department, said.' The implications here are for the development of remote-sensing technologies.

3. Things should be varied. Monoculture (whether of software, buildings or products) makes for vulnerability. The virtual ubiquity of the Microsoft Windows operating system makes its users prone to attack. This was instanced by one respondent in a survey of burglars who specialized in petrol stations, where uniformity of design relieved him of the responsibility for finding anew at each station where valuable goods were kept and how protected (see Ashton *et al.* 1998).

4. To be adaptable, things need to be simple. 'Phylogenetic constraint' occurs where an evolved system becomes so complicated that radical redesign is impossible (see Raup 1993).

Ecology has attracted other prevention-minded criminologists (see, for example, Eck and Weisburd 1995), but that interest has not to the writer's knowledge proceeded to the point where the algorithmic nature of evolution (see Dennett 1995; Morin 1999) is taken advantage of in modelling crime trends and types. An early sally in this direction might be to adapt some of the common evolution simulation software (such as *Evolution Lab*) to crime simulation purposes.[17]

The second science instanced is behaviour genetics. Its relevance to crime reduction may be primarily via the demand for opportunities route (see Walsh and Ellis 2003). In her admirable, unfashionable classic *The Nurture Assumption*, Judith Rich Harris (1998) contends that the contributions which parents make to their children's development primarily comprise their genes and where they decide to set up home. She points out that in the socialization literature, the effects of parenting styles are confounded with those of shared genes. She reviews the literature on the relationship between parent characteristics and child characteristics and demonstrates that either the same characteristics must have different and largely unpredictable effects on children, or that those influences are largely illusory. Is poor parenting a risk factor in a child's development, or do parents tending to (for example) impulsivity transmit that attribute through the conventional genetic means? Familial inheritance is always both the result of genetic endowment and environment, but environments are made, and are often correlated with the dispositions of those who inhabit them. The implications of Rich Harris's work are profound. They should be no surprise to those familiar with the earlier literature on criminality and biology (see, for example, Shah and Roth 1974; Mednick and Christiansen 1977). The latter authors demonstrated that criminality in the *biological* parent is reflected in a higher prevalence of criminality in the child, whatever the criminal record status of the *adoptive* parent. The importance of genetic factors is lent support by the work of Terrie Moffitt and her collaborators (see Moffitt 1993, 1997, 2003) whose distinction of adolescent-limited and life-course persistent offenders casts the latter as predisposed as a result of inherited and/or early acquired neuropsychological deficit. Of particular current interest is the gene variant MOAO which lowers the activity of the enzyme monoamine oxidase A and which seems implicated in violence. This relationship is stronger amongst maltreated children (see Caspi *et al.* 2002). Of course, reflecting Rich Harris's insights, it is not necessarily the case that maltreatment activates the propensity to violence. Equally plausible is the notion that MOAO and other as yet to be identified violence-relevant genes drive both parental violence (in the form of maltreatment) and child aggression. In path terms, the message is simply that one ignores at one's peril genetic or other early factors disposing to preferences. Equally, care in interpretation must be taken, given the saga of the XYY chromosome complement and its link to criminality (see Fox 1971).

Before leaving the notion of intrinsic path preferences, mention should be made of the work of Donohue and Leavitt (2000, 2003). They persuasively show rates of crime to be inversely related to earlier abortion rates, the time lag reflecting time to age of maximum criminality. The suggestion is thus that attributes (for example, of impulsivity) which yield unwanted pregnancies, possibly genetically shared with the resulting foetus, combined with parental styles reflecting both the same impulsivity which led to the pregnancy and possible resentment felt towards the resulting child, results in a greater likelihood of criminal involvement. The Leavitt and Donohue work does not disentangle the skein of causal routes. Still less does it argue for abortion rather than less troubling modes of fertility control. However, it does suggest that an unwanted pregnancy may be, for whatever reasons, a marker for future criminality. Any of the plausible causal routes would be closed off by the avoidance of such pregnancies. This way does not lie eugenics. Phenylketonuria is a disorder of genetic origin whose expression is controlled by environmental means.[18] What it must mean is that the deep-seated and understandable reluctance to admit genetic factors to a contributory role in the demand for criminal opportunities has to be put aside. The physiology of nutrition could also have been used to illustrate a neglected discipline. Whilst the current fad is for herbal tea in reducing prison violence[19] there is a much more substantial research literature linking diet and criminality which merits re-examination. (See Schoenthaler et al. (1997) for an example of a pristine double-blind trial demonstrating the efficacy of diet supplementation in reducing prison violence and anti-social behaviour.)

The final example of neglected science is presented with the most diffidence. It concerns evolutionary psychology. This is concerned with behaviours which can plausibly be regarded as adaptive, favouring the survival of one's own offspring (more relevantly one's own genes) over those of others. This has both obvious and more arcane forms of expression. Straightforwardly, it accounts for the much higher incidence of child abuse by carers who are not biologically related to the child victim, the ratio of 100:1 being mooted. Daly and Wilson's (1998) book The Truth about Cinderella makes the point fully and disarmingly (one would say entertainingly were the topic they treat not so painful).

The more subtle criminal pathway choices derive from the notion of discounting. Organisms discount the future when they value imminent goods over future goods. If you aren't going to be around tomorrow, you prefer even risky rewards today. Worker bees assume more dangerous foraging activities as their wings wear and in response to life-truncating infection (Woyciechowski and Kozlowski 1998). The notion that offenders find deferral of gratification difficult has a very long history (see, for example, Herrnstein's (1983) review). The phenomenon is now known as time discounting. Wilson and Daly

(1997), noting that the poor, the young and the criminal discount the future steeply, contend that is what we should expect, being a rational response to information indicating a diminished probability of survival or other obstacles to reproductive success. Risk-taking is rational when the expected benefits of safer courses of action are negligible. Thus early and aggressive sexual behaviour is linked with time discounting.

Readers with long memories will recall that this section is about the second of two 'glass ceilings' which seek to illustrate that there is a range of science contributions which are not currently being mainstreamed in the crime reduction enterprise. If the reader has gone along with the argument to this point, he or she will accept that crime reduction would be well served by facilitating trickle down of military and commercial applications, and by having recourse to a wider range of science disciplines.

The farmer and the cowhand should be friends?

In the musical *Oklahoma!*, harmony between those making different uses of the same land is invoked in the rousing song of that title. In this last section of the chapter, the advantages which accrue from collaboration between the hard sciences and criminology will be sampled. This has already been instanced by the development of intruder alarms suitable for temporary deployment after burglary (Griffiths *et al.* 1998; PSDB 2004c). This is done by providing brief accounts of two projects which illustrate the benefits to be gained.

There now exists a method of anticipating the distribution of local crime in the short term. Hotspotting is close to ubiquitous in the work of police analysts, but all extant methods are essentially retrospective, using the historical pattern of crime as the benchmark. The method of prospective mapping significantly outperforms the most sophisticated historical method available. This method is currently under trial in the English East Midlands region. It is not a finished product, being capable of refinement in terms of calculation and optimizing police patrol patterns in the light of the information it conveys. However, it is an exciting innovation. Its discipline origins should be explained. Traditional quantitative criminology established that a recently victimized home or person was more likely to suffer repetition of the crime in the short term (see Farrell and Pease 2001). Application of techniques from epidemiology developed to study contagious disease showed that risk of victimization spread spatially (Townsley *et al.* 2000; Townsley 2001). Putting these data together allowed the calculation of risk surfaces (Bowers and Johnson 2004). In short, it allowed the use of the crime event's predictive power. Incorporating this with mapping expertise yielded the technique under discussion (Bowers *et al.* 2004). Thus the technique is a result of a marriage of geography, epidemiology and criminology.

The second direction of work concerns a consideration of how DNA and fingerprints might be used in a novel way. Historically the informing spirit of these techniques is the striving for unique identification of individuals. As this chapter has sought to show, unique identifiability remains a goal of much police science strategy. However, that is not the only way of thinking about

DNA and allied technologies. Indeed, the notion that a day will dawn where all active offenders are to be found on the DNA database is naïve. This is because of the high churn rate in active offending, with many offenders desisting, and many neophytes starting a criminal career. At a rough guess, no more than two thirds of active offenders will be found on the database, and no more than two thirds of those on the database will be active offenders. A different way of thinking about these technologies is in terms of restriction of the suspect pool. This approach is already employed in the investigation of major crime (see Wilson *et al.* 2003 for the relevant statistics). Criminologists will be familiar with the Farrington and Lambert (2000) approach to offender profiling. They identify those personal characteristics of offenders about which witnesses are least often mistaken, and show that small suspect pools result if the presenting combination of such attributes in witness statements is considered. This approach can be equally applied to genetic markers. Thus, one can tell something about the phenotype from appropriately directed genetic assay. Put simply, one call tell something about how someone looks from particular genetic markers. For common characteristics, this can be done with accuracy for eye colour and skin tone/ethnicity, with hair colour also being the subject of research (McDonald and Foy 2004).[20] This work could reasonably be put alongside other work on pathologies, so that (for example) rare tooth anomalies (Tabata 1998) or shortness of stature (Mullis *et al.* 1991) could be candidates for inclusion. Considering enough rare pathologies should in principle allow a huge reduction in uncertainty, it would of course not matter for this approach whether the person concerned was on the national DNA database. A similar logic applies for partial fingerprints. Combining witness statements with DNA assay and other sources of evidence extends the scope of the Farrington and Lambert perspective on offender profiling.

Endnote

The message of these two projects, along with others, sounds hackneyed. It is that the insights afforded by considering the contributing disciplines, and combining them in institutions and research groups which contain diverse crime-relevant expertise, are valuable and potentially of enormous practical importance. The broadening of the police science strategy, the work of the Foresight group and the initiatives which it (or the Zeitgeist) spawned is welcome and represents movement in the desired direction. However, everywhere silos are strong. That, after all, is why silos are used to contain things. Watching the Jill Dando Institute and the Home Office struggling against silo organization of science disciplines makes their strength clear. The ESPRC Ideas Factory,[21] the Jill Dando Institute and other silo-averse enterprises should be strengthened. Other research councils should follow the ESPRC lead. Exchange arrangements between scientists with crime-relevant expertise should be multiplied. The Exchequer should consider fiscal means of facilitating the bringing to market of science-inspired crime-reductive products. The European Commission could, along with its more arcane crime-funding initiatives, develop the pan-science vision. Even if the cowhand and the farmer don't get along, the forensic entomologist (see Catts and Goff 1992) and the criminologist should try.

Acknowledgements

I'm grateful to Michael Horner, Head of the Home Office Science Secretariat, and to Paul Wiles, Chief Scientific Adviser to the Home Office, for valuable comments and suggestions on an earlier draft of this chapter.

Selected further reading

Melissa Smith and Nick Tilley's book of readings, *Crime Science: New Approaches to Preventing and Detecting Crime* (2004), shows how researchers at the Jill Dando Institute, mostly social scientists, are striving to integrate science effort for the purposes of crime reduction. This could profitably be read alongside Joe Nickell and John F. Fischer's book, *Crime Science: Methods of Forensic Detection* (1999), which provides a traditional, detection-oriented view of crime science. Paul Ekblom's (1999) lengthy piece characterizing offending and its prevention as an evolutionary struggle (*Studies in Crime Prevention 8*) provides an illustration of a conceptual carry-over from zoology to criminology. Integrative attempts are increasing in number and sophistication. Amongst the websites on which such material is likely to appear are those of the Jill Dando Institute (www.jdi.ucl.ac.uk), the Engineering and Physical Science Research Council (www.epsrc.ac.uk/) and the Home Office's Police Scientific Development Branch (www.homeoffice.gov.uk/crimpol/police/scidev). When the PSDB changes its name, searchers on that site will be redirected appropriately.

Notes

1. In the weeks before writing this, these aims were complemented and will in due course be replaced by 'objectives', of which the overarching crime-related one is to ensure that 'people are and feel more secure in their homes and daily lives'.
2. http://www.homeoffice.gov.uk/inside/aims/index.html, accessed 20 January 2005.
3. It is of interest that local authorities are mentioned as such, and that local Crime and Disorder Reduction Partnerships remain invisible. Furthermore, the local authority links to the police are mediated through the police authority, which is foreign to the spirit of the Crime and Disorder Act 1998.
4. In passing, the relevance of detection to the prevention of the (next) crime is acknowledged. Indeed the writer has elsewhere argued that instead of the traditional duality of crime prevention and detection, there is really only one, prevention, to be achieved by deflection or detection (Pease 2001).
5. By asserting that moderate access makes for stealability, the writer is more dogmatic than Felson. Rare objects have limited saleability by the thief, and universally owned items are not worth stealing.
6. See David and Sakurai (2003) for a discussion of the sub-problem of cyber-terrorism.

7. See the website of the Information Assurance Advisory Council which 'addresses the challenges of information infrastructure protection' (http://www.iaac.org.uk/, accessed 31 January 2005).
8. http://www.nhtcu.org/ (accessed 31 January 2005).
9. Or as being an early indication of a Zeitgeist which spawned these develop-ments.
10. See the Association for Payment Clearing Services (APACS) at http://www.apacs.org.uk (accessed 31 January 2005).
11. http://www.epsrc.ac.uk/default.htm (accessed 27 January 2005).
12. An interesting marginal activity of EPSRC is its 'Ideas Factory', which is 'designed to combine new ways of generating research directions with new approaches to peer review'.
13. http://www.delarue.com/ (accessed 28 January 2005).
14. http://www.jdi.ucl.ac.uk/ (accessed 28 January 2005).
15. http://www.smokecloak.com/general/msshistory.asp (accessed 28 January 2005).
16. http://www.cnn.com/2004/TECH/science/12/30/quake.animals.reut/ (accessed 28 January 2005).
17. http://www.biologyinmotion.com/evol/ (accessed 29 January 2005).
18. http://www.geneclinics.org/profiles/pku/ (accessed 29 January 2005).
19. http://www.ukcjweblog.org.uk/2005/01/26.html#a1942 (accessed 29 January 2005).
20. This work resulted from discussion at the Foresight Crime Panel.
21. http://www.epsrc.ac.uk/ResearchFunding/Programmes/Cross-EPSRCActivities/IDEASFactory/default.htm (accessed 30 January 2005).

References

Armitage, R. (2000) *An Evaluation of Secured by Design Housing in West Yorkshire. Briefing Note 7/00.* London: Home Office.

Ashton, J., Senior, B., Brown, I. and Pease, K. (1998) 'Repeat victimisation: offender accounts', *International Journal of Risk, Security and Crime Prevention*, 3: 269–80.

Bowers, K.D. and Johnson, S.J. (2004) 'Domestic burglary repeats and space-time clusters: the dimensions of risk', *European Journal of Criminology*, 2: 67–92.

Bowers, K.J., Johnson, S.J. and Pease, K. (2004) 'Prospective hot-spotting: the future of crime mapping?' *British Journal of Criminology*, 36: 1–18.

Caspi, A., McClay, J., Moffitt, T.E., Mill, J., Martin, J., Craig, I., Taylor, A. and Poulton, R. (2002) 'Evidence that the cycle of violence in maltreated children depends on genotype.' *Science*, 297: 851–4.

Catts, E.P. and Goff, M.L. (1992) 'Forensic entomology in criminal investigations', *Annual Review of Entomology*, 37: 253–72.

Cochrane, P. (1998) *108 Tips for Time Travellers.* London: Orion.

Cornish D. and Clarke R.V. (eds) (1986) *The Reasoning Criminal.* New York: Springer-Verlag.

Daly, M. and Wilson, M. (1998) *The Truth about Cinderella: A Darwinian View of Parental Love.* London: Weidenfeld & Nicolson.

David, M.W. and Sakurai, K. (2003) 'Cyber-terrorism in context', *Computer Security*, 22: 188–92.

Dennett, D. (1995) *Darwin's Dangerous Idea: Evolution and the Meanings of Life.* Harmondsworth: Penguin Books.

Donohue, J.J. and Leavitt, S.D. (2000) *The Impact of Legalised Abortion on Crime. NBER Working Paper* 8004. Cambridge, MA: National Bureau of Economic Research.

Donohue, J.J. and Leavitt, S.D. (2003) *Further Evidence that Legalised Abortion Lowered Crime: A Reply to Joyce. NBER Working Paper* 8004. Cambridge, MA: National Bureau of Economic Research.

DTI Foresight Crime Prevention Panel (2000a) *Just Around the Corner*. London: DTI.

DTI Foresight Crime Prevention Panel (2000b) *Turning the Corner*. London: DTI.

Eck, J. and Weisburd, D. (1995) *Crime and Place*. Monsey, NY: Criminal Justice Press.

Ekblom, P. (1999) 'Can we make crime prevention adaptive by learning from other evolutionary struggles?', *Studies in Crime Prevention. Vol. 8*. Stockholm: National Council for Crime Prevention.

Ekblom, P. (2004). 'How to police the future: scanning for scientific and technological innovations which generate potential threats and opportunities in crime, policing and crime reduction', in M. Smith and N. Tilley (eds) *Crime Science: New Approaches to Preventing and Detecting Crime*. Cullompton: Willan Publishing.

Farrell, G. and Pease, K. (2001) *Repeat Victimisation*. Monsey, NY: Criminal Justice Press.

Farrington, D.P. and Lambert, S. (2000) 'Statistical approaches to offender profiling', in D. Canter and L.J. Alison (eds) *Profiling Property Crimes*. Abingdon: Ashgate.

Felson, M. (1998) *Crime and Everyday Life* (2nd edn.) Thousand Oaks, CA: Pine Forge Press.

Field, S. (1990) *Trends in Crime and their Interpretation: A Study of Recorded Crime in Post-war England and Wales. Home Office Research Study* 119. London: HMSO.

Fox, R.G. (1971) 'The XYY offender: a modern myth', *Journal of Criminal Law, Criminology and Police Science*, 62: 59–73.

Future Times (1998) 'Bethesda: world future society', Summer.

Futurist (1998) 'Bethesda: world future society', June–July.

Giles, J. (2003) 'The lab arm of the law', *Nature*, 422: 13–14.

Griffiths, A., Head, L. and Todd, I. (1998) *Using Alarm Technology to Tackle Repeat Victimisation: An Operational Requirement. PSDB Publication* 26/04. Sandridge: Home Office.

Herrnstein, R.J. (1983) 'Some criminogenic traits of offenders', in J.Q. Wilson (ed.) *Crime and Public Policy*. San Francisco, CA: Institute for Contemporary Studies.

Home Office Science Policy Unit (2003) *Police Science Policy 2003–2008*. London: Home Office.

Home Office Science Policy Unit (2004) *Police Science Policy 2004–2009*. London: Home Office.

Mann, D. and Sutton, M. (1998) '>>Netcrime', *British Journal of Criminology*, 38: 201–229.

McDonald, P. and Foy, C. (2004) *Potential Genetic Markers for the Identification of Forensically Useful Morphological Traits*. London: Police Foundation.

Mednick, S.A. and Christiansen, K.O. (eds) (1977) *Biosocial Bases of Criminal Behaviour*. New York: Gardner Press.

Moffitt, T.E. (1993) 'Adolescence-limited and life-course-persistent antisocial-behavior – a developmental taxonomy', *Psychological Review*, 100: 674–701.

Moffitt, T.E. (1997) 'Adolescent-limited and life-course persistent offending: a complementary pair of developmental theories', in T. Thornberry (ed.) *Developmental Theories of Crime and Delinquency. Advances in Criminological Theory*. New Brunswick, NJ: Transaction Books.

Moffitt T.E. (2003) 'Life-course-persistent and adolescent-limited antisocial behavior', in B.B. Lahey *et al.* (eds) *Causes of Conduct Disorder and Juvenile Delinquency*. New York, NY: Guilford Press.

Moore S. (ed.) (1996) *The Fortean Times Book of Inept Crime*. London: John Brown.

Morin, P.J. (1999) *Community Ecology*. Oxford: Blackwell Science.

Moss, K. (2005) 'Crime prevention and law: rhetoric or reality?', in K. Moss and M. Stephens (eds) *Crime Prevention and the Law*. London: Routledge.

Mullis, P.E., Patel, M.S., Brickell, P.M. and Brook, C.G. (1991) 'Constitionally short stature: analysis of the insulin-like growth factor-I gene and the human growth hormone gene cluster', *Paediatrics Research*, 29: 412–15.

Muraskin, R. and Roberts, A.R. (1996) *Visions for Change: Crime and Justice in the Twenty-first Century*. New York, NY: Prentice Hall.

Nickell, J. and Fischer, J.F. (1999) *Crime Science: Methods of Forensic Detection*. Lexington, KY: University of Kentucky Press.

Olander, J.D. and Greenfield, H. (1977) *Criminal Justice through Science Fiction*. New York, NY: Franklin-Watts.

Pease, K. (2001) 'Crime reduction', in M. Maguire *et al.* (eds) *The Oxford Handbook of Criminology*. Oxford: Clarendon Press.

Phillips, D. (1977) *Crime and Authority in Victorian England: The Black Country 1835–60*. London: Croom Helm.

PSDB (2004a) *PSDB Business Plan 2004/5. PSDB Publication 26/04*. Sandridge: Home Office.

PSDB (2004b) *PSDB: An Introduction. PSDB Publication 60/04*. Sandridge: Home Office.

PSDB (2004c) *Police Radio Alarms for Crime Reduction and Repeat Burglary. PSDB Publication 60/04*. Sandridge: Home Office.

Raup, D. (1993) *Extinction: Bad Genes or Bad Luck?*. Oxford: Oxford University Press.

Rich Harris, J. (1998) *The Nurture Assumption*. London: Bloomsbury.

Rogerson, M., Ekblom, P and Pease, K. (2000) 'Crime reduction and the benefit of foresight', in S. Ballintyne *et al.* (eds) *Secure Foundations: Key Issues in Crime Prevention, Crime Reduction and Community Safety*. London: IPPR.

Schneider, J. (2005) 'Hiding in plain sight: an exploration of the illegal (?) activities of a drugs newsgroup', *The Howard Journal of Criminal Justice*, 42: 374–89.

Schoenthaler, S., Amos, W., Doraz, M.-A., Nelly, G. and Wakefield, J. (1997) 'The effect of randomized vitamin-mineral supplementation on violent and non-violent antisocial behaviour among incarcerated juveniles', *Journal of Nutritional and Environmental Medicine*, 7: 343–52.

Shah, S.A. and Roth, L.H. (1974) 'Biological and psychophysiological factors in criminality', in D. Glaser (ed.) *Handbook of Criminology*. New York, NY: Rand McNally.

Smith, M. and Tilley, N. (2004) *Crime Science: New Approaches to Preventing and Detecting Crime*. Cullompton: Willan Publishing.

Tabata, K.K. (1998) 'Hereditary diseases with tooth anomalies and their causal genes', *Kaibogaku Zasshi*, 73: 201–8 (article in Japanese, abstract at http://www.ncbi.nlm.nih.gov/entrez/query.fcgi?cmd=Retrieve&db=PubMed&list_uids=9711025&dopt=Citation).

Townsley, M.T. (2001) 'Statistical modelling of crime hot spots and repeat victimisation distributions.' Unpublished PhD thesis, Griffith University, Brisbane.

Townsley, M., Homel, R. and Chaseling, J. (2000) 'Repeat burglary victimisation: spatial and temporal patterns', *Australian and New Zealand Journal of Criminology*, 33: 37–63.

US Department of Defense (2001) *Global Positioning System Standard Positioning Service Performance Standard*. Washington, DC: Department of Defense.

Walsh, A. and Ellis, L. (eds) (2003) *Biosocial Criminology*. New York, NY: Nova.

Wilkins, L.T. (1973) 'Crime and criminal justice at the turn of the century', *Annals of the American Academy of Political and Social Science*, 408: 13–29.

Wilson, I.J., Weale, M.E. and Balding, D.J. (2003) 'Inferences from DNA data: population histories, evolutionary processes and forensic match probabilities', *Journal of the Royal Statistical Society: Series A (Statistics in Society)*, 166: 155–88.

Wilson, M. and Daly, M. (1997) 'Life expectancy, economic inequality, homicide, and reproductive timing in Chicago neighbourhoods', *British Medical Journal*, 314: 1271.

Woyciechowski, M. and Kozlowski, J. (1998) 'Division of labour by division of risk according to worker life expectancy in the honeybee (*Apis mellifera* L)', *Apidologie*, 29: 191–205.

Part III

Means of Preventing Crime

Nick Tilley

Whilst the chapters in Part II of this volume were concerned with some very broad approaches to crime control, Part III focuses more specifically on families of tactics that can be used to pre-empt or reduce crime problems. The first three chapters in Part III (Chapters 8, 9 and 10) each consider ways in which crime might be designed out.

Paul Ekblom has been attached to the Home Office research department, with a major interest in crime prevention and reduction, since the late 1970s. His CCO (conjunction of criminal opportunity) and related 5Is (intelligence, intervention, implementation, involvement and impact) attempt to provide a framework for describing and capturing the full range of forms of preventive intervention. This work has been highly influential. Ekblom has also pioneered understanding of the 'arms race' in crime, as preventers and offenders adapt to one another in moves and countermoves respectively to inhibit and achieve the successful commission of crimes. Drawing on these ideas and a long history of research on product design and crime going back to a 1985 paper on designing crime out of cars (Southall and Ekblom 1985), in Chapter 8 Ekblom lays out both some general principles of and processes in designing against crime, and some specific ideas about the role of product design in the generation and control of particular crime problems. He points out the potential of design in preventing crime, as well as 'troublesome trade-offs' that often have to be made between this and other considerations that go into product design.

In Chapter 9, Henry Shaftoe and Tim Read, both long experienced in research on crime prevention and reduction using a variety of approaches, take a sceptical look at the potential for reducing crime through environmental design. Though acknowledging that some planned environments may have had criminogenic side-effects, like Ekblom they note that environmental design needs to meet a range of objectives of which reducing or minimizing crime opportunities is but one. They are concerned that some types of environmental design to control crime may operate through the exclusion of some classes of person. They are highly critical of environmental determinism – the notion that behaviour simply and mechanically reflects the way the physical environment is laid out. Some areas with environmental designs not conducive to crime have high crime levels, they tell us, and some with environmental designs that are conducive to crime have low levels. This leads Shaftoe and Read to remind us that social and demographic factors are important in the development of areas of high crime. They argue that community consultation and involvement are crucial in creating liveable environments meeting human needs including those for safety and security.

Most of the literature on design and crime has focused on products and places, the subjects of Chapters 8 and 9. Nick Tilley is a sociologist and in view of this it is unsurprising that his interest in design and crime relates instead to social systems and social processes, and their unintended crime consequences. In Chapter 10, Tilley discusses a range of ways in which patterned and intentional (systemic) human behaviour can produce crime consequences that are not anticipated by those involved in them. He also considers, with examples, ways in which it has been possible to (re)design systems in ways that reduce or prevent crime. As with Ekblom's discussion of products and Shaftoe and Read's of the physical environment, he acknowledges that system designs often have to meet a range of needs and that crime minimization may need to be balanced with other factors.

Mike Sutton has pioneered the study of differing stolen goods markets and the scope there might be for reducing crime by making more difficult the conversion of stolen items into utilities wanted by the thief. Attempting to reduce property crime by focusing on stolen goods markets is termed the 'market reduction approach' (MRA). Since Sutton's first study published in 1993, there has been growing interest in the MRA. In Chapter 11, Sutton reviews the opportunities to intervene, and the experience of evaluated efforts to apply the MRA. He discusses the legislation relating to the receipt of stolen property, and the problems there are in applying it in practice. He highlights the routine complicity between consumer and seller of stolen goods, both of whom benefit from the transaction. He unpicks details of the ways in which stolen goods markets operate. Drawing on the literature of situational crime prevention, he discusses the mechanisms through which a range of methods of reducing the market in stolen goods might lead to falls in property crime. Finally, he acknowledges the practical difficulties that have been encountered so far in effectively implementing the theory behind the MRA approach.

Martin Gill has a long-term interest in security. He has also conducted various studies of offenders as well as victims and their experiences of crime. In Chapter 12 he indicates what can be learnt by looking at how offenders commit crimes and in particular what can be learnt about this for preventive purposes. Whilst many may wish to commit offences of various kinds they may be inhibited for lack of the wherewithal to follow through on their dispositions. Contrariwise, motivated offenders may be enabled with ready access to the means needed. Gill catalogues the sorts of resources needed for the commission of crimes. He also discusses various ways in which we can come better to understand how offenders commit crime and the resources they depend on. This is ground-breaking work. Rather little has been done so far in examining systematically the scope for crime prevention by undermining access to the resources needed to commit crime. Yet it may in future hold much promise, since opportunity is a function both of the situation facing the potential offender and the capacity of the offender to use that opportunity or to overcome obstacles laid in his or her path.

Publicity has been widely used in efforts to reduce crime. This has surface plausibility, not least because the ways in which we define situations is consequential for our behaviour, and publicity offers a means for trying to influence the ways in which potential victims, offenders and guardians define risks, responsibilities and opportunities for crime and crime control. Kate Bowers and Shane Johnson, who across a range of studies relating for instance to displacement, diffusion of benefits and near repeats, are emerging as major researchers in crime reduction and crime prevention. In Chapter 13 they provide an overview of types of publicity, categories of audience and mechanisms of influence. They also review the evidence relating to the effects of publicity of varying types. They note some of the studies which have shown the potential for publicity to impact significantly on likely offender behaviour. They pay attention to the ways in which the effects of crime prevention measures can be stretched temporally beyond their operational period by judicious use of publicity to produce anticipatory effects, a particular form of diffusion of benefits. They also note some of the potential risks of ill-judged publicity as well as the benefits that can be gained from publicity that is well designed.

Because of the ubiquitous over-representation of youth as offenders, efforts to deal with those who offend or are at risk of offending are a common part of the crime prevention and crime reduction diet. In Chapter 14, Tim Newbum, who has over a period of years conducted substantial research relating to youth offending, and Anna Souhami summarize what is known about youth diversion efforts. They show the different emphases on diversion at different periods. In the 1980s there was a broad consensus that diversion from the criminal justice system was desirable, on the basis that drawing young people into it was criminogenic. Doing little or nothing was assumed to be preferable to doing harm by labelling people delinquent. It was thought better to delay as long as possible formal entry into the criminal justice system with a variety of alternative ways of dealing with those who were found to have offended. This view had changed by the mid-1990s. A new era ushered in targeted formal interventions relating to offenders and those at risk of offending. Newburn and Souhami paint a rather bleak picture of what has been achieved. They find rather few rigorous evaluation studies and suggest that such robust evidence as there is rarely shows consistent, significant preventive effects from the types of measure applied. The most promising approaches, they conclude, include some restorative justice, cognitive and community-based mentoring programmes, though they also speculate that a return to minimal intervention for first-time and less serious offenders might make sense.

The last chapter in Part III differs in focus from the earlier ones. It relates less to interventions that might reduce crime than to interventions that might be made to persuade third parties who are in a position to intervene to reduce crime, that they should do so. Michael Scott has been a leading figure in the USA facilitating the effective implementation of problem-oriented policing. Once a student of Herman Goldstein, who founded problem-oriented policing, then a police chief, and now a faculty member at the University of Wisconsin–

Madison, Scott in Chapter 15 reviews ways in which the police can engage agencies able to reduce crime so that they should do so. He draws heavily on a framework devised by Goldstein to present a series of examples, drawn from both the USA and Britain, showing how the police have succeeded in applying levers to those whose actions were deemed necessary in order that particular local crime and disorder problems could be removed or ameliorated. This approach is rooted in recognition that there is generally little that the police can do directly or alone to deal effectively and in a sustainable manner with crime problems. They can, though, help define problems, work out what might be done and by whom, and mobilize others to act differently in ways likely to reduce crime.

Reference

Southall, D. and Ekblom, P. (1985) *Designing for Car Security: Towards a Crime Free Car. Crime Prevention Unit Paper* 4. London: Home Office.

Chapter 8

Designing products against crime

Paul Ekblom

Introduction

Design against crime (DAC) uses the processes and products of design to reduce crime and promote community safety. As will be seen, the focus in this chapter is specifically on the design of 'movable' products as opposed to places, systems and messages, although, in so doing, many general issues are covered. The aim is less to review in detail the range of product design, to cover implementation issues in much depth or to assess the limited hard evidence of impact and cost-effectiveness, and more to communicate designers' ways of thinking and acting to researchers and practitioners of crime prevention. In earlier papers I have urged designers to *think thief* about their products (Ekblom 1995, 1997). Here, the emphasis is more on encouraging crime preventers to *draw on design*, both practically and conceptually. Mapping out the nature and diversity of design is important, too, because preventers have a range of assumptions about what it means.

The obvious relationship between DAC and situational crime prevention means that much that can be said about the latter will not be restated here (see Chapter 3, this volume). Instead, the chapter will focus in turn on defining and cross-linking terms and concepts in both crime and design; identifying what is distinctive about design; examining design processes; discussing replication and adaptation; and looking at cyclical processes in the life of designs, including 'arms races' with offenders. The chapter is able to draw on a range of 'first generation' reports and publications derived from DAC work funded from, and stimulated by, the UK government's recent Crime Reduction Programme and, to a lesser extent, the UK Foresight programme's Crime Prevention Panel.[1] Since the DAC field is rapidly evolving in terms of products, concepts and processes, the ideas set out here will not be the last word – rather, a contribution to that evolution. Indeed, a 'futures'-oriented approach to the topic informs the whole chapter.

The format of this book (and the tradition of criminological publications in general) places limits on illustrations. This is a serious constraint on communication of design ideas, as Gamman and Pascoe (2004b) note, and attempt to remedy. Some of the concepts and examples presented here are, though, illustrated in several websites.[2]

Defining crime, prevention and design

Crime (and disorder) itself is, of course, extremely varied in nature, methods, offenders, targets and consequences, as the examples throughout this chapter illustrate. But design against crime is relevant to all: instrumental versus expressive or ideological; stealthy versus confrontational and perhaps violent; organized or individualistic; and professional versus opportunist.

Crime reduction is, simply, any activity to decrease the frequency and/or seriousness of criminal and related events. Mostly this is delivered by crime *prevention* – intervening in the causes of crime and disorder events to reduce the risk of their occurrence and the potential seriousness of their consequences. Prevention (or reduction) can be done in two broad contexts. *Enforcement/ judicial prevention* acts, as implied, through police detection and investigation and the criminal justice and penal systems. Although triggered in response to past crimes, it is intended to make future ones less likely – a function distinct from retrospective *justice per se. Civil prevention* acts through changes in everyday life. Enforcement/judicial prevention focuses on individual and occasionally corporate offenders; civil prevention covers both offender-oriented and situational interventions, acting at a range of ecological levels from individual victim, offender or place to family, peer groups, institutions and communities.

Causal frameworks

The causes intervened in can be simple or complex, remote (such as early childhood experiences or the market price for vehicle spares) or immediate. The latter are easier to capture and map out in a uniform framework. Familiar frameworks include the Routine Activities Theory of Cohen and Felson (1979), covering likely offender, suitable target and absence of capable guardians; the rational offender approach (Cornish and Clarke 1986) focusing on the offender's decision agenda of perceived risk, effort, reward and guilt; Wortley's (2001) additions of provocation and other forms of 'precipitation';[3] and various kinds of environmental criminology – for example, the 'crime generators and crime attractors' approach of Brantingham and Brantingham (1995). The Conjunction of Criminal Opportunity (CCO) (Ekblom 2000, 2001a) will be used here to bring together the above approaches,[4] and more. This is because it goes into greater detail on each cause (*'why* is the target suitable?'), and offers a more differentiated picture of the offender than someone who is merely 'likely' or 'rational'. It thus provides an integrated framework to describe how factors in the crime situation come together with those associated with the offender to generate criminal events, catering, too, for both civil and enforcement/ judicial prevention. The result is a map of 11, generic, immediate causes of criminal events and 11 corresponding families of intervention principle aimed at blocking those causes.

Criminal events and their prevention are relatively narrow concepts and aims. *Community safety*, in contrast, has been defined in terms of the quality of life, a state of existence centring on people's individual and collective freedom from certain real or perceived hazards, their ability to cope with those that remain and their consequent ability to get on with life's social and economic necessities and pleasures. Delivering community safety obviously depends on reducing crime, but beyond this includes actions specifically aimed at intervening in the additional causes of fear (such as lighting levels), or mitigating the wider consequences of crime such as reduced enjoyment of local amenities.[5]

Design: scope and nature

The phrase 'design against crime' or equivalents such as 'designing out crime' have been in common currency in the crime prevention field since at least the publication of Poyner's book in 1983, initially covering architecture and environmental layout ('Crime Prevention Through Environmental Design', initiated by Jeffery 1977) and, more recently, embracing products and systems. But the full scope of *design* is enormous, potentially embracing all human productive and artistic activity in every material and immaterial medium. Focusing here on the applied rather than artistic side, design is a generic *process* of creating some new or improved product which 1) is materially possible to make (e.g. it does not fall apart, obeys the laws of science and respects the behaviour of its constituent materials); 2) is fit, or fitter than predecessors, for some specified primary purpose; and 3) does not significantly interfere with other purposes or with wider requirements of social and economic life and the environment, including in cost terms (adapted from Booch 1993). Under this broad definition there is much variety amongst processes or approaches to design. At one end of the scale, say, we could envisage someone hastily stripping a branch of leaves to fashion an impromptu defensive weapon; at the other, a complex and sophisticated vehicle immobilizer system developed over several years by several large professional teams whose work has to be integrated by explicit managerial processes. Links with *problem-solving* and a focus on *abusers* as well as *users* are obvious and will be discussed below.

The *purpose* of the designed product can vary from entirely utilitarian to aesthetic and the conveyance, for the owner, of image, lifestyle and value (see Cooper and Press (1995) for a comprehensive discussion of these definitional and functional issues). Playful and subversive designs are also possible.[6] The classic principle of 'form following function' can at times be supplanted by 'form following emotion'.

Certainly, which of these principles a given product emphasizes increasingly becomes a matter of designers' choice rather than engineering constraint. New materials continually emerge and blend with in-board electronics and actuators to detach form from function unless deliberately intended (as with retro-styled radios).

Process is discussed in more detail below; its outcome is *a* design. The noun has two interpretations. A design can mean some form of stored information – concept, blueprint, plan or 'genotype' (in biological terms – Ekblom 2002a) for *replicating* and defining real-world products. More loosely speaking it can be the tangible, manufactured *end product* itself (or 'phenotype') which realizes the blueprint. Some designs are replicated industrially, on a mass scale and in high-fidelity detail, as discussed below; but at the opposite extreme, other designs are realized as a single instance, such as an individual building or landscape.

Designed products (and corresponding fields of professional competence) encompass:

- places, buildings and environments (both exteriors and interiors – see Press *et al.* 2001);

- electronic, procedural and organizational systems (see Chapter 10, this volume);[7]

- the 'two-dimensional' material of fabrics, banknotes and messages, such as posters; and

- solid 'three-dimensional' objects (although the boundary between the last two is increasingly blurred, with interactive website graphics, packaging and labels, fashion clothing bearing messages or, soon, 'wearable' IT, and graphical interfaces on items like music players).

Problem-solving processes and end products are not the only foci of design. Alternatives include the engineering approach, centring on how to exploit new technology (such as radio-frequency ID chips or new materials like kevlar) and user-centred approaches such as helping the elderly to avoid certain crime risks.

Given this wide understanding, *any* intervention in the causes of criminal events (or of feelings of insecurity) can, in principle, be improved by explicit and professional attention to design; conversely, any design which neglects crime prevention or poorly attempts it can be criminogenic. DAC's contribution to crime reduction, prevention and community safety can equally serve enforcement/justice and civil prevention, act at any of the ecological levels of intervention, realize and refine any of the 25 techniques of situational prevention (Clarke and Eck 2003), and more broadly, act through any of the 11 generic families of intervention of the CCO. Wootton and Davey (2003) extend CCO to provide a 'life-cycle' approach to DAC, as part of a programme of professional support for designers, which explicitly includes both post-crime *enforcement* issues such as design of products or places to capture fingerprints, and mitigation of the *consequences* of crime.

DAC can thus have a variable 'preventive scope', from making an individual item (or place) crime resistant, to stopping a wider set of future crimes. Thus it can deter or discourage people from stealing a given class/make/model of object (e.g. because they now know it is effectively property marked or becomes useless when stolen because of a dye-release fixture); or contribute to making them give up crime altogether because it no longer offers a niche or career where risk, effort and reward are acceptably balanced against the resources they have available to manage or exploit them.

Good design from a DAC perspective can make a better forensic field-kit, courtroom, prison, teaching pack for literacy (i.e. supplying criminals with resources to avoid offending), body armour for police, computerized criminal record system or burglar alarm; a less criminogenic shopping mall, car or mobile phone; a youth shelter that diverts young people from crime situations and legitimately satisfies their motivation for somewhere to gather and entertain themselves whilst being resistant to mistreatment and misuse; a market resistant to the resale of stolen goods; a less fear-inducing car park; a chemical which changes colour in swimming pools to shame those for whom 'P is silent as in bathing'; a street that feels safe to walk down at night, thanks to products and landscapes which effectively favour legitimate activities; and an intelligently put-together set of laws and regulations which, say, control corruption in the construction and planning field *without* seriously hindering legitimate building work, or which help regulate excessive tobacco consumption *without* sparking smuggling (the aim of crime-proofing legislation).

Bad design from a crime reduction perspective can produce a housing estate where the facilities and shared spaces available mean that young people are seen as a nuisance when they hang about, or (as with 'Radburn' estates; Town *et al.* 2003) make it easy for criminals to slip between buildings and hard to watch over parked cars; offer provocative targets such as blank aluminium surfaces on trains receptive for unwanted graffiti, or anti-graffiti posters that merely challenge offenders to greater excess; provide convenient 'mushroom heads' for interior car-door locks that are easy to snare and lift with wire loops; frustrate users and provoke damage (as with some older public telephones), leave loopholes in financial systems or computer operating systems that can be widely exploited; produce highly valuable products which are pocketable or otherwise vulnerable, or which can easily be driven away under their own power; and build courtrooms where prosecution witnesses and defendants' supporters have to wait in each others' company. In both good and bad instances, of course, the design is not the only contributor to raised or lowered crime risk, but adds to, or interacts with, other social and physical influences – 'design determinism'[8] is not being advocated here.

The rest of this chapter narrows the view. Although, strictly, all successful exercises of design yield a product in the wider sense, here the focus is largely on 'movable', and mainly industrially produced, material products of two and three dimensions (Chapters 9 and 10, this volume, consider places and management systems, respectively). Within products it gives less emphasis on security products – i.e. those whose primary purpose is crime prevention (such as removable locks for steering wheels, 'lock it or lose it' posters, handcuffs for prisoners or defensive weapons) – and centres on those where security is a secondary consideration.[9] For simplicity these are henceforward referred to as plain 'products'. They are made secure through a subset of situational approaches – that is, designing the product to make crime riskier, more difficult, more guilt-inducing and less provocative for offenders (Clarke and Eck 2003; Chapter 3, this volume). The emphasis also lies with *civil* prevention, although many of the perceived risks induced by situational prevention may draw part of their strength from enforcement/justice-based approaches. After all, the triggering of a car alarm or the designed-in capacity of a surface to capture fingerprints can sometimes lead to a prison sentence.

How products feature in crime

Unsurprisingly, products can feature in crime in a myriad of ways. Approaching this systematically requires two linked frameworks. The CCO defines products' roles in causing criminal events, and the 'Misdeeds and Security' framework (Ekblom 2005; devised to identify crime and crime reduction implications of scientific and technological innovations) describes how, in those events, they feature as subject, object, tool or setting for criminal behaviour. Products can serve as:

- a *target* of crime. *Misappropriated* (stolen for itself, its parts or its materials), *mistreated* (damaged) or *mishandled* (counterfeited, copied, sold when stolen or smuggled);

- a *target enclosure* such as a car, shipping container or retail packaging. Mistreated by being broken into or even carried off for its contents; and

- a *resource* for offenders or crime promoters (Ekblom and Tilley 2000) or a 'facilitator' (Clarke and Eck 2003). *Misused* or *misbehaved* with for crime (a tool for burglary, a getaway vehicle or joy-ridden danger on the road, a mobile phone used in drug-dealing or taking illicit pictures of young swimmers, a weapon, an aerosol paint can spraying graffiti on a wall, a computer program that controls the re-chipping of stolen phones, a prop in a confidence trick). Some of these abuses involve design by criminals themselves or by 'backroom' crime promoters – such as mechanical tools for extracting cash from phone boxes, or artful add-ons to cash machines which harvest the card particulars and the PIN number.[10]

How product design can prevent crime

There are four broad ways of securing these products against crime. In most cases, such security is about reducing the *risk* of criminal events to a greater or lesser degree, not blocking them entirely; in each case this may work either by making the products *objectively* harder, riskier or less rewarding to exploit, or *perceived as such* by the offender. They can be secured by the following means:

- Designing the products themselves to be *inherently secure* – less distinctive, attractive or provocative targets to offenders; more resistant to attack or to misuse as *resources for crime*; more likely to attract *legitimate* use and hence being unavailable for attack or misuse; useful as aids to *crime preventers* protecting their own property (e.g. café chairs with slots on the front edge of the seat to park handbags securely under the owner's knees;[11] indicative of loss or tampering; or recoverable/restorable to owner.

- Adding on *security products* – *securing* against theft by anchor-cables for laptops, safes or after-market car alarms; *safeguarding* against damage by grilles; and *scam-proofing* by hard-to-copy packaging or identity chips (although these may sometimes count as designed-in components rather than add-ons).

- *Restricting the resources of offenders – when the product is the target*: locking any specialist tools used to damage or remove it, limiting knowledge of where the target products can be found and what their vulnerabilities are. *When the product itself is the tool or weapon*: *shielding* this resource from misuse by making once-only syringes, tamper-evident medicine containers (Design Council 2000; Clarke and Newman in press a) or colour copiers that recognize banknotes and decline to reproduce them.

- Otherwise *securing the situation* in which they are located – changing the target enclosure or the *wider environment* of CCO to limit access or facilitate surveillance; acting against *crime promoters* such as cracking down on handlers of stolen goods or alerting careless owners; mobilizing people in various kinds of *crime preventer* roles – guardians of targets particularly but also handlers of potential offenders or managers of places (Clarke and Eck 2003). How mobilization is achieved is discussed under 'design as process' below.

Securing the situation, of course, goes well beyond the design of the product in which we are interested – particularly in mobilizing preventers. This requirement may either be an on-cost of bad design, as with cars that are so vulnerable to theft that they need guarding, or a realistic admission of design's limitations in particular circumstances. But wider forms of design can intentionally help preventers, empowering them (e.g. through the design of a CCTV system) or directing them by a set of rules designed to promote acceptable behaviour of door attendants and guests at a club. (These are examples of *crime-preventive* design which are not in themselves *crime-resistant*.) And the preventers' presence, empowerment or direction could themselves be the result of some higher-level exercise in designing an entire *integrated security system*. An example is a retail security environment with an interior designed for surveillance, and where products or their packaging are fitted with tags which activate detectors at the exit if the sales staff have not removed or neutralized them, which bring security staff running and which provide legal evidence of ownership.[12]

In immediate prospect are cheap connections to Internet-based networks and 'pervasive computing' or 'ubiquitous intelligence' facilities which monitor, report, identify location, make decisions and exercise control of products or their environments.[13] The catch-phrase for the fairly near future is 'if my coffee cup needs a chip and an Internet connection, it will have one' (adapted from Department of Trade and Industry 2004b). In this, the boundary of the *product* and the *system* in which it is embedded becomes increasingly blurred. Indeed, with products increasingly able to configure and adapt, chameleon-like, to physical and electronic environments, what has seemed like a clear boundary between products, environments and systems (not least to the editor of this volume!) may not remain so.

A more loosely integrated approach can work in market reduction approaches to crime prevention (Sutton *et al.* 2001), where various actions on or through buyers, sellers, second-hand shops, etc., are explicitly combined with product identification techniques (which themselves could involve product or packaging design). (Other examples of system design are in Tilley's chapter (Chapter 10), this volume.

Inherent security, at one extreme, is an essential quality of a product[14] – for example, the massive inertia[15] of current home-cinema televisions means they are unlikely to be carried off by many opportunist burglars. This could hardly be accredited to deliberate design as the weight is simply a by-product of other considerations such as the requirement to use cathode-ray or plasma screens.[16] In the middle of the range inherent security can be achieved via simple and clever system design, such as the lighting tubes on London Underground trains which use a different voltage from domestic supply, and hence are unattractive to (moderately intelligent) thieves, embodying the situational technique of lowering the value of stolen goods. At the other extreme one can include specialized security components, such as a holographic label for brand protection of vodka (Design Council 2000), or an anchor point on a laptop designed to receive an add-on security cable to take the force from thieves' tugging without being wrenched loose; or the integration of a security function into, say, a vehicle engine management computer.

Human preventers can be unreliable. Some security functions have been designed to take people out of the loop: for example, the car radio aerial that is built into the window glass, and that does not require the driver to remember to telescope it shut on leaving the vehicle. Removing human intermediaries more generally may be cheaper or more convenient, but is not always beneficial.[17]

Design as process

The *problem-oriented approach* (POA – see Chapter 23, this volume) is a process for identifying future crime risks and efficiently targeting, shaping, evaluating and improving interventions on these. In brief, POA tackles future risks based on past patterns of crime, which are characterized as the 'problems' to be solved – that is, reduced in frequency and/or seriousness. The name itself was coined (Goldstein 1990) to convey the central message that the response to a given crime (or policing) problem should not be determined by the nature of the solutions readily to hand – such as police squads or patrols – but by careful study of the problem itself, followed by a broader consideration of interventions. This 'preventive process' (Ekblom 1988, 2002a) has been variously characterized as a number of steps. The widest-known formulation is SARA (Scanning, Analysis, Response, Assessment – cf. Clarke and Eck 2003), but a more detailed latecomer is the 5Is (Ekblom 2002b, 2004a, 2004b), which will be used here to relate it to design:

- *Intelligence* is the collection and analysis of information on the crime problem and its perpetrators, causes and consequences.

- *Intervention* is applying generic principles (such as reducing the value of target products) through practical methods (such as by property marking).

- *Implementation* is making the intervention happen on the ground (e.g. by manufacture and distribution).

- *Involvement* is *mobilizing* other individuals or organizations to act as responsible crime preventers and to implement the intervention (e.g. getting people to buy secure cars and use the security features; getting designers to design in security; getting manufacturers and other *design decision-makers* (Design Council 2000) to accord crime sufficient priority); working in *partnership* with the 'professional' preventers (e.g. getting designers to work with police and others to make more secure products); and wider *climate-setting* to align expectations of, and pressures on, stakeholders such as manufacturers and consumers.

- *Impact* is whether the intervention succeeds in reducing crime on the ground, and how cost-effectively and acceptably.

Although these activities have been described as discrete stages, in reality there will be much iteration as a problem is understood in greater depth, thinking about solutions reveals new partners to be involved (who may bring fresh concerns and ideas) and initial monitoring of implementation or evaluation of impact suggests modifications are required.

The product design process

Many commentators on design, too, have emphasized its problem-solving side (e.g. Cooper and Press 1995),[18] although noting the tension between functionality and aesthetics (but, in effect, merely a different kind of problem to solve). Exploring the relationship of problem-solving in design and crime prevention is a fruitful way of trading ideas.

The product design process can be very simple and intuitive or extremely elaborate and explicitly structured (see, for example, Design Council 2000, and Clarke and Newman in press a), especially in the automotive industry, with diverse specialist teams, explicit protocols, decision gateways and so on. In explicitly attempting to draw design and crime prevention processes together, Gamman and Pascoe (2004c) describe what they call an 'iterative design process' for DAC of 'Understand, Observe, Visualise, Evaluate use, [unintentional] misuse and [deliberate] abuse, and Implement'. Cooper and Press (1995) distinguish a number of perspectives of the design process. More restrictive views centre on the *'internal creative process'* of design – the 'black box' of starting with problem and coming up with solution. More global, inclusive views cover the *'external productive process'*, involving strategic planning of product research and development, upgrading and perhaps disposal. The inclusive perspective maps across quite well to the preventive process as a whole; the internal creative process onto devising the intervention and (shading into implementation) converting concept into marketable product.[19]

A fairly generalized description of the design process is as follows:

- 'Market needs' are identified.

- Broader research is conducted into users and their context, and the requirements of manufacture, distribution and marketing.

- A product specification is drawn up (whether entirely new or an improvement on existing designs).

- Knowledge of materials, components and pre-existing usable design elements (such as gear trains) is brought together to generate trial solutions using a range of tools and techniques (see Design Council 2000) – first as concepts, then sometimes as computer simulations, and then detailed prototypes that are lab or field tested and adjusted or abandoned.

- Finally, prototypes are converted to products that are manufactured and put on the market.[20]

Many of these stages have (or should have) crime prevention counterparts, or are otherwise relevant to prevention, and the 5Is version of the preventive process can be used to explore the relationships step by step. The most distinctive and informative steps for present purposes are Intelligence and Intervention, which receive relatively greater coverage below.

Product design process: intelligence issues

Defining the scope of 'the problem'
Often in crime prevention, the 'presenting problem' as reported to the police may not be the real, underlying one. Designers are trained in various techniques for eliciting needs, trade-offs and constraints from users at various stages of the design process – via simulations, mock-ups, focus groups, etc. A determined (but selective) effort to apply these techniques to solving crime problems may be rewarding, informing not only the preventive intervention but also its implementation and the involvement of other stakeholders (e.g. will they actually *use* the alleygates?).

But this critical approach to problem definition can be pursued at more radical levels. The Design Council research (Design Council 2000) drew an interesting lesson from 'eco-design', an approach trying to accomplish something similar to DAC in that it seeks to address environmental impacts of products without unduly compromising other criteria like performance and appearance. Eco-design distinguishes between an immediate focus on *products* – making existing products (such as washing machines) more resource efficient; results – producing the same outcome in different ways; and *systems* – questioning the need fulfilled by the object, service or system, and how it is achieved. These alternatives are ranged on scales of 1) increasing benefits, at the cost of 2) *increasing difficulty of implementation* due to the progressively more pervasive and fundamental changes in the market and wider society needed to bring them about.

From a DAC perspective this could translate into, say, improving the immobilizer on cars; choosing alternative ways of reducing car crime (e.g. focusing on the design of car parks or even where appropriate concentrating on catching offenders); or reducing the number of cars to be stolen by boosting public transport – 'dematerializing' the target product and providing the function through services. (Another example is replacing vehicle excise licence discs, vulnerable to counterfeiting, with higher fuel tax.) In effect, whilst the outcome focus is the embodiment of POA itself (let problem determine solution), the system focus is more radical – zoom out to see if the problem itself should be redefined. In this respect it is worth noting that, whilst over-zealous adherence to *product* design may fall foul of the injunction to put problems before types of solution, applying this wider *design process* does not.

To some extent this represents the scale of tactics to strategy, which links nicely to recent UK moves to embed POA within the police's National Intelligence Model, where the scope and priority of crime problems can be assessed and addressed by regularized organizational arrangements in the form of tasking and co-ordinating groups. But there is also a qualitative difference, which the authors of the *Design Council Report* (2000) propose can be reflected as follows: *reducing criminal events* (within DAC, a product focus, based, I would suggest, on correcting their revealed vulnerabilities); to *crime control* (outcome focus); to wider *community safety* (system focus).[21] A community safety approach might even occasionally lead to interventions which renounce the attempt to prevent crimes (where such efforts appear impossible or too costly or have serious side-effects) but concentrate on mitigating consequences and supporting victims.[22]

Intelligence for targeting action

Some types of property are misappropriated, mistreated or misused more than others. Crime prevention efforts (design based or otherwise) can efficiently be targeted on these, whether generic types (all portable music players) or specific makes and models. Those at consistently higher risk of theft were identified by Clarke (1999), from a thorough analysis of items stolen based on statistical and crime survey data, as *hot products*.[23] They include items such as banknotes, jewellery and compact consumer electronic goods.

Important information to guide the targeting is the 'exposure base', the number of products at risk of the relevant kind of crime at any one time (Clarke and Eck 2003). Without this, a high frequency of crimes associated with a particular product may not just reflect its characteristic vulnerability to crime but also the numbers of individual exemplars out there, and the kinds of situations in which they are placed. The UK Car Theft Index (Home Office 2003) uses readily available and reliable disaggregate data on individual vehicle crimes (the great majority of which are reported to the police). For the exposure base it uses, it filters out the numbers of each make and model, which are obtainable from motor industry and licensing data. (It cannot, though, allow for when and where different types of car are parked.) Unfortunately, this represents a uniquely convenient combination of circumstances, and serious obstacles thwart aspirations to emulate it in, say, consumer electronics. In ten years' time, widespread adoption of consumer electronics linked to and registered on the Internet may alter this; and satellite geolocation may supply when and where exposed and stolen. The time for trying to get security functions based on these facilities into the product specifications is, however, now.

Intelligence for designing products – MOs
One of the most useful kinds of information for designers of crime prevention interventions in the widest sense is the modus operandi (MO) of offenders. Gamman and Hughes (2003) describe how a range of secure handbags was designed explicitly to tackle the MOs identified with the aid of the police, namely 'dipping, lifting, slashing and grabbing'.[24] Obtaining feedback from MOs and on revealed vulnerabilities of design is often a haphazard process, and more could be done to channel the information systematically to designers. One example where it has worked (see Design Council 2000) is with the network of police liaison engineers set up through the UK Motor Insurance Repair Research Centre at Thatcham, to scout expertly for information on MOs and vulnerabilities to pass on to security testers and ultimately vehicle designers.

Product design process: intervention issues

Intervention, recall, covers the stage of designing what it is that actually blocks, weakens or diverts one or more of the causes of criminal events, as these converge on the Conjunction of Criminal Opportunity. It is therefore the core task of design and of wider problem-solving against crime.

Importance of a clear rationale
Criticisms of how the POA is applied in practice often centre on lack of analysis and evaluation (e.g. Leigh *et al.* 1993; Read and Tilley 2000; Bullock and Tilley 2003). However, another shortcoming has been the lack of a clear rationale from *problem to cause to intervention*. Personal experience of assessing entries both for the Tilley Award in Problem-Oriented Policing, the Student Design Award of the Royal Society of Arts[25] and in capturing good preventive practice for knowledge transfer (Ekblom 2002b, 2004b) reveals the 'leap to a solution', or at least the poorly articulated trail, to be a widespread shortcoming.[26] A similar point is made Laycock's chapter (Chapter 23), this volume. The consequences of an inadequate rationale are, obviously enough, solutions that are difficult to realize in practice, to communicate to stakeholders, to evaluate and to replicate. Supplying pressure to declare this rationale has been one of the aims of the Tilley Award and extensive efforts were made to do likewise as the Student Design Award gained experience on crime. But articulation is helped in both cases by developing a clear and consistent crime prevention language, and CCO, 5Is and their design variants aim to contribute here (Ekblom 2002a, 2002b).

Creativity
The most obscure part of the POA is the 'black box' in which candidate solutions (strictly, interventions) are generated, selected and modified. The equivalent internal creative process of DAC is the stage at which requirements and other intelligence about the crime problem are brought together with knowledge of materials, techniques and design elements to generate the concept, and then the realization, of a crime-resistant design. Much has been written on creativity in design (see Cooper and Press 1995 for an introduction), and undoubtedly this is something that designers are explicitly trained for – and 'ordinary'

professional crime preventers could learn from. (They could also learn from the understanding of management structures, organizational settings and procedures such as 'innovation sets' to support and channel creativity.)

Lawson's (1990) description of the process is typical – insight (formulating the problem), preparation (understanding it), incubation (relaxation to allow subconscious thought), illumination (emergence of the idea) and verification (idea development and testing). As a sketch map this is adequate, but gets us no nearer opening the black box than restating the mystery of 'subconscious thought'.[27]

Generation, articulation and selection can be helped by causal frameworks such as the 'crime triangle' (Clarke and Eck 2003), and the more detailed CCO and its 'life-cycle' development (Wooton and Davey 2003), which could almost be seen as a generative, combinatorial grammar for describing, inventing and judging preventive interventions during and after the creative process. (This issue is revisited under 'replication', below.) It can also be aided by *theory* of criminal behaviour and an understanding of how specific theories interact to generate crimes.[28] But the challenge (or, rather, the *design* challenge) is to find ways of communicating these frameworks and organizationally supporting their use, so designers and problem-oriented preventers alike are willing and able to use them as a matter of course, in ways that boost, not stifle, their creativity. As a counterpoint, it is worth noting that creativity and innovation are not so much *restricted* by requirements and physical constraints, as given a defining *'fitness space'* in which to work.[29] The next section takes this theme further.

Troublesome trade-offs

Despite public concern about crime as a whole, when it comes to everyday priorities of consumers, crime prevention is often way down the list. People want a car that is stylish, high performance, economical, safe, cheap and swift to repair – and oh, by the way, that does not get stolen or broken into. A major challenge, therefore, is how to design products that are secure without jeopardizing their main purpose or interfering with a range of other criteria. These cover its manufacture, safe and economic delivery through the supply chain, marketing, installation and ultimate disposal. Recognizing, and reconciling, a range of potentially conflicting requirements at (and between) all these stages is at the heart of the industrial designer's skill.

Aesthetics A familiar critique of design against crime as a generic approach is aesthetic – that it leads inevitably to the 'fortress society'. This originally applied to the built environment (blockhouses, heavy shutters, etc.) but could equally apply to movable products – hideous armoured computer cases, ugly moneybelts (which also scream 'my cash is here!'), chains on music players that signal 'uncool' concern about risk and so on. This can happen, of course, but again it is a question of thoughtless commissioning and bad or compartmentalized design. Perfectly aesthetic handbags can be designed which are secure in diverse ways against quite brutal damage such as slashing (Gamman and Hughes 2003), car radios can be designed without obvious protective engineering features (they can be distributed in parts around the car, or concealed with panels when out of use). To cite some place-based examples, many local planning criteria now specify aesthetically acceptable designs for shutters on shops; many banks have abandoned their heavy screens without sacrificing security; and as Poyner (1983) noted, it is possible to make positive ornamental features of things like window grilles.[30]

Notwithstanding these points, fitness for purpose and context remain the leading principle in applied design. But in some circumstances it may be appropriate to go beyond *being* responsive and robust to crime, and deliberately *signalling* it – influencing offender perceptions as well as objective difficulty. Deterrent anti-theft lights wink in car interiors, warning off offenders with the aim of avoiding crime rather than resisting it and suffering damage, much like wasps' coloration (Ekblom 1995, 1999) deters predators. Street furniture may be designed to signal robustness and discourage vandals (Design Council 2000) and designed so that legitimate use is promoted, denying offenders unhindered access.

Legal and ethical issues   Designers against crime must also consider whether their design violates privacy or unacceptably constrains freedom in some way – for example, a mobile phone which reports on someone's movements, whether tracking him or her for his or her own good or for other people's, without his or her awareness or free consent. Communicating lack of trust may also be an issue – whether it is the 'spy in the cab' tachometer or the often elaborately secure toilet-paper dispensers that seem to be installed in government buildings presumably to prevent civil servants walking off with the entire roll. In some cases such lack of trust serves only to provoke and perhaps to diminish guilt feelings. *Social inclusion* values dictate that designers should ensure the security features on their products do not exclude certain groups, such as the elderly or disabled who have difficulty operating certain kinds of lock or anti-tamper mechanism, or the poor who cannot afford them. Marketing-driven design practices which make people yearn for the latest fashion and status-conferring products which some cannot legally afford remain tabled for moral debate.

Environmental considerations   Crime prevention requirements have to sit alongside environmental considerations. One approach to preventing shoplifting of small, pocketable goods is to put them in a big package, which militates against conservation of resources. One item to receive this treatment (Design Council 2000) was a small torch but, cleverly, the material for the package had come from spare plastic from producing the product itself. This example also makes a more general point – that there is far greater scope to handle troublesome trade-offs when crime is considered *simultaneously* with other design requirements rather than as a later add-on. Nuisance is another trade-off in the quality of the social environment. Whereas designing insecure cars may export costs of *crime* on to victims and the rest of society (Roman and Farrell 2002; Hardie and Hobbs in press), poorly designed car alarms export the costs of crime prevention.

Safety   With efforts to stop drink-driving or to restrict weapon use, safety and crime prevention are on the same side (intelligent cars recognize and act on drink-diminished skills and intelligent weapons fire only for their registered owner). But safety (and failsafe) considerations often collide with security. Nobody wants a crime-proof car or a building that occupants cannot escape or be rescued from. In all but extreme risks such as armoured cash-in-transit vehicles this is not really a trade-off with crime – there is no possibility of compromise. (In any case, this imbalance is reinforced by the existence of powerful fire safety regulations unmatched by crime prevention counterparts, as described for example in the *Design Council Report*.) But it is possible to make creative leaps which optimally serve safety *and* crime prevention. The last five metres of typical American fire escape stairs are normally drawn up from street level, and slide down under the weight of fleeing occupants.

Convenience   Design against crime needs to be simultaneously user friendly whilst *abuser unfriendly* (Ekblom 2001b). A major troublesome trade-off is security versus convenience, an issue taken up at various points below.

Cost   Every additional feature incorporated within a design imposes some extra cost on the design process and/or in manufacture – and in fiercely competitive sectors such as automotive design even a few additional pence on the latter may be unacceptable. Costs of money, time and attention also fall on those who buy and use secure designs (or reject and neglect them). Some security features are expensive, of course – but others need only involve a little thought at the design stage. An example is the road sign for the River Uck, Sussex, which (as can be imagined) is quite provocative of graffiti. Presumably after wearying experience, the local council devised a rectangular sign with notches cut out of the bottom corners that denied graffiti space for the offending additional letter.

Optimizing trade-offs   Ingenuity apart, the earlier in the design process that crime considerations are raised, the easier it may be to optimize or even to resolve troublesome trade-offs. Security features will be less obtrusive (and thus more aesthetic and less vulnerable to counterattack), operation may be more user-friendly, constraints on design freedom will be less, technical conflicts such as over 'electromagnetic compatibility' (Southall and Ekblom 1985) may be avoided, and costs may be reduced (if, for example, security functions can be incorporated into features required for other purposes, such as the engine management computer for cars). But sometimes even remedial design can be made to reduce crime at little cost. One of the Design Council case studies on DAC[31] relates to the prevention of a scam whereby large and expensive paint cans were bought, then returned for money-back, after the contents had been covertly replaced by water. The preventive principle selected was to help shop staff act as crime preventers by making the container tamper-evident. The practical design problem was that a remodelling of the can lid would normally require hugely expensive replacement of the metal injection mould. However, virtually zero-cost ingenuity came in the realization that shaving a microscopic layer off the surface of the mould in the right place would leave a thin telltale plastic membrane over the part of the lid where a screwdriver is pushed in to lever it off.

Sometimes, new technology can appear, or be developed on request, which relaxes these trade-offs. In cars, the arrival of cheap, reliable miniature electric motors has allowed the separation of the discriminant function of locks to be physically detached from the devices that latch the doors, removing all kinds of size, space and reliability constraints on the design of door security. But technology and engineering must be subordinate to wider design requirements, not dominant, as the next section makes clear.

When is a design not a design?

The implication in the crime prevention literature has sometimes been that DAC is simply that part of prevention which is realized through *any* material changes in products – but professional designers would dispute this. When is a design not a design? When crime resistance is incidental rather than a deliberate adaptation (as with the heavy TV screens above); a *'techno fix'*; or an *'engineering solution'*.

A *techno fix* could comprise a superficial, add-on, security product such as a D-lock holding a bicycle to a railing, where neither bike nor railing have been modified to facilitate the security function, and where only a single, exposed, line of defence is employed. In such circumstances, the defence is more likely to be defeated whether by attacking the exposed security lock itself, or its less than optimal anchorage on the protected product or the ground. Ekblom (1995) refers to this as the 'bolt-on, drop-off' syndrome. Another common kind of techno fix could involve simply sticking a security component such as a radio frequency identification chip on to an otherwise vulnerable product or engraving a property mark on it, and hoping that it will deter or discourage offenders. If the rest of the security system was in place – detectors, registers of ownership, etc. – such a chip could be part of a perfectly well designed solution whose effectiveness was substantive and sustainable beyond the initial deterrent impact on offenders' perceptions; but otherwise it would not. One example of a superficial techno fix (Design Council 2000) was the video recorder protected by a simple PIN code, introduced by one manufacturer at the instigation of the police. The crime reduction benefits were never assessed, but there were costs to users who lost their code, and to the manufacturer's service engineers who were bombarded with requests to help with lockouts (to such an extent that the usual response was to tell callers – perhaps even enterprising thieves – how to bypass the control).

An *engineering solution* would not be superficial – technically, it would do the job well and might be sophisticated in design and materials. It might even reflect an anticipation of offenders' countermoves (see below) and of efficient and reliable manufacturing requirements (from an industrial design perspective); but (like Sinclair's notorious C5 electric vehicle of the 1980s) it may have neglected its homework on marketing and use. Where techno fixes are shallow, engineering solutions are narrow – clunky, clumsy designs that are not convenient or user-friendly. They fail to respect troublesome trade-offs such as aesthetics, weight, environmental requirements or even humanitarian priorities (the infamous example being the South African car which shot flames from underneath to scorch hijackers crouching beside the door to menace the driver). Designers of engineering solutions may also fail to set up an equitable division of responsibility for making the wider system work. Some of the entries in the Royal Society of Arts' Student Design Awards under the 'Less crime, by design' theme sought to protect property from theft principally by incorporating tracker devices. As such, they would export costs of location and pursuit on to the police; thus they are 'bad' designs even if they had been technically successful at preventing crime.

It may sometimes appear that an engineering or technological approach happens to be exactly what is needed – such as more resistant glazing on vehicles to prevent illegal entry (e.g. Design Council 2000). However, this does not imply a bypassing of design – rather, much of the design task is shifted to that domain of technology – the glass itself has to be properly designed by materials technologists to allow for optimized impenetrability, visibility, cleanability, safety, weight, manufacturability and cost.

Replication, innovation and design

Studies of the POA in practice (Tilley 1993; Ekblom 2002a; Bullock and Tilley 2003; Chapter 23, this volume) have indicated serious limitations in the ability to replicate 'success stories', and in particular to mainstream such projects in wider programmes. Apart from commonplace shortcomings such as practitioners' lack of project management skills, two related issues appear to underlie this. First, the interventions that appear to work in crime prevention are often highly *context sensitive* in their implementation and/ or impact. Uniform solutions cannot be 'sprayed on' like pesticide. For example, Neighbourhood Watch may only succeed in getting implemented in communities where there is trust between neighbours (Laycock and Tilley 1995); and street lighting may depend for any tangible effect on crime, on how it interacts with street layout, pedestrian and traffic flow. Secondly, there is a distinction to be made between replicating an *end-product* 'cookbook' fashion, such as exactly copying the specific details of what was done in a successful burglary prevention project, and replicating the intelligent *process* of combining generic principles (such as 'creating a target enclosure') with practical methods (such as how to construct alleygates) and method 'elements' (e.g. how to survey victims, design locks or mobilize users) in the light of knowledge of problem and context. In fact, the 5Is framework was an attempt to redesign the POA so that the knowledge of 'what works' in one context can be captured and replicated in other contexts, and generic, transferable good practice lessons learnt. In this, replication is far from literal and detailed – it is more like *innovation* from generic principles (Ekblom 2002a, 2002b). As such, an injection of professional designers' developed, applied and controlled creativity can only be helpful to crime prevention practitioners. Interestingly, the analytical approach to capturing and describing knowledge through principles, methods and interchangeable elements could be exactly the basis needed to support a *generative*, 'combinatorial' approach to creativity that is both fruitful and disciplined (who would want a microwave cooker or a building designed by a team that was creative and *un*disciplined?).

In environmental and architectural design terms, the context/process issue translates into the need to configure places to their unique circumstances and use, by drawing together a range of principles and practical elements including crime prevention and other requirements (see ODPM/Home Office 2004). Product design, however, has to confront the question of mass production.

Mass production and adaptation to crime risk

Mass production could be said both to contribute to crime and to make its prevention harder. On crime, mass production has created more products to steal; and their identical and often (re)movable nature has made them readily disposable.[32] Arguably, it has also made the concept of property *per se* less respected. The capacity to exploit and respond to *fashion* industrially amplifies the attractiveness of products to legitimate and illegitimate owners alike. On prevention, if matching of solution to context is key, how do we nevertheless design *movable* products that are crime resistant in *most* circumstances? The earlier description of 'how product design can prevent crime' provided some answers from the crime prevention angle (from add-on security products to human and cybernetic protection); but further insights can come from the perspective of industrial design itself, and from wider consideration of the issue of adaptation.

Adaptation in the biological sense is about how living organisms are anatomically, physiologically and behaviourally fit for their purposes of survival and reproduction in the conditions they typically encounter in their natural habitat. In the case of products, it is ultimately about their survival as manufactured designs in the market, which depends on their fitness for their intended function, and a range of other requirements including (in fewer circumstances than we would like) their resistance to crime. The adaptation of individual products to crime can take several forms, in a kind of scale of sophistication:

- First, thorough research into offenders' MOs, and vulnerability and attractiveness of products, can lead to some designs for some products that are exposed to crime in sufficiently similar contexts, for a *fixed-design* approach to work and to be marketable. However, this may leave such products over or under-engineered to meet crime risks that depart significantly from the average, incurring unnecessary cost, inconvenience or weight, on the one hand, or excessive vulnerability on the other.

- Secondly, individual products can be designed for particular *niches* – to meet specific levels and kinds of crime risk – for example, fittings for public buildings may need to be more robust and better-anchored than those in private homes.

- Thirdly, *mass customization* (cf. Pease 2001) offers scope for incorporating progressively more secure components as 'optional extras' into the individual product exemplars as the judged risk increases or its nature becomes clearer to the individual purchaser and user – anchor points, armour, alarms, trackers and so on.

- Fourthly, designing *programmability* into the product after it leaves the factory. Here, the owner can activate or inactivate a security function according to perceived risk – e.g. activating a pin code on a mobile phone or – in a shorter decision cycle – the momentary decision in a particular situation whether or not to lock a vehicle or arm its alarm. One winner of the RSA Student Design Award (Ekblom 2001b) was a diamond ring with a platinum housing which slid round to hide the jewels when prudence dictated, illustrating fine adaptive discrimination between showing off wealth and style (why have jewellery otherwise?) and concealing it for security – allowing dynamic adjustment of the troublesome trade-off, as circumstances, and priorities, change. Dynamic trading-off can be found in the natural world – for example, where gaudy and conspicuous male ducks retire into dowdy, but safer, 'eclipse plumage' after the mating season. Note, though, that designed-in capacity for post-production changes can also make prevention harder – swappable covers for mobile phones, for example, render recognition of stolen property difficult. But we have been here before – horse thieves often painted out characteristic features of stolen steeds until clear of the area.

- Fifthly, designing *active discrimination* into the product itself. This requires the capacity a) to sense and judge rightful and wrongful possession, appropriate and inappropriate locations, and patterns of use and misuse (which may be quite similar); and b) to make a decision and take some sort of action – whether simply shutting down and refusing to work, sounding an alarm, sending an Internet rescue-me message, or (with a fashion garment) destroying its own value by ink-flooding. In many cases this level of adaptability can at least partially rely on the human user to have the right fingerprint, possess and use the key or security code; or even to take the decisions and make the response. However, the more complex products become, especially as they incorporate active ICT with sensors, processor, actuators and perhaps locational and communications facilities, the more they move away from being simple targets of crime towards being *active preventers* themselves. (Ekblom 1997 notes the resemblance to the giant's magic harp which cries 'Master, Master, he's stealing me!' as Jack bears it off to the beanstalk.)

Additional adaptive strategies go beyond individual products, for example involving fostering *variety* of designs; these are covered below.

Active or passive discrimination is pivotal to all the above levels of adaptation to crime, whether this is achieved though a plain lock and key, the requirement for specialist tools for opening or removing a product, hi-tech sophistication or clever design related to differential value and enjoyability of the product to legitimate and illegitimate possessors (such as a mobile phone customized to fit the contour of the user's own ear). Badly designed discriminant functions can undoubtedly be inconvenient – Internet shopping sites with elaborate and time-consuming security procedures (Design Council 2000), the frustrating loss of video or car radio security code, and the annoyance to owners and others of false alarms. These annoyances may be sufficient to motivate people to bypass the security – by neglecting to lock the car or link the laptop to the library table whilst leaving them unattended for a brief moment, disabling electronic security functions or resorting to back-street workshops that recode locked radios.

Developing the means of discrimination and realizing it in ways appropriate to the product are therefore vital. However, it is challenging, since there is usually little to distinguish between criminal and legitimate behaviour towards a given product (and in the case of car or burglar alarms, the simpler discrimination between a thief, a gust of wind or the attentions of a cat). In a sense, getting discrimination right is almost more important with the lowest, 'dead reckoning' level of adaptation, because as far as the product itself is concerned there is only one opportunity available (at the factory) to make it inherently crime resistant – or otherwise reliant on other forms of protection discussed above. Once produced, it can't learn.

Well designed discriminatory features do exist – and developments in ICT and sensory technology promise to make them better, such as biometrics and integration of multiple signals like vision and sound. But 'sensory' capacity alone, and a focus on 'who you are', are insufficient to support discrimination. 'Where you are' and 'what you are doing' information may also need taking into consideration. The designer may therefore have to build in knowledge of legitimate and illegitimate use patterns, extending their expertise from predicting and blocking 'dumb user' behaviour (e.g. by incorporating safety interlock switches on power tools or raised safety prongs on carving forks to compensate for ignorant or risky usage), to something more subtle. An example is the colour photocopier designed to detect when someone is trying to misuse it to copy banknotes as opposed to, say, holiday brochures. The false positive rate is critical to usability.

To maximize discrimination between use and abuse of products requires a step up in the kinds of intelligence described in a previous section. Designers must go beyond obtaining detailed and comprehensive information about the crime risk and its distribution, and assemble knowledge about subtle differences between use and misuse, and identity of legitimate users. This information unfortunately may not always be available, reliable or up to date; nor command sufficient priority from the designer and design decision-makers to incur the effort and expense of acquisition. Cost and implementation issues also figure in discrimination – location and registration systems need considerable infrastructure to make them work beyond a superficial and short-lived deterrent effect. In turn manufacturers need confidence that enough users will buy their product for them to justify investing, individually or collectively, in such systems (market failure in this area may require government intervention to kick start the process); and police will have a range of concerns both technical and relating to the equitable management of demand on their time.

Product design process: implementation and involvement

These issues are well-covered for DAC in the *Design Council Report* (2000) and in Clarke and Newman (in press a); and more generically in Laycock's chapter (Chapter 23, this volume). Product manufacture, marketing, distribution, sales and servicing are implementation fields in their own right and will not be covered here, although they each constrain DAC and may introduce crime risks of their own (e.g. hijacking of goods in transit or shoplifting).

On Involvement, DAC is frankly starting from a pretty low baseline. The *Design Council Report* (2000) showed that although there were best practice examples in the automotive and transport sector, very few designers or their clients even considered crime in the development of new products, and there was only limited use of DAC principles by interior and architectural designers. Subsequent efforts since that work have begun to raise the profile and provide some of the know-how in designer-friendly form.[33]

On the mechanics of Involvement, the 'CLAMED' framework (Ekblom 2001a; Pease 2001) describes the generic process of mobilizing crime preventers, including designers and manufacturers, to take responsibility for implementing *any* kind of intervention.[34] CLAMED in fact arose from a reading of the *Design Council Report* (2000) and its rich discussion of enablers and constraints on DAC. It comprises several steps:

- **Clarify** the crime prevention tasks or roles that need doing (e.g. the intervention itself, alleviating constraints and supplying enablers).

- **Locate** the individuals or organizations best placed to undertake them, including designers, manufacturers, marketers and consumers. Then:

- **Alert** them that their product could be causing crime, or that they could help stop unrelated crimes.

- **Motivate** – by hard or soft incentives including an image of corporate social responsibility, naming and shaming, 'polluter-pays' taxes (Roman and Farrell 2002), awakening consumer expectations and pressures and imposing insurance costs, and legislation (Design Council 2000; Clarke and Newman in press a). Hardie and Hobbs (in press) and Laycock (Chapter 23, this volume) give good descriptions of how a combination of many of these pressures led to radical improvements in car security; the *Design Council Report* (2000) also reports results of focus groups on consumer motivation for, and expectations of, security in product design.

- **Empower** – by supplying designers with education, guidance on intervention (e.g. Design Council 2003), information on risks, and tools (Design Council 2000) and other resources, and opportunities for influencing designs at the right stage; and by alleviating a range of constraints (Design Council 2000).

- And, perhaps **Direct**, in terms of standards (such as BSI or CEN) and targets.

These specific actions to increase the take-up of DAC and the motivation and performance of designers cannot be undertaken in isolation. All the enablers and constraints interlock and may form a self-reinforcing system which is hard to shift from one state to another. And specific actions must be done in step with public and commercial understandings and expectations – hence the importance of climate-setting activities such as setting the tone for who is responsible for the diverse causes of crime.[35]

Such 'joining-up' has to take place *within* the design and manufacturing sphere too. Competition between companies inhibits collective solutions and governments must step in to alleviate such market failures (as happened with mobile phone security – see Clarke and Newman (in press a). Fragmentation of design organization and the design process has happened (e.g. through privatization). The *Design Council Report* (2000) well describes the case of UK railway carriage security, which was formerly the responsibility of in-house designers and builders within British Rail, but which after privatization was divided between the railway operating companies and the manufacturers of rolling stock. In some cases the existence of third-party carriage-leasing companies raised further barriers to the flow of concern and information about crime, the balancing of trade-offs, and feedback on crime-preventive performance from passengers to designers.

More generally there is a responsibility and requirements gap for security standards that has to be bridged between the final manufacturers of products such as cars and the suppliers of its components. (Vehicle manufacturers seem to have succeeded here, under sustained pressure from government and insurance incentives, an awakened consumer market and legislation.) With consumer electronics, too, large multinational manufacturers in a global market may find it difficult to familiarize with, and adjust to, local crime contexts for their products – especially if their designers are in Italy or Japan, for example. Incentives available to national-level governments may be puny relative to the global market – hence the importance of acting at a collective international level, as with the EU directive on mandatory vehicle immobilizers. Government action of any kind to boost DAC is complicated by the very different constraints, enablers and working arrangements of different industries, and sometimes even of different companies within a given industry.

The position of designers themselves must also be taken into account. Whether or not crime resistance is incorporated into a product may indeed depend on the designer's own awareness, expertise and attraction to the issue (as in the wider movement towards 'socially responsive design'). But it depends even more on how the designer relates to the *design decision-maker* (Design Council 2000). Artisan designer-manufacturers apart, whether professional designers work as freelancers, in consultancies or as employees of product manufacturers, it is normally clients or employers who determine the priorities or set the specifications.

Product design process: impact

Assessment and feedback from studio tests, field trials, and user and service engineer experience are of course an inherent part of the evolutionary process that is product design – and especially with ongoing product lines they are seamlessly linked to the intelligence issues described above. In traditional evaluation and cost-effectiveness terms, however, there is unfortunately little hard evidence to report that relates to product design as opposed to 'target-hardening' and other situational approaches in general (see, for example, Clarke 1997; Ekblom 1998; Welsh and Farrington 2000). Circumstantial evidence (Sallybanks and Brown 1999) points to the contribution of vehicle security technology to the substantial and sustained reduction of theft of cars in the UK in recent years and the concentration of the dwindling loss on older, less protected vehicles. Other evidence is much more anecdotal in conventional terms but, as Clarke and Newman (in press a) note, almost entirely *self-evident*

– or would be, with evidence from images and models (Gamman and Pascoe 2004b). For example, remedial plastic housing was recently put on the buffer beams of commuter trains, to stop boys from riding there, at mortal peril. The most superficial glance reveals that there is now simply nowhere for them to stand. One research project currently under way[36] is, however, attempting a rigorous field evaluation of anti-theft grips to clip customers' bags to café tables. The more such hard evidence can be obtained, the better DAC will fare in securing sustained funding and attention from government; and the evidence may also help convince manufacturers to use DAC and consumers to prefer products so designed, although any such benefits must of course be aligned with their interests.[37]

Product design in wider processes

So far, we have treated the DAC process as a more or less linear activity (albeit involving 'internal' iterations of testing and improvement) which progresses from identifying a problem to devising and implementing a solution adapted to crime. But this is only part of what can best be understood as a series of wider processes and cycles of dynamic adaptation that link products and manufacture, crime and its prevention over more or less extended timescales. Several kinds of cycle exist:

• An individual product exemplar (such as someone's mobile phone) has a criminal career of its own. It is manufactured, sent down the supply chain, purchased, used and disposed of. Different kinds of crime can befall it at different stages, from trouble associated with obtaining raw materials (such as the 'coltan' alloy used for the magnet, which has been associated with environmental damage and even illegal eating of gorillas by freelance miners), hijacking of deliveries, commercial burglary, shoplifting and returned goods fraud at the supply chain stage; robbery, fraudulent use of services, misuse for drug dealing, football hooliganism or terrorism at the user stage; and fraudulent new-for-old exchange, littering or illegal dumping at the end of the product's life.

• The design itself has a lifecycle as a unit of marketing and manufacture (discussed below), as does the more generic concept of the mobile phone itself. (Perhaps the invention and spread of the motor vehicle over the last century or so introduced the most marked criminal lifecycle of all – which now seems to be waning. Whether we will have private motor vehicles, and thus vehicle crime, in 50 years' time is not certain.)

• Beyond individual criminal events *offenders* have their own crime careers, as do criminal networks or organizations which grow to exploit particular niches.

• And as will now be seen, wider social and technological changes and coevolution between crime preventers and offenders also drive the changing nature and scale of crime.

Crime harvests – criminal career of a product

The simplest cyclical issue is that of timing and lack of foresight by designers, a problem familiar to the military who have often failed to predict new forms of attack. A historical example was the world's first prepaid postage stamp, the Penny Black of 1840, which was initially cancelled with red franking ink. But at the time, red ink was soluble – so people started washing off the stamps and reusing them. The only indelible ink then available was black – so the Post Office had to do a quick about-face, and in 1841 came up with the Penny Red, which was franked with indelible black, and had the additional advantage of value reduction when immersed in water. Eventually, new technology in the form of synthetic dyes relaxed this constraint, but the striking design of the Penny Black was consigned to stamp albums (there, ironically, to become a target of high-value theft).[38]

Pease (2001) describes a related, and depressingly familiar, process which begins when a commercial product is designed naïve to its risk of being a target or tool for crime. The product comes on the market and, as its legitimate popularity grows (Felson 1997), there is also a rush to steal it to meet unscrupulous demand – a *crime harvest*. Finally, if the crime harvest is significant enough to people with influence, it is followed, sooner or later, by retrofit solutions. Meanwhile, once every household possesses the product, the demand, and the theft, taper off unless manufacturers are able to revive honest and dishonest interest alike by 'must have latest version' tricks, or locking the item into cycles of fashion.

The classic modern example is the mobile phone. When these first arrived in significant numbers the handsets and the system were revealed to be extremely vulnerable to frauds such as cloning. As the theft rate took off, a host of technical, procedural and legal changes were brought in to stem the enormous financial losses, and they eventually worked (Clarke *et al.* 2001).

But (as the discussion of trade-offs above made clear) retrofit solutions are never as good as those done at the original point of design. More strategic problems must also be faced. The Penny Black problem was short lived and easily rectified; but vulnerabilities on cars and houses, say, have a *crime legacy* of years or decades. By then the problem may have become self-perpetuating through the emergence of a market for that particular kind of stolen goods, a 'tooled-up' set of offenders (Clarke 1995) and crime promoters with requisite skills and contacts, and perhaps the involvement of organized crime (Clarke and Newman in press a). One could also add that, over this timespan, means of coping with the problem and diffusing the risk (e.g. through insurance) may also evolve which harden the eventual task of motivating and focusing responsibility for change when it becomes public policy to do so. And arguably, manufacturers may come to depend on the demand for replacement goods generated by theft and lubricated by insurance policies.

Getting ahead – forecasting crime risk of particular products

Anticipation could avoid many of these problems of retrofit solution. Clarke's (1999) 'hot products' concept was conceived not merely as a means of explaining, but of predicting which new products were likely to be at risk of theft. This locates it firmly within the product development cycle – whether of entirely new products or of variants of existing types. Hot products are those which are Concealable, Removable, Available, Valuable, Enjoyable and Disposable (CRAVED). Clarke and Newman (in press b) subsequently embodied this approach in a proposal for a code of practice for 'crime proofing' new products, in work for the UK Foresight Programme's Crime Prevention Panel. Research is currently under way (the EU-funded project Marc) to examine possibilities for an EU-wide system of crime proofing products alongside new legislation.

The hot products approach in principle seems a useful way to forecast and feed theft risk considerations into the DAC process, and (combined with modus operandi information) to focus designers' thoughts on the kinds of risk they may face for a given product (concealment, etc.). Complementary arrays of risk factors could be identified to cover the other generic misdeeds that products may face (mistreatment, misuse, mishandling and misbehaviour, as discussed above). And to match the largely empirical process of identifying such risk factors that led to the development of CRAVED, the more theoretical/ analytical approach of routine activities theory (Cohen and Felson 1979; Felson 1997; Pease 1997) and the CCO (Department of Trade and Industry 2004a; Ekblom 2002c, 2005) can be applied. Forecasting of crimes involving products in a wider context of 'pervasive' or 'ubiquitous' computing is currently under way in an EU-funded project on 'Future Threats and Crimes in an AmI [Ambient Intelligence] Domestic Environment'.

All forecasting approaches, however, face a serious practical consideration in handling the *uncertainty* which by definition surrounds the estimated risk. It is pretty likely that on average, some broad types of product will be riskier than others. But can the forecast be estimated and particularized to a type or model of product, in its anticipated environment of use, with sufficient confidence for design decision-makers to say 'we accept this product is at exceptional risk of theft (and it is in our interest to reduce that risk) – we must raise its security specification in the following ways'? And can the nature and scale of the risk be further particularized to guide any available choice of adaptation strategy (fixed, niche, programmable design, etc.; inherent, add-on, rely on rest of situation, as above)?

The automotive industry has gone some way towards this ideal, with its systematic approach to intelligence gathering and product testing – especially at the UK Motor Insurance Repair Research Centre.[39] Its engineers are sufficiently confident to supply firm risk assessments and advice, and manufacturers sufficiently confident to use them (although in practice this readiness may not be directly motivated by awareness and concern for the reality of crime but by the more immediate pressure of raised or lowered insurance premiums for their model, determining which was the *raison d'être* for the centre in the first place). But as for other product areas such as consumer electronics, there is clearly far to go before a skeletal framework of principle can be fleshed out with such strategic information. And circumstances may change (a point taken up below), sometimes in quite volatile ways, invalidating assumptions and decisions on cost and benefit. A few years ago, it emerged that 'set-top boxes' would soon appear on the market to enable current televisions to receive the new digital stations. Compact, lightweight, transferrable, with a wide market in many households and apparently to cost around £100, these were obvious candidates for hot products. Until, that is, the television companies decided to do what turned out to be an exercise in inadvertent system-level design against crime – and offer the box free, whilst making their profit from service subscription payments. The extent to which products in general merge into services and licensing (including supply of material or software upgrades) is a major trend with wider implications for the definition of property, as is the whole issue of illegal copying and *intellectual* property (Department of Trade and Industry 2004a). The explosive growth of music downloads and peer-to-peer file copying suggests that 'natural' cultural controls on theft do not apply in the cyberworld.

Clarke and Newman (in press a) doubt the achievability of specific forecasting with entirely new products, and suggest that a problem-oriented approach might be better – i.e. to wait and see which products cause problems before reacting. But we may go some way towards a more forward-looking, yet still practical, approach to crime risk by developing improved ways of testing for vulnerability (including by simulation) and designing in higher levels of adaptability to cope, relatively economically, with a range of possible futures. Building up an intelligence and testing system, a body of generic experience of crime risks, MOs, etc., and a sustained working relationship with manufacturers has also proved fruitful within a specific field such as vehicle crime.

Whatever the case, some simulation or demonstration studies with designers and decision-makers might help to get a better understanding of what is needed to support the process. And perhaps we should not be too concerned about the uncertainties of forecasting *crime* risk, because this would be just one of a great number of imponderables that manufacturers routinely have to judge and take a chance on when launching any product into a competitive market. (Indeed, part of the designer's and manufacturer's role in creating is to anticipate and encourage particular modes of *use* – so the same skillset could readily be used to avert *misuse*.) Government efforts to get manufacturers to acknowledge and respond to this risk may be best received and acted on if they meshed with this process. Rather than specify some fixed strategy, the government (if it so decided) should simply set manufacturers some objective of reducing crime risk, advise them of the strategic alternative approaches and ensure a level playing field amongst competitors – and then it is over to them to analyse their uncertain market, make their risk-taking decisions and do it their way. As is well documented (Design Council 2003; Clarke and Newman in press a), wherever commercial companies or industries have been strongly motivated to address a crime problem (as with the rapid loss of revenue that occurred with mobile phones, or credit card fraud, described below), they have usually solved it one way or another.

Other product-related changes in crime
Products as targets of crime are not the only things that change. Products can also act as new sources of *readiness* or motivation to offend, such as conflicts over noisy music players in trains. Advances in technology (and even basic science) are also producing a steady stream of new *tools* or resources for crime

– the cordless drill, pocketable 12 V batteries (which can be used to energize car door locks – ingeniously, in one case, through the exposed power leads of the external rear-view mirror) and so on. Things that were once secure become vulnerable overnight. One fairly widespread DAC strategy uses esoterically shaped nuts and bolts to secure fittings in public buildings. The business end of the 'Gator Wrench' consists of a bundle of steel rods that can slide up and down to conform to the outline of *any* bolt head. At a stroke it disabled, and may render obsolete, an entire preventive technique. Tools as a whole become increasingly available – no longer confined to a limited professional 'guild' but easily obtained from DIY superstores and hire companies; ever more portable (oxyacetylene cutters used to come with huge and heavy gas cylinders, now some of them fit in a shoulderbag); and ever more 'universal' or adaptable. Interestingly, tools are frequent targets for theft – perhaps then to commit further crimes? Enterprising offenders have anecdotally been known to make false fire calls to steal bolt cutters from fire engines.

Nor are changes confined to the crime products themselves. Changing social patterns make for new opportunities and motives for crime. Twenty years ago, most homes were occupied for at least part of the day – now many whole neighbourhoods are empty from 8 till 8. Some of the opportunities that were once closed off by human presence and intervention now need technological solutions, offering fresh scope but also fresh challenges for design. Because human crime preventers are not immediately available to contribute to a secure system, this leads to greater reliance on inherently secure or even, in the near future, artificially intelligent designs. By the same token, the assumptions made by designers about the presence of guardians or managers of places may no longer hold true in future, perhaps putting excessive load on the design.

Some attempts to forecast changes in crime stand in contrast to the very specific hot products approach, aiming to cover the broadest field of possibilities, often rendered as 'PESSTLE' or some anagram thereof (Political, Economic, Social, Scientific, Technological, Legal and Environmental). Two recent exercises of this kind in the crime prevention world have been led by the UK government's Foresight Programme – a wide-ranging Crime Prevention Panel (Department of Trade and Industry 2000) and a later, more specific, project on Cyber Trust and Crime Prevention (e.g. Department of Trade and Industry 2004a, 2004b). Another current group chaired by the UK Home Office (Ekblom 2005) is focusing on scientific and technological innovations and their implications for crime and crime reduction in the context of a policing science and technology strategy;[40] and more widely there is growing interest across the UK government in developing horizon-scanning approaches to policy, delivery and practice. Designers, for their part, should aim to make their products robust to a range of crime futures. All designs are a bet on the future – explicit 'futures' work just makes that bet a bit more explicit and robust, exploring assumptions about the present and questioning whether those conditions will continue to apply. At its simplest this could involve as straightforward a process as asking, for example, of each of the features of hot products, 'in future, will this product remain concealable? Removable? Available...?' and so forth, with reference to forecast trends and events such as 'increasing elderly population' or 'more power outages'.

Offenders fight back

People who design toasters certainly face problems, including the need to build in protective safety measures to allow for inexperienced users or children who try to toast toys, but at least the bread doesn't fight back. Criminals, of course, do, introducing an added loop to the cycles and changes already discussed. As every discussion of displacement acknowledges, offenders are potentially adaptable – able to circumvent crime prevention measures by changing location, target or (most relevant to DAC) tactics. The word *potentially* is significant, because reviews of the more conventional kinds of displacement over the shorter term (e.g. Hesseling 1994) show that it does not always happen, and if it does is never complete. In the DAC field, however, the wider picture of offender adaptation is not so clear, although it must be said at the outset that there is currently no *quantitative* evidence of the prevalence of the problem or its typical time course.

Offenders can respond to crime-resistant design at several levels. They can *make tactical countermoves in situ* – such as spraying quick-setting foam in a car alarm to deaden the sound. Offenders can also *turn crime prevention measures* to their own advantage – anti-shoplifting mirrors work both ways; communal CCTV in blocks of flats has been used not merely to spot who is coming into the building, but which neighbours are going out and leaving an empty flat.

Offenders can also turn designer themselves and undertake *strategic development of tools* and other resources as described above. Some even do sophisticated *reverse engineering*. Back in the nineteenth century, an American bank burglar called George Bliss grew tired of struggling with the new-fangled, and very successful, combination locks on safes. So he bought a lock and carefully dissected it to see how it worked. He then constructed a bent wire device he called the 'Little Joker'. He would break in and unscrew the dial of the combination lock, fit the Joker beneath it, and break out again. A couple of days later he would revisit the bank, recover the Joker and from the pattern of scratches on it, identify which numbers were dialled, drastically shortening the time to open the safe.

That was in the days of the clockwork revolution. Curiously, there is a close equivalent of grabbing the code in today's electronic world. A currently available watch memorizes the infrared signals from any TV remote-control device and plays them back when the zapper is lost behind the sofa. Some enterprising car thieves covertly used it during demonstration drives at a car showroom. They returned later to play the signals back, unlock the car and neutralize its alarms. Cars now have to use rolling codes that reset in a quasi-random sequence, like the spy's one-time pad.

The arms race

Social and technological change and offender adaptation make knowledge of what works in crime prevention a wasting asset. This applies to all kinds of situational prevention (and even to some offender-oriented methods), but especially to those involving design. This may simply be because design in most cases has been something that is 'created and left to do its job' rather than continually adapted as with live human guardianship (although even here, even fairly alert humans can be parted from their money by unfamiliar forms of confidence trickery and fraud).

It is now widely acknowledged that crime prevention is a kind of arms race (Ekblom 1997, 1999) between those who aim to prevent crime and adaptive, and sometimes organized, offenders who innovate, exploit social and technical change and enjoy the obsolescence of familiar crime prevention methods. This is the most challenging cycle of all those described. A good illustration of an arms race is that cited by Shover (1996) who relates the unfolding technological history of safes and safe-crackers. A more recent one concerns techniques of credit-card fraud (Levi and Handley 1998) where the game shifts from one modus operandi (such as theft and misuse of card) to another (e.g. 'card not present', as with telephone or Internet ordering of goods) as each successive loophole is closed off, often with new technology such as, now, 'chip and PIN' identification.

But the term 'arms race' implies some steady progression towards greater complexity and sophistication on both sides – which may not always occur. Many of the countermoves adopted by offenders rely on spotting and exploiting security weaknesses and devising quite elementary countermeasures, such as shoplifters wrapping metal foil around products protected by radio-frequency security stickers. (This applies even to potentially sophisticated offenders like some terrorists (Roach *et al.* in press), who often engage national forces in 'asymmetrical warfare' using elementary equipment applied in unexpected ways and places.) Perhaps this co-evolution between offenders and preventers might be better described as an innovation race rather than an arms race. In the medium to longer term, crime levels depend on which side is innovating, and mainstreaming their innovations, faster than the other.[41]

Whatever the case, the process is accelerating – whereas in former times offenders would often learn their techniques in prison, now it is straightforward to find detailed guides on making bombs or picking locks on the Internet. Crime preventers often have to struggle to keep up for several reasons: the initiative is often with the offender; offenders have only to find one chink in the armour whilst preventers must cover all eventualities;[42] and preventers must confine themselves to civilized methods. But we can get ahead by being clever and learning from other 'evolutionary struggles' (Ekblom 1999), which all have a design aspect:

- The *military* is pretty obvious – stealth versus sensors, design of forts and how to undermine them; electronic countermeasures and counter-countermeasures. Capture-proofing weapons is another principle which could usefully be applied to restricting offenders' resources. Military designers are probably the only ones used to flipping perspective between attackers versus defenders, and these high-level skills would also transfer usefully to crime prevention (see Design Council 2000). Another struggle is *predator versus prey* – and it is not just about bigger claws and fleeter hooves. Sensors are important here too. If gazelles relied on the equivalent of contemporary burglar alarms to protect them from cheetahs they would be long extinct. They do not wait to feel the proximal crash of the cheetah leaping upon them but use distal sensing. Vision has independently evolved many times in evolutionary history (Ekblom 2002a). But nor do the gazelles want to starve to death, unable to feed due to constant false alarms – so they use intelligent integration of multiple sensory modalities.

- *Pest versus farmer* and *bacteria versus antibiotics* both illustrate the impermanence of what seemed, at first, to be wonder solutions. There are simply huge numbers of bugs out there, constantly trying out new techniques against our countermeasures. But these are all a pale echo of the sophisticated evolutionary war that goes on all the time in our own bodies – that is, the immune system. Interestingly, companies like IBM have been developing so-called 'artificial immune systems' in their fight against computer viruses.

We might learn three kinds of lessons from these struggles: engineering lessons – trade-offs between weight and mobility, design details, materials; entirely new design against crime principles; and high-level ideas on how to run, and avoid, arms races.

Engineering lessons

Consider the case of seashells. It transpires that their glorious spines and flanges are defences against the crab – with whom they are in a co-evolutionary race in which progressively bigger spines are matched by bigger claws. Advertising brochures for secure containers for desktop computers speak of a hardened case, anti-jemmy flanges and bolt heads flattened to prevent prising off and bevelled to defeat pliers. This could equally be a prospectus for ambitious parent crabs interested in genetically engineering super-offspring. It certainly suggests that biomimetics is worth applying to crime-resistant design.

New technology can bypass trade-offs that have long put a brake on further improvements. In war, the trade-off between armour and mobility used to mean a stark choice between heavy castles and sluggish mounted knights, versus lightly protected but agile infantry. Then along came the internal combustion engine, the trade-off relaxed and it was suddenly possible to have armour and mobility combined – in the form of the tank. Such a major leap in crime prevention could be achieved, say, by central locking for homes. The arrival of remote wireless control systems, cheap processors, effective encryption, reliable miniature actuators can together support the development of a package which can relax the trade-off between security and convenience – also illustrating the need in forecasting to take simultaneous account of multiple and interacting trends. More generally, the shift from natural human controls to physical and electromechanical ones, and now to local and Internet-embedded cyber-controls, has begun radically to change the nature of the security game given that the constraints of space, material and inertia no longer inevitably apply to offenders and preventers (Department of Trade and Industry 2004a, 2004b; Wall 2005).

New principles

We might assume that we could learn many entirely new principles from nature to apply to crime prevention. After all, nature has had at least 600 million years, since the Cambrian explosion of life forms, to experiment with designs for defence against predation, parasitism and grazing. In fact, although the search continues, it has proved almost impossible to identify any strategy that human society, in its ingenuity, had not already reinvented. One might think, for example, that the principle of the lizard's detachable tail (used to divert and distract predators) was novel, but the police have already designed clip-on ties to prevent strangulation by criminals.

Running and avoiding arms races

What these other evolutionary struggles do teach, though, is something of far more strategic importance than isolated bright ideas, or even detailed engineering principles. They indicate how to run the arms race and even, perhaps, how to avoid it. Avoidance is important, of course, because of the wasted effort and adverse impact on other aspects of life.

Running arms races   There will always be arms races to run in design and technology – preventers have to be faster, smarter, more resilient, more scientific and more systematic at innovation and deployment, than the opposition. Ekblom (1997, 2002a) describes this process as gearing up against crime, which involves action at several levels:

- *Catching up* with existing crime problems that we cannot yet adequately control. Applying evidence of what we already know is cost-effective, innovating, evaluating to extend the evidence base and mainstreaming the successful innovations.

- *Spotting emergent crime problems* and new modus operandi, like new diseases, and nipping them in the bud.

- Setting up *learning paths* by systematically collecting information on the vulnerability of products and feeding it back to designers and manufacturers.

- Through *foresight* or *horizon-scanning* forecasts of technological and social change (as discussed above), anticipating new causes of crime and preventing or mitigating them; or at least making explicit the assumptions the design makes about future circumstances and thereby ensuring the designs are *robust* to a range of possible futures. Anticipating entirely new possibilities for prevention, and making them happen.

- Building innovative, *evolutionary capacity* (in this case) amongst designers by devising and extending frameworks such as Clarke's (1999) 'hot products', professional guidance for designers (Design Council 2003), and techniques like crime proofing or crime-impact statements, similar to environmental impact statements (Ekblom 2002c).

- Building similar capacity in *science and technology*, and alerting, motivating and empowering hard scientists to contribute to prevention (Ekblom 2005).

- Fostering *variety*. People, and especially officialdom, like norms and standards – but these equally appeal to offenders. If, for example, landlords fit similar locks on all the homes in a housing estate, it is often a case of 'crack one, and you've cracked them all'. Agricultural equivalents abound – like the crop monoculture where the entire harvest falls prey to an invading fungus. So standardization must be tempered by variety. (Imagine if burglars had to obtain, familiarize with and carry 20 different kinds of picklock.) Standards are necessary; however, those that foster variety and upgradeability are not rigid construction standards but performance standards. This flexible approach is, sensibly, adopted by institutions like the UK Loss Prevention Certification Board. They may have the added advantage of allowing *design freedom* – enabling designers to optimize trade-offs with other functional, aesthetic and marketing requirements, and discouraging them from *designing down* to meet bare minimum requirements which will probably lag behind offenders' capabilities. But even performance standards – like the '10-second delay in entry' to cars that 'police believe is sufficient to discourage spontaneous theft'[43] – are so far probably based on little hard evidence.

- Developing and applying an understanding of *durability* issues by distinguishing between those products which have a short and disposable lifecycle (and can thus be remedially redesigned at point of production, as with mobile phones), and those with a longer existence (as with cars, trains or buildings, where inherent vulnerability can leave an enduring legacy of crime – but which can be adapted during their post-production lifetime).

- Related to the last, and to foresight above, *future-proofing* product designs by specifically making them adaptable and *upgradeable*. Imagine being left with a complex, costly and now obsolete security system that thieves have learnt to bypass, and that is impossible to update further. This is reminiscent of the biological concept of 'phylogenetic constraint' – highly specialized species often become extinct because they head too far down an evolutionary blind alley. Although superbly adapted now, when conditions change they cannot back out and advance along a different path. It may even be necessary to develop a succession of preventive measures in the pipeline, as do the banks and credit-card institutions, and the satellite TV companies. New ones can be swung into action as soon as offenders learn to defeat the old ones.

- As an alternative, encouraging the facility for designers to undertake 'turnabouts' in finding radical new solutions to replace those already 'done to death' in one direction.

Avoiding arms races? The contest between crabs and seashells described above only took off on one coast of North America. On the other coast, close-relative species have only modest claws and shells. Why the difference? Biologists are still arguing, but the answer will be worth knowing. Overuse of our most powerful antibiotics merely forces bacteria to evolve immunity, whereas restrained application and quite mild doses may paradoxically put a sufficient brake on infection to enable the immune system to overcome them, without triggering a new evolutionary spiral. On the crime side, some electronic service providers decided *not* to go for state-of-the-art encryption systems for fear of provoking hackers into technological breakthroughs of their own. There are concerns (if no hard evidence yet) that effective security systems on cars and financial systems have precipitated a move from stealthy theft towards 'social engineering' including obtaining codes by deceit or even confrontational methods such as 'carjacking', where the human operator, who knows the security system, is taken along with the vehicle.

Tenner (1996) makes a general case for using low-intensity approaches to solving human problems, because high-intensity ones inevitably 'bite back' with unforeseen consequences. For the same reason Wortley (1996) argues for greater use of 'soft' approaches in situational prevention – involving the awakening of shame and guilt as much as hardening against attack. The aesthetics and semiotics side of product design could perhaps be turned to advantage here to signal emotion and personalized value (who would want to buy a stolen iPod with someone else's family photos embedded in the case?).[44]

The 'system failure' analysis of Chapman (2004) makes a related, but wider, point about the difficulties of influencing 'complex adaptive systems' (Bullock and Cliff 2004) – a whole ecosystem of adapting, adjusting and calculating agents who react to the policy-maker's or practitioner's attempt to move things in a certain desired direction. (A familiar example is the counterproductive effects of setting targets for hospital waiting lists.) Living with displacement and the longer-term forms of adaptation such as arms races requires, as Chapman would put it, a systems approach whereby our attempts to control (in this case) crime must be guided by an understanding of how the various agents and roles (preventers, offenders, crime promoters, victims) pursue goals of their own, perceive and handle risks, incentives, etc., interact and co-evolve. Obviously, this sets the pursuit of DAC through resistant products in a far wider and more demanding context than the above discussion of 'climate setting' implied, and warns us off reliance on any kind of 'design determinism' equivalent to architectural determinism (see Chapter 9, this volume).

To return to biological parallels, co-evolution between predator and prey, or grazer and grazed, has been likened to the Red Queen's Game, from *Alice through the Looking Glass* – you have to keep running just to stay on the same spot. Applied to crime prevention, we could take this to mean that coming up with new preventive measures is ultimately futile because, in time, criminals will inevitably find a way to defeat them. At the *tactical* level DAC and other situational prevention approaches are undoubtedly a wasting asset. Nevertheless, they cannot be abandoned. The long term can only ever be influenced via a succession of actions in the short term provided they are intelligently concerted. Viewed *strategically*, crime control is *not* about individual innovations and their sometimes limited shelf life; it *is* about maintaining a dynamic imbalance between creativity and innovation by preventers and that by offenders. To take a military parallel, in World War Two the Allies chose to deploy a particular radio navigation system for bombers, despite knowing that in six months the enemy would work out how it operated and develop countermeasures. The system was considered worth while because it bought time before a successor was needed. Finally, natural limits on arms races are imposed by trade-offs – cheetahs cannot get any lighter and thus faster, or they become too weak to defend their bloody prize from hyenas; trees competing for light hit a height limit imposed by the physics of water columns.

Conclusion

Designing products against crime is a topic, the study and practice of which lets us view the familiar with fresh eyes. It also leads us into unfamiliar territory. Design against crime as a whole (including movable products plus environments, interiors, systems and messages) is simultaneously a relatively narrow domain of intervention within situational crime prevention, and a broad approach that can contribute to every kind of intervention and indeed to every stage of the preventive process.

Exploring the narrower domain of DAC *interventions* suggests that they can never be the complete answer to crime (although hard evidence either way is sorely needed). Implementation, too, is a major issue – how to get producers and users alerted, motivated and empowered to make the crime-resistant choice, and to realize it well. However, DAC is likely to continue to make major contributions within situational prevention, reducing all kinds of crime in ways which complement place management or offender-oriented interventions. The boundaries of its competence will surely undergo some drastic shifts as new technology and, especially, inbuilt or ambient, web-based intelligence increasingly make their presence felt in everyday products and the systems and places they are embedded in.

Exploring the wider territory of *design as process* has revealed interesting and challenging lessons for developing the *creativity* that needs to be exercised within crime prevention as a whole, and understanding the related strategic importance of *innovation, adaptability* and *foresight*.

Acknowledgements

I am grateful to Dr Lorraine Gamman, Marcus Willcocks, Prof. Rachel Cooper, Dr Caroline Davey and Prof. Nick Tilley for helpful comments and information.

Selected further reading

Literature in this new field is rather sparse. All publications described are cited in the references for this chapter. A good contemporary set of readings covering product design against crime and how to implement it is *Designing out Crime from Products and Systems* by Clarke and Newman (in press c). Gamman and Pascoe (2004a) have edited, and contributed to 'Seeing is Believing', a recent special issue of *Crime Prevention and Community Safety Journal* with an emphasis on visual communication and design process. An older overview of mine which bridges product and environmental design is 'Less crime, by design' (1995). An illustrated overview with the same title is www.e-doca.net/Resources/Lectures/Less%20Crime%20by%20Design.htm. Ken Pease's (2001) gallop round the field for the Design Council, *Cracking Crime through Design,* is a good and pleasurable way of acquiring the flavour of the field. 'Classic' studies in this area are Ron Clarke's (1999) *Hot Products* and Southall and Ekblom's (1985) *Designing for Vehicle Security: Towards a Crime Free Car.* Research on the state of DAC in the UK by the consortium funded by the Crime Reduction Programme through the Design Council (Cambridge, Sheffield Hallam and Salford universities) provides an authoritative view of DAC issues in a range of industrial and educational sectors covering both product and environmental design. It is downloadable from www.shu.ac.uk/schools/cs/cri/adrc/dac/designagainstcrimereport.pdf.

As part of a follow-up 'how to do' package the Design Council (2003), drawing on the same team, produced *Think Thief. A Designer's Guide to Designing out Crime.* This is at www.designcouncil.org.uk/resources/assets/assets/pdf/Publications/Think%20Thief.pdf. Some accompanying case studies are at www.designcouncil.org.uk/webdav/servlet/XRM?Page/@id=6016&Session/@id=D_5tNN7DzIbDAh8FVsL8C5&Document/@id=1250.

Contemporary websites on DAC include that of Central St Martin's College of Art and Design (www.designagainstcrime.com) and www.designagainstcrime.org – the Design Policy Partnership involving members of the team that produced the original Design Council studies and material.

Futures-oriented works in this field include *Turning the Corner,* the Report of the UK Foresight Programme's Crime Prevention Panel (Department of Trade and Industry 2000) (downloadable from www.foresight.gov.uk/previous_rounds/foresight_1999_2002/crime_prevention/reports/index.html). Some specifically design-related reports are available from the same location. My own futures papers include 'Gearing up against crime: a dynamic framework to help designers keep up with the adaptive criminal in a changing world' (1997), 'Can we make crime prevention adaptive by learning from other evolutionary struggles?' (1999) and 'How to police the future: scanning for scientific and technological innovations which generate potential threats and opportunities in crime, policing and crime reduction' (2005).

Notes

1. Principally the *Design Council Report* (Design Council 2000), summarized in Learmont (in press) and www.foresight.gov.uk/previous_rounds/foresight_1999__2002/crime_prevention/reports/index.html. A number of these, plus some independently initiated studies, are summarized in Clarke and Newman (in press c). Other relevant work appears in Gamman and Pascoe (2004a) and, with a more technological flavour, Lester (2001).

2. Ekblom (2001b); further examples from the Royal Society of Arts Student Design Awards at www.rsa-design.net/sda/oe2003/20.htm and www.rsa-design.net/directions/2003-04/exh/awards.htm; Central St Martins' DAC Initiative www.designagainstcrime.com; and Design Council case studies at www.shu.ac.uk/schools/cs/cri/adrc/dac/casbrw.html.

3. See Ekblom (in preparation) on a wider understanding of the offender in situational prevention.

4. Further work is required explicitly to incorporate Wortley's precipitating factors.

5. Fuller statements of all these definitions are in Ekblom (2001a, 2002a, 2004a).

6. A creative crime preventive example was one entry to the Royal Society of Arts' Student Design Award, which disguised the real openings in a rucksack with false ones revealing apparent dirty underwear, etc.

7. A Council of Europe working group advocated a design approach to establishing crime prevention partnerships (Ekblom 2004a), and even *laws* can be considered the products of design, especially since they are shaped with the intention of coping with a range of future, potentially criminal, events whilst respecting a series of constraints on reasonableness, quality of evidence, etc.

8. As in 'architectural determinism', the simplistic and exclusive attribution of causation to architectural features, as opposed to taking simultaneous account of social factors – see Chapter 9, this volume.

9. Security *components* such as locks for incorporating in otherwise insecure products, however, blur the distinction – although this remains useful as a conceptual axis.

10. See Ekblom (2001b) and http://news.bbc.co.uk/1/hi/business/4101391.stm.

11. Gamman and Pascoe (2004c); see also www.designagainstcrime.com/researchprojects.

12. The Chipping of Goods initiative (www.chippingofgoods.org.uk) piloted the use of RF chips to protect products right through the supply chain. Bryson (1994) notes an earlier, more modest, example. In the nineteenth century prices began to be set at, say, $5.99, less to convince customers they were cheaper than they really were, and more to require sales staff to give change. Therefore they opened the new-fangled cash registers and by the resultant 'ping!' alerted the manager to the transaction. This would reduce the opportunity for them to pocket the money themselves. Thanks to Mike Sutton for this example.

13. For an authoritative review, see the Cyber Trust and Crime Prevention project website at www.foresight.gov.uk/Cyber_Trust_and_Crime_Prevention/index.html.

14. One over-used term in situational prevention is *target-hardening*. The target in question has come to include both targets and target enclosures, and inherent and added-on security.

15. Cf. Cohen and Felson's (1979) 'VIVA' concept, incorporating inertia as a theft-reducing feature of products.

16. Flat-screen technology is changing that – in future, displays could perhaps be rolled up and carried off under the arm. But even large and heavy products such as central heating boilers or antique fireplaces may be carted off if their value is high enough and demand is sufficient. Reliance on such natural security features would then have to be supplanted by deliberately designed-in ones.

17. As Pease (2001) notes, the move from chemical to digital photography removes the employee-based surveillance from photographic development services which once kept some paedophilic activities in check.

18. And see also 'user-centred' approaches to design as illustrated on the Design Council website at www.designcouncil.org.uk/webdav/servlet/XRM?Page/@id=6046&Session/@id=D_xFxoe6lL1pNBvSoWwa8f&Document/@id=1109 (or search the site on 'user centred').

19. It is worth pointing out that *the* problem (i.e. the crime to be tackled) is not the only problem to be solved through application of design and creativity – every stage of the preventive process requires solving a succession of ever more tactical problems.

20. Advances in materials science may even mean that designers can specify materials with desired sets of properties (e.g. meeting weight v. toughness trade-offs). But as with POA, deviations often occur from this ideal process. For example, many a solution has been devised before looking for an application to meet, demand to satisfy or problem to solve. A classic case was the 'Post-it' note which was inspired by the desire to exploit a weak adhesive that had been unintentionally invented, and went on to demonstrate the power of 'latent demand' (i.e. that which people didn't

know they wanted until they were shown the product). Whilst in the POA world, such solution-led success is likely to be far outweighed by solution-led oblivion, in the technological end of DAC particularly, the whole field of industrial innovation is more evenly balanced between which leads – scientific discoveries, new technologies and new applications or carefully researched requirements. Whether there are any transferable 'process' lessons for POA on *how* to start successfully from solutions is not certain, but this is important to follow up given the stream of new technologies becoming available. Criminals are surely scrutinizing these as potential resources for offending; crime preventers need a trained mind (with a stock of problems awaiting solutions at the back of their thoughts) to see the promise for prevention without getting seduced by the technology (cf. Ekblom 2005).

21. See Ekblom (2000) for an earlier discussion of crime control, etc.
22. Here, there are some links with the concept of primary, secondary and tertiary safety (World Health Organization 2004) – respectively prevent the event occurring; if it nevertheless happens, stop it and limit the harm; and stop it happening again.
23. Not all hot items are products – raw materials such as precious metals, or even rare and exotic animals and their products such as ivory can unfortunately be popular with criminals, with far less risk than dealing drugs.
24. See also www.arts.ac.uk/research/dac/web/techniques.htm.
25. See note 2.
26. The worst offenders in this respect are often those in 'social' crime prevention who sometimes can go no further than describing their intervention as 'working with young people'.
27. Detailed exploration of this fascinating but frustrating issue is not for this chapter. But I suggest that neuropsychological studies of how the brain generates thoughts are relevant and increasingly feasible, and the related evolutionary approaches to the generation and selection of ideas (cf. Blackmore 1999; Aunger 2000; Ekblom 2002a) can yield practical applications. To take a specific illustration, Lawson neglects what it is that helps designers generate good ideas (as an extreme example, Mozart generated streams of music that were brilliant first time and needed little revision – and lesser humans effortlessly utter streams of largely perfect grammatical sentences albeit not quite to the same high standard). Nor does he mention the competitive or selective processes that filter out less promising alternative solutions, or the 'prepared mind' that spots, and seizes upon promising solutions and lifts them out of the contest, refines them and repeats the generative process. This natural human process has been emulated in the 'artificial selection' embodied in genetic algorithms.
28. See Hapgood (1993) and Ekblom (2002a) on the generative role of a theory-based 'engineering science'.
29. If all designs are possible, and all equally valid, one could argue that what is being done is not design but random composition.
30. But even fortress design can be subtle. Designers of castles ensured the spiral stairs wind clockwise upwards, to force the attackers to use their left hands and enable defenders, coming down, to wield their swords in their right (equivalent attempts to incorporate asymmetry in castle design are seen in Japan, where many castle steps are set at 1.5 paces to hinder attackers coming up whilst offering no problem to defenders, running down with the aid of gravity; and where wooden 'nightingale floors' squeak to betray tiptoeing assassins). Englishmen's homes were built like castles, too – uneven 'burglar steps' were also apparently incorporated to trip intruders in the dark.
31. See note 2.

32. Unfortunately for crime prevention, even houses are often now mass produced, with only surface reconfiguration to meet local stylistic requirements – see the *Design Council Report* (2000).

33. The principal activities are viewable at www.designcouncil.org.uk/webdav/servlet/XRM?Page/@id=6016&Session/@id=D_5tNN7DzIbDAh8FVsL8C5&Document/@id=1250, www.designagainstcrime.com/, www.rsa-design.net.

34. Note that *designers* and industrial colleagues themselves Implement crime-resistant design interventions through manufacture, marketing, etc., whilst the government's task is to Involve these designers, and design decision-makers, through the CLAMED process, mobilizing them to act as crime preventers.

35. Sir John Stevens and Nick Ross (2000) memorably described mobile phone providers as 'pimping for crime'. A more radical view of the problematic nature of arriving at mutually agreed understandings of crime, and responsibility for dealing with it, is supplied by Vaughan (2004).

36. At Central St Martin's College, evaluated by the Jill Dando Institute.

37. An extreme counter-example is where manufacturers get more benefit from replacement sales of stolen products than they could from selling more secure versions.

38. For further historical examples, see Ekblom (1995, 2001a).

39. See www.thatcham.org/html/mspages/security/securmain.htm and *Design Council Report* (2000).

40. www.policereform.gov.uk/implementation/scienceandtech.html.

41. There are factors which make co-evolution a 'snakes and ladders' game. Besides the disturbances of new technology, changes in business models have design implications. The design of the traditional shop had reached a pinnacle of optimization between preventing shoplifting and facilitating trade (Ekblom 1997); the arrival of the supermarket overturned this and required the evolution of a new equilibrium. The cycle of fashion and style, and the detachment of form from function referred to above, also serve to attenuate the steady accumulation of permanently valid knowledge in the form of an ever more crime-resistant design – except, of course, at the level of generic principles and combinatorial elements. Further discussion of the 'evolutionary epistemology' of good practice and good design in crime prevention is in Ekblom (2002a).

42. Rather like the 'life:dinner' asymmetry between the consequences of encounters between prey and predator. The selective pressure is greater on the prey, which loses its life if it is unsuccessful, than on the predator, which only loses its dinner if it fails.

43. See www.solutia-autoglass.com/documents/pdfs/99IBECG-1.pdf.

44. Respecting troublesome trade-offs, note that deliberately spoiling the second-hand value of products goes against attempts to increase sustainability.

References

Aunger, R. (ed.) (2000) *Darwinising Culture. The Status of Memetics as a Science.* Oxford: Oxford University Press.

Blackmore, S. (1999) *The Meme Machine.* Oxford: Oxford University Press.

Booch, G. (1993) *Object-oriented Analysis and Design with Applications* (2nd edn). Boston, MA: Addison-Wesley Professional.

Brantingham, P.L. and Brantingham, P.J. (1995) 'Criminality of place: crime generators and crime attractors', *European Journal of Criminal Policy and Research*, 3: 5–26.

Bryson, B. (1994) *Made in America: An Informal History of the English Language in the United States.* New York, NY: Avon Books.

Bullock, K. and Tilley, N. (eds) (2003) *Crime Reduction and Problem-oriented Policing* (Jill Dando Institute Crime Science Series). Cullompton: Willan Publishing.

Bullock, S. and Cliff, D. (2004) *Complex and Emergent Behaviour in ICT Systems*. Foresight Intelligent Infrastructure Systems project (available at www.foresight.gov.uk/ Intelligent_Infrastructure_Systems/emergent_behaviour.pdf).

Chapman, J. (2004) *System Failure: Why Governments Must Learn to Think Differently* (2nd edn). London: Demos.

Clarke, R. (1995) 'Situational crime prevention', in M. Tonry and D. Farrington (eds) *Building a Safer Society: Strategic Approaches to Crime Prevention. Crime and Justice: A Review of Research. Vol. 19*. London and Chicago, IL: University of Chicago Press.

Clarke, R. (1997) *Situational Crime Prevention: Successful Case Studies* (2nd edn). New York, NY: Harrow & Heston.

Clarke, R. (1999) *Hot Products: Understanding, Anticipating and Reducing Demand for Stolen Goods. Police Research Series Paper* 112. London: Home Office.

Clarke, R. and Eck, J. (2003) *Become a Problem Solving Crime Analyst in 55 Small Steps*. London: Jill Dando Institute, University College London (available at www.jdi.ucl. ac.uk/publications/manual/crime_manual_content.php).

Clarke, R., Kemper, R. and Wyckoff, L. (2001) 'Controlling cell phone fraud in the US: lessons for the UK "Foresight" prevention initiative', *Security Journal*, 14: 7–22.

Clarke, R. and Newman, G. (in press a) 'Modifying criminogenic products – what role for government?', in R. Clarke and G. Newman (eds) *Designing out Crime from Products and Systems* (provisional title). *Crime Prevention Studies. Vol. 18*. Monsey, NY: Criminal Justice Press and Cullompton: Willan Publishing.

Clarke, R. and Newman, G. (2005b, in press b) 'Secured by design. A plan for security coding of electronic products', in R. Clarke and G. Newman (eds) *Designing out Crime from Products and Systems* (provisional title). *Crime Prevention Studies, Vol. 18*. Monsey, NY: Criminal Justice Press and Cullompton: Willan Publishing.

Clarke, R. and Newman, G. (eds) (in press c) *Designing out Crime from Products and Systems* (provisional title). *Crime Prevention Studies. Vol. 18*. Monsey, NY: Criminal Justice Press and Cullompton: Willan Publishing.

Cohen, L. and Felson, M. (1979) 'Social change and crime rate changes: a routine activities approach', *American Sociological Review*, 44: 588–608.

Cooper, R. and Press, M. (1995) *Design Agenda: A Guide to Successful Design Management*. Chichester: Wiley.

Cornish, D. and Clarke, R. (1986) *The Reasoning Criminal*. New York, NY: Springer-Verlag.

Department of Trade and Industry (2000) *Turning the Corner. Report of Foresight Programme's Crime Prevention Panel*. London: Department of Trade and Industry (available at www.foresight.gov.uk/previous_rounds/foresight_1999__2002/crime_ prevention/reports/index.html).

Department of Trade and Industry (2004a) *Foresight Cyber Trust and Crime Prevention Project – Executive Summary*. London: Department of Trade and Industry.

Department of Trade and Industry (2004b) *Foresight Cyber Trust and Crime Prevention Project – Technology Forward Look: User Guide* (available at www.foresight.gov. uk/Cyber_Trust_and_Crime_Prevention/Reports_and_Publications/technology_ forward_look.pdf).

Design Council (2000) *Design against Crime. A Report to the Design Council, the Home Office and the Department of Trade and Industry*. Cambridge, Salford and Sheffield Hallam universities (available at www.shu.ac.uk/schools/cs/ cri/adrc/dac/designagainstcrimereport.pdf; see also case studies at www. designcouncil.org.uk/webdav/servlet/XRM?Page/@id=6016&Session/@id=D_ 5tNN7DzIbDAh8FVsL8C5&Document/@id=1250).

Design Council (2003) *Think Thief. A Designer's Guide to Designing out Crime.* London: Design Council.

Ekblom, P. (1988) *Getting the Best out of Crime Analysis. Home Office Crime Prevention Unit Paper* 10. London: Home Office.

Ekblom, P. (1995) 'Less crime, by design', *Annals of the American Academy of Political and Social Science*, 539: 114–29 (special review edition edited by Wesley Skogan, Northwestern University).

Ekblom, P. (1997) 'Gearing up against crime: a dynamic framework to help designers keep up with the adaptive criminal in a changing world', *International Journal of Risk, Security and Crime Prevention*, 214: 249–65.

Ekblom, P. (1998) 'Situational crime prevention' in P. Goldblatt and C. Lewis (eds) *Reducing Offending: An Assessment of Research Evidence on Ways of Dealing with Offending Behaviour. Home Office Research Study* 187. London: Home Office.

Ekblom, P. (1999) 'Can we make crime prevention adaptive by learning from other evolutionary struggles?', *Studies on Crime and Crime Prevention*, 8: 27–51.

Ekblom, P. (2000) 'The Conjunction of Criminal Opportunity – a tool for clear, "joined-up" thinking about community safety and crime reduction', in S. Ballintyne, K. Pease and V. McLaren (eds) *Secure Foundations: Key Issues in Crime Prevention, Crime Reduction and Community Safety.* London: Institute for Public Policy Research.

Ekblom, P. (2001a) 'The Conjunction of Criminal Opportunity: a framework for crime reduction toolkits – crime reduction] (available at www.crimereduction.gov.uk/learningzone/cco.htm).

Ekblom, P. (2001b) 'Less crime, by design.' Illustrated website version of a paper presented at the Royal Society of Arts, London, October 2000 (available at www.e-doca.net/Resources/Lectures/Less%20Crime%20by%20Design.htm).

Ekblom, P. (2002a) 'From the source to the mainstream is uphill: the challenge of transferring knowledge of crime prevention through replication, innovation and anticipation', in N. Tilley (ed.) *Analysis for Crime Prevention. Crime Prevention Studies. Vol. 13.* Monsey, NY: Criminal Justice Press and Cullompton: Willan Publishing.

Ekblom, P. (2002b) 'Towards a European knowledge base – the 5 Is.' Paper prepared for the EU Crime Prevention Network Conference, Aalborg, Denmark (available from the author).

Ekblom, P. (2002c) 'Future imperfect: preparing for the crimes to come', *Criminal Justice Matters*, 46: 38–40.

Ekblom, P. (2004a) 'Shared responsibilities, pooled resources: a partnership approach to crime prevention', in P. Ekblom and A. Wyvekens (eds) *A Partnership Approach to Crime Prevention.* Strasbourg: Council of Europe Publishing.

Ekblom, P. (2004b) 'Le cadre des 5 I', in P. Bruston and A. Haroune (eds) *Réseau européen de prévention de la Criminalité (REPC): Description et échange de bonnes pratiques.* Paris: Délégation Interministérielle à la Ville.

Ekblom, P. (2005) 'How to police the future: scanning for scientific and technological innovations which generate potential threats and opportunities in crime, policing and crime reduction', in M. Smith and N. Tilley (eds) *Crime Science: New Approaches to Preventing and Detecting Crime.* Cullompton: Willan Publishing.

Ekblom, P. (in preparation) 'Enriching the offender', in G. Farrell *et al.* (eds) *Imagination for Crime Prevention: Essays in Honour of Ken Pease. Crime Prevention Studies.* Monsey, NY: Criminal Justice Press.

Ekblom, P. and Tilley, N. (2000) 'Going equipped: criminology, situational crime prevention and the resourceful offender', *British Journal of Criminology*, 40: 376–98.

Felson, M. (1997) 'Technology, business, and crime', in M. Felson and R.V. Clarke (eds) *Business and Crime Prevention.* Monsey, NY: Criminal Justice Press.

Gamman, L. and Hughes, B. (2003) '"Thinking thief" – designing out misuse, abuse and "criminal" aesthetics', *Ingenia*, 15 (available at www.raeng.org.uk/news/publications/ingenia/issue15/Gamman.pdf).

Gamman, L. and Pascoe, T. (eds) (2004a) 'Seeing is believing', *Crime Prevention and Community Safety Journal* (special issue), 6/4.

Gamman, L. and Pascoe, T. (2004b) 'Seeing is believing: notes toward a visual methodology and manifesto for crime prevention through environmental design', *Crime Prevention and Community Safety Journal*, 6: 9–18.

Gamman, L. and Pascoe, T. (2004c) 'Design out crime? Using practice-based models of the design process', *Crime Prevention and Community Safety Journal*, 6: 37–56.

Goldstein, H. (1990) *Problem-oriented Policing*. New York, NY: McGraw-Hill.

Hapgood, F. (1993) *Up the Infinite Corridor. MIT and the Technical Imagination*. Reading, MA: Addison-Wesley.

Hardie, J. and Hobbs, B. (in press) 'Partners against crime – the role of the corporate sector in tackling crime', in R. Clarke and G. Newman (eds) *Designing out Crime from Products and Systems* (provisional title). *Crime Prevention Studies. Vol. 18*. Monsey, NY: Criminal Justice Press and Cullompton: Willan Publishing.

Hesseling, R. (1994) 'Displacement: an empirical review of the literature', in R.V. Clarke (ed.) *Crime Prevention Studies. Vol. 3*. Monsey, NY: Criminal Justice Press.

Home Office (2003) *The Car Theft Index 2003*. London: Home Office (available at www.crimereduction.gov.uk/cti2003.pdf).

Jeffery, C.R. (1977) *Crime Prevention through Environmental Design*. Beverly Hills, CA: Sage.

Lawson, B. (1990) *How Designers Think*. London: Butterworth Architecture.

Laycock, G. and Tilley, N. (1995) *Policing and Neighbourhood Watch: Strategic Issues. Crime Detection and Prevention Series Paper 60*. London: Home Office.

Learmont, S. (in press) 'Design against crime', in R. Clarke and G. Newman (eds) *Designing out Crime from Products and Systems* (provisional title). *Crime Prevention Studies. Vol. 18*. Monsey, NY: Criminal Justice Press and Cullompton: Willan Publishing.

Leigh, A., Read, T. and Tilley, N. (1993) *Brit Pop II: Problem-oriented Policing in Practice. Police Research Series 93*. London: Home Office (available at www.homeoffice.gov.uk/rds/prgpdfs/fprs93.pdf).

Lester, A. (2001) *Crime Reduction through Product Design. Trends and Issues in Crime and Criminal Justice 206*. Canberra: Australian Institute of Criminology (available at www.aic.gov.au/publications/tandi/tandi206.html).

Levi, M. and Handley, J. (1998) *The Prevention of Plastic and Cheque Fraud Revisited. Home Office Research Study 182*. London: Home Office.

Office of the Deputy Prime Minister/Home Office (2004) 'Reconciling evidence of what works, knowledge of crime reduction and community safety principles, and values', Annex 2 of *Safer Places: The Planning System and Crime Prevention*. London: ODPM.

Pease, K. (1997) 'Predicting the future: the roles of routine activity and rational choice theory', in G. Newman *et al.* (eds) *Rational Choice and Situational Crime Prevention: Theoretical Foundations*. Dartmouth: Ashgate.

Pease, K. (2001) *Cracking Crime through Design*. London: Design Council Publications.

Poyner, B. (1983) *Design against Crime*. Boston, MA: Butterworths.

Press, M., Erol, R. and Cooper, R. (2001) *Off the Shelf: Design and Retail Crime* (report commissioned by the Design Council). Sheffield: Sheffield Hallam University (available at http://www.shu.ac.uk/schools/cs/cri/adrc/dac/offtheshelf.pdf).

Read, T. and Tilley, N. (2000) *Not Rocket Science? Problem-solving and Crime Reduction. Crime Reduction Series Paper 6*. London: Home Office.

Roach, J., Ekblom, P. and Flynn, R. (2005, in press) 'The conjunction of terrorist opportunity', *Security Journal*.

Roman, J. and Farrell, G. (2002) 'Cost-benefit analysis for crime prevention: opportunity costs, routine savings and crime externalities', *Crime Prevention Studies*, 14: 53–92.

Sallybanks, J. and Brown, R. (1999) *Vehicle Crime Reduction: Turning the Corner. Police Research Series Paper* 119. London: Home Office.

Shover, N. (1996) *Great Pretenders: Pursuits and Careers of Persistent Thieves*. London: Westview Press/HarperCollins.

Southall, D. and Ekblom, P. (1985) *Designing for Vehicle Security: Towards a Crime Free Car. Home Office Crime Prevention Unit Paper* 4. London: Home Office.

Stevens, Sir J. and Ross, N. (2000) 'Police Foundation lecture 2000.' London: Police Foundation.

Sutton, M., Schneider, J. and Hetherington, S. (2001) *Tackling Theft with the Market Reduction Approach. Crime Reduction Research Series Paper* 8. London: Home Office.

Tenner, E. (1996) *Why Things Bite Back: Technology and the Revenge of Unintended Consequences*. New York, NY: Alfred A. Knopf.

Tilley, N. (1993) *After Kirkholt: Theory, Methods and Results of Replication Evaluations. Crime Prevention Unit Paper* 47. London: Home Office.

Town, S., Davey, C.L. and Wootton, A.B. (2003) *Design against Crime: Secure Urban Environments by Design – Guidance for the Design of Residential Areas*. Manchester: Pelican Press.

Vaughan, B. (2004) 'The greening and governance of crime control', *Criminal Justice*, 4: 5–28

Wall, D. (2005) 'The internet as a conduit for criminals', in A. Pattavina (ed.) *Information Technology and the Criminal Justice System*. Thousand Oaks, CA: Sage.

Welsh, B. and Farrington, D. (2000) 'Monetary costs and benefits of crime prevention programs', in M. Tonry (ed.) *Crime and Justice: A Review of Research. Vol. 27*. Chicago, IL: University of Chicago Press.

Wootton, A.B. and Davey, C.L. (2003) *Crime Lifecycle. Guidance for Generating Design Against Crime Ideas*. Salford: University of Salford.

World Health Organisation (2004) *Handbook for the Documentation of Interpersonal Violence Prevention Programmes*. Geneva: WHO (available at www.who.int/violence_injury_prevention/publications/violence/handbook/en).

Wortley, R. (1996) 'Guilt, shame, and situational crime prevention', *Crime Prevention Studies*, 5: 115–32.

Wortley, R. (2001) 'A classification of techniques for controlling situational precipitators of crime', *Security Journal*, 14: 63–82.

Chapter 9

Planning out crime: the appliance of science or an act of faith?

Henry Shaftoe and Tim Read

Can good urban design improve community safety? In this chapter we will look at the evidence for and against a link between physical design and crime and we will then propose some practical measures where town planning and urban design can have a contributory role in the creation of safer communities.

Crime and the built environment

'Crime' is both a mundane and complex phenomenon. A measure that can explain and resolve one type of crime problem may have no effect on, or may even exacerbate, another crime problem. The only common link between drunken brawls outside city-centre pubs, shop-lifting, drug-dealing and graffiti-spraying is that they could all be defined as criminal and they all occur in a 'location'. Some crimes, such as credit card fraud and business corruption, have only the most tenuous links to location. But the crimes which are quantitatively (if not qualitatively) the most substantial, i.e., burglary, assaults, criminal damage and vehicle crime, are neighbourhood or location specific. It is these crimes therefore that may be amenable to control via changes in the physical environments where they occur, and we will appraise this hypothesis shortly in this chapter. Before we do that, we need to clarify three interlinked background issues that can inform our response: fear, levels of risk and the geography of crime.

Fear of crime may be a big and separate problem from actual victimization (Home Office 1989). Often fuelled by sensationalist media reporting, many people (particularly women, the elderly and people from ethnic minorities) live in fear for their safety (see Shapland and Vagg 1988; Grabosky 1989; Ferraro and LaGrange 1992; Hale 1996; Simmons and Dodd 2003). Although fear is a subjective condition, it has very real consequences, as fearful people avoid using certain areas and impose their own curfews. For example, a crime audit of Nottingham (KPMG 1990) estimated that £24 million of annual turnover was being lost by the city-centre retail and leisure sector as a result of people avoiding the area for fear of crime.

Fear may be a realistic response to actual risk, as levels of crime vary dramatically according to area. Official figures show that people living on a run-down council estate are 14 times more likely to have their homes burgled than if they live in a rural area (Mayhew and Maung 1992; Mirrlees-Black 1998). And risks of robbery can vary dramatically between various locations – British Crime Survey data indicate that the number of muggings per 10,000 adults in London is more than five and a half times higher than the figure in Wales (Simmons and Dodd, 2003).

One of the clear conclusions we can draw from the statistics is that crime is an overwhelmingly urban phenomenon. Generally speaking the highest recorded crime rates are in the Metropolitan Police Force and other police forces that include conurbations; the lowest are mainly in the more rural areas (Simmons and Dodd 2003). One method of reducing crime might therefore be to disperse the population into small rural centres; but as 80 per cent of Europe's population now lives in urban areas this would be an uphill struggle even if it were politically acceptable! However, there may be other ways that smaller 'communities' can be created within big cities, as we shall see later.

What went wrong?

Crime and insecurity rose steadily in the postwar period and even though crime rates have stabilized or reduced in the last few years, levels of fear do not appear to have decreased correspondingly (Simmons and Dodd 2003). Politicians, journalists and the general public have sought a number of scapegoats for the unacceptable levels of crime and insecurity in most Western countries, one of which has been the brutalizing and criminogenic quality of many postwar buildings and their surroundings.

A number of planned environments of the last 50 years have produced unforeseen crime-generating side-effects. Notable examples of this are single-use area zoning, which has resulted in various parts of conurbations being unoccupied at certain times of the day or week, and traffic/pedestrian segregation schemes (such as 'Radburn'[1] housing layouts and pedestrian subways) which have provided more opportune locations for street crime and offender escape routes. In response to this, various theories have emerged that suggest ways of 'designing out' crime from *existing* developments and building *new* 'crime-free' developments. Some theories are complementary but some are conflicting. Broadly speaking, the theories and the approaches emanating from them can be positioned along a continuum with 'exclusion' at one end and 'inclusion' at the other. Table 9.1 illustrates this continuum, identifying where various approaches aimed at preventing crime in the built environment lie upon it.

Within the design/crime arena there are broadly two opposing camps: those who argue for more 'closure' (strategies towards the left of Table 9.1) and those who argue for more openness/permeability (towards the right of the table). This is a practical reflection of the two major theory groupings about crime causation: classical rational choice theories and psychosocial positivist theories.

Table 9.1 The various approaches to preventing crime in the built environment, ranged according to their degree of exclusivity or inclusivity

Exclusion ←————————————————————————————————→ Inclusion

Fortification	CPTED	Secured by Design		New urbanism	'Café culture' and urban revitalization
Gated communities	Opportunity reduction	Situational crime prevention	Urban villages and actual neighbourhoods	Design for community control and social cohesion	Social crime prevention
Target-hardening	Closed layouts (e.g. cul-de-sacs)	'Living over the shop'	Mixed use	Permeable layouts	'Crowding out crime'
	Defensible space	Natural surveillance	Identifiable neighbourhoods		
		Symbolic barriers	Human scale		

The theories supporting closure assume that most criminals are opportunists who, as they go about their routine daily activities, will commit a crime if they spot a suitable target and the absence of a capable guardian who would intervene to stop or arrest them[2] (see Cohen and Felson 1979; Cornish and Clarke 1986; Felson 1987; Felson and Clarke 1998).

On the other hand, theories supporting more open neighbourhoods assume that it is the conditioning influence of our social and psychological environments that determines whether we behave illegally or not. Thus the building up of social cohesion (Hirschfield and Bowers 1997), community control (Bursik and Grasmick 1993), collective efficacy (Sampson et al. 1997), social capital (Putnam 1995) and positive peer pressure in neighbourhoods will ensure that we all will behave pro-socially rather than anti-socially.

This continuum between exclusion (or repression) and inclusion (or integration) is mirrored in the broader policy debate about the best ways to prevent crime (see Shaftoe 2004). Repressive approaches are generally favoured in divided societies, such as Brazil, South Africa and the USA (although it should be pointed out that 'New Urbanism' is an American idea), whereas integrative approaches tend to be preferred in societies aiming for greater equality, such as France and the Scandinavian countries.

At the extreme pole of 'closure' lies the phenomenon of 'gated communities'. These are the contemporary version of the old citadel concept where the rulers and their faithful followers retreated at times of threat (Schneider and Kitchen 2002). Although now emerging with a vengeance in socially and economically divided countries such as the USA and South Africa, as the preferred residential locations of the better-off, gated communities built in the eighteenth and nineteenth centuries still exist in Paris and other large European cities (see Figure 9.1). Gated communities are premised on the simplest and oldest form of opportunity reduction – keeping criminals away from crime targets by physical barriers. However, evaluations of gated communities in the USA (Blakely and Snyder 1997) have found that victimization risk is not necessarily reduced in the long term, and they have also come under criticism for depleting the public realm, undermining equal opportunities and creating ghettoes for the rich (Minton 2002; Blandy et al. 2003).[3]

These strategies are primarily based on 'situational' theories of crime prevention, which in turn are based primarily on principles of opportunity reduction (Clarke 1980, 1995). Specifically in relation to the planning and design of the built environment, 'crime prevention through environmental design' (CPTED) has been widely promoted as a cure to so-called 'design disadvantagement' (see Coleman 1985) and, in the wake of this, a number of design advice guides have been produced by local authorities and government departments. Terms such as 'defensible space', 'natural surveillance' and 'symbolic barriers' are liberally used by specialists in this field as though they were proven scientific techniques. Yet, as Atlas pointed out in 1992, CPTED had not been systematically tested and evaluated to any great extent and, over a decade later, the picture is not much different (although see Newman 1995; Armitage 2000).

CPTED as a concept started with the eponymously titled book by Jeffery (1971), but it really took off with the publication, the following year, of

Figure 9.1   A gated enclave in Pigalle, Paris

Defensible Space (Newman 1972). Based on the findings from a controlled design-improvement programme on a high-crime housing estate in the New York area, Newman proposed a system of 'defensible spaces' designed to encourage householders to supervise, and take on responsibility for, the areas in which they lived. He distilled this into four key design measures to overcome the failures of existing mass-housing provision:

1. *Territoriality* – the subdivision of buildings and grounds into zones of influence to discourage outsiders from entering and to encourage residents to defend their areas.

2. *Surveillance* – the design of buildings to allow easy observation of the related territory.

3. *Image* – the design of public housing to avoid stigma.

4. *Environment* – the juxtaposing of public housing projects with safe zones in adjacent areas.

Although he stressed the parallel importance of social issues such as family networks, community development and good housing management in creating and maintaining safer neighbourhoods (Newman 1974, 1995), it was Newman's first two 'commandments' that people latched on to. These notions of territoriality and surveillance were further refined by Alice Coleman (1985), a geographer at King's College London, who, after studying numerous English

249

housing estates produced a 'design disadvantagement' index against which one could measure and then rectify design faults which were supposedly 'causing' crime and anti-social behaviour. Design disadvantagement proved to be a seductive theory for politicians desperate to find a 'cure' for rising crime rates, so they authorized a multi-million pound 'Design Improvement Controlled Experiment' (DICE) to remodel a number of English housing estates. A subsequent evaluation for the Department of the Environment found that 'none of the DICE schemes can be judged to have been effective in meeting the (admittedly ambitious) objectives set for it by Professor Coleman' (DoE 1997).

The concept of 'defensible space' was refined by Poyner (1983), whose research suggested that it could be applied not only to residential areas, but to city centres, schools and public transport. Further research into residential layouts (primarily low rise) and their link to crime rates was undertaken by Poyner and Webb (1991). In this study they attempted to untangle the conflicting claims of social causation and design causation as explanations for the differing levels of crime in residential neighbourhoods.

In the wake of these theories about the possibility of 'designing out crime', a number of guides have subsequently been produced for developers (often jointly prepared by local authority planning departments and the police). Starting in the South East of England, the police-sponsored 'Secured by Design' accreditation scheme for new homes has spread rapidly throughout Britain. If a new house meets the requirements on a police-inspired checklist (which specifies standards of lock fittings, door strengths, window construction, etc.) then the building is awarded a 'Secured by Design' endorsement, which is supposed to be an attractive selling point for the property.[4] The key reference work upon which this approach is based is the *Police Architectural Liaison Manual of Guidance* (Home Office Crime Prevention Centre 1994). Secured by Design schemes applied to a sample of housing developments in Yorkshire were evaluated by Armitage (2000), with generally favourable conclusions. These positive findings were a useful update for the proponents of CPTED who, up until then, had still been primarily dependent on Oscar Newman's 30-year-old evaluation to justify their recommendations.

There is much common sense in a 'designing out crime' approach, but also a danger of overstating its impact and slipping into a design determinist philosophy whereby people are seen as mere automatons whose behaviour is entirely conditioned by the environment they find themselves in. There are examples of 'well designed' environments where crime levels have been high (for example, Southmead, Bristol – Figure 9.2 – Meadowell on Tyneside and Kirkholt in Rochdale) and 'badly' designed environments where the disadvantagement of the surroundings has not manifested itself in high levels of crime (for example, Lillington Gardens in Victoria, London – Figure 9.3 – and many housing estates in continental Europe). Merry (1981) found undefended 'defensible spaces' and Hillier and Shu (2002) challenged the concept by asking 'do burglars understand defensible space?'

The principle of 'symbolic barriers' (where potential miscreants understand and respond to the visual cues of surface texture changes and gateway features) has not been evaluated in any systematic way. Indeed, a modest

Figure 9.2   A 'well designed' neighbourhood, with high crime (Bristol)

Figure 9.3   Successful high-rise social housing – Lillington Gardens, Victoria, London

study (Shaftoe and James 2004) suggested that symbolic barriers might only deter the law-abiding. The whole theory that 'bad design breeds crime' becomes even shakier when we look beyond Britain and the USA, to eastern and southern Europe and Asia. In these cultures, for better or worse, extended family and neighbour support networks and inculcated moral values such as shame, pride, respect and empathy seem to over-ride the opportunities for crime provided by vulnerable building designs and layouts (see, for example, Thornton and Endo 1992).

Other theorists, mostly from the social-psychology area (but see Hillier and Shu 2002, from a spatial design perspective), have proposed more inclusive and permeable strategies for preventing locational crimes. Crudely put, these people propose 'crowding out' crime, rather than keeping out criminals. Based on Jane Jacobs' (1961) notion of 'eyes on the street' and informal social control, the integration theorists propose designs that encourage maximum use of public space by the law-abiding public, through the provision of open circulation patterns and mixed uses. They also suggest that we should design for 'community', where people in a neighbourhood know, trust and support each other, so that through a build-up of social cohesion and collective efficacy they exert control over 'their' neighbourhood and are prepared to intervene to prevent anti-social or criminal behaviour. There is also a notion of pro-social peer pressure in this concept of crowding out crime. Although not primarily crime preventative in concept, the 'Urban Villages' movement in the UK (Urban Villages Forum 1992; Neal 2003) and 'New Urbanism' in the USA (Katz 1994) represent the apotheosis of permeability. As such they have come under considerable criticism from the exponents of 'designing out crime' (see Knowles 2003; Town 2004).

In 1994, for the first time, the government issued guidelines to local authority planning departments on crime prevention (*Circular* 5/94) and suggested a broader approach to 'planning out crime' than merely security design and layout principles. It stressed the importance of a strategic approach based on the needs and demands of an area as a whole, collaboration with other public service agencies and the recognition of the importance of appropriate management of buildings and open spaces. The Scottish Office proselytized this principle of 'planning in a broader context' for crime prevention in their planning advice note (PAN 46, 1994).

This stated that:

> environmental improvement alone or in conjunction with improved security measures is unlikely to be successful in preventing crime in areas which suffer from profound social and economic distress where fundamental issues such as housing management and maintenance, job creation and community development also require to be addressed. In the regeneration of these areas a wider multi-agency approach including planners and the police is required. The same principle applies in areas such as town centres or industrial estates/business parks, where effective liaison arrangements between planning authorities, the police, town centre managers, chambers of commerce, local traders, selling and letting agents can be productive (PAN 46, 1994: 9).

The latest two items of guidance emanating from the government in England and Wales (*Planning Policy Statement 1 – Creating Sustainable Communities and 'Safer Places'*), published jointly by the Home Office and the Office of the Deputy Prime Minister (2004), offer ambivalent attitudes to crime prevention, caught as they are between the countervailing pressures to, on the one hand, 'design out' crime using exclusionary principles and, on the other hand, 'design in' sustainable communities.

As we have discussed earlier, security and safety problems are not just associated with actual crime, but with fear of crime. Fear can restrict people's activity and use of environments. Fear and actual risk of victimization do not necessarily correspond to one another (Mirrlees-Black and Maung 1994). Therefore, depending on the context, we may have to introduce measures that will make people feel safer, reduce actual chances of victimization, or both. For example, improved street lighting is generally welcomed as a fear reducer but may or may not reduce actual crime levels (Ramsay 1991; Crouch et al. 1999; Farrington and Welsh 2002; Marchant 2004). Creating fortified environments (such as high boundary walls and solid metal shutters) may reduce the opportunities for crime, but may raise levels of fear by producing environments with reduced surveillance opportunities. In many cases it may be best to encourage increased use of public and communal spaces, along with the installation of see-through shutters and fences, in the hope that there will be informal social control by the law-abiding majority (see Walop 1996).

Social planning is as important as physical planning. It will be necessary to work in collaboration with other professions and users to achieve plans that integrate the social with the physical. It is no good developing a beautiful town centre plaza if the majority of citizens avoid it because it has been taken over by homeless alcoholics and disaffected youths with nowhere else to go. Some environmental measures introduced in one area may displace crime problems to other areas or may prompt different approaches to offending. Although the impact of displacement has been exaggerated in the past (see Hesseling's 1994 review of literature on the subject; also Town 2001), it can occur to some degree whether it takes the form of 'crime switch' (Allatt 1984; Hesseling 1995), target displacement (Chaiken et al. 1974; Mayhew et al. 1976), change in modus operandi (Rengier 1985), temporal displacement (Hunt and Weiner 1977) or geographical displacement (Burrows 1980; Allatt 1984). However, in some cases there can be a beneficial displacement, termed a 'diffusion of benefits', when an intervention or design change has a positive impact on surrounding areas (Poyner and Webb 1992).

In some cases a heightened sense of security generated by the design of one environment (e.g. an enclosed shopping mall) may exacerbate the fear generators in its surroundings (e.g. pedestrian access routes, car parks and service bays) where formal and informal surveillance is not so prevalent. Closed circuit television networks often have to be expanded as they 'chase' crime from a previous hotspot to a new one. Burrows, in his 1980 study of the installation of CCTV on the London Underground, found evidence of crime displacement to those stations where cameras had yet to be installed. A case study in the financial centre of Copenhagen, Denmark, which examined, inter alia, the effects of camera surveillance on robbery concluded that whilst robbery had reduced for those able to afford the prevention measures, it had increased for those who could not (Carstensen and Frederiksen 1997).

As we noted earlier, incidents of crime, per head of population, are much higher in urban areas. The reasons for this seem to be primarily social and demographic (e.g. anonymity, greater population flow) rather than design led (e.g. number of entrapment spots and opportunistic layouts) (see Shaftoe 2000). Indeed, from a purely design perspective, rural areas, with their unlit villages and isolated houses would appear to be *more* vulnerable to crime than urban neighbourhoods. In the light of consistently lower offence rates in rural environments, an obvious move towards a solution of our crime problems would therefore be to relocate people back into the country. There are clear political and practical obstacles to this, and planning controls on rural development further inhibit this possibility. Given that the majority of people, through destiny or choice, are likely to remain in large conurbations, the challenge is to recreate the village sense of community in towns and cities, so that people know and support their neighbours and feel they have a stake in 'their' locality (see Bursik and Grasmick 1993; Shaftoe 2000).

Community control can work in residential areas but in town centres, with transient users, a different approach to the stewardship of the environment is needed. One response has been the appointment of 'town-centre managers' who have a cross-boundary remit to look after both local authority and commercial interests in their areas. Town-centre managers are able to co-ordinate (or at least consider) the range of factors that can contribute to safety in areas predominantly designed for shopping and entertainment. These factors can range from design and technology (e.g. lighting and CCTV) to deployment of neighbourhood and city-centre wardens or provision of diversionary facilities. An example of the latter can be found at the Dufferin Shopping Mall in Canada, where the manager not only introduced design changes to the communal areas but helped to set up outreach and support services for the disaffected young people and drug users who were frequenting the mall and making it feel 'unsafe' for other customers (see Wekerle and Whitzman 1995; Hall 1997).

Below are four examples of how good planning can contribute to safer environments.

Designing for the optimum mix of uses

Balanced, stable neighbourhoods with a heterogeneous mix of demography and activity may reduce crime and fear, through informal social control networks and round-the-clock surveillance. This was the approach espoused by Jane Jacobs (1961), who was scathing about the single-use zoning methods adopted by planners. Such zoning means that residential areas can be underused by day and retail areas deserted at night. In a number of British cities planners have encouraged small city-centre infill sites to be redeveloped with various types of residential accommodation rather than the usual commercial developments. Apart from issues to do with physical sustainability, such 'living over the shop', policies ensure that inner cities are well populated at all times with residents who know the area and are aware of what should and should not be happening in it (Oc and Tiesdell 1997).

Many large council estates with identical family housing types were built in the interwar or immediate postwar period, and a number of these estates became high-crime areas (Bottoms and Wiles 1986). This is at least partly to do with the concentration in these areas of families living in poverty with bored children and disaffected young people (SNU 1993; Osborn and Shaftoe 1995). These areas are usually isolated from central social and recreational facilities so some young people make their own (illicit) entertainment or take out their frustration on the built environment.

Commercial/leisure areas with concentrations of pubs and clubs will increase the risk of certain types of crime or anti-social activity, particularly those that are fuelled by alcohol, such as assaults and vandalism (Stubbs, 2002). As with many regional towns, the centre of Newport in South Wales was a drinking and entertainment attraction for people not only from the rest of the city but for many of the outlying villages. There were so many problems of disorder on weekend nights that the council and the police introduced strict controls on the development of further central entertainment facilities and critically reviewed the alcohol licences of existing premises. Ironically, the best approach would probably be to encourage good-quality social and recreational facilities on the outlying estates and villages. Potentially this would also reduce levels of car theft as late night revellers would not have to seek motorised transport to get home!

Designing and maintaining to give the right psychological signals and cues

A high-quality, cared-for environment will encourage respect for that environment and its users – Newman's (1972) third key factor of 'image'. Conversely, harsh, fortified and neglected environments may reinforce fear and actual risk. There is evidence to suggest that brutal surroundings may provoke brutal behaviour (Kuo and Sullivan 2001 – Figure 9.4), and there is a risk that increased fortification may just raise the stakes of the force and ingenuity adopted by determined miscreants.

Many modernist housing estates and urban plazas have found themselves in a deteriorating spiral of decline, precipitated at least in part by the

Figure 9.4 Council estate shopping centre, south Bristol

stigmatizing visibility of their streaked precast concrete panels and other, poor-quality finishes which signal cheap municipal design. Such areas have been gradually abandoned by those with sufficient wealth and influence to move elsewhere, leaving behind the poor, the powerless and the desperate (Skogan 1992; Morton 1994). However this spiral of physical and social decline can be reversed. Despite general rising levels of theft, robbery and drink-related violence, many banks, shopping centres and pubs have successfully gone against the grain by offering high-quality, welcoming environments in previously unpromising locations. In Haarlem in the Netherlands, as part of a strategy to improve safety and security, the municipality banned further fitting of closed roll-down shutters for shops and offered shopkeepers a subsidy to install see-through ones. At the same time they encouraged more landlords to rent out rooms above shops for residential occupation. The result of these two moves to create a city centre that was more 'transparent', welcoming and lived-in, was a reduction in insecurity and criminal behaviour (Walop 1996).

Some housing areas have also been transformed, at great expense, by combined physical and social improvements (see SNU 1993; Osborn and Shaftoe 1995). In view of the number of radical housing designs that have rapidly declined into unpopular 'sink' estates, designers of social housing have stopped experimenting on the poor and started to provide housing that will please their future occupants rather than their professional peers. Sir James Stirling's award-winning futuristic housing development at New Southgate in Runcorn had to be demolished some years ago, such was its unpopularity. In its place a housing association has built mundane (but well liked) pitch-roofed brick- clad houses, whilst the local authority is still paying off the loan on the previous housing (see Morton 1994).

Designing for control of environments by users

This concept is not just about 'ownership' and surveillance of space, but engaging users/residents in the design and development process so that they have a personal 'investment' in a designed or redesigned environment that they will wish to safeguard. Planners and urban designers may claim they do this as a matter of course through the required consultation mechanisms. However, open consultation sessions and displays of plans will often only attract and engage an unrepresentative minority of users/residents. Also, in many cases the professionals have already predetermined their short-list of design options and users/residents may rightly feel that all they are doing is 'rubber-stamping'. A genuinely participatory approach is time consuming and requires the professionals to relinquish their directorial role in favour of an 'enabling' one. These are difficult changes to make for experts who are working to deadlines and who have heartfelt visions of what good buildings and their environments should look like. On the plus side, participatory exercises can be very satisfying, particularly when they employ creative methods such as 'planning-for-real' developed by the Neighbourhood Initiatives Foundation. Planning-for-real enables lay people to visualize their own design preferences, and to reconcile these with the priorities of others, by constructing and manipulating simple three-dimensional scenarios (Neighbourhood Initiatives

Foundation 1999). It is becoming increasingly possible to develop computer simulations of three-dimensional environments as a consultation tool, but one has to be careful that the medium does not overwhelm the message.

The participatory approach to neighbourhood design and urban regeneration is supported by the British government and its success can be seen at the Royds Community Association in Bradford, Eldonians' Co-operative Housing Scheme in Liverpool and the Pembroke Street Redevelopment and Estate Management Board in Plymouth, amongst others. Such schemes have, through the active involvement of their residents in design, redevelopment and ongoing management, transformed high-crime 'sink' estates into attractive neighbourhoods with far fewer problems of insecurity. In Edinburgh, the Niddrie House Planning and Rehabilitation Group was a resident-led organization which, with council support, masterminded a multi-million pound estate regeneration programme which has transformed the area physically and socially. Two tower blocks were demolished, 1970s tenement blocks were remodelled, playgrounds were built, a new housing co-operative developed homes on the sites vacated by the tower blocks, a community centre and even a community shop were opened. Crime, although not vanquished, diminished (SNU 1994).

The above examples are of existing neighbourhoods that have been rehabilitated through community consultation and involvement, but what about new-build? It *is* possible to consult potential residents or buyers, using citizens' panels or other sampling systems that reflect the type of people likely to end up living in or using the new development. With the wisdom of hindsight, it could be argued that many of the disastrous high-rise and modernist estates of the 1960s and 1970s would not have been built if the planners and developers had consulted with potential occupiers, who generally would have preferred cosy traditional homes (of the type that we are now having to build in place of demolished tower blocks!) (Taylor 1973).

Right-sizing

As we saw earlier when comparing urban/rural victimization rates, crime flourishes in large anonymous environments. Small, identifiable communities seem to offer better mutual support and security to their residents and public services seem to work better when they are decentralized to manageable neighbourhoods (see Ward 1989). There appear to be a number of reasons why right-sized neighbourhoods are safer: people can identify with 'their' community and feel they have a stake in its well-being; they are more likely to observe and respond to inappropriate or offensive behaviour; and they are more likely to know and support their neighbours and know whom to go to for help (Bursik and Grasmick 1993; Hirschfield and Bowers 1997).

Therefore the idea of dividing big cities into clusters of 'villages' is not just a whimsical pastoral notion, but has a sound crime preventative basis and has the potential for delivering more responsive and appropriate public services. This approach was attempted in Islington and Tower Hamlets in London, and, somewhat controversially, in Walsall. This approach to creating viable and supportive small communities is espoused by Christopher Alexander in his seminal work *A Pattern Language* (1977), in which he proposes that each identifiable neighbourhood should contain a population of no more than 7,000 people. Alexander and his colleagues argue that in its evolution, the human race has developed a natural set of living 'patterns' that have stood the test of time. If we do not accord to these patterns in the way we design and manage the built environment, then problems and conflicts are more likely to arise. Alexander also believes that people should design for themselves their own houses, streets and communities, having observed that most of the most successful places in the world were not made by architects but by the people.

On the downside, one approach to planning for security is the 'ghetto of privilege' whereby certain areas are designed to be self-contained reserves which can exclude undesirables. Enclosed shopping malls with security guards and CCTV could represent 'the thin end of the wedge' of privatizing public space. In California there is a downtown commercial centre which can only be reached by car – there is no pedestrian or public transport access (Ellin 1997), and in Toronto the Eaton Centre, which takes up the majority of the downtown retail area, has a list of 12,000 residents who are classified as undesirable and are banned by the 50-strong rota of security guards (Poole 1994). The American-style fortified suburb is now being replicated in a number of new upmarket residential developments in the Home Counties of England (Minton 2002). This private response to a growing sense of insecurity, if allowed by the planners to escalate, will further polarize our built environment into a patchwork of areas which are 'no-go' for rich and poor respectively – surely not a desirable long-term outcome?

In summary

Although they can make a significant contribution to the safety and security of built environments, planning and urban design measures *alone* cannot significantly and durably reduce crime and insecurity. In some cases they may exacerbate or displace the problem. Layouts and designs that work in some areas can be a criminogenic disaster in others. The Tuscan hill village concept of stuccoed clusters of housing, walled gardens and winding alleyways has not worked the way the architect intended at the Maiden Lane Estate in Camden, north London. The design of the upper west-side skyscraper appartments in Manhattan does not prove to be so appealing when it is realized on a cloud-scraping hillside above Dundee. Even the nicest 'Tudorbethan' developments such as St Mellon's in Cardiff can become ghettoes of fear and discontent if their residents live in poverty and boredom.

It is not possible entirely to 'design out' crime. We have, in the past, concentrated too much on environmental and physical security at the expense of other social and developmental issues that are impervious to design remedies (Osborn and Shaftoe 1995). At best, good design can reduce some of the opportunities for committing certain categories of offence (such as burglary and vehicle crime). Physical and spatial planning are unlikely to have much direct impact on offences such as domestic violence, child abuse, fraud and white-collar crime. The results of physical planning and urban design provide the *backdrop* against which changing social activities and dynamics evolve. Clearly we should be designing pleasant human-scale environments where people can interact, look out for each other and where buildings have a reasonable level of security and lack of entrapment spots.

However, there is little evidence to suggest that the design of the physical environment 'determines' people's behaviour in a direct cause and effect relationship. Social planning (involving other disciplines and agencies) should complement physical planning, so that other human needs, not necessarily directly related to shelter and the use of space, are catered for:

- Design guidance for security and crime prevention is valuable but limited if it is not augmented by user consultation and anticipation of variations in use and side-effects. People are adaptable and innovative in how they respond to built environments, but they will also over-rule attempts by designers to alter their preferred use of space. Many implemented landscaping and circulation plans have been undermined by local people who discovered that paths do not follow their favoured routes (desire lines) and landscape features block short cuts to where they want to go (Brand 1994). In such cases, users will sooner or later impose their own wishes, even if it involves breaking down fences or trampling muddy paths across flower beds and shrubberies. Skateboarders in plazas and homeless alcoholics colonizing benches in enclosed shopping malls are other examples of a failure to integrate design with user need and the lack of other local facilities. Putting up signs to ban certain activities or using security officers to move people on is an inadequate response to bad planning and lack of integration.

- Built environments need to be robust but adaptable enough to accommodate changing social dynamics and demographics. Cheap-finish, mass solutions have proved to be costly (both financially and criminogenically) in the long run. Good-quality materials and 'human' building scales signal a respect for the intended users, and this respect is generally reciprocated (see Alexander 1977 for an explanation of scale).

- Planners and designers should resist the creation of a divided society wherein the better-off (and allegedly law-abiding) exclude the less privileged (and so-called 'criminal classes') from large tracts of the environment by privatizing what were formerly public spaces. Quite apart from the social ethics of such an approach, this polarization of space can raise levels of fear and mutual suspicion (Ellin 1997).

- Planners and the planning process can provide valuable components in effective approaches to preventing crime and improving community safety, which almost inevitably require long-term, strategic and multi-disciplinary interventions (cf. DoE 1993; Osborn and Shaftoe 1995).

- Crime prevention is not the only goal of enlightened social and urban policy. A crime-free environment (even if we could achieve it) would probably be sterile and unappealing. We have to balance security with both mundane considerations (such as fire service access and public rights of way) and overarching concepts such as sustainability, human rights and equal opportunities.

So how can we design an optimum environment for community safety – where both actual crime and fear of crime are not major problems? First, we can refer to the guidelines that have been produced and are based on research, but we should not be dogmatic in interpreting them. These guidelines should recommend the following process:

- If possible, carry out research and consultation with people who use, intend to use or avoid the identified environment.

- Appraise the context: current and intended use, variations in use according to time of day, week and season, levels and types of crime in the area, external influences from adjacent areas and transport patterns.

The best that can be achieved will be a built environment, supported by the optimum number of users, which is robust and adaptable enough to accommodate and absorb activities and uses which may change over time.

There is no one blueprint for a safe community but there are many pitfalls to be avoided. For example, town centre areas which have become blighted by occurrences of vandalism, theft and predatory crime may need to be revitalized by improved supervision (say, by a combination of CCTV and uniformed centre wardens), new facilities or accommodation to attract citizens back into the area (including integrative activities for people who might otherwise be threateningly 'hanging around' in the centre), as well as good urban design that avoids vulnerable locations or predatory opportunities.

Finally, there is a view that crime adds a certain 'frisson' to the vigorous dynamics of urban living (the 'mean streets' of Raymond Chandler and *film noir*), but it would appear that most city-dwellers prefer to experience such excitement vicariously rather than through direct risk of victimization. Perhaps in a utopian crime-free future, people will pay to go to theme parks where, instead of being scared on ghost trains, they can wander down deserted alleys with flickering street lamps and the silhouettes of sinister-looking characters outlined in the dim distance!

Selected further reading

The two classic books that launched the whole topic are Jane Jacobs' (1961) *The Death and Life of Great American Cities: The Failure of Town Planning* and Oscar Newman's (1972) *Defensible Space: People and Design in the Violent City*. They are both highly readable, probably due to the fact that they were written by a journalist and architect, respectively. Another architect, Barry Poyner, researched and wrote *Design against Crime: Beyond Defensible Space* (1983), which does exactly what it says on the tin. Interestingly, the recommendations made in this book are directly at odds with the new urban agenda of accessibility, mixed use and inclusivity. Along with psychologist Barry Webb, Poyner subsequently produced the ambitiously titled *Crime Free Housing* (1991) which offered

31 'patterns' to enable designers to reduce all types of crime in residential layouts. Paul and Patricia Brantingham, in their works *Environmental Criminology* (1981, 2nd edn 1991) and *Patterns in Crime* (1984), developed the theory that offenders' life patterns influenced the location of their offending behaviour, positing that offenders tended to commit crime in 'known' areas'.

For a rather less penetrable (ironically) account of the theory and research that supports permeable urban layouts as a means of preventing crime, Bill Hillier and Julienne Hanson's (1984) *The Social Logic of Space* is the seminal work. Schneider and Kitchen's (2002) *Planning for Crime Prevention* brings the permeability discussion up to date by linking it to new urbanism. Steven Town's 2004 report, *Permeability, Access Opportunities and Crime*, presents the opposing argument. For a useful discussion about the general design principles that can help to create safer neighbourhoods, Paul Stollard's (1991) *Crime Prevention through Housing Design* is worth a read while, for a more technically detailed coverage, Crouch *et al.*'s (1999) *Design for Secure Residential Environments* gets right down to nuts and bolts. Finally, Gerda Wekerle and Carolyn Whitzman's (1995) *Safe Cities: Guidelines for Planning, Design and Management* gives useful comments and information about creating safer public places and spaces.

Notes

1. The Radburn layout is based on the laudable principle of separating traffic from pedestrians in housing developments. An access road and garaging would be provided down one side of a row of houses which on the other side would front on to a purely pedestrian area characterized by gardens, communal spaces and footpaths. Unfortunately this has resulted in making many houses vulnerable to burglaries on one side and car theft on the other, and as a result many Radburn estates have been reorientated to turn them back into conventional 'houses on streets'.

2. Evidence cited to support this view is found, for example, in Budd's (1999) analysis of the BCS which suggested that a lower proportion of properties on culs-de-sac suffered burglary than properties on main or side roads.

3. A more measured application of closure theory is often suggested by architectural liaison officers, police officers responsible for advising planners and developers about the importance of 'designing out crime', under the aegis of 'secured by design' (SBD). Secure car park schemes, badged by the police, are another example of these theories being put into practice. SBD is discussed in greater detail later in this chapter.

4. See www.securedbydesign.com. Secured by Design (SBD) is a police initiative to encourage the building industry to adopt crime prevention measures in development design to assist in reducing the opportunity for crime and the fear of crime, creating a safer and more secure environment. It is intended to achieve a better quality of life by addressing crime prevention at the earliest opportunity in the design, layout and construction of homes and commercial premises. In doing so Secured by Design supports one of the government's key planning objectives; that is, 'the creation of secure, quality places where people wish to live and work' (Home Office crime reduction website – http://www.crimereduction.gov.uk/securedesign8.htm).

References

Alexander, C. (1977) *A Pattern Language – Towns, Buildings, Construction*. New York, NY: Oxford University Press.

Allatt, P. (1984) 'Residential security: containment and displacement of burglary', *Howard Journal*, 23: 99–116.

Armitage, R. (2000) *Evaluation of Secured by Design Housing in West Yorkshire. Home Office Briefing Note 7/00*. London: Home Office.

Atlas, R. (1992) 'The alchemy of CPTED: less magic, more science!' Paper presented at International Designing Out Crime Association Conference, Mississauga, Canada.

Blakely, E. and Snyder, M. (1997) *Fortress America: Gated Communities in the United States*. Washington, DC: Brookings Institute Press.

Blandy, S., Lister, D., Atkinson, R. and Flint, J. (2003) *Gated Communities: A Systematic Review of the Research Evidence*. Bristol and Glasgow: ESRC Centre for Neighbourhood Research, Universities of Bristol and Glasgow.

Bottoms, A. and Wiles, P. (1986) 'Housing tenure and residential community crime careers in Britain', in M. Tonry and N. Morris (eds) *Crime and Justice: A Review of Research. Vol. 8*. Chicago, IL: University of Chicago Press.

Brand, S. (1994) *How Buildings Learn – What Happens after They're Built*. New York, NY: Viking Penguin.

Brantingham, P. and Brantingham, P. (1981) *Environmental Criminology* (2nd edn 1991). Beverly Hills, CA: Sage.

Brantingham, P. and Brantingham, P. (1984) *Patterns in Crime*, New York, NY: Macmillan.

Budd, T. (1999) *Burglary of Domestic Dwellings: Findings from the British Crime Survey. Home Office Statistical Bulletin 4/99*. London: Home Office.

Burrows, J. (1980) 'Closed circuit television and crime on the London Underground', in R. Clarke and P. Mayhew (eds) *Designing Out Crime*. London: HMSO.

Bursik, R.J. and Grasmick, H.G. (1993) *Neighbourhoods and Crime – The Dimensions of Effective Community Control*. San Francisco, CA: Lexington Books.

Carstensen, N. and Frederiksen, K. (1997) 'Situational crime prevention', in R. Lene (ed.) *Kriminalistisk Arbog*. Copenhagen: Criminal Procedure Institute.

Chaiken, J.M., Lawless, M.W. and Stevenson, K.A. (1974) *The Impact of Police Activity on Crime: Robberies on the New York City Subway System*. New York, NY: Rand Institute.

Clarke, R. (1980). 'Situational crime prevention: theory and practice', *British Journal of Criminology*, 20: 136–47.

Clarke, R. (1995) 'Situational crime prevention', in M. Tonry and D. Farrington (eds) *Building a Safer Society: Strategic Approaches to Crime Prevention*. Chicago, IL: University of Chicago Press.

Cohen, L. and Felson, M. (1979) 'Social change and crime rate trends: a routine activity approach', *American Sociological Review*, 44: 588–608.

Coleman, A. (1985) *Utopia on Trial*. London: Hilary Shipman.

Cornish, D. and Clarke, R. (1986) *The Reasoning Criminal: Rational Choice Perspectives on Offending*. New York, NY: Springer-Verlag.

Crouch, S., Shaftoe, H. and Fleming, R. (1999) *Design for Secure Residential Environments*. Harlow: Longman.

Department of the Environment (1993) *Crime Prevention on Council Estates*. London: HMSO.

Department of the Environment (1997) *An Evaluation of DICE Schemes. Regeneration Research Summary 11*. London: DoE.

Department of the Environment and the Welsh Office (1994) *Planning Out Crime. Circular 5/94*. London: Home Office.

Ellin, N. (ed.) (1997) *Architecture of Fear*. New York, NY: Princeton Architectural Press.

Farrington, D. and Welsh, B. (2002) *The Effects of Improved Street Lighting on Crime: A Systematic Review. Home Office Research Study* 251. London: Home Office.

Felson, M. (1987) 'Routine activities and crime prevention in the developing metropolis', *Criminology*, 25: 911–31.

Felson, M. and Clarke, R. (1998) *Opportunity Makes the Thief: Practical Theory for Crime Prevention. Police Research Series Paper* 98. London: Home Office

Ferraro, K.F. and LaGrange, R. (1992) 'Are older people most afraid of crime? Reconsidering differences in fear of victimisation', *Journal of Gerontology*, 47: s233–44.

Grabosky, P. (1989) 'Elderly persons; vulnerability and involvement in crime', in *Sydney University, Institute of Criminology Proceedings*, 47: 35–50.

Hale, C. (1996) 'Fear of crime: a review of the literature', *International Review of Victimology*, 4: 79–150.

Hall, D. (1997) *The Dufferin Papers*. Toronto: Marathon Realty Company.

Hesseling, R. (1994) 'Displacement: a review of the empirical literature', in *Crime Prevention Studies. Vol. 3*. Monsey, NY: Criminal Justice Press.

Hesseling, R. (1995) 'Theft from cars: reduced or displaced?', *European Journal of Criminal Policy and Research*, 3: 79–92.

Hillier, B. and Hanson, J. (1984) *The Social Logic of Space*. Cambridge: Cambridge University Press.

Hillier, B. and Shu, S. (2002) *Do Burglars Understand Defensible Space?* London: Space Syntax Laboratory, Bartlett School of Architecture (available at www.spacesyntax. com).

Hirschfield, A. and Bowers, K. (1997) 'The effect of social cohesion on levels of recorded crime in disadvantaged areas', *Urban Studies*, 34: 1275–95.

Home Office (1989) *Report of the Working Group on the Fear of Crime. Home Office Standing Conference on Crime Prevention*. London: Home Office.

Home Office Crime Prevention Centre (1994) *Police Architectural Liaison Manual of Guidance*. London: Home Office.

Home Office and ODPM (2004) *Safer Places: The Planning System and Crime Prevention*. Tonbridge: Thomas Telford.

Hunt, A.L. and Weiner, K. (1977) 'The impact of a juvenile curfew: suppression and displacement in patterns of juvenile offences', *Journal of Police Science and Administration*, 5: 407–12.

Jacobs, J. (1961) *The Death and Life of Great American Cities: The Failure of Town Planning*. Harmondsworth: Penguin Books.

Jeffery, C.R. (1971) *Crime Prevention through Environmental Design*. Beverly Hills, CA: Sage.

Katz, P. (1994) *The New Urbanism: Towards an Architecture of Community*. New York, NY: McGraw-Hill.

Knowles, P. (2003) 'The costs of policing new urbanism', *Community Safety Journal*, 2: 33–8.

KPMG Peat Marwick and the Safe Neighbourhoods Unit (1990) *Counting out Crime: The Nottingham Crime Audit*. London: KPMG/SNU.

Kuo, F. and Sullivan, W. (2001) 'Aggression and violence in the inner city: effects of environment via mental fatigue', *Environment and Behaviour*, 33: 543–71.

Marchant, P. (2004) 'A demonstration that the claim that brighter lighting reduces crime is unfounded', *British Journal of Criminology*, 44: 441–7.

Mayhew, P., Clarke, R.V., Sturman, A. and Hough, M. (1976) *Crime as Opportunity. Home Office Research Study* 34. London: HMSO.

Mayhew, P. and Maung, N. (1992) *Surveying Crime: Findings from the 1992 British Crime Survey. Home Office Research and Statistics Department, Research Findings* 2. London: Home Office.

Merry, S. (1981) 'Defensible space undefended: social factors in crime control through environmental design', *Urban Affairs Quarterly*, 16: 397–422.

Minton, A. (2002) *Building Balanced Communities: The US and UK Compared*. London: Royal Institute of Chartered Surveyors.

Mirrlees-Black, C. (1998) *Rural Areas and Crime: Findings from the British Crime Survey. Home Office Research and Statistics Directorate Research Findings* 77. London: Home Office.

Mirrlees-Black, C. and Maung, N.A. (1994) *Fear of Crime: Findings from the 1992 British Crime Survey. Research Findings* 9. London: Home Office.

Morton, J. (1994) *From Southgate to Hallwood Park: 25 Years in the Life of a Runcorn Community*. Liverpool: Merseyside Improved Houses.

Neal, P. (ed.) (2003) *Urban Villages and the Making of Communities*. London: Spon.

Neighbourhood Initiatives Foundation (1999) *Do-ers' Guide to Planning for Real*. Telford: NIF.

Newman, O. (1972) *Defensible Space: People and Design in the Violent City*. New York, NY: Macmillan.

Newman, O. (1974) *Community of Interest: Design for Community Control*. NACRO Conference Paper, London.

Newman, O. (1995) 'Defensible space – a new physical planning tool for urban revitalisation', *Journal of the American Planning Association*, 61: 149–55.

Oc, T. and Tiesdell, S. (1997) 'Housing and safer city centres', in T. Oc and S. Tiesdell (eds) *Safer City Centres – Reviving the Public Realm*. London: Paul Chapman Publishing.

Office of the Deputy Prime Minister (2004) *Planning Policy Statement 1: Creating Sustainable Communities*. London: ODPM.

Osborn, S. and Shaftoe, H. (1995) *Safer Neighbourhoods? Successes and Failures in Crime Prevention*. York: Safe Neighbourhoods Unit/Joseph Rowntree Foundation

Poole, R. (1994) *Operation Columbus: Travels in North America*. Birmingham: West Midlands Police.

Poyner, B. (1983) *Design against Crime: Beyond Defensible Space*. London: Butterworths.

Poyner, B. (1995) *Design for Inherent Security: Guidance for Non-residential Buildings*. London: CIRIA.

Poyner, B. and Webb, B. (1991) *Crime Free Housing*. London: Butterworths.

Poyner, B. and Webb, B. (1992) 'Reducing theft from shopping bags in city center markets', in R.V. Clarke (ed.) *Situational Crime Prevention: Successful Case Studies*. Albany, NY: Harrow & Heston.

Putnam, R. (1995) 'Bowling alone: America's declining social capital', *Journal of Democracy*, 6: 65–78.

Ramsay, M. (1991) *The Effect of Better Street Lighting on Crime and Fear: A Review. Home Office Crime Prevention Unit Paper* 29. London: Home Office.

Rengier, R. (1985) 'Kriminologische Folgen der Bekampfung des Bankraubs durch technische Pravention', *Monatsschrift fur Kriminologie and Strafrechtsreform*, 68: 104–18.

Sampson, R., Raudenbush, S. and Earls, F. (1997) 'Neighbourhoods and violent crime: a multilevel study of collective efficacy', *Science*, 277: 918–24.

Schneider, R. and Kitchen, T. (2002) *Planning for Crime Prevention: A Transatlantic Perspective*. London and New York: Routledge.

Scottish Office (1994) *Planning for Crime Prevention. Planning Advice Note* 46. Edinburgh: Scottish Office.

Shaftoe, H. (2000) 'Community safety and actual neighbourhoods', in H. Barton (ed.) *Sustainable Communities: The Potential for Eco-neighbourhoods*. London: Earthscan.

Shaftoe, H. (2004) *Crime Prevention: Facts, Fallacies and the Future*. Basingstoke: Palgrave Macmillan.

Shaftoe, H. and James, S. (2004) 'Do Symbolic Barriers Prevent Crime and Offer an Increased Sense of Security?' *Planning Practice and Research*, Vol 19: 4: November 2004. 441–51.

Shapland, J. and Vagg, J. (1988) *Policing by the Public*. New York, NY: Routledge.

Simmons, J. and Dodd, T. (eds) (2003) *Crime in England and Wales 2002/3. Home Office Statistical Bulletin 07/03*. London: Home Office.

Skogan, W. (1992) *Disorder and Decline: Crime and the Spiral of Decay in American Neighbourhoods*. Berkeley, CA: UCLA Press.

SNU (1993) *Crime Prevention on Council Estates*. London: Safe Neighbourhoods Unit.

SNU (1994) *Housing Safe Communities: An Evaluation of Recent Initiatives*. London: Safe Neighbourhoods Unit.

Stollard, P. (1991) *Crime Prevention through Housing Design*.

Stubbs, D. (2002) 'The town centre tipping point: regeneration or degeneration.' Masters dissertation, University of the West of England, Bristol.

Taylor, N. (1973) *The Village in the City*. London: Temple Smith.

Thornton, R. and Endo, K. (1992) *Preventing Crime in America and Japan: A Comparative Study*. New York, NY: Sharpe.

Town, S. (2001) *Crime Displacement: The Perception, Problems, Evidence and Supporting Theory*. Bradford: West Yorkshire Police (also available on the Home Office Crime Reduction website).

Town, S. (2004) *Permeability, Access Opportunities and Crime*. Bradford: West Yorkshire Police.

Urban Villages Forum (1992) *Urban Villages: A Concept for Creating Mixed Use Urban Development on a Sustainable Scale*. London: Urban Villages Group.

Walop, M. (1996) 'Improving the inner city.' Paper presented at the Towards World Change – Setting the Stage for Community Safety Conference, Vancouver, Canada.

Ward, C. (1989) *Welcome, Thinner City: Urban Survival in the 1990s*. London: Bedford Square Press.

Wekerle, G. and Whitzman, C. (1995) *Safe Cities: Guidelines for Planning, Design and Management*. New York, NY: Van Nostrand Reinhold.

Chapter 10

Crime prevention and system design

Nick Tilley

Crime is the intentional consequence of unintended opportunity. If we take the distribution of opportunity as given we could calculate expected rates of crime given variations in levels of crime intention. Or we could take the distribution of intentions as given and calculate expected rates given variations in levels of opportunity. In practice, opportunity and intention are liable to interact. In particular, easy opportunities can reinforce or reward intention. Unintended opportunities are created in many different ways. Some are dealt with in other chapters.

New products may unintentionally create opportunity by increasing the capacity to commit crime (Ekblom and Tilley 2000). Handguns are an obvious example, but so too are battery-powered screwdrivers, cars and mobile telephones. New products may also comprise attractive new targets of theft. Innovations may create opportunity by making products lighter, smaller and more anonymous, hence more easily concealed, transported and sold on. Here examples are legion. Think of video-recorders, laptop computers, flat-screen televisions, and iPods. Some products, such as cars and mobile phones, act as both crime enablers and suitable targets for crime. Clarke has tried to capture the attributes of goods that are suitable targets for theft with his acronym, 'CRAVED' – Concealable, Removable, Accessible, Valuable, Enjoyable and Disposable (Clarke 1999). Felson refers to crime targets that are, from the likely offender's point of view, 'VIVA' – they have Value, show low Inertia, are Visible and are Accessible with easy exit chances (Felson 1998). Pease has discussed the chronic need to retrofit solutions to crime problems created by the design of products, and has advocated foresight and forethought to build in crime resistance from the start with new products that are liable to become crime targets (Pease 1997). (The issue of crime and product design is the main focus of Chapter 8, this volume.)

The criminogenic side-effects of environmental design have likewise been the focus of a good deal of attention and are discussed in Chapter 9, this volume. Oscar Newman's pioneering work on territoriality, design and crime (Newman

1973), Alice Coleman's work on design attributes and crime (Coleman 1990), C. Ray Jefferys' *Crime Prevention through Environmental Design* (Jeffery 1971), Barry Poyner's work on physical design and layout (Poyner 1983; Poyner and Webb 1991) and Paul and Patricia Brantingham's work on environment and crime pattern analysis (Brantingham and Brantingham 1981, 1984) are all arguing in various ways that the shape of the physical environment can inadvertently encourage or enable crime, by producing opportunities, but likewise might be designed or modified in ways that lessen opportunity and discourage crime. There are accusations of environmental determinism (see Chapter 8, this volume), on the grounds that it is people who take advantage of crime opportunities, but the counterpoint, as noted in the opening paragraph to this chapter, is that for people disposed to commit crime the opportunities have to be there for them to follow through on their dispositions.

This chapter draws together an array of literature that relates to a third and so far less fully articulated area of design and crime: that which relates to the creation or modification of regulation, policy, procedure and contrived routine. The less-than-perfect portmanteau term used here to capture these is 'system'. 'System' refers for present purposes to any set of organized or consciously developed habitual human behaviours.[1] The implicit contrast is with unorganized, though not necessarily unstructured, human action. Unorganized but structured actions would include, for example, economic markets that generate patterns as emergent outcomes of a multitude of discrete decisions rather than following any particular person's or group's designs or intentions. System attributes are knowingly designed, rather than unknowingly created.

There is much unsystematic behaviour that is relevant to crime opportunities and crime patterns, for example holidaymaking, pub-going, clubbing and so on. Such activities will be relevant to the production of crime patterns but are not 'systematic' in the sense of that word used here in that they are not orchestrated, planned, intended, designed or consciously habituated. Vulnerable, carefree and careless holidaymakers, unknowing about the riskiness of areas they visit, for instance comprise easy targets, and their patterned victimization is a predictable consequence of behaviours each engages in, independently but not repeatedly. What we have here is just the result of aggregates of individual choices that collectively constitute observably structured, but unplanned, patterns of behaviour. This is not to say that these unstructured patterns are beyond engineering. Incentives of various sorts, taxes, signs, information and exhortation can all be used to try to manipulate unplanned patterns of behaviour, but they are after the event and contrast with the humanly designed systems of behaviour focused on in this chapter. This chapter is not, thus, concerned with patterned crime-related behaviour as an emergent unintended consequence of aggregated individual actions. Rather its focus is on patterned unintended crime consequences of systems that are purposively designed, even though the design is rarely primarily directed at crime. It is about ways in which systems can be configured in ways that facilitate crime and may be reconfigured, or managed, to inhibit it. It is also about opportunities to think crime in the design of new systems.

How systems unintentionally create crime

There are several ways in which systems can be conducive to crime.

Systems can furnish rewards for crime

The presence of systems can provide incentives for criminal behaviour. Take smuggling. The existence of variations in levels of excise duty has for hundreds of years provided rich rewards for smuggling goods across national borders.

Systems can make crime easy

The development of some systems unintentionally facilitates crime. Take fuel drive-offs. The method by which petrol is dispensed at service stations makes driving off without payment easy. Customers serve themselves, garage staff remain inside the service station building, payment is supposedly made after the tank is filled and means of escape are at hand (see La Vigne 1994; Tilley 2005).

Systems can facilitate crime planning

Where there are predictable systems, risks, rewards, effort needed and the tools needed for offending can all, in principle, be gauged in advance. Take robbery. Regular security patrols can better be avoided than random ones. Regular patterns of cash delivery can better be targeted than random ones. Standard staffing patterns can inform plans about needs for weapons or numbers of offenders, although in practice much planning of robbery seems at best rudimentary (Matthews 2002).

Systems can disinhibit and provoke crime

Those who might not otherwise be intending to commit crimes may be disinhibited and provoked by virtue of systems in place. Take late-night city-centre violence. Happy-hour sales promotions in bars can create a supply of disinhibited drunks, who are liable to be violent and to be victims of violence (see Homel *et al.* 1997). Specified closing times and restricted transport systems can create large numbers competing for means to get home late at night, provoking friction and potential clashes between disinhibited groups trying to access buses and taxis.

Systems can generate need

Though need and relative deprivation may drive some crime which may thereby be a function of economic systems, there are more immediate ways in which systems can create needs that in turn facilitate crime. Take electricity and gas cash-prepayment meter breaks, which became an increasing problem in Britain in the 1980s, as a specific instance (see Hill 1986). Meter breaks were found to take place disproportionately in relatively poor areas, and at mid-week (Hill 1986; Forrester *et al.* 1988, 1990). Systems for the payment of social security payments to all on the same day each week may reduce the scope for mutual borrowing when money runs out, creating patterns of need that may be met by meter breaks the day before welfare payments are made.

Systems can create crime networks

Provisions for young offenders or those at risk of offending can bring them together. This may be the case for motor projects for those involved on the fringes of vehicle crime and also for holiday play-schemes in high-crime neighbourhoods. In particular if sent home at the same time these groups can crystallize. Local authority housing allocation systems can likewise unintentionally lead to concentrations of networked offenders in particular areas (Bottoms *et al.* 1992).

Systems can teach crime

To commit many crimes techniques have to be learnt. Take drug-related rapes. Internet websites that are designed to allow potential victims to recognize when they might be at risk and the precautions that they can take also indicate the properties of specific drugs and the methods that can be used to take advantage of suitable victims. Likewise, reports of offences and the easy ways in which they can be committed, on the Internet, in newspapers or on television, can all transmit crime technique (see Matthews 2002). A recent example relates to the slashing of curtains to curtain-sided trucks parked overnight at service areas. A description of the modus operandi, and the names and addresses of a gang of offenders who had been convicted, were published by the police on the Internet. Following this there was an explosive growth in the number of similar incidents (Tilley 2005).

Systems can legitimate crime

The routine non-enforcement of rules can lead to their perceived illegitimacy (see Sherman 1990). Take littering for example. There is little or no enforcement of the law surrounding the dropping of litter. It then becomes widespread and quite normal. This process of growth in crime and disorder is at the heart of the broken windows theory (Wilson and Kelling 1982).

Systems can supply likely offenders

Both the creation of those without interests in behaving lawfully and the reduction of controls over those who might otherwise be prevented from criminal behaviour can contribute to the supply of offenders. Take youth offending. School exclusions practices and policies that aim to deal with difficult and disruptive pupils remove controls from them in school hours. They may also attenuate these children's attachment to institutions that promote lawful behaviour, and provide one route to lawful means of income generation.

Systems can supply suitable targets.

Individuals who are 'out of place' appear to be at heightened risk. Take travellers, truckers, tourists and foreign students. Their elevated risk springs in part because they go unawares into offenders' 'awareness space'. They lack self-protection routines or habits. That is, the offenders are familiar with the territory and its potential spoils whilst the visiting victim is unfamiliar with the territory and its potential dangers, and has hence no systems to adapt to it. Offenders look out for those who look naïve, lost and unprotected. They comprise easy prey (see Tilley *et al.* 2004). Potential victims, who are 'at home' in a neighbourhood, are better placed to take routine precautions: they better know how to avoid being or seeming to be suitable targets. In some cases systems may help flag up non-locals. One example comprises the car licence plates in Florida which indicated 'tourist' to robbers, or those in Germany that indicated 'British soldier' to the IRA.

Some systems may be criminogenic simultaneously in a variety of ways. Take imprisonment. The criminogenic potential of prisons is well recognized. Prisons are institutions where legitimate sources of income can be lost, excuses for crime vindicated, techniques for crime transmitted and networks between offenders fostered.

The specific systems mentioned in this section are well intentioned. They develop to meet specific needs or to serve specific purposes. Excise duty is a valuable source of tax revenue. Self-service petrol stations provide for lower running costs for garages, and ultimately lower fuel prices for consumers. Regular patrols can more easily be organized and monitored than random ones. Cheap drinks are popular with customers and draw them in. Same-day welfare benefits systems for all are presumably easier to administer than ones spread across the week or month. Holiday play-schemes and motor projects are intended to provide constructive and healthy activities to those who attend them. Crime-related Internet websites are intended to provide warnings to potential victims. Inattention to minor incivilities is intended to provide authorities with the time to deal with more serious crimes. Difficult children are excluded from schools in the interests of allowing the others better to flourish. And provisions for geographic movement serve a multitude of commercial, social and personal needs. In each case the criminogenic legacy is an unintended side-effect.

Unintended crime side-effects are generated, it needs to be stressed, not just by systems that are oriented to offending and offenders, but also by other systems not ostensibly concerned with offending at all. Where new systems are found to be criminogenic, it may be necessary to retrofit solutions just as retrofit solutions have been sought where the designs of products and places have been criminogenic (see Pease 1997). Many self-service clothes stores, for example, now employ a member of staff to greet customers at the door, largely to alert them to the fact that they have been noticed, and thereby to counter the designed-in vulnerability to crime that comes with self-service retailing.

Systems and the inhibition of crime

An audit of the activities of any organization would throw up a myriad of ways in which the systems making up the organization are relevant to the generation or inhibition of crime. Take a university, for instance. Here are some examples of ways in which university systems may inhibit crimes. Clearly, if these systems are not in place then crime opportunities are to that degree more available:

- *Fraudulent expenses claims*: Requirements for evidence that tickets have been purchased, journeys undertaken and conferences attended.
- *Fraudulent sick-pay claims*: Return-to-work interviews following all days off sick to ensure employee fit to resume work.
- *Internal theft*: Systems to take up references, systems to audit goods purchased, systems to check deliveries, internal audit arrangements.
- *Burglary of student properties*: Systems to approve landlords and the properties they propose to let to students.
- *External theft*: Systems to vet those entering and leaving the university.
- *Plagiarism*: Changing titles for coursework questions, requirements that all sources used are cited and rule-setting at submission of coursework.
- *Sexual harassment, and accusations of it*: Open-door conventions for one-to-one meetings.
- *Theft from libraries*: Entry and check-out arrangements.
- *Graffiti*: Procedures for the prompt removal of new items.
- *Cycle theft*: Systems for marking cycles and keeping records of marked bikes.
- *Motor vehicle crime*: Patterns of (randomized) security patrol round the university estate.
- *Attacks on late-night ancillary staff*: Allocating staff to work in pairs; provision of escorts at quiet periods and at high-risk locations.
- *Student robbery*: Provision of transport for students at night, when they are at heightened risk.

Of course, universities as physical spaces may also enable or inhibit crime. Provision of secure bike parking, the location and design of car parks, locks and bars giving access to university buildings and university student accommodation, safes to contain exam papers, patterns of walkways through universities, levels of illumination, CCTV systems and orchestrated natural surveillance over areas of potential risk and so on may all, of course, help shape the vulnerability of the university and of those who work in it. The point here is that the way the university operates, as with any other organization, will also shape vulnerability to crime.

Moreover, at least some physical crime prevention measures require human routines if they are to be operative. Locks on doors are subverted if not used, if doors are left propped open or if they remain unrepaired when damaged; window locks only reduce opportunities for gaining entry if used; planting arrangements may only maintain scope for natural surveillance if pruning occurs regularly; CCTV systems lose their operational effectiveness unless the equipment is maintained and images are at least sometimes used; raised levels of illumination are undermined if bulbs are not replaced when they fail; and so on. Moreover, systems for the installation of physical measures may also affect their crime prevention effectiveness. For example, the use within the university of the same window locks, the same door locks, the same code for entering car parks or buildings, or the same type of safe and so on all increase certainty for the potential offender (see Ekblom 1997). They make criminal learning and tooling up for crime more straightforward. Systems for variation and random allocation of security provision can help increase the effectiveness of physical measures.

What goes for universities goes for any social unit: family, local authority, retailer, school, manufacturer, hospital, club, government department, bar, voluntary organization, military outfit, hotel and so on. The systems in place will be critical to the crime opportunities created or contained.

How systems can de designed to reduce crime

The following comprises a variety of ways in which system design can reduce crime. In most of the examples that are given system modifications have been introduced specifically to address crime problems, though in one or two cases system changes introduced for quite other reasons have had an unintended crime-reducing effect analogous to the unintended forms of system criminogenesis mentioned earlier in this chapter.

Systems can make crime more risky or at least make it seem more risky to potential offenders

There are several examples of system changes that have been introduced with a view to increasing the risk or perceived risk to the prospective offender. An Australian one relates to the introduction of random breath-testing in New South Wales as a means of reducing drunk-driving and the casualties that are associated with it. Ross Homel (1993) found that quite large numbers of random police stops and tests for alcohol, in the context of growing public intolerance of drinking and driving, produced a substantial and sustained fall in the numbers of people killed through drink-driving incidents. Lawrence Sherman (1990; see also Tilley 2004) has written likewise about the effects of crackdowns – short-term substantially concentrated and intensified police enforcement in relation to a specific crime and or location – that reduce the certainty with which potential offenders can calculate the risks of being caught committing the crime targeted in the crackdown. Sherman notes that crackdowns have quite a strong record in reducing crime and that their effect tends to outlast their application. There is temporal 'diffusion of benefits' – an extension of effectiveness beyond the time when the crackdown was in place – as those subject to the crackdown fail to realize when it has been withdrawn. Sherman speculated about the possibility of a crime prevention strategy comprising revolving and returning crackdowns. This would be a means of addressing some offences which would otherwise never come to the top of enforcement agencies' agendas. It would also be a means of maximizing offender uncertainty about whether or not they face a significant and uncontrollable risk.

Mayhew *et al.* (1989) discuss an interesting case where a change in regulation brought with it an unintended crime reduction harvest. They describe the fall in thefts of motorcycles that followed when wearing motorcycle helmets became compulsory in Germany, and when the regulation was also conscientiously enforced. In these circumstances, unless the prospective offender happened to be carrying a helmet or came prepared to commit the theft by carrying one, he or she faced substantial risks of being caught driving off on a stolen motorcycle.

Systems can make crime more difficult or make it appear more difficult

Across quite a wide range of problems, system modification appears to be a way to make crime more difficult. The first example, from Sweden, relates to cheque frauds in the 1970s (Knuttson and Kuhlhorn 1997). The problem was one of cheque books being obtained illicitly and then individual cheques being presented fraudulently. This generated a large number of crime incidents per cheque book used. Each incident typically involved only a small sum of money: less than 300 Swedish kroner. The reason for the high numbers of low-value cheque crimes was that the bank guaranteed payments below 500 kroner, and at less than 300 kroner the recipient was not even required to obtain any evidence of the identity of the person paying by cheque. The system-change response was withdrawal of the bank guarantee and a requirement that evidence of the identity of the person paying the cheque be obtained in all cases, regardless of the amount payable. This was instituted in July 1971. Figure 10.1 shows the pattern of all reported cheque crime in Sweden from 1965 to 1978. It appears that an immediate, dramatic and sustained fall took place following the change in system.

A second example, this time from the Netherlands, relates to fare evasion on buses (van Andel 1997). In 1963 conductors were withdrawn from the buses in the interests of cost reduction, and the driver sold and checked tickets. In 1966 automated ticket-stamping machines were introduced, creating easier opportunities for fare-dodging. In the mid-1980s systems were changed to try

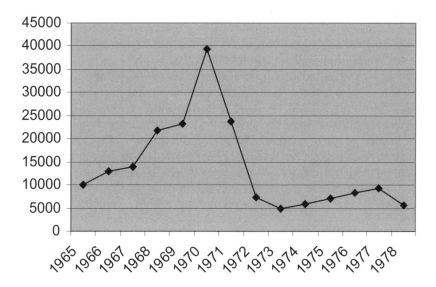

Figure 10.1 Reported cheque crimes in Sweden, 1965–78

to reduce the amount of evasion. This involved reverting to the driver selling and checking tickets as passengers boarded the buses. In Amsterdam rates of evasion went down from 9.2 per cent to 1.7 per cent, in Rotterdam from 3.8 per cent to 1.3 per cent and in The Hague from 14.1 per cent to 2.1 per cent. Though the scheme was evidently popular, unfortunately the reductions in loss were not sufficient to offset the increased operating costs.

A third example, from Britain, relates to British car-licensing arrangement (Webb *et al.* 2004, Smith and Webb 2005; see also Chapter 17, this volume). Vehicle licensing in Britain goes back to 1903. Webb *et al.* note that changes had already taken place in efforts to contain crime problems. They cite first the move from local authority to national vehicle licensing in 1974, with the creation of the Driver and Vehicle Licensing Centre (DVLC). This move was associated with the apparent ease with which those disqualified from driving in one area had been able successfully to apply for a licence to drive from another. Secondly, they quote a report from the Metropolitan Police Commissioner in 1921, which highlighted the ease with which thieves were able to steal cars and then register them as if previously unregistered, and the subsequent tightening up of procedures. The link between crime and registration arrangements evidently has quite a long history.

Webb *et al.* were commissioned to look at contemporary licensing arrangements and ways in which they might be altered with a view to reducing crime. They focus in particular on continuity and discontinuity in vehicle registration. The system in operation was allowing cars, in effect, to disappear. Both sellers and buyers were responsible for informing the DVLC of a change in keepership. However, those selling had few incentives to do so. Moreover, new owners might also delay informing DVLC for a period, during which time the vehicle–owner link became lost to the authority, and during which Vehicle Excise Duty (VED), parking fines, insurance and MOT payments could be evaded. This discontinuity in registration also facilitated vehicle theft and vehicle dumping. The failure to track the scrapping of vehicles, by informing the DVLA, fostered opportunities both to create new vehicle identities that could be attached to stolen vehicles for resale, and to dump cars at the end of their lives where they had no commercial value.[2]

Webb *et al.* suggested a simple system change for securing continuity of registration. This involved making the old owner liable for the vehicle and what is done with it until the DVLA is informed of change of ownership. This system would remove the opportunity that had previously existed, for vehicle crimes of various sorts. Webb *et al.* also made other suggestions for administrative changes. One was that proof of ownership be required to obtain replacement registration documents, as a means of removing a facilitator of vehicle theft. Another was that the vehicle registration document be required to relicense a vehicle, as a means of making it more difficult to sell stolen vehicles.

Alongside system alterations, Webb *et al.* also advocate some other complementary changes, including ones for product design (notably electronic vehicle identification) and enforcement activity (for example, use of automated number plate recognition – ANPR). These would help accurately identify and chase up unregistered vehicles, to add teeth to the suggested administrative changes. In terms of impact, Webb *et al.* estimated that VED evasion would reach £300 million by 2007 in the absence of the suggested measures, but could be expected to fall to £100 million with their full implementation.

Systems can make crime less rewarding or appear potentially less rewarding

The most celebrated case of systems development to deny reward probably relates to the rapid removal of graffiti. Sloan Howitt and Kelling (1997) describe the issue of graffiti on New York subway trains. It had been a persistent and knotty problem, involving multiple offences. Though each was trivial in itself, collectively they impacted significantly on the quality of life of millions of people. Graffiti artists evidently get their crime rewards from seeing the results of their labours on display. The simple system development that eventually cracked the problem was the quick withdrawal from service of cars covered in graffiti, so that images could never be seen publicly. Essentially, the reward that motivated the offender was removed. The New York City Transit Authority strategy was to clean a car and then ensure that it never again went into service with graffiti on it. Over a period of five years (1984–89) all cars became free from graffiti, and new graffiti more or less stopped appearing. The cleaning was backed by enforcement with police riding clean cars, and targeting efforts at detection on repeat offenders who were recognizable from their tags. However, as the cleaning regime developed numbers of arrests for graffiti/vandalism actually fell. Those for felonies went down from 237 in 1984 to 114 in 1988, whilst those for misdemeanours declined from 2681 to 974 over the same period.

A second example of system reward removal again comes from the USA, this time from Charlotte Mecklenburg. The issue here was theft of plug-in white goods from newly constructed dwellings at construction sites, prior to their occupation (Clarke and Goldstein 2002). The lack of residents, and large numbers of comings and goings at the building sites, provided for little effective guardianship. Moreover, new plug-in appliances were presumably especially attractive to thieves because they were easy to remove and were readily disposable. The response was to persuade developers to delay installation of the relevant appliances until the residences were to be occupied. That is, the potential rewards for the offender would no longer be available for them. An experiment, with co-operating developers, ran from May to October 2000. In the part of Charlotte where the initiative ran, the rate of burglary involving the targeted appliances fell from 5 and 4 per cent, respectively, in 1998 and 1999 to 1.6 per cent in 2000, and for all appliances from 5.4 and 5.3 per cent in 1988 and 1999 to 2.5 per cent in 2000. The same reductions were not found in other parts of the city, and there was scant evidence of displacement. Reduced burglary rates in the experimental area were, however, found amongst non-participating developers as well as participating ones, suggesting that there may have been some diffusion of benefits from participants to non-participants.

Systems can create offender uncertainty

Several of the examples given under the preceding three headings involve systems heightening offender uncertainty. This was the case with police crackdowns (Sherman 1990) and random breath testing (Homel 1993). It may also have been the case with the non-installation of plug-in white goods in newly built dwellings in Charlotte Mecklenburg (Clarke and Goldstein 2002). In a more general way, the significance of uncertainty creation is seen in 'anticipatory benefits', which are often obtained before crime prevention measures are installed or become operational. Smith *et al.* (2002) found that of 52 crime prevention evaluations, where adequate time-course data and detail were provided, 22 showed 'prima facie evidence of an anticipatory effect' (Smith *et al.* 2002: 74). Thus 40 per cent of those studies that were capable of showing an anticipatory effect did so. The authors stress the importance of 'publicity/disinformation' as a means by which such an effect may be produced. This relates to reduction in the confidence with which offenders can commit crimes, when they are made unsure of the difficulty, risk or reward of committing them during the period before the measures are in place. This comprises a special case of diffusion of benefits effects, which are found more broadly where potential offenders are uncertain as to the scope of place, time or crime type covered by preventive interventions.

Offender uncertainty produced from publicity had been previously noted in Laycock's finding that high-publicity property-marking had a preventive effect beyond the operational range of the property marking itself (Laycock 1997). It has been noted subsequently in Johnson and Bowers' findings, across 21 burglary prevention schemes funded through the British Home Office Crime Reduction Programme, that preventive effects were greatest during periods when the publicity created by projects was at its most intensive (Johnson and Bowers 2003, see also Chapter 13, this volume).

Systems can reduce crime provocation

The apparently 'mindless' violence and disorder that are found in some entertainment and city centre areas late at night may be reduced by a number of system changes. A notable example involved reducing the widespread availability of cheap alcohol through special promotions. Special promotions with cut-price drinks can lead to the congregation of large numbers of easily provoked inebriates, who are apt to confront one another violently as well as to behave in disorderly ways. A major demonstration project addressing this problem was undertaken in 1993 in Surfers Paradise, at the heart of the Gold Coast region in Queensland (Homel *et al.* 1997).

In the small central business district of Surfers Paradise, there were 187 licensed premises and 22 nightclubs. Numbers of violent and disorderly incidents were rising, the reputation of the area was suffering and some businesses were leaving as a consequence. Competition between bars for custom led to drinks promotions providing cheap liquor, and cost-minimizing methods of management. A Venue Management Task Group devised a checklist for assessing the policies at each individual bar, covering the following:

1. Discounting, including 'happy hours' and other binge-drinking incentives.

2. Pricing practices for low and standard alcohol beers.

3. Information for staff about serving under-age and intoxicated customers.

4. Information given to customers, promoting the bar and its use.

5. Under-age policies about admission and serving those under age.

6. Low-alcohol and non-alcoholic drink availability.

7. Instructions about response to and serving practices for those who are intoxicated.

8. Times and ranges of food available.

9. Entertainment used to promote the bar, and clientele targeted – from all-male to mixed.

10. Transport provision.

11. Serve sizes.

12. Policies relating to staff drinking, during and outside working hours.

13. Strategies to deal with problem, drinking customers.

14. Extent and nature of community and stakeholder group involvement

15. Personnel practices, including preferred staff style, recruitment, management, etc.

16. Security style, recruitment and training.

Out of these assessments came individual 'Model House Policies' for each licensee. The issues were discussed collectively by bar owners, who shared a sense of responsibility for their practices and recognized that they needed to change. A common code of practice emerged, which was eventually agreed by all but one licensee.

Adherence to the code of practice was monitored. Breaches were reported, for example, with free drinks offers, 'specials' for alcohol sales or overcrowding. They were then discussed informally with the licensee – though it became apparent that informal mutual pressure needed to be backed with action by formal police and licensing authorities.

The overall changes in management practices were striking. There were statistically significant changes in all but two of the 16 areas of assessment listed above (staff drinking and personnel were the exceptions). There appeared to be real changes in management policies and procedures. Various outcome data suggested that there was also a substantial drop in violence and disorder. For example, the numbers of incidents recorded by security companies fell at a growing rate: from 235 to 192 incidents for January to March from 1992 to 1993, respectively (–18 per cent); from 215 to 115 for April to July (–47 per cent); and from 241 to 50 for August to November (–79 per cent). Bars were evidently managed in ways producing less drunkenness and less provocation, leading to fewer problems of violence and disorder.

Systems can remind potential offenders of rules

The infraction of formal rules constitutes crimes and misdemeanours. Such transgressions, however, often involve forms of denial by offenders, so called 'techniques of neutralization' (Sykes and Matza 1957). Rule reminders prompt potential offenders, at the point of offending, to be aware that they are about to undertake a breach.

One example relates to the fraudulent return of goods to shops in exchange for cash. This is made easier where there are 'no questions' returns policies in place. Challinger (1997) discusses ways in which rule reminders were used by Coles Myer in Australia to reduce fraudulent returns. Measures included the following:

- Signs informing customers that proof of purchase would be required.
- A requirement that proof of purchase be presented when goods were returned.
- Where there was no proof of purchase:
  o a requirement of proof of personal identity when the goods were returned;
  o a requirement for a handwritten and signed statement giving identity, address and details of the purchase;
  o beyond specified sums, refunds by cheque only; and
  o reimbursement to the alleged purchaser who paid by cheque only once the cheque had cleared.

There was scope for flexibility in the application of this policy, for example when known and long-term customers were concerned.

Across the company's 500 supermarkets, 391 discount stores and 70 department stores Challinger reports an indexed fall from 100 to 17 in the number of detected fraudulent returns and a fall from 100 to 37 in the dollar value following the system changes. He reports the largest reductions in the discount stores and lowest in supermarkets, reflecting the different types of good sold in each store format.

Rule reminders have also been used in the UK in relation to reported thefts of Jobseekers' Allowance giro cheques (Dyson and Trevains 2000), and reports of thefts of mobile phones (Tilley *et al.* 2004), in relation to both of which there have been suspicions of fraud. In the case of the giro cheques claimants were required to complete and sign a form at the benefit office giving details of themselves, their National Insurance number and the alleged incident. The form was countersigned by an employee of the Employment Service. The claimant had then to take the form to a police station formally to report the theft, where it was stamped, a crime number was added and it was photocopied and returned to the claimant to take back to the Jobcentre. A low-level 'desktop' investigation followed. The idea was 'to commit the claimant to declare that a certain event has occurred and to tie that person to a story' (Dyson and Trevains 2000: 3). Over the first five months of these new procedures, the authors of the report state that the number of cheques reported stolen fell from 59 to 10, and the number reported as being subject to fraud from 38 to seven over the equivalent period in the previous year.

Systems can deny resources for crime

Offending often calls for resources. However much someone may want to commit a crime, if he or she lacks the wherewithal to do so the offence will not take place (Ekblom and Tilley 2000).

The most obvious denial of resource for offending occurs where there are restrictions to the sale of firearms, and most particularly handguns (see Chapter 3, this volume). Handguns are clearly very useful in the commission of many serious crimes, including murder, robbery and rape. Where they, and ammunition for them, can readily be purchased then offending is facilitated.

In the USA the crime rates for most offences are lower than those in the UK. A major exception relates to homicide, in particular where firearms are used. This can largely be explained by firearms availability. Though the statutory controls relating to firearms availability in the UK are far from perfect, the widespread use of replicas and air weapons (Morrison and O'Donnell 1996; Schneider *et al.* 2004) suggests that offenders are not easily able to obtain 'real' guns. And where substitutes are used, the potential injury during the conduct of the offence is much less.

In the USA, the ready availability of and increasing power, capacity and speed of handguns (specifically semi-automatics) can be used to explain rises in handgun-related homicides from the mid-1980s to the early 1990s. Then, control over the supply of these weapons in some measure explains the subsequent decline in gun-related homicides (Wintermute 2000). Control over supply was achieved partly by police operations but more significantly by the Bureau of Alcohol, Tobacco and Firearms (ATF), which tightened the oversight of federally licensed dealers (including, for example, substantial checks on new applicants), leading to a reduction from 287,000 licensees in 1993 to 86,180 in 1999. Local jurisdictions added further controls. Wintermute gives the example of Oakland, California, where the number of licence holders fell from 57 to seven in 1997 following the introduction of screening and background checks. Additional controls were also made on buyers, when checks before sales to them could be completed. A host of systems have been put in place, at least in some parts of the USA, reducing the supply of firearms as crime resources.

Systems can facilitate detection

The nature of systems can sometimes be modified or exploited to increase the chance that offenders will be detected. Kuhlhorn (1997) discusses an example of system developments to provide for the detection of welfare cheats in Sweden. In Sweden estimated annual income returns were required separately for housing benefit and for sickness benefits: the lower the income the higher the potential housing allowance; the higher the income the higher the potential sickness allowance. The 12-month periods for income estimates differed for housing allowances and for sickness benefits. There was scope, thus, for some legitimate discrepancy. Linking the data sets for the two estimates provided enabled the size of discrepancies to be seen so that cases that looked suspicious could be followed up. This move enjoyed very widespread public support: 94 per cent of 16–69 year-olds thought that the checks should be made. It turned out that welfare criminality was 'considerably less than asserted in debates about economic crime or the extent of demoralisation in Swedish society' (Kuhlhorn 1997: 240), though rates did fall from 2.7 per cent in 1979 to 1.2 per cent in 1980. The increased scope for detection was, thus, associated with a fall in the rate of identified fraud.

Systems can reduce the supply of likely offenders

As well as breaking rules regarding school attendance, truanting children are widely believed to comprise a significant supply of likely offenders. Burgess (1999) submitted an entry for a British policing award, describing a project aiming to reduce absenteeism in a high-truancy school in Whitehaven. Passes were issued to children who had permission to be absent from school for specific purposes. This was complemented with regular sweeps looking out for truanting children in the town, whose legitimate absence from school could be checked. Local education authority figures showed truancy to have reduced from 2.8 per cent in 1996–7 to 0.9 per cent for 1997–8. The weekly loss in the town centre from shop theft went down £689 to £240, according to the Whitehaven Chamber of Commerce. Though the data do not allow these improvements to be attributed unequivocally to the truancy-reducing measures, they are plausibly related to them, at least in part.

Systems can identify problems and stimulate attention to them

Systems may in various ways provide for organizations routinely to identify, analyse and formulate responses to emerging crime problems. Problem-oriented policing requires that the police deal with recurrent police-relevant problems rather than simply react to the individual incidents one by one as they take place (Goldstein 1979, 1990). The frequently used SARA model, developed by Eck and Spelman for a demonstration project in the USA in Newport News, incorporates the routine *scanning* of crime problems, followed by their *analysis*, efforts to formulate a preventive *responses* and *assessments* of the effectiveness of those responses (Eck and Spelman 1987; see also Read and Tilley 2000; Bullock and Tilley 2003). The National Intelligence Model in the UK provides a nationally mandated business model for the police systematically to identify crime problems and develop strategies to deal with them (John and Maguire 2003; Tilley 2003). Likewise, the COMPSTAT process pioneered in New York is designed routinely and recurrently to direct attention to emerging crime problems, and to hold officers to account for addressing them (see Eck and Maguire 2000). The British Crime and Disorder Act 1998 requires local partnerships, involving the police, local authority, probation service, health authority and other invitees, to attend collaboratively to local crime problems. It also requires a triennial 'audit and strategy development' process, in which crime patterns and problems are identified for preventive attention using a wide range of data sources.

Systematic attention to patterns of crime problem may occur in the private sector as well as the public sector, where losses through high-volume crime may significantly reduce profit. Masuda (1997) discusses an example of shrinkage in a rapidly growing group of four electronics discount stores based in New Jersey. The problem he focused on was internal theft. The aim was to eliminate examples of shrinkage within three months. This objective was achieved by frequent selective stock counts – in effect tracking the problem in detail. The idea was to create the *impression* of control to achieve *actual* control. In particular potential offenders would be persuaded that risks to them were high because any loss of stock would be quickly noticed and would be attributable to them. Stock losses of targeted goods (camcorders and VCRs) were, indeed, reduced to zero. There was, however, also some 'diffusion of benefits', in this case to the prevention of thefts of goods not targeted through the intervention, presumably in part due to the perceived broader risk from offending.

Theory and crime prevention through system design

A focus on system design and development sits well with a variety of crime and crime prevention theories.

Situational crime prevention theory and techniques

The theory and techniques of situational crime prevention can include systems, as well as product design, environmental design, and physical devices developed and installed in the interests of security. Some examples have already been given. Table 10.1 shows all 25 types of situational crime prevention technique as classified by Cornish and Clarke (2003) and Clarke and Eck (2003). In the version of that classification set out here, however, the examples in each cell are all of systems as understood here. Some of these are drawn directly from Cornish and Clarke's and Clarke and Eck's earlier work, and some are added. It is not known whether or not all these techniques 'work', nor are the conditions in which they could be effective well understood. The research is not there to provide the evidence needed to make an informed judgement. All, however, are recognizable system means to try to reduce crime problems or to prevent their emergence.

Environmental criminology, crime generators and crime attractors

Brantingham and Brantingham (1995) use the terms 'crime attractor' and 'crime generator' to describe places that have high numbers of crimes respectively because of the benefits promised to offenders by going there with the intention of committing crime, or because of the crime opportunities available to any who go there even though they do not do so specifically with crime in mind. Some places, such as shopping centres, may be both crime attractors (because people go there in order to steal readily accessible goods) and crime generators (because likely offenders frequenting them for legitimate purposes may spot ready opportunities for crime). Systems may likewise attract or generate crime. In effect they comprise varying non-spatial environments in which offenders, preventers, victims and crime promoters interact and gain tactical advantage over one another through exploiting some of their features. Fraudsters will be attracted to accounting systems from which they can siphon money because of predictable concentrations and flows of money and other

Table 10.1 Twenty-five techniques of procedural situational prevention

Increase the effort	Increase the risks	Reduce the rewards	Reduce provocations	Remove excuses
1. *Target harden*	6. *Extend guardianship*	11. *Conceal targets*	16. *Reduce frustrations and stress*	21. *Set rules*
• Locking and alarm-setting routines	• Taking routine precautions: go out in group at night	• Gender-neutral phone directories	• Efficient queues	• Rental agreements
• RV repair policies and services	• Leaving signs of occupancy	• Unmarked bullion/hot products trucks	• Polite service	• Harassment codes
• Randomized security devices	• Carrying phone	• Carrying computer in unmarked haversack	• Efficient service	• Hotel registration
2. *Control access*	7. *Assist natural surveillance*	12. *Remove targets*	17. *Avoid disputes*	22. *Post instructions*
• Baggage/person screening	• Countersigning cheques/key documents	• Regular collection of cash from tills	• Reduce crowding in pubs	• 'No parking'
• Handing in weapons at bars in old west	• Mobilizing postal workers	• Timetabled truck unloading	• Fixed cab fares	• 'Private property'
• Ticket checking at entries	• Informing neighbours of movements	• Clearing goods from view when parking car	• Clear pricing of goods	• 'Extinguish camp fires'
3. *Screen exits*	8. *Reduce anonymity*	13. *Identify property*	18. *Reduce emotional arousal*	23. *Alert conscience*
• Ticket checking at exits	• Badge-wearing	• Putting name in books	• Clear and efficient complaints procedures	• Roadside speed display boards
• Randomized worker bag checking	• Customer greeting	• Naming school clothes	• Providing entertainment/services at queues	• Signatures for customs declarations
• Checking if alcohol is being carried in open bottles on leaving pub	• Taking deposits	• Naming hospital property	• Separate facilities for conflicting groups	• Signatures for crime reports

4. *Deflect offenders*
- Checking and taking unique identifiers on goods transfers
- Stamping hands for event re-entry
- Provide complaints books/videos/audios

5. *Control tools/weapons*
- Housing allocation
- Weapons licensing and records of striations on bullets
- Ladder storage

9. *Utilize place managers*
- Two clerks for convenience stores
- Responsibilization of doormen/concierges
- Services in high-crime areas (e.g. taxi ranks in car parks)

10. *Strengthen formal surveillance*
- Randomised patrols
- Regular and random audit
- Use of inspectorates

14. *Disrupt markets*
- Monitor pawn shops
- Randomized trading standards inspections
- Continuous car registration

15. *Deny benefits*
- Quick graffiti cleaning
- Allow traffic jams
- Supervised single-dose drug-taking

19. *Neutralize peer pressure*
- Different day welfare payments
- Discredit crime leaders
- Re-channel peer pressure

20. *Discourage imitation*
- Rapid repair of vandalism
- Non-publication of details of modus operandi
- Disinformation about crime methods

24. *Assist compliance*
- Easy library checkout
- Public lavatories
- Regular emptying of litter bins

25. *Control drugs and alcohol*
- Breathalysers in pubs
- Server intervention
- Avoiding happy-hours

resources that criminals like to exploit. Likewise potential offenders will use opportunities that systems throw up – for instance loopholes where expenses are inadvertently repaid more than once and beneficiaries learn that they have a ready source of additional income when they need it.

Routine activities theory

Routine activities theory (Cohen and Felson 1979; Felson 1998) applies to much more than systems. It deals with the conditions for crime and the ways in which they are unintentionally created through everyday life. The everyday conditions giving rise to crime include any that throw together likely offenders and suitable targets without intermediaries either to hold back the likely offender or plausibly to protect the otherwise suitable target. Systems describe just one of the sources creating an unintended confluence of crime conditions. The systems surrounding late-night city centres comprise one example. Alcohol sales policies, licensing laws and their local use, transport systems, drinking habits, wage payment practices and queuing arrangements at pubs and fast-food restaurants all contribute to the supply of likely offenders and suitable targets, in circumstances where intermediaries will be absent or incapable. The results are relatively high rates of violence and property crime.

Crime evolution theory

Paul Ekblom has described an 'arms race' between those trying to prevent crime and those wanting to commit it, each innovating and adjusting according to the other's moves (Ekblom 1997; Chapter 8, this volume). This process can occur for systems means of thwarting crime as it can for any other (Smith and Burrows 1986). Challinger (1997) provides an example in relation to fraudulent returns of goods to stores. In relation to the policy measures described above – requirements of proof of purchase or of identity on returning stolen goods – Challinger describes how, mindful of the company's preoccupation with customer satisfaction, fraudsters began to become increasingly disruptive and aggressive when returning goods to try to coerce managers into exercising their discretion in favour of over-ruling normal procedures. He also describes how offenders would buy one item and steal another of the same kind, returning one with the receipt in exchange for cash. If the receipt was returned this activity could then be repeated. This provides further challenges for preventer system adjustment.

Systems in practice: a case study

Martha Smith (2004) looks in detail at systems used to reduce crime risks to taxi-drivers. Her work follows a study of cab drivers in Cardiff. The preventive measures identified had not on the whole been formulated by crime prevention specialists. Rather, they developed over time, presumably from experience and the folk wisdom of those involved.

Taxi-drivers are clearly an at-risk group, working on their own, known to be carrying cash (that most attractive of targets of theft), transporting strangers and also expecting payment for their services. Moreover, much taxi-drivers' custom comes late at night when travellers may be drunk and abusive or are liable to soil the cab by being sick. It is, in this sense, not surprising that the drivers and operators are attentive to potential crime situations, and have developed ways of working that attempt to minimize them.

The table of preventive techniques produced by Smith is reproduced here as Table 10.2. In this version, two distinctions are made in each cell. First, measures are subdivided into those that refer to environmental design (E), those that refer to product design (P) and those that refer to system design (S), with mixes shown with combinations of letters. Secondly, those techniques that are primarily reactive – means of dealing with an offence once it is occurring – are shown in italics whilst those that are designed to prevent them from taking place in the first place are shown in Roman. Taxi-drivers evidently use a range of routines to reduce their own risks, for instance keeping windows rolled up, prebooking bar pick-ups, limiting the amount of cash carried and making eye contact with passengers. There are also others whose systems can reduce risk to taxi-drivers – for example the police may provide decoy drivers or taxi-control centres may give accurate dispatch times, in the one case increasing risk and in the other reducing provocations to the potential offender.

What is clear from this table is the wide range of means by which taxi-drivers can and do reduce their risks of victimization, and may also have them reduced by third parties. Most of the measures Smith identifies involve preventive procedures, policies or routines, at least in part. Even where product design or environmental design is at issue, human action may be needed also, as is often the case with central door locks and making use of well lit areas. Some examples do not require individuals to activate the preventive potential, for instance safety shields between passenger and driver compartments, but they are the exception.

Policy, procedure and routine appear to be critical in crime prevention for taxi-drivers, and to have developed over time spontaneously to manage the risks faced.

The ethics of crime prevention and system design

This chapter has emphasized crime as an unintended consequence, amongst other things, of system designs that often have purposes quite unrelated to crime. In this, system designs are akin to designs of spaces and products. Many enjoy shopping in stores where they can browse the goods for sale. Most of us rejoice in the supply of cheap lightweight electrical products. But the crime legacy respectively of such retail layouts and high-tech goods is pretty clear. Similarly, as already argued, systems have their own logic, whatever the crime by-products. Crime reduction policy and practice need to acknowledge the reasons for and benefits from systems that generate crime legacies, to balance these against the costs of crime reduction modifications that may be proposed, and to devise systems that either bring additional side-benefits or do not sacrifice other advantages brought by the system (see also Chapter 8, this volume).

Table 10.2 Possible situational techniques used by taxi-drivers – routine precautions and reactive techniques

Increase the effort	Increase the risks	Reduce the rewards	Reduce provocations	Remove excuses
1. *Target harden* P Safety shields S Keep windows rolled up S Stay inside cab – *unless escaping attack from within*	6. *Extend guardianship* P Have GPS and alarm P Have radio, alarm code, or 'open mike' S Keep dispatch informed P Have CB radio, mobile phone S Use buddy system P Carry an extra key	11. *Conceal targets* S Limit funds carried S Never flash cash S 'I just started.' 'It's been ticking over' S Keep cash in more than one place	16. *Reduce frustrations and stress* ES Have supervised ranks S Have honest dispatch time S Make eye contact SS Be courteous	21. *Set rules* S Regulate the industry S Provide explicit provisions about how fare disputes are to be handled
2. *Control access* S Limit number of passengers E Move ranks to 24-hour stores or other locations S Do not obstruct windows S Prebook all bar pick-ups ES Screen passengers PS Use central door locks	7. *Assist natural surveillance* E Move ranks to 24-hour stores or other locations S Do not obstruct windows ES Use street lighting well S Travel main routes	12. *Remove targets* PS Use farecards P Sticker re: limited money PS Use safe or drop off money S Look for escape opportunity	17. *Avoid disputes* ES Display driver photo and licence S Require knowledge tests S Ask for money up front S Inform passenger of route	22. *Post instructions* S Hand out taxi rules and regulations at key venues (e.g. airports) S List rules, regulations and fares in passenger area
3. *Screen exits* S Ask rowdies to get out PS Use central door locks ES *Park to prevent door opening prior to payment* S Prevent runner from exiting by grabbing	8. *Reduce anonymity* S Keep passenger trip book PS Use caller ID S Have regular riders	13. *Identify property* P Use cab locator system (GPS)	18. *Reduce emotional arousal* S Exclude violent drivers (vet) S Control the industry to reduce driver abuses S *Do not threaten non-payers with violence* S *Do not resist a robber*	23. *Alert conscience* S Post notices re: community awareness and 'cab safe' programmes at ranks and in cabs

4. *Deflect offenders*
PS Limit seating options
S Get destination up front
ES Avoid dark places
ES Avoid alleys and deadends

5. *Control tools/weapons*
PS Don't carry a weapon
PS Put all bags in the boot

9. *Utilize place managers*
E Supervise ranks
EP Have security cameras
S Have second person ride up front with driver

10. *Strengthen formal surveillance*
E CCTV at ranks
P Trouble lights on cabs
S Authorized police stops
S Decoy police (as drivers)

14. *Disrupt markets*

15. *Deny benefits*
P Disable-vehicle capacity
P Have insider boot release
P Have first-aid kit

19. *Neutralize peer pressure*
S Ask troublemakers to get out

20. *Discourage imitation*
S Censor details of modus operandi in press releases and interviews
S Keep crime prevention tips during training 'in house'

24. *Assist compliance*
PS Use multiple payment systems
P Provide sick bag

25. *Control drugs and alcohol*
S Increase passenger sobriety prior to pickup
S Prohibit drug or alcohol consumption in cab

Note:
What Smith classifies as driver *reactive* techniques are shown in italics. The others are preventive.
Source: From Smith (2004).

The development of policies and practices to prevent the unintended crime consequences of existing conditions might seem least problematic where those conditions are already thought undesirable anyway. To the extent to which criminality, for example, is the consequence of poverty, social exclusion, child neglect and lack of legitimate opportunity, intervening both to ameliorate them for their own sake and to reduce their criminogenic side-effects, seems at first sight unproblematic. On the other hand, introducing crime-related rationales for changing policies, practices and routines that are beneficial in other ways may appear unwarranted.

Making potential crime reduction effects the major grounds for dealing with intrinsic injustices could, however, be risky. Would we want any less to reduce poverty, social exclusion, child abuse and neglect, or absence of opportunity if doing so were found to have to have no actual effect on levels of criminality? I doubt it. Attaching too much weight to secondary arguments about their expected but far from certain crime reduction effects jeopardises attention to much stronger arguments of principle in favour of such reforms. This is not, though, to deny either that there are hitherto unrecognized needs for systematic attention to emerging life-problems for likely offenders, disregard of which may produce rather specific crime legacies of the sort vividly described by Homel in Chapter 4, this volume[3] or that inequitable social conditions may be significant in producing many crime problems.

There are, at the same time, at least three good reasons for intervening in relation to policies and practices that bring significant benefits, but also a crime legacy. First, those producing crime legacies may have a duty of care in relation to those they serve, for instance universities and their students. Secondly, those whose routines produce crime legacies may not know that they are doing so, and may have an interest in changing their behaviour, especially where they are the victims, for instance where taxi-drivers practices inadvertently but avoidably put them at risk. Thirdly, crime comprises a social and personal externality – an avoidable cost borne by third parties – for instance, the patterns of alcohol-related violent incidents that are produced where groups of bars sell cut-price alcohol with consequential costs for victims, health services and the police.

As Ekblom emphasizes in Chapter 8, this volume, any good design involves balancing a range of considerations: maximizing the chance of achieving objectives, trying to create beneficial side-benefits where possible and avoiding unwanted side-effects. This is as much the case for system design as it is for product or place design. In all design settings this will involve looking at the ways in which individuals interact with the design. And part of this needs to consider crime.

Conclusion

This chapter has argued that systems, broadly understood to include regulation, policy, procedure and routine, are important to the production and reduction of crime problems. Moreover system attributes are often, in Ekblom's terms, proximal causes (Ekblom 1994). That is, rather than comprising some distant 'root cause' of criminality that may be difficult to alter, and slow burning in effect, systems are often relevant in the ways described to the immediate circumstances for offences to be committed, and bring their effects straight away. Moreover, the examples given in this chapter show that systems may, in various ways, be relevant to a very wide range of offences – for example, car crime, shop theft, frauds of various kinds, homicide, robbery, assault, disorder and burglary.

System designs or developments offer early opportunities to think crime and crime prevention rather than waiting for crime harvests to follow, just as is the case with new products or the design of new estates or buildings. The Crime and Disorder Act 1998 provides a mandate for this in local authorities, police authorities and parks authorities, and there is no reason why other public, private and voluntary sector bodies cannot follow suit. Any new large-scale development – a town, housing estate, shopping complex, government organization, business, hospital, airport, railway station, road network, holiday resort, library, university, entertainment centre, car park, motorway service area, form of taxation, benefit entitlement – will potentially create crime opportunities, provocations and incentives. It makes sense to try to take account of this in the design of systems as well as of any physical space. The effort is, however, unlikely ever to be fully successful. Systems are often complex, balance a range of considerations and are probably not entirely predictable in their outworkings (Chapman 2002). Moreover, offenders innovate, both in their efforts to find loopholes and in their use of new tools to exploit them. To inform modifications to try to nip in the bud fresh crime problems arising from systems already in place, it makes sense to scan the horizon for ways in which new loopholes emerge.

Selected further reading

There is no single source where a comprehensive account of system design as a means of crime prevention can be found. The best general account of crime as the unintended consequence of everyday life, including systems of various kinds, are the various editions of Marcus Felson's *Crime and Everyday Life* (1994, 1998 and 2002). For various studies that show how local system redesign can lead to reductions in a range of crime types and in a range of different jurisdictions, see Ron Clarke's edited collection, *Situational Crime Prevention: Successful Case Studies* (1992 and 1997). Barry Webb, Melissa Smith and Gloria Laycock's 'Designing out crime through vehicle license and registration systems' (2004) provides an account of how system redesign at a national level can reduce crime. For the most up-to-date situational crime prevention classification that will help think through multiple opportunities to reduce crime through system design, see Derek Cornish and Ron Clarke's 'Opportunities, precipitators and criminal decisions: a reply to Wortley's critique of situational crime prevention' (2003). The chapter by Ross Homel (Chapter 4) in this volume shows how system redesign is relevant not only to situational crime prevention but also to developmental prevention. Paul Ekblom's chapter (Chapter 8), which focuses mainly on product design, also contains a useful discussion of general issues of design and crime.

Notes

1. *Consciously developed* habitual behaviour is distinguished from habitual behaviour that is reproduced without intention. It is a product of design, rather than of instinct, affect or after-the-event reinforcement.
2. The value of spent vehicles fluctuates with scrap metal prices. When prices are high it pays to sell the vehicle. When low it pays to dump, if you can get away with it.
3. Homel raises interesting and important issues of system design relating to developments in criminality that are not considered in this chapter.

References

Bottoms, A., Claytor, A. and Wiles, P. (1992) 'Housing markets and residential community crime careers: a case study from Sheffield', in D. Evans *et al.* (eds) *Crime, Policing and Place.* London: Routledge.

Brantingham, P. and Brantingham, P. (1981) 'Notes on the geometry of crime', in P. Brantingham and P. Brantingham (eds) *Environmental Criminology.* Beverly Hills, CA: Sage.

Brantingham, P. and Brantingham, P. (1984) *Patterns in Crime.* New York, NY: Macmillan.

Brantingham, P. and Brantingham, P. (1995) 'Criminality of place: crime generators and crime attractors', *European Journal of Criminal Policy and Research,* 3: 5–26.

Bullock, K. and Tilley, N. (eds) (2003) *Crime Reduction and Problem-oriented Policing.* Cullompton: Willan Publishing.

Burgess, S. (1999) 'Operation ACNE.' Unpublished entry for the 1999 Tilley Award for Problem Oriented Policing. Cumbria Constabulary.

Challinger, D. (1997) 'Refund fraud in retail stores', in R.V. Clarke (ed.) *Situational Crime Prevention: Successful Case Studies.* New York, NY: Harrow & Heston.

Chapman, J. (2002) *System Failure.* London: Demos.

Clarke, R. (ed.) (1997) *Situational Crime Prevention: Successful Case Studies.* New York, NY: Harrow & Heston.

Clarke, R. (1999) *Hot Products: Understanding, Anticipating and Reducing Demand for Stolen Goods. Police Research Series Paper* 112. London: Home Office.

Clarke, R. and Eck, J. (2003) *Become a Problem-solving Crime Analyst in 55 Small Steps.* London: Jill Dando Institute of Crime Science.

Clarke, R. and Goldstein, H. (2002) 'Reducing theft at construction sites', in N. Tilley (ed.) *Analysis for Crime Prevention.* Monsey, NY: Criminal Justice Press.

Cohen, L.E. and Felson, M. (1979) 'Social change and crime rate trends: a routine activity approach', *American Sociological Review,* 44: 588–608.

Coleman, A. (1990) *Utopia on Trial.* London: Hilary Shipman.

Cornish, D. and Clarke, R. (2003) 'Opportunities, precipitators and criminal decisions: a reply to Wortley's critique of situational crime prevention', in M. Smith and D. Cornish (eds) *Theory for Practice in Situational Crime Prevention. Crime Prevention Studies. Vol. 16.* Monsey, NY: Criminal Justice Press.

Dyson, T. and Trevains, S. (2000) 'Jobseekers Allowance girocheque fraud.' Unpublished report, Devon and Cornwall Police, Benefits Agency and the Employment Service.

Eck, J. and Maguire, E. (2000) 'Have changes in policing reduced violent crime: an assessment of the evidence', in A. Blumstein and J. Wallman (eds) *The Crime Drop in America.* Cambridge: Cambridge University Press.

Eck, J. and Spelman, W. (1987). *Problem Solving: Problem-oriented Policing in Newport News*. Washington, DC: Police Executive Research Forum.

Ekblom, P. (1994) 'Proximal circumstances: a mechanism-based classification of crime prevention', in R. Clarke (ed.) *Crime Prevention Studies. Vol. 2*. Monsey, NY: Criminal Justice Press.

Ekblom, P. (1997) 'Gearing up against crime: a dynamic framework to help designers keep up with the adaptive criminal in a changing world', *International Journal of Risk, Security and Crime Prevention*, 2: 249–65.

Ekblom, P. and Tilley, N. (2000) 'Going equipped: criminology, situational crime prevention and the resourceful offender', *British Journal of Criminology*, 40: 375–98.

Felson, M. (1998) *Crime and Everyday Life* (2nd edn). Thousand Oaks, CA: Pine Forge Press.

Forrester, D., Chatterton, M. and Pease, K. with the assistance of Brown, R. (1988) *The Kirkholt Burglary Prevention Project, Rochdale. Crime Prevention Unit Paper* 13. London: Home Office.

Forrester, D., Frenz, S., O'Connell, M. and Pease, K. (1990) *The Kirkholt Burglary Prevention Project, Phase II. Crime Prevention Unit Paper* 23. London: Home Office.

Goldstein, H. (1979) 'Improving policing: a problem-oriented approach', *Crime and Delinquency*, 25: 236–58.

Goldstein, H. (1990) *Problem-oriented Policing*. New York, NY: McGraw-Hill.

Hill, N. (1986) *Prepayment Coin Meters: A Target for Burglary. Crime Prevention Unit Paper* 6. London: Home Office.

Homel, R. (1993) 'Drivers who drink and rational choice: random breath testing and the process of deterrence', in R.V. Clarke and M. Felson (eds) *Routine Activity and Rational Choice. Advances in Criminological Theory. Vol. 5*. New Brunswick, NJ: Transaction.

Homel, R., Hauritz, M., McIlwain, G., Wortley, R. and Carvolth, R. (1997) 'Preventing drunkenness and violence around nightclubs in a tourist resort', in R.V. Clarke (ed.) *Situational Crime Prevention: Successful Case Studies* (2nd edn). New York, NY: Harrow & Heston.

Jackson, M. (2002) 'Family group homes.' Unpublished entry for the 2002 Tilley Award for Problem Oriented Policing. Avon and Somerset Constabulary.

Jeffery, C.R. (1971) *Crime Prevention through Environmental Design*. Beverly Hills, CA: Sage.

John, T. and Maguire, M. (2003) 'Rolling out the National Intelligence Model: key challenges', in K. Bullock and N. Tilley (eds) *Crime Reduction and Problem-oriented Policing*. Cullompton: Willan Publishing.

Johnson, S. and Bowers, K. (2003) 'Opportunity is in the eye of the beholder: the role of publicity in crime prevention', *Criminology and Public Policy*, 2: 201–28.

Knuttson, J. and Kuhlhorn, E. (1997) 'Macro measures against crime: the example of check forgeries', in R.V. Clarke (ed.) *Situational Crime Prevention: Successful Case Studies* (2nd edn). New York, NY: Harrow & Heston.

Kuhlhorn, E. (1997) 'Housing allowances in a welfare society: reducing the temptation to cheat', in R.V. Clarke (ed.) *Situational Crime Prevention: Successful Case Studies* (2nd edn). New York, NY: Harrow & Heston.

La Vigne, N. (1994) 'Gasoline drive-offs: designing a less convenient environment', in R. Clarke (ed.) *Crime Prevention Studies. Vol. 2*. Monsey, NY: Criminal Justice Press.

Laycock, G. (1997) 'Operation identification, or the power of publicity?', in R. Clarke (ed.) *Situational Crime Prevention: Successful Case Studies* (2nd edn). New York, NY: Harrow & Heston.

Masuda, B. (1997) 'Reduction of employee theft in a retail environment: displacement vs diffusion of benefits', in R.V. Clarke (ed.) *Situational Crime Prevention: Successful Case Studies* (2nd edn). New York, NY: Harrow & Heston.

Mayhew, P., Clarke, R. and Elliot, D. (1989) 'Motorcycle theft, helmet legislation and displacement', *Howard Journal*, 28: 1–8.

Matthews, R. (2002) *Armed Robbery*. Cullompton: Willan Publishing.

Morrison, S. and O'Donnell, I. (1996) 'An analysis of decision-making practices of armed robbers', in R. Homel (ed.) *The Politics and Practice of Situational Crime Prevention. Crime Prevention Studies. Vol. 5*. Monsey NY: Criminal Justice Press.

Newman, O. (1973) *Defensible Space: Crime Prevention through Urban Design*. New York, NY: Macmillan.

Pease, K. (1997) 'Predicting the future: the roles of routine activity and rational choice theory', in G. Newman *et al.* (eds) *Rational Choice and Situational Crime Prevention*. Aldershot: Dartmouth.

Poyner, B (1983) *Design against Crime*. London: Butterworths.

Poyner, B. and Webb, B. (1991) *Crime Free Housing*. Oxford: Butterworths.

Read, T. and Tilley, N. (2000) *Not Rocket Science? Crime Reduction Research Series Paper 6*. London: Home Office.

Schneider, J., Rowe, N, Forrest, S. and Tilley, N. (2004) 'Biting the bullet: gun crime in Greater Nottingham.' Unpublished report to Nottinghamshire Constabulary.

Sherman, L. (1990) 'Police crackdowns: initial and residual deterrence', in M. Tonry and N. Morris (eds) *Crime and Justice: A Review of Research. Vol. 12*. Chicago, IL: University of Chicago Press.

Sloan Howitt, M. and Kelling, G. (1997) 'Subway graffiti in New York City: "getting up" vs. "Meanin' it and cleanin' it",' in R.V. Clarke (ed.) *Situational Crime Prevention: Successful Case Studies* (2nd edn). New York, NY: Harrow & Heston.

Smith, L. and Burrows, J. (1986) 'Nobbling the fraudsters', *Howard Journal*, 25: 13–24.

Smith, M. (2004) 'Routine precautions used by taxi-drivers: a situational crime prevention approach.' Paper presented at the American Society of Criminology meeting, Nashville, Tennessee, November.

Smith, M., Clarke, R. and Pease, K. (2002) 'Anticipatory benefits in crime prevention', in N. Tilley (ed.) *Analysis for Crime Prevention. Crime Prevention Studies. Vol. 13*. Cullompton: Willan Publishing.

Smith, M. and Webb, B. (2005) 'Vehicle excise duty evasion in the UK', in M. Smith and N. Tilley (eds) *Crime Science: New Approaches to Preventing and Detecting Crime*. Cullompton: Willan Publishing.

Stanko, E. (1990) *Everyday Violence*. London: Virago.

Sykes, G. and Matza, D. (1957) 'Techniques of neutralisation', *American Sociological Review*, 22: 664–70.

Tilley, N. (2003) 'Community policing, problem-oriented policing and intelligence-led policing', in T. Newburn (ed.) *Handbook of Policing*. Cullompton: Willan Publishing.

Tilley, N. (2004) 'Using crackdowns constructively in crime reduction', in R. Burke (ed.) *Hard Cop, Soft Cop*. Cullompton: Willan Publishing.

Tilley, N. (2005) 'Driving down crime at motorway service areas', in M. Smith and N. Tilley (eds) *Crime Science: New Approaches to Preventing and Detecting Crime*. Cullompton: Willan Publishing.

Tilley, N., Smith, J., Finer, S., Erol, R., Charles, C. and Dobby, J. (2004) *Problem-solving Street Crime*. London: Home Office.

van Andel, H. (1997) 'The care of public transport in the Netherlands', in R.V. Clarke (ed.) *Situational Crime Prevention: Successful Case Studies* (2nd edn). New York, NY: Harrow & Heston.

Webb, B., Smith, M. and Laycock, G. (2004) 'Designing out crime through vehicle license and registration systems', in M.G. Maxfield and R.V. Clarke (eds) *Understanding and Preventing Car Theft*. Monsey, NY: Criminal Justice Press.

Wilson, J. and Kelling, G. (1982) 'Broken windows', *Atlantic Monthly*, March: 29–38.

Wintermute, G. (2000) 'Guns and gun violence', in A. Blumstein and J. Wallman (eds) *The Crime Drop in America*. Cambridge: Cambridge University Press.

Chapter 11

Complicity, trading dynamics and prevalence in stolen goods markets

Mike Sutton

The purpose of this chapter is to explore the dynamics of handling stolen goods by looking at the ways markets operate. Looking at who does what with/to whom, where, when, why, how and with what effect enables us more finely to tune policing initiatives and crime reduction policy-making to fit better the social systems or interpersonal interactions that cause and shape crime problems.

Handling stolen goods carries a higher maximum penalty than domestic burglary – the intention of the legislation (s. 22 of the Theft Act 1968) being to punish and deter those who create a demand for stolen goods. And yet this intention has been strangely neglected by all but the handful of social commentators, police officers, lawyers and criminologists who have raised the issue of stolen goods from time to time. Compared with other areas of offending such as burglary and robbery, there has been relatively little research into who buys stolen goods and the factors that influence demand for them. One thing is certain though: if goods are stolen from people's houses and cars, then they are normally purchased by others to be enjoyed in their houses and cars. This very fact is at the root of earlier accounts of stolen goods markets (e.g. Colquhoun 1796; Hall 1952) where the writers focus upon the level of complicity amongst buyers in the stolen goods markets. These writers see complicity as important because it reflects the fact that knowing buyers, or reckless buyers, of stolen goods are at the very least anti-social with regard to the impact of their buying behaviour – which creates demand for more stolen goods – on the victimization of others.

Complicity in dealing or buying stolen goods

The current law in England and Wales treats the offence of handling stolen goods with particular caution. Section 22 (1) of the Theft Act 1968 requires guilt to be established on the basis of 'knowledge' or 'belief' that goods are stolen and the jury or magistrate must infer from the circumstances of the case whether the defendant had such 'knowledge' or 'belief'. Judicial interpretation of the statute has been such that a mere suspicion that goods are stolen is not enough to lead to a conviction for handling unless the defendant either knows or is virtually certain that they are stolen (Hall 1952). In this connection, Glanville Williams (1985) stressed the need to understand the meaning of *belief* within s. 22 that goods are stolen as 'the sort of belief we would associate with a devout religious believer', not as a belief that they are probably stolen. In supporting such a strictly narrow interpretation Williams argues:

> people must be allowed a margin of safety. If they cannot buy goods that they know to be probably stolen then they cannot safely buy goods when there is an appreciable possibility that they are stolen, because no one knows when lawyers, judges and juries between them may not turn possibilities into probabilities.

This consideration, above all others, places severe constraints on what can be achieved in the way of controlling theft and burglary by purely legal measures aimed at receiving. Perhaps police services should make more use of the little-used section 27 of the Theft Act 1968 when dealing with known and previously convicted prolific thieves and handlers. This section of the Act allows for joint prosecution of those suspected of stealing and/or handling stolen goods. More importantly under s. 27 it is possible, for the purpose of proving that a person knew or believed goods to be stolen, to present evidence of earlier convictions for theft or handling stolen goods. In this way s. 27 can be used to streamline the process of proving criminal intent of theft or handling for those who have been convicted of theft or handling within a five-year period prior to a current charge – and who have in their possession stolen goods from a theft occurring no more than 12 months prior to that current charge.

Where stolen goods are purchased directly from a thief the buyer is more likely to face the risk of coming within the ambit of s. 22, since such buying at the doorstep, workplace, pub or friend's house has less of the outwardly legitimate qualities associated with the type of retail outlet used by a professional fencing operation. When buying stolen goods from a seemingly legitimate retail establishment, even if they know or believe the goods to be stolen, customers face less risk of prosecution. As Klockars (1974) writes: 'one may obtain a bill for whatever one buys...such a bill serves as a ticket to legitimize the purchase.' In other more dubious situations, when selling and buying items which they know or believe to be stolen, people tend to use a number of linguistic guilt-neutralization clichés such as:

- It fell off the back of a lorry.
- It's bankrupt stock.
- Ask no questions and get told no lies.
- It came from a friend of a friend who works in the business.
- Don't look a gift-horse in the mouth (Ditton, 1977; Henry 1977, 1978, 1981; Hobbs 1989).

Foster's (1990) study of hidden economy crime amongst regular drinkers at a south London pub includes the following quotation from an interview: 'If someone came up and offered me a suede coat for £20 and it fitted, I wouldn't ask no questions, I'd take it. But then most people are like that, aren't they?'

To add to the complexity of stolen goods markets and issues of complicity – ironically, sellers sometimes pass goods off as stolen when they are not. The street hawker sells goods out of a suitcase on London's Oxford Street – talks rapidly and acts nervously, employing lookouts to stand on wastebaskets to see above the heads of the crowd to warn of approaching police officers. He sells cheap, gold-looking necklaces and chants: 'All stolen, they're all stolen.' According to Henry (1978): 'He is in fact a conman who buys second-rate, inferior goods in order to sell them at a price higher than their true value. He does this by falsely claiming that the goods are stolen and relies on this to explain their cheap price.' The same point is picked up by Walsh (1977): 'Once the greed of the customer takes over, his own perceptions of the situation will make him more interested in striking a bargain than in inspecting the quality of the merchandise at issue' (for other examples, see also Klockars 1974; Steffensmeier, 1986).

Perhaps the first writer on this theme is the London magistrate Patrick Colquhoun (1796) who set out to examine the degree to which eighteenth-century buyers of stolen goods had guilty knowledge regarding the provenance of their purchases. Noting the existence of professional *Criminal Receivers* as dealers in stolen goods, Colquhoun also distinguished between *Careless Receivers* and *Innocent Receivers*. The first of these three types of buyer is the most serious offender – the middleman of the theft business and knowing crime facilitator. The second type have a reckless disregard for the origin of goods – asking no questions and purchasing whatever they want that is on offer. As the name states, the last type innocently purchase stolen goods – believing them to be legitimately bought by the seller.

Years later, the important distinction between 'professional fences' and those who purchase stolen goods in the workplace or over the doorstep was again emphasized in Jerome Hall's (1952) three-fold typology:

1. The *Lay Receiver* – 'one who knowingly buys stolen property for his own consumption'.

2. The *Occasional Receiver* – 'one who buys stolen property for resale but very infrequently'.

3. The *Professional Receiver* – 'the dealer in stolen goods'.

Hall's aim was to reform the law in the USA by emphasizing the role of the professional receiver in the marketing of stolen goods and his typology has been criticized because of this (Klockars 1974): 'his images of lay and occasional receivers are unduly sparse and flat. They suggest nothing of the trade in stolen property among amateur thieves and dabbling dealers which thrives in bars, schools, factories and neighbourhoods.' Whilst 150 years before Hall's work on complicity, Colquhoun's description of receivers probably better described the fuller picture of the type of buyer in stolen goods markets. What is needed, however, is a description that includes an understanding of complicity and that is based upon systematic research into the variety of stolen goods markets and how they actually operate. This description and understanding of the dynamics of the stolen goods business, in terms of its impact upon theft, is examined in the remainder of this chapter.

Prevalence

The 1994 British Crime Survey (Sutton 1998) findings that over 10 per cent of those questioned admitted that they had knowingly bought stolen goods in the past five years show clearly that a significant proportion of the public are engaging in offending that carries a maximum penalty of 14 years.

As well as needing to know the prevalence of this type of offending we also need to know information that will enable detection and crime reduction initiatives to pinpoint where best to focus resources to reduce crime and tackle offending. This chapter has described the characteristics of those who admit to this type of offending and perhaps more importantly those who support demand for theft by knowingly buying stolen goods such as mobile phones. What we now need to focus upon in terms of crime markets are the questions: who does what with/to whom, where, when, why, in what way and with what effect?

The impact of stolen goods markets on theft

At the time when I first began researching the role played by stolen goods markets in theft generation, two very simple questions concerned me most (Sutton 1993):

1. Does demand for stolen goods explain the rate of theft and does an increase in demand cause an increase in theft?

2. What happens to stolen goods? In particular, how are they sold by the thief and what is the role, if any, of the middleman in stolen goods markets?

Eleven years later, having reviewed all the available literature, interviewed over 100 prolific thieves and written the stolen goods questions and analysed their answers for the 1994 British Crime Survey and the 2004 Crime and Justice Survey (forthcoming) (Sutton 1998) – in which 9,646 and 7,375 respondents, respectively, were asked about buying stolen goods – these questions have been answered.

The answer to the first question is that it is impossible to say that theft is demand led – or supply led for that matter. Rather than simply stealing to order my research reveals that prolific thieves such as burglars, shoplifters and car thieves also frequently *steal to offer*. More local research in this area, which I am currently undertaking in the Nottingham area, is likely to reveal new ways to reduce theft by reducing demand for stolen goods or by reducing criminal opportunities at the outlets where thieves sell them. Whilst some thieves do steal to order (Sutton 1998) this does not mean that individual burglaries, for example, are simply the direct result of a burglars' knowledge of what high-demand items are inside a particular home. In fact, research shows that individual ownership of 'suitable targets' (Cohen and Felson 1979) is a poor predictor of burglary risk because many burglars do not know what items a dwelling contains before breaking in (Mieth and Meier 1990). Therefore, in cases where burglars do not know their victim, the reasons why particular houses are selected for burglary – e.g. less risk of detection or apprehension (Bennett and Wright 1984) – are not the same as those that influence a burglar's decision to steal particular items from people's homes once they are inside. That said, the increase in things worth stealing in people's homes over the past few decades is likely to be important (Witte 1993; Sutton 1995) because, as Johnson *et al.* (1993) and Clarke (1999) point out, offenders have a hierarchy of goods that they prefer to take. And most houses contain at least some of those hot products (Sutton 1995). Since most burglars steal because they want money, top of their list is cash, followed by items that can be easily sold for relatively high prices such as jewellery and hi-technology home-entertainment equipment or media such as DVD collections. All this suggests that it is stolen goods markets, then, and knowledge of what can be sold in them, that motivate thieves because most steal goods to sell for cash, irrespective of whatever they want to spend that cash on.

It seems reasonable to suggest that the general increase in ownership of lightweight consumer durables and associated products such as CDs and DVDs is leading burglars and other thieves quite rightly to assume that many properties are likely to contain these 'suitable targets' for theft. In addition to increased numbers of things worth stealing from people's homes over the past four decades or so, levels of acquisitive crime have been linked both to recessions in the economy and high numbers of young males in the population (Field 1990). At such times, these factors may have an impact on offender motivation via their customers' decreased financial resources and increased material wants and needs, coupled with higher numbers of motivated offenders. For this reason, amongst others, theft rates regularly show overall patterns of increase and decline that have little to do with successful policing or crime reduction measures.

If there is a greater demand for cheap second-hand goods amongst new families or during a recession, more people will – innocently, recklessly or knowingly – buy stolen property (Sutton 1995). In recent years the UK economy has been stronger and more stable and stolen goods markets may not have been so driven by sudden increases in relative deprivation. However, we can be relatively certain of one thing and that is that demand for drugs amongst those with problem drug 'habits' does have an important role since some 29 per cent of arrested thieves are heroin or cocaine users. These are the most prolific offenders, probably responsible for more than three fifths of illegal income generated by thieves selling stolen goods in England and Wales (Bennett *et al.* 2001). It is not surprising therefore that so many crime experts now see drug use as the root of the theft problem. However, in-depth interviews with prolific thieves (Sutton 1998; Sutton *et al.* 2001) also reveal that drug dealers are often reluctant to exchange goods for drugs. Thieves know they can get more drugs if they sell their stolen booty to buy drugs with cash, rather than taking hot goods to their drug dealer. With drug dealers, the exchange rate for stolen goods is at best poor and more usually the dealer will not be interested in trying to sell the goods on when drugs offer a higher margin of profit.[1] This means that stolen goods markets play as important a part as regular hard drug use in explaining high theft rates. Therefore, these markets represent an important opportunity for crime reduction initiatives.

Clearly, then, the most valid predictor of items that burglars will choose is whether or not they believe they can be easily sold for a good price because they know other people want to buy them. Whilst weight and portability of items will be considered by thieves, this will only happen if they believe the goods to be saleable once removed (Sutton 1995). Considerations regarding weight and portability will be balanced against prices. Motivation to remove more difficult objects is likely to rise along with demand for particular products. By way of example, many new widescreen television sets outweigh models of a few years ago but are being stolen because they are valuable. As more expensive and desirable lightweight, flat, plasma screen sets come on to the market they will be very high up the thieves 'shopping' list – along with laptop computers, jewellery, credit cards and CD/DVD collections. Similarly credit cards may become an increased target for theft for use in Internet fraud – as chip and pin technology makes point of sale frauds more difficult to perpetrate. This is likely to be compounded by the desirability of powerful portable MP3 players, increasingly the target of street crime, and the immense popularity of websites selling downloadable music tracks for such equipment – all occurring at a time when the music industry is cracking down upon websites facilitating illicit, free music downloads.

Both Ron Clarke and Marcus Felson had in their highly influential earlier work on situational crime prevention (SCP) and routine activities theory (RAT) (Cohen and Felson 1979) 'taken for granted' the existence of motivated offenders (Sutton 1995). So in their earlier work they had not capitalized on the fact that stolen goods markets could be tackled with a series of strategies to increase the risks and reduce the rewards of selling and buying stolen goods. Yet reducing opportunities in stolen goods dealing fits perfectly with, and builds upon, the philosophy of both SCP and RAT. This is an important point because tackling theft in this way might satisfy the demands of writers and crime prevention practitioners who wish to deal with the underlying causes of criminal motivation as well as the vulnerability of victims' possessions (Sutton 1996). The ways that this can be achieved are set out in more depth in the next subsection of this chapter.

What do stolen goods markets look like and how useful is this knowledge?

Although they might share some of the characteristics of legitimate markets, stolen goods markets are different because they are illegal. Stolen goods markets are small and fragmented – just like many other types of illicit market. By focusing on particular types of illicit markets in the USA, such as bootlegging and gambling operations, Reuter (1985) explains the reason why they cannot expand in the same way as legal operations:

> The most immediate consequence of product illegality, stemming from the costs of asset seizure and arrest, is the need to control the flow of information about participation in the illegal activity. That is, each participant must structure his or her activities, particularly those involving other participants, so as to assure that the risk of the police learning of his or her participation is kept low.

As Reuter's (1985) important work goes on to explain, legitimate markets, on the other hand, are able to expand their enterprise by recruiting employees – a difficult thing to do in illegal operations because employees may have knowledge of their employer's criminal activities. This puts crime bosses in a particularly vulnerable position since employees can provide the police with enough information to make an arrest and put together a prosecution case.

Stolen goods markets are also similar to the heroin markets studied by Reuter in that they involve transactions that are conducted at *arm's length*. Both types of market operate at different levels – rather than as large integrated organizations of stealing, dealing, warehousing, wholesaling and retailing (Reuter 1990). Although Reuter never looked at stolen goods markets, my own research reveals that they share many of the same characteristics of the various illegal markets he studied. As the Home Office Handling Study (Sutton 1998) found, there are five main types of stolen goods market:

1. *Commercial fence supplies*: Goods are sold by thieves to business owners (fences) with shops or other businesses. Here business owners are most usually approached directly by thieves where sales are made in private – away from customers and CCTV security cameras.

2. *Commercial sales*: The fence for a profit sells goods – either to the consumer or to another distributor who will seek to sell on goods for additional profit. Consumers buying in this market are unlikely to know or believe that goods are stolen because commercial fences, being able to use legitimate retail outlets or dealerships, usually sell to innocent members of the public.

3. *Residential fence supplies*: Fences operating out of their own houses are approached directly by thieves or their associates. All transactions are conducted in private.

4. *Network sales*: An initial friend (who may charge a small commission) is approached and the item for sale is shown or described. Word is then passed on along friendship networks until a consumer is found and the sale is made in private. Many residential fences sell stolen goods in this way.

5. *Hawking*: Thieves approach and sell directly to consumers of the stolen goods. Transactions in pubs and on the streets are semi-private. Doorstep sales are private.

The need to understand the dynamics of demand and stealing to offer

Concentrating on the arrest and incarceration of local thieves often makes only short-lived improvements in local levels of crime. Reductions often do not even last until the remanded or sentenced offenders are released because other offenders take their place (Sutton and Simmonds 2004). The same is true of drug treatment programmes. Even though more and more criminally active illegal drug users enter and remain in treatment programmes and are reported to reduce their drug intake, there is rarely a corresponding reduction in local crime rates. This raises some important theoretical questions:[2] does this point to an *Archimedes principle* dynamic at work? Or the equivalent of nature disliking a vacuum? If so, then what sets the water level? Or what causes the vacuum that sucks in new offenders to take the place of inactive ones? As part of the answer, research (Sutton 1998) suggests that demand for stolen goods and the vibrancy of local markets (Sutton and Simmonds 2004) may be a force that influences the activity of local thieves and subsequent crime levels. And, as Harris *et al.* (2003) point out, there is evidence to suggest that tackling stolen goods markets to reduce theft is based on sound theoretical principles.

In deciding what to do about stolen goods markets – in particular which markets to tackle to reduce specific theft problems – it is important to understand how different local markets are operating. With such knowledge it is possible to design operations and policies that have a clearly defined mechanism by which the intervention will be expected to reduce crime. As the findings from the Home Office Handling Study show, it is wrong to think in terms of a single market for stolen goods (see also Walsh 1977; Maguire 1982; Reuter 1985). A thief selling to a fence constitutes one market; a thief selling directly to consumers represents another market; and a fence selling to consumers is another market again. Understanding the dynamics of how these markets operate, namely: who does what to/with whom, in what way, where, when, why and with what effect enables us to think of likely ways to reduce stolen goods markets – with an aim to reduce theft by impacting upon the social mechanisms that are essential in motivating people to steal. In order to gather this important information it is necessary to interview local thieves and dealers. Once the local information has been gathered and systematically examined (see Sutton *et al.* 2001), then tailor-made market reduction approach (MRA) measures can be devised to operate at the local level.

Building upon existing theories and approaches to crime control – the MRA

One of the most popular crime reduction methods in the UK is situational crime prevention (SCP). SCP involves the deployment of discreet managerial and environmental change to reduce the opportunities for crimes to occur and is particularly useful for designing solutions to prevent specific crime problems in the places where they usually happen (Clarke 1997). This approach is part of the foundation of the MRA (Sutton 1998). In addition, most crimes require convergence in space and time of likely offenders, suitable targets and the absence of capable guardians (Cohen and Felson 1979). The MRA fits the philosophy of Cohen's RAT in the following ways:

1. *Motivated offenders*: Motivated *thieves* (selling stolen goods), *dealers* (buying/selling), *consumers* (buying/owning)

2. *Suitable targets*: Stolen goods for sale – and when sold, similar goods become suitable targets for theft.

3. *Absence of capable guardians*: Low level of policing (public and private policing or citizen control) of stolen goods markets.

From what has been discussed above, stolen goods markets clearly motivate thieves, because most thieves steal to sell goods and thus obtain cash. Market demand[3] for particular goods clearly plays a role in motivating some people to steal items that they know others will buy. In the UK, new knowledge of the importance of the practice of *stealing to offer* in maintaining local stolen goods markets was first used to create an initial menu of *situational* tactics designed to reduce theft through the MRA (Sutton 1998). The menu was further developed to form the core element of a report that provides a strategic and systematic 'toolkit' for reducing stolen goods markets (Sutton *et al.* 2001). The influence of Clarke's work can be seen in the following matching of the MRA to three of the main elements of SCP philosophy:

1. *Increasing the effort of offending – focusing upon the*:
- *Thief*: making it as hard to sell stolen goods as it is to steal them.
- *Dealer (fence)*: Making it difficult 'safely' to buy and sell stolen goods.
- *Consumer*: Reducing opportunities to buy and thereby deflecting consumers to legitimate markets – or alternative illegitimate markets where they will have to work harder to find the items they want – to the point where at the least attrition is introduced in turnover and at the best the expense/effort of searching becomes intolerable.

2. *Increasing the risks of offending – focusing upon the*:
- *Thief*: Making it at least as risky to transport and sell stolen goods as it is to steal them.
- *Dealer*: Making it much more risky knowingly to buy, transport, store and trade in stolen goods.
- *Consumer*: Making it much more risky knowingly to buy, transport and own stolen goods.

3. *Reducing the rewards of offending – focusing upon the*:
- *Thief*: Reducing the price received for stolen goods because they are no longer so desirable – due to the impact of moral exhortation and increased risks (no longer a seller's market).
- *Dealer*: Reducing the profit margin on stolen goods due to the increased risks faced in inter-trader dealing and the perceived risks that the consumers face. Fewer stolen goods in circulation – no longer core source of income.

- *Consumer*: Risks/guilt of purchasing and ownership outweigh the enjoyment of possession and use of stolen goods.

Conclusion and the way forward

The MRA should be seen as a theft-reduction strategy, not simply as a way to reduce illicit trading, because each essential attempt to reduce illicit markets is also essentially targeting both the theft process and loot-trading process. Detecting those engaged in handling stolen goods and applying legal sanctions against them also ensures that offenders have less chance of profiting from the misery of victims of burglary and other thefts – which is arguably an important end in its own right and not one we should lose sight of in our pursuit of measurable theft reduction.

Harris *et al.* (2003) undertook an independent evaluation of two MRA projects that were funded under the Home Office Targeted Policing Initiative (TPI). They found that whilst the theory behind the MRA is clearly not flawed, some of the recommended MRA tactics nevertheless proved difficult to implement and that the police services involved had not always adopted the most promising tactics that are recommended by Sutton *et al.* (2001): 'The problems encountered by the projects all related to operationalising the theory…While implementation has been difficult there is certainly not sufficient evidence from the two projects to suggest that the compelling logic of the theory of market reduction is unsound.'

Harris *et al.* (2003) conclude that the two projects evaluated should be seen as forerunners for future MRA initiatives. Others can now draw upon their experiences: 'Perhaps in this light, progress should be viewed less in terms of crime reduction outcomes but more in terms of lessons about the process through which market reduction approaches should be implemented.'

Building upon the valuable lessons that Harris *et al.* have identified, and taking on board a series of recommendations from their evaluations, MRA projects are currently under way in Derby and in Mansfield in the East Midlands. Hopefully, these projects will prove cost effective in terms of reducing the extent of handling – with an aim to reduce acquisitive offending. The valuable information from the Crime and Justice Survey regarding the demographic and social characteristics of offenders at the national level will most certainly guide local decision-making in these, and other, second-generation MRA projects (see Forrest *et al.* in press).

Selected further reading

Influential very early social commentary and legal writings on stolen goods dealing can be found in the following works: Colquhoun (1796) *A Treatise on the Police of the Metropolis* and Hall (1952) *Theft, Law and Society* (2nd edn). Useful ethnographic studies can be found in Klockars (1974) *The Professional Fence* and Steffensmeier (1986) *The Fence: In the Shadow of Two Worlds.* Useful representative quantitative accounts and official crime statistics can be found in Sutton (1998) *Handling Stolen Goods and Theft: A Market*

Reduction Approach. Home Office Research Study 178 and Clarke (1999) Hot Products: Understanding, Anticipating and Reducing Demand for Stolen Goods. Police Research Series Paper 112. Informative ethnographic studies include Ditton (1977) Part-time Crime: An Ethnography of Fiddling and Pilferage, Hobbs (1989) Doing the Business: Entrepreneurship, the Working Class and Detectives in the East End of London and Foster (1990) Villains: Crime and Community in the Inner City. Other useful work on the dynamics of stolen goods markets and associated crime include Henry (1978) The Hidden Economy: The Context and Control of Borderline Crime, Reuter (1985) The Organization of Illegal Markets: An Economic Analysis and Bennett et al. (2001) Drug Use and Offending: Summary Results from the First Year of the NEW-ADAM Research Programme. Findings 148.

Notes

1. Interestingly thieves regularly report that when drug dealers do accept goods in exchange for drugs it is when they want the goods – such as gold jewellery and designer wear – for their own use (Sutton 2004).
2. Thanks are due to Sergeant Dave Simmonds of Derbyshire Constabulary for posing these questions.
3. Or, more accurately, the saleability of certain items.

References

Bennett, T. Holloway, K. and Williams, T. (2001) Drug Use and Offending: Summary Results from the First Year of the NEW-ADAM Research Programme. Findings 148. London: Home Office.

Bennett, T. and Wright, R. (1984) Burglars on Burglary. Aldershot: Gower.

Clarke, R.V. (1997) 'Introduction', in R.V. Clarke (ed.) Situational Crime Prevention: Successful Case Studies (2nd edn). Guilderland, NY: Harrow & Heston.

Clarke, R.V. (1999) Hot Products: Understanding, Anticipating and Reducing Demand for Stolen Goods. Police Research Series Paper 112. London: Home Office Policing and Reducing Crime Unit, Research Development and Statistics Directorate.

Cohen, L. and Felson, M. (1979) 'Social change and crime rate trends: a routine activity approach', American Sociological Review, 44: 580–608.

Colquhoun, P. (a Magistrate) (1796) A Treatise on the Police of the Metropolis; Containing a Detail of the Various Crimes and Misdemeanours by which Public and Private Security are, at Present, Injured and Endangered: and Suggesting Remedies for their Prevention (3rd edn). London: C. Dilly.

Ditton, J. (1977) Part-time Crime: An Ethnography of Fiddling and Pilferage. London, Macmillan.

Field, S. (1990) Trends in Crime and their Interpretation: A Study of Recorded Crime in Post-war England and Wales. Home Office Research Study 119. London: Home Office.

Forrest, S., Levi, M. and Sutton, M. (forthcoming) Handling Stolen Goods: Findings from the 2003 Crime and Criminal Justice Survey. Home Office Research Study. London. Home Office.

Forrest, S., Levi, M. and Sutton, M. (in press) Stolen Goods: Findings from the 2002/3 British Crime Survey and 2003 Crime and Criminal Justice Survey. Home Office Research Study. London: Home Office.

Foster, J. (1990) Villains: Crime and Community in the Inner City. London. Routledge.

Hall, J. (1952) Theft, Law and Society (2nd edn). Indianapolis, IN: Bobbs-Merrill Co.

Harris, C., Hale, C. and Uglow, S. (2003) 'Theory into practice: implementing a market reduction approach to property crime', in K. Bulock and N. Tilley (eds) *Crime Reduction and Problem-Oriented Policing*. Cullompton: Willan Publishing.

Henry, S. (1977) 'On the fence', *British Journal of Law and Society*, 4: 124–33.

Henry, S. (1978) *The Hidden Economy: The Context and Control of Borderline Crime*. London: Martin Robertson.

Henry, S. (ed.) (1981) *Can I have it in Cash? A Study of Informal Institutions and Unorthodox Ways of Doing Things*. London: Astragal Books.

Hobbs, D. (1989) *Doing the Business: Entrepreneurship, the Working Class and Detectives in the East End of London*. Oxford: Oxford University Press.

Johnson, D., Mangai, N. and Sanabria, H. (1993) '"Successful" criminal careers: towards an ethnography with the rational choice perspective', in R.V. Clarke and M. Felson (eds) *Routine Activity and Rational Choice: Advances in Criminological Theory*. New Brunswick, NJ: Transaction.

Klockars, C. (1974) *The Professional Fence*. New York, NY: Free Press.

Maguire, M. (1982) *Burglary in a Dwelling: The Offence, the Offender and the Victim*. London: Heinemann.

Mieth, T.D. and Meier, R.F. (1990) 'Opportunity, choice and criminal victimization: a test of a theoretical model', *Journal of Research in Crime and Delinquency*, 27: 243–66.

Reuter, P. (1985) *The Organization of Illegal Markets: An Economic Analysis*. Washington, DC: National Institute of Justice, US Department of Justice.

Reuter, P. (1990) *Money from Crime: A Study of the Economics of Drug Dealing in Washington DC*. Santa Monica, CA: RAND Corporation, Drug Policy Research Centre.

Steffensmeier, D.J. (1986) *The Fence: In the Shadow of Two Worlds*. Totowa, NJ: Rowman & Littlefield.

Sutton, M. (1993) *From Receiving to Thieving: The Market for Stolen Goods and the Incidence of Theft*. Research Bulletin 34. London: Home Office.

Sutton, M. (1995) 'Supply by theft: does the market for second-hand goods play a role in keeping crime figures high?', *British Journal of Criminology*, 38: 400–16.

Sutton, M. (1996) *Implementing Crime Prevention Schemes in a Multi-Agency Setting: Aspects of Process in the Safer Cities Programme*. Home Office Research Study 160. London: Home Office.

Sutton, M. (1998) *Handling Stolen Goods and Theft: A Market Reduction Approach*. Home Office Research Study 178. London. Home Office.

Sutton, M. (2004) 'How burglars and shoplifters sell stolen goods in Derby: describing and understanding the local illicit markets. A primary research paper', *Internet Journal of Criminology* (www.internetjournalofcriminology.com).

Sutton, M., Schneider, J. and Hetherington, S. (2001) *Tackling Theft with the Market Reduction Approach*. Home Office Crime Reduction Series Paper 8. London: Home Office.

Sutton, M. and Simmonds, D. (2004) 'Tackling burglary and other theft with the market reduction approach', *Criminal Justice Matters*, 55: 28–9.

Walsh, M. (1977) *The Fence: A New Look at the World of Property Theft*. Westport, CT: Greenwood Press.

Williams, G. (1985) 'Handling, theft and the purchaser who takes a chance', *Criminal Law Review*, 432–39.

Witte, A.D. (1993) 'Some thoughts on the future of research in crime and delinquency', *Journal of Research in Crime and Delinquency*, 30: 513–25.

Chapter 12

Reducing the capacity to offend: restricting resources for offending

Martin Gill

Introduction

Newcomers to criminology, and specifically the study of crime prevention/ reduction and criminal justice policy, may be surprised to learn that the subject has not been dominated by studying offenders and gaining insights from them to inform policy. It might seem a strange omission; a parallel might be the army failing to learn about the skill and resources of the opposition before deploying soldiers. The military may have good reasons for not being able to do so: their threat or adversary is not always easy to engage and not always willing to impart information, but offenders provide a captive audience and a range of studies have shown that they are often willing to engage in meaningful research. The problem is that they are rarely asked and as a consequence we know much less than we could about how to prevent crime.

This chapter will argue that if the commitment to reducing offending is serious, then more attention needs to be focused on understanding offenders' capacity to commit offences successfully. This will involve listening to what offenders themselves have to say, not just why they do it but what they do and how they acquire and use whatever skills or knowledge is needed. Indeed, it shall be argued that committing crime and getting away with it involves resources – that is, a set of skills and different types of knowledge.[1] By and large the importance of resources are not recognized, but by understanding them we can acquire important crime prevention information. Ultimately the aim here is to discuss ways of reducing the capacity to offend by identifying the best means of 'restricting resources for offending'.[2] The chapter will not be drawing upon a discrete body of literature but rather a range of criminological studies which help to highlight some key points.

This chapter will review theoretical perspectives that have focused on the criminal 'event', and then summarizes the evidence available on what offenders' capacities are and how these are created. In fact there is not a great deal of research and so the chapter then reviews ways in which this gap might be filled by collecting information from offenders and recognizing the limitations of these data. The final part consists of a case study to illustrate some of the points raised.

Theory

A study of offenders' capacities focuses attention on what they do at the scene of their crimes. However, within the study of crime prevention there has not been widespread interest in the sorts of decisions made by offenders at the scene. At least part of the reason is that criminology has often had a broad social focus at the macro level; certainly there has been less interest in the micro level at which 'event' decisions are analysed (see below). Furthermore, its sociological base has framed a reformist agenda which has sidelined the situational approach. Even where criminology has been interested in 'causes' this has mostly not then extended to thinking about how understanding those causes feeds into prevention. And even the parts of the discipline that have focused on the reactions to crime have focused on the police, probation, prisons and other aspects of criminal justice rather than opportunity reduction.

In looking at causal factors for crime, there has been rather more interest in what Ekblom (2002) calls distal factors, such as the influence of family background, than proximal factors such as the impediment posed by security measures. Indeed, the interest in the motivations of offenders and the causes of crime, what might be termed the initial 'involvement decisions', has somewhat overshadowed the 'event decisions'[3] which are made at the scene. Clarke (1995: 98) states: 'Involvement decisions are characteristically multi-stage and extend over substantial periods of time. Event decisions, by contrast, are frequently shorter processes, using more circumscribed information largely relating to immediate circumstances and situations.' This would suggest that 'event decisions' would be more accessible to researchers but the subject has received relatively little attention and there has not been a major focus on the capacities of offenders. Even though it is recognized that many offenders are rational, at least to some degree, there has been little research to help understand how that rationality is informed by a crime skills and knowledge base.

Any future research on offenders' capacities will be informed by approaches that have focused on event decisions. There are three that are of particular relevance:[4] Ron Clarke's situational prevention with its emphasis on opportunity reduction, Marcus Felson's routine activities theory and Paul Ekblom's conjunction of criminal opportunity. Space permits only a brief discussion of each where the focus will be on outlining their contribution to a better understanding of the value of studying offenders' resources as a route to reducing crime.

Most attention here will be devoted to situational prevention which involves manipulating the context in some way to reduce the opportunities for crime, thereby rendering situations more risky for offenders and less rewarding for them. It may include installing security devices, making areas more visible, ensuring that offenders are less able to enjoy the benefits of crime by property marking, for example.[5] Sometimes the objective will be to take away the opportunity for the offence – and this includes facilitators for crime and precipitators of it (Wortley 1997, 1998, 2001) – on other occasions to increase the amount of time it would take for an offender to be successful and thereby increasing his or her risks. Just how difficult and risky a potential offence can be made for offenders will depend not just on the range of measures that are implemented, but the extent to which they match or challenge the specific range of resources offenders have (Ekblom and Tilley 2000). An open safe with money in it is only an opportunity to someone who can access the safe and has the emotional preparedness to steal.

The lack of understanding of offenders' resources means that measures to tackle offending are not operating on a complete knowledge base – no wonder there has been question marks about whether situational measures are effective.[6] There are at least three issues here. First, there is concern that situational measures don't work and could never fully do so, partly because it is argued crime is merely displaced, partly because there are doubts about how rational offenders really are, and partly because there is scepticism that responses that fail to tackle what Ekblom referred to as 'distal' causes could ever have any long-term benefits. Secondly, it is suspected that measures work in the interests of offenders. My own work with robbers concluded that some favoured premises with security screens because they protected them from enthusiastic staff who were a significant risk factor (Gill 2000), whilst Beck and Willis (1995) are amongst those who have found that the very presence of security may make staff less conscientious as they rely on situational measures to do the job for them. Thirdly, and in a business context (see Gill 2003a), there is the view that situational measures are counterproductive – for example, whilst they may impact on offending they deter the honest customer too. This is often the case in retailing where the object is to make goods attractive to customers, which at the same time makes it easier for thieves too.

For its part routine activities theory seeks to explain the minimum conditions necessary for a crime to be committed. In its simplest and original form these conditions include a suitable target, a likely offender and the absence of a capable guardian. More recent commentaries on this approach have highlighted the need for more than just a motivated offender. For Reiner (2000: 79), for example:

> Criminal behaviour can only occur if five necessary conditions are satisfied. There must be: *labelling* of the behaviour as criminal; at least one *motivated* offender; the *means* for the offender to commit the crime; criminal *opportunities*; and the absence of effective controls, both formal and informal. By definition if one of these factors is absent a crime cannot occur.

Just as Reiner refers to the need for offenders to have the means to commit crime, Ekblom and Tilley (2000: 394), writing in a slightly different context, have noted the advantages in 'construing the offender not merely in terms of predispositions and motives, but also in terms of capacities, capabilities and resources'. Indeed, one of the problems with the routine activities theory approach is that it assumes a motivated offender can be prevented by a capable guardian, but in practice a potential offence may be prevented when a motivated offender lacks the skills and knowledge to commit the offence. This weakness in the routine activities approach, which is frequently unacknowledged, was in part responsible for the development of the 'conjunction of criminal opportunity' (CCO) approach by Ekblom (2001, 2002).

The CCO began as an extension and combination of routine activities, the rational choice theory and environmental criminology. It is a good framework for emphasizing the importance of resources. Whilst there is not the space here to discuss the approach in detail it is worth emphasizing that the CCO attempts to combine explanations of the causes of crime, both 'distal' and 'proximal', to lay a foundation for thinking about the most appropriate prevention methods. In future revisions it will hopefully take on a more active consideration of offender resources. In so doing it may become an influential framework for guiding crime reduction.

There is one other important aspect here, and something that theory can help us with, and that is the way in which offenders learn the skills that enable them to be successful at crime. If one accepts that there is a distinct knowledge base or skill-set for some crimes then it is important to trace the process by which these skills are acquired not least because it provides another way of impacting upon crime. Indeed, it may be easier to disrupt the process of skill acquisition than it is to develop techniques for disarming a skilled and knowledgeable offender.

The process by which knowledge about crime is transferred between people has been discussed by theorists. Sutherland (1949) introduced the theory of 'differential association' whereby he argued that crime was learnt from associating with offenders, and that where people are influenced by more offence-oriented opinions over law-abiding ones then they become offenders. Since then many theory books, dating back many years, have variously questioned the extent to which it adequately explains crime (see Wheeler 1992) and underlined the similarity and overlaps with social learning theory, cultural and subcultural theories and anomie (for example, see Cloward and Ohlin 1960; Cohen 1957, 1985). There is not the space here to do justice to the many good research studies on such theories, but they are important in helping to understand how offenders' capacities are generated.

So how knowledgeable and skilled are offenders?

The key argument being posited in this chapter is that even if an offender is motivated and there are opportunities to commit crime, and the latter may determine the former, the offender will still need the 'means' according to Reiner (2000) and the 'resources' according to Ekblom and Tilley (2000). Resources are crucial because they help offenders to manage all types of risks and to exploit more and different opportunities, something that Ekblom (2001) has discussed in more detail in his work on the CCO. More specifically, Ekblom and Tilley (2000: 378) have considered 'how crucial the resources available to potentials offenders are to explaining their behaviour'. They do this by developing a list of different types of resources that offenders may utilize to commit crime. The list, or classification, includes personal resources; cognitive resources; moral resources including overcoming moral scruples; facilitatory resources such as tools and weapons; and collaborative resources such as other offenders. This classification is certainly helpful in terms of developing a framework but on its own it is not especially helpful for policy or practice purposes. For example, whilst 'cognitive resources' highlights the need for offenders to learn things that enable them to commit crimes, the real issue for policy purposes is knowing precisely how they acquired that knowledge (providing an intervention point) or what precisely the knowledge is which will give clues to prevention.

However, having identified the resources necessary for a crime to take place, Ekblom and Tilley then move on to classify how offenders use resources to commit crimes. Starting with the beginning of the event decision, they work through the various stages that offenders pass through as they commit crime, discussing the resources needed along the way. Thus they begin by suggesting that offenders need skill to spot good areas for crime, and they focus on various measures that need to be tackled and the resources needed to do so and so on. Their framework is extremely helpful in recognizing what makes an offender effective and what can make him or her ineffective. On a theoretical level Ekblom and Tilley (2000) are seeking to bring the offender centre-stage, and underlining the link between situational prevention and displacement (helping to understand the forms of displacement that are most open to offenders), about how knowledge is disseminated and how offenders become organized. Of course, it gives a range of clues to crime prevention.

What emerges from this work is the realization that the answer to the question 'what resources are needed to commit offences?' leads to an answer 'a lot'. True as it is this is not an especially helpful one for practical purposes, and a more user-friendly guide would be beneficial. Indeed, one of the great advantages of the routine activities approach, and one that has made it attractive to students, is that it is fairly simple to follow, something that in no way undermines its value. However, it is a new theory and more work needs to be done linking in other elements that render a crime possible, and the resources of offenders is a case in point. Here it is possible to develop Ekblom and Tilley's (2000) work and learn from other event theories and approaches and especially situational prevention.

So what are the core 'resources' that offenders need to commit a crime? Or, to put it another way, what makes motivated offenders capable of committing an offence and enables them to believe they will be successful? Immediately the question is complicated by the fact that in some cases the motivation will be derived from the discovery or emergence of a resource. For example, an offender may meet someone who is committed to offending and he or she is persuaded to take part. But for that chance meeting the offence would not have taken place or at least it would not have involved the invited individual.

It is possible to identify perhaps seven different types of resources or capabilities. The classification of offenders' resources is presented in Box 12.1. In practice the elements overlap, but they aim to identify types of resources offenders use which provide points at which prevention efforts may be focused.

Box 12.1 A classification of offenders' resources

1. *Resources for handling emotional state*. Offenders will need to be emotionally prepared to break the law. This may follow from a scant disregard for the rules being broken, or because there are disinhibitors at work, for example, the influence of drugs or alcohol. Offenders may need to employ 'techniques of neutralization' (Sykes and Matza 1957; see also Wortley 1996) to enable them to justify the offence.

2. *Resources derived from personality traits*. Essentially what is being referred to here are the characteristics or features of a personality that make an offence possible. Ekblom and Tilley (2000) included these under 'personal resources' incorporating attributes like the intelligence to match the threat, or the courage needed to commit the crime. Some robbers have argued that they need 'bottle' (Ball *et al.* 1978). According to Wright and Decker (1994: 110), 'The ability to project a calm appearance under pressure is a requisite skill' for residential burglaries, and it could be argued that this is a feature of some people's personality.

3. *Knowledge-based resources*. This refers to the facts (often based on experience) that provide them with the knowledge to commit the offence. Walsh (1986: 44) found that, 'The most typical way for all robbers to choose their victim was through knowledge acquired through employment; residence, observation or gossip'. They need knowledge about how to commit the offence. The quality of this knowledge base will help determine the relative success of the offence, including the size of the haul and avoiding capture. Carroll and Weaver (1986: 27) divided their sample of shoplifters into experts and novices and found that 'experts were far more efficient in analysing shoplifting possibilities'. There is a knowledge base associated with weighing up risks, and these will vary with the offence, and it can help some middle-class (Clarke (1990) and white-collar offenders (Box 1983).

4. *Skills-based resources*. Whereas knowledge is about the facts that are known to offenders, skills are about the techniques needed to apply that knowledge. Clearly different skills will be needed by different offenders: confidence tricksters needs skills of charm and guile, computer hackers will need some IT skills, and taking and driving away will require at least some rudimentary driving skills.

5. *Resources derived from physical traits*. This will include the physical strength that may be needed to force open a door, or to carry out the stolen stereo system from a store or house. It may include the need to be able to run fast to facilitate an effective getaway. Sometimes physical prowess is important. Some robbers mentioned that size intimidates and so padded their clothes both for this reason and also because it helped conceal their identity (Gill 2000).

6. *Tools or 'crime facilitators', including weapons*. Some offences cannot be committed without tools; sometimes tools makes offences easier to commit. Tools could include obtaining the right clothing to commit the crime. Jackets with hoods can be favoured for street robbery so that offenders can easily cover their faces, some shoplifters like baggy clothes or clothes with plenty of pockets because they are ideal for concealing stolen goods and some commercial burglars wear oversize shoes to disguise their identity (Wiersma

1996). Some robbers carry guns because they believe that they are more likely to make the offence easier by increasing victim compliance with their demands, and most disguise themselves.

7. *Associates and contacts.* As noted above, crimes sometimes only occur because they are motivated by someone else, or are only possible because an already-motivated offender was able to find a partner which is certainly the case for some robbers (Feeney 1986) and, as Felson (1998: 27) has noted, 'delinquency thrives on delinquent friends'. As Wright and Decker (1994) note of burglars, working with others has practical and psychological advantages, but also generates a risk in that someone else could provide information for the police. Wright and Decker (1997) note that some street robbers use female accomplices, especially prostitutes, to disguise their intentions. So the more chances there are for offenders to meet each other the more criminal opportunities will result (Tremblay 1993). And contacts are similarly important, differentiated from associates because they do not take part in the offence and indeed may be innocent providers of information. An important element of success at instrumental crime is disposing of the goods and so contacts/associates in the illicit market can be crucial (see Sutton 1998; Schneider 2003; Gill *et al.* 2004). The main point here, though, is that there is a difference between knowing how to commit a crime and being able to do so. As Levi's (1981: 91, emphasis in original) research on long-term fraud clearly illustrated: 'Knowing *how* to do a long-term fraud does not mean, of course, that one is *able* to do one: one has to have the necessary contacts for financing the business and disposing of the goods.' Criminals can benefit from organizing in that they can pool resources and add capabilities including specialists (see Ekblom 2003).

These features do not apply to a specific moment in time but to several moments, or several scenes where different combinations of the capacities may be needed. For example, preparing for crime may require one set of skills (obtaining a gun from the illicit market), the crime itself a different set (a robbery where agility is needed to storm across the counter before the rising screen is activated), exiting the scene (driving skills) another, and realizing the value of goods stolen goods (knowing a trustable fence) yet one more. And as Ekblom (1997) has noted, offenders are very adaptive, they learn quickly.

Offenders' tactics are rarely unique (Cusson 1993), and there are inevitably differences between different types of offenders (see Tarling 1993) such as those between the experienced and inexperienced; between different offences and also within offences. For example, it takes considerably more skill to rob from a moving cash-in-transit van than to rob by walking up to a counter and demanding money from staff advised to give it away when threatened (Gill 2001). Clearly, there is scope for more research on resources acquired and used by offenders, and the next section considers how this might be approached.

How do we research offenders' capacities?

A main point of this chapter is that a lot more needs to be known about how offenders approach their offending. There is a big knowledge gap.[7] And one of the principal sources for information about offenders' resources is offenders themselves. It is not the only one, of course; it would be possible to watch videos of offences, glean evidence from witnesses, victims and a range of experts including the police. Nevertheless, offenders can provide important insights.

Talking to offenders

Although the British Home Office advice is to 'think thief' when contemplating tackling instrumental offences, it is far from clear how people are supposed to know how thieves think. And why should anyone suppose that thieves' skills are open to interpretation by an untrained amateur or for that matter a professional in another field? What has been suggested above is that there are skills and a knowledge base to committing crime, and these are frequently underestimated. They are, though, crucial to understanding why crime occurs and why most prolific offenders are able to avoid capture most of the time.

Offenders have the potential to provide a lot of information. Via self-report they can provide an alternative measure of levels of offending. They can provide insights into different aspects of criminal justice, not least prisons, probation and treatment programmes. Incredible as it may seem there are still few studies of prison treatment programmes that have systematically followed up prisoners after they have completed their sentences. We can also find out how security measures are perceived; certainly they have sometimes been used as resources by offenders. For example:

- Bars on windows on the ground floor of a maisonette, installed to protect against burglaries, can be used to climb to the second floor where security may be less in evidence (Wojcik *et al.* 1997).

- Signs telling would-be robbers and other thieves that money was located in a safe via the sign, 'Beware safe', in fact informed offenders that a safe meant that there were goods worth stealing (Gill 2000).

- The presence of CCTV in-store may mean that front-line staff are less security aware and thereby make things easier for thieves (Beck and Willis 1995).

- Security screens installed to protect staff from bank raids can be favoured by some robbers because they protect them from staff tempted to intervene in the offence (Gill 2000).

There are many other examples and their significance should not be underestimated. In the language of routine activity theory, the point being made is that the crime was possible because the motivated offender had the resources to render the capable guardian ineffective. So what are the best ways of learning more about these resources?

At least one reason why offenders have not been approached for information is that some feel that they are an unreliable source. As Johnson *et al.* (1993: 203) note:

the offender's description of their actions after the event may miss too much. For too many different factors may influence the offender's action in the environment, especially the many avoided victims or targets which... will provide critical insights about why targets are selected.

One of the principal concerns about learning from offenders is that they might lie. Hirschi (1986: 116) has argued that we must 'be careful not to believe everything that is heard when talking to offenders'. And Indermaur (1995: 147) reported that 'offenders construct or remember their violence in a way that minimizes their guilt or culpability'. Thus, not being accurate may not be completely deliberate but, of course, offenders do have at least two reasons to lie. First, they may not trust the interviewer and worry that anything they say may be passed on to the police or other enforcement authorities.[8] Secondly, on the face of it some may query why they would wish to give away their 'trade' secrets when it will most likely contribute to providing better information to make their offences more difficult in future. Indeed, Crawford (1998) is sceptical about the rational choice approach precisely because it is based on views of convicted career criminals who are most likely to conform to the rational choice model, and in explaining crime they are more likely to rationalize events with the benefit of hindsight.[9]

Yet, there are benefits that can be gained from talking to offenders (see Walsh 1986; Ekblom 1991; Indermaur 1995; Gill 2000; 2001), and there is a lot to learn, as Clarke (1995: 132) has suggested:

> We need to learn more about ways that offenders obtain and process information about preventative initiatives and what role is played in this process by their own direct observation, their relationship with other offenders, and information obtained through the media. Such research would be of broader theoretical interest if it were to be conducted within a larger program of work on how offenders perceive and evaluate the opportunity structure for crime and how they learn about ways in which this expands as well as contracts.

And we need to know more about what conditions are necessary, from offenders' perspectives, to make an offence possible. There are in fact a number of ways of studying offenders, each with its own advantages and drawbacks. It is perhaps worth reviewing some of the most common methods here, starting with the interview.[10]

There have been a number of studies which have been based on interviews with offenders although the advantages and disadvantages of the different locale for interviews have never been fully explored. People engage with systems in different guises and each of these has an implication for their status. Patient, pupil, student, client, customer imply different relationships to the 'professional', to the 'state' and to the 'researcher' too. And this is the same within the criminal justice system, not just between 'witness', 'victim' and 'offender', although these are all different, but also between offenders whose status can be reflected in varied descriptions such as 'ex-prisoner', 'prisoner', 'probationer', 'convicted', 'accused', 'defendant', 'charged', 'arrested', and each of these may have a consequence for what they know, and more importantly for research purposes how confident they feel about reporting it. In each of the examples given there are implications for the levels of access and therefore the type of methodological approach that is appropriate.

Prison-based studies have been quite popular over the years, although Polsky (1971: 123) has called these interviews 'partial' and 'suspect', because offenders provide information which 'the criminal thinks you want to hear' and which cannot be checked.[11] Against this Levi (1981) has argued one advantage of the prison setting is that it does leave scope for 'serious soul searching' which adds validity to prisoners' accounts. It is possible to check validity with reference to the accounts of other offenders and with details recorded in official records (for example, see Levi 1981; Indermaur 1995; Gill 2000). And dangers implicit in false co-operativeness can be managed by good interview design, ensuring that proper permissions have been sought for the research, that the objectives are clearly outlined and understood by the interviewee, and that any concerns or reservations they have are dealt with before the interview begins. One final point here: it could be argued that the problem with speaking to offenders in prison is that one is always speaking to the failures because they have been caught, the assumption being that the clever ones get away. The sample will inevitably be biased, the researcher needs to recognize these limitations but it does not render the method useless.

In addition the prison interview invariably takes place some time after the event, and there will inevitably be concerns about selective recall. There are a variety of techniques that can be used to overcome this. Bennett and Wright's (1982) classic study of burglars in prison tried to get around this to some extent by filming potential crime scenes, and showing offenders pictures of them asking them to comment on their potential for crime. Of course the relative value of the interview compared with other methods will depend on the information being sought. If offenders are being approached for details about the number of offences they have committed many will need help to remember. In order to help interviewees recall events some researchers are using the 'calendar method'. This is where the interviewer takes the interviewee through a process of recalling a month or period of time first – one must ask about holidays in the summer – and then ask him or her to think about offending around that time (a form of memory recall).

So whilst there are definite limits to the prison interview, whatever its purpose, there are ways that at least some of these can be managed. A variation of the one-off interview method is to interview offenders repeatedly over time in a longitudinal or career study. Perhaps one of the main advantages of career studies is that researchers can begin to understand people's lives, and the influences that lead them to start, continue and stop offending. But as Farrington (2001: 13) has argued: 'The key issue is validity: How far do self-reports produce an accurate estimate of the true number of offences committed? How accurately do self-reports measure the prevalence, frequency and seriousness of offending?'

Tests of validity are usually arrest or conviction records, and Farrington concedes that it is somewhat ironic that self-reports are validated against official records, the deficiencies in which they were designed to overcome. The jury is still out on whether self-reports surveys are valid, though they appear quite strong for young males (Painter and Farrington 2001). Perhaps what career studies could tell us, if the information was systematically sought, is how resources needed for offending were acquired, how they were developed and how they were used and with what success for different offences against different types of obstacles. But the problem here is that they still rely on interviews and many of the limits of interviews still apply.

Thus some researchers have adopted an ethnographic approach – that is, studying offenders in the context in which their offending takes place. Good examples include studies of robbery and burglary (Wright and Decker 1994, 1997) and staff dishonesty (Ditton 1977). To date the primary focus of this work has not been on the resources necessary to commit offending, although there is little doubt that this type of study offers real insights into the nature of offending and there is much to be gained from this approach.

Before finishing this brief review of methodologies, there are at least four other approaches which are rarely mentioned but which offer a good opportunity to learn about resources acquired and used by offenders. The first is to return offenders to 'their' crime scenes.[12] This is not a new approach, and Cromwell et al. (1991: 197) produced genuine insights leading the authors to criticize methods which rely on gaining information from offenders divorced from the scene: 'The findings suggest that burglars interviewed in prison, or those recalling crimes from the past, may engage in "rational reconstruction", reinterpreting past behaviour in a manner consistent with "what should have been" rather than "what was".'

Recently the author, working with colleagues (see Hart 2003: 2004), has taken shoplifters back to crime scenes (stores) and reconstructed their offending with a view to learning about how they circumvent security measures. It seems clear that offenders use a range of very straightforward techniques to avoid capture and more of these will be discussed later. The findings here have been used to make a training video to help raise staff awareness of shoplifters' techniques.

The second approach concerns the number of autobiographies and biographies of habitual offenders or those who have committed serious or high-profile offences since. Clearly some stories will be sensationalized but accounts of events and lives offer important opportunities to learn (see Morgan 1999; Goodey 2000; Wilson and Reuss 2000; Nellis 2002). One way would be to start with a set of theories and see to what extent the content of these publications supports the theories identified.

The third approach, and mentioned above, would be to study approaches from video evidence. As the surveillance society becomes more apparent (see Gill 2003b) it is likely more will be captured on camera and this may be of a better-quality facilitating this type of post-incident analysis. Fourthly, it may be possible to use crime scene visitors, such as scene of crime officers (SOCOs), to identify the types of resources offender used. This will sometimes be used for investigation purposes but the information gleaned can be useful for crime prevention too.

What can we learn from offenders?

Whatever the method adopted, and there is merit in all the above approaches, there are some general areas of interest that would help us to understand more about offenders' resources. This list is not intended to be exhaustive – there is not the space for that. Rather, some salient questions that could usefully be included are the following:

- What features of a target if any make it attractive or unattractive? Specific information is needed here. Sometimes offenders state 'because it is easy' or 'too tough' without being able to specify why. They will need help to articulate their thoughts. By knowing about these features it is then possible to obtain some insights into why they were easy (what resources made this the case) or why it was difficult (and what resources offenders used to manage them).

- What features of the environment, if any, helped or hindered the offence? Again, precise details are needed. A good description of the threat is important and so are the specific features and characteristics of it.

- What precise problems did different security measures pose (and combinations of them)? It is important to know why this was the case; what skills or knowledge did offenders lack that could have reduced or eliminated the threat?

- How were measures/threats they encountered tackled? Here specific details are needed to understand the type, depth and breadth of the knowledge and skill base that made this possible.

- Exactly what tools are needed to get around security measures? Where did the tools come from and what are the characteristics or features of tools that make them useful, and what skills are needed to use them and how are these acquired?

- What combinations of security measures pose the most threat? This will be context specific but can contribute to the building up of a good information base over time.

- Which measures would they always or mostly avoid and why?

- How did they learn about different measures? And how did they acquire any skills to overcome them? Also important here is their success rate at circumventing the threat that was posed.

A lot can be learnt about offenders' resources by asking questions such as: how did you get caught and what lessons did you learn from this? What if anything made the crime easy and what made the crime difficult? These questions are much more fact based and offer a good chance that people will know the answers even if they have to be teased out by a skilful researcher.

The issues of knowledge, skills and competencies are important. National Occupational Standards are statements of competence and most industries have them. It would be a very useful exercise to develop a National Occupational Standard for committing different types of crime, to be used for crime prevention purposes, of course. Ekblom (2002) was on to a similar idea in his discussion of 'performance standards'. There is a need to think carefully about the skills that are needed to commit crimes, how they differ between different offence types, where they are acquired and how they evolve in use. This will provide a better base to respond in a more focused and targeted way.

The main point being posited here is that it is not possible to come to any sort of conclusion about the effectiveness of security or crime prevention measures if offenders' perceptions and behaviour are not understood, and this includes the skills and knowledge that they have to enable them to be successful. It may be possible to improve situational measures, but to do so it is crucial that the threat is fully understood.

Case study: Jo, the shoplifter

Jo[13] has qualifications from school and might have achieved more had she been the slightest bit interested in her lessons. For Jo socializing and spending money were more important than qualifications and study. So she left school as soon as she could and before long found herself in a social setting that resulted in her experimenting with drugs. She became hooked quickly and all her offending has been related to the drug habit. She says sometimes that she wants to come off drugs but she has not convinced even herself. It is a way of life. She is used to it and she can live with the consequences and indeed quite enjoys the respect she has within her immediate networks. Her two short periods in custody may have shamed her parents but not Jo. In what follows Jo's core resources for shop theft are examined. The following case study helps illustrate what might be learned from studying offenders' views.

Resources for handling emotional state

Jo needs money for drugs, so she embarks on a theft spree in the morning to get hold of goods that can easily be sold later, to members of the local community, small shopkeepers and known fences (or even direct to dealers in exchange for drugs). Within hours the stolen goods are been passed on for about a half the retail selling price. Within another hour or two Jo has the drugs she needs and the next morning the process starts again.

Jo is too desperate to feed her habit to worry much about the consequences. She is rarely 'on' drugs when she steals, she wants to be alert to avoid capture. Desperation gets rid of all disinhibtors. She does not feel guilty. The desire to succeed though does mean she is focused, very determined, she knows what she wants, what the risks are and how these will need to be managed. She has not calculated these in any considered way but she has considerable personal experience, and she has gleaned information from other thieves, drug addicts and prisoners.

Resources derived from personality traits

Jo is an intelligent person, she is very focused and she has over time learnt how to assess risks. People find Jo likeable, she is a friendly person, and she is known as being reliable. This means that fences and others to whom she passes goods want to work with her, and those selling drugs know that she can be trusted. Her criminal network consider her a good client. Her ability to relate well to others, their perception of her as reliable and her commitment and determination to get what she wants mean that she is able to continue as a thief and support her habit much longer than others. People don't mess with Jo because they do not need to and because they like her and value her custom.

Knowledge-based resources

Jo is what Carroll and Weaver (1986) would call an 'expert'. Jo knows how and what to steal. She knows the types of goods that can sell and the type of places where the goods can be obtained easily. To Jo it has always been an advantage that retailers organized their stores in a similar way. This made it easier for honest customers but also thieves too. Stealing from a store varied little from town to town and anywhere she went she could feel safe that she would be successful. She knew what to look for and where to look for it and this applied to both goods and security measures. She always practised some golden rules: always identify the exits, always ensure that no one is watching without making that obvious, concentrate on stealing, and if spotted abort and move somewhere else.

Jo steals things that can easily be concealed and therefore removed and which have value to potential black-market buyers – for example, razors, toothbrushes, batteries, small electrical goods, perfumes, make-up or even food and alcohol. She understands how security works and this does not put her off. She knows to check for the presence of security guards. When they are not by the exit, all well and good; when they are, prepare to run. Her experience is that most do not want a chase and those that do don't run either fast or for very long – a source of encouragement. She knows that most tags can be removed easily, and cameras can be mitigated by discovering blind spots. In any event she had trained herself to bend her head slightly forward when she walks around a store making it more difficult for camera operators to get a good picture of her face. Even store detectives are not much of a threat; her approach was never to steal with someone watching, be they another shopper, member of staff or store detective.

Skills-based resources

Jo has several techniques which she feels make it easier for her to steal. She always steals in blind spots, in aisles where there are no cameras and never in front of people who could be watching, or by keeping her back to the cameras and standing close to the counter. She finds is easy to remove tags or secrete goods in clothing without in anyway looking suspicious: anyone looking at her would assume she was looking at the product and reading about it. She sometimes steals with a friend, John. She knows she can trust him, and he acts as a distraction and decoy purposefully attracting attention to himself leaving her to focus on thefts. Sometimes John's role is lookout to offer extra protection.

Mostly, though, Jo works alone, and is able to fool anyone who may be watching her. Sometimes she picks up two goods and then puts one back while she secretes the other up her sleeve. She works at pace and it would not be easy for anyone to tell what she was doing. Just in case someone was watching she would always pull forward the goods on the shelf to make it look like nothing was missing. Sometimes she makes a point of picking up two goods and dropping one of them. She then picks this up and puts it on the shelf hiding the other one in clothing. She has used a 'magic' bag, specially lined to disarm tag readers but the bag was stolen by another thief and she had not considered it necessary to make or obtain another. Sometimes she will purchase a product just to make it look like she is a normal shopper, something small that can be retuned a few days later for a refund is all that is needed to give the impression she is a genuine shopper. Sometimes she will play with her mobile phone when she is in the queue – she pretends she is sending a text message. This is to prevent her body language giving herself away and to make her look like a real shopper. Indeed, Jo's aim when stealing was always to look like an honest customer.

Resources derived from physical traits

Jo would probably be viewed as 'plain', not especially attractive or un-attractive, not overweight nor slight, and about average height. She was not distinguishable in a crowd and these characteristics were advantageous for stealing. That she was once a fast runner and could still run fairly quickly over short distances (and usually faster than security officers sometimes weighed down by inappropriate uniforms) was always useful if a quick getaway was required, although it rarely was. Jo was also able to move her hands quickly, a bit like a magician, someone had once told her, and this trait enabled her to be skilful at stealing.

Tools or 'crime facilitators' and this includes weapons

Shop thieves do need tools: they need to be able to conceal goods. Jo often used bags. She always carried a handbag although this was small and she liked to make every trip count. Mostly, though, she wore baggy clothing. She found that she could steal a lot and secrete a lot under a baggy coat. Pockets could be useful too, the deeper the better but many clothes are made this way. Some of the thieves she knew wore reversible jackets so they could change appearance quickly but Jo never felt the need. Jo always wore a hat or cap, she found them a useful disguise and made it more difficult for cameras to take a good picture of her face. She changed her hair style a lot, and she also had three wigs, all stolen, so that if she returned to stores where she had previously been caught or she felt might be looking for her, she was less recognizable. Jo also carried a small perfume spray in her hand bag; she always felt that if she was ever in a tussle with a security operative she would spray him or her in the eyes and run away. She had not yet done this, she was not a violent person but it was an option.

She also carried a rape alarm. If she was ever chased by someone not in uniform and caught she would activate the alarm. She hoped it would throw her pursuer off guard, but might also attract passers-by to stop him or her whilst she got away. Jo felt she was prepared for every eventuality.

Associates and contacts

Jo knew a few people that made her stealing viable. In addition to those to whom she sold her stolen goods, and the drug dealers, were other associates from whom she could learn and refine new techniques and learn about ways of circumventing the latest security measures. In addition were two shop assistants who colluded in her work. One worked in a small local shop, another in a garage; they worked long and unsociable hours and considered themselves badly paid. Jo was 'allowed' to steal a limited amount of goods, so as not to look too suspicious, and then paid a £50 commission each week to each of them. Although this halved Jo's earning it was easy money with little risk and she considered it worthwhile.

Stopping Jo

Jo was an able thief. She had learnt to maximize the most of her abilities and learn about the art of theft so as to maximize returns and reduce the chances of getting caught. She knew what to steal to obtain a quick return and how to limit the risks posed by different types of security. Jo had 'resources' which made her successful at crime and if anyone had taken the time to assess these they would have found lots of clues to prevent her stealing (as much) and increase the chances of catching her.

Jo would no longer be a thief if she could be cured of her drug habit. This is the only long-term solution. However, she is in no rush, she is respected and liked in community, those she knows want to work with her, they consider her a good thief and a valued client or contact. Jo has standing and respect whereas the alternative legitimate world seems to judge her harshly and critically, there is not much that appeals to her in it. She is now an expert, and the rewards are high. Jo is conscious that she would have to work very hard in the legitimate world to make as much money and then she would lose large chunks in tax, and be accountable to bosses who were less intelligent than she was. And what sort of job can you get with a record like Jo's?

There were things Jo did not like. When stores change layouts, which was not a significant event very often, she worried. She never stole from a store until she was comfortable with the new arrangements. She often wondered whether stores monitored those who window shopped for long periods. The lower the height of the shelves the more difficult it was to behave surreptitiously because it increased surveillance from overhead cameras; fewer pylons meant fewer obscured lines of vision; and lots of help points and lots of staff meant more surveillance opportunities. So fewer staff helped Jo – one of the few things that was an advantage to her as a thief that was not also an advantage to the honest shopper. She did not like being asked if she would like any help, a good customer service tip perhaps, but awkward for Jo because it drew attention to her.

Static guards were mostly not a threat, they wore uniforms and so she knew who they were and she just had to make sure they were not watching, but guards who wandered about the store were a concern: she always felt uncomfortable not knowing where they might be, especially when there were a lot of them and they looked like they were conscientious about their work. Although not put off by cameras Jo was more concerned when she knew there were lots of them covering all parts of the store because that reduced the number of blind spots. A favourite trick was to put some goods in a basket covered up by bigger ones. She would move to an aisle where there were no cameras and secrete the small goods under her clothing but reappear with her basket. The bigger goods were still on show and it was not obvious anything was amiss. A saving grace for Jo was the knowledge that cameras were not monitored most of the time and often not by people who were fully trained and dedicated to catching thieves. And even if they did they would have to communicate this to someone on the shop floor who would have to respond proactively. She was aware that most involved in security were poorly trained, if at all. Did they really know anything about the techniques thieves used? She doubted it. Too many thieves she knew stole with abandonment and so there was every chance that even a theft caught on camera would not be noticed, but she knew things could change, a professional security operation could make life awkward for Jo.

Cameras that could match up faces with pictures of suspects would be a problem to Jo, but she was not aware of any. But if stores shared pictures of suspects, and had cameras that could spot faces and alert staff, that would be unwelcome. She had heard about cameras that can identify someone by his or her gait but had not yet heard of their deployment in retailing. Some thieves would not worry too much, they would just take their chances, but Jo always wanted to avoid capture and would find this off-putting.

Some goods were more difficult to steal because they were kept behind counters. This certainly made them unattractive to Jo (but honest customers too), but this did not worry Jo too much as she would just steal other goods instead. She always wondered why tags were so accessible: if they were hidden it would make her task harder. And often tags did not work. Were they to be more reliable it might at least make her think. On one occasion she walked through an exit with lots of stolen goods, many tagged, and the alarm was sounded. The security officer on the door said to a woman with a push chair, 'sorry madam, baby buggies are always sending off the alarm'.

Jo had a ready supply of goods to be stolen. Fortunately for Jo retailers are geared up to making goods easily available. They want to help customers buy and these are so often the very things that make theft easy too. She also had staff who colluded with her. 'Thank goodness for employers who do not pay much and treat employees badly,' she thought. And there was a thriving illicit market; even 'honest' people could not resist a bargain. If law enforcement intervened in this area it could be awkward, but mostly they don't bother and she felt that she had little to worry about.

Conclusion

This chapter has discussed a range of issues relating to an aim of reducing the capacity to offend by reducing the resources available to offenders. This aim entailed a review of what offenders do at the scene of their crimes, a focus on the event rather than the offender which led to a brief review of some elements of situational prevention and to a lesser extent routine activities theory and the conjunction of criminal opportunity. It was suggested that situational prevention has not taken full account of offenders' resources, whilst a limit of routine activities is that it assumes a motivated offender can be prevented by a capable guardian, but in practice an offence may be prevented if a motivated offender lacks the resources, say the skills and knowledge to commit the offence. Routine activities theory has not asked what makes motivated offenders capable of committing an offence and getting away with it. The conjunction of criminal opportunity has exposed some weaknesses in current thinking about crime prevention but has not yet tackled the issue of offenders' resources fully.

The chapter then moved on to review some of the available literature on 'resources' and concluded that there was something of a knowledge gap. There are a range of practical problems associated with gleaning information from offenders. It was suggested that there may be legal and ethical considerations, and certainly offenders may not always be reliable: they have a reason to lie, and may not always recall their offending precisely. These are real problems but it was suggested that the threats to reliability could be managed by good interview techniques and responsive research strategies. Yet we still know very little about the best ways of getting information from offenders nor the most reliable ways of doing so, and this is another area which merits more research. Certainly it is possible to think of more imaginative research ideas such as recreating offences at the same or similar crime scenes.

In reviewing information that was available the chapter suggested that there were perhaps seven core resources that offenders have. These were resources for handling emotional state, resources derived from personality traits, knowledge-based resources, skills-based resources, resources derived from physical traits, tools or 'crime facilitators' (and this includes weapons, associates and contacts). Identifying the resources offenders use gives clues as to how offences can be thwarted. Put simply, demotivating an offender is problematic in practice, but impacting on their use of resources may be a more realistic way of making an offence less likely, more difficult (and thereby increasing the chances of offenders getting caught) or stopping it altogether. This point was illustrated via a case study of a shoplifter, Jo. This illustrated how a shoplifter might use different types of resources to commit shop thefts. Some of these were then briefly analysed to highlight how prevention may benefit from the insights.

Ultimately there is a need to find new ways of preventing crime and perhaps new ways of finding out about how offenders behave, which is likely to require revisions in traditional theories, including even some mergers, and perhaps the development of new ones. What is clear is that offenders get away with crime a lot of the time, they adapt quickly, and they are innovative; they must be doing something right and it is easy to miss some of their tricks. This chapter has suggested that we have not been looking closely enough at the right things. If we focus on 'restricting resources for offending' we may be surprised, and we may generate some new ideas for reducing offenders' capacity to offend.

Acknowledgements

I would like to thank Paul Ekblom, Nick Tilley, Claire Taylor and Hilary Coplestone-Crow for their comments on the draft of this chapter, and Marcus Felson who helped me develop some of the ideas.

Selected further reading

As noted, this is an area which has not received a great deal of coverage. Much of the work relating to resources can be found in studies about different aspects of crime prevention, such as opportunity reduction and routine activities (e.g. Clarke and Felson 1993; Felson and Clarke 1998), and the conjunction of criminal opportunity (see Ekblom 2001). Then there are studies of offenders, and career studies make an important contribution here (e.g. Farrington 2001), as do studies of specific offence types – for example, burglary (Wright and Decker 1994), robbery (Wright and Decker 1997; Gill 2000) and fraud (Levi 1981). A very good scholarly discussion of offenders' resources is provided by Ekblom and Tilley (2000) in the *British Journal of Criminology*.

Notes

1. A classification of 'resources' is provided in the chapter and refers to the range of capabilities available to an offender to enable him or her to be successful at offending.
2. In discussing the conjunction of criminal opportunity framework (discussed below), Ekblom advocates using the terminology 'restricting resources for offending'. 'Restricting' rather than 'reducing' is preferred because it also implies restricting *access* to the resources. Clearly, this is not the only way of reducing the capacity to offend, and it has not received a great deal of discussion.
3. Although usually referred to as a single decision, it invariably involves a sequence of decisions and ought to be plural.
4. Although several approaches focus on the criminal event. For example, Clarke and Felson (1993: 9) have noted the relevance of 'environmental criminology', 'hotspots', 'lifestyles', 'defensible space', 'crime prevention through environmental design' (CPTED) and 'problem-oriented policing'.
5. It may involve tackling the 'niche of offending', which is where offenders identify a source from which they can earn a living and exploit this by using resources to

manage any risks in doing so (see Ekblom 2003).

6. The whole area of 'what works' (and what doesn't) is another knowledge gap. Recently there has been a drive to redress this, by quantitative social scientists acting under the umbrella of the Campbell Collaboration (see Welsh *et al.* 2002), and interest has been fuelled by advocates of the 'realist' approach (Pawson and Tilley 1997). Work on 'reducing the capacity to offend' may also help inform theory and practice here.

7. This is despite the fact that we form opinions about offenders at an early age: Goldilocks was a burglar, Hansel and Gretel's guardians were child abusers and the wolf who blew down the piglets' houses was a murderer!

8. In addition there are legal and ethical considerations (see Ekblom 1991).

9. Similar criticisms that are made of techniques of neutralization.

10. It is worth remembering that offenders are already interviewed by the police albeit, of course, for a different purpose. How much more could be made of these interviews for crime prevention purposes? Is a great opportunity being lost to develop good crime prevention data?

11. See Walsh (1986) for good discussion of some of the methodological problems associated with interviewing incarcerated offenders.

12. A variation on the theme here is to use role plays (see Butler 1994).

13. Jo is a fictional character although all the characteristics have been derived from work with shoplifters (see Gill and Loveday 2002; Hart 2003).

References

Ball, J., Chester, L. and Perrott, R. (1978) *Cops and Robbers*. London: André Deutsch

Beck, A. and Willis, A. (1995) *Managing the Risk to safe Shopping*. Leicester: Perpetuity Press.

Bennett, T. and Wright, R. (1982) *Burglars on Burglary*. Aldershot: Cromer.

Bennett, T. and Wright, R. (1994) *Burglars on Burglary*. Aldershot: Cromer.

Box, S. (1983) *Power, Crime and Mystification*. London: Tavistock.

Butler, G. (1994) 'Commercial burglary: what offenders say', in M. Gill (ed.) *Crime at Work: Studies in Security and Crime Prevention. Volume 1*. Leicester: Perpetuity Press.

Carroll, J. and Weaver, F. (1986) 'Shoplifters' perceptions of crime opportunities: a process tracing study', in D. Cornish and R.V. Clarke (eds) *The Reasoning Criminal; Rational Choice Perspectives on Offending*. New York, NY: Springer-Verlag.

Clarke, M. (1990) *Business Crime: Its Nature and Control*. Cambridge: Polity Press.

Clarke, R.V.G. (1995) 'Situational crime prevention', in M. Tonry and D. Farrington (eds) *Building a Safer Society: Crime and Justice – A Review of Research. Volume 19*. Chicago, IL: University of Chicago Press.

Clarke, R.V.G and Felson, M. (1993) *Routine Activity and Rational Choice*. New York, NY: Transaction Publishers.

Cloward, R. and Ohlin, L. (1960) *Delinquency and Opportunity: A Theory of Delinquent Gangs*. Glencoe, IL: Free Press.

Cohen, A. (1957) *Delinquent Boys*. Glencoe, IL: Free Press.

Cohen, A. (1985) *Visions of Social Control: Crime, Punishment and Classification*. Oxford: Polity Press.

Crawford, A. (1998) *Crime Prevention and Community Safety: Politics, Policies and Practitioners*. London: Longman.

Cromwell, P.F., Olson, J.N. and Avary, D.W. (1991) 'How residential burglars choose targets: an ethnographic analysis', *Security Journal*, 2: 195–9.

Cusson, M. (1993) 'A strategic analysis of crime: criminal tactics as responses to precriminal situations', in R.V. Clarke and M. Felson (eds) *Routine Activity and Rational Choice*. New York, NY: Transaction Publishers.

Ditton, J. (1977) *Part-time Crime: An Ethnography of Fiddling and Pilferage*. London: Macmillan.

Ekblom, P. (1991) 'Talking to offenders: practical lessons for local crime prevention', in O. Nello (ed.) *Urban Crime: Statistical Approaches and Analyses. Proceedings of an International Seminar, Barcelona 1990*. Barcelona: Institut d'Estudis Metropolitans de Barcelona.

Ekblom, P. (1997) 'Gearing up against crime: a dynamic framework to help designers keep up with the adaptive criminal in a changing world', *International Journal of Risk, Security and Crime Prevention*, 2: 249–66.

Ekblom, P. (2000) 'The conjunction of criminal opportunity – a tool for clear, "joined-up" thinking about community safety and crime reduction', in S. Ballintyne *et al.* (eds) *Secure Foundations: Key Issues in Crime Prevention, Crime Reduction and Community Safety*. London: Institute for Public Policy Research.

Ekblom, P. (2001) 'The conjunction of criminal opportunity: a framework for crime reduction toolkits', crime reduction website (www.crimereduction.gov.uk/learningzone/cco.htm).

Ekblom, P. (2002) 'From the source to the mainstream is uphill: the challenge of transferring knowledge of crime prevention through replication, innovation and anticipation', in N. Tilley (ed.) *Analysis for Crime Prevention. Crime Prevention Studies. Vol. 13*. Monsey, NY: Criminal Justice Press.

Ekblom, P. (2003) 'Organised crime and the conjunction of criminal opportunity framework', in A. Edwards and P. Gill (eds) *Transnational Organised Crime: Perspectives on Global Security*. London: Routledge.

Ekblom, P., Law, H. and Sutton, M. (1996) *Safer Cities and Domestic Burglary. Home Office Research Study 164*. London. Home Office.

Ekblom, P. and Tilley, N. (2000) 'Going equipped: criminology, situational crime prevention and the resourceful offender', *British Journal of Criminology*, 40: 376–98.

Farrington, D.P. (2001) *What has been Learned from Self-reports about Criminal Careers and the Causes of Offending?* Report to the Home Office (www.homeoffice.gov.uk/rds/pdfs/farrington.pdf).

Farrington, D. (2003) 'A short history of randomized experiments in criminology', *Evaluation Review*, 27: 218–27.

Feeney, F. (1986) 'Robbers as decision-makers', in D. Cornish and R. Clarke (eds) *The Reasoning Criminal: Rational Choice Perspectives on Offending*. New York, NY: Springer-Verlag.

Felson, M. (1998) *Crime and Everyday Life* (2nd edn). Thousand Oaks, CA: Pine Forge Press.

Felson, M. and Clarke, R.V. (1998) *Opportunity Makes the Thief: Practical Theory for Crime Prevention. Police Research Series 98*. London: Home Office.

Gill, M.L. (2000) *Commercial Robbery: Offenders' Perspectives on Security and Crime Prevention*. London: Blackstone Press.

Gill, M.L. (2001) 'The craft of robbers of cash-in-transit vans: crime facilitators and the entrepreneurial approach', *International Journal of the Sociology of Law*, 29: 277–91.

Gill, M.L. (ed.) (2003a) *Managing Security. Crime at Work Series. Volume III*. Leicester: Perpetuity Press.

Gill, M.L. (ed.) (2003b) *CCTV. Crime at Work Series. Volume IV*. Leicester: Perpetuity Press.

Gill, M., Burns-Howell, T., Hemming, M., Hart, J., Clarke, R.V.G. and Wright, A. (2004) *The Illicit Market in Stolen Fast-moving Consumer Goods: A Global Impact Study.*

Leicester: Perpetuity Research and Consultancy International Ltd.

Gill, M. and Loveday, K. (2003) 'What do offenders think about CCTV?', in M.L. Gill (ed.) *CCTV. Crime at Work Series. Volume IV*. Leicester: Perpetuity Press.

Goodey, J. (2000) 'Biographical lessons for criminology', *Theoretical Criminology*, 4: 473–98.

Grabosky, P. and Duffield, G. (2001) *Red Flags of Fraud. Trends and Issues in Crime and Criminal Justice* 200. Canberra: Australian Institute of Criminology.

Harding, R.W. (1993) 'Gun use in crime, rational choice and social learning theory', in R.V. Clarke and M. Felson (eds) *Routine Activity and Rational Choice*. New York, NY: Transaction Publishers.

Hart, J. (2003) 'What the offenders say', *Security Management Today*, October: 47–9.

Hart, J. (2004) 'Shoplifters on shoplifting – raising the awareness of frontline staff', in *British Retail Consortium Yearbook 2004*. London: HMSO.

Hirschi, T. (1986) 'On the compatibility of rational choice and social control theories of crime', in D. Cornish and R.V. Clarke (eds) *The Reasoning Criminal: Rational Choice Perspectives on Offending*. New York, NY: Springer-Verlag.

Indermaur, D. (1995) *Violent Property Crime*. Sydney: Federation Press.

Johnson, B.D., Natarajan, M. and Sanabria, H. (1993) '"Successful" criminal careers: toward an ethnography within the rational choice perspective', in R.V. Clarke and M. Felson (eds) *Routine Activity and Rational Choice*. New York, NY: Transaction Publishers.

Levi, M. (1981) *The Phantom Capacitalist*. London: Tavistock.

Morgan, S. (1999) 'Prison lives: critical issues in reading autobiography', *Howard Journal*, 38: 328–40.

Nellis, M. (2002) 'Pros and cons: offender auto/biographies, penal reform and probation training', *Howard Journal*, 41: 434–68.

Painter, K. and Farrington, D. (2001) 'Evaluating situational crime prevention using a young people's survey', *British Journal of Criminology*, 41: 266–84.

Pawson, R. and Tilley, N. (1997) *Evaluation*. London: Sage.

Polsky, N. (1971) *Hustlers, Beats and Others*. Harmondsworth: Penguin Books.

Read, P.P. (1979) *The Train Robbers*. London: Cornet Books.

Reiner, R. (2000) 'Crime and control in Britain', *Sociology*, 34: 71–94.

Scheinder, J. (2003) 'Shoplifting: patterns of offending among persistent burglars', in M. Gill (ed.) *Managing Security. Crime at Work Series. Volume III*. Leicester: Perpetuity Press.

Sutherland, E. (1949) *White-collar Crime*. New York, NY: Holt, Reinhart & Winston.

Sutton, M. (1998) *Handling Stolen Goods: A Market Reduction Approach. Home Office Research Study* 178. London: HMSO.

Sykes, G. and Matza, D. (1957) 'Techniques of neutralization: a theory of delinquency', *American Journal of Sociology*, 22: 664–70.

Tarling, R. (1993) *Analysing Offending*. London: HMSO.

Tilley, N. (1997) 'Realism, situational reality and crime prevention', in G. Newman *et al.* (eds) *Rational Choice and Situational Crime Prevention: Theoretical Foundations*. Dartmouth: Ashgate.

Tremblay, P. (1993) 'Searching for suitable co-offenders', in R.V. Clarke and M. Felson (eds) *Routine Activity and Rational Choice*. New York, NY: Transaction Publishers.

Walsh, D. (1986) 'Victim selection procedures among economic criminals: the rational choice perspective', in D. Cornish and R.V. Clarke (eds) *The Reasoning Criminal; Rational Choice Perspectives on Offending*. New York, NY: Springer-Verlag.

Wiersma, E. (1996) 'Commercial burglars in the Netherlands: reasoning decision-makers?', *International Journal of Risk Security and Crime Prevention*, 1: 217–28.

Wheeler, S. (1992) 'The problem of white-collar crime motivation', in K. Schlegel and D. Weisburd (eds) *White-Collar Crime Reconsidered*. Boston, MA: Northeastern University Press.

Wilson, D. and Reuss, A. (eds) (2000) *Prison(er) Education: Stories of Change and Transformation*. Winchester: Waterside Press.

Wojcik, D., Walklate, S., Ostrihanska, Z., Mawby, R.I. and Gorgenyi, I. (1997) 'Security and crime prevention at home: A comparison of victims' response to burglary in England, Poland and Hungary', *International Journal of Risk, Security and Crime Prevention*, 2(1): 38–50.

Wortley, R (1996) *Guilt, Shame and Situational Prevention. Crime Prevention Studies*. Monsey, NY: Criminal Justice Press.

Wortley, R. (1997) 'Reconsidering the role of opportunity in situational crime prevention', in G. Newman *et al.* (eds) *Rational Choice and Situational Crime Prevention*. Aldershot: Ashgate.

Wortley, R. (1998) 'A two-stage model of situational crime prevention', *Studies on Crime and Crime Prevention*, 7: 173–88.

Wortley, R. (2001) 'A classification of techniques for controlling situational precipitators of crime', *Security Journal*, 14: 63–82.

Wright, R. and Decker, S. (1994) *Burglars on the Job: Street Life and Residential Breakins*. Boston, MA: Northeastern University Press.

Wright, R. and Decker, S. (1997) *Armed Robbers in Action*. Boston, MA: Northeastern University Press.

Chapter 13

Using publicity for preventive purposes

Kate Bowers and Shane Johnson

Introduction

Our perception of the world has a strong impact upon how we behave and interact. This can be affected in a variety of ways. For instance, the successful advertising of a consumer item has the power to encourage people to buy it, whilst unsuccessful campaigns can have an undesirable effect, sentencing a product to live out its remaining life on the 'everything must go' shelf. Consider also, for instance, the way in which the price of stocks and shares can be influenced by traders' perceptions. In a scenario where one or more trader(s) rapidly buys more and more shares of a particular company, this can generate a signal that the company concerned is a good prospect, which can easily influence the behaviour of other traders. Here, a change in the intrinsic value of the company is not required (although it will probably be desired) to catalyse a reaction from the traders – a change in their perception of the value of the company or shares is all that is needed.[1]

Research conducted within the discipline of psychology also illustrates a range of situations over which people's perceptions influence their behaviour or decisions made, and how this can be influenced by information provided. For instance, Kebbell and Johnson (2002) examined the impact of post-event information on mock-witnesses perceptions of an incident. Participants in the experiment were shown CCTV footage of a police car travelling down a road with its lights flashing and siren wailing. All participants viewed the same film but, after watching, one group were shown a picture of the car intact with no damage, whereas a second group saw a picture of the same car, but in this case the vehicle had sustained considerable damage to the bonnet and bumper. All participants were told that the picture was an accurate representation of how the car looked immediately after filming stopped, and were subsequently asked to estimate how fast they believed the vehicle had been travelling. The results indicated that those who saw a picture of the damaged vehicle consistently overestimated the speed of the vehicle, believing it to be travelling over 20 kmph faster than the other group. They also reported that they believed it had been driven more dangerously. This study and many others illustrate how providing people with information can affect their perceptions of risk even where this is incongruent with reality.

Not surprisingly then, perhaps, there has recently been an increase in the frequency with which publicity has been used to amplify the effects of crime reduction interventions or to reassure the public. The purpose of this chapter is to assist practitioners who wish to exploit the power of publicity by reviewing current practices and providing recommendations concerning the situations in which particular types of publicity are likely to have a positive impact. Considering the structure of the chapter, we begin by discussing a framework that categorizes the different types of publicity that have been used in crime reduction.[2] We also then discuss the mechanisms through which these different types of advertising should help reduce crime or reassure the public and, where possible, provide examples of the relative successes of the different approaches. We also endeavour to provide advice on how practitioners might go about planning publicity campaigns. Finally, since it is certainly the case that not all publicity is good publicity, we also discuss some of the problematic issues concerning the use of publicity.

Defining and categorizing publicity

In relation to the crime reduction enterprise, various forms of publicity can be used to realize different aims and objectives. For instance, publicity may be used with the intention of persuading offenders to stop offending, trying to make vulnerable groups adapt their behaviour so that they are less likely to become victims, or it might aim to combine these approaches. Therefore, the first major distinction between different types of publicity is whether it is aimed at offenders, victims or the public more generally – that is, the population to whom it is directed. A second major distinction concerns the geographic coverage of a campaign – is it pitched at the local, regional or national level? For instance, members of local Crime and Disorder Reduction Partnerships are likely to want to promote what is going on at the local level, to the local population. In contrast, the Home Office, or other national agencies, might be more interested in getting a message across to a wider audience. Thirdly, there is a distinction between specific and generic publicity. For instance, a magazine advert which features the slogan 'watch out there's a thief about' is a general message, whereas an article covered in a local paper that celebrates the success of a specific initiative in a particular neighbourhood or even town is more specific in nature.

Having considered where, to whom and generally what may be publicized, we next consider how information may be communicated. Publicity can be either formal or informal in nature. By 'formal' publicity we mean that which is communicated through a particular media or formal event. Examples of this form of publicity might include newspaper articles, television programmes, leaflets or posters concerned with an intervention. A focus group or a community meeting is another example of formal publicity.

In contrast, informal publicity is that which is transmitted through a community or population by word of mouth; through a conversation in a pub, for example. Such informal publicity might occur as a consequence of a formal event which has got people talking. Other possibilities clearly exist. Relevant to this type of communication is research concerned with small-world phenomenon (e.g. Milgram 1967) or scale-free networks (e.g. Watts 2003). This suggests that everyone in the world is connected through a short chain of social acquaintances, typically six. One explanation for this finding is that rather than networks of people being randomly connected, there are particular nodes or people who have a wider network than the average person (see Watts and Strogatz 1998). The idea is that these people act as hubs linking a variety of seemingly unrelated people to each other in an efficient way. The possibility exists that the average chain between two offenders is much shorter than this. Thus, it is easy to see how word of mouth alone could proliferate a suitably provocative message, particularly across short distances (rather than around the entire globe). In relation to this point, Smith *et al.* (2002) have suggested that the role of informants might usefully be extended to include the provision of information to, as well as from, offenders. In this case, informants would be used to implement a form of direct marketing, getting (dis)information directly to the target audience.

It is also important to note that publicity is not always generated by the agency directly concerned. In this sense, publicity may be considered to be intended or unintended. If the failure of a particular initiative to reduce crime is somehow leaked to the press, for instance, this will certainly be unintended publicity (at least to those who were not the informant). This is an example of our last criterion: whether the publicity is controlled or uncontrolled. Here the criterion is whether the publicity was initiated by the scheme or by an outside source, such as the local press. All the factors discussed are likely to affect the impact of any publicity associated with an intervention or policy and, as such, require consideration.

Some examples of different types of publicity that have been used in crime prevention are shown in Table 13.1. For the purposes of illustration, we also indicate how each type of campaign would generally be classified within some of the elements of our framework. We do, of course, acknowledge that the classification will vary for particular schemes. For instance, the communication of victimization statistics could be part of a national campaign or a more local initiative depending on the specific intervention. Here, we indicate what we believe would typically be most representative, whilst acknowledging that this will not always be the case. Thus, what follows should not be seen as prescriptive but rather a framework for thinking about the role of publicity in the crime reduction enterprise.

In Table 13.1 the examples are classified into four broad types. The first are informant strategies which encourage the public to provide information that leads to the capture or conviction of offenders. Secondly are offender-targeted strategies that aim to alert offenders to the possibility that they may be at an increased risk (real or not) of being caught. Thirdly, there are strategies that aim to encourage public action regarding safety, and the avoidance of behaviours that increase victimization risk. These strategies encourage residents to take certain safety precautions or make themselves safer by

Table 13.1 Some different types of publicity

	Aimed at offenders?	Aimed at the (rest of the) public?	Specific or generic?	Local or national?
Informant strategies				
CrimeWatch UK	Yes	Yes	Specific	National
CrimeStoppers	Yes	Yes	Either	Either
Neighbourhood Watch	Yes	Yes	Generic	Local
Police appeals for information	Yes	Yes	Specific	Either
Offender-targeted strategies				
Personal communications with offenders (e.g. letters, cards)	Yes	No	Specific	Local
Public signs aimed at offenders (e.g. posters advertising numbers of thieves caught)	Yes	Yes	Specific	Local
Strategies encouraging public action regarding safety				
Crime prevention advice	No	Yes	Either	Either
Public reminders/cues	No	Yes	Either	Either
Communication of victimization statistics	No	Yes	Specific	Local
Crime prevention intervention publicity				
Publicity concerning the existence of an initiative or agency	Yes	Yes	Specific	Local
Publicity concerning the success of an initiative	Yes	Yes	Specific	Local

upgrading their home security, for instance. These also include strategies to raise the public awareness of risk, such as the communication of victimization statistics. Rather than simply increasing fear of crime, publicity of this kind can encourage the public to be vigilant in particularly risky situations, or locations where, for instance, there have been a large number of bag or wallet thefts. Finally, there is publicity for which the primary purpose is to advertise the existence of crime prevention interventions. This can purely act to inform residents and offenders that there are agencies in the area that aim to reduce levels of crime. This type of publicity could also include news stories that concern the effectiveness of different crime prevention schemes.

Mechanisms

In planning any crime reduction publicity campaign (or intervention), it is important to consider carefully the mechanism(s) through which the publicity (or intervention) will lead to crime reduction. If there is no clear link between what is proposed and the desired outcome, it will be wise to rethink the campaign. Each of the four broad publicity strategies defined above aim to reduce crime, or the fear of crime, through at least one mechanism. For illustration purposes, some of the basic mechanisms are shown in Figure 13.1.

The first mechanism involves increasing the risk to offenders. The logic of this mechanism is that as a result of eliciting important information from the public, the *actual* probability of arrest and consequent prosecution of offenders will be increased. This, of course, may have a feedback effect, increasing both the perceived and actual risk to other offenders.

The second mechanism involves the manipulation of the *perceived* risk to offenders. Offenders do not have accurate data on the probability of apprehension. In fact, even with such data, the calculation of the risk of capture for any specific crime would be complicated as it depends on a variety of factors, including the presence of police officers in the area at the time, levels of natural surveillance, the precise target selected and so on. Thus, in the absence of detailed data and a complex statistical model, offender's beliefs regarding the risk of apprehension are likely to be based on a more general perception of risk. Thus, even where risks remain constant, publicity may be used to manipulate offenders' perception of the risk of detection in a specific area, or even more generally. This idea is central to rational choice theory (Cornish and Clarke 1989) which highlights an offender's assessment of risk as being one key factor considered in the decision to commit a crime or not. Simply put, where the benefits to an offender of committing a crime outweigh the perceived risks, a crime will occur; where they don't, the likelihood of a crime taking place is significantly lowered. Offender-targeted strategies such as personal communications with offenders or public signs aimed at offenders are likely to manipulate offenders' perceived risk of apprehension. Publicity about the existence of (successful) crime prevention practices is also likely to manipulate this factor.

A third mechanism through which publicity may impact upon victimization risk is by encouraging the public to reduce risky behaviour. Giving residents crime prevention advice, for instance, will hopefully encourage them to act on this advice if it highlights weaknesses in their current security measures and recommends appropriate plausible action. Public reminders, such as signs in car parks that carry the slogan 'Lock your Vehicle', can act as a cue to the public to use existing security measures appropriately. Highlighting areas of high risk with messages such as 'Thieves are operating in this area; there were one hundred bag thefts in this area last month' may also encourage people to be extra vigilant.

A fourth mechanism through which publicity can have an impact is through the reassurance of the public, which can have a reductive effect on the fear of crime. One criticism that is sometimes directed towards the use of publicity exercises is that they have the potential to increase the fear of crime. However, in the absence of supportive data, we suggest that this will only be true in specific cases. Consider, for instance, that if the public are exposed to signs that warn offenders that they are at an increased risk of being caught, or news

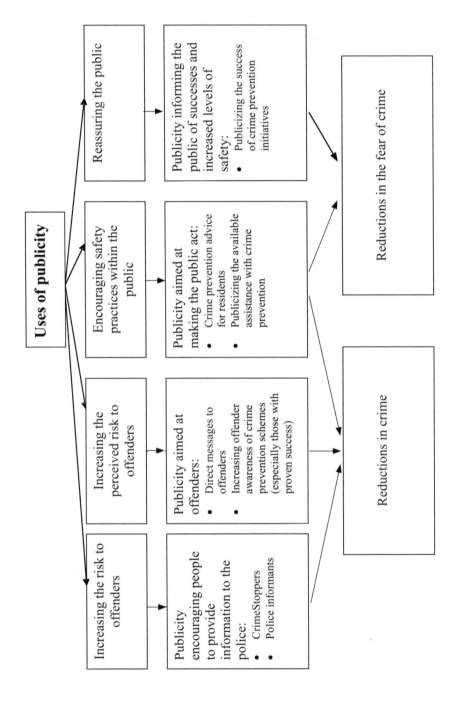

Figure 13.1 The different mechanisms associated with publicity

stories regarding the success of a crime prevention scheme, this is likely to reassure them that things can and are being done to reduce offending. It is difficult to see why this would have a negative effect on residents' fear of crime. However, the possibility exists that the publication of victimization statistics, if not done in a responsible way, could increase fear of crime. We pay more attention to this and other examples later in the chapter.

It should be noted that there is rarely a one-to-one mapping between the different types of publicity campaign and the various mechanisms. Most types of campaign are likely to have an impact by triggering multiple mechanisms, although they may have a primary mechanism. For example, informant strategies that appeal for information from witnesses might also encourage the public to be more vigilant, as the appeal will highlight the fact that a particular type of crime occurred in a specific geographic location. The principal aim of showing a reconstruction on CrimeWatch concerned with a series of crimes in a particular area is to gain information on the offender, but in all likelihood this will also encourage those passing through the area to be cautious. Additionally, the appeal may influence an offender's perception of risk if he or she assumes that an informant may come forward, or that committing further offences will increase the chances of getting caught. Considering a different type of campaign, publicizing the success of a particular crime prevention intervention (e.g. target hardening) might reassure the public and increase the perceived risk of apprehension to offenders, but might also encourage the public who have not received that treatment to install it themselves.

A final point to consider here is that there is a difference between publicity and actual implementation (and, indeed, success) of a prevention or detection strategy. The two are so often linked that it is easy to get them confused. Here, we are discussing the extent to which publicity has an effect over and above what is being done on the ground in terms of physical implementation. Let us take the example of a simple target-hardening scheme. A number of different scenarios exist:

- A scheme could be present or absent.
- A scheme could be successful at reducing crime or not.
- A scheme could be successful at reducing fear of crime or unsuccessful.
- The publicity associated with the scheme could be positive, negative or neutral.

Different configurations of these outcomes, summarized in Table 13.2, raise a number of issues. First, even if the physical implementation of a scheme is unsuccessful at reducing crime or the fear of crime, subsequent positive publicity about the scheme has the potential to reduce the fear of crime. In the simplest situation, this could occur because residents become aware of, and are reassured by, the presence of the scheme. Other possibilities exist.

Secondly, whilst negative publicity *cannot* take away any crime reductive effect a scheme has already experienced, it *could* have a negative impact upon people's fear of crime. For instance, if residents who were previously reassured by an intervention were exposed to incorrect or misleading information (e.g. sensational uncontrolled publicity) about a scheme this may bias their

Table 13.2 Possible impacts of publicity

Impact of scheme	Fear of crime reduction			Impact of scheme	Crime reduction		
Unsuccessful at reducing recipient fear	None/–	None/–	+	Unsuccessful at reducing recipient victimization	None	None	+
Successful at reducing recipient fear	++	+	+++	Successful at reducing recipient victimization	++	++	+++
No scheme	n/a	–	+	No scheme	n/a	n/a	+
Publicity	None	Negative	Positive	*Publicity*	None	Negative	Positive

Notes:
+ positive impacts.
– negative impacts.

perception of risk in their area. One type of message that might lead to such an effect would be a news item that highlighted that an area had an unusually high crime rate, without commenting that, as a result of crime prevention activity, this was falling.

Thirdly, theoretically, it is possible to reduce crime and the fear of crime by publicizing a scheme that has not, nor will, actually be implemented in practice. The ethics of publicizing such 'phantom' schemes obviously need to be considered, but the potential of such a strategy to reduce fear of crime should be apparent. A phantom scheme might also reduce crime *per se* by, for example, convincing offenders that the new 'phantom' measures would put them at an increased risk of getting caught.

Case studies

Having discussed how publicity might theoretically impact upon the actual and perceived risks of crime or apprehension, in the following sections we review some of the current evidence concerning the effectiveness of the use of publicity in crime reduction. The sections are divided into each of the four different categories of publicity defined above, and we begin with informant strategies.

Informant strategies

CrimeStoppers is an intervention that provides the public with free anonymous telephone access to the police and hence encourages them to share information concerning crimes. Callers are offered cash rewards of between £50 and £500 for information that leads to a detection. Gresham *et al.* (2001) undertook an evaluation of the CrimeStoppers scheme using information from three CrimeStopper regions in London, Tyne–Tees and Dorset. Across the three regions, CrimeStoppers received over ½ million calls in 2000. Of these, 85 per cent were successfully connected to a telephone operator and 11 per cent were considered to be sufficiently useful that action was taken. The results of the evaluation showed that of the calls for which action was taken, around 17 per cent resulted in an arrest, charge or caution. Overall this means that for the period of time studied, just over 1 per cent of all incoming calls lead to a successful detection. Considering the financial costs and benefits of the scheme, the evaluators estimate that CrimeStoppers was responsible for the recovery of stolen property valued at over £3.7 million, and that this figure was greater than an estimate of the cost of implementation. Thus, there was evidence that CrimeStoppers was also cost-effective.

Importantly, Gresham *et al.*'s evaluation found that there was variation in the effectiveness of CrimeStoppers in the different regions in which it was implemented. Those that were most effective tended to be better resourced, to be open for longer and outside normal working hours, concentrated on logging the details of actionable calls and, were better publicized. Their analysis showed that 21 per cent of all actionable calls across the three regions examined were in response to media appeals for information.

Other evaluations of CrimeStoppers programmes have been undertaken in the USA (Rosenbaum *et al.* 1987), Canada (Carriere and Ericson 1989) and Australia (Challinger 2003). Challinger's evaluation showed that 94 per cent of the public are aware of CrimeStoppers. However, when questioned concerning the main functions of CrimeStoppers, it was apparent that only 72 per cent were really aware of what the organization did. Of the sample questioned in Australia, 93 per cent said that they would definitely contact CrimeStoppers if they had relevant information, compared to 73 per cent in the UK. The evaluation also found that more dramatic crimes, such as robberies, were over-represented in requests for information, and that the police tended to use CrimeStoppers as a last resort tactic. Thus, there would appear to be greater scope for the way in which such schemes are routinely used by the police. Considering the impact of other CrimeStopper schemes, it is interesting to note that Challinger (2003) found that an Austrailian scheme outperformed its UK counterpart, with more calls answered successfully (94.5 per cent), more calls actioned (28.2 per cent) and almost twice as many arrests per call (1.9 per cent).

Thus, it would appear that schemes such as CrimeStoppers can lead to the successful prosecution of offenders. It also seems apparent that publicity relating to the scheme is important not only to encourage the public to come forward with information but also to educate them regarding the role of the organization. What remains unclear from the evaluation literature is how these kinds of scheme impact upon offenders. If offenders are aware of the benefits of CrimeStoppers this could plausibly have a deterrent effect, increasing their perceptions of the risk of being identified or successfully prosecuted. Thus, as noted by Gresham *et al.* (2001), effort should be made to raise awareness of the effectiveness of this type of scheme within the offending population and across the public more generally.

Offender-targeted strategies

Perhaps the most famous recent example of an offender-targeted publicity strategy was the Boston gun project (Kennedy et al. 2001). As part of this project, local law enforcement agencies and their crime reduction partners aimed to reduce firearm trafficking and youth homicide in the area. To do this, they implemented what is known as a 'pulling levers' deterrence strategy. The rationale of the approach was based on the finding that a large proportion of crime is committed by a small number of offenders, and hence that because of this concentration, directing resources towards these groups can have a large impact upon crime. As well as implementing a rapid zero-tolerance policy in relation to violent behaviour, a significant feature of the intervention was the clear communication of the policy to the target groups – namely, gang members. The message communicated was 'a promise to gang members that violent behaviour would evoke an immediate and intense response' (Kennedy et al. 2001). The message was delivered in a variety of ways including sit-down meetings with certain gangs, assemblies in schools and discussions with inmates of juvenile correctional facilities. As explained by Kennedy et al., the reason for the implementation of the offender-targeted publicity campaign was that, in the absence of awareness of the policy, the deterrent effect of the scheme would be limited, particularly at the beginning of implementation. Alternatively, it is possible that, in the absence of publicity, gang members would be unclear about what (e.g. violent behaviour or just membership of a gang) triggered particular law enforcement responses. Confusion of this kind would again limit the impact of the policy on the behaviour targeted, as offenders would not know which specific behaviours received what responses.

As highlighted in Figure 13.2, the very first meeting of the Boston gun project's working group with gang members was held on 15 May 1996. The pattern of results show that following the very first meeting, there was an immediate decline in the rate of youth homicides in Boston. The no-tolerance message was continually communicated throughout the implementation period of the project. The subsequent evaluation of the scheme showed impressive successes including a 63 per cent decrease in youth homicides per month, a 32 per cent decrease in shots-fired calls for service and a 25 per cent decrease in gun assaults per month following the intervention. As reductions in youth homicide were realized immediately after the policy was publicized, this suggests that publicity regarding the intervention generated a deterrent effect, as it is simply implausible that the intervention itself could have had any impact at this stage. In relation to this point more generally, as Zimring and Hawkins (1973) observe, 'the deterrence threat may best be viewed as a form of advertising'.

Strategies encouraging public action regarding safety

One publicity campaign which aimed to affect the way the public behave was

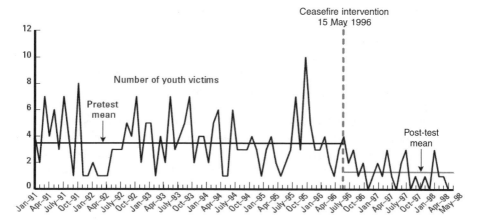

Figure 13.2 Monthly counts of homicide in Boston
Source: From Kennedy *et al.* (2001).

the 'Get Home Safe' campaign, implemented in South Belfast in 2002.[3] It was set up to reduce anti-social behaviour and alcohol-related violence and to reassure the public. A problem profile focusing on assaults in the area indicated that the main problems tended to occur at local bars and nightclubs, especially around closing time. To address this issue, the partnership established a number of schemes, including a door registration scheme, the enforcement of by-laws relating to the drinking of alcohol in the street, a 'Pub Watch' radio link, the introduction of CCTV cameras within the problem areas and an alcohol referral scheme. In addition, a very important element of the scheme was the development of a strategic marketing campaign. The aim of the campaign was to encourage 18–24-year-olds socializing in Belfast to drink sensibly, get home safely and to convey the message that drunken assault was unacceptable behaviour. To drive the campaign, the partnership developed the marketing slogan 'Think Twice – Get Home Safe', and a strong set of visuals that were used in Adshel bus stop posters, washroom posters, advertising on the rear of buses and adverts in the local press. More innovative methods were also employed including beer-mats, heat-sensitive urinal stickers and pocket-sized information leaflets. A media campaign also targeted newspapers, magazines, radio and television.

The evaluation of the Get Home Safe campaign showed that, relative to the previous year, during the period of implementation, there was a 19.2 per cent reduction in the total volume of assaults in the South Belfast area. The reduction in the number of serious assaults was greater still at 33 per cent relative to the previous year. As part of the evaluation, the impact of the marketing activity on the target population also was assessed. The results indicated that 87 per cent of a sample of pubbers/clubbers could remember something about the campaign, with 40 per cent stating that it had positively influenced their behaviour. Furthermore, the campaign appeared to have had a positive effect on respondents' perceptions of the partnership's reaction to the problem, with only 33 per cent of repondents believing that nothing was being done about alcohol-related violence following the campaign, compared to a pre-implementation figure of 55 per cent. Considering which types of publicity had the greatest impact, those surveyed reported that the posters, radio advertising and material in pubs/clubs were remembered the most. Thus, it would appear that the campaign penetrated the consciousness of those targeted and that a positive impact also was realized.

As well as local initiatives, a variety of national campaigns have been implemented that try to encourage people to behave cautiously and act in a safe manner. These are, however, notoriously difficult to evaluate. For instance, Laycock and Tilley (1996) point out that not only is there the problem of attributing reduction to one of many different schemes, but there also exists the problem of how to isolate any effects. For example, in the absence of detailed data on victims of crime and those exposed to a particular campaign (micro-level data), the displacement of risk from those who respond to publicity campaigns to those who do not can mask micro-level changes in patterns of risk. Notwithstanding these issues, Webb and Laycock (1992) report persuasive evidence of the impact of publicity campaigns on the behaviour of car owners, reporting that the proportion of cars in which doors had been left unlocked fell from 22 per cent in 1971 to 4 per cent in 1992. They raise the possibility that this change in behaviour could have been due to the influence of the various publicity campaigns concerned with car security that were implemented over the same period.

In support of this, Laycock and Tilley (1996) discuss the 'Hyena' campaign, which 'aimed to present car offenders as preying on the vulnerabilities of the community. The image used was a hyena, which market research had shown was not a popular animal, and which was seen as a scavenger and a cowardly acquisitive creature'.

Unpublished Home Office research on the impact of the 'Hyena' campaign, which cost £3 million and ran nationally in 1992, found an increase (from 23 to 28 per cent) in the proportion of motorists who set an alarm or used a crook-lock when parking, along with a 9 per cent increase in those who chose a safer place to park. It was also found that awareness of the campaign was very high – 96 per cent of motorists who took part in a survey understood the security messages of the campaign and 84 per cent were familiar with the 'Hyena' logo.

Thus, the existing research demonstrates that publicity campaigns that focus on a specific problem can be used effectively to communicate information regarding the risk of crime and what can be done to prevent it. The research discussed also provides evidence, albeit indirect in some cases, to suggest that publicity which aims to encourage the public to reduce opportunities for crime or to behave in a more acceptable manner can have a crime reductive effect.

Crime prevention intervention publicity

This section examines some case studies where publicity has been used in relation to a particular crime prevention initiative. Laycock (1991) examined the effectiveness of a property-marking scheme, which initially was not accompanied by publicity. The results of this study indicated a reduction in burglary in the first year of implementation of property marking, after which the burglary rate rose sharply. However, there was also an unexplained drop in the burglary rate in the second year of the scheme, although levels of implementation had remained constant. After conducting further research, Laycock (1991) discovered that the unexplained drop in the burglary rate occurred just after intense local and national press coverage regarding the success of the scheme. In the absence of plausible rival explanations, Laycock concluded that the publicity associated with the scheme appeared to have had a positive effect on the crime rate.

In an earlier study by the current authors (Bowers and Johnson 2003), the impact of publicity on crime reduction was examined using data collected for 21 (and in some cases 42) burglary reduction schemes evaluated as part of the Home Office's Reducing Burglary Initiative (RBI). Analyses were conducted to see whether or not the schemes that were the most successful tended to publicize their efforts, and whether the timing of burglary reduction was coincident with publicity events. The study showed that for the 21 schemes located in the north of England, there was a clear relationship between the timing and intensity of publicity and burglary reduction. This was true even when other factors, such as the degree to which measures had actually been implemented, were taken into account. Furthermore, approximately one half of the schemes evaluated implemented standalone publicity campaigns (those that ran over some time and that were seen as an intervention in themselves), and these schemes tended to be the most successful in terms of burglary reduction.

Interestingly, across the 42 schemes located in the north of England and the Midlands, there was evidence of a significant reduction in burglary in the three months that immediately preceded implementation, an effect referred to as an 'anticipatory benefit' (see also Smith et al. 2002). For the schemes for which detailed data were available, the analyses suggested that this effect was a consequence of pre-implementation publicity. Overall, the results of the study suggest that publicizing crime prevention activity can, in itself, reduce burglary. Hence, the findings concerned with anticipatory benefit suggest that publicizing crime reduction effort may have crime reduction implications even before implementation begins, or even in the absence of crime prevention activity at all.

In a further study, Stockdale and Gresham (1995) undertook an evaluation of three police force strategies that aimed to combat burglary. The results of the evaluation had some clear lessons concerning publicity. They suggested that a high public profile can accelerate the organizational changes necessary to focus resources for the particular strategy and produce a more active response to burglary. An effective publicity campaign and positive media coverage were identified as one of the key elements of successful anti-burglary strategies. The results of the research suggested that having a 'brand named' operation (their examples being Operation Bumblebee and Operation Gemini) can be advantageous because it provides a unifying focus and helps to make operations understandable to the public, which in turn helps reassure them. On a cautionary note, they warn against over-optimistic publicity that promises impacts that are simply undelieverable, and the over-use of a brand name, or use of an outdated brand name, as this has the potential to reduce the impact of the campaign.

What does and doesn't make effective publicity?

In this section we aim to provide some food for thought for practitioners aiming to implement a publicity campaign with crime reduction in mind. Where possible we have tried to include examples of good (or not so good) practice. What we cannot do here is identify what will work best in specific situations. That will very much depend upon the context in which you are implementing your campaign (see Verrill and Bentley 2003). Instead, to provide some more general guidance, we have laid out this section as a series of questions and issues that need addressing when planning a campaign.

Coverage: who/where are the targets?

Deciding whom to target with a campaign and where the campaign will run will shape the aim and scope of the entire venture. As we have seen the main focus of some campaigns is to target offenders whilst others aim to target victims. However, there are other decisions to be made such as where exactly to aim the publicity and over what area. Recent research has recommended that publicity works best in a *specific local context* and, in particular, if it tackles *specific local issues* (Bowers and Johnson 2003; Verill and Bentley 2003). It is probably better to target a particular estate, for example, or a defined neighbourhood where people are likely to talk to each other rather than an entire city or county. Informal publicity generated within a community is a very powerful way of making the most of publicity.

The people who will ultimately be exposed to a campaign will obviously depend on the type of publicity chosen, and the receptiveness of different individuals to certain types of message. A radio interview might be broadcast across an entire region, for example, but only a certain percentage of the households will be listening at any one time. Thus, careful consideration should be given to how many people the campaign will need to reach and how this can be achieved. In any event, you should plan for an element of loss with all campaigns, and it might be worth reinforcing the message by having at least one follow-up event.

When publicizing specific crime prevention campaigns, it is important to reinforce the message that you are active in the area by targeting all the recipients of the scheme. However, it is possible that publicizing over a wider area will cause a 'diffusion of benefit' (also known as the free-rider effect; Miethe 1991). This occurs when a crime prevention scheme has a positive effect not only on recipients of the intervention but also for those who are close by or associated in some way. Figure 13.3 shows one way in which the potential crime reductive effect of diffusion of benefit could be maximized using publicity. Imagine the square is an area or neighbourhood. Within this, the actual recipients are located within the white parts of the square. Publicizing the activity across the entire area – in both the white and grey parts (where there are no resources) – could increase the likelihood of a diffusion of benefit, with crime reducing over the entire square not just within the areas receiving the treatment. An evaluation of this type of strategy has not yet been done and would be more than welcome.

Timescale: when will the campaign operate relative to implementation?

It is, of course, important to consider when to publicize as well as where. Research suggests that publicity is an effective and relative cheap way of enhancing the effect of crime prevention schemes (for more details, see Bowers and Johnson 2003), but it is unlikely that you will have the resources constantly to publicize, or that such unrelenting publicity will remain as effective over time. Indeed, constant publicity has the potential to result in overexposure and people tiring of the messages you are conveying. It is therefore recommended that publicity is done in 'bursts' or 'pulses' (see also Riley and Mayhew 1980). Furthermore research concerned with advertising more generally indicates that the effects of advertising campaigns extend beyond the period during which they are active (Berkowitz et al. 2001). This suggests that people will remember your messages for some time after their delivery and that there is no need constantly to flood people with a particular campaign.

When considering the timing of publicity associated with local crime prevention activity, the findings concerned with anticipatory benefit suggest that the impact of a scheme may be enhanced by advertising what is going on before implementation begins. In a similar way it is also plausible that, in the case of initiatives that operate over a limited period of time such as police

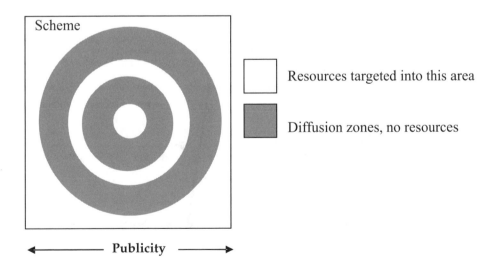

Figure 13.3 Extending the impact of crime prevention using publicity

crackdowns or sting operations, publicizing scheme activity after a scheme has terminated may have an additional effect. In relation to the latter, in an evaluation of a police crackdown, Sherman (1990) report that reductions in crime were realized during the implementation of the initiative, but that these also endured after implementation had ceased. In the absence of alternative explanations they attribute this effect to a temporary change in offenders' perceptions of the risk involved in committing crime, an effect that can extend beyond the lifetime of an operation and which they labelled 'residual deterrence'.

To punctuate the importance of these findings, an implementation timeline for a fictitious scheme is shown in Figure 13.4, along with the periods over which publicity could be used to enhance the impacts realized.

Medium: what type of publicity – newspapers, stickers, television ...?

When deciding which medium to use, a number of different factors will need to be considered. These include the cost, how effective it is likely to be at delivering the message and who would be most likely to see it. The Home Office's Communication Crime Reduction website[4] has a thorough section on selecting appropriate media. Consideration is also given to some of the advantages and disadvantages of each form of media. One example of the different strengths and weaknesses of different formats is that TV and radio adverts are more emotionally involving than printed media, but that printed media may be understood more easily on a rational level (Chauduri and Buck 1995).

There exist very few evaluations that have focused on the impacts of different media on the success of crime prevention campaigns. In a study conducted in the Netherlands, VanDijk and Steinmetz (1981) found that of

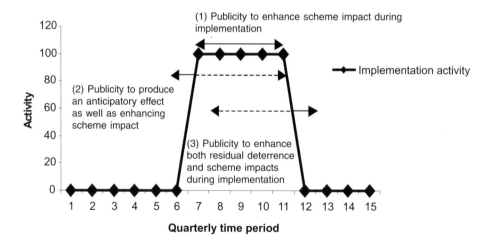

Figure 13.4 The timing of publicity

those that recalled a campaign, the majority of people remembered television adverts (82 per cent). Considerably fewer respondents recalled newspapers articles (27 per cent) or posters (9 per cent). A similar pattern of results was also reported in a more recent evaluation conducted in the UK (see Verrill and Bentley 2003). Whilst these findings are useful, the most appropriate media for a particular campaign will depend on the particular context in which an intervention is implemented.

Message: what message do you want to convey?

As we have seen, messages can be aimed at victims or offenders, and can be specific or more generic. In their review of the available data at the time, Riley and Mayhew (1980) found no effect of generic campaigns that aim to change the potential behaviour of victims. The same conclusion appear to be warranted on the basis of a recent survey conducted by Verril and Bentley (2003). In that study, over two thirds of those interviewed reported that they 'switched off' to general messages regarding crime prevention. Thus, whilst exceptions to the rule may exist, it would appear that publicity campaigns that are more general in nature are less likely to impact upon the population which they aim to affect. Commensurate with this view, Riley and Mayhew (1980) suggest that the most effective campaigns are those that are more specific; that is, those that concentrate on a particular crime type and/or those that give specific advice about how to combat the problem. This also chimes with our finding that publicity which is focused on local areas, and the specific crime prevention activities implemented within them, is effective at reducing crime. In summary, it appears that the more specific and focused the message, and the more it is tied into the local situation in terms of crime prevention, the more effective publicity is likely to be.

In terms of the actual content of the message conveyed, lessons from advertising research are relevant. Some key findings are as follows: adverts should be novel or interesting; they should be relevant to the audience they are aimed at; perhaps use 'figures of speech' that will be familiar to people; and, possibly, they should incorporate humour or metaphors that make people think (for a further discussion, see Hallahan 2000). The use of logos is also useful as it can increase people's familiarity with, and hence encourage them to remember, a campaign (Brosius and Bathelt 1994). For the purposes of illustration, some examples of different types of message associated with crime reduction are shown in Table 13.3. The table also shows how the various messages have different purposes. For instance, we see that some promote security practices, others are appeals for information and others still, give an identity to an operation or organization.

It is also important to think about the point at which individuals are likely to stop taking notice of advertising because of overexposure. It is important therefore to consider changing the format or information provided on posters, or changing their physical location. To illustrate this consider the positioning of goods in a supermarket. To increase the variety of products purchased, or to promote certain items, the location of goods is often changed so that there will be new or different products on the shelves that shoppers routinely visit.

Table 13.3   Different types of crime prevention message and examples of each

Type of message	Examples
Police operation names	Bumblebee (Met), Trident (Met), Payback (Met), Magpie (Greater Manchester), Hawk (Greater Manchester), Crystal (Merseyside), Magnet (Strathclyde), Wheel (Bradford), Target (Cambridgeshire), Cracker (Sussex), Twilight (Sussex), Deep (Nottinghamshire), Phoenix (Northumbria), Scorpion (Bedfordshire)
Crime prevention practitioner 'logos'	LANPAC (Lancashire Partnership Against Crime), Safer Merseyside Partnership, Secure by Design
Offender-orientated messages	'Burglars beware: police operations in this area' (Chiswick), 'Are you responsible? Bottles and glasses are used as offensive weapons in one out of ten assaults' (Crystal Clear)
Communication of risk messages	'Thieves are operating in this area', 'At least two women a week are killed as a result of domestic violence' (Safer Merseyside Partnership Worst Kept Secret Campaign)
Security practice prompts	'Shut it, lock it' (Cleveland Police), 'Park your stuff out of sight' (HO website), 'Be streetsafe' (Merseyside Police), 'Call time on mobile crime' (Met)
Existence of crime prevention initiatives	'You are entering a Neighbourhood Watch area', 'Burglars you're marked' (Smartwater), 'Smartwater: the solution to theft'
Appeals for information	'Drug dealers ruin lives: rat on a rat' (Merseyside Police), 'CivicWatch: don't tolerate anti-social behaviour, report it!', 'CrimeStoppers: say no and phone' (SNAP)
Success of crime prevention initiatives	'Fact: 1,842 arrests for street crime since April 2002: Merseyside Police tough on street crime' (Be Streetsafe campaign)
Motivational/reassurance messages	'Crime, together we'll crack it', 'Crime, let's bring it down' (Home Office)

Furthermore, it might be important to re-emphasize the same message in different ways. It is often useful to stick with a message or phrase with which people are familiar, but to vary the way in which you display it in successive campaigns (Zajonc 1980). To illustrate this approach, consider some of the consumer advertising campaigns with which you are familiar. Good examples might include Carlsberg (e.g. 'Carlsberg don't make X but if we did we'd probably make the best X in the world') and KitKat ('Have a break, have a KitKat'). Across a series of adverts, different scenes will be shown but the same slogan is typically used.

Planning: can you foresee any implementation problems?

Publicity campaigns should be planned much like any other crime prevention initiative. One important part of this process is to attempt to iron out any potential problems before the launch of a campaign. There have been cases where better planning could have led to a more effective campaign, and an example from the Home Office's Burglary Reduction Initiative illustrates this point nicely. In this particular scheme, a series of posters were attached to lamp-posts to advertise the activity taking place. Unfortunately, these were placed too far up the lamp-posts for the writing to be legible to passers-by, or even to be noticed by many people. Consequently, irrespective of how effective the message might have been, it is unlikely that the campaign would have had the desired effects.

There are a number of different issues that should be considered at the planning stage:

1. Consider the *context* in which the message will be communicated. In the case of posters, where will they be located? How big should the lettering be? Can you make use of the fact that your audience will be in a particular place (e.g. communicate safety on public transport at bus stops)? Will the posters need to be protected against the elements or vandalism? For television advertising, when is the communication likely to take place? Can you capitalize on this? For example, TV adverts are often scheduled so that they appear after programmes that the target audience are likely to watch. If you are targeting young people in pubs and clubs, will you be communicating to people under the influence of alcohol? If so, the message needs to be simple and easy to understand!

2. Consider the *complexity* of the message you are trying to convey. It is a general rule that to gain attention a message needs to be simple, understandable and interesting; it is also best to keep it fairly short. It is highly recommended that you 'road test' your message on members of the general public. Sometimes, in an attempt to keep the message short and snappy, it becomes too cryptic for the general public to understand. Consequently, the clarity of the message should be tested in advance of the launch of a campaign and any problems addressed.

3. Consider the *target audience*. For instance, do you need to have the message translated into another language? What type of message will appeal to your audience? Will they appreciate humour, for example?

Innovation: how can you maximize the impact?

One way of ensuring that a message is noticed is by delivering it in an innovative way. Technological innovation offers a variety of new opportunities for delivering messages and there are increasing numbers of examples of the use of new media in the field of crime prevention. Some examples already have been discussed; in this section we highlight a few more.

Student safety website

In 2003 the Home Office launched the good2besecure website.[5] This aimed to provide security advice to students on a number of different issues (McCreith and Parkinson 2004). As part of the website there are infectious or 'viral' games. For example, in one of the games the player's task is to close open windows before a burglar has the opportunity to steal the exposed goods inside. This is a fun way of reinforcing the message that taking basic precautions such as locking windows and doors can prevent incidents from occurring. McCreith and Parkinson (2004) explain that: 'Viral marketing is used to get information, such as these games, across to as many people as possible. The idea is that awareness of the game [and the crime prevention content] will grow as individuals forward the games on to fellow students'.

Talking signs

The Metropolitan Police have placed ten 'talking' signs on lamp-posts in the London Borough of Lambeth. These have been erected in railway and bus stations. The signs have eight different crime prevention messages and new messages can be recorded if new problems emerge. An example is a railway sign at Streatham station that says 'Police warning: keep your mobile phones safe, robbers operate in this area'. The talking signs are triggered by motion sensors, and operate on a two-minute delay system so that they don't start continuously when someone is standing nearby. The signs clearly have the potential to startle people, but this is also likely to make them listen. A further advantage of using something that is based on audio recordings is that they are difficult to ignore if you are within hearing range. The locations of the signs have also been carefully considered here. The public often use their mobile phones whilst travelling home on public transport and hence this is a useful time to prompt them to be cautious.

Crime prevention trailer

Cleveland Police regularly use a crime prevention advertising trailer. The rationale is that this allows them to target current hotspots of crime with crime prevention advice using minimal human resources. The trailer is 'A' frame in design, and the sides are used to display the crime prevention advice. There is also a built-in cassette player for audio messages. The advantage of the trailer is that it is mobile but it can still display the messages whilst moving. Uses for the trailer have included an anti-burglary 'Shut it and lock it' campaign and acting as a cue to motorists to lock their vehicles with the slogan 'Leave your valuables on show so I know which window to smash to grab them', signed 'A. Car Criminal'. An evaluation of the trailer found that on the 70 occasions it was used in car parks, only one crime was committed whilst it was present.

Text messaging

Dorset Police have set up a new crime prevention information service that uses text messaging. The service is called 'Safetex' and aims to give young people tips on how they can keep their night out in Bournemouth enjoyable and safe. The service gives a number of different options that people can sign up to. By texting the words 'bar', 'club' or 'street' to a certain number, it is possible to subscribe to a service that texts you tips about how to keep safe in these environments. The service is not for profit and there is no charge except the initial cost of a standard text message to set it up. Dorset Police are promoting the scheme by distributing leaflets to students, using window stickers and flyers and by offering subscribers the chance to win competitions.

In a different kind of initiative, the German police successfully piloted a scheme which aimed to help track and catch suspects. Volunteers, typically public transport employees, taxi-drivers and city workers, were sent text messages concerning suspects (descriptions, car licence plates or even pictures via multi-media messaging) the police were trying to locate. A hotline was provided for those with relevant information and a financial incentive was offered for information that led to a successful conviction. The system is currently being implemented on a national scale.

In addition to reaching people who register to participate in a particular scheme, the development of location-based telecommunication technologies means that text messages can be broadcast to all mobile phones within fairly specific geographical areas. Whilst this technology has received little attention within the field of crime prevention, potential applications, such as informing people and appealing for information about missing persons, or advertising the presence of a particular crime prevention scheme, are clear.

Caution: publicity – the residents' friend or foe?

It is important to point out that it is not the case that all crime prevention publicity is necessarily good publicity. For instance, as part of the Reducing Burglary Initiative, one of the schemes publicized an offender-based intervention, one facet of which involved sending offenders on holiday. Perhaps not surprisingly there was significant negative feedback from residents regarding this and as a consequence the intervention was abandoned. Thus, it is important to consider what the public's reaction might be to certain messages. One of the problems that needs to be faced here is that the way in which advertising or publicity affects people is likely to be a very subjective thing – what offends one person may please another. Hence, it can be very difficult to determine which instances of publicity have negative or positive effects, or both.

Possible negative effects could occur if publicity leads to an increase in fear of crime in an area or results in the public erroneously interpreting publicity as an indication that crime is on the increase. It is unlikely that messages which promote the success of crime prevention initiatives will instil fear – the public are more likely to feel safer because crime has been reduced, but there are other types of publicity that have the potential to do so. Those particularly prone are likely to be messages that concern incidents of crime that fail to point out that the risk of crime is uniformly low. To illustrate why this is likely to occur, consider that stories reported in the media are typically rare events; hence their intrinsic news value. Unfortunately, in the absence of access to reliable and accurate data sources concerning crime risk, the public are unlikely to be aware of how low the risk of crime is. After all, the media are not noted for their enthusiasm to run stories that highlight the fact that crimes did not occur! Because of this, the public can easily form a variant of what is known as an 'illusory correlation'. These occur as a consequence of an overemphasis on rare events and the lack of coverage or knowledge of common ones. This leads to people routinely seeing patterns where none exist. For example, some people believe that strange things happen when the moon is full. This is usually based on the fact that on one or a small number of occasions they are aware that something odd happened at this time. If these people gave appropriate consideration to the fact that on all the other times that the moon was full nothing unusual occurred (which will be many more occasions), they would reach a different conclusion. Thus, in relation to perceptions of the risk of crime, the coverage in the media of crime events is likely to distort people's views, generating the impression that crime is a much more frequent event than is actually the case.

In relation to this, a study conducted in Trinidad found that crime reporting by the media was skewed in the direction of more sensational types of serious crime (Chadee 2001). Incidents of murder, wounding and rape were more heavily emphasized, and less emphasis was given to property crime – which constituted over 80 per cent of serious crime in any one year. In this study, the mass media were identified as a major source of the public's information concerning crime. Thus, it is hypothesized that this overemphasis on sensational incidents could contribute to a higher fear of crime and an unrealistic perception of crime risk.

Other research suggests that information concerning localized events, often spread through word of mouth, can be more significant in influencing anxiety than the media (Roberts 2001). To a degree, this fits in with the finding that it is the promotion of local initiatives to combat crime that successfully assists in reducing crime. People are particularly interested in their own area and as a consequence will talk about whatever they find out about it. If publicity is used to communicate victimization statistics, it is advisable to include advice on how to act in the best way to avoid the problem or issue reassurance messages that something is being done about the problem.

A further concern is the extent to which publicity could cause changes in the behaviour of offenders. Practitioners using publicity should thus carefully consider what messages they are aiming to convey and ensure that these do not provide information that would encourage offenders to adapt their offending behaviour to circumvent crime reduction activity. For instance, promoting the fact that one street has been 'target hardened' as part of an initiative might highlight the fact that another street has not. This could lead to crime being displaced to the second location. Alternatively, calls for information about a particular offender with a distinctive or successful modus operandi could lead to copycat crimes being committed by others. Thus, thought needs to be given to what information is released and the potential costs and benefits of doing so.

Thought also should be given to how a particular campaign might impact upon the behaviour of those at risk. For instance, signs warning that pickpockets operate at a particular Underground station may lead to passengers checking that they still have their wallets. One potential negative consequence of this behaviour would be that any pickpockets observing passengers' reactions to the signs would subsequently know in which pockets passengers kept their wallets! Thus, care needs to be given to how people may react to a specific message and whether this may put them at a greater rather than lower risk of crime.

There are also examples of where crime prevention agencies have received bad press or criticism about how they have handled particular situations. For example, Rob Mawby (2001) points out that the public image of the police has been negatively influenced by scandals concerning racism, incompetent investigations and corruption. This is as a result of the fact that, through the media, the police have become intensely watched and highly visible. The police have to 'manage this visibility' by promoting and protecting their image. As a result of this organizations such as the Association of Chief Police Officers' Media Advisory Group have been established. Whilst our aim here is not to give advice to police forces concerning their image, it is obvious that any publicity that is used – even that promoting crime prevention – should be considered carefully before it is disseminated.

Conclusions and recommendations

In this chapter we have discussed the use of publicity for crime prevention purposes. We began by suggesting a way of classifying the different types of publicity that may be used. We also have discussed the crime prevention theory underlying the different approaches and provided some examples of campaigns that have been implemented and, where possible, considered their impacts on crime or people's behaviour. To the authors, the role of well planned publicity campaigns in crime reduction seems clear and we hope that our review equally persuades readers of this book.

However, many questions remain unanswered. For instance, what types of media work best and in what situations? To examine these sorts of questions requires the availability of good data. In addition to data on levels of crime, data on what sort of publicity was used, when, and what else was going on at the same time, would be required. Having evaluated a variety of different crime prevention schemes, the authors are well aware of the problems associated with obtaining such data, but have managed to do this in the past and know the benefits of doing so.

As discussed above, the research concerned with anticipatory benefits shows that reductions in crime can be realized even before crime prevention activity commences, particularly where forthcoming activity is publicized prior to implementation. Thus, the question exists as to whether publicizing 'phantom' schemes (fictitious interventions that are never implemented) could reduce crime. The ethics of adopting such a strategy would, of course, require careful thought. In any event, the timing of pre-scheme publicity and the implementation of an intervention should be carefully considered to maximize the potential effects of anticipatory benefit. More research in this area could provide useful insights into specifically when such benefits are realized and how they might be extended.

Selected further reading

For a clear illustration of the effect of publicity on crime prevention initiatives, the reader is referred to Gloria Laycock's (1991) 'Operation identification or the power of publicity?' Details of evaluation research that has looked at evidence of a more general effect of publicity (over 21 crime prevention schemes) can be found in our *Home Office Research Series Report* 272 (2003). For an in-depth account of the definition and the possible causes of anticipatory benefit, see Marti Smith, Ron Clarke and Ken Pease's (2002) 'Anticipatory benefit in crime prevention'.

For a more general discussion of the relationship between crime and the media, the reader is referred to the special issue of *Criminal Justice Matters* (Number 42, 2001), 'Crime and the media' (available from the Centre for Crime and Justice Studies, King's College London).This includes the discussion of issues such as public opinion and crime, newspaper crime reporting and the consequences of the way in which the media report certain types of crime (for example, violence and white-collar crime). Finally, for practical advice on implementing publicity campaigns and communicating effectively with the community, see the guidance available on the Home Office's crime reduction website (http://www.crimereduction.gov.uk/learningzone/comm_strat/home-page. htm).

Acknowledgements

The authors would like to thank Professors Ken Pease and Gloria Laycock for discussions and inspiration concerning the role of publicity in crime prevention.

Notes

1. Interestingly, Johnson *et al.* (2003) compare the behaviour of successful investors to that of burglars.
2. This represents an extension of that developed by Riley and Mayhew (1980).
3. See http://www.psni.police.uk/index/advice_centre/get_home_safe.
4. http://www.crimereduction.gov.uk/learningzone/comm_strat/pp6p1.htm.
5. http://www.good2besecure.gov.uk.
6. Source: http://www.msnbc.msn.com/id/4407538.
7. Source: http://www.clevelandpolice.uk/policing_cleveland/districts/ middlesbrough.
8. Sources: http://www.safeinbournemouth.org.uk/safex/what.html; http://www. xiam.com/news/business-gets-the-message/b2c/policing.shtml.

References

Berkowitz, D., Allaway, A. and D'Souza, G. (2001) 'The impact of differential lag effects in the allocation of advertising budgets across media', *Journal of Advertising Research*, 41: 27–36.

Bowers, K.J. and Johnson, S. (2003) *Reducing Burglary Initiative: The Role of Publicity in Crime Prevention. Home Office Research Series* 272. London: Home Office.

Brosius, H. and Bathlet, A. (1994) 'The utility of examplars in persuasive communication', *Communication Research*, 21: 48–78.

Carriere, K.D. and Ericson, R.V. (1989) *Crime Stoppers: A Study in Organization of Community Policing*. Toronto: Centre of Criminology, University of Toronto.

Chadee, D. (2001) 'Fear of crime and the media: from perception to reality', *Criminal Justice Matters*, 43: 10–12.

Challinger, D. (2003) *Crime Stoppers: Evaluating Victoria's Program. Trends and Issues in Crime and Criminal Justice 272*. Canberra: Australian Institute of Criminology.

Chauduri, A. and Buck, R. (1995) 'Media differences in rational and emotional responses to advertising', *Journal of Broadcasting and Electronic Media*, 39: 109–25.

Cornish, D.B. and Clarke, R.V. (1989) 'Crime specialization, crime displacement and rational choice theory', in H. Wegner *et al.* (eds) *Criminal Behavior and the Justice System: Psychological Perspectives*. New York, NY: Springer-Verlag.

Gresham, P., Stockdale, J., Bartholomew, I. and Bullock, K. (2001) *An Evaluation of the Impact of CrimeStoppers. Briefing Note 10/01*. London: Home Office.

Hallahan, K. (2000) 'Enhancing motivation, ability, and opportunity to process public relations messages', *Public Relations Review*, 26: 463–80.

Johnson, N.F., Jeffries, P. and Hui, P.M. (2003) *Financial Market Complexity*. Oxford: Oxford University Press.

Kebbell, M.R. and Johnson, S.D. (2002) 'The influence of belief that a car crashed on witnesses's estimates on civillian and police car speed', *The Journal of Psychology: Interdisciplinary and Applied*, 136: 597–607.

Kennedy, D.M., Braga, A. and Piehl, A.M. (2001) *Reducing Gun Violence: The Boston Gun Project's Operation Ceasefire. National Institute of Justice Research Report*. Washington, DC: US Department of Justice.

Laycock, G. (1991) 'Operation identification or the power of publicity?', *Security Journal*, 2: 67–71.

Laycock, G. and Tilley, N. (1996) 'Implementing crime prevention', in M. Tonry and D.P. Farrington (eds) *Building a Safer Society: Strategic Approaches to Crime Prevention*. Chicago, IL: University of Chicago Press.

Mawby, R. (2001) 'Promoting the police? The rise of police image work', *Criminal Justice Matters*, 43: 44–6.

McCreith, S. and Parkinson, S. (2004) *Crimes against Students: Emerging Lessons for Reducing Student Victimisation. Home Office Development and Practice Report 21*. London: Home Office.

Miethe, T.D. (1991) 'Citizen-based crime control activity and victimisation risks: an examination of displacement and free-rider effects', *Criminology*, 29: 419–39.

Milgram, S. (1967) 'The small world problem', *Psychology Today*, May: 60–7.

Riley, D. and Mayhew, P. (1980) *Crime Prevention Publicity: An Assessment. Home Office Research Study 63*. London: Home Office.

Roberts, M. (2001) 'Just noise? Newspaper crime reporting and the fear of crime', *Criminal Justice Matters*, 43: 12–14.

Rosenbaum, D.P., Lurigio, A.J. and Lavrakas, P.J. (1987) 'Crime stoppers: a national evaluation of CrimeStoppers programs', *Crime and Delinquency*, 35: 401–20.

Sherman, L. (1990) 'Police crackdowns: initial and residual deterrence', in M. Tonry and N. Morris (eds) *Crime and Justice: A Review of Research. Volume 12*. Chicago, IL: University of Chicago Press.

Smith, M.J., Clarke, R.V. and Pease, K. (2002) 'Anticipatory benefit in crime prevention', in N. Tilley (ed.) *Analysis for Crime Prevention. Crime Prevention Studies 13*. Monsey, NY: Criminal Justice Press.

Stockdale, J.E. and Gresham, P.J. (1995) *Combating Burglary: An Evaluation of Three Strategies. Crime Detection and Prevention Series Paper* 59. London: Home Office.

VanDijk, J.J.M. and Steinmetz, C.H.D. (1981) *Crime Prevention: An Evaluation of the National Publicity Campaigns.* Netherlands Ministry of Justice Research and Documentation Centre.

Verrill, J. and Bentley, J. (2003) *Informing the Effective Use of Publicity and Media Campaigns to Reduce Crime and the Fear of Crime.*

Watts, D.J. (2003) *Six Degrees: The Science of a Connected Age.* New York, NY: Norton.

Watts, D.J. and Strogatz, S.H. (1998) 'Collective dynamics of "small-world" networks', *Nature*, 393: 440–2.

Webb, B.A. and Laycock, G. (1992) *Tackling Car Crime. Crime Prevention Unit Paper* 32. London: Home Office.

Zajonc, R. (1980) 'Feeling and thinking. Preferences need no inferences', *American Psychologist*, 35: 151–75.

Zimring, F. and Hawkins, G. (1973) *Deterrence: The Legal Threat in Crime Control.* Chicago, IL: University of Chicago Press.

Chapter 14

Youth diversion

Tim Newburn and Anna Souhami

Like so many terms in criminology and criminal justice, 'diversion' defies easy definition. As a philosophy or set of practices, it has its roots in the radical critiques of penal welfarism that emerged in the 1960s and 1970s. Much influenced by labelling theory, at the heart of much diversionary activity has been the aim of minimizing the extent of contact between young offenders and the formal apparatus of the state, thereby reducing the stigmatizing effects of involvement with the criminal justice system and preventing the reoffending that follows from the establishment of delinquent identities (e.g. Goldson 2000; Pitts 2001).

As we describe below, 'diversion' has at different times focused on different aspects of the criminal justice system and criminal careers. Thus the broad ambit of diversion might include a range of activities and programmes aiming to reduce the extent of imprisonment of juvenile offenders (diversion from custody); the formal processing of young offenders in the criminal justice system (diversion from courts); and the extent of juvenile offending or the length of juvenile criminal careers (diversion from crime). A fourth area of diversion is that of pre-emptive measures to prevent the onset of a criminal career, and indeed considerable governmental attention is focused on such measures. However, our focus here is upon efforts made to reduce or prevent reoffending by young people, particularly where these involve processes or programmes that are alternatives to formal processing in the criminal justice system.[1]

The relationship of 'diversion' and crime prevention is not straightforward. As recent youth justice policy in England and Wales demonstrates, efforts have been made to achieve the broad aim of 'reduction' of youth offending both by attempting to minimize contacts between young people and the criminal justice system (what might broadly be thought of as 'diversion') and by attempting to increase opportunities for formal intervention (more commonly thought of as 'prevention'). These two approaches incorporate very different assumptions and principles about work with young offenders, and different measures of efficacy. Though elements of both approaches are visible at any one point, by and large these two approaches dominated different periods in youth justice in the UK. In this chapter we explore these two very different ways in which ideas of 'diversion' and 'prevention' have been incorporated into youth justice policy in England and Wales. Drawing on research evidence from the UK and USA, we then examine whether, and in what ways, they might be considered to be 'effective'. We begin with a brief outline of the recent history of diversion and prevention with young offenders in England and Wales.

Diversion

Diversion emerged as a dominant strategy in youth justice policy and practice in England and Wales in the 1980s. The decade has come to be seen as a distinctive period in which there was a 'quiet consensus' (Haines and Drakeford 1998) amongst policy-makers and practitioners that, wherever possible, minor and less experienced offenders should be diverted from the formal criminal justice interventions, and more serious offenders from prison. In part, this was a reflection of a dominant mode of thinking about problems of youth offending. Theoretically grounded in labelling perspectives (e.g. Becker 1963; Lemert 1970) and informed by arguments that offending by young people is relatively 'normal' and, if left alone, young people would 'grow out' of crime (e.g. Rutherford 1986), it was held that not only did state intervention not prevent reoffending, it had the potential to reinforce patterns of offending through the establishment of delinquent identities. Consequently it was argued that interventions by the formal criminal justice system had the potential to cause more harm than good and should thus be avoided or minimized wherever possible. Guidelines from the Home Office were unambiguous: diversion from the criminal justice system could reduce reoffending and prevent the onset of an offending career: 'It is recognised both in theory and in practice that delay in the entry of a young person into the formal criminal justice system may help to prevent his entry into that system altogether' (Home Office 1985).

For those young offenders who did enter the criminal justice system, prison was seen as a particularly harmful option. Consequently, a policy of diversion from incarceration was advocated for more serious young offenders by both government and practitioners. For example, the 1988 Home Office green paper stated:

> Most young offenders grow out of crime as they become more mature and responsible. They need encouragement and help to become law abiding. Even a short period in custody is quite likely to confirm them as criminals, particularly as they acquire new criminal skills from the more sophisticated offenders. They see themselves labelled as criminals and behave accordingly.

Indeed, as late as 1990 the Home Office was describing prison as 'an expensive way of making bad people worse' (Home Office 1990a).

Further, diversion from the courts and from custody had an ideological and pragmatic appeal. It chimed with an influential ideological and philosophical movement amongst practitioners to minimize state intervention in the lives of young people who offend. This coincided with the 'back to justice' movement, a critique of penal welfarism which held that through the guise of 'treatment' and 'welfare' objectives, young people were frequently subject to 'justice' interventions which were not warranted by their behaviour alone. Instead, it was argued that young people needed protection from the criminal justice system, and a policy of 'progressive minimalism' was advocated. At the same time, the diversion of minor offenders from the formal justice system corresponded with the priorities of the Conservative government, who had made a commitment both to minimize state spending and state interference and to crack down on youth crime through an emphasis on 'law and order'. Diverting offenders from the formal justice system rationalized the reach of state apparatus whilst simultaneously allowing the government to appear 'tough' by concentrating resources on more serious or persistent offenders (Pitts 1999, 2005).

In this way, the official endorsement of diversion from the courts and alternatives to custody encouraged and consolidated the emerging anti-custody and pro-diversionary 'orthodoxy' amongst youth justice practitioners (Haines and Drakeford 1998). As a result, developments at the levels of both practice and policy throughout the decade saw an increasingly bifurcated youth justice system, in which minor or less experienced offenders were diverted away from the criminal justice system and subjected to minimal intervention, whilst more serious and persistent offenders were dealt with via tightly focused community programmes. This was largely influenced by two major areas of diversionary activity: diversion from formal intervention through the use of cautioning and multi-agency practice; and diversion from custody through the refocusing of intermediate treatment.

Cautioning

The 1980s saw a huge expansion in the use of cautioning as a way of dealing with relatively minor offences by young people. Between 1980 and 1987, the proportion of girls aged 14–16 who received a caution rather than being prosecuted rose from 58 per cent to 82 per cent; for boys from 34 per cent to 82 per cent (Pitts 2005). The use of cautioning was officially endorsed in a series of Home Office circulars (1985, 1990b) which recommended that the courts should only be used as a 'last resort' and encouraged the use of cautions or informal action wherever possible and for 'a wide range of offences and offenders' (Home Office 1990b). The assumptions about youth crime that underpinned the endorsement of diversionary strategies – that formal intervention re-enforced offending behaviour and should be avoided wherever possible – were explicit. Indeed, the 1985 Home Office Circular warned that cautioning might also serve to pull people into the formal criminal justice system and recommended that cautioning should be used only where 'strict criteria' were met, warning that young people should not necessarily be cautioned simply because they were brought into a police station: instead, less formal action could be given, or no further action at all (para. 7).

The growth in cautioning and other pre-prosecution disposals is also linked with developments initiated by agencies and youth justice practitioners, in particular the development of multi-agency work through the establishment of diversion panels, such as the influential Juvenile Liaison Bureaux (JLBx) in Northamptonshire.[2] These generally consisted of representatives of the police, social services, education, youth service and voluntary sector. The panels would assess young people apprehended by the police and advise on whether further action should be taken, and if so whether this should be a caution, some further intervention or prosecution, attempting wherever possible to recommend a caution or no further action. Diversion panels also became a site of informal intervention, wherever it was decided that 'additional help should be offered to encourage the young person not to re-offend' (NACRO 1987: 16). Such interventions could involve elements of reparation, addressing offending behaviour, or focusing on other aspects of the young person's educational or social needs. Unlike the interventionist approach adopted in the late 1990s (see below) however, interventions were primarily intended only for a small number of those considered by the panel, and were directed by the principle of minimum appropriate intervention (NACRO 1987; Bell et al. 1999; Smith 2003).

Evaluations of the Northamptonshire JLBx suggest that they had a significant impact on the numbers of young people diverted from the courts. The JLBx considered all cases involving young offenders, apart from those involving the most serious offences (such as rape, murder or endangering life) and its recommendations were accepted by the police in 97 per cent of cases (Bell et al. 1999). In the first five years of its operation, the county saw a rise in cautioning from 49 per cent in 1981 to 84 per cent in 1985 (Bell et al. 1999). Further, JLBx encouraged the police to use 'no further action' – by 1985 nearly a quarter of all cases were dealt with informally, thereby affecting the number of prosecutions and formal cautions. Bell et al. report that in 1992 the JLBx dealt with 1,389 young people in 2,399 referrals, of which only 9 per cent were prosecuted. As a result, there was a marked decline in custodial sentences which fell by 65 per cent over the first six years of the JLBx (Stevens and Crook 1986).

Intermediate treatment (IT)

At approximately the same time that cautioning began to expand there also emerged a number of community-based alternatives that sought to provide fairly intensive supervision in combination with a number of other intervention programmes primarily as an alternative to custody. Developing initially in the USA and the UK in the late 1970s (Feld 1988), they became relatively common internationally during the course of the 1980s (Junger-Tas 1994) and in the UK there was a rapid expansion of intensive intermediate treatment schemes.

The term 'intermediate treatment' (IT) was introduced in England and Wales in the 1968 white paper *Children in Trouble*, which identified a need for 'intermediate treatment' for children and young people who did not need to be removed from home, but who needed greater support than that provided by straightforward social work supervision. IT was broadly envisioned as a 'preventative' programme available to children and young people of any age. Whilst it could be a formal requirement of a court order, it was largely undertaken informally with young people – both offenders and non-offenders

– whom social workers felt were 'at risk' in some way (NACRO 1991). As such, the range of interventions employed and young people involved were seemingly limitless. As Haines and Drakeford describe, 'almost anything that was done with children…could be, and was, called IT' (1998: 62).

IT was sharply refocused with the launch of the (then) Department of Health and Social Security's Intermediate Treatment Initiative in 1983. This established IT as a direct alternative to custody through the provision of £15 million to create an additional 4,500 'places in the community' for young people involved in serious or persistent offending. Despite some variation in the use of IT amongst local practitioner teams (Bottoms *et al.* 1990), its use became refocused in ways which stood in stark contrast to its 1970s incarnation. First, intervention became tightly defined and minimized. Interventions were now solely for adjudicated offenders. They were time-limited in proportion to the length of custodial sentence that might otherwise have been given. They now focused primarily on offending behaviour, rather than the young person themselves. This was consistent with the influential arguments amongst youth justice practitioners which held that 'welfare' objectives should not be used as a justification for 'justice' interventions. However, it led to some concerns that the welfare needs of young people were being neglected (Haines and Drakeford 1998). Secondly, a number of initiatives followed which aimed 'to relocate intermediate treatment at a higher point in the tariff' (Bottoms *et al.* 1990). To establish IT programmes as an alternative to custody, they now were expected to demonstrate similar levels of 'toughness' as custodial sentences, for example, by demanding more stringent conditions of attendance and more extensive monitoring (Smith 2003).

Evaluating 'diversion'

The consistency and consensus about the prioritizing of diversionary strategies throughout the 1980s, and the extent of the changes that followed, led the decade to be described as a 'successful revolution' in juvenile justice (Jones 1984). Jones (1989: i) described the optimism amongst youth justice practitioners at the end of the decade:

> The 1980s have seen a revolution in the way the juvenile justice system operates in England and Wales. There are few areas of criminal justice practice of which we can be proud but this is an exception…Many notions, which once seemed totally unrealistic, such as the abolition of juvenile imprisonment, are now viewed as achievable.

For some, this 'success' is demonstrated by the marked decline in the numbers of young people who were processed by criminal justice agencies. By such a measure the developments over the 1980s were undoubtedly successful. There was a significant and sustained decline both in the numbers of children and young people entering the courts, and in the use of custody for young people (see Table 14.1). Indeed, as some commentators note (Haines and Drakeford 1998; Smith 2003), taken together these trends indicate that the decline in

Table 14.1 Numbers of young people aged 14–16 processed and sentenced to custody, 1981–91 ('000s)

Date	Cautioned/found guilty (A)	Sentenced to custody (B)	(B) as proportion of (A)
1981	113.7	7.7	6.8%
1986	99.8	4.4	4.4%
1991	75.2	1.4	1.8%

Source: Criminal Statistics for England and Wales (1991) cited in in Smith (2003).

custody over the 1980s may be more significant than the figures suggest. The increase in the use of cautioning for minor and younger offenders meant that the courts would have seen a higher proportion of more serious offenders. Consequently, the use of custody was also declining not just in absolute terms but was also being used more sparingly in relation to serious and persistent offending.

Empirical evidence on the impact of cautioning during the 1980s suggests that it was generally successful in reducing reoffending, particularly with young people who had previously had relatively little contact with the criminal justice system. Thus, for example, the reconviction rate for offenders receiving a caution who had no previous cautions or court appearances was only a little over one tenth. Indeed, it was approximately one fifth for those who had one previous caution (see Table 14.2) which, notwithstanding that this is undoubtedly a relatively low-risk group, counts as a relatively high success rate when compared with many other diversionary activities.

The decline in the proportionate use of imprisonment for juveniles between 1985 and 1990 suggests that IT did serve as an effective diversionary alternative to custody (though see Parker *et al.* 1989). The impact of IT on reoffending is perhaps harder to assess. Bottoms *et al.*'s (1990) evaluation of IT involved a comparison of four groups of young offenders: 'heavy end' IT provided

Table 14.2 Reconviction rates for offenders cautioned in 1991

Criminal history before sample caution	% of offenders subsequently convicted within 2 years
No previous court appearance, and	
no previous cautions	11
one previous caution	22
two or more previous cautions	45
Previous court appearances, and	
no previous cautions	24
one previous caution	33
two or more previous cautions	46

Source: Home Office (1995).

compulsorily; those receiving custodial sentences; IT for those on supervision orders; and supervision orders without IT. A quasi-experimental design was used and outcomes were evaluated using crime records and self-report data. The reconviction rates a little over a year after the end of the intervention were 81 per cent for custody compared with 74 per cent for heavy-end IT, and 65 per cent of IT within supervision orders compared with 61 per cent for supervision orders without IT. The differences were not statistically significant though there was some evidence that high-end IT did have an effect on levels of both officially recorded and self-reported offending.

Prevention

The 'uneasy alliance' (Pitts 1999) between practitioners, policy-makers and politicians during the 1980s was broken with a dramatic shift in the climate of youth justice policy in England and Wales in the 1990s, which radically altered the way in which crime by young people was understood and managed.

The 1990s saw a 'repoliticization' (Pitts 1999) of youth justice and the emergence of a new populist punitiveness. Following a series of high-profile and politically potent events such as disturbances in a number of English and Welsh cities, a major campaign about the threat of 'persistent offenders' and, perhaps most importantly, the abduction and murder of James Bulger by two 10-year-old children, problems of youth crime were thrust to the centre of national debate and the attention of the emergent Labour government (Newburn 1996). This concern with serious and prominent offences by young people was accompanied by a preoccupation with low-level incivilities or 'anti-social behaviour' in which young people were seen to play a central part, and which were considered by the middle-class constituents that Labour wooed to be particularly threatening to their quality of life (Pitts 2000, 2001). As a result, youth crime became a matter of priority for the new Labour government, and their frenetic activities in this area culminated in the 'radical overhaul' (Straw and Michael 1996) of the youth justice system with the Crime and Disorder Act 1998, an ambitious and wide-ranging programme of legislative and organizational change, and one to which a particular notion of 'crime prevention' was central.

Alongside the increasing political resonance of youth crime, there was a shift in the dominant mode of thinking about its management. An increasing emphasis was being paid by governments on both sides of the Atlantic to actuarial techniques in the management of the criminal justice system, in which policy and practice were to be directed through notions of risks, outcomes and evidence. So, drawing on the influential Audit Commission report *Misspent Youth* (1996), the delivery of youth justice services in the UK were to be targeted towards selected 'risk conditions' associated with offending, such as poor parenting; inadequate discipline; truancy and school exclusion; and associating with delinquent peers (Home Office 1997).

The Crime and Disorder Act 1998 established 'preventing offending by children and young persons' as the principal aim of the youth justice system. This approach to the reduction of youth crime stood in stark contrast to the dominant orthodoxy of diversion in the 1980s. First, instead of attempting to reduce the likelihood of establishing criminal careers by reducing contact with the criminal justice system, it is assumed that prevention can be achieved by targeting young people thought likely to offend, and by drawing them into the system at an early stage. As a consequence of a series of reforms reflecting this perspective, the youth justice system is now characterized by a 'robust interventionism' (Pitts 2001: 169) in which, for example, formal intervention now applies to children as young as 10, for a second (or, in some cases, their first) offence; and pre-emptive measures provide for intervention with children below the age of criminal responsibility, including those who haven't committed an offence but are thought to be 'at risk' of doing so, or thought by others (such as neighbours or police) to be causing trouble. As Muncie points out, 'virtually any intervention, monitoring and scrutiny of young people's lives can be justified in the name of crime prevention' (2002: 151). Indeed, policies and practices that divert young people from the formal criminal justice system have effectively been abandoned (Goldson 2005) – ss. 65 and 66 of the Crime and Disorder Act 1998 put an end to cautioning and replaced them by the more interventionist and formal reprimand and final warning scheme, described below.

Secondly, the new approach also contains a different understanding of protection and intervention. The dominant ethic amongst practitioners in the 1980s was that, in order to minimize intervention and protect young people from the formal apparatus of the state, the 'welfare' needs of the young people should not properly be the concern of the criminal justice system. By contrast, the white paper which preceded the Crime and Disorder Act 1998 argued that 'there is no conflict between protecting the welfare of a young offender and preventing that individual from offending again' (Home Office 1997). Indeed, not to intervene was viewed as harmful, and as allowing '[young people] to go on wrecking their own lives as well as disrupting their families and communities'. Thus, within this approach, preventing offending by intervention through the criminal justice system is seen as a means of promoting the welfare of the young person. The intervention of the youth justice system is presented as an enabling opportunity, even an entitlement (Muncie 2002), very much in line with the operation of one of the core characteristics of what Feeley and Simon (1992) have termed the 'new penology'. In a similar vein, Leacock and Sparks (2002) argue that the extension of the vocabulary of risk characteristic of current penal policy reinforces the notion of such an obligation to intervene. Notions of risk no longer just describe 'riskiness' – the risks that young people who offend present to the public – but 'at-risk-ness': the ways in which young people might be at risk of offending, being offended against or of social exclusion. They argue that such notions contain an implicit moral imperative for intervention: risk factors become a 'checklist' of triggers to action.

'Evaluating' prevention

Perhaps unsurprisingly, the new mode of thinking about youth justice has brought with it new terms of evaluation. As outlined above, the 'success' of diversion in the 1980s was assessed in part by its marked impact on the numbers of young people processed in the criminal justice system. In these terms, an increasingly interventionist youth justice system inevitably heralds failure, and some commentators have argued that the 'new interventionism is at odds with established theory, research findings and practice experience' (Goldson 2000: 42).

As outlined above, the rise of actuarially focused strategies in the UK and the USA has brought about an emphasis on the idea of evidence-based policy and practice, and this has seen increasing attention paid to the 'what works' agenda (in the USA see Sherman *et al.* 1999). For example, in the UK, the Audit Commission (1996) emphasized the need to give primacy to methods that can demonstrate efficacy, and a Home Office review of the 'what works' literature (Goldblatt and Lewis 1998) recommended that new policy initiatives should be continually monitored and evaluated. Consequently, governments on both sides of the Atlantic have sought to invest significantly in research and evaluation with the aim of promoting programmes and policies that have been demonstrated to 'work'. As we describe below, evidence of efficacy has now been refocused on attempting to measure the extent to which different interventions affect levels and types of offending by young people.

The emphasis on such measurements in shaping youth justice interventions is not uncontentious. Some argue that this is not an appropriate thing to attempt, as standardized evaluation cannot capture the individualism and discretion that are key principles of work with young offenders (e.g. Rojek *et al.* 1988; Nellis 1995).[3] Consequently, the concern with demonstrating that interventions 'work' necessarily leads to the prioritizing of those activities that more easily lead themselves to measurable, quantifiable outcomes, and side-step ideological questions about the purpose and process of intervention. For example, Muncie argues that instead of principles of welfare, diversion or progressive justice, the youth justice system has become structured by 'the rather less philosophically defensible aim of preventing offending by any pragmatic means possible' (2002: 145). Nevertheless, the rise of the 'what works' movement has brought an increasing interest in evaluation of youth justice interventions and it is to this research evidence that we turn next. We begin by examining the impact of interventions with first-time offenders (or those with limited previous contact with criminal justice) including final warnings and restorative justice-influenced programmes, before moving on to consider more intensive, generally community penalty-based programmes and techniques including cognitive behaviourism, targeted youth interventions and intensive surveillance. The chapter concludes with an extended consideration of community-based programmes, such as mentoring, designed to challenge problematic or 'risky' youthful conduct.

Final warnings

Consistent with the new emphasis on early intervention, the 1980s diversionary orthodoxy has now been replaced by a more interventionist approach. The significantly poorer reconviction rates in cases of multiple cautioning, concerns about the relatively slight nature of cautioning as an experience for a young offender and, crucially, missed opportunities for intervention led the Audit Commission (1996) to recommend, and the Labour government to implement, a fairly radical overhaul of the system in the aftermath of the Crime and Disorder Act 1998. The Act scrapped the caution (informal and formal) and replaced it with a reprimand (for less serious offences) and a final warning. As the name implies, one of the crucial characteristics of the final warning is that, except in unusual circumstances, it may only be used once. In addition to the change of nomenclature, and the more sparing manner of usage, the new system of reprimands and final warnings also set in motion a set of other activities – such as those previously associated with 'caution plus' – involving more frequent and often earlier intervention than previously had been the case. By contrast with the old cautioning system, under the Crime and Disorder Act all young offenders receiving a final warning are referred to a youth offending team (YOT). Offenders are then expected, 'unless [the YOT] consider it inappropriate to do so', to participate in a rehabilitation programme (in which reparation is expected generally to be present). Development funding from the Youth Justice Board (YJB) set in motion a number of final warning projects which ran a broad range of intervention programmes for young offenders (see Table 14.3).

Research from the Home Office in the early years of the new disposals suggests that there has been little change in reconviction rates for pre-court diversionary measures. In July 2000 the reconviction rate for reprimands was 18.5 per cent and for final warnings 24 per cent (Jennings 2002). More recent work by the YJB found that 31 per cent of young offenders on YJB intervention programmes reoffended within a year of receiving their final warning (Holdaway and Desborough 2004). More recently still, the Criminal Justice and Court Services Act 2000 removed the requirement that a police reprimand or final warning be given to a young offender only at a police station. This introduced the possibility of 'conferences' at which parents, victims and other adults could be present – what has sometimes been referred to as 'restorative cautioning' (Young and Goold 1999).

Table 14.3 Nature of interventions within YJB-funded final warning projects

	Project sample		
	Number of projects	% of projects	% of cases
Restorative justice	13	43.3	71.5 (506)
Mentoring	8	26.7	22.2 (157)
Drugs and alcohol	3	10.0	3.1 (22)
Final warnings	1	3.3	1.4 (10)
Education	1	3.3	0.3 (2)
Prevention	1	3.3	0.1 (1)
Parenting	1	3.3	0.0 (0)
Cognitive behaviour	2	6.6	1.4 (10)
Total	30	99.8	100.0

Source: Holdaway and Desborough (2004).

Restorative justice

Though there are many competing definitions and versions of 'restorative justice' (RJ), at heart it is generally taken to involve greater recognition of the harms to victims of crime, increased participation by victims and offenders in processes of resolution and a greater emphasis on repairing the harms done. The particular version of RJ promoted by the Labour government after the 1997 election involved what they referred to as the '3Rs' of 'restoration' (young offenders apologizing and making amends), 'reintegration' (young offenders paying their debts to society) and 'responsibility' (young offenders and their parents facing the consequences of the offending behaviour).

Since 1998, the Thames Valley Police in the UK have been at the forefront of an experiment to introduce RJ principles to the process of cautioning young offenders (Pollard 2000). Officers in the force have been trained to facilitate a discussion – following a script – about the nature of the offence and how the harm caused might in some way be repaired. Although there is some evidence that such an approach to cautioning may have benefits beyond the specific goal of crime reduction, initial research findings suggest that restorative cautioning was no more effective than traditional cautioning in terms of reducing the likelihood of further sanctions being imposed or on the frequency or seriousness of offending (Wilcox *et al.* 2004) – though as we noted above, by many standards cautioning itself may be considered to be relatively successful as a form of diversion. However, the methodology used in this research doesn't allow for anything like definitive conclusions to be drawn, for the comparison of traditional and restorative cautioning was not based on random allocation and, potentially therefore, may have hidden the actual impact – positive or negative – of such processes. However, the researchers do report what appears to be 'a causal link' between such RJ-influenced processes and desistance in about a quarter of cases studied (see Hoyle *et al.* 2002), though it seems clear that this is an area – like others we will come to below – where considerably more research is necessary.

Following the Youth Justice and Criminal Evidence Act 1999 a new primary sentencing disposal was introduced in England and Wales – the referral order. It is mandatory for 10-17-year-olds pleading guilty and convicted for the first time by the Youth Court, unless the crime is seriousness enough to warrant custody or the court orders an absolute discharge. The disposal involves referring the young offender to a youth offender panel (YOP). Informed by restorative justice ideas the intention is that the panel will provide a forum away from the formality of the court. Panels consist of one YOT member and (at least) two community panel members, one of whom leads the panel. A parent or both parents of a young offender aged under 16 are expected to attend all panel meetings in all but exceptional cases. The offender can also nominate an adult to support him or her and in order to encourage the restorative nature of the process a variety of other people may be invited to attend given panel meetings including the victim or a representative of the community at large; a victim supporter; and a supporter of the young person and/or anyone else that the panel considers to be capable of having a 'good influence' on the offender.

The aim of the initial panel meeting is to devise a 'contract' and, where the victim chooses to attend, for him or her to meet and talk about the offence with the offender. It is intended that negotiations between the panel and the offender about the content of the contract should be led by the community panel members. The contract should always include reparation to the victim or wider community and a programme of activity designed primarily to prevent further offending.

Early reports from the evaluation of referral orders indicated mixed success. Unfortunately, as yet there is little indication of impact on reoffending. Concerns have also been raised about the potential for such interventions to have 'net-widening' or 'mesh-thinning' effects – drawing increasing numbers of young people into the formal justice system and, through the imposition of tough standards of compliance, ensuring that a significant proportion of young offenders subject to such orders are returned to court for re-sanctioning (with all the potential for increasing the severity of the punishment) (Haines 2000; Morris and Gelsthorpe 2000; Ball 2000, 2004).

On the positive side, however, the youth offender panels appeared initially at least to have established themselves within a year of operation as deliberative and participatory forums in which a young person's offending behaviour can be addressed (Crawford and Newburn 2003). The informal setting of youth offender panels appeared to allow young people, their parents/carers, community panel members and YOT advisers opportunities to discuss the nature and consequences of a young person's offending, as well as how to respond to this in ways which seek to repair the harm done and to address the causes of the young person's offending behaviour. In addition, the successful integration of a large number of volunteers within the youth justice process provides an opportunity for a potentially powerful new exterior voice to participate and influence this arena.

Intermediate sanctions/community penalties

Beyond cautioning systems and RJ-based initiatives aimed at first-time offenders, there is a range of non-custodial penalties (and within these, an array of different interventions and programmes that may go to make up particular penalties) used with more persistent or serious young offenders. A meta-analysis of research on interventions with serious and violent juvenile offenders by Lipsey and Wilson (1998) reviewed over 200 experimental and quasi-experimental programmes. The review suggests that, on balance, intervention programmes can work to reduce reoffending rates amongst 'serious delinquents'. However, identifying which types of programme are the more effective they found much more difficult. The most impressive effects were found in programmes that involved individual counselling, interpersonal skills and behavioural programmes. Much less success was found in connection with employment-related and academic programmes and what they describe as deterrence and vocational programmes (see Table 14.4)

Despite the apparent popularity of increasingly harsh and punitive measures for responding to youth crime the research evidence on programmes that target serious, violent and chronic offenders is far from impressive. Targeted arrest

Table 14.4 Mean effect sizes for different treatment types for non-institutionalized juvenile offenders

Treatment type	Number of programmes	Observed effect size
Interpersonal skills	3	.46[1,2]
Individual counselling	8	.52[1,2]
Behavioural programmes	7	.49[1,2]
Multiple services	17	.26[1]
Restitution, probation/parole	10	.16[1,2]
All other	14	.08
Employment related	4	.13
Academic programmes	2	.10
Advocacy/social casework	6	.11
Group counselling	9	.02
Family counselling	8	.24[1]
Reduced caseload, probation/parole	12	−.09[1]
Wilderness challenge	4	.13[2]
Early release, probation/parole	2	.10[2]
Deterrence programmes	6	−.03[2]
Vocational programmes	4	−.17[2]
Overall	117	.14[1]

Notes:
1. p = <.05 (statistical significance); 2. Q > .05 (homogeneity).
Source: Lipsey and Wilson (1998).

and prosecution programmes in the USA have been hampered by resistance from within local juvenile justice systems as well as poor research design and, by and large, have not demonstrated sizeable effects. Although a 1996 study (Rasmussen and Yu) appeared to indicate that increased incarceration of habitual young offenders could prevent a significant amount of crime, Krisberg and Howell (1998: 353) conclude that 'we know little more today about the efficacy of targeted enforcement and suppression programs than we did two decades ago'.

There is also bad news on this front in the area of intermediate sanctions more generally. According to Altschuler (1998: 385–6), 'some very basic questions concerning implementation, impact, and costs associated with intermediate sanctions remain unanswered' and such research 'has generally suffered from too few participants, so that it becomes exceedingly difficult to generate any statistically significant differences in the analysis'. Some relatively small successes have been demonstrated in intensive supervision programmes in the USA, with reductions in recidivism of between 10 per cent and 20 per cent, though the absence of experimental research design in this area leaves us some way short of being able to demonstrate any direct link between the programmes and the measured outcomes. In fact some of the strongest evidence in the area of intermediate sanctions is arguably that with a negative message. Reinforcing what we have had to say elsewhere about the paucity of evidence supporting the more punitive interventions with young offenders, evidence on the impact of boot camps on recidivism suggests that boot camps may actually worsen the problem they are designed to tackle (Mackenzie and Souryal 1994). An overview of youth violence prevention by the US Surgeon General concluded:

> Compared to traditional forms of incarceration, boot camps produced no significant effects on recidivism in three out of four evaluations and trends toward increased recidivism in two. The fourth evaluation showed significant harmful effects on youths, with a significant increase in recidivism (http://www.surgeongeneral.gov/library/youthviolence/chapter5/sec6.html).

Guerra (1998), in her overview of the field, notes that 'as offending becomes more serious, the effectiveness of intervention strategies tends to diminish' and, moreover, that interventions with young offenders tend only to demonstrate strong effects under optimal conditions, with the effects being virtually eliminated when such conditions don't exist. She goes on:

> on the one hand, given that no single factor is likely to cause [serious, violent juvenile] offending, the impact of single-component, single-context programs is limited. On the other hand, long-term, multi-component, multicontext programs can become difficult to manage with a number of unintended 'interventions' (e.g. policy changes, demographic shifts) occurring, and some contexts (e.g. political and economic forces) unamenable to change via the planned intervention.

Cognitive-behavioural interventions

The rise of the 'what works' movement on both sides of the Atlantic has seen considerable time and money invested in programmes influenced by cognitive behaviourism. In the UK cognitive skills programmes were introduced in the early 1990s (Porporino and Fabiano 2000) with the aim of affecting the ability of offenders to engage in consequentialist thinking in order to avoid those strategies that lead towards offending and enhance those that direct them elsewhere. Most work in this area has been undertaken with adult offenders, though there is some evidence from meta-analyses that suggests that such programmes may be more effective than interventions that don't include a cognitive-behavioural element (Lipsey 1992). Existing UK evidence is only available for prison-based programmes though such evidence may provide some insight for future community-based interventions.

A Home Office study (Cann et al. 2003) in the UK examined the impact on a sample of 1,534 young offenders (aged 21 or less) who had participated in one of two cognitive-behavioural programmes between 1998 and 2000: the

Enhanced Thinking Skills and the Reasoning and Rehabilitation Programmes. Matched against a comparison group, the young offenders on the programmes were subject to both one-year and two-year reconviction studies. The study found a statistically significant difference in reconviction between those that had completed the programme and the comparison group. However, such positive results need to be set in context. There were relatively high non-completion rates in the programmes and when all 'programme starters' were included in the analysis no significant differences in outcome were found. Moreover, the positive results found for programme completers after one year were not maintained after two, with no statistically significant differences in reconviction being maintained. This led the researchers to conclude that such programmes can have an impact – so long as young offenders can be persuaded to complete the course – and that post-release 'booster programmes' might also be beneficial.

A similarly inconclusive picture is painted by cognitive programmes run by the Youth Justice Board. Costing £3.9 million, 23 projects focused on moral reasoning, problem-solving and self-management, with the aim of 'encouraging offenders to understand the impact of their offending and to equip them with the skills and knowledge they need to go on to lead law-abiding lives'. As with so much YJB activity the projects were very varied in their focus with some working with persistent offenders, some working with sex offenders and others focusing on education, restorative justice or mental health. Completion rates varied from 47 to 86 per cent and were particularly low for the persistent offender projects (where the greatest impact would potentially be possible). Unfortunately, the reconviction studies conducted as part of the evaluation for these studies shed little light on 'what works': numbers of participants are extremely low and there is little in the way of useful comparison (see Feilzer *et al.* 2004 for details). Reconviction data were only available on 129 programme participants, across 17 projects in all. The overall reconviction rate was a little over 60 per cent, though it was nearer 80 per cent for those persistent offenders for whom information was available. As with so much else in this field, despite the optimistic talk in the 'what works' field, we remain some distance from any clear picture of effective interventions.

Targeted youth interventions

In the UK one of the largest sets of activities in this area has been the Youth Inclusion Programme (YIP) run by the Youth Justice Board since early 2000. Comprising 70 Youth Inclusion (YI) projects in mainly deprived areas of England and Wales, the work has focused on young people between 13 and 16 years of age at highest risk of offending. Modelled on the 'Youth Works' initiative, the programme signalled something of a shift from universal provision of youth work to more targeted provision. As with perhaps the majority of initiatives aimed at young people over the past 5–10 years, YI projects focused on risk and preventative factors, aiming to identify the 'top 50' most at-risk young people in the areas in which the programme was being run, with the aim that these young people were 'included in mainstream activities by offering support to them to overcome a variety of social problems'. The intention was that interventions should be tailored to meet the particular risk factors identified in this 'top 50' and in sufficient 'dosage' to be effective. A range of interventions were run by YI projects within the following broad categories:

- Education and training.
- Sport.
- Arts, culture and media.
- Group development.
- Mentoring.
- Environment.
- Health and drugs.
- Personal assessment.
- Motor projects.
- Family projects.
- Outreach and detached work (Morgan *et al.* 2003).

Early evaluation appears to show some impact. Thus, amongst those actively engaged by the projects there was a two thirds (65 per cent) reduction in arrest rates and a similar decrease in levels of offending. However, three fifths of the 'top 50' had never been arrested and only a quarter (27 per cent) went on to be arrested during the course of the programme. Of the two fifths that had been arrested prior to the programme, most exhibited reduced arrest rates thereafter, together with reduced levels of seriousness of offending (see Figure 14.1).

The evaluators conclude that:

> after accounting for changes in arrest rates in each project's 'host' police force, 61 [out of 67] projects experienced a decrease in the average number of offences for which the top 50 were arrested. The decreases ranged from 1 per cent to 117 per cent. The other six projects saw an increase, ranging from 1 per cent to 24 per cent (Morgan *et al.* 2003: 11).

However, some of the other measures used to assess the impact of the programme are less positive. Although temporary and permanent exclusions from school were found to have dropped, the level of unauthorized absences from school (truancy) increased markedly. Moreover, crime levels in the neighbourhoods in which the programmes were situated – regarded as a principal measure of impact – show an aggregate increase of between 6 and 11 per cent. In particular it appears that local projects simply did not recruit the more prolific offenders in sufficient numbers, nor work with those that were recruited sufficiently intensively, to stand a chance of achieving the targets set. Once again a set of interventions influenced by the what-works philosophy appears to have foundered somewhat on a programme design that in all likelihood was never capable of achieving the objectives handed it. Community-based preventive interventions are by their very nature difficult both to implement and to evaluate. The great danger of overambition and under-theorization is that any residual faith that there is in such approaches to prevention and diversion will be undermined.

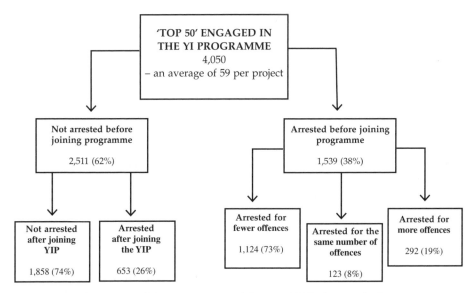

Figure 14.1 Summary of the arrest rates of the 'top 50' before and after engagement with the Youth Inclusion Programme
Source: Morgan *et al.* (2003).

Intensive surveillance

Intensive supervision programmes with young offenders are relatively new but have a somewhat longer track record in the adult criminal justice sphere. Intensive probation programmes were run in the USA from the early 1960s and became more common in the UK from the mid-1980s as demands for more 'credible' community punishments grew (Mair *et al.* 1994; Worrall and Mawby 2004). We reported above the general experiences of intermediate treatment which offered a more intensive model of supervision than that generally provided within the juvenile justice system hitherto. More recently, Intensive Supervision and Surveillance Programmes (ISSP) have been established by the Youth Justice Board in England and Wales focused on persistent and serious juvenile offenders and described by one evaluator as 'the most rigorous, non-custodial intervention available for young offenders and [claimed by YJB to be] founded on the best evidence as to what will reduce the frequency and seriousness of offending' (Moore 2004: 159).

The ISSP projects in the UK had ambitious objectives – ranging from reducing reoffending to tackling the underlying problems faced by serious and persistent offenders. Programmes were wide ranging in content including, in the bulk, some form of educational provision, together with offender behaviour programmes, restorative justice, interpersonal skills training and family support work. In terms of impact, one reviewer's summary of similar work in the adult field was that it has had 'little impact' to date (Gendreau *et al.* 2000) and US experience in this area has also noted high levels of non-compliance (Petersilia and Turner 1992) though they distinguish between programmes in terms of the extent of their treatment component, arguing that those with the greatest treatment component have the greatest impact on offending.

Evidence of impact in the UK is limited, with outcome data – as in other projects discussed here – being somewhat inadequate. Once again, completion rates were far from high with only about one half (47 per cent) of young offenders completing the ISSP – rates being higher for young offenders qualifying for such programmes because of the *seriousness* of their offending rather than its *persistence*. Worrall and Mawby (2004: 275) review existing evaluations on intensive supervision projects and, even allowing for the inclusion of work with adult offenders (which is more plentiful than that on juveniles), conclude that 'the body of evaluation research on prolific offender schemes is neither large nor unequivocal in its findings'. They describe three evaluated projects: the Burnley/Dordrecht initiative (Chenery and Pease 2000); a programme in Newcastle (Hope *et al.* 2001); and a project in Stoke-on-Trent (Worrall *et al.* 2003). The outcomes in the second and third of these studies include some positive results – the authors of the Newcastle evaluation concluding that they were '90 per cent confident that the project has had an effect in the direction of reducing re-offending rates of participants by over 50 per cent when compared with similar non-participants'. In most studies, however, numbers of participants remain small, programme effects are generally not sizeable (where they are detectable at all) and although there are some promising indications of positive engagement with persistent and serious young offenders there is little as yet that we could confidently describe as evidence of 'what works' within criminal justice-based interventions/programmes for young offenders.

Community crime prevention

Beyond the criminal justice system there are, of course, a cognate set of programmes that aim to challenge problematic or risky youthful conduct (many of which may also be accessed via the criminal justice system). Once again, however, research evidence is generally slight. An overview of community-based interventions with young people undertaken for the National Institute of Justice by Lawrence Sherman and colleagues in the late 1990s found relatively little robust evidence of substantial impact in relation to crime reduction and prevention (Sherman *et al.* 1999). In particular, they say, there is little evidence to be found in support of the 'most visible community-based crime prevention strategy in the latter twentieth century' – community mobilization (Hope 1995). There appear to be a number of reasons for the apparent absence of impact including a lack of appropriate impact evaluations and a series of problems related to difficulties of faithful implementation.

Educational programmes

Programmes based on an analysis of risk factors tend to have a broad focus – their assumption being that interventions focusing on any single factor are unlikely to be successful. However, much of the literature on interventions with juvenile offenders suggests that the majority of programmes aimed at teenage children tend to involve an educational component that focuses on the young person 'in isolation' rather than within the family context, especially in universal rather than targeted programmes (Wasserman and Miller 1998).

At best these tend to demonstrate small effects. Two educational programmes that have demonstrated some impact on offending both focused on young high-school students deemed to be high risk for anti-social behaviour or behavioural problems. In Project STATUS, Gottfredson and Gottfredson (1992) found that, compared to a control group, intervention students reported lower levels of delinquency and drug use and higher levels of self-esteem (though for a more sceptical review of work on self-esteem, see Emler 2001). Similarly, an evaluation of a violence prevention programme amongst African-American students conducted by Gabriel (1996), which involved classroom activities such as conflict resolution and mediation and field trips focusing on non-violence, appeared to demonstrate some reduction in levels of fighting and the carrying of weapons amongst programme participants compared with matched controls. Most strikingly in this area, however, is the general absence of significant impacts demonstrable in the bulk of programmes.

Gang violence

One of the areas in which there is some evidence of impact, though confined to the USA, is that of gang violence. That said, Sherman *et al.* (1999) note that most programmes have not been evaluated and some of those that have been assessed have noted occasional increases in gang violence. Nevertheless, there are a couple of notably successful illustrations of interventions which may have wider application. There appears to be little evidence in support of gang membership prevention. However, by contrast, there are some reasonably successful evaluations of interventions in active gangs, many of them based on the model adopted by the Chicago Area Project in which a 'detached worker' seeks to engage active gang members on the streets and 'to redirect gang energy towards legitimate activity, including school and work, as well as to discourage crime'. Greatest success appears to have involved work with individual gang members rather than the gang as a group (Klein 1971, 1995), with impact on both offending levels and gang cohesion.

The most solid findings about gangs come from a somewhat different angle and concern gun-related violence (Sherman 2001). Operation Ceasefire, in Boston, applied the principles of problem-oriented policing (Goldstein 1990) in the area of youth violence. Enforcement responses included conducting probation checks, changing community supervision conditions, serving outstanding arrest warrants, focusing special prosecutorial attention on crimes committed by violent gang members, increasing disorder enforcement and disrupting street-level drug markets (Braga and Kennedy 2002). After the implementation of Operation Ceasefire in 1996, there was a marked reduction in youth homicide in Boston. From a level of 44 youth homicides per year in the early 1990s the number fell to 26 in 1996, 15 in 1997, from where it remained roughly stable (18 in 1998 and 15 in 1999).

Community-based recreation programmes

One of the oft-repeated suggestions in the field of youth diversion is that recreational activities may have an important role in preventing or reducing crime. Once again, however, evidence in support of this hypothesis is far from plentiful. There is, for example, relatively little evidence of success in school-based activities aimed at preventing crime and delinquency (Sherman *et al.* 1999; Graham 2002) though research on community-based recreational interventions is also slight but possibly more positive. Sherman *et al.* report a Canadian study based in a public housing project which compared an after-school programme for low-income children with a public housing project that had only minimal services. During the course of the programme juvenile arrests declined markedly (by three quarters) in the 'treatment' site where, by contrast, they rose by two thirds in the comparison site. That the programme was an important factor in this was demonstrated by the fact that these effects were no longer visible a little over a year after the intervention had ceased. Although there is little other robust empirical support for such programmes, Sherman *et al.* conclude that they 'merit further research and development for their potential crime prevention benefits'.

Mentoring

Although Sherman *et al.* (1999) note that mentoring provides the highest 'dosage' of adult–child interaction of all formal community-based programmes, the results from extant research are far from unequivocally positive. As in other areas the greatest problem is the paucity of rigorous research. Sherman *et al.* assessed seven evaluations of mentoring programmes (see Table 14.5).

The most positive results were drawn from a controlled experiment evaluating the Big Brothers/Big Sisters (BBBS) programme in eight cities (Tierney *et al.* 1995). The study, described as 'tightly randomized', found that although it was unclear as to whether BBBS reduces criminality in later life, it was positively associated with substantial benefits for young people after one year:

> After spending around 12 hours monthly with their volunteer adult mentors, the treatment group children had 45 per cent less reported onset of drug abuse than the control group children, who had been put on the waiting list. They also had 27 per cent less onset of alcohol use, and 32 per cent less frequency of hitting someone. The program also reduced truancy: treatment group children skipped 52 per cent fewer days of school and 37 per cent fewer classes on days they were in school (http://www.ncjrs.org/works/chapter3.htm).

Moreover, the programme appeared to be highly cost-effective. The fact that it used volunteer mentors kept the costs down (though some cost-benefit calculations would include an opportunity cost for volunteers' time), the major financial burden being the process of matching mentors and young people. Though the potential long-term savings have not been calculated, according to Sherman and colleagues even the short-term benefits might justify government support for the programme.

Crucially, however, four of the seven projects reviewed by Sherman failed to show any evidence of success and of those that did show 'promise', most were successful at curbing the propensity for drug use, and not delinquency

Table 14.5 Selected community-based mentoring evaluations (USA)

Primary source (secondary)	Scientific methods (score)	Programme content	Programme effects
McCord 1978, 1992 Powers and Witmer 1972	5	2 visits monthly by paid male counsellors for 5.5 years with 253 at-risk boys under 12 in 1937–42; WW2 end	No effect on criminal record; treatment group did worse on diagnosed mental health
Tierney *et al.* 1995	5	Big Brothers and Sisters, 1 year for 10–14-year-olds, 60% minority and 27% abused; 3 hrs wkly	46% reduction in drug use onset, 32% reduction in hitting people, relative to controls
Green 1980 (Howell 1995)	4	Big Brothers for fatherless white boys, 1/2 day weekly for 6 months	No effects on disruptive class behaviour; no measures of drug use
Goodman 1972 (Howell 1995)	2	College student mentors of 10–11-year-old boys 6 hrs wkly over 2 years	High control group attrition; programme effects on crime unknown
Dicken *et al.* 1997 (Howell 1995)	3	College student mentors for 6–13-year-olds, 6 hrs wkly, 4 months	No difference in teacher-rated behaviour of mentees
Fo and O'Donnell 1974 (Howell 1995)	5	12 weeks of paid community mentors with at-risk 11–17-year-olds; N = 26	Truancy reduced significantly under some conditions
Fo and O'Donnell 1975 (Howell 1995)	5	1 year of paid community mentors meeting weekly with at-risk 10–17-year-olds	Lower recidivism for treatment groups with priors, higher without

Key (scientific methods score):
5-point scale:
1 = No reliance or confidence should be placed on the results of this evaluation because of the number and type of serious shortcomings(s) in the methodology employed.
3 = Methodology rigorous in some respects, weak in others.
5 = Methodology rigorous in almost all respects.
Source: Sherman *et al.* (1999).

or offending, in the 10–14 age group only. Moreover, success was linked to the level of 'dosage' that the young person received from his or her mentor. Thus, even in the USA, where there has been greater investment in experimental and quasi-experimental social science research in the last two to three decades, the research evidence on the potential of mentoring remains remarkably slim. The UK lags even further behind with, as yet, no randomized experiments having been conducted. Until recently, the available empirical evidence was restricted to evaluations of two main programmes: the Dalston Youth Project (DYP) and CHANCE. A lot of publicity surrounded a third, Youth At Risk (YAR), but to date this has not been subject to independent published research and any claims to the contrary should be treated with considerable scepticism.

Working with young disaffected youth from one of the most deprived boroughs in England and Wales, DYP runs programmes for 11–14-year-olds and 15–18-year-olds. Both sets of programmes have been the subject of small-scale evaluative research. Research on the older age group suggests some possible impact on self-reported offending and truancy – though not drug use – but, unfortunately, the numbers involved in the study are far too small to allow for the results to be treated with anything other than considerable caution (Webb 1997). Further evaluative research (Tarling et al. 2001) on the DYP 11–14 programme found mixed results. Using fairly broad criteria of 'success' and 'failure' (relating to engagement with the programme and subsequent functioning), small numbers of interviews with participants and no comparison or control, the authors suggest that DYP worked successfully with about half those involved. However, about half 'did not engage with the project in any meaningful way' and perhaps not surprisingly therefore the impact on offending behaviour was disappointing and gains in other areas such as behaviour, attitudes and learning were modest.

The second significant UK mentoring programme subject to evaluation – over three years – was CHANCE, established in 1996 to work with primary school-aged children with behavioural problems. The evaluation was again extremely small scale, involving interviews with only 16 children and similar numbers of mentors and parents (St James-Roberts and Samlal Singh 2001). A more recent, and robust, study in the UK evaluated 10 mentoring programmes focusing on highly disadvantaged young people (Newburn and Shiner 2005). Combining a longitudinal survey of a large group of participants, a sizeable comparison group and considerable qualitative research, the study found that mentoring had the potential to effect substantial changes in the lives of disaffected young people, particularly in relation to engagement with education, training and employment. Results in relation to offending were more mixed. Fairly sizeable reductions in offending were measured during the course of the one-year mentoring programmes (see Figure 14.2) and these were maintained during the six-month follow-up period. However, substantial and in some cases more marked reductions in offending were reported by non-participants in the programme with the consequence that the changes that were apparent amongst those young people involved in mentoring could not with any confidence be attributed to the programme. The research also found little evidence of impact on participants' use of illicit drugs. At the start of the

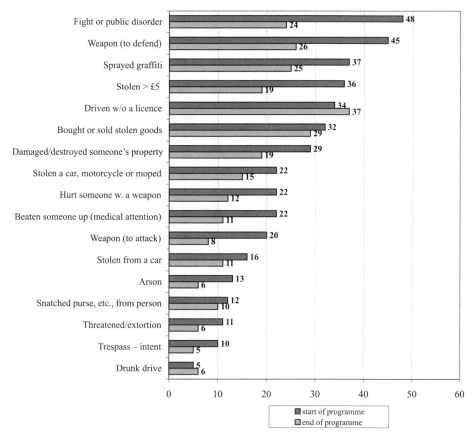

Figure 14.2 Levels of offending at the start and end of the programme (per cent in cohort)
Source: Shiner *et al.* (2004).

programme drug use was more widespread amongst participants than non-participants and these differences continued to be evident during the period covered by the programme as overall levels of use remained very stable amongst both participants and non-participants.

Current research evidence suggests that mentoring is, to borrow Sherman *et al.*'s terminology, a 'promising approach'. Indeed, there are indications that it has real potential to improve individual functioning. However, the spread of programmes without rigorous evaluation runs a number of risks. One is simply that in the same way that the stock of mentoring rose so it will fall; in the short to medium term the fashion may change and attention may turn away from mentoring towards another untested intervention. The opportunity to assess the benefits of mentoring will have been lost. Secondly, and more dangerously, it is possible of course that interventions such as mentoring do more harm than good. It is this possibility, at least as much as the positive potential, that should concentrate the mind of the policy-maker and practitioner on the need for rigorous evaluation.

Conclusions

In the UK at least there has been something of a sea change in the primary ways in which youth 'diversion' or, perhaps more accurately, youth crime prevention is conceived. Where 20–30 years ago the dominant philosophy sought to minimize the level of contact between the young offender and the formal justice system, now it is the case that early intervention and, increasingly, more extensive intervention in the lives of young offenders, is the preferred approach. Not only do the approaches differ but, perhaps predictably, the ways in which their 'success' is assessed also varies. Although attention has always in part focused on recidivism rates, for many proponents of 1980s-style diversion, success was often measured by declining numbers of young offenders processed by criminal justice agencies or, at the most serious end, in the declining use of incarceration. In other words, rather than a means to an end (crime prevention) diversion progressively became an end in itself. However, the rise of the 'what works' movement has focused attention firmly on attempting to measure how and why different measures affect levels and types of offending by young people. This is far from uncontested within academic criminology, where there is considerable debate about the appropriateness both of increasing formal interventions with young offenders and the centrality given to the measurement and evaluation of these interventions.

In fact, even in its own terms, research evidence about 'what works' with young offenders remains slight and in most cases rather inconclusive. Much of the research that has been undertaken is poorly equipped to provide the kinds of evidence that is sought, with the vast majority of what has been done in the name of 'evaluation' in this area being small in scale, slight in ambition or poor in execution.[4] The consequence, as the review above demonstrates, is that we remain some distance from having clear and robust messages for those attempting to design interventions that will prevent youthful offending or mitigate criminal careers. There are some promising signs emerging from research on restorative justice-influenced programmes, from some cognitive approaches and from community-based mentoring programmes. However, it is difficult not to conclude without a somewhat clichéd plea for more, and for more robust, research. We might finish, however, by returning to some of the diversionary ideas of the 1980s. Nor did such cautions bring with them all the interventionist accoutrements of the current final-warning system. There is perhaps some case, therefore, for the return to a more obviously bifurcated system in which interventions with first-time and the least serious young offenders are minimized, whilst engaging in a more robust attempt to identify evidence-based community and criminal justice interventions for the more serious and more persistent young offender.

Selected further reading

Good overviews of developments in youth justice since the 1970s can be found in John Muncie's *Youth and Crime* (2004) and Roger Smith's *Youth Justice: Ideas, Policy, Practice* (2003). Further useful analyses and critiques can be found in Barry Goldson's

The New Youth Justice (2000) and John Pitts' The New Politics of Youth Crime: Discipline or Solidarity (2003). Those interested in the vast literature on what used to be called 'juvenile delinquency' and is now more often referred to as offending and/or anti-social behaviour should read Michael Rutter and colleagues' Antisocial Behaviour by Young People (1998). The two best reviews of interventions in this area are that produced by Lawrence Sherman and colleagues for the National Institute of Justice, Preventing Crime: What Works, What Doesn't, What's Promising (1999) and the parallel Home Office collection edited by Goldblatt and Lewis, Reducing Offending: An Assessment of Research Evidence (1998), recently updated by Harper and Chitty as The Impact of Corrections on Re-offending: A Review of 'What Works' (2005).

Notes

1. Developmental preventive measures are covered in Chapter 4, this volume.
2. The Northamptonshire model was later commended by the Audit Commission (1996) and influenced the shape of the Final Warning Scheme and even youth offending teams introduced by the Crime and Disorder Act 1998.
3. Further, the somewhat intangible connection of practice and outcomes in social work (Meyerson 1991) arguably makes efficacy of interventions with young offenders extremely difficult to define and assess.
4. An extreme example of the inadequacy of much current research in the UK is to be found in a recent Youth Justice Board publication. Outlining a generic reconviction study of 16 crime prevention projects the report offered the following description of the method adopted in its reconviction study: 'Nine of the sixteen projects were excluded from the study for a number of reasons. This was either as a result of no young people being directly worked with or inappropriate groups of young people being targeted, i.e. classes of school pupils. A total of 216 cases were initially sent by the seven projects – this decreased to 168 as a result of the Home Office being unable to match 48 of the young people on the PNC [Police National Computer]. This declined further, with a sample of only 26 being involved in the study. This was due to data being both patchy and incomplete, and including young people starting an intervention outside the sample period. This is clearly a significantly low number, and the results should be interpreted with caution; however, it does provide some insight into the impact of the programme and adds weight to the data and information presented already on the effectiveness of the projects.'

References

Altschuler, D.M. (1998) 'Intermediate sanctions and community treatment for serious and violent juvenile offenders', in R. Loeber and D.P. Farrington (eds) Serious and Violent Juvenile Offenders: Risk Factors and Successful Interventions. Thousand Oaks, CA: Sage.

Audit Commission (1996) Misspent Youth. London: Audit Commission.

Ball, C. (2000) 'The Youth Justice and Criminal Evidence Act 1999, Part I', Criminal Law Review, 211–22.

Ball, C. (2004) 'Youth justice? Half a century of responses to youth offending', Criminal Law Review (50th anniversary edition).

Becker, H. (1963) Outsiders: Studies in the Sociology of Deviance. New York, NY: Free Press.

Bell, A., Hodgson, M. and Pragnell, S. (1999) 'Diverting children and young people from crime and the criminal justice system', in B. Goldson (ed.) *Youth Justice: Contemporary Policy and Practice*. London: Ashgate.

Bottoms, A.E., Brown, P., McWilliams, B., McWilliams, W. and Nellis, M. (1990) *Intermediate Treatment and Juvenile Justice: Key Findings and Implications from a National Survey of Intermediate Treatment Policy and Practice*. London: HMSO.

Braga, A. and Kennedy, D. (2002) 'Reducing gang violence in Boston', in W. Reed and S. Decker (eds) *Responding to Gangs: Evaluation and Research*. Washington, DC: US Department of Justice.

Cann, J., Falshaw, L., Nugent, F. and Friendship, C. (2003) *Understanding What Works: Accredited Cognitive Skills Programmes for Adult Men and Young Offenders. Findings 226*, London: Home Office.

Chenery, S. and Pease, K. (2000) 'The Burnley/Dordrecht Initiative final report'. Burnley: University of Huddersfield/Safer Cities Partnership, unpublished.

Crawford, A. and Newburn, T. (2003) *Youth Offending and Restorative Justice: Implementing Reform in Youth Justice*. Cullompton: Willan Publishing.

Dicken, C., Bryson, R. and Kass, N. (1977) 'Companionship therapy: a replication in experimental community psychology', *Journal of Consulting and Clinical Psychology*, 45: 637–46.

Emler, N. (2001) *Self-esteem: The Costs and Causes of Low Self Worth*. York: Joseph Rowntree Foundation

Feeley, M. and Simon, J. (1992) 'The new penology', *Criminology*, 30: 452–74.

Feilzer, M., Appleton, C., Roberts, C. and Hoyle, C. (2004) *Cognitive Behaviour Projects*. London: Youth Justice Board.

Feld, B. (1988) 'The juvenile court', in M. Tonry (ed.) *The Handbook of Crime and Punishment*. New York, NY: Oxford University Press.

Fo, W.S.O. and O'Donnell, C.R. (1974) 'The Buddy system: relationship and contingency conditioning in a community intervention program for youth with nonprofessionals as behavior change agents', *Journal of Consulting and Clinical Psychology*, 42: 163–9.

Fo, W.S.O. and O'Donnell, C.R. (1975) 'The Buddy system: effect of community intervention on delinquent offenses', *Behavior Therapy*, 6: 522–4.

Gabriel, R.M. (1996) *Self-enhancement, Inc. Violence Prevention Program*. Portland, OR: RMC Research.

Gendreau, P., Goggin, C. and Fulton, B. (2000) 'Intensive supervision in probation and parole settings', in C.R. Hollin (ed.) *Handbook of Offender Assessment and Treatment*. Chichester: Wiley.

Goldblatt, P. and Lewis, C. (1998) *Reducing Offending: An Assessment of Research Evidence on Ways of Dealing with Offending Behaviour. Home Office Research Study 187*. London: HMSO.

Goldson, B (2000) 'Whither diversion? Interventionism and the new youth justice', in B. Goldson (ed.) *The New Youth Justice*. Lyme Regis: Russell House Publishing.

Goldson, B. (2005) 'Beyond formalism: towards "informal" approaches to youth crime and youth justice', in T. Bateman and J. Pitts (eds) *The RHP Companion to Youth Justice*. Lyme Regis: Russell House Publishing.

Goldstein, H. (1990) *Problem-oriented Policing*. New York, NY: McGraw-Hill.

Goodman, G. (1972) *Companionship Therapy: Studies in Structured Intimacy*. San Francisco, CA: Jossey-Bass.

Gottfredson, D.C. and Gottfredson, G.D. (1992) 'Theory-guided investigation: three field experiments', in J. McCord and R.E. Tremblay (eds) *Preventing Antisocial Behaviour*. New York, NY: Guilford Press.

Graham, J. (2002) 'What works in preventing criminality', in P. Goldblatt and C. Lewis (eds) *Reducing Offending: An Assessment of Research Evidence on Ways of Dealing with Offending Behaviour*. London: Home Office.

Green, B.C. (1980) 'An evaluation of a Big Brothers' program for father-absent boys: an eco-behavioral analysis.' PhD dissertation, New York University.

Guerra, N.G. (1998) 'Serious and violent juvenile offenders: gaps in knowledge and research priorities', in R. Loeber and D.P. Farrington (eds) *Serious and Violent Juvenile Offenders: Risk Factors and Successful Interventions*. Thousand Oaks, CA: Sage.

Haines, K. (2000) 'Referral orders and youth offender panels: restorative approaches and the new youth justice', in B. Goldson (ed.) *The New Youth Justice*. Lyme Regis: Russell House Publishing.

Haines, K. and Drakeford, M (1998) *Young People and Youth Justice*. London: Macmillan.

Harper, G. and Chitty, C. (2005) *The Impact of Corrections on Re-offending: A Review of 'What Works'*. London: Home Office.

Holdaway, S. and Desborough, S. (2004) *The National Evaluation of the Youth Justice Board's Final Warning Projects*. London: Youth Justice Board.

Home Office (1985) *The Cautioning of Offenders. Home Office Circular 14/1985*. London: Home Office.

Home Office (1988) *Punishment, Custody and the Community* (Cm 424). London: HMSO.

Home Office (1990a) *Crime, Justice and Protecting the Public*. London: Home Office.

Home Office (1990b) *The Cautioning of Offenders. Home Office Circular 59/1990*. London: Home Office.

Home Office (1995) *Cautions, Court Proceedings and Sentencing, England and Wales 1994*. London: Home Office.

Home Office (1997) *No More Excuses: A New Approach to Tackling Youth Crime in England and Wales*. London: HMSO.

Hope, T. (1995) 'Community crime prevention', in M. Tonry and D.P. Farrington (eds) *Building a Safer Society. Crime and Justice. Vol. 19*. Chicago, IL: University of Chicago Press.

Hope, T., Worrall, A., Dunkerton, L. and Leacock, V. (2001) 'The Newcastle Prolific Offenders Project final evaluation report.' Keele: Keele University/Staffordshire Probation Area, unpublished.

Howell, J.C. (ed.) (1995) *Guide for Implementing the Comprehensive Strategy for Serious, Violent, and Chronic Juvenile Offenders*. Washington, DC: OJJDP.

Hoyle, C., Young, R. and Hill, R. (2002) *Proceed with Caution: An Evaluation of the Thames Valley Police Initiative in Restorative Cautioning*. York: Joseph Rowntree Foundation.

Jennings, D. (2002) *One Year Juvenile Reconviction Rates: July 2000 Cohort*. London: RDSD.

Jones, D. (1989) 'The successful revolution', *Community Care*, 30 March.

Jones, R. (1984) 'Questioning the new orthodoxy', *Community Care*, 11 October.

Junger-Tas, M. (1994) *Alternatives to Prison Sentences: Experiences and Developments*. Amsterdam: Kugler.

Kemp, V., Sorsby, A., Liddle, M. and Merrington, S. (2002) *Assessing Responses to Youth Offending in Northamptonshire. Research Briefing 2*. London: Nacro.

Klein, M.W. (1971) *Street Gangs and Street Workers*. Englewood Cliffs, NJ: Prentice Hall.

Krisberg, B. and Howell, J.C. (1998) 'The impact of the juvenile justice system and prospects for graduated sanctions in a comprehensive strategy', in R. Loeber and D.P. Farrington (eds) *Serious and Violent Juvenile Offenders: Risk Factors and Successful Interventions*. Thousand Oaks, CA: Sage.

Leacock, V. and Sparks, J.R. (2002) 'Riskiness and at-risk-ness: some ambiguous features of the current penal landscape', in N. Gray *et al.* (eds) *Criminal Justice, Mental Health and the Politics of Risk.* London: Cavendish.

Lemert, E. (1970) *Social Action and Legal Challenge: Revolution within the Juvenile Court.* Chicago, IL: Aldine.

Lipsey, M.W. (1992) 'The effect of treatment on juvenile delinquents: results from meta-analyses', in F. Losel *et al.* (eds) *Psychology and the Law: International Perspectives.* Berlin: de Gyuyter.

Lipsey, M.W. and Wilson, D.B. (1998) 'Effective intervention for serious juvenile offenders', in R. Loeber and Farrington, D.P. (eds) *Serious and Violent Juvenile Offenders: Risk Factors and Successful Interventions.* Thousand Oaks, CA: Sage.

MacKenzie, D.L. and Souryal, C. (1994) *Multisite Evaluation of Shock Incarceration.* Washington DC: National Institute of Justice.

Mair, G., Lloyd, C., Nee, C. and Sibbett, R. (1994) *Intensive Probation in England and Wales: An Evaluation.* London: Home Office.

McCord, J. (1978) 'A thirty-year followup of treatment effects', *The American Psychologist,* 33: 284–389.

McCord, J. (1992) 'Understanding motivations: considering altruism and aggression', in J. McCord (ed.) *Facts, Frameworks, Forecasts: Advances in Criminological Theory.* New Brunswick, NJ: Transaction.

Meyerson, D.E. (1991) '"Normal" ambiguity? A glimpse of an occupational culture', in P.J. Frost *et al.* (eds) *Reframing Organizational Culture.* Newbury Park, CA: Sage.

Moore, R. (2004) 'Intensive supervision and surveillance programmes for young offenders: the evidence base so far', in R. Burnett and C. Roberts (eds) *What Works in Probation and Youth Justice: Developing Evidence-based Practice.* Cullompton: Willan Publishing.

Morgan, Harris, Burrows (2003) *Evaluation of the Youth Inclusion Programme.* London: Youth Justice Board (available at http://www.youth-justice-board.gov.uk/NR/rdonlyres/535965FD-508A-4838-B890-4E4F9E337B2B/221/YIPevaluation2003.pdf).

Morris, A. and Gelsthorpe, L. (2000) 'Something old, something borrowed, something blue, but something new? A comment on the prospects for restorative justice under the Crime and Disorder Act 1998', *Criminal Law Review,* 18–30.

Muncie, J. (2000) 'Pragmatic realism? Searching for criminology in the new youth justice', in B. Goldson (ed.) *The New Youth Justice.* Lyme Regis: Russell House Publishing.

Muncie, J. (2002) 'A new deal for youth? Early intervention and correctionalism', in G. Hughes *et al.* (eds) *Crime Prevention and Community Safety: New Directions.* London: Sage.

Muncie, J. (2004) *Youth and Crime* (2nd edn). London: Sage.

Nacro (1987) *Time for Change: A New Framework for Dealing with Juvenile Crime and Offenders.* London: Nacro.

Nacro (1991) *Seizing the Initiative: Nacro's Final Report on the DHSS Intermediate Treatment Initiative to Divert Juvenile Offenders from Care and Custody: 1983–1989.* London: Nacro.

Nellis, M. (1995) 'Probation values for the 1990s', *Howard Journal,* 34: 19–44.

Newburn, T. (1996) 'Back to the future? Youth crime, youth justice and the rediscovery of "authoritarian populism"', in J. Pilcher and S. Wagg (eds) *Thatcher's Children? Politics, Childhood and Society in the 1980s and 1990s.* Lewis: Falmer Press.

Newburn, T. and Shiner, M. (2005) *Dealing with Disaffection.* Cullompton: Willan Publishing.

Parker, H., Sumner, M. and Jarvis, G. (1989) *Unmasking the Magistrates: The 'Custody or Not' Decision in Sentencing Young Offenders.* Milton Keynes: Open University Press.

Petersilia, J. and Turner, S. (1992) 'An evaluation of intensive probation in California', *Journal of Criminal Law and Criminology*, 83: 61–58.

Pitts, J. (1999) *Working with Young Offenders* (2nd edn). London: Macmillan.

Pitts, J. (2000) 'The new youth justice and the politics of electoral anxiety', in B. Goldson (ed.) *The New Youth Justice*. Lyme Regis: Russell House Publishing.

Pitts, J. (2001) 'The new correctionalism: young people, youth justice and New Labour', in R. Matthews and J. Pitts (eds) *Crime, Disorder and Community Safety*. London: Routledge.

Pitts, J. (2003) *The New Politics of Youth Crime: Discipline or Solidarity*. Lyme Regis: Russell House Publishing.

Pitts, J (2005) 'The recent history of youth justice in England and Wales', in T. Bateman and J. Pitts (eds) *The RHP Companion to Youth Justice*. Lyme Regis: Russell House Publishing.

Pollard, C. (2000) 'Victims and the criminal justice system: a new vision', *Criminal Law Review*, 1–17.

Porporino, F.J. and Fabiano, E.A. (2000) *Theory Manual for Reasoning and Rehabilitation*. Prepared for the Joint Prison Probation Service Accreditation Panel.

Powers, E. and Witmer, H. (1972) *An Experiment in the Prevention of Delinquency: The Cambridge–Somerville Youth Study*. Montclair, NJ: Patterson Smith.

Rasmussen, D. and Yu, Y. (1996) *An Evaluation of Juvenile Justice Interventions in Duval County, Florida*. Tallahassee, FL: Florida State University.

Rojek, C., Peacock, G. and Collins, S. (1988) *Social Work and Received Ideas*. London: Routledge

Rutherford, A. (1986) *Growing out of Crime*. Harmondsworth: Penguin Books.

Rutter, M., Giller, H. and Hagell, A. (1998) *Antisocial Behaviour by Young People*. Cambridge: Cambridge University Press.

Sherman, L. (2001) 'Reducing gun violence: what works, what doesn't, what's promising', *Criminal Justice*, 1: 11–25.

Sherman, L., Gottfredson, D., MacKenzie, J.E., Reuter, P. and Bushway, S. (1999) *Preventing Crime: What Works, What Doesn't, What's Promising – a Report to the United States Congress*. National Institute of Justice, Department of Criminology and Criminal Justice, University of Maryland.

Shiner, M., Young, T., Newburn, T. and Groben, S. (2004) *Mentoring Disaffected Young People: An Evaluation of Mentoring Plus*. York: Joseph Rowntree Foundation.

Smith, D.J. (1997) 'Race, crime and criminal justice', in M. Maguire *et al.* (eds) *The Oxford Handbook of Criminology*. Oxford: Clarendon Press.

Smith, R. (2003) *Youth Justice: Ideas, Policy, Practice*. Cullompton: Willan Publishing.

Stevens, M. and Crook, J. (1986) 'What the devil is intermediate treatment?', *Social Work Today*, 8 September.

St James-Roberts, I. and Samlal Singh, C. (2001) *Can Mentors Help Primary School Children with Behaviour Problems?* London: Home Office.

Straw, J. and Michael, A. (1996) *Tackling Youth Crime: Reforming Youth Justice: A Consultation Paper on an Agenda for Change*. London: Labour Party.

Tarling, R., Burrows, J. and Clarke, A. (2001) *Dalston Youth Project Part II (11–14): An Evaluation*. London: Home Office

Tierney, J.P., Baldwin Grossman, J. and Resch, N.L. (1995) *Making a Difference: An Impact Study of Big Brothers/Big Sisters*. Philadelphia, PA: Public/Private Ventures.

Wasserman, G.A. and Miller, L.S. (1998) 'The prevention of serious and violent juvenile offending', in R. Loeber and D.P. Farrington (eds) *Serious and Violent Juvenile Offenders: Risk Factors and Successful Interventions*. Thousand Oaks, CA: Sage.

Webb, J. (1997) *Dalston Youth Project Programmes 1, 2, and 3 for Young People Aged 15–18 Years: Summary of the Evaluations*. Report prepared for Crime Concern and the Dalston Youth Project.

Wilcox, A., Young, R. and Hoyle, C. (2004) *An Evaluation of the Impact of Restorative Cautioning: Findings from Reconviction Study. Home Office Findings* 255. London: Home Office.

Wonnacott, C. (1999) 'The counterfeit contract – reform, pretence and muddled principles in the new referral order', *Child and Family Law Quarterly*, 11: 271–87.

Worrall, A. and Mawby, R.C. (2004) 'Intensive projects for prolific/persistent offenders', in A. Bottoms *et al.* (eds) *Alternatives to Prison: Options for an Insecure Society.* Cullompton: Willan Publishing.

Worrall, A., Mawby, R.C., Heath, G. and Hope, T. (2003) *Intensive Supervision and Monitoring Projects. Home Office Online Report* 42/03. London: Home Office.

Young, R. and Goold, B. (1999) 'Restorative police cautioning in Aylesbury – from degrading to reintegrative shaming ceremonies?', *Criminal Law Review*, 126–38.

Chapter 15

Shifting and sharing police responsibility to address public safety problems

Michael S. Scott

The police throughout developed nations are held responsible for addressing a very wide range of social problems[1] that affect public safety. Dealing with the whole of these problems and with each particular problem is, in and of itself, complex, both in understanding the social conditions that give rise to them and in meeting the legal requirements for responding to them. Problems fall to the police for attention for various reasons. Some problems, such as murder, robbery of shops and house burglary, being serious crimes, fall squarely within widely assumed areas of police responsibility. That police should assume some responsibility for addressing these sorts of problems is nearly uncontestable. Other problems, however, such as clearing away abandoned vehicles, rounding up stray animals or taking care of inebriated persons, are only marginally police responsibilities. The argument that police should bear the primary responsibility for addressing them is weaker, although often these duties fall to the police, none the less.

The police are but one institution established to deal with breaches of law and order. But unlike other institutions whose job in maintaining order is rather narrowly prescribed, the police have a residual function. In addition to being seen as the agency of first call when a crime has been committed, they are called on to handle a wide array of other situations in which something has gone wrong – matters that do not clearly fall within the purview of others and where an immediate response is required. To a large extent, problems become police responsibilities when other formal and informal social mechanisms for controlling them have failed; when some degree of coercive authority is deemed necessary for control (Bittner 1970). Historically, this has left the police in a reactive posture, their role defined largely by the default of others in adequately addressing problems.

Precisely what duties and responsibilities police agencies assume varies considerably across jurisdictions. Each police agency's mandate evolves over time through a complex process involving legislation, judicial rulings, labour contract negotiations, budget deliberations, executive orders, community demands and political pressures. This is particularly the case in the USA where control of the police rests largely with local governments. Consequently, there can be no universal objective standard by which to determine what are the proper duties and functions of any one police agency: each agency negotiates this within the context of its political and legal environment.

Whilst the volume and complexity of matters the public expects the police to handle accumulate, the capacity of the police, in the form of resources, authority and tactics, remains limited. They cannot assume responsibility for an endless volume and variety of problems. Were police to attempt to assume sole, or even primary, responsibility for addressing such a wide range of problems, such an overwhelming mandate would jeopardize their effectiveness, their efficiency and their capacity to deliver their service in a fair and equitable fashion.

The police must have a means to reverse or minimally control the usual process by which they inherit responsibility for problems; to identify such matters and turn to those within society who are better positioned to take on the responsibility for dealing with them. Where there is reliable knowledge that certain problems can be more effectively controlled by those entities that most directly control the conditions giving rise to those problems, the police have an interest in seeing the responsibility for doing so shifted accordingly. Where it becomes clear that police resources are being disproportionately consumed by reacting to a high volume of incidents, the police are obliged to seek out more efficient methods of either preventing the incidents or, at a minimum, seeing that they are more efficiently handled. And where conventional responses to problems are producing inequitable distributions of police resources and subjecting certain groups disproportionately to the coercive powers of the police, the police are obliged at least to contribute to a public discussion about an equitable apportionment of costs and responsibilities.

Historically, the police have not been adept at marshalling arguments for shifting and sharing responsibility for addressing many public safety problems. For a variety of reasons, the police have endeavoured to meet most new demands placed upon them, however futilely, and at great cost to particular police agencies and the police institution. The police institution lacks a strong tradition for analysing data to bolster arguments as to who ought to do what to control public safety problems. The police are only recently beginning to explore this issue and to adopt a role as broker of responsibility.

Popular conceptions of community policing (or partnership policing) produce images of community groups poised and willing to assist the police in any fashion to fight crime and disorder. Whilst this is sometimes the case, nearly as often it is the case that the community, or some segment thereof, stands reluctant to assume any greater responsibility for crime and disorder, particularly when its own interests, practices or policies are challenged.[2] And so, the police increasingly find themselves in the position of brokering and apportioning the duties and responsibilities of the various entities that have a stake or interest in problems.

In the parlance of economics, the police must find ways to get those who create or contribute to crime and disorder to internalize those costs, to create incentives to shift the costs currently borne by the police (and consequently, by the general tax-paying public) to those who control the conditions that give rise to crime and disorder, and who sometimes profit under the existing arrangements for addressing the problems (Hough and Tilley 1998; see also Chisolm 2000; Hornick *et al.* 2000 for discussions of the economic analysis of crime prevention).

That the police should take the initiative in redistributing responsibility for addressing public safety problems makes sense largely because it is to them that the consequences of societal failures to address problems so often fall. The individuals, groups or agencies contributing to a problem may not even know the problem exists until it is called to their attention by the police; and they may not have any idea as to its magnitude and social costs without the police telling them. And even if they do have a full awareness of the problem, they may have no knowledge about the options for dealing with it, whereas the police bring a much greater body of knowledge and experience to bear.

Effective crime control

Only in the past 30 years has research shed much light on the effect of various police practices on crime and disorder problems (Tonry and Farrington 1995; Sherman *et al.* 1997; Goldblatt and Lewis 1998; US Department of Justice, Office of Community Oriented Policing Services 2000 et seq.; National Research Council 2003; Weisburd and Eck 2004). Whilst the research evidence is far from conclusive with respect to many – indeed, most – police practices, some reasonably reliable conclusions are beginning to emerge. Where the police seek to control problems through the direct exercise of their authority or through their visible presence (that is, where police action serves as the mechanism by which problems are prevented or controlled), the police can have a positive impact on problems to the extent their actions are highly focused on particularly problematic locations and/or persons. Where police actions are unfocused – diffusely applied to many places and persons – their effectiveness is rather limited (National Research Council 2004). This conclusion should lead the police to become more focused in their direct actions.

Direct police actions – most typically in the form of visible police presence, stopping and questioning suspects, arresting or warning violators, building prosecutable cases against offenders, etc. – are all grounded in classical deterrence theory. They seek to control crime and disorder by making potential offenders believe they are likely to be apprehended by the police and, if apprehended, subjected to swift, certain and severe punishment. In many instances, however, the deterrence model fails because the certainty of apprehension is not sufficiently high for the consequences of apprehension to have much effect on offenders' decision-making.

Indirect police action, whereby the police seek to convince or compel others to take actions which in turn will control particular crime and disorder problems, holds significant promise for controlling crime and disorder problems (Laycock and Tilley 1994; Buerger 1998). Increasingly, it is in this realm of activity that the police should improve their knowledge and skill. This notion is reinforced by criminological theories that stress the importance of opportunity (Felson and Clarke 1998). If the opportunities for problems can be controlled, the problem behaviour itself stands to be better controlled. For the most part, the police themselves have limited control or influence over the social and environmental conditions that create these opportunities for problem behaviour: others often have more.

Methods for achieving a shift in responsibility for public safety problems

The police can apply a range of methods to get others to assume greater responsibility for public safety problems (Goldstein 1996). A range of methods varies in terms of the degree of pressure or coercion the police apply to achieve their objectives.

In its ultimate form, police efforts to shift responsibility for public safety problems would entail the police assisting others to develop a capacity to identify and rectify problems without the need for police intervention. A prime example occurs where the police work at the neighbourhood level to help residents develop what sociologists term 'collective efficacy' or 'the ability of neighbourhoods to realize the common values of residents and maintain effective social controls' (Sampson *et al.* 1997). Short of a complete shift in responsibility for a public safety problem, in most instances the police will look to shift part of the responsibility (or share it) with regard to a specific problem or set of problems, bounded in time and location.

The methods described in Box 15.1, originally conceived by Goldstein (1996), are not intended to be exhaustive or definitive, but rather illustrative. The methods begin with those that generally are the least coercive measures and proceed to those that are generally increasingly coercive.

Assigning responsibility for addressing problems

There are few firm rules that dictate who is primarily responsible for addressing particular public safety problems. What rules, for example, dictate who bears primary responsibility for a retail theft problem: the police, the shop, consumers, the insurance carrier? For every problem there are several entities that contribute to the problem and therefore plausibly bear some responsibility for its remediation. The factors that determine legal and moral responsibility for public safety problems, as well as the processes and sources of authority under which such determinations are made, merit further discussion, but are beyond the scope of this chapter.

Factors determining the appropriate degree of pressure the police ought to bring to bear

Much of the art of policing is in determining the appropriate degree of pressure or coercion that ought to be brought to bear on a situation in order to resolve it. Police officials who elect to try to shift responsibility for public safety problems

Box 15.1 Methods of police pressure on others to accept responsibility for community problems (from least degree of pressure to greatest)

- Educating others regarding their responsibility for the problem.

- Making a straightforward informal request of some entity to assume responsibility for the problem.

- Making a targeted confrontational request of some entity to assume responsibility for the problem.

- Engaging another existing organization that has the capacity to help address the problem.

- Pressing for the creation of a new organization to assume responsibility for the problem.

- Shaming the delinquent entity by calling public attention to its failure to assume responsibility for the problem.

- Withdrawing police services relating to certain aspects of the problem.

- Charging fees for police services related to the problem.

- Pressing for legislation mandating that entities take measures to prevent the problem.

- Bringing a civil action to compel entities to accept responsibility for the problem.

must consider, amongst other factors: the justification for the pressure in the first instance (including the costs borne by the police and the community in the status quo); the reasonableness of the police requests of others (including the standards of proof the police must carry to establish that reasonableness); the probability that a new set of responses to the problem will have long-term preventive value; the likelihood that key constituents will endorse or accept the new police proposals (which is influenced by the complexity of the issue at hand); and the nature and degree of, and consequences for, resistance to police attempts to share or shift responsibility (including the potential risks and costs to the police organization and its officials for pressing controversial proposals).[3]

A central theme that emerges from reviewing problem-oriented policing initiatives is that in most instances the police do not set out with an overriding objective to divest themselves of responsibility for various and sundry tasks, but rather their efforts to shift responsibility for addressing particular problems is the direct product of a careful analysis of the factors giving rise to problems with the objective of developing a new response to the problem that is more effective. It is on the basis of careful exploration of problems that the police are led to conclude that somebody ought to be doing something different to control that problem better. And whilst some individuals will not question the basis on which the police make such requests, police requests are greatly strengthened if they can explain persuasively the rationale for the request, including how compliance with the request will address the problem, the basis for police knowledge about the effectiveness of the proposed response, what measures the police have already taken to resolve the problem, the limitations of those measures and the benefits to all concerned if new practices are adopted voluntarily.

Increased usage of this process for brokering responsibility is the result of several factors in policing: the new emphasis on being proactive and on prevention; the new emphasis on and capabilities to conduct detailed analysis of the police workload; the resulting recognition that incidents often cluster around a concentrated source which, if dealt with effectively, has the potential greatly to reduce the magnitude of the problem; and the new emphasis that police agencies deliver value for money.

The process leading up to police efforts to shift or share responsibility typically involves documenting the magnitude of the specific problem, identifying the conditions contributing to the problem and establishing the link between those conditions and the individual, business or organization deemed responsible for them. Thus, the gathering of detailed information, including statistical data, is an integral part of the process *before* it moves forward. Emphasis is placed on the accuracy and fairness of the documentation in order to present the strongest possible case.

Some might express discomfort with the police dealing with citizens in so heavy-handed a manner. Those concerns are certainly justified if requests are made, with the threat of more serious action, without supporting facts. A high standard of care in putting together those facts is an effective protection from such abuse. In-depth inquiry into a specific problem may clearly identify the problem and even point to specific preventive measures that seem warranted and are potentially effective. The collection of hard data about a specific problem plays a central role in establishing the need for the organization in the first instance, in convincing others as to the seriousness of the problem, and as evidence where the prevention strategies involve taking legal actions. Ideally, data would also be collected in order to evaluate the effectiveness of the strategies employed. The police must realize that efforts to shift responsibility can become an adversarial process in which they had best be prepared to document thoroughly both the conditions being exposed and the evidence they have that the person being named is indeed responsible for them. And they should be confident that the measures that they are pressing to be adopted are likely to be effective. Particularly when the proposed shift in responsibility has a major economic impact, the police can anticipate that the proposed action will be challenged in the courts, and that judges will become involved in weighing the adequacy of the evidence offered in support of adoption of the regulation.

Emerging trends in police efforts to shift responsibility for public safety problems

As the police increasingly adopt a problem-oriented approach to their work, an approach which emphasizes the careful analysis of the causes and conditions for crime and other public safety problems, and which encourages the police to seek alternatives to criminal arrest as means of preventing crime and controlling problems (Goldstein 1990), some new patterns regarding police actions are emerging. Amongst the more interesting new patterns is the increasing tendency of the police to leverage their knowledge, influence and authority to shift and share responsibility for addressing public safety problems by getting others to take actions that lead to more effective responses to problems and that alleviate the burden on the police continually to respond to repetitive incidences of crime and disorder.[4]

In the absence of systematic studies of police efforts to shift responsibility for public safety problems, it is possible to gain some cautious insights into this emerging pattern by examining cases in which the police have done so. One source of information about what the police are doing that they themselves deem innovative is police agency submissions to award programmes that recognize innovation in problem-oriented policing. The two most prominent award programmes are the Herman Goldstein Award for Excellence in Problem-oriented Policing (administered in the USA)[5] and the Tilley Award (administered in the UK)[6].

Whilst it should come as no surprise that police reports submitted to these award programmes would highlight police efforts to share and shift responsibility for public safety problems (doing so is strongly encouraged under a problem-oriented approach), one does get the impression that police agencies are finding some measure of success in their efforts to do so (Read and Tilley 2000; Scott 2000; Rojek 2003).

How one defines and measures such claims is tricky because it is often the case that the police apply several different responses to address a problem, some of which are direct actions (e.g. police enforcement, police presence) and some of which are indirect actions of the sort listed above. Teasing out the effects of each response in isolation of others is methodologically challenging. Moreover, in most instances, project reports of the type submitted to these award programmes provide an evaluation or assessment that falls short of rigorous social science standards. The evidence offered of the effectiveness, efficiency and equity of the new responses usually satisfies the standards to which the police are held, which are not always the standards of scientific research.

Much of the body of knowledge the police rely upon is based on insights the police acquired through years of experience. The value of this expertise is underestimated by those who rely only on the highest standards of social science and policy analysis to inform policy decisions and, conversely, overestimated by those who believe that 'street smarts' trump research-based knowledge. Although much police knowledge about how to prevent and control many problems is largely untested, it does not totally diminish its value. That this knowledge is sometimes packaged and presented in polished form does give it an imprimatur that carries the impression it is more scientific than is warranted. There remains a critical need to capture, test and refine police expertise, and thereby contribute to a more formal body of knowledge to support police practice. And so, whilst advocating that the police increasingly shift responsibility for public safety problems has not definitively been proven to be the correct course of action, the examples to date are none the less suggestive of a promising new direction for policing.

A discussion and examples of the successful application of each method, primarily drawn from the Goldstein and Tilley Award programmes, follow. In many instances, the police and others employ a variety of methods to address a problem, thereby complicating efforts to understand precisely what effect each method had on the overall problem. Moreover, the methods employed are not mutually exclusive. For example, where the police succeed in encouraging another agency to make confrontational requests to persons causing problems, or the police persuade a legislative body to enact a law charging special fees for police services, in effect a combination of methods has been employed.

Educating others regarding their responsibility for the problem

The police have long been involved in systematically conveying information to the public on how they can prevent crime. They do this through presentations, brochures and a variety of programmes. Some of these efforts are aimed broadly at the general public; others targeted at specific constituencies. Educational messages and programmes are directed either at potential victims (i.e. how to avoid being victimized) or potential offenders (i.e. how to avoid offending). A central theme in all these efforts is that those to whom the message is delivered are in a position to take actions that will protect themselves either from victimization or legal sanction. The educational material and presentations are generally low key: one can take the advice or ignore it. Educational messages to potential offenders adopt a helpful tone rather than a warning tone: they are aimed at people who are inclined to obey the law, but who might offend out of ignorance or carelessness:

- San Diego police analysis of the total volume of sexual assault cases drew attention to the high percentage of such cases that were acquaintance rapes involving teenagers. Using the detailed reports on each case, the sexual assault unit identified the patterns of conduct that led to the assaults. They then constructed a curriculum designed to be taught in the schools, using the facts and statistical information they derived from their study to inform students how they can reduce their risk of victimization. The initiative produced brochures – different ones for male and female students – that sought to inform students, in language and using scenarios familiar to them, about what constitutes acquaintance rape and how women can avoid being victimized by it and men avoid being accused of it (San Diego Police Department 2001).

- Collecting and analysing their experiences in dealing with crime and disorder problems in apartment complexes, police agencies are increasingly developing manuals for both landlords and tenants, and are sponsoring seminars at which such material is presented (Bureau of Justice Assistance 2000). The goal is to encourage both the tenants and the landlords to assume more of the responsibility for conditions in their housing units, and to take specific prevention measures, such as enforcement of occupancy as set forth in the leases, control over entry, locking systems, control over public areas, prohibitions against illegal activity on the premises, etc. Persuading rental property owners and managers to lease only to responsible tenants, to enforce rules governing proper behaviour on the premises, and to design and maintain properties in ways that discourage problems can be more effective than criminal law enforcement in many instances.

- The police in Plano, Texas, developed an informational presentation for the owners and managers of stores that were licensed to sell alcoholic drinks about the problem of underage drinking and what measures could be taken to help store clerks comply with the law prohibiting sales of alcohol to minors. Although sterner warnings and enforcement were essential components of this initiative, the police did learn that some clerks were confused about the law and about how to detect fraudulent attempts to purchase alcohol. Consequently, the informational programmes were more than a polite way of issuing warnings; they in fact helped some people inclined to obey the law to do so (Plano Police Department 2003).

- Police in Lancashire and in Portland, Oregon, have conducted or supported programmes to educate hotel and motel owners about methods for recognizing and preventing common crimes – ranging from burglary to prostitution to drug manufacturing – from occurring in their establishments (Lancashire Constabulary 2000; Campbell Resources, Inc. n.d.).

- To address the problem of children being hit by cars, the police in Hamilton-Wentworth, Ontario, spearheaded an initiative to develop educational materials and programmes to teach children how to cross streets safely. The materials and programmes were built upon a careful understanding of how young children best learn and apply new rules and skills and was informed by advice from traffic engineers, child educators, child-care professionals, parents and public health officials (Hamilton-Wentworth Police Department 1994).

- The police in Blackpool, UK, helped develop an educational campaign to inform visitors to this seaside resort community how to behave properly in and around licensed establishments and thereby avoid becoming either an offender or a victim (Lancashire Constabulary, n.d.).

Making a straightforward informal request of some entity to assume responsibility for the problem

The use of straightforward requests is quite naturally the first step to which the police turn when they want specific individuals to take responsibility for reducing specific problems. A positive response obviates the need for increased pressure.

Here, the police are not simply broadcasting prepared advice on prevention to a large audience. Rather, they are much more targeted in asking citizens to resolve a problem of immediate concern to them by taking a specific action. And because the request is made by the police, it carries the implication that there may be some consequences if it is ignored. Often, the police are simply informing the citizen of something he or she was not aware, and the citizen gratefully and graciously complies with the request:

- In Chula Vista, California, the police concluded that new housing developments were vulnerable to burglary because many homes were not properly designed to safeguard against it. The police developed a presentation based upon their analysis of the problem, complete with recommendations for how new homes could be designed and built to deter burglary. They made their presentation to the corporate executives of the largest housing development companies in the target area and ultimately entered into a memorandum of understanding with the developers in which developers agreed to install recommended locks and windows in all new houses, and assist the police with other burglary prevention measures. The police did not persuade the developers to agree to all their recommendations, but they achieved some improvements without resort to confrontation or coercion. Early indicators were that the new measures were contributing to significantly improved burglary rates in the target area compared to control areas (Chula Vista Police Department 2001).

- After exhaustive analysis of the problem of thefts of appliances from houses under construction, the police in Charlotte-Mecklenburg, NC, reached the conclusion that the best method of preventing such thefts was for builders to delay installing the appliances until after the house purchase had been completed and the house could be properly secured by the new owner. The police prepared a detailed presentation of their crime analysis findings to house builders and secured voluntary agreements from several builders to adopt the proposed policy. Thefts of appliances in the target area were reduced significantly (Clarke and Goldstein 2003).

Making a targeted confrontational request of some entity to assume responsibility for the problem

One of the clearest results of recent changes in policing is the increased tendency of police agencies to confront aggressively those judged to have some responsibility for a large volume of incidents that fall to the police to handle. The police typically resort to this more confrontational mode after they find that straightforward requests are ignored.

Community policing efforts, which place so much emphasis on cultivating relationships with citizens affected by problems, also contribute to increased use of confrontational requests. In having to deal with a drug house, a troublesome bar or disorderliness in a park, for example, the police may feel empowered to be more confrontational by virtue of the support they receive from aggrieved citizens.

Typically, the police document evidence of the problem and how it is caused or aggravated by the actions or inactions of certain parties. The resulting documentation is presented to the party deemed responsible, along with a request that preventive measures be taken. The hope is that, confronted with the overwhelming nature of the documentation, the party will agree to assume responsibility for taking preventive measures – out of a sense of obligation to do so. But, depending on the specific situation, the confrontation may be bolstered by subtle implications or more overt threats that failure to comply will result in more coercive measures. The potential for more coercive measures argues for a high standard of accuracy by the police in documenting conditions:

- The Peel Regional Police in Ontario made a practice of determining where persons arrested for drunken driving had their last drink. The police identified licensed establishments with a high incidence of serving persons subsequently arrested for drunken driving and forwarded this information to the local liquor-licensing board. Armed with these data, the liquor-licensing officials then confronted the owners of the problem licensed establishments, advising them to take measures to prevent recurrences. The licensing officials offered detailed advice and training for licensed establishment staff as to how to meet their legal obligations. These confrontational requests were made prior to the initiation of a formal investigation in order to give the proprietors of licensed establishments the opportunity to come into voluntary compliance with the law (Peel Regional Police 1996).

- The St Louis police informed a finance company that a residential property it financed was being used for illegal drug trafficking. This indicated to the finance company that their investment might be at risk, perhaps of being seized by the government. Realizing that an outright foreclosure and eviction of the elderly resident might bring adverse publicity for the finance company, they instead opted to pay the resident to relinquish the property and move out. The finance company then took possession of the property, thereby eliminating the drug trafficking problem (Hope 1994).

- The Miami police persuaded wholesale fruit and vegetable stallholders to improve their practices for disposing of discarded produce, to clean up and improve the appearance the commercial area in which they operated, and to improve the traffic flow and parking of commercial vehicles, all as part of an effort to reduce crime and disorder in a large commercial produce market. These improvements helped reduce the population of transient criminals in the area and alleviated traffic congestion (Miami Police Department 2002).

Engaging another existing service agency that has the capacity to help address the problem

This method involves arranging a shift of responsibility for one or more crime prevention strategies to another agency of government or to a non-profit organization providing service in the community.

Much of police business consists of handling problems and cases that fall through the cracks in the 'social net' or constitute an overflow stemming from the limited resources of other agencies – for example, mentally ill persons who are not adequately cared for in the community; drug addicts who do not receive treatment services; parks, playgrounds and housing developments that are not adequately maintained; and cars and homes that are abandoned, etc.

In-depth inquiry of the type called for in problem-oriented policing often identifies a default or a gap in service that, if corrected, would potentially reduce the problem. Initially drawn to police attention as a crime or law enforcement problem, penetrating inquiry often redefines the problem and more clearly identifies the conditions contributing to it. Thus, a problem initially reported as disorderly, threatening teenagers may, on analysis, turn out to be a problem of strained relationships between senior citizens and teenagers brought on by the policies of a neighbouring school. Engaging the school authorities in exploring preventive strategies may well result in their taking responsibility for them.

When the police identify preventive strategies which they then broker to other agencies, this can cause tensions with those agencies. Other agencies often resent what they perceive as police efforts to set their agendas or to off-load work on to them. This is particularly so during periods of retrenchment in government spending when budgets are limited.

The health, streets and building inspection departments in local authorities, and the not-for-profit organizations serving, for example, the mentally ill, battered women and run-away children must weigh the initiatives recommended by the police against other priorities. The documentation of the case by the police, and the links they are able to establish between what they find and what they recommend, are critically important.

Equally important is for the police to try to establish an atmosphere of trust and mutual understanding between themselves and the agencies whose interests overlap those of the police. The whole movement towards greater institutional partnerships has been tremendously important in this regard. Whether partnerships are mandated by legislation, as is the case in the UK, or are either wholly voluntary or compelled by executive decrees, as is more common in the USA, police requests that other agencies change their policies and practices are much better received if the members of those other agencies understand and trust the police perspective. Indeed, some agencies may not see such police requests as coercive at all but, rather, helpful. Police documentation of a problem has been used by local authorities and other statutory organizations to justify programmes they have long advocated. Non-profit private groups have used police documentation to help them justify expansions in their programmes and supporting budgets:

- A police constable in Lancashire succeeded in resolving a longstanding problem in which a scrapyard was used by local criminals to sell stolen vehicles and generally was a source of nuisance to the community. The constable did so, not by enforcing the criminal law as had been done so often before, but rather by referring the matter to the local Environmental Protection Agency. That agency found, upon inspection, that the scrapyard was inadequately protected against the emission of hazardous pollutants. By imposing new environmental protection requirements, the scrapyard operator opted to close the business instead (Lancashire Constabulary 1999b).

- The police in Blackpool, through careful data analysis, made a persuasive case to outside agencies that the most prolific drug-addicted criminal offenders ought to receive immediate and intensive drug treatment and social services immediately upon release from incarceration. This ran counter to conventional practices whereby many newly released offenders had to wait long periods for drug treatment, by which time most had resumed using drugs and committing crimes. The police engaged with probation officials, prosecutors, social workers and drug treatment providers to ensure that qualifying offenders who are willing to accept such services receive them in a timely and reliable fashion. A twelve-month evaluation indicated that the initiative had yielded a 30 per cent reduction in reported crime in the target area with no evidence of geographical displacement (Lancashire Constabulary 2003).

- Similarly, the police in Fremont, California, succeeded in persuading the local domestic violence victim assistance programme to accept direct referrals from police officers. The police demonstrated through analysis that there was a critical need to give high-priority services to repeat victims of domestic violence. Previously, victims themselves had to seek out the services. An assessment of the intervention indicated a demonstrable reduction in repeat calls for police service to assist victims of domestic violence. In this instance, whilst the police themselves assumed greater responsibility for dealing with chronic domestic violence, through their closer working relationship with other service providers, they were able to concentrate limited police and social service resources on the most problematic individuals (Fremont Police Department 1997).

- The police in Charlotte, NC, initiated discussions with the Mexican consulate and with local banks to persuade recent Mexican immigrants to use secure financial services (e.g. bank and chequing accounts, wire transfers) in order to reduce the amount of cash carried by, and often stolen from, immigrants. The police recognized that immigrants' lack of trust and understanding of American financial institutions discouraged them from adopting safer, and often less expensive, financial practices (Charlotte-Mecklenburg Police Department 2002).

Pressing for the creation of a new organization to assume responsibility for the problem

The police are not always in a position themselves to implement the measures that they conclude will best address the problem, and there may not be any other appropriate entity to do so. The police may then find themselves in the role of advocate for the creation of a new entity with the mandate and resources properly to address the problem.

With the increase in efforts to organize neighbourhoods, especially in large urban areas, it is frequently not necessary for the police to be the primary catalyst. They can often retreat to a supportive role. And there are situations in which the community organization grows on its own out of a concern about a given problem, with the police enlisted by them in support of their objectives. However, as the organizations come into existence and are sustained, the police find that they are gradually transferring responsibility for specific prevention strategies to them:

- In an effort to reduce the large demand upon police resources by divorced parents seeking assistance with the enforcement of child custody court orders, Fresno, California, police helped establish and promote the use of a privately owned and operated programme called the Child Custody Program. The programme assists parents with child custody exchanges by providing a safe facility in which both parents can come to exchange the child without need to interact with one another. The Child Custody Program helps mediate disputes between parents about custody orders. The police also worked with the courts to develop a process by which parents could file their own reports to the court alleging breaches of custody orders. This new programme and new procedures reduced the volume of calls for police service for this problem by about half. The police interest in preventing domestic disputes and violence related to child custody was met in a more efficient manner (Fresno Police Department 1999).

- Glendale, California, police organized an effort to create a new centre for day labourers as a means of eliminating the disorder, drunkenness, fighting, loitering, noise, litter and traffic congestion attendant to an unregulated day labourer market. Police secured commitments from private charitable organizations to operate the centre and its programmes (including social services, language improvement classes, and legal and labour negotiation services). The local transport authority agreed to provide the land and a local building-supply company agreed to donate the materials to construct the new facility and staff to help operate it. An advisory board comprising representatives of all stakeholders was created to oversee the centre. The police then persuaded the local authority to pass an ordinance requiring all day labourers to go through the day labourer centre to secure employment. The net result was a dramatic reduction in all aspects of the problem; a marked improvement in the employability, wages and working conditions of labourers; and a substantial reduction in demand on police and other emergency services (Glendale Police Department 1997).

- Racine, Wisconsin, police concluded that part of the solution to cleaning up drug-infested neighbourhoods was to purchase problem properties and convert them either for police use as community police stations or refurbish them and sell them to responsible occupants. In order to accomplish this, the police convinced local business leaders to establish a new private not-for-profit organization that could buy and sell real estate for the purposes established by the police and city government. This new arrangement led to the purchase and rehabilitation of a significant number of residential properties and inspired other private redevelopment in troubled neighbourhoods. The initiative yielded dramatic reductions in violent and property crime, and calls for police service and substantial improvements in the housing stock in the target areas (Racine Police Department 1999).

- Police in Fontana, California, worked with over 20 local charities, churches and businesses to form a new network of services for homeless individuals, many of whom were creating extraordinary problems for the police by their criminal and disorderly behaviour. The so-called 'Transient Enrichment Network' consolidated services for homeless individuals, providing a central facility where each homeless individual's special needs – whether mental or physical health, job placement, housing, food and shelter or substance abuse – could be diagnosed and addressed. This new network inspired police officers to deal more directly with homeless individuals, confident that doing so in many cases would lead to improvements in the individuals' behaviour and life circumstances. Early results were overwhelmingly positive with over 500 individuals benefiting from the programme in its first two years of operation. Moreover, crimes and calls for police service attributed to homeless individuals declined substantially (Fontana Police Department 1998).

Shaming the delinquent entity by calling public attention to its failure to assume responsibility for the problem

This is often an intermediate step between the type of private confrontation described earlier and resort to legal action. The stakes in resorting to public shaming are high. For many individuals, businesses and agencies their public reputation is of great value to them; having the police publicly discredit them can have significant long-term consequences. In some instances this method of shifting responsibility might be perceived as the most coercive. Consequently, the police typically use this method after more private methods of persuasion have failed. The police goal is to call to public attention the nature of the problem, the factors that cause or contribute to the problem, the reasonableness of police requests of others, the refusal of others to co-operate and the arguments for holding others to account for their contributions to the problem:

- The police in Lancashire sent official letters to registered owners of vehicles spotted cruising around areas in which street prostitution was a problem (Lancashire Constabulary 2003). Although the tone of the letters was purely educational, the unspoken effect (and no doubt, intention) of the letters was to expose kerb crawlers to possible shame by creating a risk that other persons might open and read the letters. Alternatively, the police in many jurisdictions collaborate with local media outlets to publicize the arrests of persons caught soliciting prostitutes (Buffalo Police Department 2001).

- Police officers in Green Bay, Wisconsin, sought local media coverage to expose the irresponsible practices of certain publicans, as well as the reluctance of certain public officials properly to enforce alcohol-licensing sanctions, in their effort to reduce alcohol-related problems in a neighbourhood. These actions, in combination with other actions, resulted in the closing of several problem pubs and bars through stricter enforcement of alcohol-licensing provisions and a significant reduction in calls for police service to the area, all of which inspired new economic development in and a nearly complete transformation of the area (Green Bay Police Department 1999).

- The police in a number of jurisdictions have developed ranking or rating schemes by which they communicate to the general public the relative security of different vehicles, alarm systems, houses, apartment complexes or parking facilities (Clarke and Goldstein 2003). The 'Secured by Design' scheme operated by the British police is a prime example of how publicity for meeting safety and security standards can become institutionalized. This sort of publicity both rewards the manufacturers and operators of responsibly designed and managed products and properties with favourable ratings as well as penalizes those with unfavourable ratings.

• The police in Delta, British Columbia, sought to persuade a reluctant video-arcade owner to redesign and improve management of the arcade to reduce problems associated with disorderly youth in and around the arcade. The police recruited the assistance of a local university's environmental criminology students who conducted a detailed study comparing this arcade with others in the area not having the same problems. The findings, which clearly demonstrated the inadequacies of the problematic arcade's design and management, were presented to local government officials, and reported in the mass media. As a result of this adverse publicity and persuasive findings the arcade owner agreed to the requested changes and the city council enacted a new by-law requiring minimum safety and security provisions for all arcades in the jurisdiction. Attendant calls for police service declined substantially. Perhaps the ultimate measure of success was achieved when the arcade owner began advertising that his arcade was safe and secure because it adhered to the highest standards of the industry (Delta Police Department 1997).

Withdrawing police services relating to certain aspects of the problem

The police occasionally seek to force adoption of a prevention strategy by refusing to respond, investigate, arrest or take other official actions after police requests of involved parties to take measures to reduce their likelihood of victimization have been rebuffed. Typically, this occurs in the context of a business operation when the evidence is overwhelming that the problem can be eliminated if the affected party were to implement certain measures, but which they have proclaimed they will not implement, usually out of concern that doing so would reduce their sales.

A decision to withdraw services must be sensitive to the disparate impact on those who may not be in a position to afford the most elementary steps required to prevent the offence; when imposing that cost may force an individual out of business; and, as an additional consequence, deprive a depressed neighbourhood of a vital business or service.

This method is only rarely employed by the police, most likely because they are reluctant to be seen as an agency that refuses to perform what many persist in seeing as 'their job'. The police continue to worry that failure to respond to any request for assistance might result in their failing to attend to a more serious infraction than that which was originally reported.

Most types of cases in which the police withdraw service are those in which the offence arises out of a commercial transaction that is arguably a civil matter rather than a criminal one. A few such examples are follows:

• Some police agencies refuse to respond to reports of motorists who drive away from a self-service petrol ('gasoline' in the USA) station without paying if the station has experienced a high volume of drive-offs and has been requested to require prepayment, but has refused to install such a system. Alternatively, the police might merely refuse to send out a police officer to take a report of a petrol drive-off, but instead require petrol station staff to file a form with the police.

- The police might refuse to investigate cases in which diners leave a restaurant without paying, particularly if the restaurant has a poor system for monitoring customers and collecting their payments.

- The police might advise shops which have cheques returned to them for lack of sufficient funds that the police will not take the responsibility to go after the cheque passer, especially if the outlet does not require proper identification or maintain a registry of those from whom cheques will and will not be accepted. Or a police agency might require that any merchant expecting the police to process bad cheque cases must obtain a fingerprint on the back of the cashed cheque.

- The police might refuse to record as thefts failures to return rented property such as videotapes, tools, appliances or furniture, knowing that the posting of a credit card or other security will eliminate the practice. So-called 'rent-to-own' stores can generate a high volume of reported thefts in some jurisdictions where reporting requirements are relaxed.

Other than commercial transactions, the most common type of incident for which the police might refuse to provide service is for intrusion alarms that have not been verified as suspicious (see the example and reference under 'Pressing for legislation', below).

Charging fees for police services related to the problem

This method seeks to recoup the costs to the police for providing a particular service from the individuals who directly benefit from that service. The rationale for such cost-recovery schemes is that certain individuals make an excessive claim upon public police resources; that they consume more than their fair share or more than their tax payments reasonably entitle them to. In some jurisdictions legislation authorizes the police to seek the recovery in court of the actual costs of police investigations from defendants (see Oakland Police Department 2003 whereby the police successfully recovered $35,000 in investigative costs from the owners of a problem motel). Elsewhere, police and other emergency rescue agencies charge thrill-seeking adventurers for the costs of rescuing them when their adventures go awry. Increasingly, the police are extending the cost-recovery principle to property owners whose premises generate an inordinate volume of calls for police service (e.g. bars and apartment complexes).

Although fee schemes are not intended as penalties, and therefore typically are limited to recovering no more than the actual marginal cost to the police agency, they nonetheless provide an economic incentive to individuals and businesses to keep their costs for police services under control by keeping problem behaviour under control.

- Amongst the most common problems the police must deal with are alarms from security systems installed in businesses and especially residences. They account for an extraordinarily large percentage of police business in commercial areas, in wealthy suburban areas, in resort areas out of season and even in large urban areas. Well over 90 per cent of all such alarms are false, resulting from malfunctioning of the system, animals or error on the part of the alarm's owner. This is an example of a situation in which the business person or resident has taken responsibility for a prevention strategy but has reimposed a major cost associated with that strategy back on the police. In response, the police in many jurisdictions have arranged for the enactment of an escalating set of fees that are assessed after a set number of false alarms are handled, thereby pressuring the owner to take actions that will prevent the alarms from registering falsely. In still other areas, a fee is also assessed annually in anticipation of whatever services the police may be called upon to render in connection with the alarm, including simply maintaining their readiness.

- The police in Halton, Ontario, successfully addressed chronic problems involving alcohol-related crime and disorder (and several large riots) at a large dance club in part by shifting some of the costs for police service back to the club's owners. Strict law enforcement and efforts to close the club had proven impractical and ineffective. The police successfully lobbied for a change in the liquor-licensing law so that liquor licences carry a stipulation that excessive consumption of police resources to ensure safety and security will result in the costs of those excess police resources being charged to the licence holder (Halton Regional Police Service 2003).

Pressing for legislation mandating that entities take measures to prevent the problem

In addition to having recourse to the many laws that directly proscribe illegal and harmful conduct by individuals, the police have long been aided by a variety of regulations (including city or county ordinances, by-laws, state statutes, administrative regulations, etc.) that are designed to regulate various conditions that have potential to foster offending and harm. They reflect a legislative judgement that certain businesses, organizations or individuals, by virtue of the activities in which they are engaged, have certain responsibilities to assure that those activities are carried out in ways that are safe and orderly. The prime example is the extensive regulation of premises dispensing alcoholic drinks. Primary responsibility for the measures to prevent disorder and crime within licensed premises rests with those who dispense it. The police role is secondary – to reinforce the responsibility of the owners through regulatory enforcement. The police are often in a position, by virtue of special knowledge they acquire by analysing problems, to propose specific new laws and regulations that assign responsibility for controlling criminogenic conditions to certain individuals, businesses or groups, and provide penalties for failing to do so.[7]

Adoption of such measures is typically preceded by discussion in the public forum and, somewhat more formally, in hearings held on a piece of legislation. The police may be amongst the proponents. Occasionally, they are the initiators. And in the typical scenario, the individuals on whom the burden of any new mandates will fall are the opponents. The evidence in support of adoption is more often anecdotal than rigorously acquired. Some efforts are made to introduce data of varying quality. One exception to this pattern are the heated debates over the requirement that convenience stores be required to maintain two or more staff on duty at specified hours of the day. Those debates have drawn heavily on the studies that have sought to measure the value of this strategy, and have been made especially contentious because of the conflicting results of those studies:

- To reduce residential burglaries, some cities have incorporated into their building codes certain design and construction features that prevent burglary. Some such codes go well beyond simply requiring locks on doors and windows and govern such features as lighting, natural surveillance, and door and window strength (see, for example, Overland Park, Kansas 2003).

- As part of an initiative to reduce injury from assaults with glass objects on the streets of Liverpool, Merseyside Police persuaded Liverpool City Council to enact a new requirement that the proprietors of licensed establishments be responsible for preventing glass (drink glasses and bottles) from being removed from the premises. The police then persuaded the Home Office to approve new legislation that would authorize police to confiscate any glass containers carried on the streets in Liverpool city centre. This combination of legislative acts helped produce a dramatic reduction in the volume of glass-related injuries occurring in the target area (Merseyside Police 2001).

- Salt Lake City, Utah, police persuaded its city council to enact an ordinance requiring companies that sell home and business intrusion alarm systems to provide the initial response to and investigation of all alarm activations prior to summoning the police. This policy, known as 'verified response', nearly entirely eliminated police responses to false intrusion alarms. Evidence to date suggests that this policy has had no adverse effect on the underlying problem intrusion alarms are intended to address – burglary – and have yielded substantial savings in police resources that are then available for other, more productive, activities (Salt Lake City Police Department 2001). Interestingly, the 'verified response' policy supplanted a more commonly used measure to shift responsibility for false alarms – that of charging alarm customers fees to offset the costs of police response. The fee system has demonstrated some effect in reducing the volume of false alarms, but not to the degree of 'verified response'.

Bringing a civil action to compel entities to accept responsibility for the problem

Several avenues are open by which the police and others can bring actions in the courts to force individuals or an organization to take responsibility for implementing preventive measures (see generally, Mazerolle and Roehl 1998).

This process is normally reserved for the most egregious conditions and as a last resort because, with some exceptions, the process is difficult and the costs are high. Amongst the numerous forms of civil actions the police might either initiate or support are nuisance abatement orders (in the USA), anti-social behaviour orders (in the UK), civil injunctions and restraining orders, civil asset forfeitures, civil fines, enforcement of codified regulations and evictions.

Studies relating to the problem of drugs inevitably focus attention on drug houses. The search for an alternative simply to acquiring evidence and making arrests has led the police to dust off largely unused abatement proceedings and to obtain new, specifically tailored legislation that enables them, through a court proceeding and upon presentation of adequate evidence, to seize properties associated with a high incidence of crime. Their authorization to do so, punctuated by some successful efforts, is intended to pressure landlords to take greater responsibility for control of activities on their properties. It is the threat of an abatement action that often renders targeted confrontational requests effective.

In one of the more novel uses of civil actions, the Safe Streets programme, based in Oakland, California, trains local citizens in acquiring the evidence needed to petition in small claims court for the abatement of a drug house, with no requirement of a lawyer and with any receipts from the sale of the premises to be distributed amongst the petitioners. Police involvement in this process is limited to co-operation with community members as they seek police documentation, in support of their case, of criminal activity occurring in or near the premises.

An emerging, although as yet unsettled, development in the USA is for the police to support civil lawsuits against gun manufacturers or distributors as a means of controlling gun-related violence. If such suits succeed, it will prove an extraordinary example of how the police and their local governments can compel a large industry to assume significantly greater responsibility for the harm associated with its products:

- The police in Oakland, California, filed a civil suit against the parent corporation of an international motel franchise for failure to control drug dealing, prostitution and assorted crime and disorder on its property (Oakland Police Department 2003). The suit followed repeated attempts by the police to educate the property manager and corporate executives about the problems at the motel, request improvements and warn them of possible legal consequences. In this case, the police worked progressively towards more coercive methods in a careful, measured manner. Indeed, the special unit of the Oakland Police Department that brought the civil action had developed a formal process for documenting such problems and bringing increasing levels of pressure to bear upon property managers and owners.

- Royal Canadian Mounted Police in Burnaby, BC, collaborated with government tax, fire, building, health, immigration and licence inspectors to inspect and file code violation charges against the owner of three blocks of flats which police had found were being used for organizing large-scale illegal immigrant drug trafficking. The owner resisted government efforts to improve the management of the properties and consequently they were closed by the government and emptied of tenants. This led to geographic displacement of the drug market to a nearby public transport station (where the police persuaded the managers to make design improvements to deter drug dealing) and the displacement of the base of operations to other nearby blocks of flats (where the police helped property managers form an information-sharing network to prevent problem tenants from securing leases) (Royal Canadian Mounted Police 2002).

Conclusion

Amidst the seemingly perpetual debate as to what role the police can play in controlling and preventing crime and disorder – from the pessimistic view that police actions are largely inconsequential in the face of larger social conditions, to the optimistic (perhaps hubristic) view that the police can control crime rates almost unilaterally (Bratton 1997) – there is a growing body of evidence that, indeed, the police can play a central role in crime and disorder control, though perhaps more through indirect than direct action. And so, if societies are seriously interested in purposely controlling crime and disorder rather than reactively hoping for improvements in the large social conditions that influence offending, they would do well to reconsider how best to capitalize upon their investments in the police. Rather than viewing the police institution as the institution of first and last resort when matters pertaining to public safety go awry, societies might better view the police as an informed early-warning system, an institution with the mandate, resources and opportunities to identify and understand threats to public safety and the professional expertise to recommend corrective courses of action that ought be taken. To be sure, there is much about the police institution to be improved to fully justify this role as broker of public safety responsibilities, but much to suggest that this is the direction worth taking.

Selected further reading

Readers are especially encouraged to read two publications cited in this chapter, both of which explore similar themes: Gloria Laycock and Nick Tilley's chapter 'Implementing crime prevention' in Tonry and Farrington's volume (1994) and Michael Buerger's article, 'The politics of third-party policing' in Mazerolle and Roehl's volume (1998). The best and most complete articulation of the problem-oriented policing approach is to be found in Herman Goldstein's seminal work, *Problem-oriented Policing* (1990).

Acknowledgements

Credit is due to Professor Emeritus Herman Goldstein of the University of Wisconsin Law School who originally articulated the themes of this chapter in an unpublished paper presented at the Sixth International Seminar on Environmental Criminology and Crime Analysis in Oslo, Norway, 23–25 June 1997 and in subsequent presentations. Professor Goldstein further contributed new insights, research and critiques to this chapter.

Notes

1. The term 'problem' has assumed a precise definition in policing: 'the broad range of troublesome situations that prompt citizens to turn to the police' (Goldstein 1979); 'a cluster of similar incidents, whether crime or acts of disorder, that the police are expected to handle' (Goldstein 2001); 'a group of incidents ... similar in some way ... (that are) of direct concern to the public ... (and which) fall within the broad range of the police function' (Eck and Spelman 1987); 'repetitive harmful events in the community that the public expects the police to address (Eck and Clarke 2003).
2. The British Crime and Disorder Act 1998 obliged the police to work in partnership with others on public safety concerns, but perhaps more importantly, other government agencies were reciprocally obliged to work in partnership with the police. Many British police officials have come to view this reciprocal obligation as amongst the most significant developments towards better control of crime and disorder.
3. See Buerger (1998) for an interesting discussion of the new political landscape that the police will find themselves in as they press for indirect action to control crime and disorder.
4. Set aside from this consideration are those problems or duties that the police seek to transfer to others because the police believe they do not properly fall to the police to handle in any respect. Many police agencies find themselves, for various reasons, performing all manner of duties that have little to do with their core functions. Some argue that tasks such as providing funeral and banking escorts, teaching moral values to schoolchildren, guarding construction sites, transporting probation violators to jail, investigating intrusion alarms, etc., should not be police duties. This chapter is primarily concerned with those problems that the police widely accept as falling within their public mandate and which the police feel obliged to do something about. But, police acceptance of some measure of responsibility for dealing with a problem does not and should not automatically burden the police with the sole responsibility to fix it.
5. The Herman Goldstein Award for Excellence in Problem-oriented Policing was initiated in 1993 by the Police Executive Research Forum in Washington, DC and is currently administered by the Center for Problem-oriented Policing. To date there have been some 700 submissions to the programme.
6. The Tilley Award programme was initiated in 1999 by the Home Office Policing and Reducing Crime Unit (now the Crime and Policing Group). To date there have been some 250 submissions to the programme.
7. Legislative enactments of this sort are to be distinguished from those which merely give the police more authority to arrest offenders, provisions which, whilst potentially useful, reinforce the notion that the police bear primary responsibility for controlling problems.

References

Bittner, E. (1970) *The Functions of the Police in Modern Society*. Chevy Chase, MD: National Institute of Mental Health.

Bratton, W. (1997) 'Crime is down in New York City: blame the police', in W. Bratton *et al*. (eds) *Zero Tolerance: Policing a Free Society*. London: Institute of Economic Affairs Health & Welfare Unit.

Buerger, M. (1998) 'The politics of third-party policing', in L.G. Mazerolle and J. Roehl (eds) *Civil Remedies and Crime Prevention. Crime Prevention Studies. Volume 9*. Monsey, NY: Criminal Justice Press.

Bureau of Justice Assistance (2000) *Keeping Illegal Activity out of Rental Property: A Police Guide for Establishing Landlord Training Programs*. Washington, DC: US Department of Justice, Bureau of Justice Assistance.

Campbell Resources Inc. (n.d.) *Clandestine Drug Labs: What Every Hotel and Motel Operator Should Know*. Portland, OR: City of Portland and Campbell Resources Inc.

Charlotte-Mecklenburg Police Department (2002) 'Hispanic Robbery Initiative: reducing robbery victimization and increasing trust of police and financial institutions in a Hispanic community.' Submission to the Herman Goldstein Award for Excellence in Problem-oriented Policing.

Chisolm, J. (2000) *Benefit-cost Analysis and Crime Prevention. Trends and Issues in Crime and Criminal Justice Paper 147*. Canberra: Australian Institute of Criminology (available at http://www.aic.gov.au/publications/tandi/ti147.pdf).

Chula Vista Police Department (2001) 'Designing out crime: the Chula Vista residential burglary reduction project.' Submission to the Herman Goldstein Award for Excellence in Problem-oriented Policing.

City of Overland Park (2003) 'Ordinance no. BC-2459, Section R328 (Physical Security)', in *Overland Park Municipal Code*. City of Overland Park, Kansas.

Clarke, R.V. and Goldstein, H. (2003) *Reducing Thefts at Construction Sites: Lessons from a Problem-oriented Project*. Washington, DC: US Department of Justice, Office of Community Oriented Policing Services (available at http://www.popcenter.org/Library/RecommendedReadings/ConstructionTheft.pdf).

Clarke, R.V. and Goldstein, H. (2003) *Theft from Cars in Center City Parking Facilities – a Case Study*. Washington, DC: US Department of Justice, Office of Community Oriented Policing Services (available at http://www.popcenter.org/Problems/Supplemental_Material/Car%20Thefts/clarkegold.pdf).

Delta Police Department (1997) 'The elite arcade: taming a crime generator.' Submission to the Herman Goldstein Award for Excellence in Problem-oriented Policing.

Eck, J. and Clarke, R.V. (2003) 'Classifying common police problems: a routine activity approach', in M.J. Smith and D.B. Cornish (eds) *Theory for Practice in Situational Crime Prevention. Crime Prevention Studies. Volume 16*. Monsey, NY: Criminal Justice Press.

Eck, J. and Spelman, W. (1987) *Problem-solving: Problem-oriented Policing in Newport News*. Washington, DC: Police Executive Research Forum.

Felson, M. and Clarke, R.V. (1998) *Opportunity Makes the Thief: Practical Theory for Crime Prevention. Police Research Series Paper 98*. London: Home Office Policing and Reducing Crime Unit.

Fontana Police Department (1998) '"Ten-4": the Transient Enrichment Network. A community collaboration to reduce homelessness'. Submission to the Herman Goldstein Award for Excellence in Problem-oriented Policing.

Fremont Police Department (1997) 'Domestic violence revictimization prevention. Improving police response to repeat calls of domestic violence.' Submission to the Herman Goldstein Award for Excellence in Problem-oriented Policing.

Fresno Police Department (1999) 'A multiagency approach to a community problem: stemming calls-for-service related to child custody.' Submission to the Herman Goldstein Award for Excellence in Problem-oriented Policing.

Glendale Police Department (1997) 'Day Laborer Project: a community's response to the problems of casual laborers.' Submission to the Herman Goldstein Award for Excellence in Problem-Oriented Policing.

Goldstein, H. (1990) *Problem-oriented Policing*. Philadelphia, PA: Temple University Press.

Goldstein, H. (1996) 'Establishing ownership of inquiries and responses to problems in the context of problem-oriented policing.' Unpublished draft.

Goldstein, H. (1997) 'The pattern of emerging tactics for shifting the ownership of prevention strategies in the current wave of change in policing: their implications for both environmental criminology and the police.' Unpublished draft.

Goldstein, H. (1997) 'Improving policing: a problem-oriented approach', *Crime and Delinquency* (April).

Halton Regional Police Service (2003) 'Let's dance: a community's collaborative response to the problems created by an all ages nightclub.' Submission to the Herman Goldstein Award for Excellence in Problem-oriented Policing.

Hamilton-Wentworth Police Department (1994) 'Kidestrian: child pedestrian safety.' Submission to the Herman Goldstein Award for Excellence in Problem-oriented Policing.

Home Office (n.d.) *Crime Reduction Toolkits* (available at http://www.crimereduction. gov.uk/toolkits/index.htm).

Hope, T. (1994) 'Problem-oriented policing and drug-market locations: three case studies', in R.V. Clarke (ed.) *Crime Prevention Studies. Vol. 2*. Monsey, NY: Criminal Justice Press.

Hornick, J., Paetsch, J. and Bertrand, L. (2000) *A Manual on Conducting Economic Analysis of Crime Prevention Programs*. Ottawa: National Crime Prevention Centre.

Hough, M. and Tilley, N. (1998) *Getting the Grease to the Squeak: Research Lessons for Crime Prevention. Crime Detection and Prevention Series Paper 85*. London: Home Office Police Research Group.

Lancashire Constabulary (1999a) 'The Tower Project. Blackpool Community Safety Project.' Submission to the Herman Goldstein Award for Excellence in Problem-oriented Policing.

Lancashire Constabulary (1999b) 'The Nook Scrap Yard: a POP's initiative.' Submission to the Tilley Award Programme for Excellence in Problem-oriented Policing.

Lancashire Constabulary (2000) 'Operation Adelphi: a problem-oriented approach to hotel burglary reduction.' Submission for the Tilley Award Programme for Excellence in Problem-oriented Policing.

Lancashire Constabulary (2003) 'Operation Kerb: multi-agency problem solving approach to street prostitution in Preston.' Submission to the Tilley Award Programme for Excellence in Problem-oriented Policing.

Lancashire Constabulary (n.d.) 'Nightsafe: reducing alcohol related violence and disorder' (available at http://www.lancashire.police.uk/nightsafe.html).

Laycock, G. and Tilley, N. (1994) 'Implementing crime prevention', in M. Tonry and D. Farrington (eds) *Building a Safer Society: Strategic Approaches to Crime Prevention. Crime and Justice: A Review of Research*. Chicago, IL: University of Chicago Press.

Mazerolle, L.G. and Roehl, J. (1998) *Civil Remedies and Crime Prevention. Crime Prevention Studies. Vol. 9*. Monsey, NY: Criminal Justice Press.

Merseyside Police (2001) 'Operation Crystal Clear.' Submission to the Tilley Award Programme for Excellence in Problem-oriented Policing.

Miami Police Department (2002) 'Allapatah Produce Market Power Play: revitalizing a produce market through cooperation.' Submission to the Herman Goldstein Award for Excellence in Problem-oriented Policing.

Oakland Police Department (2003) 'The Oakland Airport Motel Program. Eliminating criminal and nuisance behavior at a motel.' Submission to the Herman Goldstein Award for Excellence in Problem-oriented Policing.

Peel Regional Police (1996) 'The Last Drink Program: targeting licensed premises to reduce impaired driving.' Submission to the Herman Goldstein Award for Excellence in Problem-oriented Policing.

Plano Police Department (2003) 'Underage drinking: more than a minor issue.' Submission to the Herman Goldstein Award for Excellence in Problem-oriented Policing.

Racine Police Department (1999) 'The power of partnerships: revitalizing neighborhoods through community policing houses.' Submission to the Herman Goldstein Award for Excellence in Problem-oriented Policing.

Read, T. and Tilley, N. (2000) *Not Rocket Science? Problem-solving and Crime Reduction. Crime Reduction Research Series Paper 6*. London: Home Office Policing and Reducing Crime Unit.

Rojek, J. (2003) 'A decade of excellence in problem-oriented policing: characteristics of the Goldstein Award winners', *Police Quarterly*, 6: 492–515.

Royal Canadian Mounted Police (2002) 'Project Metrotown: reducing drug trafficking and related crime through multiagency cooperation and community partnerships.' Submission to the Herman Goldstein Award for Excellence in Problem-oriented Policing.

Salt Lake City Police Department (2001) 'The false alarm solution: verified response.' Submission to the Herman Goldstein Award for Excellence in Problem-oriented Policing.

Sampson, R., Raudenbush, S. and Earls, F. (1997) 'Neighborhoods and violent crime: a multilevel study of collective efficacy', *Science*, 277: 918–24.

San Diego Police Department (2001) 'Sexual assault: educating a community about non-stranger sexual assault.' Submission to the Herman Goldstein Award for Excellence in Problem-oriented Policing (see http://www.popcenter.org/Problems/PDFs/men_web%20rev.pdf and http://www.popcenter.org/Problems/PDFs/women_booklet.pdf for the brochures).

Scott, M. (2000) *Problem-oriented Policing: Reflections on the First 20 Years*. Washington, DC: US Department of Justice, Office of Community Oriented Policing Services.

Sherman, L., Gottfredson, D., MacKenzie, D., Eck, J., Reuter, P. and Bushway, S. (1997) *Preventing Crime: What Works, What Doesn't, What's Promising*. Washington, DC: US Department of Justice, Office of Justice Programs.

Tonry, M. and Farrington, D. (1995) 'Strategic approaches to crime prevention', *Crime and Justice: A Review of Research*, 19: 1–20.

US Department of Justice, Office of Community Oriented Policing Services (2000, et seq.) *Problem-oriented Guides for Police*. Washington, DC: US Department of Justice.

Weisburd, D. and Eck, J. (2004) 'What can police do to reduce crime, disorder, and fear?', *Annals of the American Academy of Political and Social Science*, 593: 42–65.

Part IV

Prevention in Practice

Nick Tilley

This part of the handbook moves away from general approaches and families of tactic to prevent and reduce crime regardless of type, and looks instead at what has been done in relation to a series of problems that have commonly been a focus of preventive efforts.

As shown in Figure IV.1, burglary and vehicle crime (the subjects of Chapters 16 and 17) together came to account for just over half of all recorded crime in England and Wales in the early to mid-1990s, though the proportion has now fallen to about a third. The high share of burglary and vehicle crime largely explain the attention devoted to them. Such systematic research as there has been on patterns of business victimization suggests much higher rates of crime against businesses than those found against households and individuals. Hence crime against business is the focus of Chapter 18. Though it is much more common than would be suggested from recorded crime statistics, it is the seriousness of violent and sexual crime that explains the widespread preventive attention given to it (see Chapter 19). Drug and alcohol misuse, and illicit drug trafficking, comprise, of course, problems in themselves. They have equally been a focus of attention because of the crime and disorder problems associated with them. They are discussed in Chapter 20. Finally, it is not just crime itself that has concerned policy-makers and practitioners. The fear of crime (Chapter 21) has been identified as a significant, separate and distinctive problem warranting interventions focused on it alone.

Niall Hamilton-Smith and Andrew Kent work within the Home Office and were part of the team there responsible for evaluations of the domestic burglary reduction element in the Crime Reduction Programme (CRP), which ran in England and Wales from 1999 to 2002. In Chapter 16 they provide an overview of research evidence about patterns of burglary. They then move on specifically to prevention. Though they refer to other research also, they draw heavily on the burglary-related work of the CRP, a large component of which was undertaken by three research consortia looking respectively at suites of projects in the North, Midlands and South. Hamilton-Smith and Kent distil from the research evidence the apparent impact of a wide range of types

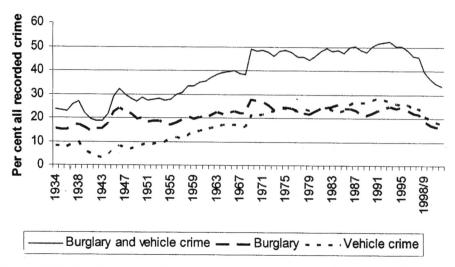

Figure IV.1 Burglary and vehicle crime as a proportion of all recorded offences in England and Wales, 1934–2003
Note: Vehicle crime here excludes theft of cycles. This offence alone accounted for 14–15 per cent of all recorded crime during the Second World War, but now represents only about 2 per cent

of measure that have been put in place to try to reduce domestic burglary, distinguishing between strength of evidence about effects, effect sizes, rate of success and cost-benefit estimates. They organize many of these findings about differing measures amongst the five major classes of technique used in situational crime prevention, though they also discuss 'complementary measures' that fall outside this schema.

Barry Webb has for many years been interested in design and crime and has undertaken a wide variety of studies that have looked at ways in which design modifications of varying types can reduce levels of crime. These studies have related to such diverse problems as theft of purses in markets, crime on housing estates and fly-tipping, as well as vehicle theft, which he focuses on in Chapter 17. Webb stresses the need to obtain a good grasp of specific vehicle crime problems to work through potential interventions to deal with them. He looks historically at how different types of vehicle crime have changed over time. Different forms of vehicle crime problem call for different preventive responses. Webb discusses three aspects of design and the reduction of vehicle crime. The first relates to the vehicle itself and its vulnerability to crime. The second relates to the environment on which the car is parked. And the third concerns the vehicle registration and licensing system which may or may not facilitate the commission of crime. These three design areas correspond to the families of measure discussed in Chapters 8–10.

Crimes against businesses are hard to distinguish for the most part in recorded crime statistics. Non-domestic burglary is differentiated from domestic burglary but includes, for example, sheds, schools and hospitals as well as commercial premises. Figure IV.2 shows the proportion of all burglaries represented by those not against domestic premises since 1898. It

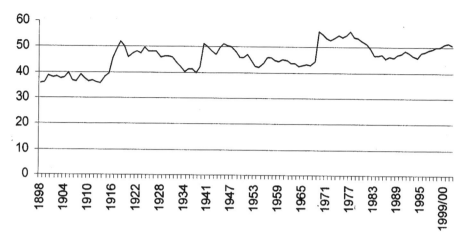

Figure IV.2 Non-domestic burglaries as a percentage of all recorded burglaries in England and Wales, 1898–2003

can be seen that the proportions are consistently quite high, and now run to just over half. Shop theft has been a specific category of recorded crime since 1934, but generally depends for its identification on shop workers and recorded figures are likely substantially to underestimate the problem. As Figure IV.3 shows, numbers of recorded offences grew steadily from the late 1950s to early 1980s, perhaps reflecting the increases in self-service shopping. There have been only two sweeps of the Commercial Victimization Survey (CVS), the counterpart to the British Crime Survey, providing an alternative estimate of crime levels not dependent on public crime reporting and police crime recording practices. However, the CVS sweeps have covered only a subset of commercial premises, excluding for example all those offering services. Thus what we know from official sources about patterns of crime against businesses is rather limited. Matt Hopkins and John Burrows, who have been major contributors to the literature about patterns of crime against business and about attempts to lessen it, review what is known in Chapter 18. They discuss methods that have been used to measure crime against businesses, estimates of costs of crime against business, observed patterns of crime against business and explanations for them, and initiatives that have been tried to reduce it. They provide a detailed account of one project, the 'Small Business and Crime Initiative' using Paul Ekblom's 5Is framework to do so.

Mike Maguire, with wide interests in criminology including as part of it substantial work on alcohol-related violence and its prevention and on violent offenders, and Fiona Brookman, with a recent book on homicide, discuss violent and sexual crime in Chapter 19. They point out that the issues revolving around these problems are potentially wide-ranging. They make two important points that are relevant also to the remainder of the book. The first is that there are significant differences in subtypes of problem that call for different preventive responses. The second is that for the most part the range of problems looked at are circumscribed. They are largely

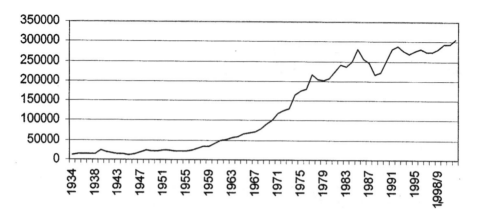

Figure IV.3   Recorded incidents of shop theft in England and Wales, 1934–2003

confined to those ordinarily dealt with by the police and courts in the western world, which are discussed by and generally familiar to criminologists. Large-scale atrocities and potential responses to these, however, are not discussed. Maguire and Brookman provide an overview of patterns of violent and sexual crime in England and Wales. They discuss three major families of problem: those relating to domestic violence and sexual abuse, those relating to alcohol-related violence in public places and those relating to 'predatory violence'. They argue that the suite of attributes associated with each of these major classes suggests qualitatively different opportunities for preventive intervention.

In Chapter 20, Tim McSweeney and Mike Hough, who individually and jointly have contributed much of that which is known about drugs, drug problems and responses to drugs issues, address the tricky problem of drugs, alcohol and crime. The problem is tricky on at least two different counts. First, the relationship between crime and drugs and alcohol is a difficult one clearly to unpick and evidence. Secondly, finding interventions effectively to address drug and alcohol-related problems has also proven to be very difficult. McSweeney and Hough present recent data on patterns of drug use, alcohol consumption and offending behaviour both in general and amongst a number of different key population subgroups. They provide an overview of theories that explain some of the quite complex interactions at work that may link drugs, alcohol and offending. They also look at the effectiveness of differing strategies that have been adopted to try to reduce alcohol and drug-related crime. Using Ekblom's 5Is framework they examine in some detail the use of Drug Treatment and Testing Orders (DTTOs) as a particular form of intervention aiming to reduce drug-related crime. They conclude that treatment constitutes but one element of change processes that may be involved in desistance from drug misuse and associated crime.

The last chapter of Part IV turns away from problems of crime and their genesis and addresses instead fear of crime. Chapter 21 brings together Jason Ditton, who has written widely on measurement issues relating to fear of crime and has also pointed out that fear is neither the only nor the commonest the way of responding to crime, and Martin Innes, who has played a key part in research relating to the British police's 'reassurance agenda', which is substantially concerned with addressing issues relating to the fear of crime. As Ditton and Innes note there has been a major concern with fear of crime as a problem *sui generis*. Specifically, it has been assumed that it is a bad thing, that there is too much of it and that it should be lessened measurably. Yet Ditton and Innes question these assumptions. For them some fear is sometimes good, and some fear is sometimes bad. It might be good, for example, where it encourages sensible precautions against victimization amongst those otherwise at risk. It depends on the situation. Taking this view, the right policy is one which produces an optimal distribution of fear. Ditton and Innes also raise serious concerns over the ways in which fear of crime has been measured. They then go on to review the literature on efforts to reduce fear of crime. They describe the National Reassurance Policing Programme (NRPP), launched in April 2003. This at the same time mobilizes visible, accessible and familiar police officers, focuses on dealing with 'signal crimes' (those events and states that precipitate public anxieties) and attempts to engage the community in solutions to problems using informal social control, as means of managing fear of crime. Ditton and Innes use the notion of 'perceptual intervention' to capture what can be done to alter the way crime is experienced and how it is seen. It is this which may be achieved with the NRPP work relating to signal crimes, and which may enable the reduction of corrosive and dysfunctional fear of crime. Finally Ditton and Innes discuss various measurement issues in the evaluation of efforts to deal with fear of crime.

Chapter 16

The prevention of domestic burglary

Niall Hamilton-Smith and Andrew Kent

Introduction

Domestic burglary is one of the most common and serious property crime offences. In England and Wales domestic burglary currently accounts for around 6–8 per cent of all crime (Dodd *et al.* 2004), although this represents a historic low after a sustained fall over a number of years. Domestic burglary is also commonly a significant problem across much of the developed world (Van Kesteren *et al.* 2000).

Reducing levels of burglary has long been a key priority for law enforcement and government agencies in England and Wales. This is unsurprising in view of high levels of public concern associated with the offence (Dodd *et al.* 2004), and the serious emotional impacts often resulting from victimization (Simmons and Dodd 2003). The imperative to tackle burglary has also been reinforced by studies that have quantified the financial costs of this offence. Brand and Price (2000) estimated that the average domestic burglary offence, including costs to the victim as well as costs to official agencies, was £2,300 per offence, amounting in 1999–2000 to a total cost for England and Wales of £2.7 billion.

In England and Wales a number of central government programmes have aimed to sponsor burglary prevention activity. Notably, burglary prevention was one of the major components of Safer Cities (Ekblom *et al.* 1996), a programme that invested additional funds in crime reduction in cities with the highest crime rates. Subsequently, the investment in burglary reduction was increased still further as part of the Crime Reduction Programme (CRP), a multi-initiative programme which ran between 1998 and 2002 (Homel *et al.* 2004). The Reducing Burglary Initiative (RBI) was one of the largest of these initiatives, involving over 240 locally based projects being given grants totalling over £25 million. The first phase of 63 projects was launched in October 1999 and was subject to a full independent evaluation that was intended to elicit not only what worked in burglary reduction, but also what was cost-effective. To this end three evaluation consortia were formed (the 'southern', 'midlands' and 'northern' consortia), with each being given the task of evaluating 21 phase-one projects.[1]

This chapter focuses on evidence regarding the effectiveness of the different crime prevention techniques that have come to be employed to address domestic burglary. International evidence is included in this discussion, although evidence is primarily from the RBI evaluations. Before assessing 'what works' in burglary prevention, this chapter will briefly review some key generic project issues that often have a particular bearing on whether burglary prevention techniques are effective.

The grounds for prevention

Criminological research provides a wide range of empirical insights and theoretical 'tools' for understanding burglary and devising preventative responses. There is not the space here to discuss these in any detail, though Lamm Weisel (2002) can be recommended as providing an excellent summary. Briefly, the common basis behind crime prevention approaches is that the motivation to offend is limited and suppressible and that motivation is inextricably linked to the availability of opportunities for committing crime (Mayhew *et al*. 1976) (see Figure 16.1). If opportunities are removed or blocked in some way then crimes will not occur. A key supporting theory here is that offenders make a rational decision to offend, weighing up the costs and benefits of exploiting a particular opportunity (Cornish and Clarke 1986). Thus, if the real or perceived costs of exploiting an opportunity can be manipulated so that they outweigh the perceived benefits for the offender, then the offender will make the rational decision not to commit that offence.

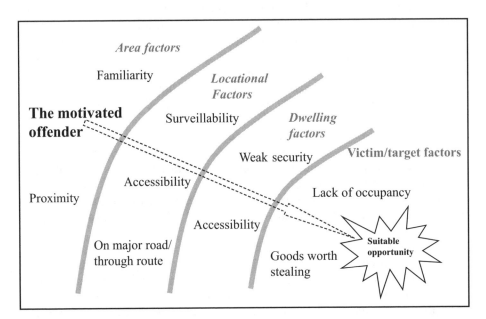

Figure 16.1   Assessing burglary opportunities

However, crime opportunities are super-abundant, and if offenders were fully rational then they would adapt to the blockage of one opportunity by simply identifying an alternative. Fortunately, though, offenders generally act with only a limited amount of rationality when committing an offence (Cornish and Clarke 1986). The majority of burglary offenders do not engage in elaborate pre-offence planning (Wright and Decker 1994), but typically exploit criminal opportunities that they come across 'in passing' (Wiles and Costello 2000). Whilst offenders may employ some degree of conscious rational decision-making, much of their behaviour is in fact guided by routines and by internalized 'rules of thumb' for identifying, assessing and exploiting criminal opportunities (Cromwell *et al.* 1991; Cornish 1994).

Other factors also 'frame' or 'bound' the rational decision-making of offending (Cornish and Clarke 1987). Principally, offenders need a variety of resources to commit an offence. These can range from physical resources required in the commission of the offence (Ekblom and Tilley 2000), through to social resources such as co-offenders to help in the commission of the offence or to provide encouragement. Burglars also typically require a fence to buy stolen goods off them (Sutton *et al.* 1998). Finally, offenders need to have the individual resources to successfully exploit opportunities such as skill, nerve and the ability to identify suitable opportunities.

Routines also effectively limit offending and lend a vital element of predictability to patterns of offending. Where offenders live, and areas which they routinely visit and are familiar with, determine to a significant extent where crimes occur (Brantingham and Brantingham 1984). The location, characteristics and concentration of suitable opportunities are also critical here, and it is the 'coming together' of offenders and suitable opportunities that can generate high concentrations of crime. What typically makes an opportunity 'suitable' when it comes to burglary includes the presence of valuable and removable goods,[2] the absence of household security that might frustrate or deter the offender and the absence of a 'capable guardian' (i.e. typically a house being unoccupied).

'Routine activities theory' (Cohen and Felson 1979) formalizes the interplay of these different elements in the construction of the criminal event (see Figure 16.2). At its most basic formulation the theory asserts that criminal events occur when a motivated (or 'likely') offender comes across a suitable opportunity in the absence of a capable guardian. This highlights the fact that the level and distribution of a given crime can partially be explained by the distribution of offenders, suitable targets and capable guardians. As offenders and suitable opportunities are not distributed evenly in time or space, crime is also distributed unevenly. Crime prevention practitioners have therefore generally focused their efforts on addressing high-crime concentrations, identifying and addressing the particular characteristics that generate a crime problem in a specific context. Common foci in burglary prevention work have included:

- 'hot spots' of burglary, typically geographic areas or communities that have enduringly high levels of burglary;

- distinct social or demographic groups who share a heightened risk of victimization (for instance students – see Barberet *et al.* 2004); and

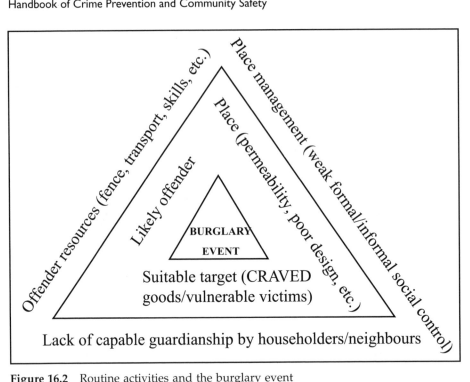

Figure 16.2 Routine activities and the burglary event

- preventing repeat victimization by offering protection to victims of burglary. A strong body of research has demonstrated that once a household has been burgled it is at greater risk of being burgled again than houses that haven't been burgled in the first place (Forrester *et al.* 1988). Repeat victimization accounts for a disproportionately large share of all burglaries (Budd 1999), and a common protective strategy is to offer assistance to first-time victims after the initial incident to reduce the risk of a repeat. Assistance is usually required quickly because the risk of repeat victimization is greatest in the first few weeks after the first incident (Polvi *et al.* 1991).

Such burglary prevention work often falls outside the routine day-to-day work of relevant agencies such as the police and local government. Whilst these agencies are usually at the forefront of prevention activity, typically programmes of work are organized on a temporary 'project' basis, with a particular high-burglary concentration being targeted. There are a number of generic issues that commonly arise in relation to such project-based work.

General issues in developing burglary prevention work

Before moving to consider the effectiveness of specific burglary prevention techniques, it is worth considering some of the issues that commonly have a bearing on whether appropriate techniques are identified in the first place, and whether they are implemented effectively. Many of these issues are generic to crime prevention work generally, are exhaustively covered in pre-existing literature and will therefore not be reiterated here. For example, weaknesses in undertaking problem analysis (see Bullock and Tilley 2003), difficulties experienced in delivering work through partnerships (see Jacobson 2003) and the frequent inadequacy of arrangements for monitoring or evaluating prevention work (Read and Tilley 2000) are all recurrent themes. However, the RBI evaluations also drew attention to a number of issues that – whilst applicable to other crime prevention work – proved particularly pertinent when developing burglary prevention work.

Complementary packages of interventions

Where projects were implementing multiple measures for reducing burglary it was important that they complemented each other (Hope *et al.* 2004; Millie and Hough 2004). For instance, under the RBI a number of projects planned to introduce measures that – on the one hand – looked to deter or repel offenders from crime targets, whilst at the same time employing these alongside measures that aimed to apprehend offenders who were attempting to exploit those targets. These approaches, when combined, are clearly incompatible, with the former liable to undermine the effectiveness of the latter.

Prevention packages over standalone measures

A consistent finding across all three RBI evaluation consortia was that the majority of projects opted for implementing packages of measures rather than single standalone measures. This is unsurprising in so far as guidance literature prepared from RBI projects encouraged a problem-solving approach which addressed the different factors that can combine to generate burglary risk (Tilley *et al.* 1999). The multi-faceted nature of burglary problems in turn recommended a range of measures to address different aspects of the problem.

However, this is not to imply that the more measures projects employed the more effective they were. Indeed the Midlands evaluation consortium found that projects that implemented fewer interventions, but implemented them well, were more effective than other projects (Hope *et al.* 2004). Aside from the obvious difficulties of successfully managing and co-ordinating greater numbers of interventions, doing 'a bit of everything' sometimes testified to a weak problem analysis and/or basing a work programme on 'thin-spreading' resources between a range of project partners.

'High unit spend'/high dosage

Consistent with Ekblom *et al.*'s (1996) earlier findings, the Northern RBI evaluation consortium found that projects that spent more – in terms of financial spend per household in the project area – were more likely to have an impact on burglary (Hirschfield 2004). The Southern evaluation consortia also supported these findings, but refined them further with their concept of 'dosage' (Millie and Hough 2004). They concluded that projects that implemented work at a 'higher dosage' were more likely to be effective. However, they recognized that high dosage normally involved a combination of different, potentially competing elements, and that an effective balance between them would have to be achieved on a case-by-case basis.

To explain these elements in terms of the provision of security equipment to households, dosage consists of 'coverage' (the size of area covered by a project); 'intensity' (the proportion of households targeted within an area and the amount of 'intervention' and/or spend each targeted household receives); and 'duration' (the amount of time an intervention lasts). Clearly with a limited resource, maximizing one of these elements can only come at the expense of the others. This leads to the question of what sort of considerations might a crime prevention practitioner bring to bear to decide on what constitutes an effective balance. There is little in the way of empirical evidence to provide guidance here, though Ekblom *et al.* (1996) does provide unit cost-per-household figures for burglary reduction work which give some indication of the levels of expenditure associated with more effective burglary reduction work. The extent to which a burglary problem is concentrated geographically might also help determine appropriate 'coverage' and 'intensity' in so far as problems that are focused on a small subset of heavily victimized/at-risk properties *may*[3] recommend a low-coverage–high-intensity approach. In terms of duration as well, projects which seek to trigger a deterrent impact through being highly visible may be more effective if they implement a high volume of work over a short duration.

Forecasting demand

RBI projects often failed to implement a high dosage of activity because the demand from communities proved less than anticipated. Errors in forecasting demand were sometimes due to poor consultation processes and a failure to offer communities services that they actually wanted and/or a concomitant failure to create demand for what was being offered (Hearnden *et al.* 2004).

A common cause of forecasting error was a failure – when work was based on the take-up of services from victims – to factor in the likely 'drop off' in demand that would occur if projects successfully reduced the number of victimizations. Another issue facing some projects was their failure to account for the fact that the burglary trend in the targeted area was already on a downward trajectory. Yet another difficulty was that some projects launched their work during a seasonal low point in burglary levels. This could be problematic for projects that were looking to 'hit the ground running' and generate a high profile through implementing a high volume of work from the outset.

A lack of demand for project services could also be due to more fundamental problems with the appropriateness of chosen interventions. In one respect interventions represent hypothetical solutions to problems that may be disproved when implemented on the ground (Hearnden *et al.* 2004). Hope *et al.* (2004), in using the term 'problem-solving implementation', allude to the important finding that effective RBI projects were not projects that stuck rigidly to the recommendations of their original problem analysis.

Rather, effective projects adapted their work intelligently to cope with any implementation difficulties that were encountered. However, an ability to adapt work intelligently to emerging developments in turn depended on projects monitoring their performance effectively, something that many projects struggled to do (Jacobson 2003).

Preventing burglary: situational crime prevention techniques

In looking at ways in which to prevent burglary, this chapter will predominantly focus on 'situational' crime prevention techniques and their effectiveness. Although clearly there are a range of other types of interventions that may have an impact on burglary offending, such as efforts to incarcerate or rehabilitate offenders through conventional criminal justice system mechanisms, such interventions are rarely burglary specific. Where funding has been channelled in the UK to address burglary specifically, or to address a range of crime problems at the area level, situational crime prevention techniques have generally been to the fore. The attraction of situational techniques in these contexts is that their underlying theoretical framework lends itself to a practical problem-solving focus. Situational crime prevention is based on reducing crime through identifying and 'blocking' the fairly immediate circumstances that generate crime opportunities.

Clarke, as the leading exponent of situational crime prevention, has developed a framework of 25 techniques for blocking opportunities. These can in turn be organized around five 'headline' categories of technique. Although burglary prevention measures do not commonly span all 25 techniques they do commonly encompass these five headline categories. Therefore, in reviewing effectiveness, techniques will be organized under each heading and will be accompanied by a table summarizing the key evidence.

The set of tables in this section requires some explanation. This is provided in Box 16.1. Before turning to the evidence tables a number of qualifications should also be made:

- The evidence collated here is principally drawn from the Reducing Burglary Initiative (RBI) evaluations, though other evaluation material is introduced in cases where it can evidence the potential 'standalone' benefits of a specific technique.

- Although many of the interventions detailed here generally fit fairly well under one particular 'technique', some interventions could clearly span two or more types of technique or headline 'categories' depending on how they are implemented.

- The presentation of results here represents a collation and aggregation of evidence on what *can* work in burglary prevention. It is not an attempt to make definitive judgements of the comparative effectiveness of one technique against another (in 'academic speak' this is not a meta-analysis). On the contrary, it could be argued that any attempt to present such a definitive

Box 16.1   Key for situational crime prevention tables

'Standalone evidence'   Where evidence does exist on the standalone impact of a given technique the number of studies are indicated and the studies referenced.

'Type, implementation and use'   Under the RBI the vast majority of interventions were implemented within a broader package. This column indicates whether, *on average*, a given intervention represented a significant part of this package (in terms of expenditure). The number of RBI projects where this intervention was employed are also indicated. Cases where projects largely failed to implement an intervention are excluded.

Key to success ratings
✓✓✓   Strong evidence (both RBI package and isolated) that method works.

✓✓   Moderate evidence (both RBI package and/or isolated) that method works.

✓   Minimal evidence (RBI package only) that method works.

?✓   Promising – mixed evidence but overall associated with positive results.

?✗   Disappointing – mixed evidence but overall associated with negative results.

✗   No evidence that this works (from RBI and/or isolated evaluation results).

'Range of net change in RBI studies'   Under the RBI, the precise impacts of individual techniques were generally impossible to assess because they were part of a broader package of measures. Therefore, the figures given here relate to the average impact – and the range of impacts – achieved by *projects as a whole* where a specific technique was employed. Only projects where the relevant techniques were implemented partially or fully are included in this measure.

'% of RBI projects where intervention is associated with positive outcome'   This column details the percentage of projects where a technique was implemented (partially or fully) and was also judged to have a positive impact.

Key to cost-effectiveness ratings
✗✗✗   Associated with packages where input (costs) are substantially greater than the output (savings).

✗✗   Associated with packages where input (costs) are moderately greater than the output (savings).

✗   Associated with packages where input (costs) are marginally greater than the output (savings).

=   Associated with packages where output (saving) is roughly equal to the input (costs).

✓   Associated with packages where output (savings) are marginally greater than the input (costs).

✓✓   Associated with packages where output (savings) are moderately greater than the input (costs).

✓✓✓   Associated with packages where output (savings) are substantially greater than the input (costs).

'Cost-benefit average and number of cost beneficial RBI studies'   This measure reports the cost-effectiveness of projects as a whole, and is only based on instances where the technique in question was viewed as having been implemented.[4] Cost-benefits are reported in terms of how much money was saved (or lost) for each pound of project money invested. Thus a cost-benefit ratio of 1:1.8 indicates that for each £1 invested £1.80 was saved in terms of the benefits derived from the project. This would therefore indicate that a project was cost-effective. A cost-benefit ratio of 1:0.5 would indicate that for each pound invested only 50p was saved, thus indicating that the project was not cost beneficial. Negative cost-benefit ratios reported here related to a limited number of instances where projects were judged to have led to 'net increases' in crime (see Hope *et al.* 2004).

judgement is of limited value because prevention techniques are heavily context dependent – that is, the techniques are only effective when they are deployed in the right problem context. This can be readily seen in the tables that accompany the discussion, as even some of the techniques that have *on aggregate* proven to be most effective have proven to be ineffective and/or cost-effective in certain instances.

'Increase the effort'

This category encompasses prevention measures that quite literally make it physically more difficult for an offender to access houses or to access semi-public or private areas around households. Typical burglary prevention measures within this category include target-hardening households on the basis of some criteria, or impeding offender movement or access to private or semi-public property surrounding houses through measures such as fencing and alleygating.

    As can be seen in Table 16.1, the majority of these interventions were associated with some measure of effectiveness – though the cost-effectiveness of some interventions was more variable. There were also a number of additional non-RBI studies that provided evidence that some of these measures – principally target-hardening households through the provision of security equipment such as door and window locks or providing households with alarms – could be effective on a standalone basis.

Locks on doors and windows (target-hardening households)
A large number of pre-existing studies have demonstrated that providing households with security enhancements such as good-quality door and window locks can reduce the risk of victimization (Forrester *et al.* 1990; Tilley and Webb 1994; Ekblom *et al.* 1996; Osborn *et al.* 2004). Other studies have demonstrated that offenders are particularly perceptive to changes in locks to houses (Wright *et al.* 1995). As well as providing improved locks, other common target-hardening measures include providing 'anti-carding' deadbolts, providing laminated or strengthened glass, and door chains and viewers (commonly

Table 16.1 The evidence on interventions reducing burglary through 'increasing the effort'

Intervention	Standalone evidence of reduction (no. of studies)	Type, implementation and use within RBI studies	Success ratings for combined RBI and standalone results	Range of net change in RBI studies (average and range)	Percentage associated with positive outcomes when implemented	Cost-benefit rating for RBI studies	Cost-benefits for RBI studies (average in no.)
Locks on windows and doors (area wide)	Gross increase of 30%, but a net reduction of between 24 and 29% compared to control area and BCU wider area respectively in one study (Allatt 1984)	Large component in 3 RBI studies	✓✓✓	*17% net reduction* (−10% to −27%)	100	✓✓✓	*1:3.87* (*2 studies cost-beneficial*)
Alley gating	50–60% gross reductions noted across 4 studies (Armstrong 1999; Young 1999; University of Liverpool 2003)	Large component in 7 RBI studies	✓✓✓	*15% net reduction* (+5% to −59%)	63	=	*1:1.17* (*3 studies cost-beneficial*)
Locks on doors and windows (targeted)	Gross increase of 30%, but a net reduction of between 24 and 29% compared to control area and BCU wider area respectively in one study (Allatt 1984)	Large component in 26 RBI studies	✓✓	*9% net reduction* (+44% to −34%)	66	=	*1:1.18* (*13 studies cost-beneficial*)

Fencing	No evidence available	Large component in 5 RBI studies	✓	12% net reduction (+21% to −59%)	40	✗	1:0.21 (2 studies cost-beneficial)
Barrier plants	No evidence available	Small component in 3 RBI studies	?✓	19% net reduction (+16% to −43%)	67	✗	1:−0.02 (1 study cost-beneficial)

employed to help elderly residents avoid distraction burglary). Grilles or bars on groundfloor windows are also occasionally employed, though as Lamm Weisel (2002) has noted these can be unpopular on aesthetic grounds.

It can be readily observed that under the RBI the effectiveness of target-hardening varied widely both within and between different target-hardening approaches. Beyond generic project management factors, the following issues appear to have had a critical bearing on the effectiveness of target-hardening approaches:

- The criteria for target-hardening households. RBI projects employed a variety of criteria for determining which households within a project should receive target-hardening services. Many focused on assisting burglary victims (a 'targeted' approach), on the basis that these victims were likely to be at heightened risk of a further victimization. Other projects applied broader criteria, target-hardening households that they perceived to be vulnerable or even simply target-hardening households on a 'first come first served' basis within the context of a project area (an 'area-wide' approach). The appropriateness of these approaches seems to have been determined by a combination of two key factors.

  The first factor was whether a project had correctly defined a group of recipient households that were 'at risk.' As discussed by Millie and Hough (2004), project-defined criteria for assessing 'vulnerability' were often vague and impressionistic and did not necessarily equate to actual 'risk'. Moreover, many projects target-hardened existing burglary victims on the basis that they were likely to be victimized again. However, many did not independently assess – or struggled accurately to assess – whether repeat victimization was actually a problem in their project area (see Hope *et al.* 2004). A further difficulty was that projects, in target-hardening burglary victims, often failed to target-harden their premises within the short time frame that repeat victimization studies suggest is critical if the risk of a further victimization is to be minimized (Polvi *et al.* 1991).

  The second factor relates to the discussion in the previous section on project dosage. It would appear that the effectiveness of target-hardening could be limited if too narrow a group of households were targeted. For instance, some projects overestimated the number of burglary victims that they would have to help during the project period. This left them in the position of sometimes target-hardening only a very small percentage of households within a target area (Millie and Hough 2004). This may in part account for the finding in Table 16.1, namely, that area-wide approaches were, on aggregate, more effective than target-specific ones, as some target-specific interventions resulted in very low dosages of crime prevention activity.

- The presence of 'suitable recipients'. The effectiveness of target-hardening also appears to have been affected by the characteristics of recipient households and whether they utilized, or were able to utilize, the security equipment provided effectively. Certain household types, such as student or ethnic minority households, may require additional support if they are to access or utilize security measures effectively.

- The presence of 'suitable infrastructure'. The effectiveness of target-hardening is also dependent on households having the necessary infrastructure to support high-quality security devices. For instance, one RBI project had to scale back its proposed target-hardening activities when it found that the rental properties that it planned to secure had door frames that could not support the locks that were to be installed (Hearnden *et al.* 2004).

- Finally, target-hardening packages may obviously be less effective if they fail to cover the key household access points that are being exploited by offenders, or which might easily be exploited if the current favoured access points are blocked. Here a key supporting element of many successful target-hardening schemes was assessing the needs of recipient households through conducting a detailed security survey first.

Alleygating

This was a popular RBI intervention, providing a potentially effective way of blocking offender access to vulnerable rear areas of certain types of housing (in particular Victorian terraced properties and Radburn-style housing). Alleygates can also help households 'reclaim' control and ownership of these rear areas (whether they be private gardens, communal alleyways or paths). In many deprived neighbourhoods such areas had come to be seen as not only access routes for offenders but also areas which were being used for offending activity in their own right owing to the natural cover they provided.

A wide range of studies have testified to the effectiveness of alleygates (Armstrong 1999; Young 1999; ODPM 2002; Bowers *et al.* 2003). More recently, Hirschfield (2003) has identified a range of additional benefits that gates can bring to high-crime communities, including environmental improvements to gated areas with residents taking greater ownership of these areas and, con-comitantly, improved resident satisfaction with the area in which they live.

The cost-effectiveness of alleygating schemes under the RBI was more variable. This was in part due to the general complexity of the implementation processes involved, with the installation of gates often requiring detailed community consultation, together with extensive legal, planning and design work. Variable cost-effectiveness could also result from considerable variations in the unit costs of different manufactured gates. Whilst good procurement practice could limit costs, projects could also be constrained by local social and infrastructural characteristics which resulted in a requirement for more expensive gates.

Covering all the relevant access points to a residential block was potentially important if alleygates were to be effective. This issue of effective coverage was common, and there were three key factors that determined whether full coverage was successfully attained:

- If one or more residents refused permission to have gates installed then this could undermine or seriously delay proceedings.

- Effectiveness was also dependent on the presence of a suitable supporting infrastructure, in terms of walls and fences being adequate to support the weight of the gates and to also block offender access (see fencing below).

- The long-term efficacy of alleygating also depended on local residents continuing to use gates appropriately. Effectiveness could be undermined if residents failed to lock gates or propped gates open. For instance, in one RBI project the effectiveness of installed alleygates was potentially threatened by the high number of students living in the area (Kay *et al.* 2004). The project managed to anticipate this threat and procured gates that were self-closing and locking (thus alleviating the need for students to remember to close them). The chosen gates also had to shut quietly, as it was considered that gates slamming as a result of students returning home late at night would lead to residents propping gates open to prevent such disturbances.

Fencing/barrier plants

Fencing and barrier plants (typically 'prickly' varieties of bushes) were employed by a variety of RBI projects – though they appear to have been most effective where they were used to support and complement other interventions. For instance, projects that sought to protect the backs of houses with alleygates often needed to erect fencing as well to close 'gaps' in the protective coverage caused by low walls or damage to existing walls and fences. Fencing, however, could appear a deceptively simple option for projects, as in reality installing effective fencing was expensive and time-consuming, necessitating as it did extensive consultation, planning and design processes. Fencing could also be compromised in instances where existing 'gaps' afforded residents with convenient shortcuts to access local amenities, and in instances were local authority planning guidelines imposed height restrictions on what could be erected.

'Increase the risks'

Leaving aside conventional police strategies for apprehending offenders, there is a range of measures than can either increase risk for offenders or at least increase their perception of risk (see Table 16.2). An important caveat however is that many of these measures – if they are actually to increase risk – are dependent on the police having the capacity and will to back up them up (for instance, through being able to respond effectively to burglary alarms if alarm coverage is increased).

Burglar alarms

Whilst some offenders do claim an ability to circumvent alarms, few seem inclined to take the risk. Burglar alarms can be an effective burglary prevention measure both as a visual deterrent that increases an offender's perception of risk and as a measure that increases their risk of apprehension (Mayhew 1984; Wright *et al.* 1995; Chenery *et al.* 1997; Coupe and Kaur in press). Different types of alarms have different strengths. Alarms that are immediately audible will maximize the deterrent value of the measure, whilst also potentially alerting neighbours and residents who may assist in the subsequent apprehension of the offender(s). Alarms that are inaudible but which alert the police (or a commercially run intermediary monitoring service) that an offence may be in progress maximize the potential for apprehending the offender at or near the scene (Coupe and Kaur in press). Finally, alarms which have a time lapse before emitting an audible signal potentially combine the advantages of both. A further observed advantage of audible systems is that, when alarms do sound, if offenders still commit the offence, fewer goods are subsequently stolen (Coupe and Kaur, in press).

Where alarms do alert the police either directly – or through an intermediary source – that an offence is in progress, evidence shows that an offender is far more likely to be apprehended at, or near, the scene if the police respond quickly and with a greater number of patrol units[5] (Coupe and Griffiths 1996). However, the ability of the police to resource such a response has traditionally been impeded by the high number of false alarm reports received. However, recent research – albeit research based on examining non-residential premises – has suggested that the police could respond to activations more effectively if they filter out the minority of premises which account for the majority of false alarms (Coupe and Kaur in press).

A variety of other alarm systems were utilized in the RBI to target the vulnerability of particular groups. For instance pendant alarms, which were given to vulnerable elderly householders in some projects, could be activated by the householder if they felt threatened or suspected that a bogus caller was trying to burgle him or her. Such alarms also had the advantage that they could provide ancillary functions, such as allowing elderly occupants to activate the alarm if they had a fall or accident. In other projects, cluster alarms were employed. These were police-linked alarms which could be installed on a temporary basis into a group of houses that were viewed as at risk of victimization. Some projects employed this on the basis that an alarm cluster was centred around a house that had been recently victimized, with neighbouring households also being protected on the basis that they were also at a heightened risk of victimization. This accords well with the notion of isomorphic repeat victimization,[6] and in essence offers a formal surveillance alternative to 'Cocoon Watches'.

Although alarm installation work in RBI projects generally appears to have been effective, it is unclear whether certain alarm types were more effective than others. Moreover, the cost-effectiveness of many of these interventions was poor. Alarm systems are expensive to install, and also come with annual service charge costs. These considerations may make long-term alarm installations unsuitable for areas with a high residential turnover, or areas where residents will struggle to afford service charges.

Street lighting, security lighting, 'occupancy' lighting

Enhancing lighting whether at the street or individual household level offers a range of options for improving surveillance, thereby increasing the risk that offenders will be identified, or at least increasing their perception of risk. Moreover, street lighting may boost surveillance not only by making it easy for people to observe offending behaviour but also – through encouraging more people to move around at night – increasing the number of potential observers (Painter and Farrington 1997; Pease 1999).

Individual studies have presented a mixed picture, with some street-lighting schemes clearly having a significant impact on burglary and a range of other crimes (Painter and Farrington 1997, 1999). Results from 10 RBI projects where

Table 16.2 The evidence on interventions reducing burglary through increasing the risks

Intervention	Standalone evidence of reduction (no. of studies)	Type, implementation and use within RBI studies	Success ratings for combined RBI and standalone results	Range of net change in RBI studies (average and range)	Percentage associated with positive outcomes when implemented	Cost benefit rating for RBI studies	Cost benefits for RBI studies (average in no.)
Street lighting	Note there is still debate over the effect. USA – gross reduction of 10% relative to 33% increase in the control area (Atlanta Regional Commission 1974); UK – 40% gross reduction relative to 15% reduction the control area (Painter and Farrington 1997); UK – 15% reduction relative to 1% increase in control area (Painter and Farrington 1999)	Large component in 10 RBI studies	✓	*8% net reduction* (+16% to –59%)	50	✗✗	*1:-0.5 (4 studies cost beneficial)*
Alarms	55% gross reduction relative to 8% in a control area in one study. Note not residential	Small component in 9 RBI studies	✓	*8% net reduction* (+44% to –41%)	67	=	*1:0.91 (4 studies cost beneficial)*

but commercial burglary study (Rubenstein *et al.* 1980)

Neighbourhood Watch	None apparent but may reduce fear of crime in the area (Bennett 1990)	Large component in 7 RBI studies	?✓	14% net reduction (+5% to −30%)	86	✓	1:1.58 (4 studies cost beneficial)
Dawn-to-dusk lighting	No evidence available	Small component in 5 RBI studies	?✓	6% net reduction (+16% to −41%)	40	✗✗✗	1:-1.23 (1 study cost beneficial)
Cocoon hardening/ Watch	Gross reduction of 30% in one study (Chenery *et al.* 1997)	Small component in 5 RBI studies	?✗	11% net increase (+44% to −14%)	33	✗✗✗	1:-2.15 (2 studies cost beneficial)
Foliage height reduction	No evidence available	Small component in 6 RBI studies	?✗	2% net reduction (+16% to −59%)	33	✗✗✗	1:1.64 (1 study cost beneficial)

street lighting was introduced were variable, with roughly half the schemes being associated with reductions in burglary. The cost-effectiveness of schemes was more doubtful, however, with the majority of schemes being assessed as cost-ineffective. Such mixed results however are perhaps unsurprising in view of widely ranging unit costs for different types of lighting and the complexity of lighting effects.[7]

Security lighting and 'occupancy' lighting work at the level of individual households. The former consists of external lights, typically working on a movement-sensor basis, which either provide residents and neighbours with enhanced surveillance over offenders who are approaching a property, or which deter an approaching offender who may perceive a risk of surveillance. An offender may also interpret security lighting as an indicator that a house is occupied. This is also the intended effect of 'occupancy' lighting which is internal household lighting, typically operated either on a timer basis or on a light-sensor basis ('dusk to dawn' lighting), to give the impression that someone is at home. There is limited evidence on the effectiveness of such lighting under the RBI (but see below), though BCS figures suggest that the ownership of such items is associated with lower household burglary risk (Dodd *et al.* 2004).

Other environmental measures

RBI case studies provide limited evidence on the effectiveness of other environmental measures that predominantly focused on enhancing surveillance. However, whilst RBI studies appear to cast doubt on the effectiveness of measures such as 'dawn to dusk' lighting and 'foliage reduction' (cutting back vegetation to improve surveillance), these results appear to be primarily due to 'project level' characteristics associated with the implementation of such measures, rather than the effectiveness of the measures themselves. Those projects that typically implemented these measures tended also to adopt a 'doing a bit of everything' approach to project planning and implementation. As was observed earlier, these types of projects appear to have been generally less successful in reducing burglary than projects which implemented a smaller, more focused, package of measures.

Conversely, pre-existing studies have shown that undertaking a more comprehensive strategy to modify the environmental characteristics of an area to reduce criminal opportunities can be effective. One such strategy, which evidence has shown can be effective (Brown 1999; Pascoe 1999; Armitage 2000) and which seeks comprehensively to 'design out crime' from residential areas is 'secure by design' (SBD) (SBD is discussed in detail in Chapters 8 and 9, this volume).

Neighbourhood Watch/Cocoon Watch

Neighbourhood Watch groups are groups of residents who – with some measure of support from the police – come together to enhance informal surveillance, thus deterring or contributing to the apprehension of offenders. Groups, however, can also act as a conduit for the police to pass on crime prevention advice and provide updates on emerging crime problems. The police and other groups may also distribute crime prevention equipment such as property-marking kits to groups. Finally, the deterrent value of groups is usually enhanced through the placement of window stickers in members houses, and the erection of street-based signs, alerting offenders to the fact that they are in a Neighbourhood Watch area.

A wide range of studies from both the USA and UK have concluded that such groups have little effect on crime rates (Rosenbaum 1988; Bennett 1990; Brown 1992; Matthews and Trickey 1994), in part because schemes tend to flourish most in areas which already have low crime rates. However, although groups may rarely have an impact on crime, some studies have noted other benefits. For instance, Hussain's (1988) survey of UK-based groups found that schemes were good at instilling a sense of security and improving relationships between the police and residents, whilst Dowds and Mayhew (1994) noted that group membership could increase motivation to report incidents to the police. Moreover, RBI projects did provide evidence that groups – when placed within a wider package of project interventions – could complement and support other interventions by acting as a channel for communication and a mechanism for generating community engagement.

Cocoon Watches work with the same basic premise as Neighbourhood Watch generally, but they are essentially organized on an informal basis. Cocoon Watches were developed as a measure to protect repeat victims, although they equally have the potential to protect households that may be subject to isomorphic repeat victimization. They are set up by the police or partner agencies in the wake of a house being victimized. Residents surrounding that house are subsequently asked to exert greater surveillance over their neighbour on the basis that they are at heightened risk of being victimized again. They may also be invited to exert greater surveillance over each others' properties more generally, on the basis that they are all at heightened risk. This approach has been successfully used alongside other repeat victimization measures such as target-hardening (Forrester et al. 1990; Chenery et al. 1997). Target-hardening has also sometimes been offered to cocoon members. Under the RBI Cocoon Watches and 'cocoon target-hardening' were not strongly associated with positive impacts. However, this may in part be due to the fact that these measures were often based on unevidenced assumptions regarding the significance of repeat vicitimization in the area.

CCTV

RBI projects were not permitted to use their grants for funding street-based CCTV schemes, as a separate grant scheme operated under the CRP for funding such work. However CCTV can be used overtly or covertly to provide formal surveillance of vulnerable households, and may therefore have the potential to prevent burglary. Evidence on the effectiveness of such measures, though, in explicitly reducing burglary is limited. For instance, Gill and Loveday (2003), when interviewing offenders, found that most were not deterred by the presence of cameras, partly because the typical duration of their offending was so short that they felt that the police were unlikely to respond quickly enough to apprehend them. More recently, Gill and Spriggs (in press), in their national evaluation of a dozen UK CCTV schemes, found limited evidence of positive impacts on burglary, with only 3 out of 12 schemes registering significant reductions. Even in those instances where burglary did reduce, there was evidence to suggest that it was being displaced to other areas.

The lack of effectiveness of CCTV schemes may relate to the fact that their focus is generally broader than burglary reduction. Moreover, the size of area that they typically encompass often limits the extent to which cameras can be effectively monitored, and the degree to which images can be 'actioned' by official agencies. In more controlled and specific contexts cameras may have more potential. For instance, Chatterton and Frenz's (1994) study of 15 schemes using CCTV in sheltered accommodation did find that the introduction of cameras had a significant impact on burglary, at least for the first 5–10 months after installation.

'Reduce the rewards'

This category covers interventions that either remove or reduce the value of potential targets to offenders (see Table 16.3). In burglary prevention work the technique most commonly employed under this category is property marking. Although one of the most famous UK burglary studies (Forrester *et al.* 1988) employed some measure of target removal, this measure is rarely employed in practice. More recently, a number of burglary prevention schemes have employed a range of interventions aimed at reducing the opportunities for selling goods by regulating the sale of second-hand goods. Whilst under the RBI these strategies tended to be associated with some measure of success, they tended not to be burglary specific, but rather aimed to reduce the opportunities for selling stolen goods more generally. As such market reduction techniques are discussed elsewhere in this volume (Chapter 11), they will not be covered here.

Property marking

The evidence on the effectiveness of property marking is mixed. Although Laycock (1985) did demonstrate that property marking could be associated with a 38 per cent reduction in burglary in one pilot scheme, this impact was notably higher than in other studies (for instance, Heller *et al.* 1975; Knuttsson 1984). Under the RBI a number of projects attempted to implement property marking with the aim that a high level of marked property would allow the police not only to recover more property but also to arrest more offenders and handlers caught in possession of stolen items. The ultimate aspiration was that this would in due course deter offenders from stealing goods that they thought might be marked. However, such a design proved unrealistic in view of the fact that the police traditionally recover only a small percentage of stolen property (Coupe and Griffiths 1996). Few RBI schemes achieved high levels of property-marking coverage and, even where they did, there was little evidence of any schemes successfully mobilizing the police or their partners to change their practices so as to recover more stolen items.

Where higher levels of property-marking coverage were achieved by RBI projects, attaining that coverage generally proved resource intensive. In some schemes the use of police officers to deliver property-marking kits was viewed as a questionable use of resources. However, the costs of deploying police in

Table 16.3 The evidence of interventions reducing burglary through 'reducing the rewards'

Intervention	Standalone evidence of reduction (no. of studies)	Type, implementation and use within RBI studies	Success ratings for combined RBI and standalone results	Range of net change in RBI studies (average and range)	Percentage associated with positive outcomes when implemented	Cost benefit rating for RBI studies	Cost benefits for RBI studies (average in no.)
Property marking	Little evidence of stand-alone effectiveness (Heller *et al* 1975; Knuttsson 1984; Laycock 1985, 1991)	Small component in 20 RBI studies	✓	*14% net reduction* *(+16% to –43%)*	67	✓	*1:2.08* *(8 studies cost beneficial)*
Covert trackers/ cameras	No evidence available	Small component in 6 RBI studies	?✓	*2% net reduction* *(+16% to –27%)*	50	✗✗	*1:0.32* *(no studies found to be cost beneficial)*

this way may have been justified if – in delivering property-marking kits – the police also fulfilled a number of other functions. For instance, Laycock (1985, 1991) noted that the police delivery of property-marking kits could be combined to good effect with a general high-visibility policing operation (see below).

The unit costs of property marking varied considerably under the RBI. Cost was dependent not only on how kits were delivered but also on the type of kit used. Whilst stickers and UV pens proved a relatively cheap way of marking property, more expensive high-tech options were also pursued, such as the utilization of microscopic dot stamps and SmartWater.[8] Whilst the potential of such high-tech techniques cannot be dismissed, their value, in schemes where little if any property was actually recovered, was limited.

Property marking has been seen to work when it is combined with related publicity which alerts the offender to the presence of property-marked items (Laycock 1991). Offenders may be deterred on this basis because they perceive there to be less value, or a greater risk, in stealing property from covered households. The conventional way of conveying this message is for property-marked households to alert offenders through placing stickers in the window of their dwelling advertising the fact that they have marked goods. The relative lack of effectiveness of many RBI property-marking schemes appears in part to be due to the fact that, generally, schemes failed to publicize their efforts in this (or in any other) way.

Covert cameras/trackers

Under the RBI, cameras and hi-tech tracking technology were used in a number of schemes. Although in some instances this technology was used, with limited effect, to increase the detection of burglary offenders, a more common ambition was to utilize the technology as a way of gathering intelligence on, and then blocking, markets for stolen burglary items. There was limited evidence that these measures were either effective or cost-effective. These failures can be related to a variety of factors:

- Such technology was highly expensive to procure and using such equipment required a degree of staff training that was often absent. The resources required to undertake accompanying sting or undercover operations could also be formidably high.

- A common strategy for utilizing this equipment was to place it in high-value electronic items in households that were perceived to be at risk of victimization, usually households that had just been burgled. However, it often proved difficult to find households to volunteer to act as bait for this sort of operation.

- Projects did not operate with realistic probabilities, in terms of thinking through how many trackers were likely to be stolen and what sort of impact this in turn would have on levels of burglary. Projects typically could only afford a small number of trackers and in most projects employing this approach no trackers were stolen during the project period.

- Even in the rare instances where trackers were stolen it was difficult to capitalize on such an event in terms of making significant inroads into the market for stolen goods. This difficulty in part reflects the fact that many projects appear to have operated with an oversimplified view of stolen goods markets. Their expectation that in tracking a few stolen goods they would in turn be able to 'crack' a distinctive local stolen goods markets, runs counter to research which shows that stolen goods are disposed of, and sold on, through a flexible, fast-moving and varied network of offender–handler–buyer relationships (Sutton *et al.* 1998).

Target removal

Forrester *et al.* (1988) document one of the few well-known examples of burglary prevention being driven through removing an item of property that was attracting offenders. However, the property in question (electricity coin meters) are increasingly uncommon within a UK context, and few projects since have had a property-removal element. A notable exception to this in the RBI was the establishment in one project of safe storage facilities for student property during the holiday period (Northern Consortium 2002). This allowed students, who might otherwise leave such property in their term-time residencies, to store valuable electronic items, etc., in secure storage provided by the university. Whilst the evaluators concluded that this intervention was unlikely to have contributed to a reduction in burglary owing to the fact that it had not been publicized to offenders, they hypothesized that it could have contributed to a reduction in the number of goods stolen by offenders when houses were broken into.

'Reduce provocations'

Burglary prevention interventions that sought to reduce provocations focused on limiting the influence amongst youths of peers who might encourage them to become involved in burglary offending (see Table 16.4). Often, a related objective of many RBI projects was physically to limit the availability of youths to get involved in offending (by taking up their spare time with more constructive activities).

Education/outreach work and diversionary activities

A number of RBI projects sought to implement a variety of measures that aimed to persuade/educate youths about the perils and consequences of involvement in offending. Other projects sought to provide diversionary activities for youths on the basis that youth involvement in burglary was a result of boredom and peer influence, and that the provision of constructive activities would reduce or prevent their involvement in burglary.

The RBI evaluations were unable to find compelling evidence of the impact of such measures on burglary. However, in most instances the evaluations were too short term to be able to identify an impact on the predisposition of young people to be involved in crime. Nevertheless, RBI projects exposed a number of common limitations with these types of interventions. First, these approaches often appeared unevidenced in so far as it was unclear whether

Table 16.4 The evidence of interventions reducing burglary through 'reducing provocation'

Intervention	Standalone evidence of reduction (no. of studies)	Type, implementation and use within RBI studies	Success ratings for combined RBI and standalone results	Range of net change in RBI studies (average and range)	Percentage associated with positive outcomes when implemented	Cost benefit rating for RBI studies	Cost benefits for RBI studies (average in no.)
School awareness programmes	No evidence available	Large component in 4 RBI studies	✓	*5% net reduction (+16% to −21%)*	75	✓	*1:0.62 (1 study cost beneficial)*
Youth diversion schemes	Mixed results (Loxley et al. 2002)	Large component in 15 RBI studies	✓	*17% net reduction (+5% to −43%)*	79	✓	*1:1.5 (9 studies cost beneficial)*
Outreach work	No evidence available	Small component in 1 RBI study	?✓	*6% net reduction*	100	✓	*1:1.54 (1 study cost beneficial)*

local youths significantly contributed to burglary levels. Secondly, the targeting, timing and intensity of diversionary activities, in particular, were often such that it was implausible that they would have a significant impact on burglary. This is consistent with Loxley *et al.*'s (2002) earlier evaluation findings on the potential effectiveness of standalone youth diversionary activities in the UK. Whilst not dismissing the potential for other types of benefits, the evaluators concluded that it was implausible that diversionary schemes impacted substantially on burglary. This is because they were not targeted sufficiently at 'high risk' youths, and the limited time periods in which they operated meant that potential offenders still had plenty of 'availability' during peak burglary periods in which they could commit offences.

The evidence on the effectiveness of these approaches 'in reducing provocations' is therefore limited. However, it does appear that such activities could play a valuable supporting role for a wider package of interventions, generating trust and engagement within deprived communities that could help enhance the take-up and effectiveness of other interventions. Furthermore, educational and outreach work could be utilized to increase security-conscious behaviour not only amongst targeted youths but also – through encouraging them to take prevention materials home – amongst their parents (Ekblom *et al.* 1996).

'Remove excuses'

This category of techniques in burglary prevention terms typically covers interventions that seek to limit offending by stimulating the conscience of the offender, or through controlling the behaviour of potential offenders through place-specific rules (see Table 16.5).

Deterrent publicity
Aside from many of the types of publicity which have already been covered in our discussion of preceding interventions such as property-marking, window stickers or Neighbourhood Watch signs, some RBI projects utilized publicity that was deliberately targeted at catching the conscience of offenders. Approaches employed included street-based signage and directly sending deterrent messages to offenders commonly in the form of Christmas cards that informed them that the police were keeping an eye on them. Evidence on the effectiveness of these approaches appears to be mixed, though the key considerations in determining their success are similar to those governing the use of publicity more generally (see section below). Specific problems relating to street-based signage included problems with the positioning and visibility of signage, as well as issues around the clarity of the messages conveyed (see Flockenhaus *et al.* 2002 for a good example of this).

Rental agreements
One method for controlling the behaviour of known burglary offenders who are resident in social housing is to use rental agreements and the potential threat of eviction as leverage to reduce offending behaviour. In one project (Adamson 2002) persistent offenders were issued with warnings about their

Table 16.5 The evidence on interventions reducing burglary through removing excuses

Intervention	Standalone evidence of reduction (no. of studies)	Type, implementation and use within RBI studies	Success ratings for combined RBI and standalone results	Range of net change in RBI studies (average and range)	Percentage associated with positive outcomes when implemented	Cost benefit rating for RBI studies	Cost benefits for RBI studies (average in no.)
Media broadcasts and handouts targeted at offenders	No evidence available	Supportive component in 8 RBI studies	✓	16% net reduction (+5% to −42%)	75	✓	1:2.04 (4 studies cost beneficial)
Landlord registration	No evidence available	Small component in 5 RBI studies	✓	10% net reduction (+16% to −27%)	60	✗	1:0.19 (2 studies cost beneficial)
Tenant-based approaches	No evidence available	Small component in 8 RBI studies	?✓	12% net reduction (+44 to −55%)	88	✓✓	1:2.38 (3 studies cost beneficial)
ASBOs	No evidence available: ASBO use for burglars is relatively new – hence there are no current evaluation data	Small component in 3 RBI studies	?✓	16% net reduction (−5% to −27%)	67	=	1:0.55 (0 studies cost beneficial)
Signs (including posters and stickers) targeted at offenders	No evidence available	Supportive component in 3 RBI studies	?✗	2% net increase (+16% to −10%)	67	✗✗	1:−0.45 (0 studies cost beneficial)

burglary offending. They were then evicted if they continued to offend and were banned from returning to any property within a given radius. Empty properties were then filled, ideally with relatives of existing reliable tenants, and applications from families of unreliable tenants were given a low priority. In short, the method represents an almost conscious attempt to reverse the sort of 'area tipping' effect identified by Baldwin and Bottoms (1976), whereby areas decline as more and more well behaved tenants are driven out by 'problem tenants' (only to be replaced in turn by more problem tenants). Although the use of such methods may raise ethical issues, they do appear to be effective.

Anti-social behaviour orders

In the UK, one key development has been the development of anti-social behaviour orders (ASBOs) as a means of controlling or preventing offending behaviour. ASBOs only require a lower civil burden of proof[9] to be imposed upon an individual – but their breach can result in criminal sanctions. ASBOs can impose on an individual a range of behavioural restrictions such as exclusion from a geographic area or a night-time curfew. Although successfully applying for and enforcing an ASBO typically requires strong multi-agency co-operation (Campbell 2002), they would appear to have potential as a method of burglary prevention. Although the use of ASBOs explicitly to reduce burglary offending has been rare to date, Bullock and Jones (2004), in their study of similar behavioural contracts in one area of London, found that many of the targeted youths had had previous contact with the police in relation to burglary. Similarly some RBI projects also utilized ASBOs though they were usually targeted at individuals who were engaged in a range of criminal and anti-social behaviours not just burglary. Evidence on the possible long-term consequences of such measures is not yet available.

Private rental sector measures

Many conventional offender and victim-oriented situational crime prevention measures in a UK context have proven easiest to administer within the context of social housing. However, the private rented sector also has a large number of tenants who are vulnerable and/or engaged in offending. A particular growth area has been the student rental market, with university expansion fuelling a growth in multi-let student houses in inner-city areas. More generally, a large number of young, often vulnerable, people also reside in large multi-let households, commonly termed as 'houses in multiple occupancy' (HIMOs). HIMOs frequently have poor standards of physical security, exacerbated by tenants with poor security behaviours.

A number of RBI properties attempted to address issues of poor security in the private rental sector. Two principal methods were used for doing this, and in at least one project they were used in combination:

- *Incentivizing landlords*. A number of RBI projects sought to engage landlords to improve the security of their housing stock. Some projects tried to do this through at least part funding security equipment. However, many landlords proved uninterested in such offers. Moreover, projects often struggled to identify and contact absentee landlords in the first place. Other projects utilized more 'stick' in their tactics of persuasion, setting up 'registered landlord lists' which either rated landlords on their security provision or simply excluded landlords who did not meet a minimum level of security. Such lists could work well, particularly if they were backed up by the relevant institutions or agencies responsible for directing individuals towards rented accommodation (such as university accommodation offices). However, a key factor in the effectiveness of these approaches is the characteristics of the underlying rental market. Incentivizing landlords appears to be more achievable in areas where there is an excess supply of rented properties relative to demand, thus providing leverage over landlords anxious to attract tenants.

- *Tenant vetting.* In one RBI scheme (Bowers 2002) private landlords were encouraged to improve the security of their housing stock in return for the police vetting prospective tenants. The theory behind this approach is that it would prevent offenders and other potentially problematic tenants moving in to participating landlords' properties, thus presumably helping to protect existing tenants from victimization and protecting landlords from possible financial losses. Such an approach, though it showed some potential to contribute to burglary reduction, required careful management in view of the range of ethical and legal issues it raised.

Supporting/complementary measures

Although situational crime prevention measures formed the core of the majority of RBI projects, many projects also employed other measures that might be seen as either supporting or complementing situational approaches (see Table 16.6). As already discussed, this chapter is not going to attempt to encompass the more routine (and well evidenced) of these, such as enhanced police detection activities or the extended provision of drug treatment services for burglary offenders. However, there were four additional types of interventions that were commonly employed to complement situational approaches which merit some mention here.

General publicity (broadcasts, newsletters, handouts, crime prevention packs, etc.)

The inherent importance of publicity to the effectiveness of interventions such as property marking has been discussed in the preceding sections. However, in addition to these intervention-specific forms of publicity, RBI projects employed a wide range of different types of publicity, utilizing different messages and mediums. Within the RBI, publicity generally contributed to one or more of the following purposes. To:

- facilitate the engagement of residents with project interventions;
- facilitate behavioural change amongst residents or specific populations, with the aim of lowering their risk of victimization. A related purpose – though

one rarely pursued under the RBI – is for publicity to change attitudes and/or emotions, and in particular for it to help reduce fear of crime; and

- change the perceptions of potential offenders in terms of the opportunities for exploiting criminal opportunities.

A wide range of studies have demonstrated that publicity is frequently a critical component in successful crime reduction work (Vader 1979; Sacco and Silverman 1981; Lavakras *et al.* 1983; Bowers and Johnson 2003). Indeed, Bowers and Johnson's analysis of the impact of publicity on 21 RBI projects in the north of England concluded that publicity was a successful intervention in its own right. Bowers and Johnson, in particular, noted that publicity could effectively 'extend' a project either temporally or spatially by stimulating a perception amongst offenders that schemes covered a wider area or time period than they actually did.

RBI projects employed a wide range of publicity measures, including radio interviews, newspaper articles, television slots, leaflets/flyers/letters, posters, stickers and community events. However, the majority of these activities were locally based and locally focused, and Bowers and Johnson's work suggests that such publicity is more likely to be both effective and cost-effective. This is not only because it can be tailored tightly to context-specific problems, issues and perceptions but it can also utilize formats and media which best fit local preferences.

Locally based publicity is also likely to be more cost-effective in that it can exploit not only cheaper, formal publicity media, but also a range of informal media that may be free (not least word of mouth). However, the choice of medium appears frequently to have been dictated by convenience and familiarity rather than an informed assessment of whether that medium was best suited to accessing a particular audience. Research into the use of publicity in the Tees Valley in the UK found that precisely those groups whom one might wish to reach the most (such as deprived communities and ethnic minority residents) are in fact the least likely to 'pick up' and recall publicity messages (Research Solutions UK 2003).

Weaknesses in choosing and targeting media under the RBI are reflected in a wider lack of media skills evident amongst practitioners running RBI projects (Hough *et al.* 2004). Nevertheless, under the RBI some innovative attempts were made to reach target audiences. Difficulties in communicating with ethnic minority groups were resolved in one project through the direct use of ethnic minority liaison officers to engage with residents (Keele University 2002a). In influencing students, RBI projects employed a range of unconventional tactics, notably targeting parents as a way of reaching students. The Home Office also sponsored centrally, in co-operation with the National Union of Students, a website that included games designed vicariously to inform students about burglary risk factors and good security behaviours.[10]

Tenant support

In a couple of RBI projects, measures were adopted to try to support new tenants, and in particular single parents, moving into the area. The reasoning

Table 16.6 The evidence on supporting/complementary interventions in burglary reduction projects

Intervention	Standalone evidence of reduction (no. of studies)	Type, implementation and use within RBI studies	Success ratings for combined RBI and standalone results	Range of net change in RBI studies (average and range)	Percentage associated with positive outcomes when implemented	Cost benefit rating for RBI studies	Cost benefits for RBI studies (average in no.)
Media approaches – broadcasts, newsletters, posters and handouts (community focused)	No evidence available	Supportive component in 15 RBI studies	✓	*14% net reduction (+16% to –41%)*	80	✓✓	*1:2.36 (8 studies cost beneficial)*
Crime prevention advice packs	No evidence available	Supportive component in 18 RBI studies	✓✓	*12.6% net reduction (+16% to –43%)*	72	✓	*1:2.51 (11 studies cost beneficial)*
Tidy up appearances of area	No evidence available	Small component in 5 RBI studies	✓✓	*27% net reduction (–1 to –43%)*	100	✓	*1:1.39 (3 studies cost beneficial)*
Target prolific offenders/zero-tolerance policing	Reduction of 62%, relative to 41%, and by 18% in other areas (diff of benefits) in one study (Farrell *et al.* 1998)	Large component in 9 RBI studies	✓✓	*17% net reduction (+16% to –59%)*	80	=	*1:1.14 (4 studies cost beneficial)*

| High-visibility patrolling | Domestic gross reduction between 16 and 21% in the target areas (city) but relative to a 25% gross reduction in the control area in one study (Jones and Tilley 2004) | Small component in 8 RBI studies | ?✓ | 18% net reduction (+16% to −59%) | 75 | = | 1:1.09 (5 studies cost beneficial) |

behind these approaches accorded well with pre-existing research which shows that single parents (Budd 1999) and new tenants moving into an area (Ellingworth and Pease 1998) are at a heightened risk of burglary victimization. In one scheme tenant support was linked to an area-based policy that sought to reduce the growing number of void properties, to settle new families on to the estate and to stabilize the high turnover of residents (Keele University 2002b). This was to be achieved not only through offering these new tenants the 'carrot' of extensively improved and renovated properties (including high-quality security equipment) but also through offering them structured support to minimize their social isolation and vulnerability. The project partly sought to do this by moving new tenants in 'on bulk' into distinct blocks of housing in co-ordinated 'moving-in days' with the idea that this would encourage new tenants to support each other. This approach enjoyed some measure of success, at least in the short term, attracting and retaining a number of new tenants. However, the evaluators were less certain that the longer-term aim of stabilizing the area through reducing the number of void properties had been achieved, partly because the intervention appears to have become progressively 'diluted' and less focused around its original principles.

Area 'clear ups' and other aesthetic improvements

RBI projects utilized a range of other measures that were intended to build up the overarching capacity of communities both to engage with projects and also to take ownership of their burglary problem. Such measures included setting up formal structures such as community groups and residents' associations, whilst others sought to stimulate community confidence and motivation through aesthetic improvements. In particular, area-based 'clear-ups' contributed to a couple of successful burglary projects. Although it is hard to attribute to such measures a direct impact on burglary, it appears plausible that the removal of rubbish and graffiti helped give projects credibility and encouraged residents to engage with project work. It might also be reasonably hypothesized that clear-ups could – through increasing community confidence – result in residents exerting stronger guardianship over their local areas thereby reducing offending opportunities. This would be loosely consistent with Wilson and Kelling's (1982) 'broken windows' hypothesis.

Crackdown and consolidation/high-visibility policing

This approach is based on the police initially targeting key local burglary offenders and then following this up with a package of 'consolidation' measures which might typically include community-based work and situational crime prevention measures. A key rationale is that whilst police crackdown work on its own can be particularly effective in the short term, gains decay rapidly over time (Sherman 1990; Scott 2003). Consolidation mentions are therefore intended to help sustain and even extend these gains (Wright and Pease 1995). In particular, the removal of key offenders from an area may create a window of opportunity for working with a community, as residents may feel more confident to engage in crime reduction work and may feel more positive about agencies like the police.

In Farrell *et al.* (1998), a pilot project implemented this approach – targeting active prolific offenders. These offenders were identified on the basis of formalized criteria, and were then targeted using a range of tactics including bail enforcement, stop and search, and covert observation. This crackdown phase was then followed up with a consolidation phase which centred around target-hardening households that had been burgled in the previous six months. The pilot achieved a significant reduction in burglary across both stages of the project. Only one 'cycle' of crackdown and consolidation was undertaken in this project, though Tilley and Laycock (2002) have also suggested that applying crackdown and consolidation cycles randomly, at different times and in different areas, could maximise offender uncertainty and their perceptions of risk. A number of RBI projects also attempted to follow a crackdown and consolidation approach, though most struggled to resource sufficiently the crackdown element. In one instance where, at least the initial crackdown phase was well implemented, there was evidence that it had had a marked impact on burglary, and that consolidation activities had delayed any subsequent decay in that impact (Millie in press).

One potential element of any crackdown phase is the use of 'high-visibility policing' (HVP). This may entail putting into an area a significantly strengthened *visible* uniformed police presence for a short period of time. HVP was often implemented as an intervention in its own right under the RBI, although the resources for such work often weren't forthcoming or weren't sustained. The RBI provides limited evidence to suggest that HVP was an effective intervention for specifically reducing burglary, though as a supporting intervention it could have a range of positive impacts. These could include providing community reassurance, improving police–community relations, generating intelligence on offenders through enhanced contact with residents and helping to deliver other RBI interventions (typically property marking).

Concluding remarks

Both the RBI and a diverse range of other evaluation studies provide a substantial evidence base on what can be effective in preventing burglary. The reader may feel though that less has been said here about how one might tackle emerging or future burglary patterns. The omission is deliberate in so far as current social, demographic, consumer and technological trends provide no clear indications as to where burglary 'may be heading'. This uncertainty within a UK context is reflected in the recent loss of predicative power of the Home Office's previous model (see Dhiri *et al.* 1999) for estimating burglary trends. Whilst some of the key variables that contribute to the 'supply' of offenders have retained a degree of predicative power (notably the number of unemployed young males – see Simmons and Dodds 2003), the contribution of other variables has become uncertain. It is beyond the scope of this chapter to discuss in detail the many possible contributory factors that have led to this uncertainty. However, even a cursory consideration of some recent social and consumer trends demonstrates that the implications of such trends – in terms of their impact on burglary – are far from clear. For example:

- Within the UK there has been a steady increase in the number of single adult households.[11] This trend may result in lower levels of household occupancy and consequently greater burglary opportunities. However, this trend has also put immense pressure on the UK's housing stock, leading to a requirement to initiate a large building programme to supply affordable new housing. This new housing may counter the negative consequences of low occupancy *if* improved standards of physical and design security are adopted by developers. Current housing shortages are also leading to more young adults staying longer in the parental home, which may also reduce offending opportunities. Finally, assumptions about lower levels of household occupancy may prove invalid if current trends towards increased home working continue and accelerate.

- It is unclear what the implications of future consumer trends will be. For instance, the growth in the market for high-value portable goods in recent years, notably mobile phones, has been widely seen as having contributed to the growth in street robbery (Smith 2003). This has coincided, at least in the UK, with a clear drop-off in the desirability of certain household electrical products for thieves (Dodd *et al.* 2004). Whether these trends continue, say with iPod and 3G mobile phone technology continuing to fuel street crime, is debatable. Conversely, will the increasing ownership of new household products such as flat-screen televisions fuel greater offending, or will many offenders find large flat screens too cumbersome to constitute an attractive opportunity?

- The accessibility of new products to thieves also depends on the technological attributes of these products. For instance, the prospect of more disposable income being spent on 'intangible products' (for instance membership or access to Internet-based or digital services) may limit offending opportunities. Equally, technology that allows personal electronic goods to be tracked or immobilized[12] if stolen is rapidly becoming available. The extent to which they are actually commercially adopted, and whether that availability is reinforced by consumer demand for such services, is open to question.

Regardless of these uncertainties, within the context of the current situation there are still some clear opportunities for extending and refining existing burglary prevention practices. Leaving aside more generic crime reduction developments such as targeting prolific offenders and tackling the market for stolen goods, these opportunities include the following:

- In the light of the last point made above, there is some scope for government to engage with private industry and retailers to develop and promote products which include security features such as immobilizers.

- Burglary reduction projects in England and Wales have started to pay more heed to the vulnerabilities of high-risk demographic groups. To date attention has focused on examining burglary against students and against the elderly, but there is clearly scope for more work to be done with other groups identified as being at high risk (see Budd 1999), notably with ethnic minority households in low-income areas and with single parents.

- A related development under the RBI is the increasing range and sophistication of work being done to prevent burglary through utilizing a diverse range of 'levers' drawn from the area of housing management. These include behavioural 'contracts' such as tenancy agreements designed to deter offenders, through to co-ordinated support arrangements for new tenants at risk of victimization. More ambitiously still, some areas have also started to remodel housing allocation policies effectively to 'engineer out' offending cultures from high-crime areas.

- Similar work has also been undertaken with private sector landlords. However, security standards in the private rented sector are still often very poor. A promising development within England and Wales has been the introduction of 'enabling' legislation which opens the door for minimum security standards to be specified within building regulations for both domestic and non-domestic premises. More generally, there has been a concerted effort to ensure that security considerations are more routinely included within planning decisions, and guidance to facilitate this has recently been published.[13]

- The potential of 'isomorphic repeat victimization' (see note 6 for an explanation) has yet to be fully explored or tested. The isomorphic model has recently been utilized to help produce more accurate 'prospective hotspot' maps to target burglary reduction resources at emerging burglary concentrations (Bowers *et al.* 2004). A pilot is currently being developed to explore the practical utility of this approach.

- Finally, the RBI evaluations in particular have thrown up a range of findings that relate not so much to the efficacy of particular techniques but to how burglary reduction work can best be developed and managed. Whilst this may seem mundane, the RBI findings would suggest that the most rapid improvement in burglary prevention performance is to be found in this area.

Selected further reading

Due to the relative prominence and frequency of domestic burglary, the general crime prevention and crime reduction literature draws heavily upon studies that have either assessed the efficacy of burglary reduction techniques or have explored the characteristics and patterns of burglary offending. In terms of literature that exclusively focuses on domestic burglary, Lamm Weisel's (2002) *Burglary of Single-family Houses* can be readily recommended as a comprehensive summary covering the patterns of burglary, the decision-making and preferences of offenders, the analysis of burglary problems and the selection of effective reduction measures. Curtin *et al.*'s (2001) *Developing Crime Reduction Plans: Some Examples from the Reducing Burglary Initiative* also provides a useful guide to analysing burglary problems and developing tailored responses.

In terms of evaluation results from the UK's Reducing Burglary Initiative, readers are advised to go to Kodz's *et al.*'s online report at: http://www.homeoffice.gov.uk/rds/pdfs04/rdsolr3904.pdf. From here readers can find links to the online impact reports produced by the three evaluation consortia as well as links to a number of short case study summaries detailing the findings from some of the individual project evaluations. More practitioner-focused guidance on burglary reduction together with links to key Home Office reports are also available at: http://www.crimereduction. gov.uk/burglaryminisite01.htm. Readers wishing to read more on burglary trends and patterns within a UK context are recommended to refer to the 2003/4 British Crime Survey report available at: http://www.homeoffice.gov.uk/rds/crimeew0304.html. Budd's earlier (1999) study *Burglary of Domestic Dwellings: Findings from the British Crime Survey* – which extensively analyses burglary data from the 1998 British Crime Survey – can also be highly recommended. Her summary of the main practitioner implications deriving from this study is excellent and can be found at: http://www.homeoffice.gov. uk/rds/prgpdfs/brf501.pdf. A summary of international burglary patterns and trends, based on the 2000 International Crime Victim Surveys, can be found at: http://www. unicri.it/icvs/publications/pdf_files/CriminalVictimisationUrbanEurope.pdf.

The studies above predominantly examine patterns of burglary utilizing victim data. A number of studies – which explore burglary in terms of the behaviour, decision-making and reasoning of offenders – can also be recommended. These include Wright and Decker's (1994) *Burglars on the Job: Street Life and Residential Break-ins*, Cromwell *et al.*'s (1991) excellent and very readable *Residential Burglary: An Ethnographic Analysis* and Bennett and Wright's (1989) *Burglars on Burglary: Prevention and the Offender*. A recent (2004) and accessible study on burglary offender decision-making by Hearnden and Magill can be found at: http://www.homeoffice.gov.uk/rds/pdfs04/r249.pdf.

Notes

1. If the reader wishes to pursue the detailed findings of these evaluations they can be found at Kodz *et al.* (2004) http://www.homeoffice.gov.uk/rds/pdfs04/ rdsolr3904.pdf.

2. See Clarke (1999) for a fuller consideration of the different characteristics of consumer goods that make them desirable to a thief.

3. This presupposes that this subset of properties have enduring characteristics that put them at greater risk compared to other houses in the surrounding area.

4. The cost-effectiveness estimates produced under the RBI evaluations are based on a number of assumptions, such as assumptions about the lifespan of capital items and the longevity of burglary reduction impacts. Readers should read Bowles and Pradiptyo (2004) for further details.

5. Coupe and Griffiths (1996) found that improvements in detection did not simply derive from a quick response alone, but from a combination of speed and a higher number of police patrols attending. They recommended that one way this could be resourced would be for the police to deploy more 'single-crewed police' vehicles.

6. 'Isomorphic repeat victimization' refers to an observed pattern of burglary victimization where, after a house is victimized, houses either side of this first house – up to a certain distance – are at heightened risk of victimization for a period of time (Townsley *et al.* 2003; Johnson and Bowers 2004).

7. Painter's (1992) earlier discussion of lighting within the wider context of the female use of public space is recommended as illustrating some of these issues.

8. SmartWater is a water-based solution with a unique forensic code designed to protect household property whilst being almost invisible to the naked eye. It glows under UV light and is practically impossible to remove entirely.

9. Under English law a defendant can be found guilty in civil cases if it is considered that on 'the balance of probabilities' he or she has committed the act with which

he or she is charged. In criminal cases the burden of proof is higher, requiring that the accused by proven guilty 'beyond reasonable doubt'.

10. The website can be viewed at www.good2bsecure.gov.uk.
11. See http://www.statistics.gov.uk/cci/nugget.asp?id=818.
12. See http://www.crimereduction.gov.uk/target.htm for a description of one immobilizing product.
13. This guidance can be viewed at http://www.odpm.gov.uk/stellent/groups/odpm_planning/documents/page/odpm_plan_028449.pdf.

References

Adamson, S. (2002) 'Grovehill, Middlesborough Strategic Development Project: final report.' Upublished paper.

Allatt, P. (1984) 'Residential security: containment and displacement of burglar', *Howard Journal*, 23: 99–116.

Armitage, R. (2000) *An Evaluation of Secured by Design Housing within West Yorkshire. Home Office Briefing Note 7/00.* London: Home Office.

Armstrong, Y.A. (1999) 'Evaluation of the Forest Fields Gating Project.' Unpublished manuscript, University of the West of England, Bristol.

Atlanta Regional Commission (1974) *Street Light Project: Final Evaluation Report.* Atlanta, GA: Atlanta Regional Commission.

Baldwin, J. and Bottoms, A. (1976) *The Urban Criminal: A Study in Sheffield.* London: Tavistock.

Barberet, R., Fisher, B.S. and Taylor, H. (2004) *University Student Safety in the East Midlands. Home Office Online Report 61/04.* London: Home Office.

Bennett, T. (1990) *Evaluating Neighbourhood Watch. Cambridge Studies in Criminology.* Aldershot: Gower.

Bennett, T. and Wright, T. (1984) *Burglars on Burglary: Prevention and the Offender.* Aldershot: Gower.

Bowers, K.J. (2002) 'Morecombe Strategic Development Project: final report.' Unpublished paper.

Bowers, K.J. and Johnson, S.D. (2003) *The Role of Publicity in Crime Prevention: Findings from the Reducing Burglary Initiative. Home Office Research Study 272.* London: Home Office.

Bowers, K.J., Johnson, S.D. and Hirschfield, A. (2003) *Pushing Back the Boundaries: New Techniques for Assessing the Impact of Burglary Schemes. Home Office Online Report 24/03.* London: Home Office.

Bowers, K.J., Johnson, S.D. and Pease, K. (2004) 'Prospective hot-spotting: the future of crime mapping?', *British Journal of Criminology*, 44: 641–58.

Bowles, R. and Pradiptyo, R. (2004) *Reducing Burglary Initiative: An Analysis of Costs, Benefits and Cost Effectiveness. Home Office Online Report 43/04.* London: Home Office.

Brand, S. and Price, R. (2000) *The Economic and Social Costs of Crime. Home Office Research Study 217.* London: Home Office.

Brantingham, P.L. and Brantingham, P.J. (1984) *Patterns in Crime.* New York, NY: Macmillan.

Bridgeman, C. and Hobbs, L. (1997) *Preventing Repeat Victimisation: The Police Officer's Guide.* London: Home Office.

Brown, L. (1992) *Neighbourhood Watch: A Literature Review. Central Research Unit Paper.* Edinburgh: Scottish Office.

Brown, J. (1999) 'An evaluation of the Secured By Design Initiative in Gwent, South Wales.' Unpublished MSc, Scarman Centre for the Study of Public Order, University of Leicester.

Budd, T. (1999) *Burglary of Domestic Dwellings: Findings from the British Crime Survey. RDS Statistical Bulletin Issue 4/99.* London: Home Office.

Bullock, K. and Jones, B. (2004) *Acceptable Behaviour Contracts Addressing Antisocial Behaviour in the London Borough of Islington. Home Office Online Report* 02/04. London: Home Office.

Bullock, K. and Tilley, N. (2003) 'Introduction: problem-oriented policing, the concept, implementation and impact in the UK and USA', in K. Bullock and N. Tilley (eds) *Crime Reduction and Problem-oriented Policing.* Cullompton: Willan Publishing.

Campbell, S. (2002) *A Review of Anti-social Behaviour Orders. Home Office Research Study* 236. London: Home Office.

Chatterton, M.R. and Frenz, S.J. (1994) 'Closed circuit television: its role in reducing burglaries and the fear of crime in sheltered accommodation for the elderly', *Security Journal,* 5: 133–9.

Chenery, S., Holt, J. and Pease, K. (1997) *Biting Back II: Reducing Repeat Victimisation in Huddersfield. Crime Detection and Prevention Series Paper* 82. London: Home Office.

Clarke, R.V. (1999) *Hot Products: Understanding, Anticipating and Reducing Demand for Stolen Goods. Home Office Police Research Series Paper* 112. London: Home Office.

Cohen, L.E. and Felson, M. (1979) 'Social change and crime rate trends: a routine activity approach', *American Sociological Review,* 44: 588–608.

Cornish, D. (1994) 'The procedural analysis of offending and its relevance for situational prevention', in R.V. Clarke (ed.) *Crime Prevention Studies. Volume* 3. Monsey, NY: Criminal Justice Press.

Cornish, D.B. and Clarke, R.V. (eds) (1986) *The Reasoning Criminal: Rational Choice Perspectives on Offending.* New York, NY: Springer-Verlag.

Cornish, D.B. and Clarke, R.V. (1987) 'Understanding crime displacement: an application of rational choice theory', *Criminology,* 25: 933–47.

Coupe, T. and Griffiths, M. (1996) *Solving Residential Burglary. Crime Detection and Prevention Series Paper* 77. London: Home Office.

Coupe, T. and Kaur, S. (in press) *The Role of Alarms and CCTV in Detecting Non-residential Burglary.*

Cromwell, P.F., Olson, J.N. and Avary, D'Aunn (1991) *Residential Burglary: An Ethnographic Analysis. Studies in Crime, Law, and Justice,* 8. London: Sage.

Curtin, L. *et al.* (2001) *Developing Crime Reduction Plans: Some Examples from the Reducing Burglary Initiative. Crime Reduction Research Series Paper* 7. London: Home Office.

Dhiri, S., Brand, S., Harries, R. and Price, R. (1999) *Modelling and Predicting Property Crime Trends. Home Office Research Study* 198. London: Home Office.

Dodd, T., Nicholas, S., Povey, D. and Walker, A. (2004) *Crime in England and Wales 2003/2004. Statistical Bulletin* 10/04. London: Home Office.

Dowds, L. and Mayhew, P. (1994) *Participation in Neighbourhood Watch: Findings from the 1992 British Crime Survey. Home Office Research Findings* 11. London: Home Office.

Ekblom, P., Law, H. and Sutton, M. (1996) *Domestic Burglary Schemes in the Safer Cities Programme. Home Office Research Study* 164. London: Home Office.

Ekblom, P. and Tilley, N. (2000) 'Going equipped criminology, situational crime prevention and the resourceful offender', *British Journal of Criminology,* 40: 376–98.

Ellingworth, D.M. and Pease, K. (1998) 'Movers and breakers: household property crime against those moving home', *International Journal of Risk, Security and Crime Prevention,* 3: 35–42.

Farrell, G., Chenery, S. and Pease, K. (1998) *Consolidating Police Crackdowns: Findings from an Anti-burglary Project. Police Research Series Paper* 113. London: Home Office.

Flockenhaus, M., Mille, A., Mallender, J. and Kingsworth, R. (2002) 'Harringay Strategic Development Project: final report.' Unpublished paper.

Forrester, D.P., Chatterton, M.R. and Pease, K. (1988) *The Kirkholt Burglary Prevention Project. Crime Prevention Unit Paper* 13. London: Home Office.

Forrester, D.P., Frenz, S., O'Connor, M. and Pease, K. (1990) *The Kirkholt Burglary Prevention Project: Phase II. Crime Prevention Unit Paper* 23. London: Home Office.

Gill, M. and Loveday, K. (2003) 'What do offenders think about CCTV?', *Crime Prevention and Community Safety: An International Journal*, 5: 17–25.

Gill, M. and Spriggs, A. (in press) *Assessing the Impact of CCTV. Home Office Research Paper* 292. London: Home Office.

Hearnden, I., Millie, A., Hamilton-Smith, L.N. and Willis, J. (2004) 'From action to reaction: delivery and management in reducing burglary initiative projects', in L.N. Hamilton-Smith (ed.) *The Reducing Burglary Initiative: Design, Development and Delivery. Home Office Research Study* 287. London: Home Office.

Heller, N.B., Stenzel, W.W., Gill, A.D., Kolde, R.A. and Schimmerman, S.R. (1975) *Operation Identification Projects: Assessment of Effectiveness. National Evaluation Program, Phase I, Summary Report.* National Institute of Law Enforcement and Criminal Justice.

Hirschfield, A. (2003) Plenary presentation on the evaluation of Reducing Burglary Initiative Projects in the north of England, Home Office/Greater Manchester Police burglary reduction event, Old Trafford, December.

Hirschfield, A. (2004) *The Impact of the Reducing Burglary Initiative in the North of England. Home Office Online Report* 40/04. London: Home Office.

Homel, P., Nutley, S.N., Tilley, N. and Webb, B. (2004) *Investing to Deliver. Reviewing the Implementation of the UK Crime Reduction Programme. Home Office Research Study* 281. London: Home Office.

Hope, T., Bryan, J., Crawley, E., Crawley, P., Russell, N. and Trickett, A. (2004) *Strategic Development Projects in the Yorkshire and the Humber, East Midlands and Eastern Regions. Home Office Online Report* 41/04. London: Home Office.

Hough, M., Hedderman, C. and Hamilton-Smith, L.N. (2004) 'The design and development of the reducing burglary initiative', in L.N. Hamilton-Smith (ed.) *The Reducing Burglary Initiative: Design, Development and Delivery. Home Office Research Study* 287. London: Home Office.

Husain, S. (1988) *Neighbourhood Watch in England and Wales: A Locational Analysis. Crime Prevention Unit Paper* 12. London: Home Office.

Jacobson, J. (2003) *The Reducing Burglary Initiative: Planning for Partnership. Home Office Development and Practice Report* 4. London: Home Office.

Johnson, S.D. and Bowers, K.J. (2004) 'The stability of space-time clusters of burglary', *British Journal of Criminology*, 44: 55–65.

Jones, B. and Tilley, N. (2004) *The Impact of High Visibility Patrols on Personal Robbery. Research Findings* 201. London: Home Office.

Kay, C., Hearnden, I., Millie, A., Mallender, J. and Kingsnorth, R. (2002) 'Selly Oak Strategic Development Project: final report.' Unpublished paper.

Keele University (2002a) 'Luton, Dallow Ward Strategic Development Project: final process/outcome report.' Unpublished paper.

Keele University (2002b) 'Lincoln, St Giles Strategic Development Project: final process/outcome report.' Unpublished paper.

Knuttsson, J. (1984) *Operation Identification – a Way to Prevent Burglaries? Report* 14. Sweden: Office of Community Oriented Policing Service, National Council for Crime Prevention.

Kodz, J., Pease, K. and Stephens, M. (2004) *Explanatory Note for Online Reports OLR 40/04 to OLR 43/04. Home Office Online Report 39/04.* London: Home Office.

Lamm Weisel, D. (2002) *Burglary of Single-family Houses. Problem-oriented Guides for Police Problem-specific Guides Series Guide* 18. Washington, DC: Department of Justice.

Lavakras, P.J., Rosenbaum, D.P. and Kaminski, F. (1983) 'Transmitting information about crime and crime prevention to citizens: the Evanston newsletter quasi-experimental experiment', *Journal of Police Science and Administration*, 2: 463–73.

Laycock, G. (1985) *Property Marking – a Deterrent to Domestic Burglary? Crime Prevention Paper* 3. London: Home Office.

Laycock, G. (1991) 'Operation Identification or the power of publicity?', *Security Journal*, 2: 67–71.

Loxley, C., Curtin, L. and Brown, R. (2002) *Summer Splash Schemes 2000: Findings from Six Case Studies. Crime Reduction Research Series Paper* 12. London: Home Office.

Matthews, R. and Trickey, J. (1994) *The Eyres Monsell Crime Reduction Project.* Leicester: Centre for the Study of Public Order, University of Leicester.

Mayhew, P. (1984) 'Target-hardening: how much of an answer?', in R. Clarke and T. Hope (eds) *Coping with Burglary.* Boston, MA: Kluwer-Nijhoff.

Mayhew, P., Clarke, R.V., Sturman, A. and Hough, J.M. (1976) *Crime as Opportunity.* London: HMSO.

Millie, A. (in press) 'Reducing burglary by crackdown and consolidation', *Policing.*

Millie, A. and Hough, M. (2004) *Assessing the Impact of the Reducing Burglary Initiative in Southern England and Wales* (2nd edn). *Home Office Online Report 42/04.* London: Home Office.

Northern Consortium (University of Liverpool, University of Huddersfield, University of Hull and Matrix, MHA Research and Consultancy) (2002) 'Final report: Annex 14: Rusholme.' Unpublished paper.

ODPM (2002) Solving the problem. Alley-gating. Renewal.net online document (available at http://www.renewal.net/).

Osborn, J., Thompson, M., Hearnden, I., Millie, A., Mallender, J. and Kingsnorth, R. (2004) *Reducing Burglary Initiative Project Summary Fordbridge, Solihull. Supplement 2 to Home Office Research Findings* 204. London: Home Office.

Painter, K.A. (1992) 'Different worlds: the spatial, temporal, and social dimensions of female victimisation', in D. Evans *et al.* (eds) *Crime, Policing, and Place: Essays in Environmental Criminology.* London: Routledge.

Painter, K.A. and Farrington, D.P. (1997) 'The crime reducing effect of improved street lighting: the Dudley project', in R.V. Clarke (ed.) *Situational Crime Prevention: Successful Case Studies* (2nd edn). Guilderland, NY: Harrow & Heston.

Painter, K.A. and Farrington, D.P. (1999) 'Street lighting and crime: diffusion of benefits in the Stoke-on-Trent project', in K. Painter and N. Tilly (eds) *Surveillance of Public Space: CCTV, Street Lighting and Crime Prevention. Crime Prevention Studies. Volume 10.* Monsey, NY: Criminal Justice Press.

Pascoe, T. (1999) *Evaluation of Secured by Design in Public Sector Housing. Final Report.* Watford: BRE.

Pease, K. (1999) 'A review of street lighting evaluations', in K. Painter and N. Tilly (eds) *Surveillance of Public Space: CCTV, Street Lighting and Crime Prevention, Crime Prevention Studies. Volume 10.* Monsey, NY: Criminal Justice Press.

Polvi, N., Looman, T., Humphries, C. and Pease, K. (1991) 'The time course of repeat burglary victimisation', *British Journal of Criminology*, 31: 411–14.

Read, T. and Tilley, N. (2000) *Not Rocket Science? Problem-solving and Crime Reduction. Crime Reduction Research Series Paper* 6. London: Home Office.

Research Solutions UK Ltd (2003) 'Informing the effective use of publicity and media campaigns to reduce crime and the fear of crime' (Research Solutions Paper). Unpublished.

Rosenbaum, D. (1988) 'A critical eye on neighbourhood watch: does it reduce crime and fear?', in T. Hope and M. Shaw (eds) *Communities and Crime Reduction*. London: HMSO.

Rubenstein, H., Murray, C., Montoyama, T. and Rouse, W.V. (1980) *The Link between Crime and the Built Environment: The Current State of Knowledge. Volume 1*. Washington, DC: National Institute of Justice.

Sacco, V. and Silverman, R. (1981) 'Selling crime prevention: the evaluation of a mass media campaign', *Canadian Journal of Criminology*, 23: 191–201.

Scott, M.S. (2003) *The Benefits and Consequences of Police Crackdowns. Problem-oriented Guides for Police Response Guide Series* 1. Washington, DC: US Department of Justice.

Sherman L.W. (1990) 'Police crackdowns: initial and residual deterrence', in M. Tonry and N. Morris (eds) *Crime and Justice: An Annual Review of Research*. Chicago, IL: University of Chicago Press.

Simmons, J. and Dodd, T. (eds) (2003) *Crime in England and Wales 2002/2003. July 2003. Home Office Staistical Bulletin 07/03*. London: Home Office.

Smith, J. (2003) *The Nature of Personal Robbery. Home Office Research Study* 254. London: Home Office.

Sutton, M., Johnston, K. and Lockwood, H. (1998) *Handling Stolen Goods: A Market Reduction Approach. Home Office Research Study* 178. London: Home Office.

Tilley, N. and Laycock, G. (2002) *Working Out What to Do: Evidence-based Crime Reduction. Crime Reduction Research Series Paper* 11. London: Home Office.

Tilley, N. and Webb, J. (1994) *Burglary Reduction: Findings from Safer Cities Schemes. Home Office Crime Prevention Unit Paper* 51. London: Home Office.

Tilley, N., Pease, K., Hough, M. and Brown, R. (1999) *Burglary Prevention: Early Lessons from the Crime Reduction Programme. Crime Reduction Research Series Paper* 1. London: Home Office.

Townsley, M., Homel, R. and Chaseling, J. (2003) 'Infectious burglaries. A test of the near repeat hypothesis', *British Journal of Criminology*, 43: 615–34.

University of Liverpool (2003) *Closing off Opportunities: The Impact of Alleygating*. Liverpool: University of Liverpool Civic Design Department.

Vader, R.J. (1979) *Crime Prevention through National Publicity Campaigns: Emerging Insights. Home Office Research Bulletin* 7. London: Home Office.

Van Kesteren, J., Mayhew, P. and Nieuwbeerta, P. (2000) *Criminal Victimisation in Seventeen Industrialised Countries – Key Findings from the 2000 International Crime Victims Survey*. The Hague: WODC.

Wiles, P. and Costello, A. (2000) *The 'Road to Nowhere': The Evidence for Travelling Criminals. Home Office Research Study* 207. London: Home Office.

Wilson, J.Q. and Kelling, G.E. (1982) 'Broken windows: the police and neighborhood safety', *Atlantic Monthly*, 249: 29–38.

Wright, A. and Pease, K. (1995) 'Making use of the crackdown and consolidation cycle', *Policing Today*, October.

Wright, R. and Decker, S. (1994) *Burglars on the Job: Street Life and Residential Break-ins*. Boston, MA: Northeastern University Press.

Wright, R., Logie, R. and Decker, S. (1995) 'Criminal expertise and offender decision making: an experimental study of the target selection process in residential burglary', *Journal of Research in Crime and Delinquency*, 32: 39–53.

Young, C. (1999) *The Smithdown Road Pilot 'Alleygating' Project: Evaluated on Behalf of the Safer Merseyside Partnership*. Liverpool: University of Liverpool, Department of Civic Design.

Chapter 17

Preventing vehicle crime

Barry Webb

Introduction

Sir Alec Issigonis, considered one of the great innovative car designers, decided, it is said, not to include a radio in his new mini because he thought it would be distracting to the driver and never catch on. Which just goes to show that designers can't always get it right. It is important, therefore, that manufacturers and designers can respond rapidly to problems or unanticipated consequences of their new products as they emerge. The way in which the motor industry has responded to consumer demand for radios and cassette players in their cars is an example, with a whole separate industry developing to provide ever increasingly sophisticated in-car entertainment systems. Rapid recall of cars when a fault is discovered in a component is also testimony to the industry's capacity to respond rapidly to safety issues. The history of vehicle crime in Britain is a tale of unanticipated consequences of the new product but, alas, not rapid response so that by the end of the twentieth century theft of and from vehicles had developed into a feature of everyday life. This chapter examines the growth of vehicle crime through the twentieth century in Britain, describing both the scale and nature of the problem, its evolution and the different approaches taken to its prevention.

The rise and fall of motor vehicle crime

There is now a substantial research literature showing how the design of goods and products can facilitate and introduce new forms of crime through the opportunities created. The credit card (Levi and Handley 1998), the Internet (Newman and Clarke 2003) and the mobile phone (Tilley *et al.* 2004) are all relatively recent examples of new products and services which have brought with them new forms of crime and new ways of committing old forms of crime. The opportunities for crime, particularly theft, emerge and are exploited as products enter the mass market, for a number of reasons. First, there are more products around to steal. Secondly, there is more demand so it is easier to sell stolen products; and, thirdly, as the product becomes part of everyday life, rather than a rare luxury item, it is easier to hide or disguise a stolen item.

This pattern can be seen in the way vehicle crime has developed over the last 100 years. The early twentieth century saw a step change in motor vehicle production, to take it from a rare luxury item to a mass-market product. By 1914, Herbert Austin's factory in Birmingham had increased production ten-fold since its opening in 1906. In 1913, William Morris opened his factory in Oxford, and the Ford company introduced the mass production line in Michigan. Figure 17.1 shows the remarkable growth in vehicle ownership since, with the mass market for vehicles really taking off after the Second World War during which many people learnt to drive.

Problems of vehicle crime began to develop and be recognized as an emerging problem quite quickly, as this extract from the 1918–19 Metropolitan Police annual report illustrates:

> Amongst other crime, larcenies of motor-cars and vans have been frequent. These, again, are in large measure due to the carelessness of owners. The best remedy in this case is an improvement in the system of registration which might be so arranged as to make the disposal of a stolen vehicle extremely difficult (from the *Report of the Commissioner of Police of the Metropolis for the Years 1918 and 1919*, p. 12).

Subsequent annual reports contain similar comments, signifying that although the police were providing an early warning of a problem, little was being done about it. This particular extract shows how the police recognized the need to get to grips with two issues quite quickly – the security of the vehicle itself and

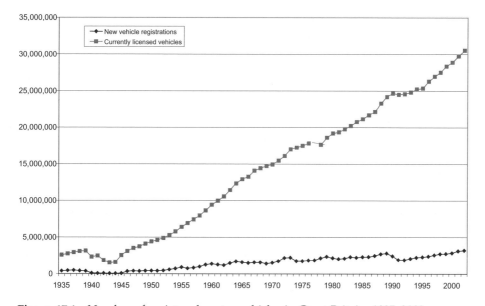

Figure 17.1 Number of registered motor vehicles in Great Britain, 1935–2002

the effectiveness of the vehicle registration and licensing system. Yet it is really only relatively recently that either of these has been seriously tackled with crime prevention in mind. We will examine these approaches to prevention later in this chapter.

Over the course of the next 70 years, as a consequence of the failure to respond to these problems early on, vehicle crime continued to grow rapidly. By the 1990s there were over 1 million recorded thefts of and from vehicles taking place in England and Wales annually, peaking in 1992 with 1.5 million such thefts making up nearly a third of all recorded crime. Estimates from victimization surveys in the UK suggest the true figure is closer to 2.5 million vehicle-related thefts, as thefts from vehicles are particularly poorly reported to the police.

This growth in vehicle crime is not simply due to more cars being on the road but reflects the fact that the vehicle was becoming an increasingly attractive target for thieves, with risk per 1,000 vehicles growing massively. In 1935 there were 6.8 thefts from vehicles per 1,000 registered vehicles. At its peak in 1992, the risk was 39 thefts per 1,000 vehicles on the road. Thefts of vehicles show similar increases in risk. The problem, moreover, seemed particularly a British one. An international crime victimization survey showed that the risk of vehicle crime in 1996 in England was the highest in Europe and higher even than in the USA (Mayhew and White 1997).

Taking the problem apart

One of the principles of effective crime prevention is that it should focus on clearly specified and specific behaviours, which often means breaking down larger problems into smaller and more specific subsets of problem. Police recorded crime figures enable us to make a start on this process, as figures for theft from vehicles and theft of vehicles have been recorded separately for England and Wales since 1934. In addition, 'unauthorized taking of a motor vehicle without the owner's consent' incidents, where the vehicle is taken but recovered shortly after, have been recorded separately since 1969 when it became an indictable offence. These are three very different problems, as Figure 17.2 shows. The figure indicates that all three vehicle crime problems have two broad patterns in common – large increases since records began and large reductions since 1992. They also differ in some important ways.

Theft from vehicles

Numerically, thefts from vehicles have consistently been the biggest motor vehicle crime problem, and particularly from 1980 since when these have grown massively to make up around two thirds of all vehicle crime. But this is only the tip of the iceberg. The British Crime Survey (BCS) reveals that thefts from vehicles are particularly poorly reported to and recorded by the police with just 36 per cent of thefts from vehicles ending up in police records compared with over 90 per cent for thefts of vehicles (Dodd et al. 2004). The true scale of the problem is therefore much larger than even the dramatic pattern shown by police records in Figure 17.2.

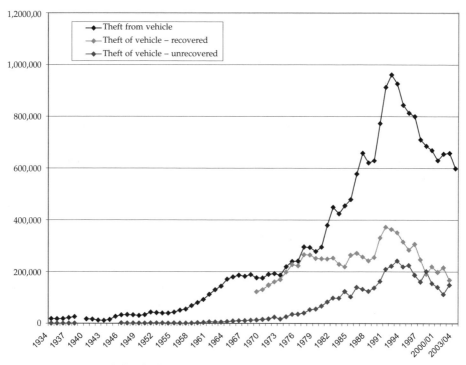

Figure 17.2 Recorded vehicle crime in England and Wales, 1934–2004

Thefts from vehicles include a variety of behaviour, such as siphoning fuel from petrol tanks, removing car batteries, wheels and other external components as well as stealing items from inside the car. In-car entertainment (ICE) systems have become a particular target. It is argued (Webb and Laycock 1992) that the dramatic rise in thefts from vehicles during the 1980s was in part fuelled by ICE systems entering the mass market, making them more available to steal and stimulating demand for the latest ICE system. By 1991, ICE systems were taken in 33 per cent of incidents. The reduction in thefts since 1992 is equally as dramatic, due in part to increased vehicle security, discussed later, and particularly the practice of spreading the various ICE parts throughout the car and embedding them in the fabric of the vehicle, making it very much more difficult to steal a complete system.

The problem of theft of external components continues, however, with the BCS showing that these were taken in 37 per cent of thefts in 2000 (Kershaw *et al.* 2000), up considerably from the figure of 20 per cent which a survey of thefts in six forces in 1991 produced (Webb and Laycock 1992). The cost of spare parts may be a driver for this problem, as it is for some thefts of cars which are stolen to be broken up for spares.

Permanent theft of vehicles

Cars are the target in 81 per cent of thefts of vehicles where the vehicle is permanently lost, with motor cycles and light commercial vehicles each making up 9 per cent of thefts and HGVs 1 per cent (Sallybanks and Brown 1999). These kinds of statistic, however, hide a great deal of variation in risk between different types, makes and models of vehicle. For example, 56 per 1,000 registered livestock carriers were stolen and permanently lost in 1994 compared with the average for HGVs overall of 6, and 24 for vehicles as a whole (Brown 1995). Their much smaller number, however (156 stolen in 1994), means they affect the national crime statistics hardly at all and so don't attract much crime prevention attention. Construction plant also has a very high rate of theft where the plant is never recovered, higher than that for vehicles as a whole, but again small numbers. Both these high-risk problems reflect increased opportunity to steal and conceal the stolen vehicle, being left unattended for long periods on farmland, building sites and other relatively unsupervised areas and also being used in similar environments where they are unlikely to attract the attention of the police or other law enforcement agencies. The importance of supervision of parking areas generally is discussed later in this chapter.

The recorded crime figures for vehicles stolen and not recovered shown in Figure 17.2 reflect a number of rather different problems:

- The theft of vehicles for financial gain, changing the identity of the vehicle and using it or selling it on as a legitimate vehicle.
- Stealing the vehicle to break up and sell as spare parts – HGV thefts are thought to be particularly targeted for this.
- Exporting the stolen vehicle to sell in other countries – construction plant is considered at risk here.
- Owners fraudulently reporting the car as stolen in order to claim the insurance.

Each of these problems requires a rather different set of opportunities and skills and, therefore, will have different implications for crime prevention. Very little, however, is known about the nature and even size of these subsets of problem. A committee set up by the British government to reduce vehicle crime reported the police view that stealing cars to sell or break for parts accounted for about 65 per cent of all vehicles stolen and never recovered (VCRAT 1999). In relation to the export of stolen vehicles, Brown and Clarke (2004) estimate that this is likely to be around 0.2 per cent of unrecovered vehicles, much less than the police estimate of between 10 and 20 per cent of unrecovered stolen vehicles. Insurance fraud has been estimated as being as much as 20 per cent of all reported permanent thefts (Webb and Laycock 1992). The fact that older vehicles are more at risk of permanent theft than newer ones suggests that this is a particular problem worth looking at more closely.

Theft resulting in permanent loss of the vehicle generally has, until relatively recently, been a much smaller problem than either theft from vehicles or theft where the vehicle is later recovered. It has, however, developed so that it is now a more significant part of the vehicle crime problem. Prior to 1970, permanent theft of vehicles was of little significance. In 1935, there were just 0.09 thefts per 1,000 vehicles, and even in 1969 the vehicle was permanently lost in just 10 per cent of all vehicle thefts. By 2003, however, the risk of permanent theft was 50 times greater than in 1935, at 4.9 per 1,000 vehicles, with such thefts now making up 47 per cent of all vehicle theft.

One explanation for the growth in the 1970s and 1980s is that the increased number of vehicles on the road presented the vehicle registration and licensing system with such a workload that it was unable to keep track as effectively of vehicle and keeper identities, making it easier for thieves to change the identity of stolen vehicles and pass them off as legitimate vehicles. The role of the vehicle registration and licensing system is examined later in this chapter. Reductions post-1992 are likely due to the introduction of more sophisticated electronic immobilizing devices in cars, again discussed further below.

Temporary thefts of vehicles

The recorded figures for thefts of vehicles which are subsequently recovered reflect a number of very different problems. These include taking the car to:

• get home at night when the last train has gone;
• use in another crime;
• show off to your mates; or
• see how fast you can drive.

Again, we know very little about the size of these various problems, although so-called joy-riding will make up a substantial proportion. Research shows that this is likely to involve juveniles more than other forms of vehicle crime, that it is a very prevalent activity amongst juveniles in some areas (at least it was in 1990) and that sporty models of car are the car of choice (Spencer 1992). Spencer's report indicates the extent to which it had become part of the juvenile culture on the estate she examined. The fact that the problem persisted in Northern Ireland in the face of very violent punishment from paramilitary organizations if perpetrators were caught reveals young boys' almost addiction to fast cars and showing off. It is perhaps, therefore, no surprise that probation service motor projects that aim to divert young offenders away from joy-riding show disappointing results (Smith 1999).

Figure 17.2 shows that the pattern for these thefts is very different from that for permanent theft of vehicles and more similar to that for theft from vehicles, at least for the first decade of official figures. This suggests that offenders committing temporary theft and theft from vehicles are likely to be more similar than offenders involved in permanent theft. Spencer's research confirms that the young boys she spoke to were involved in these two forms of crime much more than permanent theft, although some 'graduated' to making money from stealing cars. Secondly, post-1980 temporary theft shows little growth in a period when thefts from and permanent theft of vehicles rose massively. It therefore seems to have been the first of the three problems to come under some control, likely due to the impact of steering column locks introduced some ten years earlier into newer cars, discussed later in this chapter.

These two patterns are much clearer in Figure 17.3. Whilst national figures for unauthorized takings are available only since 1969, such figures are available in some police forces prior to this. Figure 17.3 shows the pattern for all three problems in London between 1923 and 1997.

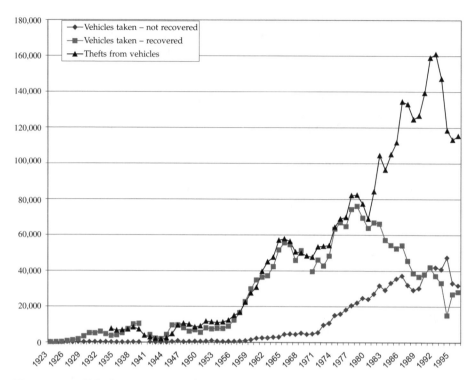

Figure 17.3 Vehicle crime in London, 1923–97

The long-term similarity between temporary thefts and thefts from vehicles is striking, suggesting the two problems and offender populations are indeed closely related. In support of this, analysis of police records shows that about 10 per cent of cases recorded as theft from a vehicle prior to 1969 also involved the unauthorized taking of the vehicle. Secondly, whilst the national data show a levelling-off for unauthorized takings post-1980, in London the change is much more dramatic with temporary thefts reducing so sharply that by 1992 they are outnumbered by the traditionally much smaller problem of permanent vehicle theft. One explanation for this is the additional impact of road congestion in London which simply removes the reason for joy-riding – if you can't drive fast, what's the point?

Approaches to prevention

In the course of setting out this broad picture of vehicle crime, we have begun to introduce some possible explanations for the various rises and falls in different problems. For example, we have mentioned the role of improved vehicle security a number of times. Further analysis of risk factors associated with vehicle crime has highlighted two other areas – where the vehicle is parked and the effectiveness of the vehicle registration and licensing system. Crime prevention work has, consequently, focused on the three key areas of:

- enhancing the security of the vehicle itself;
- making the parking environment safer; and
- improving the effectiveness of the vehicle registration and licensing system.

These are not alternative approaches but complementary, targeting different levels of the problem. Enhancing the designed-in security of the car itself can be seen as action at the micro level, whilst targeting the parking environment is meso-level activity and enhancing the national administrative system to keep better track of who owns what vehicle is macro-level work. Greater impact is, therefore, likely to be achieved if all three strands are pursued together and, indeed, it has been suggested that the low level of vehicle theft in Germany is due to more robust approaches to vehicle security *and* registration and licensing than in the UK (Webb *et al.* 2004).

These crime prevention approaches have been led at national level, although action is required at the international level in relation to vehicle security, and at the local level in relation to car parking security, making implementation of change complex. Generally speaking, most effort to date has focused on improving the security of the vehicle itself and this is also where most change has taken place. Currently, the vehicle registration and licensing system is receiving a lot of government attention and undergoing change. Whilst there has been some effort to improve the security of public car parking, this has been less robust and provision of safe and secure residential car parking remains a topic of debate and a difficult issue for planners, as we shall see.

Improving vehicle security

The dominant approach to reducing vehicle crime has been to improve the security of the vehicle itself, through perimeter security to make it harder to get into the vehicle, and through systems that disable the car from being moved. There have been gradual improvements in both forms of security throughout the twentieth century. In the early days of the motor vehicle, there was very little in the way of either form of security with vehicles being open cabs and engines started using crank handles or push buttons. Perimeter security improved as cabs became enclosed and glass windows fitted. T-shaped handles on doors were replaced with D-shaped handles and locks to prevent thieves from using pipes to lever open doors. Eventually the door lock was incorporated into the door itself. Engine start-up was protected with locks being built into ignition switches, until 1949 when Chrysler developed the key-operated ignition switch.

These developments were slow, however, and increasing levels of vehicle crime prompted governments and consumer organizations to press manufacturers to do more, and faster. Pre-empting EU legislation which took effect in 1974, the vehicle manufacturers negotiated an agreement with the British government resulting in steering column locks being fitted to all new cars from 1970 onwards. This was followed, in the 1980s, by a good deal of government-sponsored activity examining ways in which both engine immobilization and perimeter security might be improved (Southall and Ekblom 1995). It was hoped the manufacturers would take on the ideas flowing from this work. Their slowness in doing so prompted more robust confrontation in the early 1990s, with the Consumers Association highlighting very publicly the ease with which vehicles could be broken into, and the Home Office publishing the first Car Theft Index – a league table exposing those makes and models of car most at risk. The pressure on manufacturers was kept up with the introduction of EU legislation in 1995 requiring all new cars to be fitted with electronic immobilisers from 1998 onwards.

Figure 17.4 shows three key events following government intervention which each marked a step change in levels of vehicle security in the UK – steering column locks in 1969, the publication of the first Car Theft Index in 1992 and electronic immobilizers in 1998.

Steering column locks

It is not immediately clear from Figure 17.4 that steering column locks have had the desired effect. However, detailed evaluation shows that they have been very effective in Germany, and that they probably had some effect in the UK but the way they were introduced in the UK substantially weakened their impact (Webb *et al.* 2004).

In the UK, steering column locks were fitted only in new cars and indeed the risk of theft of new cars did substantially reduce (Mayhew and Hough

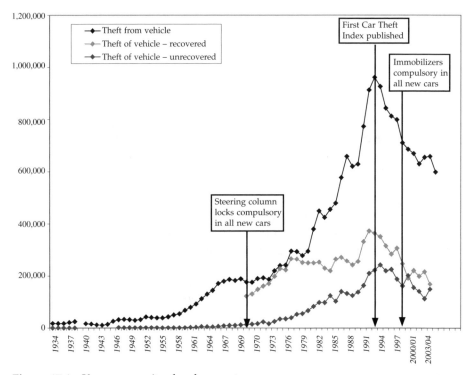

Figure 17.4 Key car security developments

1976). However, research has consistently shown that older vehicles are much more at risk of theft than younger ones, which meant that this particular policy did not provide any immediate protection to those vehicles most at risk. Moreover, Mayhew and Hough showed that the risk to these older, unprotected cars actually increased, more than cancelling out the gains made in relation to new cars.

It takes about 10 years for the vehicle parc in Britain to be replaced, so by 1980, it was argued, the impact of the steering column lock would be more noticeable since a sufficiently large proportion of vehicles would be protected by the device. Remarkably, this is the point at which thefts of vehicles for temporary use stopped rising and stabilized so it could be argued that steering column locks have helped bring temporary theft of vehicles under control. It made no dent, however, in permanent thefts of vehicles. Whilst the steering column lock seems to deter some of the more opportunistic thieves, it does not seem to have presented a challenge to the more determined thieves who steal the car for financial gain – and insurance fraud by vehicle owners would not be affected by improved vehicle security of any kind.

The impact of steering column locks in the Federal Republic of Germany, in contrast, was much more dramatic, largely as result of the more stringent requirement that all vehicles, new and old, be fitted with steering column locks by 30 June 1962. Figure 17.5 shows that the result was that a problem which was roughly on the same scale as England and Wales in 1961 reduced immediately and has continued at a much lower level ever since. The rate of

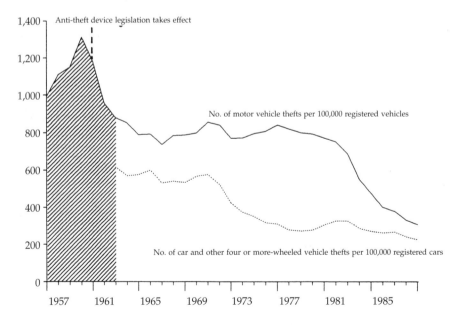

Figure 17.5 Impact of steering column locks in Germany
Source: Webb (1994).

theft in Germany in 2001 was still less than a fifth of that in the UK despite the large reductions achieved in England and Wales since 1992. Clarke and Harris (1992) suggest this more powerful effect was achieved because the 'big bang' approach wiped out a culture of car theft amongst juveniles almost overnight, whereas the more modest approach in Britain allowed such a culture to continue and grow, as Spencer's research with young people showed it did. Theft from vehicles, however, remained a problem in Germany and developed in the same way as in Britain – clearly vehicles still attracted the attention of thieves in Germany, just not joy-riders.

Figure 17.5 shows that steering column locks had a much bigger impact on thefts of four-wheeled vehicles than for vehicles as a whole in Germany. The reason for this is that 'all vehicles' includes mopeds and motorcycles, and thefts of these vehicles in Germany increased three-fold after the introduction of steering column locks, rising from 2 per 100 registered vehicles to 6 per 100 by 1980. Although mopeds and motorcycles were also fitted with steering column locks, these devices offered less protection from thieves, being easily disabled by using the handlebars as a lever to break the lock. Moreover, Webb (1994) argues that some of the car theft may have displaced to these less well protected targets. This particular vehicle theft problem in Germany reduced equally as dramatically after 1980 when motor cycle helmet legislation was introduced (Mayhew et al. 1989). Importantly, there was no displacement back to car theft.

The Car Theft Index

The Car Theft Index appears, from Figure 17.4, to have had a major impact on all three major forms of vehicle theft. Methodologically this was an incredibly detailed and precise piece of work – it had to be since the government aimed to use it as a lever to change the behaviour of the motor manufacturers who were still not particularly interested in the security (Laycock 2004). For them, security was not an issue for their customers in the same way that comfort, safety or speed was. To put it bluntly, there was no incentive for them to take security and crime prevention seriously.

The Car Theft Index changed all that, and made security a marketing issue. By exposing those makes and models of car most at risk, customers were empowered to make informed decisions about their choice of vehicle. Coupled with the great deal of publicity generated by this first index, and the noise the Consumers Association was making (e.g. *Which?* 1991), the manufacturers began to design more sophisticated devices such as deadlocks and engine immobilizers into the more numerous economy vehicles. The extent to which vehicle security improved after 1992 is revealed in the British Crime Survey (Kinshott 2001) which shows that by 2000, 49 per cent of respondents said their car had an alarm compared with 23 per cent in 1992, 67 per cent had central locking in 2000 compared with 35 per cent in 1992, and 62 per cent had immobilizers compared with 23 per cent in 1992. In-car entertainment security had also markedly improved.

Laycock (2004) is careful not to attribute the reductions in vehicle crime since 1992 solely to the Car Theft Index and the subsequent changes in vehicle security levels, but it is hard to point to anything else that could explain these large crime reductions. In addition, more detailed evaluation of specific devices such as immobilizers supports the view that vehicle crime has reduced as a result of these very substantial improvements in vehicle security (Brown 2004).

Immobilizers

One of the issues for physical security devices is that offenders eventually find ways around them, requiring manufacturers to be alert and to respond to early signs of such adaptation. We have seen so far in this discussion offender adaptation is manifested in two ways – first, through displacing their attention to targets not yet protected by the new device and, secondly, through the development of new modus operandi to overcome the new device (for example, using a pipe to lever open T-door handles). Brown (2004), in his evaluation of vehicle immobilizers, develops a more sophisticated picture of the way in which offenders adapt to these new conditions.

Brown's evaluation shows that the introduction of EU legislation requiring all new cars to be fitted with electronic engine immobilizers has been effective in reducing the risk of both temporary and permanent thefts of vehicles. Although the drop in theft predates 1998, when the legislation actually came into force, many manufacturers were fitting immobilizers well before this, anticipating the legislation in the same way they did for steering column locks. The legislation required only new cars to have this protection and so it is little surprise that, as with the experience of the steering column lock in Britain, Brown finds evidence of displacement of theft to older, unprotected vehicles. But such displacement was found only in relation to temporary theft. Permanent theft showed no such displacement, and why would it? If new vehicles are being stolen for their intrinsic resale value, it makes little sense to target older and less valuable vehicles. It makes more sense to work out how to overcome the security devices protecting the valuable cars. And there is indeed some evidence of this.

Rates of permanent theft of new vehicles have been increasing recently in contrast to the continued downward trend for the rest of the vehicle parc. Temporary thefts show a similar but less marked pattern, and lagging behind by a year or two. This suggests that more determined thieves, who have the financial incentive to do so, are beginning to find ways to beat immobilizers, and that these new techniques are being picked up a little later by 'joy-riders'. Essentially, the skilled and committed thieves make the technological breakthrough, and this is then learnt and 'mainstreamed' by the larger population of thieves involved in temporary theft. The evidence for this is thin, but if this is an early warning of such a process and it continues, it could soon and quite quickly reverse the downward trend in vehicle theft.

Two new modus operandi have been suggested as being used increasingly by thieves to overcome immobilizers. The first is car-jacking. This is a very rare crime indeed, and whilst it is possible that car thieves may resort to such measures, there is no evidence that they have done so on the scale needed to show an upward trend in theft rates for newer vehicles nationally. Moreover, it wouldn't explain the increase in temporary theft rates for new cars – joy-riders are unlikely to adopt this 'MO'. The second theory, for which there is more evidence, is that thieves are making greater effort to obtain car keys through house burglaries. Using keys obtained from house burglaries to steal cars seems quite common. Levesley *et al.* (2003) found that keys were used in 85 per cent of cases where the 'MO' was known, and in 37 per cent of these the keys were obtained from house burglary. However, they do show that this 'MO' has become more common over time, with the proportion of cars stolen using keys from house burglary rising from 19 per cent in 1998 to 44 per cent in 2000 (Figure 17.6). Use of keys stolen during robberies also increased. There are lessons here for manufacturers – for example, to prevent car engines from being restarted once they have been reported stolen, and making greater use of bio-metrics in vehicle security.

Summary

There are a number of lessons from the vehicle security and crime experience that are worth drawing out at this point. First, clearly, improved vehicle security can reduce vehicle crime. Evidence from both the Car Theft Index and the British Crime Survey is that vehicles with lower levels of security are more at risk, and more detailed evaluations have shown how different security measures can impact effectively on different kinds of vehicle crime.

Secondly, a problem in the past with security devices is that, whilst they can be effective, often people forget to engage them or don't use them because of the inconvenience. One of the reasons for the effectiveness of vehicle security systems is that they have become increasingly automated, being engaged and disengaged much more easily than devices in the past. Webb and Laycock (1992) report many fewer parked cars left insecure in 1992 compared with 20 years earlier, and attribute this not only to drivers taking more care but also to more automated systems such as central locking that enable owners to secure their vehicle fully more easily. Electronic immobilizers that engage automatically when the vehicle ignition is turned off and the vehicle locked add to this level of automated protection.

Thirdly, the issue of displacement is an important one. Although not inevitable or total, we have seen evidence of displacement of some forms of

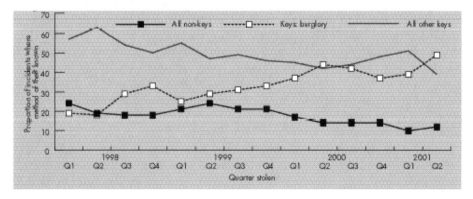

Figure 17.6   Use of keys in car theft
Source: Levesley *et al.* (2003).

vehicle crime following an increase in vehicle security and manufacturers, the police and governments need to be able to respond rapidly to new trends as they emerge.

Fourthly, implementation strategies are important and can affect outcomes. The most effective strategies have required governments to press the motor manufacturers and traders quite hard. More subtle approaches don't appear to be sufficient when there is little payoff for the manufacturers.

One of the more important risk factors revealed by the Car Theft Index is the age of the car and this has been consistent in every sweep of the index. Older vehicles are much more at risk of theft than newer ones – for both temporary and permanent theft. This could be because older vehicles have less sophisticated security devices than newer ones, and what they do have may be broken or not in good working order. It may, however, also be because they are owned by less well off people and thus parked in higher-risk areas where offenders are more likely to live, and where more secure parking is less available. It is to the role of the parking environment in vehicle crime that we now turn.

The parking environment

There is now a considerable body of evidence showing how environmental design can contribute to the control of crime (see Chapter 9, this volume). Indeed, some would argue that its role has been undervalued and that getting the design and management of the environment right to make sure crime doesn't happen in the first place should be the prime focus of crime prevention practitioners and policy-makers. In relation to vehicle crime, this means the parking environment. Two areas have received some attention from researchers and policy-makers in this respect – public car parks and residential parking around the home.

Public car parks

As vehicle ownership has grown, so has the requirement for an infrastructure that can accommodate the vehicle, particularly in town and city centres. The scale and speed of growth of car ownership have, and indeed continue, to put enormous pressure on planners and engineers to keep up with demand. An early example of this comes from London where, although places had begun to be specified for parking in the 1920s, demand exceeded supply to the extent that, in 1928, the government made it illegal for drivers in London to lock their cars when parked so that cars causing an obstruction could be moved if necessary. In 1931 the private sector moved in, and National Car Parks was created.

It was after the Second World War that the real boom in car ownership got underway, prompting much greater effort and attention to controlling urban car parking and congestion. The availability of many bomb-damaged sites as car parks helped relieve the immediate problem during the 1950s and traffic wardens and parking meters were introduced in 1960. It was the 1960s and

1970s, however, that saw a massive growth in the provision of designated town-centre car parking. The high-capacity multistorey car park was seen as the design solution and planning authorities now required any new urban developments to include the building of a car park, for use privately or to be handed over to the local authority as 'planning gain'. By the end of the 1960s, the car park construction and management industry had developed sufficiently to sustain its own professional association, and the British Parking Association was formed in 1967.

Up to now, the priority had been to provide sufficient parking accommodation for cars coming into urban centres. Policy during the 1970s, however, began to shift to promoting initiatives that kept cars out of congested urban centres. Such initiatives included providing more car parking at train stations to encourage greater use of public transport, creating out-of-town shopping centres providing parking for many thousands of cars and introducing park-and-ride schemes.

It is easy to see how the new public car park, with so many cars parked in one place and sometimes unsupervised for many hours, provided increased opportunities for vehicle crime. Yet, again, little was done and it was not until the early 1990s that security and safety in these settings became a national issue. The AA and the RAC as well as the Consumers Association (in a paper called 'Pay and dismay', *Which?* 1990) began to complain very publicly about the problems and how these were being neglected by car park operators and owners. As we discussed in relation to car manufacturers, there was simply no financial incentive for car park operators to deal with these problems since demand for parking was at a premium. The question of the car park operators' liability for what happened in their car park, therefore, became a key issue, with these organizations lobbying for changes in regulation which would increase operators' liability. By altering the way in which the costs of vehicle crime were borne, it was hoped this would provide an economic incentive for car park organizations to do more to reduce crime in their car parks. At the same time, the police were also concerned about these settings for crime, and had begun to develop a 'secured car park' scheme whereby car parks which met specified standards would be given an award and a plaque denoting its status as a 'secured car park'. This was taken up nationally in 1992 and heavily promoted. A recent evaluation of the scheme, however, is disappointing. A particular problem has been the take-up of the scheme which, as the scheme is voluntary, is low (1,000 car parks out of an estimated 20,000 nationally) and tends to involve mainly car parks which were already pretty safe, requiring little change to meet the scheme standards (Smith *et al.* 2003).

The design problem

The 2003/4 British Crime Survey shows that, overall, public car parks account for just 16 per cent for all theft of and from vehicles (Dodd *et al.* 2004). This statistic does not reflect risk, however. It may be that more cars are stolen or broken into when parked on the street near the owner's home because that's where they spend most of their time.

The most sophisticated analysis of risk, taking into account how long cars spend at different locations, was carried out by Clarke and Mayhew (1998) using 1994 British Crime Survey data. Table 17.1 reveals a very different picture, showing that public car parks present the highest risk for theft of and from cars – nearly four times that for street parking around the home.

Table 17.1 Risk of vehicle theft by parking location in England and Wales

Location	Thefts per 100,000 cars per 24 hours
Home garage	2
Home carport/drive	40
Home street	117
Housing estate garage	(38)
Housing estate car park	(101)
Work garage	(48)
Work street	118
Work car park	37
Work other	62
Other street	327
Public car park	454
Other	143

Note: Vehicle theft refers to theft of and from vehicles.
Source: Clarke and Mayhew (1998).

Locally, public car parks can vary enormously in crime rate. An analysis of car parks in Nottingham city centre showed, for example, a range from being completely crime free to one car park which suffered 547 vehicle-related crimes per 1,000 spaces in one year (Smith *et al*. 2003). Public car parks vary enormously in their design (multistorey, surface, underground) and in their operation (pay and display, coin-operated entry/exit systems, manned entry/exit systems, pay on foot and valet parking). These differences will affect the level of supervision of parked cars, and control of vehicular access and exit, and consequently the level of vehicle-related crime.

Webb *et al*. (1992) were able to demonstrate how the design of a car park and the system used to operate it interact to influence crime rates, and how these variously affected theft of and theft from cars. They showed in particular the following:

- Unmanned car parks using a pay-and-display operating system were the riskiest places to leave cars. Surface car parks using this operating system, especially at commuter train stations where cars are left for long periods of time, presented the highest car-crime rates of all car parks examined in the study.

- Exit barriers control theft of cars but not theft from cars. All 14 of the central London multistorey cars parks examined had exit barrier controls. In 1991, only two car thefts were recorded from these car parks, compared with 430 thefts from cars.

- The presence of people to supervise the parking floor is required to control theft from cars. In surface car parks, this can be provided by having entrances and exits manned, and by encouraging businesses such as taxis, fast-food vans and flower stalls to operate on or near the car park. Multistorey car parks present more of a challenge, but examples were found where the presence of staff to control and direct parking and offer services such as car cleaning created crime-free environments.

These are fundamental aspects of car park design and operation and show, therefore, how important it is to get the design and operating system right in the first place. Once established, these are expensive and difficult characteristics to change and are therefore unlikely to be implemented in the absence of any economic incentive to do so, as the poor take-up of the secured car-park scheme demonstrates.

Partly for this reason, CCTV has been a popular initiative in car parks, encouraged and supported financially by government funding. Evaluations (Poyner 1992; Tilley 1993) show that CCTV can help to reduce crime in public car parks, especially if accompanied by other measures which help generate in the mind of offenders increased risk of capture. But CCTV-driven crime reductions may be hard to sustain. Tilley's (1993) study suggests that it is the illusion of, rather than actual, increased risk that has been the crime-reducing mechanism. Experience on the London Underground (Webb and Laycock 1992) suggests that once this has been realized by offenders, the crime reduction effect will wear off. All of which points to the need to get the design of these settings and systems right in the first place, so that crime control is achieved as part of the everyday operation of the car park and not as an 'add-on' which is hard to sustain.

Residential car parking

Of all vehicle-related theft, 65 per cent takes place in and around the home (Dodd *et al.* 2004). Although public car parks are the *riskiest* places to leave cars, it is the residential parking environment that needs to be attended to if any substantial impact on the *number* of vehicle-related crimes is to be made.

Like town centres, residential developments have also had to deal with ever-increasing levels of car ownership. Car-parking arrangements are one of the top issues for house buyers. The typical and preferred design solution has been to provide parking within the curtilage of the house, with a garage if possible. Such arrangements, however, become more difficult as housing density gets greater – and clearly impossible for flat-dwellers – so that street and communal car parks become more common in these settings. These parking arrangements have consequences for crime, with some providing more opportunity for theft of or from cars than others. It is, however, not just the detailed parking arrangements that influence car crime rates but also wider design characteristics of the housing area.

Poyner and Webb (1991) remains one of the most detailed studies of residential crime, and one of the earliest to reveal the extent of residential vehicle crime. By making detailed comparisons of crime rates in neighbouring housing areas that differed in design and layout, they were able to demonstrate the relationship between design and various aspects of residential crime, including car crime. Table 17.2 summarizes the car crime rates found in the housing areas with different parking arrangements. The table shows a similar pattern for both theft of and theft from cars, suggesting that similar principles for prevention will apply to both. Clearly, communal parking bays are to be avoided. Even street parking is safer than these parking lots, to the extent that Poyner (forthcoming) observes that residents have now started to avoid using these parking areas and are parking their cars on estate approach roads. Adaptation to problematic environments like this is not uncommon. Cars parked within the curtilage of the house are the safest.

Table 17.2 Impact of parking arrangements on residential vehicle crime

	Theft of cars (no. per 1,000 households)	Theft from cars (no. per 1,000 households)
Communal parking bays unsupervised from houses	40	39
Parking in streets overlooked by houses	16	15
On private driveways in front/at side of house	8	16

Source: Calculated from data published in Poyner and Webb (1991).

The protection afforded from theft from cars by private driveways, however, is not as great as for theft of cars. The reason for this is that the effect of driveways on this particular problem is compromised by wider characteristics of the area – the presence of networks of footpaths, segregated from the road system. Table 17.3 shows that private driveways have little control over theft from cars in areas which are permeated with such footway networks, although theft of cars remains low.

Table 17.3 Effect of segregated footway systems on residential vehicle crime in areas where parking is provided on private driveways

	Theft of cars (no. per 1,000 households)	Theft from cars (no. per 1,000 households)
Extensive foothpath network throughout area	7	32
No separate footpath network	10	7

Source: Calculated from data published in Poyner and Webb (1991).

This all makes logical sense, if you think about it from the thief's point of view. Stealing a car is a more difficult, lengthier and possibly noisier task than stealing from it. Rapid, surreptitious escape is also more difficult, being confined to the road and possibly having to deal with more obstacles such as junctions and other road users which slow down escape. It doesn't take much, therefore, to deter offenders and having the car parked close enough to the house to enable owners to be able to see and hear suspicious activity seems sufficient. Networks of segregated footpaths, however, facilitate escape on foot and enable offenders to disappear from sight of the house quickly. These networks, therefore, negate any advantage of the car being parked close to the house and promote theft from cars.

Private driveways, however, are not always possible in so-called 'affordable' housing, where units are built at higher density. In this sense, the car has always presented housing designers and planners with a challenge, and continues to do so. It takes up space, which is a problem when the pressure is to build at higher density. It also makes the place look untidy and gets in the way of more aesthetically pleasing and philosophically driven design solutions. For example, whilst recent government guidance on planning and crime prevention acknowledges that private driveways are the safest form of parking arrangement, it goes on to say: 'However, this is not always possible, especially when seeking to design higher density residential or mixed use developments. Garages and driveways can also lead to "inactive frontages"' (Office of the Deputy Prime Minister 2004). Courtyard parking is seen as a solution, although the guidance does advise against courtyards 'not adequately overlooked by capable guardians', and that these should be close to the home where the cars can be seen. The trouble with this is that Poyner's updated detailed research work shows that even shared parking bays or courts in front of houses are at high risk, still higher than street parking (Poyner forthcoming).

The challenge for designers, therefore, is to come up with a design solution to car crime in the context of higher-density housing. In order to do this, though, they need to understand more about crime and the design principles to use to minimize crime risk. One of the difficulties for designers, in this respect, is that crime prevention design guidance is often drafted in vague terms, and is certainly not crime specific.

Although the House Builders Federation supported the original work by Poyner and Webb, it has never been adopted or included in any formal guidance. Providing designers with more insight into the specific crime problems they need to design against, and the current evidence about what does and does not work, might enable designers to tailor design solutions better to the context, and to experiment more rationally to develop more innovative solutions to what is clearly a still unresolved problem of how to provide safe parking in high-density housing areas.

Improving the effectiveness of the vehicle registration and licensing system

The approaches discussed so far have both been focused on how to 'design out' crime. This third approach is also about design, but in relation to an administrative system rather than a product or a physical environment.

The UK vehicle registration and licensing system is aimed at ensuring compliance by vehicle keepers with various vehicle regulations, specifically to enforce the collection of vehicle tax, compulsory levels of insurance, standards of driving and standards of vehicle roadworthiness. It does this by keeping and maintaining a register of all vehicles and keepers in the country, containing information about their identity, location and status, and enabling vehicles and their owners to be linked so that one can be identified from knowledge of the other.

If the system is not secure and the databases do not contain accurate and up-to-date information on the identity, address and status (e.g. licensed or not) of vehicles and their keepers it enables keepers to evade these various regulations, because they know they can't be traced. For the same reason, it also creates opportunities for other forms of anti-social behaviour, such as keepers dumping vehicles when they reach the end of their useful life. Opportunities to steal vehicles for selling are also created if it is hard to verify the true identity of a vehicle and its keeper, especially if key documents can be fraudulently obtained, allowing the vehicle to be passed off as legitimate. The task, therefore, is to create unique identifiers for vehicles that are difficult to tamper with, and a system that enables any changes to vehicle and keeper to be recognized and verified and the national register updated quickly.

The need for such a system emerged as early as 1903 when worries about public safety prompted the need to be able to identify and punish bad drivers. Unique vehicle identifiers were created in the form of the vehicle number plate, drivers had to be licensed and locally maintained registers of all vehicles and their keepers introduced so that owners could be identified from the vehicle number plate.

As vehicle ownership grew, the system began to strain and offenders, including vehicle thieves, found loop-holes. Bad drivers disqualified by one licensing authority, for example, soon discovered they could apply fraudulently but probably successfully for a new licence from another licensing authority. In relation to vehicle theft, the Metropolitan Police Commissioner made this observation as early as 1921:

> Unfortunately the new system of registration introduced by the Ministry of Transport, which it was hoped would render the disposal of stolen cars very difficult has not yet had the desired results, arising chiefly from the ease with which thieves have been able to re-register their cars by representing that they had never been registered before. Amended instructions to remedy the defect have, however, been issued by the Authority concerned.

Since then, demands on the system have increased enormously, not only because of the massive growth in car ownership but also because the system became the vehicle for ensuring compliance with additional vehicle regulations – compulsory third-party insurance was introduced in 1930, driving tests made compulsory in 1935 and MOT tests introduced in 1960. Webb *et al.* (2004) argue that one plausible reason for the growth in permanent theft of vehicles in the 1970s could be that a critical mass in vehicles on the road and workload of the system had been reached, and offenders discovered the opportunities created by a system struggling to keep up.

Various efforts have been made to close down such opportunities. Locally based registers were replaced, in 1974, by a national system, and more tamper-proof vehicle identification numbers, stamped into the fabric of the vehicle, were introduced. Despite these changes, problems continued:

- A review by the Vehicle Crime Reduction Action Team (VCRAT 1999) concluded that vehicle theft could be reduced by 100,000 offences per year if the registration and licensing system were tightened up. Proposals included requiring proof of ownership before issuing replacement vehicle registration documents, requiring the salvage and motor insurance industries to notify DVLA of scrapped and written-off vehicles, and requiring proof of vehicle ownership before replacement number plates are issued. The effect of these changes would be to improve the accuracy of information on the national vehicle register and make it harder for thieves to steal the identities of other cars, particularly scrapped vehicles, and apply these to stolen vehicles – processes known as 'ringing' (where the identity is taken from a scrapped vehicle) and cloning (where the identity is taken from a 'live' vehicle).

- Some 238,000 vehicles were abandoned in 2000, representing 12 per cent of all vehicles reaching their end of life in that year. This problem is predicted to increase as a result of EU legislation and slumps in the price of scrap metal, which increase the costs of legitimate disposal to the keeper (Smith *et al.* 2004).

- Some 5.1 per cent of vehicles were driven on the road without tax in 1999/2000, representing a loss of £183 million to the exchequer (Smith and Webb 2005).

- Around 5 per cent of cars on the road have no insurance (Greenaway 2004), imposing a cost of around £30 per year on the premiums of honest motorists. This compares with an incidence of as low as 1 per cent reported in some EU member states.

- Evaluation of the use of automated number plate readers to stop vehicles apparently in breach of registration and licensing regulations reveals variations in the accuracy of the DVLA database for non-payment of tax from 19 per cent in one force to 67 per cent in another (PA Consulting 2004).

The main problem with the way the system had evolved was that it had changed in a very piecemeal fashion. Recognizing this, the government commissioned a review of the whole system, seeking proposals for modernizing and making it fit for the twenty-first century.

The subsequent report (Laycock and Webb forthcoming) took the view that the problem was systemic, that it was not about particular procedures or inefficiencies on DVLA's part, but was an issue of system design. The report identified five key strategic problems which it felt could be addressed relatively quickly and would make substantial impact. They were:

- database inaccuracy;
- insecurity of vehicle identification systems;

- inadequate enforcement;
- lack of strategic overview; and
- crime prevention as a priority.

Eleven recommendations were proposed which, together, aimed to design a system that would deal with these problems. These are summarized in Box 17.1. Seven of these focused on the first problem, indicating the vital importance attached to database accuracy.

The first recommendation is an example of systemic thinking. The current system relies on both sellers and buyers of vehicles to each notify the licensing authority of change of ownership. There is, however, little incentive for either to do this, especially for those buyers inclined to avoid tax, insurance and MOT payments. Making current owners liable for the vehicle until the licensing authorities have been notified of change of ownership (continuous liability) would create that incentive, and consequently improve the accuracy

Box 17.1   Modernizing the UK vehicle registration and licensing system

Database inaccuracy

1. Registered keepers remain liable for their vehicle until change of keepership is notified to DVLA.
2. Buyers to show reliable proof of identity when registering as a new keeper.
3. Move to a single or virtual database by 2004.
4. Key details of vehicle and keeper verified and updated at each relevant contact with vehicles/keepers.
5. Police and other appropriate enforcement agencies to have secure, online access to relevant parts of the database, leaving an audit trail for data protection purposes.
6. Insurance industry and motor trade to supply relevant information to the database electronically within one working week by 2004 and move to real time by 2007.
7. Commission an independent review of insurance arrangements with respect to whether the person or the vehicle should be insured.

Insecurity of vehicle identification systems

8. Introduce electronic vehicle identification before the end of 2007.

Inadequate enforcement

9. Establish an enforcement capability, funded out of increased tax and insurance receipts.

Lack of strategic oversight

10. Establish a Vehicle Licensing Implementation Group and Vehicle Licensing Futures Group.

Crime prevention not a priority

11. Crime prevention to take a higher priority within DVLA.

of the vehicle record. A similar system operates in Germany, where continuous insurance liability means that vehicle owners cannot cancel their insurance until they prove they have sold the vehicle and the registration authority has checked details of the new owner and his or her insurance arrangements. It has been argued (Webb *et al.* 2004) that this more robust approach to both vehicle control and security has helped keep vehicle theft to a minimum in Germany and much less than in the Britain.

These proposals also make the most of new technology. For example, technologies now exist that enable more fraud- and tamper-proof vehicle identifiers to be created (recommendation 8). Electronic chips in vehicles would enable vehicle identity to be confirmed reliably at various contact points (e.g., in garages when being tested for roadworthiness), would enable stolen or unlicensed vehicles to be detected via roadside readers, and facilitate electronic relicensing. Technologies that enable separate motor vehicle databases to update each other when a vehicle has contact with one also provide an opportunity to modernize the current system and improve accuracy of information.

Technological advances also aid the business of enforcement. Recommendation 9 reflects the review's findings that the risk of getting caught driving without tax, insurance or an MOT was low and was not considered a high priority by the police. One solution suggested was to create a separate, self-financing enforcement agency to address licensing-related transgressions. However, the introduction of automated number-plate recognition (ANPR) in many police forces has increased considerably police capacity and interest in enforcement for these offences. Targeting offenders for registration and licensing offences results in arrests for more serious crimes. In a recent evaluation of the use of ANPR to stop vehicles flagged by DVLA as either not being taxed or having a current keeper, 17 per cent of such stops resulted in an arrest for burglary or theft, with other arrests for vehicle crime, drugs and robbery (PA Consulting 2004). Other work has also shown the value of targeting minor traffic offences as a means of identifying and capturing more serious criminals (Chenery *et al.* 1999). The effect of this is to raise the interest of the police in traffic-related crimes, and ANPR allows them to do this relatively efficiently and effectively.

Finally, the whole system approach is advocated in recommendation 10, both to ensure that the impact of initiatives focused on one part of the system are considered in relation to the system as a whole, and to identify new technologies that might be taken advantage of in keeping the system up to date, and consequently one step ahead of, rather than behind, offenders.

These proposals were accepted in principle by the government and implementation has begun, although this has been patchy and compromises inevitably made (Laycock and Webb forthcoming). A series of papers produced as part of the review showed what might be achieved if these proposals were implemented in full. In relation to theft of vehicles, for example, it was estimated that vehicle theft could reduce by as much as 50 per cent from its current state by 2007 (Jill Dando Institute 2002). This was rather greater than the outcome VCRAT predicted would arise from such changes, for two important reasons. First, the context in which these measures were being introduced had changed since the VCRAT report. In particular, the level of designed-in vehicle security had greatly improved, as we discussed earlier. The impact of tightening up the registration and licensing system, it was argued, would be enhanced by, as well as enhance, the impact arising from improved vehicle security as offenders found it both more difficult to steal vehicles *and* to sell them. The long-term low rates of vehicle theft in Germany were pointed out as an example of such combined rather than independent impact. Secondly, whilst VCRAT had assumed such changes would impact only on problems of ringing and cloning, it was argued that the changes proposed would actually reduce both permanent and temporary theft. Table 17.4 shows how some of the key measures were designed to work, and reveals that some would impact on temporary thefts directly. In addition, as we discussed earlier, evidence was emerging that controlling permanent theft could cut off the supply of new modus operandi to overcome vehicle security devices, thus indirectly impacting on temporary thefts.

Table 17.4 How the licensing changes will work

Initiative	How will it impact on vehicle theft	What we would expect to see
Keepers remain liable for their vehicle until it is registered with another keeper, or reported scrapped or stolen	Improves information on vehicles that have been scrapped, making it harder for thieves to steal their identities and apply them to stolen vehicles	Reduced theft for financial gain
Greater enforcement through widespread use of automatic number plate readers	Increases the risk of being detected driving a stolen vehicle, or vehicles wanted for other reasons	Reduced theft for financial gain and temporary use
Various motor vehicle databases linked in real time to each other	Improves accuracy of vehicle record, making it harder for thieves to steal the identities of scrapped vehicles	Reduced theft for financial gain
Chips in vehicles and roadside readers enable vehicle details to be checked	Increases the risk of being captured driving a stolen vehicle	Reduced theft for financial gain and temporary use

Conclusions

This chapter has focused on three main approaches to car crime prevention. There is clearly a strong rationale for each, and evidence that working together they would have a more powerful effect than individually.

Whilst each has been pursued, more or less vigorously, at national level, implementation strategies and success have varied. Each has had a different government department in the lead. Efforts to improve vehicle security and public car parks have been led by the Home Office, guidance for safe and secure residential layout and design is led by the Office of the Deputy Prime Minister, and the vehicle registration and licensing system is the responsibility of the Department for Transport. Some of these, although being led at national level, require local implementation (for example, public and residential car parking). The vehicle licensing changes require action at the national level, whilst vehicle security improvements require action from the motor manufacturers at the international level. Whilst the government has direct managerial control of the vehicle registration and licensing system, it has no direct power in the other two areas, and has had to rely on 'levering' action from those that do. In relation to vehicle security, the government had to resort to using the robust levers of legislation and engineering consumer demand to get the manufacturers to take the issue of vehicle security seriously. Efforts to improve car park security, however, have not progressed beyond the encouragement of voluntary take-up of recommendations and good practice. It is perhaps not surprising, then, that it is designed-in vehicle security that has seen most change and improvement in the last ten years or so.

One area which continually attracts local interest, and is therefore worth mentioning here, is motor projects for young offenders or those at risk of offending. The idea is that young offenders get involved in vehicle crime because they are interested in vehicles and want to see how fast they can drive them and show off to their mates. If this energy and interest could be satisfied in more controlled and non-criminal ways, then they wouldn't need to steal cars. Such projects may also provide them with skills as, for example, a mechanic, which might stand them in good stead when seeking employment.

Providing such outlets for youngsters is appealing, and motor projects sprung up all over the place during the 1970s and 1980s as a result of probation service involvement. Theoretically, however, whilst it makes some sense, others argue that such projects could well stimulate interest in vehicles rather than sating it. Moreover, it could provide young offenders with the opportunity to work out how to overcome security devices, start cars without keys or generally make them familiar enough with vehicles to facilitate stealing them. Smith's (1999) review of independent evaluations of motor projects concludes that outcomes in terms of reconviction rates are disappointing. In practice, it is difficult to attract and keep the right people on the scheme – it is hard to match the level of excitement offered by joy-riding, and completion rates are typically low. Smith also shows that how the scheme is supposed to work to reduce crime is often not thought through. These results and practical problems are not confined to motor projects but to more generic diversionary schemes for young people (e.g. Loxley *et al.* 2002).

In summary, it is clear that situational crime prevention measures have brought about, and have the potential to bring about, further substantial reductions in vehicle crime in Britain. Most of this is the result of improved designed-in vehicle security, brought about by considerable leverage applied to the motor manufacturers to get them to take vehicle security as seriously as vehicle safety. Further reductions in vehicle crime can be expected from the introduction of changes to the vehicle registration and licensing system, and associated improved enforcement of driving offences. Improving secure car parking has some way to go yet. Whilst there is now available considerable guidance on how to make parking, both in public and residential areas, more secure, there is little evidence to date of much take-up of this advice in high-crime car parks. In relation to new build, the widespread introduction of pay on foot as opposed to pay and display car parks seems a good move, since these control vehicular exit and are therefore likely to be safer from theft of cars. The layouts advocated by the current design fashion of New Urbanism for residential environments, however, have come in for some criticism as likely to produce higher rather than low residential car crime rates (Town and O'Toole 2005), and need to be carefully watched.

Selected further reading

In *Understanding and Preventing Car Theft* (2004), Michael Maxfield and Ron Clarke pull together an impressive array of papers on various aspects of car crime from the USA, the UK and Australia. The book is the product of an international conference, designed to present the most up-to-date and significant research with the aim of increasing both attention to the problem and the knowledge base in the USA.

Vehicle crime often means car crime to many, but cars are not the only target and sometimes not the most at risk. A series of papers produced by the Home Office (the *Police Research Group* papers) by various authors covers the full range, including light commercial vehicles, heavy good vehicles, construction plant and motor cycles as well as cars. Together, these papers provide a much fuller picture of vehicle crime. They are all available on the Home Office website.

Car parks have attracted a good deal of attention as risky locations for car crime. Ron Clarke's problem-oriented guide *Thefts of and from Cars in Parking Facilities* (available at www.cops.usdoj.gov) nicely summarizes the risk factors and effectiveness of practical responses from the research. More recent evaluation of a national UK car park security scheme is provided by Smith *et al.* in *Between the Lines: An Evaluation of the Secured Car Park Award Scheme* (2003).

In 1998, the British government announced a national target to reduce vehicle crime by 30 per cent over five years. The subsequent strategy is described in *Tackling Vehicle Crime: A Five Year Strategy* (available on the crime reduction website – www.crimereduction.gov.uk/vcrat1.htm) and the evidence-base behind that strategy is described in *Vehicle Crime Reduction: Turning the Corner* by Joanne Sallybanks and Rick Brown (1999).

An important source of research evidence on environmental design and vehicle crime is Barry Poyner's work. *Crime Free Housing* (1991) and *Design for Inherent Security: Guidance for Non-residential Buildings* (1995) provide essential reading for anyone interested in designing out residential and non-residential car crime.

Finally, Claire Corbett's book *Car Crime* (2003) provides a wide-ranging view of car crime, including cultural, historical and legal perspectives and car-related offences such as speeding, bad, drunk and unlicensed driving.

References

Brown, R. (1995) *The Nature and Extent of Heavy Goods Vehicle Theft. Crime Detection and Prevention Series Paper* 66. London: Home Office

Brown, R. (2004) 'The effectiveness of electronic immobilisation: changing patterns of temporary and permanent vehicle theft', in M. Maxfield and R.V. Clarke (eds) *Understanding and Preventing Car Theft. Crime Prevention Studies. Vol. 17.* Cullompton: Willan Publishing.

Brown, R. and Clarke, R.V. (2004) 'Police intelligence and theft of vehicles for export: recent UK experience', in M. Maxfield and R.V. Clarke (eds) *Understanding and Preventing Car Theft. Crime Prevention Studies. Vol. 17.* Cullompton: Willan Publishing.

Chenery, S., Henshaw, C. and Pease, K. (1999) *Illegal Parking in Disabled Bays: A Means of Offender Targeting. Briefing Note* 1/99. London: Home Office.

Clarke, R.V. and Harris, P.M. (1992) 'Auto theft and its prevention', in M. Tonry (ed.) *Crime and Justice: A Review of Research. Vol. 16.* Chicago, IL: University of Chicago Press.

Clarke, R.V. and Mayhew, P. (1998) 'Preventing crime in parking lots: what we know and what we need to know', in M. Felson and R. Peiser (eds) *Reducing Crime Through Real Estate Development and Management.* Washington, DC: Urban Land Institute.

Corbett, C. (2003) *Car Crime.* Cullompton: Willan Publishing.

Dodd, T., Nicholas, S., Povey, D. and Walker, A. (2004) *Crime in England and Wales 2003/2004. Home Office Statistical Bulletin* 10/04. London: Home Office.

Greenaway, D. (2004) *Uninsured Driving in the United Kingdom. A Report for the Secretary of State for Transport.* London: Department of Transport.

Jill Dando Institute (2002) *Measuring the Impact of MVRIB Initiatives on Vehicle Theft.* London: JDI (available at www.jdi.ucl.ac.uk).

Kershaw, C., Budd, T., Kinshott, G., Mattinson, J., Mayhew, P. and Myhill, A. (2000) *The 2000 British Crime Survey. Home Office Statistical Bulletin* 18/00. London: Home Office.

Kinshott, G. (2001) *Vehicle-related Thefts: Practice Messages from the British Crime Survey. Research Briefing Note* 6/01. London: Home Office.

Laycock, G. (2004) 'The UK Car Theft Index: an example of government leverage', in M. Maxfield and R.V. Clarke (eds) *Understanding and Preventing Car Theft. Crime Prevention Studies. Vol. 17.* Cullompton: Willan Publishing.

Laycock, G. and Webb, B. (forthcoming) 'Designing out crime from the UK vehicle licensing system', in R.V. Clarke (ed.) *Crime Prevention Studies. Vol. 18,* pp. 201–228. Mosby, New York: Criminal Justice Press.

Levesley, T., Braun, G., Wilkinson, M. and Powell, C. (2003) *Emerging Methods of Car Theft – Theft of Keys. Research Findings* 239. London: Home Office.

Levi, M. and Handley, J. (1998) *The Prevention of Plastic and Cheque Fraud Revisited. Home Office Research Study* 182. London: Home Office.

Loxley, C., Curtin, L. and Brown, R. (2002) *Summer Splash Schemes 2000: Findings from Six Case Studies. Crime Reduction Research Series Paper* 12. London: Home Office.

Maxfield, M. and Clarke, R. (2004) *Understanding and Preventing Car Theft.* Cullompton: Willan Publishing.

Mayhew, P., Clarke, R.V. and Elliott (1989) 'Motor cycle theft, helmet legislation and displacement', *Howard Journal of Criminal Justice,* 28: 1–8.

Mayhew, P. and Hough, J.M. (1976) *Crime as Opportunity. Home Office Research Study* 34. London: HMSO.

Mayhew, P. and White, P. (1997) *The 1996 International Crime Victimisation Survey. Research and Statistics Directorate Research Findings* 57. London: Home Office.

Newman, G.R. and Clarke, R.V. (2003) *Superhighway Robbery: Preventing E-commerce Crime.* Cullompton: Willan Publishing.

Office of the Deputy Prime Minister (2004) *Safer Places: The Planning System and Crime Prevention.* London: HMSO.

PA Consulting (2004) *Driving Down Crime: Denying Criminals the Use of the Road*. London: HMSO.

Poyner, B. (1992) 'Situational crime prevention in two parking facilities', in R.V. Clarke (ed.) *Situation Crime Prevention: Successful Case Studies*. New York, NY: Harrow and Heston.

Poyner, B. (1995) *Design for Inherent Security: Guidance for Non-residential Buildings*. London: CIRIA.

Poyner, B. (forthcoming) *Designing Crime-free Housing: The Research Evidence*. London: Jill Dando Institute.

Poyner, B. and Webb, B. (1991) *Crime Free Housing*. Oxford: Butterworth

Sallybanks, J. and Brown, R. (1999) *Vehicle Crime Reduction: Turning the Corner. Police Research Series Paper* 119. London: Home Office.

Smith, A. (1999) *Motor Projects Reviewed: Current Knowledge of Good Practice. Ad Hoc Policing and Reducing Crime Unit Paper*. London: Home Office.

Smith, D.G., Gregson, M. and Morgan, J. (2003) *Between the Lines: An Evaluation of the Secured Car Park Award Scheme. Home Office Research Study* 266. London: Home Office.

Smith, M., Jacobson, J. and Webb, B. (2004) 'Abandoned vehicles in England: impact of the End of Life Directive and new initiatives on likely future trends', *Journal of Resources, Conservation and Recycling*, 41: 177–89.

Smith, M. and Webb, B. (2005) 'Vehicle excise duty evasion in the UK', in M. Smith and N. Tilley (eds) *Crime Science: New Approaches to Crime Detection and Prevention*. Cullompton: Willan Publishing.

Southall, D. and Ekblom, P. (1995) *Designing for Car Security: Toward a Crime Free Car. Crime Prevention Unit Paper* 4. London: Home Office.

Spencer, E. (1992) *Car Crime and Young People on a Sunderland Housing Estate. Crime Prevention Unit Series Paper* 40. London: Home Office.

Tilley, N. (1993) *Understanding Car Parks, Crime and CCTV: Evaluation Lessons from Safer Cities. Crime Prevention Unit Series Paper* 42. London: Home Office.

Tilley, N., Smith, J., Finer, S., Erol, R., Charles, C. and Dobby, J. (2004) *Problem-solving Street Crime: Practical Lessons from the Street Crime Initiative*. London: Home Office.

Town, S. and O'Toole, (2005) 'Crime-friendly neighbourhoods: how "new urbanist" planners sacrifice safety in the name of "openness" and "accessibility"', in *Reason: Free Minds and Free Markets*, 36: 31–6.

VCRAT (1999) *Tackling Vehicle Crime: A Five Year Strategy. Report by the Vehicle Crime Reduction Action Team*. London: Home Office.

Webb, B. (1994) 'Steering column locks and motor vehicle theft: evaluations from three countries', in R.V.G. Clarke (ed.) *Crime Prevention Studies. Vol. 2*. New York, NY: Willow Tree Press.

Webb, B., Brown, B. and Bennett, K. (1992) *Preventing Car Crime in Car Parks. Crime Prevention Unit Series Paper* 34. London: Home Office.

Webb, B. and Laycock, G. (1992) *Reducing Crime on the London Underground. Crime Prevention Unit Paper* 30. London: Home Office.

Webb, B. and Laycock, G. (1992) *Tackling Car Crime: The Nature and Extent of the Problem. Crime Prevention Unit Paper* 32. London: Home Office.

Webb, B., Smith, M. and Laycock, G. (2004) 'Designing out crime through vehicle licensing and registration systems', in M. Maxfield and R.V. Clarke (eds) *Understanding and Preventing Car Theft. Crime Prevention Studies. Vol. 17*. Cullompton: Willan Publishing.

Which? (1991) *Car Security League*, February: 107–9.

Chapter 18

Business and crime

John Burrows and Matt Hopkins

Introduction

This chapter focuses upon the extent and nature of crimes against business and the prevention of crime in this area.[1] It has been observed that, despite the overall losses business sustain from crime and the impact that crime can have upon business turnover, crime against businesses has been subject to relatively little attention by academics and practitioners alike (Hibberd and Shapland 1993; Burrows 1997). There are a variety of reasons for this. One contributory factor may be that a large proportion of the research in this area has developed in line with the policy and funding of the Home Office, which has tended to focus upon individuals and households as victims of crime, rather than businesses. Coupled with this, crime prevention efforts have tended to be targeted towards individuals and households because they are victims of a far greater proportion of overall crime than businesses. There are far more households than businesses so it follows that attempts to prevent crimes against households are likely to have a greater impact on overall crime figures and the fear of crime.

Shapland and Vagg (1988) argue that it has also been assumed by many that crime against business is not 'as serious' as crime against the individual, although their own research clearly confounds this view, showing crimes against business may have serious consequences. Allied to this, it has often been perceived that all businesses are large entities that can either control crime or budget for its consequences (Burrows 1997). However, the reality is that 94 per cent of UK businesses are small concerns employing fewer than ten people (Burrows 1997). Many are economically marginal and research has shown that many of these smaller businesses are not able to survive the cost of crimes such as burglary (see Wood *et al.* 1996).

The relative lack of interest in crimes against business may also be partly attributable to the inadequacies of police recording systems in identifying businesses as victims. The police service has never been required to provide the Home Office with statistics separating those where businesses, and those who work in them, have been victimized, and – as a result – few of the recording systems operated by the police service require such a distinction to be drawn. For example, a burglary against a house is recorded as 'burglary of a dwelling', whereas a burglary against a business will be recorded as 'burglary other than a dwelling': a classification that embraces burglaries against all non-residential buildings, from schools to garden sheds. In short, current British crime-recording conventions provide no marker of the extent of crime affecting business.

The chapter is structured into three main sections. First, the major research that has been conducted in this area is summarized. The commentary then examines some of the research that has tried to explain why certain types of business experience high rates of victimization. The next section then looks at the prospects for preventing crimes against business and presents a case study of a major crime reduction initiative that aimed to reduce crime against small businesses in an English city. In the final section, there is a discussion of the major issues raised by the research evidence.

Research into crime against business

The dearth of research considering crimes against businesses has long been noted (Felson and Clarke 1997). But it is apparent that in recent years there has been a growth of interest in the area and attention has started to be directed at both the extent of crime against businesses and the subsequent financial cost of victimization. Generally, the work conducted on crimes against business can be categorized into four main types, namely:

1. *Surveys of crime against business*: studies that measure the proportion of business that are victims of crime, the number of incidents they are victims of and the costs of crime to business. The two sweeps of the Commercial Victimization Survey (or CVS: Mirrlees-Black and Ross 1995; Taylor 2004) provide the primary example.

2. *Studies focused on a particular crime problem*: a number of studies have explored the frequency or severity of a particular crime problem experienced by businesses, such as racial harassment (Ekblom and Simon 1988). Farrington and Burrows (1993), for example, sought to establish explanations for the dramatic rise in recorded shop theft in the late 1980s/early 1990s.

3. *Theoretical investigations of what 'drives' crime against business*: a number of studies theorize about why business are victims, or question why certain patterns of crime emerge. Examples are the application of routine activity theory to business crime patterns (Felson 1996) or the study of changing victimization patterns within a panel sample of small businesses (Hopkins and Tilley 2001).

4. *Evaluations of crime prevention initiatives or crime prevention advice to business*: there have been a number of studies of the impact of particular initiatives taken by a single company, or a consortium of businesses (see Farrington *et al.* 1993; Gill 1998a), and others that have evaluated the impact of crime

reduction mechanisms implemented by businesses in a particular area (Wood *et al.* 1996; Tilley and Hopkins 1998). In addition, crime prevention guidance for businesses has been published (see, for example, Health and Safety Executive 1995).

It is evident that the work conducted in these four areas is beginning to make a significant contribution to the knowledge base in relation to crimes against business. However, most of this work has generally been conducted by only a few institutions: in particular, the Home Office, the British Retail Consortium (BRC)[2] and academic institutions such as the Scarman Centre[3] at Leicester University.[4]

The Home Office research has considered a number of aspects of business crime, such as burglary (Laycock 1985; Tilley 1993), shop theft (Ekblom 1986), robbery (Ekblom 1987; Austin 1988), crime and racial harassment against Asian-run small shops (Ekblom and Simon 1988) and fraud (Levi 1988; Levi *et al.* 1991). Since 1992, the BRC has published 11 national surveys of retail crime. There have also been several collections of specific research studies in the area, with the most notable contributions contained in two collections of papers edited by Gill (1994, 1998a) and arising from a conference on business crime organised by the US National Institute of Justice in 1996 (see Felson and Clarke 1997).

Surveys exploring the extent and range of crime against business

The successful implementation of crime reduction measures is dependent upon knowing what the problem is, where the problem exists and why it occurs. This is as relevant for businesses as for households. As a response to the growing desire to understand both the spatial and temporal patterns of crimes against businesses, a number of surveys have been commissioned. These surveys can be broken down into a number of categories. They include national and local studies considering a number of crimes against business. The national studies (and one international survey) have generally considered the rates of victimization against businesses for a range of crimes, whereas localized studies have often concentrated on a specific offence. Finally, there have also been a number of studies conducted that have given advice on the prevention of specific types of crime, such as credit card fraud (Levi *et al.* 1991) and violence against staff (Poyner and Warne 1988). A brief outline is given below of some of the main methodological challenges faced by such surveys. Consideration is then given to some of their main findings.

Methodological challenges

Crime surveys represent a way of measuring all crime incidents against businesses (rather than just crime reported to the police) and they also offer the potential to ask business managers/owners about the fear of crime and perceptions of crime risks within their local area. There are three key issues, however, that need to be addressed in undertaking such surveys, and that also need to be considered in evaluating their findings.

The first relates to establishing the size of the business population under review so that researchers, and subsequently those weighing up their evidence, can be sure of how 'population' estimates extrapolated from the sample have been drawn. The key to judging the overall problem of crimes against business in England and Wales – for example – is to start with a firm understanding of how many businesses operate in England and Wales, how many people they employ and what their turnover is. Table 18.1 provides broad *estimates* of the number of firms, by key sector, in the UK in 2000, the number of employees and their turnover.

The table does not provide a comprehensive list of all businesses in the UK, but it does serve to enforce a number of points. It is clear that the number of companies within each sector is not representative of the number of employees or turnover overall. For example, 19 per cent of businesses are manufacturers, but they employ 33 per cent of all staff and account for 31 per cent of turnover. It follows that surveys that may be representative of the number of firms may not be representative of the number of employees or turnover. To complicate matters, the business database lists used as a sampling frame for national surveys often underestimate the number of trading businesses. For example, the Yell business database estimates the size of the manufacturing population to be 82,107; Dun and Bradstreet estimate it to be 75,120; whereas the NOS data, drawn on in Table 18.1, provide a figure of 152,235.

The second issue relates to the most reliable way to measure crimes against business. Surveys can either interview those working at business premises directly, or collect data through the head offices of businesses and rely on their account of crime incidence/losses across the different outlets they operate. Both the 'premises' and 'head office' approaches have their relative advantages and disadvantages; they are considered in more detail below.

The third issue is to determine the range of crimes to be explored. Most surveys of business crime clearly define the range of crimes under review. But whilst it is useful to determine parameters in this way, this of course inhibits any claim to have covered all aspects of crime to which businesses might be subjected.

Table 18.1 Number of firms, employees and turnover in 2000

	Firms (VAT reg.)		Employees		Turnover (billions)	
Manufacturing	152,235	(19%)	3,958,000	(33%)	£469.1	(31%)
Construction	171,085	(21%)	1,188,000	(10%)	£121.5	(8%)
Wholesale/retail	313,685	(39%)	4,095,000	(34%)	£730.3	(48%)
Hotel/restaurants	105,225	(13%)	1,413,000	(12%)	£47.4	(3%)
Transport/communication	73,185	(9%)	1,451,000	(12%)	£167.8	(11%)
Total	815,415	(100%)	12,105,000	(100%)	£1536.1	(100%)

Note:
The data sources are all from the National Office of Statistics; the data on firms from size analysis of UK businesses statistics; employee data from Annual Abstract of Statistics; and turnover data from Annual Business Inquiry (all 2001).

International comparisons

The first (and, to date, only) international survey of crimes against business (Van Dijk and Terlouw 1995) compared the results of victimization surveys completed by retail premises across nine countries: Hungary, the Czech Republic, the Netherlands, Germany, the UK, Australia, France, Switzerland and Italy.[5] The survey addressed various crime types – such as burglary, vandalism and robbery – over a 12-month recall period. It was found that 'theft by persons' was the most common crime type with the highest prevalence rate in Hungary (83 per cent) and the lowest in Italy (45 per cent). The second most common crime was burglary (with rates ranging from 40 per cent in the Czech Republic to 14 per cent in Italy), except in France and Italy where fraud by outsiders was the second most common crime. The least common crimes were theft of company vehicles, fraud by personnel and corruption. UK businesses experienced the highest prevalence rates of theft from, and of, company vehicles (23 per cent and 10 per cent, respectively), and the second highest rates of burglary (37 per cent) and assault (18 per cent).

National surveys

In the UK a number of national studies have considered crimes against business; the key studies are outlined in Table 18.2.[6] They range from the CVS (Mirrlees-Black and Ross 1995; Taylor 2004), eleven 'Retail Crime Costs' surveys conducted by the BRC (e.g. Burrows and Speed 1994 or Speed *et al.* 1995), two surveys by the British Chambers of Commerce (BCC)[7] and a number of one-off surveys, such as the Scottish Business Crime Survey (Burrows *et al.* 1999). Two of the surveys – those by the BRC and the Home Office CVS – are considered in detail here as they serve to illustrate the two main differing methodological approaches to measuring business crime.

The annual BRC surveys have all been 'head office' surveys where the participating retailers were either BRC member companies or identified through allied trade associations or local Chambers of Commerce. The data was collected through postal questionnaires. This method enables the survey to represent a large proportion of the sector – by sales, if not by businesses – at relatively low cost. In the 2002 survey a total of 20,902 retail outlets were covered (which accounted for 43 per cent of UK retail sales).[8] Each survey asks businesses about the *number* of incidents experienced over the period of a year for a number of crime types (burglary, criminal damage, robbery, fraud, violence and abuse), and also about the costs of such crime.

Table 18.3 outlines some of the main findings of the 2002 'Retail Crime Costs' survey. The eleven reports have consistently shown that shop theft accounts for the highest numbers of incidents against retail premises. In 2002 there were 3,066 incidents of shop theft per 100 outlets (compared to 3,790 in 2001) and this amounted to 8.5 million incidents recorded nationally (compared to 306,000 recorded in the Home Office Criminal Statistics). In comparison, there were 37 incidents of staff theft per 100 outlets, 36 incidents of abuse and violence and 34 burglaries (including attempts) per 100. Whilst the average shop theft is not costly, for incidents such as criminal damage/arson, burglary and robbery, the average cost per incident is particularly high and can represent a heavy financial burden on businesses (e.g. £3,963 per incident of criminal damage/arson).

Table 18.2 Key national studies of crimes against business (surveys covering a number of crime types)

Name of survey	Key sectors covered	Year of publication and area covered	Organization commissioning the work
Commercial Victimization Survey (1)	Retail (1,666 premises) and manufacturing (1,259 premises)	1995 – England and Wales	Home Office
Commercial Victimization Survey (2)	Retail (3,955) and manufacturing (2,561) premises and 181 head offices	2004 – England and Wales	Home Office
BRC Surveys	Head offices of retail businesses representing an average of around 45,000 premises	Eleven surveys completed annually from 1994 to present – UK	British Retail Consortium
Forum of Private Business Survey	Transport, retail, hotel and caterers, construction and agriculture, wholesalers and services – a total of 2,618 businesses	1996 – United Kingdom	Forum of Private Business (FPB)[1]
Scottish Business Crime Surveyed	Manufacture, construction, wholesale and retail, transport and communications – 2,500 premises surveys and 148 head office interviews covering 3,680 premises	1999 – Scotland	Scottish Business Crime Centre[2]
BCC (1)	All sectors – over 3,000 businesses	1997 – UK	British Chambers of Commerce
BCC (2)	All sectors – 2,914	2001 – UK	British Chambers of Commerce
Survey of UK co-operative retailers	Co-op retail businesses. 2003 survey included 16 co-operative societies and 1,995 premises	Three surveys completed from 2000	
Survey of retail newsagents	Retail businesses – 482 premises	2002 – UK	National Federation of Retail Newsagents

Notes:

1. The FPB is a pressure group representing over 25,000 businesses in the UK and 75,000 in Europe. It conducts a range of research and represents business interests at local, national and European levels to policy-makers.
2. The Scottish Business Crime Centre was created under the Business Crime Reduction Strategy for Scotland. It is a partnership between the police, Scottish Executive and Scottish business. The main function of the centre is to provide practical advice to the business/commercial sectors on how to develop business crime reduction and prevention strategies.

Table 18.3 Key findings of the British Retail Consortium Report, 2002

Incident type	Incidents per 100 outlets	Average cost per incident (£)
Shop theft	3,066	88
Abuse and violence	36	–
Criminal damage and arson	23	3,963
Burglary (including attempts)	34	2,722[1]
Staff theft	37	541
Robbery	5	1,967

Note:
1. Figure is for stock loss and damage repair in a completed burglary.

The BRC surveys also assess risk rates within the different parts of the retail sector. The 2002 survey showed that department stores, DIY stores and food/drink outlets tended to experience the highest risks. Department stores had the highest incidence rates for customer theft (9,461 per 100), staff theft (406 per 100), criminal damage/arson (127 per 100) and robbery (26 per 100). DIY stores had the highest risk of burglary (43 per 100) and food/drink stores the highest risk of till snatches (12 per 100).[9]

The 1994 CVS represented the first attempt by government to conduct a national survey to measure crime against business. The CVS adopted the 'premises approach' and directly interviewed the managers/owners of individual business premises rather than relying on data that had been collated at head offices. To the extent that managers running parts of multi-site business may not report all crime incidents to the centre, the CVS is likely to provide a more accurate assessment of crime rates against business than the BRC surveys.

The CVS focused on retail and manufacturing businesses.[10] The sample was selected from the BT Businesses database, which provides telephone numbers, standard industrial classification (SIC) codes and the number of employees within each company. The database does have limitations as it registers only those who opt to be in the *Yellow Pages* and it can quickly become outdated (as businesses close and others open). The overall sample for the study was 2,925, of which 1,666 were retail and 1,259 were manufacturing concerns.

In total, 80 per cent of retailers interviewed had been a victim of at least one crime in 1993. The most common crimes were theft by customers (which 47 per cent of retailers had experienced), burglary (24 per cent), theft from vehicles (23 per cent) and vandalism (22 per cent). The overall rates of victimization were lower for manufacturers. The survey found that 63 per cent of manufacturers had experienced at least one incident of crime. The most prevalent crimes for manufacturers were thefts from vehicles (25 per cent), burglary (24 per cent) and vandalism (16 per cent). Manufacturers were just as likely to be burgled as retailers.

The different methodologies used by the BRC and CVS research make it difficult to draw straightforward comparisons between the two surveys. However, it is possible to compare incidence rates recorded in the CVS and

BRC surveys for retail premises for 1993/94.[11] These data are presented in Table 18.4.

The table indicates that, in both surveys, burglary and employee theft are the most common crimes to occur against retail premises. However, it should be noted *that, for each category, the average number of incidents recorded by the CVS was higher than those recorded by the BRC survey.* Whilst other factors may be at play here, this suggests that premises surveys may give a more reliable account of business crime as they deal directly with the business outlets (the potential victim). It would be expected that individual premises would be more aware of the number of crimes they had experienced than head offices.

The national surveys summarized above give an interesting insight into patterns of business crime, although it is clear that more research is required to consider crime rates against businesses beyond the retail or manufacturing sectors. Gill (1998b) started to do this by considering data from an FPB survey of some 2,618 businesses, embracing a range of business sectors such as retail, manufacture, wholesale, construction, agricultural, transport and hotels. This study represented a step forward in understanding business crime beyond the retail and manufacturing sectors but Gill acknowledged that more needed to be done to understand why specific types of business experience high rates of victimization. This key issue was explored further by the first Scottish Business Crime survey, or SBC (Burrows *et al.* 1999). The SBC combined the methodology of both the CVS and BRC surveys by conducting premises and head office surveys, and it was also considerably wider in its scope – covering businesses in the manufacturing, wholesale/retail, construction, transport/telecommunications and hotels/restaurants sectors.[12]

Some interesting victimization patterns resulted. The hotel/restaurant sector, for example, proved to have the highest incidence rate of overall crime (716 incidents of crime per 100 premises) and the transport sector the lowest (453 incidents per 100 premises). There were also clear intra-sector variations in patterns of victimization. For example, businesses in the hotel/restaurant and post/telecommunications sector tended to experience high rates of violence, threats and assaults. Particularly high-risk businesses included public transport businesses (432 incidents of violence per 100), post/telecoms (429 per 100) and restaurants/takeaways (387 per 100). In contrast businesses in the manufacturing, construction and wholesale/retail sector tended to experience the highest rates of property crime. For example, food/beverage businesses experienced 71 burglaries per 100 premises, motor/fuel businesses

Table 18.4 A comparison of incidence rates (per 100 businesses) reported in the BRC and CVS surveys for 1993/4

Crime type	Commercial Victimization Survey	British Retail Consortium (1993/4)
Burglary	93	53
Employee theft	93	65
Vandalism	87	28
Robbery	8	3

experienced 255 incidents of vandalism and retailers 246 incidents of theft by outsiders.[13]

Repeat victimization

Repeat victimization has been highlighted as a predictor of future risk in residential burglary (Farrell and Pease 1993; Pease 1998) and the CVS (Mirrlees-Black and Ross 1995) also considered repeat victimization for retailers and manufacturers across crime types such as burglary, vandalism and fraud. For retailers, 10 per cent of respondents were repeat victims of burglary: they constituted 38 per cent of all victims and had 66 per cent of all incidents. A similar picture was found for manufacturers. In total, 11 per cent were repeat victims of burglary: they constituted 48 per cent of victims and had 71 per cent of incidents. Similar proportions were recorded for other incident types.

The CVS did not, however, explore the time course of incidents in order to establish repeat victimization patterns. The first survey carried out by the Small Business and Crime Initiative project (or SBCI; Wood *et al.* 1996) did, however, explore this issue. It found patterns similar to the previous studies on repeat domestic burglaries. Over a quarter of repeat burglaries took place within the first month of the previous incident and 43 per cent took place within the first two months.

Comparisons with rates of personal/household crime

Making comparisons of the rate of crimes against businesses to crime against households or individuals can be difficult because of the different ways that incidents are measured and because certain crimes (such as shop theft) are not committed against both groups. However, comparisons can be made between the CVS and BRC and the British Crime Survey (or BCS, for households and individuals) and these generally suggest that businesses experience higher rates of crime than households or individuals. For example, 80 per cent of retailers and 63 per cent of manufacturers had been victims of crime in 1994, according to the CVS, compared to 34 per cent of individuals in the 1998 BCS (Mirrlees-Black *et al.* 1998).

Crime 'prevalence' is however different from crime 'incidence',[14] and the latter measure helps to give an indication of the extent of repeat victimization. By using BRC data some comparison can also be made between the household and retail incidence rates for crimes such as burglary: in 1997 there were 4.4 burglaries per 100 households (including attempts), compared to 34 per 100 retail premises recorded by the BRC.

The costs of crime

Various research studies have indicated that the financial impact of crime can affect the future trading prospects of many businesses. Making accurate assessments of the cost of crime to businesses can, however, prove difficult and differences can arise between surveys using *premises* and *head office* approaches. There are also many costs of crime that are hard to assess (such as loss of orders, delayed delivery and staff absence).

The methodology employed in the CVS enabled the overall costs of crime to be calculated for retailers and manufacturers. The survey estimated that in

1994 retailers lost £780 million to crime and manufacturers £275 million: this represented 0.7 per cent of retail turnover and 0.2 per cent of manufacturing turnover. Expressed in monetary terms for individual premises, a small retailer could expect to lose on average £1,850 per year though crime and a large retailer £12,450. Small manufacturers on average lost £1,740 and large manufacturers £7,730. For both business sectors the highest average costs were sustained through the theft of vehicles: on average this crime cost £3,940 per incident for a retailer and £3,980 for a manufacturer.

Whilst the first CVS found the overall cost of crime to retailers to be £780 million, this was very much less than the £2,149 million estimated by the BRC survey for 1993/4. Closer analysis however revealed that the difference lay entirely in the fact that the BRC sought to measure 'shrinkage' and, using estimates provided by respondent firms, apportioned £1,207 million of these losses to customer theft and employee theft. The BRC survey also asked retailers about the consequential and indirect losses they sustained through crime, and attributed an additional £42 million to such losses. Finally, the coverage of the two surveys was different, and in the case of the BRC costs from businesses in Scotland and Northern Ireland (including £226 million attributed to terrorist acts) served to boost the total. In terms of direct losses attributable to crime the BRC survey actually produced *lower estimates* than the CVS.

Local surveys

The commentary so far has focused on national victimization surveys but a number of localized studies have also been conducted to try to understand the crime problems businesses face. These studies – such as the SBCI (Wood *et al.* 1996), Camden Three Streets Project (Hopkins and Tilley 1998) or Holborn Business Partnership Crime Survey (MHB 2002) – have included surveys that have addressed a number of crime-related issues against businesses. Table 18.5 summarizes their coverage. A number of local surveys have also been carried out addressing specific issues such as burglary against small shops (Tilley

Table 18.5 Key 'local/thematic' studies of crimes against business

Name of survey	Key sectors covered	Year of publication and area covered
Small Business and Crime Initiative	Retail, manufacturing, wholesale, services	1996 and 1998 – two surveys of over 800 businesses including a 'panel' sample element
Camden Three Streets Project	All businesses	1998 – 87 businesses in three north London streets
Crime on industrial estates	Manufacturing	1994 – over 400 premises on industrial estates
Crime in Asian-run shops	Retail	1988 – survey of 296 shops across London
Holborn Business Partnership Crime Survey	All sectors	2002 – postal survey of 162 businesses including surveys with 248 employees.

1993), shop theft (McCulloch 1996), robbery at sub-post offices (Ekblom 1987), ram-raiding (Jacques 1994), crime and nuisance problems in shopping centres (Phillips and Cochrane 1988) and on industrial estates (Johnston *et al.* 1994) and racially motivated crime (Ekblom and Simon 1988).

It is difficult to determine whether local victimization surveys or national surveys provide the most accurate data on business victimization rates. Local surveys tend to adopt the 'premises approach', which the commentary above has suggested will tend to produce more accurate crime counting, but it is possible that 'head office' surveys provide a more comprehensive account of crime costs.[15] However, victims can forget about the numbers of incidents they have been a victim of (especially shop theft that, for some, is a daily occurrence) and are often unsure about the actual time of year when incidents occurred (i.e. the month).

The SBCI (Wood *et al.* 1996; Tilley and Hopkins 1998) represents the best resourced, and most detailed, example of a local survey. It comprised two survey sweeps – one carried out before implementation of preventive activities and one after – which produced the largest localized sample of small business interviewed so far in the UK.[16]

The first SBCI survey was completed in September 1995 and the second in September 1997. Both surveys recorded data for a recall period of 12 months. They found that 74 per cent of businesses had experienced at least one incident of crime in sweep one and 60 per cent in sweep two. The overall prevalence rate for the first sweep was similar to that recorded in the CVS (this was 74 per cent), and the prevalence rates recorded for a number of crime types are not dissimilar: for example, the most prevalent crime in both sweeps was burglary. The highest concentration rate, in both sweeps, was for incidents of abuse (4.5 incidents per victim in sweep one and 3.6 in sweep two), whilst the highest incidence rates (in both sweeps) were recorded for fraud.

Overall, the SBCI echoed the findings of many of other local studies that have shown businesses have high rates of crime when compared to residential premises. Whilst most have primarily sought to establish the rates of crime experienced by business, others have explored wider issues. Hopkins and Tilley (1998), for example, reported on the findings of interviews with 87 businesses in three north London streets. They found that 30 per cent of businesses had considered relocating because of the effect of crime and 29 per cent had considered ceasing trading.

Summary

Although this review has been far from exhaustive, it has sought to summarize the principal research on crimes against business. Many of the findings are difficult to compare because of the different ways data have been collected and analysed. Several consistent patterns have, however, emerged. In relation to *crime risks* for business it is apparent that:

- businesses tend to have higher rates of victimization when compared to households and individuals for a number of crime types. For example, the CVS showed that the chances of retail or manufacturing premises being burgled was six times higher than for a household, and that there were four times as many thefts of vehicles per hundred owners;

- businesses sustain heavy financial losses from crime;

- repeat victimization is a significant problem for businesses, across a number of crime types. This has been highlighted at a national and local level through CVS data, the Safer Cities programme (Tilley 1993) and the SBCI (Wood *et al.* 1996). The patterns identified here are similar to those for residential premises, but the overall number of repeats per business premises is obviously much higher; and

- crime risks vary substantially by sector and subsector. The SBC, in particular, shows that crime is heavily targeted at a relatively small proportion of businesses and that most broad business sectors have their own 'crime profile' with one or more forms of crime to which they are particularly vulnerable.

The evidence also demonstrates that, whilst it is frequently suggested that businesses should be able to protect themselves from crime, not all businesses are able to afford to do so. Indeed it is not an exaggeration to state that crime threatens the existence of many businesses (see Wood *et al.* 1996).

Explaining crime patterns against businesses

Whilst national surveys of crime against business have made progress in measuring the number and rate of crimes against businesses, there has been little explanation as to why crime is often concentrated against particular businesses within each sector. A small but growing number of studies have started to explain why some business premises have higher risks than others. Felson (1996) applied routine activity theory, which suggests that for any direct-contact predatory violation to occur there has to be a convergence in time and space of a likely offender and suitable target in the absence of a 'capable guardian' (Cohen and Felson 1979), to business crime. It was conjectured that businesses where high crime rates were observed would have a 'ready supply of offenders' in the locality (or passing through the business), 'target suitability' in terms of the consumer durables available on the premises and an 'absence of capable guardianship' at times when offences are likely to occur.

Such a theoretical stance is easily applied to acquisitive crime, such as burglaries of business premises. For example, data from the BRC surveys highlight that there are high rates of burglaries in department stores. This is hardly surprising when considering that there are lots of potential offenders and lots of lightweight expensive consumer durables to take. Hopkins (1998) also used routine activity theory to develop an understanding as to why certain business types experience high rates of violent crime. He suggested that some businesses develop routine active patterns and have certain 'lifestyle' attributes that generate incidents of violence. Data were analysed from over 150 incidents of violence in small businesses. It was observed that typical characteristics of businesses where high rates of violence are observed included operating in the retail or service sector, late opening hours, the serving of alcohol and the experience of high rates of shop theft.

Although routine activity theory has been used to help develop an understanding of why some business experience high rates of victimization, some research has also tried to explain variation in risk *within the same types of business activity*. The variation in the crime experience for certain business premises was explored in some detail as part of the SBC (Burrows *et al.* 1999). Having completed the crime surveys, researchers made follow-up visits to selected premises. In total, ten pairs of businesses[17] were visited: in each pair one business was selected which had experienced high crime rates and another with low crime rates. Clarke's 'opportunity reducing' typology of the techniques of situational crime prevention (Clarke 1992) were then used to give examples of how businesses 'increased the effort' for offenders to commit crime, 'increased risks' for offenders and 'reduced rewards' for offenders (see Burrows *et al.* 1999).

It was found that there was a clear division in the crime profile of businesses according to the degree of contact they had with customers. For those businesses *with little customer contact* (manufacturing, construction) the focus of their problems tended to be burglary, criminal damage and staff theft. In these businesses the following patterns were observed:

- *Location/supply of offenders*: high-risk businesses tended to be located next to problem housing estates, whereas low-risk premises were not.

- *Surveillance/guardianship*: risks were increased by the absence of surveillance for long periods – particularly over weekends. Often the low-risk premises were protected by security guards and CCTV.

- *Target suitability*: often high-risk premises were surrounded by a yard area where there were a number of potential entry points. Typically the yard would be full of waste and rubbish that would often be set alight.

For those with a high degree of customer contact (retail, hotel, transport) the focus of their problems tended to be customer theft, abuse and violence:

- *Location/supply of offenders*: most types of business with a high degree of customer contact were located in town centres. However the highest-risk businesses (pubs, restaurants and taxi firms) were dependent upon late night working and often came into contact with drunken customers.

- *Surveillance/guardianship*: the risk of burglary/criminal damage would be increased by a lack of surveillance around the business at night.[18]

- *Target suitability*: most businesses offered considerable rewards for those inclined to commit crimes such as burglary. Many stocked items that were lightweight and expensive, such as alcohol and electrical goods.

The prevention of crimes against business

The wide diversity of businesses means it is very difficult to make generic statements about the overall impact of crime upon the profitability of businesses or their ability to trade, or what help can be given to businesses to try to reduce crime. At one end of the scale, some businesses have entire security departments dedicated to loss-reduction activities and these businesses are likely to have up-to-date security equipment, security guards and sophisticated payment systems. To such businesses, the control of crime can constitute an everyday, mainstream, business activity. At the other end of the scale many smaller and medium-sized enterprises will be unable to afford hi-tech security equipment and indeed a single incident of crime could represent a threat to their future existence. Moreover the absolute scale of loses incurred is often not directly indicative of the priority that will be accorded to crime control. Burrows (1991) cites the fact that spiralling credit card losses in the late 1980s and early 1990s were not initially viewed by the credit card industry as a particular cause for concern, simply because losses as a percentage of turnover were decreasing.

There are no comprehensive data on the extent to which businesses invest in preventing crime. Many national and local studies have sought to explore the extent of this expenditure. The 2003 BRC survey, for example, suggests the retail industry alone spends £54 million per annum.[19] There can be no doubt that the investment is very large, and whilst many costs are borne in terms of the recruitment of additional staff and security devices, the exponential growth of the private security industry might be seen as something of a barometer of this investment (although the industry does of course serve public sector clients as well). It has long been remarked that the number of personnel employed in the industry exceeds the number of police officers. A current estimate is that over 350,000 people work in the security industry, and of these 125,000 are security officers.[20]

The absence of data on the investment in prevention by businesses themselves is matched by lack of any real understanding of what impact this investment has upon reducing crime. Businesses may evaluate the impact of such investment on crime reduction but there is no incentive for them to disseminate the findings of any such work.[21] This section turns instead to assess the national and local attention given to the prevention of crime against businesses. It initially considers government policy on crime against businesses. It then considers local partnership activities.

Government policy on crimes against business

The question of who should take prime responsibility for the management of crime against business has long been a 'political football' and this position is unlikely to change. The polar positions are well known: the business perspective is that crime control is the responsibility of the state, and there is nothing to separate crime against business from any others that the police and criminal justice system address. In contrast, the position of successive governments has been that all potential victims of crime have a responsibility to protect themselves. Moreover it is argued that the marketing and operation of many business concerns effectively 'create' new opportunities for crime and that it is therefore the responsibility of the businesses concerned to control any unintended consequences: the 'externalities' of their 'creations'.

In reality both sides have operated from compromise positions and partnership arrangements constitute the only practical way forward. In broad terms, there is some consensus that businesses must take prime responsibility for taking precautionary measures and then identifying crimes against their interests, to instigate initial investigations and do all they can to identify suspects and set out the nature of the crime they have committed. With this support, the police will then be in a position to call on their additional powers of investigation (where appropriate) and initiate proceedings that will bring the perpetrators of business crime to justice. In short, partnership is fundamental to effective action.

There have been many 'ebbs and flows' around this compromise position over the years, but the signs are that in recent years there has been a more concerted effort by central government to tackle issues relating to business crime.

Current government thinking is shaped around consultation with businesses on key issues relating to crime reduction (Home Office 2003). This has been coupled with a development of policy based around partnership working (with groups such as the British Chambers of Commerce and Federation of Small Businesses) and a desire to involve businesses in crime reduction. Steps were made in this direction in 2003 through the Capital Modernization Fund, which granted £15 million to help reduce crime in small businesses in deprived areas. The government strategy 'Developing Crime Reduction Advice and Support Services for Business' led to the appointment of business crime reduction advisers in the latter half of 2003. Business crime advisers were appointed in each government region with the key remit of:

- conducting a mapping exercise of all existing activities around business-related crime in their region;
- promoting business involvement in crime reduction activity;
- assessing where the gaps are, and where focus is needed for future work; and
- submitting a three-year strategy on business crime (in June 2004).

It is clear from the current direction in central government policy that businesses are likely to receive greater attention in the future. At present, however, it is unclear what the crime reduction advisers are likely to deliver in terms of crime reduction, or where the main focus of their attention is likely to be.

Local initiatives to reduce crimes against business

The advent of the Crime and Disorder Act 1998 made it a statutory obligation for local authorities to conduct audits of crime and disorder problems and, although the primary focus of such work has been on crimes such as burglary from dwellings, vehicle crime and anti-social behaviour/disorder, there is evidence that this has fostered some interest in business crime.[22]

It is evident, however, that the work conducted by crime and disorder partnerships with businesses has assumed a rather narrow focus. It has typically been directed at crimes against retail premises and licensed premises within city/town centres with the key aim of promoting city centres as areas where people can feel safe in partaking in day and night-time leisure activities. This has been primarily driven by changes in the economy of most cities over the last 20–30 years and a movement from the manufacturing sector to retail and services. Most of the larger cities across the UK are now reliant upon both retail and service sector business located in the city centre to sustain the local economy. It has become more important than ever for most cities to attract large well-known retailers to their city centres and to try to develop a 24-hour economy. In tandem to this has been the growth of the large out-of-town retail parks that are also essential to the economy of many larger towns.

There are dangers in looking to these town-centre initiatives as a guide to 'good practice' in preventing business crime generally. Focusing attention on city centres will often translate into working with the larger multinational companies that, to a large extent, are able to protect themselves from crime. Conversely this prioritization generally means that smaller retail businesses, and business from other sectors that are not located with town/city centres – often those most in need of help – are frequently not the focus of crime reduction activity. There is therefore some advantage to be gained from examining, as a case study, a project that was implemented to reduce crimes against business within two inner urban areas of an English city (rather than the city centre). The project was known as the 'Small Business and Crime Initiative', or SBCI, and it focused upon medium and small enterprises from all business sectors and commenced in September 1995.

This case study is presented as it outlines a number of the key challenges faced in both the delivery and evaluation of cross-business crime prevention initiatives, and it highlights a number of lessons for future projects. The case study is presented by using Ebklom's 5Is as a framework (Ekblom 2002). Ekblom developed the 5Is as a conceptual approach that might be used by crime prevention practitioners in addressing crime problems and as an aid to the transfer of crime prevention knowledge. The key elements presented below have been tailored towards understanding crime problems faced by businesses:

- *Intelligence*: how was information gathered on the crime problems faced by businesses in the area? How was it analysed and what does it tell us about the causes of crime?
- *Intervention*: what possible interventions were considered to reduce and prevent crime?
- *Implementation*: what 'in-principle' interventions were converted into practical methods? How were they shaped by the local context?
- *Insertion*: how was the implementation put in place? What agencies, companies and individuals were involved?
- *Impact*: what was the impact of intervention?

Case study: the Small Business and Crime Initiative

Presented in terms of the 5Is, the SBCI progressed as follows.

I   Intelligence: gathering information on the crime problem faced/analysing the data and searching for causes

The SBCI was immediately faced with a number of challenges in addressing the 'intelligence' issue. The first problem involved actually ascertaining the size of the business population in the two areas. Various business population databases are available but such databases are seldom comprehensive.[23] To remedy the problem, a comprehensive audit of the local business population was carried out by getting researchers to 'walk' the two areas and count the number of businesses:[24] this suggested that there were 1,381 operating businesses premises.

The second challenge was to ascertain the extent of the crime problem against businesses in the two areas. As indicated earlier, using police data to determine the extent of victimization within the business community can be highly problematic. The initiative team rapidly reached the view that a survey of crimes against businesses in the two areas would prove to be the only means by which intelligence on the extent and patterns of crime against business could be understood. A survey, involving face-to-face interviews with business owners/managers, was conducted in September 1995. The questionnaire focused on a number of issues affecting businesses over the preceding year and included the following:

- *Experience of crime and the costs arising from victimization.* Respondents were asked if they had experienced a range of crime types (burglary, criminal damage, customer theft, staff theft, robbery, fraud, transport loss, violence and abuse) over a 12-month recall period. The questionnaire allowed for up to four incidents to be logged for each crime type. For each, the date and cost of each incident were noted.

- *Actions taken to reduce crime.* Businesses were asked about the security measures they had installed and other precautions taken against crime (such as limiting the amount of cash in the till or having something available for self-defence).

- *Perceptions of the local environment and fear of crime.* The surveys examined the perceptions of crime and disorder problems in the local area (such as vandalism, drinking on the streets and drug dealing) and specific problems relating to the workplace (such as fear of crime when working alone, going to the bank, cashing up and closing up at night).

The owners/managers of 894 businesses, employing over 7,000 staff, were interviewed, which represented a response rate of 65 per cent. A total of 72 different types of businesses were interviewed. Most could be categorized into the retail, manufacturing, wholesale or 'other services' sectors. Critically, more than 90 per cent of the businesses surveyed employed under 10 staff.

Table 18.6 The most prevalent crimes in each business sector in the Small Business and Crime Initiative survey

	Manufacture (*n* = 122)	Wholesale (*n* = 89)	Retail (*n* = 365)	Service (*n* = 316)
Most prevalent crime	Burglary (49%)	Burglary (39%)	Burglary (43%)	Burglary (36%)
Second most prevalent	Transport loss (35%)	Transport loss (36%)	Fraud (43%)	Criminal damage (27%)
Third most prevalent	Criminal damage (29%)	Fraud (28%)	Customer theft (35%)	Fraud (23%)
Overall prevalence rate	*74%*	*75%*	*82%*	*70%*

The survey results highlighted that a total of 76 per cent of businesses were victim of at least one incident of crime over the 12-month recall period. The highest prevalence rates were for burglary (experienced by 41 per cent), fraud (31 per cent) and transport losses (24 per cent). The overall prevalence rates for each sector and the three most prevalent crimes with each sector are highlighted in Table 18.6. There was also evidence that crime was heavily concentrated against a small number of businesses. A total of 15 per cent of businesses (135 overall) were victims of 58 per cent of all incidents (1,600).

2   Intervention: considering possible interventions to reduce and prevent crime
There is growing evidence that, whilst many crime reduction projects are able to obtain a thorough understanding of the problems facing them, many are not able to develop workable ideas for interventions that address the causes (Laycock and Webb 2000). Moreover, the evidence from several decades of crime prevention/community safety activity is that partnership is often critical in mounting effective countermeasures against crime, but businesses do not naturally form a community. Whilst many are members of trade groups, at a local level there may be strong rivalry between businesses aiming to secure business in competition with each other.

To tackle this challenge, the SBCI took a proactive, and inclusive, approach to developing crime reduction strategies. As well as conducting the survey, representatives of the police, city council and local chambers of commerce actively took part in the initiative steering group and two consultation forums with local businesses were organized. These consultations (one in each area) aimed both to gauge the views of owners/managers on the results of the survey and to try to establish some idea as to how the major crime and anti-social behaviour problems could be addressed. Many business owners were surprised by results of the survey and the high rate of crime against businesses. This had the immediate impact of many suggesting that there was almost a state of 'lawlessness' in the community and a breakdown in discipline amongst many people. This also led to calls for action by the police and SBCI, including:

- more police on the beat to deter offenders;
- quicker responses from the police to incidents;
- use of weapons for protection (such as baseball bats);
- greater use of CCTV;
- the naming and shaming of offenders in the local media; and
- tougher sentences for offenders (including boot camps, birching and capital punishment).

Many of these suggestions were beyond the scope and remit of the SBCI, though they do begin to give an idea as to the sense of fear and desperation some business owners expressed.

3 Implementation: translating ideas for interventions into practical methods

Many crime reduction projects suffer from implementation failure. This may be a result of a range of factors, such as not having the financial resources to implement adequate reduction mechanisms, not having the support of partners, or not having the right calibre of staff or the number of staff to implement measures (Laycock and Webb 2000).

Whilst the forums had given the SBCI project team a flavour of the type of approaches local businesses would ideally like to see, many were beyond the remit and power of the SBCI. However a number of approaches – developed from both experience of 'what works' elsewhere and ideas generated from local forums – were put forward by the team. These approaches focused upon the chronic victims of crime, burglary, fraud and customer theft. The actual methods used, and the way they were expected to impact crime, are outlined in Table 18.7.

These methods were shaped by a number of practical considerations, and particularly the fact that the implementation period was restricted: the project had to try and focus upon problems where there might be easily identifiable solutions, upon problems where something could be achieved within the project timescales and on businesses with the most severe crime problems.

4 Insertion: how the implementation plan was put in place

The SBCI interventions were generally implemented by the project staff. They would conduct visits to business premises and where possible the police would also send a representative. A number of other agencies (such as the local chambers of commerce, city council, etc.) were also aware of the project and had an input at various stages. There were, however, a number of issues encountered with the implementation that are likely to be relevant to all projects of this nature. They included the following:

- *Cost/resources*: a generic problem with many crime reduction projects is that resources are limited. Many of the remedies to the problems faced pointed to the need to purchase and maintain security hardware, but such hardware is costly and often businesses could not find the capital or sustain the regular overheads. In addition to this, giving advice to business (such as fraud packs) only 'facilitated' crime prevention activity rather than ensuring advice was pursued.

Table 18.7 Crime reduction mechanisms developed

Crime problem addressed	Method
Chronic victimization (businesses that were victims of 10 or more incidents – excluding shop theft and fraud)	Visits to the appropriate businesses were made by a SBCI staff member and a crime prevention officer. A full audit was completed and a report on crime prevention measures recommended were submitted to the business. The key aim was to tailor prevention mechanisms to reduce crime within the context of each chronic victim
Burglary	Visits were made by SBCI staff to victims to determine the risk of repeat victimization and develop mechanisms to prevent further incidents from occurring
	Covert CCTV (aimed at recording offences in progress and identifying offenders) was installed in high-risk premises
	Proactive use of forensic science techniques: aimed at linking suspects to a scene of crime
	The installation of silent 'auto-diallers' to alert the police and business manager/owner that there is an intruder and ensure a quick response
Fraud	Information packs to businesses aimed at encouraging businesses to adopt practices that would limit risk in the future
Customer theft	Information packs to businesses to heighten knowledge of how to prevent further incidents

- *The complex nature of crime*: developing 'simple' solutions to crime problems is often difficult. This became apparent to the SBCI when visits to businesses with crime problems commenced. Often incidents were interlinked (shop theft to violence, criminal damage to burglary, etc.) and crime and disorder was related to a number of factors external to the business: for example, being located next to a problem estate, next to void properties or schools. Therefore, partnerships needed to be developed with the relevant agencies to discuss such issues.[25]

- *The changing nature of crime*: victimization surveys take a 'snapshot' of crime over a fixed period. However, crime problems are fluid and continually change. Therefore as the project developed strategies to tackle problems identified from the survey, it had to be mindful of the patterns of victimization that emerged during the project and be responsive to them.

- *Cultural barriers*: there was a perception amongst project researchers that some businesses from the Asian community were reluctant to tell the SBCI about crime problems they had faced. There appeared to be some suspicion of outsiders and many saw it as a dent to their pride to ask for outside help.

- *Getting businesses interested*: some business owners/managers were delighted that the SBCI had been developed and that somebody was taking an interest in issues relating to small businesses. However, many other businesses had a more hardened attitude and were sceptical about the likely impact that the SBCI would have upon crime. It was therefore difficult to get such businesses involved with the project.

5   Impact: assessing the impact of intervention(s)

The impact of the SBCI interventions was measured by researchers from Nottingham Trent University (see Tilley and Hopkins 1998). The provision for outcome evaluation was built into the project from its start, enabling the evaluators to have both close contact with the project and a detailed knowledge of the process of implementation.

The impact was primarily evaluated by using data from a second survey sweep conducted in September 1997, two years after the original sweep, and comparing findings with the first. It was recognized that reliance on such data alone was problematic as it was not possible to interview exactly the same cohort of businesses as in the previous sample (a number of these businesses had closed and new businesses had opened). In addition to this, such a method does not take into account general trends in crime across the area that might be responsible for the changes in patterns observed (rather than project impact). Therefore, where possible, comparison were made to other areas by using available police data.

The second survey sweep was a replication of the first (with a few additional questions – for instance, on whether businesses had any contact with the SBCI). In total 965 interviews were completed, which – like the first survey – constituted a response rate of 65 per cent (1,489 trading businesses were identified in sweep two). Table 18.8 presents the main 'headline' figures from the second survey sweep.

The overall picture to emerge from the evaluation of the SBCI was mixed. There were substantial falls in chronic victimization, commercial burglary fell and there were falls in the incidence rate for fraud. However, whether it was the mechanisms implemented by the project or other external factors that generated the observed outcomes was sometimes less than clear. When the data are considered in more detail for the chronic victims they indicated the following:

- A total of 26 were *not* visited by the project. Of these, 16 were interviewed in both sweeps. These experienced 447 incidents in sweep 1 and 49 in sweep 2 (a fall of 89 per cent).

- A total of 30 businesses *were visited but no intervention followed*. Of these, 16 were interviewed in both sweeps. These experienced 171 incidents in sweep 1 and 38 in sweep 2 (a fall of 77 per cent).

- A total of 26 businesses *were visited and changes were implemented*. Of these, 15 were interviewed in both sweeps. These experienced 174 incidents in sweep 1 and 58 in sweep 2 (a fall of 66 per cent).

Table 18.8 Crime types targeted and 'actual' impact on crime

Crime issue addressed	Patterns found in sweep 2	Was there any evidence of project impact?
Chronic victimization	The majority of chronic victims in sweep 1 were not highly victimized in sweep 2. A fall in crime (in the 29 sweep 1 chronic victims also interviewed in sweep 2) of 86% was observed (675 incidents to 95)	Some evidence that SBCI activity helped reduce chronic victimization, though a number of business 'inherited' chronic victimization in sweep 2
Overall commercial crime	Rates fell substantially across all crime types except customer theft. Incidence rates fell by 33%, concentration by 4% and prevalence by 19%	Suggests there was heightened awareness of business crime overall in the business community and for offenders
Commercial burglary	The rate of non-domestic burglary fell at around twice the rate in the target areas compared to the rest of the force area. Incidence rates fell by 41%, concentration by 6% and prevalence by 36%	Unclear; the fall in non-domestic burglary in a neighbouring beat area was similar to that in project area
Fraud	There was a fall in prevalence by 37%, incidence by 17%, though an increase in concentration of 30%	Unclear, fall in prevalence and incidence, though increase in concentration
Customer theft/ violence	Data on incidence are weak as respondents were often unable to say how many crimes they had suffered. Figures suggested a slight increase	No impact

The striking pattern that emerges from the outcome data is that there was little variation in the fall in crime for businesses visited or not visited by the SBCI, and the reductions observed were higher for businesses where there was no visit made or no intervention made. This suggests that direct action by the SBCI had little impact upon victimization. However, all businesses that were identified as chronic victims in sweep 1 were contacted by the SBCI and there was some evidence that this prompted businesses to address their victimization problems (often the decision not to visit businesses or intervene was due to the fact that businesses had made efforts to address their problems). This was supported by output data on the average number of crime prevention measures the panel sample of businesses (those interviewed in both sweeps) had in sweep 1 compared to sweep 2. For the panel sample of 476 businesses, the number of crime prevention devices increased from an average 4.7 to 4.8, though for chronic victims interviewed in both sweeps the number increased from an average of 5 to 5.4.

Summary and discussion

Whilst most will see a clear distinction between crimes against personal victims and those against business – based on the simple distinction of 'who loses' – in reality the boundaries are far from straightforward. Indeed it could be argued that one of the first prerequisites for promoting any coherent publicly co-ordinated strategy against business crime is to recognize the blurred lines between these supposedly different forms of criminality, and to work within a more coherent conceptual framework.

The question of 'who loses', for example, is seldom one dimensional, especially in the context of the huge number of very small businesses operating in the UK (many operating directly from residential premises). There may be little doubt in respect of – say – the overnight burglary of business premises, but the theft of a company car proves a little more complicated: nominally the company is the loser, but the employee and his or her family may lose possessions left in the vehicle and will certainly be affected until a replacement vehicle is provided. Moreover, losses sustained in business crime do not 'disappear into the ether': any losses will either impact the company's overall profitability (and, for public companies, its dividends to shareholders, which will sometimes include pension funds) or the salaries paid to its employees. Even if losses are made up by insurance, they will – in time – be redeemed by increased insurance premiums. Alternatively, and in extreme circumstances, losses from crime may cause a business to collapse, thus affecting employment prospects and the facilities or choice available to the public (a point that almost certainly influences the current flush of crime prevention schemes to assist businesses in town centres).

Whilst these consequential costs may appear a little too far removed really to affect short-term public policy decisions, the impact on victims should be more easily grasped. To the extent that incidents of crime involve more than financial consequences, it has to be remembered that business crime affects 'real people'. When the burglary of business premises is targeted against a small retail concern and the owner and his or her family 'live over the shop', for example, there is no reason to believe the sense of intrusion and anxiety caused will be any different from a residential burglary.[26] Indeed it has been argued that, even if the premises are unoccupied at the time of the incident, the impact can affect all staff working there so that, whilst the sense of 'personal intrusion' might be less, this is counteracted by the fact that many more people may be involved (see Johnston *et al.* 1994; Tilley and Hopkins 1998). There is also evidence that some crimes against business premises can create a ripple effect on public anxiety and fear about crime. Research has shown how news of this sort of crime can spread quickly – through customers using business services – and have an impact on perceptions of local safety (Hibberd and Shapland 1993).

If many of the costs of 'business crime' are directly or indirectly borne by the public, and indeed much of this crime has more than financial implications and impacts 'real people', it then has to be asked if the separation between personal and business crime has any justification in analysing offending behaviour and determining how to prevent offending. It is hard to imagine why this should be the case. The available research evidence suggests that offenders are at best 'target blind' in terms of this separation and that target selection is based primarily on the opportunity, the potential rewards, the effort that has to be made to complete the crime successfully and the risk of getting caught (Clarke 1992). Businesses can offer more attractive rewards than many households, especially retail concerns (e.g. electrical stores and off-licences are targeted because the goods are easy to sell on) and – for some crimes – they offer the possibility that the offenders' actions may go undiscovered. The latter argument applies classically to offences like credit card fraud and shoplifting, and this is probably one reason why a number of 'cohort' studies show that the latter is typically the first offence committed by those who embark on 'criminal careers' (see West and Farrington 1977).

Whilst these various arguments, coupled with parallel arguments about the scale and severity of the problem facing businesses (especially in some sectors), point to the need to address business crime seriously, there can be little doubt that it has been allocated a relatively low priority. The recent Home Office consultation on business crime (2003) noted that there was some dissatisfaction conveyed by those businesses taking part about the lack of attention paid to the subject by central government. It was also felt by businesses that this was directly related to the lack of reliable information on the subject and that there are no specific police targets on business crime. Whilst there has been no shortage of advice provided for businesses, the closest the UK has come to providing guidance on business responsibilities in relation to crime has been through the Turnbull report (ICA 1999), which states that crime *could be* included as a specific risk that directors of public limited companies (PLCs) need to address and report on to their shareholders. And whilst some businesses do take vigorous action against crime, in the main the business reaction to this issue has recently been described as 'unmentionable: a kind of corporate halitosis' (Levi *et al.* 2003).

Policing priorities are largely dictated by government targets – which all relate to personal crime. It might be facetious to argue that, as shoplifting constitutes the start of the learning curve for many offenders, it should warrant prioritization by the police and others. 'Theft from shop' is also a crime that has a very heavy impact on the courts. Whilst the offence 'theft from shop' accounts for around a quarter of all incidents of theft it accounts for around a half of all *offenders* dealt with for theft. However a more compelling argument is that the high crime rates experienced by businesses represent a significant missed opportunity, as they offer the police service a much greater chance of apprehending offenders. Not only does survey work indicate the high risks faced by businesses, but it also shows that the levels of repeat victimization are high when compared to households. The CVS shows that the percentage of victims for burglary with entry is six times higher for retail and manufacturing premises as compared to households – and when repeats are taken into account the number of incidents is nine times higher.

The new government strategy for business crime, and in particular the appointment of business crime advisers in each government region, suggests there may be some more momentum – at a local level – for crime and disorder partnerships to work with businesses to initiate preventive strategies. To date, however, it appears that the business-related work conducted by partnerships has assumed a rather narrow focus. It has typically been directed at crimes against retail premises and licensed premises within city/town centres, with the key aim of promoting the safety of city centres: a means to an end. This is probably symptomatic of the view that 'business crime is for business to address' is pervasive in public sector thinking.

There is of course no real likelihood that governments will radically change their priorities, and indeed most will argue that probably the best driver of preventive action – the self-interest of the potential victim – will continue to ensure that those businesses that are able to protect themselves will do so. But this 'incentivization' mechanism does not operate so well in those circumstances when business (or households) do not have the resources to take remedial action, and particularly in those circumstances when these same parties are also the most at risk. Here the SBCI – set up to explore whether a co-ordinated drive to tackle crime against small to medium-sized businesses can be effective – provides a useful example of what can be achieved. The initiative strongly suggested that the establishment of a dedicated, and independently funded, team can be a key catalyst for reducing crime against business. There have, however, been few comparable, and properly evaluated, initiatives of this kind – and undoubtedly there is much yet to learn.

Selected further reading

There are a growing number of general texts that focus on a number of issues relating to business and crime. Particularly useful are Martin Gill's *Crime at Work* series: *Crime at Work: Studies in Security and Crime Prevention* (1994), and *Crime at Work: Increasing the Risk for Offenders* (1998). Another useful collection of papers on general business crime issues is Marcus Felson and Ron Clarke's *Business and Crime Prevention* (1997). In addition to this, Matt Hopkins gives an account of some of the main areas where future research should focus in 'Crimes against business: the way forward for future research' (2002).

There have been two Home Office surveys of business crime: Catriona Mirrlees-Black and Alec Ross's *Crime against Retail and Manufacturing Premises: Findings from the 1994 Commercial Victimisation Survey* (1995) and Taylor's *Crime against Retail and Manufacturing Premises: Findings from the 2002 Commercial Victimisation Survey* (2004). The only other regular surveys are carried out by the British Retail Consortium (BRC) and are of course restricted to the retail sector only (details can be found on the BRC website: www.brc.org.uk). The Scottish Business Crime Survey (1999) is also worth looking at here as it builds upon the methodology developed in the CVS and BRC surveys (see Burrows *et al.*, *Counting the Cost: Crime against Business in Scotland*, 1999).

There are numerous studies that focus on specific crime issues faced by businesses. Malcom Hibberd and Joanna Shapland's *Violent Crime in Small Shops* (1993) and Paul Ekblom and Frances Simon's *Crime and Racial Harassment in Asian-run Small Shops* (1988) are good examples.

In relation to understanding what drives crime against businesses, three texts are useful. Marcus Felson applies routine activity theory to business crime in 'Preventing retail theft: an application of environmental criminology' (1996), and Martin Gill considers the relationship between business characteristics and victimization in 'The victimization of business: indicators of risk and the direction of future research' (1998). Matt Hopkins's paper, 'Developing a framework for understanding patterns of abuse and violence against businesses' (2002), draws some of the main themes of these papers together.

Finally, for those looking to learn more about evaluations of business crime reduction projects, key publications include *Crime against Small Business: Facing the Challenge* (Wood *et al.* 1996) and Nick Tilley and Matt Hopkins' *Business as Usual: An Evaluation of the Small Business and Crime Initiative* (1998).

Notes

1. The focus is on crimes against business premises and employees in small and medium-sized enterprises rather than crimes often associated with larger multinational businesses such as transnational financial crime, fraud or computer crime. It does not examine crimes committed *by business*.
2. The BRC is a trade association representing the retail sector, from the large multiples and department stores through to independents.
3. Now the Department of Criminology.
4. It is not suggested that these are the only institutions to conduct research in this area: businesses themselves conduct internal research and other external bodies such as Crime Concern, the Police Foundation and local authorities have conducted surveys, though not all this work is published.
5. Although this represents the only international 'premises' survey, it is not the only comparison of business crime across state boundaries. Ernst and Young, and PriceWaterhouseCoopers, regularly conduct 'head office' global surveys on fraud (see, for example, Ernst and Young 2001; PriceWaterhouseCoopers 2003), and Bamfield uses a similar method to produce the 'European Theft barometer on theft and retail shrinkage' (Bamfield 2003).
6. Other national studies have been conducted, but these tend to be crime specific – for example, NOP conducted a survey of hi-tech crime in 105 UK-based organizations in 2002.
7. The British Chambers of Commerce comprise nationally a network of quality-accredited Chambers of Commerce, all uniquely positioned at the heart of every business community in the UK. Over 135,000 businesses are represented from all sectors across the UK.
8. The surveys cover the financial year (April to April). The sample has been as high as 54,000 in 1992/3 and 52,000 in 1993/4.
9. It should be noted here that these patterns are remarkably similar to previous years.
10. The comparison here relates to the 1994 CVS as, at the time of writing, a summary of the findings of the 2002 CVS had just been published (Taylor 2004), but the full report of the survey was not available.

11. These are the only two CVS/ BRC surveys that can be compared. The CVS is for 1994, the BRC survey for April 1993 to April 1994.
12. In total, 2,501 'premises' surveys were conducted and 148 head offices took part (covering 3,680 business premises).
13. Some of the reasons why these patterns emerge are considered in more detail later in the chapter.
14. Prevalence rates indicate the proportion of businesses (or other targets) that have suffered from crime, or a particular type of crime. Incidence rates express the number of incidents (rather than the number of victims) recorded per 100 business premises.
15. The analysis above suggest 'direct' costs are counted in much the same way under either approach, but many consequential and indirect costs are better recorded via head office surveys (typically, for example, the individual outlets of retail multiples will look to their head office to arrange windows/door replacement, overnight guards, etc., after an overnight break-in).
16. There were 865 respondents in sweep one and 945 in sweep two.
17. Two from the following sectors: manufacturing, construction, wholesale/retail, hotel/restaurants and transport/communication.
18. In late-night incidents there would often be bystanders present at incidents but generally few would intervene.
19. The total losses from crime were £1.70 billion, costs of crime prevention were £0.54 billion and thus the costs of crime totalled £2.25 billion.
20. These figures are drawn from the British Security Industry Association website.
21. There are exceptions: the 'crime at work' articles (Gill 1994, 1998a) often draw on the lessons of experiments and trials carried out by businesses, as do small research studies like that by Farrington *et al.* (1986). Burrows (1991) draws on a number of case studies, often involving collaboration across different businesses, showing where crime prevention initiatives have 'paid for themselves'.
22. Examples are given in the BRC *Retail Crime Costs* report 2002 of schemes such as Wigan Town Centre partnership, Leicester City Watch and from Northampton Crime and Disorder partnership.
23. See 'Methodological challenges', above. The high turnover of businesses is a root cause of the inaccuracy of most databases.
24. It is accepted that street observations will not serve to identify businesses that are run from home, etc.
25. It should also be noted that the project was implemented before the advent of the Crime and Disorder Act 1998 and the concept of partnership in crime reduction was not as well developed as it has since become.
26. By the same token, many 'personal crimes' will take place on business premises. The third BCS, for example, found that seven out of ten thefts of workers' property took place at work (Mayhew *et al.* 1989).

References

Austin, C. (1988) *The Prevention of Robbery at Building Society Branches. Crime Prevention Unit Paper* 14. London: Home Office.

Bamfield, J. (2003) *The European Theft Barometer III*. Third Report to the Retail Industry. Nottingham: Centre for Retail Research.

British Chambers of Commerce (2001a) *Securing Enterprise: A Framework for Tackling Business Crime*. London: BCC.

British Chambers of Commerce (2001b) *Business Crime Survey 2001*. London: BCC.

British Retail Consortium (2003) *Retail Crime Costs Survey 2002*. London: British Retail Consortium.

Buckle, A. and Farrington, D. (1984) 'An observational study of shoplifting', *British Journal of Criminology*, 24: 63–73.

Buckle, A., Farrington, D., Speed, M. and Burns-Howell, T. (1992) 'Measuring shoplifting by repeated systematic counting', *Security Journal*, 3: 137–45.

Budd, T. (1999) *Violence at Work: Findings from the British Crime Survey*. London: Home Office and Health and Safety Executive.

Burrows, J. (1991) *Making Crime Prevention Pay: Initiatives from Business. Crime Prevention Unit Paper 27*. London: Home Office.

Burrows, J. (1997) 'Criminology and business crime: building the bridge', in M. Felson and R.V. Clarke (eds) *Business and Crime Prevention*. Monsey, NY: Criminal Justice Press.

Burrows, J. and Speed, M. (1994) *Retail Crime Costs, 1992/93 Survey*. London: British Retail Consortium.

Burrows, J., Anderson, S., Bamfield, J., Hopkins, M. and Ingram, D. (1999) *Counting the Cost: Crime against Business in Scotland*. Edinburgh: Scottish Executive.

Clarke, R. (1992) *Situational Crime Prevention: Successful Case Studies*. New York, NY: Harrow & Heston.

Cohen, L.E. and Felson, M. (1979) 'Social change and crime rate trends: a routine activity approach', *American Sociological Review*, 44: 588-607.

Co-operative Movement (2003) *Retail Crime Survey*. London: Cooperative Movement.

Ekblom, P. (1986) *The Prevention of Shoptheft: An Approach through Crime Analysis. Crime Prevention Unit Paper 5*. London: Home Office.

Ekblom, P. (1987) *Preventing Robberies at Sub-post Offices: An Evaluation of a Security Initiative. Crime Prevention Unit Paper 9*. London: Home Office.

Ekblom, P. (2002) 'From the source to the mainstream is uphill: the challenge of transferring knowledge of crime prevention through replication, innovation and anticipation', in N. Tilley (ed.) *Analysis for Crime Prevention, Crime Prevention Studies. Vol. 13*. Monsey, NY: Criminal Justice Press.

Ekblom, P. and Simon, F. (1988) *Crime and Racial Harassment in Asian-run Small Shops. Police Research Group Crime Prevention Paper Series 15*. London: Home Office.

Ernst and Young (2001) *Fraud – the Unmanaged Risk*. London: Ernst and Young.

Farrell, G. and Pease, K. (1993) *Once Bitten, Twice Bitten: Repeat Victimisation and its Implications for Crime Prevention. Crime Prevention Unit Series Paper 36*. London: Home Office.

Farrington, D.P., Bowen, S., Buckle, A., Burns-Howell, T., Burrows, J. and Speed, M. (1993) 'An experiment in the prevention of shoplifting', in R.V. Clarke (ed.) *Crime Prevention Studies. Vol. 1*. Monsey, NY: Criminal Justice Press.

Farrington, D. and Burrows, J. (1993) 'Did shoplifting really decrease?', *British Journal of Criminology*, 33: 57–69.

Felson, M. (1996) 'Preventing retail theft: an application of environmental criminology', *Security Journal*, 7: 71–5.

Felson, M. and Clarke, R.V. (1997) *Business and Crime Prevention*. Monsey, NY: Criminal Justice Press.

Gill, M. (1994) *Crime at Work: Studies in Security and Crime Prevention. Crime at Work Series. Volume I*. Leicester: Perpetuity Press.

Gill, M. (1998a) *Crime at Work: Increasing the Risk for Offenders. Crime at Work Series. Volume II*. Leicester: Perpetuity Press.

Gill, M. (1998b) 'The victimisation of business: indicators of risk and the direction of future research', *International Review of Victimology*, 6: 17–28.

Health and Safety Executive (1995) *Preventing Violence to Retail Staff.* London: Health and Safety Executive.

Hibberd, M and Shapland, J. (1993) *Violent Crime in Small Shops.* London: Police Foundation.

Home Office (2003) *Business and Crime Consultation Paper.* London: Home Office.

Hopkins, M. (1998) 'Abuse and violence within the workplace: a study of small businesses in Leicester', *International Journal of Risk, Security and Crime Prevention*, 4: 293–306.

Hopkins, M. (2002) 'Developing a framework for understanding patterns of abuse and violence against buinsesses', in M. Gill *et al.* (eds) *Violence at Work: Causes, Patterns and Prevention.* Cullompton: Willan Publishing.

Hopkins, M. (2002b) 'Crimes against business: the way forward for future research', *British Journal of Criminology*, 42.

Hopkins, M. and Tilley, N. (1998) 'Commercial crime, crime prevention and community safety: a study of three streets in Camden, north London', in M. Gill (ed.) *Crime at Work: Increasing the Risk for Offenders. Crime at Work Series. Volume II.* Leicester: Perpetuity Press.

Hopkins, M. and Tilley, N. (2001) 'Once a victim always a victim? A study of how crime patterns may change over time', *International Review of Victimology*, 8: 51–65.

ICA (1999) *Internal Control: Guidance for Directors on the Combined Code.* London: Institute of Chartered Accountants for England and Wales.

Jacques, C. (1994) 'Ram raiding: the history, incidence and scope for prevention', in M. Gill (ed.) *Crime at Work: Studies in Security and Crime Prevention. Crime at Work Series. Volume I.* Leicester: Perpetuity Press.

Johnston, V., Leitner, M., Shapland, T. and Wiles, P. (1994) *Crime on Industrial Estates. Crime Prevention Series Paper* 54. London: Home Office.

Laycock, G. (1985) *Reducing Burglary: A Study of Chemist Shops. Crime Prevention Unit Paper* 1. London: Home Office.

Laycock, G. and Webb, B. (2000) 'Making it all happen', in S. Ballintyne *et al.* (eds) *Secure Foundations: Key Issues in Crime Prevention, Crime Reduction and Community Safety.* London: Institue for Public Policy Research.

Levi, M. (1988) *The Prevention of Fraud. Crime Prevention Unit Paper* 17. London: Home Office.

Levi, M., Bissell, P. and Richardson, T. (1991) *The Prevention of Cheque and Credit Card Fraud. Crime Prevention Unit Paper* 26. London: Home Office.

Levi, M., Morgan, J. and Burrows, J. (2003) 'Enhancing business crime reduction: UK directors' responsibilities to review the impact of crime on businesses', *Security Journal*, 16: 7–29.

Mayhew, P., Elliott, D. and Dowds, L. (1989) *The 1988 British Crime Survey. Home Office Research Study* 111. London: HMSO.

McCulloch, H. (1996) *Shoptheft: Improving the Police Response. Crime Detection and Prevention Series Paper* 76. London: Home Office.

MHB (2002) *Crime and Anti-social Behaviour Survey of Business Premises and Employees in the Holborn Business Partnership Area.* London: Morgan Harris Burrows.

Mirrlees-Black, C. and Ross, A. (1995) *Crime against Retail and Manufacturing Premises: Findings from the 1994 Commercial Victimisation Survey. Home Office Research Study* 146. London: Home Office.

Mirrlees-Black, C., Budd, T., Partridge, S. and Mayhew, P. (1998) *The 1998 British Crime Survey: England and Wales. Home Office Statistical Bulletin* 21/98. London: Home Office.

National Federation of Retail News (2002) *Crime in Cornershops – 2002 Crime Survey.* London: NFRN.

National Hi-tech Crime Unit (2002) *Hi-Tech Crime: The Impact on UK Business*. London: NHTCU.

Pease, K. (1998) *Repeat Victimisation: Taking Stock. Crime Detection and Prevention Series Paper* 90. London: Home Office.

Phillips, S. and Cochrane, R. (1988) *Crime and Nuisance in the Shopping Centre: A Case Study in Crime Prevention. Crime Prevention Unit Paper* 16. London: Home Office.

Poyner, B. and Warne, C. (1988) *Preventing Violence to Staff*. London: Health and Safety Executive.

PriceWaterhouseCoopers (2003) *Economic Crime Survey 2003*. London: PWC in association with Wilmer, Cutler and Pickering.

Shapland, J. and Vagg, J. (1988) *Policing by the Public*. London: Tavistock.

Speed, M., Burrows, J. and Bamfield, M. (1995) *Retail Crime Costs 1993/94 Survey*. London: British Retail Consortium.

Taylor, J. (2004) *Crime against Retail and Manufacturing Premises: Findings from the 2002 Commercial Victimisation Survey. Home Office Findings* 259. London: Home Office.

Tilley, N. (1993) *The Prevention of Crime against Small Businesses: The Safer Cities Experience. Crime Prevention Series Paper* 45. London: Home Office.

Tilley, N. and Hopkins, M. (1998) *Business as Usual: An Evaluation of the Small Business and Crime Initiative. Police Research Series Paper* 95. London: Home Office.

Van Dijk, J.J.M. and Terlouw, G.J. (1995) 'Fraude en Criminaliteit Tegen het Bedrijfsleven in Internationaal Perspectief', *Justitiele Verkenningen*, 4: 119–42.

West, D. and Farrington, D. (1977) *The Delinquent Way of Life. Cambridge Studies in Criminology*. London: Heinmann.

Wood, J., Wheelwright, G. and Burrows, J. (1996) *Crime against Small Business: Facing the Challenge*. Swindon: Crime Concern.

Chapter 19

Violent and sexual crime

Mike Maguire and Fiona Brookman

Introduction

Looked at globally, both the scale and the range of 'violent and sexual crime' are immense. Quite apart from the millions of isolated acts of violence and sexual abuse that appear in official crime statistics, large numbers of people are killed, injured, abused or exploited in clearly criminal acts (though they are rarely recorded as such) associated with political conflicts, terrorism, the 'war on terror', despotic governments, civil wars, organized crime and so on. It is not difficult to find recent examples of large-scale atrocities against civilians: mass rape, trafficking in human beings, slavery and even genocide. Violence against women within the household is also widespread – and even culturally acceptable – in many societies.

Clearly, at least in the foreseeable future, the prospects of a significant reduction in the totality of violence are remote. Inasmuch as plausible strategies can be formulated, they require expertise in fields such as international politics, human rights law or anti-poverty action. Even if we had such expertise (which we do not), it would be foolish to attempt to cover the whole picture in one short chapter, and the discussion here will be restricted to territory more familiar to criminologists. Nevertheless, it is important to remain aware of the broader picture, and that the kinds of preventive strategies most commonly discussed or evaluated within the criminological literature are relevant only to a fraction of the overall problem of violence.[1]

Whilst not losing sight of the wider context, then, this chapter will be structured mainly around a more conventional understanding of the range of behaviour covered by the term 'violent and sexual crime' – in essence, the kinds of interpersonal offences routinely dealt with by the police and courts in the developed western world. Even limited in this way, the prevention (or reduction[2]) of violent and sexual crime presents difficult and complex challenges. The nature, circumstances and locations of offences vary widely, as do the motives of those who commit them. They are often committed on the spur of the moment, and a high proportion involve people without a previous criminal record. Many, too – especially those that take place within households – remain hidden from public view. Prediction of where, when and by whom they will be committed is therefore particularly difficult. Moreover, unlike many forms of property crime, their 'targets' (people's bodies) are extremely mobile and cannot readily be protected, for example, by locks and bolts or constant CCTV surveillance. Hence it is by no means easy to determine which basic strategies and methods of prevention are likely to be effective: should the main focus be, for example, on increasing environmental safety in possible violence 'hotspots', on encouraging self-protection, on reducing public tolerance of abusive behaviour, or on deterring, 'treating' or 'incapacitating' potential offenders?

It is argued in this chapter that there is no simple answer to this question. Different preventive strategies have to be developed in relation to different forms of violent and sexual crime, in each case based on an understanding of their temporal and spatial patterns, the characteristics and inter-relationships of those most frequently involved as offenders and victims and, as far as possible, their key 'drivers': the particular social and cultural contexts with which they are associated, as well as psychological factors, which may help to explain *why* they occur.

Of course, criminal behaviour can be divided up into 'types' in many different ways, based on criteria such as legal categories, social circumstances, locations, motives, victim–offender relationships and so on. No one classificatory system is fully satisfactory, and there are always overlaps. The approach we have adopted is to identify three broad 'clusters' of violent and/or sexual crime, which will be discussed separately. These are:

- domestic violence and sexual abuse;
- alcohol-related violence in public places; and
- predatory violence.

Each cluster has a number of core characteristics, found in a large proportion of incidents within it, which have to be prime considerations when devising preventive strategies. For example, the first is characterized by a prior or continuing relationship between offender and victim, and is most likely to take place – often on a recurring basis – within the privacy of a shared household. The second is likely to involve spontaneous, one-off incidents between strangers (in some cases initiated as much by the 'victim' as the 'offender') and tends to occur in licensed premises or on town-centre streets in the late evening or early hours of the morning. The third – again, mainly involving assaults on strangers – is more likely to be carried out by repeat offenders, who seek out and attack victims for a variety of motives, including financial gain, racial hatred and sexual or sadistic desires.

In each case, we shall look at distinctive types of incident within the main 'cluster', considering briefly their extent and distribution and any social, cultural or psychological factors strongly associated with them, before discussing strategies and methods which are, or might be, used to reduce their incidence and any research evidence on effectiveness. In order to keep the chapter manageable, although we shall draw on the international crime prevention literature, most of the specific patterns of offending and statistical data presented will be from England and Wales. To help orient the reader and avoid repetition, we begin with some broad statistical data on violent and sexual crime in England and Wales, to which individual sections will add appropriate comments and material.

Before doing so, there are two other important introductory points to add. First, it is emphasized that, although 'sexual' and 'violent' offences are often discussed under separate subheadings (and are counted separately in official court and police statistics), this does not imply that they are mutually exclusive terms: on the contrary, most sexual crime can be considered violent in some sense.

Secondly, it should be noted that, although the prevention and reduction of homicide are included within the discussion, they are not treated here as a separate subject. It has been argued by the authors elsewhere (Brookman 2005; Brookman and Maguire forthcoming) that most homicide can be seen as the peak of a 'pyramid' of violent crime, in the sense that very similar incidents can result either in death or in serious injury, depending to a large extent on fortuitous circumstances (what part of the body a knife hits, the intervention or not of bystanders, a quick or a slow medical response and so on) and hence that effective strategies to reduce serious violence should also result in a reduction in homicide. However, it is also recognized that some cases of homicide involve a clear intention to kill, and to make sure that the victim is dead. It is likely that few such cases, especially those which involve preplanning, are preventable by most of the general violence reduction strategies discussed here.

Violent and sexual crime in England and Wales: an overview

Overall numbers and trends

The two main sources of data about the extent of violent and sexual crime in England and Wales are official statistics on offences recorded by the police and estimates based on responses to the British Crime Survey (BCS). Both sources, however, have well-known limitations in terms of any claims to reflect 'real' totals of violent crime (Coleman and Moynihan 1996; Maguire 2002) and have lately diverged in terms of the trends they depict (Smith and Allen 2004; Allen *et al.* 2005).

In the official crime statistics, violent and sexual offences are currently presented under three main headings, based on legal classifications: violence against the person (VAP), robbery and sexual offences. In 2003/4 in England and Wales, these together totalled around 1.1 million offences, the great majority of them in the VAP category (see Table 19.1). This represents under 19 per cent of all offences recorded by the police, and the volume of violent crime remains small in comparison with property offences. It is also important to note that only 44,000 of the 955,000 offences of VAP – and less than 1 per cent of all recorded offences – were classified as involving 'more serious' violence. Indeed, over half of all offences recorded as VAP involved no physical injury,

Table 19.1 Crimes recorded by the police, 2003/4

	n (thousands)	%
Violence against the person (VAP)	955.8	16.1
More serious VAP	*43.9*	*0.7*
Other offences against the person – with injury	*433.4*	*7.3*
Other offences against the person – without injury	*478.5*	*8.1*
Robbery	101.2	1.7
Sexual offences	52.1	0.9
Property offences	4,610.3	77.7
All other recorded offences	215.2	3.6
Total recorded crime	5,934.6	100.0

Source: Adapted from Dodd *et al.* (2004).

being made up mainly of cases of common assault, 'harassment' or possession of weapons.

Prior to 1998, less serious offences of these kinds were not included in the official crime statistics, and this and other changes in recording practice have made it more difficult than ever to draw firm conclusions about trends in violence from police figures. The change in counting rules produced a sudden artificial increase in violent crime, recorded offences of VAP almost doubling between 1997/8 and 1998/9. Further 'inflation' was caused by the introduction of the National Crime Recording Standard (NCRS) in 2002, whereby the police were obliged to follow stricter rules in recording incidents as crimes (Simmons *et al.* 2003). However, even allowing for these changes, police figures suggest a fairly strong upward trend, particularly in the last two years.

By contrast, responses to the BCS indicate a substantial and continuing *fall* in violent incidents since the mid-1990s. As shown in Table 19.2, these contradictory trends are apparent in serious violence as well as in more minor cases. Part of the explanation for the difference seems to be a rapid growth in public willingness to report violent incidents to the police: according to the BCS, the reporting rate for woundings rose from 40 per cent in 1995 to 57 per cent in 2003/4. Even so, there remains something of a puzzle here.

Where robbery is concerned, police and BCS messages about trends are in closer accord, both indicating a rise between the late 1990s and 2001/2, followed by a fall over the next two years. Police figures now distinguish between robbery of business and of personal property. The latter – which accounts for over 90 per cent of recorded robberies – is made up predominantly of street robberies or 'muggings' (Smith 2003; Tilley *et al.* 2004). In 2003/4, just over 91,000 personal robberies were recorded by the police, while estimates from BCS interviews (combining reports of robberies and 'snatch thefts') suggest a total of around 400,000 'muggings' (Dodd *et al.* 2004: ch. 2).

The kinds of personal crimes for which it is most difficult to obtain credible official data about numbers or trends are sexual offences. Victims are often reluctant to report them to general crime surveys like the BCS (which does

Table 19.2 Trends in more serious violence, as measured by the police and the BCS

Year	n	n
Offences of 'wounding' as estimated by BCS		
1995	914,000	
1997	804,000	
1999	650,000	
2001/2	648,000	
2002/3	708,000	
2003/4	655,000	
'More serious' offences of violence against the person recorded by the police		
1995	19,151*	
1997	23,581*	
1998/9	26,900*	27,047
2001/2		32,366
2002/3		38,274**
2003/4		43,850**

Notes;
* Old counting rules.
** Following introduction of NCRS.

The categories of 'wounding' and 'more serious' violence are not directly comparable.

not include them in its estimates), and many are afraid or unwilling to report them to the police. Changes in the social climate (for example, in attitudes towards, and knowledge about, child sexual abuse) or police response (such as improved services to rape victims) may also significantly affect the numbers of offences that come to light. For what it is worth, the total numbers of sexual offences recorded by the police in England and Wales increased from 30,274 in 1995 to 52,070 in 2003/4. In recent years, over half all recorded sexual offences have involved indecent assault, a quarter rape and around 8 per cent gross indecency or sexual intercourse with a child. The largest increases have been seen in rape of a female (from 4,986 in 1995 to 12,354 in 2003/4).

This rapid review of police and BCS statistics provides the bare bones of 'official' portrayals of violent and sexual crime in England and Wales. In brief, these concur that the most common types of such offences are 'less serious' assaults (many of them involving no physical injury) and – to a much lesser extent – personal robbery. Both sources also suggest that personal robbery is declining. However, there are contradictory messages about whether violent and sexual crime more generally is rising or falling.

Uncertainty about the reliability of measurement has obvious implications for crime reduction efforts. Neither personal crimes as a whole, nor many individual categories within them, are easily and reliably counted, whether by the police, by other agencies (e.g. hospitals) or by survey research. This is particularly true of offences committed by acquaintances or family members (which form a large proportion of both violent and sexual crime – see the next section), where existing and future relationships have a major influence on decisions about whether to report them. Moreover, in such circumstances, it may be that one of the positive effects of preventive interventions is to persuade victims to overcome unwillingness to report: as a result, the numbers of recorded offences may actually rise rather than fall, giving the false impression that the intervention has failed.

'Clusters' of violent and sexual offending: implications for preventive strategies

Although there have been moves to make them more directly useful to policy-making and practice (Simmons 2001), official statistics still focus primarily on legal categories of crime and tell us relatively little about the different social contexts in which violence against the person takes place – vital information for the formulation of preventive responses. For example, published police statistics do not even routinely distinguish between 'street' and 'domestic' violence, nor separate out assaults which are 'alcohol related' (though such information can be extracted from police records at a local level). Equally, incidents of what is commonly understood as 'mugging' are still often hidden amongst figures on both robbery and 'theft from the person'. The BCS is more helpful in this regard, but at the same time tends to distort the relative frequency of some types of crime – for example, grossly underestimating sexual offences and domestic violence – owing to differences in the kinds of incident that victims are willing to mention in a survey interview (although this problem has been ameliorated by the use of portable computers into which respondents enter confidential data themselves – see below).

As mentioned earlier, we have here divided the discussion into three main sections, each covering a 'cluster' of broadly cognate types of criminal behaviour – *domestic violence/sexual abuse, alcohol-related violence in public places* and *predatory violence/sexual assault*. Which of the three should have highest priority in terms of preventive responses is a matter for argument; indeed, it is not even clear which contains the highest numbers of offences or serious injuries. According to the BCS, for example, assaults by strangers or acquaintances (which are mainly 'street' crimes) outnumber domestic assaults by about five to one (Dodd *et al.* 2004: Table 2.01), but it is likely that the latter are undercounted to a much greater extent. Where police statistics are concerned, figures are hard to come by and there is considerable variation between forces but, overall, domestic assaults seem to account for about a third of all recorded offences of violence and over half of those against women (various police forces, pers. comm.; see also Maguire 1997: 155).

Preventive strategies are often divided, following Brantingham and Faust (1976), into 'primary', 'secondary' and 'tertiary' approaches, aiming respectively to reduce opportunities for crime, to divert 'at risk' (mainly young) people from possible future pathways into offending and to prevent reoffending by people who are already involved in crime. Traditionally, the police have taken the lead in primary prevention, youth services in secondary prevention, and probation and prisons in tertiary prevention. This three-way classification reflects a somewhat narrow view of crime reduction activity. For example, it largely omits strategies aimed at altering or ameliorating structural conditions (such as social inequality or social exclusion) or cultural forms (such as assumptions about male control over women) which are considered to be criminogenic. Nevertheless, it can be extended and adapted to encompass a wider vision of the field. In the following discussion, we shall distinguish broadly between approaches that aim to:

1. create *safer environments* in which opportunities or incentives to use violence are reduced (by means of, for example, surveillance of violent 'hotspots', better design of pubs and clubs, or protection of potential victims);

2. cut off the 'production lines' of *potential new offenders*, by a variety of approaches, including:

   • targeting interventions at specific 'at-risk' children and families (for example, through parenting orders); or

   • improving conditions and services in selected high-crime neighbourhoods (e.g. through targeted regeneration strategies, educational programmes or the provision of alternative activities for young people); or

   • changing social or economic conditions thought to 'foster' violence and/or challenging cultures and attitudes tolerant or approving of it (e.g. through fiscal, health or educational policies aimed at reducing social inequality, reducing drug-taking or 'binge drinking', or combating negative aspects of 'youth culture')

3. 'treat', 'rehabilitate', deter or control/'manage' *known offenders*.

In essence, approaches under (1) and (3) correspond largely to Brantingham and Faust's 'primary' and 'tertiary' forms of crime prevention, respectively, whilst (2) combines their 'secondary' prevention with a much wider range of social policies and interventions.

We shall suggest in the following sections that the particular characteristics of offences in each of the three 'clusters' of incident types make them more suited to some rather than other of these types of interventions, and that the focus of preventive strategies should vary accordingly. For example, most domestic violence and sexual abuse takes place behind closed doors and is likely to involve repeated assaults on the same victim. Arguably, therefore, the main focus should be on bringing more cases to light and protecting the victims from further abuse. Alcohol-related violence in public places tends to be committed in easily observable fashion at predictable times and locations, often by 'one-off' offenders. It is therefore well suited to 'environmental' or 'situational' crime reduction strategies. Predatory violence, by contrast, is often committed by offenders known to the police, but is much less predictable in terms of times and locations. It is therefore perhaps best reduced by offender-centred interventions including deterrence, 'treatment' or, arguably, in high-risk cases by preventive detention or individual surveillance, 'tagging' and so on.

Arguing for a different *focus* should not be taken to mean that each type of crime should be addressed by just one type of intervention. On the contrary, preventive strategies are generally considered likely to be more effective if they are 'multi-pronged', integrating a mix of aims and methods in a coherent fashion – ideally in the context of effective multi-agency partnership (see, for example, Bullock and Tilley 2003). The key point is that the mix, and the core focus, should be determined by careful analysis of the nature and patterns of the behaviour, as well as consideration of possible reasons behind these patterns.

Finally, it will be argued that it is important to retain a long-term as well as a short-term perspective, and to pay attention to all three of the main theoretical frameworks within which criminologists have discussed the 'causes of crime' – what Pease (2002: 948) neatly terms 'the 3 S's, at least if you say them aloud': 'structure', 'psyche' and 'circumstances' (in other words, those highlighting structural conditions in society, those emphasizing the 'pathology' of individual offenders and those focusing on the immediate circumstances and environment in which offences take place). Because of the insecure nature of funding for crime reduction and the emphasis placed on measurable 'performance', many strategies are aimed only at short-term reductions in crime figures or reoffending rates (see, for example, Maguire 2004; Tilley 2004 on the Home Office Crime Reduction Programme). Longer-term initiatives and those with less easily measurable objectives (such as cultural change or combating 'social exclusion') tend to be less politically attractive. However, whilst situational approaches, which are aimed primarily at changing 'circumstances', are the most likely to deliver short-term gains, these are unlikely to be sustained unless linked to efforts to promote wider 'structural' change – ideally, where crime prevention objectives are integrated with wider social policies such as public education or the regeneration of deprived areas.

We now move to a more detailed discussion of preventive strategies in relation to each of the three main 'clusters' of violent and sexual crime that have been identified.

Domestic violence and sexual abuse

Offences in this 'cluster' will be discussed under two separate headings: 'partner violence' and 'child abuse'. The former includes most cases of 'domestic violence' as defined by the Home Office (2000), namely, 'threatening behaviour, violence or abuse (psychological, physical, sexual, financial or emotional) between adults who are or have been intimate partners or are family members, regardless of gender'. Whilst this definition is gender neutral, we shall generally concentrate on male violence against female partners (or former partners), in keeping with the bulk of evidence indicating the gendered nature of most adult violence within the home. We shall also say little about domestic violence against adults other than partners (for example, 'elder abuse', which usually involves mistreatment of ageing parents), although this is not an insignificant problem. The second heading includes any form of victimization of infants or children within the domestic setting. It is, however, important to note that abuse of both adults and children quite often occurs within the same household, with estimates of the overlap ranging from 30 to 60 per cent (Paradine and Wilkinson 2004: 4).

Partner violence

Extent and distribution

It is well established that domestic violence is particularly susceptible to under-reporting to – and under-recording by – the police. Even so, it has been estimated that the police in England and Wales receive a call about it every minute (HMCPSI/HMIC 2004) and assaults by intimate partners or ex-partners make up a significant proportion of all recorded violent crime.[3]

According to the 2003/4 BCS, 16 per cent of violent incidents against adults – and 31 per cent of those against women[4] – were domestic assaults, although these are also likely to be underestimates owing to victim reluctance to reveal sensitive matters to a survey (Upson *et al.* 2004: 73). Perhaps the best British data come from the 2001 BCS, which included a detailed self-completion questionnaire and made every effort to reassure respondents about confidentiality. This specialized survey produced estimates of domestic violence five times higher than the main BCS (see also Barnish 2004). Even so, significant undercounting is still likely, owing to factors such as the presence of partners in the house whilst the questionnaire is completed, failure to address the full range of abusive behaviour and absence from the survey of individuals who have fled from domestic violence and live in refuges or temporary accommodation (Mirrlees-Black 1999; Walby and Myhill 2001a; Walby and Allen 2004).

BCS findings suggest that higher proportions of domestic violence incidents (70 per cent) result in injury compared with acquaintance violence (50 per cent), stranger violence (48 per cent) and muggings (29 per cent). Moreover, there is evidence that very high proportions of victims of domestic violence are repeatedly victimized (Morley and Mullender 1994).

Women are clearly at greater risk of domestic violence than men. Prevalence research in the UK suggests that it has been experienced by between one quarter and one third of women, depending upon the breadth of definitions and particular methodologies used (Paradine and Wilkinson 2004: 5).

Homicide represents the most extreme manifestation of interpersonal violence and homicide data provide further insight into the extent and nature of partner violence. Domestic homicide accounts for approximately 25 per cent of all homicides in England and Wales (Brookman 2005; see also MPS 2003: 5) and, once again, victimization varies significantly by gender. Of all women aged 17 or above who were victims of homicide between 1995 and 2000 in England and Wales, 57 per cent were killed by their current or former partner, boyfriend or lover (a rate of about two such homicides per week). In contrast, only 6 per cent of male victims were killed by a female partner or ex-partner. It is also significant that a high proportion of female victims of domestic homicide – and, incidentally, of female *offenders* – have experienced a history of abuse at the hands of their intimate male partners (Brookman 2005: 161), suggesting a strong link between domestic violence and domestic homicide.

Preventing partner violence

Because domestic violence generally takes place behind closed doors, many of the 'situational' preventive methods associated with crimes that take place in public spaces (such as CCTV monitoring of violence 'hotspots') are not normally an option. Instead, preventive strategies have traditionally been aimed either at changing the behaviour of known offenders (i.e. through 'tertiary' crime reduction methods such as deterrent sentences and rehabilitative programmes) or, especially since the success of the feminist movement in the 1970s in bringing the problem of domestic violence on to the political agenda, at the protection of victims and potential victims (for example, through the provision of women's refuges, or seeking court injunctions to prevent contact from former partners – strategies that might be broadly classified as 'primary' prevention). However, offender and victim-focused approaches are increasingly being combined, and there are many examples of more integrated and holistic approaches. The latter tend to have two key characteristics: they generally involve multi-agency partnership and incorporate a growing focus on risk assessment and risk management. We now briefly comment in turn on (1) offender-focused, (2) victim-focused and (3) more integrated (multi-agency, risk-based) approaches to the prevention of partner violence.

Offender-focused responses   Looking first at interventions which focus primarily on offenders, these include automatic arrest policies; standard sentencing responses (such as straightforward prison or community sentences); exclusionary orders or injunctions to prevent or regulate contact between offenders and their (current or former) partners; and rehabilitative programmes designed especially for people convicted of domestic violence.

Whilst automatic arrest policies may remove the immediate risk of further violence after the police have left, they are unlikely achieve more than this unless followed up by some other form of action. Equally, 'tough' sentencing and exclusionary orders may have some (probably temporary) deterrent effect, but neither is likely on its own to effect lasting change in perpetrators' attitudes and behaviour.

This is now widely recognized, and the UK has followed the lead from North America in viewing rehabilitative interventions with men as a critical component in the effort to reduce domestic violence (Gilchrist and Kebbell 2004). However, there has been considerable disagreement about the principles on which they should be based, as well as about their effectiveness. For example, many domestic violence perpetrator programmes have focused upon anger control (as do many more general rape and violent recidivist programmes). Yet the links between anger and violence are far from clear (Loza and Loza-Fanous 1999, for instance, found no differences in scores on anger scales between violent and non-violent offenders). Moreover, the unthinking use of 'anger management' programmes for violent offenders has been criticized for its failure to recognize that violence – and especially domestic violence – is not necessarily about being angry and out of control; on the contrary, it can be used instrumentally to establish or maintain control (Gilchrist and Kebbell 2004; Brookman 2005). Other perpetrator programmes focus more on attitudes and beliefs – including beliefs about women – that support or promote the use of violence, and use a variety of psycho-dynamic, psycho-educational or cognitive-behavioural approaches to challenge these.

The effectiveness of offender programmes in reducing reoffending by perpetrators of domestic violence is still far from clear. Amongst recent positive evidence is a study by Lewis (2004), based on in-depth interviews with 134 women (as survivors) and 122 men (as perpetrators) as well as postal questionnaire responses. It was found that sanctions which embodied rehabilitation (abuser programmes) were significantly more effective than sanctions which embodied deterrence (fine, jail, etc.). For example, women's accounts (suggested by Lewis to be the best measure of subsequent violence) indicated that only 33 per cent of men who completed an abuser programme, in comparison to 70 per cent of men who received a traditional sanction, committed a subsequent violent act against their partner in the 12 months after sentencing (Lewis 2004: 209). Other positive results have been reported for a variety of programmes by, for example, Burton et al. (1998), Skyner and Waters (1999), Dobash and Dobash (2000) and Dobash et al. (1999, 2000).

However, methodological problems, including selection effects, small sample sizes and difficulty in measuring reoffending, make research in this area notoriously difficult, and several researchers have reached cautious conclusions about the effects of offender programmes. Gilchrist and Kebbell (2004: 236) also warn against simplistic generalizations about whether programmes 'work' or 'do not work'. They note a welcome shift of emphasis in recent years from global questions of these kinds to questions such as 'which groups work best for which type of perpetrator'? In short, there is increasing evidence that perpetrators of domestic violence are far from a homogeneous group and that, at the very least, we should be thinking in terms of 'typologies of batterers' and what sorts of programmes best fit different sorts of offenders. For example, Holtzworth-Munroe and Stuart (1994) suggest that male perpetrators of domestic violence vary on four dimensions, namely:

1. severity/frequency of violence;
2. generality of the violence;
3. psychopathology/personality disorder characteristics; and
4. distal/proximal antecedents to the violence.

Based on variations along these dimensions, they identified three distinct types of 'batterer' (see also Holtzworth-Munroe et al. 2000; Waltz et al. 2000). Similarly, recent UK research by Gilchrist et al. (2003) identified two main types of domestic violence offenders: 'borderline/emotionally dependent' offenders (characterized by high levels of jealousy and stormy, intense relationships, high levels of interpersonal dependency, high levels of anger and low self-esteem); and 'anti-social/narcissistic' offenders (described as having hostile attitudes towards women, low empathy, high rates of alcohol dependence and multiple previous convictions). Even within these categories, however, the research found offenders to be a diverse group with a wide variety of needs, making it difficult to recommend specific courses of action that would be effective with a significant proportion of them.

Victim-focused responses   One of the main responses to domestic violence advocated and developed – mainly by feminist groups – in the 1970s was to protect (female) victims by encouraging them to leave abusive partners and, where necessary, to offer them temporary accommodation in the safe haven of a women's refuge (Pizzey 1974). Such groups also often campaigned for automatic arrest policies, heavier sentences for assailants and more effective legal mechanisms to stop harassment, 'stalking' and so on. In one sense, these may be seen as 'offender-focused' responses to violence, but the core interest of most of those demanding them was the protection of 'battered' women from further abuse. Generally speaking, such initiatives were developed by campaigning groups and the voluntary sector, and had little official support. However, domestic violence has gradually come to be seen by the government and the major criminal justice agencies as a priority issue, and the protection of victims as a core policy consideration. With this change in attitude, there is now much more co-operation between community groups and the formal criminal justice system in attempting to achieve this aim.

One example is what is generally referred to as 'victim advocacy', one of the main aims of which is to support victims through court processes and to improve their confidence and participation in the system, thus helping to 'bring to justice' more perpetrators – the assumption being that this will reduce future domestic violence. A key campaigning and co-ordinating organization in the promotion of advocacy in the UK is the Co-ordinated Response and Advocacy Resource Group (CRARG 2003). A government-supported initiative is also currently underway to provide accredited training for 'advocates' nationwide.

A linked development is the creation of specialized domestic violence courts (SDVCs). A recent evaluation of five of these courts in England and Wales identified three key ways in which the SDVCs were beneficial: 1) clustering and fast-tracking domestic violence cases enhanced the effectiveness of court and support services for victims; 2) advocacy and information-sharing was easier to accomplish; and 3) victim participation and satisfaction were improved (Cook *et al.* 2004). The report concluded that specialist courts enable the development of best practice in ways of working that place the victim at the heart of the process. SDVCs are now beginning to be established on a wider scale across England and Wales.

Integrated and risk-based approaches   As noted earlier, offender-focused interventions – both punitive and rehabilitative – are increasingly being combined with attention to the protection of, and support for, potential victims (principally, any current or recent partners) of the offender in question. These more holistic approaches to the problem of domestic violence have two important characteristics, also typical of the direction of crime reduction policy more generally: the growing weight placed upon risk assessment and the involvement of multi-agency partnerships. Comments will be made on each of these features in turn, before presenting some brief examples of integrated, multi-pronged approaches to domestic violence reduction.

Risk assessment
Risk assessment is made somewhat easier in domestic violence than in many other forms of violent crime by the fact that it is often a highly repetitive offence with discernible patterns of behaviour, mainly directed against the same victim. There has been a considerable amount of research aimed at improving methods of predicting both serious partner assaults and homicide. Table 19.3 summarizes the key risk factors that have been identified in relation to each. As many of these overlap – for example, the profiles of men who kill their partners do not differ greatly from those who use non-lethal violence (Aldridge and Browne 2003) – the risk factors have been combined. However, those that have been associated particularly strongly with an elevated risk of lethal harm are italicized.

Table 19.3 Key risk factors for domestic (partner) violence and partner homicide

Nature of risk	Key risk factors/markers
Situational/contextual	*Previous violence within the relationship*
	Separation or threat of separation
	Escalation of violence
	Child custody issues
Perpetrator characteristics and behaviour relating to current relationship	*Obsessive and excessive possessiveness/sexual jealousy*
	Stalking
	Threats to kill
	Suicide threats
	Forced sex/sexual assault
	Extreme dominance
	Minimization/denial of assault history
Perpetrator related (historic/ outside this relationship)	Violence outside the family
	Drug/alcohol misuse/dependence
	Child abuse
	Animal abuse
	Recent employment problems
	Childhood abuse/witnessing domestic violence
	Past assault of stranger, acquaintances, family and/or police officers
Victim related	Self-predictions of assault and level of harm
	Pregnancy/new birth
	Isolation
	Drug/alcohol abuse
	Ill-health/disability
	Childhood abuse/witnessing domestic violence

Note: Factors strongly associated with an elevated risk of homicide are italicized.
Sources: Walby and Myhill (2001b), Barnish (2004), Paradine and Wilkinson (2004), Brookman and Maguire (2005).

Factors found to be most strongly and consistently associated with domestic (partner) homicide include previous domestic violence within the same relationship; separation or the threat of separation instigated by a female partner; sexual jealousy; and stalking (Johnson and Grant 1999; Aldridge and Browne 2003; Brookman and Maguire 2005). Other features of a male perpetrator's behaviour towards a particular female partner that increase the risk of homicide include threats with weapons, threats to kill, infliction of serious injury, threats of suicide in response to the woman's wish to leave, forced sex and extensive dominance (Barnish 2004). In addition, male partners' violence outside the family, and/or a history of drug or alcohol misuse, have been found to increase the risk of lethal violence, although Dobash *et al.* (2001, 2002) concluded from their research with inmates serving life sentences for murder in Britain that factors relating directly to the relationship (such as separation and possessiveness) were stronger risk indicators than those external to it. Finally, an important finding for practitioners to take account of is that women's own predictions of future serious harm against them are also amongst factors predictive of homicide (Weisz *et al.* 2000).

In relation to domestic violence more generally, Riggs *et al.* (2000) concluded that the best and simplest risk marker was previous domestic violence, whilst – as with homicide – separation has also consistently been identified as a key risk factor (Walby and Myhill 2001b). Hence, whilst for many women separation brings relief from violence, for a significant minority it risks an escalation of violence and abuse (Barnish 2004: 28).

Formal risk prediction tools, and even simply guidance on spotting 'warning signs', are clearly useful in assisting practitioners to make decisions about whether and when to intervene, and are a valuable management aid for setting priorities and making the best use of scarce resources. However, risk prediction in relation to human behaviour is not an 'exact science' and in practice is undermined by problems such as incomplete or inaccurate information and lack of skills or understanding amongst those undertaking it. Moreover, where one is seeking to prevent what are relatively rare events such as grave violence or homicide, it suffers from the problem of overprediction. The presence even of all the most salient risk factors, such as separation or threats to kill, does *not* lead to serious violence in the great majority of cases. Hence translating risk assessment into effective risk *management* is anything but straightforward, and any form of targeting that involves expensive and/ or intrusive interventions faces the risk of expending considerable resources on high proportions of 'false positives' (i.e. those predicted to reoffend who would not in fact have done so).

It also has to be recognized that, whilst violence in hotspots such as city-centre entertainment areas or football grounds is relatively predictable in terms of time and location and may be managed – at least at key times – by the constant presence of police officers or private security staff (often aided by CCTV) who can intervene almost immediately, the scope for closely monitoring even the highest-risk domestic violence victims and offenders, let alone intervening in incidents as they are happening, is much more limited. Efforts can be made to encourage both early calls for assistance (e.g. by special alarm systems provided for high-risk victims) and rapid police responses to calls. However, the main focus of risk management in this area has to be on more generalized forms of surveillance and longer-term interventions with known offenders and known victims.

Multi-agency partnership

The second prominent characteristic of current approaches to domestic violence prevention, as with crime reduction as a whole, is that of multi-agency partnership. As discussed at length in this volume and elsewhere (e.g. Crawford 1998; Hughes 1998; Pease 2002), multi-agency approaches have the advantage of tackling problems in more depth and from a variety of angles, but the drawback that getting agencies to work together with the necessary degree of shared purpose, harmony and effective communication is a major task. Specifically in relation to domestic violence, the main deficiencies identified in UK attempts to introduce co-ordinated community responses have been failures to secure commitment from key agencies; shortage and insecurity of funding; imbalance of power between statutory and voluntary sector representatives; lack of consultation systems with domestic violence survivors; and inadequate evaluation provision (Gilchrist and Blissett 2002; Barnish 2004; Paradine and Wilkinson 2004).

There is no space here to cover the range of integrated, multi-agency initiatives that have been implemented at national, regional and local levels, but it may be helpful to give a few illustrative examples.

A common approach is to tie in offender programmes with victim support. One of the oldest and most strongly established models here is the Duluth Domestic Violence Programme, a psycho-educational groupwork programme for perpetrators linked with concurrent support for women and children. It is based on a project set up in Duluth, Minnesota, in the 1980s, which developed a comprehensive community-based programme designed to co-ordinate responses amongst the many agencies and practitioners who typically respond to domestic violence cases. The model was used by the National Probation Service in England and Wales as the basis for the development of the Integrated Domestic Abuse Programme (IDAP), which was piloted as a Pathfinder and is now being used more widely in community sentences. As in the original model, this combines treatment of offenders with support for their victims. It normally includes probation, police, women's groups and social services.

The research evidence is largely unclear on the effectiveness of the Duluth model. Shepard (1992) found that no combination of interventions studied (civil or criminal court intervention, perpetrator programme completion, number of sessions attended or imprisonment) was significantly related to reconviction within five years of the intervention: the best recidivism predictors were the individual characteristics of perpetrators, rather than the characteristics of the intervention system. Other studies have been more encouraging, though several emphasize that effectiveness may vary according to many factors, including community conditions, presence of children and local police–community relations (Hague 2001; Mears 2003). The IDAP programme has not yet been evaluated in terms of outcomes, but some important delivery issues have been identified, including heavy demands on staff and administrative time, the value of mixed-sex teams (to set positive examples of male–female relationships) and the importance of clear and formal protocols of communication, both within probation and between probation and outside agencies (Bilby and Thatcher 2004).

A somewhat different kind of interagency response, focused strongly on the protection of victims, is that represented by specialist women's safety units (WSUs), which offer a sort of 'one-stop shop' for dealing with issues around domestic violence and bring together seconded (or part-seconded) staff from a variety of agencies. The WSU in Cardiff is considered a leading example in this field in the UK, and includes a seconded police officer working within the unit. A recent evaluation of the unit, based on structured interviews with a random sample of 120 of the 3,000 or so women who had sought its assistance, found that all agreed or strongly agreed with the idea that meeting with the WSU would result in a reduction in the violence in their lives (Robinson 2005).

Another experiment associated with the current cluster of innovative domestic violence initiatives in Cardiff is directly based on risk assessment and risk management. This uses multi-agency risk assessment conferences (MARACs) to identify high-risk domestic violence victims and put in place plans and responsibilities for monitoring and protecting them (for example, regular visits or special alarm systems – with an eye also, of course, on the offenders from whom the threats may come). These are, as it were, the flipside of the statutory multi-agency public protection arrangements (MAPPA) that have been in place for some years to assess, monitor and manage sexual and violent offenders (Maguire *et al.* 2001; Kemshall and Maguire 2001, 2002 – and see below). A recent evaluation of MARACs in Cardiff reported positive findings in relation to the safety of victims, measured by the numbers of complaints and call-outs to the police post-MARAC, and data from telephone interviews with victims. All three indicators revealed that the majority of victims (about 6 in 10) had not been revictimized since the MARAC. Further benefits reported included enhanced information-sharing (Robinson 2004).

In the USA, particularly, multi-agency forums are becoming a popular means of monitoring and improving responses to domestic violence at community level. They variously aim to exchange information, identify and address service provision problems, co-ordinate agency activities, promote good practice through training and guidelines, track cases and carry out audits to assess individual agency practice, and promote community awareness and prevention. Most have received no outcome evaluation, although there is some US evidence that they can lead to increases in the proportion of calls to the police resulting in arrests and prosecutions (WHO 2002).

A significant proportion of US states now also conduct fatality reviews of deaths resulting from domestic violence. These often look at the actions (or inaction) of a range of agencies in the lead-up to the homicide, in order to establish whether there are any lessons to be learnt and to formulate recommendations to improve interagency working. They also tend to focus on risk assessment issues. Similar reviews have been conducted in London by local multi-agency domestic violence forums since 2002. Findings from one of these generated 13 recommendations for health services as a result of warning signs of escalating violence going unheeded, or receiving an inadequate response. Other recommendations from reviews have included a 24-hour independent advocacy service for victims, charging offenders with separate offences against children when children witness domestic violence and a common domestic violence risk assessment tool for all agencies (Barnish 2004: 133). The government is proposing to establish a statutory basis for domestic violence homicide reviews in the UK (Home Office 2003).

Finally, a good example of turning research on risk factors into practice can be found in work by the Metropolitan Police Service in conjunction with a range of partner agencies. The service conducted its own analysis of risk factors associated with homicides in London, identifying six as the most important: separation, pregnancy, escalation of violence, cultural issues (e.g. in relation to 'honour killings'), stalking and sexual assault (MPS 2003). The research has informed the construction of a risk assessment model ('SPECSS'), intended to focus police officers' attention on danger signs. Risk management guidelines have also been developed (with yet another mnemonic, 'RARA'), based on 1) removing the risk (e.g. arresting the perpetrator); 2) avoiding risk (e.g. re-housing the victim); 3) reducing the risk (e.g. victim safety planning and use of protective legislation); and 4) 'accepting' the risk (e.g. through multi-agency intervention planning).

Child abuse

Not surprisingly, there is no generally agreed definition of child abuse. Three problems have hampered efforts to define it (and ultimately assess its prevalence): 1) identifying the boundaries between abuse (or more broadly maltreatment) and other forms of harm such as the consequences of poor parenting or severe social deprivation; 2) known differences between cultures and countries and generations over acceptable ways to treat children; and 3) achieving 'single measures' of abuse or neglect which have any meaning (see Cawson *et al.* 2000).

Abuse is generally categorized into three types: physical, sexual and emotional (or psychological) – though the latter is a relative newcomer to the research literature. These categories are clearly not mutually exclusive: sexual abuse can be regarded as a special category of physical abuse, whilst all forms of abuse involve an element of emotional abuse (Cawson *et al.* 2000). Of course, 'child abuse' in its broadest sense can include general abuses suffered by children in a particular society or social class which are created by wider social and economic conditions and events, such as war, famine, poor public health or housing services and so on, and the prevention of such abuse may be sought in social change outside the purview of the criminal justice system or conventional crime prevention practices (see, for example, Erlich 1996; NCIPCA 1996; Wattam 1999).[5] However, we are here concerned with individualized child abuse within the household – abuse which may well have its roots in wider social problems, but which involves a clear 'offender' within or closely associated with the household.

Extent of child abuse

Using the following definition of physical abuse, some 8,000 children's names appeared on the Child Protection Register in England under the physical abuse category, during the year ending 31 March 2001. This translates to a recorded incidence of 7 per 10,000 children, or 0.07 per cent (Creighton 2002: 2): 'Physical abuse may involve hitting, shaking, throwing, poisoning, burning or scalding, drowning, suffocating, or otherwise causing physical harm to the child. Physical harm may also be caused when a parent or carer feigns the symptoms of, or deliberately causes, ill health to a child whom they are looking after' (Department of Health 2001: 41). This figure is severely limited in that it relies upon reports from professionals. Yet there is consistent evidence that this is an activity that is rarely reported to any authorities. Studies based on surveys of victims or offenders are somewhat more reliable, though again there will be a significant dark figure. The largest-scale UK study to address the issue comprehensively (including physical, sexual, emotional abuse and neglect) is that by Cawson *et al.* (2000). In a large random probability sample of the general population, 2,869 young adults aged between 18 and 24 were surveyed to explore their childhood experiences of maltreatment. The researchers found that the family was the primary arena for physical abuse and hence concentrated their analysis in this area.

A quarter of the sample reported having experienced some physical abuse. However, when a stricter definition of serious physical abuse was applied and restricted to parents or carers, the proportion in the serious abuse category fell to 7 per cent. These figures represent a lifetime prevalence rather than annual incidence. They are not greatly dissimilar to those produced from a survey by Ghate *et al.* (forthcoming, cited in Creighton 2002: 3), who found that some 6 per cent of parents had used physically abusive methods – defined as 'hitting with an implement, punching, kicking, beating up or burned or scalded on purpose' – with their child (aged 0–12 years) in the last year and 11 per cent during the child's lifetime.

The extent of child sexual abuse is equally difficult to measure. It was not until the broadcast of BBC's *ChildWatch* in 1986 (which attracted 16.5 million viewers) and the 1987 Cleveland Inquiry (Butler-Sloss 1988) that serious concerns about its extent and damaging effects were publicly aired and debated in the UK (Cawson *et al.* 2000: 73). Since then, there have been numerous attempts to determine its prevalence, with somewhat confusing results owing to both its hidden nature and variations in definitions.

Finkelhor (1994), in a review of 21 national studies, found victimization prevalence rates ranging from 7 per cent to 36 per cent for females and between 3 per cent and 29 per cent for males (see also LaFontaine 1990). He concluded that a prevalence figure of around 20 per cent for females and 10 per cent for males was realistic. The most recent attempt to gauge the extent of child sexual abuse in the UK was undertaken as part of the aforementioned wider study of child maltreatment by Cawson *et al.* (2000). This found that 1 per cent of the sample has been abused by parents/carers, 3 per cent by other relatives and 11 per cent by other people known to them (4 per cent had been abused by strangers). Females were more likely than males to have been victims, and between a quarter to a third of abusers were thought to have been juveniles.

Preventing child abuse
Strategies to reduce child abuse within households have much in common with

those for partner violence and, owing to limited space, only a brief outline will be presented, focusing mainly on ways in which they differ.

Particularly since the growth of media coverage and hostile public feeling about 'paedophiles', the main response to sexual abuse of children, whether by parents, relatives or others close to the household, has been to punish and control the offender by long prison sentences, attendance at sex-offender treatment programmes, registration as a sex offender and, in many cases, exclusion from further close contact with children (see, for example, Kemshall and Maguire 2001; Cobley 2005; Matravers 2005). Physical abuse – which appears to be much more common than sexual abuse where parents or carers are the offender(s) – also attracts exclusionary responses (perpetrators are listed as Schedule 1 offenders and Social Services often use their powers to prevent children living with them), although there is considerably more flexibility and much depends on 'expert' assessments and judgements about the risk to the child.

These 'tertiary', offender-focused forms of crime reduction – with a strong focus on incapacitation and deterrence – appear to be quite effective, albeit sometimes at high emotional cost to those involved, in terms of preventing reoffending by individuals (particularly against the same victims). However, it is clear that only a small proportion of violent or sexual abusers of children close to them come to the notice of the authorities and hence become subject to such controls. More general preventive strategies are therefore necessary to protect children from abuse that has not yet come to light (or, though latent, has not yet started).

Two kinds of strategies can be quickly mentioned which attempt to do this. First, those that target specialist services at, or try to build up 'social capital' in, particular deprived areas where there is thought to be a higher than average risk of (especially physical) child abuse; and, secondly, those which try to promote general awareness of the problem.

A great deal of the most recent research in the area of child protection focuses upon the importance of adopting what is generally termed a community level approach. This sees the problem of child abuse as part of wider health problems and family stresses within disadvantaged communities, caused by a combination of the large structural inequalities that exist in the distribution of income and other resources and services. As Cawson et al. (2000: 104) point out, 'Strategies for protecting children will need to be quite different if the problems result from situational pressures such as illness or poverty than if they result from fundamentally pathological, aggressively dominant relationships'. Whilst social inclusion and anti-poverty policies may bear some fruit in the long term, writers such as Jack (2004) argue that they have as yet had little impact on the wider structural disadvantage, and that there are other strategies which can help ameliorate some of the pressures in the shorter term. One is to assist in building up the social networks of parents and the social capital of the wider community (i.e. overall social relations between people and the norms of trust and reciprocity upon which they are based). This can be attempted through, for example, the development and/or support of a wide range of community groups such as preschool playgroups, children's clubs, youth clubs, women's groups, parenting programmes and home visiting, a strategy for which there is some evidence of positive results (Eastham 1990; Holman 2000). Equally, home-visiting services that use trained professionals or volunteers (often experienced mothers from the same deprived communities) to provide advice and support to families on child-care issues, as well as focusing on the mothers' health and well-being, have been found in some studies to raise the self-esteem, parenting skills and confidence of disadvantaged parents, as well as reducing rates of childhood injury (Elkan *et al*. 2000; Wiggins *et al*. 2002; McAuley *et al*. 2004). A well-known community project with some of these aims is SureStart, a government-funded initiative in which the National Society for the Prevention of Cruelty to Children (NSPCC) is also involved. This is targeted at the parents of babies and young children in disadvantaged communities, and sets out where possible to support parents right from the birth of their children.[6]

Finally, organizations like the NSPCC have for many years used publicity campaigns in an effort to reach a wide audience and educate the public about the risks of child abuse. The NSPCC has developed five 'Full Stop' action programmes focusing upon 'the child in the family, school, the community, child protection and the child in society'. For example, practical advice in user-friendly magazine formats has been targeted at new parents (about how to deal with the stresses of a newborn, how to appreciate their fragility and how and where to get help). Publicity also has a broad surveillance function, in that the NSPCC tries to encourage members of the public to report suspicions about child abuse. For example, it ran a national public education campaign in March 2002 entitled 'Someone to turn to'. Sponsored by Microsoft, this used TV and billboard advertising and a public information leaflet in order to improve public knowledge about what to do in the event of suspecting abuse. A broadly similar approach can be found in relation to child sex abuse in 'Stop it Now', a public education campaign aimed at preventing such abuse by increasing public awareness and empowering people to act responsibly to protect children (see below for further discussion).

Alcohol-related crime in public places

We turn now to a very different 'cluster' of violent offences, those committed in public places under the influence of alcohol. These occur predominantly in the late evening or early hours of the morning, in or outside pubs and clubs in city and town centres. Unlike domestic violence and child abuse, most incidents are between strangers and occur on a one-off, rather than repeated, basis. Indeed, local research indicates that the majority of the offenders who are arrested – typically, young men – have no previous convictions for violent or public order offences (Maguire and Nettleton 2003).

Extent and trends

Measurement of the scale of 'alcohol-related violence' is difficult and raises considerable definitional problems, particularly if incidents of 'disorder' are included (Tierney and Hobbs 2003; though see Maguire and Hopkins 2003;

Maguire and Nettleton 2003 for examples of innovative attempts using a variety of data sources). The 'best estimate' from the 1999 BCS of the total number of alcohol-related assaults by strangers or acquaintances in England and Wales was 860,000 (Budd 2003).[7] In the case of 'stranger to stranger' assaults, more than half the perpetrators are described by BCS respondents as under the influence of alcohol; equally, respondents who visit nightclubs or discotheques at least once a week have been found to be nearly eight times more likely to be assaulted than the national average (Mattinson 2001; see also Allen *et al.* 2003). There is also broad agreement that alcohol-related violence and disorder have been increasing in Britain with the relaxation of the licensing laws and the growth of the 'night-time' or '24/7' economy, built around attracting large numbers of young people to concentrations of pubs, clubs, discotheques and fast-food outlets in city centres. These developments have led to concerns about a growing culture of violence and 'binge drinking' (Light 2000; LGA 2002; Hobbs *et al.* 2000, 2003; Strategy Unit 2004). On Friday and Saturday nights in some of the larger cities, well over 100,000 people may be crowded into such areas. At the same time, the number of police officers available to deal with any trouble is often surprisingly small. In fact, most of the policing is undertaken by private security staff attached to individual licensed premises – usually referred to as 'door staff' or 'bouncers'. Whilst the situation is undoubtedly improving (see below), such staff have themselves often been 'part of the problem'. Until relatively recently, they were subject to very little regulation and the job, poorly paid and offering little training, has tended to attract people who are quick to resort to violence and in some cases engage in drug dealing or other criminal activity (Morris 1998; Lister *et al.* 2001; Hobbs *et al.* 2002).

Preventive strategies

Despite an accumulation of knowledge over some time about the nature of the problem, the implementation of strategies to prevent or reduce these kinds of violence and disorder has generally been sporadic and *ad hoc*, and there has been little rigorous evaluation of what actually 'works' in this regard. Most commentators have reached the conclusion that it is only through partnership working – especially between the police, local councils, licensees and the drinks industry more generally – that a more sustained grip on the problem will be achieved (Deehan 1999; NACRO 2001; Maguire and Nettleton 2003). Although it figured fairly low on the agenda of Crime and Disorder Reduction Partnerships (CDRPs) in their first three-year plans covering 1999–2002 (Deehan and Saville 2000; SIRC 2002), there has been a considerable surge in interest over the last three or four years, and many CDRPs have since highlighted and addressed alcohol-related violence as a priority issue in their crime audits, strategies and plans (Richardson and Budd 2003; Richardson *et al.* 2003). Importantly, too, there has been a major push from central government on the issue, including the development in 2004 of the national Alcohol Harm Reduction Strategy for England (Strategy Unit 2004), discussed further below.

Whilst some preventive interventions – such as arrest referral schemes or court sentences which channel offenders into educational or treatment programmes to combat alcohol abuse – are targeted at individuals who have committed assaults, and there are moves to increase punishment and deterrence (for example, through fixed penalty fines and exclusion orders) for drunken 'anti-social behaviour' on the streets, the focus of most current strategic thinking about the reduction of alcohol-related violence tends to be less on its perpetrators than on the locations, environments and 'cultures' within which it takes place. This includes, on the one hand, attention to the physical layout, bar-staff practices and security arrangements of pubs and clubs, as well as to flows of people on the streets and congregations that occur at particular times as they attempt to buy 'fast food', find transport home and so on. It also includes attention to broader questions about the 'culture of drinking' – and especially 'binge' drinking by young people – which appears to be more prominent in Britain than in most other European countries. In other words, this is a type of violent crime that appears to be well suited to both 'primary' (especially 'situational') and 'secondary' (especially education and 'climate changing') crime prevention methods, though probably less so to 'tertiary' methods based on targeting 'known offenders' for rehabilitation, surveillance, deterrence or exclusion.

Situational approaches

The most promising situational methods in this field can be broadly divided into those aimed at improving the environment and management of individual licensed premises, and those aimed at effective management of late-night entertainment areas as a whole. The latter include not only direct management of drinkers on the streets but also city-centre management at a much broader level (including more co-ordinated thinking about infrastructure, planning and licensing policies and so on).

Individual premises   Several studies have found that violence inside (or just outside) licensed premises, although by no means absent from others, tends to occur disproportionately in or around certain pubs and clubs, many of which acquire something of a reputation for fights. Factors identified as increasing the risk of violence in individual premises are almost all associated with weak or inadequate management. These include poor design (for example, insufficient seating, lack of quiet areas or difficult bar access); poor physical maintenance of buildings; overcrowding; lack of ventilation; and high noise levels – all of which can increase feelings of annoyance or bring people into competition for services or space. They also include weaknesses in the day-to-day supervision and control of customers: most importantly, poorly trained bar staff who engage in irresponsible serving practices or undisciplined and aggressive door staff who attract or instigate violence themselves (see, for example, Tuck 1989; Homel and Clark 1994; Graham and Homel 1997; Purser 1997; Deehan 1999; Hobbs *et al.* 2003).

A number of studies in the mid-1990s produced evidence to suggest that efforts to address these problems and improve the management and physical environment of specific premises could help to reduce incidents in those locations (Graham and Homel 1997; Purser 1997; see also Deehan 1999). However, such changes were rarely enforced, and it was not until the problem of alcohol-related violence began to attract serious media and government attention in the early 2000s that more systematic approaches began to be adopted to 'clamp down' on poorly managed venues.

An important early example was the Tackling Alcohol-related Street Crime (TASC) project in Cardiff city centre, funded and evaluated under the Home Office Crime Reduction Programme. This involved partnership between the police, county council, local hospital and representatives of pub and club owners and managers (the Licensees' Forum). Whilst also aimed at broader methods of violence reduction (see next section), the TASC project paid close attention to hotspot premises with high rates of violent incidents. It was helped in this by the creation of a dedicated database, maintained by a full-time analyst, which held detailed records of every known violent incident in the city centre. These were extracted from a variety of sources including police incident, crime and custody records, CCTV operators' records and the accident and emergency department of the local hospital (Maguire and Nettleton 2003). The database was used for a variety of purposes, but proved particularly useful to police licensing officers, who were able to visit premises and confront managers with a comprehensive record of recent incidents, the underlying threat being that, if they did nothing to correct the problems, the same data could eventually be used as evidence to persuade magistrates not to renew their licence. Other interventions aimed at improving the quality of management and control of premises included targeted policing operations directed at particular clubs, a training and registration scheme for door supervisors and a training programme for bar staff. The Licensees' Forum was also active in promoting good management practice and acted as a positive channel of communication between the police and licensees. The evaluation found significant and sustained reductions in violent incidents in and around specific clubs which were the target of coordinated interventions, in contrast to increases in violence in the city-centre area as a whole, suggesting that sharply focused situational methods can be effective in reducing alcohol-related violence at the level of individual premises, but that they may not have a wider impact on the surrounding area (Maguire and Nettleton 2003; see also Maguire and Hopkins 2003 and next section).

Over the last three or four years, police and local authorities have generally tightened up formal controls over licensed premises. This has been undertaken partly through increases in licensing officers and the establishment of regular dialogue about security with representatives of the brewing and entertainment industries – resulting, for example, in the regulation and reduction of 'happy hours', which can encourage young people to drink large amounts of alcohol within a short period. Importantly, too, in October 2004 a compulsory national registration scheme was introduced for door supervisors, administered by the Security Industry Association (SIA 2004).[8]

Managing city centres Whilst initiatives to regulate individual premises appear to have had some success in reducing highly localized violence, they are unlikely (at least in the short term) significantly to reduce the numbers of intoxicated or semi-intoxicated young people moving around city centres late at night. Any attempt to reduce incidents of violence and disorder across entertainment areas as a whole – a large minority of which occur on the streets or at public gathering points such as fast-food outlets or bus stops, rather than in or around specific licensed premises (Matttinson 2001; Maguire and Nettleton 2003) – has therefore to take into account wider issues.

Broader factors in the local environment that have been identified as increasing the risk of violence include problems of overcrowding and access to services, in some ways paralleling those causing friction inside pubs and clubs. For example, Tuck (1989) noted over a decade ago that alcohol-related violence is often generated at 'congestion' and 'cluster' points within cities. Congestion points are particularly busy spots or bottlenecks at which revellers may pass each other on public thoroughfares between pubs and nightclubs. Cluster points are areas where crowds of people may gather when waiting for (and sometimes competing for) service, such as fast-food outlets, taxi ranks and at the bars of public houses. Both offer the potential for incidents to be triggered as people jostle each other or argue over access to the services.

Whilst sensitive and well targeted policing (assuming that enough officers can be made available), assisted by CCTV, can help to regulate behaviour and reduce violence at hotspots of these kinds, much more effective, less costly and sustainable solutions to such problems lie in the hands of local authorities and agencies involved in town-centre management, public transport, planning and licensing, where possible working in partnership with commercial stakeholders. These include changes to street layout and design to remove congestion points. They include staggering closing times to prevent major surges of customers leaving several large venues at once. They include providing easier access to both public and private transport late at night. Importantly, too, they include taking a longer-term and strategic, rather than individualized, approach to licensing and planning issues, in order to ensure that licensed premises and fast-food outlets are not clustered too densely in areas with limited space or adequate infrastructure (Maguire and Hopkins 2003).

Of course, managing city centres is expensive, and an important recent development, which is likely to give situational interventions a considerable boost, is the introduction by central government, as part of its broader strategy on alcohol harm reduction (see below), of proposals to ask the owners of licensed premises in late-night entertainment areas to pay towards the cost of managing crime and disorder created by excessive alcohol consumption. This proposal – which has echoes of debates about the extent to which football clubs should pay for the policing and prevention of hooliganism in and around stadiums – includes funding the creation of 'city-centre marshals' to patrol areas such as taxi ranks and late-night bus stops (Strategy Unit 2004).

'Secondary' approaches

In addition to the above situational approaches aimed at creating a safer environment, there is also increasing interest in broader preventive approaches to tackle the social and cultural roots of the problem of excessive drinking – especially so-called 'binge' drinking (or frequent 'drinking to get drunk'), which appears to be particularly strongly associated with violence (Richardson *et al.* 2003). Current government strategies in this area have as their goal the reduction not just of violent crime and disorder, but of a whole range of harms – including lost days at work, road accidents, and deaths and illness from liver damage – caused by the excessive consumption of alcohol. The lead in England (Wales has its own strategy, led by the Welsh Assembly) has been taken by the Strategy Unit of the Cabinet Office, which in 2004 introduced the Alcohol Harm Reduction Strategy for England (Strategy Unit 2004).

In addition to 'tougher' policing and punishment policies, and assistance to local authorities with town-centre management, the main planks of the strategy include major investment in alcohol education programmes, research and publicity (funding contributions to which will be sought from the drinks industry); tighter regulation of alcohol advertising (by Ofcom); better labelling of alcohol levels in drinks; advice to employers on how to deal with staff who appear to have alcohol problems; training to help NHS staff identify alcohol problems and refer people for treatment at an early stage; and improvements to alcohol treatment services. The overall effect of such policies, in some ways similar to long-established campaigns against smoking, should be to focus more attention on the risks of alcohol consumption and, hopefully, to generate long-term cultural and attitudinal change which will discourage excessive (including 'binge') drinking.

'Predatory' violence and sexual assault

The third and final 'cluster' of offences to be considered here are various forms of what we shall call 'predatory' violence and sexual assault: in essence, crimes in which the offender (with varying degrees of conscious planning) seeks out and attacks victims, often strangers who have done little or nothing to provoke the assault. The motives for such attacks vary widely, and in many cases are difficult to determine. They are sometimes categorized as either instrumental (typically, in personal robbery) or expressive (as in beating people up 'for kicks'), but the two frequently overlap. For example, research suggests that robbery is often motivated as much by enjoyment of obtaining 'control' over victims as by financial gain (Topalli et al. 2002). Moreover, the term 'predatory' is itself problematic, inasmuch as it suggests a planned and deliberate 'stalking of prey'. Whilst there are cases in which this is a fair description of the activity – as where rapists look out for lone women walking home at night, or paedophiles 'target' or 'groom' children for sexual assault – these are fairly rare. More common are scenarios in which someone with few inhibitions about using violence or sexual aggression responds to a 'trigger' such as someone's clothes or appearance, and then targets that particular person for attack: the response may be cold and controlled, or it may be marked by anger and loss of control. Of course, the boundary between such a scenario and some of the 'alcohol-related violence' discussed in the previous section is blurred – indeed, both can be committed by the same people, and some offenders become 'predatory' only when under the influence of alcohol (or, for that matter, drugs). However, the main difference is that whereas most alcohol-related violence and disorder is intrinsically related to the culture of 'binge drinking' and all kinds of people can become caught up in it when drunk, 'predatory' violence is more directly linked to the personal history and psychological make-up of particular individuals, for many of whom acts of violence *per se* (or assaults on specific types of people) hold a special attraction.

The latter point is important in that it largely explains why preventive strategies aimed at 'predatory' violence tend to have a very different focus from those aimed at alcohol-related violence. Primarily, they involve 'tertiary' crime prevention approaches, based on the risk management of 'dangerous' individuals, as opposed to monitoring or altering particular locations or environments. However, as will be described, some recent thinking has begun to shift the focus a little from the individual alone to the community in which he or she lives. The following discussion of predatory violence will be divided into two parts: the first a general account of policies aimed at protecting the public and reducing the risks of serious harm by 'dangerous offenders'; and the second a look at a particular form of predatory violence, the phenomenon of 'hate crime' (violence motivated by racial, homophobic or other prejudice against particular social groups). Whilst interventions with convicted offenders remain a prominent feature of responses to hate crime, it is widely agreed that these will be effective only if underpinned by strong 'secondary' forms of prevention, including policies to challenge racist and homophobic attitudes at a national and community level.

'Dangerous' offenders

It is important to note at the outset that policies relating to so-called 'dangerous' offenders are often highly controversial, and over the last decade or so the whole topic has become increasingly politicized and the subject of intense media and public concern (some would say 'hysteria'). This is especially true of concerns about 'predatory paedophiles'. Although, as has often been pointed out, the risks of sexual or violent attacks on children by strangers are very small in comparison with those by family members and acquaintances, fears of 'stranger-danger' have been relentlessly reinforced by massive media coverage of particularly disturbing cases of child abduction and homicide (Worrall 1997; Thompson 1998; Kitzinger 1999; Wilczynski and Sinclair 1999; Cobley 2000; Walters 2001; Kemshall and Maguire 2001, 2005). In just a few years, it has been argued, the 'spectre of the mobile and anonymous sexual offender' preying on the young has become a terrifying and ever-present concern for many people (Hebenton and Thomas 1996: 249) and the paedophile has been constructed as a 'demon' to be 'put under surveillance, punished, contained and constrained' (Young 1996: 9). Current concerns about international terrorism, of course, have further ratcheted up general fears about dangerous 'strangers in our midst'.

In such a charged atmosphere, it is difficult to construct considered and ethically justifiable policies to protect the public from what are undoubtedly real risks of serious harm, but greatly exaggerated in terms of frequency of occurrence. The argument that there is a category of people so dangerous that special 'incapacitative' measures (breaching normally accepted human rights and principles governing the degree to which a democratic state can restrict citizens' freedom) are justified in order to protect the public from them is by no means new, but has become increasingly accepted by government and put into practice with minimal opposition.[9] Indeed, it is probably fair to say that the main governmental response to fears about 'dangerous offenders' since the early 1980s has been to devise ways of keeping them in prison for longer and longer periods, either through restricting release on parole (Maguire 1992) or by passing legislation to allow 'exceptional' sentences for those so defined (e.g. Criminal Justice Act 1991; Crime (Sentences) Act 1997; see Nash 1999; Power 1999; Cobley 2005). More recently, too, the government has shown itself increasingly willing to propose the use of preventive detention for people suspected of being 'dangerous' but against whom there is insufficient evidence for a criminal conviction (as in the draft of the Mental Health Bill put forward in 2002, which proposed indefinite detention of some 'psychopaths', and in recent attempts to increase powers of detention of suspected terrorists[10]).

There is no space here to rehearse these major debates. However, whatever one's view about the use of long-term imprisonment or detention for people considered dangerous, it is clear that this can only be part of any effective public protection strategy and that many such people will continue to live in, or be released into, the community. It is therefore important to examine strategies that have been, or are being, developed for their 'risk management' in the community.

MAPPA

In England and Wales, the central plank of such strategies in recent years has been the use of 'multi-agency public protection arrangements' (MAPPAs). These are statutory arrangements, governed by the Criminal Justice and Court Services Act 2000, and based on formal partnership at a local level between police forces, probation services, social services, prisons, housing, health and other agencies which may have a useful part to play. Their core functions are the risk assessment and risk management of 'relevant' sexual and violent offenders (in essence, virtually all sex offenders and those violent offenders sentenced to a year or more in custody).[11] Risk assessment is assisted by the sharing of information about individual offenders, authorized by interagency protocols. Offenders are normally classified as 'low', 'medium' or 'high' risk, although a small number of exceptionally high-risk offenders – usually referred to as the 'critical few' (Bryan and Doyle 2005) – are singled out for special attention. In the case of high-risk offenders, risk management measures may be implemented and overseen by a 'multi-agency public protection panel' (MAPPP), made up of senior managers from each organization, but in more routine cases it is usually undertaken by a lower-tier, more local committee (a 'multi-agency risk assessment conference', or MARAC). This process generally involves the formulation, implementation and review of a plan for each individual offender. Depending upon the level of risk, such plans may range from no action beyond an occasional case review, through routine police or probation home visits, to covert police surveillance or the seeking of a sex offender order to restrict the offender's movements (Home Office 2001; Maguire et al. 2001; Bryan and Doyle 2005). In many cases – and particularly in the case of sex offenders – strategies to maintain control and surveillance are given 'teeth' by extra powers that have been legislated over recent years to impose conditions upon high-risk offenders in the community. These include extended licence periods for those released from prison; sex offender registration, which entails an obligation on most convicted sex offenders to register their address with the police for at least five years; and sex offender orders – civil orders with conditions attached, breach of which is a criminal offence punishable by a substantial period of imprisonment (Power 1999; Plotnikoff and Woolfson 2000; Kemshall and Maguire 2001; Cobley 2005).

An evaluation of the work of the first statutorily constituted MAPPPs, set up under the Crime and Disorder Act 1998, found that there were wide variations in skills and practice between areas and that, whilst very high-risk cases were handled thoroughly, many areas were experiencing difficulties in coping with the volume of cases, and especially in maintaining effective risk management of medium or low-risk offenders over sustained periods. This included problems in record-keeping, in 'ownership' of cases, and in following up and reviewing decisions and actions systematically. More generally, little systematic thought had been given to how best to 'risk manage' offenders who were not under formal licence: most areas relied on periodic home visits or surveillance from police officers, or reports or observations of suspicious behaviour (Maguire *et al.* 2001; see also Kemshall and Maguire 2001, 2002). However, more recent accounts suggests that there have been considerable improvements in terms of consistency, record-keeping, accountability and monitoring (Bryan and Doyle 2005).

Engaging the community? Emerging agendas

It is likely – though by no means 'proven' – that, particularly as a result of improved information-sharing and interagency co-ordination (e.g. linking housing decisions with surveillance considerations), the advent of MAPPA has provided a greater degree of public protection than single-agency responses to 'dangerous' offenders. However, no matter how well MAPPAs 'work', they face the problem that whenever (as is inevitable) a serious incident occurs, the already-fragile public trust in 'agencies' and 'experts' as guarantors of community safety diminishes a little more, and populist calls for more draconian measures against violent or (especially) sexual offenders increase in volume. Such calls include persistent demands for a British version of the American 'Megan's Law', whereby the local community would have a right to be informed of the names and addresses of people with convictions for sexual offences. In 2000 and 2001, following the murder of Sarah Payne and the subsequent arrest of her killer (a man already on the sex offenders register and known to the local MAPPP), this became the core theme of a campaign by the *News of the World* to 'name and shame paedophiles'. The campaign fuelled a spate of public disorder and vigilante action, some against wrongly identified people, in several towns (Thomas 2001).

Home Office ministers, supported by the police, resisted robustly the demands for 'community notification' (as it is referred to in the USA), arguing that a 'Sarah's Law' would be 'unworkable' in the UK; worse, it would be likely to create more mobility amongst offenders, driving them 'underground' and making them more difficult to monitor and control.[12] They did, however, make some concessions, including placing an obligation on local MAPPPs to publish annual reports with basic statistics on registered sex offenders living in the area, and establishing a system whereby representatives of local communities are appointed as members of MAPPPs, thus having a say in strategic decision-making about risk management (though not individual cases). Nevertheless, the whole episode helped to open up a broader and better informed debate about whether and to what extent local communities should be informed about, consulted about or actively involved in the risk management of sex offenders (for further discussion, see Kemshall and Maguire 2005).

Generally speaking, the message from American research is that community notification *per se* – for example, simply posting the names and addresses of sex offenders on a website – is unlikely to prevent reoffending, and may have negative effects. Zevitz and Farkas (2000) argue that it increases community anxiety; Prentky (1996) describes a marginalizing impact which can be detrimental to offenders' reintegration and avoidance of reoffending; and Schram and Milloy (1995) found no statistically significant difference in reoffending between offenders subject to community notification and those who were not (for further discussion, see Rudin 1996; Freeman-Longo and Blanchard 1998). On the other hand, there is growing enthusiasm for (although as yet no conclusive evidence about the effectiveness of) a variety of initiatives that are aimed at informing and involving local communities in a more positive fashion, some of which are also beginning to attract attention in the UK. These fit well with, and hence derive extra impetus from, a broader central government agenda of 'civil renewal' and community engagement (Blunkett 2003).

One of the best known is 'Circles of Support', originally imported into Britain from the USA via the Wolvercote specialist clinic for sex offender treatment and now being piloted in several areas. In brief, the idea stemmed from recognition that many sex offenders are socially isolated and thus have no one to support any efforts they make to avoid reoffending or to recognize signs that they may be about to do so. Indeed, such isolation may be used in a perverse way by sex offenders to sustain their offending behaviour, thus increasing the risk to the community. In the words of one convicted paedophile: 'In order for a sex offender to succeed he needs secrecy, isolation… He needs to feel unwanted, pathetic, of low self-esteem, unloved, self-pitying and rejected by "normal" adults.'[13]

The intervention attempts to counteract the social isolation of individual offenders by providing a 'circle' of local volunteers who maintain regular contact with them. In addition to providing social support, the volunteers are trained to provide relapse prevention help and to identify 'warning signals' for risky behaviour. They will also inform the statutory authorities if the risky behaviour appears to warrant it (Kemshall and Maguire 2005).

Another important community-based initiative is 'Stop it Now', through which partnerships of voluntary and statutory agencies provide a combination of education, awareness raising and a helpline to offer advice and support, both to people who suspect abuse and to offenders or potential offenders who want to stop their own abusive thoughts and behaviour (Freeman-Longo and Blanchard 1998). A small number of similar projects have been set up in the UK (see www.stopitnow.org.uk). As in the USA, public education is emphasized, information is disseminated to train members of the public to identify 'warning signs' and sex offenders are urged to come forward for treatment and advice.

Both the above approaches recognize that sex offenders are members of communities and aim to broaden the responsibility for 'policing' them beyond statutory agencies like police and probation. Thus, Circles of Support uses selected volunteers to create a 'pseudo-community' around the offender, combining reintegration and support with community surveillance. 'Stop it Now' goes further, theoretically locating responsibility for dealing with sex offenders within the whole community, as well as offering treatment and other services for those prepared to self-disclose. Importantly, too, both seek to redress the demonization of sex offenders and to offer constructive community-based techniques for their long-term management. Although not yet evaluated, they appear to offer some promising solutions to the problem of how to engage in a constructive dialogue with the public on the deeply emotive subject of sex offenders and risk (Maguire and Kemshall 2004; Kemshall and Maguire 2005).

Whilst the above kinds of initiatives have so far developed piecemeal and on a small scale in England and Wales, a more holistic approach has been evident in Scotland, where the Cosgrove Report set out an integrated and multi-pronged strategy for reducing the risk of sex offending, at the heart of which is an emphasis on communicating with and involving the public. The report (Cosgrove 2001: 20) stated:

> We have noted the concerns expressed by local communities about sex offenders living in their area. Emotive responses may be understandable but they are counter-productive. It is important for lead agencies to engage local communities by helping them to understand the risks posed when a sex offender goes underground, making it more difficult for the police to keep track of him. It is far better for communities to be involved in finding solutions as part of a strategic plan than feeling that they themselves must take on what is likely to be a less effective response in a way that does not reduce the risk posed by the offender ... The aim should be to harness the concerns of local communities through open dialogue.

The above examples all reflect to some extent what seems to be a gradually emerging consensus about the basic ingredients necessary for a successful strategy to manage the risk from known sex offenders in a particular community. The same thinking applies whether or not 'community notification' (the release of offenders' names and addresses) is practised. Key ingredients appear to include the following:

- Inclusionary strategies such as 'Circles of Support' to reduce the social isolation of offenders and enhance risk management, community surveillance and reintegration.

- Direct engagement of communities in risk management.

- A strong emphasis on public education and developing public awareness.

- Frequent face-to-face contact and dialogue between professionals (particularly the police) and the local community.

- Support to those who receive information.

- Assistance to parents, children and communities to 'self-risk manage'.

It is now widely recognized that information dissemination and school education must be handled with care to avoid creating either fearful children or vigilante action. An important principle seems to be that if a significant item of 'risk knowledge' is passed to the public (and with it the burden of anxiety, fear and resentment), then this should be supported with practical advice on risk management techniques and responsible use of the information. This kind of thinking underpins many of the better managed community notification schemes in the USA, which combine dissemination of information about high-risk sex offenders with the provision of advice and written material on child sex abuse prevention. In the words of a police officer responsible for the register and notification in Seattle: 'Doing community notification without doing community education is like smoking a cigarette while you're standing in a pool of gasoline. You are setting yourself up for a disaster' (Freeman-Longo and Blanchard 1998: 110).

Concluding comments
Over the past two or three decades, policies in relation to 'predatory' violent and sexual offending have generally speaking conformed to what Connelly and Williamson (2000) term a 'community protection model', whereby high priority is given to the safety of the general public (in many cases, children), and there is an emphasis on exclusionary interventions (including lengthy imprisonment, 'tagging' and restrictions on movement in licence conditions), particularly for sex offenders. Although 'partnership' working has become a core feature of these policies, this has been largely restricted to state agencies, and a highly secretive, closed professional expert system of risk management has evolved. This general approach has not on the whole made communities feel 'safer': on the contrary, it has been associated with rises in fear of crime, and increasingly punitive attitudes towards (and in some cases, 'demonization' of) offenders. There has also been observed a growing sense of distance – and sometimes mistrust – between professionals and the public (Kemshall and Maguire 2001, 2005). In the long term, this is an unproductive and ineffective approach to risk management. Particularly where sex offenders are concerned, it leads to considerable numbers of socially isolated and rejected ex-offenders subject to little natural community surveillance, who will require ever-increasing resources to 'manage' them.

However, partly in response to populist challenges to this 'professional monopoly', serious attention is beginning to be paid to ways of genuinely involving communities in risk management. At the extreme, these involve what has been described as a 'public health' (as opposed to 'community protection') model of responding to potentially dangerous offenders – ideally, developing a partnership between professionals and public, in which *whole communities* have an active and appropriately regulated part in their risk management, alongside professionals (Kemshall and Mackenzie 2004; see also Mercy *et al.* 1993). 'Circles and Support', 'Stop it Now' and the Cosgrove Report proposals are good examples of such moves in relation to sex offenders. Of course, this raises the very real question – pertinent to community involvement in responses to all forms of crime and anti-social behaviour, but particularly acute in the case of sex offenders – of whether communities can be persuaded away from virulently punitive or vigilantist responses to people thought to pose a risk, and 'educated' to see the problem and its 'solutions' in similar ways to the 'experts'.

Hate crime: racist and homophobic violence

The term 'hate crime' was coined in America, where it was originally applied to racist violence. It has been used to embrace, at the extreme, genocide, ethnic cleansing and serial killing, but in its more common forms in western societies it manifests itself in assaults, name-calling, harassment and vandalism. The concept has been widened over time to include crimes committed for motives related to differences in sexuality, religion or culture (see Bayley 2002). In the UK, most attention has been paid to racially motivated crime, particularly in the aftermath of the Steven Lawrence Inquiry. That said, recent years have also seen growing attention to homophobic crime and religion-related offences.

Extent and nature of hate crime

Racially aggravated offences were introduced under the Crime and Disorder Act 1998. As a result, nine existing offences in the areas of assault, harassment, criminal damage and public order now have racially aggravated versions which carry higher maximum sentences. The Anti-terrorism Crime and Security Act 2001 added specific offences of religiously aggravated assault, criminal damage, public order and harassment.

The number of racist incidents reported to the police in England and Wales over the last decade or so has risen steadily, apart from a dramatic rise of 300 per cent between 1998 and 2000, half of which took place in the Metropolitan Police Service area. Smith *et al.* (2002) note that the publication of the Macpherson Report on the Lawrence Inquiry had profound effects on both the reporting and recording of racist incidents. Even so, they argue that the recorded figures are still likely to be a fraction of the 'real' total. The number of racially motivated incidents in 2002/3 estimated from BCS data was 206,000, two thirds of these involving personal (as opposed to 'household') crime. Moreover, findings from the 2000 BCS indicate that around 1 in 6 of all incidents of criminal victimization against Asians and African-Caribbeans are believed by the victim to be racially motivated (Clancy *et al.* 2001).

A total of 4,728 individuals were implicated as suspects in racially motivated offences in 2003/4, of whom 3,616 (76 per cent) were prosecuted – predominantly for racially aggravated public order offences (CPS 2004).

Smith *et al.* (2002) argue that violence and racism intertwine and trigger one another in complex configurations of social memory, exclusion and scapegoating. They suggest both cultural and economic dimensions to committing offences involving violent racism, pointing out that most perpetrators they identified in Greater Manchester had few resources, little cultural capital and were excluded from good-quality housing, employment and life changes. They found few 'hard-core racist' offenders *per se* and almost two thirds of their sample reported convictions for other offences – mainly theft, assault and drugs – suggesting that racist offending is often part of a wider pattern of criminal behaviour.

Less is known about hate crime based on the sexual orientation or gender identity of the victim, partly because many victims of, or witnesses to, assaults on lesbian, gay, bisexual or transgender (LGBT) people lack confidence in the criminal justice system and are reluctant to report them to the police. Official figures on reported incidents, therefore, are particularly unreliable as a guide to levels and trends in this kind of crime. The BCS is also relatively unhelpful in this respect. There are, however, a number of useful surveys to draw on. For example, a survey of over 2,500 LGBT people by the National Advisory Group/Policing Lesbian and Gay Communities (1999) found that 21 per cent had suffered physical abuse and 5 per cent had been raped in the last year. A similar figure of 18 per cent (compared to 3 per cent of males in the general population) emerged from a survey of 300 gay men living in Edinburgh (Morrison and MacKay 2000). The latter study also indicates that most anti-gay assaults are committed by strangers, mainly near known gay venues or in the street late at night. Of those gay men experiencing violent attacks, 37 per cent said that they had reported them to the police.

It has further been estimated that 30–50 per cent of same-sex-attracted young people in secondary schools will have directly experienced homophobic bullying (Warwick *et al.* 2004). Such bullying has been associated with high levels of absenteeism and truancy in secondary school (Rivers 2000, 2001).

Finally, there has been little data-gathering until very recently on hate crime with a religious motive. As part of the Crown Prosecution Service (CPS) Racial Incident Monitoring Scheme, 'religiously aggravated' incidents are now being monitored. In 2003/4, just 49 such incidents were recorded by the police. The actual or perceived religion of the victim was Muslim in half these cases, and Jewish in 11 per cent.

Preventing hate crime

As with predatory violent offending more generally, strategies to reduce hate crime pay strong attention to 'tertiary' approaches – i.e. interventions to risk assess, change or control individual known offenders. However, this is an area of offending in which it seems especially important to combine these with wider and more long-term strategies aimed at, for example, public education and improved community relations, in order to tackle the social 'roots' of the problem. Here we briefly discuss examples of a variety of complementary approaches, under the headings of offender control and change; education; situational approaches; and community and multi-agency-based approaches.

Offender control and change   Hate crime has become a priority area in policing over the last few years and a number of enforcement strategies have been developed and recommended. The Association of Chief Police Officers (ACPO) (2000) suggests that arrest and fast-track prosecution, anti-social behaviour orders, active acquisition of CCTV and photographic images of activities, and automatic number-plate recognition (ANPR) of vehicles should all be considered in an effort to target known perpetrators. They also discuss the potential for evicting perpetrators of hate crime from their homes under the Housing Act, as well as advocating use of the media to 'name and shame' those implicated.

Where convicted and sentenced offenders are concerned, the main direction of policy appears to be a combination of tougher sentences (especially longer terms of imprisonment) and efforts to change their behaviour, thinking and attitudes. Whilst the latter includes, in some cases, attendance at cognitive-behavioural or anger management programmes designed for violent offenders generally, it has been argued that some racist and homophobic offenders are unlikely to benefit from these (indeed, they may even be counterproductive) and may require specially designed programmes attended only by those involved in hate crime (HMIP 2005: 34).

Education The longer-term prevention of hate crime should clearly involve education of young children in schools about diversity, as well as efforts to tackle behaviour such as name-calling and bullying, which is often directed against people who are perceived as 'different'. Warwick *et al.* (2004) state that there is emerging good practice in preventing homophobic bullying in schools, quoting evidence to suggest that both a whole-school approach (with a clear anti-hate ethos) and specific classroom activities are needed to prevent homophobic incidents. Approaches that have been successful in encouraging learning about sexual orientation include drama-based videos, talks by external visitors and theatre-based education. Identifying opportunities across the curriculum for pupils to reflect on rights, fairness and discrimination are also highlighted by the authors as important means of tackling homophobic sentiment. Kohatsu and Sasao (2003: 157) likewise view schools as a key arena within which to disseminate anti-hate sentiment. They suggest that classes on the psychology of race be made an integral part of the school curriculum and argue that race education programmes must be seen as much more than merely the 'theme of the day'. They also advocate extending education regarding race and racial identity beyond the academic setting to include the family and community via the use of community workshops and seminars. Other means of promoting anti-hate sentiment include the media as well as the use of advertising and marketing – such as beer mats, till receipts, tax discs, stationery, wrist bands, stickers, posters – to make it 'cool' to be anti-racist and anti-homophobic, 'uncool' to be a hater (ACPO 2000).

Situational approaches There is also considerable scope for 'primary' (situational) approaches, where the main focus is on identifying the locations of prevalent hate offences and taking steps to change the environment or conditions surrounding them. For example, ACPO (2000) have suggested the installation of high-profile CCTV cameras in identified hate-crime hotspots, together with improved lighting and crime-aware design of bus shelters and telephone boxes. Some forms of hate crime are closely associated with particular activities or events and allow for a more focused intervention strategy involving close surveillance. An obvious example is racist chanting and violence inside football grounds, which was quite prevalent in England in the 1990s, but has been greatly reduced through a variety of measures including CCTV surveillance and large-scale police officer presence at matches. Such arenas also offer the potential for 'secondary' prevention strategies such as intensive anti-racist campaigns. ACPO (2000) suggested anti-racist and anti-homophobic messages in programmes and brochures, together with slogans on static display and on the garments of stewards, officials and players. Since then, the 'Kick Racism out of Football' slogan has been widely displayed in these ways, and players (and indeed the broadcast media) have played a prominent part in reinforcing the message. There is no direct research evidence to show that it has had an impact, but anecdotally there appears to have been something of a cultural shift and, for example, the once common practice of racist groups using football grounds as recruiting areas is no longer readily visible.

Preventive measures aimed at protecting individual victims (or potential victims) have also been used quite widely. It is possible, for example, to 'target harden' homes at risk of arson attack through measures such as anti-arson mailboxes, fire extinguishers, fire-resistant door mats, and smoke and flame detectors. Ways of facilitating access to assistance when violent attacks are threatened – as well as providing reassurance to people fearful of attack – include panic-button telephone units and telephone helplines staffed by volunteers who speak different languages. ACPO (2000) also suggests that 'Ringmaster' (a computer-controlled telephone message system normally used to pass information to Shopwatch, Pubwatch and Neighbourhood Watch) could be adapted to send information to potential victims of hate crime and organizations representing their interests. However, in discussing victim-focused interventions the authors stress that care should be taken to avoid restrictions of lifestyle that would themselves constitute a form of victimization (ACPO 2000: 67; see also Kohatsu and Sasao 2003).

Community and multi-agency approaches   Finally, potentially the most effective approach to the reduction of hate crime (and, indeed, most other forms of crime) is one that involves a variety of agencies, engages the local community and integrates a number of different preventive strategies. In the UK, such multi-pronged initiatives are increasingly being co-ordinated and implemented under the 'community safety' agenda pursued by Crime and Disorder Reduction Partnerships (CDRPs).

As Bayley (2002) emphasizes, the successful maintenance of community safety depends largely on the willingness of the public to assist the authorities, and especially the police, by reporting crime and giving information: arbitrary and abusive policing alienates the public and reduces their willingness to come forward. This is particularly relevant to hate crime, as it has long been recognized that police attitudes to both ethnic minorities and gay people – and perceptions by members of those communities of police attitudes towards them – have hindered the communication and co-operation that are vital to tackling it effectively. However, in the UK, both the Lawrence Inquiry and sustained government attention to gay rights have provided opportunities for senior police management to drive through policies aimed at significantly changing the organization's culture, attitudes and responses in relation to 'diversity' issues. As a consequence, considerable success has recently been claimed by the police – especially in collaboration with other agencies through CDRPs – in engaging the trust and co-operation of both minority ethnic and LGBT communities in efforts to reduce hate crime. McGhee (2003: 27), who notes that such offences have become a high-priority target for many police forces and local authorities, argues that:

> Policing is no longer concerned with driving sexual minority communities (such as gay men) underground. Rather, new policing styles and practices are emerging in relation to the LGBT community where the primary objective is that of attempting to open and improve channels of communication between this community and the police.

McGhee reviewed the success of the Hidden Targets Multi-agency Group that was established in October 2001 in Southampton (see also Southampton Gay Community Health Service 2001). The group includes representatives from 17 statutory and voluntary organizations and agencies across Hampshire. Positive findings were reported suggesting that greater outreach and publicity were creating greater confidence amongst the LGBT community in the reporting process and court services. In addition, work completed during the first year had enabled services to respond more effectively to people experiencing homophobic and transphobic harassment. However, attention was drawn to a failure to engage ordinary (non-agency affiliated) LGBT individuals in the running of the project – a problem common in multi-agency community safety initiatives of all kinds (Ballintyne and Fraser 2000).

Finally, in reviewing five multi-agency projects in the USA designed to prevent hate crime, Wessler (2000) found that the most effective approaches included co-ordination amongst all components of the criminal justice system, combined with focused efforts to address the needs of victims, diversion programmes for young people and activities encouraging hate crime prevention in schools. He singled out as a particularly good model the Los Angeles County District Attorney's JOLT (Juvenile Offenders Learning Tolerance) programme, a hate crime initiative aimed at young people that combines prevention, early intervention and prosecution and, critically, is community based. JOLT incorporates education and training for school staff to explore issues of bias, prejudice and hate violence, as well as in reconciliation techniques. At the same time, it incorporates a pre-prosecution diversion programme for juveniles 12–18-years-old who have engaged in 'bias-motivated misconduct' or have committed low-level hate crimes. Most are given the option of being suspended or expelled from school or participating in the diversion programme. The latter involves signing a JOLT contract stipulating that they must complete an intensive anti-hate curriculum; attend a programme focusing on anger management and conflict resolution; write letters of apology to the victims; fulfil a restitution agreement, if appropriate; and attend school, receive satisfactory grades and demonstrate good citizenship. Those considered as 'hard core' offenders and unsuitable for diversion are prosecuted.

Concluding remarks

This chapter has covered only a small proportion of the wide variety of forms in which sexual and violent crime is manifested, but has illustrated a number of the key general points which we set out to make. These include the following:

1. The importance of recognizing this variety, including the variety of underlying factors which help to explain why certain patterns of crime emerge in different areas and circumstances, and involve people with particular characteristics. The examples we have given clearly suggest that there is no 'one size fits all' preventive strategy to reduce 'violence', but that strategies must be based on understanding and analysis of the key features and social context of the specific type (or 'cluster') of violent or sexual behaviour that one seeks to reduce.

2. Recognition that, although any preventive strategy against violent crime (as against almost any form of crime) needs a core focus, it is more likely to be effective if part of an integrated, co-ordinated and 'multi-pronged' set of interventions to attack the problem from a variety of angles. This usually necessitates multi-agency partnership and collaboration, ideally with each partner being clear about how their work contributes to an overall plan; critically, too, it necessitates thought-about ways of genuinely involving 'the community' in the enterprise.

3. The importance of maintaining a long-term as well as a short-term perspective. This entails attention to 'structure' as well as to 'psyche' and 'circumstances', and recognition that early achievements in crime reduction (especially those gained through methods such as enforcement, exclusion or surveillance) are likely to be sustained only if crime reduction interventions are seen as part of much broader, long-term policies aimed at tackling fundamental problems such as social exclusion or cultures which condone oppressive behaviour against particular social groups.

As noted at the outset, 'violent and sexual crime' is a slippery concept, very difficult to quantify with any confidence. Despite considerable amounts of research, there are few conclusive statements that can be made about the effectiveness – and especially the long-term effectiveness – of any specific way of responding to 'it'. Nevertheless, it is argued that, in the absence of certainty, the kinds of analytical approach outlined here offer the most logical way forward.

Selected further reading

There are relatively few discussions of the prevention of violence as a whole. Two exceptions are James Gilligan's *Preventing Violence* (2001) and Reiss and Roth's *Understanding and Preventing Violence* (1993). There is also a useful short booklet published in 2002 by Betsy Stanko *et al. – Taking Stock: What do we Know about Interpersonal*

Violence? Most often, however, the prevention of violence is discussed either within general texts on crime prevention or in publications focusing on specific forms of violence. An example of the former is Ken Pease's chapter 'Crime reduction' in the *Oxford Handbook of Criminology* (M. Maguire, R. Morgan and R. Reiner eds, 2002).

Where specific forms of violence are concerned, there is a considerable literature on homicide, much of which is summarized in Brookman and Maguire's (forthcoming) review, 'Reducing homicide: a review of the possibilities'. Brookman's (2005) book *Understanding Homicide* (specifically chap. 11) also covers some of this ground. Other recommended texts are *Homicide: Patterns, Prevention and Control* (Strang and Gerull 1993), 'Intervention in lethal violence' (Hall 1999) and 'The police role in preventing homicide: considering the impact of problem-orientated policing on the prevalence of murder' (White *et al.* 2003). Finally, Jenny Mouzos' *Homicidal Encounters: A Study of Homicide in Australia 1989–99* (2000) contains a useful section on the prevention of homicide.

Probably the most comprehensive literature reviews on preventing domestic violence are Part 2 of Mary Barnish's *Domestic Violence: A Literature Review* (2004) and Paradine and Wilkinson's *A Research and Literature Review: Protection and Accountability: The Reporting, Investigation and Prosecution of Domestic Violence Cases* (2004). Other very useful sources include the Metropolitan Police Service's (2003) *Findings from the Multi-agency Domestic Violence Murder Reviews in London,* the Home Office's (2003) *Safety and Justice: The Government's Proposals on Domestic Violence* and Gilchrist and Kebbell's 'Domestic violence: current issues in definitions and interventions with perpetrators in the UK' (2004). Finally, for discussions and evaluations of some of the most up-to-date techniques for reducing domestic violence and protecting victims, see Cook *et al.*'s *Evaluation of Specialist Domestic Violence Courts/Fast Track Systems* (2004) and Amanda Robinson's *Domestic Violence MARACs (Multi-agency Risk Assessment Conferences) for Very High-risk Victims in Cardiff, Wales: A Process and Outcome Evaluation* (2004).

On street robbery, useful sources are Tilley *et al.*'s (2004) *Problem-solving Street Crime: Practical Lessons from the Street Crime Initiative* and Jonathan Smith's (2003) *The Nature of Personal Robbery.*

Much of the work on sex offending has concentrated on ways of 'managing' high-risk offenders. Two edited books with several useful chapters are Kemshall and MacKenzie's (2004) *Managing Sex Offender Risk* and Matravers' (2005) *Sex Offenders in the Community: Contexts, Challenges and Responses.* For a detailed study of practice in this area, see Maguire *et al.*'s (2001) *Risk Management of Sexual and Violent Offenders: The Work of Public Protection Panels.*

There is very little written on the prevention of hate crime in the UK. The main sources recommended are ACPO's (2000) *Identifying and Combating Hate Crime,* McGhee's (2003) 'Hidden targets, hidden harms: community safety and sexual minority communities' and Bayley's (2002) 'Policing hate: what can be done'.

Notes

1. There are, of course, important exceptions, notably Stan Cohen's (2001) book, *States of Denial: Knowing about Atrocities and Suffering.*
2. The terms 'prevention' and 'reduction' are used interchangeably throughout the chapter. Generally speaking, 'reduction' has been replacing 'prevention' over recent years in both academic and practice literature, although there appears to be no strong reason for this beyond a desire to reflect more modesty about what is achievable.

3. As noted earlier, police figures are not routinely separated into domestic and non-domestic offences, but a special analysis of assaults recorded in 1990–2 indicated that 52 per cent of violent attacks on women (and 19 per cent of those on men) took place in their own or the offender's home (Maguire 1997: 155).
4. Similar rates, ranging from 23 to 28 per cent, have been identified in the Netherlands, the USA, Australia, New Zealand and Canada (Mirrlees-Black 1999).
5. For example, the National Commission of the Inquiry into the Prevention of Child Abuse defines child abuse as consisting of 'anything which individuals, institutions or processes do or fail to do which directly or indirectly harms children or damages their prospects of a safe and healthy development into adulthood' (NCIPCA 1996: 4).
6. www.surestart.gov.uk; see www.nspcc.org.uk/html/home/informationresources/CDtilbury.htm and Wright (2004) for information about the Safe Kids project.
7. There were estimated to be a further 66,000 alcohol-related muggings and 320,000 alcohol-related incidents of domestic assault, but the latter figure is likely to be a gross underestimate for reasons described earlier.
8. See http://www.the-sia.org.uk/licences/doors-transition.asp.
9. It is interesting to compare the ease with which legislation such as the 'two strikes and you're out' sentences for serious sexual and violent offenders in the Crime (Sentences) Act 1997 passed through Parliament, compared with the fierceness of the principled debates about proposed 'dangerousness' legislation in the 1970s (following concerns about 'dangerous psychopaths': see Butler Committee 1975; Bottoms 1977; Floud and Young 1981; Radzinowicz and Hood 1981a, 1981b; for more recent discussion, see Kemshall and Maguire 2001).
10. On the Mental Health Bill, see http://www.markwalton.net/04/reform/index.asp; on terrorism, see Brandon (2004).
11. It is also open to those responsible for MAPPA to take action in respect of other offenders, and even unconvicted people, who come to notice as potentially posing a risk of serious harm to the public.
12. See, for example, comments by Home Office minister Beverley Hughes at www.bbc.co.uk/news ('Sarah's Law unworkable', 13 December 2001).
13. 'Stephen', quoted at www.bbc.co.uk/news ('Paedophiles may go underground', (13 December 2001).

References

ACPO (2000) *Identifying and Combating Hate Crime*. London: ACPO.

Aldridge, M.L. and Browne, K.D. (2003) 'Perpetrators of spousal homicide', *Trauma, Violence and Abuse*, 4: 265–76.

Allen, C., Dodd, T. and Salisbury, H. (2005) *Crime in England and Wales: Quarterly Update to September 2004. Home Office Statistical Bulletin* 03/05. London: Home Office.

Allen, J., Nicholas, S., Salisbury, H. and Wood, M. (2003) 'Nature of burglary, vehicle and violent crime', in C. Flood-Page and J. Taylor (eds) *Crime in England and Wales 2001/2002: Supplementary Volume. Home Office Statistical Bulletin* 10/03. London: Home Office.

Ballintyne, S. and Fraser, P. (2000) 'It's good to talk, but it's not good enough', in S. Ballintyne *et al.* (eds) *Secure Foundations: Key Issues in Crime Prevention, Crime Reduction and Community Safety*. London: Institute of Public Policy Research.

Barnish, M. (2004) *Domestic Violence: A Literature Review*. London: HM Inspectorate of Probation (available at http://www.homeoffice.gov.uk/docs3/thematic_dv_literaturereview.pdf).

Bayley, D. (2002) 'Policing hate: what can be done', in *Policing and Society*, 12: 83–91.

Bilby, C. and Thatcher, R. (2004) *Early Stages in the Development of the Integrated Domested Abuse Programme (IDAP): Implementing the Duluth Domestic Violence Pathfinder. Online Report 29/04*. London: Home Office (available at http://www.homeoffice.gov.uk/rds/pdfs04/rdsolr2904.pdf).

Blunkett, D. (2003) *Civil Renewal: A New Agenda*. London: Home Office (available at http://www.homeoffice.gov.uk/docs2/civilrennewagenda.pdf).

Bottoms, A. (1977) 'Reflections on the renaissance of dangerousness.' *Howard Journal of Criminal Justice*, 16: 70–96.

Brandon, B. (2004) 'Terrorism, human rights and the rule of law: 120 years of the UK's legal response to terrorism', *Criminal Law Review*, 981–97.

Brantingham, P. and Faust, F. (1976) 'A conceptual model of crime prevention', *Crime and Delinquency*, 22: 284–96.

Brookman, F. (2005) *Understanding Homicide*. London: Sage.

Brookman, F. and Maguire, M. (2005) 'Reducing homicide: a review of the possibilities', *Crime Law and Social Change*. Vol. 42, nos. 4–5, pp. 325–403.

Bryan, T. and Doyle, P. (2005) 'Developing multi-agency public protection arrangements', in A. Matravers (ed.) *Sex Offenders in the Community: Contexts, Challenges and Responses*. Cullompton: Willan Publishing.

Budd, T. (2003) *Alcohol-related Assault: Findings from the British Crime Survey. Home Office Online Report 35/03*. London: Home Office (available at http://www.homeoffice.gov.uk/rds/pdfs2/rdsolr3503.pdf).

Bullock, K. and Tilley, N. (eds) (2003) *Crime Reduction and Problem-oriented Policing*. Cullompton: Willan Publishing.

Burton, S., Regan, L. and Kelly, L. (1998) *Supporting Women and Challenging Men: Lessons from the Domestic Violence Intervention Project*. Bristol: University of Bristol and Policy Press.

Butler, Lord (1975) *Report of the Committee on Mentally Disordered Offenders* (Cmnd 6244). London: HMSO.

Butler-Sloss, E. (1988) *Report of the Inquiry into Child Abuse in Cleveland*. London: HMSO.

Cawson, P., Wattam, C., Brooker, S. and Kelly, G. (2000) *Child Maltreatment in the United Kingdom: A Study of the Prevalence of Child Abuse and Neglect*. London: NSPCC (an executive summary is available at www.nspcc.org.uk/inform).

Clancy, A., Hough, M., Aust, R. and Kershaw, C. (2001) *Crime, Policing and Justice: The Experience of Ethnic Minorities. Findings from the 2000 British Crime Survey. HORS 223*. London: Home Office.

Cobley, C. (2000) *Sex Offenders: Law, Policy and Practice*. Bristol: Jordans.

Cobley, C. (2005) 'The legislative framework' in A. Matravers (ed.) *Sex Offenders in the Community: Contexts, Challenges and Responses*. Cullompton: Willan Publishing.

Cohen, S. (2001) *States of Denial: Knowing about Atrocities and Suffering*. Cambridge: Polity Press.

Coleman, C. and Moynihan, J. (1996) *Understanding Crime Data: Haunted by the Dark Figure*. Philadelphia, PA: Open University Press.

Connelly, C. and Williamson, S. (2000) *Review of the Research Literature on Serious Violent and Sexual Offenders. Crime and Criminal Justice Research Findings 46*. Edinburgh: Scottish Executive Central Research Unit.

Cook, D., Burton, M., Robinson, A. and Vallely, C. (2004) *Evaluation of Specialist Domestic Violence Courts/Fast Track Systems*. London: Crown Prosecution Service and Department of Constitutional Affairs (available at http://www.cps.gov.uk/publications/reports/index.html).

Cosgrove, Lady (2001) *The Report of the Expert Panel on Sex Offending*. Edinburgh: Scottish Executive.

CRARG (2003) Website of Co-ordinated Response and Advocacy Resource Group (http://www.crarg.org.uk/about.htm).

Crawford, A. (1998) *Crime Prevention and Community Safety: Politics, Policies and Practices*. Harlow: Longman.

Creighton, S. (2002) *Physical Abuse*. NSPCC information briefing (January) (available at www.nspcc.org.uk/inform).

Crown Prosecution Service (CPS) (2004) *Crown Prosecution Service Racist Incident Monitoring Annual Report 2003–2004*. London: CPS.

Deehan, A. (1999) *Alcohol and Crime: Taking Stock. Crime Reduction Research Series Paper 3*. London: Home Office.

Deehan, A. and Saville, E. (2000) *Crime and Disorder Partnerships: Alcohol Related Crime and Disorder in Audit and Strategy Documents. Briefing Note 9/2000*. London: Home Office.

Department of Health (DOH) (2001) *Children and Young People on Child Protection Registers, Year Ending 31 March 2000: England*. London: Department of Health.

Dobash, R.E. and Dobash, R.P. (2000) 'Evaluating criminal justice interventions for domestic violence', *Crime and Delinquency*, 46: 252–70.

Dobash, R.E., Dobash, R.P., Cavanagh, K. and Lewis, R. (2000) *Changing Violent Men*. Thousand Oaks, CA: Sage.

Dobash, R.P., Dobash, R.E., Cavanaugh, K. and Lewis, R. (1999) 'A research evaluation of British programmes for violent men', *Journal of Social Policy*, 28: 205–33.

Dobash, R.P., Dobash, R.E., Cavanagh, K. and Lewis, R. (2001) *Homicide in Britain: Risk Factors, Situational Contexts and Lethal Interventions* (ESRC violence research programme. Final report). Manchester: Manchester University.

Dobash, R.P., Dobash, R., Cavanagh, K. and Lewis, R. (2002) *Homicide in the Family–New Findings Revealed* (available at http://news.man.ac.uk/1020610359/index_html).

Dodd, T., Nicholas, S., Povey, D. and Walker, A. (2004), *Crime in England and Wales 2003/2004. Home Office Statistical Bulletin 10/04*. London: Home Office.

Eastham, D. (1990) 'Plan it, or suck it and see', in G. Darvill and G. Smale (eds) *Partners in Empowerment: Networks of Innovation in Social Work*. London: National Institute of Social Work.

Elkan, R., Kendrick, D., Hewitt, M., Robinson, J., Tolley, K., Blaim, R., Dewey, M., Williams, D. and Brummell, K. (2000) 'The effectiveness of domiciliary health visiting: a systematic review of international studies and a selective review of the British literature', *Health Technology Assessment*, 4.

Erlich, A. (1996) 'The home-work reality and its effects on children', in *Childhood Matters: The Report of the National Commission of Inquiry into the Prevention of Child Abuse. Volume 2. Background Papers*. London: HMSO.

Felson, M. (2002) *Crime and Everyday Life* (3rd edn). London: Pine Forge.

Finkelhor, D. (1994) 'The international epidemiology of child sexual abuse', *Child Abuse and Neglect*, 18: 409–17.

Floud, J. and Young, W. (1981) *Dangerousness and Criminal Justice*. London: Heinemann.

Freeman-Longo, R.E. and Blanchard, G.T. (1998) *Sexual Abuse in America: Epidemic of the 21st Century*. Brandon, VT: Safer Society Press.

Gilchrist, E. and Blissett, J. (2002) 'Magistrates' attitudes to domestic violence and sentencing options', *Howard Journal*, 41: 348–63.

Gilchrist, E. and Kebbell, M. (2004) 'Domestic violence: current issues in definitions and interventions with perpetrators in the UK', in J.R. Adler (ed.) *Forensic Psychology: Concepts, Debates and Practice*. Cullompton: Willan Publishing.

Gilchrist, E., Johnson, R., Takriti, R., Weston, S., Beech, A. and Kebbell, M. (2003) *Domestic Violence Offenders; Characteristics and Offending Related Needs. Findings* 217. London: Home Office Research, Development and Statistics Directorate.

Gilligan, J. (2001) *Preventing Violence*. London: Thames & Hudson.

Graham, K. and Homel, R. (1997) 'Creating safer bars', in M. Plant *et al.* (eds) *Alcohol: Minimising the Harm – What Works?'* London: Free Association Books.

Hague, G. (2001) 'Multi agency initiatives', in J. Taylor-Browne (ed.) *What Works in Reducing Domestic Violence? A Comprehensive Guide for Professionals*. London: Whiting Birch.

Hall, H. (1999) 'Intervention in lethal violence', in *Lethal Violence: A Sourcebook on Fatal Domestic, Acquaintance and Stranger Violence*. Boca Raton, FL: CRC Press.

Hebenton, B. and Thomas, T. (1996) 'Tracking sex offenders', *Howard Journal*, 35: 97–112.

HMCPSI/HMIC (2004) *Violence at Home: A Joint Thematic Inspection of the Investigation and Prosecution of Cases Involving Domestic Violence*. London: HM Crown Prosecution Inspectorate/HM Inspectorate of Constabulary.

HMIP (2005) *An Inspection of National Probation Service Work with Racially Motivated Offenders* (thematic report, HM Inspectorate of Probation). London: Home Office.

Hobbs, D., Hadfield, P., Lister, S. and Winlow, S. (2002) '"Door Lore": the art and economics of intimidation', *British Journal of Criminology*, 42: 352–70.

Hobbs, D., Hadfield, P., Lister, S. and Winlow, S. (2003) *Bouncers: Violence and Governance in the Night-time Economy*. Oxford: Oxford University Press.

Hobbs, D., Lister, S., Hadfield, P., Winlow, S. and Hall, S. (2000) 'Receiving shadows: liminality, governance and the night-time economy' *British Journal of Sociology*, 51: 701–17.

Holman, R. (2000) *Kids at the Door Revisited*. Lyme Regis: Russell House.

Holtzworth-Munroe, A. and Stuart, G.L. (1994) 'Typologies of male batterers: three sub-types and the differences among them', *Psychological Bulletin*, 116: 476–97.

Holtzworth-Munroe, A., Meehan, J.C., Herron, K., Rehman, U. and Stuart, G.L. (2000) 'Testing the Holtzworth-Munroe and Stuart (1994) batterer typology', *Journal of Consulting and Clinical Psychology*, 68: 1000–19.

Home Office (2000) *HOC 19/2000 Domestic Violence: Revised Circular to the Police*. London: Home Office.

Home Office (2001) *Initial Guidance to the Police and Probation Services on Sections 67 and 68 of the Criminal Justice and Court Services Act 2000*. London: Home Office.

Home Office (2003) *Safety and Justice: The Government's Proposals on Domestic Violence*. London: Home Office.

Homel, R. and Clarke, J. (1994) 'The prediction and prevention of violence in pubs and clubs', in R.V. Clarke (ed.) *Crime Prevention Studies. Vol. 3*. Monsey, NY: Criminal Justice Press.

Hughes, G. (1998) *Understanding Crime Prevention: Social Control, Risk and Late Modernity*. Buckingham: Open University Press.

Jack, G. (2004), 'Child protection at the community level', *Child Abuse Review*, 13: 368–83.

Johnson, S.L. and Grant, B.A. (1999) *Review of Issues Associated with Serious Spouse Abuse among Federally Sentenced Male Offenders* (Research Branch, Correctional Service of Canada) (available at www.csc-scc.gc.ca).

Kemshall, H. and MacKenzie, G. (eds) (2004) *Managing Sex Offender Risk*. London: Jessica Kingsley.

Kemshall, H. and Maguire, M. (2001) 'Public protection, partnership and risk penality: the multi-agency risk management of sexual and violent offenders', *Punishment and Society*, 5: 237–64.

Kemshall, H. and Maguire, M. (2002) 'Community justice, risk management and the role of multi-agency public protection panels', *British Journal of Community Justice*, 1: 11–27.

Kemshall, H. and Maguire, M. (2005) 'Sex offenders, risk penality and the problem of disclosure to the community', in A. Matravers (ed.) *Sex Offenders in the Community: Contexts, Challenges and Responses*. Cullompton: Willan Publishing.

Kitzinger, J. (1999) 'The ultimate neighbour from hell: media framing of paedophiles', in B. Franklin (ed.) *Social Policy, Media and Misrepresentation*. London: Routledge.

Kohatsu, E. and Sasao, T. (2003) 'Perceived racism, racial environments, and hate violence against Asian Americans: research, clinical issues and prevention', in B. Wallace and R. Carter (eds) *Understanding and Dealing with Violence*. London: Sage.

LaFontaine, J. (1990) *Child Sexual Abuse*. Cambridge: Polity Press.

Levi, M. and Maguire, M. (2002) 'Violent crime', in M. Maguire, R. Morgan and R. Reiner (eds) *The Oxford Handbook of Criminology* (3rd edn). Oxford: Oxford University Press.

Lewis, R. (2004) 'Making justice work: effective legal interventions for domestic violence', *British Journal of Criminology*, 44: 204–24.

LGA (2002) *All Day and All of the Night? An LGA Discussion Paper*. London: Local Government Association.

Light, R. (2000) 'Liberalising liquor licensing law: order into chaos?', *New Law Journal*, 23: 926–9.

Lister, S., Hadfield, P., Hobbs, D. and Winlow, S. (2001) 'Accounting for bouncers: occupational licensing as a mechanism for regulation', *Criminal Justice*, 1: 363–84.

Loza, W. and Loza-Fanous, A. (1999) 'The fallacy of reducing rape and violent recidivism by treating anger', *International Journal of Offender Therapy and Comparative Criminology*, 43: 492–502.

Maguire, M. (1992) 'Parole', in E. Stockdale and S. Casale (eds) *Criminal Justice Under Stress*. London: Blackstone Press.

Maguire, M. (1997) 'Crime statistics, patterns and trends: changing perceptions and their implications', in M. Maguire, R. Morgan and R. Reiner (eds) *The Oxford Handbook of Criminology* (1st edn). Oxford: Oxford University Press.

Maguire, M. (2002) 'Crime statistics: the "data explosion" and its implications', in M. Maguire, R. Morgan and R. Reiner (eds) *The Oxford Handbook of Criminology* (3rd edn). Oxford: Oxford University Press.

Maguire, M. (2004) 'The crime reduction programme: reflections on the vision and the reality' *Criminal Justice* (special issue), 43: 213–37.

Maguire, M. and Hopkins, M. (2003) 'Data analysis for problem-solving: alcohol and city centre violence', in K. Bullock and N. Tilley (eds) *Crime Reduction and Problem-oriented Policing*. Cullompton: Willan Publishing.

Maguire, M. and Kemshall, H. (2004) 'Multi-agency public protection arrangements: key issues', in H. Kemshall and G. MacKenzie (eds) *Managing Sex Offender Risk*. London: Jessica Kingsley.

Maguire, M., Kemshall, H., Noaks, L., Wincup, E. and Sharpe, K. (2001), *Risk Management of Sexual and Violent Offenders: The Work of Public Protection Panels. Police Research Series Paper* 139. London: Home Office.

Maguire, M. and Nettleton, H. (2003) *Reducing Alcohol-related Violence and Disorder: An Evaluation of the 'TASC' Project. Home Office Research Study* 265. London: Home Office.

Matravers, A. (ed.) (2005) *Sex Offenders in the Community: Contexts, Challenges and Responses*. Cullompton: Willan Publishing.

Mattinson, J. (2001) *Stranger and Acquaintance Violence: Practice Messages from the British Crime Survey. Home Office Briefing Note* 7/01. London: Home Office.

McAuley, C., Knapp, M., Beecham, J., McCurry, N. and Slead, M. (2004), *Young Families Under Stress: Outcomes and Costs of Home-start Support.* York: Joseph Rowntree Foundation.

McGhee, D. (2003) 'Hidden targets, hidden harms: community safety and sexual minority communities', *Crime Prevention and Community Safety: An International Journal*, 5: 27–40.

Mears, D.P. (2003) 'Research and interventions to reduce domestic violence revictimization', *Trauma, Violence and Abuse*, 44: 127–47.

Mercy, J.A., Rosenberg, M.L., Powell, K.E., Broome, C.V. and Roper, W.L. (1993) 'Public health policy for preventing violence', *Health Affairs*, 12: 7–29.

Metropolitan Police Service (MPS) (2003) *Findings from the Multi-agency Domestic Violence Murder Reviews in London.* London: HPS.

Mirrlees-Black, C. (1999) *Domestic Violence: Findings from a New British Crime Survey Self-completion Questionnaire. Home Office Research Study* 191. London: Home Office Research, Development and Statistics Directorate.

Morley, R. and Mullender, A. (1994) *Preventing Domestic Violence to Women. Crime Prevention Unit Series Paper* 48. London: Home Office Police Research Group.

Morris, S. (1998) *Clubs, Drugs and Doormen. Crime Detection and Prevention Series Paper* 86. London: Home Office Police Research Group.

Morrison, C. and MacKay, A. (2000) *The Experience of Violence and Harassment of Gay Men in the City of Edinburgh.* Edinburgh: Scottish Executive Central Research Unit.

Mouzos, J. (2000) *Homicidal Encounters: A Study of Homicide in Australia 1989–99.* Canberra: Australian Institute of Criminology.

NACRO (2001) *Drink and Disorder: Alcohol, Crime and Anti-social Behaviour.* London: National Association for the Care and Resettlement of Offenders.

Nash, M. (1999) *Police, Probation and Protecting the Public.* London: Blackstone Press.

National Advisory Group (1999) *Breaking the Chain of Hate: A National Survey Examining Levels of Homophobic Crime and Community Confidence towards the Police Service.* Manchester: National Advisory Group/Policing Lesbian and Gay Communities.

National Commission of Inquiry into the Prevention of Child Abuse (1996) *Childhood Matters. Vol. 1. The Report.* London: HMSO.

Paradine, K. and Wilkinson, J. (2004) *A Research and Literature Review: Protection and Accountability: The Reporting, Investigation and Prosecution of Domestic Violence Cases.* Hook, Hampshire: National Centre for Policing Excellence, Centrex.

Pease, K. (2002) 'Crime reduction', in M. Maguire, R. Morgan and R. Reiner (eds) *The Oxford Handbook of Criminology.* Oxford: Oxford University Press.

Pizzey, E. (1974) *Scream Quietly or the Neighbours Will Hear.* Harmondsworth: Penguin Books.

Plotnikoff, J. and Woolfson, R. (2000) *Where Are They Now? An Evaluation of Sex Offender Registration in England and Wales. Police Research Series Paper* 126. London: Home Office.

Power, H. (1999) 'The Crime Disorder Act, 1998: sex offenders, privacy and the police', *Criminal Law Review*, 3–16.

Power, H. (2005) 'Disclosing information on sex offenders: the human rights implications', in A. Matravers (ed.) *Sex Offenders in the Community: Contexts, Challenges and Responses.* Cullompton: Willan Publishing.

Prentky, R. (1996) 'Community notification and constructive risk reduction', *Journal of Interpersonal Violence*, 11: 295–8.

Purser, R. (1997) *Prevention Approaches to Alcohol Related Crime – a Review of a Community Based Initiative from a UK Midlands City.* Birmingham: Aquarius.

Radzinowicz, L. and Hood, R. (1981a) 'A dangerous direction in sentencing reform', *Criminal Law Review*, 713–24.

Radzinowicz, L. and Hood, R. (1981b) 'Dangerousness and criminal justice: a few reflections', *Criminal Law Review*, 756–61.

Reiss and Roth (1993) *Understanding and Preventing Violence*. Washington, DC: National Academy Press.

Richardson, A. and Budd, T. (2003) *Alcohol, Crime and Disorder: A Study of Young Adults. Home Office Research Study* 263. London: Home Office.

Richardson, A., Budd, T., Engineer, R., Phillips, A., Thompson, J. and Nicholls, J. (2003) *Drinking, Crime and Disorder. Research Findings* 185. London: Home Office (available at http://www.homeoffice.gov.uk/rds/pdfs2/r185.pdf).

Riggs, D.S., Caulfield, M.B. and Street, A.E. (2000) 'Risk for domestic violence: factors associated with perpetration and victimization', *Journal of Clinical Psychology*, 56: 1289–316.

Rivers, I. (2000) 'Social exclusion, absenteeism and sexual minority youth', *Support for Learning*, 15: 13–17.

Rivers, I. (2001) 'The bullying of sexual minorities at school: its nature and long-term correlates', *Educational and Child Psychology*, 18: 33–46.

Robinson, A. (2004) *Domestic Violence MARACs (Multi-agency Risk Assessment Conferences) for Very High-risk Victims in Cardiff, Wales: A Process and Outcome Evaluation*. Cardiff: School of Social Sciences, Cardiff University (available at http://www.cardiff.ac.uk/socsi/whoswho/robinson.html).

Robinson, A. (2005) *The Cardiff Women's Safety Unit: Understanding the Costs and Consequences of Domestic Violence*. Cardiff, School of Social Sciences, Cardiff University (available at http://www.cardiff.ac.uk/socsi/whoswho/robinson.html).

Rudin, J. (1996) 'Megan's Law: can it stop sexual predators – and at what cost to constitutional rights?', *Criminal Justice*, 11: 2–10.

Schram, D. and Milloy, C. (1995) *Community Notification: A Study of Offender Characteristics and Recidivism*. Seattle, WA: Urban Policy Research.

Shepard, M. (1992) 'Predicting batterer recidivism five years after community intervention', *Journal of Family Violence*, 7: 167–78.

Simmons, J. (2000) *Review of Crime Statistics: A Discussion Document*. London: Home Office.

Simmons, J., Legg, C. and Hosking, R. (2003) *National Crime Recording Standard (NCRS): An Analysis of the Impact on Recorded Crime. Part One. The National Picture. Online Report* 31/03. London: Home Office (available at http://www.homeoffice.gov.uk/rds/pdfs2/rdsolr3103.pdf).

Skyner, D.R. and Waters, J. (1999) 'Working with perpetrators of domestic violence to protect women and children: a partnership between Cheshire Probation Service and the NSPCC', *Child Abuse Review*, 8: 46–54.

Smith, D., Ray, L. and Wastell, L. (2002) *Racial Violence in Greater Manchester. ESRC Research Findings*. London: ESRC Violence Research Programme.

Smith, J. (2003) *The Nature of Personal Robbery. Home Office Research Study* 254. London: Home Office.

Smith, J. and Allen, C. (2004) *Violent Crime in England and Wales. Home Office Online Report* 18/04. London: Home Office (available at http://www.homeoffice.gov.uk/rds/pdfs04/rdsolr1804.pdf).

Social Issues Research Centre (SIRC) (2002) *Counting the Cost: The Measurement and Recording of Alcohol-related Violence and Disorder*. London: The Portman Group.

Southampton Gay Community Health Service (2001) *Hidden Targets: Lesbian Women and Gay Men's Experiences of Homophobic Crime and Harassment in Southampton*. Southampton: Southampton City Council.

Southampton Gay Community Health Service (2002), *Hidden Targets: Lesbian Women and Gay Men's Experiences of Homophobic Crime and Harassment in Southampton – Progress Report*. Southampton: Southampton City Council.

Stanko, B., O'Beirne, M. and Zaffuto, G. (2002) *Taking Stock: What do we Know about Interpersonal Violence? ESRC Violence Research Programme.* London: Royal Holloway, University of London.

Strang, H. and Gerull, S. (1993) 'Homicide: patterns, prevention and control', in *Australian Institute of Criminology Conference Proceedings.*

Strategy Unit (2004) *Alcohol Harm Reduction Strategy for England.* London: Cabinet Office Strategy Unit (available at www.strategy.gov.uk).

Thomas, T. (2001) 'Sex offenders, the Home Office and the Sunday papers', *Journal of Social Welfare and Family Law,* 23: 103–4.

Thompson, K. (1998) *Moral Panics.* London: Routledge.

Tierney, J. and Hobbs, D. (2003) *Alcohol-related Crime and Disorder Data: Guidance for Local Partnerships.* London: Home Office (available at www.homeoffice.gov.uk/rds/onlinepubs1.html).

Tilley, N. (2004) 'Applying theory-driven evaluation to the British Crime Reduction Programme: the theories of the programme and of its evaluations', *Criminal Justice,* (Special Issue), 4: 255–76.

Tilley, N., Smith, J., Finer, S., Erol, R., Charles, C. and Dobby, J. (2004) *Problem-solving Street Crime: Practical Lessons from the Street Crime Initiative.* London: Home Office.

Topalli, V., Wright, R. and Fornango, R. (2002) 'Drug dealers, robbery, and retaliation: vulnerability, deterrence, and the contagion of violence', *British Journal of Criminology,* 42: 337–51.

Tuck, M. (1989) *Drinking and Disorder: A Study of Non-Metropolitan Violence. Home Office Research Study* 108. London: Home Office.

Upson, A., Povey, D. and Gray, A. (2004) 'Violent crime' in T. Dodd *et al.* (eds) *Crime in England and Wales, 2003–2004. Home Office Statistical Bulletin* 10/04. London: Home Office (available at http://www.homeoffice.gov.uk/rds/pdfs04/hosb1004.pdf).

Walby, S. and Allen, J. (2004) *Domestic Violence, Sexual Assault and Stalking: Findings from the British Crime Survey. Home Office Research Study* 276. London: Home Office Research, Development and Statistics Directorate.

Walby, S. and Myhill, A. (2001a) 'New survey methodologies in researching violence against women', *British Journal of Criminology,* 41: 502–22.

Walby, S. and Myhill, A. (2001b) 'Assessing and managing risk', in J. Taylor-Browne (ed.) *What Works in Reducing Domestic Violence? A Comprehensive Guide for Professionals.* London: Whiting and Birch.

Walters, A. (2001) *Acid Row.* London: Macmillan.

Waltz, J., Babcock, J.C., Jacobson, N.S. and Gottman, J.M. (2000) 'Testing a typology of batterers', *Journal of Consulting and Clinical Psychology,* 68: 658–69.

Warwick, I., Chase, E., Aggleton, P. and Sanders, S. (2004) *Homophobia, Sexual Orientation and Schools: A Review and Implications for Action. Research Report* 594. London: Department for Education and Skills.

Wattam, C. (1999) 'The prevention of child abuse', *Children and Society,* 13: 317–29.

Weisz, A.N., Tomlan, R.M. and Saunders, D. (2000) 'Assessing the risk of severe domestic violence: the importance of survivors' predictions', *Journal of Interpersonal Violence,* 15: 75–90.

Wessler, S. (2000) *Promising Practices against Hate Crimes: Five State and Local Demonstration Projects.* Washington, DC: US Department of Justice.

White, M. *et al.* (2003) 'The police role in preventing homicide: considering the impact of problem-orientated policing on the prevalence of murder', *Journal of Research in Crime and Delinquency,* 40: 194–225.

Wiggins, M., Oakley, A., Roberts, I., Turner, H., Rajan, L., Austerberry, H., Mujica, R. and Mugford, M. (2002) *The Social Support and Family Health Study: A Randomised Controlled Trial and Economic Evaluation of Two Alternative Forms of Postnatal Support for Mothers Living in Disadvantaged Inner City Areas. Final Project Report for the NHS*

R&D Health Technology Assessment Programme. London: Social Research Unit, Institute of Education.

Wilczynski, A. (1997) *Child Homicide.* London: Greenwich Medical.

Wilczynski, A. and Sinclair, K. (1999) 'Moral tales: representations of child abuse in the quality and tabloid media', *Australian and New Zealand Journal of Criminology,* 32: 262–83.

World Health Organization (2002) *World Report on Violence and Health: Summary.* Geneva: World Health Organization.

Worrall, A. (1997) *Punishment in the Community: The Future of Criminal Justice.* London: Longman.

Wright, S. (2004) 'Child protection in the community: a community development approach', *Child Abuse Review,* 13: 384–98.

Young, A. (1996) *Imagining Crime: Textual Outlaws and Criminal Conversations.* London: Sage.

Zevitz, R. and Farkas, M. (2000) 'Sex offender community notification: managing high risk criminals or exacting further vengeance?', *Behavioural Sciences and the Law,* 18: 375–91.

Chapter 20

Drugs and alcohol

Tim McSweeney and Mike Hough

Introduction

Drug-related crime began to emerge as a significant policy issue in Britain during the late 1980s. Since then it has become progressively more visible as a social and political problem. Alcohol-related crime and disorder have tended to attract policy attention in phases. The intense concern about 'lager louts' in the late 1980s abated, but has now re-emerged as a policy issue – with more explicit associations with the late-night economy. As a result, there is now a consensus that there are clear forms of *association* between both drug and alcohol use and crime, and a degree of consensus, at least, that there are causal links between some forms of drug or alcohol use and some forms of crime. However the nature of these links is complex and the direction of these links remains the source of much debate (Best *et al.* 2001a; Simpson 2003; Alcohol Concern 2004). Nevertheless this association now forms a key tenet underpinning recent drug, alcohol and crime reduction strategies in Britain.

In keeping with much of the contemporary debate, we have focused here mainly upon the links between drug use and property offences such as burglary, shoplifting and robbery. We consider the links between alcohol and crime (particularly those offences involving violence) but we have not explored the drugs and violence nexus. Violence clearly occurs in many types of drug market, and for some drugs there are relationships between intoxication and violence (see Goldstein 1985; Dobinson and Ward 1986; Anglin and Speckart 1988; Jarvis and Parker 1989; Harrison and Backenheimer 1998). We have avoided this terrain simply because of constraints of space.

This is not an exhaustive review. The research evidence exploring and describing the links between drug use, alcohol and crime has already been comprehensively reviewed elsewhere.[1] It is not our intention to duplicate this work. Instead, by focusing predominantly on recent British research, we aim to do three things:

- Present the latest data on the nature and extent of drug use, alcohol consumption and offending behaviour amongst different sections of the population.

- Overview the key theories that have been developed to help explain some of the different interactions and links between drugs, alcohol and offending that have been observed.

- Consider the effectiveness of different strategies aimed at reducing drug and alcohol-related crime.

Finally we apply Ekblom's (2003) '5 Is' framework and focus in more detail on one recent intervention aimed at reducing drug-related crime: the drug treatment and testing order (DTTO). In using the 5 Is to explore the effectiveness of the DTTO as a crime reduction measure we consider:

- the rationale for introducing the orders;
- how they have been implemented, developed and delivered; and
- the evidence for their effectiveness.

We end by discussing some recent developments and offer our conclusions about the prospects of the DTTO and similar forms of coerced treatment as a strategy for reducing crime.

Drug taking, alcohol use and offending in the overall population

A large number of people engage in illicit drug use in developed countries throughout the world. Most do so in a fairly controlled way, with cannabis being the most widely used drug. According to United Nations' estimates, 185 million people worldwide – approximately 5 per cent of those aged 15 years and over – have consumed an illicit drug (UNODC 2004). The 2002/3 British Crime Survey (BCS) estimates that 36 per cent of the adult (16–59) population in England and Wales have used illicit drugs at some stage in their life, and 12 per cent have used illicit drugs during the previous 12 months. This represents around 4 million people using illicit drugs over a year. Around 1 million will have used Class A drugs. Use is largely concentrated amongst the young: 47 per cent of people between the ages of 16 and 24 have used an illicit drug at some time in their life and 28 per cent will have done so during the last year (Condon and Smith 2003). The early/mid-20s are the peak age for drug use.

Cannabis is by far the most frequently consumed illicit drug in England and Wales, with around 3 million users in 2004. Amphetamines, cocaine and ecstasy are the next most commonly used drugs. All three drugs show similar levels of use, according to the BCS: 2 per cent of the adult population. Use of heroin and crack is rarer. There has been an increase in the use of cannabis, crack and cocaine since the mid-1990s.

Alcohol use is, of course, much more widespread. Over nine out of ten adults in Britain, around 40 million people, consume alcohol, with the majority experiencing no problems most of the time (Cabinet Office 2004: 9). Findings from the BCS (2000) suggest that there were 1.2 million incidents of alcohol-related violence during 1999; approximately 23,000 incidents each week where the victim considered the perpetrator to be under the influence of alcohol (Budd 2003). Consistent with an overall downward trend in violence, the BCS data suggest that the rate of alcohol-related violence fell between 1995 and 1999. However, Budd also notes that most alcohol-related incidents involving strangers and/or acquaintances go unreported to the police. Those most at risk are unemployed men under 30 who themselves drink heavily. Recent research has also explored the role of alcohol in relation to violence and the night-time economy – the context in which most crime of this nature occurs (Finney 2004a); alcohol-related sexual violence (Finney 2004b); and alcohol-related intimate partner violence (Finney 2004c).

The 2003 Crime and Justice Survey (Budd and Sharp 2005) sampled around 12,000 people aged 10–65 in England and Wales about the nature and extent of their offending: 41 per cent had committed a core offence at least once in their lives whilst one in ten had done so during the last year. The survey estimates that there were 3.8 million active offenders and confirms that young people, particularly males, are responsible for a disproportionate amount of crime. Drug use was rarely a factor in offending within the general population though the role of alcohol was more prominent. However, serious offenders and problematic drug users are under-represented in these household-based surveys.

Drug and alcohol use and offending amongst young people

A national survey of over 10,000 secondary school children aged 11–15 years questioned during 2003 revealed that 21 per cent had taken an illicit drug during the last year; 12 per cent had done so during the last month. Cannabis was the most frequently used drug with 13 per cent of pupils aged 11–15 having used it during the last year. One per cent had used heroin and/or cocaine at some point during the last 12 months. Four per cent had taken a Class A drug during this period. The likelihood of being offered drugs appears to increase sharply with age, from 19 per cent amongst 11-year-olds to 65 per cent amongst 15-year-olds. One in four pupils reported having drunk alcohol during the last week (Department of Health 2004).

The Youth Lifestyle Survey (YLS) provides an estimate of the extent, frequency and nature of drug and alcohol use and self-reported offending amongst a sample of 12–30-year-olds in England and Wales, taking into account background and lifestyle factors (Flood-Page et al. 2000; Harrington 2000; Richardson and Budd 2003). It makes broadly similar but slightly higher estimates than the BCS.

Harrington (2000) used the YLS to explore the underage drinking behaviour of 1,790 young people aged 12–17. Most (84 per cent) had drunk at some point in their lives; half of those aged 16–17 reported that they drank at least once a week with 62 per cent having done so in the week before interview. Although unable to identify a causal relationship between offending and underage drinking the YLS revealed that a higher proportion of offenders aged 12–17 were frequent drinkers (36 per cent) than non-offenders (20 per cent).

More recently, Richardson and Budd (2003) used findings from the same survey to consider the association between binge drinking and offending behaviour. They described how 39 per cent of the 1,376 young adults aged between 18 and 24 years qualified as 'binge drinkers' (those who got very drunk at least once a month). These binge drinkers were found to be more likely to report involvement in crime or disorderly behaviour (60 per cent) than other young adults in the sample described as 'regular' drinkers (25 per cent). Richardson and Budd note that the link between drinking and offending was particularly strong for violent crimes. Related research by Engineer *et al.* (2003) identified an array of factors that young adults felt contributed to alcohol, crime and disorder. These included:

- the effects of binge drinking;
- attitudes and motivations;
- social and peer group norms; and
- the drinking environment.

The YLS has also identified the family, school and peer group as being important influences on a young person's likelihood of offending and highlights lifestyle factors such as drug use and frequent drinking as the most important predictors of offending (Flood-Page *et al.* 2000). About a fifth of young people admitted to some form of offending, and self-reported drug use was found to be the strongest predictor of serious or persistent offending, with the odds of offending for drug users being nearly five times higher than for non-drug-using respondents. Drug use (at least once a month) was also found to be the most predictive factor of involvement in offending for older men (aged 18–30 years).

Recent research also suggests that young people identified as 'vulnerable' are much more likely to experiment with drugs at an earlier age. Their circumstances may also expose them to the range of risk factors associated with the problematic use of substances (Goulden and Sondhi 2001). A number of other studies have addressed the prevalence and nature of substance use amongst these vulnerable groups including: young offenders (Newburn 1998; Hammersley *et al.* 2003), excludees (Powis *et al.* 1998), children looked after by local authorities (Biehal *et al.* 1995; Ward 1998; Ward *et al.* 2003), the homeless (Klee and Reed 1998; Wincup *et al.* 2003) and children of parents who misuse drugs (Lloyd 1998).

For the majority of young people, there is no persuasive evidence that there is any direct causal linkage between offending and drug or alcohol use. Both minor offending and alcohol use are very prevalent, and illicit drug use is far from rare. However, the association between substance use and offending in surveys like the YLS is perhaps better understood as being 'deeply embedded in other social processes since…drug use is both about risk taking…[and]…about using "time out" to self-medicate the impact of the stresses and strains of both success and failure in "modern" times' (Parker *et al.* 1998: 151–2).

Parker and colleagues' longitudinal study described evolving patterns of drug use amongst young people in the north west of England (Measham *et al.* 2001; Williams and Parker 2001). Experience of illicit drugs was widespread in their sample and most funded drug use through legitimate means. In developing their concept of normalization, Parker *et al.* explain the extensive growth in availability, experimentation, use and acceptability of illicit drugs by today's youth with their respondents making a sharp distinction between acceptable and unacceptable drugs – with heroin and crack falling into the latter group, and use of these drugs was low. There was only a very small minority who were heavily involved in crime, dependent drug use and other forms of delinquency.

Subsequent research has since described how 55 per cent of 18–34-year-olds accept that using drugs is a normal part of some people's lives whilst two thirds report having a friend or family member who uses illicit drugs (Stratford *et al.* 2003).

Drug and alcohol use amongst known offenders

There were just under 1.5 million offenders sentenced by the courts during 2003 (Home Office 2005), whilst earlier government estimates indicate that a group of around 100,000 offenders are currently active and might be considered as prolific (MacLeod 2003). As will become clear, illicit drug use and heavy drinking are much more prevalent amongst known offenders than the wider population. Dependent or problematic[2] use of drugs is also much more common. A large number of offenders have been identified as regular users of illicit drugs and many regard themselves as dependent, often attributing their offending behaviour to their use of drugs.

Research has consistently shown how the criminal justice systems of developed countries throughout the world have disproportionate levels of contact with drug users. For example, a large proportion of arrestees in England and Wales, the USA and Australia test positive for one or more drugs at the time of arrest (59, 68 and 69 per cent respectively) (Taylor and Bennett 1999; Fitzgerald and Chilvers 2002).

The NEW-ADAM survey (Bennett 1998, 2000; Bennett *et al.* 2001; Holloway and Bennett 2004) involved drug testing and interviewing samples of arrestees in different locations throughout England and Wales. The final sweep of the survey interviewed 3,091 arrestees across 16 locations (equivalent to around 28 per cent of the estimated 11,000 arrestees processed by these sites and half those deemed eligible). Sixty-nine per cent of all tested arrestees were positive for some form of illicit drug, with 38 per cent testing positive for opiates and/or cocaine (including crack). The average weekly expenditure on drugs, for heroin and crack and cocaine users, was £323. The main sources of illegal income during the last 12 months were property crime (theft, burglary, robbery, handling stolen goods and fraud/deception) followed by undeclared earnings whilst claiming social security benefits and drug dealing. Heroin and crack/cocaine users had an average annual illegal income of around £24,000 – compared to an average annual illegal income of £6,000 for non-drug using arrestees. Most (89 per cent) of those using heroin, cocaine or crack in the last year acknowledged a link between their drug use and offending. Bennett has concluded that drug use and in particular the use of heroin and crack/cocaine is associated with higher levels of offending.

Alcohol use is clearly widespread amongst the offender population. In the NEW-ADAM survey, just under three fifths (58 per cent) of the arrestees interviewed reported using alcohol in the three days prior to arrest (Holloway and Bennett 2004). It should be noted that NEW-ADAM specifically excludes those arrested for alcohol-related offences (such as drink driving and disorderly drunkenness).

Arrest referral schemes have existed in some UK locations since the late 1980s. By 2002, all 43 police force areas in England and Wales were operating these schemes, though most were still in early stages of development. National estimates indicate that around 180,000 problematic drug users enter the criminal justice system through custody suites each year (Sondhi et al. 2002). Between October 2000 and September 2001, arrest referral workers in England and Wales screened 48,810 drug-using offenders and revealed an estimated expenditure of £550 million per year on illicit drugs (£11,000 per individual). In London these schemes contacted 10 per cent of all arrestees (11,793 contacts from a total of 121,021 arrests made) between April 2000 and March 2001 (Oerton et al. 2003).

In addition, an evaluation of new powers available to the police in England and Wales to drug-test arrestees in specific target offence groups found that at least half of all arrestees in six of the nine pilot areas tested positive for heroin and/or cocaine use. In one London site 65 per cent of arrestees tested positive for heroin or cocaine use (Deaton 2004).

Man et al. (2002) examined 1,575 custody records from three metropolitan police areas in an attempt to understand the extent to which arrestees were involved in alcohol-specific offences or had been drinking at the time of their arrest. Just under one third of the records sampled revealed that alcohol was a factor in the arrest: being either an alcohol-specific offence like drunkenness or drink driving (15 per cent) or alcohol-related where the arrestee had being drinking or was drunk prior to arrest (16 per cent). They discovered that those arrested for these offences spent significantly longer in custody, over half required medical attention and they were more likely to be aggressive or violent whilst in custody. They concluded that drunkenness and related anti-social behaviour represented a considerable burden on police resources.

A significant minority of offenders subject to community supervision have also been identified as problem users. Estimates from various English probation areas range from 7 per cent in north east London to 16 per cent in Cheshire (May 1999). For example, drug-using offenders on probation in London were found to be spending an average of £362 per week on drugs prior to arrest primarily raised by committing acquisitive crime, notably shoplifting. In the month before arrest, over half (51 per cent) of these probationers were using both heroin and crack (Hearnden and Harocopos 2000). In the USA, nearly 70 per cent of probationers report past use of illicit drugs and just under a third had used in the month before their most recent offence (BJS 1998).

Hearnden and Magill (2004) interviewed 82 burglars to discover why they first became involved in crime and how they selected potential targets. Just under one in four stated that they had become involved in burglary in order to fund their drug use. Raising money for drugs was also reported as the main motivation for more recent burglaries. Of 57 offenders asked, 34 recalled that at its height their daily expenditure on drugs was costing them more than £100.

Similarly, different sections of the prison population in England and Wales experience higher levels of drug use than the general population (Strang *et al.* 1998; Singleton *et al.* 1999). Recently the Home Office commissioned an extensive programme of research that described high levels of drug dependence amongst women, young male and minority ethnic prisoners (Ramsay 2003). The research also revealed that 73 per cent of 1,900 recently sentenced male prisoners interviewed during 2000 had used an illicit drug in the year before imprisonment, and more than half these considered themselves to have a drug problem. A similar number were able to establish a link between their drug use and offending behaviours.

Such trends are consistently replicated across US (Robins and Reiger 1991; CASA 1998; Peters *et al.* 1998), Australian (Butler 1997; Kevin 2000) and European (Turnbull and McSweeney 2000; Stover *et al.* 2001) prison populations.

A report by the Prison Reform Trust (Solomon 2004) highlighted concerns about an estimated 20,000 prisoners who are thought to have severe alcohol dependency problems and noted that over two thirds of the 74,000 prisoners in England and Wales are hazardous drinkers. Their prognosis is that much bleaker given the limited opportunities for appropriate throughcare on release, exacerbated by a chronic shortage of community-based alcohol services.

Offending amongst the 'problem drug-using' population

Only a small minority of illicit drug users go on to develop potentially problematic patterns of use (Hough 1996; Godfrey *et al.* 2002). Problematic use tends to focus on – but is not exclusive to – drugs of dependency such as heroin, cocaine (especially when smoked as crack) and amphetamine. Gauging the number of problematic users is difficult because of the various definitions and measurement used, and thus estimates have varied (Meltzer *et al.* 1995; Edmunds *et al.* 1998, 1999; Bramley-Harker *et al.* 2000; Frischer *et al.* 2001). One of the more recent estimates (Godfrey *et al.* 2002) suggests that there are between 280,000 and 500,000 problem Class A drug users in England and Wales – at least 7 per cent of the 4 million who use illicit drugs each year. It is also apparent that the circumstances of many of these problematic drug users expose them to a range of risk factors associated with other forms of social exclusion: increasing susceptibility to major physical and psychological health problems and often exacerbating personal, economic and legal difficulties (Gossop *et al.* 1998; MacGregor 2000).

Whilst there is no persuasive research evidence of any causal link between drug use and crime for the vast majority of illicit drug users (Hough 1996,

2002), the large amount of money spent by the minority of problematic or chaotic users to finance consumption has been consistently highlighted by several studies, in different locations and over a number of years. The largest prospective longitudinal cohort study of treatment outcome for drug misusers ever conducted in the UK, the National Treatment Outcome Research Study (NTORS), estimated that the 1,075 users it tracked were, prior to intake, buying drugs with a street value of £20 million per year. Sixty-one per cent of the NTORS sample reported committing crimes other than drug possession in the three months before they started treatment; in aggregate they admitted to 71,000 crimes in this period. The most commonly reported offence was shoplifting (Gossop *et al.* 1998). Ten per cent of the sample accounted for three quarters of the total acquisitive crimes committed. By contrast, half reported that they had not committed any acquisitive crime in the three months prior to starting treatment (Stewart *et al.* 2000).

A smaller study of 221 methadone reduction and maintenance clients in London found over four fifths had been arrested for some criminal offence in the past (Coid *et al.* 2000). However, offending prior to treatment had not always been undertaken solely to fund drug taking. Despite this, two thirds believed there was a strong link between their current offending and their drug habit and half claimed that their current offending served solely to fund their drug use. Best *et al.* (2001b) examined 100 people entering drug treatment in London. Consistent with NTORS and Coid *et al.*, they found slightly more than half the sample reported funding drug use through acquisitive crime. This study also demonstrated how those involved in crime often report more frequent use of crack and a greater expenditure on drugs.

Harocopos *et al.* (2003) tracked a cohort of 100 London crack users over an 18-month period. At intake, levels of drug use and involvement in crime were high. In the month before interview these crack users reported an average daily expenditure of £100 and most financed their use through crime. However, those respondents who were abstinent from drugs at follow-up were significantly less likely to offend than those who continued to use. These findings are consistent with results to emerge from 4–5 year follow-up interviews completed with NTORS participants, suggesting that crack users report a greater involvement in acquisitive crime than non-users (Gossop *et al.* 2002).

There is also an extensive research literature in the USA which suggests that many problematic users are involved in criminal activity (Nurco *et al.* 1995; Anglin and Perrochet 1998; Lurigio 2000; NIJ 2000).

Patterns of drug use and offending amongst criminally involved problem drug users

There is now quite a significant body of research examining patterns of crime and drug use amongst problem users who are identified as such as they pass through the criminal process. Much of this work has involved evaluations of criminal justice-based referral and treatment programmes targeting this group. The studies show that these problem drug users commit large amounts of acquisitive crime. For example, the evaluation of a range of arrest referral schemes designed to refer offenders to treatment also found similar levels of expenditure on drugs funded through property crimes such as burglary. Again most reported polydrug use, with 97 per cent using either opiates or stimulants or both (Edmunds *et al.* 1999). More recently, Oerton and colleagues (2003) described the characteristics of 12,000 problem drug users identified by arrest referral workers in London. The offence profile of these arrestees varied and included shoplifting (21 per cent), drug offences (17 per cent), other theft (12 per cent) and burglary (10 per cent). Four fifths (80 per cent) had previous convictions. Many had used heroin (55 per cent) and crack cocaine (49 per cent) in the month before their arrest. Average weekly expenditure was £391. For those using both heroin and crack cocaine weekly expenditure rose to £632. Half (51 per cent) reported no previous contact with treatment services.

Explaining the links between substance use and offending

In summarizing what this body of research evidence tells us about the links between drugs and crime, the first point to emphasize is that there are different explanations for the *association* between illicit drug use and crime for different groups of drug user. In considering the links it is essential to be specific about these different groups.

The literature suggests that 'lifestyle' and 'subcultural' factors are important in explaining why those who try illicit drugs are also more likely than others to get involved in other forms of law-breaking. The search for novelty and excitement, and enjoyment of the rewards of risk-taking, are defining aspects of youth culture. It is hardly a surprise that large minorities of the population engage in the – relatively controlled – risks of both recreational drug use and minor crime at some stage of their adolescence and young adulthood.

For those whose offending – and drug use – is more persistent and less controlled, other explanatory factors also need to be called into play. In the first place, chaotic drug users and persistent offenders – in contrast to controlled drug users and occasional petty offenders – have limited social and economic resources, and limited exposure to legitimate 'life opportunities'. The majority are from deprived backgrounds, with inconsistent parenting, poor access to housing and health care, low educational attainment and limited employment prospects. *Controlled* drug use has no obvious association with social exclusion; how could it, given the scale of participation? *Chaotic* or *dependent* use, by contrast, shares that constellation of risk factors that also predict heavy involvement in crime – and exposure to many forms of social exclusion.

If these factors *predispose* people to both uncontrolled drug use and to involvement in persistent offending, Walters (1998) and De Li Periu and MacKenzie (2000) have discussed how reciprocal causal relationships can begin to emerge, whereby criminal involvement both facilitates and maintains drug use, and drug use maintains involvement in crime. Whilst some researchers, such as Hammersley and colleagues (1989) and Dunlap and colleagues (2002), have argued for subcultural explanations of the close linkage, the accounts of the offenders themselves are more consistent with a pathological perspective, where dependence provides the motive for acquisitive offending.

A 'war on drugs' is one of the most persistent of political metaphors. In mobilizing their troops, drug warriors point to drug-related crime as one of the worst consequences of drug use. The research evidence calls into question the simple 'addiction model' of the relationship between drugs and crime whereby illicit drug use leads inexorably to dependence and thence to crime. The relationships are actually more complex. Most drug users are – and remain – in control of their use; many such users are also involved in crime, but drugs are not to blame for this. There is a small minority of drug users who are dependent on their use and chaotic in their lifestyles; there is a strong probability that these will finance their drug use through property crime. The inter-relationships between illicit drug use, problematic drug use and regular offending are set out schematically in Figure 20.1. This is intended to be illustrative rather than precise.

It makes sense to think of chaotic or dependent drug use and persistent offending sharing causal roots; but it is also important to understand how, once established, the two behaviours can be mutually sustaining. Drug dependence tends to *amplify* the offending rates of people whose circumstances may predispose them to becoming persistent offenders. There are important policy implications here. It makes excellent sense to provide treatment services for drug-dependent offenders; if successful, it should substantially reduce levels of crime. However, to maintain the lifestyle changes, which treatment may enable, it will also be necessary to address the factors that drew this group into persistent offending in the first place.

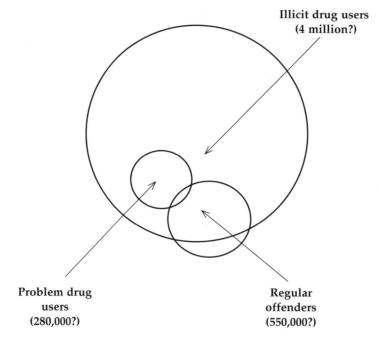

Figure 20.1 Illicit drug use, problem drug use and persistent offending

Effective strategies to reduce drug and alcohol-related crime

Criminal policy was slow to recognize the distinctive relationship between drug dependence and acquisitive crime that is now commonplace in developed industrialized societies. In Britain it was only in the mid-1990s that there was widespread recognition that conventional strategies of deterrence and incapacitation were poorly suited to the problem. By the turn of the century a broad policy consensus had emerged that the provision of community-based treatment alternatives for drug-dependent offenders was a more cost-effective approach to tackling drug-related crime than the use of custody, and carried fewer detrimental effects (ACPO 2002; Allen 2002; Home Affairs Committee 2002; Social Exclusion Unit 2002).

Reflecting this, from 1995 onwards, and especially since 1997, there has been increasing investment in treatment targeting those involved in crime. Indeed, much of the growth in investment in drug services has been motivated by the desire to reduce crime rather than the risks more directly associated with dependent drug use such as the problems posed by blood-borne viruses. Legislation introduced since 1997 has substantially extended the ability of the criminal justice system to coerce drug-dependent offenders into treatment.

The question whether coerced treatment is effective can be broken down into two constituent parts. The first is whether treatment *of any sort* is effective. The consensus here – based largely but not exclusively on North American research – is that several different types of treatment can reduce both dependent drug use and involvement in crime, and can lead to improved health and social functioning. There are several British reviews of this body of work (e.g. Department of Health 1996; Hough 1996; Marsden and Farrell 2002).

The second question is whether *coerced* treatment works. The position here is less clear. Received wisdom amongst treatment agencies – at least until recently – has been that without motivation to change, dependent drug users will not benefit from coerced treatment. However, the idea has gained ground over the last decade that skilled workers can use motivational interviewing techniques to accelerate dependent users though the 'cycle of change' to a point where they find motivation to change their behaviour. The American research broadly supports this position – with some exceptions – suggesting that coercion provides a viable mechanism for *retention* in treatment and that retention in treatment is a precondition for success. The evidence is summarized succinctly by Farabee *et al.* (1998). Anglin's (1988) study of the California Civil Addict Program (CAP) remains one of the best demonstrations that legally coerced treatment can provide long-term benefits. However, European research is more equivocal. For example, Hunt and Stevens (2004: 336–7, citing Stevens *et al.* 2003) describe how a recent review 'found evidence suggestive of a positive impact on retention, and equivalent outcomes to voluntary treatment (USA and Switzerland); that coerced treatment is ineffective in reducing crime (the Netherlands); and that coercive approaches are largely ineffective, and with potential adverse effects on voluntary treatment services (Germany)'.

Taken as a whole, the international research evidence suggests that coerced treatment will be effective under some conditions but not under others. The context in which measures are applied is probably a critical factor in determining outcome. It may well be that the alternatives to coerced treatment faced by offenders in the USA are substantially less palatable than those in European countries that have found less encouraging outcomes. The quality of treatment – whether it is coerced or not – will also affect outcome, of course; and variations between countries in quality of treatment could explain the international differences.

Certainly the quality of treatment in many British initiatives targeting criminally involved drug users has been a source of concern. Many have had difficulty in effectively engaging and retaining clients referred via the criminal justice system (Sondhi et al. 2002; McSweeney et al. 2004a). The Audit Commission (2002) highlighted how those offered or seeking help often encounter difficulties when attempting to access support, and identified a number of potential barriers:

- Problems accessing appropriate treatment because of limited options and long waiting lists.
- Care packages which fail to meet individual needs.
- Poor care management and co-ordination.
- Poor links with primary care, different treatment agencies and other services.

The Audit Commission (2004) has since described how, despite the significant expansion in drug treatment provision during recent years, a lack of integrated support often hampers its effectiveness and threatens to undermine any progress made as a result of engagement with treatment services. As part of a wider attempt to overcome these problems the British government has recently launched a major Drug Interventions Programme designed to get statutory and voluntary sector agencies working together to tackle the social factors associated with substance misuse and crime. It has recently allocated almost £0.5 billion to this programme over three years; if successful, it has the potential substantially to reduce levels of substance misuse and crime.

However, an evaluation of a London-based programme designed to integrate drug and alcohol treatment with mental health services, and education, training and employment support, described some of the challenges and difficulties encountered when attempting to integrate services in this way. In doing so it highlighted important lessons for central and regional government on funding and working with the voluntary sector to deliver services (McSweeney et al. 2004a). With over half the 2,187 clients contacting the programme engaging with only one service – despite being identified as having several areas of need at assessment – it stressed the need for funding regimes that reward good partnership working as well as delivering targets. Without this, the goodwill and commitment shown towards any enterprise will quickly erode.

By comparison, research evidence about the effectiveness of various initiatives to tackle alcohol-related crime remains limited and, although there are a number of programmes across the country focusing, for example, on problems in and around licensed premises, most have not yet been evaluated. One exception is the TASC project which aimed to tackle alcohol-related street crime and violence in Cardiff (Maguire et al. 2003). The evaluation identified a number of good practice points to ensure the long-term success of future crime prevention in this area:

- Establishing and sustaining effective links with managers of licensed premises.
- Ensuring a well resourced project team is fully integrated into police objectives and priorities.
- Maintaining an up-to-date and dedicated database to monitor trends.
- Developing standard training, registration and disciplinary systems for door staff.
- Promoting project objectives widely using a number of innovative sources.
- Engaging public and private sector stakeholders in broader dialogue about the strategic management of the late-night economy.

Sondhi *et al.* (2002) also noted the potential for delivering brief health interventions undertaken in criminal justice settings that might be effective in reducing alcohol consumption. In June 2004, drug testing of arrestees was expanded in a number of pilot areas in an attempt to identify those who also abuse alcohol. Work is currently being undertaken around alcohol arrest referral provision, specifying alcohol assessment and treatment as a bail condition and creating an opportunity for diversion away from the criminal justice system.

Coerced treatment and the 5 Is

Using Ekblom's (2003) 5 Is framework we now focus on the court sentence which provides the main paradigm of coerced treatment in Britain – the drug treatment and testing order (DTTO). Using this approach we shall consider the impact of DTTOs as a crime reduction measure by describing:

- the rationale for introducing it (Intelligence);
- how it has been implemented, developed and delivered (Intervention, Implementation, Involvement); and
- the evidence for its effectiveness (Impact).

DTTOs have been subsumed within the new 'generic' community order which was established through the Criminal Justice Act 2003 and introduced in April 2005. The order enables sentencers to 'tailor make' community sentences, imposing any of a wide range of conditions, including those that constitute the DTTO. The DTTO has become a community order with drug rehabilitation requirements (DRR). Sentencers are expected to continue to use DRRs broadly in the same way as they had used DTTOs in the past, but there is now scope for more flexibility.

Intelligence

Self-report studies consistently indicate that a small proportion of offenders are responsible for a disproportionate amount of crime. For example, Budd and Sharp (2005: 3) note that although prolific offenders (defined as those who committed six or more offences in the last year) 'formed only 2% of the sample and 26% of active offenders, they accounted for 82 per cent of all offences measured'. Earlier estimates from the Home Office (2001: 21) using data from the Offenders Index suggested that in any given year there were around 1 million active offenders: 100,000 of them were thought to be responsible for committing a significant proportion of all crime. Half were believed to be under 21. Nearly two thirds were thought to be hard drug users and three quarters had no work and little or no legal income. Similarly, 10 per cent of the NTORS sample accounted for three quarters of the total acquisitive crimes committed prior to engaging with treatment (Stewart *et al.* 2000).

During 2003/4, there were estimated to be between 125,900 and 154,000 problem drug users in contact with drug treatment services and general practitioners in England (Druglink 2004; National Treatment Agency 2004a). It is estimated by Godfrey *et al.* (2002) that up to one third of all problematic drug users will never contact treatment services and there is evidence from the NEW-ADAM survey of arrestees to support this: 37 per cent of drug-misusing repeat offenders reported never having received drug treatment (Holloway and Bennett 2004). The Audit Commission (2004) and Sondhi *et al.* (2002) have described a range of possible reasons for drug users not contacting treatment services. These include:

- a lack of motivation and 'not being ready';
- past negative experiences of treatment;
- concerns about confidentiality and suspicion of criminal justice-based initiatives like arrest referral;
- denial, stigma and fear of exposure;
- for women, childcare and protection issues;
- low self-esteem and peer pressure to maintain a drug-using lifestyle; and
- limited choice, inflexible appointment systems and restricted opening hours.

Whilst increasing the provision of voluntary treatment places is clearly important, for the various reasons outlined above it could be argued that simply inviting criminally involved problem drug users to utilize these additional spaces is unlikely to be entirely successful. One of the potential merits of interventions like the DTTO is the assumption that the coercive influence exerted by the criminal justice system can act as an effective catalyst for engagement with treatment services. Evidence from qualitative interviews with drug-using offenders certainly supports this notion:

> I've all the best intentions there to do it [engage with treatment voluntarily] but as I said to you that will take up my whole day. You wake up ill, so the first priority is just to get myself not ill, yeah. So I'll have to go out shoplifting, yeah, which is going to take a whole morning, even an afternoon sometimes. The afternoon you've got to sell the stuff you've nicked, that might take another couple of hours. Then you've got to score the gear, then you've got to use the gear and by that time the

day's done, you know. And you're thinking 'oh I'll do it tomorrow', but tomorrow you have to do exactly the same thing. I mean I say 'I'll do it today, not tomorrow', but before you know it that day's leading to a week, that week's leading to a month, and I suppose if you do get arrested and you've got that chance to do something about it then you'll take it.

Intervention

DTTOs were high-tariff community penalties available to the courts when custody would otherwise have been a serious consideration.[3] Introduced by the Crime and Disorder Act 1998, the order targeted offenders aged 16 years and over, identified as dependent on drugs and committing high levels of acquisitive crime to support their use. The orders were intensive. Contact, including treatment, took place over five days a week, for a total of 20 hours per week, for the first 13 weeks of the order. Orders were imposed for a minimum of six months to a maximum of three years. An offender had to consent before an order could be made.

As a criminal justice intervention, the main aim of the DTTO was to reduce offending using a harm-reduction approach to tackle substance misuse. However, legislation did not stipulate what form or approach treatment should take. Consequently, individual treatment programmes had largely been developed at a local level by probation services and treatment agencies on the basis of the range of treatment available locally and individual offender needs. Drug testing at specified periods was mandatory throughout the duration of the order. Treatment was reinforced through probation supervision and progress was monitored through regular court reviews. National Standards (2000) for the supervision of offenders in the community aimed to promote a number of objectives by regulating the nature and extent of contact as part of the DTTO. They stipulated that for offenders on court orders, breach proceedings should be instigated as a result of a second unacceptable failure to attend, with a first failure leading to a final-warning letter.

Turnbull *et al.* (2000) described the selection processes offenders usually had to pass through before a DTTO could be made:

- being referred to a DTTO worker/team for an assessment;
- being accepted by the worker/team as appropriate for an assessment;
- consenting to a DTTO assessment and proposal;
- being assessed as suitable; and
- the recommendation of the assessors being accepted by the courts.

Government guidance stated that an individual's suitability for a DTTO must be assessed against the following criteria:

- type and seriousness of the offence(s);
- seriousness of drug problem and susceptibility to treatment;
- motivation to change; and
- volume of drug-related offending.

In addition, the court must have been satisfied of the following:

- An offender had been assessed by probation and treatment staff as being dependent on or misusing drugs and was susceptible to the kind of treatment being proposed.
- A treatment plan had been drawn up which included the name and address of the treatment provider, and indicated whether the proposed treatment was residential or non-residential.
- Confirmation that arrangements for this treatment were in place (i.e. funding and availability).
- The length of the order had been agreed taking into account the views of the treatment provider.

McSweeney *et al.* (2004b) noted that probation staff were typically involved in determining whether an order should be made (conducting a standalone assessment or participating in multi-agency assessment and the subsequent presentence reporting), in supervising the offender and assuming responsibility for the administrative maintenance of the order (periodically meeting the offender and liaising with the court to report progress and identify situations when conditions of the order have been breached or a decision has to be made as to whether it should be revoked). By contrast, treatment staff were involved in direct treatment provision (keyworking and directly running therapeutic activities such as 'group work'). In some cases they also managed routine drug testing and had a liaison role in which progress and deviations from the requirements of the order were reported to probation. More rarely, treatment staff were involved in reporting directly to the courts on progress.

Between October 2000 and December 2003, 18,414 orders had been made by the courts (NAO 2004). National targets for DTTO commencements doubled from 6,000 in 2002/3 to 12,000 in 2004/5 (or 13,000 if an extra 1,000 DTTOs with lower-intensity care plans are included).

Implementation

Inevitably with an ambitious enterprise like this, there were likely to be a range of wider issues that impacted upon the overall effectiveness of the approach as a crime reduction measure. For example, there has since the late 1990s been a number of structural and organizational changes to both health services and criminal justice agencies with the DTTO being developed and delivered alongside a number of new criminal justice-based initiatives, such as arrest referral schemes and youth offending teams. This was also a period of fundamental change to the way in which health, criminal justice and welfare agencies were required to work together and the manner in which treatment services were commissioned. At around this time a number of new structures were emerging or in the early stages of development. These included Drug Action Teams (DATs), Crime and Disorder Reduction Partnerships (CDRPs) and Primary Care Trusts (PCTs).

During 2001 the Probation Service in England and Wales was fundamentally restructured. This followed changes already implemented to staffing structures and the content of programmes being delivered by the service. In addition, it was announced at the start of 2004 that the Prison and Probation Services were to be merged to form the National Offender Management Service (NOMS). Indeed, even before this radical announcement the Probation Inspectorate recalled how the orders had been rolled out under 'the most challenging of circumstances' and described a climate of 'organisational exhaustion' which has left the service 'under strain and not effectively delivering all that is currently expected of it' (HMIP 2003a; 2003b).

An unintended – but perhaps predictable – consequence of this rapid and ongoing change is that a number of serious organizational and procedural problems remain in some areas (McSweeney *et al.* 2004b: 52). These include, for example, backlogs in processing and completing presentence reports and assessments; inadequate training for new community assessment teams; and delays in submitting completed reports for consideration. Cumulatively these factors have understandably strained the relationships between probation staff, treatment providers and the courts. Excessive delays also prolong the length of time it takes to access appropriate support and could potentially jeopardize the chances of being offered this type of intervention (Falk 2004). There have been widespread reports of low morale, problems of staff retention and recruitment, increased workloads and a growing emphasis on bureaucracy and accountability within both health and criminal justice fields (DrugScope 2004; Farrow 2004). There are, in addition, problems providing consistent forms of DTTO provision across different areas and locations, each with their own organizational structure and system for funding.

One of the strategies to reduce the prison population has involved enhancing sentencer and public confidence in community sentences. This has seen a greater emphasis being placed on compliance with the conditions of community penalties and might partially explain successive increases in DTTO commencement targets. However this downward pressure placed increasing emphasis on probation management and staff to generate and sustain appropriate rates of referrals to DTTO programmes. As a consequence there was a perceived emphasis being placed on 'quantity over quality' which in turn distorted the approach taken in some areas when it came to identifying suitable candidates, as the following quotation from a probation manager illustrates:

What matters at the moment, and again it is something that I have challenged and been criticized for, that the impact in reducing offending behaviour is not reflected in programme commencement rates. So we could have 100 people and it has happened in some areas where you get them on to the programme but they are breached within the first week but that actually means that you meet the target and that is the important thing at the moment. I think if one is more professional, if I can use that word, and actually propose DTTOs for the offending community who can actually use and benefit from it and it will actually have a future impact on their offending behaviour, you will not be actually … you would be more selective. And that is what is happening with us here now; we are actually being discouraged from being selective.

This has led to a degree of uncertainty, confusion and lack of clarity about suitability for the order. Another important factor to emerge is the pressure on probation services to find available treatment at the earliest opportunity. The drive to meet increased commencement rates has led to an expansion of the target group and increases the likelihood that less serious offenders are being placed on orders. This has posed particular problems for probation staff, as these lower-tariff offenders are often reluctant to engage in intensive forms of treatment. The problems created by target setting are exacerbated further still by a perceived lack of appropriate treatment facilities in some areas to meet this increased demand: 'If we actually meet targets, which went up fifty per cent this year and the proposal is that they will go up fifty per cent again next year, the care management teams won't have enough money to fund residential treatment' (senior probation officer).

In a recent review of the 'what works' evidence, Harper and Chitty (2004: 48) identified three main implementation problems that are likely to affect both the delivery and success of interventions in reducing offending: the rapid expansion of programmes; targeting programmes ineffectively; and higher than expected attrition rates. All these problems have hampered the effective implementation and delivery of DTTOs. Furthermore it is widely acknowledged that the rigorous enforcement of DTTO national standards is inconsistent with emerging evidence and the accepted notion of dependent drug use as a 'chronic relapsing condition'. There is also little evidence to suggest that the rigorous enforcement of these standards makes such disposals more effective (Hedderman and Hough 2004).

The research evidence also emphasizes the importance of matching treatment approaches to the specific needs of different drug-using populations (i.e. young people, women, black and minority ethnic groups, and stimulant users). However, attempts to match clients with suitable forms of treatment can be determined as much by individual preferences, resources and treatment availability as by any shared or agreed model of good practice, with DTTO completion rates ranging widely across England and Wales (from 71 per cent in Dorset to 8 per cent in Kent) (NAO 2004).

Using and exploiting the coercive potential of the criminal justice system to act as a conduit to treatment for criminally involved problem users is one of the most controversial issues in the addictions field today and raises a number of philosophical and empirical concerns (Wild *et al.* 1998). Clearly, providing drug treatment within a criminal justice context has presented a number of important issues and challenges: around system capacity and funding (Parker 2004); the responsiveness and appropriateness of treatment to different typologies of problem user (Howard League 1999); information sharing and confidentiality (Barton and Quinn 2002); and the impact on voluntarism and existing service provision (Hunt and Stevens 2004). Other potential stumbling blocks have been identified, relating to procedures, service delivery and organizational issues. In order to negotiate these hurdles those involved in developing and delivering interventions like the DTTO need to ensure that they refine referral and assessment procedures, provide appropriate and responsive interventions, clarify treatment objectives and offer consistency around procedures for testing, reviews and enforcement. Without sufficient attention, these factors threaten to undermine the overall effectiveness of the orders (Turnbull *et al.* 2000; Eley *et al.* 2002; Best *et al.* 2003; Bean 2004; Falk 2004). Despite these considerable challenges and pressures, some models of good practice have emerged (NAO 2004).

Involvement

The main advantages of the DTTO reported by a sample of those recently mandated by the courts in London and Kent (McSweeney *et al.* 2004b: 55) included:

- the level of structure and support offered – including out-of-hours support;
- the information and advice available;
- access to holistic support around housing, benefits, and education, training and employment provision;
- the professionalism of staff; and
- rapid access to substitute prescribing which in turn eliminates the need for continued involvement in crime.

Whilst the nature and extent of contact required by the order are demanding, it is nevertheless perceived by many as a positive aspect of the DTTO, especially during the crucial early stages of the order. Almost regardless of the therapeutic content, the simple requirement to get up each morning and spend a large fraction of the day engaged in purposeful activity can be experienced as both novel and therapeutic. Successfully complying with a routine of this kind is also often experienced by participants as progress. The way that the programme structures and fills time is important because it can create an effective barrier to the use of drugs as a way of filling time and providing purpose and recreation (McSweeney *et al.* 2004b: 55).

From the perspective of professionals involved, an important strength of the DTTO appeared to be its ability (potentially) to engage in treatment a group of criminally involved drug users who may have previously lacked either the opportunity or inclination to access appropriate support as an alternative to imprisonment. Speed of access to treatment, the level of structure and intensity offered, and the dedicated funding allocated to provide this kind of support appear to constitute other important aspects of the approach. DTTOs can also offer a more manageable treatment package and place more accountability upon the client. Involvement in DTTOs had also led to improvements in a number of other areas for both health and criminal justice professionals. These include improvements to staff knowledge and development; client perceptions of treatment and probation; and joint working between professionals.

A common concern amongst judges and magistrates is that they often have little or no feedback on the effectiveness or impact of most of the sentences that they pass. An innovative feature of the DTTO is the court review process, whereby offenders are returned to court, initially on a monthly basis, for an assessment of progress. The feedback provided through this process is generally welcomed by sentencers (Turnbull *et al.* 2000; Hough *et al.* 2003). In

581

some cases the review process has also enhanced offenders' experience of the DTTO; they have responded positively to the interest shown by judges and magistrates and to the encouragement and praise they have received for good progress.

Whilst the development of a criminal justice focus to providing treatment for problem drug users raises a number of fundamental and practical dilemmas for both criminal justice agencies and treatment services (Barton 1999a, 1999b; Stimson 2000), this does not rule out the possibility that multiple objectives – in this case relating to public health and crime reduction – are achievable through a single intervention (Hough 2001). In order to implement these programmes successfully in the British context, establishing and sustaining effective partnerships emerge as one of the single most important obstacles to overcome (Turnbull *et al.* 2000; Eley *et al.* 2002; Best *et al.* 2003). Effective interagency working is often compromised by conflicts of approach and treatment philosophy or difficulties in bringing together health and criminal justice workers with different working styles, organizational priorities, traditions and values (Hough 1996; 2002).

Impact

Since being made available nationally there have been a number of studies examining the processes and effectiveness of DTTOs).[4] Many of the studies focusing on outcomes suggest that drug-dependent offenders can be effectively coerced into treatment, with those successfully retained on programmes reporting reductions in drug use and offending.

That said, much of this outcomes-based research can be criticized on methodological grounds: most have relied on self-report measures; some have relied on urine test data for the period covering the treatment programme only; and few collected reliable outcome measures relating to reoffending, and fewer still ran for periods of time stretching beyond engagement with the programme, comparing treatment groups with comparison samples. Findings may also have been distorted to some degree by both sampling and response bias. Like much of the research on drug treatment outcomes, this growing body of evidence has not always made clear exactly how treatment works and which treatment modalities work best with whom (Audit Commission 2002; Bean 2004). We can therefore say very little with any certainty about the effectiveness of DTTOs over the long term in tackling substance misuse and improving individual and social functioning.

In the short term, findings from a two-year reconviction study of the first 210 offenders to receive a DTTO on pilot schemes proved disappointing (Hough *et al.* 2003). Programme completion rates were low (30 per cent) and two-year reconviction rates high (80 per cent). However, these findings did reveal substantial differences in reconviction rates between those successfully completing their orders and those who were revoked: 53 per cent of completers were reconvicted within two years compared to 91 per cent of those revoked. Given the very extensive involvement in offending reported by the completers before the order, there are some grounds for optimism – if only the retention rates could be improved. The research concluded that if DTTOs were to be a viable option, it was essential to develop effective strategies for engaging and retaining offenders in treatment, deploying timely, responsive and appropriate services. However, statistics for 2003 suggest that the position has not improved following the national roll-out: completion rates have fallen slightly from 30 per cent in the pilots to 27 per cent, and the overall two-year reconviction rates have risen by 10 percentage points to 90 per cent (Home Office 2004a).

High attrition rates have also emerged as a common feature of court-based initiatives in other countries, particularly for those schemes targeting problematic drug users and persistent, high-level offenders (Freeman 2003). The international research evidence suggests that efforts to enhance programme engagement and retention rates could improve the overall effectiveness of court-mandated treatment since the coercive influence exerted by the criminal justice system has been shown to be an effective 'catalyst for commencing treatment rather than an effective motivation for remaining in treatment' (Murphy 2000). Cahill *et al.* (2003) describe previous research which suggests that, whilst external forms of pressure like legal coercion might increase treatment entry and short-term retention, it appears to have little impact on longer-term outcomes. In doing so they note that motivation for treatment is not the same as motivation for change. This is broadly consistent with the sentiments of Fiorentine *et al.* (1999) who have suggested that the characteristics of individuals when they enter treatment (i.e. referral source and motivation) are frequently less important for predicting retention and outcome than external factors like the quality and perceived utility of treatment being offered and the client–worker relationship. Recent analysis of the National Drug Treatment Monitoring System (Millar *et al.* 2004: 4) also found that 'the strongest predictor of retention or completion of treatment was not the characteristics of the client, but related to the agency they had attended'.

There are also some interesting findings to emerge from an ongoing study involving eight organizations from six countries examining the processes and effectiveness of drug treatment motivated, ordered or supervised by the criminal justice system.[5] An interim report (McSweeney *et al.* 2004b) described data from 157 drug users (a mix of 'voluntary' and DTTO clients) accessing treatment across 10 sites in London and Kent between June 2003 and January 2004. One of the main findings was that over 80 per cent of the sample described an internal pressure to engage in treatment (i.e. they were there because they wanted to be), whilst 56 per cent also reported experiencing some form of external pressure affecting their decision (usually from a partner, family or friends). In fact, just under half (48 per cent) the 'volunteers' reported experiencing some form of pressure to enter treatment. Perhaps unsurprisingly, the only item on which there was a significant difference observed between the two groups related to pressure from legal authorities, with 43 per cent of the DTTO sample experiencing this. It is interesting that only a minority of people in the DTTO group reported feeling pressure from legal authorities to enter treatment, given that they are under study as a group who have supposedly entered treatment under legal coercion. Similar findings have been recorded in American studies (Marlowe *et al.* 1996).

The findings also highlight a number of important differences between those mandated to treatment by the courts and those assumed to be seeking treatment 'voluntarily'. Compared to these volunteers, people who entered treatment as part of a DTTO at the research sites were:

- more likely to be male;
- using a wider range of drugs;
- making more frequent use of heroin and crack;
- injecting more frequently;
- spending more on drugs;
- more criminally active;
- less likely to suffer psychological problems; and
- more likely to be at an earlier stage in the 'cycle of change'.

These differences imply that the people on a DTTO are likely to find it more difficult to succeed in treatment than those who enter voluntarily (except for their less severe psychological problems, which might increase the chances of retention). It also suggests that gains in terms of reduced drug use and crime are likely to be greater in the DTTO group.

Conclusions

This chapter has summarized the research literature that sheds light on the links between substance misuse and crime, and has examined strategies for responding to the resultant problems. One of the key conclusions to draw from this body of work relates to the nature of the links between illicit drug use and crime. There can be little doubt that such links exist, but they are more complex than public and political debate usually recognizes. Most of those who use illicit drugs do so in moderate and controlled ways; there is no evidence that their drug use triggers other forms of crime. But for a small minority, chaotic, dependent drug use and chaotic, persistent offending are heavily intertwined, and this group undoubtedly commits a very large amount of crime.

Responding to the needs of this group and to the problems that they create for themselves and others is one of those 'wicked issues' that cuts across the jurisdictions of several agencies at national and local level. Clearly treatment for drug dependency has to remain an important component of the response. However, perhaps the most important of our conclusions is that expectations of coerced treatment should be *realistic*. Treatment – whether or not coerced – has both failures and successes, and the latter are often partial: 40 per cent of those followed up in NTORS were still using heroin at least once a week four years after entering treatment (Gossop *et al.* 2001a). Coerced treatment options such as DTTOs are clearly not a panacea for tackling the wider problems of drug use and drug-related crime. The findings we have presented here are consistent with the growing desistance literature which suggests that treatment forms a crucial but also only a minor aspect in the larger process of recovery 'which does not preclude community, familial or voluntary interventions or self-change processes' (Maruna *et al.* 2004: 10).

For McNeill (2004: 244), these 'studies suggest that this process of change, as well as being inherently individualised, is also rich and complex, sometimes ambivalent and contradictory, and not reducible to the simplicities of applying the right "treatment" at the right "dosage" to cure the assessed "criminogenic needs"'. It would appear that the challenge for those involved in delivering drug treatment within a criminal justice context is to recognize 'this "natural" process of reform and design interventions that can enhance or complement these spontaneous effects' (Maruna *et al.* 2004: 16).

We have discussed the political and popular appeal of the idea that 'addiction' is an important driver of crime. However, privileging drug treatment as the central solution to crime problems could prove a serious policy error. Drug dependence is only one of a constellation of factors that draw people into chaotic, persistent offending. Drug-dependent persistent offenders are likely to face a series of well entrenched – and well researched – problems associated with housing, employment and employability, social skills and family relationships and mental health problems. Entwined drug dependence and persistent offending are centrally problems of social exclusion. Dealing with problems of dependence in isolation will never be more than half a solution.

With these caveats, the current governmental investment in drug treatment for persistent offenders is to be welcomed. Using the criminal justice system as a conduit to treatment is a more humane and intelligent solution than the alternative pursued in the USA – mass imprisonment. The treatment provided through the criminal process must obviously be of sufficient quality to have an impact on a very intractable group. The drug rehabilitation requirement (DRR), replacing the DTTO from April 2005, offers some cause for cautious optimism.[6] If well resourced, targeted and appropriately designed drug treatment and integrated support is given to the recipients of the DRR, it should be possible to achieve higher rates of retention in treatment than with DTTOs, and a significant minority can be expected to reduce their substance use and offending levels.

In developing strategies for responding to drug-dependent persistent offending, the government faces several challenges. First, in the rush to provide treatment resources for offenders, provision must not be compromised for the large proportion of dependent drug users who do *not* fund their drug use through crime. Secondly, the principles underpinning provision for those who *are* involved in crime must remain principles of treatment, not of crime control. Thirdly, as it becomes more widely understood that treatment is only a partial solution to problems of drug-related crime, it will be important to work to retain public confidence in the approach (cf. Stead *et al.* 2002: Hough *et al.* 2003). Finally it is essential that policies relating to substance misuse address alcohol as well as illicit drugs, and that problems of alcohol-related crime are not overshadowed by crime problems associated with the dependent use of illicit drugs.

Selected further reading

Recent reviews by Mike Hough (2003) and Philip Bean (2004) provide comprehensive overviews of the theoretical assumptions and models underpinning much of the drugs–crime debate. Both also explore the rationale for, and effectiveness of, 'coercive' drug treatment and consider the ethical and practical concerns raised by exploiting the coercive potential of the criminal justice system as a means of identifying and diverting increasing numbers of criminally involved problem drug users into treatment.

Relevant US reviews include the work of David Farabee and colleagues ('The effectiveness of coerced drug treatment for drug-abusing offenders', 1998) and Douglas B. Marlowe ('Effective strategies for intervening with drug abusing offenders', 2002 and 'Integrating substance abuse treatment and criminal justice supervision', 2003). Marlowe ('Assessment of coercive and noncoercive pressures to enter drug abuse treatment', 1996) and Cameron Wild ('Perceived coercion among clients entering substance abuse treatment: structural and psychological determinants', 1998) have also examined the perceived pressures and motivations of those accessing drug treatment from various referral sources.

Alex Stevens and colleagues have recently published an article ('Quasi-compulsory treatment of drug dependent offenders: an international literature review', 2005) reviewing the international (including non-English language) literature on the processes and effectiveness of court-ordered drug treatment. The European literature appears more equivocal about the prospects for reducing crime and drug use through the use of 'coercive' treatment. The review is part of a wider study that represents the first systematic, comparative, cross-national research project of its kind conducted in Europe, and is tracking the progress of 845 people who have entered drug treatment in five European countries, half having been mandated by the courts. More details of the study and its findings can be found at http://www.kent.ac.uk/eiss/projects/qct-europe/index.htm.

Notes

1. See Hough (1996), Deehan (1999), Seddon (2000), Hough et al. (2001), Bean (2004) Stevens et al. (2005) for recent reviews.
2. The ACMD (1982) define problematic users as those experiencing social, psychological, legal or physical problems arising from their use of drugs.
3. With effect from April 2005, DTTOs were subsumed within a generic 'community order' introduced by the Criminal Justice Act 2003. A court can now make a community order with a drug rehabilitation requirement, which can be specified so as to be functionally equivalent to a DTTO.
4. See Turnbull et al. (2000), Barker et al. (2002), Eley et al. (2002), Ricketts et al. (2002), Best et al. (2003), Finch et al. (2003), HMIP (2003), Hough et al. (2003), McIvor (2004), NAO (2004).
5. Details of the QCT Europe study can be found at http://www.kent.ac.uk/eiss/projects/qct-europe/index.htm.
6. DRRs are intended to be more flexible than DTTOs, and more consistent with the principles enshrined in Models of Care (2002). There is some evidence that this is already happening with the introduction of interim measures to ensure greater flexibility in terms of the level of contact required and overall management of the orders (Home Office 2004b). This includes the introduction of a stabilization period in an effort to improve engagement, retention and completion rates.

References

Advisory Council on the Misuse of Drugs (1982) *Treatment and Rehabilitation*. London: HMSO.

Alcohol Concern (2004) *Alcohol and Crime. Factsheet* 10. London: Alcohol Concern.

Allen, R. (2002) 'What does the public think about prison?', *Criminal Justice Matters*, 49: 6–7.

Anglin, M.D. (1988) 'The efficacy of civil commitment in treating narcotic addiction', in C.G. Leukfield and F.M. Tims (eds) *Compulsory Treatment of Drug Abuse: Research and Clinical Practice. NIDA Research Monograph* 86. Rockville, MD: National Institute on Drug Abuse.

Anglin, M.D. and Perrochet, B. (1998) 'Drug use and crime: a historical review of research conducted by the UCLA Drug Abuse Research Center', *Substance Use and Misuse*, 33: 1871–914.

Anglin, M.D. and Speckart, G. (1988) 'Narcotics and crime: a multi-sample, multi-method analysis', *Criminology*, 26: 197–233.

Association of Chief Police Officers of England, Wales and Northern Ireland (2002) *A Review of Drugs Policy and Proposals for the Future*. London: ACPO.

Audit Commission (2002) *Changing Habits: The Commissioning and Management of Community Drug Services for Adults*. London: Audit Commission.

Audit Commission (2004) *Drug Misuse 2004. Reducing the Local Impact*. London: Audit Commission.

Ball, J.C., Schaffer, J.W. and Nurgo, D.N. (1983) 'The day to day criminality of heroin addicts in Baltimore – a study in the continuity of offence rates', *Drug and Alcohol Dependence*, 12: 119–42.

Barker, V., Horrocks, C., Kelly, N. and Robinson, D. (2002) *Experiencing Drug Treatment and Testing Orders in Wakefield: Taking a Narrative Approach*. Huddersfield: University of Huddersfield.

Barton, A. (1999a) 'Breaking the crime/drugs cycle: the birth of a new approach?', *Howard Journal of Criminal Justice*, 38: 144–57.

Barton, A. (1999b) 'Sentenced to treatment? Criminal justice orders and the health service', *Critical Social Policy*, 19: 463–83.

Barton, A. and Quinn, C. (2002) 'Risk management of groups or respect for the individual? Issues for information sharing and confidentiality in drug treatment and testing orders', *Drugs: Education, Prevention and Policy*, 9: 35–43.

Bean, P. (2004) *Drugs and Crime* (2nd edn). Cullompton: Willan Publishing.

Bennett, T. (1998) *Drugs and Crime: The Results of Research on Drug Testing and Interviewing Arrestees. Home Office Research Study* 183. London: Home Office.

Bennett, T. (2000) *Drugs and Crime: The Results of the Second Development Stage of the NEW-ADAM Programme. Home Office Research Study* 205. London: Home Office.

Bennett, T., Holloway, K. and Williams, T. (2001) *Drug Use and Offending: Summary Results of the First Year of the NEW-ADAM Research Programme. Home Office Research Findings* 148. London: Home Office.

Best D., Man, L., Gossop, M., Harris, J., Sidwell, C. and Strang, J. (2001a) 'Understanding the developmental relationship between drug use and crime: are drug users the best people to ask?', *Addiction Research and Theory*, 9: 151–64.

Best, D., Man, L., Rees, S., Witton, J. and Strang, J. (2003) *Evaluating the Effectiveness of Drug Treatment and Testing Orders in London. A Report to the London Probation Area*. London: National Addiction Centre.

Best, D., Sidwell, C., Gossop, M., Harris, J. and Strang, J. (2001b) 'Crime and expenditure among polydrug misusers seeking treatment', *British Journal of Criminology*, 41: 119–26.

Biehal, N., Clayden, J., Stein, M. and Wade, J. (1995) *Moving On. Young People and Leaving Care Schemes*. London: HMSO.

Bramley-Harker, E., Hickman, M. and Turnbull, P. (2000) *Sizing the UK Market for Illegal Drugs. A Report to the Home Office*. London: National Economic Research Associates.

Budd, T. (2003) *Alcohol-related Assault: Findings from the British Crime Survey. Home Office Online Report* 35/03. London: Home Office.

Budd, T. and Sharp, C. (2005) *Offending in England and Wales: First Results from the 2003 Crime and Justice Survey. Home Office Research Findings* 244. London: Home Office.

Bureau of Justice Statistics (1998) *Substance Abuse and Treatment of Adults on Probation, 1995.* NCJ 166611. Washington, DC: BJS.

Butler, T. (1997) *Preliminary Findings from the Inmate Health Survey of the Inmate Population in the New South Wales Correctional System.* Sydney: New South Wales Department of Corrective Services.

Cabinet Office (2004) *Alcohol Harm Reduction Strategy for England. Prime Minister's Strategy Unit.* London: Cabinet Office.

Cahill, M.A., Adinoff, B., Hosig, H., Muller, K. and Pulliam, C. (2003) 'Motivation for treatment preceding and following a substance abuse program', *Addictive Behaviors,* 28: 67–79.

Centre on Addiction and Substance Abuse (1998) *Behind Bars: Substance Abuse and America's Prison Population.* New York, NY: Columbia University.

Coid, J., Carvell, A., Kittler, Z., Healey, A. and Henderson, J. (2000) *Opiates, Criminal Behaviour, and Methadone Treatment.* London: Home Office.

Condon, J. and Smith, N. (2003) *Prevalence of Drug Use: Key Findings from the 2002/03 British Crime Survey. Home Office Research Findings* 229. London: Home Office.

Deaton, S. (2004) *On-charge Drug Testing: Evaluation of Drug Testing in the Criminal Justice System. Home Office Development and Practice Report* 16. London: Home Office.

Deehan, A. (1999) *Alcohol and Crime: Taking Stock. Briefing Note. Crime Reduction Series* 3. London: Home Office Policing and Reducing Crime Unit.

De Li Periu, H. and MacKenzie, D. (2000) 'Drug involvement, lifestyles and criminal activities among probationers', *Journal of Drug Issues,* 30: 593–620.

Department of Health (1996) *The Task Force to Review Services for Drug Misusers. Report of an Independent Review of Drug Treatment Services in England.* London: Department of Health.

Department of Health (2004) *Drug Use, Smoking and Drinking among Young People in England in 2003.* London: Department of Health.

Dobinson, I. and Ward, P. (1986) 'Heroin and property crime: an Australian perspective', *Journal of Drug Issues,* 16: 249–62.

Druglink (2004) 'Minister "misled" over numbers in drug treatment', November/December.

DrugScope (2004) *Guide to UK Drug Policy.* London: DrugScope.

Dunlap, E., Golub, A., Johnson, B. and Wesley, D. (2002) 'Intergenerational transmission of conduct norms for drugs, sexual exploitation and violence: a case study', *British Journal of Criminology,* 42: 1–20.

Edmunds, M., Hough, M., Turnbull, P.J. and May, T. (1999) *Doing Justice to Treatment: Referring Offenders to Drug Services. Drug Prevention Advisory Service Paper* 2. London: Home Office.

Edmunds, M., May, T., Hough, M. and Hearnden, I. (1998) *Arrest Referral: Emerging Lessons from Research. Drugs Prevention Initiative Paper* 23. London: Home Office.

Ekblom, P. (2003) *5 Is: A Practical Tool for Transfer and Sharing of Crime Prevention Knowledge.* London: Home Office (available at (http://www.crimereduction.gov.uk/learningzone/5isprint.doc).

Eley, S., Gallop, K., McIvor, G., Morgan, K. and Yates, R. (2002) *Drug Treatment and Testing Orders: Evaluation of the Scottish Pilots.* Edinburgh: Scottish Executive Central Research Unit.

Engineer, R., Phillips, A., Thompson, J. and Nicholls, J. (2003) *Drunk and Disorderly: A Qualitative Study of Binge Drinking among 18 to 24-year-olds*. Home Office Research Study 262. London: Home Office.

Falk, C. (2004) 'Are DTTOs working? Issues of policy, implementation and practice', *Probation Journal. The Journal of Community and Criminal Justice*, 51: 398–406.

Farabee, D., Prendergast, M. and Anglin, M.D. (1998) 'The effectiveness of coerced treatment for drug-abusing offenders', *Federal Probation*, 62: 3–10.

Farrington, D. (1997) 'Human development and criminal careers', in M. Maguire *et al.* (eds) *The Oxford Handbook of Criminology*. Oxford: Oxford University Press.

Farrington, D. (2002) 'Developmental criminology and risk focussed prevention', in M. Maguire *et al.* (eds) *The Oxford Handbook of Criminology*. Oxford: Oxford University Press.

Farrow, K. (2004) 'Still committed after all these years? Morale in the modern-day probation service', *Probation Journal. The Journal of Community and Criminal Justice*, 51: 206–20.

Finch, E., Brotchie, J., Williams, K., Ruben, S., Felix L. and Strang, J. (2003) 'Sentenced to treatment: early experience of drug treatment and testing orders in England', *European Addiction Research*, 9: 131–7.

Finney, A. (2004a) *Violence in the Night-time Economy: Key Findings from the Research*. Home Office Research Findings 214. London: Home Office.

Finney, A. (2004b) *Alcohol and Sexual Violence: Key Findings from the Research*. Home Office Research Findings 215. London: Home Office.

Finney, A. (2004c) *Alcohol and Intimate Partner Violence: Key Findings from the Research*. Home Office Research Findings 216. London: Home Office.

Fiorentine, R., Nakashima, J. and Anglin, M.D. (1999) 'Client engagement with drug treatment', *Journal of Substance Abuse Treatment*, 17: 199–206.

Fitzgerald, J. and Chilvers, M. (2002) *Multiple Drug Use among Police Detainees. Contemporary Issues in Crime and Justice. Bulletin* 65. Sydney: New South Wales Bureau of Crime Statistics and Research.

Flood-Page, C., Campbell, S., Harrington, V. and Miller, J. (2000) *Youth Crime: Findings from the 1998/99 Youth Lifestyles Survey. Home Office Research Studies* 209. London: Home Office.

Freeman, K. (2003) 'Health and well-being outcomes for drug-dependent offenders on the NSW Drug Court Programme', *Drug and Alcohol Review*, 22: 409–16.

Frischer, M., Hickman, M., Klaus, L., Mariani, F. and Wiessing, L. (2001) 'A comparison of different methods for estimating the prevalence of problematic drug misuse in Great Britain', *Addiction*, 96: 1465–76.

Godfrey, C., Eaton, G., McDougall, C. and Culyer, A. (2002) *The Economic and Social Costs of Class A Drug Use in England and Wales, 2000. Home Office Research Study* 249. London: Home Office.

Goldstein, P. (1985) 'The drugs/violence nexus: a tripartite conceptual framework', *Journal of Drug Issues*, 15: 493–506.

Gossop, M., Browne, N., Stewart, D. and Marsden, J. (2003) 'Alcohol use outcomes and heavy drinking at 4–5 years among a treatment sample of drug misusers', *Journal of Substance Abuse Treatment*, 25: 135–43.

Gossop, M., Marsden, J. and Stewart, D. (1998) *NTORS at One Year. The National Treatment Outcome Research Study. Changes in Substance Use, Health and Criminal Behaviour at One Year after Intake*. London: Department of Health.

Gossop, M., Marsden, J. and Stewart, D. (2001a) *National Treatment Outcome Research Study (NTORS) after Five Years: Changes in Substance Use, Health and Criminal Behaviour During Five Years after Intake*. London: National Addiction Centre.

Gossop, M., Marsden, J., Stewart, D. and Kidd, T. (2002) 'Changes in use of crack cocaine after drug misuse treatment: 4–5 year follow-up results from the National Treatment Outcome Research Study', *Drug and Alcohol Dependence*, 66: 21–8.

Gossop, M., Marsden, J. *et al.* (2001b) 'Outcomes after methadone maintenance and methadone reduction treatments: two-year follow-up results from the National Treatment Outcome Research Study', *Drug and Alcohol Dependence*, 62: 255–64.

Goulden, C. and Sondhi, A. (2001) *At the Margins: Drug Use by Vulnerable Young People in the 1998/99 Youth Lifestyles Survey. Home Office Research Study* 228. London: Home Office.

Hammersley, R.H., Forsyth, A., Morrison, V. and Davies, J.B. (1989) 'The relationship between crime and opiod use', *British Journal of Addiction*, 84: 1029–43.

Hammersley, R., Marsland, L. and Reid, M. (2003) *Substance Use by Young Offenders: The Impact of the Normalisation of Drug Use in the Early Years of the 21st Century. Home Office Research Study* 261. London: Home Office.

Harocopos, A., Dennis, D., Turnbull, P.J., Parsons, J. and Hough, M. (2003) *On the Rocks: A Follow-up Study of Crack Users in London. A Report of an Independent Study Funded by the Community Fund and the National Treatment Agency for Substance Misuse.* London: Criminal Policy Research Unit, South Bank University.

Harper, G. and Chitty, C. (eds) (2004) *The Impact of Corrections on Re-offending: A Review of 'What Works'. Home Office Research Study* 291. London: Home Office.

Harrington, V. (2000) *Underage Drinking: Findings from the 1998–99 Youth Lifestyles Survey. Home Office Research Findings* 125. London: Home Office.

Harrison, L.D. and Backenheimer, M. (1998) 'Research careers in unravelling the drug-crime nexus in the US', *Substance Use and Misuse*, 33: 1763–2003.

Hearnden, I. and Harocopos, A. (2000) *Problem Drug Use and Probation in London. Home Office Research Findings* 112. London: Home Office.

Hearnden, I. and Magill, C. (2004) *Decision-making by House Burglars: Offenders' Perspectives. Home Office Research Study* 249. London: Home Office.

Hedderman, C. and Hough, M. (2004) 'Getting tough or being effective: what matters?', in G. Mair (ed.) *What Matters in Probation.* Cullompton: Willan Publishing.

HM Inspectorate of Probation (2003a) *A Long Way in a Short Time. Inspection of the Implementation of Drug Treatment and Testing Orders by the National Probation Service.* London: Home Office.

HM Inspectorate of Probation (2003b) *2002/2003 Annual Report. Independent Scrutiny of the National Probation Service.* London: Home Office.

Holloway, K. and Bennett, T. (2004) *The Results of the First Two Years of the NEW-ADAM Programme. Home Office Online Report* 19/04. London: Home Office.

Home Affairs Committee (2002) *The Government's Drugs Policy: Is it working? Vol. 1. Report and Proceedings of the Committee.* London: HMSO.

Home Office (2000) *National Standards for the Supervision of Offenders in the Community 2000.* London: Home Office.

Home Office (2001) *Criminal Justice: The Way Ahead* (Cm 5074). London: Home Office (available at (http://www.archive.official-documents.co.uk/document/cm50/5074/5074.pdf).

Home Office (2002) *Probation Statistics for England and Wales.* London: Home Office (available at http://www.homeoffice.gov.uk/rds/pdfs2/probation2002.pdf).

Home Office (2004a) *Offender Management Caseload Statistics 2003* (15/04, RDS NOMS). London: Home Office.

Home Office (2004b) DTTOs/DDRs. *Advice and Information about Changes and Future Arrangements. Probation Circular* 55/2004. London: Home Office.

Home Office (2005) *Sentencing Statistics 2003* (05/05, RDS NOMS). London: Home Office.

Hough, M. (1996) *Drug Misusers and the Criminal Justice System: A Review of the Literature. Drugs Prevention Initiative Paper* 15. London: Home Office.

Hough, M. (2001) 'Balancing public health and criminal justice interventions', *International Journal of Drug Policy*, 12: 429–33.

Hough, M. (2002) 'Drug user treatment within a criminal justice context', *Substance Use and Misuse*, 37: 985–96.

Hough, M. (2003) 'Drug-dependant offenders and justice for all', in M. Tonry (ed.) *Confronting Crime: Crime Control Policy under New Labour.* Cullompton: Willan Publishing.

Hough, M., Clancy, A., McSweeney, T. and Turnbull, P.J. (2003) *The Impact of Drug Treatment and Testing Orders on Offending: Two Year Reconviction Results. Home Office Research Findings* 184. London: Home Office.

Hough, M., Jacobson, J. and Millie, A. (2003) *The Decision to Imprison: Sentencing and the Prison Population.* London: Prison Reform Trust.

Hough, M., McSweeney, T. and Turnbull, P. (2001) *Drugs and Crime: What are the Links? Evidence to the Home Affairs Committee Inquiry into Drug Policy.* London: DrugScope.

Howard League for Penal Reform (1999) *A Chance to Break the Cycle: Women and the Drug Treatment and Testing Order.* London: Howard League.

Hunt, N. and Stevens, A. (2004) 'Whose harm? Harm reduction and the shift to coercion in UK drug policy', *Social Policy and Society*, 3: 333–42.

Jarvis, G. and Parker, H. (1989) 'Young heroin users and crime: how do the "new users" finance their habits?', *British Journal of Criminology*, 29: 175–85.

Kevin, M. (2000) *Using Drugs in Prison. Research Summary. Research and Statistics Unit.* Sydney: New South Wales Department of Corrective Services.

Klee, H. and Reid, P. (1998) 'Drugs and youth homelessness: reducing the risks', *Drugs: Education, Prevention and Policy*, 5: 269–80.

Lloyd, C. (1998) 'Risk factors for problem drug use: identifying vulnerable groups', *Drugs: Education, Prevention and Policy*, 5: 217–32.

Lurigio, A. (2000) 'Drug treatment effectiveness and availability', *Criminal Justice and Behaviour*, 27: 495–528.

MacGregor, S. (2000) 'The drugs–crime nexus', *Drugs: Education, Prevention and Policy*, 7: 311–16.

MacLeod, J. (2003) *A Theory and Model of the Conviction Process in Modelling Crime and Offending: Recent Developments in England and Wales. Home Office Occasional Paper* 80. London: Home Office.

Maguire, M., Nettleton, H., Rix, A. and Raybould, S. (2003) *Reducing Alcohol-related Violence and Disorder: An Evaluation of the 'TASC' Project. Home Office Research Study* 265. London: Home Office.

Man, L., Best, D., Marshall, J., Godfrey, C. and Budd, T. (2002) *Dealing with Alcohol-related Detainees in the Custody Suite. Home Office Research Findings* 178. London: Home Office.

Marlowe, D.B. (2002) 'Effective strategies for intervening with drug abusing offenders', *Villanova Law Review*, 47.

Marlowe, D.B. (2003) 'Integreating substance abuse treatment and criminal justice supervision', *Science and Practice Perspectives*, August.

Marlowe, D.B., Kirby, K.C., Bonieskie, L.M., Glass, D.J., Dodds, L.D., Husband, S.D., Platt, J.J. and Festinger, D.S. (1996) 'Assessment of coercive and noncoercive pressures to enter drug abuse treatment', *Drug and Alcohol Dependence*, 42: 77–84.

Marsden, J. and Farrell, M. (2002) *Research on What Works to Reduce Illegal Drug Misuse in Changing Habits: The Commissioning and Management of Community Drug Services for Adults.* London: Audit Commission.

Maruna, S., Immarigeon, R. and LeBel, T.P. (2004) 'Ex-offender reintegration: theory and practice', in S. Maruna and R. Immarigeon (eds) *After Crime and Punishment: Pathways to Offender Reintegration.* Cullompton: Willan Publishing.

May, C. (1999) Explaining reconviction following a community sentence: the role of social factors. Home Office Research Study 192. London: Home Office.

McIvor, G. (2004) *Reconviction Following Drug Treatment and Testing Orders*. Edinburgh: Scottish Executive Social Research.

McNeill, F. (2004) 'Supporting desistance in probation practice: a response to Maruna, Porter and Carvalho', *Probation Journal. The Journal of Community and Criminal Justice*, 51: 241–47.

McSweeney, T., Herrington, V., Hough, M., Turnbull, P.J. and Parsons, J. (2004a) *From Dependency to Work: Addressing the Multiple Needs of Offenders' with Drug Problems. Researching Criminal Justice Series*. Bristol: Policy Press.

McSweeney, T., Stevens, A. and Hunt, N. (2004b) *The Quasi-compulsory Treatment of Drug Dependent Offenders in Europe*. A national interim report (England) prepared for the European Commission.

Measham, F., Aldridge, J. and Parker, H. (2001) *Dancing on Drugs. Risk, Health and Hedonism in the British Club Scene*. London: Free Association Books.

Meltzer, H., Gill, B., Petticrew, M. and Hinds, K. (1995) *Prevalence of Psychiatric Morbidity among Adults Living in Private Households*. London: OPCS.

Millar, T., Donmall, M. and Jones, A. (2004) *Treatment Effectiveness: Demonstration Analysis of Treatment Surveillance Data about Treatment Completion and Retention*. London: National Treatment Agency for Substance Misuse.

Murphy, T. (2000) 'Coercing offenders into treatment: a comprehensive diversion strategy.' Paper presented to the Society for the Study of Addiction, annual symposium, Leeds, October.

National Audit Office (2004) *The Drug Treatment and Testing Order: Early Lessons*. London: National Audit Office.

National Institute of Justice (2000) *1999 Annual Report on Drug Use among Adult and Juvenile Arrestees. Arrestee Drug Abuse Monitoring Program (ADAM)*. Washington, DC: National Institute of Justice.

National Treatment Agency for Substance Misuse (2002) *Models of Care for Substance Misuse Treatment: Promoting Quality, Efficiency and Effectiveness in Drug Misuse Treatment Services*. London: NTA.

National Treatment Agency for Substance Misuse (2004a) *Key Statistics on Drug Misusers in Treatment, England 2003/04*. London: NTA.

National Treatment Agency for Substance Misuse (2004b) '54 per cent more drug misusers get treatment in England.' London: NTA (available at http://www.nta.nhs.uk/).

Newburn, T. (1998) 'Young offenders, drugs and prevention', *Drugs: Education, Prevention and Policy*, 5: 233–43.

Nurco, D.N., Kinlock, T.W. and Hanlon, T.E. (1995) 'The drugs–crime connection', in J. Inciardi and K. McElrath (eds) *The American Drug Scene: An Anthology*. Los Angeles, CA: Roxbury.

Oerton, J., Hunter, G., Hickman, M., Morgan, D., Turnbull, P., Kothari, G. and Marsden, J. (2003) 'Arrest referral in London police stations: characteristics of the first year. A key point of intervention for drug users?', *Drugs: Education, Prevention and Policy*, 10: 73–85.

Parker, H. (2004) 'The new drugs intervention industry: what outcomes can drugs/criminal justice treatment programmes realistically deliver?', *Probation Journal. The Journal of Community and Criminal Justice*, 51: 379–86.

Parker, H., Aldridge, J. and Measham, F. (1998) *Illegal Leisure: The Normalisation of Adolescent Recreational Drug Use*. London: Routledge.

Peters, R.H., Greenbaum, P.E., Edens, J.F., Carter, C.R. and Ortiz, M.M. (1998) 'Prevalence of DSM-IV substance abuse and dependence disorders among prison inmates', *American Journal of Drug and Alcohol Abuse*, 24: 573–87.

Powis, B., Griffiths, P., Gossop, M., Lloyd, C. and Strang, J. (1998) 'Drug use and offending behaviour among young people excluded from school', *Drugs: Education, Prevention and Policy*, 5: 245–56.

Ramsay, M. (2003) *Prisoners' Drug Use and Treatment: Seven Research Studies. Home Office Research Study* 267. London: Home Office.

Richardson, A. and Budd, T. (2003) *Alcohol, Crime and Disorder: A Study of Young Adults. Home Office Research Study* 263. London: Home Office.

Ricketts, T., Bliss, K., Murphy, K. and Brooker, C. (2002) *The Life-course of the DTTO: Engagement with Drug Treatment and Testing Orders*. Sheffield: School of Health and Related Research, University of Sheffield.

Robins, L.N. and Reiger, D.A. (1991) *Psychiatric Disorders in America: The Epidemiologic Catchment Area Study*. New York, NY: Free Press.

Seddon, T. (2000) 'Explaining the drug–crime link: theoretical, policy and research issues', *Journal of Social Policy*, 29: 95–107.

Simpson, M. (2003) 'The relationship between drug use and crime: a puzzle inside an enigma', *International Journal of Drug Policy*, 14: 307–19.

Singleton, N., Farrel, M. and Meltzer, H. (1999) *Substance Misuse among Prisoners in England and Wales*. London: ONS.

Social Exclusion Unit (2002) *Reducing Re-offending by Ex-prisoners*. London: Social Exclusion Unit.

Soloman, E. (2004) *Alcohol and Re-offending – Who Cares?* London: Prison Reform Trust.

Sondhi, A., O'Shea, J. and Williams, T. (2002) *Arrest Referral: Emerging Findings from the National Monitoring and Evaluation Programme. DPAS Paper* 18. London: Home Office.

Stead, M., MacFadyen, L. and Hastings, G. (2002) *What do the Public Really Feel about Non-custodial Penalties? Rethinking Crime and Punishment*. London: Esmée Fairbairn Foundation.

Stevens, A., Berto, D., Heckmann, W., Kerschl, V., Oeuvray, K., van Ooyen, M., Steffan, E. and Uchtenhagen, A. (2005) 'Quasi-compulsory treatment of drug dependent offenders: an international literature review', *Substance Use and Misuse*, 40: 1–15.

Stewart, D., Gossop, M., Marsden, J. and Rolfe, A. (2000) 'Drug misuse and acquisitive crime among clients recruited to the National Treatment Outcome Research Study', *Criminal Behaviour and Mental Health*, 10: 13–24.

Stimson, G.V. (2000) 'Blair declares war: the unhealthy state of British drug policy', *International Journal of Drug Policy*, 11: 259–64.

Stover, H., Von Ossietzky, C. and Merino, P.P. (2001) *An Overview Study: Assistance to Drug Users in European Union Prisons. EMCDDA Scientific Report*. Lisbon: European Monitoring Centre for Drugs and Drug Addiction.

Strang, J., Heuston, J., Gossop, M., Green, J. and Maden, T. (1998) *HIV/AIDS Risk Behaviour among Adult Male Prisoners. Home Office Research Findings* 82. London: Home Office.

Stratford, N., Gould, A., Hinds, K. and McKeganey, N. (2003) *The Measurement of Changing Public Attitudes towards Illegal Drugs in Britain*. London: Economic and Social Research Council.

Taylor, B. and Bennett, T. (1999) *Comparing Drug Use Rates of Detained Arrestees in the United States and England*. Washington, DC: National Institute of Justice.

Turnbull, P.J. and McSweeney, T. (2000) *Drug Treatment in Prison and Aftercare: A Literature Review and Results of a Survey of European Countries*. Stasburg: Pompidou Group, Council of Europe.

Turnbull, P.J., McSweeney, T., Hough, M., Webster, R. and Edmunds, M. (2000) *Drug Treatment and Testing Orders: Final Evaluation Report. Home Office Research Study* 212. London: Home Office.

United Nations Office on Drugs and Crime (2004) *World Drug Report 2004*. Geneva: United Nations Publications.

Walters, G. (1998) *Changing Lives of Drugs and Crime*. Chichester: Wiley.

Ward, J. (1998) 'Substance use among young people "looked after" by social services', *Drugs: Education, Prevention and Policy*, 5: 257–67.

Ward, J., Henderson, Z. and Pearson, G. (2003) *One Problem among Many: Drug Use among Care Leavers in Transition to Independent Living. Home Office Research Study* 260. London: Home Office.

Wild, T.C., Newton-Taylor, B. and Alleto, R. (1998) 'Perceived coercion among clients entering substance abuse treatment: structural and psychological determinants', *Addictive Behaviors*, 23: 81–95.

Williams, L. and Parker, H. (2001) 'Alcohol, cannabis, ecstasy and cocaine: drugs of reasoned choice amongst young adult recreational drug users in England', *International Journal of Drug Policy*, 12: 397–413.

Wincup, E., Buckland, G. and Bayliss, R. (2003) *Youth Homelessness and Substance Misuse: Report to the Drugs and Alcohol Research Unit. Home Office Research Study* 258. London: Home Office.

Chapter 21

The role of perceptual intervention in the management of crime fear

Jason Ditton and Martin Innes

[Fear] of crime has become a major problem in our nation. Left unchecked, it can destroy the fabric of civilised society, causing us to become suspicious of each other, locking ourselves in our homes and offices, and relinquishing our streets to predators. The level of fear, however, is often far out of proportion to the objective risks of crime (Williams and Pate 1986: 53).

Introduction

The supports of current UK government policy towards crime-related fear appear to be fourfold. One, it is a bad thing. Two, there is too much of it. Three, it should be reduced. Four, this reduction should be measurable.

The relationships of the fear reduction policy to the crime reduction one (and the switch from crime prevention to crime reduction) are artefacts of policy manoeuvrings of the late twentieth century although, in the British context, the former can be traced to at least the Grade Report (Grade 1989: 1) and the philosophical sentiments to earlier American statements (Williams and Pate 1986). Although the Americans were the first to see the potential in crime fear and its lack of symmetry with crime itself (Brooks 1974: 244, being one of the first clear statements of the difference between the two), the British have now overtaken them in the degree to which fear reduction has become the cornerstone of preventative policy if a recent American review (Weisburd and Eck 2004) is allowed to set the tone.

That crime and fear should be yoked together in this way – as if they were somehow two sides of the same coin – is slightly surprising as they have been recognized as separate entitites, and ones for which different ameliorative policies are believed appropriate, for at least 20 years. That they are still seen as somehow conjoined may well be, as Garofalo and Laub (1978: 246) put it, because the way that the question is worded demands a particular answer:

When research is oriented in terms of the fear of crime, the implicit policy question is: How can the fear of crime be reduced? But phrasing the question in this way implies an answer: If the problem is the fear of crime, then the solution is to reduce crime, or at least to convince people that crime has been reduced...Specifically, questions are asked or problems are posed in such a way that the 'answer' is contained within the question or the problem statement. This creates a cognitive bind which limits the possibility of finding a solution: [then they quote from an unpublished paper by Leslie Wilkins] 'The specification of the problem in terms of the answer is always a specification for failure.'

Considering the four supports in turn, first and secondly, is fear of crime a bad thing, and is there too much of it? Clearly, it cannot absolutely be bad. A citizenry with no such fear would have a nasty, brutish and short existence. Each member would throw away his or her front door key (for ease of ingress), pin his or her money on the outside of his or her clothing (for ease of access) and make a point of publicly insulting large young men with shaven heads carrying hatchets (for ease of egress). Conversely, a citizenry paralysed with such fear would never leave the house, buy any food or speak to anybody, and thus have a life equally nasty, brutish and short. This point, or some version thereof, has been recognized, even by the Home Office, who commented in 1989:

An element of fear can be considered helpful in persuading people to guard against victimisation. Arguably, however, being mentally prepared in this way is better defined as awareness or concern, not fear. Fear itself can slide into hopelessness or terror, either of which can be counter-productive in terms of taking reasonable precautions (quoted in Lee 2004: 42).

We have a different view. The support for the current philosophy seems to be that some fear is a good thing, but people have too much of it, which is bad. Even this deduction is somewhat conjectural: it isn't really clear whether or not the problem is the amount of fear, or the rate and direction of change in fear rates when compared to recorded crime rates. In any event, how on earth has a consensus been arrived at wherein it can confidently be said that there is too much fear? What seems to have happened, and this is necessarily speculative, is that during a sustained period (roughly from 1993) UK recorded crime fell annually. However, national crime surveys didn't pick up on any equivalent (indeed, any) fall in levels of fear of crime.

The failed search for this is presumably based on the untested idea that prior to 1993 levels of fear were somehow 'correct', or at least were a baseline against which future levels could be measured. It is hard to find evidence to choose between the latter two interpretations. There is some evidence that people think crime is increasing when it isn't, and that more crime is violent than is, in fact, the case (Hough and Roberts 1998).[1]

However, Warr (1980, 1982) suggests that public beliefs about the frequency of various crimes are remarkably accurate, although the least frequent crimes are overestimated and the most frequent ones underestimated, which is something consistent with general findings in studies of judgemental processes. He further suggests (and we shall return to his key concept of 'perceptual intervention' towards the end of this chapter):

> strategies designed to reduce the social consequences of crime by altering public perceptions of crime are unlikely to succeed unless they are accompanied by true reductions in crime. Put another way, it seems unlikely that the public can be 'fooled' about crime. Though they may deny such intention, advocates of perceptual intervention have not demonstrated the need for such intervention (Warr 1982: 199).

Leaving aside the well-known research-evidenced knowledge that there has never been much relationship between levels of crime and levels of fear, and that reductions in crime have rarely led to reductions in fear of it, reducing measured fear became the cornerstone of policy. Needless to say, the difficulty of measuring emotions has not received much attention although, when it has, difficulties have been noted: 'we are not suggesting here that emotions cannot be measured. We believe, however, that such measurement is difficult when the emotion is fear, the object is crime, and the method is survey' (Gibbs and Hanrahan 1993: 387). Unfortunately, what appears to have happened is that an appreciation of the disjunction between objectively and subjectively measured risk of victimization was transferred to fear of victimization (which has no alternative and objective index). It is certainly the case that subjective and objective victimization measurements do not usually equate. For example, in the first two waves of a three-wave Trinidadian longitudinal survey (reported in part in Ditton *et al.* 2003), 60 per cent of respondents claimed to expect to be a crime victim in the 12 months following first interview, but 12 months later at second interview, only 12 per cent had indeed been victims. Looked at simply, some 48 per cent had what might be called 'false riskiness'. Considering the four two-wave possibilities, 9 per cent thought victimization likely, and indeed were victimized; 3 per cent thought victimization unlikely, but were victimized; 53 per cent thought victimization likely, and but were not victimized; and 35 per cent thought victimization unlikely, and were right.

For some reason, the disjunction between objective and subjective risk (a large percentage of any surveyed population think they are likely to become a victim, but only a small percentage ever do) is seen to be indicative of something to which policy should attend. However, it isn't clear whether it is recommended that many people should reduce their subjective risk rating a little, or whether a few people should reduce it a lot. The problem is that the disjunction is illusory. It is in no sense individually or collectively irrational for all a given population to feel that there is some degree of likelihood that they will become a victim even though only a tiny proportion will actually become so. Until victimization is inflicted on the few to which it eventually is, how can anybody know who should predict it for themselves?

But it is fear, rather than risk, to which policy currently attends. An additional policy difficulty is based on translating the illusion that false riskiness is a problem into one where 'false feariness' is one too. Here the problem deepens as fear has no objective index. Indeed, a feature of the fear of crime which distinguishes it from perceived risk of victimization (and from crime itself) is that there is only one way of measuring people's fear (unless psychological measures are introduced) and that is by asking them self-rating questions about it. With risk of victimization we at least have self-reported or other-counted victimizations as an objective comparison:[2] with fear of victimization, we have nothing.[3]

However, instead of immersing ourselves in such epistemological issues, we feel that fear of crime is neither good nor bad *per se*, nor is there an appropriate amount of it that all citizens should possess, but rather that fear is a situational rather than relativistic issue. It isn't that people don't have the 'right' amount of fear, but rather that sometimes fear is good (some fear is good) and sometimes fear is bad (some fear is bad). Put simply, from here on we refer to positive and negative fear of crime. From this perspective, policy should be directed to defining the optimal or ideal level of positive fear (Garofalo 1981: 856–7) and practice oriented to achieving it.

Next, thirdly and fourthly, should we reduce fear and can we measure that reduction? It is by no means obvious that reducing fear is necessarily a good thing. It is certainly the case that the police have spent more of their history increasing rather than reducing fear in the citizenry, from their imposition on the UK populace in the middle of the nineteenth century (Silver 1967, 1970; Storch 1975, 1976), through the American riots of the 1960s (Block 1971) where extreme fear of crime was manufactured to become a dominant cause of support for the police, to the fall of the Berlin wall in the 1990s, following which fear of crime there began gradually to replace fear of the police (Łoś 2002; see also Korinek 1997; Ewald 2000).

At one exquisite moment in the past, police as fear-creators bumped into police as fear-reducers. The fear-creators were trying to exaggerate the risks of crime in a local competition for scarce municipal funds at the same time as the US Police Foundation was experimenting with alternative policing strategies, one of whose goals was the reduction of crime (Pate *et al.* 1986; Skogan 1986; Williams and Pate 1986; Moore and Trojanowicz 1988). Most recently, of course, the general increase in recorded crime in the last quarter of the twentieth century seems to have been accompanied by a decline in fear of the police (first noticed by Thomas and Hyman 1977). Although deliberately increasing fear may not now be the most frequently cited policing policy it certainly remains the leitmotif of commercial advertising campaigns for privately purchasable domestic security equipment (Crawford 1998: 12).

A typically unexamined difficulty here is that the philosophical basis of emotional reduction is seated uncomfortably on two mutually exclusive propositions. On the one hand, it is assumed that fear is a stable individual personal phenomenon, in the sense of being neither chimeric nor contingent (neither fleeting nor dependent on the context – participation in a criminological survey – which is the sole type of occasion on which it is articulated). Put another way, and using a distinction first applied to fear of crime by Archer and Erlich-Erfer (1991: 344), it is 'chronic' rather than 'acute'. This proposition is rarely tested, but on the only occasion when it has been (Farrall and Gadd 2004) the precise opposite was found. On the other hand, it is simultaneously assumed to be an unstable general societal phenomenon in the sense that it is believed that an appropriately targeted policy can affect reductions. Again, there is, hitherto, no conclusive evidence that this can be done. That fear of crime is the reverse of this, viz.: an unstable individual yet stable general thing (see Ditton *et al.* 2003, 2005) is an equally tenable, yet, as far as the prospects for successful fear reduction go, a monumentally disastrous alternative.

Let us assume that reducing overall fear might be a wise prescription for some people, but that the reverse might be true for others. A general policy to reduce fear seems absurdly insensitive to the fact that many different problems concern different people in different ways and to different degrees in different places (and even to the same people at different times of the day, week or year). In this sense, a national policy (whether to reduce or increase fear) seems particularly out of place, and a micro-local policy of examining its contours appears far more appropriate.

Finally, whatever we decide to do, can the effect of doing it be measured? Two further problems collide here. On the one hand, it can be demonstrated that for every well-known finding in the field of the fear of crime, there is an equally well established and entirely opposite one. As a relevant example, Allatt (1984) found that improved residential security positively affected fear of burglary, but not burglary itself, but Ekblom *et al.* (1966) found precisely the opposite. Typically, as in this example, it cannot easily be established whether contradictory findings exist because the situations to which the same intervention is applied differ sufficiently to reverse the effects, whether the measuring instrumentation is at fault (or whether it is a mixture of the two; or of one or more of them and one or more completely different variables).

Until now the only exception to this ironic general rule has been the finding that women are more fearful than men. Recently, however, Sutton and Farrall (2005) had the foresight to include a lie scale in their question set, and can now show that women lie in one direction (pretending to be more fearful than they are) and men in the other (pretending to be less fearful than they are).[4] They conclude, by the way, that with data thus controlled, men are slightly more fearful than women, rather than less so.

To be sure, there have been many attempts to develop superior instrumentation, but most represent merely office doodling rather than field research, wherein 'experts' earnestly consult a sample of one, and then dreamily compose what they consider to be model questions. Consequently, there are so many different question types that it was possible to list 14 pages of them nearly 20 years ago (Ferraro and LaGrange 1987: 83–96), but there is no obvious way of discerning which is 'better' than any other, although it has been shown that different question wording (Kury 1994), and different methods of contacting respondents (Kury and Wurger 1993) affect responses.

Crime victimization, as a contrast example, shows how having two separate types of measurement can assist. We have officially recorded crime statistics, and problems with them are well known. We also have, increasingly, informally collected victimization statistics from crime surveys. Although too little attention is typically paid to the deficiencies of the latter (amongst many are the more serious the victimization, the less reliable the self-report of feelings (Biderman 1981)), respondent negligence in reporting victimizations to researchers that they had reported to the police is as frequently discovered as is reporting them to researchers having neglected to report them to the police (Sparks *et al.* 1977); and the number of self-reported victimizations is a function of the persistence of the interviewer and the patience of the respondent rather than of any objectively discoverable frequency of victimization (Clarren and Schwartz 1976: 129) – at least they are independent of the former. No such luxury exists with fear statistics.

The foregoing seems to set a pessimistic agenda. Not so. We recognize that academics can criticize, but that practitioners need to do something. Accordingly, we now review attempts (local ones rather than national ones, and these are inevitably police partnership ones rather than governmental ones) to reduce fear, and, noticing – rather than ignoring – the problems we have detailed, look to the emergent National Reassurance Policing Programme (NRPP) and its focus on signal events as sources of fear before, in the penultimate section, suggesting what we feel is a suitable evaluation strategy for the future.

Policing attempts to reduce fear

> there remains the danger that attempts to convince people their fears are groundless will be instrumental in convincing them that their fears are justified (Henig and Maxfield 1978: 310).

American enthusiasm for experiments in policing designed to reduce crime (reducing the fear of it was very much a by-product) began in the 1970s, more than a decade before the first British experiments. Although fear of crime was 'discovered' in America in 1967 – some 15 years before being found in Britain (Ditton and Farrall 2001) – the reason for this seems to have more to do with the fact that some key American police chiefs were criminologists (such as Lee P. Brown, the Police Chief of Houston; see Brown 1984; Brown and Wycoff 1987), with a few, such as Gary W. Cordner, Police Chief of St Michaels, even holding PhDs in the subject (see Cordner 1986). Their understanding and appreciation of experimentation and quasi-experimentation presumably derived from this expertise, and their application of it at the local rather than national level from the fact that policing in America is wholly local rather than merely superficially so as in Britain.

The backdrop for this had been hung by Charles Bahn (1974: 343) who was one of the first to consider the value of police visibility, and was the first, as far as we are aware, to use the term 'reassurance'. He was also the first (and perhaps the last) to point out that 'very tall, strikingly red-haired, or otherwise memorable' police officers (who would be at something of a disadvantage in undercover work) should be stationed at fixed posts in urban locations rather than prowl around so as better to reassure the citizenry. Somewhat stipulative at that point, although Balkin and Houlden (1983: 25) were later to find that 'the type of person most likely to reduce fear of crime is one employed in the public sector or employed in the private sector and wearing a uniform'. The sheer size of any particular police force relative to the number of citizens for which they are responsible is not related to fear of crime (Krahn and Kennedy

1985), and simple increases in the numbers of police officers (the dose-response problem to which we return shortly) are unlikely to do the trick. Even Bahn was aware that a plethora of laughing policemen might unnerve the citizenry, as efforts to convince them that crime had fallen might create more problems than it solved 'since fear does not readily dissipate, some people might suspect that the figures are being manipulated' (1974: 341), a finding much later supported by Winkel (1986: 384–5) who notices what he terms a 'boomerang effect' if increased police presence is introduced too rapidly. He comments: 'the abrupt and unannounced introduction of intensive foot and contact patrols in a neighbourhood can easily stimulate the impression among the residents that there must really be something wrong: otherwise why would there be so many policemen around.' A series of American crime-reducing city experiments picked up Bahn's gauntlet, although some were under way while he was drafting his article. He was clearly aware of the Kansas trials, although they were not mentioned in his bibliography.[5]

It is difficult to come to any solid conclusions from these experiments (brutal simplicity has it that increased foot patrol reduces measured fear, but that nothing else does) as they all had different bases, sampling logics, time-frames and so on. It is also unnecessary to review them in detail here, as they, and others (totalling 26 undertaken between 1974 and 1999), have been the subject of a recent and exhaustive review (Zhao et al. 2002). Those authors conclude that in sites with mere additional police presence, 59 per cent saw a decrease in fear (with 38 per cent no change and 3 per cent an increase). In sites with some additional proactive policing component, 75 per cent saw a decrease in fear (with 36 per cent no change and none an increase). Dubious stuff. However, they conclude (2002: 296):

> some studies conducted significance tests while others did not. Based on the information available, it is unclear whether the studies that found a decline in fear may have turned out to be insignificant if significance tests had been conducted … how can you compare the levels of significance among time-series studies, panel data analysis, and cross-sectional studies? Are these significance tests the same? We doubted whether they were.

Little experimental research on policing initiatives and their effect on fear has been conducted in Britain, although Allatt (1984), Bennett (1991, 1994) and Ekblom et al. (1996) are exceptions, and this provides the recent burst of keenness for police-driven fear reduction little relevant theoretical or implementation pedigree. The main difficulty is that available evidence creates a dilemma. On the one hand, those fear-reducing interventions that have been shown to be relatively successful (increased police foot patrols) are prohibitively expensive. By which we mean, not the incremental and possibly affordable cost of additional police officers, but a sufficient number of additional police officers to make a generally appreciated perceptual difference in numbers. This dose-response problem is one to which more attention might usefully be given in future. On the other hand, those interventions which are cost-effective (newsletters, media-reassurance campaigns) have ambiguous results in the sense that sometimes they appear to reduce fear, sometimes they have no effect and, on other occasions, they seem to increase it.

The latter, however, is only a problem if fear is viewed monodimensionally, that is, if only reductions in it are seen as desirable.[6] A slight detour might indicate why such an approach is insufficiently subtle. Noticed increases in crime itself, for example, when reductions are sought, are not always viewed inevitably as problematic. Crime reduction projects naturally seek statistical evidence of reduction (although as Hope 1995 points out, a general reduction in crime might even make things worse comparatively for some because of victim concentration), but are usually sensitive to misinterpretations of increases, which may be because 'a reduction in victimisation is masked by a corresponding increase in the proportion of crime reported' (Clarren and Schwartz 1976: 122) and/or for many other well-known reasons. As for fear reduction:

> some approaches aimed at fear reduction may actually increase fear among certain people, while other strategies may increase the incidence of crime itself. This may occur in two ways: (1) the policies which are designed to attract people to downtown areas may also attract criminals, and (2) the increased feelings of security which follow from successful fear reduction campaigns attract more potential victims and may result in carelessness (Henig and Maxfield 1978: 310).

That crime prevention programmes can, by increasing security consciousness, also increase measurable fear is well established (Norton and Courlander 1982; Winkel 1987, 1988). Indeed, the mere fact of being interviewed as part of a crime-reducing or fear-reducing research project can create rather than defuse or have no effect on crime fear. Rosenbaum provides a delightful example from an otherwise unpublished randomized experimental design study wherein an experimental group of burglary victim respondents were given a home security survey, and both experimental group and control group burglary victim respondents were later examined via a telephone survey. He:

> found that burglary victims who were given a home security survey by an experienced crime prevention officer were significantly more fearful of revictimisation, felt less control over their chances of revictimisation, were more upset and angry about the incident, and reported less emotional and psychological recovery than victims who did not receive a home security survey (Rosenbaum 1987: 120).

We mentioned earlier that fear of crime needn't be a bad thing. Here we go further: fear of crime is both good and essential. Those unconvinced by arguments advanced so far might choose to consider an analogy between crime prevention and tobacco-smoking cessation campaigns. Who would voluntarily cease smoking if the financial benefits and health disbenefits were not the twin pillars of cessation recommendation? Fear of lung cancer and other medical problems, together with the promise that cessation will gradually return the ex-user to almost the same life chances enjoyed by nonsmokers, offer an enviable and successful behavioural control model, but one, we stress, for which fear is an essential and positive component (Peto *et al.* 2000; Doll *et al.* 2004). A negative fear of lung cancer might persuade a smoker that cessation was pointless and that increased consumption would permit some guilty additional pleasure whilst dying. A positive fear of it promotes cessation. Rosenbaum again:

> the goal of fear reduction that moved to the forefront of national policy on community crime prevention may need to be re-examined. Fear reduction may not be possible or even desirable given the objective of increasing citizen crime prevention behaviors. While large increases in fear of crime would be dysfunctional, models used to predict preventive health behaviors suggest that moderate increases in perceived vulnerability may be necessary to induce behavior change directed at minimizing the risk of victimization. Fear arousal is unlikely to be destructive if it can be channeled into action that is perceived to be efficacious (Rosenbaum 1987: 129).

The restriction of attention within the fear of crime field to monodimensionality implies, as Rosenbaum (1987) later nicely suggested, recognition of the distinction between theory-failure, implementation-failure and measurement-failure. We do not feel that the enhanced policing projects described briefly above represent implementation-failure (although they may do: only resolution of the measurement problems will tell). They certainly represent theory-failure, and on at least two levels.

First, the already noted failure to recognize that fear might be an essential good; and secondly, that fear is neither the only, nor even the most likely, response to either crime victimisation, or to the prospect of it.[7] A more significant confusion is that between personal fear of future victimization and general concern about crime in society (Garofalo 1981). Those who are generally concerned might not be fearful of personal future victimization, and those fearful of personal future victimization might not be generally concerned. Others might be worried about both, and still others worried about neither. Typical analysis of traditional survey questions elides four response types confusingly into two, and that misses the point (Brantingham *et al.* 1986: 140–1).

Reassurance as perceptual intervention

It should be evident from this review that police crime reduction programmes tend to be associated particularly with the range of practices labelled 'community policing'. Arguably the most sophisticated, current and long-term contemporary example of community policing is the Chicago Alternative Policing Strategy (CAPS).

Established in April 1993, CAPS was based upon a quasi-experimental research design, with implementation and measurement activities initially focused upon five prototype districts, each of which had a matched comparison site. Following early successes across a range of indicators in the prototype districts (Skogan 1996; Skogan and Hartnett 1997), CAPS was expanded to all Chicago's police patrol divisions in 1995. The original aims of the programme included crime reduction, increasing public trust and confidence in the police and improving the general quality of life for citizens in Chicago.

Informed by previous community policing experiments and programmes, the Chicago version sought systematically to implement community policing principles in order to focus the police department's resources on the city's chronic crime and disorder 'problems', rather than simply responding to more acute criminal 'incidents' (Goldstein 1987). To resource this shift, nearly one thousand extra police officers were hired and all the city's uniformed officers were trained in problem-solving techniques (Skogan 1996). CAPS encouraged public involvement in policing, sought to engage problem-solving by police officers, and to foster new and better partnerships with other agencies. Police officers were given relatively long-term assignments to a beat, and were encouraged to spend as much time as possible 'on the ground' responding to calls, interacting with members of the public and engaging with preventative projects.

Of particular consequence for our present concerns is the fact that alongside a systematic implementation effort, CAPS has been subject to a well designed measurement and evaluation regimen. Over a ten-year period, a large number of cross-sectional and longitudinal surveys have been employed by the programme evaluators to document and track a variety of change processes associated with the policing reforms. As part of this more general evaluation approach, surveys have been used to monitor changes in Chicagoans' fear of crime and to infer the role of policing in inducing these changes.[8]

Data reported by Skogan and Hartnett (1997) drawn from the wave-one 'baseline' (April–May 1993) and wave-two (June–September 1994) surveys give a sense of the early impact that CAPS had upon public opinions and attitudes in the five prototype areas. Controlling for a variety of factors, they identified positive effects from raising the visibility of police activities and by engaging problem-solving techniques against the public's priority problems. Focusing upon fear and concern in particular, they note that the activities of the police have played an important 'reassurance' function, which contributed to changes in people's perceptions (Skogan and Hartnett 1997; Skogan and Steiner 2004).

The emerging findings from Chicago are being watched carefully by senior police officers and politicians around the globe. This is due not only to the systematic nature of the reform programme that has been implemented, but also because the impacts of these reforms are being carefully evaluated. In England and Wales, CAPS has had a direct influence upon what has come to be labelled 'reassurance policing'. This influence reflects the fact that, at a time when politicians and some senior police officers were becoming increasingly concerned by an apparent reassurance 'gap', the research evidence from CAPS served to remind them that levels of fear of crime were not a constant about which nothing could be done, and that, under the right conditions and notwithstanding the philosophical and analytical problems noted above, measured fear of crime can be reduced with a sufficiently well designed and implemented 'boots on the ground' policy coupled to a rigorous 'state of the art' project evaluation design.

In an effort to address this problem, and building upon pilot work conducted by Surrey Police, the Metropolitan Police Service and the University of Surrey, the Association of Chief Police Officers and the Police Standards Unit of the UK Home Office launched the National Reassurance Policing Programme (NRPP) in April 2003. Involving 16 trial sites based in eight police forces in England, the NRPP was designed to develop and test a style of policing explicitly intended to reduce levels of public fear of crime whilst simultaneously improving levels of public trust and confidence in the police.[9] The NRPP model of reassurance policing is based upon three interlinked and mutually reinforcing components:

1. Ensuring police officers are visible, accessible and familiar.
2. Using aspects of the signal crimes perspective as a local problem identification and targeting methodology,
3. The co-production of solutions through engaging community-based informal social control wherever possible.

A more detailed description of these components can be found in Innes (2004a) and in Innes *et al.* (2004a) and will not be reproduced here. However, it is important to contrast the NRPP model of reassurance policing with an earlier and less developed version proposed by Her Majesty's Inspectorate of Constabulary (HMIC) (Povey 2001). The HMIC version of reassurance postulated that, in order to serve a reassurance function, officers merely need to ensure they are simply visible, accessible and familiar. However, this presumes – erroneously in our view – that seeing a familiar police officer will over-ride any fear that is generated by that person's negative experiences or his or her perceptions of the environmental conditions in which he or she is situated.

As we have already evidenced, just seeing police officers isn't necessarily reassuring. Furthermore, and as was also detailed in an earlier section, previous evaluative studies suggest that changes in the nature and volume of fear are more likely to be achieved by those policing programmes that have incorporated forms of problem-solving intervention alongside enhanced visibility, accessibility and familiarity. It is for these two reasons that the NRPP highlights the role of acting against signal crimes and signal disorders, and for encouraging where possible the deployment of informal social control. The signal crimes methodology essentially provides a rationale for reassurance policing in terms of identifying where to focus interventions and problem-solving efforts in order to maximize their impact upon public perceptions. In what follows, we are referring to the NRPP model of reassurance policing.

In its current form, one of the key objectives of reassurance policing is cast as fear reduction. In line with our broader argument, we would suggest that this would be better articulated as fear management.[10] This is not just semantic revisionism, but conveys an important dimension of the reassurance agenda and in particular its role in informal social control. Under the right conditions, fear of crime is a key stimulus that encourages people to join together and actively engage in community governance of a sort that fosters informal social control. In effect, then, in order to promote this dimension of the reassurance programme, the police are relying upon there being a certain amount of citizen fear of crime (not of policemen) present, as without it, there is no motivation for shared active citizenship.

Of course, it has to be the right amount of the right type of fear. For as previous research has demonstrated, under certain conditions, fear of crime functions to degrade informal social control (Hunter and Baumer 1982). As such, what the concept of fear management does is produce a suitable amount of the right type of fear in the context of local social order. Where there is too much fear, the police must work with the community to reduce it. Where there is the right amount but the wrong type of fear, they need to change its form.

Just as it is important to clarify which version of reassurance policing is being supported, it is equally important to be clear how it differs from community policing and the CAPS programme that influenced it. For whilst it shares much of the 'genetic make-up' of community policing, and is most definitely part of its genealogical lineage, there is an important difference between reassurance policing and its antecedents. This relates to the fact that reassurance is based upon a more conceptually sophisticated understanding of how impact upon crime risk perception and fear of crime is achieved. It is this understanding that animates many of the core processes and systems of NRPP. Here we return to, and significantly develop, the analytic purchase of Warr's (1982) notion of perceptual intervention.

Concerned as Warr was to demonstrate that public beliefs about the prevalence of crime are actually more accurate than is often credited, he stresses that reductions in fear of crime require beliefs in reductions in actual rates of offending.[11] Implicitly, then, he identifies two key causal routes via which perceptual interventions work. First, one can change *what* is perceived – that is, alter some objective aspect of the situation concerned and this is the route Warr emphasizes. Alternatively, one can change *how* something is perceived, where the material situation remains constant, but the subjective interpretation and definition of it are manipulated in some fashion. The problem for Warr's 'materialist' approach and its emphasis upon crime reduction as a necessary precursor to widespread change in public perceptions of risk is that recent experience in the UK does not correspond to this logic. As we noted earlier, despite year-on-year reductions in recorded crime in the UK, since the mid-1990s, over 75 per cent of the public when questioned as part of the British Crime Survey repeatedly thought that crime was static or rising when, as objectively measured, it was falling.

In part this public disbelief may be a symptom of how, although recorded crime in the UK has been reduced, public policing has been rendered increasingly invisible to the public. The overarching operational trend, driven by a rationality of efficiency and effectiveness, has been to reduce uniform patrol work and thereby to limit the capacity to intervene against the low-level disorders that ordinary people encounter routinely in their everyday lives. Instead, police resources have been increasingly focused upon collecting intelligence about recidivist offenders who commit a significant proportion of the more serious offence types and disrupting their activities and, in the process, providing an increasingly limited, motorized, reactive service to emergency calls from the public. However, 'running' informants, manipulating intelligence databases and disrupting criminogenic networks are not something that is ordinarily visible to most citizens (Innes 2004a). As such, whilst incident-based policing may be effective, and recorded crime may fall, the visible symbols of formal social control in many communities have been rendered more remote. So whilst the objective conditions in terms of risk of criminal victimization may be gradually improving, some of the symbolic mechanisms that are crucial to how people subjectively construct an impression of their security have been rendered increasingly fragile. These counteracting trends explain, at least in part, how it is that crime rates may be declining, but people do not perceive this to be the case.

It is our contention that effective perceptual interventions, and thus effective fear management programmes, are those that succeed in manipulating both *what* is seen, and *how* it is seen. This is because, although the common adage is that 'I'll believe it when I see it', in actual fact, people will often only 'see it when they believe it'.[12] In terms of perceptual interventions this indicates that very often, in order to alter what is seen, a necessary precursor is changing how the object itself is perceived. On this basis, the reductions in crime are not seen or believed by the public, because they have not been confronted by evidence that challenges how they generally interpret the crime problem. In short, it is not so much that recorded crime has further to be reduced, but rather that people have to perceive that much reduction has already occurred.

Drawing upon this approach, a perceptual intervention can be defined as an action (or connected set of actions) performed with the intention of altering or manipulating in some defined way how a particular aspect of the world is seen and understood by another individual or group. Very often the reason for performing a perceptual intervention is the belief that it will induce a form of behavioural modification. Presented in this way, social life is suffused with perceptual interventions of different kinds, ranging in intensity and scale from the whispered rumours and innuendos passed between individuals, through advertising and marketing, on to mass education, war-time propaganda, peace-time political 'spin doctoring' and, perhaps the most intense type, 'brain-washing'. As forms of social action, these interventions are designed to shape perception, employ different methodologies and are underpinned by distinct purposes, but they share a common objective of changing how the world is seen in some fashion.[13]

Introducing the notion of perceptual intervention provides a real insight into how and why some forms of policing are able to manipulate or change people's fears. It also articulates something important about the emerging reassurance policing style. By making police officers more visible, accessible and familiar, by targeting those signal crimes and disorders that have a disproportionate impact upon collective risk perception, and by catalysing informal social control, reassurance policing is based upon a logic of perceptual intervention. That is, it seeks to alter what is seen, particularly by focusing upon those signal crimes and disorders that are especially generative of the more negative forms of fear of crime, whilst simultaneously manipulating how they are seen by enhancing the visibility and efficacy of formal and informal social control processes, so that crime and disorder events assume the status of transgressive aberrations in the local order, rather than as the norm.

The NRPP approach to reassurance policing is focused upon a particular type of perceptual intervention: control signals. A control signal occurs when an act of social control is performed in order deliberately to shape public perceptions of risk and security by emphasizing and exploiting the symbolic qualities of social control. Thus the signal relates to the communicative properties that inhere in all acts of social control (Innes 2003). From the point of view of reassurance policing, control signals are enacted in order to counteract or at least ameliorate negative fear that is generated in particular by signal crimes and signal disorders.

The concepts of signal crime and signal disorder are crucial to the conduct of the NRPP, because they provide an explanation of how fears about crime and disorder are generated. Put simply, the key idea is that certain events and incidents have a disproportionate impact upon levels of fear in a community, because they are interpreted as warning signals about the distribution of risks and threats. Thus not all crimes and disorders are equivalent in terms of their impact upon levels of fear of crime, and the degree of impact may not be related at all to legally defined hierarchies of relative seriousness. Ostensibly similar incidents can generate markedly different responses, legalistically serious ones little impact and legalistically insignificant ones dramatic and major negative local reverberations.

This reflects wider social processes in contemporary social life, where people are routinely assailed by high volumes of information as they navigate their way through social space. In order to manage this flood of data, much is effectively ignored by people on the basis that little is of any consequence to the ordering of routine conduct – it functions as little more than 'white noise'. In contrast to this noise, though, signals are the units of information that have salience and significance to people because they convey important data about appropriate modes of conduct and attitude given the conditions of the situations in which they are located. Crimes and disorders, and the physical traces of such acts, are frequently important in this regard because they are events that communicate relevant information about potential threats to safety in the social environment. Scanning the environment for indicators of risk and potential threat is a basic instinct of most organisms and, in human group life, the diverse range of acts that tend to be generically labelled as crimes and disorders are amongst the most regularly encountered threats to security.

The notion that certain crimes and incivilities function as signals and that the signalling process is useful in explaining the distribution of fear and risk perception has a number of diverse precedents, including the work of Goffman (1972), Ferraro (1995) and Slovic (1992, 2000). However, where the current work on signal crimes differs from these earlier uses of signalling, is that by combining aspects of the sociological work of Goffman (1972) and the semiotics of Eco (1976), a formal methodology for diagnosing signal crimes and signal disorders from the public's crime talk has been established. A full account of the conceptual apparatus that underpins the signal crimes perspective and examples of its use in analysing empirical data can be found in Innes (2004b); here we will simply highlight some of its more pertinent dimensions.

Informed by the theoretical work of both Goffman and Eco, the key feature of a signal is that it is identified by an individual or group as having had an effect upon them in some way. It is this effect that serves to mark out an event as a signal, distinguishing it from mere noise. In terms of operationalizing the signal crimes concept in order to inform and direct the conduct of reassurance policing, it is this formal methodology that enables the separation of those events which function as signals to people from those events which constitute noise. This thereby identifies which problems to target police problem-solving and enforcement activities at in order for them to function as a successful perceptual intervention.

All signals comprise three components: an expression, a content and an effect (Innes 2004b). The expression is the event or problem that generates a content and effect. So, for example, if someone said he or she were walking in the town centre and he or she saw a mugging, the mugging would constitute the expression. The content relates to the risk that is perceived as a result of experiencing or hearing about a particular expression. Thus the person encountering the mugging might say he or she interpreted it as posing a risk to him or herself, and that risk would constitute the content of the signal.

Importantly, the research conducted to date has identified that people do not account for risks only in terms of their own safety; they also regularly focus upon risks to their property, to significant others,[14] to co-residents in a neighbourhood and to social order more generally. Then finally the expression and content must generate an emotional, cognitive or behavioural effect. An emotional effect involves a change in how the person feels, a cognitive effect changes how he or she thinks and a behavioural effect involves a change in his or her behaviour. Thus seeing the mugging might cause someone to feel afraid, or to change his or her behaviour – for example, he or she may not go into town alone any more. It is the conjoining of an expression, content and effect that serves to establish the presence of a signal. If any of these components are missing then a signal is not evident.

Using these three constructs, people's talk about their experiences of crime and disorder can be analysed to establish what incidents are functioning as signals for them. For example, Innes (2004b) gives the following example of an interviewee's detailed account of recent events in the interviewee's neighbourhood:

R: Yes, they have had a car pinched at the end house here and there were a couple of people burgled, there was a car last week or the week before with three tyres slashed.
I: Really, and how does that make people feel?
R: Sick … well people lock the door and they won't come out.[15]

In this extract, there are three expressions present: the theft of the car, the burglaries and the damage to the car tyres. The risk that is connoted by these expressions is to the co-residents in the neighbourhood identified by the word 'people', and the effect is a change in behaviour in that they lock the door and 'won't come out'. By using this analytic methodology it is possible to identify the different signal crimes and disorders that people identify, and by comparing their accounts it is possible to identify which incidents and problems are especially impactive in terms of shaping collective risk perceptions and thus causing fear of crime. It is these signals that are targeted by the formal social control interventions enacted under the auspices of reassurance policing.

Reflecting the broadly interactionist thrust of Goffman's writings, the signal crimes perspective holds that the signalling properties associated with an incident do not inhere in the incident, nor indeed in particular offence types. Rather a signal only becomes a signal to somebody because of how it is interpreted by him or her. Thus recent empirical work has shown that some murders function as signals to some people but not others, and some burglaries function as a signal to a particular individual but other burglaries do not. Similarly, certain incidents of vandalism function as signals but not all people will necessarily see the same incident as a signal. Whether an event has an effect on an individual or group will depend upon how it is interpreted by that person or group, and the situated context in which it is located.

The operational implication of this is that the police or other agencies, if they want to manage fear of crime effectively, cannot simply decide upon what their priorities for action are. This approach, although typical of the way that 'problem' estates were dealt with in the 1970s, is now outmoded (Rock 1988). Then, external professionals decided what the problems and solutions were; now, internal amateurs are surveyed, and they decide what the problems are. Preliminary research has strongly suggested that the signals that cause fear vary considerably by area (Innes *et al.* 2004a). Consequently the police have to capture data from the public in order to identify what the key signals in different localities are. As such, in terms of identifying the causes of fear – a prerequisite for managing it – what is required are locally oriented data-capture mechanisms, in the form of local fear-of-crime surveys that are sufficiently sensitive to reflect local conditions and local problems.

Although there are a number of notable examples of locally oriented fear-of-crime surveys, the field remains dominated by large-scale national examples. But whilst extrapolating findings from national fear-of-crime surveys will provide an estimate of the distribution of fear in a population, if one is engaged in attempts to manage fear, this requires a greater precision and granularity to the data. Fear management requires a knowledge of what is triggering the problem in the first place. Even if fear in different areas is caused by what ostensibly appear to be similar problems, such as 'drugs' or 'mugging', these issues are likely to demonstrate considerable situational variation on the ground. Variation that is important in understanding how fear is being caused, why it is being caused and thus what interventions might be employed to reconfigure it so as to minimize its negative effects and maximize its positive ones.

Under the auspices of the NRPP a multi-method approach to identifying signal crimes and disorders has been used, employing a combination of local fear-of-crime surveys and qualitative techniques at the micro level. The survey is used to identify broad patterns and trends in terms of what the local problems are perceived to be according to various sociodemographic and sociogeographic variables. These data on the distribution of fear in a population and how it is segmented are then augmented by more detailed qualitative research using in-depth interviews and field observation to establish a more textured, complex and subtle understanding of the particular signals that are causing these fears. As such, the more quantitative data are used to provide some sense of what the key signals are likely to be and where they might be occurring, and the qualitative data 'drill down' into the issues to supply more detailed contextual information in terms of what precisely is causing the fear, when and where these activities are taking place, and who is perceived as being involved in causing the problems. This more detailed information about the contours of the signals has high operational value to police and other agencies as it is this that can be used to design appropriate interventions and to target their activities towards those problems where they are likely to achieve a disproportionate perceptual impact.

In adopting this approach, early data from signal crimes research strongly suggest that in terms of understanding how fear is generated in communities, social and physical disorders are often as important, if not more important than crimes (Innes 2004b). In terms of what they interpret as signals of criminogenic risk, ordinary people do not clearly differentiate between crime, social disorder and physical disorder. Rather they seem to construct their perceptions of insecurity around a combination of these signals. This tends to confirm a sense that the reason why some events come to function as signals has less to do with the qualities inhering in the incidents themselves than what they symbolize and stand for in the eyes of the person perceiving them. As such it provides a coherent explanation of why it is that incivilities demonstrate such a capacity to induce fear in people despite the fact that they rarely encapsulate any immediate and direct objective threat to safety. However, the presence of incivilities (and other crimes) in an area is interpreted as a general signal about the overall state of local social order and social control.

In emphasizing the salience of incivilities there are obvious potential similarities that could be drawn with the more established broken windows hypothesis and its usage in justifying a form of police practice that has sometimes been labelled 'zero-tolerance policing' (ZTP). In fact, the incorporation of a signal event logic into the operating principles of reassurance policing helps to distinguish it from zero tolerance on at least two grounds. First, whereas the orienting objective of reassurance policing can be understood as fear management, in contrast, ZTP identifies fear reduction as a route to crime reduction. Secondly, the latter approach, informed by Wilson and Kelling's (1982) hypothesis about the role of physical and social disorder in establishing a trajectory of generalized community decline, postulates that police need to engage aggressive interventions against incivilities and to have zero tolerance for such disorders.

In contrast, the signal crimes perspective argues contrary to this position by claiming that communities can and do tolerate a certain amount of certain types of low-level disorder and crime without these problems wholly undermining social order. However, they cannot tolerate all sorts of problems, nor can they tolerate an infinite amount of disorder. Consequently, what effective reassurance policing has to do is identify and intervene against those signal events that disrupt the extant local social order. This can be illustrated by reference to an example described in Innes *et al.* (2004b). In one ward in

London, interviews with residents of the area uncovered highly developed social networks that were routinely involved in informal social control to enforce widely shared normative boundaries of conduct. Moreover, there was agreement that to some degree most people in the area were 'at it' in some way or another, engaged in minor acts of criminality, and this was accepted and acknowledged as part of community life in this area.

Because of this situation, the respondents interviewed were not particularly concerned by the fact that there were high rates of mugging in the area, on the basis that there was an informally enforced understanding that 'you didn't mug locals' and if this did occur the local social network would be activated and would prove highly effective in recovering property and punishing the perpetrators. Consequently, the reported fear of crime amongst the respondents was unexpectedly low in respect of street robbery. The exception to this low level of fear was connected to issues related to a crack house that had opened in the area. This had functioned as a powerful warning signal to the residents and was a source of concern and worry to several people spoken to. Whilst for a range of issues the community was able almost to be self-policing, confronted with a more complex and difficult problem the engagement of formal social control was required.

Thinking in terms of signalling processes and how acts of deviance and social control are interpreted by people as signals about the state of local social orders offers new insights into understanding how fear of crime is generated and how such issues are involved in the symbolic construction of social space. Equally importantly, the signal crimes perspective proposes a formal methodology for analysing how people talk about crime and disorder and for using this to separate the things that act as signals for them from mere noise. Incorporated into the systems and processes of reassurance policing, it is an approach that identifies which incidents should be targeted for enforcement and/or problem-solving efforts in order that the presence of control is signalled to communities. In so doing, reassurance policing takes seriously the logic of perceptual intervention as effective fear management often requires a combination of objective and subjective change.

Enacting control signals against signal crimes and signal disorders is an approach that aims to neutralize the more corrosive forms of fear that flow from particular signal events. These are identified through a combination of local fear-of-crime surveys together with the broad patterns identified by micro-level qualitative work that serve to illuminate the specificities of a situation and its signals. The theory is clear. The practice is problematic. There is a growing suspicion that our ability to measure phenomena and changes in them has failed to keep up with our ability to understand them.

Measuring and understanding

So how might these problems of measuring change be resolved? They arrive at two levels. First, has there been a valid and reliable change of *Affect* at post- compared with pre- time points? Secondly, whatever the empirical direction of change (or lack of it), is this to be seen as a positive or negative *Effect*?

First, then, *Affect*.

At the outset, whether or not whatever change is pinpointed has internal validity depends on the degree to which research design moves towards the upper, sophisticated end of the five-point scale modified by, *inter alia*, Sherman *et al.* (1997), and from non-experimental through quasi-experimental to full experimental. However, all too often, this latter opportunity randomly to allocate respondents to control and experimental groups is not even considered, although past experience shows that this is possible (in ways far more contentious for subjects than forcing them to experience enhanced policing, see Berg *et al.* 1978). In addition, it would also, we feel, add considerably to the weight of published reports of intervention evaluations if a sixth point was added, and the analyst was also 'blind' as to which group was the experimental one and which the control one.

Longitudinal panels (for both control and experimental samples) are essential. A culture of selecting instead repeat cross-sectional samples in the evaluation of local interventions has grown up in Britain, possibly as imitation of the structure of the British Crime Survey. Panels should be to criminologists what separated identical twin studies are to geneticists.[16] Panels obviously imply no need to match pre- and post- samples, nor to weight them when unmatched (with the attendant problem of deleting real respondents and substituting fictitious ones) unless general population extrapolations are sought.

In practice, because of sample 'attrition' (of those initially interviewed respondents who, for various reasons, cannot be interviewed in subsequent waves), panels are best intentionally embedded in a repeat cross-sectional longitudinal design. In practical terms, sample attrition can be reckoned at about 30 per cent per wave. That is (and see Figure 21.1), from 614 respondents contacted in wave one (the left-hand bar) from an address list of around 877, about 70 per cent (430) are still there in wave two, with 70 per cent of them (300) still there at wave three. Following this model, a fresh 184 replacement respondents are added at wave two to make up for those lost from wave one. Of the original 614, 300 make it to wave three; and of the 184 added at wave two, 129 survive to wave three. At the third wave, 185 replacements are added to those lost from wave two to bring the wave three total back up to 614. The 614 were recruited at wave one to offer the likelihood of retaining 300 of them at wave three: 300 respondents being the target panel size.

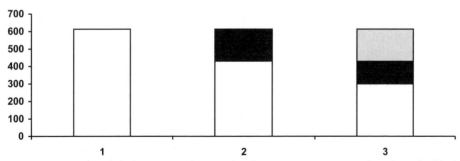

Figure 21.1 A model, three-wave longitudinal repeat cross-sectional with embedded panel design

Why bother with these replacement respondents? Sampling a population generally has at least two purposes. In the model described here, the longitudinal panel (the 300 who took part in all three waves) can illuminate change over time and, for them to do this, they have to answer the same questions three times. These repeat questions might amount to, say, about half those asked at each wave.

However, each wave can separately be defined as a one-off cross-sectional survey. In this sense, the other half of the questions might be a different set for each of the three waves. For some issues, the mere 300 who survived all three waves might be adequate for panel analysis purposes, but insufficient in number to resolve satisfactorily the issues posed by the questions asked for the first time at wave two or three. Weighting procedures might well come into play when each wave is considered as a one-off cross-sectional survey, but only if there is an intention to generalize the results to the population from which the sample was drawn.

Analysis of panel-derived data permits two crucial evaluation dimensions denied those working with data from repeated cross-sectional samples. First, consider data from the first two waves of a longitudinal panel sample conducted in Trinidad. In the first wave of the pilot survey, 63.7 per cent of the sample claimed that they felt safe when walking alone at night in the area where they lived. In the second wave, an identical 63.7 per cent claimed to feel safe in the same circumstances. Had this been two cross-sectional surveys (i.e. asking the same questions, but of different samples), then the conclusion would have been that there had been no change in perceived safety. However, comparing answers over time, and on a case-by-case basis, it was found that 18.4 per cent of those who were originally safe had become unsafe, and that 18.4 per cent of those who had originally claimed to be unsafe had, one year later, become safe. In all, some 36.8 per cent of the panel had changed their self-ascribed safety status in 12 months – indicative of high 'level' but low 'normative' stability (Ditton *et al.* 2003: 57).

Analysis of third-wave contact with these Trinidadian respondents is reported elsewhere (Ditton *et al.* 2005), but showed that instability of response to questions on degree of respondent fear of crime had not diminished 24 months into the project. Some of those who had been unfearful on the two previous occasions that they had responded remained that way, and some of those who had been consistently fearful when asked before also didn't change their minds. Some of those who had become more fearful at wave two stayed that way, and some of them became less fearful again. Some who had become less fearful remained so, but some of them went back to being fearful.

As an example of the second benefit, recall that the traditional response options to standard safety questions ('very safe', 'safe', 'unsafe', 'very unsafe') are typically collapsed into two ('safe' and 'unsafe') prior to analysis and report. With longitudinal panel data, the original four options can be retained and analysis may choose to plot movements between, for example, 'safe' to 'very safe', and from 'very unsafe' to 'unsafe', which would be indicative of benefits invisible to binary analysis. This permits reinstatement of the idea of safe-to-unsafe as a continuum rather than as a binary alternative, with fear thus being a scalar rather than oppositional variable – something to which theoretical underpinning has recently been provided by Gabriel and Greve (2003).

Secondly, *Effect*.

This Trinidad-exampled longitudinal surveying illustrates that people's expressed crime fears are not nearly as consistent or immutable as research based on cross-sectional surveying unwittingly implies. But what are we to make of it? Is their fear (or lack of it) – even when unchanging – a good or bad thing? Is change of feeling (and, for some, changing it back again) a positive or negative thing? Within the quantitative database thus assembled, respondent demographic discriminators cannot assist much as they are typically constant (e.g. gender) changing slightly and consistently and identically for the whole sample (e.g. age) or subject to broadly similar slight changes (e.g. income). The explanatory effect of non-demographic independent variables (chiefly victimization) between response collection points was inconsistent, and affected only a small minority of respondents.

Because the Trinidad research team had had no expectation that respondents would change their minds about their levels of crime fear (wave-three data had been collected before that from waves one and two had been analysed), it had not occurred to them to seek reasons for change or non-change contemporaneously. Future instrument design might wisely choose to cater for this distinct possibility. Accordingly, those involved in the Trinidad study returned to a sample of respondents, with some from each of the possible change or non-change types mentioned above, and tape-recorded a number of qualitative interviews which sought explanations for their previous responses. Analysis of this interview data indicated that some of those who change their minds about their levels of fear have good reasons to, and some don't (or can't) remember. The qualitative interviews, it has to be admitted, were held a long time after the final quantitative response was recorded (something else that future studies following this lead might choose to repair). And some of those who don't change their minds have good reason not to, but, again, some others don't.

We have hinted that research in this field is typically monophasal, and even when multiphasal is typically non-panel. However, for those considering adopting the longitudinal quantitative plus follow-up qualitative design that we recommend, there are enough examples of good longitudinal designs.[17]

Conclusion

In this chapter, we have tried to do two things. One, indicate that there is nothing particularly mysterious or odd about the frequently discovered fact that conventionally measured respondent crime fear may increase following their involvement in some sort of police-driven fear reduction programme. Indeed, our aim is to show that far from being a peripheral or marginal (and perhaps unwanted) finding, this should be the central focus of the type of future research that we feel will yield the most useful and informative results, and that across-time patterns of increases–decreases–increases (or whatever) in reported fears should be the clay from which future conceptual models must be fashioned rather than, as in the past, linger as uncomfortable and undesirable findings which are rationalised away or brushed under the evaluation carpet.

However, and this represents our second aim, what passes for the traditional approach to research design in this area (repeated cross-sectional quantitative surveys) will neither adequately contour the dimensions of fear and non-fear, nor supply sufficient context for analysis to decide whether increased or reduced fear is a good or bad thing. Our recommended research design (at least two phase-panel quantitative surveying followed by selective qualitative interview) is a minimum requirement for cost-effective future evaluation in this field.

Selected further reading

The best summary of the voluminous research literature on fear of crime is to be found in Chris Hale's (1996) article 'Fear of crime: a review of the literature'. A number of the key studies on the subject of fear of crime are brought together in the collection edited by Jason Ditton and Stephen Farrall (2001), *The Fear of Crime*. Kenneth Ferraro's (1995) book, *Fear of Crime: Interpreting Victimization Risk*, provides a theoretically interesting approach to the topic and an extended attempt to interpret some empirical data. The theoretical links between fear and levels of crime and disorder are best dealt with by Ralph Taylor in his *Breaking away from Broken Windows* (2000), and a helpful summary of the evidence of policing impacts upon fear, crime and disorder is provided in Weisburd and Eck's (2004) article 'What can police do to reduce crime, disorder, and fear?'.

Acknowledgements

The authors are indebted to Stephen Farrall, Murray Lee, Ken Pease, Natasha Semmens, Wesley Skogan, Nick Tilley and Frans Winkel for comments on an initial draft of this chapter.

Notes

1. Hough and Roberts (1998: 8, emphasis in original) claim 'whilst three-quarters thought that there was more crime nationally, just over half (54%) thought that crime *in their area* had increased'. Close inspection of the data (Hough, pers. comm.) indicates that 96 per cent thought the national crime rate went up or stayed the same, and 89 per cent thought this of the local rate. However, 75 per cent thought the national rate went up a little or a lot (only 55 per cent for the local rate), and only 20 per cent thought the national rate stayed the same (but 34 per cent thought the local rate had). This is in line with findings reported in Brantingham *et al.* (1986: 141), where they suggest that reflections on the national rate may relate to general concern about crime and those on the local rate to specific fear of becoming a victim.
2. Although, of course, self-reported victimization data tend to be victim based, but official criminal statistical data tend to be victimization based. This can usually be corrected for comparative purposes, but is usually ignored.

3. Archer and Erlich-Erfer (1991) have suggested that it might be possible to collect archival traces of general population gross crime fear changes against which to calibrate gross question responses (in their case, the traces were increases in handgun purchase and reductions in hitch-hiking after a series of brutal local murders), but nobody has followed their lead. This may be because behavioural measures typically fail to yield persuasive data.

4. An empirical proof of a possibility previously predicted by Smith and Torstensson (1997).

5. The cities involved were Kansas (Kelling *et al.* 1974); San Diego (Boydstun 1975); Cincinnati (Clarren and Schwartz 1976); Hartford (Fowler *et al.* 1979); Baltimore (Cordner 1986); Houston and Newark (Pate *et al.* 1986; Skogan 1986; Williams and Pate 1986; Brown and Wycoff 1987; Skogan and Wykoff 1987); and Flint (Moore and Trojanowicz 1988).

6. These remarks set aside Murray Lee's scholarly demonstration of the possibility that creating the 'fearing subject' is the aim of government policy (Lee 1999, 2001, 2004).

7. On anger as a more typical response, see Ditton *et al.* (1999a, 1999b); on the typical confusion between fear and anxiety, Croake and Hinkle (1976), Fattah (1993); and between anger and anxiety, Sarnoff and Zimbardo (1961).

8. Four waves of telephone surveys were conducted and figures reported are weighted to correct for multi-telephone homes and multi-adult families. During 1994–6 the surveys included 1,300–1,800 respondents. The 1997–9 surveys involved 2,800–3,000 respondents. In 2001 over 2,500 individuals were interviewed and in the final 2003 wave, 3,140 participated. Response rates varied between 35 and 60 per cent depending upon the area, and declined somewhat over time.

9. The eight police force areas involved in the NRPP are Surrey; the Metropolitan Police; Lancashire; Merseyside; Greater Manchester; Thames Valley; West Midlands; and Leicestershire. Further details on the NRPP are available at www. reassurancepolicing.co.uk.

10. Mark Warr (1987: 30) mentioned that fear should be 'managed' but did not develop the idea in the way suggested here.

11. As Smith *et al.* (2002) have shown, crime prevention initiatives can succeed before implementation if people erroneously believe them to be in place.

12. This phrase, and a particularly telling example of its salience, is to be found in Diane Vaughan's (1996) incisive account of the *Challenger* space shuttle disaster.

13. The conceptual apparatus for developing Warr's concept of perceptual intervention in this fashion can be traced back to the more 'strategically' oriented aspects of Erving Goffman's work on disrupted impression management and its impacts upon the conventions and rituals of the interaction order (cf. Goffman 1959, 1961, 1972).

14. Fishman and Mesch (1996) have established that some people's victimization fears, particularly that of mothers, is concern about their children, but the signal crime approach is the first to include public property in the list of things that people can fear to be at risk.

15. R denotes respondent, I denotes interviewer.

16. In an ideal world, criminologists would use identical twin respondents, with one of each pair in the experimental group and the other of each in the control group.

17. The following is an inevitably incomplete list of those relevant research reports which have at least a panel element, if not an entire panel structure: Kelling *et al.* (1974), Burgess and Holmstrom (1978), Cutler (1979–80), Feinberg (1981), Kilpartick *et al.* (1979a, 1979b, 1981), Atkeson *et al.* (1982), Becker *et al.* (1982), Calhoun *et al.* (1982), Allatt (1984), Frank and Stewart (1984), Cordner (1986), Pate *et al.*

(1986), Skogan (1986), Brown and Wycoff (1987), O'Keefe and Reid-Nash (1987), Rosenbaum (1987), Norris and Johnson (1988), Resick *et al.* (1988), Norris *et al.* (1990), Bennett (1990, 1991), Kaniasty and Norris (1992), Riggs *et al.* (1992), Norris and Kaniasty (1992, 1994), Perkins and Taylor (1996), Denkers and Winkel (1998), Robinson *et al.* (2003).

References

Allatt, P. (1984) 'Fear of crime: the effect of improved residential security on a difficult to let estate', *Howard Journal of Criminal Justice*, 23: 170–82.

Archer, D. and Erlich-Erfer, L. (1991) 'Fear and loading: archival traces of the response to extraordinary violence', *Social Psychology Quarterly*, 54: 343–52.

Atkeson, B., Calhoun, K., Resick, P. and Ellis, E. (1982) 'Victims of rape: repeated assessment of depressive symptoms', *Journal of Consulting and Clinical Psychology*, 50: 96–102.

Bahn, C. (1974) 'The reassurance factor in police patrol', *Criminology*, 12: 338–45.

Balkin, S. and Houlden, P. (1983) 'Reducing fear of crime through occupational presence', *Criminal Justice and Behaviour*, 10: 13–33.

Becker, J., Skinner, L., Abel, G., Howell, J. and Bruce, K. (1982) 'The effects of sexual assault on rape and attempted rape victims', *Victimology*, 7: 106–13.

Bennett, T. (1990) 'Tackling fear of crime', *Home Office Research Bulletin*, 28: 14–19.

Bennett, T. (1991) 'The effectiveness of a police-initiated fear reducing strategy', *British Journal of Criminology*, 31: 1–14.

Bennett, T. (1994) 'Confidence in the police as a mediating factor in the fear of crime', *International Review of Victimology*, 3: 179–94.

Berg, I., Consterdine, M., Hullin, R., McGuire, R. and Tyrer, S. (1978) 'The effect of two randomly allocated court procedures on truancy', *British Journal of Criminology*, 18: 232–44.

Biderman, A. (1981) 'Sources of data for victimology', *Journal of Criminal Law and Criminology*, 72: 789–817.

Block, R. (1971) 'Fear of crime and fear of the police', *Social Problems*, 19: 91–100.

Boydstun, J. (1975) *San Diego Field Interrogation: Final Report*. Washington, DC: Police Foundation.

Brantingham, P., Brantingham, P. and Butcher, D. (1986) 'Perceived and actual crime risks', in R. Figlio, S. Hakim and R. Renegert (eds) *Metropolitan Crime Patterns*. New York, NY: Criminal Justice Press.

Brooks, J. (1974) 'The fear of crime in the United States', *Crime and Delinquency*, July: 241–4.

Brown, L. (1984) 'Strategies to reduce the fear of crime', *The Police Chief*, June: 45–6.

Brown, L. and Wycoff, M. (1987) 'Policing Houston: Reducing fear and improving service', *Crime and Delinquency*, 33: 71–89.

Burgess, A. and Holmstrom, L. (1978) 'Recovery from rape and prior life stress', *Research in Nursing and Health*, 1: 165–74.

Calhoun, K., Atkeson, B. and Resick, P. (1982) 'A longitudinal examination of fear reactions in victims of rape', *Journal of Counselling Psychology*, 29: 655–61.

Clarren, S. and Schwartz, A. (1976) 'Measuring a program's impact: a cautionary tale', in W. Skogan (ed.) *Sample Surveys of the Victims of Crime*. Cambridge, MA: Ballinger.

Cordner, G. (1986) 'Fear of crime and the police: an evaluation of a fear-reducing strategy', *Journal of Police Science and Administration*, 14: 223–33.

Crawford, A. (1998) *Crime Prevention and Community Safety*. London: Longman.

Croake, J. and Hinkle, D. (1976) 'Methodological problems in the study of fears', *Journal of Psychology*, 93: 197–202.

Cutler, S. (1979–80) 'Safety on the streets: cohort changes in fear', *International Journal of Aging and Human Development*, 10: 373–84.

Denkers, A. and Winkel, F. (1998) 'Crime victims' well-being and fear in a prospective and longitudinal study', *International Review of Victimology*, 5: 141–62.

Ditton, J., Bannister, J., Gilchrist, E. and Farrall, S. (1999a) 'Afraid or angry? Recalibrating the "fear" of crime', *International Review of Victimology*, 6: 83–99.

Ditton, J., Farrall, S., Bannister, J., Gilchrist, E. and Pease, K. (1999b) 'Reactions to victimisation: why has anger been ignored?', *Crime Prevention and Community Safety: An International Journal*, 1: 37–54.

Ditton, J. and Farrall, S. (2001) 'Introduction', in J. Ditton and S. Farrall (eds) *The Fear of Crime*. Aldershot: International Library of Criminology, Criminal Justice and Penology.

Ditton, J., Chadee, D. and Khan, F. (2003) 'The stability of global and specific measures of the fear of crime: results from a two wave Trinidadian longitudinal study', *International Review of Victimology*, 9: 49–70.

Ditton, J., Khan, F. and Chadee, D. (2005) 'Fear of crime quantitative measurement instability revisited and qualitative consistency added: results from a three wave Trinidadian longitudinal study', *International Review of Victimology*, forthcoming.

Doll, R., Peto, R., Boreham, J. and Sutherland, I. (2004) 'Mortality in relation to smoking: 60 years' observations on male British doctors', *British Medical Journal*, 328: 1519–28.

Eco, U. (1976) *A Theory of Semiotics*. Bloomington, IN: Indiana University Press.

Ekblom, P., Law, H. and Sutton, M. (1996) *Safer Cities and Domestic Burglary* (HORS 162). London: Home Office.

Ewald, U. (2000) 'Criminal victimisation and social adaptation in modernity: Fear of crime and risk perception in the new Germany', in T. Hope and R. Sparks (eds) *Crime, Risk and Insecurity*. London: Routledge.

Farrall, S. and Gadd, D. (2004) 'The frequency of the fear of crime', *British Journal of Criminology*, 44: 127–32.

Fattah, E. (1993) 'Research on fear of crime: some common conceptual and measurement problems', in W. Bilsky *et al.* (eds) *Fear of Crime and Criminal Victimisation*. Stuttgart: Ferdinand Enke Verlag.

Feinberg, N. (1981) 'The emotional and behavioural consequences of violent crime on elderly victims', *Victimology*, 6: 355–7.

Ferraro, K. (1995) *Fear of Crime: Interpreting Victimisation Risk*. Albany, NY: SUNY Press.

Ferraro, K. and LaGrange, R. (1987) 'The measurement of fear of crime', *Sociological Inquiry*, 57: 70–101.

Fishman, G. and Mesch, G. (1996) 'Fear of crime in Israel: a multidimensional approach', *Social Science Quarterly*, 77: 75–89.

Fowler, F., McCalla, M. and Mangione, T. (1979) *Reducing Residential Crime and Fear: The Hartford Neighborhood Crime Prevention Program*. Washington, DC: US Department of Justice, LEAA and NILECJ.

Frank, E. and Stewart, B. (1984) 'Depressive symptoms in rape victims', *Journal of Affective Disorders*, 7: 77–85.

Gabriel, U. and Greve, W. (2003) 'The psychology of fear of crime: conceptual and methodological perspectives' *British Journal of Criminology*, 43: 600–14.

Garofalo, J. (1981) 'The fear of crime: causes and consequences', *Journal of Criminal Law and Criminology*, 72: 839–57.

Garofalo, J. and Laub, J. (1978) 'The fear of crime: broadening our perspective', *Victimology*, 3: 242–53.

Gibbs, J. and Hanrahan, K. (1993) 'Safety demand and supply: an alternative to fear of crime', *Justice Quarterly*, 10: 369–94.

Goffman, E. (1952) 'On cooling the mark out: some aspects of adaptation to failure,' *Psychiatry: Journal for the Study of Interpersonal Processes*, 15: 451–63.

Goffman, E. (1959) *The Presentation of Self in Everyday Life*. New York, NY: Doubleday, Anchor.

Goffman, E. (1961) *Asylums: Essays on the Social Situation of Mental Patients and Other Inmates*. New York, NY: Doubleday, Anchor.

Goffman, E. (1970) *Strategic Interaction*. Oxford: Basil Blackwell.

Goffman, E. (1972) 'Normal appearances', in E. Goffman, *Relations in Public: Microstudies of the Public Order*. New York, NY: Harper Colophon.

Goldstein, H. (1987) 'Toward community-oriented policing: potential, basic requirements, and threshold questions', *Crime and Delinquency*, 33: 6–30.

Grade, M. (1989) *Report of the Working Group on the Fear of Crime*. London: Home Office.

Hale, C. (1996) 'Fear of crime: a review of the literature', *International Review of Victimology*, 4: 79–150.

Henig, J. and Maxfield, M. (1978) 'Reducing fear of crime: strategies for intervention', *Victimology*, 3: 297–313.

Hope, T. (1995) 'The flux of victimisation', *British Journal of Criminology*, 35: 327–42.

Hough, M. and Roberts, J. (1998) *Attitudes to Punishment: Findings from the British Crime Survey* (HORS 179). London: Home Office.

Hunter, A. and Baumer, T. (1982) 'Street traffic, social integration, and fear of crime', *Sociological Inquiry*, 52: 122–31.

Innes, M. (2003) *Understanding Social Control: Deviance, Crime and Social Order*. Buckingham: Open University Press.

Innes, M. (2004a) Re-inventing tradition? Reassurance, neighbourhood security and policing', *Criminal Justice*, 4: 151–71.

Innes, M. (2004b) 'Signal crimes and signal disorders: notes on deviance as communicative action', *British Journal of Sociology*, 55: 335–55.

Innes, M. *et al.* (2004a) *The Signal Crimes Perspective: Interim Findings*. Guildford: Surrey Police (available at www.reassurancepolicing.co.uk).

Innes, M. *et al.* (2004b) *Signal Crimes and Reassurance Policing: Year One Final Report*. Guildford: Surrey Police.

Kaniasty, K. and Norris, F. (1992) 'Social support and victims of crime: matching event, support and outcome', *American Journal of Community Psychology*, 20: 211–41.

Kelling, G., Pate, T., Dieckman, D. and Brown, C. (1974) *The Kansas City Preventive Patrol Experiment: A Summary Report*. Washington DC: Police Foundation.

Kilpatrick, D., Resick, P. and Veronen, L. (1981) 'Effects of rape experience: a longitudinal study', *Journal of Social Issues*, 37: 105–22.

Kilpatrick, D., Veronen, L. and Resick, P. (1979a) 'Assessment of the aftermath of rape: changing patterns of fear', *Journal of Behavioral Assessment*, 1: 133–48.

Kilpatrick, D., Veronen, L. and Resick, P. (1979) 'The aftermath of rape: recent empirical findings', *American Journal of Orthopsychiatry*, 49: 658–69.

Korinek, L. (1997) 'Fear of crime: a contemporary example from the former "Eastern Bloc"', *EuroCriminology*, 11: 81–8.

Krahn, H. and Kennedy, L.W. (1985) 'Producing personal safety: the effects of crime rates, police force size, and fear of crime', *Criminology*, 23: 697–710.

Kury, H. (1994) 'The influence of the specific formulation of questions on the results of victim studies', *European Journal of Criminal Policy and Research*, 2: 48–68.

Kury, H. and Wurger, M. (1993) 'The influence of the type of data collection method on the results of the victim surveys: a German research project', in A. del Frate *et al.* (eds) *Understanding Crime: Experiences of Crime and Crime Control*. Rome: UNICRI.

Lavrakas, P. and Lewis, D. (1980) 'The conceptualisation and measurement of citizens' crime prevention behaviours', *Journal of Research in Crime and Delinquency*, July: 254–72.

Lee, M. (1999) 'The fear of crime and self-governance: towards a genealogy', *Australian and New Zealand Journal of Criminology*, 32: 227–46.

Lee, M. (2001) 'The genesis of "fear of crime"', *Theoretical Criminology*, 5: 467–85.

Lee, M. (2004) 'Governing "fear of crime"', in R. Hil and G. Tait (eds) *Hard Lessons: Reflections on Governance and Crime Control in Late Modernity*. Aldershot: Ashgate.

Los, M. (2002) 'Post-communist fear of crime and the commercialisation of security', *Theoretical Criminology*, 6: 165–88.

Moore, M. and Trojanowicz, R. (1988) 'Police and the fear of crime', *Perspectives on Policing*, 3: 1–7.

Norris, F. and Johnson, K. (1988) 'The effects of "self-help"– precautionary measures on criminal victimisation and fear: Implications for crime-prevention policy', *Journal of Urban Affairs*, 10: 161–81.

Norris, F. and Kaniasty, K. (1992) 'A longitudinal study of the effects of various crime prevention strategies on criminal victimisation, fear of crime, and psychological distress', *American Journal of Community Psychology*, 20: 625–48.

Norris, F. and Kaniasty, K. (1994) 'Psychological distress following criminal victimisation in the general population: cross-sectional, longitudinal and prospective analyses', *Journal of Consulting and Clinical Psychology*, 62: 111–23.

Norris, F., Kaniasty, K. and Scheer, D. (1990) 'Use of mental health services among victims of crime: frequency, correlates, and subsequent recovery', *Journal of Consulting and Clinical Psychology*, 58: 538–47.

Norton, L. and Courlander, M. (1982) 'Fear of crime among the elderly: the role of crime prevention programs', *The Gerontologist*, 22: 388–93.

O'Keefe, G. and Reid-Nash, K. (1987) 'Crime news and real-world blues', *Communication Research*, 14: 147–63.

Pate, A., Wycoff, M., Skogan, W. and Sherman, L. (1986) *Reducing Fear of Crime in Houston and Newark: A Summary Report*. Washington, DC: NIJ.

Perkins, D. and Taylor, R. (1996) 'Ecological assessment of community disorder: their relationship to fear of crime and theoretical implications', *American Journal of Community Psychology*, 24: 63–107.

Peto, R., Darby, S., Deo, H., Silcocks, P., Whitley, E. and Doll, R. (2000) 'Smoking, smoking cessation, and lung cancer in the UK since 1950: combination of national statistics with two case-control studies', *British Medical Journal*, 321: 323–9.

Povey, K. (2001) *Open All Hours*. London: Her Majesty's Inspectorate of Constabulary.

Resick, P., Jordan, C., Girelli, S., Hutter, C. and Marhoefer-Dvorak, S. (1988) 'A comparative outcome study of behavioural group therapy for sexual assault victims', *Behavioural Therapy*, 19: 385–407.

Riggs, D., Cancu, C., Gershuny, B., Greenbert, D. and Foa, E. (1992) 'Anger and post-traumatic stress disorder in female crime victims', *Journal of Traumatic Stress*, 5: 613–25.

Robinson, J., Lawton, B., Taylor, R. and Perkins, D. (2003) 'Multilevel longitudinal impacts of incivilities: fear of crime, expected safety and block satisfaction', *Journal of Quantitative Criminology*, 19: 237–74.

Rock, P. (1988) 'Crime reduction initiatives on problem estates', in T. Hope and M. Shaw (eds) *Communities and Crime Reduction*. London: HMSO.

Rosenbaum, D. (1987) 'The theory and research behind neighborhood watch: is it a sound fear and crime reduction strategy?' *Crime and Delinquency*, 33: 103–34.

Sarnoff, I. and Zimbardo, P. (1961) 'Anxiety, fear, and social affiliation', *Journal of Abnormal and Social Psychology*, 62: 356–63.

Sherman, L., Gottfredson, D., MacKenzie, D., Eck, J., Reuter, P. and Bushway, S. (1997) *Preventing Crime: What Works, What Doesn't, What's Promising*. Washington, DC: USDOJ.

Silver, A. (1967) 'The demand for order in civil society: a review of some themes in the history of urban crime, police and riot', in D. Bordua (ed) *The Police: Six Sociological Essays*. New York, NY: Wiley.

Silver, A. (1970) 'Social and ideological bases of British elite reactions to domestic crisis, 1829–1832' *Politics and Society*, 1: 179–201.

Skogan, W. (1986) 'The impact of victimisation on fear', *Crime and Delinquency*, 33: 135–54.

Skogan, W. (1996) *Evaluating Problem-solving Policing: The Chicago Experience* (available at www.northwestern.edu/ipr/publications/policing_papers/caps17, accessed 26/07/04).

Skogan, W. and Hartnett, K. (1997) *Community Policing, Chicago Style*. New York, NY: Oxford University Press.

Skogan and Steiner (2004) *CAPS at 10*. Evanston, IL: Northwestern University, Institute for Policy Research.

Skogan, W. and Wycoff, M. (1987) 'Some unexpected effects of a police service for victims', *Crime and Delinquency*, 33: 491–501.

Slovic, P. (1992) 'Perceptions of risk: reflections on the psychometric paradigm', in S. Krimsky and D. Goulding (eds) *Social Theories of Risk*. Westport, CT: Praeger.

Slovic, P. (2000) *The Perception of Risk*. New York, NY: Earthscan.

Smith, M., Clarke, R. and Pease, K. (2002) 'Anticipatory benefits in crime prevention', in N. Tilley (ed.) *Analysis for Crime Prevention*. Monsey, NY: Criminal Justice Press.

Smith, W. and Torstensson, M. (1997) 'Gender differences in risk perception and neutralising fear of crime', *British Journal of Criminology*, 37: 608–34.

Sparks, R., Genn, H. and Dodd, D. (1977) *Surveying Victims: A Study of the Measurement of Criminal Victimisation*. Chichester: Wiley.

Storch, R. (1975) 'The plague of blue locusts: police reform and popular resistance in northern England, 1840–1857', *International Review of Social History*, 20: 61–90.

Storch, R. (1976) 'The policeman as domestic missionary: urban discipline and popular culture in northern England, 1850–1880', *Journal of Social History*, 9: 481–509.

Sutton, R. and Farrall, S. (2005) 'Gender, social desirable responding and the fear of crime: are women really more anxious about crime?', *British Journal of Criminology*, forthcoming.

Taylor, R. (2000) *Breaking away from Broken Windows*. Boulder, CO: Westview Press.

Thomas, C. and Hyman, J. (1977) 'Perceptions of crime, fear of victimisation, and public perceptions of police performance', *Journal of Police Science and Administration*, 5: 305–17.

Vaughan, D. (1996) *The Challenger Launch Decision*. Chicago, IL: University of Chicago Press.

Warr, M. (1980) 'The accuracy of public beliefs about crime', *Social Forces*, 59: 456–70.

Warr, M. (1982) 'The accuracy of public beliefs about crime: further evidence', *Criminology*, 20: 185–204.

Warr, M. (1987) 'Fear of victimisation and sensitivity to risk', *Journal of Quantitative Criminology*, 3: 29–46.

Warr, M. (1990) 'Dangerous situations: social context and fear of victimization', *Social Forces*, 68: 891–907.

Warr, M. and Stafford, M. (1983) 'Fear of victimisation: a look at the proximate causes', *Social Forces*, 61: 1033–43.

Weisburd, D. and Eck, J. (2004) 'What can police do to reduce crime, disorder, and fear?', *Annals of the American Academy of Political and Social Science*, 593: 42–65.

Williams, H. and Pate, A. (1986) 'Returning to first principles: reducing the fear of crime in Newark', *Crime and Delinquency*, 33: 3–70.

Wilson, J.Q. and Kelling, G. (1982) 'Broken windows', *The Atlantic Monthly*, March: 29–38.

Winkel, F. (1986) 'Reducing fear of crime through police visibility: a field experiment', *Criminal Justice Policy Review*, 1: 381–98.

Winkel, F. (1987) 'Response generalisation in crime prevention campaigns', *British Journal of Criminology*, 27: 155–73.

Winkel, F. (1988) 'The police and reducing fear of crime: a comparison of the crime centred and the quality of life approaches', *Police Studies*, 11: 183–9.

Zhao, J., Scheider, M. and Thurman, Q. (2002) 'The effect of police presence on public fear reduction and satisfaction: a review of the literature', *The Justice Professional*, 15: 273–99.

Part V

The Preventive Process

Nick Tilley

The final part of this volume includes chapters laying out the 'preventive process'. This takes the reader through the process of identifying crime and crime-related problems for preventive attention, the analysis of those problems, decisions about what might be done about them, the evaluation of the effectiveness of strategies and tactics used, and the operation of partnerships in relation to whose work these activities are supposed to take place. The chapters presented here assume that evidence-based policies and practices have better prospects of success than ones disregarding evidence, however difficult in practice it might be to obtain evidence, analyse it and persuade decision-makers to attend to it. These chapters do not, though, assume that evidence alone can determine priorities or appropriate responses. Whilst decisions about these may be informed by evidence, other issues of politics, ideology and aesthetics will always also be important.

Alex Hirschfield, for many years at Liverpool University though now at Huddersfield University, has long been involved in the analysis of large data sets to inform the work of local crime reduction partnerships, especially in Merseyside. In Chapter 22, he brings his expertise in geographic information systems to bear on the local analysis of patterns of offending, in order to inform preventive priorities. Hirschfield explains the theory informing analyses of crime patterns for preventive purposes. He then distinguishes between crime-centred analysis (CCA – looking at patterns across space and time, and changes in them) and crime environmental analysis (CEA – making linkages between crime and the social and physical environment in which it takes place). He also distinguishes between analyses of aggregate data and disaggregate data and discusses their use in CCA and CEA. He considers the appropriate use of varying data sets. He provides illuminating worked examples of some of the sorts of analysis that can be undertaken to inform decisions about what to prioritize and what sorts of intervention will be appropriate.

Problem-solving methodologies have come to be widely used in crime prevention and crime reduction. In Chapter 23, Gloria Laycock, who was for some 30 years a member of the Home Office bringing evidence-based problem-solving to crime prevention, and has more recently been directing the Jill Dando Institute of Crime Science, takes the reader through the processes needed to formulate effective responses to specific crime problems. Laycock highlights some key theoretical ideas that can inform problem-solving crime prevention. These include 'crime pattern theory', 'routine activities theory', 'the crime triangle', 'the rational choice perspective' and 'mechanisms and contexts'. In formulating a response she advocates that problem-solvers 'think thief'; use 'crime scripts'; look out for 'crime chains'; conduct problem-solving iteratively; combine overlapping concepts from varying theories; focus on generic motivating factors that operate within sets of offences; identify opportunities quickly to nip emerging problems in the bud; identify crime facilitators; take account of ethical issues; attend to project implementation issues; and adopt a strategic approach to achieve sustainable effects without unwanted side-effects. She works through what this might mean in practice by taking the example of the kinds of crime and disorder problem often found in a city centre.

Weaknesses in the evaluations of initiatives have often been noted in reviews of efforts to prevent and reduce crime. There have also been major disagreements about the standards and methods that are needed if evaluations are to be informative. John Eck has over many years in the USA been at the heart of developments in situational crime prevention and problem-oriented policing, and their evaluation. He also took part in Sherman *et al.*'s influential 1997 report to the US Congress, *Preventing Crime: What Works, What Doesn't and What's Promising* (Sherman *et al.* 1997). In Chapter 24, he discusses what is needed if evaluations of crime prevention initiatives are to provide informative results that can appropriately be generalized in application to further work. His chapter is peppered with examples, mostly relating to place management as a method of crime prevention. Eck highlights the crucial importance of theory and of understanding the causal processes through which crime prevention measures may work. The critical elements in this he identifies as interventions (what's done), outcomes (what results), cases (what is affected) and setting (the context for the intervention). Each of these has to be properly understood and specified. In order for findings to be applicable, evaluations have to deal with questions of mechanism (how effects are brought about), association (the statistical connection with the intervention and outcome), temporal order (that the intervention preceded the outcome), rival causes (elimination of plausible alternative explanations) and generalizability (that the findings are relevant to a class of interventions and relevant cases). What is involved in each of these is discussed in some detail. Eck goes on to discuss a number of research designs and their strengths and limitations. He then considers what it is we can learn from evaluation studies and how. The telling heading for Eck's concluding section is, 'No theory, no lesson'!

The need for partnership in crime prevention has by now become taken for granted in most western jurisdictions. It has been officially advocated in England and Wales at least since 1984, when an interdepartmental circular was issued recommending it. Daniel Gilling's doctoral thesis, awarded in 1992, discussed multi-agency work in crime prevention and he has maintained this as a significant research interest. He has, thus, followed in some detail over a long period the trials and tribulations of this difficult aspect of crime reduction activity, which he discusses in Chapter 25. Gilling reviews the findings of studies that have been directed at understanding obstacles to the effective operation of partnerships, and at finding ways in which these might be overcome. These refer to such issues as structure, leadership and resources. However, Gilling highlights the need to set partnership working in a wider context. This implies that the complex interactions involved in partnerships' operations within and between micro (interpersonal), meso (interorganizational) and macro (political, economic and structural) levels, need to be unpicked. According to Gilling, of particular importance for partnerships, government support for them and their operation, has been the apparent transition from 'government' (supposedly achieving co-ordination through hierarchy and bureaucracy) to 'governance' (supposedly achieving co-ordination through markets and networks). The New Public Management, with performance indicators stressing crime reduction and crime control has, he suggests, contributed to police dominance in partnerships, privileging its agenda over those of other members. At the same time strategies of 'responsibilization' are diffusing responsibilities for crime prevention more widely.

Reference

Sherman, L.W., Gottfredson, D., MacKenzie, D., Eck, J., Reuter, P. and Bushway, S. (1997) *Preventing Crime: What Works, What Doesn't, What's Promising.* Washington, DC: US Department of Justice, Office of Justice Programs.

Chapter 22

Analysis for intervention

Alex Hirschfield

Introduction

This chapter examines the types of analyses that need to be undertaken to inform decisions about how, where and when to intervene to reduce and prevent crime. There are many different types of decision to be made and a plethora of analyses that can be deployed to support them and to monitor their impact on crime.

Knowing how, where and when to intervene requires both an understanding of the nature of the crime problem and an appreciation of what is available in terms of interventions and crime prevention strategies for tackling crime. The relevance and effectiveness of crime prevention measures necessitate not only that these two sets of knowledge are readily available, but also that the inter-relationships between them are fully understood.

Thus there needs to be a clear understanding of which crimes occur at which locations, what the crime generators are likely to be in terms of opportunities, how offences are committed (e.g. modus operandi) and when they take place. But data are also needed on which interventions are appropriate to each situation, what are the tactical, organizational and environmental conditions for their successful implementation and what are the likely economic and opportunity costs of their deployment.

This chapter begins by mapping out what we mean by 'intervention' in terms of preventing crime and how this concept translates into different types of activity and decision-making. Particular attention is paid to the types of analyses needed to inform decisions. Links between crime theory and crime analysis are also explored.

This is followed by a discussion of the different types of analysis that are carried out to identify the nature, size and distribution of crime problems so that appropriate action can be taken. A crime analysis framework is presented that distinguishes analyses by their breadth and choice of scale. The former concerns whether or not they focus solely on crime or on links between crime and the physical and social environment whilst the latter relates to their level of resolution: how far they utilize aggregate or disaggregate crime data.

The next section introduces the different types of secondary data required to inform the prevention process. The notion of hypothesis-driven data collection as a means of avoiding 'data overload' is presented. Variations in the scale and level of resolution of existing data sets, their quality, access and availability are discussed and gaps in data are identified. Particular attention is paid to data on recorded crime and calls for service to the police. Data on contextual factors, such as sociodemographics, infrastructure and landuse, are also discussed.

The following section sets out the types of aggregate data analysis typically used to profile crime problems within local authorities at the area level. Particular attention is focused on identifying areas of significantly high and significantly low crime, on profiling the crime mix in different communities and on measuring whether or not crime is concentrated into a relatively small number of areas or more widely distributed. Methods used for relating the geography of crime to that of other problems (e.g. deprivation) are also discussed.

The chapter then examines the types of analysis that are possible using disaggregate data on crime and other topics. Pin mapping, the derivation of crime hotspots, the use of residential neighbourhood classifications and digital aerial photography are covered. Particular attention is paid to the role of geographical information systems and spatial analysis. A series of practical examples are then used to describe the data and analytical techniques required for different forms of resource targeting (e.g. households, properties and places). The construction of 'resource targeting tables' that can guide where crime prevention measures should be located is explained and examples given of their use. The chapter concludes by summarizing the knowledge and skills needed by practitioners to conduct analyses for intervention.

Crime theory, decision-making and analysis

There are many different ways to intervene to prevent crime. Some involve making targets less vulnerable by strengthening them in some way (e.g. fitting bolts to doors and locks to the windows of vulnerable properties); others focus on improving surveillance (using CCTV cameras or improving street lighting) or by boosting guardianship (e.g. introducing neighbourhood wardens, encouraging more people to use town centres and setting up business watch schemes). Others raise awareness of crime risks through publicity campaigns or directly target offenders through assertive policing.

A number of stakeholders are involved. They include persons with an interest in and responsibility for making decisions on how to respond to crime. These can broadly be described as 'policy deciders', a mix of policy-makers who determine priorities about how resources should be used and policy implementation teams who are responsible for selecting and implementing appropriate interventions on the ground. Whilst the former may be made up of government ministers, local politicians and senior executives in service delivery agencies, for example constabularies, and Crime and Disorder

Reduction Partnerships (CDRPs), the latter typically comprise practitioners ranging from police basic command unit (BCU) and divisional commanders, project managers, through to crime analysts, project workers, wardens, community support officers and individual police officers.

Questions and decisions

The effectiveness with which crime prevention measures are deployed depends, to a great extent, on how far interventions are appropriate for tackling the types of crime that a community faces and, if appropriate, how accurately they are targeted, how well they are implemented and how receptive local communities are to having them in their area.

Different types of analysis are required to support activities such as targeting, project implementation and community engagement. The issue of appropriateness or fitness for purpose implies a solid understanding of the local crime problem(s) coupled with knowledge about specific tactics or interventions that are likely to do the job. The targeting of resources needs to be guided on where, when and how crime incidents take place. What else is happening in an area in terms of other policing or crime prevention measures may also be relevant. Effective implementation needs to be informed by an understanding of the physical and social characteristics of the affected areas (street layouts, housing design, community cohesion, concentration of offenders), as well as knowledge and experience of project management, partnership working and data sharing.

There are clearly a number of decisions that need to be made. These require different types of learning and expertise that, in turn, are informed by different types of analysis at different stages in the decision-making process. Inevitably, a number of questions arise about the nature and purpose of intervening to prevent crime. For example, there are questions about how to:

- get a clear understanding of local crime problems;
- choose interventions to tackle them;
- determine whether or not the chosen interventions are appropriate to the problems;
- articulate the ways that they are expected to prevent crime. What is the theory that underpins their use? And
- find out about local conditions that may influence effectiveness.

These questions have implications for the nature and sophistication of supporting analyses.

There is also the question of where analyses fit into this picture. For example:

- What aspects of the intervention process need to be analysed and why?
- Which types of analysis need to be undertaken?
- At what point in time are they needed?
- Which data sets need to be collected?
- How can the results from the analyses be used?

Taken as a whole, the 'intervention process' needs to be seen as part of the policy-making cycle. This begins with problem analysis followed by policy options appraisal and then progresses to policy implementation, continuous monitoring, evaluation and policy review. Analyses in support of the intervention process can be undertaken at each stage of this cycle or throughout the process. Relevant analyses in the initial stages would focus on crime problems and the socioenvironmental contexts in which they occur. Halfway through the cycle, the emphasis would be on monitoring and reviewing the implementation of projects. The analyses in later stages would be concerned with the measurement of policy impacts, the attribution of observed changes to interventions and the search for any policy side-effects such as displacement, crime switch or the diffusion of benefits (i.e. where crime reduces in areas not subjected to the intervention).

The concern in this chapter is with analyses to support interventions in the initial stages. The monitoring, evaluation and review of crime prevention programmes are covered elsewhere in this handbook (see Chapter 24).

Even the initial tasks require a breadth of knowledge and analytical skills. A holistic approach to analysis for intervention would involve learning not only about patterns of crime and disorder within a community, but also about other factors that affect the targeting, implementation and ultimately the effectiveness of crime prevention measures. These include an understanding of the following:

- The distribution of crime opportunities (i.e. the underlying contextual factors that facilitate, generate or protect against crime).
- Crime prevention strategies and their appropriateness.
- Methods for resource allocation and targeting.
- Prerequisites for the deployment of crime prevention on the ground (partnership working, engagement and support of communities).
- Funding.
- Likely sustainability of crime prevention measures.

Knowledge about each of the above cannot be acquired solely through an analysis of recorded crime data. Knowing about the types of communities into which crime prevention measures are being introduced is crucial. Not all areas are equally receptive to crime prevention. Some may be less socially cohesive than others, making the task of gaining community support for initiatives that much harder. There will be differences in street layout, landuse, housing management practices, transport routes and accessibility of neighbourhoods to offenders, all of which will influence the size and nature of the challenge ahead.

Understanding crime patterns

Understanding patterns of crime and the mechanisms that generate them is a good starting point. Crimes are not unique random events but rather share a number of common characteristics or features reflecting the activities both of victims and offenders. These common characteristics might include a tendency for incidents to occur in the same areas (spatial clustering), to afflict the same households or individuals (repeat victimization) or to occur at certain times of the day. They may also feature specific modus operandi, affect particular types of property or be perpetrated against victims with similar demographic and social characteristics (e.g. unemployed single people).

The fact that discernible patterns of crime can be identified is helpful when deciding how to intervene. Thus, the concentration of crime on particular days of the week or at specific times of day (e.g. assaults on Saturday nights between 11 pm and 2 am) means that the same level of resources need not be deployed at all times. Likewise, the fact that some individuals are at greater risk of being a victim of crime or indeed an offender (e.g. young males aged 19–24) than others (middle-aged couples) means that interventions aimed at protecting vulnerable people or deterring offenders need not be targeted at everyone within the population. Similarly, the fact that some locations (e.g. areas of multi-occupied housing in inner-city areas) are more prone to crime than others (e.g. semi-detached dwellings in affluent suburbs) means that we can be selective as to where we target initiatives to reduce crime. Not everywhere will need the same attention.

Thus three main components of the manifestation of crime, namely timing, target/perpetrator characteristics and location, can be used to inform how best to respond. If crime were a random phenomenon, then the power of robust analysis in formulating and targeting appropriate responses to crime would be much diminished. Indeed, it is the regularities and systematic patterns in the distribution of crime that ensure the value and benefits of robust analyses.

Crime theory and analysis

Theories of crime can help us to make sense as to why crimes do not occur randomly. These can be used not only to explain why crimes occur, where they occur and when but also to indicate how to intervene to prevent them or to reduce them. The two are inextricably linked in that crime prevention, to be successful, needs to be based on sound theory, whereas theory needs to be constructed from empirical evidence of the nature, scale and distribution of crime, including the insights provided through successful and unsuccessful attempts to prevent and reduce it.

Table 22.1 identifies some of the main theories that have been advanced to explain crime patterns, the implications of these for analysis and the crime prevention interventions implied by them.

Routine activities theory (Cohen and Felson 1979) explains crime in terms of the convergence, in time and space, of a motivated offender, a suitable target for the offender (e.g. a vulnerable person or unprotected property) and the absence of capable guardians against crime (e.g. a lack of surveillance and intervention by those who can prevent or disrupt the commission of an offence).

Suitable targets for crime may be a person or an item of property whose position in space or time puts that person or object at more or less risk of criminal attack. Capable guardians are not restricted to police officers or security guards but include anyone whose presence or proximity discourages

Table 22.1 Theories used to explain regularities in the distribution of crime

Theory	Crime mechanism	Implication for analysis	Relevant interventions
Routine activities theory (Cohen and Felson 1979)	Convergence in space and time of suitable targets, motivated offenders and absence of capable guardians against crime	Need to identify times and locations where guardianship is poor. How, where and when potential crime targets are unprotected	Situational crime prevention measures – target hardening, target removal, improved surveillance
Rational choice theory	Deliberate targeting decisions of offenders based on objective assessment of benefits and risk	Need to focus on how crimes are committed and how this varies by offence type. Include modus operandi in analysis of crime incidents. If this is not done interventions may be irrelevant to the way crimes are committed	Raise the risk to offenders through situational measures informed by MO analysis. Targeted policing of crime hotspots. The targeting of known offenders (especially prolific offenders). Crime prevention publicity
Crime attractors, crime generators, crime detractors (Brantingham and Brantingham 1995)	Situations (venues, service provision, events) that create crime opportunities by bringing people together	Need to identify locations, situations and events that attract and generate crime. Implies incorporating into an analysis data on the landuse and functions of particular properties and areas	Excluding offenders from the crime situation: keeping crowds of children out of sweet shops. Qualified door staff at bars and clubs. Extra patrols and surveillance at public transport termini. Radios and CCTV on buses. Setting rules for behaviour in shopping centres and clubs or on public transport
Crime pattern theory	Patterns of movement down paths, across nodes and along edges	Emphasizes the need for maps and analyses of crime for different hours of the day and days of the week, and to link this to commuter flows: school children being released from school, bars closing, or any other process that moves people amongst nodes and along paths	Automatic number-plate recognition systems. Police presence at strategic points on arterial roads (corridors of crime)

a crime from happening and may include families at home during the day, neighbours, visitors and employees who, by just being present at a given place and time serve as guardians against crime. Motivated offenders are those who respond to criminal opportunities.

Routine activities theory implies that the solutions would be to protect targets (e.g. by fitting window locks, strengthening doors and other forms of 'target hardening'), to increase guardianship (e.g. by improving surveillance through CCTV or setting up business watch schemes) and by raising the effort and risk for the offender in carrying out a crime (Clarke 1997; Felson and Clarke 1998).

For crime analysis, routine activities theory suggests that it is important not only to identify the location and timing of a crime but also to look at the context in which an offence takes place in terms of natural surveillance, the presence of people in and around the vicinity at different times of day and in relation to existing crime prevention measures protecting people and properties (e.g. alarms, window locks).

Although it is possible to gather such information through a detailed survey at the scene of a crime, this level of data would not be available to the crime analyst looking at several hundred burglaries across a sizeable area and trying to make sense of it all. However, the relevance of the context in which crimes occur does raise an important point, namely, that understanding crime patterns requires more than crime data.

Rational choice theory looks at the offender's decision in selecting a target based on his or her perceptions of the costs and benefits of committing a crime and how these compare against the chances of apprehension, the costs associated with the journey to crime and the expected reward from a particular offence. The theory assumes that the target with the highest net benefit will be chosen and can be used to understand patterns of offending, particularly how the modus operandi can vary with motivation and offence type (e.g. whether to steal a car for joy riding, for selling on or for stripping to parts). Thus joy riders are more likely to select a vehicle with good acceleration that is fun to drive, dismantlers may pick an older car whose parts may be valuable for resale and those simply wanting to drive home may pick the car most convenient to steal (Felson and Clarke 1998).

Once again, this theory has implications for crime analysis. The emphasis here is on the need to look at the modus operandi (MO) of the offence as well at timing and location. Unlike information on guardianship or the prevalence of existing levels of protection against crime, data on MO can be obtained from recorded crime incidents available to the analyst. The identification of how crimes have been committed can be an important step in ensuring that appropriate interventions are deployed. If the majority of burglaries to terraced houses are a result of offenders gaining entry to the rear of properties, then this is where protective measures are needed.

Two additional theories extend the range of factors that explain the manifestation of crime. Brantingham and Brantingham (1995) recognized that places can generate crime as well as attract crime. 'Crime generators' are places that create opportunities for crimes to take place because they bring large numbers of people together. Offenders confronted with abundant opportunities may commit crimes in these areas even though their presence there is for other reasons. Examples include shopping centres, bus stations, schools, venues for sporting events and concerts. These are the settings for opportunistic crime.

Crime attractors are locations, sites and properties that are well known to offenders (e.g. because of the criminal activities that occur there) and, as such, are specifically targeted by them. Examples include red-light districts, drug-dealing areas and run-down housing estates.

A crime detractor refers to a location that discourages offenders and offending. A stable business, the presence of middle-aged women, mixes of activities or easy natural surveillance can have such a positive consequence. Urban areas can be viewed as a 'patchwork of crime generators, crime attractors, crime detractors and neutral areas'.

Finally, crime pattern theory explains how people involved in crime move about in space and time. Central to the theory are the notions of 'nodes', 'paths' and 'edges'. Nodes are departure and arrival points (e.g. stations, bus stops, home, work, school or leisure facility locations). Paths are the journeys between nodes. Edges are boundaries of areas where people live, work, shop or seek entertainment. Some crimes are more likely to occur at the edges – such as racial attacks, robberies or shoplifting – because people from different neighbourhoods who do not know each other come together there.

The recognition that there are mechanisms such as crime attractors, crime generators, nodes, paths and edges adds considerably to the list of factors that need to be taken into account when conducting analyses for intervention. Changes in the functions of areas and flows of people by time of day point to a need for analysts not only to generate crime maps for different hours of the day and days of the week, but also, to link these to pedestrian flows amongst nodes and along paths, to the opening and closing of schools, shops, bars, clubs and other activities. Identifying properties and sites that serve as crime attractors and generators can inform the targeting and retargeting of crime prevention efforts. However, much more is needed than crime data to take these factors into account.

Theories are helpful because they explain what puts people, property and places at risk. If the conditions that promote or hinder the commission of an offence are known, then action can be taken to boost factors that protect against crime and to remove or reduce those that facilitate crime.

Knowing how to intervene also means understanding the distribution of crime opportunities and how they arise as well as familiarizing oneself with crime patterns. Although crime theories tell us a great deal about crime opportunities, analyses for intervention normally focus upon historic patterns of crime – identifying 'hotspots' and concentrating on what has already taken place.

The extent to which neighbourhoods experience different crime problems will also be influenced by differences in the social and demographic composition of target areas, levels of poverty and disadvantage, housing type and tenure, street layout, urban design, accessibility and levels of social cohesion within communities. These factors influence the number of offenders and those at risk of offending living within such areas and the supply of suitable crime targets (vulnerable people, properties and items of property). They also affect the ability of communities to protect themselves against crime through securing property, increasing surveillance, forming coalitions against crime (e.g. residents associations) and through supervising and exerting control over children and young people.

The crime analysis framework

It is clear from the above discussion that the mechanisms that generate crime patterns are shaped by the physical and social environment. The point was made that crime data alone are not sufficient fully to account for all the factors that analyses for the purposes of intervention need to cover.

However, it is not essential always to include environmental data in the analysis of crime problems. Indeed, much can be achieved solely through analysing crime incidents in terms of their location, timing and the extent to which they affect the same households or individuals (repeat victimization). However, when crime patterns are placed into their social and physical environmental context, additional questions about their manifestation can be explored (e.g. which types of neighbourhood have the highest crime? Do assaults cluster around particular bars?).

Crime analysis can be classified by its breadth (i.e. the degree to which the attributes of the crime alone is the focus of the analysis) and by its scale. The latter refers to the level of resolution used to explore crime patterns. For example, this may be at the level of the individual incident using disaggregate data for individuals or properties or at a higher level using aggregate crime data for zones (e.g. wards or police beats).

Crime-centred analysis and crime environment analysis

It is useful to break down analyses for scanning and profiling crime into the following two categories:

1. Crime-centred analyses (CCA).
2. Crime-environment analyses (CEA).

CCA uses a range of measurements and statistical techniques to identify the manifestation of crime and how it is changing over time. It would include analyses of its spatial distribution, its temporal patterns and how crime within one area compared with that elsewhere.

CEA examines the relationship between crime and aspects of the physical and social environment. This would include exploring links between crime and community-level characteristics (e.g. disadvantage, community cohesion) and between crime and other factors such as landuse, transport routes, the distribution of crime generators, crime attractors and, if available, crime prevention measures.

Each type of profiling can be carried out using individual-level data, aggregate data or a combination of the two. This crime analysis framework is shown in Figure 22.1. Some analyses will be entirely based on aggregate crime data (A, Figure 22.1). At the other extreme, there will be analyses only featuring crime data but carried out at the individual incident level (B, Figure 22.1). In between, will be those that combine aggregate and disaggregate crime data (C, Figure 22.1). Other analyses will bring crime data together with social and physical environmental data. Once again these may be carried out at the aggregate scale (D), at the disaggregate scale (E) or using some combination of the two (F).

Relevant questions to ask in relation to CCA would include the following:

- Where do crimes occur?
- When do crimes occur?
- When crimes occur, *where* do they occur?
- Where crimes occur, *when* do they occur?
- How do crimes occur (MO analysis)?
- Do areas with one crime problem have other crime problems?
- Where are these areas?
- Which and how many crimes do they have?
- How much of the population is affected (prevalence)?
- How concentrated is crime (socially, temporally, over space)?
- To what extent are there repeat crimes?
- What is the time interval between repeats?
- Where are repeat crimes concentrated?

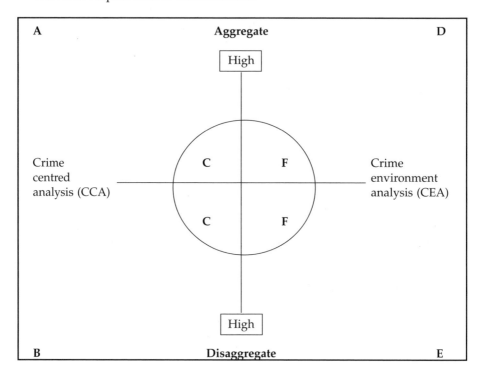

Figure 22.1 The crime analysis framework

- Who are the victims? Who are the offenders?
- Do offenders live in the areas with the highest crime rates?
- Do offence locations relate to those of previous offences?

Some of these questions (where and when do crimes occur?) are relatively straightforward to answer. Others are more complex. Thus answers to the question 'when crimes occur, *where* do they occur?' implies a different analysis from addressing the question 'where crimes occur, *when* do they occur?'. In the former, the emphasis is on subsetting the incidents according to their time of occurrence, perhaps by hour of the day, and then displaying their location. In the latter, incidents are mapped irrespective of the time of day in which they occur and their temporal distribution is then analysed. More sophisticated analyses utilize both the temporal and locational attributes of crime incidents to explore the relationship between the timing and location of crimes. Thus analyses of the space-time clustering of crime would explore the extent to which offences are linked or form part of a series as a result of their location and timing (Rossmo 1999; Canter 2003).

The arithmetic of CCA also includes the derivation of different measures of incidence and crime rate. Three can be distinguished, namely, incidence, prevalence and concentration. Incidence expresses the number of crimes committed in relation to the number of residents or households in the area (for example, the number of domestic burglaries per 1,000 households). Prevalence relates the number of victimized households to the total number of households (for example, burgled households per 1,000 households) and concentration measures the number of incidents per victim. In short, incidence counts crimes, prevalence counts victims and concentration counts the number of crimes per victim. The phenomenon of repeat of victimization explains why the number of crimes will often exceed the number of victims (Farrell and Pease 1993; Pease 1998).

Where consistent crime data (i.e. recorded in the same way for the same areas) are available for two or more time periods additional CCAs are possible that focus on the dynamics of crime. Thus it is then possible to ask the following:

- Is the volume of crime decreasing or increasing?
- Are crimes affecting the same areas or new areas?
- Are crimes diffusing or concentrating?
- Is there evidence of displacement or crime switch?

Variations in the accuracy of recorded crime data will affect the reliability of all these analyses. Locations are often poorly defined, especially for crimes against the person. The timings of incidents are often crude estimates. Whilst errors in the former can be reduced by better geo-referencing, the impact of those in the latter can be minimized through estimating the most likely time of occurrence using probability theory (Ratcliffe 2002).

CCA can be explored for total crime, specific crime categories (e.g. acquisitive property crime, violence and assault) or for individual offences (e.g. domestic burglary and theft of vehicle).

Widening the scope: crime environment analysis

The extensive list of questions outlined above demonstrates that a considerable amount of analysis can be carried out solely using crime data, without any reference to physical or social environmental factors. Inclusion of the latter opens up the prospect of carrying out a wide range of additional analyses whereby crime patterns are explored within different physical, social and policy environments and comparisons in crime between them are studied.

Thus CEA places crime patterns into a broader context revealing some of the social and physical environmental factors associated with them. These very factors will also have implications for the effectiveness of crime prevention measures on the ground. The types of question addressed in a CEA would include the following:

- What types of area have high crime?
- Are they student areas or deprived estates?
- Do they have particular types of housing or built environment?
- Are they policy priority areas?
- What types of transport and communications do they have?
- Are they accessible to offenders?
- Do they have poor natural surveillance?
- Do they have a large number of potential crime attractors?
- Do they have crime prevention measures already? If so, which?

Aggregate versus disaggregate analysis

The level of resolution at which crime data are made available can vary considerably. If the data are in the form of total counts by type of crime for police beats or BCUs, then it will only be possible to carry out analyses at the aggregate territorial zone level. Both CCA and CEA can be undertaken at the aggregate level but the ability to look for patterns in the distribution of individual offences will be lost. It would also be impossible to identify repeat victimization at this scale.

The supply of individual crime records enables the analyst to adopt a far more flexible approach. It enables the distribution of individual offences within police beats and BCUs to be identified. The space-time clustering of crimes can be examined. Hotspots can be identified. The individual addresses can be used to identify repeat crimes within a 12-month period and these can subsequently be mapped as points with a high degree of precision (e.g. down to a one-metre resolution).

Disaggregate crime data can also be used to produce aggregate crime statistics, although not vice versa. For example, if appropriate area identifiers (e.g. BCU, police beat and ward codes) are included on each individual record, then crime counts can easily be produced by small area for subsequent aggregate analysis. If not, then is it possible, by using a geographical information system (GIS), to 'intersect' points (e.g. burglaries with a one-metre grid reference) and 'polygons' (e.g. police beat boundaries). This procedure will append an area code to each individual record and these can then be used to aggregate offences by small area.

Release of individual-level crime data for processing and analysis will require both a data-processing and a data-sharing agreement to be signed by the external agency or researcher. This is not always a straightforward procedure and will vary considerably from one police force area to another.

Whatever the scale and breadth of the analysis, thought has to be given to the range of data sets required. These are now discussed.

Informing prevention: data requirements and sources

A range of existing or secondary data sets is available in Britain, as in most other countries, for profiling local crime problems and for identifying contextual factors that either facilitate or pose obstacles to implementing crime prevention measures on the ground. Some of these are comparable across different areas because they are collected using a consistent coding framework (e.g. recorded crime data broken down by Home Office crime codes and 2001 Population Census data). Others (e.g. calls for service to the police) are subject to local variations in how they are categorized and grouped together.

Notwithstanding how data on offences or incivilities are categorized, there are still differences in data quality reflecting inconsistencies in the accuracy of the location and timing of incidents. There are also variations by crime type in the extent to which recorded crime data reflect actual levels of victimization because of the widespread under-reporting of crime. (Dodd *et al.* 2004).

Dimensions of crime

Recorded crime only reflects one of several problems that crime prevention interventions seek to influence. There are many dimensions to the 'crime problem' and not all these can be measured or profiled using secondary data sources (Rogerson and Christmann 2004). The following illustrates the range:

* Area crime level (recorded crime – police statistics).
* Actual victimization (unreported plus reported – survey data).
* Crime opportunities within an area (secondary and survey data).
* Perceptions of crime within an area (survey data).
* Perceptions of crime opportunities (survey data).
* Fear of crime (survey data).
* Anger about crime (survey data).
* Shock about crime (survey data).
* Perceptions of safety (survey data).

The above is not an exhaustive list but serves to illustrate subtle, but important, differences in how crime may be viewed.

Area crime levels identified from police statistics give an indicative picture of crime within a community but are affected by under-reporting. On average around 42 per cent of crimes that takes place are reported and roughly 74 per cent of those reported end up on police computers as recorded crime. Levels of both reporting and recording vary by offence. Domestic burglary and theft of vehicles have relatively high levels of reporting (78–95 per cent) usually for insurance purposes and most are recorded. By contrast, only 30 per cent of all common assaults are reported to the police and around 68 per cent of these end up being recorded. This represents an improvement in recent years following the introduction of the National Crime Recording Standard in Britain (Dodd *et al.* 2004).

Victimization surveys, such as the British Crime Survey (BCS), are essential for estimating how much crime is committed because they identify both reported and unreported incidents. Thus the extent of under-reporting and under-recording of crime is revealed by comparing BCS data with recorded crime. Without the BCS it would be difficult to identify how far recorded crime underestimates the true picture.

Thus although recorded crime data can be used as baselines to measure change over time or to benchmark one area against another they do not measure total victimization or the number and distribution of likely crime opportunities. Neither do they measure perceptions of crime.

Perceptions of crime may be a particularly important barometer of how residents perceive their neighbourhood and may directly influence their lifestyle, behaviour and quality of life. Other responses to crime (experienced or perceived) can also be identified. Fear of crime and its reduction is a key performance indicator for the police and CDRPs, but cannot be measured from recorded crime data. Other emotions and responses to crime such as anger and shock are often overlooked but may be crucial when publicizing crime prevention or formulating other policy responses. Dealing with anger may require a different response from tacking fear.

Perceptions of safety may be instrumental in influencing people's mobility, social networking and their use of local services (e.g. public transport). In common with fear of crime these perceptions may not relate to the actual risk of victimization or improve when crime falls.

Other incidents not regarded as criminal offences *per se*, for example, disorder, incivilities and anti-social behaviour, can be also be strong drivers of anxiety and fear and can influence perceptions of crime and safety as well as neighbourhood satisfaction and quality of life (Rogerson and Christmann 2004). Disorder and anti-social behaviour incidents cannot be analysed using recorded crime data but indications of levels of concern by the public about incivilities can be gleaned by examining calls for service to the police.

Each of these measures has some relevance to the design and delivery of crime prevention interventions but the data on them are patchy, dependent on surveys that include questions on each phenomenon (perceptions, fear, anger, etc.) and are not available at small-area level. The point in highlighting them is to place recorded crime data into the broader analytical framework needed to understand fully the impact of crime on communities and the impact of crime prevention on perceptions.

Relevant secondary data sets

There is an abundance of secondary data on crime, disorder and the physical and social environment. The problem that confronts most analysts is that of becoming overwhelmed by what is available. A key consideration here is to be clear about how secondary data are to be used and to avoid selecting numerous data sets that effectively measure the same phenomenon.

Most analysts would seek information on volume crime and other key crime categories (e.g. burglary, theft of and from vehicles, robbery, theft, assault, violence and so on). Selected data on the social and physical environment as a framework for CEA require the analyst to be more cautious.

A systematic approach is needed to distinguish between relevant and superfluous data and to avoid 'data overload'. The way forward is to identify and assemble data on a hypothesis-driven basis. Thus the starting point would be to prioritize data sets that identify the following:

- Crime-related outcomes that are amenable to change through crime prevention interventions. The question here is 'what would one expect to see change at the community level if the interventions are effective'?

- Contextual factors (visible at the community/area level) that one would expect might influence the choice of an intervention and its likely success.

Examples of 'crime-related outcomes' would include levels of crime, crime mix, offending behaviour, disorder and anti-social behaviour and, if feasible, resident perceptions of each problem. Data on these would be needed both initially, to identify local crime problems, and at subsequent points in time, to measure change.

Examples of 'contextual factors' would include landuse (e.g. residential versus town centre), crime generators and attractors (housing, schools, road junctions, public transport termini) and data on demography, guardianship (people's presence in an area) and community cohesion.

Each data set and each variable within each data set should then be assessed for its relevance in respect of the hypothesized outcomes and contextual factors. If data are not relevant then time and resources should not be spent on assembling them. If they are relevant, then priority should be given to data that are accessible, have consistency and can be updated over time.

A range of secondary data that are typically used for crime analysis are listed in Box 22.1. The data sets have been allocated to one of two categories: crime and disorder, and physical, social and policy environment.

Crime and disorder

The data sets on crime and disorder are listed as either aggregated data or disaggregated data. The former refers to crime counts or rates that are available for geographical areas such as CDRPs, police force areas, BCUs, wards or census output areas. Disaggregated crime data refer to individual crime records that have an address, postcode and may contain an easting and northing grid reference denoting the precise location of the recorded incident.

Disaggregate crime data can be mapped using a geographical information system (GIS). However, recorded offences can be highly variable in the way in which addresses and locations are geographically referenced. The precision of the locational reference is highly dependent upon the crime category. Pinpointing the location of residential burglaries is, for example, in theory,

Box 22.1 A selection of data sets for profiling crime problems

---

Crime and disorder

Command and control
Aggregate:
Total incidents; Total disorder; Juvenile disturbances; CDRP; PFAs; BCUs; WARDS

Disaggregate:
X, Y (100 m); time; date; incident code; primary; secondary; tertiary

Denominators
Aggregate:
Population (MYE); households; residential properties; non-residential props; CDRP; PFAs; BCUs; wards

Disaggregate:
OS address points (1 m)

Recorded crime
Aggregate:
Total crime; Main crime categories; CDRP; PFAs; BCUs; wards

Disaggregate:
X, Y (1 m, 10 m); time; date; Crime code; MO

Offenders (aggregate)
Offence X; age X; area; [CDRP; PFAs; BCUs; wards]

Physical, social and policy environment

Infrastructure
Street network; OS OSCAR; motorways; A roads; B roads; railway stations; bus stations; bus stops; bus routes

Admin/policy boundaries
CDRPs; police force areas (PFAs); BCUs; wards; EDs; 2001 output areas; NDCs; SRBs; NRF; CRP target areas; EU objective 1, 2; DAT areas; Probation petty session divisions

Landuse
Digital aerial photography; residential areas; housing estates; town centres; 'districts' (e.g. CBDs, 'Theatreland', 'Chinagown', red-light districts, etc.); parks; playgrounds; cemetaries; shopping malls; retail parks; industrial estates; car parks

Social exclusion (aggregate)
[CDRP; PFAs; BCUs; wards]; Index of Deprivation 2004; domain scores/ranks; adult unemployment; youth unemployment; unemployment duration; school exclusions; truancy; HMOs; voids

Facilities/policy instruments
Police station; fire stations; prisons; courts; hostels; GPs; hospitals; hotels; schools, colleges, HEIs; youth clubs/facilities; leisure facilities; garages; pubs, night clubs; CCTV; alleygates; N wardens; Home/Business Watch; off-licences; public WCs

Demography/social structure (aggregate)
[wards, EDS]; ACORN group category [CDRP; PFAs; BCUs; wards]; age groups; household type; ethnic groups; housing type; housing tenure

---

Notes: MYE = Mid Year Population Estimates; N Wardens = Neighbourhood Warden Schemes; NCDs = New Deal for Communities areas; CDRP = Crime and Disorder Reduction Partnership areas; SRB = Single Regeneration Budget project areas; NRF = Neighbourhood Renewal Fund eligible areas; CRP = Crime Reduction Programme; HEIs = Higher Education Institutes; CBDs = Central Business Districts.

easier than identifying burglaries affecting corner shops, pharmacies and small businesses with 25 or fewer employees. This is primarily because non-residential properties are not coded consistently by their function, use and number of employees in police data (Bowers *et al.* 1998).

Crimes against the person, in particular robbery, theft and assault, are more difficult to map because of the often high degree of uncertainty about where they occur. In many information systems, their location is assigned to the nearest landmark or street intersection but in many cases it is difficult to obtain a reliable spatial reference for them. These problems are compounded when it comes to pinpointing the location of crime and anti-social behaviour on public transport.

Disaggregated crime data are not in the public domain and usually can only be accessed by agreement with the supplier, typically the police force. They are most useful for identifying crime hotspots, for producing crime profiles for non-standard user-defined areas and for monitoring changes in crime patterns following the implementation of crime prevention measures (e.g. checking for geographical displacement).

Command and control data are useful as a barometer of public anxiety and concern about crime and anti-social behaviour, especially in relation to juvenile disturbances, neighbour disputes and other forms of minor disorder. Their strengths include the facts that:

- they are continuous over time;
- the recorded incidents are not restricted to criminal events;
- many reports are by observers overcoming non-reporting by victims;
- they are subjected to only minimal screening by the police;
- they tend to be highly correlated with data on recorded crime; and
- errors of over-reporting tend to be counterbalanced by those of under-reporting.

The principal weaknesses with the data are that:

- they are subject to both under-reporting and over-reporting (e.g. where several telephone calls reporting the same incident appear in the data);
- a single incident may generate more than one call;
- updates about an incident may be recorded as a separate call;
- there may be a significant time lag between the time of the incident and the logging of the call;
- the location of the event's occurrence and that of the caller may not be recorded; and
- large volumes of data are generated which are only kept for short periods.

In common with recorded crime data, calls for service to the police can also be supplied in aggregated or disaggregated form.

Denominators

Although the volume of recorded crimes and command and control incidents provides an indication of the overall size of the problem in an area and enables some analysis of where clusters of crime occur and how they vary over time, they need to be related to appropriate denominators in order to construct crime rates.

Population denominators (total number of persons, total number of households) are typically obtained from the decennial population census and are available for administrative zones (e.g. wards) but not for *ad hoc* user-defined areas (e.g. a particular housing estate or a 500-metre radius around a public house or school). In these cases they need to be constructed by adding together the populations using small areas as building blocks (e.g. census output areas).

In the UK, the Ordnance Survey provide a one-metre grid reference for every address in the country. The product, called AddressPoint, is a gazetteer that distinguishes residential from non-residential properties at the address level. By using a GIS to sum all the addresses located within particular boundaries, it is possible to estimate the total number of residential and non-residential properties located in each zone. This information can then be used as denominators for crime rates (e.g. the number of non-domestic burglaries per 1,000 non-domestic properties). As the gazetteer is regularly updated, it can be used to identify new buildings and development and to produce more up-to-date estimates of the population in an area (i.e. based on the number of addresses) than the census.

Although these methods will generate a residential population they do not provide any indication of the numbers of persons present in non-residential areas and, more importantly, how these fluctuate by time of day. Therefore, they cannot be used to construct assault rates or theft rates in town centres on Saturday nights because they will inevitably underestimate the number of persons present in those areas at that time. Some measure of the present or 'available population' in these areas is required to identify the risk and prevalence of street crime, although this is not currently available on a consistent basis across all non-residential areas.

Physical, social and policy environment

The second half of Box 22.1 identifies non-crime data sets that can be used in a CEA to identify the context within which crimes occur. The spatial manifestation of crime is the result of a complex web of inter-relationships between demographic, social, cultural, lifestyle and landuse characteristics. Research has shown, for example, that there are strong links between the distribution of crime and the levels of deprivation and social cohesion found in different areas (Hirschfield and Bowers 1997). It is also important that spatial patterns of crime are not viewed in isolation from the functions of different areas (Wikström 1991).

Similarly, crime prevention initiatives do not operate within a closed system. An intervention that generates a successful outcome in one location at one time may be unsuccessful elsewhere. Therefore, analyses for intervention need to identify not only which types of crime to tackle but also how the characteristics of an area (e.g. its housing, street network, social composition, landuse and policy environment) might influence the deployment and effectiveness of the proposed crime prevention measures.

Landuse is potentially a very important contextual factor. Data on landuse can provide important clues about potential crime risks but they are seldom used for this purpose. For example, maps showing the juxtaposition of different types of buildings, different street layouts, the bordering of poor and affluent areas or the distribution of shrubs, trees and foliage that obscure natural surveillance would be particularly useful in identifying crime opportunities.

A secondary school next to a shopping parade may create opportunities for shoplifting, vandalism and truancy. One or two drugs houses or badly run pubs can affect the whole complexion of a neighbourhood. New roads or bus routes may create new crime risks in areas they touch whilst closing down crime opportunities in areas they cut off.

Situations and opportunities for crime also vary by time of day. A given location may be unfavourable for crime at one time but ideal for crime at another. For instance, an area that is primarily a business district during the day (with low crime) may become an entertainment area during the night (with a higher risk of theft and assault).

Other environmental contextual factors include the ones listed below:

The type and distribution of housing
Areas with subdivided, multiply-occupied, privately rented dwellings owned by indifferent landlords will be more difficult to protect than elsewhere. Such areas attract transient populations with low levels of social cohesion and are more accessible to actual/potential offenders.

Street layout and design of the built environment
Some designs provide very poor natural surveillance and easy and concealed access to the rear of properties that can create opportunities for burglars, drug dealers and muggers.

Accessibility of the area
Highly accessible areas (served by arterial roads, railways and bus routes) are more vulnerable to travelling criminals than those with poor communications.

Social, ethnic and demographic characteristics
Vulnerability to crime and the way preventive action is targeted will be affected by the level of deprivation, the age structure of the population, the ethnic mix in the area, unemployment levels, the number of single-parent families and student/migrant populations.

Community cohesion/co-operation
The community might be more or less inclined to participate in the implementation and planning of schemes. The effectiveness of a crime prevention initiative can be jeopardized where there is apathy on behalf of the community for whatever reason (e.g. because of a lack of trust in the implementation agency, a lack of ownership of or involvement in the scheme, or a perception that the scheme is irrelevant or will not work). Apathy and non-participation are more likely to occur in less socially cohesive communities.

Crime prevention measures

The presence and distribution of existing crime prevention measures (e.g. CCTV, alley-gate schemes, target-hardened properties, and street and warden initiatives) need to be analysed in conjunction with the need/demand for crime prevention (for example, existing levels of crime and disorder) so that the mismatch between the two can be identified. Once this is achieved any changes or gaps in the existing deployment of resources to combat or prevent crime can be defined.

The presence of other regeneration and crime prevention initiatives

Interventions are seldom implemented in a policy vacuum. Crime prevention strategies can be more effective if they can build upon other local initiatives implemented by the police, local authority, schools or local residents. It is desirable to ensure that the aims of any new initiatives complement and do not compete with or contradict those of existing projects

Geodemographic classifications provide a useful means for contextualizing residential areas. These identify similar types of residential neighbourhood in terms of their demographic, socioeconomic, ethnic and housing composition. They enable researchers to gain a better understanding of geographical variations in the occurrence of victimization and offending problems, medical conditions, lifestyle characteristics and consumer behaviour.

It has been long recognized that certain types of residential neighbourhood are more criminogenic than others. The British Crime Survey (BCS), using the ACORN geodemographic classification, showed that the areas of highest risk for residential burglary included low-income areas (i.e. including social housing) and areas with a mixed social status and an over-representation of single people. Burglary rates in these areas were over twice the national average (Dodd *et al.* 2004). In short, area classifications provide a better spatial framework than purely administrative units (e.g. electoral wards and census tracts), which are unlikely to contain socially homogeneous populations.

However, administrative and policy boundaries also have their uses. First, they can be displayed on a map upon which individual offences and command and control incidents can be superimposed. This will give a visual impression of the concentration of crimes within particular areas (e.g. wards and police beats) and how it is spread across several zones. Secondly, boundaries can also be used to perform data aggregations as discussed earlier.

The extent to which the data sets in Box 22.1 will be accessed by the analyst depends on the degree to which a CCA, CEA or mixed approach is required and on the balance between aggregate and disaggregate analysis.

Scanning and profiling crime problems I: aggregate analyses

Introduction

Disaggregate crime data are not universally available to all stakeholders involved in analyses for intervention. Nor are they needed for all CCAs and CEAs. Much can be done using aggregated data for CDRPs, BCUs, wards, police beats and other spatial units. Even where individual-level crime data are provided it often makes sense to produce crime counts for wards and other zones for which denominators for crime rates and other demographic and social indicators are available.

Aggregate-level crime-centred analyses

CCAs using data that are aggregated to specific zones (e.g. wards) are different from micro-level analyses using point data since everything is constrained by the use of bounded territorial units. Notwithstanding these limitations, there are a number of useful analyses that can be performed to facilitate the planning of when and where to intervene to reduce crime. Some examples for CCAs, albeit by no means exhaustive, would include the following:

- Tabulation of crime counts and derivation of crime rates.
- Identification of areas with significantly high and significantly low crime.
- Benchmarking of area crime rates against comparison areas.
- Identification of crime mix and its variation across areas.
- Identification of areas falling into the worst percentile on one or more crime types.
- Derivation of composite crime indices for ranking of areas.
- Calculation of the concentration of crime at area level.
- Identification of changes in the concentration of crime in one area compared with another (e.g. in the target area compared with the rest of the police force area).
- Identification of repeat crime by area.
- Identification of temporal variations in crime by area.

In common with the analysis of disaggregated data, CCAs for predefined zones can be performed for each crime type. Some of these analyses are best illustrated by means of examples. Tables 22.2 and 22.3 show a selection of offences occurring in the 22 wards of a northern English town that has been renamed as Barchester to preserve confidentiality. The figures in Table 22.2 are the number of offences in each ward and those in Table 22.3 are the crime rates expressed as either per 1,000 persons or households.

Additional information has been provided in Table 22.3 to enable Barchester wards with significantly high crime and those with significantly low crime to be identified. This has done by calculating the standard deviations across the 22 wards from the Barchester mean for each offence rate. The standard deviations are then added to the mean values to identify high-crime wards (defined as those exceeding one but below two standard deviations above the mean) and wards with significantly higher crime (those with crime rates that exceed two standard deviations above the mean). Deducting the standard deviations from the means defines low-crime areas and wards with significantly lower crime (i.e. those with rates of less than two standard deviations below the mean).

This analysis is beneficial because it enables the reader to pinpoint immediately where the significantly high and significantly low-crime areas are located. In this case, the reference area is Barchester but it could easily have

Table 22.2 Crime counts in Barchester

Ward	Pop.	House-holds	Burglary	Burglary other	TOV	TFV	Sex offences	Robbery	Violence	Criminal damage	Arson	Theft from person	Shop-lifting
No.1	8300	2341	99	74	49	112	5	12	108	276	12	8	65
No.2	7200	2196	57	34	23	48	2	9	49	107	13	4	2
No.3	5800	1975	26	30	8	76	1	4	22	46	5	1	0
No.4	6500	2312	45	41	29	113	1	9	41	143	7	5	11
No.5	6700	2569	51	86	27	115	5	5	51	162	6	1	6
No.6	2100	1021	8	10	6	15	0	0	2	20	1	0	0
No.7	6900	2712	90	62	26	148	6	12	134	205	15	6	33
No.8	6800	2469	88	88	38	140	4	3	54	203	13	5	9
No.9	8000	3367	115	82	25	99	7	5	52	191	8	4	20
No.10	6600	2474	29	37	9	37	3	2	14	54	5	0	4
No.11	6700	2267	23	50	33	63	1	1	19	111	7	0	2
No.12	6400	2607	51	28	14	42	4	5	33	117	4	3	0
No.13	6600	2752	98	53	30	102	7	14	77	240	13	6	38
No.14	4200	1459	31	18	18	44	1	0	13	34	4	0	0
No.15	6500	2366	70	70	36	106	5	4	76	162	26	9	90
No.16	6100	2394	31	26	15	73	0	3	26	76	2	4	17
No.17	6800	2284	119	74	24	70	14	4	94	167	16	3	0
No.18	7900	2149	31	115	42	218	8	36	434	243	14	69	524
No.19	6500	2839	70	61	39	90	5	3	76	259	12	2	6
No.20	6300	2509	63	70	49	142	6	9	121	302	12	4	47
No.21	7300	2876	136	89	57	204	3	23	220	348	13	21	51
No.22	4100	1383	25	24	22	56	0	0	25	46	0	2	3
	140300	51321	1356	1222	619	2113	88	163	1741	3512	298	157	928

Notes:
TOV = theft of vehicles; TFV = theft from vehicles.

been the police force area within which Barchester is located, the region or the nation. Although less detailed than a CCA using disaggregate crime data, this analysis does provide sufficient information for strategic decisions on which areas are likely to be strong candidates for additional crime prevention measures.

Using several years' worth of data would enable the analyst to identify whether significantly high crime afflicts the same wards or affects new areas over time. The extent to which extreme values continue to emerge or begin to lessen would provide a broad indication of convergence between the higher and lower-crime areas.

Table 22.4 identifies the contribution that each offence makes to the overall level of crime in each ward. Thus in ward 1 of Table 22.4, burglary accounted for 12.07 per cent of all the offences occurring in that ward, burglary other 9.02 per cent, criminal damage 33 per cent and so on reaching 100 per cent when all offence categories are added together.

Identifying the crime mix in this way provides an indication of the prominent problem that crime prevention agencies face in each area. For example, theft from vehicles represented over one third of all incidents in ward 3 but only 12 per cent in ward 17. Interestingly, ward 3 did not emerge with a significantly high crime rate for theft from vehicles, although there was more of this type of crime than any other. If targeting of resources was based on the prevalence of theft from vehicles, then ward 18 would have been selected even though this offence type amounted to only 12.5 per cent of all incidents in this ward.

Figure 22.2 highlights further differences in crime mix between certain wards and Barchester as a whole. Robbery and theft (including shoplifting) amounted to 37 per cent of all incidents in ward 18 compared with 10 per cent in Barchester and none in ward 14. By contrast, in the latter the dominant problem was acquisitive property crime (burglary and vehicle crime) that collectively comprised 68 per cent of all incidents. These marked differences in crime composition undoubtedly reflect differences in landuse and the functions of different areas; even without landuse data it is clear to see that ward 18 was likely to be a town centre and ward 14 a residential area.

The extent to which Barchester's crime was concentrated into each ward represents a third form of analyses. Table 22.5 reveals that 56.5 per cent of all shoplifting incidents occurred in ward 18; an area containing only 5 per cent of Barchester's population. This ward contained over 43 per cent of Barchester's theft from the person offences, one quarter of violent incidents and one fifth of robberies.

This type of crime concentration table can be easily adapted to form a resource targeting table (RTT). An RRT provides data on the extent to which an area's crime (i.e. that for an entire region or town) is concentrated in its constituent zones. A typical RTT contains four columns: the first contains a code or identifier for the zone; the second the percentage of the entire reference area's crime (e.g. the town's total crime) found within the zone; the third, the cumulative percentage of the town's crime in the first and successive zones; and the fourth, the cumulative percentage of the population. Table 22.6 contains RTTs for burglary, shoplifting and violence against the person.

Table 22.3 Crime rates Barchester: wards with significantly high and significantly low crime

Ward	Pop.	House-holds	Burglary	Burglary other	TOV	TFV	Sex offences	Robbery	Violence	Criminal damage	Arson	Theft from person	Shop-lifting
No.1	8300	2341	42.29	31.61	20.93	47.84	0.60	1.45	13.01	117.90	5.13	0.96	7.83
No.2	7200	2196	25.96	15.48	10.47	21.86	0.28	1.25	6.81	45.71	5.92	0.56	0.28
No.3	5800	1975	13.16	15.19	4.05	38.48	0.17	0.69	3.79	19.65	2.53	0.17	0.00
No.4	6500	2312	19.46	17.73	12.54	48.88	0.15	1.38	6.31	61.09	3.03	0.77	1.69
No.5	6700	2569	19.85	33.48	10.51	44.76	0.75	0.75	7.61	69.20	2.34	0.15	0.90
No.6	2100	1021	7.84	9.79	5.88	14.69	0.00	0.00	0.95	8.54	0.98	0.00	0.00
No.7	6900	2712	33.19	22.86	9.59	54.57	0.87	1.74	19.42	87.57	5.53	0.87	4.78
No.8	6800	2469	35.64	35.64	15.39	56.70	0.59	0.44	7.94	86.72	5.27	0.74	1.32
No.9	8000	3367	34.16	24.35	7.43	29.40	0.88	0.63	6.50	81.59	2.38	0.50	2.50
No.10	6600	2474	11.72	14.96	3.64	14.96	0.45	0.30	2.12	23.07	2.02	0.00	0.61
No.11	6700	2267	10.15	22.06	14.56	27.79	0.15	0.15	2.84	47.42	3.09	0.00	0.30
No.12	6400	2607	19.56	10.74	5.37	16.11	0.63	0.78	5.16	49.98	1.53	0.47	0.00
No.13	6600	2752	35.61	19.26	10.90	37.06	1.06	2.12	11.67	102.52	4.72	0.91	5.76
No.14	4200	1459	21.25	12.34	12.34	30.16	0.24	0.00	3.10	14.52	2.74	0.00	0.00
No.15	6500	2366	29.59	29.59	15.22	44.80	0.77	0.62	11.69	69.20	10.99	1.38	13.85
No.16	6100	2394	12.95	32.40	6.27	30.49	0.00	0.49	4.26	32.46	0.84	0.66	2.79
No.17	6800	2284	52.10	32.40	10.51	30.65	2.06	0.59	13.82	71.34	7.01	0.44	0.00
No.18	7900	2149	14.43	53.51	19.54	101.44	1.01	4.56	54.94	103.80	6.51	8.73	66.33

No.19	6500	2839	24.66	21.49	13.74	31.70	0.77	0.46	11.69	110.64	4.23	0.31	0.92
No.20	6300	2509	25.11	27.90	19.53	56.60	0.95	1.43	19.21	129.00	4.78	0.63	7.46
No.21	7300	2876	47.29	30.95	19.82	70.93	0.41	3.15	30.14	148.65	4.52	2.88	6.99
No.22	4100	1383	18.08	17.35	15.91	40.49	0.00	0.00	6.10	19.65	0.00	0.49	0.73
Mean			25.18	23.16	12.0	40.47	0.58	1.04	11.32	68.19	3.91	0.98	5.68
SD			12.27	10.55	5.27	20.07	0.47	1.09	11.93	39.99	2.49	1.83	14.01

Notes:

TOV = theft of vehicles; TFV = theft from vehicles.

Dark grey shading and bold = significantly high crime; light grey shading = high crime; italics left justified bold = significantly low crime.

Table 22.4 Crime mix in Barchester

Ward	Burglary	Burglary other	TOV	TFV	Sex offences	Robbery	Violence	Criminal damage	Arson	Theft from person	Shop-lifting	Total
No.1	12.07	9.02	5.98	13.66	0.61	1.46	13.17	33.7	1.46	0.98	7.93	100
No.2	16.38	9.77	6.61	13.79	0.57	2.59	14.08	30.7	3.74	1.15	0.57	100
No.3	11.87	13.70	3.65	**34.70**	0.46	1.83	10.05	21.0	2.28	0.46	0.00	100
No.4	10.11	9.21	6.52	25.39	0.22	2.02	9.21	32.1	1.57	1.12	2.47	100
No.5	9.90	16.70	5.24	22.33	0.97	0.97	9.90	31.5	1.17	0.19	1.17	100
No.6	12.90	16.13	9.68	24.19	0.00	0.00	3.23	32.3	1.61	0.00	0.00	100
No.7	12.21	8.41	3.53	20.08	0.81	1.63	18.18	27.8	2.04	0.81	4.48	100
No.8	13.64	13.64	5.89	21.71	0.62	0.47	8.37	31.5	2.02	0.78	1.40	100
No.9	18.91	13.49	4.11	16.28	1.15	0.82	8.55	31.4	1.32	0.66	3.29	100
No.10	**14.95**	**19.07**	4.64	19.07	1.55	1.03	7.22	27.8	2.58	0.00	2.06	100
No.11	7.42	16.13	10.65	20.32	0.32	0.32	6.13	35.8	2.26	0.00	0.65	100
No.12	16.94	9.30	4.65	13.95	1.33	1.66	10.96	38.9	1.33	1.00	0.00	100
No.13	14.45	7.82	4.42	15.04	1.03	2.06	11.36	35.4	1.92	0.88	5.60	100
No.14	**19.02**	11.04	**11.04**	26.99	0.61	0.00	7.98	20.9	2.45	0.00	0.00	100
No.15	10.70	10.70	5.50	16.21	0.76	0.61	11.62	24.8	3.98	1.38	13.76	100
No.16	11.36	9.52	5.49	26.74	0.00	1.10	9.52	27.8	0.73	1.47	6.23	100
No.17	**20.34**	12.65	4.10	11.97	**2.39**	0.68	16.07	28.5	2.74	0.51	0.00	100
No.18	1.79	6.63	2.42	12.57	0.46	2.08	**25.03**	14.0	0.81	**3.98**	**30.22**	100
No.19	11.24	9.79	6.26	14.45	0.80	0.48	12.20	**41.6**	1.93	0.32	0.96	100
No.20	7.64	8.48	5.94	17.21	0.73	1.09	14.67	36.6	1.45	0.48	5.70	100
No.21	11.67	7.64	4.89	17.51	0.26	1.97	18.88	29.9	1.12	1.80	4.38	100
No.22	12.32	11.82	10.84	27.59	0.00	0.00	12.32	22.7	0.00	0.99	1.48	100
Total	11.12	10.02	5.08	17.32	0.72	1.34	14.27	28.8	2.44	1.29	7.61	100

Notes:
TOV = theft of vehicles; TFV = theft from vehicles.
Bold = prominence of offence within crime mix.

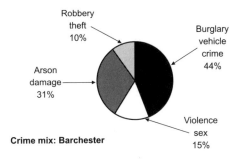

Crime mix: Barchester

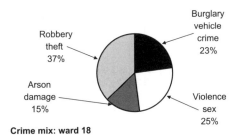

Crime mix: ward 18

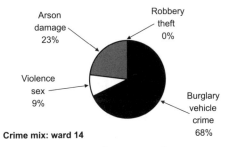

Crime mix: ward 14

Figure 22.2 Crime mix in selected Barchester wards

Burglary was the least concentrated offence in Barchester followed by violence against the person and shoplifting. Half of all burglaries could be targeted by focusing attention on 7 of the 22 wards that collectively contained just over one third of the population (Table 22.6). Directing attention to just 4 of the 22 wards would target half of all the cases of violence against the person. However, in the case of shoplifting, over half of all incidents were located in just one of the 22 wards

Taking all three analyses together it is possible to identify areas that, for certain offences, had a high prevalence (rate), a high concentration and a prominent position in terms of crime mix (prominence). The value for each ward on each measure for domestic burglary is shown in Table 22.7. The wards in Barchester have been ranked in descending order of the burglary rate (prevalence) and the ranks for crime concentration and the prominence

Table 22.5 Crime concentration in Barchester

Ward	Pop.	House-holds	Burglary	Burglary other	TOV	TFV	Sex offences	Robbery	Violence	Criminal damage	Arson	Theft from person	Shop-lifting
No.1	5.9	4.6	7.3	6.1	7.9	5.3	5.7	7.4	6.2	7.9	4.0	5.1	7.0
No.2	5.1	4.3	4.2	2.8	3.7	2.3	2.3	5.5	2.8	3.0	4.4	2.5	0.2
No.3	4.1	3.8	1.9	2.5	1.3	3.6	1.1	2.5	1.3	1.3	1.7	0.6	0.0
No.4	4.6	4.5	3.3	3.4	4.7	5.3	1.1	5.5	2.4	4.1	2.3	3.2	1.2
No.5	4.8	5.0	3.8	7.0	4.4	5.4	5.7	3.1	2.9	4.6	2.0	0.6	0.6
No.6	1.5	2.0	0.6	0.8	1.0	0.7	0.0	0.0	0.1	0.6	0.3	0.0	0.0
No.7	4.9	5.3	6.6	5.1	4.2	7.0	6.8	7.4	7.7	5.8	5.0	3.8	3.6
No.8	4.8	4.8	6.5	7.2	6.1	6.6	4.5	1.8	3.1	5.8	4.4	3.2	1.0
No.9	5.7	6.6	8.5	6.7	4.0	4.7	8.0	3.1	3.0	5.4	2.7	2.5	2.2
No.10	4.7	4.8	2.1	3.0	1.5	1.8	3.4	1.2	0.8	1.5	1.7	0.0	0.4
No.11	4.8	4.4	1.7	4.1	5.3	3.0	1.1	0.6	1.1	3.2	2.3	0.0	0.2
No.12	4.6	5.1	3.8	2.3	2.3	2.0	4.5	3.1	1.9	3.3	1.3	1.9	0.0
No.13	4.7	5.4	7.2	4.3	4.8	4.8	8.0	8.6	4.4	6.8	4.4	3.8	4.1
No.14	3.0	2.8	2.3	1.5	2.9	2.1	1.1	0.0	0.7	1.0	1.3	0.0	0.0
No.15	4.6	4.6	5.2	5.7	5.8	5.0	5.7	2.5	4.4	4.6	8.7	5.7	9.7
No.16	4.3	4.7	2.3	2.1	2.4	3.5	0.0	1.8	1.5	2.2	0.7	2.5	1.8
No.17	4.8	4.5	8.8	6.1	3.9	3.3	15.9	2.5	5.4	4.8	5.4	1.9	0.0
No.18	5.6	4.2	2.3	9.4	6.8	10.3	9.1	22.1	24.9	6.9	4.7	43.9	56.5
No.19	4.6	5.5	5.2	5.0	6.3	4.3	5.7	1.8	4.4	7.4	4.0	1.3	0.6
No.20	4.5	4.9	4.6	5.7	7.9	6.7	6.8	5.5	7.0	8.6	4.0	2.5	5.1
No.21	5.2	5.6	10.0	7.3	9.2	9.7	3.4	14.1	12.6	9.9	4.4	13.4	5.5
No.22	2.9	2.7	1.8	2.0	3.6	2.7	0.0	0.0	1.4	1.3	0.0	1.3	0.3
	100	100	100	100	100	100	100	100	100	100	100	100	100

Notes:
TOV = theft of vehicles; TFV = theft from vehicles.
Dark grey shading and bold = highly concentrated offence.

Table 22.6 Resource targeting tables for burglary, shoplifting and violence in Barchester

Ward	Burglary	CM (%)	CM (% HH)	Ward	Shoplifting	CM (%)	Ward	Violence	CM (%)
No.21	10.0	10.0	5.6	No.18	56.5	56.5	No.18	24.9	24.9
No.17	8.8	18.8	10.1	No.15	9.7	66.2	No.21	12.6	37.6
No.9	8.5	27.3	16.6	No.1	7.0	73.2	No.7	7.7	45.3
No.1	7.3	34.6	21.2	No.21	5.5	78.7	No.20	7.0	52.2
No.13	7.2	41.8	26.5	No.20	5.1	83.7	No.1	6.2	58.4
No.7	6.6	48.5	31.8	No.13	4.1	87.8	No.17	5.4	63.8
No.8	6.5	54.9	36.6	No.7	3.6	91.4	No.13	4.4	68.2
No.15	5.2	60.1	41.2	No.9	2.2	93.5	No.15	4.4	72.6
No.19	5.2	65.3	46.8	No.16	1.8	95.4	No.19	4.4	77.0
No.20	4.6	69.9	51.7	No.4	1.2	96.6	No.8	3.1	80.1
No.2	4.2	74.1	55.9	No.8	1.0	97.5	No.9	3.0	83.1
No.5	3.8	77.9	60.9	No.5	0.6	98.2	No.5	2.9	86.0
No.12	3.8	81.6	66.0	No.19	0.6	98.8	No.2	2.8	88.8
No.4	3.3	85.0	70.5	No.10	0.4	99.2	No.4	2.4	91.2
No.14	2.3	87.2	73.4	No.22	0.3	99.6	No.12	1.9	93.0
No.16	2.3	89.5	78.0	No.2	0.2	99.8	No.16	1.5	94.5
No.18	2.3	91.8	82.2	No.11	0.2	100.0	No.22	1.4	96.0
No.10	2.1	94.0	87.1	No.3	0.0	100.0	No.3	1.3	97.2
No.3	1.9	95.9	90.9	No.6	0.0	100.0	No.11	1.1	98.3
No.22	1.8	97.7	93.6	No.12	0.0	100.0	No.10	0.8	99.1
No.11	1.7	99.4	98.0	No.14	0.0	100.0	No.14	0.7	99.9
No.6	0.6	100.0	100.0	No.17	0.0	100.0	No.6	0.1	100.0

Notes:

CM (%) = cumulative percentage of crime; CM (% HH) = cumulative percentage of households.
Dark grey shading = wards that collectively contain over half of the crime; light grey shading = wards that collectively contain over 80% of the crime.

Table 22.7 The prevalence, concentration and prominence of burglary in Barchester

Ward	Prevalence	R	Concentration	R	Prominence	R
No.17	**52.10**	(1)	**8.8**	(2)	**20.34**	(1)
No.21	**47.29**	(2)	**10.0**	(1)	11.67	(14)
No.1	**42.29**	(3)	7.3	(4)	12.07	(12)
No.8	35.64	(4)	6.5	(7)	13.64	(8)
No.13	35.61	(5)	7.2	(5)	14.45	(7)
No.9	34.16	(6)	**8.5**	(3)	18.91	(3)
No.7	33.19	(7)	6.6	(6)	12.21	(11)
No.15	29.59	(8)	5.2	(9)	10.7	(17)
No.2	25.96	(9)	4.2	(11)	16.38	(5)
No.20	25.11	(10)	4.6	(10)	7.64	(20)
No.19	24.66	(11)	5.2	(9)	11.24	(16)
No.14	21.25	(12)	2.3	(16)	**19.02**	(2)
No.5	19.85	(13)	3.8	(13)	9.9	(19)
No.12	19.56	(14)	3.8	(13)	16.94	(4)
No.4	19.46	(15)	3.3	(14)	10.11	(18)
No.22	18.08	(16)	1.8	(20)	12.32	(10)
No.18	14.43	(17)	2.3	(16)	1.79	(22)
No.3	13.16	(18)	1.9	(19)	11.87	(13)
No.16	12.95	(19)	2.3	(16)	11.36	(15)
No.10	*11.72*	(20)	2.1	(18)	**14.95**	(6)
No.11	*10.15*	(21)	1.7	(21)	7.42	(21)
No.6	*7.84*	(22)	0.6	(22)	12.9	(9)

Notes:
R (10) = rank of ward within Barchester.
Figures in bold = high score.

of burglary in the area's crime mix are also shown in the column labelled 'R'. In Barchester, there was a close, albeit not perfect, correlation between the burglary rate and the extent to which burglary was concentrated in a particular ward (Spearman's rank .953, p = .000). However, the prominence of burglary in each ward's crime mix was not related to either its burglary rate or its degree of concentration (Spearman's rank .320 and .242, respectively, both non-significant).

Tabulating all three measures for an offence category will help inform resource allocation decisions at the strategic (aggregate) level. For example, ward 17 was the only area to score highly on all three measures (prevalence, concentration and prominence) for domestic burglary. Not only did it have a significantly high burglary rate that exceeded two standard deviations above the Barchester mean, it also contained 9 per cent of the town's burglaries and burglary represented over one fifth of all crime in the area. As such, it would be a strong candidate for targeting burglary reduction measures. Burglary also accounted for around one fifth of all crime in ward 14 but its prevalence rate was not significantly high and it had a relatively low concentration of all Barchester's burglaries making this less of a priority for action, although further intelligence would need to be used (e.g. about offender MOs, residents' fears and concerns) before making a final decision.

Each measure provides a different insight into the burglary problem – prevalence denotes how much of the community is affected by crime and by deduction how many households are free from crime. Concentration informs the analyst about how much of the crime problem will be targeted if action is taken in the area of interest. Finally, 'prominence' indicates how much burglary features amongst the crime problems that the police and other agencies have to tackle in the area.

The term 'concentration' as discussed above in relation to aggregate CCA refers to the geographical concentration of crime as distinct from the concentration of crimes per victim used in the measurement of repeat victimization. Both refer to concentrations, the former focusing on how many victims account for how much of the crime and the latter on how many areas account for how much of the crime.

All these examples are of CCAs at the aggregate level. No social or physical environmental data have been involved.

It is also often the case that different types of crime occur at different times of the day. This is important to know. For instance, if there were a large number of thefts in an area, and these tended to occur at night, it may be sensible to install improved street lighting. However, if they occurred during the day, it may be a waste of money to install new lighting. Thus, it is important to understand the main problems in an area before attempting to solve them.

Figure 22.3 illustrates fluctuations in the time of the day that crime occurs in Barchester. The figures shown relate to burglary other, but a similar exercise could be undertaken for any other crime type. There is a peak in non-residential burglary at about five o'clock in the afternoon; there is also a large amount of activity between eight and ten o'clock at night. This intelligence would be useful in, for example, the deployment of security guards to areas with a large number of non-residential properties. The activity of these guards would be particularly effective if concentrated into the times of day at which non-residential burglary most often occurs.

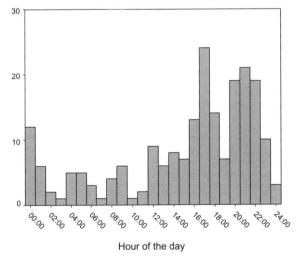

Figure 22.3 Temporal variation in the time of non-residential burglaries in Barchester

Aggregate-level crime environment analyses

The examples given above of CCA at the aggregate scale have featured the use of administrative zones such as wards. Analyses at the aggregate level can also be conducted for non-standard areas but this depends on being able to aggregate individual-level geo-coded crime records to *ad hoc* boundaries. GIS software is required to achieve this.

Once this is done, it is then possible to examine crime levels, crime mix and crime concentration for areas defined on the basis of landuse, policy delivery, cultural or ethnic factors or other criteria (e.g. 'natural communities'). Generating crime counts for boundaries that delineate particular landuses, economic activities or social characteristics represents a move away from a largely CCA towards crime environment analysis (CEA).

Comparative analysis of crime rates for non-standard areas is not commonplace but may be required to gain a strategic picture of crime levels in non-residential areas, or surrounding known crime generators and attractors. In Britain, resource allocation for crime prevention is increasingly being overseen by the Government Offices for the Regions. At a regional level it might be useful for monitoring resource allocation and performance to be able to identify the following:

- Crime levels within policy priority areas and for area-based initiatives region-wide (e.g. New Deal for Communities areas, Neighbourhood Renewal Fund areas).

- Crime profiles for town centres, out-of-town retail parks, industrial estates, transport hubs, economic development areas and urban 'cultural quarters' within a region.

- Cross-border crime (e.g. crime around police force area borders).

The minimum requirement to perform such analyses is to have consistent crime data for an entire region. In Britain, this means bringing together data from several police forces into a single database with common conventions for coding crime, handling missing data and consistent geo-referencing.

Several regions have recently or are in the process of building such systems. What is lacking is perhaps more in-depth thinking as to how to use such systems and get the most out of them.

Aggregate CEAs are more typically carried out using standard administrative boundaries for which population and social indicators are available. What distinguishes aggregate CEA from aggregate CCA is the incorporation of non-crime data. This can be achieved in a number of ways. An increasingly common approach is to map or tabulate crime rates for zones that have been ranked according to their values on a social indicator such as a poverty or deprivation index. Data presented in this way enable the analyst immediately to see whether or not there is a *prima facie* relationship between the crime rate and deprivation level.

Examples of this are shown in Figures 22.4 and 22.5. Figure 22.4 identifies wards in Greater Manchester falling into the worst 10 per cent of wards for

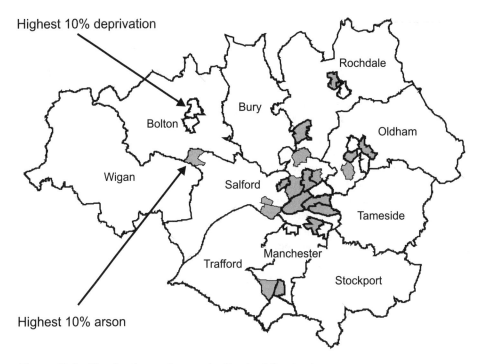

Figure 22.4 Deprivation and arson in Greater Manchester

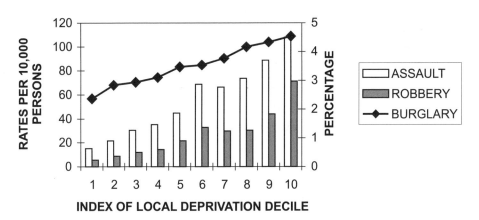

Figure 22.5 Crime rates and deprivation intensity on Merseyside

arson and those occupying the worst 10 per cent on deprivation. Although there is some overlap between the two, half the wards with the highest arson rates did not fall into the most deprived category and vice versa.

Figure 22.5 tabulates crime rates by the levels of deprivation of the areas in which they occurred. This was produced first by aggregating census enumeration districts in Merseyside into ten equal groups (deciles) according to their values on a deprivation index. The number of crimes and populations were then aggregated by deprivation decile and rates for domestic burglary, assault and robbery calculated for each decile. There is a discernible increase in crime, particularly assault, with increasing severity of deprivation. Although not evidence of a causal relationship, this information can be used to refine the targeting of crime prevention measures perhaps by levering in additional resources provided for deprived areas towards funding crime prevention.

Figure 22.6 identifies the distance in kilometres between the homes of victims of assault and the assault location and the assault rate on Merseyside, both shown by the level of deprivation in victims' area of residence (the deprivation decile). The bars for home–attack distance and those for assault rate are mirror images of each other. The assault rates rises with deprivation and the home attack distance decreases. Assault victims are more likely to be attacked closer to their home if they come from deprived areas. In other words, deprived areas are more dangerous places.

Clearly much can be gained by introducing environmental data even into an aggregate analysis. However, when the units of observation are the individual crimes, far more options are available for the ways in which they are analysed. Selected examples of these are now discussed.

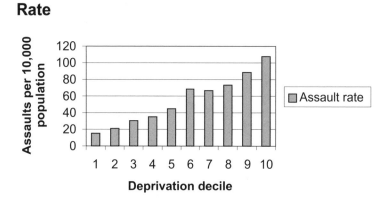

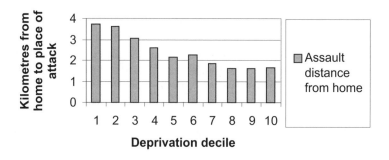

Figure 22.6   Assault: rate and distance from home

Scanning and profiling crime problems II: disaggregate analyses

The widespread availability of geographical information systems (GIS) software has opened up considerable opportunities for disaggregate CCA and CEA using individual-level crime data.

A GIS can best be described as a system of hardware, software and procedures designed to support the capture, management, manipulation, analysis, modelling and display of spatially referenced information. Such systems enable links to be established and spatial relationships to be explored between data derived from different sources (e.g. calls to the police, crime reports and census variables). They can be used in conjunction with grid-referenced crime data to undertake analyses which overcome the limitations inherent in the use of spatially aggregated data for predetermined geographical boundaries (e.g. police beats).

For example, all the data sets illustrated in Box 22.1 can be processed, cross-referenced and mapped using a GIS.

Crime-centred analyses

CCA at the disaggregate level involves distilling important information from the distribution of individual incidents. Unlike aggregate analyses where the units of observation are zones or other entities by which data are grouped, disaggregate CCA enables one to explore variations in the spatial and temporal patterning of incidents on any of the variables contained within a crime report (e.g. crime type, modus operandi (MO), value of goods stolen, etc.). Examples of disaggregate CCAs include the production of point distribution maps depicting the location of individual offences. For example, the location of domestic burglaries, assaults or residential property arson can be mapped using the grid reference as the point location.

The manner in which these offences are mapped can vary. For example, the location of domestic burglaries may be displayed by hour of the day or day of the week to reveal how patterns alter over time. The map may be restricted to burglaries where the MO is by entry to the rear of properties. Alternatively, different maps could be produced for each major MO category or by MO and time of day and so on. Each of these analyses can be classed as CCA because it does not involve the interrogation of any data sets other than crime data.

Figure 22.7 gives an example of the simplest form of disaggregate CCA. It displays incidents of criminal damage to bus stops on the Wirral peninsula on Merseyside, northwest England. Each point represents a vandalized bus stop over a one-year period.

Other applications for CCA that could be applied to refine the map in Figure 22.7 might include the following:

- Mapping the distribution of repeat incidents.

- Conducting radial analyses (e.g. counting the number of incidents in a 500 m radius of selected schools).

Figure 22.7   Criminal damage to bus stops on the Wirral, 2000
Source: Newton (2003).

- Identifying buffer zones (e.g. alongside the bus routes that the bus stops serve) and calculating the number of offences by crime type at different points along the route.

- Identifying clusters/hotspots of bus-shelter damage.

The ability of a GIS to perform spatial query operations, interrogate a database and automate the production of pin maps showing crime incidents is a flexible and fast way of gaining an initial picture of crime patterns. However, there are limitations to this approach as a means of searching for patterns in crime data because the decisions as to what to look for are made by the analyst. It is only too easy for the analyst to miss a potentially significant crime problem. Research has shown that police officers with local knowledge are often wrong in their perceptions of where both hotspots and areas of unusually low crime are located. In fact they get it wrong half the time (Ratcliffe and McCullagh 2001).

Distilling the information on a map such as that in Figure 22.7 into a smaller number of clusters or hotspots is useful as a synthesis for the recipient of this information, enabling him or her to see the wood for the trees. The rationale behind this process is to identify the grouping together of crimes within certain time periods, in specific locations that are unlikely to have occurred by chance; in other words, the non-random bunching of incidents.

The underlying reasons why clusters form may be varied. Their interpretation by the analyst will usually be informed by knowledge of an area, an appreciation of crime theory or by putting hotspots into context through adding other data layers. These might include the location of known offenders or other intelligence or information on the social and physical environment extending the CCA into a CEA.

There are a number of clustering and hotspot techniques that are now available. Figure 22.8 shows domestic burglary hotspots on Merseyside using recorded crime data for 1995. The software used to produce these hotspots was the Spatial and Temporal Analysis of Crime (STAC) software developed by the Illinois Criminal Justice Information Authority (Block 1994). STAC is one of the pioneering hotspotting programs that identifies crime clusters by representing concentrations of points as ellipses.

The advantage of STAC is that it reveals the orientation of the hotspots as well as their size. For example, hotspot A in Figure 22.8 runs north-west to south-east whilst hotspot B runs east to west.

However, the number of ellipses produced in STAC and their size can vary considerably depending on the window that is used to define the area of interest. In this analysis, the whole of Merseyside is used as the 'window'. If the analyst zooms in to this map to define a much smaller window, perhaps using only one quarter of the map in Figure 22.8, then a new set of ellipses would emerge.

A number of advances have been made in hotspotting techniques since the development of STAC in the 1990s. In recent years several GIS products have been developed that have embedded software for defining spatial and temporal hotspots. The US National Institute of Justice (NIJ) Mapping and Analysis for Public Safety (MAPS) initiative provides crime analysis freeware including the CrimeStat spatial statistics program that contains an enhanced version of STAC, the Crime Analysis Spatial Extension for ESRI's ArcGIS and other products (http://www.ojp.usdoj.gov/nij/maps/).

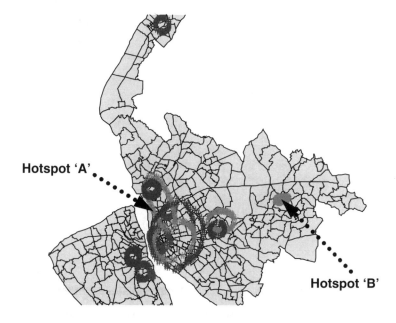

Figure 22.8 Domestic burglary hotspots on Merseyside using STAC

Figure 22.9 shows an example of hotspots generated by the CrimeStat GIS software package available through MAPS. It uses a technique called nearest neighbour hierarchical (Nnh) clustering that groups points together on the basis of their geographical proximity. The user specifies a maximum 'threshold' distance between the points and the minimum number of points that are required for each cluster. The smaller the inter-point distances the less likely it is that the points conform to a random distribution.

First-order clusters (not shown on Figure 22.9) represent groups of points that are closer together than the threshold distance and in which there is at least the minimum number of points specified by the user. The first-order clusters are themselves grouped together to form second-order clusters and the latter are grouped together to form third-order clusters in a hierarchical manner.

The value of the hierarchical approach lies in its ability to define crime clusters at different scales from a single data set. Thus relatively large (third order) clusters can be defined for strategic planning at a regional or county level and within these large clusters smaller (second order) hotspots can be identified and within these even smaller (first order) hotspots can be delineated. The latter can be used to identify crime generators and attractors at the micro level for more refined targeting.

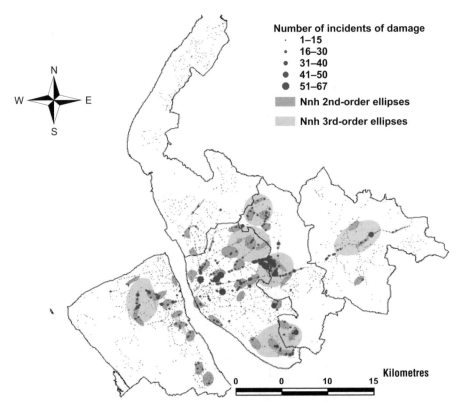

Figure 22.9 Criminal damage to Merseyside bus stops: hotspots from crime analyst
Source: Newton (2003).

The map in Figure 22.9 draws on the criminal damage to bus stops example discussed above. It shows six third-order clusters depicting criminal damage to bus stops that can be used to guide the deployment of patrols at the county level and, within these, over 40 second-order clusters for more site-specific surveillance and targeting hardening.

Crime environment analyses

As has been demonstrated, much can be gained from processing, mapping and analysing disaggregate crime data. Spatial and temporal clusters can be identified and the concentration of offences within properties (e.g. repeat burglary) or indeed affecting the same individuals (repeat personal victimization) can be explored. None of this would be possible without going down to the level of the individual incident.

The identification of crime patterns, hotspots and repeat crimes can be further enhanced by adding data on the social and physical environment. For example, when individual points (e.g. burglaries or criminal damage to bus stops) are superimposed on a map showing street layouts, building footprints, schools and public open space, the patterns that emerge make much more sense because they are put into context. Thus areas of poor guardianship become apparent when landuse data identify poor natural surveillance. Burglaries involving access by offenders to the rear of properties make more sense when street layouts reveal that it is rows of terraced housing separated by alleyways at the rear that are being victimized.

Plotting repeatedly victimized houses in relation to housing type may generate further explanations as to why certain properties are repeatedly targeted. Recent research into isomorphic victimization clearly demonstrates the need to contextualize crime patterns (Johnson and Bowers 2004). This is the added value of disaggregate CEA.

Various combinations of crime and environmental data can be cross-referenced. Typically, analyses involve superimposing crimes at specific locations (points) on a map displaying basic landuse information (e.g. built-up areas, open space, main roads and transport routes). Other environmental data may be used as a backcloth. Examples include administrative boundaries (police beats and wards), social indicators (e.g. deprivation score and unemployment rates) or geodemographic (residential area) classifications.

Figure 22.10 illustrates the cross-referencing of disaggregate crime incidents with social environmental data. Figure 22.10 (a) shows ward boundaries in central and south Liverpool. Figure 22.10(b) shows the different types of residential neighbourhood *within* each ward using data from the Super Profiles Geodemographic Classification at the census enumeration district (ED) level. ED boundaries were used for the 1991 census when there were approximately 15–20 EDs within each ward.

Three area types have been labelled on Figure 22.10 (b): 'Have Nots', the most disadvantaged areas with the greatest poverty; 'Urban Venturers', areas with over-representations of young single people, students and generally transient populations; and 'Affluent Achievers', areas of high income and owner-occupied housing.

a   b

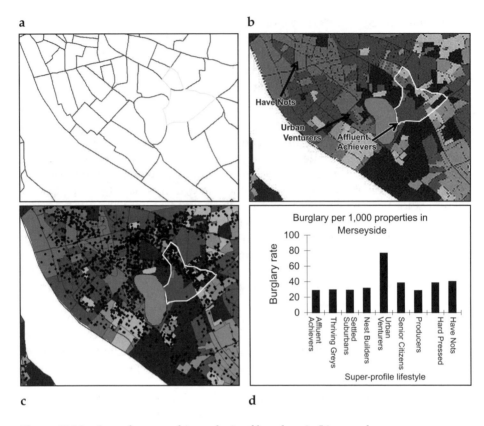

c   d

Figure 22.10 A geodemographic analysis of burglary in Liverpool

Figure 22.10 (c) is a plot of domestic burglaries within the area over a one-year period. Some geodemographic clusters appear to have concentrations of burglaries whilst others are almost entirely free of them.

To make sense of this, the GIS is used to intersect the individual burglaries with the super-profile area types. The outcome of a 'point-in-polygon intersect' in a GIS is the automatic appending of an area type code to each individual burglary incident. Thus each incident gains a code denoting the types of residential neighbourhood within which it occurred. The burglaries can then be summed for each area type to calculate a frequency or total number of burglaries for each type of neighbourhood. Since census EDs are used as the building blocks, the total populations for each area type can be calculated by aggregating the ED population counts. In this case, it has been possible to derive the total number of households in each geodemographic cluster and this serves as a denominator for calculating the burglary.

Figure 22.10 (d) shows the outcome of this analysis and identifies 'Urban Venturers' as the neighbourhood type with the highest domestic burglary rate. An inspection of the profile for 'Urban Venturers' suggests that this is a neighbourhood type with a high student population (an abundant supply of high-value goods to steal), relatively poor levels of guardianship (many single persons and fewer people around during the day) and relatively low social cohesion (ethnically mixed population, high turnover and privately rented accommodation).

The relationship between these social, housing and lifestyle characteristics and burglary would not have been possible in a purely CCA. However, it would be a mistake to infer from this association that burglaries only happened in student households or that the characteristics of Urban Venturer areas were the sole explanation as to why properties were targeted by offenders. The 'ecological fallacy', namely, inferring that an overlap of social characteristics at the neighbourhood level (i.e. in each super-profile lifestyle) means that they also coincide at the household level (i.e. all households exactly mirror the area profile) must be acknowledged and avoided. The promotion of the ecological fallacy is easy to succumb to in geodemographic analyses of crime.

Digital aerial photography

The visualization of disaggregate crime data can be further enhanced by the superimposition of digital aerial photographs. These provide valuable information about the presence of factors that can significantly increase or significantly decrease the risk of victimization. For example, the picture gained by using a GIS to plot domestic burglaries for individual properties by time of occurrence and MO can be enhanced considerably if aerial photographs identify those dwellings that back on to the open space or situations where the presence of trees and shrubs are blocking the natural surveillance of properties.

Figure 22.11 shows bus stops succumbing to criminal damage against the backdrop of a digital aerial photograph. The most victimized bus stop is labelled 'bus stop A'. This bus stop had 27 incidents of criminal damage in 2000. Bus stop B, only 120 metres away, had 8 incidents within the same period. Bus stop B is fairly close to a number of residential properties. Bus stop A, on the other hand, is not overlooked; it is shielded by trees and appears to be adjacent to more open space, perhaps, derelict land and open fields. Without the aerial photograph the differences between these environments would not have been easily identifiable. They suggest that it is the lack of natural surveillance and guardianship that may be a key factor in accounting for bus stop A's higher level of victimization. Its relocation to point C, where natural surveillance and guardianship are likely to be much stronger, may significantly reduce the number of criminal damage incidents.

Crime prevention as an additional layer

A major gap in analyses for intervention is the incorporation of data on the location, coverage and period of operation of crime prevention measures. For example, some researchers have produced maps that show the location of fixed CCTV cameras in relation to the street network depicting the direction in which they are pointing and the distance over which they can see for the collection of evidence that can be used in court (Chainey 2001). Others have mapped assaults on a university campus in relation to the area of illumination given by street lights and the presence of shrubbery and street furniture (Rengert

Figure 22.11   Minimization site appraisal using a digital aerial photograph
Source: Newton (2003).

et al. 2001). These are detailed site appraisals that combine crime data with information on landuse, buildings and the crime prevention environment.

The quantification, mapping and analysis of crime prevention are the new frontier. They will provide further evidence that crime analysts need to prioritize resources, to fill gaps (high crime and no crime prevention), to target and to reassign interventions to reduce crime successfully.

Conclusion

Crime-centred analyses and crime environment analyses, when carried out well, can help both policy-makers and policy implementation teams identify which types of crime within their areas need to be prioritized because they are significantly higher than expected, are concentrated in a small number of identifiable areas or because they are prominent amongst the incidents notified to the authorities. The CEA will also help identify factors that may facilitate or inhibit the implementation of crime prevention policy (e.g. low/high social cohesion, good/poor natural surveillance, suitable/unsuitable housing for target hardening, alley-gating, etc.).

Policy-makers and policy implementation teams need to evidence both the problem, through comprehensive crime and contextual analysis, and the solution, through selection of interventions appropriate to the crime problem and through identifying anticipated mechanisms through which crime is reduced.

To make the most of objective information on crime problems, contextual factors and policy mechanisms, there need to be good channels of communication between data analysis and decision-making. If these are non-existent or weak, then action needs to be taken to strengthen them. The extent to which decisions are informed by evidence may depend on the competence and robustness of the decision-making procedures within crime reduction agencies.

Policy implementation teams need to be aware that crime analysis may be just one of a number of factors that contribute to decisions about resource allocation.

The analysis and mapping of crime data to support decision-making in crime prevention and evaluation exercises require access to appropriate data and software but also competence and skills in a number of key areas. These include the following:

- An awareness of sources of data on crime, disorder, landuse and sociodemographic conditions.
- An awareness of data quality and data protection issues.
- Expertise in the manipulation, processing and handling of large data sets.
- Familiarity with and competence in the use of GIS.
- Knowledge of appropriate denominators for use in deriving crime rates.
- Basic skills in data analysis.
- Skills in map design and in the presentation of data as tables and graphs.
- An ability to interpret the results from data analysis.
- Writing skills.

Other areas of competence relevant to some of the functions described earlier in this chapter include the following:

- Expertise in identifying crime clusters and hotspots from disaggregate data.
- An ability to identify repeat crimes using police data and other sources.
- Knowledge of crime displacement and how to detect it.
- Competence in designing and executing crime victimization surveys.
- Expertise in consulting with local communities.

There may well be a division of labour in terms of these core skills in that crime analysts and police local research and intelligence officers may be better equipped to undertake some tasks (e.g. identifying repeat crimes) than local authority community safety officers.

Selected further reading

For an excellent guide to crime analysis that covers many of the topics discussed in this chapter, see Clarke and Eck (2003) *Becoming a Problem-solving Crime Analyst in 55 Steps*. Applications of crime analysis and GIS by researchers, community safety practitioners and policy evaluators, including examples of good practice from the UK, can be found in Hirschfield and Bowers (2001) *Mapping and Analysing Crime Data*. An in-depth discussion of methodological challenges confronting researchers and crime analysts is covered in Tilley (2002) *Analysis for Crime Prevention*.

A comprehensive overview of crime mapping written by a geographer with abundant examples of different styles of mapping can be found in Harries (1999) *Mapping Crime: Principle and Practice*. A particularly useful book for practitioners that contains a good discussion of GIS implementation issues and database design, together with case studies describing successful GIS applications, can be found in Leipnik and Albert (2002) *GIS in Law Enforcement: Implementation Issues and Case Studies*.

A series of useful guides on analyses in a policing context has been produced by the US Department of Justice. The COPS guides produced by the DOJ's Office of Community Oriented Policing Services are available from www.cops.usdoj.gov. A good general overview of analysis in policing can be found in Bynum (2001) *Using Analysis for Problem-solving: A Guidebook for Law Enforcement*.

Eck and Weiburd (1995) *Crime and Place. Crime Prevention Studies. Volume 4* includes material on crime theories, methods for defining hotspots and applications of analysis in policing. An excellent discussion on the identification of different types of hotspot can be found in Ratcliffe (2004) 'The hotspot matrix: a framework for the spatio-temporal targeting of crime reduction'.

There are several useful websites, some of which host email list servers for practitioners. Mapping and Analysis for Public Safety (MAPS), National Institute of Justice, USA, provides a plethora of material on crime mapping and analysis plus a list server (www.ojp.usdoj.gov/nij/maps/). The International Association of Crime Analysts website (www.iaca.net) houses information on conferences, publications and training materials. A list server for analysts is also provided. In the UK, the Home Office Toolkits are worth consulting, especially the page on Focus Areas (www.crimereduction.gov.uk/toolkits).

A wide range of UK social and demographic data for small areas, useful for crime environment analyses, can be downloaded from the Office of National Statistics (ONS) Neighbourhood Statistics website (www.neighbourhood.statistics.gov.uk). The Association of Geographic Information (AGI) host a Crime and Disorder Special Interest Group which can be found from www.agi.org.uk. Information on UK policy initiatives can be found at www.policyhub.gov.uk.

References

Block , C.R. (1994) 'STAC hot spot areas: a statistical tool for law enforcement decisions', in *Proceedings of the Workshop on Crime Analysis through Computer Mapping*. Chicago: IL: Criminal Justice Information Authority.

Bowers, K.J., Hirschfield, A. and Johnson, S.D. (1998) 'Victimisation revisited: a case study of non-residential repeat burglary on Merseyside', *British Journal of Criminology*, 38: 429–52.

Brantingham, P. and Brantingham, P. (1995) 'Criminality of place: crime generators and crime attractors', *European Journal of Criminal Policy and Research*, 3: 5–26.

Bynum, T.S. (2001) *Using Analysis for Problem-solving: A Guidebook for Law Enforcement*. Washington, DC: US Department of Justice.

Canter, D. (2003). *Mapping Murder: The Secrets of Geographical Profiling*. London: Virgin Publishing.

Chainey, S. (2001) 'Combating crime through partnership. Examples of crime and disorder mapping solutions in London, UK', in A. Hirschfield and K.J. Bowers (eds) *Mapping and Analysing Crime Data – Lessons from Research and Practice*. London: Taylor & Francis.

Clarke, R.V. (ed.) (1997) *Situational Crime Prevention: Successful Case Studies* (2nd edn). Albany, NY: Harrow & Heston.

Clarke, R. and Eck, J. (2003) *Becoming a Problem-solving Crime Analyst in 55 Steps*. London: Jill Dando Institute of Crime Science, University College London (downloadable from www.jdi.ucl.ac.uk).

Cohen, L.E. and Felson, M. (1979) 'Social change and crime rate trends: a routine activity approach', *American Sociological Review*, 44: 588–608.

Dodd, T., Nicholas, S., Povey, D. and Walker, A. (2004) *Crime in England and Wales 2003/2004. Home Office Statistical Bulletin 10/04*. London: Home Office.

Eck, J. and Weiburd, D. (1995) *Crime and Place. Crime Prevention Studies. Volume 4*. Monsey, NY: Willow Tree Press.

Farrell, G. and Pease, K. (1993) *Once Bitten, Twice Bitten: Repeat Victimisation and Its Implications for Crime Prevention*. London: Home Office.

Felson, M. and Clarke, R.V. (1998) *Opportunity Makes the Thief: Practical Theory for Crime Prevention. Home Office Policing and Reducing Crime Unit Police Research Series Paper 98*. London: Home Office.

Harries, K. (1999) *Mapping Crime: Principle and Practice*. Washington, DC: Crime Mapping Research Centre, National Institute of Justice.

Hirschfield, A. and Bowers, K.J. (1997) 'The effect of social cohesion on levels of recorded crime in disadvantaged areas', *Urban Studies*, 34: 1275–95.

Hirschfield, A. and Bowers, K. (eds) (2001) *Mapping and Analysing Crime Data: Lessons from Research and Practice*. London: Taylor & Francis.

Johnson, S.D. and Bowers, K.J. (2004) 'The stability of space-time clusters of burglary', *British Journal of Criminology*, 44: 55–65.

Leipnik, M.R. and Albert, D.A. (eds) (2002) *GIS in Law Enforcement: Implementation Issues and Case Studies*. London: Taylor & Francis.

Newton, A.D. (2003) 'Crime and disorder on buses: towards an evidence base for effective crime prevention.' Unpublished PhD thesis, Department of Civic Design, University of Liverpool.

Pease, K. (1998) *Repeat Victimisation: Taking Stock. Crime Detection and Prevention Series, Paper 90*. London: Home Office.

Ratcliffe, J.H. (2002) 'Aoristic signatures and the spatio-temporal analysis of high volume crime patterns', *Journal of Quantitative Criminology*, 18: 23–43.

Ratcliffe, J. (2004) 'The hot spot matrix: a framework for the spatio-temporal targeting of crime reduction', *Police, Practice and Research*, 5: 5–23.

Ratcliffe, J.H. and McCullagh, M.J. (2001) Chasing ghosts? Police perception of high crime areas', *British Journal of Criminology*, 41: 330–41.

Rengert, G., Mattson, M. and Henderson, K. (2001) *Campus Security: Situational Crime Prevention in High-density Environments*. Monsey, NY: Criminal Justice Press.

Rogerson, M. and Christmann, K. (2004) *Crime, Fear of Crime and Quality of Life*. Sheffield: CRESR.

Rossmo, D.K. (1999) *Geographic Profiling*. New York, NY: CRC Press.

Tilley, N. (ed.) (2002) *Analysis for Crime Prevention. Crime Prevention Studies. Volume 13*. Cullompton: Willan Publishing.

Wikstrom, P.-O.H. (1991) *Urban Crime, Criminals and Victims: The Swedish Experience in an Anglo-American Comparative Perspective*. New York, NY: Springer-Verlag.

Chapter 23

Deciding what to do

Gloria Laycock

This chapter considers the process of determining an appropriate response to a presenting problem of crime or disorder.[1] It begins with a discussion of some of the concepts to which reference is made in later sections. Some of these concepts are discussed more fully in other parts of this volume but are briefly considered here in the interests of making the present chapter a 'standalone' contribution. They are regarded as necessary to the development of the response element of the scanning, analysis, response and assessment (SARA) process. Although this process is frequently described as iterative rather than linear, this is often overlooked in practice. Examples are given to illustrate the response development process, but also to bring out its iterative nature and to illustrate the need for a strategic approach, which in some cases may span local, regional and national levels.

Some useful concepts

This section discusses, in two parts, some concepts that are necessary to decide upon an effective situational response to crime and disorder. The first looks at more theoretical approaches that offer ways of thinking about crime to inform response development. The second discusses a number of other issues that need to be borne in mind in the response development process.

Ways of thinking about crime

Criminology is peppered with alternative ways of conceptualizing crime and disorder. They are not necessarily mutually exclusive and vary in their applicability to crime reduction. Those discussed here come from the field of what is generally called environmental criminology. All the ideas are based on the assumption that crime can be controlled by making changes to the immediate environment and that it is characteristics of that environment that fundamentally cause the behaviour under review. They constitute a backdrop against which responses to a crime or disorder problem can be developed.

Crime pattern theory

We begin with crime pattern theory, which is at a relatively high level of analysis and much of which has been developed by Patricia and Paul Brantingham (1991) over a number of years. Crime is not randomly distributed in space – it clusters – and crime pattern theory attempts to explain why this is so. Patricia and Paul Brantingham introduced the notion of nodes and pathways in describing physical crime patterns; nodes being the special foci of offenders' lives – where they live, work, play or visit family and friends; places with which they are familiar and areas in which they feel safe and unobtrusive. Pathways are the routes between nodes and these are also vulnerable to crime and disorder (Brantingham and Brantingham 1993). These characteristics of the environment are said to influence the location and timing of offence patterns. So, for example, the routes from offenders' homes to local bars might be considered vulnerable to crime. Similarly the routes taken by schoolchildren to and from school might be susceptible to minor acts of vandalism or bullying. Even the offence and body dump sites of serial killers can be related to these concepts (Rossmo 2000).

Most crime analysts attempting to deal with volume crimes such as theft, burglary and car crime begin with an examination of these crime patterns. They are frequently mapped using techniques from geographic information science (GIS). Once established, however, the patterns need further investigation to determine what might have caused them to be where they are, when and why. This process can be thought of as 'testing hypotheses' about what might be associated with the patterns and those hypotheses can be based upon some of the concepts described in the remainder of this section.

Routine activity

One of the reasons for the crime patterns that we see is that the majority of offences are a product of the routine activities of everyday life (Felson 2002). It is both the routine activities of the offender and the victim that produce these patterns and an appreciation and understanding of that process can assist in determining what to do to prevent or reduce the problem. So, for example, the majority of burglars tend to offend close to their home address (Wiles and Costello 2000) or in areas with which they are otherwise familiar. This might contribute to an explanation of the higher rate of burglary on some public housing estates, where relatively poorer people tend to live, including burglars. We would also expect a higher proportion of those burglaries to result in 'nil taken' or to involve relatively less loss compared with losses in more affluent areas where the more professional burglars might operate, and we would expect the burglars in high-crime areas to be younger, on average, than the general population of burglars although determining that might depend on the relative sizes of the two burglar populations.

Ideas such as these can be tested against the data. If they were correct then we might expect the lower-level burglaries to be more opportunistic and this too, can be tested. If so, then some practical implications for reduction might follow. For example, reducing the opportunities for offending, perhaps by better target hardening, might be all that is needed to make a difference in a high-crime, public housing area where less determined and less skilled burglars are operating. This might be particularly true where there was shown to be a high incidence of repeat victimization. In contrast, it might be more appropriate, when considering the burglary of high-value goods from more wealthy houses some distance from the homes of known offenders, to assume that the more committed burglar planned the offences. In such cases we may be more interested in capture and it would then be appropriate, perhaps, to ensure that as much forensic evidence as possible was collected. We know, for example, that although DNA traces are only left in about 5 per cent of burglaries, resulting in only around 3 per cent being loaded on to the DNA database, where they are left, however, it is possible to identify the offender in 48 per cent of cases (Webb *et al.* 2005).

The crime triangle

As Cohen and Felson suggested (1979), three components are necessary for the completion of most crime – a suitable victim, a motivated offender and the absence of a capable guardian. If these three components come together in space and time then an offence will necessarily happen. In order to reduce crime, then, something needs to be done about one or more of these elements. It is worth noting that all three components are logically necessary and that only one need be removed to prevent the offence. It is sometimes erroneously assumed that all three elements need to be tackled, although if they are, of course, this might increase the chances of success.

All three elements were addressed in a project intended to reduce repeat domestic violence in West Yorkshire, England (Hamner *et al.* 1999). The research team, together with the police, thought systematically about ways in which the potential victims might become less vulnerable, the offender less motivated and how they might introduce more capable guardians. The resulting set of options, as set out in Table 23.1, illustrate the ways in which the responses to the problem of domestic violence were linked to the victimization risk of the victims whilst following the crime triangle framework. The intervention levels relate to the number of times the complainant contacted the police with a complaint.

Eck (2003) has elaborated on the notion of capable guardian and has illustrated the ways in which thinking about the different kinds of guardianship can lead to ideas for reduction. This has been done in the context of what is commonly called the problem analysis triangle (PAT), as illustrated in Figure 23.1. The basic triangle represents the offender, place and target or victim, which can clearly be a person or an object and which can be related very easily to Felson's crime triangle. Eck's elaboration shows that the nature of guardianship can differ when applied to the offender, the target or victim or the place. As Felson (1995) notes, the most effective guardians are 'personal', for example, parents of their young children. Their obvious concern to protect children, not only from crime but all other sorts of harm, perhaps accounts for the relatively infrequent extent to which children are victimized, despite their obvious vulnerability and the existence of some (albeit very few) highly

Table 23.1 The domestic violence repeat victimization model

Intervention level	Victim	Perpetrator (common law offences)	Perpetrator (criminal offences)
Level 1	• Gather information • Information letter 1 • Police Watch	• Reiterate force policy • First official warning • Information letter 1	• Magistrates – conditional bail/ checks • Police Watch • Information letter 1
Level 2	• Information letter 2 • Community constable visit • Cocoon and Police Watches • Target hardening property	• Reiterate force policy • Second official warning • Police Watch • Information letter 2	• Magistrates – bail opposed/ checks • Police Watch increased • Information letter 2 • Crown Prosecution Service (CPS) file jacket and domestic violence (DV) history
Level 3	• Information letter 3 • Police Watch • Domestic violence officer visit • Agency meeting • Panic button/ vodaphone	• Reiterate force policy • Third official warning • Police Watch • Information letter 3	• Magistrates – bail opposed/ checks • Police Watch increased • Information letter 3 • CPS file jacket and DV history and contact CPS

Source: From Hanmer *et al*. (1999).

motivated offenders. As children move into adolescence they are at risk of positively rejecting the level of guardianship that has kept them safe. To some extent as a consequence, they are at heightened risk and this can be seen in the relevant statistics.

The word 'capable' as a description of the kind of guardianship we are talking about is significant. It is operationally defined in the sense that a reinforcer is defined in Skinnerian psychology. Whether a particular response is reinforced by a stimulus depends upon whether or not that response is at a higher level of probability of occurring the next time that stimulus is presented. Thus it is not until after exposure to the stimulus, and an observation of the effect, that it can be said to reinforce the response and thus be called a reinforcer;

Figure 23.1   The problem analysis triangle

similarly with the notion of a capable guardian. It cannot be assumed that introducing a 'guardian' into a situation automatically renders them or it 'capable'. For example, CCTV is potentially a mechanical guardian but it is completely ineffectual unless offenders believe that there is someone watching a screen, or that there will be some consequence to any observed offending on their part. Nor can we assume that a once capable guardian will remain so in perpetuity. Returning to the example of parent/child guardianship, parents are highly effective guardians throughout childhood but as young people move into adolescence the efficacy of parental guardianship will decrease sometimes to the point of counterproductivity. This may happen when parents, keen to ensure that their adolescent children are safe, insist on collecting them following an evening out. Instead of appreciating the concern, the young people may argue to come home alone or even say that other parents are collecting them in order to ensure their freedom to do as they wish. At this point the capable guardianship, which the parent intends, becomes less capable.

The rational choice perspective
The basis of the rational choice perspective was first set out by Cornish and Clarke (1986) and has been expanded, notably by Clarke, over a number of years. It assumes that offenders tend to make rational decisions – rational in a limited sense rather than an absolute sense (Opp 1997). Clearly offenders do not necessarily have all the available information when deciding whether or not to offend and indeed they may pause only momentarily, if that, to consider the potential consequences. Nevertheless, assuming that offenders do, at some level and to some extent, weigh up the pros and cons of their behaviour has led to a wide array of potential responses that have been shown to reduce crime. Many of these examples are reported in research journals or have been published in the *Crime Prevention* series of books edited by Ron Clarke, to which reference has been made in other chapters of this volume.

In summary, Clarke and colleagues have argued that offenders consider the effort, risk and potential reward when deciding whether or not to offend. They also think about the extent to which they can justify their action – rationalize it, or make excuses. The extent to which they may have been provoked is also relevant. Irritating queues, for example, especially in crowded bars, can simply of themselves increase disorder. Through various studies a range of effective responses to crime and disorder have been shown to fit into a 5 × 5 table as set out in Table 23.2 and taken from Clarke and Eck (2003). These responses fit into the situational crime prevention framework, which assumes that immediate environments, and the opportunities they offer, cause crime.

Mechanisms and contexts

One of the most important decisions in determining what to do in response to a problem of crime and disorder is to consider the mechanism through which any planned initiative might have an effect in its physical, social, spatial and temporal context. The mechanism indicates *how* the measure will work. What exactly is it that will reduce the offending or disorder problem? These concepts are discussed fully by Pawson and Tilley (1997) and have been considered specifically in relation to crime and disorder by Tilley and Laycock (2001).

Table 23.2 Twenty-five techniques of situational crime prevention

Aim	Technique	
Increase the effort	1.	Harden targets
	2.	Control access to facilities
	3.	Screen exits
	4.	Deflect offenders
	5.	Control tools/weapons
Increase the risks	6.	Extend guardianship
	7.	Assist natural surveillance
	8.	Reduce anonymity
	9.	Utilize place managers
	10.	Strengthen formal surveillance
Reduce the rewards	11.	Conceal targets
	12.	Remove targets
	13.	Identify property
	14.	Disrupt markets
	15.	Deny benefits
Reduce provocations	16.	Reduce frustrations and stress
	17.	Avoid disputes
	18.	Reduce emotional arousal
	19.	Neutralize peer pressure
	20.	Discourage imitation
Remove excuses	21.	Extend guardianship
	22.	Assist natural surveillance
	23.	Reduce anonymity
	24.	Utilize place managers
	25.	Strengthen formal surveillance

Articulating the mechanism is essentially the same as formulating a hypothesis. Whether it works or not is an empirical question that can only be determined by trial and error. It is the mechanism that should be tested, not the response itself, which may be insufficiently explicit and not simply transferable to other contexts. For example, introducing Neighbourhood Watch into an area might be deemed an appropriate response to domestic burglary. But it is the mechanism through which it works that needs to be made explicit and tested. It is then much easier to see how it might have worked in the experimental area and whether it might work in other areas (Laycock and Tilley 1995a). There are a number of mechanisms through which it might operate. For example it might increase the perceived risk to offenders by encouraging the belief that if they are seen in the area the police will be called. The mechanism would be the perception on the part of the offender of increased risk through surveillance. In an area of middle-class housing with no resident offender population such a mechanism might be effective. Indeed it could be part of the reason why such areas have a smaller burglary rate than other places. But attempting to introduce Neighbourhood Watch into a high-crime area with a resident offender population might be very difficult and ineffectual because that mechanism cannot reasonably be expected to work in that context. Phoning the police when seeing a burglary in progress may not be lightly done in a high-crime area with a transient and disaffected resident population.

It is, then, the mechanism of a response that is being implemented and it is that mechanism that should be considered when deciding what to do. The process of thinking through how a response might work can sometimes make it clear that it is unlikely to be effective without even implementing it. For example, if an arrest policy for domestic violence offenders were to work we might assume that the mechanism would be through some sort of shaming process. This would be unlikely to work for individuals with a substantial existing arrest history for that or other offences. In such circumstances we might hypothesize that it would make things worse and lead not to a reduction in violence but to an increase. This interpretation is so plausible as to question the ethics of indiscriminately introducing such a policy on a wide scale.

As discussed by Rosenbaum *et al.* (1986), there are a number of threats when testing mechanisms in real-world situations. He considers theory failure, implementation failure and measurement failure as possible problems. The main aim is to test the mechanism that underlies the response and this, as we have discussed earlier, can be related directly to the theoretical framework that was considered in its development. We are thus testing a theory but need to guard against concluding that the mechanism failed (and therefore that the underlying theory was wrong) when in practice it may have been that the mechanism was not properly implemented or the means of measuring the intended effect was inadequate. The research literature is full of worthy attempts to evaluate plausible mechanisms which resulted in a conclusion that implementation failed (Bullock and Tilley 2003). Measurement failure seems to be less frequently discussed but is clearly a threat to the evaluation of mechanisms.

Things to bear in mind in developing a response

This section considers a number of issues that can usefully be considered in the process of response development.

Think thief

Whatever the mechanism or mechanisms adopted in response to a crime and disorder problem, they are generally assumed to work by in some way influencing the perceptions of the offender and thus his or her estimate of the chances of success, however crude that calculus might be. Clarke and Eck (2003) go so far as to suggest that all prevention schemes work through offender perceptions. It is therefore sensible to think about any planned response as it might be seen by a potential offender. To use Ekblom's words – think thief (Ekblom 1995). It is possible that following the implementation of an initiative, offenders may change their behaviour in ways that maintain a criminal lifestyle. Any initiative is vulnerable to these adverse consequences but they can be reduced if initiatives are properly thought out with due consideration given to the offenders' potential response.

One possible adverse consequence is displacement. Six different types of displacement have been identified – spatial, temporal, modus operandi, crime switch, target switch and offender switch (Barr and Pease 1990). We know from research that, in general, displacement is less likely than it is assumed to be, and although it may happen there is usually a net reduction in offending, bearing in mind that in some cases there may be an increase in seriousness (Hesseling 1994). So, for example, there has been a welcome reduction in car theft in the UK over the past ten years (Webb *et al.* 2004), but we are now seeing the more serious problem of car jacking, albeit to a much lesser extent. Whilst it is not possible to guard against all types of displacement it is worth while considering the possibility that it might happen and planning a response accordingly. To take an extreme example, some high-value cars can be opened using fingerprint identification of the owner. A ruthless offender might go as far as to cut off the owner's thumb in order to steal the vehicle. It would be comfortably within current technology to ensure that the fingerprint was taken from a digit that had a fully functioning blood supply.

Displacement is not the only potentially adverse consequence of responding to a crime problem. Depending on the nature of the initiative, some offenders might actually increase their rate of offending. So, for example, as noted above, a mandatory arrest policy in response to domestic violence might so anger the offender that he behaves even more violently towards the original victim. This might be anticipated if the offender has a history of criminal behaviour and is angered rather than shamed by arrest. Clarke and Eck (2003) describe this as defiance on the part of the offender.

The final potentially adverse consequence to be considered here is adaptation. This is a longer-term process and may happen as a consequence of the natural evolution of society more broadly. It reflects the way in which offenders as a whole might respond to the changing opportunity structures for crime. As Pease (1997) has noted, predicting longer-term changes in crime rates is a difficult challenge although in some areas not impossible. Dick Turpin may have carried out a string of successful highway robberies but there is not much prospect of robbery on horseback being successful on modern motorways. The advent of the motor car has, however, opened up a whole host of alternative offences of which the adaptive and ever vigilant offenders have been able to take advantage. Ekblom (1997) describes this process in more detail in encouraging designers to get ahead of the criminal in a constantly evolving environment. It is possible to confuse adaptation with displacement and it can be difficult to distinguish between the two. Strictly, adaptation is not a response to a planned crime reduction initiative but rather the more natural product of the evolutionary development of crime itself.

Use crime scripts

Derek Cornish (1994) discussed the idea of crime scripts, which he borrowed from cognitive science. Crime scripts describe the ways in which an offence unfolds and attempt to make explicit the series of decision points through which the would-be offender passes in the process of crime commission. To take a familiar non-crime example, when dining out in a restaurant, the diner would normally have gone through a series of necessary actions such as choosing the restaurant, entering, sitting, ordering a meal and so on (Nisbett and Ross 1980 cited in Cornish 1994). Decisions are being made at each of these necessary points. Taking this concept into the crime field we can see that the final act of committing a crime may have been preceded by a number of decisions, at any one of which the decision to offend might have been made less likely by an appropriate intervention. Furthermore the process of committing one offence can offer the opportunity to commit other related offences. Indeed some offences may be committed as a necessary consequence of committing the target offence. For example, in order to commit a burglary it may be necessary first to commit criminal damage in breaking into the house. Post-burglary, further offending might follow in the form of handling stolen goods and credit card fraud (see also the discussion below on crime chains).

Crime scripts can be useful in the response development process since they offer a mechanism for systematically working through the decision process, thus exposing a range of potential intervention points.

Crime or problem chains

As Felson and Clarke (1999) remind us, and as can be assumed from the crime script process, one crime can sometimes lead to another. There are several senses in which this is so. First, an act of burglary can include criminal damage, selling and receiving stolen goods and perhaps the fraudulent use of a stolen credit card. As the crime unfolds, so too may opportunities for other offences. A burglar who finds the sole female householder asleep in bed may go on to commit a rape or even murder. So we need to be aware of this possibility in considering how to classify and codify crimes initially. The initial classification of the offending behaviour is critically relevant to the way in which the crime problem is described and thus to the way in which any possible responses might be developed. If the problem definition is wrong to start with, and some significant problems can be missed because of the existing crime classification systems, then the whole crime reduction process can be compromised.

Secondly, one set of offences may be causally linked to another set and may also be a necessary precondition for them. So, for example, it may be the case that disorderly behaviour on Saturday night, which is caused by excess drinking, leads on to graffiti, vandalism and other damage and even assault. Dealing with, say, the graffiti, by a rapid cleaning programme, which in other circumstances might be a most effective response, would in these circumstances be quite ineffectual. All the problems subsequent to the drunkenness are contingent on it. So dealing with them in isolation, without first attending to the initial upstream problem, would not be the best use of resources.

The third sense in which offences are linked results in what are called Van Dijk chains (Van Dijk 1994). These occur when a person is victimized and he or she then victimizes someone else to make good his or her loss. So, for example, if someone steals my dustbin, and I then steal that of one of my neighbours, and he or she then takes a bin from one of his or her neighbours, and so on, we have a Van Dijk chain, which needs to be broken.

An awareness of the possibility of these various crime or problem chains might sensibly affect a crime response programme.

The iterative nature of the process

It has been mentioned several times that the process of response development is an iterative one. Ideas can be tested, modified and retested as necessary. And some ideas can be developed in parallel leading to a more complex process than is implied by the linearly described SARA process. Some hypotheses can be developed and tested in parallel, and some may be part of a package where, if one proposition is true, it probably follows that others are also true. For example, if most shoplifters are drug addicts and if drug addicts are 24 years old on average, then it follows that shoplifters are also likely to be 24 years old on average. The propositions are not independent and can be investigated in parallel in any given data set.

This iterative process applies at more than one level in the SARA scheme. For example, we might test a number of hypotheses within the crime data set before deciding on what we think to be the significant causal events, and it is these causal events that will constitute the focus of our intervention. This would require an iterative process at the analysis stage and would contribute to getting a proper problem definition, which is clearly a vital first step prior to moving on to a determination of the response. We might then try a number of responses to the problem, with varying degrees of success, which would imply the need for an iterative process at the response stage too. We are thus testing hypotheses as part of both the problem definition and response development processes.

Overlapping concepts

The ways of thinking about crime and of influencing offenders' judgements about crime are not mutually exclusive: in practice they are often found to be operating simultaneously. So, for example, on a routine journey to the public house, a man might come across a car with an open window and laptop sitting on the back seat. Having checked that nobody was about the individual may then take it. In the process he would have made a judgement on the chances of being seen, the likelihood of being caught with it before disposal and the possibility of getting rid of it, perhaps in the pub to which he is heading. Such a scenario would involve routine activities and the rational choice perspective, and crime scripts would also be relevant. In considering responses, target hardening and increasing surveillance might be productive approaches as might an initiative to discourage the sale of stolen goods in public houses at risk of such activity.

The concepts and theoretical approaches outlined in the first part of this section are meant to assist in the process of thinking about crime patterns and what might have caused them rather than as an exhaustive set of unique approaches to problem definition or problem-solving.

Facilitating compliance

When tackling a specific crime problem it is often worth while considering the motivation of offenders, following the thinking of Felson and the crime triangle. It is not the motivation of a specific individual offender that needs to be considered, however, but the motivation of the class of potential offenders relevant to the offence in question. For example, when Forrester and colleagues were attempting to reduce domestic burglary on the Kirkholt estate in Rochdale (Forrester et al. 1988), they reasoned, following the perceived wisdom of the day, that the offenders might be motivated to offend because of the need for cash to buy drugs. Bearing this in mind it was intended to introduce a drug treatment programme at the same time as the burglary initiative so as to maximize recruitment into treatment and to minimize the chances of displacement. In the event, a study of offender motivation on the estate carried out with the help of the local probation service (Forrester, et al. 1990) showed that the problem was not drugs but debt. It was therefore decided to introduce a debt-counselling service as a way of trying to reduce displacement and facilitate the transfer of offenders from an offending to non-offending lifestyle.

Although it was not felt to be appropriate to introduce a drug treatment programme on to the Kirkholt estate at that time, it may well be more relevant to local burglary prevention activities these days. Drug taking and drug addiction are more prevalent now and adopting a strategic approach to the targeting of drug treatment programmes to coincide with the introduction of other crime prevention initiatives may make sense in some areas.

To facilitate compliance with non-offending behaviour, it is also plausible to offer crime-free ways of filling time. This is particularly relevant to young people who are often characterized as 'hanging around on street corners' and thus getting into mischief. The provision of school-holiday play schemes is an example of this, although they have met with mixed success (Heal and Laycock 1987; Loxley et al. 2002). After-school clubs may fare better, but if they are to reduce crime and disorder effectively then they may need to be offered at high-risk times. A decision on this would depend upon the mechanism that was assumed to be operating. For example, if it were assumed that the offer of play schemes or some similar activities would lead to the young people feeling more socially included, and thus to have a 'stake' in society, then it may not matter when the schemes were operating. If, on the other hand, they were assumed to divert young people from crime and into the more socially acceptable activities then they would need to be available at times of high-crime risk.

Read and Tilley (2000) briefly described what is arguably one of the better examples of facilitating compliance by offering socially acceptable alternatives. They give an account of the work of a local beat officer who, concerned with the number of complaints about youths causing annoyance on a particular public housing development, established a football league. Between 1993 and 1997 there were, on average, 340 calls over the period of the school holidays (21 July–3 September). This fell to 266 complaints during the period of operation of the scheme. An important feature of this scheme was that it was highly competitive and points were deducted if any of the players were in trouble with the police. Players and managers, keen to do well, worked to dissuade team members from misbehaving. In effect the scheme introduced a system of 'informal social control', which operated beyond the time at which the youngsters were playing football.

Damping procedures

To quote a well worn cliché, nipping problems in the bud is probably more effective than waiting until they have a stronger foothold and have expanded. So the timing of a response, as well as its appropriateness, is also relevant. Early warning of emerging problems can, therefore, be valuable. This is particularly likely to be the case with relatively minor offences carried out by young people. There was, for example, a minor epidemic of the theft of Volkswagen badges off motor vehicles, which swept the UK for a short period. Although it is difficult, even in hindsight, to envisage what might have been done to dampen this spread, an early warning of the outbreak might have been helpful.

At a totally different level, there is increasing evidence that domestic (and possibly other) burglaries occur in spates. They not only cluster in space but also in time (Johnson and Bowers 2004). This provides a good example of a crime outbreak that might be successfully reduced by a timely police response, or through some other 'damping' process. In order to introduce early damping procedures there needs to be a rapid and accurate data collection exercise associated with the problem in question. In many police agencies and local authorities such good-quality data are not available.

Crime facilitators

It is clear from an analysis of the ways in which crimes manifest themselves that offenders need help. According to Clarke and Eck (2003), there are three types of facilitator – physical, social or chemical. Physical facilitators might be the tools used by the burglar, or the gun in an armed robbery, and social facilitators would include the interactions of young men in a group, where they can easily be seen to encourage the kind of roudyism so abhorred by the older generation. Chemical facilitators, which are often disinhibitors such as alcohol, are clearly implicated in many offences including domestic assault.

In tackling crime it is often useful to address the availability of the crime facilitator rather than the crime itself. This is what stores do, for example, when they refuse to sell spray cans to young people whom they suspect may be going to use the paint inappropriately.

Ethical and related issues

Presumed efficacy cannot be the only criterion upon which to base a decision to implement a response against crime. The social acceptability of the response itself obviously has to be taken into account. So, even if there were evidence that extreme sentencing policies were effective in reducing crime, they would be socially unacceptable in a modern western democracy.

The acceptability or otherwise of some responses may, however, be more subtle. For example, one of the criticisms of situational crime prevention (SCP) is that it can lead to a fortress society (Felson and Clarke 1997). This criticism arises in part because of a particularly narrow view of SCP which, as we saw in Table 23.2, goes far beyond target hardening. Nevertheless it is a pervasive view that SCP is oppressive and unwelcome. There is, however, no reason why this needs to be so. If security is considered at the design stage in the development of goods and services then an oppressive appearance is far less likely. For example, there is no apparent difference in appearance between a car with or without an immobilizer or deadlock. But the car with the security is far less likely to be stolen (Houghton 1992; Webb *et al.* 2004).

Project management/implementation

Deciding on a potentially appropriate response to a crime or disorder problem is a significant step in the right direction but unfortunately it is only a first step. Many otherwise worthy projects fail because insufficient attention was paid to the process of project management and implementation.

Some ideal responses may be far too expensive to be acceptable either in financial or social terms. It is important, therefore, that proposals are realistic and not overambitious or expensive. It is also necessary that a project manager or some other designated person has responsibility for ensuring that the implementation actually takes place. The more complex the response set, then the more important it becomes that the process is properly managed.

One of the main reasons for implementation failure is that the agency expected to carry out the implementation has no direct interest in doing so. For example, if 700,000 mobile phones are stolen in the UK each year (Harrington and Mayhew 2001), then we might expect almost as many to be bought to replace them. It is not, therefore, in the obvious interests of the mobile phone manufacturers to redesign the phones so that they do not work when stolen. Indeed there is case to be made that it is in the direct interest of the manufacturers of fashionable goods to design them in such a way that attracts theft. Whilst this view might be regarded as unduly cynical we should acknowledge that commercial companies exist to make profit and do not naturally see it as their role to contribute to crime reduction. The successful response to crime and disorder needs to take account of the contingencies under which these companies operate and design the crime response in such a way that it *is* in their interest to co-operate.

The importance of using 'levers' to achieve higher levels of co-operation is now becoming recognized (Laycock and Tilley 1995b) and there are a number of possible levers that can be applied ranging from simple requests or the provision to data to demonstrate that a problem exists, to the use of the civil or criminal law (Goldstein 1997; see also Chapter 15, this volume). Prior to the appliance of any leverage it is necessary to identify those with the competency to address the problem – i.e. the organization or agency that has the power to change the situation in the desired manner (Laycock 2004).

The need for a strategic approach

Ad hoc solutions to identified crime problems are all very well but they might be better, and more effective in the longer term, if they were set within a broader strategic framework. The British Home Office, for example, has recently made funds available to pay for neighbourhood wardens or auxiliary police officers. Indeed, there is a whole host of alternative sources of patrol in the UK ranging from the regular police through special constables, community support officers, neighbourhood and street wardens and citizen volunteers to the private security industry. In their various forms they represent an obvious opportunity to respond to the public demand for more officers on patrol. This 'mixed economy' of policing (Crawford *et al.* 2004) produces a number of problems including the exercise of authority, legitimacy and the confusion and lack of recognition by the public of these various alternative sources of local patrol. As Crawford *et al.* point out, focusing on visible security solutions as a primary response to problems of crime and disorder can heighten anxiety, foster exclusionary tendencies and reinforce intergroup differences.

In the context of this discussion the existence of so many options for the delivery of visible patrols, at no immediate cost to the local community since many are centrally funded for time-limited periods, offers a 'quick fix' solution. Adopting such a solution, in addition to the problems set out by Crawford and colleagues, illustrates the lack of longer-term strategic planning. If problems are not to recur, then there needs to be some consideration of the 'big picture'. If, for example, neighbourhood wardens are used as patrol officers on a problematic housing estate a strategic thinker might ask what the longer-term plan is for that estate. Is it intended that there will always need to be such patrols in the area? Is there an exit strategy? Who will take over the maintenance of order when or if the patrols pull out? Or is there an assumption that the patrols need only operate for a fixed period in order to 'stabilize' the community and give time for more permanent solutions to emerge? Answering questions of this type might facilitate the development of strategic planning at the local level and reduce the adoption of 'quick fix' but in the longer-term ineffectual responses.

Reducing crime and disorder in practice: some examples

Why is an understanding of crime theories relevant to the development of a response to crime and disorder? A few illustrations have been given above. As might have been inferred, the most appropriate responses will directly address the reasons for the observed patterns of crime. Establishing those reasons – better understanding of the underlying mechanisms that led to the observed patterns – will facilitate the development of a response that can be much more closely linked with those patterns. There are at least two advantages to this. First it facilitates the development of the most *appropriate* response and, secondly, it makes much clearer the *process of evaluation*. Highly specific hypotheses can be set out, which directly link the response to the presenting problem and the ways in which that response is intended to have an effect. This is particularly useful when operating in highly complex social environments with a whole range of activities being introduced or curtailed in multi-ethnic communities.

To take an example, Forrester *et al.* (1988) introduced measures on the Kirkholt estate in Rochdale to reduce the vulnerability of burglary victims to repeat victimization. There were a lot of other things happening on the estate at that time (as is often the case in the real world), including the fact that it was an estates' action area with improvements being made in the central heating systems, windows and so on. It was, therefore, plausible that the subsequent reduction in burglary was caused by these estate-level improvements rather than the very specific and targeted initiatives introduced to protect the victims from further burglaries (Safe Neighbourhoods Unit 1993). This alternative explanation becomes much less plausible, however, when it is shown specifically that the burglary of repeat victims fell to zero within seven months of the start of the project (Forrester *et al.* 1988, 1990).

The remainder of this section looks at an example of response development in practice, taking account of the theoretical ideas introduced above and the importance of considering the mechanism through which any given response might work in the context of the presenting problem. The example is a complex one of crime and disorder in the city centre including general disorder associated with pubs and clubs. Although fictitious, it draws on data from local agencies, suitably anonymized, and illustrates the development of multiple responses in a complex environment.

Crime and disorder in the city centre

This fictitious example considers a problem of crime and disorder in a typical city centre. A brief to tackle crime and disorder on such a scale is ambitious and the first action might be to break the problem down by day and night. Typically the offence profile for each of these timeframes would be very different (Chainey and Ratcliffe 2005). We might find that the daytime crime profile was characterized by shop theft, snatch theft or 'dips' and youths hanging around whilst the night-time problems might be disorder, vandalism, criminal damage and street urination. The offence patterns associated with each time period need to be considered separately. Although this is a hypothetical example the data presented draw on published research or information that has been provided from other local projects.

Daytime crime and disorder
Let us assume that in our hypothetical city centre the scanning process reveals problems of shop theft, snatch theft and 'dips' and young people 'hanging around and causing annoyance'. Beginning with *shop theft*, and using the data from Ekblom (1986) as an example, he found that the police data were

not good enough to provide more than a broad-brush look at the problem of shop theft in his study area. His 'scanning' exercise identified one shop in the shopping area which contributed 40 per cent of the shop theft problem to the local police. He then approached the store with a request for more detailed data. This was eventually provided by the store detectives who recorded where the offences were occurring and other offence characteristics including details on the offenders. This is not an untypical eventuality. Police data are often inadequate as the sole source of information on offending in an area.

From the specially collected data, Ekblom showed that the problem of theft from this store, which sold records, cassettes, videos, computer games, etc., was very specific. Not all the products were at equal risk – of 40 sections in the store, not surprisingly just three – rock 'n' pop, soul 'n' disco and computers – accounted for 73 per cent of incidents. A visit to the store quickly revealed why this was so. The records and cassettes were on live display – they did not use the 'master bag' system where an empty box or cassettes is taken to the cashier for the disk or whatever it is to be inserted. As a consequence it was very easy for young people to steal the goods. This was made even easier by the layout of the store which, because of the commercial imperative to expose as much merchandise as possible to the public, was displayed on high units which blocked visibility. The policing style of the store was based on detection. Store detectives, dressed in 'normal' clothes, would patrol and arrest shop thieves who would later be collected by the local police for charge and disposal.

A number of responses were suggested by Ekblom in consultation with the store managers, most of which involved increasing perceived risk through increased surveillance – lowering display stands and introducing highly visible guards rather than employing store detectives. In addition the computer section (from which the computer games were stolen) was closed (target removal), although this was done for commercial reasons rather than for crime prevention purposes.

Turning to the next problem, *snatch theft and 'dips'*, a similar approach needs to be adopted of defining the problem as specifically as possible. The kinds of things that might need to be considered are reviewed by Smith (2003), who used data from over 2,000 crime reports across seven police force areas. He showed how the nature of personal robbery varied and the extent to which it concentrated in specific high-crime areas. Smith addressed personal robbery in general, which includes snatch theft and 'dips'. He defines snatch thefts as those incidents where an offender snatches property away from the victim with force being applied to the property rather than the victim. In contrast, 'dips' do not involve force with property being removed furtively from a handbag, pocket or some other container.

There are a number of hypotheses that might be tested en route to finding effective solutions to this aspect of the city-centre crime problem. For example, we might suggest that snatch thefts occur around coffee bars, where handbags have been left on the floor by busy shoppers having a rest. Dips, on the other hand, might occur around bus stops or in the marketplace, where there are crowds of people and jostling is not unexpected. These hypotheses can be tested using police data or data specifically collected in order to test the ideas.

It may be necessary, for example, to ask the coffee bar managers to establish a data collection exercise to try to determine where in the bars thefts actually occur. Are they near to the door, or are there tables on the pavement with easy access by casual passers-by?

Assuming that our hypotheses prove correct, and looking at solutions, an obvious approach to the snatch theft issue might be to encourage the bar and café owners to take some responsibility for providing a safe and secure place for women to leave their bags. Note that in arriving at this suggestion we have identified the store management as having the competency to change the situation and are suggesting ways in which they can alter the environment of the restaurants and bars so as to reduce the opportunity for theft. It may be necessary to identify and exercise some leverage to encourage them to take responsibility in this way. One major chain, which has accepted responsibility, is now trialling a 'crime reduction chair'. These chairs are intended to provide a secure place for the attachment of bags, and clearly increase the effort that offenders have to go to in order to steal the bag, to the point that it becomes extremely difficult to do so without great risk. The provision of the chairs is, of course, only a first step in reducing the offending – customers have to be made aware of their existence and make use of them. This is a much more general point of educating the public to take sensible precautions against what are still relatively rare events. In the context of a bar, this may be made even more difficult because of excessive drinking by customers who become careless of their property as a result.

The problem of controlling 'dips' offers a different set of challenges. Poyner and Webb (1992) addressed this problem in a study carried out in Birmingham. They found that the problem centred on the market area and they looked at the layout of stalls as a means of reducing dips. Because the stalls were close together it was much easier to steal from the crowded shoppers in a relatively small space. In a different study, Ponyer (1983) also addressed dips at a bus stop, effectively looking in detail at the crime script – the whole process through which a group of young offenders working together managed to achieve their aims. Again they showed the relevance of crowds and jostling, which in this case required the reorganization of the queuing process when boarding the buses.

So far in our discussion we have seen how localized changes in the opportunity for committing crime can lead to plausible and often evidence-based methods of reducing it. It may be the case, however, that a more appropriate response could be made at national level, which would bring the problem under control across a much wider area. For example, in looking at robbery in general it is fairly easy to identify the mobile phone as a popular target (Harrington and Mayhew 2001). Mobile phones are stolen in a whole range of offence types including street robberies of various kinds (mugging, snatch theft, dips, 'bullying' by school children preying on each other, etc.) and other offences such as car theft and burglary. When there is a clear and popular target for crime, such as the mobile phone, it makes sense to ask whether the phones themselves could be designed so as to make them less vulnerable to theft across the whole range of offences rather than tackling each offence at hundreds of different locations in a piecemeal manner. One of the reasons for the high rate of loss of mobile phones is their popularity with young people and the prevalence of 'pay as you go' systems which facilitate the replacement of SIM cards into handsets. The design of the mobile phone is clearly not within the competency of the local crime reduction agencies to address, but it is certainly an issue for central government – not only in pressing the mobile manufacturers to deal with the problem, but also in scanning for the emergence of other high-risk goods, which might be at similar future risk. The mobile phone provides an illustration of the way in which local and central crime reduction services might need to work together in achieving the most effective and efficient response to crime.

The final problem associated with crime and disorder in our fictitious city centre is 'youths causing annoyance'. It seems that some young people, by their very existence, annoy older people! There are a number of questions to ask – or hypotheses to test – in approaching this problem. First, looking at the time of day of complaints, and using police data, we might wonder whether any incidents are occurring during school hours. In which case it makes sense to contact the local schools (having established which schools the offending children are supposed to be attending) and check on truancy reports. It also makes sense to ask whether the young people are actually committing any offences or are simply 'hanging around'. In a study of the Bullring area of Birmingham, for example, it was shown that the young people, about whom a number of complaints had been made, were not offending to any noticeable extent. Shop theft was being carried out more by older offenders, and the young ones were simply using the shopping area as a safe, warm and comfortable place to meet (Phillips and Cochrane 1988). In some respects this is something to encourage provided they are not missing school.

In considering young people and their annoyance levels, we first need to establish whether they should be in school. If they should, then this is the first issue to be dealt with – it is a 'crime' chain problem (although the behaviour falls far short of criminal). Dealing with the truancy might solve the problem. Assuming that they are not truanting to any significant extent, the next question might be whether they are committing offences, or just hanging around. If offending, then the offending itself needs to be looked at just as any other offence patterns might be – where, when and how are the offences happening, and what can be done to deal with them. If, on the other hand, the young people are simply hanging around in an area where older people would rather they didn't, what can be done about that? Is there a legitimate place for them to congregate that is safe? Can one be created? Could the voluntary sector be involved in helping to define the need and provide a solution? The approach would be characterized as facilitating compliance and removing excuses – making it easier for young people to meet and interact in a socially acceptable context. These questions do not presuppose that young people are necessarily problems, but rather that they too have legitimate needs which might need to be catered for in socially acceptable ways.

In examining aspects of daytime crime in the city centre we have seen that the process of both problem definition and response development can be quite complex. In the UK, the most appropriate locus for that effort would probably be the local Crime and Disorder Partnership. Table 23.3 sets out a range of

Table 23.3 Tackling daytime crime and disorder

Agency	Contribution to problem definition	Potential action in response to problem
Police	Data	Arrest, cautioning
Local government		
Education department	Information on truants	Improved supervision in schools to tackle truancy
Environmental services	Information on street layout	Rearrangement of street furniture
Private sector		
Shops	Data on shop theft within store	Improve store layout, review selling practices, change policing style in store
Bus operators	Bus stop layout	Redesign bus stops
Restaurants and bars	Data on location of offending	Take greater responsibility for safety of customers' goods
Voluntary sector	Liaise with young people to determine needs	Support the provision of facilities for the legitimate congregation of young people around shopping centres or elsewhere

agencies that might sensibly be involved in that process and provides, by way of illustration, some suggestions on their contribution to the definition of the problem and its solution.

Night-time crime and disorder
In our typical city centre, a scanning exercise might demonstrate problems of disorder, vandalism, criminal damage and street urination during the hours of darkness. Again the problems need to be broken down into smaller and more manageable parts, rather than trying to tackle the whole set of issues at once. An important question is the extent to which the disorder, vandalism and damage are all consequential upon the extent and style of alcohol consumption. Indeed the street urination might also be related to the excessive consumption of alcohol together with inadequate provision of public toilet facilities. An early hypothesis to be investigated would be the possible relationship between alcohol consumption and the problematic sets of behaviours.

Let us assume that the local authorities have decided that a 24-hour city centre is desirable. This might mean encouraging shopping and commercial activities during the day and turning to an entertainment and drinking culture in the evening and during the night. Such a decision brings with it the probability that there will be excessive alcohol consumption by young people, encouraged by a large number of bars and clubs offering 'happy hours' and effectively competing with each other for custom. Inevitably in such a scenario there will be disorder as the patrons spill out on to the streets at closing time, and there will clearly be a heightened risk or violence, vandalism and street urination. It should be expected and planned for.

Homel and colleagues (1997) have shown that the managers of bars and clubs can be persuaded to work together and bring excessive consumption under control by not offering cheap drinks, controlling 'pub crawling' and training door staff better to manage patrons at the time they leave premises. In academic terms this amounts to controlling a crime facilitator (alcohol). Within the establishments it was also shown that the layout of furniture, access to the bar and control of queuing all contributed to reducing alcohol-related problems.

Controlling access to fast food and to transport home can also reduce provocation and remove excuses for violence and disorder. It can also reduce the number of illegal taxi cabs that might be tempted to operate (Knutsson and Søvik 2005) and thus reduce some of the serious assaults that can be associated with their operation.

If a more orderly and less drunken departure from the bars and clubs of our fictitious city centre could be achieved then we might find that vandalism and street urination reduced in parallel. If they did not, then we may need to test other hypotheses associated with their incidence. It may be, for example, that homeless people were urinating in the streets because there were no facilities for them to do otherwise, or because those facilities that were made available to shoppers during the day were closed at night. This could then be addressed separately.

As with the daytime problems the night-time crime and disorder needs to be tackled following a thorough analysis of the problem but bearing in mind the strategic plans for the area and the kinds of behaviour that those plans necessarily will encourage. Alcohol is a crime facilitator in UK culture, and it should come as no surprise to any local authority that uncontrolled access to alcohol by young people will lead to disorder and other crime problems. The solution, rather than more policing, lies first with the design of the drinking environment, the management of the bars and clubs and the provision of sufficient services – transport, toilets, food outlets – to accommodate the expected number of people. It may then be that the crime chains that begin with excessive consumption of alcohol can be broken at an early stage.

Table 23.4 illustrates the role that some agencies might take in tackling the night-time problems of a city centre. Again, in the UK, it would probably be for the local Crime and Disorder Partnerships to take the responsibility for co-ordinating any work but it is worth noting that the list of 'players' in Table 23.4 differs from that in Table 23.3, although both groups are addressing the general problem of 'city-centre crime'. Whether or not all the players need to be around the one table, or whether they would be better organized as two groups, would be for the local authorities to determine. Given the amount of work involved, however, and the discrete nature of the two classes of offending, it might be sensible if the groups were separate. It is also worth noting the relatively minor role played by the police in this process. Although

Table 23.4 Tackling night-time crime and disorder

Agency	Contribution to problem definition	Potential action in response to problem
Police	Data	Targeted patrols
Local government		
Licensing authority	Location of pubs and clubs Information on licensees	Revocation of licences
Environmental services	Location of public utilities Data on location and timing of graffiti and vandalism	Installation of additional toilets Relocation of street furniture Rapid cleaning of graffiti Provision of litter bins
Private sector		
Licensed premises	Information on extent of alcohol consumption	Stop special offers designed to encourage drinking of alcohol Train bar and door staff Reduce queuing
Taxi firms	Location of taxi ranks	Relocate cab ranks Control queues
Bus operators	Timetable information	Operate late-night buses Control queues
Fast-food outlets		Offer a food-ordering service from late-night clubs Control queues Manage littering

detection, patrol and other routine police activities obviously have a role to play, the approach taken to the reduction of crime and disorder problems is primarily one of anticipation and prevention.

Links between national and local responses

This chapter has focused on the development of responses to crime and disorder at the local level, although it has been noted that it is sometimes much more efficient to deal with a 'hot product' (Clarke 1999) at national level. The mobile phone was given as an example. The same is true for crime facilitators such as guns, alcohol and drug abuse, all of which either facilitate or are variously involved in crimes locally. The rules governing these facilitators, and the ease with which they can be accessed, are controlled by central government. It is within the broader legislative framework governing access to alcohol, etc., that the local attempts to control crime operate. The extent to which local agencies can successfully control access to crime facilitators is constrained or supported by that framework. It is thus important that central governments are aware of the extent to which their legislation can affect local options. This awareness is developing, and we now see the European Union, for example, actively encouraging a consideration of the potential crime consequences of new legislation.

Central governments can approach the crime prevention task as discussed here from more than one direction. They can, as was noted earlier, try to anticipate the crime consequences of the development of new technologies, and encourage designers to think ahead and design goods with crime in mind (Foresight 2000), or they can keep in close touch with local crime reduction efforts and respond rapidly to deal with emerging problems. This might require them to take a more empirical approach to legislation and acknowledge that some laws may make things worse rather than better. Significant recent changes to the ways in which alcohol is controlled in the UK are a case in point (Room 2004). The overall approach to crime control at central level need not be substantially different from that advocated in this chapter as appropriate for local groups; essentially, adopting a more empirical and scientific problem-oriented approach with an open mind when looking for solutions.

Summary

This chapter has suggested that in order to develop effective and efficient responses to crime and disorder, knowledge of some basic theoretical principles of human behaviour is not only helpful but essential. This is particularly so if the responses are to be evaluated and a body of knowledge developed showing not only what works but how and where. Prior to the development of responses, and as important, is a clear statement of the problem. This might involve a number of iterations in trying to establish the correlates of crime patterns and their causes. By thinking about potential solutions using some of the concepts outlined in the earlier part of this chapter, planners will be able to suggest a wider range of approaches beyond the traditional policing preferences for patrol or recourse to the criminal justice system.

Selected further reading

For a detailed description of the development of a problem-oriented approach using the concepts of context, mechanism and outcome, see Tilley and Laycock's Home Office/National Institute of Justice report *Working out What to Do: Evidence-based Crime Reduction* (2001). This can be downloaded free of charge from the Home Office website at www.homeoffice.gov.uk. These concepts are developed and discussed fully in Pawson and Tilley's *Realistic Evaluation*, which was published in 1997. The theoretical approaches discussed in the chapter are reviewed briefly in Clarke and Eck's manual for crime analysts, *Become a Problem Solving Crime Analyst* (2003), which also takes the reader through a problem-oriented approach to crime reduction.

Almost any of the books in Clarke's *Crime Prevention* series provides examples of problem-solving in action. The earlier volumes discuss situational crime prevention in a broad context and provide examples of problem-solving in relation to selected offences. Some of the later volumes choose themes, for example violence associated with alcohol abuse was covered in Homel *et al.*'s (1997) edited volume *Policing for Prevention: Reducing Crime, Public Intoxication and Injury*.

Readily available accounts of problem-solving can be found in the COPS guides available for download from the website www.popcenter.org, which is supported by the COPS office of the US government. Each guide covers a specific crime or disorder topic and draws on research from around the world. The series is growing all the time as new topics are added.

Note

1. This chapter is seen as relevant to crime and disorder as well as to many aspects of terrorism. For the sake of brevity the word 'crime' is generally used but the reader should assume the wider relevance unless otherwise noted.

References

Barr, R. and Pease, K. (1990) 'Crime placement, displacement, and deflection', in M. Tonry and N. Morris (eds) *Crime and Justice: A Review of Research. Vol. 12*. Chicago, IL, and London: University of Chicago Press.

Brantingham, P.J. and Brantingham, P.L. (eds) (1991) *Environmental Criminology*. Prospect Heights, OH: Waveland.

Brantingham, P.L. and Brantingham, P.J. (1993) 'Environment, routine and situation: toward a pattern theory of crime', in R.V. Clarke and M. Felson (eds) *Routine Activity and Rational Choice: Advances in Criminological Theory. Volume 5*. New Brunswick, NJ: Transaction Press.

Bullock, K. and Tilley, N. (eds) (2003) *Crime Reduction and Problem-oriented Policing. Crime Science Series. Volume 2*. Cullompton: Willan Publishing.

Chainey, S.P. and Ratcliffe, J.H. (2005) *GIS and Crime Mapping*. Chichester: Wiley.

Clarke, R.V. (1999) *Hot Products: Understanding, Anticipating and Reducing Demand for Stolen Goods. Police Research Series Paper* 112. London: Home Office Research Development and Statistics Directorate.

Clarke, R.V. and Eck, J. (2003) *Become a Problem-solving Crime Analyst*. London: Jill Dando Institute of Crime Science.

Cohen, L.E. and Felson, M. (1979) 'Social change and crime rate trends: a routine activity approach', *American Sociological Review*, 44: 588–608.

Cornish, D. (1994) 'The procedural analysis of offending and its relevance for situational crime prevention', in R.V. Clarke (ed.) *Crime Prevention Studies. Volume 3*. Monsey, NY: Criminal Justice Press.

Cornish, D. and Clarke, R.V. (1986) *The Reasoning Criminal: Rational Choice Perspectives on Offending*. New York, NY: Springer-Verlag.

Crawford, A., Lister, S., Blackburn S. and Burnett, J. (2004) *'Plural Policing': The Mixed Economy of Visible Security Patrols: A Summary of Research Findings*. Abingdon: Marston Book Services.

Eck, J. (2003) 'Police problems: the complexity of problem theory, research and evaluation', in J. Knutsson (ed.) *Problem Oriented Policing: From Innovation to Mainstream. Crime Prevention Studies. Vol. 15*. Monsey, NY: Criminal Justice Press.

Ekblom, P. (1986) *The Prevention of Shop Theft: An Approach through Crime Analysis. Crime Prevention Unit Paper* 5. London: Home Office.

Ekblom, P. (1995) 'Less crime, by design', *Annals of the American Academy of Political and Social Science*, 539: 114–29.

Ekblom, P. (1997) 'Gearing up against crime: a dynamic framework to help designers keep up with the adaptive criminal in a changing world', *International Journal of Risk, Security and Crime Prevention*, 2: 249–65.

Felson, M. (1995) 'Those who discourage crime', in J.E. Eck and D. Weisburd (eds) *Crime Prevention Studies. Volume 4*. Monsey, NY: Criminal Justice Press.

Felson, M. (2002) *Crime and Everyday Life* (3rd edn). Thousand Oaks, CA: Sage.

Felson, M. and Clarke, R.V. (1997) 'The ethics of situational crime prevention', in G. Newman *et al.* (eds) *Rational Choice and Situational Crime Prevention: Theoretical Foundations*. Aldershot: Ashgate.

Felson, M. and Clarke, R. (1999) *Opportunity Makes the Thief: Practical Theory for Crime Prevention. Police Research Series Paper* 98. London: Home Office.

Foresight Programme (2000) *Turning the Corner*. London: Department of Trade and Industry.

Forrester, D., Chatterton, M. and Pease, K. with the assistance of Brown, R. (1988) *The Kirkholt Burglary Prevention Project, Rochdale. Crime Prevention Unit Paper* 13. London: Home Office.

Forrester, D., Frenz, S., O'Connell, M. and Pease, K. (1990) *The Kirkholt Burglary Prevention Project: Phase II. Crime Prevention Unit Paper* 23. London: Home Office.

Goldstein, H. (1997) *The pattern of emerging tactics for shifting ownership of prevention strategies in the current wave of change in policing: their implications for both environmental criminology and the police.* Paper presented at the Sixth International Seminar of Environmental Criminology and Crime Analysis, Oslo, Norway (available at www.popcenter.org).

Hanmer, J., Griffiths, S. and Jerwood, D. (1999) *Arresting Evidence: Domestic Violence and Repeat Victimisation. Police Research Series Paper* 104. London: Home Office Research, Development and Statistics Directorate.

Harrington, V. and Mayhew, P. (2001) *Mobile Phone Theft. Home Office Research Study* 235. London: Home Office Research, Development and Statistics Directorate.

Heal, K. and Laycock, G.K. (1987) *Preventing Juvenile Crime: The Staffordshire Experience. Crime Prevention Unit Paper* 8. London: Home Office.

Hesseling, R. (1994) 'Displacement: a review of the empirical literature', in R.V. Clarke (ed.) *Crime Prevention Studies. Volume 3*. Monsey, NY: Criminal Justice Press.

Homel, R., Hauritz, M., Wortley, R., McIlwain, G. and Carvolth, R. (1997) 'Preventing alcohol related crime through community action: the Surfers Paradise Safety Action Project', in R. Homel (ed.) *Policing for Prevention: Reducing Crime, Public Intoxication and Injury. Crime Prevention Studies. Volume 7*. New York, NY: Criminal Justice Press.

Houghton, G. (1992) *Car Theft in England and Wales: The Home Office Car Theft Index. Crime Prevention Unit Paper* 33. London: Home Office.

Johnson, S.D. and Bowers, K.J. (2004) 'The stability of space-time clusters of burglary', *British Journal of Criminology*, 44: 55–65.

Knutsson, J. and Søvik, K.-E. (2005) *Problemorienterat polisarbete i teori och praktik*. Solna: Polishögskolan.

Laycock, G. (2004) 'The UK Car Theft Index: an example of government leverage', *Crime Prevention Studies. Vol. 17*. Cullompton: Willan Publishing.

Laycock, G.K. and Tilley, N. (1995a) *Policing and Neighbourhood Watch: Strategic Issues. Crime Detection and Prevention Series* 60. London: Home Office.

Laycock, G.K. and Tilley, N. (1995b) 'Implementing crime prevention programs', in M. Tonry and D. Farrington (eds) *Building a Safer Society: Crime and Justice, A Review of Research. Volume 19.* Chicago, IL: University of Chicago Press.

Loxley, C., Curtin, R. and Brown, R. (2002) *Summer Splash Schemes 2000: Findings from Six Case Studies. Crime Reduction Series Paper* 12. London: Home Office Research, Development and Statistics Directorate.

Nisbett, R.E. and Ross, L. (1980) *Human Inference: Strategies and Short-comings of Social Judgement.* Englewood Cliffs , NJ: Prentice Hall.

Opp, K.-D. (1997) 'Limited rationality and crime', in G. Newman *et al.* (eds) *Rational Choice and Situational Crime Prevention.* Aldershot: Dartmouth.

Pawson, R. and Tilley, N. (1997) *Realistic Evaluation.* London: Sage.

Pease, K. (1997) 'Predicting the future: the roles of routine activity and rational choice theory', in G. Newman *et al.* (eds) *Rational Choice and Situational Crime Prevention.* Aldershot: Dartmouth.

Phillips, S. and Cochrane, R. (1988) *Crime and Nuisance in the Shopping Centre: A Case Study in Crime Prevention. Crime Prevention Unit Paper* 16. London: Home Office.

Poyner, B. (1983) *Design against Crime: Beyond Defensible Space.* London: Butterworths.

Poyner, B. and Webb, B. (1992) 'Reducing theft from shopping bags in city centre markets', in R.V. Clarke (ed.) *Situational Crime Prevention: Successful Case Studies.* New York, NY: Harrow & Heston.

Read, T. and Tilley, N. (2000) *Not Rocket Science? Problem Solving and Crime Reduction. Crime Reduction Series Paper* 6. London: Home Office Research, Development and Statistics Directorate.

Room, R. (2004) 'Disabling the public interest: alcohol strategies and policies for England', *Addiction*, 99: 1083.

Rosenbaum, D.P., Lewis, D.A. and Grant, J.A. (1986) 'Neighbourhood-based crime prevention: assessing the efficacy of community organising in Chicago', in D. Rosenbaum (ed.) *Community Crime Prevention: Does it Work?* London: Sage.

Rossmo, D.K. (2000) *Geographic Profiling.* Boca Raton, FA: CRC Press.

Safe Neighbourhoods Unit (1993) *Crime Prevention on Council Estates.* London: Department of the Environment.

Smith, J. (2003) *The Nature of Personal Robbery. Home Office Research Study* 254. London: Home Office Research, Development and Statistics Directorate.

Tilley, N. and Laycock, G. (2001) *Working Out What To Do: Evidence-based Crime Reduction. Crime Reduction Series Paper* 11. London: Home Office.

Van Dijk, J. (1994) 'Understanding crime rates: on interactions between rational choices of victims and offenders', *British Journal of Criminology*, 34: 105–21.

Webb, B., Smith, M. and Laycock, G. (2004) 'Designing out crime through vehicle licensing and registration systems', in M. Maxfield and R.V. Clarke (eds) *Understanding and Preventing Car Theft. Crime Prevention Studies. Volume 17.* Cullompton: Willan Publishing.

Webb, B., Smith, C., Brock, A. and Townsley, M. (2005) 'DNA fast-tracking', in M. Smith and N. Tilley (eds) *Crime Science: New Approaches to Preventing and Detecting Crime.* Cullompton: Willan Publishing.

Wiles, P. and Costello, A. (2000) *The 'Road to Nowhere': The Evidence for Travelling Criminals. Home Office Research Study* 207. London: Home Office.

Chapter 24

Evaluation for lesson learning

John E. Eck

Introduction

> The best laid schemes o' mice an' men
> Gang aft a-gley,
> An' lea'e us nought but grief an' pain
> For promis'd joy (Robert Burns).

Life is so constructed that an event does not, cannot, will not, match the expectations (Charlotte Bronte).

One of the common denominators I have found is that expectations rise above that which is expected (George W. Bush).

How do we learn from evaluations? Do we let evaluation findings vote for winners and losers, giving more votes to the rigorous evaluations than the less rigorous? Or do we learn what works from other information, in addition to evaluation findings? In particular, what is the role of crime prevention theory in learning from evaluations? Consider the following example.

In the late 1980s and early 1990s, crack cocaine dealing and its associated crimes seemed to overwhelm US police departments. As the number of crack houses and street drug-sales locations proliferated, so did the homicide rate. It became abundantly clear that standard police tactics were not up to the job of controlling, let alone reducing these problems, so local police forces were forced to innovate. And there were many innovations. Some of these were seat-of-the-pants innovations – reverse-buy operations, for example, wherein police posed as the drug dealers they had just arrested, and then arrested the buyers and seized their vehicles. The thought was that this would deter customers from using popular drug markets. There is today no evidence that such operations had their intended effect, yet they were wildly popular with US police agencies.

Some of the new anti-drug approaches were thoroughly evaluated, so now, with the ebbing of the crack epidemic, we can say we have learnt some important lessons. One of the most important lessons is that place management matters, perhaps more than any other single factor, for preventing street drug crimes. We will use this experience, particularly the evaluations and research surrounding interventions with landlords and property managers, to illustrate how we learn from evaluations.

In this chapter, we will describe how we construct evaluations and how we learn from them, using evaluations of place management interventions as an extended example. Much of the evaluation literature discusses how we can create useful comparisons through evaluation designs that give us confidence that the intervention we are evaluating really was, or was not, the cause of the crime changes we observed. We will follow that tradition. We will also see why considerations of design alone are inadequate for learning. In particular, we will emphasize the theoretical foundations of the intervention. Theory, we will see, is the hub around which all evaluation learning revolves.

The recent push to evidence-based prevention (Sherman *et al.* 2002) emphasizes the need to formulate and enact crime reduction policies based on scientific evidence. There are a number of ways of describing the use of evidence in crime prevention, but three seem particularly germane. Moving from the specific to the general, we would want evidence that shows that:

1. for a specific crime problem an intervention is the appropriate choice;

2. the application of this intervention resulted in the prevention of the type of crime we are interested in; and

3. if we applied the intervention again we will obtain similar results.

The first form of evidence helps us select an intervention. This requires a theory of crime problems, supported by evidence from empirical tests, from which it is possible to deduce interventions that are plausibly effective. The theory describes how the crime problem originates, what features of settings contribute to the problem and logically suggests ways to manipulate settings to reduce the problem. An evidence-based approach selects the intervention to be applied from the class of possible interventions that are based on sound theories. Selection of an intervention outside this class of potential interventions cannot be considered evidence based. Nevertheless, we do not require evaluation evidence at this stage. We are prepared to select an intervention that has not been tested, but comes from a theory that has survived tests.

This brings us to the second form of evidence. We have applied a plausible intervention – based on an empirically tested theory. Nevertheless, there is no guarantee that this intervention will work as well as we expect. We therefore must test the actual application of the theoretical intervention. It is to serve this function that we conduct evaluations that can tell us, with some confidence, that the intervention did or did not produce the expected outcomes.

The third form of evidence gives us licence to generalize from the specific instances of the evaluations to broader application. To do so, we would like to have multiple tests of the intervention showing that the intervention is more successful than its alternatives at reducing the crime problem in particular types of settings. But a track record of positive evaluations, regardless of their rigour, is insufficient for learning. Though we tend to believe that past performance is an indicator of future performance, we also know that things do not always work predictably. So to generalize from the isolated evaluations to broad application, we need a way of showing that these are not isolated instances at all, but part of a larger pattern that we can rely upon. The bridge from the specific to the general is theory.

The evaluation evidence provides information supporting or contradicting the original theory. It is the theory that gives us the warrant to generalize. So we have an evidence-based loop, from empirically sound theory, to tested application, which in turn provides evidence about the original theory, and which then allows us to reapply the intervention (or not). Evaluations, in short, teach us lessons because they apply and test theories.

The circumstances we have been discussing are seldom achieved in crime prevention. Often the crime problem is not thoroughly investigated. Often there is no attempt to apply a well tested theory to the problem. Typically, there is scant scientific evidence about what would work in the type of setting in question.

This chapter advocates a hard-nosed scepticism about crime prevention interventions. Despite remarkable gains in knowledge over the last few decades, there is much we do not know about crime and its prevention, and we cannot assume we know the answers. Well researched theories do not always provide effective interventions, but unresearched ideas are even less likely to. And interventions without a theoretical basis are extremely unreliable.

We will begin in the next section by examining the purposes behind evaluations of crime prevention interventions. Different decision-makers have different interests. They ask different questions and look for different types of answers. Once we have examined the purposes of evaluations, we will look at the basic elements of crime prevention evaluations. In particular, we will look at the interplay amongst the intervention, cases, setting and outcome. The following section describes the criteria we use to make general claims that an intervention is effective. Here we look at five criteria — mechanism, association, temporal order, elimination of rival explanations and generalizing – and the forms of validity that correspond to them. The fifth section provides an overview of evaluation design. Designs organize systematic comparisons between what occurred during the intervention and what might have occurred if the intervention had not been implemented. This is important to all crime prevention evaluations. In the sixth section we examine the process by which we generalize from specific evaluation findings to larger lessons. We see that theory plays an important, indeed a critical role, in learning from evaluations. In the final section we will contrast two evaluation programmes – one based on theory and the other not – as case studies in evaluation learning.

Purposes of evaluations

> Nothing has such power to broaden the mind as the ability to investigate systematically and truly all that comes under your observation in life (Marcus Aurelius).

Most evaluations attempt to establish a causal connection between an intervention (*I*) and some outcome (*O*). It is upon these evaluations we will focus our attention. Before we do so, however, it is important briefly to consider an important subclass of evaluations that are not designed to establish a strong causal connection. Instead, they are designed simply to establish that a desirable outcome has been achieved. Such evaluations are most useful for prevention efforts in which local decision-makers want to determine if a crime problem diminished sufficiently to reallocate resources to other crime problems. If crime does not diminish, then the decision-makers may change the intervention in some way to increase the odds that their goals will be achieved. If crime does diminish sufficiently, the intervention may be curtailed, as its purposes were achieved. If the decision-makers have little interest in repeating the intervention, they have little to gain from rigorously demonstrating that the reduction in crime is caused by the intervention (Eck 2002a).

The unanticipated availability of funding, for example, may prompt police officials to apply an innovative strategy against a persistent burglary problem. These funds are not expected to be available in the future, so something else will have to be done about other burglary problems. The local decision-maker has more interest in establishing that burglary has gone down than in demonstrating that the innovation is the most likely cause of the decline. Consider another common example. A particular crime spikes, leading to a hastily conceived reaction. The crime declines. Crime may have declined for other reasons, but the important thing is that it did decline sufficiently to move on to other problems (Eck 2002a). Such evaluations are useful for management of resources, but they provide little useful knowledge to guide future action.[1] In short, these non-causal evaluations are highly specific to local circumstances[2] and we learn little from them.

We will focus our attention on evaluations that teach lessons that can guide future actions. The purpose of such evaluations is to increase the stockpile of information about what is likely and unlikely to reduce crime. They help answer the question: what should we do if we face a similar crime problem again?

Elements of crime prevention evaluations

> The strongest arguments prove nothing so long as the conclusions are not verified by experience. Experimental science is the queen of sciences and the goal of all speculation (Roger Bacon).

There are four basic elements that must be considered in all evaluations: interventions, outcomes, cases and settings (Shadish *et al.* 2002). The relationships of these elements are shown in Figure 24.1. The intervention acts on the cases. As the cases are imbedded in a setting, it is the combination of these three elements that create the outcome. The process by which this takes place is the causal mechanism, which we will come back to later (Pawson and Tilley 2000). Each of these four elements has a distinct part to play in drawing lessons from evaluations. Let's look at each in turn.

Interventions

The intervention is the package of actions whose effectiveness the evaluation is supposed to determine. We think of interventions as packages because all interventions involve a collection of actions, often choreographed by a set of procedures. Sometimes the intervention is a sequence of actions (e.g. selecting the people who will take action, training these people, scheduling their work times and deploying them) and sometimes multiple tasks must occur at the same time (e.g. increasing the risk to offenders and communicating this increase in a credible manner).

Consider an evaluation of the effectiveness of landlord interventions on curbing crime at drug-dealing locations (Eck and Wartell 1998). Here, the intervention package evaluated included police enforcement at the site followed by police contact of the owner, and a meeting between a narcotics detective, a city building inspector and the owner (or representative) at the site of the building with the drug problem. Police communicated a threat of civil action to the owner if they failed to co-operate (Eck and Wartell 1998). One can imagine a group of closely related interventions, most of which were not tested:

- With or without enforcement prior to the intervention.
- With or without a building inspector.
- With or without a narcotics detective.
- With others present.
- At the site or some other location.
- By phone or by e-mail.
- With or without a threat.
- Other additions and variations.

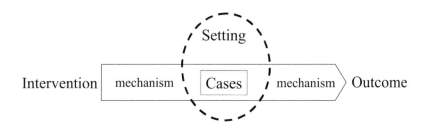

Figure 24.1 Process of causation in crime prevention programmes

The very specific intervention evaluated is an exemplar of a class of closely related interventions that could have been implemented. Consequently, we are interested in three forms of lessons about interventions. First, if we did the same intervention again, would we get the same results? Clearly we must know enough about the package of actions the intervention contains to be able to repeat it. If the intervention is poorly described, then we cannot repeat the intervention precisely and learning from evaluations becomes extremely difficult.

Secondly, we will want to generalize from one specific intervention to related interventions. We would like to know what parts of this package are essential – without which the intervention fails – and which parts we can vary. We are interested in generalizing about the essential core. Based on the Eck and Wartell evaluation, we cannot determine which, if any, of the parts of the package are not critical. To answer this question we need to compare the results of many evaluations of similar, but not identical, intervention packages.

But we also want to generalize further. What does our success at preventing drug dealing by intervening with landlords tell us about the possibility of controlling bar fights by intervening with bar owners? What does it tell us of the effectiveness of controlling college student drinking disturbances by intervening with the students' landlords? What does it tell us of the effectiveness of controlling thefts from hotel rooms by intervening with hotel managers? Or what does it tell us of the effectiveness of controlling thefts from pleasure boats by intervening with marina owners?

Outcomes

The outcome in crime prevention is the change in target crimes (or disorders). As was the case with the intervention, we can distinguish amongst levels of outcome generalizations. First, do we get the same outcome if we measure it differently? Does it matter if we measure crime by offender self-reports, interviews of victims or by crime reported to the police, for example? Secondly, we want to know if we can generalize from the specific crime type to closely related crime types. Even seemingly related crimes are sometimes differentially vulnerable to prevention tactics: for example vehicle theft and theft from vehicles (Clarke and Harris 1992).

Cases

The intervention works on the cases. Cases are the people or areas involved with crime. Place management interventions work on owners of property and the people they employ to manage their property. Since owners and places usually have a one-to-one correspondence, distinguishing between places and people is less important for place management interventions than for other interventions. When evaluating the effectiveness of forms of rehabilitation (the intervention), the cases are people (the offenders whose behaviour one is trying to change). When evaluating the effectiveness of street closures on crime, the cases are the areas containing the streets being closed. When evaluating the effectiveness of sexual assault awareness training for college women, people are the cases.

We should distinguish between micro-level and macro-level cases. Consider two different evaluations of two related but nevertheless different interventions. In the first, addresses with extremely high levels of crime are selected and the owners are induced to improve how they regulate conduct on their property. The outcome is measured by the average reduction in crime experienced by the targeted addresses. In the second, high-crime neighbourhoods are selected and community-wide crackdowns on poor management practices are undertaken to induce owners to improve how they regulate conduct on their property. The outcome is measured by the average reduction in crime experienced by the targeted neighbourhoods.

In the first instance, the case is an address, a place. This is a micro-level intervention. Specific places are singled out and targeted. They may be near each other or far apart. Connections amongst the cases are assumed to be irrelevant. Outcomes are measured at the places.

In the second instance, the cases are areas. This is a macro-level intervention. Neighbourhoods are singled out and targeted. Here crime locations and non-crime locations in the same area are treated. High-crime locations outside the selected neighbourhoods are not addressed. It is assumed that some interaction amongst the places within neighbourhoods is important for generating crime. Measurement is conducted at the neighbourhood level.

Interventions on micro cases are often based on a different theory from those based on the macro level. The interventions themselves are usually different in important ways, even if they appear superficially related. And outcomes are measured differently. For this reason, evaluations of interventions on micro cases are not easily generalized to interventions on macro cases, and vice versa.

As implied by their name, case-study evaluations are examinations of the impact of an intervention on a single case. Poyner's evaluation of the impact of the removal of connecting walkways on robberies in a housing complex is a case study (Poyner 1994). He examined a single facility and measured the change in crime for the facility before and after the intervention. Even studies with several cases are considered case studies when the number of cases is too small to generalize to a larger group. An evaluation of the impact of four separate CCTV installations in Cincinnati (Mazerolle *et al.* 2002) is best considered a case study. In contrast, if 50 locations with CCTV installations had been compared to 50 similar locations without installations, we would not have a case study. Most evaluations of interventions on places or areas are case studies of one or a few cases.

Just as we are interested in two forms of lessons about interventions, we have similar interest in learning about cases. Can we generalize from the cases used in one experiment to all cases of that type? Can we generalize from the specific type of case to related types of cases? And can we generalize from one level to another (micro to macro or vice versa). In the first instance we might be interested in generalizing from the 50 drug corners in low-income neighbourhoods where crack was sold that were involved in an evaluation, to all crack sales corners. In the second instance we might be interested in whether we can generalize from crack sales corners to crack sales in bars. In the third instance, we might want to know if we can generalize from a neighbourhood-wide intervention against drug-dealing locations to site specific interventions scattered among several neighbourhoods.

Settings

Interventions operate on cases to achieve outcomes in specific settings. Settings provide the context, and the context interacts with the intervention to varying degrees (Pawson and Tilley 2000). Interventions that affect the legal-economic incentives of private sector property owners of persistent drug locations appear to work well, but they probably only work well when property owners operate in marginal rental markets. If the rental market is flourishing, drug sites are unlikely because landlords will take the initiative to protect their locations. In extremely weak rental markets, or in rental markets that have completely collapsed, landlords are likely to abandon their properties if their costs rise, or have already done so (Eck and Wartell 1997). Consequently, interventions to compel better place management may have no effect. Notice how one aspect of the setting – rental market conditions – interacts with the intervention and sets the boundaries on effectiveness. In this example, rental market conditions provide incentives or disincentives to place managers. The intervention does not change this aspect of the setting, but leverages it to accomplish the desired outcome. In other interventions parts of the setting may be altered, as in the construction of a street barricade to alter traffic flow to disrupt a drug market.

Again, we are interested in two forms of generalization: first, from the settings observed in the evaluation to very similar settings that were not part of the evaluation; and, secondly, from the type of setting examined in the evaluation to other types of settings. The interaction between context and intervention means that some interventions will be highly context dependent. In such instances, minor variation in either the intervention or the setting can change the outcome. Context dependency inhibits valid generalization to dissimilar contexts, but promotes generalization to very similar contexts. If the interaction is modest, or if the context is common, there are fewer obvious barriers to valid broad generalization (Eck 2002a). Typically, we have little information about the context sensitivity of interventions. The fact that we can discover multiple evaluations of the same intervention that have similar outcomes suggests that many interventions have wide application, and so are probably not extremely context sensitive.[3] On the other hand, when we see multiple evaluations of the same intervention yielding widely disparate outcomes, we might be observing a consequence of context sensitivity. But we cannot be sure. Variation in the evaluation methods used could be the cause of the ambiguous results.

All four of these elements – intervention, cases, setting and outcome – should be described by the governing theory. That is, the theory should give some guidance as to what general form of intervention will work, on what types of cases and in which settings to achieve a type of outcome. However, crime prevention theories often provide little specific guidance. They almost never, for example, assert that the intervention will produce a reduction in reported crime but not in victimization survey counts.

Criteria for judging effectiveness

> Life is the art of drawing sufficient conclusions from insufficient premises (Samuel Butler).

> All inferences from experience, therefore, are effects of custom, not reasoning (David Hume).

A claim of intervention effectiveness is an assertion that when applied to members of a class of cases in a type of setting the intervention will reliably cause a reduction in crime. With the singular exception mentioned earlier, the goal of all evaluations is to make general statements from particular examples. Or, stated in the negative, we are usually uninterested in evaluations that are not exemplars of a class of interventions on a class of cases in a class of settings producing a class of outcomes. But because an evaluation of a particular intervention–case–setting–outcome combination may not be representative of the larger classes we are interested in, we require good evidence to make convincing generalizations. We also need good theory. In particular, we need evidence and theory that can contribute to answering five difficult questions:

1. Is there good reason to believe that the intervention could act on the type of cases in which one is interested; in the settings these cases are found, to achieve the desired outcomes? This is a question about *mechanism*.

2. Is there a statistical relationship between the implementation of the intervention and changes in the target crime? This is a question about *association*.

3. Does the intervention precede the changes in crime? This is a question about *temporal order*.

4. Are there plausible alternative explanations for the changes in crime that challenge claims for the effects of the intervention? This is a question about *rival causes* of the observed outcomes.

5. Do the evaluation findings support (or contradict) a general theory that asserts that if other members of the class of interventions were applied to relevant cases in the appropriate settings we would get similar outcomes? This last question is about *generalizing* from a particular evaluation to common application.

We will examine each of these questions in turn.

Mechanism

A mechanism is a process by which the intervention results in the outcome (see Figure 24.1). If we claim that throwing a switch causes a light to come on, a description of the mechanism would be the diagram of the electrical circuits involved and the theory of electricity. The mechanism, ideally, stems directly from a general theory supplemented by local conditions (the specific wiring pattern connecting the switch, power source and light bulb). Interventions based on the theory of situational crime prevention rely on a mechanism of rational choice (Clarke and Eck, 2003). 'Such interventions alter a setting so that offenders perceive an increase in effort or risk, or a reduction in reward, excuses or provocations.' Most situational-based interventions operate on only some of these perceptions. A description of a situationally based intervention mechanism would describe which parts of the setting were altered, how they were altered and how this in turn changed the way offenders perceived crime opportunities. And it would apply this general framework to the specific circumstances being investigated.

Mechanism is critically important for several reasons. First, it provides a coherent explanation as to how and why the intervention should work. This gives the intervention some plausibility, particularly if the theory upon which the mechanism is based is strongly supported by other research and thorough analysis of local conditions shows how the theory is applicable. The validity of the theory gives us confidence in the intervention. Absent a credible theory, we are justifiably sceptical of claims that an intervention will be effective. But as we discussed at the outset, even good theories can result in ineffective interventions, so strong theoretical support is not sufficient to support a claim for the intervention. Similarly, even if there is strong empirical support for an intervention, we would still be dubious of a claim that an intervention is effective if we did not have an explanation as to how it reduces crime.

The importance of mechanism is often overlooked in criminological evaluations, though Pawson and Tilley (2000) place considerable emphasis on it. This is not the case in well developed sciences, where the requirement of mechanism serves an important salutary role. Early proponents of continental drift were unable to persuade geologists that their theory of continental movement was valid, despite the considerable evidence they amassed. It was not until 1965 with the elaboration of the underlying mechanism (and evidence for that mechanism) that geology accepted the idea that the earth's crust moves (Winchester 2003). The bacterial cause of many stomach ulcers was only accepted once it was demonstrated that there was a mechanism for the process (Thagard 1999). Though it may seem that the requirement for a coherent mechanism is unduly conservative, consider the role such a requirement played in the demise of cold fusion. Much of the early, and ultimately justifiable, scepticism of physicists about cold fusion rested on the absence of a plausible mechanism for cold fusion. In fact, cold fusion violated well established theoretical mechanisms in physics (Taubes 1993). The scientific requirement that the black box between presumed cause and presumed effect needs to be opened and its contents described curbs overly enthusiastic theorizing from empirical anomalies (as in the case of cold fusion). It also adds to the fertility of valid theories by opening up new areas for scientific exploration.

The second reason we are concerned with mechanism is that we can use our knowledge of mechanism to describe evaluation results that would be observable if the intervention were acting according to theory. Results are intermediate indicators of mechanism operating between the intervention and the outcome. They are empirical findings other than the outcome that are traceable to the intervention. If the mechanism is operating, then in addition to observing a drop in the specified crime (the outcome), we will also observe other empirical regularities consistent with the theory.

This provides us with greater confidence that the intervention is the cause of the outcome, particularly if these results are unlikely to come from other potential causes of the outcome. Other possible causes of the outcome must use different mechanisms to achieve the same outcome with the same cases.[4] The ability to rule out alternative mechanisms helps establish that the intervention is the most likely cause of the outcome.

This is depicted in Figure 24.2, where the intervention being tested (I) and one or more alternative explanations (Z_j) can operate on the same cases in the same setting to produce the same outcome, but they use different mechanisms. The mechanism for I produces results R_i and the Z mechanisms produce results R_z. Observing R_i rather than R_z can help eliminate Z_j as rival hypotheses, thereby strengthening the argument that it is I that produced O.

An example of a causal mechanism is shown in Figure 24.3. The dotted boxes describe the content of their associated solid boxes. If the intervention were unable to change the incentive structure of managers, we would not expect the intervention to change the way the location is managed, so we would not expect it to reduce crime. If we found evidence that, despite the lack of changes in management incentives, crime dropped, then we would be suspicious of claims that some form of place management change caused the decline. Similarly, if place management changed but offender perceptions did not, then we could not expect crime to decline. If in this situation we found a decline in crime, then we should be more willing to believe something other than place management was the cause.

Observing these results provides a diagnostic tool, as summarized in Table 24.1. For us to claim that the intervention prevents crime we need, at minimum, to show a prevention outcome (first row) and mechanism results (first column) that are consistent with our theory. If the desired outcome (first row) is coupled with unexpected results (third column) then we should be suspicious of claims that the intervention was the cause of the outcome. If the results specified by the mechanism are found (second column), but the outcome

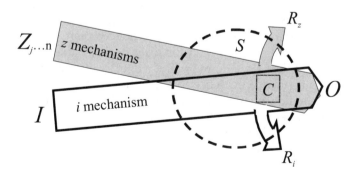

Figure 24.2 Alternatives to the intervention being tested using different mechanisms to achieve the same outcomes

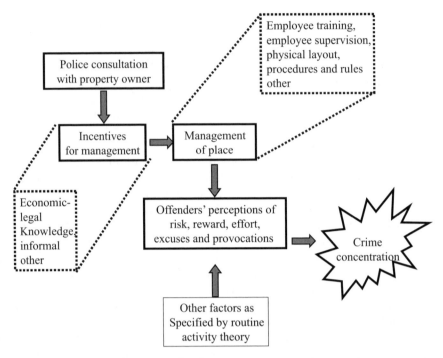

Figure 24.3 The mechanism of place management interventions on crime concentration

is not as expected (second row), then we have evidence of the interventions ineffectiveness. Failure to find the expected results (third column) as well as failure to achieve the desired outcome (second row) suggests that there may have been an implementation failure, or the theory is wrong.

Let's apply Table 24.1 to the example shown in Figure 24.3. In their evaluation of landlord interventions to curb drug-dealing-related crime, Eck and Wartell found evidence that the intervention did prevent crime. How did this happen? This required a look at the mechanism results. Eck and Wartell looked for two types of evidence that landlords acted in ways that could influence drug dealers. The first was a change in the physical environment. They found no evidence for this mechanism; landlords made very few environmental changes (Clarke and Eck, 2003). The second was the eviction of the drug dealer. Here they found that landlords who received the intervention were much more likely than those who did not to evict the drug dealer, if the drug dealer was the leaseholder (but they were no more likely to evict if someone else held the lease). These results provide evidence showing the causal path the intervention takes. The combination of outcome and results correspond to the situation described in the upper-middle cell of Table 24.1. If the results had shown no differences in evictions, then we would not know how the intervention caused the outcome (upper-right cell in Table 24.1) and we would be justified in being sceptical that this intervention was the cause of the outcome, even though it was a randomized controlled trial.

The third reason mechanism is important is that it aids in drawing larger conclusions about the intervention. The evaluator must show that

Table 24.1 Using mechanism results as diagnostics

Outcome	Mechanism results	
	Expected	Not expected
Prevention	Evidence of intervention effectiveness	Evidence that some other factor caused the outcome, or that the mechanism theory is incorrect
No prevention	Evidence of intervention ineffectiveness	Evidence of inadequate implementation of intervention, or that the mechanism theory is incorrect

the specific intervention being tested is a valid extension of the theory. This requires an elaboration of the theoretical mechanism and a demonstration that the intervention faithfully adheres to it. This is called 'construct validity' (Shadish *et al.* 2002). If the intervention has high construct validity, we can draw implications from the evaluation to the theory and to related theoretical mechanisms. With low construct validity we have extremely limited abilities to draw larger conclusions.

Owners of rental property are place managers according to routine activity theory, but the drug dealers, the neighbours of the drug dealers and police officers are not. If the evaluator had tested the effectiveness of police raids, or organizing tenants, or counselling drug dealers and claimed that these were manifestations of place management, the evaluator's claim would be (construct) invalid and the evaluation would have no implications for place management. Thus, it could provide no evidence supporting or undercutting the use of place management interventions.

In addition to doing what we think we are doing, we also must apply it in a theoretically valid context. Place manager interventions, for example, only make theoretical sense when applied to places with concentrations of crime. They make little sense when applied to places with little or no crime. Not only is it extremely difficult to detect whether crime dropped (because there is so little crime to get rid of) but, more importantly, when there is little or no crime there is no reason to believe that management practices facilitate crime (Eck 1995). Consequently, without a crime concentration, there is no reason to believe that changing management could reduce crime.

Theories describe the cases and settings for which an intervention is applicable. If the intervention is applied in situations where it is not expected to work, we should not expect it to work and, if it does, we should be suspicious. Continuing with our example of place management, let's look at the misapplication of an intervention. Repeat victimization is not synonymous with place concentration. Some repeat victimization creates spatial hotspots, but other forms do not. Assume we are interested in reducing victimization against women by estranged spouses and boyfriends. We identify women who reported threats from estranged husbands or boyfriends and find that these threats are scattered amongst many sites with little or no repeat threats at the same sites. Place theory is clearly inappropriate for developing an intervention. If a place-based intervention were used in this circumstance, and the evaluator drew conclusions about the efficacy of such interventions, these conclusions would have little construct validity. And evidence from an evaluation of such an intervention would have little bearing on the utility of place management interventions in general, or the theory these interventions are based upon.

In short, mechanism serves three critical roles. First, it makes the intervention plausible, even in advance of any evaluation. We still need to conduct an evaluation, but we would want to try this intervention before any other proposed intervention that does not have a well established mechanism. Secondly, mechanism results help us interpret findings from evaluations. Anomalous results cast suspicion on conclusions that the intervention was effective. Thirdly, mechanism aids in removing barriers to generalizing from particular evaluation conclusions to broader conclusions.

Association

In addition to demonstrating a plausible mechanism and consistent results, the evaluator must provide valid evidence that there is an association between the presence of the intervention and the drop in crime. This is called 'statistical conclusion validity' (Shadish *et al.* 2002). If the random fluctuations in crime are inadvertently attributed to changes in the intervention, then the evaluator's conclusions about the intervention's efficacy are invalid. Similarly, the conclusions are less valid if the evaluator over- or underestimates the association between the imposition of the intervention and the change in crime than if the evaluator makes an accurate estimate of the relationship.

Two types of mistakes can occur in drawing valid conclusions about association. First, one might conclude that there is an association between the intervention and the outcome when in fact there is not. Evaluations that make no attempt to rule out random fluctuations through the use of significance tests or confidence intervals are particularly vulnerable to this error. Secondly, one might conclude that there is no association between the intervention and the outcome when in fact there is an association. Evaluations with weak measures of the outcome, poor implementation of the intervention and highly heterogeneous cases run the risk of falling victim to this error (Shadish *et al.* 2002).

For example, Popkin and others failed to find an association between legal actions against landlords whose property had drug dealing and neighbourhood residents' perceptions of drug dealing. This may have been due to poor measurement. Citizens were asked *after* the intervention whether they perceived a change in drug dealing following the interventions (Popkin *et al.* 1995). Because there is no measurement of citizens' perceptions before the intervention, problems with recall could contaminate the measure of outcome. It is notable that this evaluation is the only assessment of landlord interventions to curb drug-related problems that relied solely on citizen perceptions measured after the intervention, and is the only evaluation to report no association between the intervention and the outcome (Eck 2002b).

Temporal order

Temporal order requires that the intervention precede the outcome. If there is a change in the outcome before the intervention takes place, we can reject the hypothesis that the intervention caused this change. Most evaluations that measure crime before and after the implementation of the intervention have no trouble establishing temporal order. There are two circumstances in which temporal order raises problems for evaluators. In the first, cases with and without the intervention are compared with regard to the outcome, but there is no pre-implementation measure. This means we are measuring the relative magnitude of crime after the intervention instead of what we should be measuring, the relative change in outcome amongst the cases.

In evaluations of this type, we do not know if the differences amongst the cases existed before the intervention was put into action. Measuring crime in well lit and poorly lit locations around a city would fall victim to this problem. If we found that poorly lit places had more crime than well lit places, it may be because poorer neighbourhoods receive worse public services, including lighting, and they have more crime, but the lighting does not cause a decline in crime.

Sometimes policy-makers forget to look at changes in crime prior to the implementation of an intervention. This is particularly the case when no formal evaluation is conducted but political decision-makers want to tout a particular programme. New York City police reforms of the mid-1990s are a case in point. In their efforts to exclaim the virtues of new police tactics, politicians, the press and some academics asserted that the decline in homicides was an outcome of these changes. They forgot to look at the trend in homicides in the years leading up to the police changes. Crime had been declining for several years, thus suggesting that temporal order had been violated and undercutting the conclusion that the police had a large role in the decline in homicides (Eck and Maguire 2000).

Recently, Smith *et al.* (2002) raised the issue of anticipator effects of interventions. That is, offenders anticipating a crime prevention intervention change their behaviours, thus reducing crime, before the intervention is underway. There are a number of explanations for anticipatory effects. These explanations fall into two categories: anticipatory effects that are the result of the evaluator misinterpreting the data (e.g. the effects of smoothing); and circumstances where offenders somehow heard about the intervention before it began. In neither case are these violations of temporal order. In the first instance, more careful analysis would reveal that the intervention came before the outcome. In the second instance the evaluator should include any form of communication about an intervention to be part of the intervention, particularly communications received by offenders, be the communications intentional, such as publicity campaigns, or unintentional, such as rumours. If such communications precede the change in outcome, there is no violation of temporal order. But if the change in outcome precedes these communications, there is a violation. Such communication is part of the interventions mechanism and should be made explicit through measurement during the evaluation.

Rival causes

If the evaluator has given a plausible mechanism for the intervention, shown a valid association between the intervention and the outcome, and demonstrated that the intervention preceded the outcome, there is another hurdle he or she must jump to claim convincingly that the intervention caused the outcome. The evaluator must show that there are no plausible explanations for the outcome change other than the intervention. This is a very high hurdle that most evaluations do not achieve. Here we will look at the nature of these rival causes.

Having established mechanism, association and temporal order we now have some basic facts. The rival explanations with which we should be concerned must fit these facts at least as well as the intervention being tested.

All legitimate rival explanations must have a mechanism. The rival's mechanism can be derived from the same theory that produced the intervention being tested, or it can come from a rival theory. Let's consider the first situation by way of example. An intervention based on situational crime prevention might be undertaken to make it more difficult for burglars to commit their offence (increasing effort through the use of improved locks). A rival cause might be that at the same time the intervention was implemented, but independently of the intervention, police implemented a drunk-driver crackdown in the same area. This increased offenders' perceived risk of being caught. Both the intervention and the rival explanation can be explained through situational crime prevention, but they use different mechanisms. Clearly one would not feel confident in attributing the decline in burglaries to the intervention unless one could eliminate the drunk-driver campaign as a viable explanation.

Alternatively, a theory other than that which gave rise to the intervention provides a rival explanation's mechanism. Could the decline in drug dealing in a neighbourhood be due to increased neighbourhood resistance to drug dealing rather than the use of landlord interventions? Increased neighbourhood resistance is an explanation that is usually based on some form of social disorganization theory, whilst landlord interventions are usually based on routine activity theory and situational crime prevention. It could be a viable rival because increased community resistance may have created political pressure on the police to crack down on drug dealing, which led them to implement the landlord intervention. This rival would be associated with both the outcome and the intervention we are interested in testing and it meets the temporal order criteria. But according to the rival explanation, the landlord intervention was a simple by-product and had no effect. It was the residents who caused the decline.

Note that in both these examples, the rival explanations had established mechanism, association and temporal order. If they had not, we would not be terribly concerned with them. Proposed rivals that have no known viable mechanism, are not associated with the outcome or violate temporal order can be discounted. As noted earlier, evidence that an alternative explanation's mechanism is not operating on the cases and setting can be used to reject the alternative as a valid rival.

The setting can influence which explanations are valid rivals and which are not. Let's use a police crackdown on smuggling as an example. If the smuggling is taking place at a well lit road border crossing, then the presence of a full moon on the night of the intervention may not be a viable rival explanation. But if the smuggling were in an open desert environment, or on the seacoast, a full moon might be a rival because it provides illumination and, on a seacoast, influences the height of the tides.

Over 40 years ago Campbell and Stanley (1963) classified rival hypotheses (calling them threats to validity or sources of invalidity). This list has been modified over the years, though the most recent list is relatively similar to the original (Shadish *et al.* 2002):[5]

- *Selection*: cases that receive the intervention are systematically different from cases that did not get the treatment, and these differences caused the outcome.

- *History*: about the same time as the intervention, there were other external changes in the setting of the intervention that caused the outcome.

- *Maturation*: normal changes in the cases over time were responsible for the outcome.

- *Regression*: crime was at an extreme (high or low) when the intervention was implemented. Crime, like most things, varies and extremes tend to move back to the average, even if nothing is done. So the observed improvement is due to the natural return to the normal, rather than the intervention.

- *Attrition*: cases dropped out of the evaluation, thus creating the illusion that the intervention was effective.

- *Testing*: people can change the way they report crime because of repeated exposure to surveys or other measurement. This caused the change in the outcome.

- *Instrumentation*: changes in the way crime is counted were mistaken for intervention effects.

- *Combinations of above*: a combination of these rival explanations caused the change in outcome, particularly combinations of selection and other explanations.

Evaluation designs vary with regard to which rivals they can eliminate and to which they are vulnerable. The degree to which an evaluation can eliminate rivals effects the evaluation's 'internal validity' (Shadish *et al.* 2002). Evaluations that cannot eliminate viable rival explanations have very low internal validity. Evaluations that can eliminate all of them have high internal validity. Internal validity applies to the specific intervention, cases, outcomes and setting being examined in the evaluation. As rival explanations do not have to be proved, just left as possibilities, internal validity is a measure of our confidence that the evaluation's conclusions would be found again if a stronger evaluation design (one that could absolutely eliminate all rivals) were employed.

Consequently, internal validity is a subjective measure of what would happen in a hypothetical circumstance. High internal validity provides no warrant to generalize beyond the intervention, cases, setting and outcomes actually observed in the evaluation. For that purpose, we need something else.

Generalizing

As noted earlier, we are seldom interested in a single evaluation's results for what they say about the particular intervention examined. Instead, we want to know if the results are highly predictable of what we will achieve if we routinely applied the intervention. If intervening with property owners reduced drug dealing at drug hotspots in San Diego, will it do the same in Atlanta, or Manchester, or Oslo?

Our ability to generalize is often expressed by external validity (Shadish et al. 2002). External validity expresses our confidence that an evaluation's findings are generalizable to similar cases, settings and outcomes, and even to variations in the precise form of the intervention. To the extent that the evaluations were conducted on atypical forms of the intervention, peculiar cases, in odd settings or to produce unconventional outcomes, we will not be able to generalize to normal application. The trouble is we often do not know if the evaluation's intervention, cases, settings or outcomes are typical or not.

Sometimes evaluations have characteristics that clearly call into question whether the findings could be replicated. Evaluations that are highly intrusive into the intervention mechanism raise troublesome questions about their generalizability. To the extent that the people implementing the intervention, or who are affected by the intervention, are aware of the evaluation, we should be concerned that external validity is jeopardized. So, for example, the survey of property owners in Eck and Wartell's (1998) evaluation of landlord interventions should raise questions about whether similar results could be achieved when no survey is conducted. If the evaluator has to intervene with agency personnel to assure that experimental conditions are adhered to, or that cases are included in the evaluation, then external validity is being undermined because such actions would not take place if the intervention were implemented normally (i.e. rather than as an experiment or other intrusive formal test).

Even if there is nothing obviously atypical about the form of the intervention, the cases studied, the setting of the cases or the outcomes examined we should not assume that the evaluation's results are typical of what we would find if we were to repeat the intervention with similar cases, settings and outcomes. The fact of the matter is that crime prevention theories give us very little guidance as to what interventions, cases, settings or outcomes are 'similar enough' and what are 'insufficiently' similar to establish a basis from which to generalize. This is one of the reasons both situational crime prevention and problem-oriented policing demand careful analysis of crime cases and settings before selecting an intervention.

If we could create a representative sample of cases and settings and systematically test all the variations of interventions and outcomes on this sample, our evaluation, in principle, would have very high external validity.

The impossibility of drawing such a sample, the cost of conducting such a large study and the administrative burden required to assure the integrity of the project make such an undertaking a pipe dream.

If we restrict our facts to empirical findings, then we are in a dilemma. No single study, regardless of its rigour, number of cases or its design (see next section), provides a warrant for generalization. But how many studies do we need? Over two hundred years ago David Hume argued that there is no logical method for generalizing from any number of instances to some future condition (Hume 1992 (1777)). Yet, we not only want to generalize, we must generalize.

External validity is a peculiar concept and stands apart from the three other forms of validity described by Shadish *et al.* (2002). In each other instance – construct, statistical conclusion and internal validity – we begin with a presumed association between some intervention (*I*) and some outcome (*O*) that we would like to claim is causal. Each form of validity describes a class of rival explanations for the presumed association:

- *Construct validity*: the association is not between the concepts we believe are operating.

- *Statistical conclusion validity*: the presumed association is the consequence of inappropriate statistical analysis.

- *Internal validity*: the association is spurious, and due to some other factors.

If we can eliminate each of the threats we are permitted to conclude that *I* causes *O*. Not so with external validity. We do not begin with a presumed association based on empirical observation. We simply ask what stands in the way of generalizing from a single study. Further, we can never eliminate all external threats, nor do we have a method that in principle could do so. We might be able to dispense with some obvious threats, but we can never claim they all have been eliminated or that the most important barriers to generalization have been dispelled. And even if we were able to conduct a large number of evaluations on a random sample of interventions, cases, settings and outcomes, we would still face the difficulty of generalizing from the populations from which these samples were drawn to future populations of interventions, cases, settings and outcomes.

The problem of external validity is that it is based on induction. As noted earlier, the logical foundations of induction were quite exploded by Hume. Philosophers of science have been debating the appropriate way to generalize ever since. Popper's idea of falsifying, though not the final word on the subject, is a viable, logical and practical alternative. So rather than base generalization on induction, we would be better served to use falsification. The question is, how?

In summary, external validity provides very little justification for generalizing. The most that considerations of external validity can do is to give reasons for not generalizing – suggesting obvious pitfalls we might encounter. So an evaluation with low external validity has considerable obstacles to extension and one with high external validity has no obvious barriers to extrapolation. But the absence of obvious threats to external validity does not make generalization valid, nor does it tell us the limits of valid generalizations. We are left in the dark. We will put some light on this dark place later, once we look at evaluation designs.

Choosing the right design

Eliminate all other factors, and the one which remains must be the truth (Sherlock Holmes).

...*there is no more rational procedure than the method of trial and error – of conjecture and refutation*: of boldly proposing theories; of trying our best to show that these are erroneous; and accepting them tentatively if our critical efforts are unsuccessful (Karl Popper).

An evaluation does not demonstrate an intervention works by providing evidence to support this hypothesis. Rather, an evaluation eliminates all other causes of the outcome, thus showing that the intervention is the only plausible explanation remaining. This is easily understood by imagining the classic drawing-room murder mystery in which we have a murder victim (the outcome) and a house full of suspects (potential causes of the outcome). The detective (the evaluator) in these stories systematically rules out each suspect until, at the end of the novel, he or she is left with one suspect, the guilty party. In a stereotypical novel, the detective assembles the suspects in the drawing-room and lays out his or her reasoning. Then the guilty party jumps up and confesses.

In evaluations the evaluator does the equivalent of assembling the possible suspects and giving evidence showing why they can or cannot be eliminated. But the actual cause of the outcome does not confess. And whilst the detective in these novels almost always points his or her finger at a single guilty party, it is often the case that the evaluator can only narrow the field of likely causes. If the intervention is still one of the suspects, and there are few other suspected causes, the evaluation has some internal validity.

The basic manner in which this is done is to construct an evaluation design that successfully eliminates the rivals. But this is not the only way. Alternatives can be eliminated by a number of means, including statistical analysis of data, logic and reference to well established scientific facts. We have discussed one of these approaches at some length – examination of the results of mechanism. If the pattern of results fits only one mechanism – that of the intervention being evaluated – then alternative explanations are unlikely.

However, the success of non-design approaches is highly dependent on the specifics of the intervention, outcome, cases and setting. Some features of settings are highly stable – street patterns, for example. Thus under many situations, street pattern changes are implausible rivals since they do not change often. But we must be careful about such rules of thumb. Streets do change on occasion, and in some localities they may be in great flux. Nevertheless, though we will lay great emphasis on design, we cannot forget that even if the design does not eliminate a rival that does not mean the rival is an actual cause of the outcome. It is only a possible cause. And if non-design information can dispense with this possibility, the rival can be discarded and internal validity enhanced.

Randomized experiments

Randomized experiments involve two or more treatments, one of which serves as a baseline, or control. The purpose of a control is to show what will occur if no new intervention is applied. It documents our expectations of what happens when nothing new is done. Comparisons of the control experiences to the experiences of the treatment groups give estimates of the intervention's effects. Cases, in these types of experiments, are randomly assigned to the different treatments. Thus, the group of cases in the control group is not statistically different from the group of cases in any of the other treatment groups. So the only difference between the groups is the intervention. Consequently, if the outcomes of the groups are statistically different after the intervention is applied, only the treatment could have caused it.

To examine the effectiveness of landlord interventions on crime at drug-dealing locations, Eck and Wartell used a randomize experiment. The places assigned had to meet two basic criteria for inclusion in the experiment. First, they had to have had a police enforcement action against drug dealing and the drug dealer could not own the location. Immediately following police enforcement, property records were examined, and eligible locations were randomly assigned to the three groups. Police took no further action on those places and landlords assigned to the control group. Police sent a letter to owners of places assigned to the second group. The letter informed the owner about the enforcement and offered police assistance if the owner wanted it. Unless the owner contacted the police, the police did nothing following the letter. For the third group, police demanded a meeting with the property owner and a city-code enforcement official at the drug-dealing location. At that time a plan for addressing the problem was to be drawn up. Police warned the owner that if they did not co-operate the city would take legal action against the property owner under state civil law (Eck and Wartell 1998). Because the three groups were composed by random assignment, the characteristics of the groups were statistically identical. Thus, differences in crime following treatment could only be due to the interventions.

In short, a randomized experiment can eliminate almost all rival explanations. The major rival hypothesis is that attrition from the groups caused the difference in outcomes. But if the evaluator can show that there was little or no attrition (cases assigned to the control actually received the control treatment and cases assigned to the various intervention conditions actually received their prescribed intervention), then the experiment has extremely high internal validity.

Randomized experiments require that certain conditions be met. First, the cases need to be independent of each other. That is, treating a particular case has no influence on other cases in the experiment. This prevents cross-contamination of control and intervention cases. Displacement and diffusion of crime prevention benefits are two possible sources of such contamination. So if either is likely, each case in the experiment needs to be protected from displacement or diffusion from other cases (Clarke and Eck 2003). Other examples of situations where independence is difficult to achieve include the following:

- *Transportation systems*: stations on train lines.
- *Chain businesses*: gas stations owned by the same company.
- *Proximate similar locations*: nearby parking garages.
- *Networked people*: individual members of the same gang.

In all these situations, treating one case can have an influence on other cases that are not supposed to receive the treatment.

Secondly, randomized experiments require tight managerial controls. This includes assuring that cases assigned to various groups receive their assigned treatment; that the interventions are applied exactly as prescribed; and that measurements are taken in precisely the same manner for all cases. These managerial controls are applied to achieve high levels of internal validity. But they also create artificial conditions that are unlikely to occur when the intervention is used normally. In everyday application the crime prevention workers are unlikely to be closely monitored; interventions will vary in intensity, quality and duration; and outcome measurement will be limited. To the degree that these factors influence outcomes, we can expect experimental outcomes to be highly divergent from everyday outcomes. So the artificial conditions required for randomized experiments create obstacles to generalizability (Eck 2002a).

Thirdly, there need to be sufficient numbers of cases available for assignment for the benefits of randomization to be forthcoming. But in many circumstances, there are not enough cases to assign randomly. Some cases are peculiar. Take Poyner's (1997) case-study evaluation of the demolition of walkways in a British housing estate. It is highly unlikely that there were a sufficient number of identically constructed housing estates with high robbery rates to be used in a randomized experiment. Felson and company's evaluation of the redesign of the New York Port Authority Bus Terminal (Felson *et al.* 1996) is another useful case study where a randomized design would be impossible to conduct: the terminal is unique in New York.

What makes these two case studies useful is not the testing of a specific intervention, but what we can learn about a general type of intervention. And randomized experiments are ill-suited for such purposes. This is because the more heterogeneous the cases, the more cases one needs for a randomized experiment. Heterogeneity increases the managerial controls required to maintain experimental conditions (Weisburd *et al.* 1993). Homogeneity aids statistical conclusion validity and internal validity, but undercuts generalizability. With a heterogeneous set of cases we can be more confident that the intervention works on a broad variety of cases in a variety of settings. We lose this ability if all the studied cases are of the same type and in the same setting.

Quasi-experiments

Quasi-experiments were developed to address the fact that randomized experiments are not always feasible. Like randomized experiments, quasi-experiments systematically manipulate the intervention. The intervention is turned on and off at prescribed times, and sometimes compared to a control group that does not receive the intervention, but cases are not randomly assigned to different treatments, so there may be important differences amongst the groups prior to treatment. They usually have less internal validity than randomized experiments, because we seldom can be sure that the comparison (baseline or control) is statistically identical to the treatment group. The differences, small though they may be, may be the cause of the outcomes, rather than the intervention. Consequently, ruling out rival explanations is often more difficult than with randomized experiments.

There are many forms of quasi-experiments, designed to provide the most internal validity possible. Consequently, the internal validity of quasi-experiments varies greatly. In general, quasi-experiments that involve a control group that is very similar to an intervention group, and measure the target crime for many time periods before and many time periods after the treatment (multiple-time series designs), yield much higher levels of internal validity than quasi-experiments with simple before and after treatment measures using control groups. At the very bottom level of internal validity are evaluations where there is no control group and only single before-treatment and after-treatment measures are taken.

The intrusiveness of quasi-experiments is highly variable. Quasi-experiments that are conducted after the intervention has been implemented, using data that are routinely collected by agencies (reported crime data, for example), are not very obtrusive, though this approach can make it more difficult to rule out rival explanations, thereby reducing internal validity. But as a group, quasi-experiments provide a great deal of flexibility and allow one to evaluate a broad range of interventions. Further, they permit evaluations that are less intrusive and therefore create fewer barriers to generalizing to other settings, cases, outcomes and interventions.

Tim Hope's evaluation of interventions with landlords used a quasi-experiment to three sites in St Louis. Hope looked at a long time series of drug-related events around each of the three sites before and after police interventions with landlords. He compared changes at these treated sites to changes in the same events in nearby control areas. Because the control areas are not identical to the intervention sites, we cannot be absolutely sure that some unexpected, unknown and unrelated change in the control or intervention settings did not produce the findings. Nevertheless, the design used by Hope eliminated almost all rival explanations in two of the three locations (Hope 1994). Because Hope evaluated the interventions after they had been carried out, it was unobtrusive. Thus Hope's evaluation design does not create obvious barriers to generalizing to other cases and settings.

Non-experiments

Non-experiments do not involve the systematic manipulation of the intervention, cases or the setting. Rather, the evaluator gathers data describing cases on which the intervention was applied and describing cases on which the intervention was not applied. These cases may be from similar or different settings. These are called cross-sectional studies. The evaluator then uses statistical methods to compare intervention cases to non-intervention cases and looks for differences in outcomes. Differences in case and setting characteristics might influence these outcomes, so these differences are rival explanations. To eliminate them, the evaluator should control for these differences. Because it is virtually impossible to control for all the differences, cross-sectional non-experimental studies usually have very low internal validity. These studies also have difficulty establishing temporal order. It is often unclear if the outcome differences amongst the cases are due to the presence of the intervention or whether the presumed outcome caused the presumed intervention.

Longitudinal studies examine cases with and without the intervention over time. Longitudinal non-experiments can have high internal validity if there is a strong theory with a high degree of scientific credibility underlying the intervention. Evaluations of economic policies typically employ longitudinal non-experimental designs because the theory describes the most likely rival explanations, thus allowing the evaluator to control for them. Crime theories are not as well developed as economic theory.

The primary advantages of non-experimental evaluations are that they are usually not intrusive and they can be applied when it is impossible to employ quasi-experiments or randomized experiments. Though non-experiments may have fewer obvious barriers to generalization, their low internal validity makes conclusions drawn from them highly suspect.

Process evaluations

Process evaluations demonstrate how an intervention was implemented and how it functioned. They are typically used to document the nature of the applied intervention and thereby enhance construct validity. They can also assist in establishing internal validity by elaborating the mechanisms by which the intervention, cases and settings interact to create the outcome. In short, they are useful as supplements to other forms of evaluation, but by themselves they cannot show that an intervention succeeded or failed.

As part of their randomized experiment testing the efficacy of landlord interventions to control drug dealing, Eck and Wartell (1998) collected a variety of process information. These came from specially designed police activity logs and interviews with landlords after the intervention. These data helped show how the intervention worked. Because the intervention was on landlords, it was important to show how pressure on landlords had an effect on the outcome. By isolating the mechanism, Eck and Wartell were able to demonstrate that the intervention being tested was the intervention doing the work.

In contrast, let's briefly examine a well-known, particularly well executed quasi-experiment that was unable to pin down the mechanism causing the outcome. Sherman and Rogan (1995) evaluated the impact of specialized police gun patrols at reducing firearms-related violence. Using several quasi-experimental designs, they were able to show convincingly that the decline in firearms-related violence was most likely due to the police intervention. However, the study could not describe how this took place.

Did the police patrols reduce crime by reducing the guns available for crimes? This seemed unlikely, as there were relatively few firearms seized. However, there may have been a few guns that were repeatedly used in crimes, and these were the ones seized. Or the people in these neighbourhoods who normally carried firearms may have left their guns at home, so they were unavailable to be used in crime. Or perhaps the police patrols created a specific deterrent effect by stopping people highly likely to engage in firearms violence. These individuals may have curtailed their risky behaviour. The evaluation was unable to shed much light on these alternative mechanisms (Sherman and Rogan 1995).

Though this evaluation made a substantial contribution by showing that it is possible to reduce gun-related homicides and other gun crimes through direct police action, it did not pinpoint the precise causal mechanism. If the mechanism was through the removal of a few hot guns, then police actions precisely tailored to such guns could be crafted. If it was a general deterrent effect, then training police how to detect guns might not be required. Simply concentrating patrols in high-gun crime areas and times might be sufficient. If the mechanism was specific deterrence of high-risk offenders, then crafting a repeat offender programme might be effective. Applying one of these mechanisms well is probably less expensive and less intrusive on civil liberties than weakly applying all three mechanisms. Fortunately, a follow-up evaluation suggest that general deterrence is probably not the active ingredient and focusing on repeat offenders is likely to be (McGarrell *et al.* 2001), though this evaluation cannot eliminate the possibility that the mechanism is the removal of a few hot guns.

Learning from evaluations

> There's an old saying in Tennessee – I know it's in Texas, probably in Tennessee ... that says, fool me once, shame on ... shame on you. Fool me ... you can't get fooled again (George W. Bush).

How do we learn from evaluations? Evaluations teach us about the validity of our theories, and it is our theories that give us licence to generalize. Let's look at this process and see why evaluations without theory have limited utility. We will use Figure 24.4 as a map of this discussion.

From a theory of crime we speculate that a particular intervention might be effective at preventing a form of crime when applied to particular types of cases in certain types of settings (arrow from theory to A). From the general theoretical intervention process we infer a particular manifestation in an actual context (downward arrow), the theory is operationalized in B and then evaluated. Operationalization determines the construct validity of

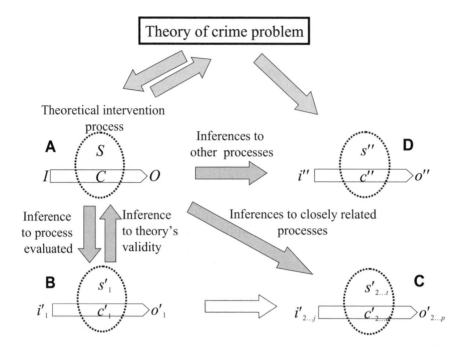

Figure 24.4   Varieties of speculative inferences

the evaluation's conclusions. If the evaluation's conclusions have reasonable construct, statistical conclusion and internal validity, it has implications for the validity of the theoretical intervention (upward arrow from B to A) as well as the original theory (arrow from A to theory). Positive results suggest the theory is correct. Negative results imply the opposite. Completely inconclusive results carry no implications.

We would like to make two types of generalizations from the evaluation. First, we want to generalize to slight variations in the intervention, cases, settings and outcomes (unshaded arrow from B to C). By slight, we mean alterations that are expected when the first intervention is applied again in other places and in other times. We can think of these as fraternal twin intervention processes. Interventions that require extreme precision in implementation and routine application will have high barriers to generalizing because modest variation in how the intervention is applied will change the results obtained. Highly context-specific interventions also will have major obstacles to generalizing because slight changes in the settings and cases can dramatically alter the outcomes. And interventions that are highly crime specific will have serious impediments to generalizing because applying them to even closely related crimes could yield different outcomes.

Though one is tempted to infer from the specific (B) to the general (C), this is not a particularly reliable inference. We never have evaluations of a representative sample of combinations of interventions, settings, cases and outcomes. In fact, we typically have a pitifully small number of evaluations from which to make such inferences – often only one or two evaluations. A more reliable method of drawing lessons from the experience of B is to make use of the theory from which it was derived. If the B is supportive of A, and if there is other evidence from other studies supporting the theory, then we can infer C from A. Following this process, we can make reasonable generalizations (arrow from A to C) from single case-study evaluations, providing the original theory is sound and the case study has reasonable construct, statistical conclusion and internal validity.

The other type of generalization we would like to make is to cousins of the process evaluated. If we were on thin ice making direct inferences from B to C, we are trying to walk on water when we make inferences directly from B to D. If the theory has sound empirical backing, an A to D or a theory to D inference is reasonable. The findings from B give us more confidence that the inference is reasonable than if the evaluation had not been conducted, or had opposite findings.

We would, for example, like to make reliable statements about interventions with place managers to reduce crimes not directly related to drug dealing. We have a limited number of case studies of interventions with bar owners to reduce assault. The number of these evaluations and their internal validity do not match the collection of drug-dealing intervention evaluations, though they consistently indicate place management works in bars too (Eck 2002b). So by themselves the bar evaluations provide modest evidence for reliable effectiveness. Yet, because of their kinship to the drug place interventions we have been discussing – a kinship through a common theory – we can be more confident that intervening with owners of drinking establishments can be an effective method for reducing crime in these places. There are no evaluations of anti-prostitution interventions focused on owners of prostitution locations. Yet it is reasonable to believe that such interventions would be effective because such interventions would be based on an empirically supported theory.

There are some important implications from this argument. First, positive conclusions from an evaluation of an intervention without strong theoretical support provide few handles for making inferences. Such conclusions are anomalies until they can be explained by a theory. Further, if an evaluation finds that the intervention is ineffective, then in the absence of a strong theory to the contrary this finding gives good reason to abandon the intervention.

Secondly, conclusions from evaluations of interventions based on theories with strong theoretical support have broad implications. If the conclusions are positive, then applying the intervention in similar situations is warranted. If the conclusions are negative, despite the theory's implications, then this suggests an urgent need to replicate the evaluation. Because it undercuts the theory, the evaluation's conclusions suggest the theory may be vulnerable. However, without further testing we cannot be sure.

Thirdly, synthesizing the results of evaluations must take into account the validity of the theory supporting the intervention, in addition to addressing the internal validity of evaluations. Ignoring the empirical support for a theory systematically biases syntheses against interventions from strong theories and for interventions from weak or non-existent theories. In short, failing to account for evidence supporting the theory discards evidence.

We have been discussing better or worse inferences, not categorically valid inferences. We can never be absolutely certain an intervention will work for a set of cases, settings and outcomes. A single case-study evaluation concluding that an intervention derived from a strong theory is effective should not end evaluations of the intervention. The more evaluation evidence we have, the more confidence we can have in our inferences. And the greater the expected costs of applying an intervention the more confidence we should require. So the more speculative the inference, the more expensive the intervention, and the worse the possible side-effects are from an intervention, the greater the need for evaluative evidence.

Nevertheless, evaluations are far more important for what they imply about an intervention's parent theory than what evaluations directly imply about the intervention's siblings and cousins. We should not forget that learning takes place when we try something innovative, and innovative interventions have far less evidence supporting them than the interventions they are to replace. This puts us in a quandary that cannot be resolved if we restrict ourselves to evaluation-based evidence. By restricting ourselves to evaluation-based evidence we stifle innovation and reduce our ability to learn. The only way out of this dilemma is through the use of a broader range of scientific evidence, particularly evidence that describes the validity of theories.

Conclusion: no theory, no lesson

> It is the tension between creativity and skepticism that has produced the stunning and unexpected findings of science (Carl Sagan).

This chapter examined how we use evidence from specific crime prevention evaluations to form general conclusions that can guide our crime reduction practices. Though many evaluations may be conducted for highly local purposes, most evaluations are conducted to teach us lessons that go far beyond the specific intervention, cases, setting and outcomes examined. Generalization is the *raison d'être* of evaluation research. Because invalid evaluation conclusions provide poor foundations for such generalizations, considerable emphasis has been placed on internal and statistical conclusion validity. As important as these considerations are, and they are very important indeed, they provide little guidance for drawing general lessons. Neither, it turns out, does external validity. By itself, accumulating evaluation findings – even when one takes into account the internal and statistical conclusion validity of various evaluations – does not teach us much.

Our current knowledge about the important role of place management in preventing crime is not simply the consequence of a number of rigorous evaluations (Eck 2002b). These are necessary, but ultimately insufficient conditions for learning. Place management is now known to be an important aid to crime control because it is derived from a well established and empirically supported set of related theories: routine activity theory, rational choice and situational crime prevention. The evaluations of place management interventions on drug dealing add evidence in support of these theories – at least the portions focused on places. And because of this mutual support – theory to evaluation, evaluation to theory – we can extend our knowledge.

The evaluation that results from interventions with place managers in drinking establishments is not as extensive as is the case with drug-dealing locations, yet it shows positive effects (Eck 2002b). Without a common theoretical base and the drug location evaluations we would have less confidence in the drinking-place evaluations. But with this external support, we have much greater confidence. Further, we can extend place management to domains where it has not been evaluated. The same theory that supports the intervention on drug places suggests it works when applied to some forms of prostitution locations (Eck 1995). Recent case studies suggest it has even wider application. Drug dealing, drinking-related assaults and prostitution are all related to consensual vices. Do interventions with place managers have an effect on non-consensual, predatory crimes? Here our willingness to generalize becomes more tenuous, yet Clarke and Goldstein (to take one example) show that intervening with property owners can reduce theft from new home construction sites (Clarke and Goldstein 2002). Though more evaluations are called for, we are more confident of the correctness of this generalization than we would be without an overarching theory that describes the mechanism by which such interventions work.

We can summarize this chapter's main argument with the following seven points:

1. We want evaluations of specific crime prevention interventions to teach us general lessons about what we can expect to achieve if we apply a related intervention.

2. Neither internal validity nor external validity can give such lessons: the first because it is not intended to and the second because it is based on refuted principles of logic.

3. We are permitted to generalize by way of theory. The process works as follows:

   • We conjecture a general theory of a crime problem.

   • This theory is tested in a variety of ways, most of which are not evaluations of interventions.

   • From a theory that has survived such tests we logically deduce a general intervention.

   • The general intervention is operationalized in the form of a specific intervention, on a concrete set of cases, in a specific setting, using particular outcome measures.

   • A strong test of an operationalization provides evidence about this specific intervention.

   • This evidence has bearing on the validity of the general intervention from which it was derived, and on the original theory.

   • A specific operationalization that does not survive evaluation undercuts the specific intervention, the general intervention and perhaps the theory itself.

- It is from either the general intervention or the theory that we generalize to variations in the intervention, setting, cases and outcome measures.

4. Our confidence in a theory to produce valid generalizations is based in part on findings from specific evaluations and in part on other (non-evaluation) tests of the theory (as well as logic, coherence and fit with other known facts about the world).

5. Generalization from any specific intervention not based on theory is without foundation.

6. Weakly supported theories, or theories from which it is difficult to deduce specific interventions, provide weak justifications for generalizing, even if a specific evaluation produces supportive evidence.

7. Finally, negative findings from an evaluation of a specific intervention are damning of interventions without sound theoretical roots.

Let's close this discussion with a negative example. Mandatory arrest policies for minor domestic assaults have been extensively evaluated with randomized experiments. Probably no police anti-crime strategy has been tested so much with evaluations with such high internal validity. Yet we probably learnt far less from these experiments than we should have. More than 10 years after the first of these experiments in Minneapolis (Sherman and Berk 1984) and several years after the last of the six replications were completed, a synthesis of the outcomes could not come to a conclusive answer to whether arresting suspects reduced crime, did nothing or increased it (Garner *et al.* 1995). A more recent analysis suggests that arrest produces weak specific deterrent effects overall, but these effects vary by type of offender (Maxwell *et al.* 2002).

Why did it take so long to come up with such equivocal findings, despite the rigour of the research designs employed? The answer is simple. There was not, and still is not, a good theory of domestic assaults. To get a glimpse of the numerous mechanisms by which arrest could influence domestic violence, consider the following example.

Nick Tilley (2000) asked a group of non-criminologists to think 'realistically' about possible mechanisms. Table 24.2 lists their suggestions, the setting (context) within which they might work and what outcomes we could expect to observe. Each is plausible; arrest could have many effects, in many contexts. Without a sound theory of domestic violence, we do not know which of these (or other) mechanisms really operate in which actual settings. A coherent, logical and empirically tested theory could have helped to narrow the field and aided the creation of rigorous experiments that could have taught important lessons.

The domestic violence experiments are a clear example of blind empiricism. If there had been a coherent, logical and empirically supported theory of domestic violence, evaluators might have even selected an intervention more powerful than arrest. The evaluations could have been focused on relevant cases and settings. They could have empirically examined multiple mechanisms. And the form of outcome for which we would expect positive results could have been specified. The evaluations would then have been tests

Table 24.2 Alternative theories for explaining the effects of arrest on domestic violence recidivism

Mechanism	Context	Expected outcome pattern
Women's shame	Membership of 'respectable' knowing communities	Reduced levels of reporting of incidents amongst those with close attachments to communities valuing traditional family life
Women's fear of recrimination	History of violence; culturally supported violence; alcoholism of offender	Reduced levels of reporting amongst the chronically victimized
Women's fear of loss of partner	Emotional or financial dependency on partner	Reduced level of reporting amongst poorer and emotionally weaker women
Women's fear of children being taken into care	Pattern of general domestic violence against whole family	Reduced level of reporting amongst families known to social services
Women's empowerment	Availability of refuges; support for women; financial resources of women	Increased levels of separation where support and alternative living arrangements available
Incapacitation of offender	Length of time held	Short-term reductions in repeat incidents
Offender shame	Membership of 'respectable' knowing community	Reduced repeat violence within 'respectable' communities
Offender anger	Cultural acceptability of male violence to women; what man has to lose from brushes with the law	Increased levels of violence amongst those violence-sanctioning communities marginal to mainstream society
Offender shock	Offender attachment to partner; self-image as law-abiding respectable person	Reduced levels of violence, and help-seeking behaviour amongst short-tempered 'respectable' men
Changed norms about propriety of domestic violence	Positive publicity	Longer-term reduced levels of reported and unreported violence

Source: Tilley (2000).

of the theory as well as the intervention, and we would now know a great deal more about reducing domestic assaults. Though still useful, the randomized experiments delivered far less than they could have if a theoretically based intervention had been tested.

Drawing broad lessons from evaluations requires sound theory and evidence. If the intervention is not a logical extension of a sound theory, then the evaluation cannot test a theory, so we learn little. If it is a logical extension of a theory, then the evaluation is first and foremost a test of the theory. It is the interaction of theory and evidence that gives us a warrant to generalize and provides us lessons for future crime prevention action.

Selected further reading

The best basic treatment of research and evaluation design issues is William R. Shadish *et al.* (2002) *Experimentation and Quasi-experimental Designs for General Causal Inference*. This is the latest in the development of a comprehensive explanation of research methods in the social sciences. The original treatment of evaluation methods is still very useful – Donald T. Campbell and Julian C. Stanley (1963) *Experimental and Quasi-experimental Designs for Research*. A well written text that does a good job with evaluation topics (and much more) is William Trochim (2001) *The Research Methods Knowledge Base*. Though the ideas expressed in these books are of fundamental importance, they provide insufficient treatment of how the treatment influences the outcome mechanism.

To learn more on the importance of mechanism in evaluating crime prevention programmes, read Ray Pawson and Nick Tilley (2000) *Realistic Evaluation*. This book provides a much needed counterweight to the experimental tradition that ignores the mechanism. Other useful readings along these lines include Nick Tilley (2000) 'Doing realistic evaluation of criminal justice'; Nick Tilley (1997) 'Realism, situational rationality and crime prevention'; Nick Tilley and Gloria Laycock (2002) *Working Out What to Do: Evidence-based Crime Reduction*; and John E. Eck (2002) 'Learning from experience in problem-oriented policing and situational prevention: the positive functions of weak evaluations and the negative functions of strong ones'.

Case studies of the applications of these ideas can be found in Martin Gill and Vicky Turbin (1999) 'Evaluating "realistic evaluations": evidence from a study of CCTV' and Jason Ditton and Emma Short (1999) 'Yes, it works, no it doesn't: comparing the effects of open-street CCTV in two adjacent Scottish town centres'.

Nick Tilley's (2002) edited volume on evaluating prevention has very useful articles on displacement, cost-benefit analysis, selecting evaluation models and partnerships: *Evaluation for Crime Prevention*. Also see Ronald V. Clarke's (1997) book, *Situational Crime Prevention: Successful Case Studies*. Finally, Ronald V. Clarke and John E. Eck (2003) *Become a Problem-solving Crime Analyst: In 55 Small Steps* and their 2005 *Crime Analysis for Problem Solvers. In 60 Small Steps* provide practical advice to crime analysts who need to evaluate crime prevention programmes.

Acknowledgements

I must thank Nick Tilley for his patience, encouragement and useful criticisms, and Tamara Madensen for her editorial assistance and quick wit. I am also in debt to my students in course 18-078-741-001 who were cleverly able to teach me more about the foundations of evaluation research than I could find in books or practice. I alone am responsible for any omissions and errors in logic or fact.

Notes

1. If crime does decline about the time the new intervention is deployed, local decision-makers may choose to assign credit to the intervention, and if they can create enough publicity, they may be able to convince others that the intervention was the proximate cause of the decline. This has little do with the evidence, however, and much to do with access to news media and opinion-makers. If crime does not decline, decision-makers are unlikely to use the evaluation results publicly.
2. For this reason, such evaluations are seldom published in academic journals and books. They are often not documented at all. But if they are documented, they are most likely to be described in government reports.
3. Or the tests have only been applied in a highly restricted range of contexts.
4. If they used the same mechanism, on the same cases and settings to produce the same outcomes, these alternatives would be indistinguishable from the intervention being tested. They would, therefore, not be alternatives, but simply alternative names for the same thing.
5. Shadish *et al.* (2002) include 'ambiguous temporal precedence' as a ninth rival explanation. Here it is dealt with separately under temporal order because of its importance and for ease of explanation.

References

Campbell, D.T. and Stanley, J.C. (1963) *Experimental and Quasi-experimental Designs for Research*. New York, NY: Houghton Mifflin.

Clarke, R.V. (1997) *Situational Crime Prevention: Successful Case Studies*. Albany, NY: Harrow & Heston.

Clarke, R.V. and Eck, J.E. (2003) *Become a Problem-solving Crime Analyst: In 55 Small Steps*. London: Jill Dando Institute of Crime Science.

Clarke, R.V. and Eck, J.E. (2005) *Crime Analysis for Problem Solvers. In 60 Small Steps*. Washington, DC: Office of Community Oriented Policing.

Clarke, R.V. and Goldstein, H. (2002) 'Reducing theft at construction sites: lessons from a problem-oriented project', in N. Tilley (ed.) *Analysis for Crime Prevention*. Monsey, NY: Criminal Justice Press.

Clarke, R.V. and Harris, P.M. (1992) 'Auto theft and its prevention', in M. Tonry (ed.) *Crime and Justice: A Review of Research*. Chicago, IL: University of Chicago Press.

Ditton, J. and Short, E. (1999) 'Yes, it works, no it doesn't: comparing the effects of open-street CCTV in two adjacent Scottish town centres', in K. Painter and N. Tilley (eds) *Civil Remedies and Crime Prevention. Crime Prevention Studies. Vol. 10*. Monsey, NY: Criminal Justice Press.

Eck, J.E. (1995) 'A general model of the geography of illicit retail market places', in J.E. Eck and D. Weisburd (eds) *Crime and Place*. Monsey, NY: Criminal Justice Press.

Eck, J.E. (2002a) 'Learning from experience in problem-oriented policing and situational prevention: the positive functions of weak evaluations and the negative functions of strong ones', in N. Tilley (ed.) *Evaluation in Crime Prevention*. Monsey, NY: Criminal Justice Press.

Eck, J.E. (2002b) 'Preventing crime at places', in L.W. Sherman *et al.* (eds) *Evidence-based Crime Prevention*. New York, NY: Routledge.

Eck, J.E. and Maguire, E. (2000) 'Have changes in policing reduced violent crime? An assessment of the evidence', in A. Blumstein and J. Wallman (eds) *The Crime Drop in America*. New York, NY: Cambridge University Press.

Eck, J.E. and Wartell, J. (1997) *Reducing Crime and Drug Dealing by Improving Place Management: A Randomized Experiment. Report to the National Institute of Justice*. San Diego, CA: San Diego Police Department.

Eck, J.E. and Wartell, J. (1998) 'Improving the management of rental properties with drug problems: a randomized experiment', in L. Mazerolle and J. Roehl (eds) *Civil Remedies and Crime Prevention*. Monsey, NY: Criminal Justice Press.

Felson, M., Belange, M.E., Bichler, G.M., Bruzinski, C.D., Campbell, G.S., Fried, C.L., Grofik, K.C., Mazur, I.S., O'Regan, A.B., Sweeney, P.J., Ullman, A.L. and Williams, L.M. (1996) 'Redesigning Hell: preventing crime and disorder at the Port Authority Bus Terminal', in R.V. Clarke (ed.) *Preventing Mass Transit Crime*. Monsey, NY: Criminal Justice Press.

Garner, J.H., Fagan, J. and Maxwell, C.D. (1995) 'Published findings from the Spouse Assault Replication Program: a critical review', *Journal of Quantitative Criminology*, 11: 3–28.

Gill, M. and Turbin, V. (1999) 'Evaluating "realistic evaluations": evidence from a study of CCTV', in K. Painter and N. Tilley (eds) *Civil Remedies and Crime Prevention. Crime Prevention Studies. Vol. 10*. Monsey, NY: Criminal Justice Press.

Hope, T. (1994) 'Problem-oriented policing and drug market locations: three case studies', in R.V. Clarke (ed.) *Crime Prevention Studies*. Monsey, NY: Criminal Justice Press.

Hume, D. (1992) (1777) *Enquiries Concerning Human Understanding and Concerning the Principles of Morals*. New York, NY: Oxford University Press.

Maxwell, C.D., Garner, J.H. and Fagan, J.A. (2002) 'The preventive effects of arrest on intimate partner violence: research, policy and theory', *Criminology and Public Policy*, 2: 51–80.

Mazerolle, L., Hurley, D. and Chamlin, M. (2002) 'Social behavior in public space: an analysis of behavioral adaptation to CCTV', *Security Journal* 15: 59–76.

McGarrell, E.F., Chermak, S., Weiss, A. and Wilson, J. (2001) 'Reducing firearms violence through directed police patrol', *Criminology and Public Policy*, 1: 119–48.

Pawson, R. and Tilley, N. (2000) *Realistic Evaluation*. New York, NY: Sage.

Popkin, S.J., Olson, L.M., Lurigio, A.J., Gwiasda, V.E. and Carter, R.G. (1995) 'Sweeping out drugs and crime: residents' views of the Chicago Housing Authority's Public Housing Drug Elimination Program', *Crime and Delinquency*, 41: 73–99.

Poyner, B. (1994) 'Lessons from Lisson Green: an evaluation of walkway demolition on a British housing estate', in R.V. Clarke (ed.) *Crime Prevention Studies*. Monsey, NY: Criminal Justice Press.

Shadish, W.R., Cook, T.D. and Campbell, D.T. (2002) *Experimentation and Quasi-Experimental Designs for General Causal Inference*. New York, NY: Houghton Mifflin.

Sherman, L.W. and Berk, R.A. (1984) 'Specific deterrent effects of arrests for domestic assault', *American Sociological Review*, 49: 261–72.

Sherman, L.W., Farrington, D., Welsh, B. and MacKenzie, D.L. (eds) (2002) *Evidence-based Crime Prevention*. New York, NY: Routledge.

Sherman, L.W. and Rogan, D.P. (1995) 'Effects of gun seizures on gun violence: "hot spots" patrol in Kansas City', *Justice Quarterly*, 12: 673–93.

Smith, M.J., Clarke, R.V. and Pease, K. (2002) 'Anticipatory benefits of crime prevention', in N. Tilley (ed.) *Analysis for Crime Prevention*. Monsey, NY: Criminal Justice Press.

Taubes, G. (1993) *Bad Science: The Short Life and Weird Times of Cold Fusion*. New York, NY: Random House.

Thagard, P. (1999) *How Scientists Study Diseases*. Princeton, NJ: Princeton University Press.

Tilley, N. (1997) 'Realism, situational rationality and crime prevention', in G. Newman *et al.* (eds) *Rational Choice and Situational Crime Prevention*. Aldershot: Ashgate.

Tilley, N. (2000) 'Doing realistic evaluation of criminal justice', in V. Jupp *et al.* (eds) *Criminology in the Field: The Practice of Criminological Research*. London: Sage.

Tilley, N. (ed.) (2002) *Evaluation for Crime Prevention. Evaluation in Crime Prevention. Vol. 14.* Monsey, NY: Criminal Justice Press.

Tilley, N. and Laycock, G. (2002) *Working out What to Do: Evidence-based Crime Reduction. Crime Reduction Research Paper* 11. London: Home Office.

Trochim, W. (2001) *The Research Methods Knowledge Base*. Cincinnati, OH: Atomicdog.

Weisburd, D., Petrosino, A. and Mason, G. (1993) 'Design sensitivity in criminal justice experiments', in M. Tonry (ed.) *Crime and Justice: A Review of Research*. Chicago, IL: University of Chicago Press.

Winchester, S. (2003) *Krakatoa – The Day the World Exploded: August 27, 1883*. New York, NY: HarperCollins.

Chapter 25

Partnership and crime prevention

Daniel Gilling

Introduction

This chapter reviews the partnership approach, regarded by many as a key ingredient of effective practice, but difficult to establish and maintain. We begin by offering a brief overview of the content of official reports which have sought to document the difficulties of the partnership approach, and to recommend various ways to improve practice. For a number of reasons, this approach is found wanting, and it becomes necessary to examine partnership working through three related and interacting levels of analysis that draw attention to the tensions, ambiguities and contradictions that flow through partnerships, providing them with many of their operational difficulties.

The empirical focus of the chapter is upon developments in policy and practice in the UK, in part because of the recognition that an understanding of the partnership context needs to be both detailed, and specific. Nevertheless, since the structure and operation of crime prevention partnerships in the UK are not that dissimilar to those operating in other advanced capitalist countries, and since many of the contextual issues are also global, it is suggested that the issues addressed have a much wider applicability. Limitations of space inhibit a full discussion of the UK policy context, and readers are referred to Hughes and Edwards (Chapter 2, this volume).

The 'what makes a good partnership?' approach (and its limitations)

From 2004 onwards, statutory Crime and Disorder Reduction Partnerships (CDRPs) in the UK will have to undertake an annual self-assessment of their 'health'. The self-assessment is informed by the accumulated wisdom of a number of studies that have sought to establish an answer to the question: 'what makes a good partnership?' These studies have routinely punctuated the development of the partnership approach to crime prevention, particularly from the report of the Morgan Committee (Home Office 1991) onwards, since this committee had been established to find out why it was that the previous decade's policy of encouraging the formation of local partnerships had failed to produce the hoped-for results (see Gilling 1997). Whilst some of the practical messages to fall out of this report were obscured in the political cloud that hung over its unwelcome reception by the then Conservative administration, a number of subsequent publications have issued and reissued guidance on a similar theme.[1]

The 'official' sources of these studies point to an orientation towards governmental concerns with the operation of crime prevention partnerships. This particularly explains the intervention of the Audit Commission, whose primary concern is with the economy, efficiency, effectiveness and value for money of local public services, such as the police and local authorities, who are now heavily involved in CDRPs. The self-assessment requirement for CDRPs is at least *suggestive* that perhaps all is not well on the partnership front, and that the advice of the guidance has been unheeded or for some other reason not followed.

There is not the space to map out all of what these studies have had to say, but at the risk of providing a generalization that applies to none, we may characterize their collective general thrust in the following way.

It is of crucial importance, first of all, that partnerships have a clear sense of mission or purpose, built around a recognition of interdependence, that partner agencies will not be able to meet their objectives without relying upon the contribution of one another. In order to develop such a mission, partners need to be frank and honest about the reasons for their involvement, and they need to have trust in one another's motives and competence.

Once we have the mission, the next important issue appears to be leadership. Leadership manifests itself in a number of ways. Senior managers must lead in terms of being able to commit resources on behalf of their agencies, being able to unblock blockages within their own agencies, being able to support their staff in developing their partnership work and holding the implemented activities of the partnership to account, through forms of monitoring and performance management. There should also be leadership in terms of the drive and enthusiasm of project managers and other 'champions' who are dynamic enough to be able to 'think outside the box' of traditional agency responses and activities, and able to 'sell' their vision to others.

Following on from leadership, there is a strong consensus in favour of partnerships developing an appropriate structure, where strategic management is divided off from operational and implementation issues (more the domain of effective project management), but where there is a clear line of communication (and accountability) between them, as well as back to 'parent' agencies. The structure must be underpinned by a strong 'process focus' on crime prevention (particularly by following the problem-oriented approach), and by good contacts between agency representatives, in turn informed by a good knowledge and understanding of one another's roles and responsibilities. There is evidence of a preference for partnership structures that are relatively small and 'business-like'.

Next, it is apparent that partnerships require appropriate resources in order for them to function. One vital resource is information, and it is often recommended that protocols are used to facilitate exchange, that agencies need to resist unnecessary confidentiality and that when information is exchanged it is in small enough units of resolution to overcome inevitable difficulties emanating from the lack of co-terminosity. It must be exchanged in a format that allows it to be usable, given the very different software and information systems that are in existence.

Another resource is time, which it is suggested has to be made available for personnel involved in the protracted negotiations that are a specific feature of partnership working, particularly when they are expected to fit their partnership working around 'the day job'. Finance is also important to allow partnerships sufficient resources to implement concrete initiatives; and expertise is necessary, in terms of a knowledge of crime prevention and the problem-oriented approach, to ensure that those initiatives are appropriately evidence based.

The final common theme is that of durability. There are clearly problems encountered when individuals, particularly visionary ones, vacate their roles and take all their knowledge, as well as their drive and enthusiasm, with them. For this reason, it is important that agencies try to provide continuity in representation, and that processes and decisions are well documented so that they survive the departure of individuals. Durability is also likely to be facilitated when funding sources are less short termist and project orientated.

There is relatively little to quibble about here. One might question the logic of requiring partnerships to be relatively small, but then there is always a tension between the demands of democracy, which might favour larger and more consultative partnerships, and efficiency, which requires business to be done. There is also relatively little that seems that complicated: to borrow a phrase, most of this is *not rocket science* (Tilley and Read 2000). Yet this begs the question of why, if it is not that difficult to construct an effective partnership, problems with the partnership approach still persist. Evidence of this can be found in the recent research of Hedderman and Williams (2001) and Phillips *et al.* (2002), who show how the majority of the projects they studied, which were financially supported by the Reducing Burglary Initiative under the Crime Reduction Programme, and which were supposed to be managed by the CDRPs, had achieved very little after 18 months of operation.

Whilst it is not beyond the bounds of possibility that there still exists considerable incompetence and inexperience in the seemingly mysterious arts of partnership working, it may be that there is something altogether more fundamental at work here, which points to the limitations of the 'what makes a good partnership?' approach, which bears certain similarities to the *what works* approach to crime prevention. There are two ways in which we can conceptualize these limitations.

First, it may indeed be possible to describe *what works* in partnership working, just as it is to describe *what works* in crime prevention; but describing what works is not the same as *understanding how it works*, nor *under what conditions*. In realist terms (Pawson and Tilley 1997), the fault of the *what works* approach is usually to abstract a crime prevention *measure* from the *context* in which it is employed, and from the *mechanism* that is responsible for firing it. This is dangerously reductionist. Consequently, we would be committing the same mistake if we treated the partnership approach like this, as some of the literature undoubtedly does. A partnership may be seen to work because of a complex constellation of factors that create a conducive environment, and the danger of any approach that seeks to establish a recipe for success is that it misses some of the more vital ingredients, perhaps because they are not so manifestly obvious.

Secondly, the 'what makes a successful partnership?' approach carries the same, mistaken *programmatic* appeal (Wilkinson and Appelbee 1999) as those management texts that occasionally make the 'best seller' lists and propel their authors to celebrity status. That is to say, they offer too simple an approach to what are actually complex social phenomena, in this case reducing the partnership approach to little more than a particular set of interorganizational arrangements. Certainly the partnership approach is about interorganizational arrangements, but it involves process as well as structure (Sydow 1998), and these may be best examined through an understanding of three related but different levels of analysis. Heuristically, it is useful to look at each in turn, but it is vital to remember that they operate through their inter-relationship, rather than in isolation, and thus issues manifest themselves at more than one level.

At its most basic, partnerships involve working relations between individuals who may have no formal authority over one another, because they belong to different agencies, or represent different bodies. At this interpersonal or *micro* level, as many observers have noted (Webb 1991), trust may be the most important commodity in establishing good working relations. But these individuals invariably bring a certain amount of 'baggage' with them, particularly emanating from their occupational or agency backgrounds. As professionals, for example, they may have been trained and socialized into certain ways of doing things and seeing the world. To some extent, phenomena such as professional ideology, occupational culture and organizational culture 'script' their action, although one should not be overdeterministic about this, for individuals often demonstrate an individual capacity to shake free from the straitjacket into which their occupational experience has placed them. Nevertheless, at this organizational, institutional or *meso* level of analysis, one can see how such factors as the incompatibility of professional ideologies, or power imbalances, impact upon the fortunes of partnership working.

Yet like individuals, organizations also bring 'baggage' with them, even if they too have some capacity for independent action. This baggage is accumulated from the wider context in which partnership working takes place. It relates to governmental action, which has a significant part to play in providing conditions conducive to partnership working, particularly via financial incentives. It also relates to wider forces, such as economic and sociopolitical changes, which impact upon relations between the state and civil society. These contextual or *macro*-level forces may then be played out in various ways in partnerships.

The contention in this chapter is that the 'what makes a good partnership?' approach fails to appreciate the complexities of interactions between different levels of analysis. It tends to concentrate more on the empirically observable micro and meso levels, and to neglect the macro context, just as some sociological paradigms focus on agency, and not structure. It is not that the micro and meso levels are unimportant, but they offer an incomplete understanding of partnership action, or inaction. Some of the reports identified above do indeed make reference to certain structural constraints (e.g. Home Office 1991; Audit Commission 2002), but the lack of a systematic analytic overview weakens their overall impact.

The apparent motivation behind the 'what makes a good partnership?' approach is to establish *successful* partnerships. There are two problems here. First, there is an implied link between successful partnerships and successful crime prevention, when actually no line of causality has been or can be established. Some avoid this problem. For example, Hedderman and Williams (2001) state at the outset that their focus is on organizational and managerial issues, and not on the question of impact.

Secondly, what is meant by success, and who defines it? A partnership that fails to deliver on central government's terms may be successful, perversely, for this very reason, if the participants have sought deliberately to thwart central government's policy ends.

The dominant view is that success should be measured in terms of crime preventive outcomes, which, in the absence of an easy measure of pure prevention (Pease 1994), tends to be crime reduction. But, notwithstanding the practical measurement difficulties, this is not the only possible criterion of success (Hughes 1996). More specifically, as the foregoing discussion intimates, and as many such as Hope (2004) have observed, whilst we refer here to crime prevention partnerships, it is apparent that there is a real difference, not to mention some degree of tension, between *crime prevention, community safety* and *crime reduction*, and their respective desirable outcomes.

One of the problems in thinking about success is that it is an inherent feature of the partnership approach, and the conditions that have brought about its existence, that the rationale for partnership may differ according to the standpoint of the participant. Governments may have one thing in mind in their promotion of the partnership approach, but those who are voluntarily or involuntarily drawn into local partnerships, whether they be local governmental agencies, private businesses or members of the local community, including their democratic representatives, may have in mind a quite different goal or purpose. This is because partnership is a part of what Crawford (1997) refers to as the decentring/recentring dialectic of late-modern governance, or what Clarke and Newman (1997) refer to, in similar terms, as centrifugal and centripetal forces. What this means is that the establishment of partnerships simultaneously implies the loss of central control and direction over their business: the direction of partnerships is decentred to the partner agencies, although the centre may use various instruments to try to recentre the control.

The problem with this from an academic point of view is that no single view should necessarily be privileged at the expense of the others. It is very tempting to presume that, notwithstanding this variety of motives and interests, ultimate authority should be ceded to the perspective of central government, which is often the 'main player' in the development of the partnership approach, in terms of providing the legislative mandate, establishing a knowledge base through promotional activities and providing the funding. However, to adopt such a statist view is to make a mistake of misunderstanding and underestimating the power of the forces unleashed by the partnership approach. In the case of policy in the UK, moreover, it would be quite wrong to presume that central government even speaks with a single voice, as we shall see below.

Whilst we have looked above at the 'what makes a good partnership?' approach, it is important to emphasize that running alongside there are more critically informed academic studies, amongst them Pearson *et al.* (1992); Crawford (1994a); Gilling (1993, 1994); Crawford and Jones (1995); Hughes (1996). The divide should not be exaggerated, since the former approach contains critical elements, and the latter is not without its practical concerns. However, overall the academic studies tend to focus more centrally on the difficulties of partnership working that derive from the power differentials between agencies and the discourses that they are able to draw upon; the consequences that such difficulties raise; and the wider ramifications of crime prevention partnerships for changing relations between the state and civil society, particularly with regard to issues of democracy and accountability.

Hughes (1996) has drawn out the main themes of this literature, and this does not need to be repeated here. However, we will access the issues these studies raise via an examination of the different levels of analysis referred to above.

The context of the partnership approach

The context provides us with the macro level of analysis for the partnership approach, identifying aspects that, whilst they do not *determine* the character of partnership working, at least have the potential to exert a significant influence. We can break this down into a number of constituent elements.

Government policy

Government policy, particularly in the form of legislative mandate and funding, is one of the things that Hudson (1987) identifies as being capable of pushing interorganizational relations from independence to interdependence, the latter being the condition that is most conducive to *interagency* partnership working. Prior to the establishment of CDRPs in 1998, government relied mainly upon a policy of exhortation, from *Home Office Circular* 8/84 onwards, backed up by the cultivation and dissemination of an evidence base by the Crime Prevention Unit, and by occasional funding initiatives, the most comprehensive of which was the Safer Cities Programme, which ran from 1988 until the mid-1990s (Gilling 1997). According to the Morgan Report (Home Office 1991), Home Office policy met with only limited success. The problem was perceived to lie primarily with the narrow emphasis that the Home Office placed upon *crime prevention* rather than *community safety*; the lack of core funding; and the fact that crime prevention was regarded only as a peripheral concern of all agencies.

The government of the day was politically disinclined to respond to the Morgan recommendation that local authorities should be given a lead statutory duty for community safety and a ring-fenced budget; and in a changed political climate, where both main political parties sought to out-manoeuvre the other over their claims to be *tough on crime*, there seemed little space for further government policy developments. Nevertheless, at the local level an increasing number of local authorities, particularly those in urban areas and under Labour control, effectively took up Morgan's recommendations to the extent that they were able, for reasons that we shall explore below.

When New Labour entered office in 1997, therefore, local government associations were already strongly behind its policy agenda of resurrecting the Morgan recommendations, albeit in a watered-down version, in so far as the Crime and Disorder Act 1998 (CDA) instituted a plan for joint leadership between the local authorities and the police, but also proposed that there would be no central funding for CDRPs, as it was anticipated that their activities could be funded out of the future savings accrued from successful crime reduction work. The lack of additional central funding, which echoed the message originally issued in *Circular 8/84*, brought with it the risk that CDRPs might be stillborn, and it is interesting how quickly the central funding began to flow, first through the Crime Reduction Programme (CRP), and latterly through a bewildering array of other short-term 'pots'.

The provision of this additional funding suggests two things. First, it attests to the impatience of central government to deliver on its own political promise of being *tough on crime and tough on the causes of crime*. Thus, the funding that has been available to CDRPs has tended to be conditional upon the pursuit of a central performance management agenda that prioritizes a specific range of higher-profile, 'volume' crimes, and an accompanying set of targets. Secondly, it suggests a degree of belated recognition that CDRPs require additional funds to support their activities.

Central government impatience for CDRPs to form and conduct their first rounds of audit, consultation and strategy-setting, all within the space of a year, belied a misunderstanding not only of the lack of technical capacity in many CDRPs, but also of the time it takes for partnerships to evolve into effective structures. As the research of Phillips *et al.* (2002) shows, CDRPs encountered a range of problems. Many of these were linked to capacity issues, such as the lack of data-sharing or ability to deal with incompatible data sets, a lack of crime audit and consultation expertise, the inability to set SMART targets in local crime reduction strategies and the tendency, when identifying possible initiatives, for practitioners to rely upon past experience rather than following the rationalistic logic of the problem-oriented approach. Some problems related more to difficulties with partnership formation, such as an over-reliance on the contributions of the two responsible authorities, namely the police and local authority (whom the statutory guidance unconvincingly suggested were *not* to be regarded as first amongst equals); the reluctance of certain agencies, notably health, probation and local authority education and social services departments, to come 'on board' the partnerships; concerns from non-statutory partnership representatives that the whole process appeared to be dominated by statutory agency concerns; and a tendency to write crime reduction strategies that effectively 'repackaged' what individual agencies were already doing by themselves.

Some problems, finally, related to the politics of centre versus locality. Thus the concerns about statutory agency domination hinted that it was a governmental agenda that drove the partnerships, rather than any genuine commitment to the rhetoric of *local solutions for local problems*; and this was manifested particularly in suggestions that local strategies reflected not the results of the local audit or local consultation, but rather the crime reduction priorities of central government, which local partnerships were urged not to forget.

This is quite an impressive array of difficulties and undoubtedly many others have been encountered since. The difficulties suggest that, whilst central government can create the conditions for the partnership approach, it cannot control how it will unfold. In part, this may reflect inconsistency in government policy (see below), since a lot of the 'push' for crime prevention partnerships has been undone by the generation of 'pull' factors from other dimensions of governmental activity; but in part it also reflects the influence of other contextual factors and the shadows that they cast over partnership working.

From government to governance

Whilst the natural focus for any discussion of crime control will tend to be the policy initiatives of central government, one cannot ignore the wider processes of sociopolitical transformation that have a direct and indirect impact upon the shape and fortunes of such policies. In terms of a direct impact, the partnership approach can be seen as a part of the reflexive governmental response to the changed conditions of late modernity; whilst, more indirectly, these changed conditions have altered the relationship between state and civil society, and in so doing have introduced a number of tensions and ambiguities into relations between those involved in the partnership approach.

The wider transformation referred to here is, broadly speaking, the shift from modernity to late modernity; from a welfare liberal state to a neoliberal state; and from government, with the predominance of hierarchical, bureaucratic modes of co-ordination, to governance, with its shift from hierarchies, via markets, to networks as the increasingly prevalent mode of co-ordination. The transformation has come about largely as a result of crisis in the modern state, which became increasingly evident with the fiscal crisis of the 1970s. The modern state failed to live up to its progressive aspirations in a succession of policy failures in fields including crime control, which witnessed steadily increasing levels of crime and insecurity, almost regardless of the efforts of those in the criminal justice system. In the process a democratic deficit emerged, adding a legitimacy crisis as statutory services were seen to fail particular groups, and to operate in ways that took scant regard of citizen needs and interests.

More specifically, modernist state services may be inappropriate vehicles for addressing social problems, as policy analysis often shows such services generating as many problems as they solve (Pierre and Peters 2000). State services, moreover, have been organized primarily around the interests of the bureau-professions who staffed them, operating with a narrow single-service orientation, and a 'deficit' model of their users, presenting them as needy and generally incapable (Wilkinson and Appelbee 1999). Such problems proved immune to reforms such as those implemented in the corporate management reorganizations of the 1960s and 1970s, which foundered on the resilient rocks of departmentalism and paternalism. Meanwhile, the claim to some specialist knowledge and skills in areas such as crime control had a hollow ring to it when confronted with the reality of rising crime and the 'nothing works' crisis that surrounded it.

The emergence of a neoliberal political orthodoxy resulted in a significant change of emphasis, and a modification of governmental ambitions, evidenced for some in the field of crime control by the arrival of a new penology (Feeley and Simon 1994) where the emphasis shifts from the elimination of crime to its efficient risk management. Such a modification also entails the rolling back of the frontiers of the state and an increasing reliance on individual responsibility, and on the capacity of the market to provide for basic needs such as welfare and security. Whilst neoliberals might have overstated the capacity of the market to provide security for all, the subsequent emergence of a third-way politics, evidenced in the UK by the arrival of New Labour as a political force, has not changed the basic dominance of neoliberal thought in terms of its predilection for a more modest role for government in service provision. One reason for this may be that neoliberalism has unleashed the forces of economic globalization, which make it hard if not impossible for nation-states, in a competitive international economy, to envisage a return to the progressive 'tax and spend' statist politics of yesteryear.

The logic of all this transformation is the emergence of a very different set of relations between state agencies and others. Rather than dominating policy domains, as perhaps they once did, state agencies become one of a number of different local 'players' in increasingly complex networks of local governance. The enhanced role accorded to others, such as the community, reflects the uncomfortable acknowledgement for statutory services that they possess neither the resources nor the expertise to tackle problems such as crime by themselves, but must work with and through others. Thus the emergence of governance is synonymous with the emergence of an 'enabling' role for the local state (Stoker 1998), working with others in networks of which crime prevention partnerships are one example.

There are a number of important questions to ask about this apparent transition from government to governance. One concerns the completeness of the transformation: is it a wholesale change, or merely a change by degree? As Rhodes (1997) has observed, the model of the unitary state used to represent government has always been something of an exaggeration, more of an organizing perspective than a reflection of reality. The state has never been completely dominant, and hierarchies have never been the only mode of co-ordination, even in the golden years of modernity. What we are seeing, then, is perhaps better seen as a shift in the balance between hierarchies, markets and networks as modes of co-ordination. Since it may be a shift in balance, what remains interesting is the relationship between the different modes. In particular, to what extent does the shift towards governance and networks represent a diminution of central state power?

As Pierre and Peters (2000) have observed, the shift towards governance should not necessarily be seen as something that has been against the will of government, and the presumption that it is a diminution of power rests on an erroneous zero-sum conception of power, where the state's 'loss' is considered only to be others' 'gain'. Rather, as they suggest, it might be an indicator of *smarter* government: 'To some extent, "letting other regimes rule" is a governance scenario which reflects a policy choice based on a strategic assessment of the consequences of economic globalisation and sub-national political assertiveness' (2000: 136). These points hold particular relevance for crime prevention partnerships. The promotion of partnerships has allowed government to avoid economically damaging allegations of the state over-reaching itself, and overstating its competence, whilst cleverly facilitating the corollary of this, namely, the off-loading of responsibility for crime and security on to others. A number of commentators (e.g. Walklate 1991), in support of this point, have identified the various 'blaming' mechanisms that lie behind the rise of crime prevention.

In addition, the accommodation of 'subnational political assertiveness' relates in particular to the rise of cities as key stakeholders in the global economy, and their concerns that crime and disorder should not be allowed to stand in the way of the pursuit of their 'urban fortunes' (Taylor 1999). Evidence of such concerns may be found in McLaughlin's (1994) portrait of urban local authorities' shift from 'police monitoring' towards a strategic concern with community safety, and the way that many local authorities developed 'voluntary' partnerships despite the government's lukewarm reception of the Morgan Report back in 1991. The capacity of the 1998 CDA to work with this tide of local community safety, despite the former's apparent emphasis on a rather different model of crime and disorder reduction, stands as testimony to this, although whether it has also succeeded in mobilizing bias in favour of crime reduction is less certain. What we may have here, then, is not so much a zero-sum transfer of power, as a win-win situation in which the different participants of the network may each gain, even if there is a subtle, simultaneous shift in emphasis.

The implication is that the arrival of CDRPs, and partnerships like them, may not signal a *decline* in the central state's power over the domain of crime control so much as its *transformation* into networks, where power is dispersed or perhaps 'hollowed out' through a complex set of relationships that the state then seeks to enable or to steer. Crawford (1997) characterizes this as neo-corporatist. So, how is this achieved? In crime prevention we have seen government fall back on its constitutional powers to mandate partnerships, but such an old, unreconstructed hierarchical approach has also quickly given way to other policy instruments that have been used to facilitate the steering of partnership business.

The most significant of these have been the techniques of performance management that are entwined in the general discourse of new public management (NPM). These techniques have allowed government to steer, rather than to row, through the central allocation of funding backed up by the expectation (now 'policed' in the UK by regional government offices) that such funding will be used to support crime reduction strategies that address the Home Office's own strategic priorities, as outlined in its own public service agreements (PSAs), and evidenced by a range of specific best-value performance indicators (BVPIs). Yet as we have seen in the research of Phillips *et al.* (2002), there can be problems with these NPM policy instruments. First, the priorities identified in the performance indicators may not be shared by all partnership participants, and if they do indeed become local priorities this can lead to resentment amongst those whose concerns have not been addressed, and growing cynicism within the community concerning the capacity of local partnerships to represent local interests. Arguably, the location of CDRPs at district council level provides a structural barrier to their being perceived as local enough, particularly in an area such as crime, which is prone to such sub-locality variation, both in criminalization, victimization and levels of concern and tolerance (Hancock 2001).

Secondly, as many other commentators have observed (e.g. Rhodes 1997; Crawford 1998b), NPM has the unwelcome effect of encouraging agencies to become inward-looking, focusing upon their own 'core business' rather than being responsive to the interests of the wider partnership. It also transforms this core business into something that may be at odds with the rationalities of others involved in the partnership approach, particularly in its imposition of a top-down model of accountability. In other words, NPM can actively undermine partnership working.

We may be witnessing this effect in the current development of CDRPs. Hope (2004) suggests that the politically motivated injection of NPM, specifically in the form of BVPIs, has propelled CDRPs towards crime reduction. The practical significance of this is that it places the police firmly 'in charge' of the local agenda (even if this agenda has in turn been imposed upon the police by central government), using new approaches such as the much-vaunted 'National Intelligence Model', which appear to have given the police a new-found confidence in crime control, perhaps not unrelated to the statistical reductions in crime that have occurred in recent years. Police dominance, which has been a commonly observed theme in other academic studies (Pearson *et al.* 1992; Gilling 1994), derives from the fact that the BVPIs that CDRPs pursue are largely *their* PIs, and that the police possess the key resources, in terms of knowledge, skills and capital, to tackle it, and to know what it is that they are tackling. In such a context, it is difficult to see CDRPs arriving at a genuinely shared vision.

The implication of the shift to crime reduction is that the partnership element is threatened if others do not wish to line up behind the 'police agenda'. Recent history suggests the police role has always been instrumental (Hughes and McLaughlin 2002). For example, the Cornish Committee's recommendations for partnership working back in the 1960s were effectively resisted by the police. The approach of the 1980s Conservative government, to attempt to persuade the police and other local agencies into partnership working, was also undermined, albeit partly from within, as the partnership policy co-existed with, and practically lost out to, a strong push which placed the police in the vanguard of a renewed emphasis on 'crime control', which to some extent was also repeated in the 1990s, following only a brief departure into an 'age of reason' in criminal justice policy.

Garland (2001) views a similar phenomenon through a somewhat different lens when he discusses the sovereignty predicament of late-modern governments, who have to face the relative normality of high crime and a generally ineffective criminal justice system. These 'facts' lead them in the direction of 'responsibilization', which is somewhat akin to governance, in dispersing the responsibility for crime control across from the state to civil society, but not wholly so. For political reasons, particularly for moral authoritarian neo-Conservative governments, it is still important for the state to be seen to be able to maintain law and order, through occasional shows of force such as those characterized by the discourse of 'crime control'. It may be, then, that the shift to police-led crime reduction may reflect this sovereignty predicament to some extent, particularly when it is accompanied by an increasingly assertive, enforcement-oriented stance against issues such as anti-social behaviour, in which other writers (Stenson 2000) clearly see the hand of a sovereign state.

If the reader is struggling to see the relevance of all this for the partnership approach, it is important to stress that the fortunes of the partnership approach are very much structured around these wider processes that are taking place, and which the foregoing account demonstrates are complex, and by no means unidirectional. Whilst such processes may manifest themselves in specific ways in the UK, they are also more general across advanced capitalist states.

The problem of inconsistent government?

In the UK, it is the police service that perhaps most obviously finds itself straddling the two responses of the sovereignty predicament identified by Garland (2001). They obviously perform a key role in sovereign crime control, but they also have a key role in responsibilization through crime prevention partnerships, which past policy has deliberately steered to be police led, and perhaps continues to do so. Yet this all leaves the police on the horns of a dilemma, for the rhetoric of partnership still pervades CDRPs, and this is even something that the police organization has signed up to by way of commitment (ACPO 1996). Yet its core business has been prescribed as crime reduction. Which way should the police service turn as a result of this apparent inconsistency? The dilemma may be sharpened in the intra-agency politics of policing, where decentralization to basic command units (BCUs) supports the localism of CDRPs (with which they are often co-terminous), against the centralized decision-making of police headquarters. The danger for the police is that they may be perceived as paying only lip service to partnership working, in much the same way, perhaps, as they did to community consultation (Morgan 1987).

Alternatively, they may seek to restrict their attention to 'serious crime', leaving CDRPs to function in what becomes a two-tier system of policing, against the disorder, incivility and anti-social behaviour which are the source of so much insecurity in late-modern society. Evidence of this may be found in the governmental decision to allocate a clear responsibility for anti-social behaviour to CDRPs, in recognition of the fact that it has hitherto been no other agency's key priority (Policy Action Team 8 2000).

Another possible example of inconsistency can be found in a comparison of policy across government departments. Whilst the Home Office exercises considerable influence over CDRPs, it is not the only body to do so, as CDRPs also fall under the purview of central departments concerned with matters of local government, such as the Office of the Deputy Prime Minister (ODPM). Whilst the Home Office pushes a tight crime and disorder reduction line over CDRPs, these other departments see the CDRP role more broadly, falling under the general theme of *neighbourhood renewal*. This is because crime, along with features of deprivation such as unemployment, educational disadvantage and poor health, is conceived as an element of social exclusion, where problems combine to bar access to participation in 'normal' social life. Social exclusion, it is believed, is best tackled by *joined-up government* where services addressing these constituent elements of exclusion are co-ordinated in an holistic way, so that the mutually reinforcing nature of these problems can be more effectively addressed. This is the logic behind the initiative, of the neighbourhood renewal strategy, to establish Local Strategic Partnerships (LSPs) as local 'meta-partnerships', drawing in a range of agencies, partnerships and programmes in order to achieve this joined-up approach. CDRPs are one such partnership to be brought under the arm of the LSP, but a great irony is that whilst the inclusion of CDRPs may represent joined-up government, it may be inconsistent with the messages emanating from the Home Office. This requires some explanation.

The inclusion of CDRPs within the networks of neighbourhood renewal has the potential to take them down a somewhat different path from crime prevention. Linking crime with social deprivation takes it in the direction of the discourse of social crime prevention, focusing on the social environmental influences on criminal motivations and dispositions. This is closer to community safety, giving non-criminal justice participants in CDRPs an alternative rationale that may accord more closely with their own interests, as well as those of marginalized or deprived groups. The existence of this alternative rationale provides potential for some *cognitive dissonance* within CDRPs.

As was noted above, many local authorities embraced community safety in the 1990s because they became aware of the impact of crime on their local communities, and thus on their own political fortunes; and because they became aware of the importance of safety in attracting inward investment in a global economy where capital is fluid. This economic development role of local authorities has been described elsewhere as civic boosterism (Cochrane 1994). The key question is, how do local authorities set about attaining security? Do they do it in an inclusionary way as implied by the welfare liberal vision of community safety, or the social crime preventive implications of neighbourhood renewal? Or do they do it in an exclusionary way, by using 'control agents' (Rose 2000), such as street wardens, CCTV systems and the like, to maintain controlled spaces, in which enterprise can flourish, and from which dangerous others can be debarred?

The latter is more consistent with the Home Office's emphasis on crime reduction, which can be pursued through a range of risk management techniques as well as more sovereign strategies such as zero-tolerance-style policing. Bauman (2000: 38) clearly suspects the latter when he argues that 'to excel in the job of the precinct policeman is the best (perhaps the only) thing state governments may do to cajole the nomadic capital into investing in its subjects' welfare'. Yet the definite answer is unclear at present, although the lack of loud noises of protest against the Home Office's crime reduction line may be grounds either for pessimism or concern that marginalized community groups are not the only ones that may be 'hard to hear'. It may be that this latter, exclusionary path also reflects the interests of the business community, who may not be key 'players' in local partnerships, but whose interests appear well heard in partnerships, even in their physical absence (Cochrane 1994). There is certainly evidence of the business agenda being vigorously pursued by some partnerships (Coleman *et al*. 2002).

Again it is important to remind the reader that this critical excursion into policy analysis is very relevant for the analysis of the partnership approach, which is not simply a technical programme that is amenable to organizational and managerial techniques of improvement. Rather, it is also a deeply political issue.

Sharpening the focus: the meso and micro levels

Partnerships are fundamentally about networked relations between organizations. However, organizations do not meet one another necessarily on equal terms, and previous research on crime prevention partnerships has indicated that there tend to be clear power differentials between partners, with the police, as we have seen, having greater power by virtue of their control over resources, including information; and their ability to frame the problem and its solution in particular ways (Smith 2000). The source of such power differentials may be found in part in the historical mandate that has given the police the lead role in local crime control, as well as the main resources, including custodianship of information about crime and disorder. Late-modern structural changes, notably the shift from (public) police to (mixed economy) policing may be challenging this primacy, but the challenge still has some way to go to alter local cultural expectations, and it faces the counter-challenge of developments discussed by Hope (2004) and above, where the Home Office has effectively pushed the role of the police to the forefront in crime reduction.

As we have seen, the Home Office performance agenda generally supposes that CDRPs are there to meet police ends. This does not seem to be a strong base upon which to build partnerships of equals, although we should not presume, despite the rhetoric, that CDRPs are there for purposes of equal representation. If we look at CDRPs more as multi-agency than interagency structures, then we can see, as Crawford (1998b) points out, that interdependence is not necessary: it merely becomes a case of seeing how different agencies can contribute to helping the police to meet their objectives. With this in mind, it is interesting to observe the advice of Her Majesty's Inspectorate of Constabulary (1998), which suggests that in order to secure the collaboration of 'reluctant partners' the police should consider using such devices as shaming, or the threatened withdrawal of services. There is not much here that is suggestive of sensitive negotiation. However, given, as we have seen, that the agenda for CDRPs is

747

not just set by the Home Office, one can imagine points of tension with other interests, although the prospects of them becoming manifest may depend to some extent upon the strength of the ideology of unity that underpins the partnership approach (Smith 2000).

As Smith points out, the danger of this ideology is that it can lead to strategies of conflict avoidance, where power differentials between agencies, and their different crime preventive programmes, are left unchallenged. Conflict avoidance may be motivated by the need to preserve the impression of unity, but also by the felt need to preserve good relations at an interpersonal level: the ideology makes it important that individuals, as well as organizations, are seen to 'get on'.

One manifestation of conflict avoidance may be to privilege the programmes of specific agencies, such as the police, because, in the absence of the kind of debate that is a healthy part of the checks and balances of government (Pearson *et al.* 1992), the police's programme is facilitated at the structural level, for reasons we have already explored. But another manifestation, where there may be no structural dominance but there is still difference between partners, may be the frequently discovered phenomenon of the talking shop, where partnerships are active in 'negotiations', but where very little of substance is ever decided or acted upon. The difference between agencies here may be encountered in different professional ideologies, of the sort highlighted by Holdaway (1986) or Thomas (1994), which tend to parallel the differences between community safety and crime reduction, or situational and social crime prevention. One way of accommodating such difference, without regressing to the talking shop (which may be less viable now that partnerships are statutorily obliged to develop their own strategies), is to adopt what Crawford (1997) nicely refers to as the *smorgasbord tactic*, where space can be found for all different ideological predilections by developing a strategy that encompasses a wide variety of approaches to crime prevention. It may be that this smorgasbord tactic has manifested itself in some CDRP strategies that are hopelessly aspirational and unrealistic, but nevertheless preserve the partnership peace.

However, whilst ideological conflict may have been a discernible feature of the 1980s, there is reason to suppose that it may be less prevalent in the new millennium. In part this may be because of the growth of the partnership approach, not just in crime prevention but across a range of policy domains. This has had the effect of institutionalizing partnership working, rather than making it an optional extra, and routinizing encounters with different professional ideologies, thus minimizing the shock. Also, the difference between ideologies itself may be on the wane, because of the erosion of professional discretion and its replacement by the universal discourse of managerialism, with its language of performance indicators, SMART objectives, project management and the like – even if all it achieves is the tacit acknowledgement of partners' own needs to concentrate on their own core business! Similarly, increasingly generic techniques of risk management (Hughes and McLaughlin 2002) also erode cultural difference, making partnership working less of a venture of unknown quantity. The relative ease with which the police and probation service have joined together into public protection panels to exercise surveillance over high-risk or dangerous offenders is a good example, which would have surprised commentators only a decade ago, given the depth of ideological difference that then appeared to exist between the two agencies (Crawford 1994b). Together these changes have done much to homogenize the public sector experience, including the familiarity with partnerships, although we should not presume that difference has simply been managed away.

Yet whilst there has been considerable change as a result of the emergence of distinctly late-modern styles of governance, we should not underestimate the potential for organizations to demonstrate a resistance to change, something that they have always been good at. Thus the shift from government to community governance, and from hierarchy to network, may well be discernible to the outsider, but inside there are still strong themes of business as usual. Academic commentators may see the necessity for trust-based networks, but some public sector agencies may persist in operating with 'deficit model' views of the community, which may explain why community consultation (and participation) has been one of the least well developed features of CDRP work in most places. Similarly, they are still inclined to see themselves as 'first amongst equals', which may explain Phillips et al.'s (2002) observation about the non-statutory sector's frustration at being effectively *frozen out* of CDRP business. In many ways this has been imposed from above, by the persistent, often short-notice interventions of new government initiatives, which have become a familiar feature of this policy terrain, as practitioners have to learn to accommodate the *permanent campaign* that now seems to be a feature of law and order politics (McLaughlin 2002), the symptoms of which read like a bad case of 'initiativitis'.

Another feature of agency resistance to change is departmentalism, also known as the *silo mentality*. Such a mentality has been hardened by the strictures of NPM and its prioritization of core business, together with its heavily top-down, vertical structure of accountability. This creates further difficulties. First, the top-down emphasis of NPM makes it much harder for accountability mechanisms to be exercised, meaningfully, from below, thus establishing a structural disregard for genuine community governance, adding to the problem of the deficit model. Secondly, the vertical control structures that are put in place to manage performance do not comfortably accommodate the horizontal linkages that are required by partnerships, as a networked form of governance. Attempts to develop cross-cutting performance indicators to address this issue have ended up, as we have seen, looking like the imposition of *police* performance indicators on to CDRPs, with obvious consequences for power differentials.

Even when partnerships have been tightly coupled, as in the case of hybrid youth offending teams (YOTs), problems have arisen as secondees to YOTs have continued to be held accountable to their 'parent' agencies, with the result that not much in the way of genuinely interagency work has been conducted (Smith 2000). And where partnerships have been more loosely coupled, as in the case of CDRPs, there has often been an accountability gap between strategic and operational partnerships, with officers in the latter being left to manage themselves (Hedderman and Williams 2001), often with negative consequences for initiative implementation. Ironically, the flexibility in organizational form that is so highly valued by NPM ends up being defeated by the inflexibility of vertical lines of accountability.

Although it cannot alone be held responsible for this, Crawford (2001) points out that NPM, with its emphasis on performance management and other tools of audit, has done a great deal to effect the 'institutionalization of distrust', when trust is supposed to be the lifeblood of the networked mode of governance exemplified by the partnership approach. Tilley (2001) suggests that the demand for evidence-led practice does much the same thing, constraining professional discretion, in effect, to the tried and tested formula of *what works*, even if this formula's validity is questionable. Obviously the erosion of trust is important if it means that there is no solid basis for partnership working, but this is not its only negative consequence. Many studies of partnership working draw attention to the importance of key individuals whose drive and enthusiasm, together with a visionary ability to make holistic connections across service areas, are held to be responsible for a range of partnership successes. Yet these qualities may be blunted by the institutionalization of distrust, which pushes practitioners back into the arms of the familiar, the routine and the measurable. Crawford (2001) also observes that the NPM agenda tends to focus more on the quantifiable and the 'do-able' features of performance, and again this may hamper the innovative practice that is required to tackle truly *wicked issues* such as crime.

Whilst trust is frequently identified as a necessary condition of partnership working, it is infrequently explored in any great depth. The Audit Commission (1998), for example, promotes trust, but has little to say about *how* it might be formed, other than through 'frank exchanges' – although these are surely a consequence, not a cause of trust. In networks, which lack the authoritative relations of hierarchies or the allocative mechanism of the market, trust is the basis of social relations. Within networks it is an expression of confidence in the reliability of others to produce or contribute towards the production of a particular outcome (Sydow 1998), and in this sense it has a predictive quality, like risk.

Sydow suggests that there is a tendency, in studies about partnerships, to assume that trust exists, as if there could be no partnerships without trust. However, where partnerships are mandated, as they are in the case of CDRPs, there is no reason to presume the prior existence of trust. Similarly, where partnership comes to be regarded as a relatively routine feature of the policy landscape, and is perceived in programmatic terms (Wilkinson and Appelbee 1999), as it arguably is at present, then again there is no reason to presume the prior existence of trust.

Trust tends to be conceived of mostly in interpersonal relations, and, perhaps to a lesser extent, in organizational terms: one trusts other individuals, and one trusts organizations. This conception is accurate to a point, but it threatens a social scientific dualism, neglecting the importance of structural conditions in facilitating the production of trust (Sydow 1998). Thus we must not forget that the trustworthiness of individuals is constituted in part from the baggage that they bring with them to the collaborative table, and the social rules that guide their actions and are reproduced when there. With this in mind, we can begin to consider the nature of trust in crime prevention partnerships.

It is often noted that trusting relations take time to form. Partnership formation is a slow process, which may begin with a succession of relatively small steps. This may be recognized implicitly by those who identify the value of measures such as joint training and placements (e.g. Holdaway 1986), that enable agency representatives to get to know one another, and their different assumptive worlds. It is implicitly recognized, also, in some of the 'what makes a good partnership?' studies that point to the value of 'quick wins' in demonstrating the potential virtue of the partnership approach (Hough and Tilley 1998). Yet if quick wins rely on implemented crime prevention measures then they are unlikely to be that quick, as implementation is a relatively advanced stage of the policy process. In the absence of 'quick wins', it may be, as Sydow suggests, that individuals look for more subtle signs that allow them to attribute the antecedents of trustworthiness (competence, benevolence and integrity) to others. But if this is so, then CDRPs may encounter problems.

First, the impatient results orientation of NPM (Crawford 1997), and the political pressure to succeed, meant CDRPs were established with indecent haste, and expected to operate at their full potential from early on. This afforded very little time for partnership formation in areas where partnerships did not previously exist, and little time for pre-existing partnerships to get used to the more business-like post-1998 orientation. Perhaps this was a strategic error by the Home Office, which overestimated the prevalence and capacity of local partnership working, but it established trust problems from the outset, not least because the haste to produce audits and strategies led to the *de facto* domination of partnerships by the two responsible authorities, namely the police and local authorities, although as we have seen there are other reasons for this. From the perspectives of those involved on the periphery, however, this made CDRPs look less than benevolent in the pursuit of their particularistic, mainly police-dominated agendas. Since, as Sydow (1998) intimates, trust is partly process based, based upon experience of past exchanges and accumulated reputations, the consequences of this haste are likely to endure well beyond the short term.

Secondly, it is clear that there are a number of organizational practices that may be taken as subtle signs of (un)trustworthiness. One of these stems from the lack of 'horizontal surveillance' of partnership working referred to above, which means that individuals often are not held to account for their contribution to partnerships. This means, in turn, that they are able to get away with what might otherwise be characterized as poor performance, such as infrequent attendance or limited contributions at partnership forums. These may be taken as signs of limited competence, and may therefore retard trust formation. The reluctance to exchange information, which has been a hallmark of some agencies' contributions to CDRPs, and which may be due to a culture of confidentiality, may have the same effect. A final example of such organizational practices is the police habit of routinely abstracting officers to perform short-term duties elsewhere, or of moving officers into different areas of police specialism, apparently for purposes of career development. From an outsider's point of views, these may be read as the actions of an untrustworthy organization.

Many of the macro-level issues that we have discussed above can be reconceived as issues of trust, although we do not have the space here to elaborate upon this. Overall, hopefully enough has been discussed and illustrated to show the centrality of trust to the partnership approach. This does not mean that trust should necessarily be the only dimension to interorganizational relations. As Lowndes and Skelcher (1998) have observed, partnerships are dynamic things, with processes that pass through a certain lifecycle. Whilst trust may be a necessary condition for what they call *the pre-partnership stage*, and may underpin other stages as well, trust by itself is an inadequate mode of governance to ensure effective partnership work. Thus, and implicit from some of the discussion had above, *partnership formation* also requires some hierarchical governance in the form of a bureaucratic structure, with a clear management structure that links the horizontal with the vertical, and that bridges the strategic and the operational. Lowndes and Skelcher assert that trust alone will not ensure a sharp enough focus for partnership working, and may exacerbate the 'talking shop' phenomenon. Once we move to the *programme delivery* phase, they suggest that markets, or perhaps more accurately quasi-markets, in the shape of contracts and service-level agreements, may become more appropriate modes of governance, for ensuring that there is some tangible output from partnerships. Again, one can see the logic of this as a way of dealing with the kind of inactivity encountered by Hedderman and Williams (2001). However, once partnerships move beyond trust as a mode of governance they enter other modes that introduce elements of structured power relations, with all the attendant baggage we have considered above.

Summary

This chapter began with a brief review of the 'what makes a good partnership?' approach, which may well have accurately described the features of good partnership working. The approach may even provide a model that can be replicated elsewhere, but by decontextualizing and oversimplifying partnerships, it provides no great understanding of why partnerships work, or often do not work, in the way they do. Such understanding requires a more critical and structurally informed view.

The chapter has examined the current operation of the partnership approach in the UK, arguing the need for specificity when seeking to understand the complex interaction of different levels of analysis, and the impact of this on partnership working. The UK example shows that there are strong forces that have stood in the way of the development of CDRPs, which means that despite the impressive partnership infrastructure, partnership working itself may be far less extensive than might be imagined.

Indeed, current developments may be such that, whilst ostensibly a case remains for partnerships in crime prevention, in practice effort is being channelled back through the police, in the form of intelligence-led policing, with partnership being more of a one-way street, in terms of CDRPs being used to address 'second order' problems, such as anti-social behaviour and the fear of crime. Of course there is likely to be considerable local variation, with some partnerships better equipped than others with advocacy coalitions that may be able to buck the trend, with truly creative responses to the wicked issue of crime. But elsewhere there is the danger of partnership becoming largely symbolic, as the state's desire to resolve its sovereignty predicament continues to undermine the prospects for genuine partnership working.

Selected further reading

The problem with partnership approaches to problems such as crime is that such approaches are means to ends, rather than ends in themselves, although many participants in partnerships probably need reminding of this fact. As means to ends, they attract rather less interest than they merit, and so the publications are inevitably sparser than they ideally should be. In terms of official publications, the study by Coretta Phillips and colleagues, *Crime and Disorder Reduction Partnerships: Round One Progress* (2002), provides a good empirically grounded account of the problems encountered by CDRPs at an early stage in their development, whilst the Audit Commission's (1998) *A Fruitful Partnership* gives a good flavour of an orthodox, managerialist perspective on partnership working.

In terms of more critical accounts, Gordon Hughes' (1996) 'Strategies of multi-agency crime prevention and community safety in contemporary Britain' provides a clear and well set-out overview of emergent perspectives on partnership working up to the period immediately before the advent of CDRPs, whilst Adam Crawford offers a solid, theoretically informed critique of the partnership approach in *The Local Governance of Crime* (1997). Finally, for a more up-to-date assessment of the partnership approach, which links it more closely to New Labour's political project, and which examines developments over a number of policy fields in addition to crime prevention, the reader would do well to consult Caroline Glendinning's (2002) edited collection, *Partnership, New Labour and the Governance of Welfare*.

Note

1. Although they do not necessarily all follow exactly the same line (some, for example, focus rather more on the problems that the solutions), the chronologically ordered work of Liddle and Gelsthorpe (1994a, 1994b, 1994c); Sutton (1996); Audit Commission (1998); Her Majesty's Inspector of Constabulary (1998); Hough and Tilley (1998); the Pathfinder Report on the early experiences of CDRPs (Home Office 1999); Hedderman and Williams (2001); again the Audit Commission (2002); Phillips *et al.* (2002) broadly all fall into this paradigm.

References

Association of Chief Police Officers (1996) *Towards 2000: A Crime Prevention Strategy for the New Millennium*. Lancaster: ACPO.

Audit Commission (1998) *A Fruitful Partnership: Effective Partnership Working*. Abingdon: Audit Commission.

Audit Commission (2002) *Community Safety Partnerships*. London: Audit Commission.

Bauman, Z. (2000) 'Social uses of law and order', in D. Garland and R. Sparks (eds) *Criminology and Social Theory*. Oxford: Oxford University Press.

Clarke, J. and Newman, J. (1997) *The Managerial State*. London: Sage.

Cochrane, A. (1994) 'Restructuring the local welfare state', in R. Burrows and B. Loader (eds) *Towards a Post-Fordist Welfare State?* London: Routledge.

Coleman, R., Sim, J. and Whyte, D. (2002) 'Power, politics and partnerships: the state of crime prevention on Merseyside', in G. Hughes and A. Edwards (eds) *Crime Control and Community: The New Politics of Public Safety*. Cullompton: Willan Publishing.

Crawford, A. (1994a) 'The partnership approach to community crime prevention: corporatism at the local level?', *Social and Legal Studies* 3: 497–519.

Crawford, A. (1994b) 'Social values and managerial goals: police and probation officers' experiences and views of inter-agency co-operation', *Policing and Society*, 4: 323–39.

Crawford, A. (1997) *The Local Governance of Crime*. Oxford: Clarendon Press.

Crawford, A. (1998a) *Crime Prevention and Community Safety: Politics, Policies and Practices*. Harlow: Longman.

Crawford, A. (1998b) 'Delilvering multi-agency partnerships in community safety', in A. Marlow and J. Pitts (eds) *Planning Safer Communities*. Lyme Regis: Russell House.

Crawford, A. (2001) 'Joined-up but fragmented: contradiction, ambiguity and ambivalence at the heart of New Labour's "Third Way"', in R. Matthews and J. Pitts (eds) *Crime, Disorder and Community Safety*. London: Routledge.

Crawford, A. and Jones, M. (1995) 'Inter-agency co-operation and community-based crime prevention', *British Journal of Criminology*, 35: 17–33.

Feeley, M. and Simon, J. (1994) 'Actuarial justice: the emerging new criminal law', in D. Nelken (ed.) *The Futures of Criminology*. London: Sage.

Garland, D. (2001) *The Culture of Control*. Oxford: Oxford University Press.

Gilling, D. (1993) 'Crime prevention discourses and the multi-agency approach', in *Howard Journal*, 21: 145–57.

Gilling, D. (1994) 'Multi-agency crime prevention in Britain: the problem of combining situational and social strategies', *Crime Prevention Studies*, 3: 231–48.

Gilling, D. (1997) *Crime Prevention: Theory, Policy and Politics*. London: UCL Press.

Glendinning, C. (2002) *Partnership, New Labour and the Governance of Welfare*. Bristol: Policy Press.

Hancock, L. (2001) *Community, Crime and Disorder: Safety and Regeneration in Urban Neighbourhoods*. Basingstoke: Palgrave.

Hedderman, C. and Williams, C. (2001) *Making Partnerships Work: Emerging Findings from the Reducing Burglary Initiative*. PRCU Briefing Note 1/01. London: Home Office.

Her Majesty's Inspector of Constabulary (1998) *Beating Crime*. London: Home Office.

Holdaway, S. (1986) 'Police and social work relations: problems and possibilities', in *British Journal of Social Work*, 16: 220–7.

Home Office (1991) *Safer Communities: The Local Delivery of Crime Prevention through the Partnership Approach*. London: Home Office.

Home Office (1999) *Statutory Partnerships Pathfinder Sites Report*. London: Home Office.

Hope, T. (2004) 'The new local governance of crime prevention', in M. Emmerich (ed.) *Public Services Under New Labour*. London: IPPR.

Hough, M. and Tilley, N. (1998) *Getting the Grease to the Squeak*. London: Home Office Police Research Group.

Hudson, B. (1987) 'Collaboration in social welfare: a framework for analysis', in *Policy and Politics*, 15: 175–82.

Hughes, G. (1996) 'Strategies of multi-agency crime prevention and community safety in contemporary Britain', *Studies on Crime and Crime Prevention*, 5: 221–44.

Hughes, G. (1998) *Understanding Crime Prevention*. Milton Keynes: Open University Press.

Hughes, G. and McLaughlin, E. (2002) 'Together we'll crack it: partnership and the governance of crime prevention', in C. Glendinning (ed.) *Partnership, New Labour and the Governance of Welfare*. Bristol: Policy Press.

Liddle, M. and Gelsthorpe, L. (1994a) *Inter-agency Crime Prevention: Organising Local Delivery. Crime Prevention Unit Paper* 52. London: Home Office.

Liddle, M. and Gelsthorpe, L. (1994b) *Crime Prevention and Inter-agency Co-operation. Crime Prevention Unit Paper* 53. London: Home Office.

Liddle, M. and Gelsthorpe, L. (1994c) *Inter-agency Crime Prevention: Further Issues. Supplementary Paper to Crime Prevention Unit Papers* 52 and 53. London: Home Office.

Lowndes, V. and Skelcher, C. (1998) 'The dynamics of multi-organisational partnerships: an analysis of changing modes of governance', *Public Administration*, 76: 313–33.

McLaughlin, E. (1994) *Community, Policing and Accountability*. Aldershot: Avebury.

McLaughlin, E. (2002) '"Same bed, different dreams": postmodern reflections on crime prevention and community safety', in G. Hughes and A. Edwards (eds) *Crime Control and Community: The New Politics of Public Safety*. Cullompton: Willan Publishing.

Morgan, R. (1987) 'The local determinants of policing policy', in P. Willmott (ed.) *Policing and the Community*. London: Policy Studies Institute.

Pawson, R. and Tilley, N. (1997) *Realistic Evaluation*. London: Sage.

Pearson, G., Blagg, H., Smith, D., Sampson, A. and Stubbs, P. (1992) 'Crime, community and conflict: the multi-agency approach', in D. Downes (ed.) *Unravelling Criminal Justice*. London: Routledge.

Pease, K. (1994) 'Crime prevention', in M. Maguire *et al.* (eds) *The Oxford Handbook of Criminology*. Oxford: Oxford University Press.

Phillips, C., Jacobson, J., Prime, R., Carter, M. and Considine, M. (2002) *Crime and Disorder Reduction Partnerships: Round One Progress. Police Research Series Paper* 151. London: Home Office.

Pierre, J. and Peters, B.G. (2000) *Governance, Politics and the State*. New York, NY: St Martin's Press.

Policy Action Team 8 (2000) *Anti-social Behaviour*. London: National Strategy for Neighbourhood Renewal.

Rhodes, R. (1997) *Understanding Governance: Policy Networks, Reflexivity and Accountability*. Buckingham: Open University Press.

Rose, N. (2000) 'Government and control', in D. Garland and R. Sparks (eds) *Criminology and Social Theory*. Oxford: Oxford University Press.

Smith, D. (2000) 'Corporatism and the new youth justice', in B. Goldson (ed.) *The New Youth Justice*. Lyme Regis: Russell House.

Stenson, K. (2000) 'Crime control, social policy and liberalism', in G. Lewis *et al.* (eds) *Rethinking Social Policy*. London: Sage.

Stoker, G. (1998) 'Governance as theory: five propositions', *International Social Science Journal*, 155: 17–28.

Sutton, M. (1996) *Implementing Crime Prevention Schemes in a Multi-agency Setting: Aspects of Process in the Safer Cities Programme. Home Office Research Study* 160. London: HMSO.

Sydow, J. (1998) 'Understanding the constitution of interorganisational trust', in C. Lane and R. Bachmann (eds) *Trust within and between Organisations: Conceptual Issues and Empirical Applications*. Oxford: Oxford University Press.

Taylor, I. (1999) *Crime in Context*. Cambridge: Polity Press.

Thomas, T. (1994) *Police and Social Workers*. London: Arena.

Tilley, N. (2001) 'Evaluation and evidence-led crime reduction policy and practice', in R. Matthews and J. Pitts (eds) *Crime, Disorder and Community Safety*. London: Routledge.

Tilley, N. and Read, T. (2000) *Not Rocket Science? Problem Solving and Crime Reduction. Crime Reduction Research Series Paper* 6. London: Home Office.

Walklate, S. (1991) 'Victims, crime prevention and social control', in R. Reiner and M. Cross (eds) *Beyond Law and Order*. Basingstoke: Macmillan.

Webb, A. (1991) 'Coordination: a problem in public sector management', in *Policy and Politics*, 19: 229–41.

Wilkinson, D. and Appelbee, E. (1999) *Implementing Holistic Government*. Bristol: Policy Press.

Glossary

Note:
Within the definitions, terms in bold refer to related definitions in the glossary.

Adolescent-limited offending
Offending that is largely confined to adolescence. This is contrasted with **life-course persistent offending**, and may have different causes and present different preventive challenges.

Anticipatory benefits
A form of **diffusion of benefits** where the effect of a crime prevention intervention is felt before it becomes operational. The effect may be brought about, for example, by publicity for a planned measure or by increased police activity before longer-term crime prevention measures are introduced.

Anti-social behaviour
Activity that causes harm or annoyance to other citizens, which may or may not be criminal (e.g. youths causing annoyance).

British Crime Survey
A victimization survey asking a randomly selected sample of individuals over 16 years of age, in England and Wales, about their crime experiences over the previous year. It covers household and individual crime but not crimes against businesses. As well as asking about crimes suffered, it also asks about fear of crime. It was first conducted in 1982 and is now carried out on a rolling programme.

Broken windows
An idea developed by James Q. Wilson and George Kelling, suggesting that the neglect of relatively minor incivilities can create a permissive environment for crime and lead to a tipping point where crime problems become serious and out of control.

Burglary

An offence in which someone enters or tries to enter premises as a trespasser with the intention of committing theft, rape, grievous bodily harm or unlawful damage. A distinction is drawn between 'domestic' burglary, where the premises are a dwelling (or connected outhouse or garage), and 'non-domestic' burglary for other kinds of premises (including detached garages, sheds, commercial premises, schools, hospitals, etc.). A burglary does not entail forced entry or actual loss of goods.

Community crime prevention

Crime prevention that involves participation of community members. Participation may involve identifying priority issues, development of preventive responses, engaging in efforts to reduce crime or a mixture of these. Community may refer to small neighbourhoods, small towns or villages, areas of a city, whole cities, the populace at large or subgroups defined by some common attribute other than shared geographic area residence (for instance, ethnicity, religion or age). It may also refer to groups of citizens, leaders of grassroots organizations or front-line locally based agency workers.

Community policing

A decentralized form of policing with a particular focus on a local neighbourhood, where local priority issues are identified and addressed often through problem-solving involving residents and businesses.

Community safety

A term used to describe a broad approach to the achievement of safety and security, generally in local authority areas. It involves focusing on a broad range of crimes and **incivilities**, both to reduce actual levels of crime and **anti-social behaviour**, and anxieties about crime impairing citizens' quality of life. It may extend also to non-crime-related hazards such as road accidents, accidents in the home and fires.

Concentration

The extent to which crime or criminality is disproportionately found amongst particular offenders, victims, places or targets. Overall levels of concentration can be calculated by dividing **incidence** by **prevalence**. The phenomenon of **repeat victimization**, for example, produces relatively high levels of concentration of crime at particular locations or affecting particular individuals.

Conjunction of criminal opportunity (CCO)

A framework designed comprehensively to map out crime causes and preventive points of intervention.

Context

Those physical, social, cultural, political and economic circumstances that are relevant to the generation of crime patterns or to the effectiveness of policies or practices aiming to reduce crime.

Crackdown and consolidation

The achievement of short-term falls in crime through intensive patrol and police enforcement activity, followed by longer-term social and environmental measures to achieve sustained reductions in crime. A series of crackdowns may be needed as longer-term measures bite.

Crime and Disorder Act 1998

Legislation covering England and Wales laying out statutory responsibilities for crime reduction in local authority areas. *Inter alia*, it requires the police and district or unitary local authorities to form local multi-agency partnerships which must conduct an audit of crime and disorder every three years, formulate a strategy and monitor progress in achieving targets. It also imposes, in **Section 17**, a responsibility on police and local authorities to consider the crime consequences of all their policies and practices.

Crime and Disorder Reduction Partnership

Local bodies in England and Wales with statutory responsibility for crime and disorder issues, set up under the terms of the **Crime and Disorder Act 1998**.

Crime events

Individual occurrences of criminal behaviour. As a focus of preventive analysis and intervention, they are contrasted with **criminality**. Patterns of crime events are understood as a function of place, time, target and victim attribute, and may be changed by altering these rather than by addressing the criminality of offenders.

Crime facilitator

Any tool or product or chemical that assists in the commission of a crime. Guns, alcohol and battery driven screwdrivers, for example, are all crime facilitators.

Crime pattern analysis

The examination of patterns of crime event by time, place, victim, target and perpetrator characteristics. This is generally undertaken with a view to informing decisions about preventive priorities or preventive interventions. It differs from much crime analysis in police services which focuses on offenders and networks of offenders with a view to targeting enforcement efforts on serious and prolific offenders or on disrupting their networks. Both forms of analysis may be undertaken within the same office and some preventive strategies (for example, involving **crackdown and consolidation** cycles) may also be informed by both.

Crime prevention

Any measure aimed at preventing crime. The term has come often specifically to connote policing and physical security measures.

Crime prevention through environmental design (CPTED)

An approach to crime prevention and crime reduction that focuses on the design of the physical environment. CPTED has become a worldwide movement. It relates to a wide range of physical environments, including buildings, car parks, housing estates, etc.

Crime reduction
Crime prevention, but without the connotations of **crime prevention**. Any of a variety of measures may be included with the purpose of reducing crime, put in place by any of a variety of agencies.

Crime science
The application of scientific method and the deployment of any scientific disciplines in the interest of crime prevention, crime reduction and crime detection. Crime science is sometimes distinguished from criminology, which has specific associations with the social sciences.

Crime scripts
The decision points involved in committing a crime – for instance, preparing to commit an offence, travelling to a crime site, selecting a target, conducting the crime, getting away and converting the crime to utilities. Different crimes have different crime scripts. They often involve several individual offences – for example, criminal damage, theft and sale of stolen property. Crime scripts may suggest several possible points of intervention in relation to a set of crimes.

Crime triangle
An analysis of crime event patterns in terms of attributes of the location, offender and victim. It is loosely related to **routine activities theory**. The purpose of the crime triangle is less to list every attribute associated with location, offender and victim, but more to identify those that are critical to the production of the patterns, and most especially those that are potentially subject to intervention. The terms **crime triangle** and **problem-analysis triangle** are used more or less interchangeably.

Criminality
A particular set of dispositions to commit crime. Some crime prevention efforts are directed at reducing criminality in the belief that this addresses more fundamental causes of crime than situational approaches that focus on crime events.

Deterrence (general)
The effective discouragement of crime by the population at large as a result of the apprehension and/or punishment of offenders. General deterrence is often distinguished from **specific or individual deterrence**.

Deterrence (specific or individual)
The effective discouragement of an individual from future criminal activity as a result of the experience of punishments received for the commission of past

crimes. Specific or individual deterrence is often distinguished from **general deterrence**.

Developmental pathways
A view of human development that sees it less as a continuous process beginning in early childhood, and more as a series of phases with **transitions** and **turning points**, when there may be changes of direction. This clearly provides potential points of intervention for those whose course of life might otherwise be leading towards criminality.

Developmental prevention
The prevention of the onset of criminality through interventions in early life. Developmental prevention may target **risk factors** that are associated to a greater or lesser extent with later criminal behaviour, even though the causal relationship may not be understood. Some developmental prevention is targeted at those who have shown themselves to be at high risk, with pre-delinquent behaviour. Other developmental prevention is more broadly based on quite wide groups of children, many of whom would not in any case become criminal.

Diffusion of benefits
The spread of crime prevention effects beyond their operational range. Types of diffusion mirror those of **displacement**, i.e. by place, target, time, crime type, technique or offender, or any combination of these.

Displacement
The substitution of a prevented crime by another. Displacement may be by place, target, time, crime type, technique or offender, or any combination of these. The converse of displacement is **diffusion of benefits**, of which there are the same types. Overall, the effects of crime prevention comprise direct preventive effect, plus diffusion of benefits effects, minus displacement effects.

Diversion
The redirection of those deemed liable to offend from criminal to non-criminal behaviour. A side-effect of diversionary behaviour may be unintentionally to bestow a criminal identity through labelling or through creating criminal groups.

Domestic violence
The deliberate infliction of physical, sexual or emotional harms on past or present members of the same household.

Drug testing and treatment orders (DTTOs)
High-tariff community penalties available to the courts targeting offenders who commit high levels of acquisitive crime to support their drug use. Contact is five days a week initially. Orders can last from six months to three years. The purpose is to reduce offending and to tackle substance misuse.

Edges

Boundaries between areas where people live, work, shop or take their leisure. They are the characteristic sites for some crime types such as racial attacks, robberies, etc., because those from different neighbourhoods unknown to each other meet there. The concepts of **node** and **path** are linked to that of 'edge'.

Effort increase

A type of **situational crime prevention**, in which the real or apparent difficulty in committing a crime is increased. There are several ways in which efforts required to commit a crime may be increased.

Evaluation

The systematic assessment of the processes, outputs and outcomes of initiatives, policies and practices. The methods used in evaluation in crime prevention are much contested. Strong evidence on outcome effects is often difficult to obtain, though is frequently requested.

Fear of crime

Anxieties about crime or the perceived prospects of victimization. The **British Crime Survey** attempts to estimate levels of fear of crime, through questions asked at every sweep.

Five Is

A series of headings to capture the essential elements of a crime prevention or reduction initiative so that lessons learnt can be clear and decisions made about replication. The 5 Is comprise: intelligence, intervention, implementation, involvement and impact.

Geographic information system (GIS)

More or less sophisticated computer packages that allow for various methods of mapping crime patterns. Most police agencies and many local authorities now have GIS systems that can be used not only to map crime but also to map its relationship to other social and physical conditions.

Guardian

A person or thing capable of, or deemed capable of, providing protection to a potential crime target. According to **routine activities theory** absence of a capable guardian is one of the essential conditions for a direct-contact predatory offence to take place. The installation of guardianship is one means of crime prevention.

Home Office

The government department in England and Wales that has overall responsibility for crime prevention/reduction. Other government departments also having a significant interest in crime prevention include the Office of the Deputy Prime Minister, the Department for Education and Skills, and the Department of Trade and Industry.

Hot products
Products that tend to be a focus for theft because of their intrinsic value or because they can be easily carried and sold to third parties.

Hotspot
Locations in which there are large numbers of crime events. Some hotspots are transitory. Others endure over long periods.

Incapacitation
Preventing crime by disabling a prospective offender from committing crime. Incarceration is the commonest form of incapacitation, though it obviously does not prevent crimes from taking place inside prisons.

Incarceration
Another word for imprisonment. Incarceration might, in principle, achieve crime prevention through incapacitation. Offenders might also be rehabilitated. On the other hand they might also learn crime techniques, form connections with criminal associates and have a criminal identity bestowed reducing their prospects of living a law-abiding life on release. Rates of reconviction following release tend generally to be high.

Incidence
The number of crimes or the number of crimes in relation to a potential victim population. Incidence comprises one measurement of crime levels alongside **prevalence** and **concentration**.

Incivility
A minor form of anti-social behaviour that may or may not be criminal, but which causes some distress to others, especially when repeated. Examples of incivilities include litter, dog mess and loud noise.

Intimate handler
A person capable of exerting restraint on a potential offender because of his or her close relationship to him or her. The mobilization of intimate handlers is a potential form of crime prevention.

Labelling
The authoritative assignment of some consequential identity to a person or group of persons. The label given may affect the life chances of those affected. They may also embrace the identity bestowed on them. This may unintentionally exacerbate criminal tendencies, where the person or group are defined as criminals or delinquents.

Leverage
Pressure applied to third parties to persuade them to act differently. Leverage is often applied in crime prevention to agencies and members of the private sector to convince them not to act in criminogenic ways, or to create potentially **hot products**.

Life-course persistent offending
Patterns of offending that extend beyond adolescence into older age. This is contrasted with **adolescent-limited offending**, and may have different causes and present different preventive challenges.

Likely offender
An individual who, by virtue of age, sex, background or group affiliation, is liable to take advantage of criminal opportunities. The term **likely offender** is used in **routine activities theory**. For a direct-contact predatory crime to take place one of the necessary conditions is the presence of a likely offender.

Market reduction approach (MRA)
The attempt to reduce property crime by focusing on the various ways in which stolen goods are disposed of.

Mechanism
The underlying, generally unseen, means by which crime prevention measures bring about their effects. 'Increased perceived risk' is an example of a crime prevention mechanism that may be activated through a number of different specific interventions. Deterrence, diversion and reduced perceived reward are other examples. The same intervention may activate different mechanisms in different **contexts**. For example, arresting perpetrators of domestic violence may shame in some conditions but anger in others. In the first it is liable to reduce the likelihood of repeat offending and in the latter to increase it.

Morgan Report
An influential Home Office report, produced under the chairmanship of James Morgan and published in 1991, that looked at local arrangements for delivering crime prevention and community safety.

National Crime Victimization Survey (NCVS)
A victimization survey conducted in the USA, with modifications, since 1972. It is the US counterpart to the **British Crime Survey**.

National Intelligence Model (NIM)
A business model used by enforcement agencies, most notably the police, providing for the analysis of intelligence to identify priority local, regional and national issues, to instigate action in relation to them and to review the results of the actions taken. The NIM was developed by the National Crime Intelligence Service (NCIS), building on what was deemed best practice in intelligence-led policing.

Neighbourhood Watch
A very widespread movement where groups of householders collaborate together and with the police to provide mutual protection and to function as the 'eyes and ears' of the police in local neighbourhoods. The term Home

Watch is sometimes used instead. In addition to Neighbourhood Watch there are now numerous other watch schemes (for example, Pub Watch, Farm Watch, Shop Watch, Forecourt Watch and so on). All work on similar principles.

Nodes
Departure and arrival points, such as stations, home, work and shopping centres. This is a key term, alongside **edge** and **path**, in crime pattern theory. Offenders tend to offend within their awareness space near nodes and on the paths between them, where they are familiar with the opportunities but are unlikely to be recognized.

Opportunity
The relative ease with which an action, in particular the commission of a crime, can be taken. In **situational crime prevention**, opportunity refers to the balance of risks, rewards and efforts that seem to be needed to commit specific criminal acts. In other criminological traditions it has referred to the openings available to subsets of people to engage in either law-abiding or criminal ways of life.

Paths
Routes along which journeys between **nodes** are taken.

Performance indicators
Measurements of achievement, often in relation to specific targets set for projects and organizations. Performance indicators can often have perverse effects. These are unintended consequences drawing those affected away from many of those functions that are not or cannot be captured with the performance measures used. The common adage used to refer to this is, 'What gets counted gets done'.

Personal crime
Crime where the target of the crime is not property (see **property crime**) but is instead the individual. Assault, murder and rape are all personal crimes. Robbery is sometimes classified as a personal crime, because the target is the person, but it can also be seen to be a property crime since the objective is to acquire money or goods.

Place manager
A person or group overseeing a location, with some interest in or responsibility for it, providing for its increased safety.

Plural policing
The involvement of the extended family of policing agencies going beyond sworn officers also to include police specials, neighbourhood wardens, police community support officers, security personnel, etc. In most western societies sworn officers comprise a minority of all those with policing responsibilities.

Policy transfer
The transmission of a policy or set or practices that have developed in one country, leading to their adoption in another.

Prevalence
The number of persons or places that are victimized once or more. The prevalence rate, for example, gives the number of persons or households per hundred, thousand or hundred thousand who are victimized once or more. Victimization surveys often report prevalence rates. The **incidence** rate divided by the prevalence rate gives the level of **concentration** of crime.

Primary crime prevention
Prevention of crime events. This is compared to **secondary crime prevention** and **tertiary crime prevention**.

Problem analysis triangle (PAT)
See **crime triangle**. The only difference is that the PAT may also be used in relation to non-crime and well as crime problems, though the terms offender and victim may not then be strictly relevant. Instead 'caller' and 'source of problem' may be used. The problem analysis triangle was developed for use in problem-oriented policing but has come to be used much more widely.

Problem-oriented policing/partnership (POP)
Originally, policing that is concerned with identifying police-relevant public and community concerns and working out effective ways of dealing with them. POP had its origins in the USA but spread to many other countries also. SARA (**scanning, analysis, response, assessment**) and PAT (the **problem analysis triangle**) are widely used in POP. In Britain, in recognition of the importance of partnership in crime prevention, the term problem-oriented partnership is often substituted for problem-oriented policing.

Prolific offender
Frequent offenders. They are sometimes referred to as persistent offenders. The terms, though, have slightly different meanings. There may be persistent occasional offenders. There may be prolific sporadic offenders. The thresholds used to identify prolific and persistent offenders are a matter of convention.

Property crime
Crime where the main target of the offence is not the person (see **personal crime**), but is instead an object. Theft, burglary and criminal damage are all property crimes. Robbery is sometimes classified as a property crime, because the object is the acquisition of property, but it can also be seen to be personal since the person is also targeted.

Prospective hotspotting
The prediction of future hotspots on the grounds that crimes against one victim (notably domestic burglary) not only increase the probability of that target being repeated but also increase the risks to those living nearby.

Provocation reduction
A technique in **situational crime prevention** which involves reducing the immediate and provocative stimulus to a criminal act.

Rational choice
The notion that some level of rationality is involved in action, even if it is limited. Rational choice models of offending, assuming no more than 'weak' rationality on the part of offenders, have been associated with **situational crime prevention**, though recent theory is questioning whether they are entailed by it.

Rehabilitation
Treatment of known offenders with a view to reducing their criminality, normally by lessening their disposition to commit crime or increasing their capacity to live law-abiding lives.

Removal of excuses
A technique in **situational crime prevention** which involves making it more difficult for the offender to disregard the harm being done or rules being breached at the point of crime commission.

Repeat victimization
The observed tendency across a wide range of crime types and targets for victimization to increase risk of revictimization, especially in the short term. There are two types of **mechanism** through which repeat patterns may be produced. 'Boost' or 'event dependent' mechanisms refer to ways in which one crime precipitates a repeat incident – for example, where the offender returns to steal goods that could not be carried the first time round. 'Flag' or 'risk heterogeneity' accounts refer to ways in which some targets are such that they show themselves to be especially vulnerable to crime and hence attract offenders repeatedly. Some repeats may be a function of 'boost', some of 'flag' and some of both.

Responsibilization
The processes through which the historically assumed duties of the state and the police to control crime are passed to other public bodies, members of the private sector, citizens and voluntary groups.

Restorative justice
Participation by victims and offenders in processes designed to repair the harms done by the offender to the victim. The term 'reintegrative shaming' is also sometime used. 'Family group conferences' are devices often used for the delivery of restorative justice. Restorative justice has most often been applied with youth offenders and in relation to relatively minor crimes although it is now being tried with more serious offending such as burglary and robbery.

Reward reduction
A technique in **situational crime prevention** which involves reducing the prospective rewards from committing specific offences.

Risk factors
Factors associated with criminality and patterns of crime events, though their causal relationships may not be understood. Risk factors are often the focus of attention in **developmental prevention**.

Risk increase
A technique in **situational crime prevention** which involves increasing the risk or perceived risk to potential offenders from committing an identified set of crimes.

Robbery
An offence in which property is demanded using either actual violence or the threat of violence.

Root causes
The underlying sources of criminality. These are far from fully understood and are hotly disputed. Amongst the candidates entertained are genetic abnormality, diet, childhood neglect, social conditions, stupidity, lack of legitimate opportunity, lack of moral guidance and crime opportunities. It is unlikely that there is any single root cause whose removal could bring crime to an end.

Routine activities theory (RAT)
The notion that direct-contact predatory crime is a function of the co-presence in time and space of a likely offender, suitable target and absence of capable guardian. Changes in crime rates can be explained by the changes in the supply, distribution and movement of these three.

Safer Cities
In England and Wales, a major Home Office crime prevention programme that ran from 1988 to the early 1990s, providing grants and staff to stimulate and fund crime prevention initiatives in a number of relatively high-crime local authority areas. In the USA, a local problem-solving crime prevention programme was pioneered in Newark, New Jersey to address crime problems there.

Scanning, analysis, response, assessment (SARA)
Phases in problem-solving used in **problem-oriented policing** and developed in a demonstration project in Newport News. Although scanning, analysis, response and assessment are sometimes represented as linear stages, in practice there have to be feedback loops between them as the definition and understanding of problems and ways of dealing with them develop and as results of interventions become clear.

Secondary crime prevention
The prevention of criminality amongst those at risk of becoming criminal. This is contrasted with **primary crime prevention** and **tertiary crime prevention.**

Section 17
That part of the **Crime and Disorder Act 1998**, that obliges local authorities, police authorities, parks authorities and broads authorities to consider the crime consequences in their policies and practices.

Situational crime prevention
An approach to crime prevention that focuses on reducing opportunities for crime by modifying the immediate circumstances surrounding criminal acts. It is associated with problem-solving and action research. The main **mechanisms** for situational crime prevention include increasing risk and effort, reducing rewards and provocation, and removing excuses.

Stranger violence
Violence committed against someone who is unknown to the perpetrator. Stranger violence is contrasted with **domestic violence** and violence between acquaintances. They present different preventive opportunities and challenges.

Targets
A term used in several different senses. It may refer to objects of crime, or to the aims of those trying to prevent crime, or to individuals who have been identified as the focus for police attention. Target can also be used in a managerial sense. Target-setting by public agencies in the UK, including those with responsibilities for crime control, became very widespread in the early 2000s as a method of giving work focus, achieving accountability and ensuring attention to government priorities.

Tertiary crime prevention
The prevention of continued criminal behaviour amongst those already involved in it. Tertiary crime prevention is contrasted with **primary crime prevention** and **secondary crime prevention**.

Transitions
Points between stages in the course of the developmental pathways through which individuals pass. Transitions can comprise **turning points**.

Turning points
Key events in a person's life which mark a change in direction. Some turning points may lead to the instigation of criminal careers amongst those who have not previously been involved in offending, and others may lead to the abrupt end to a criminal career that has already started. They often coincide with **transitions**, but not invariably.

Van Dijk chains
A series of linked offences where one precipitates another. For instance, if someone has his or her bicycle stolen he or she may take another and so on.

Volume crime
Crimes that are widely experienced and make up a high proportion of all crime. In practice, in Britain, volume crime has been taken to refer to burglary and vehicle crime. In the early 1990s this accounted for about half all recorded crime though by the early 2000s the proportion had dropped to about a third as a result of falls in commercial and domestic burglary and in theft of and from vehicles, alongside some increase in violent crime.

Index